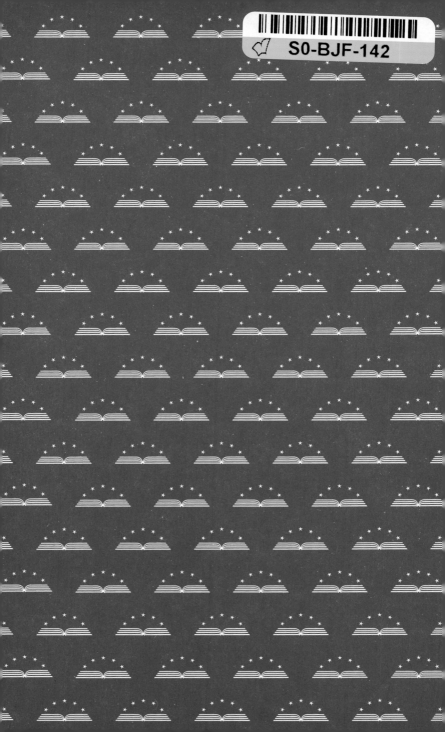

VIRGIL THOMSON

VIRGIL THOMSON
MUSIC CHRONICLES
1940–1954

The Musical Scene
The Art of Judging Music
Music Right and Left
Music Reviewed 1940–1954
Other Writings

Tim Page, *editor*

THE LIBRARY OF AMERICA

The paper meets the requirements of
ANSI/NISO z39.48-1992 (Permanence of Paper).

Distributed to the trade in the United States
by Penguin Random House Inc.
and in Canada by Penguin Random House Canada Ltd.

Library of Congress Control Number: 2013916299
ISBN 978-1-59853-309-5

————

First Printing
The Library of America—258

Manufactured in the United States of America

Virgil Thomson: Music Chronicles 1940–1954
is published with support from the

VIRGIL THOMSON FOUNDATION, LTD.

Contents

From Out of Town
From Overseas
Thoughts in Season

APPENDIX
Early Articles and Reviews 1922–1938

THE MUSICAL SCENE

Introduction

THE FOLLOWING selected essays and reviews, with one exception, appeared in the *New York Herald Tribune* between October 11, 1940 and July 23, 1944. They are not offered here as a complete picture of New York's musical life during that time but rather as a panoramic (here and there even stereoscopic) view of musical America as that has been visible to an American musician resident in New York. They have been arranged by subjects because they cover too short a period to give chronological order any specific value. They have been chosen in some cases because of what I imagine to be a general interest in the subjects covered, in others because I have wished to give a further circulation to ideas that I hope may be of use to other persons, whether professionals or laymen, whose relation to musical art is not wholly casual.

I hope, further, that in spite of all the diversity of subjects and all the variation that exists in the thoroughness with which these have been treated, a clear attitude has been expressed toward the art and a clear view taken of its place in culture. That view is the result of much reflection on my part and of long practice as a writer of music. If it fails to appear at the end as either consistent or defensible, the book will have failed of its purpose. Certainly I do not feel adequate to summing it up here in a paragraph. But I hope it will communicate itself to the reader as a straightforward and eminently sensible attitude.

This does not mean that I hold my opinions to be all true. I do not. Nor do I consider them to be permanent. I am both submissive to facts and amenable to argument. And I consider my personal biases to be facts, not opinions. I will not even hold, therefore, that these do not carry some weight in the balance of my judgment. But if my opinions are not wholly unbiased, neither are they irresponsible. They are the opinions of a man from Missouri who is also a workman. For all the faults of judgment that may be found in them, I sincerely hope that they will not be considered as frivolously arrived at or too unfairly stated, my aim in this regard having been, as you may well suppose, to inform the reader rather than to protect anybody's career or to help perpetuate any given state of affairs.

Except for a reasonable correction of typographical accidents and grammatical slips, most of the pieces are printed as they originally appeared, though occasionally a more precise word or phrase has been substituted for a hastily chosen one.

I wish to express my thanks to Minna Lederman, editor of *Modern Music*, for her kind permission to include the article entitled "Chaplin Scores."

V. T.

Denville, New Jersey, 1945

Taste in Music

A TASTE *for* music, a taste for anything, is an ability to consume it with pleasure. Taste *in* music is preferential consumption, a greater liking for certain kinds of it than for others. A broad taste in music involves the ability to consume with pleasure many kinds of it.

Vast numbers of persons, many of them highly intelligent, derive no pleasure at all from organized sound. An even larger number can take it or leave it alone. They find it agreeable for the most part, stimulating of the sentiments and occasionally interesting to the mind. But music is not for them a passional experience, a transport, an auditory universe. Everybody, however, has some kind of taste *in* music, even persons with little or no taste *for* it. No subject, save perhaps the theory of money, is disputed about so constantly in contemporary life as the divers styles of musical expression, both popular and erudite, their nature and likability.

There are often striking contradictions between what musical people admire and what they like. Admiration, being a judgment, is submission to reason. But liking is an inspiration, a datum exigent, unreasonable, and impossible by any act of the will to alter. It will frequently alter itself, however, without warning. And loyalty to things we once loved dearly brings tension into everybody's taste. Persons whose musical experience is limited may, indeed, be more loyal to old likings than persons who deal with music all the time. The latter tend to reject and to accept with vehemence; they are choosy. And their choosiness is quite independent of their judgment; it is personal and profoundly capricious. They can switch from Beethoven to boogie-woogie, from Bach to barbershop, with a facility that is possible only to those who take all music for their clothes closet. For practical living, man needs to be free in his thought and responsible in his actions. But in dealing with art, responsibility of thought, which makes for slowness of judgment, and freedom of action, which makes for flexibility of taste, constitute the mechanics of vigor.

The development of taste is not a major objective in musical education. What the young need is understanding, that whole paraphernalia of analysis and synthesis whereby a piece is broken up into its component details, mastered, restored to integrity, and possessed. Musical understanding depends not so much on the number of works one has learned in this fashion, provided examples from several schools have been included, as on the completeness with which the procedure has been carried out. Any student can be convinced by study that Mozart is a more accomplished workman than Grieg or Rachmaninoff. If he still likes Grieg and Rachmaninoff better, that is his privilege. Maturity is certain to alter, whatever they may be, his youthful predilections.

Persons unprepared by training to roam the world of music in freedom but who enjoy music and wish to increase that enjoyment are constantly searching for a key, a passport that will hasten their progress. There is none, really, except study. And how far it is profitable to spend time cultivating talent where there is no vocation every man must decide for himself. But if there is any door-opener to taste it is knowledge. One cannot know whether one likes, can use, a work unless one has some method beyond mere instinct for tasting it. The only known ways to taste a piece of music are to read it in score or to follow it in performance. And it is quite impossible to follow unfamiliar kinds of music without an analytical method, a set of aids to memory that enables one to discern the pattern of what is taking place.

But an ability to hear is not the whole of musical reception. A vote seems to be required, a yes or no as to whether one desires, for the present, further acquaintance. Now, the enjoyment of old musical acquaintance is such a pleasant thing for all and so quite sufficiently absorbing for the unskilled that nearly everybody leans toward a timid conservatism with regard to unfamiliar music. The too old, the too new, the in-any-way strange we resist simply because we do not know how to take them on. The lay public will try anything; but it will be disappointed, on first hearing, in anything it has no method for remembering. We like the idea of being musically progressive, because progress is one of our national ideals; but we do not always know how to conduct a progress.

Well, the way of that is long. It is nothing less, if one wishes to take part in America's musical growing-up, than learning to hear music correctly and learning to know one's mind. Persons who cannot follow music at all do well to admit the fact and let music alone. Persons who really hear it, whom *it* will not let alone, usually improve themselves by one means and another in their ability to hear patterns in sound; and with more and more music thus rendered available to them, they can choose at any moment their personal allegiances with a modicum of liberty. The tolerant but untrained, however, will always be a bit uncertain in their tastes. They will never know, for instance, whether they are entitled to vote publicly or not. They will consequently assume the privilege more proudly, more dogmatically, and more irresponsibly than musicians themselves are likely to do. And they will rarely know the difference between their tastes and their opinions.

It is the ignorantly formed and categorically expressed opinions of the amateur, in fact, that make the music world companionable. Professional musicians express, for the most part, responsible opinions; and these show a surprising tendency to approach, within twenty-five years, unanimity. There is not much difference of opinion any more, for instance, about either the nature or the value of Debussy's music, or of Puccini's, or of what Stravinsky wrote before 1914. But musicians' personal likings are eclectic; they imply no agreement of any kind. It is laymen who like to like together. Musicians' opinions influence nothing; they simply recognize, with a certain delay but correctly, the history of music. Lay opinion influences everything —even, at times, creation. And at all times it is the pronouncements of persons who know something about music but not too much, and a bit more about what they like but still not too much, that end by creating those modes or fashions in consumption that make up the history of taste.

There is no doubt that lay opinion is in large part organized and directed by knowledgeable persons—by critics, college instructors, conductors, publishers' employees, and leaders of fashion. It is nevertheless not wholly under their control. The leaders of taste can no more create deliberately a mode in music than advertising campaigns can make popular a product that the public doesn't want. They can only manipulate a trend. And trends follow folk patterns. Nobody connected with a trend in music—whether composer, executant, manager, critic, consumer, or even resister—is a free agent with regard to it. That is why unsuccessful or unfashionable music, music that seems to ignore what the rest of the world is listening to, is sometimes the best music, the freest, the most original—though there is no rule about that either.

And so, thus caught up on the wheel of fatality, how can anybody really know anything about music, beyond its immediate practice or perception, least of all what he likes? Learning is a precious thing and knowing one's mind is even more so. But let none of us who think we belong to music fancy too highly our opinions about it, since in twenty-five years most of these will have either gone down the drain or become every man's private conviction. And please let none imagine, either, that his personal tastes are unique, indissoluble, and free. Those who think themselves most individual in their likings are most easily trapped by the appeal of chic, since chic is no more than the ability to accept trends in fashion with grace, to vary them ever so slightly, to follow a movement under the sincere illusion that one is being oneself. And those who imagine themselves most independent as judges make up the most predictable public in the world, that known to managements as the university trade, since intellectuals will always pay for the privilege of exercising their intellectual powers. Rarities of any kind, ancient or modern, are merely stones to whet their minds against. You can always sell to the world of learning acquaintance with that which it does not know.

In the long run, such freedom as anybody has is the reward of labor, much study, and inveterate wariness. And the pleasures of taste, at best, are transitory, since nobody, professional or layman, can be sure that what he finds beautiful this year may not be just another piece of music to him next. The best any of us can do about any piece, short of memorizing its actual sounds and storing it away intact against lean musical moments, is to consult his appetite about its immediate consumption, his appetite and his digestive experience. And after consumption to argue about the thing interminably with all his friends. *De gustibus disputandum est.*

COVERING THE ORCHESTRAS

Age without Honor

PHILHARMONIC-SYMPHONY ORCHESTRA, *John Barbirolli,* conductor, last night at Carnegie Hall, performing Beethoven's Overture to *Egmont*, Elgar's "Enigma" Variations, and Sibelius's Symphony No. 2.

THE PHILHARMONIC-SYMPHONY SOCIETY of New York opened its ninety-ninth season last evening in Carnegie Hall. There was little that could be called festive about the occasion. The menu was routine, the playing ditto.

Beethoven's Overture to *Egmont* is a classic hors d'oeuvre. Nobody's digestion was ever spoiled by it and no late comer has ever lost much by missing it. It was preceded, as is the custom nowadays, by our national anthem, gulped down standing, like a cocktail. I seem to remember that in 1917 and 1918 a sonorous arrangement of *The Star Spangled Banner* by Walter Damrosch was current at these concerts. After so long a time I couldn't be sure whether that was the orchestration used last night. I rather think not. Last night's version seemed to have more weight than brilliance. It had the somber and spiritless sonority of the German military bands one hears in France these days. That somberness is due, I think, to an attempt to express authority through mere weighty blowing and sawing in the middle and lower ranges of the various orchestral instruments, rather than by the more classic method of placing every instrument in its most brilliant and grateful register in order to achieve the maximum of carrying-power and of richness. I may be wrong about the reasons for it, but I think I am right about the general effect, unless my seat was in an acoustical dead spot of the hall, which I do not think it was. The anthem, to me, sounded logy and coarse; it lacked the buoyancy and the sweep that are its finest musical qualities.

Elgar's "Enigma" Variations are an academic effort not at all lacking in musical charm. I call them academic because I think the composer's interest in the musical devices he was employing was greater than his effort toward a direct and forceful

9

expression of anything in particular. Like most English composers, Elgar orchestrates accurately and competently. Now,
when a man can do anything accurately and competently he
is always on the lookout for occasions to do that thing. In the
Continental tradition of music-writing orchestration is always
incidental to expression, to construction, to rhetoric. Many of
the greatest composers—Chopin and Schumann, for instance—
never bothered to become skillful at it in any major way. Others,
like Beethoven and Brahms, always kept its fanciness down to
the strict minimum of what expression needs. I've an idea the
Elgar Variations are mostly a pretext for orchestration, a pretty
pretext and a graceful one, not without charm and a modicum
of sincerity, but a pretext for fancywork all the same, for that
massively frivolous patchwork in pastel shades of which one sees
such quantities in any intellectual British suburban dwelling.

Twenty years' residence on the European continent has
largely spared me Sibelius. Last night's Second Symphony was
my first in quite some years. I found it vulgar, self-indulgent,
and provincial beyond all description. I realize that there are
sincere Sibelius-lovers in the world, though I must say I've
never met one among educated professional musicians. I realize
also that this work has a kind of popular power unusual in symphonic literature. Even Wagner scarcely goes over so big on the
radio. That populace-pleasing power is not unlike the power of
a Hollywood class-A picture. Sibelius is in no sense a naïf; he is
merely provincial. Let me leave it at that for the present. Perhaps, if I have to hear much more of him, I'll sit down one day
with the scores and really find out what is in them. Last night's
experience of one was not much of a temptation, however, to
read or sit through many more.

The concert as a whole, in fact, both as to program and
as to playing, was anything but a memorable experience. The
music itself was soggy, the playing dull and brutal. As a friend
remarked who had never been to one of these concerts before,
"I understand now why the Philharmonic is not a part of New
York's intellectual life."

October 11, 1940

Sonorous Splendors

BOSTON SYMPHONY ORCHESTRA, *Serge Koussevitzky*, conductor, yesterday afternoon at Symphony Hall, Boston, performing Vaughan Williams's Symphony No. 2 (*A London Symphony*) and Beethoven's Symphony No. 5.

BOSTON, OCTOBER 11.—And so, in cerulean sunshine and through indescribable splendors of autumnal leafage, to Boston —the Hub of the Universe, the Home of the Bean and the Cod. The home, as well, of the Boston Symphony Orchestra, the finest by all-around criteria of our resident instrumental foundations.

The sixtieth season of its concerts opened this afternoon with Vaughan Williams's *London Symphony*. I remember hearing the work nearly twenty years ago in that same Symphony Hall, Pierre Monteux conducting. It is the same piece it was then, too, in spite of some cuts operated by the composer. The first two movements are long, episodic, disjointed. The third is short, delicate, neatly sequential, compact, efficacious, charming. The finale is rich and varied. Its musical material is of high quality, its instrumental organization ample and solid. Also it is not without expressive power. Perhaps one is accustomed to the lengthiness and the slow reflective atmosphere of the symphony by the time one gets to this movement. The improvement in melodic material that manifests itself as the work progresses helps, too. In any case, the last two of the symphony's four movements are anything but dull, which the first two are, and more than a little.

Making a program out of only that and Beethoven, out of one live Englishman and one dead German, classic and great though he be, is an obvious reference to current events and sympathies. The reference might have turned out in its effect to be not nearly so gracious as in its intention had those last two movements of the *London Symphony* not been in themselves so impressive, the finale so moving and deeply somber. It was written in 1913, I believe. It might have been written last month, so actual is its expressive content.

The Vaughan Williams symphony served also as a vehicle for a display of orchestral virtuosity on the part of Dr. Koussevitzky and his men such as few orchestras are capable of offering their subscribers. Not that the piece itself is of any great difficulty; it is only reasonably hard to play, I imagine. But the Boston organization is in such fine fettle after its Berkshire season that every passage, any passage, no matter what, serves as a pretext for those constant miracles of precision and of exact equilibrium that a first-class modern orchestra is capable of.

Musically considered, these refinements are more of a delight in themselves than a help of any kind to the work played. They rather tend, especially in the fine molding and rounding off of phrases, to interrupt the music's continuity, to give it an exaggerated emphasis all over that obliterates any real emphasis or meaning that the score may imply. Only the toughest of the classics and the most glittery of the moderns can satisfactorily resist that kind of polish in execution.

The Beethoven Fifth Symphony resists it quite satisfactorily indeed. Dr. Koussevitzky, be it said to his credit, doesn't try to get away with too much careful modeling, either. Rather he puts his effort into a rhythmic exactitude that adds to Beethoven's dynamism a kind of monumental weight that is appropriate and good. When he tries to achieve more of that weight by forcing the strings beyond their optimum sonority, the result is not so good. The sound that comes out is less loud and less weighty than that which would have come out if the point of maximum resonance had not been surpassed.

All instrumentalists know this; and conductors, of course, know it too when they are calm enough to remember it. But at the back of every conductor's mind is a desire to make his orchestra produce a louder noise than anyone else's orchestra can produce, a really majestic noise, a Niagara Falls of sound. At some time in the course of nearly every concert this desire overpowers him. You can tell when it is coming on by the way he goes into a brief convulsion at that point. The convulsion is useful to the conductor, because it prevents his hearing what the orchestra really sounds like while his fit is on. But if you watch carefully from the house you will usually find that the sound provoked out of a group of exacerbated musicians by any gesture of the convulsive type is less accurate in pitch and less sonorous in decibels than a more objectively conducted fortissimo.

It may seem graceless on my part to mention here a fault almost no conductor is free of and to imply by so doing that there is something particularly regrettable about Dr. Koussevitzky's sharing it. I do mean to imply exactly that, however, because somewhere, some time, some conductor must get around to doing some serious work on the orchestral fortissimo comparable to the work that has already produced from our orchestras such delights of delicacy. And I think it not unfair to suggest that perhaps our finest instrumental ensembles might be just the groups to profit most by such an effort, that maybe it is even their duty to do something about correcting the inefficiency that comes from being overstrenuous.

October 12, 1940

Velvet Paws

PHILADELPHIA ORCHESTRA, *Eugene Ormandy*, conductor, last night at Carnegie Hall, performing, among other works, Mr. Ormandy's orchestration of Handel's Concerto for Orchestra in D Major, Sibelius's Symphony No. 1, and Respighi's *Feste Romane*.

THERE is a whispering campaign around New York which would pretend that the Philadelphia Orchestra has gone off too, and seriously. Do not believe it. The Philadelphia ensemble is as fine a group of orchestral players as exists anywhere, and the sounds that emerge from their instruments are in every way worthy of the superb musicians who play these instruments. Certainly last night's performance showed no evidence, to my ear, of carelessness, of indifference, or of sabotage.

Nowhere else is there such a string choir; one would like to stroke its tone, as if the suavity of it were a visual and a tactile thing, like pale pinky-brown velvet. If memory does not trick, that luxurious and justly celebrated string-tone is less forced, less hoarse and throaty than it was in the days of the all too Slavic ex-King Leopold, now of Hollywood.

There are conductors more highly paid than Mr. Ormandy, in all probability. There are certainly some more highly advertised. Very few musicians anywhere in the world, however, conduct an orchestra with such straightforwardness, such lively understanding, such dependable architectonics. No lackadaisical daisy he, and no Holy Roller, either. His every gesture is civilized, sane, effective. The resultant musical performance is in consequence civilized, sane, and effective beyond all comparison with that of his more showily temperamental colleagues.

Last night's program opened with Mr. Ormandy's own reorchestration of a Handel concerto. For once let us praise a man for tampering with the classics. The score is as brilliant and gay and Handelian as one could wish, a great deal more so than if the original text had been observed. I found it no end jolly.

I also sat through another Sibelius symphony, listening attentively. The melodic material was everywhere of inferior quality; the harmonic substructure was at its best unobtrusive; at its worst corny. The scoring seemed accurate and sure-fire.*

The formal structure, such as there was, was a smooth piecing together of oddments, not unlike what is known to the film world as "cutting." As in a well-cut film, occasions for compensating the essential jerkiness of the flow were exploited whenever they could be found; at those moments something took place not unlike the "plugging" of a theme song.

There is not space here, nor time tonight, to go into the Sibelius matter any further than this. Suffice it to say that for the present I stick to my opinion of last Friday, which was that I found his music "vulgar, self-indulgent and provincial." Respighi's brilliant but meretricious *Feste Romane* sounded last night like good clean musical fun in comparison.

October 16, 1940

Three Orchestras

THE NEW YORK PHILHARMONIC, the Boston, and the Philadelphia orchestras are justly celebrated organizations. Their personnel is tops. They are composed of expert instrumentalists, internationally trained, prepared to meet any emergency of technique or of style according to accepted formulas. These

---

*It has since come to my knowledge that Mr. Ormandy, like many another conductor, does not hesitate to alter a composer's scoring if he considers this to require improvement.

elements are as mutually replaceable and as anonymous as members of the Roman Catholic clergy. And the summum of their integrity, their consecration, and their efficacy is as beyond question.

The conductors of these orchestras, of all first-class orchestras everywhere, in fact, are, although in a pinch mutually replaceable, quite the opposite of anonymous. The modern world likes impersonal musicianship, but it will have none of impersonal conducting. The role of the orchestral conductor is therefore a dual role. He needs to be objective in rehearsal and dependable technically in performance, but he must project in the concert hall a personal and subjective interpretation of every work he conducts. If he lacks technical objectivity he is not a competent conductor, fails to draw the best from his players. If he lacks the power of personal projection, he does not hold his public. He should really be Bodanzky and Mary Garden at the same time.

Also, he must interpret an international repertory, because a resident symphony orchestra is a repertory theater. That repertory, all over the world, consists of the same fifty pieces. A small amount of playing-time a year—say five or ten per cent of it—is more flexible, consists of foreign novelties and compliments to local composers. The reasons for the standardization of symphony repertory are many, and all of them are not pretty ones. But the fact is that the standardized repertory is just another neutral background, like the standardized instrumental execution; it throws further into relief the glamour and the personality of the conductor.

Conductors' glamour and personality fall into three easily recognizable geographic types: the Slavic, the central European, and the Latin. There are excellent American conductors, but there is no such thing (not yet, at any rate) as American conducting. There is such a thing as American music, however; and most of the unhappiness that exists about it in America is due to the fact that there is no way of interpreting it in our high-powered concerts excepting a European way. An Arab or Chinese way would be more advantageous, because that would be a frank translation, comprehensible as such. But the most difficult thing in the world is to translate an American book into British. Musically we are Europe's child, just as we are linguistically Britain's; but we are already another person, just as

our language is already another thing than England's English.
It is the common grammar that deceives everybody. Still, the
literary world is not so deceived as the musical world is. We
do not try to produce plays by Odets and Saroyan and Erskine
Caldwell with English actors or in an Anglo-international manner. They would come out pretty funny if we did. In fact, there
is more to be said for playing Borodin here as if it were by Roy
Harris, which is one way of coming to understand it, after all,
than there is for the present practice of playing Roy Harris as
if it were Borodin, which is a sure way of preventing anybody's
ever understanding it.

However all that may be, the three European styles of conducting are what we have in our concert halls. Those styles,
conveniently enough, are represented by the conductors of our
three first Northeastern orchestras. Dr. Koussevitzky holds the
Slavic chair; the Hungarian Mr. Ormandy is admirably central
European, and Mr. Barbirolli, for better or for worse, is unquestionably an Italian conductor.

The characteristics of the Slavic style of playing are exaggerated dynamism and facile emotivity. It seems to be made
for Tchaikovsky and Tchaikovsky for it. There is a tendency
among all Slavs to overblow the brass and to encourage a thick
and throaty, an absorbent string-tone. That Slavic string-tone
blends the highly differentiated wind-instrument timbres unto
itself in a muddy but unified sonority that is a powerful carrying agent for the facile and rather emotional substance of the
Russian symphonists. Dr. Koussevitzky, although he has a Slavic
weakness for dynamic exaggeration, is not Slavic-minded at all
about string-tone; he is pure Parisian, the purest Parisian we
have on this coast.

The central European style of conducting is military, authoritative, and energetic. It is capable of a gentleness in soft passages
and of a nobility in loud ones that is incomparable. It is the
musical language of the great Viennese masters from Haydn
through Schönberg, although it seems to have been made up
both for and out of Handel. Perhaps the Handelian is its most
easily exportable form. Mr. Ormandy is an admirable exponent
of this style. His authority is authoritative, his tenderness tender.
He happens also to have inherited from his Slavic predecessor a superb choir of rich Tchaikovskian string-players. He has

toned down their dynamic violence and toned up their lethargic throat-tones; but he has kept their rare and finely blended dark coloration, a bright dark thing like red copper. The instruments themselves are, I am told, all from the old Cremona fiddle-makers. At present the string sound that comes from them is like nothing else I have ever heard anywhere.

Koussevitzky is better at balancing a string-chord than any-body. He always was. When he first came to Paris, after the war, he could already do it, could do it with any pick-up orchestra. The French conductors themselves could not make such an exact equilibrium, a balance in which the most neutral viola part, the most secondary second-violin part, were as clearly per-ceptible as the top-line melody or the bass. His Boston string section is a lovely thing, thinner and more brilliant, as is the Parisian taste, than that of the Philadelphia band; and his chord-balances, just because of that thinner and higher-voiced sonor-ity, are neater, more stable, more exact. The Philadelphia tone, however, in its present condition, remains a luxury product of unmatched quality, a unique experience for its delicacy and for its almost tactile sensuality.

Mr. Barbirolli is a Latin out of his natural water; perhaps, too, just a little over his head. By temperament a self-effacing accom-panist, he is not at his best in a stellar role. He might be excel-lent at the opera. He is objective and clear-minded about music; he likes and produces from his band that centrifugal sonority that Latins love, a sonority that is not so much a blend of differ-ent sounds as a simultaneity of clearly differentiated ones. One has the feeling, all the same, that he might do better in rehearsal than in concert. He gives a reading rather than a performance. He deforms a composer's wish rather less than the more spec-tacular leaders do; but he rarely possesses a work and makes it his own. And I think he is bored by the necessity of being a personality. All of which gives him an air of being out beyond his depth. His honest but elementary little breast stroke is no match for the streamlined baton technique that both his public and his players are used to. So he gets frantic and conducts with his hair, always the first refuge of an Italian when he can't think of the right next move.

The Philharmonic does not have that tradition of great con-ductors under long tenure that the Philadelphia and the Boston

have. The Philharmonic's best conductors, Mahler, Mengelberg, Walter, Furtwängler, Toscanini, have never stayed long
enough to mold the orchestra into a thing at once expressive
of its leaders and of the city and public it is supposed to honor;
not, at least, in the way that the Philadelphia Orchestra seems to
be at the same time Leopold Stokowski and Eugene Ormandy
and also an appropriate symbol of that swanky and luxurious
town. Nor in the way that the Boston seems, even after sixteen
years of Koussevitzky, still to remember the martial elegance
of Muck, the Gallic clearheadedness of Monteux, as well as
to correspond in both programs and playing to that tradition
of bourgeois dignity with intellectual open-mindedness that is
Boston, the most characteristically Victorian and inveterately
good-mannered of our intellectual centers.

I imagine the trouble with the Philharmonic is that nobody
really cares. Nobody in New York could care, because New York
is a musical market-place, a crossroads. We are not obliged to
take our nourishment from any one source of supply, to trade
with any one store. And so, whereas a really first-rate orchestra is
a necessity to a proud provincial city, it maybe isn't worth bothering about here. We don't need to keep any conductor around
all the time. We can let them come and go, because even the
best among them need our metropolitan accolade far more than
we need the steady presence of their rather terrifying tension.

And so New York takes on an Emil Paur and keeps him for
years, a Josef Stransky, a Van Hoogstraten. Under such men the
Philharmonic lies fallow, rests up, so to speak, for those terrific
combats between the podium and the desks that mark the brief
Metropolitan tenure of great conductors.

October 20, 1940

Music from Chicago

CHICAGO SYMPHONY ORCHESTRA, *Frederick Stock*, conductor, last night at Carnegie Hall, performing Weber's Overture to *Euryanthe*, Brahms's Symphony No. 3, Roy Harris's *American Creed*, and Richard Strauss's *Till Eulenspiegel*.

FLOWERS on the stage and flowers in the musicians' buttonholes, two fiftieth seasons to celebrate, that of the Chicago Symphony Orchestra and that of our own Carnegie Hall, an exchange of visits between Chicago's orchestra and our own Philharmonic—what with all this and a new work by Roy Harris, last night was indeed a sufficiently festive occasion for flowers on the stage and flowers in the musicians' buttonholes.

The Chicago Symphony Orchestra sounds like a French orchestra. Its fiddle tone, thin as a wedge, espouses by resemblance that of oboe and trumpet, absorbs nothing, stands clear in the orchestral bouquet. All the instrumental sounds stand clear and separate. Their harmony is one of juxtaposition, not of absorptive domination. As in an eighteenth-century flower picture, all is distinct, nothing crushed.

Mr. Stock won his audience last night, as he has won audiences for thirty-five years, by playing them music very beautifully, not by wowing them.

I missed the *Euryanthe* Overture, save through a crack. The Brahms Third Symphony was a dream of loveliness and equilibrium. It is the best built, the most continuous of Brahms's symphonies; and it contains, on the whole, the best melodic material of the four. With no weakness of its structure to conceal and no gracelessness in its musical content to disturb the clarity of its message, it offered Mr. Stock occasion for one of those rare and blessed readings in which the music seems to play itself. Especially the end movements, the first and the last, floated on a Viennese lilt, pastoral, poetic, and effortlessly convincing. The passage in the finale was particularly happy where the wind plays sustained harmonic progressions which the violins caress with almost inaudible tendrils of sound, little wiggly figures that dart like silent goldfish around a rock.

Till Eulenspiegel was merry, though perhaps a trifle discontinuous. Its prankiness, however, was light and gay and nearer by far to the humor of its author than those weighty readings we sometimes hear that make it sound like the ponderous pleasantries of a machine-gun.

Mr. Harris's *American Creed* invites kidding, as all of his programistically prefaced works do. If we take his music as he offers it, however, we risk refusing a quite good thing. No composer in the world, not even in Italy or Germany, makes such shameless use of patriotic feelings to advertise his product. One would think, to read his prefaces, that he had been awarded by God, or at least by popular vote, a monopolistic privilege of expressing our nation's deepest ideals and highest aspirations. And when the piece so advertised turns out to be mostly not very clearly orchestrated schoolish counterpoint and a quite skimpy double fugue (neither of which has any American connotation whatsoever), one is tempted to put the whole thing down as insincere and a bad joke.

The truth, however, is other. Mr. Harris, though the bearer of no exceptional melodic gifts and the possessor of no really thorough musical schooling, has an unquenchable passion to know and to use all the procedures of musical composition. He has pondered over the medieval French melodic line and over the problem of continuous (non-repeating) melodic development, and he has come by this road to understand where the crucial problem lies in America's musical coming-of-age. That problem would seem to be how shall we absorb all of European musical culture rather than merely that current in Vienna between the years 1750 and 1850. Harris has learned by meditation and hard work that if we expect to produce music worthy to rank with that of the Viennese masters we must go through a selective evolution comparable to that which took place in Europe for at least three centuries before the miracle of Vienna occurred.

He knows that musical material, even folklore material, is as international as musical form and syntax, that localism is no more than one man's colorful accent. He knows this so well that he avoids, as though it were of the devil, any colorful accent whatsoever. He puts his musical effort on serious problems of material and of form. He does not always get anywhere in his music; but it is serious music, much more serious music than his blurbs would lead one to believe.

He is monotonous in his material and in his form. (All his pieces begin alike.) But every now and then something really happens. It happened last night in the closing pages of both movements of his *Creed*. It was unexpected, original (in spite of the Stravinsky allusion), and beautiful. And it had exactly as much to do with America as mountains or mosquitoes or childbirth have, none of which is anybody's property and none of which has any ethnic significance whatsoever.

November 21, 1940

Community Orchestra

PIONEER VALLEY SYMPHONY, *Harold Alexander Leslie*, conductor, on April 26 at The Auditorium, Northfield Seminary, Northfield, Massachusetts, performing Haydn's Symphony No. 2 ("London"); Dvořák's Symphony No. 5 ("From the New World"), and short works by Mendelssohn and Humperdinck.

PIONEER VALLEY is a name employed locally to designate that portion of the Connecticut River valley that lies above Northampton and below the Vermont border. It is agriculturally and industrially prosperous. Tobacco, apples, and the manufacture of precision tools are the sources of its livelihood and the economic bases of its culture. It is the seat of at least three (that I know of) residential secondary schools of national repute. Through its proximity to Smith College at Northampton and to the University of Vermont at Burlington its residents are in constant touch with the major intellectual tradition. It has no submerged proletariat and no millionaire residential colony. The valley comes as near to being an integrated community, both socially and intellectually, as any district I know of in this part of the United States, excepting perhaps certain communities in New York State and in Pennsylvania that are wholly organized about a religious faith.

Three years ago Pioneer Valley caught the symphony-orchestra bug. An ambitious young violinist from Greenfield, the valley's metropolis, organized in the fall of 1939 a Young People's Symphony. Finding that there was more interest in concerted musical practice than this organization could satisfy, he got together the following season an adult group also. Managerial problems were handled during the first season by the Kiwanis Club of Greenfield. This last season the Pioneer Valley Symphony Association has managed itself. Its year's budget was $2,500. All but $500 of this has been met by the sale of tickets.

The orchestra consists of seventy-five to eighty musicians. They rehearse in Greenfield, coming from considerable distances weekly for that purpose. Those for whom the trip would constitute a financial strain receive mileage. The personnel is drawn from all walks of life. The organizer and conductor, Mr. Harold Leslie, is a Greenfield boy, a graduate of the New England Conservatory and a pupil of Dr. Koussevitzky. Five public concerts have been given this season, three in Greenfield, one in Northfield, and one in Brattleboro.

I heard the concert in Northfield last Saturday night. The program was distinguished, the playing admirable. Mr. Leslie is obviously a conductor of talent and a musician of sound knowledge. He makes no show of temperament, but his conducting gestures are obeyed. He achieves correct orchestral balances and a nice homogeneity of tone. He read all the works with complete clarity and with real musical comprehension. Rarely have I heard an amateur orchestral concert so glowing with musical life. It was even played in tune. His orchestra, his audience, and himself were all as clearly representative of the New England musical tradition as anything could be.

That tradition has always been a sound one. New England is the only region of the United States where music has been for a hundred and fifty years integrated and incorporated with the whole intellectual tradition, where music has been taught and practiced as a form of communication and not as a special activity. As a result, New England and a few communities farther west that are its cultural progeny have provided most of the backbone for whatever musical tradition we have that is transmissible as a part of our whole intellectual tradition.

It is not accident that has given to the Boston Symphony its unique role in American musical life of the last forty years. It is not accident that enabled Dr. Archibald Davison and the Harvard Glee Club to reform choral style and repertory in the United States during the 1920's. It is not accident that Boston has turned out so many well-schooled composers, from Lowell

Mason to Walter Piston. Nor is it quite by accident that the upper middle region of the Connecticut River valley should go about following the national fad for symphonic exercise in such a sound and sensible manner as it has.

Whether the expansion of orchestral interest that has caused the founding of some 30,000 symphony orchestras in the United States during the depression decade will survive this new decade so inauspiciously inaugurated with wars and rumors of wars I could not prophesy. But I am quite certain that any community feeling an urge toward such exercise would do well to observe the results, artistic and social, achieved in two years by the Pioneer Valley Symphony Association. I grant you, of course, that few communities have such natural advantages to start with in the form of cultural and social unity plus complete access to the best in intellectual and musical tradition.

April 29, 1941

It's About Time

NBC SYMPHONY ORCHESTRA, *Arturo Toscanini*, conductor, yesterday afternoon in Studio 8-H, Radio City, performing four American works: C. M. Loeffler's *Memories of My Childhood*, Paul Creston's Choric Dance No. 2, Morton Gould's *A Lincoln Legend*, and George Gershwin's *Rhapsody in Blue*. Soloists: *Earl Wild*, piano, and *Benny Goodman*, clarinet.

MR. TOSCANINI has played four American pieces in a row. He did it yesterday afternoon at a concert given before an invited audience in Studio 8-H, Radio City, the program being broadcast as the season's first of the NBC Symphony Orchestra. Whether this conductor, in his whole American career, which covers well over thirty years, has formerly played that much American music all together I am not sure. But undeniably his previous encouragement of local art has been microscopic. Well, it's never too late to mend. And yesterday's gesture, which one hopes is the beginning of some fuller amends, was gratefully received by a large hand-picked audience.

It was handsomely carried out, too, with all the attention to detail and careful effort to understand the spirit of musical works that are characteristic of Mr. Toscanini's conducting. If the renditions were not the most beautiful one could imagine, that is probably due to the fact that the NBC orchestra is not the finest instrumental group in the world. It plays with attention, as all radio orchestras do; and some of the soloists are first-class. But the ensemble is far from homogeneous, and nowhere is there much extra beauty of tone. Also there were not yesterday enough strings to balance the brass and percussion, so that the tuttis all sounded clattery. Nevertheless, the renditions, if not especially lovely, were at all times spirited, neat, and snappy.

Loeffler's *Memories of My Childhood* is old-fashioned impressionism of the Franco-Bostonian school. It is full of trick orchestration, and its contrapuntal texture is respectable. It is literate music-writing, but it doesn't get off the ground. It meanders gracefully without ever taking flight.

Morton Gould's *Lincoln Legend* takes the air a little better, but it is always having to make emergency landings in swampy places. After sitting on some vaguely Middle Western landscape for a time, it gets off to quite a promising joyride with *John Brown's Body* and *The Old Grey Mare*; but a lack of something necessary constantly pulls it back to earth. It next does some desultory hedge-hopping and then finally bogs down not far from where it started. It, too, is full of trick orchestration, though less objectionably than other works I have heard by this composer.

Paul Creston's Choric Dance No. 2 sounds to me like a fine piece. The material is interesting, the development of it imaginative, the rhythm far from banal, and the sentiment sustained. His instrumentation is sonorous, well calculated, and appropriate. The work has atmosphere, too, and personality. It sounds like a choric dance. It does not sound like somebody's memories of his musical education.

Gershwin's *Rhapsody in Blue* is a modern classic. It has stood tough treatment from lots of people, and it is still a beautiful and gay work. It got tough treatment yesterday, from Mr. Goodman's opening lick to Mr. Toscanini's final wallop. Goodman established a tone of high virtuosity. Mr. Wild, the piano soloist, carried this on and added an affetuoso radio manner that alternated brilliant and violent execution of the hotcha passages with a studied and rather boring rubato in the lyrical ones that made one wish he would stop fooling around and let the show get on. Mr. Toscanini didn't have a chance to do much to the piece till the song-like theme with horn accompaniment came in.

Mistaking this for Tchaikovsky (it does sound rather like *Romeo and Juliet*), he leaned on it heavily and then began building up a Warner Brothers finale. It all came off like a ton of bricks. It was the *Rhapsody in Blue* all right, as what rendition isn't? But it was as far from George's own way of playing the piece as one could imagine. George played it straight, kept the rhythm going, even in the passages of free recitation, which he treated as comments on the more animated parts, not as interruptions of them. He didn't moon around, and he didn't get brutal.

I don't expect every artist to do every piece just as the author used to. If a work is any good, it can stand lots of mishandling and lots of reinterpreting. But I was a little sorry yesterday to hear this gay, sweet, rhapsodical number treated to a routine glamorizing that rubbed all the bloom off it and left its surface as shining and as glittery as a nickel-plated Apollo Belvedere.

November 2, 1942

Boston's Pops

EVERY CITY has some kind of summer concert series offering a mixed repertory of music old and new from which the lighter veins of composition are not excluded. New York takes its Philharmonic concerts at the Lewisohn Stadium without much admixture of popular tunes. The Goldman Band provides us our dosage necessary of military marches, of selections from operetta, of Viennese waltzes, of popular overtures and suites no longer considered respectable to hear at two-dollar concerts or even at the Stadium.

Boston's particular version of all this is its famous Pop Concerts. These take place in Symphony Hall with the full Boston Symphony Orchestra playing (renamed for ten weeks each year "The Boston Pops Orchestra") and Arthur Fiedler leading. (I should like to add his name to those of Smallens and Barlow as excellent and thoroughly experienced American conductors.) For the Pops season all the seats are removed from the main floor and the surface of this made level so that it can be filled with tables. Food and drink is offered reasonably. The balcony seats are sold to non-consuming listeners for seventy-five, fifty, and twenty-five cents.

This set-up seems normal enough, though no other American city has ever been able to reproduce it. What the Boston customers get is all the pleasures of a Continental café plus a concert of the Boston Symphony Orchestra. There are no outdoor noises or bugs. The air-conditioning is mild. Smoking is permitted. The service is silent and satisfactory. The repertory is uninhibited. The house is packed with music-lovers of all ages, and there are lots of young men with their girls. This is the fifty-sixth season of the series and Mr. Fiedler's twelfth as conductor.

The charm of these evenings is partly due to food and tobacco and democratic assembly and partly, of course, to the music. Really it is due to the contiguity of all these. But the music itself has a charm quite rare and unexpected these days that is due to the application of the Boston Symphony's excellent musicianship to a whole range of musical repertory that seldom gets properly played at all. The standard symphonies are always getting themselves well played. The Sousa marches and the more popular overtures occasionally get themselves rendered well enough. But there is a whole section of the musical library that seems destined either to constantly inadequate execution or to complete neglect. I mean pieces like Handel's Largo, the waltzes of Strauss and Waldteufel, Schubert's *Serenade*, Saint-Saëns's *The Animals' Carnival*, Chabrier's *España*, Tchaikovsky's *Marche Slave* and *1812*, and many another work perennially loved by all.

This repertory, known to the music-publishing trades as "popular classics and semi-classics," is the bridge between simple song and the high art realms of music. It is what enables everybody to understand Beethoven and Mozart. It is the door through which young people enter into the magic domain of musical comprehension. It is infinitely touching to hear it played with loving care by such a band and listened to with lively ears by such an alert audience as Boston's.

A week ago I wandered into Symphony Hall and after some difficulty (for the house was sold out, as usual) obtained entry. The orchestra was playing the waltz scene from *Faust*. I have known the piece, as everyone else has, since I was a baby. For thirty years I haven't cared much for it. I only realized the other night that it has been at least that long since I have heard it well played. Even at the opera houses they rarely use enough strings. And besides, one isn't always willing to sit through *Faust* just to hear the Prelude and the Waltz and the final Trio. At the Pops it was perfect. So was Tchaikovsky's *Nutcracker Suite* that followed. Hearing this light but charming music from the back of the hall played with all the tonal beauty and dynamic perspective that it was intended to have, I was carried back in fancy to the brilliance of the great opera houses of thirty and more years ago. And I remembered Igor Stravinsky's description of what he had hoped to do in his ballet scores, *Le Baiser de la Fée* and *Jeu de Cartes.* "I wanted," he said, "to evoke the memory of the brilliance and the charm of the ballet spectacles of our former Imperial Opera."

Also on the program was a selection of favorite melodies from Victor Herbert. The audience was visibly transported to remembrance of light-opera days. There was also a piece about a mosquito that had to be repeated. And a set of variations on *Yankee Doodle* by Mr. Morton Gould. The latter purported to be a swing version, but only one chorus really got off the ground. That was this citizen's opinion. The rest of the audience enjoyed the piece enough to demand its repetition. But even this crochety spoil-sport is glad to have heard the work. Mr. Fiedler, in the course of putting some of every kind of music on every program, plays a great deal of serious music by living composers. He even commissions new works from time to time. Walter Piston's ballet *The Incredible Flutist* was the result of such a commission; it was given its first and, to my knowledge, only choreographic rendition at those concerts.

Koussevitzky rehearses the orchestra three times for each of his programs, and he prepares twenty-four programs during his season of thirty weeks. Fiedler has two rehearsals for every seven programs, and he plays about sixty-five concerts (with very little repeating in them) during the Pops season of ten weeks. That means that familiar symphonies and such, as at our own Stadium concerts, rarely get rehearsed at all. New pieces and revivals (I noticed Weber's *Abu Hassan* Overture on the bill for last week) get read through. This seems to be sufficient, even for most of the gramophone recordings. For the Pops Orchestra,

before a ruling of the American Federation of Musicians forbade further recordings by members of the Boston Symphony
Orchestra, has long been a favorite with record-buyers.

The Boston Pops are really a lovely success story. They have
no budget troubles. They have no audience troubles. They
have no program troubles. They just play everything and play
it beautifully, and everybody loves them and comes every night
to hear them and to eat sandwiches with beer or to sip cool
punches and juleps in the friendly ambiance of good old Symphony Hall.

June 8, 1941

Band Music

INELUCTABLE is the charm of the military band. Frequently
incorrect, however, is the military denomination. One uses it,
lacking a proper term, for ensembles like that which plays of
a summer evening in Central and Prospect Parks under the
leadership of Messrs. Goldman and son. From a military band,
strictly speaking, one expects a possibility of ambulation not
easily concordant with the use of the tubular chimes and of the
Italian harp, though no doubt our new motorized armies, did
they not consider the noises of engine and of caterpillar tread
appropriate and sufficient music for their parades, might solve
the problem of the portative harp and chime as neatly and as
elegantly as the cavalry long ago solved that of the kettledrum.
More classical, of course, is the practice whereby really military
outfits exercising in the field leave behind them in barracks all
instruments of unwarlike appearance and symbolism, though
they hesitate not to employ these indoors for celebration of the
peaceable and sedentary concert rite.

Wholly peaceable and sedentary of a summer night is our
municipality's pride, the Goldman Band. Equally peaceable is
the crowd, both sedentary and deambulant, that assists at these
musical ceremonies on the Mall. The opening concert of the
season last Wednesday night was almost too peaceable for my
taste. I should have liked more music in the military style and
less duplication of symphonic repertory. It is scarcely worth

while going out to the Mall to hear Tchaikovsky's *Romeo and Juliet* or the Sibelius *Finlandia*, both of which are plugged all winter at indoor concerts and on the radio and both of which sound infinitely better, if we must have them in the summer, played with strings by the Philharmonic at the Lewisohn Stadium.

The question of repertory for band concerts is a vexing one. It is not that the general public won't take high-class music. If that were true there would be no problem. The truth is that New York's proletarian public, which is both musical and highly literate, will take any amount of symphonic repertory or of anything else. It seems to me the duty of all musical organizations to play for this avid and absorptive public all of that organization's best and most characteristic literature. We do not put up with string quartets playing transcriptions of piano music nor with organists who insist on playing Wagner. Why military bands should fill up nine tenths of their programs with versions of symphonic stuff I do not know.

I know, of course, that the library of original band music is not large. It consists chiefly of marches, though these constitute in themselves a unique repertory. There are also a certain number of "characteristic" or "genre" pieces by bandmasters, most of which are too cute for current tastes. There is also the further and much larger field of what we call "popular" music. Such music must naturally be performed in "arrangements"; but since it is never played anywhere except in arrangements, it is legitimate to consider all arrangements of it as equally appropriate to the instruments for which they are made. Such compositions frequently contain, indeed, writing for wind ensemble that is in every way idiomatic, sonorous, and satisfactory.

I am not protesting against the *use* of *arrangements*, in so far as that term means free versions of familiar melodies. I protest against the *abuse* of *transcriptions*, by which I mean the translation to other instrumental media of works that are both satisfactory and easily available in their correct form. The fad for orchestral transcriptions of organ music and other eighteenth-century matter is so far a harmless one; it serves chiefly to prove the classical culture of conductors and of modernist composers. It does not yet occupy the major part of our orchestral

programs. Band programs are nowadays almost wholly occupied with transcriptions of orchestral music. To their detriment,
I think.

One can forgive band leaders for playing the *Lucia di Lammermoor* sextet and the Overture to *William Tell*. The snobbery that has eliminated these admirable works and others like
them from the programs of our two-dollar concerts has left us
no place to hear them save on the Mall. I fear rather that any
extension of symphonic snobbery to these frankly popular circumstances may end by eliminating from our lives altogether
the repertory of popular "classics" and "semi-classics" that gave
to band concerts formerly such charm and such power of sentimental appeal.

Among popular "classics," or among the "semi-classics," if
you prefer, that it is pleasant to hear at band concerts I place all
selections from the works of Richard Wagner. Not that these
works are unavailable at the opera. It is rather that many familiar
passages from them, having long ago extracted themselves like
nut meats from their theatrical context, lead today as independent an existence as that of any Italian overture or air. They are
constantly being played (slightly transformed) at orchestral as
well as at band concerts. I find the band versions rather more
satisfactory, on the whole. The absence of violins removes that
juicy-fruit quality that is so monotonous in the orchestral versions. This is less bothersome in the theater than at a concert
because there are usually fewer strings and because the placement of the brass instruments throws these last into still further
relief. In the versions for military band everything takes on what
seems to me ideal Wagnerian proportions. The brass becomes a
true *harmonie*, or village band, and all the woodwind and percussive sonorities simply outgrowths and accents of this, like a
daisy's petals. The out-of-doors gives to the music's substance,
too, a healthiness that is far from unbecoming. It ceases to demand from us the routine emotional responses that it seems to
need for survival in the concert hall. It stands on its own feet for
once as perfectly good music in theatrical vein, and not devoid
of a certain Teutonic dignity.

Everything, however, is trimming and filling at a band concert, except the military marches. These are the historical reason
for its existence, and they comprise the only repertory that is

unique to it. That repertory, which is neither small nor monotonous, contains almost the whole memorable work of a great and characteristically American master, the late John Philip Sousa. It comprises as well many fine pieces from the pen of Mr. Edwin Franko Goldman, our band's elder leader. It was nice to hear young Goldman's excellent transcription of Stravinsky's *Fire Bird* Lullaby and Finale. It was nice to hear Henry Cowell's original piece for band, called *Shoonthree*. It was charming indeed to hear two movements of Haydn's Trumpet Concerto executed with neatness and delicacy on the cornet by Mr. Leonard B. Smith. One sat through the Wagner with toleration of its open-air qualities and through the Tchaikovsky and the Bach and the Sibelius with what was already getting to be patience. What one really brought home from the evening was exactly what one had gone for, two marches by Goldman *père*.

Everything else, excepting Mr. Cowell's piece, can be heard to better advantage at the Stadium and during the season's course certainly will be. I find it a little excessive to have to sit through so much frankly non-essential repertory in order to hear two short works from the band's essential repertory. I do not consider that the replaying of all that classical truck shows a raising of the Goldman Band's cultural standard. Quite the contrary. It shows submission to the plugging procedures of the Appreciation Racket. The cultural result is the same as what happens to cooking when farmers stop eating what they grow because somebody on the air has told them nationally advertised canned goods are superior to the home-grown pea.

June 22, 1941

Landscape with Music

THE HOLLYWOOD BOWL is more agreeable to the eye than to the ear. Its seating space is like a fan laid against a Spanish hillside. Its slow rise in elevation from band shell to top seats is considerable, but this is continued in such a gentle slope by the concave mountain behind that the scalloped top of the land seems rather to finish off the architect's design than to enclose it. The natural advantages of the site become thus more gracefully protective than imposing; and the whole scene takes on, right in the middle of a suburb, an effect at once of openness and of isolation. That intimacy with the empyrean which Nature and the designer have offered here would be even more inspiring if it were not for cool evenings and heavy dews that turn the mind toward sweaters and perhaps a flannel belly-band.

"Symphonies Under the Stars" is the grandiose, if somewhat supersibilant, title of the concerts held in this spacious locale throughout July and August and into September. The Philharmonic Orchestra of Los Angeles constitutes the executant musical body. Guest conductors ranging from Erno Rapee through Bruno Walter and Sir Thomas Beecham lead it. Artists as solid in popular favor and as diversified in musical allegiance as Artur Rubinstein, Oscar Levant, and Gracie Allen add star quality. Programs range from the folksy to the standard symphonic type, Sunday representing the lowest common denominator of musical initiation and Thursday (servants' night out) being reserved for conductors and repertory of the intellectual, or classic, tradition. The acoustics of the place are not very good, and the orchestra did not impress me in one hearing as being quite up to Eastern or to Middle Western standards of musical refinement. But the shell of the Bowl is charming, and its public is amiable; moreover, programs are comprehensive and the visiting artists distinguished. What it seems chiefly to lack for full perfection is first-class musical sounds.

At the opening concert of the season last Sunday the program was frankly popular and, in honor of the Fourth of July, wholly of American authorship. MacDowell, Victor Herbert, Gershwin, Cadman, Sousa, and Handy (by *The St. Louis Blues*) were the standard composers represented. Ferde Grofé, Louis Alter, Morton Gould, Rodgers and Hart, and Meredith Willson—a light-theater and radio group—made up the younger contingent. There were, in addition, a medley of service songs (sung by a male chorus of ten or twelve voices plus a young lady from the night clubs, named Ginny Simms) and a work of anonymous origin entitled "Concerto for Index Finger" (of which hand was not stated), executed on a toy pianoforte by the ever delightful Gracie Allen, Mr. Whiteman conducting.

Mr. Grofé conducted his own *March for Americans* (What could the title mean? Is it orthopedic or merely exclusive?) and a movement from his *Grand Canyon Suite*. Mr. Grofé's musical intention is of a mild order, and his conducting last Sunday was not noticeably effective. Captain Willson led two movements from his symphony, *The Missions of California*, and later Sousa's *The Stars and Stripes Forever*. His own pieces, which were harmonious and faintly funereal, like the religious music in films, were neatly conducted. And his *Stars and Stripes* was a rousingly straightforward performance in the best military style I have heard employed during this war in any symphonic rendition of that superb work.

The rest of the evening belonged to Mr. Whiteman, except for what was taken of it by Miss Simms for the rendering (with crooning cadenzas) of William C. Handy's masterpiece, *The St. Louis Blues*. Miss Simms is apparently not aware that the inhabitants of that city pronounce its final "s" and that the omission of the auxiliary verb "have" in "would not gone" is both traditional and correct. Mr. Whiteman accompanied her admirably.

He did more, however, than accompany a soloist for Gershwin's *Rhapsody in Blue*. He gave the work shape and ease, in spite of Mr. Ray Turner's rather poundy piano-playing. Spontaneity is the charm of that piece, and spontaneity is about the last quality one ever encounters nowadays in its performance. It has become tense and violent and assertive. Mr. Whiteman brought it back, so far as he could with uncooperative pianism, to its original mood of meditation and (as the title says) rhapsody.

It is, of course, permissible to make any interpretation one likes of any piece. Nobody is ever patently right about music. But many musical renditions are patently wrong. Leopold Stokowski and George Balanchine, for example, were clearly in error when they fancied Bach's *Matthäuspassion* to be an appropriate accompaniment for pantomime. I believe it to be incorrect and ineffective, when conducting the *Rhapsody in Blue*, to concentrate on climax-building at the expense of spontaneous lyricism. Efforts to make *William Tell* music out of it and Holy Grail music are equally, in my opinion, doomed to failure.

As an example of what I consider a misreading of both the composer's thought and the work's expressive possibilities, I quote from the *Hollywood Bowl Magazine*, official annotated program book of the "Symphonies Under the Stars":

"Gershwin's 'Rhapsody in Blue' comes in striking contrast to the Willson music from the idyllic valleys of California. There is a passionate cry for deliverance from the cement-and-steel canyons of New York City in this deeply emotional, nervously actuated rhapsody. The bells echoed in the Gershwin opus are those of the Elevated and the Underground, are workshift bells all of which Gershwin's New Yorkers, for whom this rhapsody is written, try to forget.

"It is almost as if Gershwin were voicing all the frustrations and longings of the men and women of twentieth-century New York, in one frantically sustained almost deliriously self-forgetting heart cry for release from reality."

It is not George Gershwin's writing, it seems to me, that should be called "frantically sustained almost deliriously self-forgetting," but rather that of Mr. Bruno David Ussher, author of the program notes. Mr. Whiteman, for whose musical organization the piece actually was written, has a sounder idea both of its feeling content and of how to sustain its continuity without getting frantic than any other conductor I have ever heard lead it.

July 11, 1943

Music at the Golden Gate

SAN FRANCISCO is better off for music during the summer than most other American cities. At the moment there is fare, and plenty of it, for all appetites. The proper bars are full of sweet swing, the improper ones of hotter stuff. There are, as musical shows, something with Ethel Waters, called *Laugh Time*, and the Ballet Theater, both playing indoors. There are popular opera and orchestral concerts playing (though not every day, absolutely free, nevertheless) outdoors at the Sigmund Stern Grove. There are military bands around, also. Two major string quartets are operating in the Bay region. The London and the Budapest Quartets divide their work between, respectively, Berkeley (at the University of California) and San Francisco and Oakland (at Mills College), each giving eight or more concerts. There are solo recitals, too, with modernistic programs. And there are weekly concerts of hot music at the C.I.O. Hot Jazz Hall.

The outdoor concerts, so far as I have heard them, are, just as in Los Angeles, more notable for the beauty of their locale (all grass and trees and family picnics and no gravel or concrete anywhere) than for any especial distinction of execution or of repertory. The Budapest Quartet, however, is in fine form. The London's work is even more elegant, with John Pennington, William Primrose and C. Warwick Evans at their old places, and Laurent Halleux replacing the late Thomas Petrie as second violin. At a concert of French music given the other evening in the art museum, Virginia Morley and Livingston Gearhart revealed themselves to be not only a top-flight team of duo-pianists but musicians who understand what modern music is about. They played two great works that one rarely hears, Stravinsky's Concerto for two pianos alone and Debussy's three-movement rhapsody, *En Blanc et Noir*. It was equally a pleasure to hear serious music written for two pianos and to hear two pianists playing any music as if that were a serious occupation and not a form of badminton.

The Hot Jazz Concerts are a result of some lectures delivered last spring by Rudi Blesh at the San Francisco Museum of Art. These were illustrated by records from Mr. Blesh's own collection, as well as by non-processed executions. For the latter there was brought here from Louisiana no less an artist than Willie "Bunk" Johnson, considered by many the finest of all trumpet-players. Johnson was an original member of the earliest hot group known, the Original Superior Band, organized in 1891 in New Orleans. For many years its leader, he is celebrated in the histories of hot music not only for his integrity as an artist but for his mastery of that imperious trumpet tone chiefly familiar to laymen nowadays through the work of his pupil Louis Armstrong.

At the closing of the lecture series many lovers of the hot wished to keep Mr. Johnson around, but the local musicians' union, which, it would seem, is not favorable to the hot style, has made it difficult for him to work. Negroes and whites are not allowed to play together, for one thing, and the informal participation in public music-making of visiting artists is forbidden, for another. There is, moreover, some kind of general ruling against jam sessions. Mr. Harry Bridges, regional director of the C.I.O. and long a patron of cultural activities (the San Francisco Symphony Orchestra is playing for his membership next week), came to the rescue of hot art by arranging a place for it in his own union clubrooms. As a result, Bunk Johnson's Hot Seven play every Sunday afternoon all afternoon in an auditorium now known as the C.I.O. Hot Jazz Hall under the management of the Hot Jazz Society of San Francisco. Persons not members of this society can join at the door if properly introduced. Last Sunday there were perhaps five hundred people, a youngish but not adolescent audience consisting of well-dressed working people, professors, a goodly number of service men, both enlisted and commissioned, and one pretty young lady in a welder's uniform, complete with metal hat. Dancing was permitted in the back of the hall, and drinks were available in an adjoining bar.

The music was executed in the style known as New Orleans. The bass, a tuba, played straightforwardly and right on the beat. The drums indulged in no fancy work. Neither did the banjo. Piano, clarinet, trumpet, and trombone improvised with the greatest freedom but also with an astonishing sobriety. Nobody tried to show how fast he could play or how high. At no point was there any attempt to swing the beat or to fake a fury. Neither did any soloist try to conceal the tune. Variations were developed musically out of it and never left its expression for mere flambuoyancy, though Billy Singleton, who played piano as guest in several numbers, did plenty of expert work in thirds and chromatic octaves. Bob Barton, a youngster, played trombone with a fine dirty tone. Ellis Horne, the clarinet, is an accomplished mature artist and no show-off.

"Bunk" Johnson himself is an artist of delicate imagination, meditative in style rather than flashy, and master of the darkest trumpet tone I have ever heard. He is also the greatest master of "blue," or off-pitch, notes it has been my pleasure to encounter. The degrees of his deviation from normal pitch are infinite, and the taste with which he exploits this variety merits no less a word than impeccable. His timbres, his intonations, and his melodic invention are at all times expressive, at all times reasonable, and at all times completely interesting. His work takes on, in consequence, and so does that of those working with him, depth, ease and lucidity. Nothing could be less sentimental or speak more sincerely from the heart, less jittery or move around more freely. Certainly no music was ever less confused.

The basic rhythm of his band is so solid and so plain that its effect on players and public alike is the opposite of that nervous exasperation that is frequently a result of jazz performance. It stills, rather, the nerves and allows the mind free play in that purely auditory perception of feeling that is the alpha and the omega of music. I suspect Mr. Bridges is right. This sort of music is as cultural an activity as any and more so than most. Certainly it is more rarely to be encountered at a high degree of purity than the symphonic stuff. Both kinds of music, of course, are deplorably commercialized these days. Its purity, nevertheless, a noncommercial quality, is wherein any music's cultural value lies.

August 8, 1943

The Philharmonic Centenary

LETTERS have been arriving numerously of late protesting against the meager plans announced by the Philharmonic-Symphony Orchestra for the celebration of its hundredth anniversary next year. Why these protests should be sent to me rather than to the directors of the Philharmonic I do not know, unless perhaps it is thought that the directors of that body are impervious to suggestion and complaint, and my correspondents hope to seduce me into waging through the press a campaign doomed apparently to failure otherwise.

The centennial festivities, as announced in the press of Saturday, March 15, consist in relieving the monotony of Mr. Barbirolli's tenure, which runs for one more year, in very much the same way as has been done this year, by a parade of guest conductors. These would be Stokowski, Walter, Mitropoulos, Rodzinski, Goossens, Fritz Busch, and possibly Toscanini and Koussevitzky. The Old Man had not yet replied to the invitation; and Mr. Petrillo, president of the National Federation of Musicians, had not yet given formal consent for the Philharmonic musicians to play under the good Doctor, who is not a member of the union, though unofficial advices from union headquarters seemed to indicate that such consent would be granted without difficulty.

The chief complaints against the inadequacy of this program

are two: it honors no conductor of American birth or training, and it commissions no new compositions, American or other.

I must say that if I had been making out the list I should have put in Alexander Smallens and Howard Barlow, both American-trained and both interesting conductors; and I should have preferred Pierre Monteux and Thomas Beecham among the available European-trained to either Goossens or Busch. Under no circumstances, however, should I have made out any such list at all. A string of guest conductors, though obviously the first thing the Philharmonic management would think of, is the last thing the Philharmonic musicians need. These have been so thoroughly guest-conducted for twenty years now that they have become temperamental, erratic, and difficult as only first-class musicians can become when subjected to every known variety of browbeating and wheedling. The best birthday present the Philharmonic could offer itself and us would be a good permanent full-time conductor, somebody worthy of the job and capable of assuming all its musical responsibilities. It's no use saying such conductors don't exist. I know three out of work and at least three more who could be stepped up most deservingly from provincial posts.

As for the commissioning of musical works, both Boston and Chicago seem to have picked pretty good musical values, plus doing themselves honor, in so celebrating their fiftieth anniversaries. I hadn't really expected anything like that of the Philharmonic; but I am disappointed, all the same, at its not having been done. I hadn't expected it because I am a little cynical about that institution.

As I pointed out earlier in the season, it doesn't play a very important part in New York's intellectual life; nor has it since the days of Gustav Mahler. It was, to say the least, quiescent under Stransky from 1911 to 1922. From 1922 on, under Mengelberg and Toscanini, each of whom ranked as a regular conductor of the Philharmonic for about ten years, but who really worked here only part of the time each season, there were some brilliant performances of classic works. The whole weight of these men's prestige was thrown against living music. Guest conductors performed certain new scores on tolerance; Boston, Philadel-phia, and Cleveland brought most of them for us to hear; local societies were organized for the exposition and dissemination of others. The Philharmonic office in the 1930's made no concealment of its position. The maestro did not "like" modern music; he was under no obligation to conduct any of it at the Philharmonic. Mr. Barbirolli has played more new music than Toscanini, but little of it has been significant or striking in any way. He has been the center of much controversy, virtually none of it concerned with the æsthetics of musical composition.

Thus it has come about that the Philharmonic-Symphony Orchestra, both personnel and management, though pretty much up to the minute on conducting, has worked for thirty years on the sidelines of creative music—that is, of music as she is really writ. The personnel is not entirely on the outside, because the boys do play other music other places; and they all get brought up to date a bit summers at the Stadium, where the repertory is livelier. Yes, and Arthur Judson has other managerial irons in the fire than the Philharmonic, quite a few. But still the fact is that the current Philharmonic tradition, the tradition in force ever since its merging with the National Symphony in 1921, is one of fine instrumentalism and fancy conducting, not of intimate collaboration with the creators of music. And that is why I permit myself a certain cynicism in reply when people write or ask me why new works are not being commissioned to fête the hundredth year. The old Philharmonic is a tricky bird. Give her a good master and she'll lay you golden eggs. But don't expect those golden eggs to hatch live goslings. Above all, don't expect an organization that has for thirty years either ignored the existence of the more vigorous movements in contemporary music or snubbed them ostentatiously to suddenly start giving money away for their encouragement.

Not that a sudden change is inconceivable, provided some more fundamental change were to take place in the organization's musical policy. But this year, at least, the Philharmonic has shown, indeed, very little sign of having a musical policy. Each concert has seemed more or less fortuitous. Mr. Barbirolli, who is supposed to be the conductor, has been replaced by guests for nearly one third of the concerts. A great deal of contemporary music has been played, for a change, but selected, it would seem, from a grab-bag. Two world-famous violinists have both played the same concerto in the same season. I have found little logic in the program-making, whether the works played were ancient or modern. This applies equally to those of the conductor and to those of his guests.

It is classical to celebrate a feast by giving way for one day to one's besetting weakness. But, ladies and gentlemen who direct the destinies of the Philharmonic, do you really think another whole year of it is without serious risk? Your conductor has already accepted for this season what amounts to the status of a guest. He has accepted for next year to be one among eight. That means that for two years the musicians will have had no conductor, no unified command, hence no real discipline. For twenty years, they haven't had much, I admit; but once a year Mengelberg or the Old Man turned up and told them what was what. Barbirolli was all right, too, I suppose, as long as he conducted, or was allowed to conduct, his own orchestra. But do you really think the temperamental Philharmonic, if left for a whole year without any conductor of its own at all, won't blow sky-high one day when some equally temperamental guest says "Boo" to it?

Musical composition has gone on for some years now with small blessings from the Philharmonic; and though I could wish things were otherwise, it would be against nature to expect much more right now. But I do think, birthdays aside, that that venerable institution is tempting Providence to go on playing around with guest conductors when what she really needs is a lord and master who will take some of the jumpiness out of her and put her to work on a five-year plan of some kind, building something in America's musical life that would be worthy of her history and of the city that loves her and supports her and complains about her.

What would such a plan be? Nothing less than the building of an audience for American music and the building of an American repertory for that audience. Nothing is easier. Half the countries in Europe have accomplished a similar thing deliberately. The technique of it is known. Nothing would be a worthier job for our Philharmonic; and, of course, it could be fantastically a success. Everybody is ready. Local audience, radio executives, national public, composers even. And the naming of an American conductor, which would be necessary, because Europeans have only the vaguest conception of what American music is about, would not present the difficulty it does when we envisage, as we do now, that problem as one of naming an American to conduct a repertory ninety-five per cent European.

I'm afraid I'm dreaming about the present I should like to give the Philharmonic, one first-class, full-time American conductor complete with five-year plan and full authority to execute it. But I may as well return to my cynicism. I cannot offer such a present. And there is about as much chance of the Philharmonic offering it to itself as there is of Toscanini conducting Schönberg's *Fünf Orchesterstücke* at an NBC broadcast.

March 23, 1941

Being Odious

PHILHARMONIC-SYMPHONY ORCHESTRA, *Bruno Walter*, conductor, last night at Carnegie Hall, performing, among other works, Emerson Whithorne's *Dream Pedlar*, Schumann's Symphony No. 3 ("Rhenish"), Mozart's Violin Concerto in D major, and Smetana's symphonic poem *Vltava (The Moldau)*. Soloist: *Joseph Szigeti*, violin.

THE WHOLE EVENING invited comparisons. Mr. Whithorne's *Dream Pedlar* invited comparison with all the pieces of similar title and texture that one has ever heard, and man and boy one has heard a lot. Writing whimsy for a hundred musicians used to be considered a proper activity for composers who were both gentlemen and scholars. Arnold Bax enjoyed a certain reputation at this in the post-war decade. Mr. Whithorne does it with skill. His music is neatly calculated and rather better knit than most.

Schumann's "Rhenish" Symphony invited dual comparison with his own non-symphonic works and with the works of the other Romantic symphonists. On both counts it comes off unfavorably. It has not the technical freedom of his pianoforte and chamber writing, and it lacks the orchestral amplitude we enjoy in the symphonic writing of many a lesser personality like Berlioz or Brahms or even Tchaikovsky. All the same, it is fine music, noble and manly and full of real tunes. It was especially a pleasure to hear it in Mr. Walter's poetic and exuberant rendition.

The Mozart Violin Concerto invited comparison with Mozart's concerts for other instruments. It is less fine music than almost any of his pianoforte concertos, for example, though the last movement is first-class. The Smetana *Moldau* reminded one of pop concerts and a whole repertory of pleasantly patriotic pieces seldom heard any more, even at pop concerts. It has a fine big tune, too.

Mr. Szigeti invites comparison with other violinistic great. His tone is not so majestic as Kreisler's, and his intonation is less impeccable than that of Heifetz. His Mozart is more interesting than that of either, though it was not at its best last night. His E-string squeaked a bit. The lower ones, especially the third and fourth, were warm and pungent, however. If he exaggerated Mozart's dynamism, as if the concerto were something in the gypsy style, he did bite into the rhythmic texture of it deeper than those artists do who take such care for keeping Mozart round and gentle and, as the swing boys would say, "sweet." The Szigeti Mozart last night, though a little out of hand, was definitely on the "hot" side. For one who vigorously objects to sweets with his meat (and Mozart is certainly meat) that was a pleasure too. It didn't come off right, but Szigeti is on a good track.

Mr. Walter invites comparison, naturally, with the others who have conducted the Philharmonic-Symphony Orchestra this season. There is a German verb, *musizieren,* which means *to make music.* It applies more clearly to Mr. Walter than to either Rodzinski or Mitropoulos. These others have their excellences and their special abilities, but they don't make as good music as Mr. Walter does.

Mr. Walter has no special trick of excellence. He is excellent all over. He is not the greatest conductor in the world, though he is a very great one. His Mozart, for instance, though justly famous for its sensible tempos and its general lack of fussiness and folderol, I consider less fine than that of Sir Thomas Beecham. His Debussy is certainly less magical than that of either Monteux or Furtwängler. And Dr. Koussevitzky can no doubt beat him at Mussorgsky, though Walter need yield to none on

German music. Take him all round, he is as fine a leader as we have heard with any orchestra this year; and the Philharmonic itself sounds better than it ever has in my memory. *Walter musiziert.* And that is a pleasure for those who like music with their concerts.

January 31, 1941

Diminishing Artistic Returns

BOSTON SYMPHONY ORCHESTRA, *Serge Koussevitzky,* conductor, last night at Carnegie Hall, performing Berlioz's *Symphonie Fantastique* and Hindemith's *Mathis der Maler.*

THERE is a point in the perfection of artistic skills beyond which further progress is without artistic value. The surface becomes so shiny that nothing else can be perceived. The Boston Symphony Orchestra has been dangerously close to that point for several years now; and if last night's concert in Carnegie Hall is typical of the orchestra's present work, one may well judge that the point of optimum precision has now been passed.

Matters of musical understanding, of stylistic penetration, and of interpretative warmth all aside—for these constitute the inner substance of music—its outer substance, sound, is wholly a matter of precision. Precisions of attack, of pitch, of color, of phrasing, of force, of blending constitute the musical amenities. Ultimate perfection in any of them is unattainable, but a reasonable degree of accuracy makes it possible for the meaning of music to be transmitted. Overmeticulousness about any of them will more often than not defeat this end.

One has heard string quartets play so carefully for beauty of tone that all the attacks became tenuous and the rhythm got lost. One has observed them so preoccupied about simultaneity of attack that the repeated split second in which the players look at one another before beginning each phrase ends by destroying the music's line. One has heard all the amenities sacrificed for a relentless rhythm or a climactic effect; and on the whole this procedure is probably less injurious to musical communication than the more delicate violences.

Some of the precisions observed by the Boston Symphony

Orchestra last night were good for the music and some were not. In both the Berlioz *Symphonie Fantastique* and the Hindemith *Mathis der Maler* the instrumental colors, the mixtures and shades of sound, were more delicately differentiated and more expressively exact than this listener has ever heard them before. But their exactitude was achieved at the price of such watchfulness that both pieces seemed lacking in coherence and in continuity. In both of them, for example, Mr. Koussevitzky took such long breaths between phrases that one forgot there was supposed to be any sequence among these.

This wide spacing of phrases, plus the use of tempos rather slower than the standard French ones, dragged the Berlioz work out a good ten minutes longer than it is accustomed to last. (Forty-six minutes is the average timing of it; fifty minutes is a long version. Koussevitzky took an hour.) The first three movements seemed interminable. I did not time the Hindemith work, but it seemed slow, gasping, and overemphatic. All this was the result of too much care about phrase attacks and instrumental blending. The attacks and the blending were incredibly precise. But the beautiful and spicy sounds we heard were less a performance *of* music by Berlioz and Hindemith than they were a performance *by* the Boston Symphony Orchestra.

February 10, 1944

The Personality of Three Orchestras

ORCHESTRAS are not wholly the product of their conductors. Their conductors train them and put them through their paces in public. But the conductor is one personality, and the orchestra is another (in private life a hundred others). A good orchestral concert is really more a duet than a domination.

Our three great Eastern ensembles, for instance—the Philadelphia, the Boston, and the New York Philharmonic—are as different from one another as the cities that created them and that forged them slowly into the image of each city's intellectual ideals. Conductors from outside have been had in to aid this formation, and a few of these have left traces of their own taste on that of the cities they have worked for. But chiefly their function has been to care for a precious musical organism, to watch over it, to perfect it in the observance of the musical amenities, and to allow it to mature according to its own nature and in accordance with its community's particular temperament. The conductor is never a static participant in such a process. He matures, too, in harmony with the community if he stays a reasonable length of time, is nourished and formed by local ideas, becomes a part of the thing to which he has contributed his special abilities.

Serge Koussevitzky and Eugene Ormandy are cases in point of my thesis. They have been ripened and refined by their association with the Boston and the Philadelphia orchestras in a way that was not predictable at all during their previous careers. It was obvious always that both would go far, but it was not indicated to prophecy that Koussevitzky, the temperamental Slav, would become a master of orchestral understatement or that Ormandy, the boyish and straightforward central European, would become a sort of specialist of delicately equilibrated orchestral sensuality. These developments, I am sure, are as legitimately creditable to environmental influence as to any previously manifested characteristics. Contact with orchestras of powerful temperament and specific orientation, as well as responsibility to cities of ancient and irreducible character— Boston, the intellectually elegant and urbane; Philadelphia, where everything, even intellectual achievement and moral pride, turns into a luxury, into a sort of sensuous awareness of social differences—contact, conflict, and collaboration between their strong European and the even stronger local traditions has given to these conductors their quality of being both the creature and the guiding hand of their own orchestras.

It is surprising (and most pleasant) to observe how two orchestras as accomplished as these can differ so completely in the kind of sounds they make. Boston makes thin sounds, like the Paris orchestras, thin and utterly precise, like golden wire and bright enamel. Nothing ever happens that isn't clear. No matter what the piece, no matter how inspired or how mistaken the conductor's understanding of it, the Boston execution is always transparent. So perfectly turned out is any of its executions that, whether becoming to the work or not, it has a way of separating itself from it. It neither conceals the work nor presents it; it walks down the street beside it, rather, very much as a piece of consummate dressmaking will sometimes do with the lady who thinks she is wearing it.

The Philadelphia sonorities are less transparent, and the tonal balance is less stable. Because the sounds that make it up are all rounder and deeper and more human. They breathe; they seem almost to have sentience. They have a tactile quality, too, like a skin you might touch; yet they are never heavy nor hot. They are warm and moist and alive compared to Boston's Swiss-watch-like mechanism. As a price of this vibrancy, however, the Philadelphia Orchestra is not always easy to conduct. It is probably the most sensitive orchestra in the world. The leader can get a fortissimo out of it by lifting a finger, and he can upset the whole balance of it by any nervousness. Boston is tougher, more independent. No matter how the conductor feels or what mistakes he may make, the orchestra always plays correctly, saves its own face and his. Philadelphia is less objective, less rigidly mannered. But at its best it gives a more touching performance, achieves a more intimate contact with its audience. Boston, for all its glacial perfection, has no intimacy at all. No matter where one sits, the music seems very far away.

Our Philharmonic is a horse of another color and one that has had far too many riders. It has been whipped and spurred for forty years by guest conductors and by famous virtuosos with small sense of responsibility about the orchestra's future or about its relation to our community's culture. It has become erratic, temperamental, undependable, and in every way difficult to handle. The sound of it has of late years been more like an industrial blast than like a musical communication. By moments there has been lovely work, but such moments have had an air of being accidental, the result of one day's well-being in the life of a neurotic. When the Philharmonic has been good it has sometimes been very good, but when it has been bad it has as often gone clean out of bounds.

Mr. Rodzinski has undertaken to heal its neuroses. At least we presume that is what he has undertaken. Because improve-ment is noticeable already in tonal transparency, and a faint blush seems to be appearing on the surface of the string sounds. Rhythmic co-ordination, too, though far from normal, is definitely ameliorated. It is to be hoped sincerely that progress will continue. But let no one imagine that forty years of ill-treatment are going to be wiped out in a season. The Philharmonic will have to be restrained from the ground up, schooled for dependability, and accustomed to being able to count on its conductor. Under a steady and responsible hand it should in time develop into a team worthy of its magnificent personnel and of its nation-wide public. What specific virtues it may eventually develop are unpredictable. At present its faults, like those of any spoiled child or horse, are more easily definable than its qualities. But it would be surprising if an orchestra so carefully selected, functioning in a city so sophisticated musically as New York, did not, once convalescence from old ills is firmly established, manifest characteristics of specific originality.

October 17, 1943

CHIEFLY CONDUCTORS

Conducting Reviewed

Except for the regular visitors of the Boston and Philadelphia orchestras, New York has heard no outside symphonic ensembles this season. But we have heard conductors from everywhere. We have heard none of these (excepting Koussevitzky and Ormandy and possibly Barbirolli) under ideal conditions. By this I mean that they have mostly been heard conducting orchestras they had not selected or trained, orchestras that are not their orchestras. Under such circumstances the finer details of execution, if not absent altogether, are always lacking in the spontaneity that is a product of long association between the musicians and their leader. On the other hand, the leaders (and the musicians too) have all been heard under identical conditions, so that comparisons of musicianship and of style are more fairly based than usual. The Philharmonic and the City Symphony have been running what it is legitimate to consider as a kind of competition which, if it did not exhibit everybody at his best or anybody completely, did show them all playing the same game with the same equipment.

There is no question, I think, that with standard Philharmonic equipment Mr. Koussevitzky has produced the best all-around result of the year. His work and that of the orchestra sounded assured, sensible, eloquent, correct. No air of improvisation and no unexpected technical emergencies marred its musicality or interrupted its flow. It was calm and powerful and efficient and well bred. Its most impressive quality was its dependability. One knew from the beginning it was going to be all right, and it was. Buying a ticket to one of his concerts was like buying a ticket to a concert by Toscanini or buying a record by Beecham, a wholly calculable investment.

Everybody else who has led the Philharmonic this season has been, by comparison, a blind date. The great Stokowski, ordinarily a conductor of high technical finish, did some good work and some very bad. Rodzinski, of Cleveland, a most efficient workman on the whole, did brilliant renditions of Hindemith and of Berlioz; but having spent more time rehearsing one of these than was proportionately allowable, he gave an unprepared reading of Mendelssohn's *Midsummer Night's Dream* that was higglety-pigglety. Busch's work was neither musically nor technically quite up to big-time standards; and the same is true, I understand (I unfortunately missed his concerts), of Goossens's. Damrosch was variable in his readings, but he got the loveliest sound out of the Philharmonic I have ever heard anybody get. Mr. Barbirolli, the Philharmonic's titular conductor, was conducting his own orchestra and so not fairly admissible to the guest competition. His work was very much as it always is, competent but a little rough; and his musical conceptions were lacking in nobility.

The Mitropoulos concerts were wholly dependable technically. Musically they varied a good deal. Some of them were nervous and violent, others calm almost to the point of platitude. He played more of the important new music than any of the other leaders did, played it clearly and efficiently and for the most part convincingly. Of them all, his case remains the least decisive. He is a great workman, certainly. He is an interesting musician, certainly. The exact nature of his musical culture and personality remains, however, vague. He seems to be oversensitive, overweaning, overbrutal, overintelligent, and underconfident, and wholly without ease. He is clearly a musician of class, nevertheless, and a coming man of some sort in the musical world.

The contrary from every point of view is Bruno Walter. Musically he is most dependable, though his effective range of repertory is small, being limited chiefly to the German romantics. His specialty is the late German romantics, Bruckner and Mahler, though his Schumann is equally fine and his Beethoven has juice. At one time he enjoyed considerable prestige for his conducting of Mozart, though his readings in this repertory have never been able to stand competition with Beecham's. Nevertheless, in the narrow field of his specialization Walter is a rich musical mind, a conductor whose work has breadth and depth and a certain grand sincerity. He is also a technician of high quality. Unfortunately, he is undependable technically. His concerts, even the best of them, are marred by a sloppiness of beat and general indifference to shipshapeness of execution that tend to alienate those elements of the public that are not wholly absorbed by the music he is playing. At his best he is one of the great living interpreters of music. When not at his best, he is still an authentic musician and worth hearing. But the concentration of thought and energy that underlies his best work seems not always to be wholly at his command.

The City Symphony has worked under a great variety of leaders this year, and I have not been able to hear them all. The great ones, of course, have been Beecham and Reiner. The former is a flood, a volcano, an earthquake, and as unpredictable as any of these. The latter is as calculable as the stars and about as distant. It is too bad we didn't hear them both with the Philharmonic instead of several of the lesser musicians whom we did. But it was an invaluable privilege, of course, for the Mayor's boys to play under them. It is invaluable also to have two orchestras in New York completing each other's repertory and playing to somewhat different musical publics. The City Symphony has produced a great deal of new music and has been honored by the appearance of hitherto little-known soloists and conductors. Among the latter, all of whom I have not heard, Mr. Henri Pensis impressed me as being extraordinarily dependable both technically and musically, an artist of high intelligence and power. I fancy he, too, is some kind of coming man and that we shall be hearing more and more of him.

At orchestral concerts of less than heroic pretensions it is not fair to match conductors, because on these occasions the music itself is more the subject of everybody's interest than the executant style. But in a seasonal review of conducting one does remember, all the same, the excellent work of Stiedry and Szell at the New Friends of Music, the liveliness of Saidenberg with his Little Symphony and of Farbman with his so-called "Symphonietta," the thoroughly intelligent programing of new music by Miss Petrides at the concerts of her "Orchestrette Classique," and the elegant renditions of classic small scores by Adolf Busch and by the French flutist René Le Roy. All these one is thankful for, all these and Alfred Wallenstein, too, who plays reams of fine music, new and old, over the radio and plays it admirably.

The season's finest orchestral playing, as a whole, has been done by the Boston Symphony. The most satisfactory renditions I have heard of modern pieces were Mitropoulos's readings of

Aaron Copland's *Statements* and of Hindemith's Symphony No. 1 with the Philharmonic. The most revelatory of an older work I should say was Beecham's rendering of Haydn's Ninety-ninth at a concert of the Philadelphia Orchestra, though his playing of the Berlioz "Chasse Royale" from *The Trojans in Carthage* at the concert of the City Symphony will run his Haydn a close second for vigor and finesse and sheer musical grandeur.

The best single conducting job I heard at the Metropolitan Opera this winter was Beecham's *Faust*. The best dramatic conducting I have heard outside the Met was Smallens's *Porgy and Bess*, though Fritz Busch's *Macbeth* at the New Opera Company merits a memento. For these and all similar blessings may we ever remain duly thankful.

April 19, 1942

Pipe-Organ Obsession

PHILADELPHIA ORCHESTRA, *Leopold Stokowski*, conductor, last night at Carnegie Hall, performing Beethoven's Overture to *Leonore* No. 3, Brahms's Variations on a Theme by Haydn, "Siegfried's Death," from Wagner's *Götterdämmerung*, and Shostakovich's Symphony No. 6.

I⊤ becomes increasingly clear to this listener that Leopold Stokowski's concept of orchestral music is derived from organ-playing. He cares nothing for the spontaneous collaboration that is the joy of ensemble players, the kind of perfect concord that swingsters call being "in the groove" and that French instrumentalists refer to as "the little blue flame." He treats his men as if they were 110 stops of a concert organ, each complete with swell-box, all voiced for solo use and mutually adjusted for producing balanced chords of any timbre at any degree of loudness or softness.

His latest seating arrangement is an adaptation to orchestral uses of pipe-organ antiphony. He long ago did away with the classical symphonic antiphony of first violins on one side against seconds on the other, through both of which pierce succeeding layers of supporting woodwind, brass, and percussion. He has his musicians arranged now with all the strings massed at back center as if these were a single homogeneous body of foundation tone, like Great Organ diapasons, with woodwinds out in front, like a Choir Organ or *positif,* and with the brasses at the right and left downstage corners, like the heavy solo reeds of a French organ, the horns playing antiphonally on one side against the trumpets and trombones on the other.

This massive acoustic-architectural layout established, he proceeds to play on the whole thing with his bare fingers as if it were a solo instrument. Nothing is left to the musicians' personal taste or feeling. He even went so far last night as to mold Mr. Kincaid's flute passages by hand, an insulting procedure toward an artist of Mr. Kincaid's stature, but a necessary procedure for producing the kind of one-man musical performance that Mr. Stokowski has in mind.

He carries his pipe-organ obsession to the extent of imitating organ rhythm, even. Now the organ, a mechanical wind instrument, knows no lilt or swing. It executes an even scale and an evenly progressive crescendo or diminuendo. It can play *sforzando* and *fortepiano,* but its accent knows no beat. Its rhythm is entirely quantitative, a question of long and short note-values, never of beat-stresses varied within the measure.

To have made Brahms's Haydn Variations, with the Viennese lilt and only occasional passage of non-accentual music that sets off by contrast their otherwise steadily swinging rhythm, into something that sounded like nothing so much as a skillful organ transcription of these same Variations is a triumph of will-power as well as of conductorial skill. The thoroughness and clarity of the technical procedures by which this deformation was operated make any questioning of its æsthetic value seem like quibbling, since, as always with Stokowski, the means employed, no matter what æsthetic end is achieved by them, are a contribution to orchestral technique.

It is just as well that he chose for his technical exhibition last night music that could take it. Beethoven's *Leonore* No. 3, Brahms's Haydn Variations, and Siegfried's Death Music from *Die Götterdämmerung* are all fool-proof and virtuoso-proof. No matter how you play them, they sound.

Shostakovich's Sixth Symphony, like all the later works of that gifted and facile composer, is pretty hard to conceal, too. It is clear, obvious, effective, old-fashioned. It is not, perhaps, as successfully pulled off as his First and Fifth. Its allegiance seems to be divided between a romanticized, and hence attenuated, neo-classicism and a full-blooded Muscovite orientalism à la Boro-din. Each movement begins with a gesture of goodwill toward the lately reputable International Style and goes off as quickly as possible into the atmospheric market-place-and-landscape painting that Russians have always loved so enthusiastically. It is a pleasant piece and not without a certain concentration at moments. If it were signed by an American composer, say Harl McDonald or Walter Piston, it would be classifiable as good salable academicism.

December 4, 1940

Impeccable Musical Tailoring

BOSTON SYMPHONY ORCHESTRA, *Serge Koussevitzky,* conduc-tor, yesterday afternoon at Carnegie Hall, performing Mozart's Sym-phony No. 35 ("Haffner"), Martinů's Concerto Grosso for chamber orchestra, and two works by Tchaikovsky: Piano Concerto No. 1 and the *1812* Overture. Soloist: *Alexander Borovsky,* piano.

ONE has known New York men who always had their suits made in Boston and elderly ladies from various parts of the Eastern seaboard who would never go anywhere else for a hat. Certainly we do not produce here or import at present from any other provincial center such perfect musical tailoring as that which the Boston Symphony Orchestra exhibits for us in Carnegie Hall ten times a season and which was again displayed yesterday afternoon.

The reasons for this superiority are many, not the least of them being more ample rehearsal time per program than most other orchestras can afford. Another is Mr. Koussevitzky's long period of incumbency as conductor and drill-master of the out-fit. A third is, no doubt, Boston itself, a city whose intellectual tradition is both robust and elegant. Boston is, indeed, in no small degree responsible for what Koussevitzky is today. Always a brilliant and a powerful leader, he has grown mellower there and stronger. Boston has refined his crudities of style and deep-ened his musical culture. It has steadied a man once flashy and erratic and made of him a true musical master.

It is easy to disagree with anybody's musical interpretations, but rarely can one disagree with an artist on such clear grounds as one can with the good Doctor. This is where musical tailoring and the Boston manner become valuable beyond their mere intrinsic charm. Toscanini's musical workmanship is always of a high order. But it is opaque; one can't easily hear pieces through it. Koussevitzky's is clarity itself, the presentation of it to the audience authoritative but gentlemanly. No matter how wrong one may think him about any given musical rendition, there always seems to be room for his conception and for one's own in the same concert hall.

There is some free mental space, also, between the way he thinks a piece should be played and the Boston Orchestra's rendition. This is due, curiously enough, to the exactitude with which the orchestra renders his conception plus an observance on both his and its part of all the musical amenities. Forceful expression is never expected (at least, the oversteppings in this respect are rare) to justify vulgar tone from the brass, messy fiddle-playing, incorrect phrasing, or false tonal equilibrium. This care for what I call the musical amenities makes the Boston Orchestra very easy to listen to, even when one doesn't care much for the work one is hearing; and it makes it impossible to get angry with its leader for not being invariably of the same mind as oneself about interpretative matters.

Yesterday the Mozart was not at all my kind of Mozart; but it was lovely, all the same. It was streamlined, grave, distant. The minuet, as usual, was fast. The finale was a marvel of delicate precision in the string work. The Tchaikovsky B-flat minor (or "Juke-Box") Piano Concerto was balanced and lucid, and the orchestra actually sounded as if it were accompanying a pianoforte instead of spanking it. Mr. Borovsky, the soloist, played well enough, at least without *schmalz*, though his two hands did not always sound together. The *1812* Overture was ripsnorting and good fun. The brass was triumphantly sonorous at the end without sounding coarse. Bravos followed.

The novelty was Bohuslav Martinů's Concerto Grosso for chamber orchestra, a fine and vigorous work by a fine and vigorous composer. Mr. Martinů is a worthy heir to the tradition that produced Dvořák and Smetana. His music is Czechish in melodic character, internationalist and neo-classic in technique.

His instrumentation is fresh in sound, the usage he makes of a piano being most original and successful. The superbly rhythmic and resonant piano-playing of Messrs. Sanromá and Zighera was, I am sure, responsible in no small way for the fine effect of it all. From the spontaneous burst of applause which followed the last chord it seemed probable that Mr. Martinů may have fathered a sturdy little repertory piece. In any case he is the author of a most agreeable one.

January 11, 1942

Britain Wins

NEW YORK CITY SYMPHONY ORCHESTRA, *Sir Thomas Beecham*, conductor, last night at Carnegie Hall, performing Sir Thomas's orchestration of Handel's "The Faithful Shepherd," Mozart's Symphony No. 31 ("Paris"), Sibelius's Symphony No. 7, and Tchaikovsky's *Francesca da Rimini*. Presented by Mayor Fiorello La Guardia and the New York City WPA Music Project.

THE CONCERT that Beecham conducted last night with the New York City Symphony Orchestra proved several interesting things. It proved first of all the dictum that there are no bad orchestras, only bad conductors. No orchestra has played better this season in New York City, by any imaginable standards, than Mayor La Guardia's WPA boys played for Sir Thomas. The program was a difficult one, too, and all of it new to the ensemble. It proved also that Beecham is an A-1 man of music as well as an A-1 man of the orchestra. Such lyric grace in the interpretation of Handel and such majestic proportions in the reading of Mozart are not available, to my knowledge, in the work of any other living conductor. His excellence in the eighteenth-century repertory, indeed, is known and everywhere recognized. That he should be equally convincing in Sibelius and Tchaikovsky is news to these parts.

He won his audience with the first phrases of the Handel. It is a fine piece, in every way gracious and lovely; and the Beecham orchestration of it is neat, tasteful, and far from timid.

The Mozart "Paris" Symphony No. 31, in D major, is a noble work. Particularly noticeable in the execution of it, as in that of the Handel, were the silken sonority of the strings and their precision. Also the utterly convincing nature of the tempos. I have long wondered why Beecham's Mozart tempos were always so satisfactory. I think this is due to his preoccupation with the Grand Line of his interpretations. Whenever an artist has a reasoned conception of any musical work as a unit unrolling itself in time, rather than as a series of more or less interesting moments, the tempos naturally fall into place. It also becomes possible to refine and elaborate the detail to quite a high degree when that, too, is all in its place as a part of the Grand Line.

Pleasing indeed were the breadth and sustained continuity of the Mozart slow movement. Conductors are likely to keep these movements low in dynamics and to get moony over them. Either that or to go kittenish and break their continuity into fragments. The current conception of a Mozart andante is that of a slice of thin sugary ham, spiced up by a minuet, between two slabs of some more sustaining musical fare. Beecham played last night's slow movement as if it were the second act of a three-act opera, the one upon which the whole work turns.

A Sibelius expert informed me he had never heard the Seventh Symphony played so well. I have never heard Tchaikovsky's *Francesca da Rimini* played so well. It was eloquent and sweeping and tender. Its pianissimos and its loud work were both superior to what we currently hear from even the best orchestras. Nothing was overstated; nothing was unclear or at any time tonally vulgar.

I was not converted into a Sibelius-lover by rehearing after many years the Seventh Symphony. Beside Tchaikovsky, from whom its whole æsthetic and most of its technique are derived, it sounded pretty amateurish. I do not believe for a moment that its gray and dirty-brown orchestral coloring is a depiction of either the Finnish soul or the Finnish landscape. The Finns I have known have all been brighter and more striking in character, and the countryside of that athletic people has always been depicted to us through art and photography as blazing with clear color and with sunshine. I think Sibelius just orchestrates badly.

However that may be, we have reason to be proud of our New York City Symphony Orchestra. And though Sibelius may be a more gifted composer than I think he is, two certainties remain after last night's triumphal success. One is that nobody has to take seriously any longer the excuses of the Philharmonic for not playing any better than it currently does. Because if the WPA can play like that, the Philharmonic can too. The other certainty is that in sending us Sir Thomas Beecham as a musical ambassador, Britain has certainly delivered the goods.

April 7, 1941

More Beecham

NEW YORK CITY SYMPHONY ORCHESTRA, *Sir Thomas Beecham,* conductor, last night at Carnegie Hall, performing Haydn's Symphony No. 102, Mozart's Symphony No. 36, Delius's *Paris: The Song of a Great City,* and Dvořák's Symphonic Variations. Presented by Mayor La Guardia and the New York City WPA Music Project.

THE SECOND Beecham concert of the New York City Symphony was a triumph like the first. The house was full and loved it. Sir Thomas was in form and looked as if he were loving it. The orchestra played as if they loved both him and music.

Beecham alone of the great conductors, as Nikisch did before him, collaborates with an orchestra rather than conquers it. As a result his orchestra always sounds like an ensemble of skilled musicians rather than like a Panzer division on the march. This particular attitude toward music-making places him at once as the survivor of a vanished epoch and the hope of the next. He is the obvious rallying-point for all these musicians, young and old, who have had enough of musical Cæsarism.

Not that he is lacking in authority or discipline. He has more of both than most. But these are imposed and accepted, as such things can only be imposed and accepted in the Republic of Art, by the exercise of friendliness and human consideration. As a result of this courteous and pleasant manner, he achieves a spontaneity of collaboration that is in every musical way superior to the machine finish that makes the work of less humanely tempered men sound dead and horrid.

Noticeable in both his concerts this season has been the consistent musicality of his fortissimos. He can make the WPA boys play as softly and as loud as the musicians do in any other orchestra. But one is never conscious of any forcing of the sonority. Koussevitzky often forces his strings beyond the point of maximum resonance. Mitropoulos makes all the instruments sound powerful but husky. Walter is not infrequently sloppy, inexcusably sloppy about his tuttis. Toscanini seems not to care what kind of noise comes out of his musicians' efforts, provided there is a certain equilibrium of one kind of sound against another and provided the whole machine is kept rolling. Stokowski, of course, sacrifices everything to the production of an organlike sostenuto dominated by overplayed brasses. Beecham, on the other hand, lets the strings dominate the ensemble, keeps them in command of tonal coloration, as is undoubtedly the correct tradition of orchestral execution, as it is of orchestral writing; and yet he seems to have no difficulty about building or sustaining majestic fortissimos in which the strings sound full and easy and unforced.

In contrast to the subtlety and flexibility of his string work at all dynamic levels, he keeps his woodwinds cool and neatly precise, in the French taste. His brasses, too, are kept quietly rich, never allowed to scream. And he has a nice sense of dosage, spicy but not obtrusive, in dealing with the percussion section.

Last week I commented on the excellence of his musical interpretations both of eighteenth-century and of nineteenth-century repertory. This was again manifest last night in the brilliance and wit of his Haydn, in the majesty and mystery of his Mozart. (A Bostonian composer of my acquaintance was not entirely happy about the leisurely pace of both minuets.) The Delius piece last night was made to sound like the almost first-class impressionism it is. And the Dvořák came off as the Czechish charm-number that composer would write so prettily and so infallibly.

All this I mention simply for the record. I should like to impress on my readers that Beecham's interpretative excellence is the achievement of no mere gifted musical amateur. It is the expression not only of a sound musical culture but of a skilled orchestral technique as well. Sir Thomas makes music sound convincing because he is convinced of how it should sound. He succeeds finally, however, not only by being able to imagine the result, but by being able to convince a hundred musicians that nothing is needed for its achievement beyond intelligent goodwill and the exercise of their instrumental skill within that range of sonorities traditionally considered legitimate and beautiful.

April 14, 1941

Showy Conducting

PHILHARMONIC-SYMPHONIC ORCHESTRA, *Dimitri Mitro-poulos*, conductor, yesterday afternoon at Carnegie Hall, performing two works by Beethoven—Overture to *Lenore* No. 2 and Symphony No. 4—and Richard Strauss's *Sinfonia Domestica*.

IT was a big show, everybody showing off but Beethoven. Mr. Mitropoulos was showing how well he could make unpopular Beethoven sound and how popular he could make unpopular Strauss. Strauss was showing what he could do with a large orchestra and the most humdrum of subjects. The Philharmonic musicians were showing Mr. Mitropoulos and the audience how elaborately well they can play, if asked. The audience itself was definitely on the brilliant side.

Beethoven's Overture to *Leonore,* No. 2, was conducted by Mr. Mitropoulos with a firm mastery of what he wanted. What he mostly wanted was spectacular contrasts in the Verdi manner of *ppppp* versus *fffff*. The pauses were exaggerated, too. The effect on this listener was about what it would be if Orson Welles were to apply his invasion-from-Mars technique to the recounting of a bedtime story as familiar as "Little Red Riding Hood" or "The Three Bears." The contrary applies to the interpretation of the same composer's Fourth Symphony, an ungrateful work for the most part, which was turned into, especially at the end, quite exciting entertainment.

Strauss's *Sinfonia Domestica* is second only to his *Alpine Symphony* in unpopularity. It is very long and very elaborate, and it rather too closely resembles its subject. Twenty-five or thirty years ago there used to be found occasionally in business offices a framed motto that read: "Life is just one damn thing after another." Mr. Strauss's musical picture of an average day in his own family is rather like that. It goes on and on without anything happening musically that is in any way memorable.

Mr. Mitropoulos's conducting of it was in every way sensational. He gave it continuity; and he pulled out of his men the most sensational sonorities in order to give it, if possible, vividness. He worked very hard and succeeded beyond all imaginable success. Everybody was so worked up by the end of it that the crying of "Hurrah!" and "Bravo!" was only natural, to let

off one's steam. My neighbor remarked as the conductor took
many bows: "My! He must be tired."

We were all tired, I think. We all felt we had been through a
work-out of some kind. We had been put through our paces as
audience very much as the Philharmonic had been put through
its technical gamut.

It is not possible to chalk up a complete score for any conductor on one concert. Mr. Mitropoulos is obviously a great orchestral technician. His musical taste, as expressed in last night's
program, seems neither fresh nor particularly sound. Admitted
that he made a dull Strauss work interesting to listen to and a
dullish Beethoven symphony vaguely exciting. He didn't make
either of them sound like better or worse music than they are.
He merely lifted them out of their usual semi-oblivion and used
them as what the theatrical world calls "vehicles." It was interesting to hear what he could do *with* the Strauss, less interesting
to hear what he did *to* the Beethoven.

The program was like certain parties one has been to. The
right names were there, but all the wrong people. Nevertheless, a really good time was had. Mr. Mitropoulos conducts the
wrong pieces magnificently, shows them a whale of a time. This
listener had a whale of a time, too. Maybe that is the right way
to conduct second-class works. It will be interesting to hear
what he does *with* or *to* Mozart, Schubert, Debussy.

December 20, 1940

The Maestro

NBC SYMPHONY ORCHESTRA, *Arturo Toscanini*, conductor,
yesterday afternoon in Studio 8-H, Radio City, performing Mozart's
Overture to *Die Zauberflöte*, Haydn's Symphony No. 104, and
Beethoven's Symphony No. 8.

ARTURO TOSCANINI conducted his first concert of the winter
yesterday afternoon in the NBC's Studio 8-H. The program was
classical, and the Maestro was in good form. If the orchestra
didn't sound in any choir—strings, woods, or brasses—quite as
beautiful tonally as one might have wished, that is probably no
fault of his. It is doubtful whether real symphonic mellowness

is obtainable in that hall, anyway, which is too wide and too shallow to have an acoustic focus. Everything sounds a little raucous there except the brass instruments, and they sometimes hardly sound at all.

There is no other living conductor so unfailingly attentive as Toscanini to the music he conducts. His mind never wanders, never runs ahead of the measure or lags behind it. I fancy the quality of his own attention is in no small way responsible for the absorption with which audiences listen to him. And I think it is responsible, too, for the equalized surface tension, that solid, expensive, luxury-product feel that is one of the most striking characteristics of his performance. Whether he goes deep into the substance of a work or, in one man's opinion, misses its sense completely, he always builds its architecture soundly and fits in the detail so smoothly that the piece comes out all streamlined, like a plywood bomber or a racing yacht.

It is not merely that his tempos are all a shade fast, like those of many another elderly musician (Saint-Saëns used to play the piano so fast the ear could scarcely follow). There is an element in his beat, too, that tends to make the music go round and round. He marks the meter so clearly that every down-beat takes on a slight stress—not a pulsation or lilt, as in Viennese waltzes, but a tiny, tiny dry accent, like the click of a well-running machine. This mechanical purring both gives to his readings a great rhythmic clarity and assures the listener that all is under control. It is also, nevertheless, a little bit lulling. One gets hypnotized by the smooth-working mechanics of the execution and forgets to listen to the music as a human communication.

I do not think that any down-beat accentuation was presupposed by the classical symphonists—by Haydn, Mozart, or Beethoven. When they wanted stresses they always wrote them in, even on a down-beat. I think they made their meters clear through the contours and quantities of their musical drawing and that their accentuation patterns derive their great expressive (and surprise) value from their complete independence of the basic meter. If I am right about this, if Toscanini's addition of regular measure stresses, however small these may be, to an already indicated pattern of irregular, non-metrical stresses in classical symphonies is uncanonical, it is also a fault.

It confounds accent with meter, instead of setting meter against accent. It simplifies orchestral conducting and rather oversimplifies the exposition of a piece. It smooths down the detail and trivializes it, sacrifices personal expression to grandeur of architectural effect. This is the characteristic procedure of the best Italian opera conductors, and it is electrifying in the theater. I do not believe, however, that it gives as vivid a rendering of classical Viennese symphonies as a clear dissociation in every measure of meter versus accent does.

November 1, 1943

Absolute Theater

PHILHARMONIC-SYMPHONY ORCHESTRA, *Arturo Toscanini*, conductor, yesterday afternoon at Carnegie Hall, performing three works by Beethoven: Overture to *Fidelio*, Concerto for Piano, Violin, and Cello in C major (Triple Concerto), and Symphony No. 7. Soloists: *Ania Dorfmann*, piano, *Mishel Piastro*, violin, and *Joseph Schuster*, cello.

YESTERDAY AFTERNOON's Toscanini concert at Carnegie Hall, the fifth of his Beethoven series, revived (temporarily, I imagine) two rarely heard works, the *Fidelio* Overture and the Triple Concerto for violin, cello and piano. It also reinvigorated (rather unduly, I thought) the well-known Seventh Symphony. And it gave further opportunity for studying the approach of the most celebrated conductor in the world to the music of the greatest of all symphonic composers. A Beethoven cycle is always profoundly satisfactory, no matter who conducts it. A Toscanini concert is always stimulating to an audience, no matter what the program is. That public enthusiasm about the present series should run high is not surprising. That I am unable to share it wholeheartedly is a matter of sincere regret to me.

The Triple Concerto is a work that Beethoven experts have never much admired. Its tunes are long and lovely; but, being a little too long and lovely, they proved difficult for him to develop. Their working out is a shade laborious. Also the concerted solo instruments do not produce a sound which opposes itself advantageously to that of the orchestra. They sound poor, like a hotel trio, rather than rich, as a single instrument does, or as a group can that is chosen for its intrinsic harmoniousness, when contrasted to the more massive but less brilliant sound of an orchestral tutti. The artists did their best yesterday to produce an ensemble, but all three sounded better separately than together. Miss Dorfmann and Mr. Schuster played with fine tone, fine rhythm, and full authority. Mr. Piastro's work was less stable, his tone shifting between one of great sweetness and one of a certain acidity, the latter quality being due, I think, to an occasional fault of pitch.

The Seventh Symphony was not so much the full Seventh Symphony as a highly dramatized outline or syllabus of the Seventh Symphony. Its main melodic material, its harmonic progress, and especially the dynamic pattern, the chiaroscuro of it, were wholly clear. Unfortunately many of the rapid string passages were not audible in detail. This skimping of the fast work was probably unavoidable at the given speed, but it is not usually considered the best musical style to play non-theatrical works at a speed at which their detail cannot be executed satisfactorily by the group performing them.

The first movement was the only one that seemed comfortable in its tempo, and that got into some trouble about rhythm along in the middle. It got into trouble at the same place it nearly always gets into trouble, namely, about half-way through, where more care is required than was expended yesterday if the six-eight time is to be prevented from turning itself into two-four. The second movement came out as a barcarolle, the third and fourth rather in tarantella vein. In none of them was there any sense of mystery to make the Beethoven fury seem interiorly dramatic rather than merely of the stage.

At all times the effect, save for surface roughnesses, was certainly that desired by the conductor. No conductor I know of seems to have in his inner ear so clearly an auditory image of a piece as Toscanini does. His psychological power over his executant musicians and over his audience is due, no doubt, to the preciseness with which he knows what he wants out of both. The musical value of what he wants varies, as it does with any conductor, from work to work and even from concert to concert. What varies surprisingly little is the efficacy of his personal domination of both orchestra and public. And what is most surprising of all is that his personal assertion, unlike that

of his more romantic or poetic rivals, is very little a thing of personalized emotion. It is a kind of Latin clarity about the main
lines of tonal architecture, especially the dynamic ones, and a
ruthless insistence that the piece be accepted in terms of these.
Music is never at ease under his whip, and it rarely sings. But its
shape and progress are always wholly clear. And if his mastery of
emphasis does not always convince one of his full comprehension of a composer's meaning, the theater-like build-up of the
whole thing is both terrifyingly effective and wholly worthy of
the applause it so automatically provokes.

May 2, 1942

The Toscanini Case

ARTURO TOSCANINI's musical personality is a unique one in
the modern world. One has to go back to Mendelssohn to find
its parallel. A reactionary in spirit, he has none the less revolutionized orchestral conducting by his radical simplification of
its procedures. Almost wholly devoted to the playing of familiar
classics, he has at the same time transformed these into an auditive image of twentieth-century America with such unconscious
completeness that musicians and laymen all over the world have
acclaimed his achievement without, I think, very much bothering to analyze it. They were satisfied that it should be, for the
most part, musically acceptable and at all times exciting.

Excitement is of the essence in Toscanini's concept of musical performance. But his is not the kind of excitement that has
been the specialty of the more emotional conductors of the last
fifty years. Theirs was a personal projection, a transformation
through each conductor's own mind of what the conductor
considered to be the composer's meaning. At its best this supposed a marriage of historical and literary with musical culture.
It was derived from the conducting style of Richard Wagner;
and its chief transmitters to us have been the line that is von
Bülow, Nikisch, and Beecham. For musicians of this tradition
every piece is a different piece, every author and epoch another
case for stylistic differentiation and for special understanding.
When they miss, they miss; but when they pull it off, they evoke
for us a series of new worlds, each of these verifiable by our

whole knowledge of the past, as well as by our instinctive sense of musical meaning. Theirs is the humane cultural tradition. And if their interpretations have sometimes been accompanied by no small amount of personal idiosyncrasy and a febrile display of nerves, that, too, is a traditional concomitant of the sort of trancelike intensity that is necessary for the projection of any concept that is a product equally of learning and of inspiration.

Toscanini's conducting style, like that of Mendelssohn (if Wagner is to be believed about the latter), is very little dependent on literary culture and historical knowledge. It is disembodied music and disembodied theater. It opens few vistas to the understanding of men and epochs; it produces a temporary, but intense, condition of purely auditory excitement. The Maestro is a man of music, nothing else. Being also a man of (in his formative years) predominantly theatrical experience, he reads all music in terms of its possible audience effect. The absence of poetical allusions and of historical references in his interpretation is significant, I think, of a certain disdain for the general culture of his individual listeners. In any case, whatever he may have inherited of nineteenth-century respect for individualistic culture was sacrificed many years ago to an emphasizing of those musical aspects that have a direct effect on everybody. It is extraordinary how little musicians discuss among themselves Toscanini's rightness or wrongness about matters of speed and rhythm and the tonal amenities. Like any other musician, he is frequently apt about these and as frequently in error. What seems to be more important than all that is his unvarying ability to put over a piece. Like Mendelssohn, he quite shamelessly whips up the tempo and sacrifices clarity and ignores a basic rhythm, just making the music, like his baton, go round and round, if he finds his audience's attention tending to waver. No piece has to mean anything specific; every piece has to provoke from its hearers a spontaneous vote of acceptance. This is what I call the "wow technique."

Now, what are we accepting when we applaud a Toscanini rendition? Not personal poetry, certainly; nor any historical evocation; nor a literal and academic reading of a classic score. I think it is his power of abstraction we are acclaiming, the abstraction of a piece's essential outline. If he has reduced conducting motions to their essential outline, too, that is not mere elegance on his part, nor ostentation either; it is a systematic throwing away of all refinements that might interfere with his schematic rendition. His whole accent is on the structure of a piece. Its thematic materials are the building blocks with which that structure is erected. Expression and ornamentation are details to be kept in place. Unity, coherence, and emphasis are the qualities that must be brought out.

Both theatrical experience and bad eyesight are probably responsible for the Toscanini style. When one cannot depend on reading a score in public, one must memorize everything. And when one memorizes everything, one acquires a great awareness of music's run-through. One runs it through in the mind constantly; and one finds in that way a streamlined rendering that is wholly independent of detail and even of specific significance, a disembodied version that is all shape and no texture. Later, in rehearsal, one returns to the texture; and one takes care that it serve always as neutral surfacing for the shape. But shape is what any piece is always about that one has memorized through the eye and the inner ear. Playing a piece for shape and run-through gives (if the piece has any shape at all) the most exciting effect that can ever be produced. It is the same procedure as that of directing a melodrama on the stage, character and dialogue being kept at all times subsidiary to the effects of pure theater, to the building up in the audience of a state of intense anxiety that is relieved only at the end of the last act.

The radical simplification of interpretative problems that all this entails has changed orchestral conducting from a matter of culture and of its personal projection into something more like engineering. Young conductors don't bother much any more to feel music or to make their musicians feel it. They analyze it, concentrate in rehearsal on the essentials of its rhetoric, and let the expressive details fall where they may, counting on each man's skill and everybody's instinctive musicianship to take care of these eventually. Poetry and nobility of expression are left for the last, to be put in as with an eyedropper or laid on like icing, if there is time. All this is good, because it makes music less esoteric. It is crude because it makes understanding an incidental matter; but it is a useful procedure and one wholly characteristic of our land and century. About its auditory result I am less enthusiastic than many. I find Toscanini's work, for the most part, spiritually unenlightening, except when he plays Italian music. But that is only a personal experience; many musicians find otherwise. And those of us who like more differentiation, more poetry, and more thought in our music, who find his much advertised fidelity to the notes of musical scores to be grossly exaggerated, his equally advertised "perfection" to be more so, and both of these aims, even when achieved, to be of secondary importance, even we must admit, nevertheless, the reality of Toscanini's musicianship and achievements. For good or for ill, and most probably for good, orchestral conducting will never be the same again.

I say most probably for good, because it is noticeable already that lesser conductors analyze music better than they used to and that this simple extraction of a work's formal essence tends to facilitate rather than to obfuscate differentiations of style and expression in the conducting of men whose musical experience is more limited but whose general culture is more ample than Toscanini's. Many of his contemporaries and most of his famous predecessors have had more interesting minds. Almost none has been so gifted a natural musician and so strictly professional a showman. He has simplified the technique of the art by eliminating all the hangovers of Late Romantic emotionalism and by standardizing a basic technique of musical rendition that is applicable to any piece in the world, whether one understands its spirit or not. This may be treason to culture, or it may be merely a radical purging of culture's own fifth column. I fancy it includes a bit of both. In any case, I believe that the introduction of a new cultural understanding into orchestral rendition, as one observes this in the work of Smallens, for instance, and in that of most of the other good American conductors, is as directly traceable to Toscanini's having previously eliminated practically all cultural understanding from it as the means of their doing so have been facilitated by his radical simplifications of conducting procedure.

Toscanini's influence lies, so far, chiefly in America. Europe has its Furtwänglers and its Beechams and its great French conductors like Monteux and Munch. And it has no need of exchanging their interpretations or their working methods for anything so oversimplified as Toscanini's. The Romantic tradition has already transformed itself there into a modern tradition that is as rich and as complex and as generally satisfactory to the mind as the tradition of Wagner and Nikisch was. That tradition is too complex for us. We admire the work of the great European conductors, but we do not quite understand how it is done. A century of importing them has not revealed their secrets to our local boys. We watched Toscanini work for ten years at the Philharmonic; and now there are 30,000 symphony orchestras in the United States, practically all of them led by the local boys. He is the founding father of American conducting. Whether we like or not the way he interprets music (and I don't much, though many do), his place in our musical history is certainly an important one.

In any European sense, he is not a complete musician, as the late Karl Muck was, and perhaps not even a great technician, as Reiner is, for example. He is too completely self-taught to be wholly responsible to any Great Tradition. But he is a thoroughgoing professional, although self-taught; and he has shown our musicians how to be thoroughgoing professionals too, although self-taught. The value of this contribution to our musical life cannot be overestimated. Any influence Toscanini might possibly have on European musical life would be anti-cultural. His ruthless clearing away here, however, of Romantic weeds and unsuccessful implantations has made a space where conductors are already being grown locally. And a steady supply of good American conductors to the local market is the thing above all else needful right now to the public understanding and the autochthonous development of American musical composition.

May 17, 1942

COMPOSITIONS AND COMPOSERS

Bach Goes to Church

CANTATA SINGERS, *Arthur Mendel*, conductor, with *Ralph Kirkpatrick*, harpsichord, and *Heinz Arnold*, organ, last night at the Unitarian Church of All Souls, New York, performing Bach's complete *Weinachtsoratorium*. Soloists: *Rose Dirman*, soprano, *Jean Bryan*, contralto, *Donald Dame*, tenor, and *Paul Seymour Matthen*, bass.

THE CLOSER the performing conditions for Sebastian Bach's concerted music are approximated to those of early eighteenth-century provincial Germany the more the music sounds like twentieth-century American swing. The exactitude with which a minimum time unit is kept unaltered at all times, the persistence of this unit as one of exactly measured length rather than of pulsation, the omnipresence of the harpsichord's ping, like a brush on a cymbal, the constant employment of wiggly counterpoint and staccato bass, all make it a matter of preference between anachronisms whether one puts it that Bach has gone to town or that some of the more scholarly jitterbugs of the town have wandered into a church.

Last night's performance of the *Christmas Oratorio* was full of swing and gusto. The soloists, particularly the ladies, Miss Rose Dirman and Miss Jean Bryan, both of them possessors of lovely voices, sang their arias to the accompaniment of solo woodwinds as neatly and enthusiastically as if they were playing instrumental duets with Benny Goodman. The gentlemen sang the magnificently dramatic recitatives with clarity and dispatch. The chorus came in on the big numbers as if these were the gayest of contrapuntal merry-go-rounds, which indeed they are; the high trumpets played out of tune, as they must have in Leipzig at Bach's own Thomaskirche; and the inexorable rhythm of Mr. Ralph Kirkpatrick's harpsichord continuo sustained the whole with a vigor and a brightness rarely encountered these days.

It was Mr. Mendel's intention to reproduce as closely as possible the sonorities of what may be called the world premieres of the work, for the six Cantatas that it comprises were never executed under Bach in any one day, as these took place under

the composer's direction more than two hundred years ago.
Instrumentally the revival was highly credible, except that the
Thomaskirche organ, still playable, is more frankly bright in
sound than any modern instrument. The chorus of thirty-two
voices, a number somewhat larger than Bach had available, sang
with good rhythm and surprisingly clear German diction. But
the fuzzy, fluty quality of Anglo-Saxon vocalization bears little
resemblance to the harsh and sonorous brilliance of a Continental chorus. And when we remember that in Bach's choir,
according to Albert Schweitzer, the treble parts were all sung
by boys, whose voices are more penetrating, even, than those
of women, it is terrifying to imagine the piercing noises that
must have filled that stone-pillared and stone-walled auditorium
with rejoicing.

Even without the resonance that must have been literally
an earful for St. Thomas's congregation, the final chorus with
three high trumpets tootling for dear life in the neighborhood
of high D was as jolly a bit of Christmas cheer as has come your
reviewer's way this Nativity. God rest you merry, gentlemen!
Let nothing you dismay!

December 31, 1940

New Star Reveals Old

NEW YORK CITY SYMPHONY ORCHESTRA, *Reginald Stewart*,
conductor, last night at Carnegie Hall, performing, among other
works, Luigi Silva's orchestration of Boccherini's Concerto in D major
for Cello and Orchestra. Soloist: *Mr. Silva*, cello.

LUIGI BOCCHERINI was the greatest composer of all time for
the violoncello. Not even old Sebastian Bach nor the French
masters of the viola da gamba and the bastarda wrote so skillfully, so idiomatically, so brilliantly as he for the played-between-
the-legs bowed instruments. He was also a symphonist of renown and a great composer by almost any standard of estimate.

It has been customary, when executing his cello concertos
and his symphonies in modern orchestral circumstances, to amplify the orchestrations, to thicken them unmercifully, with the
result that only the music's characteristic melodic and harmonic

outlines remain, but none of those instrumental dispositions that are so brilliantly, so satisfyingly thin in his scores. Mr. Luigi Silva has had the wit and the sound musical sense to present the musical world with something that, if it is not completely Boccherini, is far nearer to its original than what we usually get.

He found the original score in the Library of Congress. From this he made an edition, now distributed by the New York Public Library, that is completely faithful to the original in all the string parts, the original being scored for cello solo and string orchestra. To these he has added, for performance in large halls, discreet reinforcements of the tuttis by two flutes, two oboes, two horns, and two bassoons, a normal symphonic ensemble of Boccherini's epoch. It is thus possible either to execute the concerto as chamber music, exactly according to the author's specifications, or to execute it in Carnegie Hall, as was done yesterday, with, I should say, less falsification than a literal re-inforcing of the string parts by a too large number of players would have produced.

Yesterday's effect was one of delicacy and grandeur. The concerto is in every way lovely as music. Its execution, moreover, was the only execution that this announcer has ever heard of a concerto for cello and orchestra in which the solo instrument seemed to be properly balanced against its orchestral comple-ment. Not for nothing did Boccherini so carefully write no other cello parts and virtually none even for the violas when the soloist plays. He is accompanied by violins only, for the most part, these written softly and divisi. The solo part lies high, as was Boccherini's taste; and Mr. Silva's cadenzas (he played his own) carry the tessitura to practically Himalayan heights by means of harmonics. The third of these cadenzas, an imitation of hunting-horn harmonies, was accompanied by two real horns in the most charming way imaginable.

November 3, 1941

The Gluck Case

THE JUILLIARD SCHOOL used to give modern operas. They did but they don't any more, as the ditty hath it. Their lat-est production was Gluck's *Iphigenia in Tauris*, a work that sometimes passes in the modern world for the most classic of musical classics, but that in its own day was considered a triumph of novelty and of fashion. I have no quarrel with a pedagogical policy that eschews today's modernism in favor of that of a century and a half back. I am all for bringing up young on the ancient models of things, even though this may imply glorification of the Agamemnon family. The young take more things in their stride than we do maybe, anyway, including what Mr. John Peale Bishop, I think it was, once rhymed so prettily as "Iphigenia's incestuous desires." The purpose of this article is not to correct anybody's morals but to offer a warning to whom it may concern that Gluck's operas are not quite such model matter for musical imitation as their historical prestige might suggest.

That prestige is as much a result of publicity as it is of intrinsic musical excellence, though the latter, as anyone knows, is not wholly wanting. Gluck had a gift from his prodigious early years of making himself a center of controversy and of intellectual excitement. He perfected this gift in Italy, where he learned, as well, a great deal about sheer theater and became a skilled harmonist and orchestrator. Counterpoint he never mastered, but he got to be extremely expert at musical prosody.* Arriving in Paris with this far from negligible equipment for dramatic composition, he proceeded to make himself a protagonist and eventually the victor in one of those Parisian wars about æsthetics that have always been characteristic of French intellectual life.

The Gluck-Piccinni quarrel was really a revival, or continuation, of the famous *querelle des bouffons*, which had been going on for half a century. Everybody from Rameau to Jean-Jacques Rousseau had taken part in it. Its chief point of controversy was the respective virtues of the French and Italian operatic styles. The former prized correct declamation above melodic charm and admitted symphonic interludes as desirable to full musical expression. The latter prized tunefulness and easy theatrical effect and refused to consider music as wholly subservient to

---

*Debussy, in his famous *Lettre ouverte à Monsieur le Chevalier W. Gluck (Monsieur Croche, antidilettante;* Paris, 1921), accuses the Austrian composer of incorrect French prosody. Textually, he says: *"Entre nous, vous prosodiez fort mal; du moins, vous faites de la langue française une langue d'accentuation quand elle est au contraire une langue nuancée."*

literature. The French side called the Italian school irresponsible and frivolous; the Italian defenders (Jean-Jacques among them) found the French opera static, pompous, and dull.

Piccinni was a charming composer, in many ways a more gifted and skillful musician than Gluck; and he was fabulously successful at the Opéra. Gluck's backers were mostly literary people. What they wanted was a composer who could placate the melody-fanciers without sacrificing correct declamation or obscuring the literary content of a dramatic poem. Gluck was exactly what they needed, an Italian-trained composer with a healthy German respect for the French language. And so they turned him on to the business of staging a contemporary literary movement by pretending merely to revive the past.

The latter game is old French strategy. Racine had taught manners, language, and moral conduct to the bourgeoisie and court of Louis XIV by pretending merely to retell the plots of Seneca and Euripides. The authors of the Enlightenment were busy preparing (quite consciously) a political revolution; but to conceal the novelty of their reflections about society, economics, and law they pretended that they were merely studying ancient Greece and Rome. When Greco-Roman analogies were weak or insufficient they brought the prestige of the natural sciences into play and based their argument on a wholly fictitious figment known as the "natural man." Gluck took advantage of this argument in his famous preface to *Alceste* to pretend that his music was superior to that of all other composers because, whereas theirs was merely music and perishable, like all that follows æsthetic fashion, his could never die, being a true depiction of "nature" itself. (By "nature" he meant, as any man of the eighteenth century did, what the nineteenth called "human nature" and what our own is likely to term "psychology.") I have heard Salvador Dalí defend his painting with the similar argument that it was superior to mere "art" because it was an exact picture of his own dreams (dreams being the only "reality" surrealism admits).

All this is purest sales-talk. Dalí is an intellectually fashionable painter, as Gluck was an intellectually fashionable composer. The more they try to explain this fact away, the more it becomes clear that their relation to a literary movement is fuller justification for the fame of their work than either their original power or their intrinsic skill, though in neither case is the latter element wholly negligible. For all his talk of "reforming" the opera, Gluck did nothing of the kind. Dr. Paul Henry Lang, of Columbia University, likes to maintain that he had no influence on any subsequent operatic composition. Berlioz certainly admired and studied the orchestral writing in Gluck, because he quotes liberally from it in his *Treatise on Instrumentation*. Wagner used him as a battle cry for his own career, which he also called a "reform," and rewrote some of the scores. All this has accomplished exactly what Gluck's own polemics accomplished: namely, to keep him famous, while the operas are given more and more seldom. The revival of interest in pre-Revolutionary French opera that has accompanied our own searchings among seventeenth- and eighteenth-century composers for reference points in defense of modernism has occasionally foundered on Gluck, for the simple reason that Lully and Rameau, its real masters, are not easily singable by modern voices. And so managers and conductors are likely to make a great point of reviving Gluck and pretending that it is pre-Romantic opera.

This is not true. The literary content of Gluck's librettos is the purest Classic Revivalism; and the Classic Revival, like the subsequent Medieval Revival, is one of the more sentimental and obscurantist aspects of the Romantic movement. Particularly is this true in music, where there were not even any ancient texts to revive. Gluck's choral passages are straight Protestant hymnody of the school popularized in America by Lowell Mason. His arias are watered Handel. His characters are artificial without being even symbolic. His recitative, the second-best element of his musical composition (after the instrumentation, which is tops, in spite of his abuse of string tremolando) is definitely inferior to that of Rameau, on which it is modeled. Because of his contrapuntal deficiency, his music is lacking in animation and in interior life. His melodies follow the harmony rather than generate it. The whole is lacking in surprise. Every number is predictable after four bars.

The most nearly individual note in his music is one derived from its literary and fashionable associations. That is a sort of sugary pastoral flavor that permeates his whole concept of classical antiquity. Everybody on the stage walks around as blithely as if he were about to become an ancestor, or a founding father of some future republic. The Agamemnons, even, that bloody and incestuous clan, express themselves musically with all the placidity of a prosperous agricultural family. They complain about hard times, of course, as is the habit of such families; but they are really mostly busy impressing everybody with how noble they are in their suffering.

Many people find Gluck's music enchanting. Some of these like it because they like sugar from any period. Others like it because they think they get a glimpse through it of pre-Revolutionary operatic style. To these latter I suggest that they beg, bully, and bargain with the producing agencies till they get a chance to hear the operas of Rameau and of Handel. Once acquainted with these, I doubt if they will ever take Gluck's classical antiquity seriously again, just as there is no possibility of really liking his camouflaged Romanticism with anything like the warmth we feel toward the full-blooded article in Mozart and in Beethoven.

As a career-boy, he made his fortune and got knighted by the Pope. He was a second-class composer, nevertheless. As a successor to the great of his century he was distinctly an anticlimax. As much so as the well-known line from Iphigenia's first aria in Tauris (a companion piece to our own "for God, for country, and for Yale"):

> "J'ai vu se tourner contre moi
> les dieux, ma patrie et mon père."

March 8, 1942

The Seasons *in Brooklyn*

BROOKLYN SYMPHONY ORCHESTRA, *Carl Bamberger*, conductor, with the BROOKLYN INSTITUTE CHORUS and the NEW CHORAL GROUP OF MANHATTAN, last night at the Brooklyn Academy of Music, performing Haydn's oratorio *Die Jahreszeiten*.

RARELY have I passed a pleasanter summer. I refer to the second section of Haydn's *The Seasons*, which I heard last night at the Brooklyn Academy of Music. Spring was cheerful and autumn lusty, winter lugubrious and grand. But it was the long, lazy summer that I loved most of all.

Musical literature contains no finer collection of landscape painting than Haydn's homage to the year. There is virtually one of everything. A sunrise, a frog, a quail, a storm, a harvest, a vintage, complete with love and waltzing, a communal spinning-song, every kind of weather known to the temperate regions, and finally a hymn of praise to God and truth and the reviving earth. There are people, too, nice, plain, farm people, giving the measure of man at all times to this Romantic landscape with figures.

No two pieces of it are alike. The musico-pictorial invention is constant and enormous. The accuracy of the pictures and the economy of musical notes with which they are drawn are surprising and impressive. Debussy himself was no more reticent or more powerfully suggestive. Both he and Mendelssohn were less humane.

Grand indeed is the drinking-waltz entitled "Joyful, joyful the liquor flows." The winter spinning scene is the most interesting piece of its species I have ever heard. The prelude to winter is an atmospheric piece of the most effective kind. Its title, "The Thick Fogs at the Approach of Winter," might be by Erik Satie. "The Farmer's Joyful Feeling about the Rich Harvest," another instrumental interlude, is everything its title says. The storm is as grand as Beethoven's, the sunrise as noble as Prokofiev's. But nowhere that I know is there so full and melodious an outpouring as the long summer aria for soprano, "O, how pleasing to the senses." Neither Bach nor Mozart ever uttered so steady a flow of rich song.

The chorus sang handsomely under Mr. Carl Bamberger's direction. The orchestra and soloists were a little rough. All that made no difference. The reading of the work was lucid and utterly persuasive. It so happens I had never heard it before or read it. That is why I am a bit lyrical about it now. It seems to me to present Haydn at his most imaginative and ingenious, the oratorio (or cantata) formula at its least stuffy and most gracious, and the art of musical landscape painting at its most complete. I am deeply grateful to the Brooklyn Symphony Orchestra and its assisting choral groups for this revelation of a neglected masterpiece. Please, may we hear it more often?

March 19, 1942

Haydn, Beethoven, and Mozart

LATELY I have been reading and rereading the Haydn piano sonatas. Like all of Haydn's music they represent a gold mine of melody and of instrumental imagination. There is scarcely one that does not contain some passage familiar to us all, familiar, I may add, more often than not because of Beethoven's unacknowledged quotation of it in sonata or symphony. They also represent, as do equally the piano sonatas of Mozart and Beethoven, the counterpart to the symphonies of these masters. If one wants to understand the latter, one must study the former; and vice versa.

What strikes me most about Haydn is that of the three great Viennese masters he is by far the most melodious. His thematic invention is the most varied of them all and his thematic development the most tuneful. His whole musical concept is lyrical. For this reason he is at his best in the non-lyrical movements. The first movement and the minuet are commonly his richest. The development of his first-movement themes through a cycle of sonata-form modulations gives symmetry and weight to what might be merely graceful if no such formal layout were employed. Similarly, the minuet's quality of dance music enforces a certain objectivity upon his process of composition that adds to Haydn's abundance of personal fancy the welcome solidity of a straightforward and easily understood human significance. The rondo, Haydn's most frequently observed last-movement scheme, gives too much play to his musical imagination, obliges him too little to expression. The same is true of his slow movements, which are melodious and full of incidental invention, but which do not say much.

The truth is that Haydn wrote music like an old bachelor (which, for all practical purposes, he was). A self-contained and self-sufficient lyricism is its dominant characteristic, an avuncular generosity its chief means of contact with the listener. Of humane objectivity it has virtually none save the jolly and waltz-like dance movements, where he remembers his peasant upbringing. The encounter of his native lyrical abundance with sonata-form formalities, however, as that takes place in his first movements, produces a kind of three-dimensional grandeur that is acceptable in terms of its sheer musical magnificence, without regard to what its expressive intention may be. In this respect Haydn's instrumental music looks backward to that of Domenico Scarlatti and the Bach family, just as his oratorios resemble strongly those of Handel. His technical procedures are those of Romanticism; but his thought is neither expansive, like Beethoven's, nor dramatic, like that of Mozart. It is a lyrical fountain forever overflowing and constantly inundating everybody with melody.

Beethoven really was an old bachelor. But he never liked it. All his music is cataclysmic, as if he were constantly trying to break out of his solitude. His first movements state the problem squarely. His slow movements are less interesting, because they try unsuccessfully to avoid it; they tread water. His minuets and scherzos reopen the problem and announce the hope of a solution. The finales, almost always the finest and certainly the most characteristic movements in Beethoven, are the solution that the whole piece has been working up to. That solution is usually of a religious nature. It represents redemption, the victory of soul over flesh. It varies from calm serenity to active triumph, but joy is its thesis. In the Ninth Symphony a German ode on that subject is inserted to clinch the matter. The bonds of solitude are broken because they are imagined as being broken. That breaking is of a purely mystical nature, a temporary identification of the self with God or with all humanity. The form of the musical expression is free and infinitely varied. The finales show Beethoven at his most personal and most masterful. They are grand, terribly serious, and, for the most part, inspiring.

Solitude was unknown to Mozart. Except for a short time in Paris, just after his mother died there, he was probably never in all his life alone for so much as half a day. His music, likewise, is full of dramatic animation. His themes are like people, his developments a working out of their contrasting natures. His first movements, in spite of the beauty of their material, are little more than a first act or prelude to the drama of the rest. The slow movements are always the crux of the matter, the freest, grandest, and most fanciful part of any Mozart sonata or symphony. They are impossible to interpret unless one considers them as theater, as a dramatization of real characters, a conflict among other people's emotions. The minuet which follows (in the quartets it more commonly precedes) is pure ballet. It has nothing to do with Haydn's peasant gambols. It is slow and stately and complex. It, too, shows a conflict of sentiments, as if the dramatic struggles of the preceding movement were here resolved, or at least appeased, through observance of the social amenities. It is a tense and static little affair.

The finales are not dramatic at all. They are mostly fast and always furious. Nothing in music, excepting maybe five or six of the Bach organ fugues, have that kind of power and insistence, as of an element unchained. They do not have to be played at breakneck speed. Those for piano solo definitely profit by moderation in this regard. But rhythmic tension they must have and dynamic contrast. They are the moral of the piece. They show, as Mozart was always trying to show in his operas, how marvelously vigorous life can be when people make up their minds to put their petty differences on the shelf and to collaborate in full good will at being human beings together. Their whole effect can be spoiled unless the preceding movement, whether that is an adagio or the more usual minuet, is presented at a contrasting tempo. Any speed that suggests the scherzo in rendering a Mozart minuet not only falsifies the significance of the minuet itself but steals, as well, the fire of the movement that follows.

December 21, 1941

Mozart's Leftism

PERSONS of humanitarian, libertarian, and politically liberal orientation have for a century used Beethoven as their musical standard-bearer. I employ the word *use* deliberately. Because it is hard to find much in Beethoven's life or music—beyond the legend of his having torn up the dedication of his "Heroic" Symphony to Napoleon when that defender of the French Revolution allowed himself to be crowned Emperor—to justify the adoration in which he has always been held by political liberals.

Wagner, yes. Wagner was full of political theory; and he got himself exiled from Germany (losing a good opera job at Dresden in so doing) for participating in the unsuccessful revolutionary uprising of 1848 beside his friend, the philosopher of anarchy, Mikhail Bakunin. If he had not gone pseudo-Christian and jingo at the end of his life, he would probably be venerated by members of the Third and Fourth Internationals in the same way that Beethoven is worshipped (rather than really listened to) by adherents of the Second.

Mozart, both his life and his works inform us, was more continuously occupied than either of these other composers with what we nowadays call "leftism" (not to be confused with "left wing," Community Party euphemism meaning the Communist Party).

Mozart was not, like Wagner, a political revolutionary. Nor was he, like Beethoven, an old fraud who just talked about human rights and dignity but who was really an irascible, intolerant, and scheming careerist, who allowed himself the liberty, when he felt like it, of being unjust toward the poor, lickspittle toward the rich, dishonest in business, unjust and unforgiving toward the members of his own family.

As a touring child prodigy Mozart was pampered by royalty, though he worked hard all the time. But after the age of twelve he was mostly pushed around by the great, beginning with Hieronymus Colloredo, Archbishop of Salzburg, going on through Grimm and Madame d'Epinay in Paris, and ending with the Emperor Francis I of Austria. He took it like a little man, too. Few musical lives bear witness to a more complete integrity of character in sickness and in health, in riches and in poverty, such little riches as he knew.

Mozart was not embittered by illness and adversity; he was tempered by them. Furthermore, he was acquainted with French libertarian ideas, having been fully exposed to these in Paris, where he spent his twenty-third year. But he was never at any time a revolter. He was an absorber and a builder. He never tried to throw out of the window his Catholic faith or his allegiance to his Emperor, in spite of much unpleasant treatment from both Church and State. He merely added to them his belief in human rights and the practice of Masonic fellowship as he had learned these in Paris and in Vienna.

The three great theater-pieces of his maturity, *Die Zauberflöte*, *Le Nozze di Figaro*, and *Don Giovanni*, are all of them celebrations of this faith and fellowship, of what we should call liberalism or "leftism" and what the eighteenth century called Enlightenment.

Die Zauberflöte, in spite of its obscure libretto, is the easiest of these to grasp. Mozart, like practically all other self-respecting men in those days, like the French King and his own Emperor, even, like our own George Washington and Benjamin Franklin, was a Freemason. Freemasonry was not the anti-Catholic secret society it became in nineteenth-century America, and it was far from being the conspiracy of job-holding that it developed into under France's Third Republic. It was more like Rotary than like anything else we know. Something between that, perhaps, and organized Marxism. It softened the manners and broadened the viewpoint of all classes in society. Even in Austria, the most retarded country in Europe politically, its fellowship was practiced without interference or suppression.

On account of changes that were operated upon the libretto of *Die Zauberflöte* during its composition and mounting, the fairy-story allegory it tells has always been considered obscure. Obscure it is in its details, if you like, in its mixing up of Zoroaster with Egypt and Japan. But surely its main moral, that married happiness and dignity are to be won only by renouncing pride and snobbery and by conducting oneself as an ethical being, is clear. And certainly its textual references to liberty, equality, and fraternity are unmistakable.

If this were Mozart's only work with ideas of the kind in it, we could discount its humanitarian content as we discount the stilted verses of *Idomeneo*. But it is not. *Figaro*, to Beaumarchais's satirical play, was revolutionary in its egalitarianism; and *Don Giovanni* is the most humane and tolerant piece about sacred and profane love that anybody has ever written.

In Lorenzo da Ponte, who made the libretti for *Figaro* and *Don Giovanni*, Mozart had a collaborator ideal to his taste. They worked together so closely that the libretti seem almost to have been made to fit the music, the music to come spontaneously out of the libretti. With a da Ponte text he was able to do completely what he was able later to do only partially with Schikaneder's fairy tale *Die Zauberflöte*—namely, to transform the whole thing into an expression of his own ideas.

The reason why the "meaning" of the two more naturalistic works is less easy to grasp than that of the fairy tale is that the humanitarianism of the fairy tale is its only easily comprehensible element. In the others practically everything is stated directly *but* the composer's attitude toward his characters.

Beaumarchais's play is straight social satire, a poking fun at the nobility for not being noble enough. It is closer to pamphlet journalism than it is to humane letters. It is what we might call a snappy and sophisticated little number. Mozart and da Ponte changed all the accents, made everybody human, gave to all the characters, to masters and servants alike, the human dignity of their faults and of their virtues. They produced out of a piece of propaganda that was scarcely literature one of the most touching pictures of eighteenth-century life that exists.

Don Giovanni is a tragicomedy about sacred and profane love. Its dramatic tone is of the most daring. It begins with a dirty comic song, goes on to a murder, a series of seductions, a sort of detective-story pursuit of the murderer in which one of the previously seduced ladies plays always a high comedy role; a party, a ballet, a supper scene with music on the stage, a supernatural punishment of the villain, and a good-humored finale in which everybody reappears but the villain.

The villain is charming; the ladies are charming; everybody in the play is charming. Everybody has passion and character; everybody acts according to his passion and his character. Nobody is seriously blamed (except by other characters) for being what he is or for acting the way he acts. The play implies a complete fatalism about love and about revenge. Don Giovanni gets away with everything, Donna Elvira with nothing. Donna Anna never succeeds in avenging her father's unjust murder. Punishment of this is left to supernatural agencies. Love is not punished at all. Its sacred (or at least its honorable) manifestations and its profane (or libertine) practice are shown as equally successful and satisfactory. The only unsatisfied person in the play is Donna Elvira, who is not at all displeased with herself for having sinned. She is merely chagrined at having been abandoned.

Mozart is kind to these people and pokes fun at every one of them. The balance between sympathy and observation is so neat as to be almost miraculous. *Don Giovanni* is one of the funniest shows in the world and one of the most terrifying. It is all about love, and it kids love to a fare-ye-well. It is the world's greatest opera and the world's greatest parody of opera. It is a moral entertainment so movingly human that the morality gets lost before the play is scarcely started.

Why do I call it leftist? I don't. I say the nearest thing we know to eighteenth-century Enlightenment is called today liberalism or leftism. But there is not a liberal or a leftist alive who could have conceived, much less written, that opera. It is the work of a Christian man who knew all about the new doctrinaire ideas and respected them, who practiced many of the new precepts proudly, and who belonged to a humanitarian secret society; but who had also suffered as few men suffer in this world. He saw life clearly, profoundly, amusingly, and partook of it kindly. He expressed no bitterness, offered no panacea to its ills. His life was the most unspeakable slavery; he wrote as a free man. He was not a liberal; he was liberated. And his acquaintance, through doctrine and practice, with all the most advanced ideas of his day in politics, in ethics, in music, was not for nothing in the achievement of that liberation.

December 15, 1940

The Berlioz Case

THERE are lots of books in print about the life and works of Hector Berlioz. Several of these, perhaps the best of them, are by the composer himself. All of them are preoccupied with the problem of matching up the "greatness" of his music with the nature and extent of his prestige or popularity. Some maintain that for all its world-wide dissemination and all its undeniable expertness, it is somehow or other not "great" really. Others hold that for all its undeniable "greatness" and its world-wide acceptance in orchestral repertory, certain of the larger works are unjustifiably neglected.

Leaving aside for a moment the hazy concept of "greatness" and looking at ascertainable facts, it is not possible to deny that a considerable body of Berlioz's work has enjoyed success both within and without the composer's native land for more than a century. Even during his lifetime Berlioz was recognized as an original master. His *Fantastic Symphony*, the *Roman Carnival* and *Benvenuto Cellini* overtures are still played all over the world. The first of these has even been made into a successful ballet, like the "*Pathétique*" of Tchaikovsky and the Fourth of Brahms. *Harold in Italy*, though less popular than these, holds

its place in repertory as one of the rare works of real distinction ever written for solo viola with orchestra. At least three of
the big choral works—the Requiem Mass, the Te Deum, and
a sort of opera-oratorio, *The Damnation of Faust*—are given
as frequently as the availability of the unusually large musical
forces required for their execution permits. They have probably
been heard in the musical centers as frequently during the last
century as Beethoven's *Missa Solemnis*, Verdi's Requiem, Bach's
Mass in B minor, or Haydn's oratorios.

There are certain works of Berlioz that are heard less often,
just as Beethoven's *Mount of Olives*, Mozart's Requiem and his
Mass in C minor (both unfinished), César Franck's *Beatitudes*,
Mahler's Ninth Symphony, and Boito's *Mephistopheles* are. None
of these works is more difficult to perform than the previously
named ones, but all are a little less grateful to conduct and less
satisfying to the musical public, on account of certain musical
weaknesses or, in the case of the Mozart works, their unfinished
state. Among the *grandes machines*, as the French call them,
of Berlioz that do not achieve frequent performance in their
entirety are his two operas, *The Capture of Troy* and *The Trojans
at Carthage*, his *Symphonie Funèbre et Triomphale* (written for
outdoor performance to celebrate the tenth anniversary of the
1830 Revolution), the oratorio *L'Enfance du Christ*, and the
"dramatic symphony" *Romeo and Juliet*, which Mr. Toscanini
has chosen to revive for the opening of the Philharmonic's second century of concert seasons.

The last work turns out to be one of those that deserve in
every generation a complete rehearing but that are more remarkable for the quality of certain already well-known excerpts
than for any stylistic or spiritual integrity of the whole. The
quality of these easily extractable sections, which are three,—
Romeo at the Capulet's ball, the Garden and Love scenes, and
the Queen Mab scherzo—is unique. There is nothing exactly
comparable to this kind of Berlioz elsewhere in music. For
vigor, delicacy, dramatic power, tenderness, melodic freshness,
and orchestral sophistication they are "great" music, if that
term means anything at all. Other sections of the work are suf-
fused with an original and most distinguished species of musical
poesy. Still others, especially the finale, are routine bombast. It
is of no demerit to Berlioz that he did not sustain his highest
level of creative power throughout a long work for chorus,

soloists, and orchestra. No composer ever did. It is rather to his credit that he sustained it in this work through three whole numbers of a certain length. And it is lucky for us that all three are instrumental pieces (the off-stage chorus in the Garden Scene can be omitted without grave falsification of the effect) and can thus be heard more frequently than would be possible if they required the mobilization of choral troops.

The undisputed facts about Berlioz's music are still these. It has always been admired and played, even when expensive to execute. Certain works are less frequently performed than others. The musical world, which has usually been in agreement about this master's best qualities no less than about his particular weaknesses, has always granted him world primacy in the art of instrumentation and profound originality of dramatic expression, as well as a highly personal, an inimitable approach to the procedures of musical composition. The razor edge, moreover, of his mind has never been denied. He was terrifyingly articulate both as a composer and as a critic. Also, his *Treatise on Instrumentation* is considered as fundamental a contribution to musical knowledge as Rameau's and Fux's works on harmony or Sebastian Bach's *Art of Fugue*. If worldwide admiration, both lay and professional, and a profound influence on the technique of his art do not define "greatness" in a composer, then I give up.

That Berlioz's musical production is uneven in quality is of no importance. So is everybody else's. That a just balance between expression and virtuosity is less regularly achieved in them than in the works of his classical-minded predecessors is not surprising. He was, after all, a Romantic; and the aim of all the Romantics was to produce a new kind of intensity by upsetting the classical ideal of a just balance between expression and virtuosity. They all overstepped the classic bounds of taste. Liszt's music is over-rhetorical. Wagner's is full of Germanic jingo and shameless in its exploitation of his own and his audience's erotic instincts. Schumann's is boisterous, Mendelssohn's stuffy, Brahms's timid and overrespectful of the past. Even Verdi, the purest of them all, made sometimes such pure theater that all sane sense of plot and character disappears. Only Chopin, in the whole nineteenth century, wrote music regularly, habitually according to an æsthetic that would not have shocked Mozart or Handel.

In any age, moreover, the work of the most original creators is the least even of all in quality. Perhaps "greatness" is a quality that precludes originality. In that case, respect for it is merely a worship of power and of the status quo and should be discouraged. One of the surest marks of high quality in art is the existence side by side of undeniable and universally acceptable beauty with elements that never cease to surprise. If this latter quality is absent the work is no longer alive. If it is too constantly present the work gets put away on a shelf eventually for reference use only. The music of Hector Berlioz is neither dead nor buried. Much of it is as alive and beautiful as anybody's. *Romeo and Juliet* contains three pieces that rank with the *Fantastic Symphony* and with his celebrated overtures. Even the whole work is worth reconsidering from time to time. Its revival after sixty years has done honor to the Philharmonic and to Mr. Toscanini and given pleasure to a musical public that paid as high as eleven dollars a seat to hear its opening performance.

The Damnation of Faust, which Dr. Rodzinski has promised us for next month, is an even grander work. The only real trouble about Berlioz's music is that there isn't enough of it that is written for orchestra alone. What there is is fine. But the bulk of his work requires massive concentrations that are not easy to assemble, such as full orchestra and four hundred choristers plus twenty-eight trumpets and trombones and fourteen kettledrums, as in one section of the Requiem. This effort is very much worth making from time to time. But every time it is made one finds that his really grand pieces of music are exactly the ones that everybody has always known to be grand, usually orchestral interludes that are quite playable as excerpts. I do not think Berlioz suffers from neglect. Nearly everything is played in the current concerts that is possible. And the big "machines" that constitute the bulk of his production are given, one or another of them, about as frequently as those of any other composer are. In Paris, they are given more often than here, of course. But they are, after all, French music. And the musical culture of New York has always embraced the Germano-Slavic and the Italian, just as that of London has, more readily than the products of the Gallic mind.

October 11, 1942

Theater and Religion

NBC SYMPHONY ORCHESTRA, *Arturo Toscanini*, conductor, with the WESTMINSTER CHOIR, on November 23 at Carnegie Hall, performing two works by Verdi: Te Deum and Requiem for Alessandro Manzoni. Soloists: *Zinka Milanov*, soprano, *Bruna Castagna*, contralto, *Jussi Björling*, tenor, and *Nicola Moscona*, bass.

MANAGERS refer to him as The Maestro. Orchestral players call him The Old Man in much the same spirit of reverence and healthy fear with which persons resident on the banks of the Mississippi never use any other name for that mighty stream than simply The River. This department had anticipated employing the polite but noncommittal form, Mr. Toscanini. After last Saturday night's rendition of the Verdi Te Deum and Requiem, we feel more like shouting to the city simply: "The Old Man is back!"

No better piece could he have chosen than the Verdi Requiem to make us appreciate his qualities as a master of musical theater. Gaudy, surprising, sumptuous, melodramatic and grand is Verdi's homage to Italy's poet and his own dear friend, Manzoni. No religious musical work of the last century is more sincerely or more completely what it is. Theatrical religion or religious theater? Let him answer who could tell us the same of nineteenth-century Neapolitan church architecture. Nowhere as in Naples does the eye find such constant verification of what the ear tells us when we listen to Palestrina, to Bach, to Mozart —namely, that to the sincerely religious there is no difference between sacred and secular style.

Verdi, though not a particularly pious man, was a sincere Catholic; he was also a sincere man of the theater and a sincere Italian. His Requiem is as sincere a piece of theatrical Italian Catholicism as has ever been written. Sincere Protestants often find it shocking. Sincere non-believers are likely to find it comic. But so might any one find the Dies Iræ itself who had no stomach for horror.

The only sound æsthetic standard I know of that covers all works and epochs is that anything is all right if it is enough so. That is to say that extremism in art, when it really is extreme, and middle-of-the-road normality, when it is really clear and comprehensible to all men, carry in their very extremism and universality the hallmarks of their authenticity. The Verdi Requiem has never raised any eyebrows in Naples (with which city, the seat of Verdi's greatest operatic successes, I like to identify it spiritually) or even in Milan (where it was first performed, in 1874). The question of its acceptance into the musical tradition of Protestant America is still, on account of its extreme theatricality, undecided.

As music that is not only very beautiful in itself, but that is also really "enough so," I give it my vote. I have not always been of that mind; I have long considered it an oddity of which the intrinsic worth scarcely justified the difficulties of a proper execution. After Saturday's performance I have no reserves.

The Maestro conducted it as if it were no more complicated than the "Miserere" from *Il Trovatore* and no less splendidly compelling than *Otello* or *La Traviata*. The Westminster Choir, handsomely gowned in white satin and violet velvet of ecclesiastical cut, sang perfectly. But perfectly. The soloists, Zinka Milanov, Bruna Castagna, Jussi Björling, and Nicola Moscona, sang like stars from some celestial opera house. The two ladies merit each a mark of 99 per cent for their rendition of the impossible Agnus Dei passage in parallel octaves unaccompanied. The kettledrummer, whose name I do not know, merits mention in heaven for his two-stick, unison explosions in the Dies Iræ and for the evenness of his Verdian *ppppp* rolls elsewhere.

Worthy of mention, too, is the implied homage to a regretted musician in the choice of this particular program by Mr. Toscanini to raise money for the Alma Gluck Zimbalist Memorial of the Roosevelt Hospital Development Fund. Just as the great expatriate Italian could have chosen no work more advantageous for himself to conduct, I can think of no more appropriate piece of music with which to honor the memory of a much-loved opera singer than Verdi's sincerely and superbly operatic Requiem.

November 25, 1940

The "Brahms Line"

JOHANNES BRAHMS was not during his lifetime a popular composer. Even today his works are little known and less loved
by the concert-going publics of France, Italy, Spain, Mexico,
and the South American republics. In the German-speaking
countries, in Scandinavia, in Holland, in England, and in the
United States a certain kind of musician has long borne his
music great love. But neither the Latin nor the Slavic musical
civilization has so far absorbed it at all. Its popularity among us
has been growing steadily of late until today it ranks in popular
favor with the music of Tchaikovsky and of Sibelius. This season
the Brahms symphonic works have far outnumbered in performance the works of Beethoven, of Mozart, and of Schubert.
The emergence of Brahms as a popular symphonist concords
(in time, at least) with the noticeable confluence of two musical currents; and the result of that confluence is certain to be
worth watching. These currents are the growing conservatism
of the "advanced" musical world, the world of modernism in
style and structure, and the deeply inveterate conservatism of
the non-professional music public.

A devotion to Brahms has always been, at least in our century, the mark of a quite definite musical conservatism. Even
in his own day, which is not far past, this was mostly so, too.
His whole musical program was traditionalist. He aimed to
reinvigorate the classical style rather than to transform it or
to add to it. In this he was the direct (and bitter) opponent of
Richard Wagner. Wagner considered the works of his predecessors and of his contemporaries as equally grist for his mill, and
he considered the business of his mill to be the turning out of
a new kind of music for new kinds of social usage. He called
this "the music of the future." Brahms considered his role to be
that of a preserver of the classic tradition against the destructive tendencies of Romanticism. He modeled his contrapuntal
style on the practices of Bach and of Mozart; his formal layouts
in the long works he copies directly out of works by Mozart
and Beethoven. His only voluntary concession to Romanticism
was in the direction of chromatic harmony, and that was fairly
hesitant.

Brahms was not by instinct a popular figure. He rather despised the non-professional public, and he had more gift for
tinycraft in music-writing than for sustained eloquence. He was
nevertheless obliged, even though an opponent of Wagnerian
demagogy, to do something about sustained eloquence, because no German could have success as a serious composer who
did not obviously continue in the line of Beethoven. Brahms
worked at this line assiduously, and finally, in his forties, produced a symphony. Later he produced three more. It was hard
work for him, because his musical imagination was more lyrical than heroic and his instrumental style more at home with
scrupulosities of chamber music than in the broader symphonic
manner. Neither was he any such master of the orchestra as his
more radical contemporaries, Wagner, Berlioz, and Liszt.

He succeeded by sheer determination, and by the constant
imitation of classic models, in pulling off these works most cred-
itably and in building up for himself in Germany, in En-gland,
and even in America a devoted public of musicians who considered him to be the direct heir of Bach and Beethoven. The
justice of that opinion is not a matter for present dispute, but
its existence has long been an undeniable fact. A curious recent
development in the Brahms controversy is that instead of having to wait for acceptance by the whole intellectual music world
(which would include, of necessity, the Latins and the Slavs),
the Brahms music has now achieved popular acceptance here
without benefit of clergy.

In this it has separated itself from the work of those composers who have reached the masses with all canonical benediction.
Beethoven and Wagner and Bach and Mozart our public has
been taught to love. And if the modernists have sometimes regretted their haste in throwing the weight of their prestige on
the side of Richard Wagner in his (and his widow's) campaign
to popularize his operas, the fact remains that all over the world
they did it. Brahms they nearly always resisted, as they mostly
resisted Tchaikovsky and Sibelius. In all three cases the general
public in Scandinavia, in England, and in the United States has
stepped in and offered its accolade spontaneously.

This fact might well take some of the wind out of Brahms's
academic admirers, leave them defending the lost cause that is
no longer lost and yet still not wholly won academically, if it
were not for the fact that new support has suddenly come to

them from an intellectual source, from the heart of modernism itself. Ever since about 1914 modern music has been decreasingly revolutionary in its aims and increasingly conservative in its procedures. The so-called "neo-classicism" of Stravinsky and Hindemith and other accepted leaders of the modernist movement, though by no means without value historically and even intrinsically, is none the less a position of defense rather than of attack. Its stabilizing tendencies are proved by the fact that it has enabled a great number of modernist composers to accept teaching posts in academic institutions, its cultural aim being frankly the incorporation of modern stylistic procedures into what is left, if any, of the classic tradition.

The joke of it all on the neo-classic modernists is that their program turns out to be exactly that of Johannes Brahms. Modern music has, in the words of a recent correspondent, writing of the Hindemith First Symphony, "executed a masterly retreat to the heavily fortified Brahms Line." Examine ten, almost any ten, modern symphonies and you will see, I think, that this is true. If my correspondent is right (and I think he is), it turns out that at the same time that our general public is taking to Brahms as a frankly popular symphonist like Tchaikovsky and Sibelius, the modernist intellectuals discover themselves to be following in exactly his pattern of basic traditionalism with contemporary surfacing. They also find themselves faced, as Brahms did, with the necessity of climbing down from their power of ivory tinycraft and doing something about symphonic eloquence. If they don't, the symphony public won't respect them; and if the symphony public doesn't respect them, they are likely to lose their teaching jobs.

It is sad to see official modernism turn out to be, after all, doubly conformist and wholly conservative. Maybe after the war there will be musical advance from the Brahms Line again. But for the present both the general public and most of the intellectual musicians are immured behind its surprisingly solid bastions. And if it is not pleasant to see modernist composers timidly pulling their punches and, what is worse, striking in many cases below the public's belt, it is salutary to observe that same public rising spontaneously to the work of a man who, though not a grandly original master, was a musical workman of high integrity and unquestioned nobility of thought.

April 26, 1942

Acquaintance with Wagner

About once a year your reviewer ventures to dip an ear again into the Wagnerian stream. He thinks he ought to find out whether anything about it has changed since the last time or if anything has possibly changed in him that might provoke a reversal of judgment about it all and a return of the passionate absorption with which he used to plunge himself into that vast current of sound. This season's expedition took him to hear *Die Walküre* last Tuesday evening at the Metropolitan Opera House. So far as he could tell, nothing has altered since last he heard the work.

The tunes are the same tunes as before, some excellent and some not so excellent. The symphonic development of the leitmotives continues to vary in interest according to the musical value of the leitmotives themselves. Those that contain chromatic progressions, arpeggios, or skips of a major sixth still become monotonous on repetition, while those based on narrowed skips and diatonic movement continue to support expansion without apparent strain. Wagner never learned the elementary rules of thumb that aided Bach and Handel and Haydn and Mozart and even Schubert to estimate the strength of melodic materials. His rhythmic patterns are frequently monotonous, too; and he has a weakness for step-wise modulating sequences.

The instrumentation remains rich in sound and highly personal. And if it often creates its theatrical excitement by the use of mere hubbub, that excitement is still a dependable effect and the instrumental dispositions involved are acoustically sound. It has long seemed to me that Wagner's original contributions to musical art are chiefly of an orchestral nature. Indeed, orchestration is the one element of musical composition in which Wagner had sound training, exception being made for the rules of German declamation, which he derived for himself by studying the works of Mozart and Weber and Meyerbeer. His music-writing is more varied in quality than is that of any other composer of equal celebrity, even Berlioz; but no matter what the quality, it always sounds well. It is always instrumentally interesting and infallibly sumptuous.

Sometimes the musical quality runs high, too. There are

unforgettable moments of invention in any of Wagner's operas, though the percentage of memorable pages out of his
whole production will probably be inferior to that in Verdi and
certainly far less than what one can find in Mozart. And their
excellence is not due wholly to orchestral orotundity; he wrote
often charmingly for the voice, as well. He wrote rather more
effectively, however, it seems to me, for the higher voices than
for the lower. His tenor and soprano roles are more pleasing
and more expressive than his alto, baritone, or bass writing.
His Ortruds and his Frickas are always a slight bore; and King
Marke, Wotan, Hunding, Fafner, even for habitual Wagnerians,
are proverbially great big ones. He had little feeling for the
heavier vocal timbres, and there is no real liberty in his handling
of them.

Well, all that is all that. Wagner was a gifted and original composer, though an unusually uneven one. And his lack of early
musical instruction is probably the cause of his major faults,
though I doubt if ignorance could be held responsible for any
of his virtues. He was not, as a matter of fact, an ignorant man;
he was merely an autodidact, lacking, like most autodidacts,
more in æsthetic judgment than in culture. He read voluminously and understood what he read; he reflected in a penetrating way about æsthetic matters, and he mastered easily any
musical technique he felt he needed. His troublesomeness on
the musical scene has always been due less to the force of his
musical genius (which was recognized from the beginning) than
to the fact that neither instinct nor training had prepared him
to criticize his own work with the objectivity that the quality of
genius in it demanded. As a result, every score is a sea beach full
of jewelry and jetsam. Fishing around for priceless bits is a rewarding occupation for young musicians, just as bathing in the
sound of it is always agreeable to any musical ear. But musicians
are likely to find nowadays that the treasure has been pretty well
combed and that continued examination of the remnants yields
little they hadn't known was there before.

What continues to fascinate me is not Wagner's music but
Wagner the man. A scoundrel and a charmer he must have been
such as one rarely meets. Perfidious in friendship, ungrateful in
love, irresponsible in politics, utterly without principle in his
professional life, and in business, of course, a pure confidence-
man, he represents completely the nineteenth-century ideal of

toughness. He was everything the bourgeois feared, hoped for, and longed to worship in the artist. The brilliancy of his mind, the modernity of his culture, the ruthlessness of his ambition, and the shining armor of his conceit, even the senile erotomania of his later years, all went into a legend that satisfied the longings of many a solid citizen, as they had long made him an attractive figure to aristocrats and intellectuals.

To know him was considered a privilege by the greatest figures of Europe, though many of these found the privilege costly. His conversation was stimulating on every subject; his wit was incisive and cruel; his polemical writing was expansive, unprincipled, and aimed usually below the belt. He was the most inspiring orchestral conductor and the most penetrating music critic of his century. His intellectual courage and the plain guts with which he stood off professional rivalries, social intrigues, political persecution, and financial disaster are none the less breathtaking for the fact that his very character invited outrageous fortune.

All this remains; it is available in many books. The music remains, too; and it is available at virtually every opera house in the world. It would not bring out the crowds or incite conductors and vocalists to the serious efforts it does if it did not have, in spite of its obvious inequalities, strength beneath its fustian still. To deny that strength were folly. To submit to it is unquestionably a pleasure. But what your reviewer would like most of all is to have known the superb and fantastic Wagner himself.

February 21, 1943

Dissent from Wagner

A RECENT ARTICLE of this column wherein it was suggested that the music of Richard Wagner was perhaps less interesting intrinsically than the personality of the man behind it has brought a certain amount of correspondence to the music desk, much of it, surprisingly, complimentary. The widow of a famous music critic wrote: "Your 'Acquaintance with Wagner' seems to me the last and best word on the gentleman. I read it with the greatest interest and shall keep it for future reading." A Bostonian composer mentioned Wagner's "overbearing confusion" and called him "to me the least satisfactory of the larger musical phenomena."

Many persons, of course, consider Wagner the *most* satisfactory of the larger musical phenomena. But that he *is* one of the larger musical phenomena is not disputed. What has long been argued about is the nature of the phenomenon and its value to civilization. Its value to individual persons is a private matter, and the voting or ticket-buying power of those persons is a statistical fact. Neither private pleasures, however, nor public devotions prove anything in art. Unless there is unanimous acceptance of a man's work, which is rare, it is the people who don't like it that have the last word in its evaluation.

There is no sounder proof of Shakespeare's central position in English literature, or of Dante's in Italian, than the fact that nobody objects to it. Such a position in music is occupied, through common consent, by a triumvirate—Bach, Beethoven, and Mozart. Wagner's pretensions to universal authority are inadmissible from the very fact that the music world is not unanimous about admitting them. Mozart is a great composer, a clear value to humanity, because no responsible musician denies that he is. But Wagner is not an absolute value from the very fact that Rossini denied it and Nietzsche denied it and Brahms denied it and, in our own time, Debussy and Stravinsky have denied it. This does not mean that, with the exception of Rossini, all these composers (including Nietzsche) have not stolen a trick or two from Wagner or accepted him as a major influence on their style. They have. But the fact that they have accepted his work with reservations is what proves my thesis.

Similar reservations are current about the music of Berlioz, of Gluck, of Weber, of Verdi, of Mahler, Strauss, Hindemith, Milhaud, and Aaron Copland, not to speak of the symphonists that descend from Brahms—the line of Tchaikovsky and Franck and Sibelius and Shostakovich and Roy Harris. These men represent musical values of a high order, but the values they represent are not satisfactory to all. They are therefore minor masters. J. S. Bach and Handel and Haydn and Mozart and Beethoven and Schubert and Chopin are major masters. So, very probably, are Schumann and Debussy. Richard Wagner is not. He could not be with so many musicians against him.

It is not the purpose of this essay to prove that liking Wagner's music is a low taste. Its purpose is to demonstrate that Wagner's music is a taste like any other, wholly legitimate but in no way sacred. The great masters are a bore to many people; they actively annoy almost none. But the minor masters annoy a great many people in a great many ways. There are excellent musicians who simply cannot stand the Berlioz bravura; others find it invigorating. There are those who are ravished by the sweetness of Grieg, carried away by the emphases of Verdi, or deeply shaken by the Tchaikovskian eloquence. To others all this is superficial. A Wagnerian bath is the cleansing flood for their souls. Still others find refreshment in the acidities of Stravinsky or in the dry champagne of Scarlatti and of Couperin.

All tastes are legitimate, and it is not necessary to account for them unless one finds it amusing to do so. Distastes are equally legitimate, including a distaste for music itself. If one has a distaste for the great masters of music, or a complete indifference to them, one is not a musician; that is all. But if one is a musician and if one has serious reservations about the music of any given composer, those reservations are grounds for suspicion that such music is not wholly straightforward. If the reservations are shared by other musicians, even a few, over a reasonable space of time, then that music has failed to convince the world of its purity.

It is the thesis of this reviewer that the music of Richard Wagner is an achievement somewhat less remarkable than that of the undisputed major masters of our tradition. The argument for this thesis is the simple syllogism that the canonization of a major master in any art requires a virtually unanimous vote of the initiates and that Wagner has never got anything approaching such a vote. He hoped, and many of his friends believed, that he would get it eventually, that the hesitant of spirit would come round. In the decade succeeding his death they seemed to be about to. The peak of his music's prestige within the profession occurred around 1890. The decline of this has been continuous ever since, though there was a notable rise in its popular acceptance between the two world wars. It seems now most unlikely that any thorough or intellectual rehabilitation of Wagner will take place until the wave of his box-office popularity shall have subsided.

And so for the present there is no reason why he shouldn't

provide sport for his enemies as well as delight for the faithful. Most of all, right now, his music needs debunking and deglamorizing, so that some unprejudiced analysis of its virtues may eventually be possible. The question is not whether Wagner is one of the "larger musical phenomena." Of course he is. Or whether he is one of the prime numbers in music, which he certainly is not. The question is simply how do the scores stand up page by page beside those of other standard dramatic composers from Mozart to Massenet. When the parishioners take up that little bingo game, there will be surprises for all, I promise, many of them agreeable.

March 7, 1943

Strauss and Wagner

THREE of Richard Strauss's operas—*Salomé, Elektra,* and *Der Rosenkavalier*—have provoked world-wide admiration. Their musical style has long been called by the vague term "post-Wagnerian." Their whole method, musical and dramatic, seems to me, however, to merit a more specific denomination. The German æsthetic most current in poetry, painting, and the theater arts during the epoch of their composition has always been known as expressionism or, in German, *Expressionismus.*

Considering the important role played in the very creation of these works by literary and theatrical modernism, it is only just to their composer to credit him with having something on his mind beyond a mere continuation or extension of the Wagnerian musical technique. Two of them were made in close collaboration with a poet, Hugo von Hofmannsthal. The other, *Salomé,* uses as libretto the translation of a tragedy written originally in French by Oscar Wilde. It is not to be denied, I think, that however old-fashioned this sort of literature may seem nowadays, all three plays have a linguistic style and a moral (or amoral) consistency that make them more distinguished entertainment than any of the mythological poems that Richard Wagner (who was not properly a man of letters at all, in spite of his large literary production) ran up for himself. Wagner's best works are full even of musical inequalities, and the contrast between their musical vigor and their religio-philosophico-poetic flaccidity has always been a scandal. Strauss's three great ones (I do not know his others well) are all of a piece. You can take them or leave them, but you cannot separate their music from what it expresses.

Strauss's concept of dramatic composition, though derived from Wagner's, turns out in practice to give a quite different result. It begins, of course, by accepting the Wagnerian formulas of the convulsive accompaniment and of the expansion of time. I do not know where Wagner picked up the idea of scrapping all accompanimental formality, of eschewing, I mean, all orchestral figurations of an abstract character. Neither Gluck nor Beethoven nor Weber nor Meyerbeer nor Berlioz, from all of whom Wagner appropriated theatrical procedures, ever did anything of the kind. They made their accompaniments appropriate and expressive, but it never occurred to any of them to destroy their function as a sort of auditory proscenium by whose static structure the more sensitive and personal music of the characters themselves is framed.

Characterization and all personal expression are classically the role of the vocal line and take place on the stage, just as atmosphere and dramatic emphasis are that of the orchestra and belong in the pit. In Wagner, and even more in Strauss, the orchestra takes over the work of characterization, as well as that of emotional analysis and amplification, leaving little for the singing actors to do beyond a certain amount of intoned speech-imitation in the low register, punctuated by intensely pushed-out cries in the upper. Not appearing ridiculous while they stand around waiting for their emotions to be described by the orchestra has always been the acting problem of Wagnerian singers. Nobody minds the eight to twelve minutes of relative immobility during which the Countess Almaviva in Mozart's *Marriage of Figaro* sings her "Dove sono" or Charpentier's Louise describes her own love life in an aria beginning, "Depuis le jour." But when Sieglinde, in the first act of *Die Walküre*, has nothing to do but cross the stage once while the orchestra plays a fifteen-minute footnote, it becomes evident to all that something should really be arranged to keep her occupied.

Strauss avoided this kind of situation by choosing stories about people who were not too dignified—who were, indeed, human-all-too-human (preferably outrageous)—and by putting the playwriting of these into skilled hands. He did not ask his artists either to stand around doing nothing or to do very much continuously expressive singing (they've enough to do getting the notes right). He gave them instead a literary and orchestral blueprint for acting all over the stage. Hence it is that, though the vocal line is always rather static and often musically nondescript, the visual drama, like the auditory orchestral one, is constantly and intensely convulsive. The convulsiveness all round is greater than in Wagner; can afford to be so because Strauss, a composer of much experience in the concert forms, can always make an act hold together, give it shape, progress, and conclusion, no matter how much violence goes on, even at a length, as in *Elektra*, of nearly two hours.

It is not my thesis that Strauss is the greater composer of the two. He is not. His thematic invention is too often bromidic and careless. He is a better musician than Wagner, yes, though not nearly so original or powerful a musical mind. His operas (or music-dramas) are certainly made after the Wagnerian model. But what happened to the Wagnerian model in Strauss's hands is something like this: He kept the convulsive accompaniment and the augmentation of time; but, feeling a need to correct the embarrassment to actors and to the public that Wagner had caused by taking most of its dramatic responsibility away from vocal expression, he called in expert literary men, who tightened up the plays, while they searched in legend and in abnormal psychology for subjects suitable to convulsive orchestral treatment by a master hand.

It is exactly this research into the lurid and its rendering in the cataclysmic style that constitutes the kind of German art known to its practitioners as *Expressionismus*. Musically and musico-dramatically Strauss is its world master, and the Metropolitan Opera Company's present *Salomé* I recommend as a vigorous production of one of its masterpieces. It is not incorrect to call Strauss's music post-Wagnerian; it is merely insufficient. Because expressionism represents a rebirth rather than a mere survival of the Wagnerian music-drama, the term is sufficient only if we admit, as I see no reason for not admitting, that the whole expressionist movement, which was larger than any one man's contribution to it, came into existence spiritually, as well as temporally, after Wagner.

December 13, 1942

Mahler and Boston at Their Best

BOSTON SYMPHONY ORCHESTRA, *Serge Koussevitzky*, conductor, last night at Carnegie Hall, performing Mahler's Symphony No. 9 and works by Mussorgsky, Liadov, and Rimsky-Korsakov.

GUSTAV MAHLER is to Richard Strauss as Bach to Handel or Debussy to Ravel. All such pairs of contemporaries have a common background of style and material that gives to their contrasted temperaments the ability to define and enclose an epoch, as the heads and the tails of a coin define and enclose between them its content.

Mahler's music is the more introspective. It is meditative, viscero-emotional, all about himself. Strauss's is declamatory, objective, descriptive of everything in the world but himself. Mahler's has the power of attracting fanatical devotion to itself and to the personality of its author. Strauss's gives a ripsnorting good time to all without provoking the slightest curiosity anywhere about its author's private life. Mahler wrote as if the material of Viennese music itself were so bound up with his own soul that only by integrating the two in a practically marital union could a work be created that would be a valid expression of either. Strauss wrote his pieces very much as a theatrical producer cooks up a show.

And yet the musical material and technique of the two are almost identical. Their themes might have been written by either, so characteristically do they consist of descending appoggiaturas and upward skips of the sixth. The two have an equal freedom of modulation and the same habit of playing their chromatics wild, not limiting the use of these to modulatory or to melodic purposes but throwing them in anywhere they feel like it for any reason whatsoever.

Both orchestrate, of course, with a sure hand and with wide resources of imagination and fancy. Mahler's orchestra, however, is the more elegant of the two by far, as is likewise his harmonic and contrapuntal fabric. His concentration on personal sincerity gave him an integrated manner of expressing himself, at his best, that is stylistically more noble than anything Strauss, with all his barnstorming brilliance, ever achieved. The Strauss heavy doublings and unashamed use of mere orchestral hubbub belong to a less refined and a less responsible order of musical expression. Mahler keeps his colors clean, and he never writes a middle part that hasn't in itself some intensity of expression or some grace.

The Ninth Symphony (considered by most Mahler devotees to be the finest of his works, though *Das Lied von der Erde* has its worshippers and so have the *Kindertotenlieder*) is beautifully made and beautifully thought. It is utterly German and Viennese and strangely not so at the same time. In reviewing *Das Lied von der Erde* some time back, I opined that there were some French influences in the particular contrapuntal approach Mahler employed. Naturally, I pulled down on my head a flood of abusive correspondence from the Mahlerites, who will have no analyzing of their idol and certainly no aspersions cast upon his hundred-per-cent Germanism. I suppose they don't count his Israelite birth or his professional travels (he conducted here at the Metropolitan Opera House and at the Philharmonic for something like three years) as factual evidence of a certain internationalism in his culture. Nevertheless, as I listened to the Ninth Symphony last night, I was still aware of French influences. Certain of these are technical, like the no-doubling orchestration. Others are æsthetic. I know the protest mail I shall get for saying this, but I must say it. Mahler has a great deal in common with the French impressionists. As an Italian musician to whom I mentioned the matter put it, "He comes as near being an impressionist as a German could."

Mr. Koussevitzky's reading of the work was highly satisfactory to this listener, who had only recently listened to Bruno Walter's recorded rendition of it with the Vienna Philharmonic Orchestra. Walter was slow and sentimental, and his unsteady tempos made a muddle out of Mahler's refined exactitude of notation. Koussevitzky let the piece move and kept the rhythms in place. In addition, the orchestral playing was of the beauteous kind that only Boston gives us regularly any more. Fluffy Russian savories done to a turn lightened and ended the evening's musical repast.

March 14, 1941

Close Communion

ORIGINAL BALLETS RUSSES, *Colonel W. de Basil*, general director, last night at the Fifty-first Street Theatre, New York, performing Stravinsky's *Balustrade*, ballet in four movements (based upon his
Concerto for Violin and Orchestra), conducted by *Mr. Stravinsky*, with
soloist *Samuel Dushkin*, violin; choreography by *George Balanchine*,
and design by *Pavel Tchelitcheff*. Also performed: Emmanuel Chabrier's *Cotillon* and Tchaikovsky's *Aurora's Wedding*, both conducted
by *Antal Doráti*.

THE STRAVINSKY Violin Concerto turns out to be good ballet music by the same qualities that made it a not very good
violin concerto. In no sense a conversation between soloist and
ensemble, it is rather a monologue for violin to which other
instruments play a continuous accompaniment, an insistent
monologue as of someone improvising stubbornly and not caring whether anybody is trying to accompany him or not. The
result lacks brilliance as a concerto. Toughly, hard-headedly poetic as music, it is not the least bit "grateful," as soloists would
put it, for the violin.

It is exactly because of its lack of soaring cantilena and of
sparkling passage work, cadenzas, show-off matter in general,
that it is ideal for continuous choreographic composition. It is
as tightly woven as a bird-cage. As four bird-cages, to be exact,
because it consists of four tight and tough little movements,
each of them minutely massive. Excepting the last. That is more
loose-hung, more dependent on mimicries of Tchaikovskian
charm than the other three.

These are as naïvely dogmatic as a first-prize violin student
from the Paris Conservatory, for whom, indeed, the work might
well have been composed. Its evocations of the violin classroom, combined with its willful avoidance of anything that
might possibly imply a connection with that tradition of Baroque and Romantic musical culture that is the only possible
excuse for playing the violin at all, give to the work a tense and
heartrending charm.

This concentrated emotional quality, an emotional quality
concentrated in and expressed by structural ingenuity, seems
to have given Mr. Balanchine his first chance in several years
to do what he loves to do best, to build long choreographic

"variations," as the dancing world calls them, of a tightly knit continuity. I should not care to opine regarding their æsthetic value, nor should I feel technically competent to describe them further than by saying that they seemed to me of a piece with the music. They seemed to have come out of the music and to walk in close communion beside it, the closeness of this spiritual communion providing an independence, so characteristic of Balanchine, that relieved the dancers from any pedestrian obligation to keep step with the measure.

The composer conducted handsomely and Mr. Dushkin executed the violin solo role with accuracy and comprehension, as if the piece belonged to them jointly, which, as a matter of fact, it rather does. Something in the nature of an ovation was their reward; and they shared this fraternally with Mr. Balanchine, Mr. Tchelitcheff, the decorator, being absent on account of a seasonal grippe. The whole occasion, indeed, shone with that white light of mutual artistic understanding that has made ballet as practiced by Russians in our century something a good deal more incandescent than any other kind of dancing spectacle.

I should like to add, as a footnote to my recounting of the evening, that the orchestra played extremely well under Mr. Antal Doráti for the two other ballets. Also that the score for *Cotillon,* pieced together out of Chabrier, has lost none of its loveliness since first I heard it in 1932, though I thought at the time and still think the finale needs a more sonorous instrumentation.

January 23, 1941

Stravinsky's Symphony

LAST SUNDAY AFTERNOON Mr. Leopold Stokowski and the NBC Symphony Orchestra gave us a performance that was notable in every way of Igor Stravinsky's Symphony in C major. Local musicians and music-lovers are grateful primarily to these gentlemen for the work's being done at all. But to have heard it in a rendition marked by such detailed clarity and so much over-all comprehension gives double reason for the proffering of public thanks.*

*The composer was displeased at the non-observance of his strictly marked tempos.

The piece has been in existence for more than two years; it was written to celebrate the fiftieth anniversary of Chicago's orchestra, and it has been played in various Western cities. Our local conductors have all read the score and turned it down. They have mostly considered it to be a weak work. In refusing to expose it to us, while giving us many another new symphony that has turned out to be weaker, they have presumed that a stricter standard of excellence is applicable to the work of a famous author than is appropriate to apply to that by composers of lesser prestige. This is reasonable enough, though contrary to the usual practice of program-makers. They have taken for granted also that conductors' judgments in this matter should satisfy the musical public.

It is true that we expect a high quality of musical workmanship from writers who have all their lives employed a high quality of musical workmanship, and Igor Stravinsky has never let us down in that respect. Moreover, any conductor can see from looking at the score of the Symphony in C major that it is not a piece likely to attract crowds or to win the conventional epithet "moving" (which means box-office). Neither is it, on the other hand, especially difficult of comprehension. If it had been played by everybody within the season of its Chicago première, as it most likely would have been had it been the work of Rachmaninoff or Shostakovich or Prokofiev or any other composer of world-wide fame excepting Stravinsky, an estimate of its intrinsic value would probably have been made without much delay by the musical public itself. It is difficult to understand on what grounds the Eastern conductors have neglected an obviously well-written work in large form by a composer of such high repute. Their private reserves about its spiritual or æsthetic value would seem to me interesting as opinion but hardly valid reason for refusing to expose it to general judgment.

Well, Mr. Stokowski and the radio people have finally fulfilled a cultural obligation that in former times would have been considered a privilege of the non-commercial agencies. It is not the first time this has occurred. Alfred Wallenstein, of WOR, Howard Barlow and his guest conductors at Columbia, have frequently shown more confidence in their nation-wide public than the leaders of our resident musical foundations have in the taste of their local subscribers. It may be that the country at large is more curious about new music, more open-minded and more advanced than the elite of the Eastern cities. The history of the Stravinsky symphony and also that of the Milhaud symphony, which was written at the same time and which has had many successful performances in the Middle and Far West without yet reaching us, would seem to indicate that the Atlantic seaboard has lost much of its former cultural leadership.

After all this build-up by avoidance, the Stravinsky symphony turns out to be no wild and woolly he-bear at all. It is an elegantly written piece in the author's own especial version of the neo-classic manner. It is a companion work to his Piano Concerto of twenty years back, to his Octette, to his Piano Sonata, to a whole series of compositions that aim to evoke the amenities of late eighteenth-century Vienna.

To expect an expansive rendering of his subjective emotional life is to prepare oneself for disappointment in listening to Stravinsky's music. He has never gone in for that; he has, on the contrary, for thirty years insistently expressed his disdain for it in print and in person. He has always worked objectively, directing his whole talent and mind toward as impersonal a rendering as that of a painter or of a dramatist. He has frequently varied the object of his expression, and he has invariably chosen a manner of writing suitable to that object; but his æsthetic of musical composition has not altered since he first began to write, some forty years ago.

He has always been a man of the theater, and he has always thought like one. When writing for the stage he is directly atmospheric; he makes musical décor. When writing for the concert platform he is evocative. His symphony is no less theatrical a conception than the early piece called *Fireworks* or the opera about a Chinese emperor and a mechanical nightingale. It evokes the Austrian court symphony as deliberately as *Le Baiser de la Fée* evokes the Imperial Opera of Saint Petersburg and the ballets of Tchaikovsky or as *Petrouchka* represents the sights and sounds of a village carnival. It could be made into a ballet tomorrow, and probably will be before the decade is done.

There is no question that this particular piece, like many another of Stravinsky's platform productions, is stiff and a little prim. Its thematic material is impersonal, its syntax formal, its harmony and instrumentation wholly elegant and well bred.

The author has done his best to make it as dry as champagne, as neutral as distilled water. It is not detrimental to the work, however, that in spite of his almost academic intentions, the Russian ballet-master in him does take over from time to time. Indeed, what breadth the piece has is due to the incompleteness of its voluntary stylization. It is no sugar-tit. And it has little ambition toward the *genre chef-d'œuvre*. But in its quiet way it is something of a masterpiece, all the same. When one compares it with its author's other works of the last twenty years in similar vein, one can hardly fail to recognize that it is the most ample of all his efforts to evoke the Austrian court style. Whatever the value of doing that may be, it is undeniably an achievement to have done it and to have bestowed thus on twenty years of labor so adequate a crown.

The legitimacy of the author's intention is no less open to question than is the legitimacy of any other æsthetic of our time. The intrinsic worth of the piece (aside from the clear mastery of its writing and rhetoric) and its possible influence on history are impossible of contemporary estimation. But that it presents a high degree of musical interest is undeniable. It does seem a little timorous of our Eastern conductors to have neglected it for two years while giving us constantly new works by minor Slavic symphonists (and others) that are certainly no better box-office. It was either overtimid of them, if the box-office is all they were afraid of, or overconfident about their own taste, if they thought their lack of personal liking for the work entitled them to avoid the clear responsibility of communicating it to us without delay.

February 28, 1943

Stravinsky's Late Beethoven

CELIUS DOUGHERTY and VINCENZ RUZICKA, piano duo, in recital last night at Town Hall, performing, among other works, Mr. Dougherty's *Music from Seas and Ships: An American Sonata* and Stravinsky's *Concerto per due pianoforte soli.*

DOUGHERTY and Ruzicka, who played two pianos in recital last night at Town Hall, are enlightened program-makers. It is unfortunate that irresponsible tempos and a good deal of slappy tone-production marred what might otherwise have been one of the season's musical treats. Schubert's great F-minor Fantasy, a sonata by Purcell and a Prelude and Fugue of Buxtehude gave the concert a high degree of classical interest, while a new work of Mr. Dougherty's composition on American sea chanties offered a not unpleasant repose before the modern-style severities of Stravinsky's Concerto for Two Pianos Alone. The latter work in particular needs a charming, even an urbane, interpretation if it is to be absolved by contemporary audiences from the charge of gratuitous ugliness, its very abstruseness being a sufficient unpleasantness for many.

It is abstruse because, as in most of Stravinsky's music from the last twenty-five years, its style is its subject. And the music-lovers brought up on the Romantic tradition of music, in which the style is supposed to derive from the subject, are confused by any other approach to the art. Nevertheless, the use of style as subject, the evocation of past periods, the modernistic usage of ancestral furniture and formulas, is as vigorous a practice in contemporary music as it is in contemporary theater, contemporary architecture and decoration. The whole æsthetic of Johannes Brahms, indeed, whom many consider the bulwark of musical conservatism, is based upon nothing less. Stravinsky cannot be reproached for his masterly distortions of classical shape and phraseology without the same indictment being held valid against the original neoclassic composer of them all, Brahms, who invented the looking-backward business, the taking of a style as his subject.

Brahms's preferred subject-matter was the style of Beethoven's middle period. The subject-matter of Stravinsky's Concerto for Two Pianos Alone is, if I mistake not, the style of Beethoven's later period, in particular that of the last four or five piano sonatas. It contains a stormy sonata movement, an air with coloratura ornaments, and a set of extended variations ending with a fugue. The melodic material is angular and strong, the emotional content violent. The calmer passages are static and more than a little mannered. Transitions are operated brusquely and without grace. There is a certain willful barbarism about the relation of theme to accompaniment. The whole picture of the later Beethoven music, as you can see, is complete, with all its mannerisms and all its perfectly real seriousness. And Stravinsky's music has here, just as Beethoven's did beneath the mannerisms he had inherited from Mozart and Haydn and those he had acquired in the course of his own composing life, an undeniable integrity of expression.

I should like to say also a certain grandeur of expression, were it not for the fact that grandeur, just as in many of Beethoven's later works, is as much the *modus operandi*, the conscious manner of the piece, as it is a result of inherent excellence. It is even more than in Beethoven the subject-matter, because the concerto is a study of another man's stylistic achievement. In Beethoven's case that achievement consisted in the extended expression of grandiose sentiments in a vocabulary of such astounding directness that musical scholars have never yet been able to agree how far plain rudeness, a deliberate avoidance of the amenities, was of the essence. I think last night's audience, though certainly impressed by his talent, felt equally uncertain about Mr. Stravinsky's desire to please.

March 23, 1944

Shostakovich's Seventh

WHETHER one is able to listen without mind-wandering to the Seventh Symphony of Dmitri Shostakovich probably depends on the rapidity of one's musical perceptions. It seems to have been written for the slow-witted, the not very musical and the distracted. In this respect it differs from nearly all those other symphonies in which abnormal length is part and parcel of the composer's concept. Beethoven's Ninth, Mahler's Ninth and Eighth, Bruckner's Seventh, and the great Berlioz "machines" are long because they could not have been made any shorter without eliminating something the author wanted in. Their matter is complex and cannot be expounded briefly.

The Shostakovich piece, on the other hand, is merely a stretching out of material that is in no way deep or difficult to understand. The stretching itself is not even a matter of real, though possibly unnecessary, development. It is for the most part straight repetition. The piece seems to be the length it is not because the substance of it would brook no briefer expression but because, for some reason not inherent in the material, the composer wished it that way. Of what that reason could possibly be I have only the vaguest notion. That the reason was clear to its author I have not the slightest doubt, however, because the piece all though bears the marks of complete assurance. It is no pent-up pouring out of personal feelings and still less an encyclopedic display of musical skill. It is as interminably straightforward and withal as limited in spiritual scope as a film like *The Great Ziegfeld* or *Gone with the Wind*. It could have said what it says in fifteen minutes, or it could have gone on for two hours more. The proportions of the work seem to this auditor, in short, wholly arbitrary.

They do not seem, nevertheless, accidental. Nothing seems accidental in the piece. The themes are clearly thought out and their doings are simplified with a master's hand. The harmonies, the contrapuntal web, the orchestration show no evidence of floundering or of experiment. If the music has no mystery and consequently no real freedom of thought, neither does it contain any obscurity or any evidence of personal frustration. It is as objective as an editorial, as self-assured as the news report of a public ceremony.

Heretofore this author's music, whether theatrical or symphonic, has been animated by an instinct for easy theatrical values. He has put into his works with never-failing effect crowd scenes, barcarolles, burlesques, and patriotic finales, holding these all together with a kind of neutral continuity-writing in two-part counterpoint. The most entertaining of these numbers have always been the burlesques of bourgeois musical taste, which were the more charming for their being purged, as it were, of bitterness by the optimism of the final patriotic and military passages. One could always feel in them the rambunctious but gifted boy whose heart was really in the right place. In spite of the static and not very significant character of the incessant two-part counterpoint between his "production numbers," if one may call them that in symphonic music, have always been bright, full of gusto, and genuinely characteristic of their composer. They have put us in contact with a real person.

The Seventh Symphony has the same formal structure as the rest of its author's work. It is a series of production numbers, interspersed with neutral matter written chiefly in that same two-part counterpoint. There is a mechanized military march and the usual patriotic ending, neither of them quite as interesting or imaginative as it might be. And the rest of the episodes are even tamer. The pastorale and the Protestant chorale are competent routine stuff, no more; and the continuity counterpoint, though less static than usual, just sort of runs on as if some cinematic narrative were in progress that needed neutral accompaniment. The opening passage, which is said to represent the good Soviet citizen, is bold and buoyant. But nowhere is there any real comedy, which is what Shostakovich does best.

It is no reproach to an author to say that one of his works is the kind of work it is. And this work is certainly of more sober mien than most of its author's others. It is very long and very serious, and both these qualities are certainly deliberate observances. The facile competence and the assurance of the whole thing, moreover, eliminate the possibility that any auditor find the struggle between the artist and his material a major subject of interest. It is easy to listen to the piece, equally easy to skip any part of it without missing the sense of the whole. It is excellent journalism, and some of it can even be remembered. But it will probably not make much difference to anybody's inner musical life whether he hears it or doesn't.

Shostakovich is an abundant musician, a "natural" composer. He is also an experienced and perfectly assured one. Heretofore he has manifested a boyish taste for low comedy (redeemed by patriotic sentiments) that gave gusto to his writing and made listening to it sometimes fun. The present work shows a wish to put boyish things behind him and an ability to do so without losing confidence in himself. That it is less amusing than his previous works is not to its discredit. That it is, in spite of its serious air and pretentious proportions, thin of substance, unoriginal, and shallow indicates that the mature production of this gifted master is likely to be on the stuffy side. That he has so deliberately diluted his matter, adapted it, by both excessive simplification and excessive repetition, to the comprehension of a child of eight, indicates that he is willing to write down to a real or fictitious psychology of mass consumption in a way that may eventually disqualify him for consideration as a serious composer.

October 18, 1942

More of Same

SHOSTAKOVICH's Eighth Symphony, which was performed at yesterday afternoon's broadcast concert of the Philharmonic-Symphony Orchestra in Carnegie Hall, has been hitherto surrounded by its protectors with an air of mystery. The Columbia Broadcasting System has encouraged one to believe that a certain sum was paid for the performing rights and then refused to admit or deny the figure. The Russians themselves have refused to make any formal statement about the work at all. Though performed with public success in Moscow as early as November of last year, the newspapers that reflect official opinion there, *Pravda* and *Izvestia*, have never reviewed it. The piece itself, however, is as plain as the nose on your face. Why Russian government circles should reserve judgment on it is as difficult to imagine as any loyal reason why its American backers should go all kittenish about what they have done to deserve it.

The symphony, in four movements, lasts sixty-three minutes. Its melodic material is interesting; and if this is not always of the highest expressivity in degree, there is never any doubt about the nature of its expressive intent. The formal continuity is loose, but quite sufficient for a work of broad and simple character. There is no diffuseness; there is, as in the Seventh Symphony by the same author, merely extension. The orchestration is thin but tense. Its effects, like the melodic and contrapuntal ones, are easy to follow, both because many of them employ only one or two instruments and because all of them are insisted upon at some length.

This symphony is typical of its author's recent work. It is

economical in the sense that matter ordinarily sufficient for a twenty-minute piece has been stretched out to last an hour. It has been stretched by the use of lengthy instrumental solos and other kinds of thin writing, but not by any abuse of literal repetition. There is little in the piece that need have taken very long either to compose or to score. Yet for all the spreading thin of its substance, the musical interest of this is sustained and homogeneous. Here is no carelessly thrown-together construction, but a rather remarkably stretched-out one.

The political value of launchings such as those the recent works of this composer have received is not a question requiring opinion from this department. But if symphonic music has any real value as national propaganda, it is difficult to imagine a contemporary composer better suited than Shostakovich to the producing of it for this purpose. No one else writes so seriously, so simply, so plainly. No one else makes an impression of sincerity with so little effort. Very probably length is a help to him in making this impression, since nobody ever takes a long piece for wholly meretricious. It is hard to see otherwise what that length accomplishes. Certainly it is a deliberately adopted device. Its texture is too skillfully attenuated for it to be the result of mere abundance. And anyway there is no abundance in it; but there is, on the other hand, every device of economy known to musical composition.

April 3, 1944

Smetana's Heir

BOSTON SYMPHONY ORCHESTRA, *Serge Koussevitzky*, conductor, yesterday afternoon at Carnegie Hall, performing Martinů's Symphony No. 1 and Beethoven's Symphony No. 3 ("Eroica").

WHAT a pleasure! What a pleasure to hear the Boston Symphony Orchestra again! Yesterday afternoon's concert in Carnegie Hall was substantial and delicious, with two symphonies for fare, an old and a new—the Beethoven "Eroica" and a First by the brilliant Czechish composer Bohuslav Martinů. The music was interesting, and the renditions couldn't have been more elegant. Just think of it! An ensemble that sounds like an ensemble playing music that sounds like music! It restores one's faith; it really does.

The Martinů Symphony is a beauty. It is wholly lovely and doesn't sound like anything else. Original is not the word for it, because the thematic material is not quite that. The best of this, moreover, is folklorish in the good Czech tradition. The harmonic underpinning is a little plain, too, solid enough but not imaginative. Personal or individual would describe the work better. Because these words describe style rather than substance.

Personal indeed is the delicate but vigorous rhythmic animation, the singing (rather than dynamic) syncopation that permeates the work. Personal and individual, too, is the whole orchestral sound of it, the acoustical superstructure that shimmers constantly. It doesn't glow like Debussy or glitter like Ravel. It is more like Berlioz in its translucency or like Smetana, Mr. Martinů's compatriot. It is like Smetana because the shining sounds of it sing as well as shine; the instrumental complication is a part of the musical conception, not an icing laid over it.

The shimmer I speak of is produced acoustically by mixing acid sonorities with sweet ones. There is always an oboe around, a muted trumpet or horn, violin harmonics, or light tremolos played near the bridge. Against these are sweet flutes rising in thirds, or clarinets. Often the strings play subdivided, high and tenderly; and what they play is not sugary, but a shade acidulous in its harmony. Consistently the whole is pointed up by delicately percussive harp or piano. One would not have dreamed that after fifty years' vulgarization of this kind of writing anybody could make it sound so fresh, so lovely, so varied, so entirely personal. One wouldn't have thought, either, that a composer could keep it up through a whole symphony, that he could find enough variants to make it interesting.

Martinů has kept it interesting, however, and made it deeply expressive. He has amplified his taste for acid-sweet mixtures into a full stylistic outlet for personal thoughts. He has had no need of demagogy from the brass or of sob stuff from the strings. He uses both as musical instruments of an ensemble that constantly sings. It sings in many timbres and many colors, but always the colors are clean and bright and always they are integrated into a shimmering pattern. The symphony is beautiful music and beautiful workmanship. And if, in spite of its impersonal subject-matter (I take it to be a meditation about his native land), it is highly individual music nevertheless, that fact places Martinů already above his predecessor Dvořák and in the high company of Smetana, greatest of all those symphonic composers in whose work patriotism is of the essence.

November 22, 1942

Repeating Pattern

PHILHARMONIC-SYMPHONY ORCHESTRA, *Artur Rodzin-ski*, conductor, performing Roy Harris's *March in the Time of War*, Martinů's Symphony No. 2, Beethoven's Piano Concerto No. 5 ("Emperor"), and Richard Strauss's *Till Eulenspiegel*. Soloist: *Robert Casadesus*, piano.

MARTINŮ's Second Symphony, which received its first local performance last night at a Philharmonic concert in Carnegie Hall, is less fresh than his first. Its melodic material is a little too plain and sensible for the ornate figurations in which it is embedded. The themes are immobilized, like flies in amber; they are repeated prismatically, but they do not expand or go anywhere. The piece has the stamp of high-class workmanship, but it follows a formula that is already becoming monotonous.

Like the shimmering sonorities of his master, Albert Roussel, the glittering and note-heavy textures of Bohuslav Martinů are, for all their transparency, an inflexible medium of expression. They suit best exotic or fanciful subjects. Applied to straightforward melodies of songlike character or to the semi-abstract motifs that are the basis of symphonic continuity, they create a dichotomy of style that suggests a photograph of your Aunt Sophie in front of the Taj Mahal. Neither the subject nor the background appears to advantage in such an arrangement. The background goes a little tawdry, and the subject does not express itself completely. The Second Symphony last night sounded mechanical, repetitive, overelaborate, and essentially trivial.

Far from trivial was the piano-playing of Robert Casadesus. Utterly clean without any hardness, it had no sloppy edges anywhere and no ugly tone. Alone among the great virtuosos,

Mr. Casadesus has preserved the tenderness of intimacy in the framework of power-projection. He has also preserved the French rhythmic tradition (which is the ancient and basic European one) in the rendering of German music. Never a quantity out of line; never a stress but for rhetorical reason. Many a passage of considerable length is executed, loud or soft, without any dynamic alteration of any kind; and the meter is clearer than if it had been thumped out. His was an extraordinary performance of the "Emperor" Concerto, extraordinary for its beauty, its power, its physical perfection, its intellectual distinction, its musical *élan*. Its only fault was a tendency to hurry along (largely the fault of the orchestra) in the waltz finale.

December 31, 1943

The Hindemith Case

PAUL HINDEMITH's music is both mountainous and mouse-like. The volume of it is enormous; its expressive content is minute and not easy to catch. His output is voluminous; that implies a certain facility. His tonal grammar and syntax are perfectly clear; that is evidence of care taken. His work has style also; and that is proof of its artistic integrity, of an integration between what its author feels and what his listener hears.

There is nevertheless a good deal that is obscure about it. How often has one sat through pieces by Hindemith that seem to make sense musically but little or no sense emotionally! Even so ingratiating a piece as the Third String Quartet sounds more like the work of a composer who had nothing better to do one morning than like something that had got itself born out of inner necessity. His work could hardly be called hermetic, because hermetism is usually pretty compact. I should say that the obscurity one encounters in it is due rather to the diffuseness of its thought than to any especial concentration of meaning or any rigidly novel technique.

It is not, properly speaking, academic music. It is too loosely put together for that. It is cleanly written down but not much polished, and it meanders more than is considered good "form" in academic circles. Also, its instrumentation,

though completely sure-handed, is rarely brilliant or "effective" in the way that the work of celebrated pedagogues is
likely to be. He does not seem to be interested in stylistic or
cultural showing off any more than he is in emotional expan-
siveness or emotional concentration.

His music exerts a great fascination, however, over music
students; and it is not without a certain impressiveness for
the music public in general. It is obviously both competent
and serious. It is dogmatic and forceful and honest and completely without charm. It is as German as anything could be
and farther removed from the Viennese spirit than any music
could possibly be that wasn't the work of a German from the
Lutheran North. It has no warmth, no psychological understanding, no gentleness, no *Gemütlichkeit*, and no sex-appeal.
It hasn't even the smooth surface tension of systematic atonality. It is neither humane nor stylish, though it does have
a kind of style, a style rather like that of some ponderously
monumental and not wholly incommodious railway station.

Having reflected in this vein for some years about Hindemith's non-programmatic music, it was with the hope of
maybe finding I was all wrong that I went to hear the National Orchestra from Washington play symphonic excerpts
from *Mathis der Maler* last Tuesday evening. I wanted to see
what the least picturesque composer alive would do with
the most picturesque subject imaginable. I remembered his
having tried his hand some years ago at a picturesque subject
drawn from modern life in an opera called *Neues vom Tage*,
and I remembered having been amused at the way he had
managed to write music for that work that was ponderous
and cute at the same time.

Mathis der Maler turned out to be more of same, only more
serious in tone, on account of its subject-matter, which has
to do with three religious pictures by Mathias Grünewald—
a *Descent of Angels*, an *Entombment*, and a *Temptation of
Saint Anthony*. The subject is an ambitious one and presents
a problem of musical method for which there is no precedent
in musical tradition.

There are several classic procedures for representing visual
images by means of music. There is the ancient and simple
one employed by Rameau and Handel and Sebastian Bach,

which is to imitate in the melodic contours either the sil-
houette or the characteristic motion of the thing one wishes
to describe, valleys being exalted, for instance, the crooked
being made straight and the rough places plain, Adam falling
out of paradise, troupes of angels tripping down the major
scale, and gentlemen attempting from love's sickness to fly-
y-y-y-y-y-y-y in vain. There is also the Romantic procedure
of adding to this auditive and kinetic vocabulary of visual
suggestion a subjective description of the emotional effect
of it all on some sensitive observer or participant. Bacchana-
lian routs, debauches in Venusberg, Swiss mountain weather,
graveyard ballets, and visits to hell on Walpurgisnacht are
common in nineteenth-century music.

Mendelssohn's contribution to landscape technique consisted in making the observer always the same man, himself.
In Scotland, in Italy, in fairyland, he is always Mendelssohn,
sympathetic and sensitive and strictly non-participant. The
modern French technique of musical landscape painting, of
which Debussy was the most skillful practitioner, is essentially
Mendelssohnian, though the expressive range and psychological intensity of Debussy's work are greater than those
of Mendelssohn's because it is not bound to the German
conception of thorough bass or to the idea of "developing"
the thematic material. It conceives any melodic line as a self-
sufficient expressive unit, counterpoint as a plurality of such
units, harmony and rhythm as coloristic ornamentation to
melody. "Form" in the German sense of harmonic progress
is something to be avoided, since it implies that the author
is either going somewhere or trying to make a point, instead
of receiving and transmitting a series of related impressions
from some point of view where he is supposed to remain
motionless, his will immobilized by the intensity of the visual-
auditive photographic process. Musical landscape painting
does not need "form" in the sense of progress. It needs, on
the contrary, a static musical unity based on sequential statement of all the things that need to be said in order to make
the piece a proper description of its subject.

All these procedures exist as known ways of translating
sight into sound. There is no known way of translating into
sound visual pictures that have already been translated into

so stylized a medium as painting. A composer's version of a painter's version of the Church's version of scenes from sacred history is what *Mathis der Maler* purports to be. As such it is naturally not very successful. It couldn't be. When one considers, in addition, that Hindemith has never properly liberated himself from the German bass, that his rhythm is constrained and unimaginative, that whenever he can't think what to do next he writes imitative counterpoint, that his melodic contours, though dignified enough, are inexpressive, that his creative concentration is too diffuse to allow him to write either visual music or subjective emotional music effectively, it is surprising that the *Mathis* tryptich should come off at all.

It comes off, just as all his music does, in spite of everything, by good intentions and by being playably orchestrated. The *Entombment* has a certain directly expressive quality, though the influence of Grünewald would seem to be present more as private stimulus to the composer's invention than as anything a listener need take cognizance of. The *Descent of the Angels* and the *Temptation of Saint Anthony* are not handled as convincingly, on the whole, as the Romantic masters handled similar subjects. Saint Anthony's victory over temptation, for instance, is represented by a routine Lutheran chorale harmonized for brass in a routine manner that might just as well represent Mr. Hindemith's satisfaction at getting to the end of his piece as a saint's triumph over his lower nature.

Mathis der Maler is typical of North Germany at its best and of modern scholastic facility at its worst. It is complex, ineffective, unpolished, lacking in both grace and expressive power. All the same, it has a moral elevation and a straightforward, if clumsy, honesty that make it impossible not to respect and to admire it for being at all times unquestionably "good" music.

February 9, 1941

Serious Music

BUDAPEST STRING QUARTET, with *Mordecai Bauman*, baritone,
and *Milton Kaye*, pianist, yesterday afternoon at Town Hall, performing Schubert's Quartet No. 14 ("Death and the Maiden"), Schönberg's *Verklärte Nacht*, and six songs by Charles Ives. *Josef Roismann*
and *Alexander Schneider*, violin; *Boris Kroyt*, viola, *Mischa Schneider*,
cello. Presented by New Friends of Music.

City dwellers are at their best in early winter between five
and seven of an afternoon. No time is more propitious for the
projection of high musical thought; none finds the devoted listener more completely in possession of his faculties. Yesterday's
concert of the New Friends of Music was a delight to the ear
and to the mind, and I fancy the audience at Town Hall must
have offered equal delight to the executants.

Franz Schubert's "Death and the Maiden" quartet is a
deeply tragic, lyrically impassioned meditation on the death
of Franz Schubert, provoked by his having contracted an
incurable disease. The work is Schubert at his most inspired
and most sustained. The Budapest String Quartet played it
with comprehension of its emotional poignancy as well as of
its musical values.

Chamber music in a hall that seats 1,500 people is, of
course, a contradiction in terms; and string-quartet sonorities are likely to come out pretty false under such conditions.
Even if forced fortissimos are avoided, there is a constant
temptation to make over-powerful accents and a certainty
that no matter what happens the tone of the ensemble will
have a certain deadness laid on it.

The reason why public string-quartet playing is such a difficult art is that in the clear, dead acoustic of such halls every
musical fault is audible; and at the same time no auditory
glamour, no sharpness of sensuous delight, is there to charm
the listener through a work or passage that isn't quite all it
should be in rhythm or intonation.

The Budapest Quartet has a satisfying cellist to build its
tonal structure on. Mr. Mischa Schneider's tone is never
groany, never waily, rarely hoarse. He keeps his fortes within

the limits of what can be made to sound; and his rhythm is a live thing, a breathing thing, a sustaining pulse for the whole musical musculature.

Mr. Boris Kroyt's viola and Mr. Alexander Schneider's second violin are delicate, higher distillates of the same essential timbre. The first violin does not blend so well, stands out a trifle by its too thin, acid tone and by being every now and then squarely off pitch.

Charles Ives's songs have a certain sincerity and worthiness about them. On the whole they are pretty kittenish. The texts are kittenish; the tunes are kittenish; the accompaniments are practically kitty on the keys. Only short passages of "Evening" and "Charles Rutledge" have any musical or prosodic inevitability about them, and they sound more like improvisation than like organic composition. The finale of "General Booth Enters into Heaven," however, the part built around the hymn-tune "There Is a Fountain Filled with Blood," is first-class music. The double harmonies are not just a blur, as Ives's harmonies so often are. They are like a prism that defracts, a lens that amplifies; and their notation and placing are as precise as a good job in optics.

Verklärte Nacht, far from being an isolated example of something or other in Arnold Schönberg's career, as is commonly supposed, is a work that embodies all that composer's finest and corniest qualities. The finesse of its string-writing makes it a joy to play and to hear. The seriousness of its emotional content is unquestionable. Its slithery chromaticism is the emotional and technical diving-board from which a young man of such gift and power (he wrote it at twenty-five) could only plump off square into the mud-puddle of atonality. Atonality was already being theorized about in Vienna in those days (1889). The young Schönberg slipped, plumped, embraced, stayed.

The most individual among Schönberg's many gifts as a composer is his ability to enlarge an emotional experience without going to town sentimentally about it. He blows it up, not to hit you over the head with it, but to inspect it. His *Verklärte Nacht*, no less than his *Gurrelieder* and his *Pierrot Lunaire*, is a microscopic examination, a psychic analysis of its stated poetic text. Schönberg is a late Romantic, if you will; but not for nothing did he spend his first fifty years as a fellow citizen and contemporary of Dr. Sigmund Freud.

October 21, 1940

Real Modern Music

NBC SYMPHONY ORCHESTRA, *Leopold Stokowski*, conductor, yesterday afternoon in Studio 8-H, Radio City, performing, among other works, Schönberg's Piano Concerto, Op. 42. Soloist: *Eduard Steuermann*, piano.

ARNOLD SCHÖNBERG's Piano Concerto, which received its first performance anywhere yesterday afternoon by the NBC Symphony Orchestra, Leopold Stokowski conducting and Eduard Steuermann playing the solo part, is the first original work for large orchestra by this master to be heard in New York since quite a long time back. For many of our young music-lovers it is no doubt their first hearing of any orchestral work of its kind. One cannot be too grateful to Mr. Stokowski for giving himself the trouble to prepare it and for paying his radio listeners the compliment of presuming their interest. It is an honor paid not only to one of the great living masters of music but to the American public as well; and the General Motors Corporation, which sponsored the broadcast, should be proud of the event.*

The piece, which lasts a shade under twenty minutes, consists of four sections neatly sewn together and played without pause—a waltz, a scherzo, an adagio, and a rondo. All are based on a single theme, though there is considerable development of secondary material in the scherzo. The musical syntax is that commonly known as the twelve-tone system, which is to say that the employment of dissonance is integral rather than ornamental. The expression of the work is

---

*Leopold Stokowski's contract as conductor of the NBC Orchestra was not renewed for the following year. His assiduity toward modern composition is considered in musical circles to be the chief reason for this change.

romantic and deeply sentimental, as is Schönberg's custom and as is the best modern Viennese tradition.

The instrumentation, too, is characteristic of its author. It is delicate and scattered. The music hops around from one instrument to another all the time. It sounds like chamber music for a hundred players. There is plenty of melody, but no massing of instruments on any single line for giving the melody emphasis, as is customary in oratorical symphonic writing. The work is not oratorical, anyway. It is poetical and reflective. And it builds up its moments of emphasis by rhythmic device and contrapuntal complication, very much as old Sebastian Bach was wont to do. Its inspiration and its communication are lyrical, intimate, thoughtful, sweet, and sometimes witty, like good private talk. At no point is there grandiloquence or theater. The work derives much of its impressiveness from its avoidance of any attempt to impress us by force.

Its great beauty is derived partly from the extreme delicacy and variety of its instrumentation and partly from the consistency of its harmonic structure (a result of its systematic observance of the twelve-tone syntax). Its particular combination of lyric freedom and figurational fancy with the strictest tonal logic places it high among the works of this greatest among the living Viennese masters (resident now in Hollywood) and high among the musical achievements of our century. With the increasing conservatism of contemporary composers about matters harmonic, many of our young people have never really heard much modern music. Radical and thoroughgoing modern music, I mean. It is too seldom performed. Well, here is a piece of it and a very fine one, a beautiful and original work that is really thought through and that doesn't sound like anything else.

Eduard Steuermann played the piano part with all delicacy and love. There isn't much in it to show off with (only two brief and fragmentary cadenzas, and they are not written for brilliance), but the piano is there all the time. It weaves in and out rather in chamber style, and Mr. Steuermann never overplayed it or underplayed it. Everybody gave his serious best to this serious and far from easy work. One came away

almost not minding that it had been preceded by the inexcusably long (nearly five minutes) commercial plug that is
the NBC hour's present sacrifice to commercial sponsorship.

February 7, 1944

A Wealth of Dissonance

INTERNATIONAL SOCIETY FOR CONTEMPORARY MUSIC
last night at the Church of Saint Mary the Virgin, New York, presenting,
among other works, Imbrie's String Quartet in B flat, performed by the
Bennington String Quartet (*Orrea Pernel* and *Mariana Lowell Barzun*,
violinists, *Betty Yokell*, viola, and *George Finkel*, cello), and organ works
by Schönberg, Muffat, and Lamb, performed by *Carl Weinrich*.

MUSIC of dissonant texture is a particular cult of the International Society for Contemporary Music. The music of Arnold
Schönberg is the prayer book for dissonanace-lovers, especially
those brought up in the central-European rite. The Church of
St. Mary the Virgin has long been the seat, if not of dissonance,
of dissidence from the banal in musical practice. Last night it
housed a concert of the International Society that was pretext
and framing for a new work by Schönberg, written for that most
dissonant of all instruments, the organ, and played to perfection
on New York's most brilliant-sounding organ by Carl Weinrich.

The organ is a dissonant instrument because it contains rows
of pipes tuned to furnish the entire harmonic series, or most
of it, upon the pressing down of any one key. The simplest
major chord under such an arrangement becomes a highly
complex sonority. Many churches, especially those with stone
interiors, those with more height than width and those that
contain complex sound-reflecting surfaces in the form of tran-
septs, vaults, tribunes, and side aisles, are in themselves highly
dissonant sound-boxes. The dying away of any sound in such
resonant buildings being somewhat slower than instantaneous,
the playing in them of rapid organ music, even though this be
composed according to classical harmonic syntax, produces a
complexity of reverberation that is virtually complete. Modern music does not sound one whit more discordant at St.

Mary's, for instance, and didn't last night, than a toccata by the seventeenth-century composer Georg Muffat.

This is not to say that all organ music sounds alike. Music differs in tune and rhythm and progress (or form); and one harmonic sequence differs from another in glory, as well as in significance. But since any music played on the fuller combinations of a rich and bright-toned organ in a reverberating enclosure makes all the tones of the chromatic scale all the time, the calculated dissonance of modern writing adds little to the effective dissonance that is inherent to the acoustical set-up.

Schönberg's Variations for Organ, opus 40, finished in 1943, is not a twelve-tone piece. It is squarely, though chromatically, in D minor. It is coloristic in conception and gives opportunity for diversified registration. Rhythmically it is a bit halting, like most of this author's music. Harmonically and contrapuntally it is full of fancy. The whole effect is that of musical impressionism, an accumulation of fancy being its aim rather than an impressive build-up.

Hugh Lamb's Fugue in E, on the other hand, though equally dissonant, is not a color-piece; it is a line-drawing that builds to a climax of complex sound by the march of unrelenting counterpoint. Both works are rich to the ear; but the Schönberg is lighter, wittier, more romantic in feeling, and intellectually the more distinguished. Lamb's is a sound church piece; Schönberg's is poetry.

A String Quartet in B flat by Sergeant Andrew Imbrie preceded these organ pieces. It is a skillful work, dissonant in sound, oratorical in its gesture, with good melodic material and a serious poetic tone. It, too, profited from the resonant acoustics of the church; but even in a dry concert hall I am sure it would have sounded well, because no amount of acoustical glamour can conceal musical poverty. Sergeant Imbrie's work showed no such poverty. It showed original musical thought, sound workmanship and dignified, highly personal sentiments.*

April 11, 1944

*Sergeant Imbrie's String Quartet in B flat was later awarded the New York Music Critics' Circle award as the best new piece of American chamber music first performed in New York in the 1943–44 season.

French Music Here

DARIUS MILHAUD has communicated to me the catalogue of an exhibit held recently in the foyer of the Music Building at Mills College, Oakland, California, for the two weeks from November 27 through December 11, 1940, of Erik Satie's manuscripts. These manuscripts, the property of Monsieur Milhaud, were brought by him last summer from France at some inconvenience, since the traveling facilities available at that time did not always include transportation of unlimited personal impedimenta. That Monsieur Milhaud should have made room for these at the cost of leaving behind manuscripts and orchestral material of his own for which he might have need during his stay here is evidence of the esteem in which he holds the unpublished works of the late Sage of Arceuil.

The catalogue, which contains 105 items, mentions fourteen bound booklets that average forty pages each and fourteen paperbound booklets that run as high as twenty-five pages each. In addition, there are the twenty-four-page orchestral score of *Five Grimaces for "A Midsummer Night's Dream"* and a score of fifteen pages of a piece called simply *Danse*, dated December 5, 1890, later incorporated into the longer work entitled *Three Pieces in the Shape of a Pear*. There are sketches for three ballets, *Jack-in-the-Box*, *Relâche* and *Mercure*, and for the marionette opera *Geneviève de Brabant*. Also songs, famous ones like "Le Chapelier," from *Alice in Wonderland*, and "La Statue de Bronze," and dozens of unpublished waltz-songs and other such light matter written during the eight (or was it twelve?) years that Satie earned his living by playing the piano at a small theatrical establishment called The Harvest Moon (La Lune Rousse), an enterprise of the type known as *cabaret Montmartrois* or *boîte de chansonniers*.

There are counterpoint exercises, too, and fugues and chorales from his second student days when, already forty, he enrolled at Vincent d'Indy's Schola Cantorum and for four years went through all the scholastic musical grind he had skipped in youth. And there are letters, forty-three of them, to Monsieur Milhaud, photographs, programs, clippings, and accounts. Item 47 is a first edition of *Images*, by Claude Debussy, bearing a dedication to Satie from his lifelong friend.

The collection, as one can see from the above brief digest, is an extensive one. Its importance depends on what one thinks of Erik Satie as a musical figure. This writer is in agreement with Darius Milhaud and with some of the other contemporary French composers in placing Satie's work among the major musical values of our century. He has even gone so far in print, nearly twenty years ago, as to parallel the three German B's— Bach, Beethoven, and Brahms—with the three S's of modern music—in descending order of significance, Satie, Schönberg, and Stravinsky.

That is a personal estimate, of course, though one agreed to by many musicians in France and some elsewhere. I should not wish to force my personal musical tastes on anyone, any more than I should want anybody else's forced on me. If you love Mahler, for instance, Mahler is your oyster; and the same goes for Strauss, Sibelius, Palestrina, and Gershwin. But there are certain key personalities without some acceptance of which it is impossible to understand and accept the music of the place and epoch that they dominated. Erik Satie is one of those.

French and other Parisian music of the 1930's has been but little performed in America. (That is an old quarrel of mine with the League of Composers.) Such of it as has been performed here is usually considered to be mildly pleasant but on the whole not very impressive. This estimate is justified only on the part of persons initiated to its æsthetic. And its æsthetic, as was that of Debussy, is derived directly from the words and from the works of Satie, whose firmest conviction was that the only healthy thing music can do in our century is to stop trying to be impressive.

The Satie musical æsthetic is the only twentieth-century musical æsthetic in the Western world. Schönberg and his school are Romantics; and their twelve-tone syntax, however intriguing one may find it intellectually, is the purest Romantic chromaticism. Hindemith, however gifted, is a neo-classicist, like Brahms, with ears glued firmly to the past. The same is true of the later Stravinsky and of his satellites. Even *Petrouchka* and *The Rite of Spring* are the Wagnerian theater symphony and the nineteenth-century cult of nationalistic folklore applied to ballet.

Of all the influential composers of our time, and influence

even his detractors cannot deny him, Satie is the only one whose works can be enjoyed and appreciated without any knowledge of the history of music. These lack the prestige of traditional modernism, as they lack the prestige of the Romantic tradition itself, a tradition of constant Revolution. They are as simple, as straightforward, as devastating as the remarks of a child.

To the uninitiated they sound trifling. To those who love them they are fresh and beautiful and firmly right. And that freshness and rightness have long dominated the musical thought of France. Any attempt to penetrate that musical thought without first penetrating that of Erik Satie is fruitless. Even Debussy is growing less and less comprehensible these days to those who never knew Satie.

When Satie used to be performed here occasionally, the works were found difficult to understand. French music in all centuries has been rather special, not quite like anything else. In our century it has become esoteric to a degree not currently admitted even in France. It has eschewed the impressive, the heroic, the oratorical, everything that is aimed at moving mass audiences. Like modern French poetry and painting, it has directed its communication to the individual.

It has valued, in consequence, quietude, precision, acuteness of auditory observation, gentleness, sincerity and directness of statement. Persons who admire these qualities in private life are not infrequently embarrassed when they encounter them in public places. It is this embarrassment that gives to all French music, and to the work of Satie and his neophytes in particular, an air of superficiality, as if it were salon music written for the drawing-rooms of some snobbish set.

To suppose this true is to be ignorant of the poverty and the high devotion to the art that marked the life of Erik Satie to its very end in a public hospital. And to ignore all art that is not heroic or at least intensely emotional is to commit the greatest of snobberies. For, by a reversal of values that constitutes one of the most surprising phenomena of a century that has so far been occupied almost exclusively with reversing values, the only thing really hermetic and difficult to understand about the music of Erik Satie is the fact that there is nothing hermetic about it at all.

It wears no priestly robes; it mumbles no incantations; it

is not painted up by Max Factor to terrify elderly ladies or to give little girls a thrill. Neither is it designed to impress orchestral conductors or to get anybody a job teaching school. It has literally no devious motivation. It is as simple as a friendly conversation and in its better moments exactly as poetic and as profound.

These thoughts occurred to me the other evening at a League of Composers concert of recent works by Milhaud. Not a piece on the program had a climax or a loud ending. Nothing was pretentious or apocalyptical or messianic or overdramatized. The composer's effort at all times was to be clear and true. And when I saw the catalogue of the Satie manuscripts and learned how Milhaud had brought them to America at the cost of not bringing all his own; when I remembered, also, the brilliant and theatrically effective works of Milhaud's youth, *Le Bœuf sur le Toit* and *Le Train Bleu* and *La Création du Monde*, I realized that after Satie's death he had been led, how unconsciously I cannot say, to assume the mantle of Satie's leadership and to eschew all musical vanity. That, at any rate, is my explanation of how one of the most facile and turbulent talents of our time has become one of the most completely calm of modern masters; and how, by adding thus depth and penetration and simple humanity to his gamut, he has become the first composer of his country and a leader in that musical tradition which of all living musical traditions is the least moribund.

January 5, 1941

Better Than It Sounds

LEAGUE OF COMPOSERS presenting a concert of new music by South American composers yesterday afternoon at the New York Public Library, with works by José María Castro, José Ardévol, Domingo Santa Cruz, Francisco Mignone, Luis Gianneo, Héctor Tosar, and Camargo Guarnieri performed by American and Latin-American musicians including *Mr. Mignone*, piano, *Liddy Mignone*, soprano, and *Hugo Balzo*, piano.

THE LEAGUE OF COMPOSERS concert of works by living South American composers at the Public Library yesterday afternoon was a good deal of a disappointment. Both the works and their execution were animated by the best intentions and pulled off in some cases with no small skill, but somehow a proper ambiance for musical acceptance was missing. Decidedly a new formula is needed for the presentation of South American music. I have read and heard privately a great deal of this music. There is a large repertory of interesting stuff, but every time it is staged in the North American concert manner it is a flop. My acquaintance with the music leads me to believe that the fault is ours.

The South Americans seem to have a functional conception of music, as all the Latin peoples do. Their music is written to be used rather than to be inspected. A great deal of it is reflective. This kind is pleasant to read or to play for two or three musical friends; it loses its intimacy and its gentle communication when it is subjected to concert expounding. Most of the Brazilian work is in popular vein. Miss Elsie Houston has made a success of this kind of music by singing it with its own kind of vocalization, keeping all flavor of the vocal studios out of it. Every time the works of Villa-Lobos and his school are performed without an air of informality and of spontaneity, they lose the quality of spontaneity that is their chief charm.

Between the frankly popular style and the wholly intimate style South Americans seem to have found no middle ground save that of virtuosity. Their theater music and their night-club music and their carnival music and their magic incantations are in every way admirable. The Brazilians are especially good at all these. The intellectual music of Uruguay, Argentina, Chile, and Peru is of a sincerity and a gentle loveliness unmatched, to my knowledge, elsewhere in the world. I have never yet heard a piece of South American music from anywhere that was written with any obvious awareness of a concert public, however intelligent that public might be, that did not fall into the ways of virtuosity and end by sounding hopelessly provincial. Because virtuosity is always provincial unless it is the flower of a decaying great tradition.

Now, South America, like North America, is musically very young. It has not had time yet to go to seed and fluff. Musical expression in this hemisphere is still a serious matter, even when it is gay and folksy. The concert hall is at best a mortuary chamber, most of all for living music. When that music is written, as the northern Europeans do it, with full consciousness of

audience psychology, it becomes as formal a thing as a mythological opera or a learned lecture. Now, mythological operas
and learned lectures are perfectly good things; but they both
presuppose a public, or at least a patron and his guests. They are
objective. The constant tendency of South American music to
go either popular (which implies no public, only participants) or
utterly intellectual, reflective, and private (which shows a clear
indifference to impressiveness) makes me think that perhaps
there isn't much public down there for any intellectual product
more profound than salon meditations and facile virtuosity. In
any case there is a great deal of music written in those parts that
has the perfume of integrity. Some of this is folklorish and some
of it is contrapuntal and abstract. None of it does itself justice
in the columbarium-like layout of our professional concerts.

March 9, 1942

Harris and Shostakovich

BOSTON SYMPHONY ORCHESTRA, *Serge Koussevitzky*, conduc-
tor, yesterday afternoon at Carnegie Hall, performing Tchaikovsky's
Overture to *Romeo and Juliet*, Roy Harris's Symphony No. 3, and
Shostakovich's Symphony No. 3.

AMERICA's most popular symphonist, Roy Harris, and Russia's
best-known one (and we gather he is as popular at home as
abroad), Dmitri Shostakovich, shared honors and applause at
yesterday's concert of the Boston Symphony Orchestra in Carnegie Hall. Both composers are disputed about in professional
circles, but the fact is scarcely controvertible that they have won
the affection of a large musical public. The fact that yesterday's
performance of Harris's Third Symphony was the thirty-third
(all told) in three seasons means that the work has passed out
of the novelty stage and that it is something more than a fillip
to the musically curious.

Since any programmatic juxtaposition renders comparison
inevitable, it is fair, I think, to consider yesterday's two symphonies and their authors as at least momentarily parallel. Mr.
Harris's work appeared to me yesterday as the more original of
the two, Mr. Shostakovich's as the more facile. Harris's Third

Symphony has goodly melodic material; but its structure and instrumentation, though in no way banal, are somewhat naïve. Their naïveté, indeed, is the source of much of their intensity of expression. Shostakovich's material is less noteworthy, and his contrapuntal style lacks tension. But he orchestrates with some brilliance, and he builds a climax with professional smoothness. The notes of Harris are more significant than they sound, for their resonance is, even in the loudest tuttis, always muffled by unidiomatic instrumental writing and ungrateful chord dispositions. The Shostakovich score sounds at all times sonorously confident; but the notes themselves, though charming enough in the animated passages, are not nearly so convincing to this listener as the sound they make is agreeable.

It is possible that my greater interest in the music of Harris is due to nothing more recondite than the fact that we are fellow countrymen and that his musical thought is consequently sympathetic to my own instincts and sentiments. Even the greatest of the Russian musicians (and I do not consider Shostakovich one of these) owe much of their power over us to certain strangenesses of thought and manner. Harris's work is not strange at all; or if it is, it is so only because of its rather unprofessional surface tension. Inside, it is as familiar and as welcome as something that oft was felt (and deeply) but never said before.

There has been a great deal of effort made to interpret Harris as an American master of the (essentially European) heroic style. I think the idea is false, because I do not consider him a master of anything, least of all of that (even in Europe) foolish and decadent manner. Grandiloquent he is, and clumsy as a technician and hopelessly lacking in objectivity. Heroics are a form of theater, and Harris is without theatrical instinct. His one film score proved that. His is a reflective nature, lyrical and introspective and quietly fanciful. My interpretation of his qualities is, of course, no better than anybody else's; but I am moved by his music, and I feel, therefore, an obligation to describe it in my own way. Whatever its exact nature is, I believe it to be beautiful and more than skin-deep. I am not so convinced in the case of Shostakovich, for all his gaiety and gusto and sound facility.

The Boston orchestra played admirably, as usual. It occurred to me, listening to the Tchaikovsky *Romeo and Juliet*, that Mr. Koussevitzky's way of playing the works of this composer is more eloquent than what the others do with them because, in addition to his consistent avoidance of forced instrumental tone, he makes practically no alterations of the basic rhythm. Such as he does make are of a formal nature, like a slight retard before a new section. He never allows the expressive nature of a Tchaikovsky melody to interrupt the firm rhythm over which it flows. This reticence seems to me to clarify the music and to augment its significance.

April 5, 1942

Superficially Warlike

BOSTON SYMPHONY ORCHESTRA, *Serge Koussevitzky*, conductor, with the HARVARD GLEE CLUB and the RADCLIFFE CHORAL SOCIETY, yesterday afternoon at Carnegie Hall performing Schuman's Secular Cantata No. 2 (*A Free Song*), Barber's Essay for Orchestra No. 1, Copland's *A Lincoln Portrait*, and Beethoven's Symphony No. 5. With *Will Geer*, speaker.

THE BOSTON SYMPHONY ORCHESTRA offered yesterday afternoon in Carnegie Hall a program without much inner unity. Such external cohesion as it had consisted of indirect references to the war. But musically the works played seemed rather to contradict one another than to set one another off.

The title of Mr. William Schuman's secular cantata, *A Free Song*, refers, I take it, since the composition is partly fugal in style, not to musical freedom but to freedom of some other kind, economic, social, religious, amorous, or political, no doubt. The times being what they are, one would probably be safe in betting it was the latter, though of certain evidence I have none, the chorus's effective enunciation of the text being zero in row U. The music's intrinsic interest seemed also to this listener to add up to a not high figure.

Private Samuel Barber's Essay for Orchestra, No. 1, is a pretty piece but not a very strong one. It resembles more a meditation than it does the kind of logical exposition one usually associates with the classical prose form of that name. Perhaps Mr. Barber thinks of the word *essay* in its contemporary sense of a reflective composition on some relatively trivial subject. Certainly his musical material here is not striking. Neither, unfortunately, is his development of it, though there is, as always in this composer's music, grace. The military note was added to this performance by the composer's presence, bowing, in uniform.

Mr. Aaron Copland's *A Lincoln Portrait* consists of a pastorale, a scherzo, and a melodrama. The first is plain but pleasant; the second, a sort of county-fair scene made up of phrases out of Stephen Foster, is brilliantly picturesque. Lincoln himself comes into the portrait only by quotation, when an actor (yesterday it was Mr. Will Geer) speaks, as finale, over a slight orchestral accompaniment selected passages from the addresses of the great President. Even if Mr. Geer had not seen fit to utter these in the flat and twangy accent used in theatrical productions to characterize Vermont storekeepers, they would still have seemed, for all their grandeur, an unhappy ending to a musical work.

It is not easy to make a portrait of a person no longer living, as any artist will tell you. But the problem, difficult or not, is what it is; and Mr. Copland has chosen to essay it. By leaving off in the middle and simply inserting quotations from Lincoln's speeches, he has achieved a result comparable to what a painter would achieve if, after sketching in a period background of some kind, he were to substitute for a full rendering of his subject a half-dozen snapshots taken at various epochs of the latter's life, including something from the war period, of course.

The afternoon ended with an excellent performance of Beethoven's Fifth Symphony, of which the principal motif is currently thought to resemble the letter V in Morse code— three dots and a dash. This motif really consists, in its most frequent statement, of four dots, and in its initial, or motto, form of three dots and something the length of about fifteen dashes, a signal not admitted, so far as I know, in any telegraphic alphabet. Yesterday's rendition was a fine one, all the same.

April 4, 1943

More Barber

BOSTON SYMPHONY ORCHESTRA, *Serge Koussevitzky*, conductor, last night at Carnegie Hall, performing Mozart's *Eine Kleine Nachtmusik*, Barber's Symphony No. 2, Brahms's Symphony No. 3, and selections from Berlioz's *Damnation de Faust*.

NOT in several years has your announcer heard Serge Koussevitzky in such fine form as at last night's concert of the Boston Symphony Orchestra in Carnegie Hall. The orchestra itself is always in such perfect condition that one gets to thinking it doesn't make much difference how the conductor feels. It does, though. Because with him, too, at his best and well cast as to repertory, the music he plays can be as memorable an experience as the sound it makes.

Mozart's *Kleine Nachtmusik* is not perfect casting for the good Doctor. The rhythm of Mozart, his meter, his varied phraseology, the relation of ornament to melodic line, the function of off-beat accents and of surprise modulations all seem to escape him. The music comes out, in consequence, pallid and more than a little nervous. But once this work was out of the way, the concert took on color. I have seldom heard a reading of the Brahms Third Symphony (by far his best, in my modest opinion) that was at once so poetic, so gracious and so transparent. The Berlioz selections, ending as usual with the *Rakoczy March*, were so happily equilibrated in every way and so utterly delicious as sheer sound that their memory will remain, I am sure, for many years as a model of the way they can and should be performed.

Samuel Barber's Second Symphony is a broadly conceived work full of variety and emphasis. I admit some uncertainty as to what it is all about. If his First, which we heard on Wednesday at the Philharmonic, represents, as I think it does, a Hamlet-like backward yearning toward the womb of German Romanticism, this one may well be Hamlet in modern dress. I've a suspicion they are really the same piece. The new one is modernistic on the surface; at least an effort has been made to write in the dissonant style. But the melodic material would have been set off just as well, probably better, by a less angular harmonic texture. Also, Mr. Barber does not handle dissonant counterpoint with freedom.

The work seems to lack striking melody and contrapuntal life. There is lots of emphasis, but it is all of inferior material; and it is operated chiefly by instrumental weight rather than led up to by logic or by tonal rhetoric. Even the instrumentation, though competently calculated, is lacking in character. The constant abuse of instrumental doublings for purposes of emphasis has produced a muddiness of texture that weighs down further a piece already top-heavy with oratorical paraphernalia. Mr. Barber at his best is songful and elegiac. His harmonic instincts and training, though elegant, are conventional. Pending further acquaintance with his Second Symphony, I am inclined to think that the commission to write a work glorifying the Army Air Forces has led him to try his hand at a publicity task for which he had little taste and less preparation.

March 10, 1944

Bernstein in Boston

BOSTON SYMPHONY ORCHESTRA, *Serge Koussevitzky* and *Leonard Bernstein*, conductors, yesterday afternoon at Symphony Hall, Boston, performing Schumann's Symphony No. 3 ("Rhenish"), Mr. Bernstein's Symphony No. 1 ("Jeremiah"), and Copland's *El Salón Mexico*. Soloist: *Jennie Tourel*, mezzo-soprano.

THE BOSTON SYMPHONY ORCHESTRA at home seems always less ostentatious than on tour. In the hall where it has rehearsed (a hall of well-focused rather than diffuse acoustic properties) and in front of its own well-washed and well-mannered audience, it strikes one as only natural that the cultural amenities should have taken on so high a polish, as of good wood long regularly waxed and rubbed. Not the least of this orchestra's cultural amenities is its gracious hospitality to that which is novel and of good report in the world of music.

Leonard Bernstein, who conducted his own First Symphony today, is nationally of good report as a conductor. He is less well known as a composer, though the present work, which has already been received well by both press and public in Pittsburgh, will no doubt go far toward correcting this situation. It is not a masterpiece by any means, but it has solid orchestral qualities and a certain charm that should give it a temporary popularity, not the least of its charms in today's concert being Mr. Bernstein's excellent directing of it and Jennie Tourel's resonant intoning of its Hebrew text.

Unlike Robert Schumann (his Third, or "Rhenish," Symphony was played just before the new work, Mr. Koussevitzky conducting), who composed with genius but who was not a master of instrumentation, Mr. Bernstein orchestrates like a master but does not compose with either originality or much skill. His piece lacks contrapuntal coherence, melodic distinction, rhythmic progress, harmonic logic, and concentration of thought. On the other hand, it has by moments a certain lyrical intensity; and at the beginning of the middle, or scherzo, section there is a sort of dance passage that evokes most poignantly the Jewish Near East. Also, the instrumentation makes lovely sounds. The loud and soft contrasts are probably more extreme than they need be, but the placement of the instruments is at all times sonorous.

There is no useless instrumental doubling anywhere. Solo passages are placed in grateful ranges for each instrument. And in the tuttis he writes his brass a little high, just as Berlioz did. The result is one of shining brilliance and vibrant juxtapositions of color. Aaron Copland's *El Salón Mexico*, which Mr. Bernstein conducted at the end, itself a fairly brilliant piece of orchestration, sounded muddy by comparison with the Bernstein score. Neither his sure-handed scoring, however, almost too sure-handed for a young man of twenty-five who is going to be a real composer, nor the diffuse and improvisatory character of the composition inspires the confidence in Mr. Bernstein's original gifts that this reviewer entertains towards his genius as an executant and an interpreter.*

February 19, 1944

*The "Jeremiah" Symphony received, nevertheless, the award of the Music Critics Circle of New York City as the most distinguished new orchestral work of American authorship played there during the season of 1943–44.

Our Musical Tom Sawyer

NBC SYMPHONY ORCHESTRA, *Leopold Stokowski*, conductor, yesterday afternoon in Studio 8-H, Radio City, performing, among other
works, Antheil's Symphony No. 4.

GEORGE ANTHEIL, whose Fourth Symphony was given its
first performance anywhere by Leopold Stokowski and the
NBC Symphony Orchestra yesterday afternoon, has long been
a problem child among musicians. Extravagantly gifted but
imperfectly trained, he was publicized in Germany, in France,
and in the United States during the 1920's as a boy genius; and
some of the most influential literary figures of the time—notably James Joyce and Ezra Pound—hailed him as a musical messiah. Of late years he has been engaged in diversified journalistic
activity (he has written musical criticism, a syndicated column
about endocrinology for the lovelorn, political prophecy, and
military analysis), as well as the composition of film scores. Yesterday's performance of the Fourth Symphony marks his return
to the serious music world. At forty-four, though a far more
expert workman than he used to be, he is still something of a
problem child, because his qualities are unusual.

He is also a problem child because he is not quite aware of his
qualities. Twenty years ago he posed as the heir of Igor Stravinsky; today he is clearly making a bid for the Shostakovich trade.
But he is not any kind of a Russian composer. He is an American composer, probably the most thoroughgoing American of
us all. He is a musical Tom Sawyer, gay, fanciful, ingenuous,
self-confident, and comical. It is the courageous comicality of
his work, in fact, that has long endeared it to the literary mind.
He is not in the stuffy sense an imitator of anybody; he is a
humorist, a parodist, a clown.

The Fourth Symphony, though surely this was not its author's
intention, is about the most complete musical picture of an
American circus that has ever been made. There is everything
in it—military band music, waltzes, sentimental ditties, a Red
Army song, a fugue, eccentric dancing, every kind of a joke,
acrobatic turn, patriotic reference, and glamorous monstrosity.
It is bright, hard, noisy, busy, bumptious, efficient, and incredibly real. It is "Columbia, the Gem of the Ocean" orchestrated

in red, white, and blue, with three cheers for the same every
five minutes and plenty of pink lemonade. By moments it is
thin of texture, but at its best and busiest it makes a hubbub
like a live crowd and five brass bands. And its tunes can all be
remembered.

This is not to say that the work is a masterpiece. But it is
hard, clean, humane, outdoor fun and not at all timid in its
manipulation of the higher musical skills. If you like your music
sanctimonious, or even logical, you will probably be shocked by
it. But if you like tunes, rhythms, discords, and bright sounds
for themselves alone, you will find its brash complexity as rewarding as yesterday's audience seemed to do. Myself, I have
always found Antheil's serious music (excepting his operas) invigorating. I consider him a powerful musician and a healthy
spirit. And once again Mr. Stokowski and the General Motors
Corporation merit our thanks for giving us music that makes
sense here and now.

February 14, 1944

Levant Tough and Tender

NBC SYMPHONY ORCHESTRA, *Alfred Wallenstein*, conductor,
last night in Studio 8-H, Radio City, performing Louis Spohr's Symphony No. 2, Ravel's *La Valse*, and Oscar Levant's Concerto for Piano
and Orchestra. Soloist: *Mr. Levant*, piano.

IT is amazing the amount of good music-writing and careful
music execution that gets lost over the radio. I listened last
night to a concert of the NBC orchestra from one of those seating arrangements where one sees the performance through glass
but hears it through an electrical receiving mechanism. This
mechanism gives normally a result not inferior to that of the
bedside box and truer acoustically than what most household
receiving sets produce. I heard the strings most of the time,
excepting for the cellos, which were rarely audible. I heard the
flutes and clarinets pretty regularly and the trumpets. Oboes,
bassoons, and trombones were never audible except in solo
work. Horns and double basses came into the softest passages
like added atmospheric pressure on the eardrums. The whole

auditory effect was so distorted, so false to reality, that I don't wonder at the necessity radio companies seem to feel of sort of excusing the whole serious music business and of bolstering it up with unashamed sales-talk before and after.

The Spohr Symphony No. 2 is inoffensive. Its lively scherzo and schottische finale would make good background music in a refined beer hall or in any American home. Ravel's *La Valse* is known to most of my readers, though few, I suspect, would have recognized it through the fog of radio distortion that made it sound less like *La Valse* than like an orchestra tuning up to play *La Valse*.

Oscar Levant's Piano Concerto is a rather fine piece of music. Or rather it contains fine pieces of music. Its pieces are better than its whole, which is jerky, because the music neither moves along nor stands still. The themes are good; and if they are harmonically and orchestrally overdressed, they are ostentatiously enough so that no one need suspect their author of naïveté. The rhythm is lively, too, and the expression, for the most part, direct and easily comprehensible.

I suspect its piecemeal character of being due to lack of a central musical idea or dominating emotional urge. Its most obvious single communication is the composer's desire, determination, even, to write a piano concerto. Maybe a too long working over destroyed its original unity. As music it is honest and charming and, for all its pseudo-complexity, straightforward. At least, each passage is straightforward. It is the spiritual isolation of the passages one from another that gives the whole a reserved and compartmental quality that weakens its impact.

Nevertheless, the impact of Mr. Levant's battling personality is not absent. His music, like his mind, is tough and real and animated by a ferocious integrity. Its off moments are like the Sunday afternoon of a pugilist, all dressed up and no place to go. But even so, biceps are visible through the flimsy suiting of Hollywood atonality; and whenever he makes a spontaneous movement, he bursts the none too solid ready-made seams. I have mentioned all the faults I could find in the Piano Concerto, because he would expect that of me, as I should of him. But the same professional loyalty impels me to dwell also for a brief paragraph (though strength is far harder to describe than weakness) on its real excellence, because, for all its not being,

I think, a completely successful work, it is friendly music and good music, all of it. It is even, beneath its trappings of school-boy homage to Gershwin and Schönberg, hard and lonely and original music, full of song and solitude. I sometimes wish Levant would not work so hard at being a composer. He seems afraid to relax and let music write itself. But every man must scale Parnassus in his own way. Maybe the hard way is the only one he would feel right about taking.

February 18, 1942

The Budding Grove

FOURTH ANNUAL CONCERT OF STUDENT COMPOSITIONS last night at the New York High School of Music and Art, New York, presenting four pieces for piano, five chamber works, three choral works, and three orchestral works conducted and performed by the students of the school.

NEW YORK's High School of Music and Art is a public high school to which students, stemming from all classes of society and resident in all neighborhoods, are admitted on a basis of musical or artistic aptitudes. This is not to say that literary and scientific studies are neglected or that any deficiency in these is tolerated. On the contrary, the academic work of this admirable institution ranks higher than that of most high schools. But its work in music and art is, of course, its specialty; and this must be seen to be believed. Yesterday afternoon in the assembly hall a fourth annual concert was given of original compositions written and performed by students.

These varied from simple pianoforte pieces to works for full orchestra. There were duets, trios, a wind sextet, a piece for string ensemble, and others for choir, including a full anthem for chorus, soloists, and organ. The soloists played and sang beautifully; the conductors led with vigor and exactitude; the orchestra performed in excellent style and with lovely tone, and the chorus sang real English words with all beauty of sound and with correct intonation. The young people seemed, moreover, to understand and to believe in one another's work. From the beginning to the end there was pleasure in being present at the skillful accomplishment of sincere musical acts. There was joy and friendliness and spontaneity of collaboration and no lack whatever of an intelligently critical attitude in the reception of the different works.

The pieces were by students aged thirteen to eighteen, at all different stages of advancement from the first to the ninth semester of theory instruction. They were not classroom exercises but free compositions, uncorrected by any instructor and chosen competitively for this performance. Their musical language was the basic musical language of educated America, roughly the language of European Romanticism from Schumann to Tchaikovsky. There was little of Wagnerian insistence or of Brahmsian introversion. Mozart and Beethoven, however, had certainly been consulted as models of formal procedure. The choral pieces were based on less classic models, though in no case was there any departure from acceptable style. The farthest any piece strayed from mid-nineteenth-century harmonic syntax was the moderate but wholly neat and charming French impressionism of Mr. Meyer Kupferman's Wind Sextet.

All this is normal and usual. Youth is conservative, and mild Romanticism is its oyster. One does not expect consistent revolutionism or radical research from adolescents. Neither does one expect to encounter much unconscious influence of backwoods American folklore in the music of urban New York. The spirit of yesterday's work was one of respect for classic methods and the emulation of classic beauties. What one had not quite expected was the air on everybody's part, both authors and interpreters, of being completely at home in the writing and performing of music. It was all as natural as a school play or magazine. And when Americans, even a few hundreds of them in New York City, can express themselves in music as easily and as well as that, we may rest assured that America's musical future is as solidly based as her present distinction in the divers branches of literature.

April 17, 1942

OPERA

Mozart on Love

THE POPULARITY of the New Opera Company's *Così Fan Tutte* performances and the general acknowledgment of their musical excellence have stimulated the following reflections on the part of this reviewer.

First of all, let it be reiterated that the singing itself is, by any standard of contemporary opera singing, very good singing indeed. Paris, Dresden, Vienna, Milan, and our own Metropolitan are lucky when they can get together a Mozart cast of that quality. Miss Milanov, who sang Donna Anna last year in *Don Giovanni*, is not the mistress of her voice nor of the musical content of her roles that Miss Ina Souez is, for instance, who sings Fiordiligi in the present production. And that role, written for Madame Ferrarese del Bene, demands a compass far from ordinary. Miss Kuzak is not so good a singer as the Metropolitan's Miss Sayao, but she has a distinguished personality. Mr. Marshall, whom I heard on the opening night in the tenor role, has a voice not unfavorably comparable to that of the Met's Mr. Kullman. And Fritz Busch, who conducted, is a better conductor and a far finer musician than most of those Thirty-ninth Street has been offering. Even the scenery and the costumes and the heavy-handed stage direction were better than what new productions get at most of the big houses nowadays. For all their carelessness and crudity, they were high art beside what was exhibited last year with Gluck's *Alceste*. There is no getting around it or laughing it off, *Così Fan Tutte* at the Forty-fourth Street Theater, though far from ideal, is none the less a high-class operatic performance.

The pleasure it has been giving, let me repeat, is nearly one hundred per cent musical. (Or, at least, musico-literary, since da Ponte's libretto constitutes a far from negligible element in the enjoyment to be derived from Mozart's psychologically quite elaborate setting of it.) And the person obviously responsible for the high musical level of the production is Mr. (or, in the German style, Dr.) Fritz Busch. One can scarcely overemphasize the pleasurable effect of witnessing an opera that has been really rehearsed; and one can never be too grateful to a conductor who nursemaids six soloists, at least one of whom has never been on a stage before, through the opening night of an extremely difficult work without any of them either losing his head or taking the bit in his teeth. With a smallish and not really first-rate orchestra, with inexperienced soloists, with scenery so carelessly designed and executed that nobody could tell what any of it was going to do next, with none of the ladies' costumes capable of being got through any of the doors without the skirt having to be tipped up on its side, with all these stimuli to pity and terror and with a show to be got across of a work fantastically famous and difficult, Mr. Busch produced a performance in which all the orchestral notes were in their proper places and in which no singer trembled or got tight in the throat. More than that, he gave a rendition that was good entertainment and that was dramatically convincing.

Making convincing dramatic entertainment out of *Così Fan Tutte* has not been one of the specialties of our century. Indeed, it has long been considered impossible to do anything approaching this. One is used to seeing the play treated as a bit of not very funny eighteenth-century smut and the music as a set piece of the Rococo charm school. The libretto has rarely been interpreted for what it is, a serious farce-comedy in the Molière vein by an extremely gifted poet whom Mozart had already honored twice with his collaboration. But unless the libretto is so interpreted, it is impossible to give to the musical rendition of it a dramatic expression any more profound than what one might give to a musical version of *Twin Beds*.

Fritz Busch knows better. He knows that Wolfgang Amadeus Mozart did not waste his music on trash. Mozart never, in fact, wrote an opera of which the theme was not a plea for tenderness, for humane compassion, and for an enlightened and philosophic toleration of human weakness. And, although some of his librettists were more skillful littérateurs than others, Mozart himself manifested no small sense of literary values in his choice of subjects and of authors. His first opera, *La Finta Semplice*, was written at the age of twelve to a play by Goldoni. *Mitridate* is made from an Italian translation of Racine. *La Clemenza di Tito* is by Metastasio. And *Le Nozze di Figaro* is both Beaumarchais and da Ponte. Even if *Così Fan Tutte* were not the work of Mozart's favorite librettist, one should be able to tell from the complexity of the musical fabric that the composer had a certain interest in what he was doing.

What he was doing was showing that infidelity can strengthen love. He had reason to know, whose own wife's conduct was definitely on the promiscuous side. And he was showing also that one needn't be especially high-minded in order to be both loving and sensible. His characters are people of quite conventional mentality who behave as almost any of us might. Also, like almost any of us, they learn from jealousy, torment, and amorous disillusionment that love can go on just the same (perhaps even better) when pride has been got out of the way.

Now, the trouble with the representation of all this in music is that as Mozart's carefree young lovers draw closer to the real facts of life, their music becomes progressively less brilliant. His second act runs richer and deeper than the first, but it is at no time so sparkling. The first is all concerted pieces, the second mostly arias. It is customary to knock the audience cold by the speed and precision of the first and to let the second bog down into sentiment. Mr. Busch has sacrificed the brilliance of the concerted pieces in order to build up to a genuinely moving quality in the heart pains the young men suffer at proving their mistresses false.

This novel attitude toward the story helps to save for us some of Mozart's finest music at no disadvantage to the always delightful first act. Not that Busch's first act tempos aren't more than a bit on the slow side. I think they are mostly slower than is really necessary. But, as I explained in reviewing the performance a week ago last Tuesday night, I don't think Mr. Busch is particularly good at finding perfect tempos anyway. What he has done here is to find the sense and the seriousness in this beautiful work and to show them to us with the aid of his vocal collaborators. Now that he has shown us that *Così Fan Tutte* can be made to make sense all the way through by not allowing it to run away with itself at the beginning, it should be not at all difficult for other conductors to adjust this conception to a pace (a pacing, rather) that will preserve the very high level at once of animation and of expressivity that makes Mozart's operas different from all the other operas in the world and far more powerful than most.

October 25, 1941

Confusion Ordered

THE MAGIC FLUTE, opera in two acts, libretto in English by *Edward J. Dent* (after the German original by *Emanuel Schikaneder*), music by *Wolfgang Amadeus Mozart*, performed last night at Juilliard Concert Hall by the Juilliard School Opera Department, *Albert Stoessel*, conductor, *Alfredo Valenti*, Stage Director, with *Rita Doubet* (Queen of the Night), *Estelle Hoffman* (Pamina), *Davis Cunningham* (Tamino), *Vivienne Simon* (Papagena), and *William Gephart* (Papageno).

MUCH has been said about the stupidity and the useless complexity of *The Magic Flute*'s libretto. It has certainly never made much sense to this reviewer. Last night's performance at the Juilliard School made it seem as simple as a Sunday-school pageant. And when all is said and done, that is about what *The Magic Flute* is. It is an allegorical fairy tale in praise of Freemasonry and the brotherhood of man.

The locale of the action and the identity of the characters have usually been represented as fanciful. Tamino, being a Japanese prince, has been put into every imaginable kind of Oriental armor. Zoroaster is classically got up Persian. Pamina is likely to be vague in style. And the scenery is normally Biedermeier Egyptian. Is it any wonder we don't quite get the plot?

Frederick Kiesler has taken for granted that calling the high priest Zoroaster and at the same time having him pray to Isis and Osiris was not necessarily an anachronism on the part of the authors, but was rather simply the routine language of the Masonic Lodges, which pretended to trace their origin to Egypt and which certainly welcomed into their fold believers from all religions. The prince's Japanese birth he takes to be a simple literary masquerade, since it is highly probably that he represents the Emperor Joseph II, recently inducted to the Lodge, as the Queen of the Night represents Joseph's mother, Maria Theresa, who never approved of Freemasonry.

Kiesler has taken everybody out of masquerade except the Queen.* Tamino, Pamina, and the Priests are represented as eighteenth-century gentlefolk. The Bird-Man and Bird-Woman he has left in their feathers, as indeed they were left by the plot

---

*Mr. Kiesler informs me that his original project required that the Queen of the Night be dressed to represent Maria Theresa.

to live out their simple lives without the enlightenment of Masonic initiation.

He has used a permanent stage-set, indicating changes of locale by changing painted pictures that are framed in a sort of late eighteenth-century pavilion, upstage center, and indicating changes of weather by projecting clouds, flames, and other atmospheric effects on a cyclorama at the back. As a result we know not only that we are dealing with real people in the chief characters, but that these are living through a series of adventures and trials that take place in various real sites and climatic conditions, rather than merely going through a series of pretexts for singing on a stage a diversified series of songs in fancy dress.

It has long been a conviction of this reviewer that the best theatrical results are rarely obtained from professional stage designers, but rather from artists who practice professionally the more basic plastic techniques. To be specific, from oil painters, sculptors, and architects. The only real renovations of staging that have taken place in the last thirty years have been due to the collaboration of constructivist sculptors, cubist and post-cubist painters with opera and ballet. Kiesler has approached *The Magic Flute* as an architect. He has made the decorations clear and functional, and he has given them an unbelievable architectural solidity and a high seriousness of expression. Their lack of meretriciousness is astounding.

There is no malice in my spending my space today on the visual aspects of last night's *The Magic Flute*. The singing was excellent, the orchestra excellent, the whole auditory presentation an honor to the school and a pleasure to its hearers (and hearing *The Magic Flute* is no mean pleasure). But it does seem to me that there is more news value in Kiesler's having made the opera make sense than there could be in anybody's having sung it no matter how well.

December 12, 1940

Two-Star Matinee

LA TRAVIATA, opera in four acts, libretto by *Francesco Maria Piave*, music by *Giuseppe Verdi*, yesterday afternoon at the Metropolitan Opera House, *Cesare Sodero*, conductor, *Désiré Defrère*, stage director, with *Licia Albanese* (Violetta) and *Lawrence Tibbett* (Germont).

IF the coronation of stardom for male actors is *Hamlet*, that for actresses is certainly *La Dame aux Camélias*. Licia Albanese won for herself a royal crown in that role yesterday afternoon at the Metropolitan Opera House, the version used being the best known of all the musical ones, Verdi's incomparable *La Traviata*. Her triumph was shared with Cesare Sodero, who conducted the work more beautifully than I have heard any other conductor conduct any opera in many, many years. The supporting cast and ensemble did good work, too; but the intensity and the delicacy and the animation of the whole were unquestionably centered in Miss Albanese and Mr. Sodero, and it was obvious during the curtain calls that the audience was fully aware of this.

Miss Albanese began by looking beautiful but singing with a tremolo that was no doubt due to nervousness. She had never sung the role before, I believe. After fifteen minutes the tremolo disappeared, leaving only beauty, both personal and vocal. She was as deeply touching in her gaiety as in her heartbreaks and in her tubercular agony. She used her limpid voice, her delicate person, and her excellent musicianship to equal effect in creating the character Violetta. I use the word *create* for her achievement because that is what she really did. She did not play or imitate or sketch. She created a complete personality that lived and loved and drank champagne and made decisions and died. She did this with skill, with art, with conviction, with beauty, and with all loveliness.

She lived her "Ah, fors'è lui" as she sang it. And how well she sang it! As if she had no doubt of its musical and dramatic sincerity, as if she knew it were a part of the play. In the last scene her transition from low speaking (and what rich speaking!) to the full high B flat on which she dies was one of the most accomplished bits of vocalism it has been my pleasure to hear in some time. That it was as deeply moving as it was skillful to observe and lovely to hear is proof of Miss Albanese's high standards of musical and dramatic integrity. One has heard many Violettas. Miss Albanese's is, I should think, one of the great ones, because, like all the great ones, it resembles no other yet is wholly convincing.

That it was so convincing and pleasurable is due in large measure to the identity of conception that was manifest between herself and Mr. Sodero about the opera itself. From the delicate prelude to the last tragic chord, the conductor kept the whole piece lacy and light and sweet. Its background is the waltz, the Second Empire French waltz, sparkling and tender. And the oom-pah-pah of waltz accompaniment is both the abstract musical material of the opera's continuity-foundation and the theme of which the work is an expressive development. Only Beethoven, among all the other composers of opera, knew as Verdi did the gamut of drama that lies in abstract musical formulas, in scales, arpeggios, and neutral accompanying figures. He filled *Fidelio* with them, played with them as freely as if they had been the equally abstract Fifth Symphony theme.

It was clear from the care with which Mr. Sodero brought in the first statement of the oom-pah-pah basic chords, as they first appear wholly uncovered in the prelude, that he knew what Verdi was up to. Mysterious and dramatic they were, a first foreshadowing of the merry waltz motifs that permeate the opera and give it its special tone of mundanity and of penetrating personal sentiment. On a basis like that anything can happen. For four acts on that basis drama did happen, and personal sentiments grew into personal tragedy.

Always the waltz was present; always Mr. Sodero knew it was present and each time for what reason. The whole moved expressively and with animation. The tempos were always right for the drama, the rhythm always right for the music, the orchestral and vocal balances always right for full clarity and emphasis. I have rarely heard opera directed so satisfactorily. One could hear everything that went on in the pit and on the stage. Neither seemed assertive or subservient. And neither made any special effort at loudness. I do hope we shall have lots more of Mr. Sodero before the season is out and of Miss Albanese, too. This reviewer could do without the radio introduction that still holds up the Saturday matinee curtain for ten minutes to read the cast out loud and to recount a bowdlerized version of the plot.

December 6, 1942

Negro Traviata

LA TRAVIATA, opera in four acts, libretto by *Francesco Maria Piave*, music by *Giuseppe Verdi*, performed last night at Madison Square Garden by the National Negro Opera Company, *Frederick Vajda*, conductor, with *Lillian Evanti* (Violetta) and *William Franklin* (Germont).

THE NATIONAL NEGRO OPERA COMPANY, which made its first local appearance last night in Madison Square Garden before an audience estimated at 10,000 persons, looks like a praiseworthy singing group. What it sounds like is more difficult to say, since any opera company working under what amount almost to outdoor conditions, including the use of electrical amplification, sounds very much like any other opera company. What it would sound like in a theater of reasonable proportions is even harder to imagine. About all one could hear in undistorted form was rhythm and pitch. Nevertheless, it was clear that two, at least, of the soloists are singers of some value and that the choral work was solid.

Lillian Evanti, who sang the role of Violetta, has certainly a voice of wide range and many colors. Her control of those colors appeared to be at times a little precarious, but she has an ear for pitch and an instinct for dramatic expression. I should like to hear her sing without microphonic aid or interference. I fancy that Miss Evanti, though perhaps not fully mistress of her extraordinary vocal resources, is capable of brilliance and beauty.

William Franklin, who sang Germont, has a ringing baritone voice of excellent placement; and his enunciation of words is unusually clear. He has an unaffected dignity of presence, too, though his personal dramatic projection is not great. I have not seen his Porgy, but I can imagine it as more convincing than his Germont, who is a bit of a stuffy character anyhow.

It has never seemed to me that Negroes had much to gain from attempting to adopt the theater of Romanticism. They are not a Romantic people, and they do not understand bourgeois violence. The Baroque in tragedy, in comedy, and in religion is their home town. They understand its afflatus and its pageantry, its conventions, its excesses, and all its humane elegance. The operas of Handel are made for them. They could make real spectacles out of these, and they could sing their grandiloquent airs and choruses with the most touching dignity.

If there is any future for Negro opera (and I am convinced there is a great one), that future depends on the choice of a repertory that is congenial to Negro thought and attitudes, that exploits the Negro's gift for noble sentiments and sustained vocal outpourings. Nineteenth-century Italian opera does not do justice to his enormous but somewhat impersonal dramatic and musical talents. It is as unsuitable to him and as difficult for him to do convincingly as the Baroque repertory has become for contemporary white people.

March 30, 1944

The Verdi Case

HEARING last Monday Verdi's *The Masked Ball* at the Metropolitan Opera House has led me to wonder why that work, so satisfying orchestrally and so brilliant in its vocal writing, has never moved much the layman's simple human heart and why, even among musicians, it is more admired than deeply loved.

It is easy enough to pick flaws in the book, for these are many and grave. The heroine has no character; she is a lay figure. The hero has little more, not enough to make him interesting. An opera can get away with a vague tenor (Mozart's *Don Giovanni* does) if the heroine is a real live woman and the villain sufficiently wicked. It is hard to interest an audience in two lovers whose personalities are so imprecise and whose passion itself is so trivial.

The lovers are further thrown into shadow by the lady's husband, Renato. This future regicide is an extremely interesting person. He is kind, loyal, and passionate. All one's sympathy goes out to him. It seems a pity that such a tactful and forbearing spouse, once he had got his silly wife home from a midnight expedition where she had gone to gather a magic herb some fortune-teller had told her about and where she had ended by compromising her husband in front of his political enemies, it seems really too bad that after their long walk home in the snow he didn't sit down with her and quietly, by some straight-from-the-shoulder questioning, find out what really had or hadn't been going on and then decide on some sensible course of action. I was sorry to see a good man's home broken up so uselessly.

Oscar, the king's frivolous page, whose indiscretions betray his master's interests every time he opens his mouth, was a favorite of Verdi himself among his dramatic creations. Musically this preference is understandable, because rarely has a composer expressed so well pretty frivolity and light-hearted empty-headedness as they are implied in Oscar's staccato coloratura airs. The trouble with this role nowadays is the necessity of its being sung by a woman. Italian stage conventions are more precise than ours about femininity and masculinity. Consequently travesty is easier to get away with in Italy than here. It is virtually impossible on the Anglo-Saxon stage for a woman to represent an effeminate youth without seeming merely to be playing a male role ineffectually.

The opera's libretto is not its only fault. Its very musical strength is its weakness. The expressive nature of the orchestral accompaniments, the appropriateness of the contrapuntal writing, the sustained characterization of individual parts in the concerted numbers, the thematic unity of the whole work, are justly celebrated. Neither Meyerbeer nor Rossini ever etched a theatrical design more deeply. Richard Wagner himself, though a more sumptuous painter of psychological traits, was less accurate in his timing. Verdi did an A-1 professional job on *The Masked Ball*.

But music never lives by its professional quality. It lives by its tunes. And the tunes in *The Masked Ball* are every one of them tricky. Let us except the baritone aria "Eri tu," Oscar's "Saper vorreste," and just possibly the Laughing Chorus. All the others fall somewhere between broad simplicity and full, complex expression.

La Traviata and *Il Trovatore* are full of simple melodies that depict character and feeling in elementary but universally acceptable music. Wagner, at his best, and Mozart wrote melodies that express the same broad values but that comment more profoundly on the drama at the same time.

The orchestral accompaniment of *The Masked Ball* is a more elaborate auditive picture of the play than is the orchestral accompaniment of any opera Verdi had previously written. It sounds like the best French contemporary work, bearing little resemblance to the previously current Italian style that Wagner describes as "making the orchestra sound like a big guitar." The trios, quartets, and other ensemble pieces are equally fine. The melodic materials all these are made out of is simply not good enough. The tunes are pretty—little more. They lack the grand and elementary plainness of those in the earlier works. And they lack the penetrating accuracy of great stage music. They are affected and soft, like the libretto.

One could put the blame for the whole trouble on the libretto if one didn't know that Verdi's career was always dominated by the same problem. In *Aïda* he went back to broad writing. But he was obsessed by the desire to make Italian operas that would be as penetrating psychologically as French operas and as sumptuous musically as the German. He mastered psychological penetration instrumentally and wrote, in *Otello* and *Falstaff*, two of the most sumptuous musical works of the century. He could write big simple melodies and magnificent vocal bravura passages. He never learned how to build a melodic line that would be at the same time monumental and penetratingly expressive of the text. This inability to interpret character delicately is what gives to *Otello* and *Falstaff* a certain air, in spite of their instrumental delights, of banality. The same inability gives to *La Traviata* its rough and massive grandeur.

The lack of really delicate delicacy in Verdi's melodic contours, compensated though it be by pungent orchestration and the soundest dramatic building, makes the whole body of his work seem just a bit commercial. One is more often tempted, in fact, to take off one's hat to his triumphs of pure musical theater than one is to bare one's head before any revelations of the subtleties of human sentiment or of the depths of the human heart.

December 8, 1940

Hokum and Schmalz

LA FORZA DEL DESTINO, opera in a prologue and four acts, libretto by *Francesco Maria Piave*, music by *Giuseppe Verdi*, yesterday afternoon at the Metropolitan Opera House, *Bruno Walter*, conductor, *Herbert Graf*, stage director, with *Stella Roman* (Donna Leonora), *Frederick Jagel* (Don Alvaro), *Lawrence Tibbett* (Don Carlos), *Ezio Pinza* (Abbot), and *Salvatore Baccaloni* (Friar).

THE METROPOLITAN OPERA's first broadcast performance of the season was a thoroughly uninspired walk-through of Verdi's *La Forza del Destino*. Not that the work itself is particularly inspired, either. It suffers from a libretto that is little more than a stringing together of all the nineteenth-century Italian theater hokum that its author, Piave, had ever heard of; and that means practically all there was. There are murders and maledictions and tavern gaieties and transvestitism and mistaken identity and a battle and a storm and an eating scene and a comic monk and a paternal abbot and a male chorus dressed up as Franciscans and several duels and at the end a general carnage of all the principal persons. Underneath all this there is no real conflict of character and no general theme beyond that suggested in the title, which might well be translated, "Tough Luck."

Verdi wrote some skillful and rather grand music to this hodgepodge, though not his most touching by any means. It is hard and brilliant theater music, and unless it is performed with a hard and brilliant timing it sounds absurd. A few moments yesterday were so performed, notably the duet between Pinza and Baccaloni, as Abbot and friar. Stella Roman gave the stage a lift, too, whenever she was on it, through the strange and commanding beauty of her voice. It is too bad that an interesting and highly personal timbre should be almost her whole stock in trade as a star. I say *almost* because she does sing on pitch, too. But she has no personal warmth on a stage and no tension. She creates no drama. Also, her work lacks continuity. She doesn't sing in phrases, only in single notes. These she exploits with her own spectacular technique of crooning and crescendo; and very agreeable they are to hear, I must say. But her work has no architectural line, either as drama or as music.

Architectural line is what Bruno Walter's reading of the score seemed chiefly to lack, too. Instead of pathos and emphasis, he achieved only sentimentality and clatter. Rarely have I heard the Metropolitan orchestra sound so ill-balanced, its strings so thin, its brasses so tinny. And that exactitude of timing that is the very essence of melodrama was nowhere present, save in the Baccaloni-Pinza duet.

Frederick Jagel and Lawrence Tibbett were ineffective, to say the least. The former sang throatily and without rhythm, the latter painfully and constantly flat. I am afraid Mr. Tibbett has become in recent years a vocal liability to whatever opera he appears in. The resonance is gone; he is almost never up to pitch; it makes one's throat ache to hear him. Even his dramatic power seems to have deserted him. Yesterday he moved about with as little of ease and freedom in his limbs as in his voice, though his static appearance was that of youth.

The full telling of yesterday's sad story requires my recording that the chorus work was ragged, unresonant, and frequently off pitch. Also that the crowd scenes contained too much milling around for either musical accuracy or dramatic significance. On the whole, however, I am inclined to blame the general ineffectiveness of the performance on the conductor. I felt no radiation of power from him except during the playing of the Overture; and the singers gave no evidence of being held firmly to the rocket-like trajectory that the work requires in order to be convincing. It is possible, of course, that Mr. Walter had felt impelled out of loyalty to management and public to go through with his seasonal début at a time when he was not yet fully recovered from his recent illness.

November 28, 1943

Vocalism Victorious

DIE WALKÜRE, opera in three acts by *Richard Wagner*, last night at the Metropolitan Opera House, *Erich Leinsdorf,* conductor, *Lothar Wallerstein,* stage director, with *Lauritz Melchior* (Siegmund), *Julius Huehn* (Wotan), *Lotte Lehmann* (Sieglinde), *Helen Traubel* (Brünnhilde), and *Kerstin Thorborg* (Fricka).

WAGNER continues to bring out the vocalism fans. Last night's *Walküre* was heard by a full house at the Metropolitan with many standing, and applause ran high. Vocalism ran pretty high, too, with Lotte Lehmann leading the field, Lauritz Melchior placing. Helen Traubel ran well. Julius Huehn, limping vocally from the start, was about to run in the third act, in spite of his disabilities, when your reviewer went off to write his piece.

The first act was the more satisfactory of the two that he heard, partly because the singing was more expert and partly because it is a better piece of music than the second, which, in spite of the pleasant bravura of the Valkyries' whoop and some most ingenious storm music, is long, labored, and fragmentary. The first contains some of the best musical conversation there is anywhere. This is quiet and delicately varied; and last night Miss Lehmann and Mr. Melchior enunciated it with all clarity, intoned it with all beauty of sound. The tenor cavatina, or Spring Song, too, was delivered with a rhythmic alacrity most agreeable to follow; and the final curtain was built up to with great skill and much restraint by both artists.

Mr. Leinsdorf's conducting of the orchestra under all this was of no small aid to the protagonists on the stage. He kept the accompaniment alive and mostly soft all the way through, a beautiful job. Naturally, since singing was the subject of the evening, it didn't occur to anyone to offer the conductor even a teensy-weensy curtain call.

The second act was loud and coarse, as is its nature. Miss Traubel's handsome voice was displayed *grosso modo* without much refinement of expression, and so was Miss Thorborg's. The former lady wore a flat coiffure and an exasperated expression not unlike those of a comic-strip character named Inna Minnie. The latter looked angry and acid in her yellow silk wrapper. Mr. Huehn looked well, but his throat was in no state to sing Wotan. The orchestra was raucous, the trombones being particularly unpleasant in their inability to achieve a round tone or a correct balance in chords.

Wagner as a young man was angry against Donizetti's music and jealous of its success. It is one of the neater ironies of fate that his own operas, after a hundred years, have come to fulfill the exact function in repertory that Donizetti's used to. They are vehicles for vocalism and nothing else. Nobody cares who conducts them or very much what the orchestra sounds like, provided it remains subservient to the singers and makes a clatter at the climaxes.

Vocalism is the thing sought, not dramatic sense nor vicarious emotional experience nor any kind of audio-visual spectacle. Stage direction and scenic effects are unimportant. Even symphonic pacing has ceased to count. But the whole art of singing, as that is understood today, is exemplified in the work of the great Wagnerian vocalists. People go to hear Flagstad and Traubel and Melchior and Lehmann exactly as they used to go to hear Melba and Sembrich and Caruso and Adelina Patti.

They listen raptly and applaud with vigor. They get their money's worth, too, because the Wagner productions nowadays, though often carelessly conducted, have more good throat work on display than we are likely to find in the productions of Italian pieces that were written with vocal display in mind. These have become virtually impossible of correct execution in the present decline of vocal art. But Wagner can still be sung.

February 17, 1943

Carmen à l'Aimable

CARMEN, opera in four acts, libretto by *Henri Meilhac* and *Ludovic Halévy*, music by *Georges Bizet*, yesterday afternoon at the Metropolitan Opera House, *Wilfrid Pelletier*, conductor, *Désiré Defrère*, stage director, with *Gladys Swarthout* (Carmen), *Licia Albanese* (Micaela), *Thelma Votipka* (Frasquita), *Helen Olheim* (Mercedes), *Charles Kullman* (Don José), *Leonard Warren* (Escamillo), *Alessio de Paolis* (Remendado), *Louis D'Angelo* (Zuniga), and *Wilfred Engelman* (Morales).

YESTERDAY's matinee, being a broadcast performance, would seem to have been cast for vocal effect. Very successfully, too. Such an abundance of beautiful singing is not to be heard every day. The acting was not much, though the climaxes were solid, thanks to Mr. Kullman; and the spectacle in general was sumptuous.

Miss Swarthout's voice is warm and beautiful and friendly, and her usage of it is far from unrefined musically. In the role of Carmen that friendliness seems to get in her way, excepting for the passages of pure anger, which she does well. Carmen is classically considered to be a sexy role, and it is not easy to be friendly and sexy at the same time. She is jolly; she is athletic; she grins constantly. She is as pretty as a moving picture and, in the "healthy" American sense, attractive; but she has about as much direct sex-appeal as a Chesterfield cigarette advertisement. She is all charm and innuendo, and she has far too much energy.

She has, however, a fine and full stage presence whenever she manages to keep still; and her deadpan is utterly beautiful and terrifying. She overdresses the part less than most stars, and some of her studied "business" is excellent. Her card scene is good. The death scene is good too, though a shade violent. She might have been quieter and left the violence to Don José. Her dancing in the second act was more convincingly Spanish and more distinguished than anything the ballet troupe did yesterday. Her whole rendition, in addition to its auditory opulence, showed evidence of great pains and much sincere effort to get things right. Working thus against nature to achieve melodrama, the result could hardly be expected to rank among the world's great Carmens. It was due purely to Miss Swarthout's vocal warmth that a characterization otherwise fairly frigid ended by being acceptable as the cause of so much amorous conflagration.

Mr. Kullman sang well and looked well. Also, as I mentioned before, it was due to his dramatic foresight that the climaxes all came off adequately. Miss Albanese's French is of the sketchiest and her comprehension of French style equally so. So she did the only thing possible with the rule of Micaela; she sang it in the Italian style. But being a singer of refinement in the Italian style, nothing she did was offensive. She took every occasion to display her beautiful voice, even adding a *messa di voce* on high B flat in the third-act aria; but at no time did she destroy the cantilena or falsify the expression of Bizet's lovely music. Her singing was distinguished and, as always, beautiful.

Equally distinguished and beautiful was that of Mr. Leonard Warren as Escamillo. He neither looked nor even pretended to act the part; but oh, how beautifully he sang! What vigor of musical line! What refreshing variety of *demi-teints*! What constantly accurate resonance, at all times placed squarely in the upper part of the face! The Misses Votipka and Olheim, the Messrs. Cehanovsky, De Paolis, D'Angelo, and Engelman did solo bits and the celebrated concerted numbers with style and full resonance.

The stage direction was mostly not very good, especially for the chorus. The Joseph Urban scenery is still excellent. The conductor gave us a real French *Carmen*, but a second-class one. That is to say that his conception was correct but that the adjustments of tempos one to another were often a bit crude. The delicate ones came out overemphasized, the sharper ones a little fuzzy. The tempos were mostly on the fast side, a fault that did little harm to the performance except in a few places— animated it rather. The orchestra itself sounded well. On the whole, a vigorous performance of a vigorous work, a *Carmen* memorable for real singing in every role.

March 16, 1941

Paris Forever

LA VIE PARISIENNE, opera in four acts, libretto by *Felix Brentano* and *Louis Verneuil*, music by *Jacques Offenbach*, lyrics by *Marion Jones Farquhar*, performed last night at the Forty-fourth Street Theatre by the New Opera Company, *Antal Doráti*, conductor, *Mr. Brentano*, stage director, with *Clifford Newdahl* (Mr. Hutchinson), *Ruby Mercer* (Evelyn Hutchinson), *Carolina Segrera* (Metella), and *Ann Lipton* (Gabrielle).

IN the French version, a Swedish family is the protagonist of that love affair with Paris that seems to come once into the lives of so many people from so many lands. In the A. P. Herbert version it is an English household. Messieurs Felix Brentano and Louis Verneuil have for the present adaptation brought their visitors from Chicago, which is appropriate and charming of them. The real subject of the piece, however, is the homage that Offenbach himself, a German from the Rhineland, was offering to the city which he loved and which loved him.

Paris has always been good for foreign musicians and some-times good to them. To none was ever it more generous than to Jacques Offenbach, né Levy, from Offenbach-am-Main. And no musician, foreign or French, not even the Gustave Charpen-tier of *Louise*, ever placed at the feet of his mistress a fresher or a lovelier tribute than *La Vie Parisienne*. It is a crown of waltzes picked out with polkas and quadrilles and interwoven with melodies that distill the tender sentiment, the whole tied up with a great big lacy ribbon in the form of a cancan. And the melodies are as fresh as the day they were picked; the rhythm pops like champagne; the gaiety is as genuine as anything I have ever seen on a stage. Every company that acts that operetta has the time of its life and communicates its effervescence. This production is certain to sell lots of fizz-water for the tonier bistros of the town. And to leave happy memories with all. The grand quadrille and cancan that end the third scene are a very ocean of lace and of legs. As Jean Cocteau, himself no mean lover of the Lutetian strand, once said of such an occasion, "Venus herself, nascent, could not have kicked up more foam."

One has one's reserves about any transformation of a text one loves. I regret the omission, on silly moralistic grounds presumably, of the flirtatious wife. I regret the omission of the traditional gesture with which the nymphomaniac widow ends her number, "Es-tu content, mon colonel?" which is a lifting high of the hoopskirt to expose black panties worn in memory of the departed mate. I regret the omission of the patter song, "Repeuplons les salons du Faubourg Saint-Germain," and of the father's chop-licking, "Je veux m'en fourrer jusque-là." Also the virtual omission of the theme song: "Je serai votre guide dans ce ville splendide." Nevertheless, this version is a good one. The spoken text is less ingenious than Mrs. Farquhar's rhymed lyrics, which are tiptop. All in all, it is difficult to imagine a better adaptation and translation job of a musical play, or to remember one.

The star of the cast is Clifford Newdahl, who both sings and really troops. The others are better vocally than dramatically, though Miss Ruby Mercer does her love stuff with much charm, and Miss Carolina Segrera has a genuinely powerful stage personality. Miss Ann Lipton, the soubrette, is my favorite among the ladies of the cast, both vocally and personally. The men are all right but sort of stuffy, like all singing heroes.

From the specially hand-painted curtain in the Chéret manner to the last detail of gloves and footwear, the stage-sets and the costumes are sumptuous and witty, rich in material, designed and combined with both taste and brilliance. So are the dancing and the stage movements. As a musical show *La Vie Parisienne* makes the rest of Broadway both look and sound silly; and this applies to the Thirty-ninth Street crematorium as well, whenever that ancient and honorable institution tries to do light opera. I do hope the New Opera Company can keep the show running. Or possibly sell it to a producer. It would not surprise me if there should turn out to be gold in those trills and furbelows.* If the Paris of Offenbach, which is, after all, about as near to the eternal Paris as any, not excepting that of the late Third Republic, can sell bubbly in the bars and put other operas at the Forty-fourth Street over the spring, she will have made a pretty return for the love that New Yorkers and musicians have long borne her.

November 6, 1941

Melody and Tears

LA BOHÈME, opera in four acts, libretto by *Giuseppe Giacosa* and *Luigi Illica*, music by *Giacomo Puccini*, yesterday afternoon at the Metropolitan Opera House, *Gennaro Papi*, conductor, *Désiré Defrère*, stage director, with *Annamary Dickey* (Musetta), *Armand Tokatyan* (Rodolfo), and *Jarmila Novotná* (Mimi).

YESTERDAY's performance was a ripsnorter for gaiety, vigor and general run-around. Few effects in the theater are more thoroughly delightful than that of chorus ladies' maternal physiques in gamins' wigs and trousers. Everybody loves it, even the chorus ladies themselves, who cavort and tussle enthusiastically. Few theatrical devices are so completely ineffective, on the other hand, as that of hiding youthful love behind a beard.

Yesterday's gamins were jolly. Yesterday's youthful lovers seemed, on the whole, more boisterous than passionate. Mr. Tokatyan sang Rodolfo on short notice in an improvised costume that consisted of a modern tail-coat such as gentlemen wear as customers to the opera and a pair of equally modern, quite snappily cut, in fact, trousers of a light, checked material. He sported above these a neat black beard trimmed in a style resembling at once that commonly associated with graphic representations of Our Saviour and that indubitably worn by Napoleon III. His singing was good, though the voice is a little harsh.

Miss Novotná was dressed in the least glamorous colors,

*This production closed shortly afterward.

excepting for a little red jacket in the first act. At the Café Momus festivities she wore an infant's hood of white lace with streamers that tied under the chin. Already tall, the get-up made her look like Charlotte Greenwood. She sang at all times handsomely, though her voice has a veil on it, a slight buzz that prevents it from being the movingly beautiful thing it would be if she could give it a clearer and more ringing sound. Her musical style yesterday and her acting were the afternoon's most distinguished. In a cast that overacted and whooped up the show incessantly, she remained calm and convincing at all times. Her death was genuinely touching, though Mr. Tokatyan's behavior with the corpse was anything but.

Miss Dickey, as Musetta, sang and acted well, in spite of a wig that suggested 1900 blondined hair more than it did anything associated with the Latin Quarter of the 1840's, and in spite also of a rather silly pink dress that stood out too much in the ensemble. Her last act was admirable.

After having been to a number of comic works at the Metropolitan this season, it was good to hear an opera with a tragic ending. The deployment of all the singers and all the instrumentalists that opera in a big house requires, the setting up of so much scenery and the designing of so many costumes, all the paraphernalia of what my colleague Mr. Richard Watts referred to last week as "so tumultuous a dramatic medium," are likely to seem futile unless the subject-matter of the work that uses them all is something more essentially serious than what can be arranged into a happy ending.

In the case of *La Bohème* the touching quality of the work is not due to the mere presence of death. It is due as well to the genius of Giacomo Puccini. I call his musico-dramatic gift genius because no one has ever been able either to analyze its power away or to laugh it off. Say what you will, and present that opera how you like, it is a truly sad story that makes people cry. After all, is anything in the world more poignant than youth and love and tuberculosis?

January 4, 1941

Mildly Dissenting

DER ROSENKAVALIER, opera in three acts, libretto by *Hugo von Hofmannsthal*, music by *Richard Strauss*, last night at the Metropolitan Opera House, *Erich Leinsdorf*, conductor, *Désiré Defrère*, stage director, with *Lotte Lehmann* (Princess von Werdenberg), *Jarmila Novotná* (Octavian), *Irra Petina* (Annina), *Marita Farell* (Sophie), and *Emanuel List* (Baron Ochs von Lerchenau).

"THE KNIGHT OF THE ROSE," or *The Rose Cavalier*, as the Metropolitan Opera program so drolly translates it, was the operatic fare of last evening. The audience adored it and the singers seemed to be having a good time. The performance all through was remarkably even and smooth. I am sure it is a personal shortcoming that I did not find myself taking much interest in the affair.

If I may be permitted the confession, I have never been able to keep my mind on *Der Rosenkavalier*. It does not bother me and it does not amuse me. I can take a cat nap here and there without seeming to miss anything, because when I wake up the music is always doing exactly what it was when I dropped off. It is full of waltzes that all sound alike and that have nothing to do with the play, which is about mid-eighteenth-century Vienna. It is full of broken-up vocal lines that have no musical necessity, because the orchestra always has the tune anyway, and that always have to be sung loud because the orchestration is thick and pushing, owing to Strauss's constant overwriting for the horns. I think it is really an acting opera, because the vocal line is not very interesting and the orchestral writing, though elaborate, is to my ear wholly inconsequential. I make exception vocally for the final trio, which is as pretty as can be, and instrumentally for the well-known passage where the celesta comments in another key.

From the acting point of view the work has many good roles. The Marschallin, the Baron, the Knight of the Rose himself and the Italian intriguers are all well characterized by the librettist and easy to play. The Marschallin is not easy to do with distinction, but fortunately we still have Lotte Lehmann for that. Octavian, the Knight, is not easy to do with elegance, either, but Miss Novotná saved us last night from the embarrassment one so often feels at the all too feminine shape and manners of the Marschallin's young lover. My favorite actress in the cast was, as usual, Irra Petina. I love what she does with her hands. I also love the way she sings and found her vocally the most satisfactory artist in the cast. Lehmann's voice is lovely but faded. Novotná is musically stylish but sometimes lacking in tonal beauty. Miss Farell's work is not quite ripe. Emanuel List is competent but rough. And the rest of the singers hadn't enough to do to make them vocally noticeable last night. Everybody's singing was all right; but nobody's, except Miss Petina's, was anything to cherish in the memory as sheer sound.

Erich Leinsdorf conducted all right, too, though an ideal rendition would have been rhythmically more flexible. Also, if the orchestra is not to force the singers in this work to sing always loud and monotonously, especial care must be used to secure a highly transparent string tone and the woodwinds must be discreet. Otherwise the sound gets thick and absorbs the voices instead of setting them off. Leinsdorf didn't bother much about this. His work had a certain zip and go about it, however; and he got a clean response from his orchestra. Defrère's stage direction was excellent, and the thirty-year-old sets of Hans Kautsky are still acceptable. With so many quite good elements involved, and with the whole performance operating on such a high level of presentability, it seemed a shame that I couldn't get up anything like the enthusiasm about it that the audience did.

March 14, 1942

Free Love, Socialism, and Why Girls Leave Home

LOUISE, opera in four acts by *Gustave Charpentier*, yesterday afternoon at the Metropolitan Opera House, *Sir Thomas Beecham*, conductor, *Désiré Defrère*, stage director, with *Grace Moore* (Louise), *Raoul Jobin* (Julien), *Doris Doe* (Mother), *Ezio Pinza* (Father), and *Maxine Stellman* (Irma). With *Nina Youchkevich* and dancers.

YESTERDAY AFTERNOON's performance of *Louise* at the Metropolitan Opera House was one of mounting power. It began rather weakly with Mr. Jobin singing throatily and off pitch and Miss Moore posing around in attitudes derived from still photographs of Sarah Bernhardt. It picked up with the entrance of Miss Doe, and it became a real dramatic exposition when Mr. Pinza arrived. The sweeping musical conception of Sir Thomas Beecham, who conducted, and the great beauty of the symphonic passages made it evident, too, that a musico-dramatic occasion of some magnitude was in progress.

The second act belonged to the conductor and to the ensemble, as it should, with Miss Maxine Stellman adding a handsomely sung solo in the dressmaking scene. The third act was everybody's. Miss Moore began it with a good "Depuis le jour." She and Mr. Jobin then got through the conversation about socialism and their love-duet and had just gone into the house when the surprise party arrived with lanterns and dancers and a brass band. Here Sir Thomas and the chorus took over again and did a rousing "Coronation of the Muse," with Miss Youchkevitch dancing most prettily. Then Miss Doe came on; and everybody else left but Louise and Julien, the alto Mother giving at this point a well-sung and excellently acted summons for Daughter to come home and console sick Father. One felt one had been through quite a bit of excitement by this time, but the height of it was yet to come.

The last act was a triumphant rendition dramatically, vocally, and musically by Miss Moore, Miss Doe, Mr. Pinza, Sir Thomas, and the orchestra of one of the most shocking family brawls I have ever witnessed. Everybody was superb. Indeed, this climactic summary of all the reasons why girls leave home was of a sweep and power that marked the afternoon as a memorable one. It also brought to this reviewer's notice the fact that the whole plot and libretto of *Louise* are literature.

It has long been supposed that Gustave Charpentier wrote his own text for this opera; and, indeed, no other author is named on the title page of the score. I do not know exactly how much work the composer did on the libretto; but Max Jacob once told me that the plot of it was conceived and much of the dialogue written down in one evening at a dinner of Charpentier and some literary friends in a Paris restaurant, Jacob himself being present and participating in the communal creation. Also that the poet Saint-Pol-Roux was the one writer there who remembered to put his name to the work. He may also have done more on it at a later time, because Jacob assured me that Saint-Pol-Roux received performing-rights fees regularly for *Louise* from the Society of Dramatic Authors and Composers.

Whatever may be the exact history of this libretto, however, it is certainly not the work of a literary amateur. Its intrigue is tightly woven; its characterization is powerful, and the dialogue is simple, direct, and stylistically pure in a way hardly to be expected of a composer who has never shown elsewhere any unusual literary mastery. What is his and characteristic, of course, is the musical mastery, manifest throughout the opera, of all the implications of a brilliant literary text. The opera is built up with clear musical characterization, an intense expression of the atmosphere of its subject, and a sound respect for the plain language of plain people. Its musical continuity is symphonic in character without being overcomplex; and its orchestral coloration is fanciful, appropriately picturesque and expert. If it were not for the trumpery musical quality of two of the chief leitmotives—Louise's and Julien's—and the consequent monotony of their subsequent developments, the work might almost rank beside *Carmen* and *La Traviata* in operatic literature. Even so, when conducted with understanding and acted with some style, as it was yesterday (not to speak of much excellent singing), it is a pretty poignant piece of musical theater.

January 16, 1943

The Grace Moore Case

ONE has watched in the past Miss Grace Moore's operatic career with amazement and sometimes with impatience. Her faults were so abundant, her talents, musical and dramatic, so limited, that it has often been occasion for wonder that so much energy and hard work should be deployed on so seemingly hopeless an errand. After seeing her in *La Tosca* the other evening, I am inclined to think that the expenditures were not wasted, after all, and that she has "arrived," as people used to say, at a quite indisputable and authentic stardom.

Her faults have not diminished nor her qualities changed. Both, indeed, have matured. It is the complete visibility of all the factors involved that makes it possible for us to accept her as a finished artist. It is probable also that the realization by Miss Moore herself that her voice will never be any more beautiful than it is today nor her acting any more effective that causes her to give so careful, so conscientious a performance. Few, indeed, are the operatic *prime donne* whose work bears evidence of such good will toward art and such workmanlike integrity.

Miss Moore's musical gifts are modest but well schooled. Her voice, once almost overbrilliant, has lost its surface glamour but none of its real fire; and Miss Moore has improved considerably of late years at the handling of it. It always had more flame in it than sheer beauty. Nowadays this warmth is supplemented by a technical assurance that is none the less welcome for being, alas, all too rare among vocalists of the French school.

Miss Moore's musicianship is difficult to diagnose, because her roles have so far all been such as to require no especial refinement of musical understanding. She seems to have had sensible coaching, and she sings mostly on pitch and in fair rhythm. The musical instinct, I should say, is adequate and the technique solid, so far as it goes, the only element of Miss Moore's musical equipment that goes beyond good training being the very personal timbre of a voice that is the more penetratingly affecting from having lost the impersonal brilliance and bloom of its youth.

Miss Moore's shortcomings at the creating of dramatic illusion are well known. No amount of coaching has been able to make an actress out of her. And yet her performances are far from ineffective. She goes through the motions of acting with such gusto and beams at the audience with such obvious pleasure that no one can resist her wholly. I have often thought she misunderstood her talent, that she is essentially a comedienne and that her proper role is that of the buxom lass with arms akimbo, apple cheeks, and a merry wit. Certainly her stage comportment has not the somber intensity we are accustomed to associate with humorless amour and tragic outcome. In whatever role, she seems always to be playing Madame Sans-Gêne. Her physical advantages themselves are scarcely those of the tragic actress. She has a face that records no darker sentiment than that of well-being. Her arms wave cheerfully at all times. Her smile is what is known as infectious. And yet she plays *femmes fatales*. How does she get away with it?

She gets away with it by giving, however inadequate as illusion, a completely careful and studied performance. No audience can resist such a compliment. She also gets away with it because the nature of her studied performance is such as to recall a great tradition of operatic acting. She has been coached by Garden in the routine of pose and plastic attitude. Her whole concept of stage action is pre-First-World-War—1900, even. It is derived from the sculpture of Rodin. It has never heard of modern stage style, which is static and low in relief, like contemporary sculpture. Like Garden, she moves in spirals and adopts, wherever possible, robes that lend themselves to vorticism. The contrast between her rounded feminine pantomime and the angular masculinity of Mr. Sved, who plays Scarpia to her Tosca, is advantageous to the plot and to both artists.

There is no doubt that Miss Moore's face and figure are ill adapted to tragic expression. Nevertheless, the choreography of her performance is not without interest or dignity. Its very artificiality is proof of its authenticity. It is a detailed reconstruction, worked out in some of the roles under Garden's own tutelage, of the best French tradition of operatic acting. It is not animated by genius, as Garden's work was; nor has Miss Moore, for all her blandness and cheerful spirits, any erotic projection comparable to Miss Garden's somber fire and intellectual sensuality. But, for all that, her work is made after a great model.

The spirit of great workmanship can never be copied, but its technical shape and framework almost can. I am inclined to think Miss Moore's position in the operatic world, quite apart from the mere agreeableness of her performances, which, at their worst, never let one down, has something to do with her relation to a great tradition. In an epoch when operatic style is little understood and its practice more and more improvisational, Miss Moore gives a thoroughly worked-out rendition of whatever she does. That working out, moreover, is done on no eclectic precept or personal basis. It is a sincere attempt to observe a great tradition. And somehow, by sheer good will, hard work and intellectual modesty, Miss Moore manages to produce the best performance now available in that tradition.

Her work is old-fashioned, if you like. And her personal shortcomings are enormous. But these are so frankly not concealed that we can easily discount their effect on us. And her consistent avoidance of anything vocal or dramatic that might possibly be considered contemporary is proof of a passionate devotion to one of the grandest periods of operatic rendition.

I share her admiration for the operatic style of the Third Republic. And I take off my hat to a contemporary artist who has gone back to the highest decades of that period for models to copy and to emulate.

February 22, 1942

Mélisande

THE CHARACTERS in *Pelléas et Mélisande* are correct, well-to-do French people. They don't talk about their business much; but they own property, wear good clothes and seem to be running some sort of kingdom. They have strong passions, kind hearts, good manners, and an intense family life. They understand about love and approve of it. What they cannot deal with is any vagueness on the subject. Mélisande's attractiveness for them seems to be due partly to the fact that she has no family ties (they can thus adopt her completely) and partly to the fact that her affections and her amorous tendencies are both powerful and imprecise. She fascinates them; they never know what to think of her. She keeps them guessing not through any plan but simply through the fact, astounding and incredible to them, that she has no plan, no conscious motives of any sort.

This lack of project, of intention on her part does not prevent her from acting with utter straightforwardness. Her one interest in life is being loved; she demands love from everybody and gets it. She pays willingly any price asked and suffers cheerfully all the consequences involved, early marriage, childbirth and death. She will do anything to avoid not being loved. She lies about a ring she has lost; she submits to a thorough beating from her husband; she refuses to hold a grudge against anyone at any time. Her famous remark at the end of the flagellation scene reveals how egocentric is all her sweetness. "I am not happy here" is her whole comment on the incident. A lonely girl with a floating libido and no malice toward anyone can cause lots of trouble in a well-organized family.

Her husband sees trouble coming quite early, goes to bed of a minor ailment, and tries to think the situation out. "Mélisande, be reasonable!" is his last plea. She doesn't know what he means. After that, tragedy is inevitable. Attempts on the husband's part to discipline her and to spy on her friendship with his younger brother merely bring out the relentless quality in her character, her inability to accept any discipline whatsoever. He tries to murder his brother. Then he pleads with him as man to man. But by that time the brother's sentiments are sufficiently definite so that he cannot, as an honest Frenchman, go back on them. Mélisande wouldn't have collaborated on a noble renunciation, anyway. She would never have got the idea. So the young man is ordered away on a trip. When his departure provokes a real love scene (husband having impatiently shut them both out of the house one evening), there is at last a visible justification for running the deceiver through with a sword.

Nevertheless, Mélisande has the last word. She gives birth to a child, forgives her husband his violence by saying there is nothing to forgive, and dies sweetly, like Little Eva, after refusing to answer all direct questions about her love life. The husband, reasonable and logical to the end, has wanted to know whether he has killed his brother unjustly. Also, with a legitimate curiosity, whether there is any chance he is not the father of the baby. Her reply is equivocal, "We have done nothing to be blamed for." The aged father, an observer from the beginning rather than an actor in the tragedy, thereupon brings out the following pearl of wisdom and of comfort for his bereaved son: "It's terrible but it's not your fault." The French family is thus juridical-minded to the last.

This recital has one purpose only, to remind my readers and all who saw the lovely performance of this opera last week at the Metropolitan that the role of Mélisande is not an easy one to play. It has never been easy, and very few singing actresses have ever made a success of it. Mary Garden and Maggie Teyte were memorable. I have heard others do it, but none convincingly. Mélisande must be childlike on the surface and amorous underneath. She must be both affectionate and self-centered. She must radiate an unaware sexual preoccupation. And she must move delicately. The opera is her show, hers and the conductor's.

Bidu Sayao, in the present production, comes nearer to making the opera her show than any other singer I know of has done, excepting always Garden and Teyte (and I never saw Teyte in it). She has worked out a visible line of movement that is expressive, and her fragile youth is most touching. It is the first star role I have seen her carry off at all, her whole previous effectiveness having been in the domain of the soubrette. She has not learned yet to project her amorous feelings and her sorrows in heroine style, as if the future of the cosmos hung upon them. But she seems to have made a beginning. Also she has created a Mélisande that, if it is not one of the great ones, is convincing, nevertheless.

Martial Singher, as Pelléas, overpowers her in every way. His vocalism, his declamation, his stage presence, his whole musical and dramatic equipment are of another magnitude. Their scenes together are his scenes, though there seems to be no intention on his part of making them so. All the same, Miss Sayao does a good Mélisande. Her characterization represents not only a step forward for her as a serious actress but also a contribution second only to that of Mr. Singher to a beautiful performance of a great work. When one remembers how many fine sopranos have made no effect at all in the role (though they have dreamed all their lives of singing it), one is obliged to recognize Miss Sayao's achievement as being a far from minor one.

January 30, 1944

Porgy *in Maplewood*

Aꜰᴛᴇʀ sɪx ʏᴇᴀʀs George Gershwin's *Porgy and Bess* is still a beautiful piece of music. Its faults are numberless; but its inspiration is authentic, its expressive quotient high.

I went to Maplewood, New Jersey, last Monday night to hear its reopening. Cheryl Crawford has produced it with almost the original cast, Alexander Smallens conducting, as before. Happily, the Mamoulian scenery and stage movements have not been reconstituted; they were always too ponderous and too complex to be advantageous. Also, Mr. Smallens has taken occasion to diminish the thickness of the instrumentation and to make some further musical cuts. Gershwin would not have minded, I am sure. He was, if anything, too complaisant about permitting changes in his scores. And his orchestration, at best, was never very skillful or very personal, this particular score, which he probably made without assistance, being heavily overcharged with useless doublings.

As to musical cuts, a considerable number of these had already been made, with Gershwin's consent, during the opera's original run. Others have been incorporated in this production, with the purpose of speeding up certain badly timed passages and with that of eliminating, where possible, the embarrassments due to Gershwin's incredibly amateurish way of writing recitative. In some cases spoken dialogue has been substituted for intoned speech. Without being entirely certain from one hearing whether all these excisions, instrumental and textual, are exactly the right ones to have made and whether perhaps even more of them might be desirable, I approve heartily their having been made at all. It seems to me that that kind of correction, carried out by a skillful musician who knew the composer well and respected his genius, is exactly what the work needs right now. By making it as good a show as possible, as easy to execute and to listen to as is consistent with Gershwin's own writing (nobody has altered his actual notes), the work has, I fancy, more chance of becoming a part of standard operatic repertory than it would have in its original rather clumsy version. Conductors at the Metropolitan do far worse distorting of European classics. Anyway, there will always be time later to revive the original version, if anyone feels passionately about it.

Porgy and Bess is a strange case. It has more faults than any work I have ever known by a reputable composer. There are faults of taste, faults of technique, and grave miscalculations about theatrical effect. It remains, none the less, a beautiful piece of music and a deeply moving play for the lyric theater. Its melodic invention is abundant and pretty distinguished. Its expressive power is impeded by no conscious stylization of the musical means. Gershwin's lack of any intellectual orientation, even the most elementary, toward musical style and his positive ignorance about everything that makes opera opera seem only to have thrown the more into relief his ability to write beautiful and expressive melody and his childlike sincerity. When one considers one by one the new works that the world's greatest opera houses have produced with ballyhoos and hallelujahs in the past forty years and the almost unvarying pattern of their failure, one is inclined to be more than proud of our little Georgie. He didn't know much about musical æsthetics and he couldn't orchestrate for shucks; but his strength was as the strength of ten because his musical heart was really pure.

It was so pure that he could put music to a piece of phony white folklore about Negro life in Charleston, music which is itself about as Negroid as Broadway, and still get Negro artists to perform it without sticking their tongues in their cheeks. They perform it movingly and sincerely. Miss Ruby Elzy, as Serena, gives the loveliest single performance in the cast; Mr. Avon Long, as Sporting Life, replacing the original Bubbles in that role, gives the most brilliant. Miss Helen Dowdy as the Strawberry Woman is perfect both vocally and dramatically, and Miss Georgette Harvey is complete as Maria. I have never cared much for Miss Anne Brown or for Mr. Todd Duncan, who play the name parts. She is vocally not quite top-drawer and rather wooden as an actress. He is a good singer, and he has a stage personality of great sweetness and warmth. But he hams and mugs and overplays and misses most of his best effects by underestimating his own simple power. Mr. Edward Matthews, as Jake, though vocally excellent, makes the same mistake. Miss Harriet Jackson, as Clara, began a little nervously and got better; vocally she was quite lovely. Mr. Jack Carr, who played Crown, was handsome to behold; but he is both vocally and dramatically insufficient for this weighty part. The goat was the most beautiful animal of his species I have ever laid my eyes on.

Rumor hath it that the production will be brought to town. I hope so. It is a good one, and the score itself has both musical distinction and popular appeal. It has a few weak moments, always did. These are invariably the scenes in prose dialogue. The set pieces, where George was working with Ira Gershwin's neatly metrical lyrics, are all excellent. In a year when American compositions are being searched out and honored, it would be not only just, it would be, I should think, good business to expose before our eager and friendly musical public a work which not only New York, the composer's natal city, but America, his native land, might well be proud to honor and happy to love.*

October 19, 1941

---

*This revival opened shortly afterwards on Broadway, where it ran for two years. In January 1945 the company was still touring.

Blitzstein's Operas

THE MORE comprehensive and grandiose any subject-matter, the more necessary it is to treat it theatrically in a stylized and conventional manner. Symbolic and legendary histories, as of gods, demigods and heroes, involving, as they always do, the prestige of some ethnic group and a whole panoply of the supernatural, have always required for their serious exposition as spectacle the conventions of poetic diction and of ceremonial choreography. From the Greek tragic theater to the contemporary opera there is no exception. There is only the corrective of comedy, which pokes fun when serious matters and noble conventions get out of hand and go pompous.

The conventions of serious theatrical style, once established as an observance by authors and spectators, require a steady supply of serious subject-matter for their continuance. The opera, for example, has in the 340 years of its existence roamed and combed indefatigably the fields of mythology, of military and political history, of religion, sexuality, and social unrest. Embedded and fossilized in the repertories of the most conformist opera foundations are subjects that, if treated less stylistically, would be even today social dynamite. Incest, revolution, suicide, miscegenation, black magic, religious heresy, pessimism, free love, and the abolition of private property are glorified and advocated nightly at the Metropolitan Opera House. In face of such a tradition, Mr. Marc Blitzstein's advocacy of militant trade-unionism as a self-protective measure for America's unemployed, in his opera *No for an Answer*, need not surprise, though the use of a serious art form for the presentation of a serious theme would seem to have shocked some.

This work is not Mr. Blitzstein's first offense, any more than it is the opera's first offense. If Goethe's *Faust* and *Werther*, in Gounod's and Massenet's musical investitures, seem little likely to provoke nowadays much psychological dither, Mozart's Freemasonry and Richard Wagner's philosophy of revolution still peer through their operatic trappings to give us pause. Even socialism is no newcomer to the musical boards. When we remember Alfred Bruneau's *L'Attaque au Moulin* and *Le Rêve* (both after Zola), Gustave Charpentier's *Louise*, and Dmitri

Shostakovich's *Lady Macbeth of Mzensk* (in rising order of so-cialistic violence), it does seem a little foolish to be bothered by so orthodox an exposure of trade-union theory. *Louise*, for instance, not only expounds socialist principles at some length but throws in also a defense of free love and depicts the break-ing of family ties by a respectable working girl for reasons of sexual unrest as proper behavior on her part.

What makes the Blitzstein work more pungent just now than these others is the fact that its locale is here and that its language is our own. It is also of some impact that Mr. Blitzstein's musi-cal style, as contrastable with the morass of respected, academic American music-writing that bogged down our opera houses annually until these institutions got tired of losing money and stopped it, is itself pretty pungent and potent.

It is of no importance that I should esteem *No for an Answer* to be a slightly less interesting work musically than Blitzstein's earlier opera, *The Cradle Will Rock*. That is a personal estimate, and many musicians disagree with it. What is of importance to note, and very few musicians can disagree with this, is the fact that Mr. Blitzstein has proved himself in both works to be an opera composer of considerable power. I wish to insist, therefore, that no matter what happens to the present work in the way of commercial success or failure, it is a serious work on a noble subject by a major musical author. Nothing can wash that out.

As to the nature of the Blitzstein talent, the following obser-vations seem to me possible ones to make:

His dramatic sense is strong and his timing of dramatic points accurate.

His musical invention is abundant and varied, his musical characterization appropriate and often sharply expressive. He can draw laughter and tears as few living composers can.

His musical procedure in the theater is based on stylistic parody. The parody of a torch song and the parody of a lullaby are particularly effective, though in different ways. The parody of a love scene, where the girl wants to talk but the man has only one thing on his mind, is touching indeed. The parody of a workers' chorus rehearsal is carried to the point of imitating Russian choral arrangements, à la Volga Boat Song, as these are currently indulged in by worker groups more or less Slavic in racial constituency. Whether the parody is always a conscious one I could not say. I should imagine that the *No for an Answer* theme song itself was not quite intended as a take-off on Robinson's and Latouche's *Ballad for Americans*; but it comes close to being funny, all the same.

Unconscious mocking of oneself is masochistic. It is the buffoonery of the father Karamazov. It is also a characteristic trait of Yiddish comedy. Conscious parody can be tender and humane, as in the love and lullaby scenes, as well as devastatingly ironical. When Blitzstein parodies knowingly, his music has better tunes and better structure than when he is parodying unconsciously. In the latter case he gets sentimental; and the assumed vulgarity of his musical style, so really elegant at its best, comes dangerously close to the real thing.

It is not within my province or professional competence to estimate the literary value of the Blitzstein libretti. They seem sufficient to me, and I often remember whole scenes from them. To any who might opine that the characters are lay figures, I suggest that characters for musical treatment have to be pretty simple. Few operas have more than one or two real people in them. *No for an Answer* has at least two, the rich boy and the little tough, the spy.

The musical value of the Blitzstein scores I place quite high. I place that of *The Cradle Will Rock* higher than that of *No for an Answer*. I think the author got involved in handling a more complex literary situation and in consequence neglected to give the continuous build that the more complex literary situation demands. He counted too much on the drama's own build. Also, the accompaniments, especially to melodrama and action, are insufficient and inexpressive. They sound like parodies of Dwight Fiske.

I am not happy about this work, as I was about the other. There is material there, human, literary, and musical, to make a successful opera; but it needs reworking. I understand much has been done since last Sunday. Probably more will be done before next. That is good procedure. Gounod's *Faust* had to be quite radically rewritten before it became the successful work we know.

January 12, 1941

"Experimental" Opera

A RECENT production by the Columbia Theater Associates of an "operatic comedy" entitled *Pieces of Eight*, by Bernard Wagenaar and Edward Eager, has occasioned, in view of its generally unfavorable reception by the reviewing press, no small amount of reflection by all concerned. Not that there is anything grave about a group of serious artists having brought forth a work that has failed to please or even to impress. Everybody does bad work from time to time. It is rather that the results of all the autopsies, public and private, that have been performed over the piece have caused the directors of this and of many another similar artistic project to wonder, organic financial disease being not involved in this tragedy, whether there might not be some basic mental maladjustment in their own attitude toward musical theater that is capable of being corrected.

There are many establishments in the United States consecrated to the production with amateur, partly amateur, or student forces of something known as "experimental" theater. The words *experiment*, *workshop*, and *laboratory* are so frequently associated with this kind of effort that it is probably correct to assume that a pragmatic theory of style underlies the whole movement. It is my opinion that a pragmatic attitude toward style, though advantageous for audiences as a critical point of view, is not sufficiently dynamic to give force and direction to people involved in the making of art. Even for an entrepreneur such an attitude is dangerously close to the more brutal forms of commercialism. In enterprises operating under academic influence it is inevitable that a certain broad-mindedness about styles and techniques should prevail. But it is all the more necessary, hence, that the creative art projects of universities and colleges should espouse some particular æsthetic or other if they wish to avoid diffuseness. Eclecticism of taste is becoming to scholars, but eclecticism in style is not a forward-looking æsthetic for artists.

The whole concept of "experimental" art is probably a false one anyway. Certainly it is if by *experimental* is meant: "Let's try it out and see what happens." Artistic work proceeds, of course, just like any other, by trial and error. But by the time the public and the critical press are invited to witness a show, to use it, as Gertrude Stein would say, in the living that they are doing, the makers of the show, at least, should be fairly well satisfied that it makes a continuity. Performance at this point is an experiment only in the scientific sense of a demonstration, the chief hazard involved being the nature of the reception it will receive, which is not an artistic consideration.

Artists and producers are constantly risking both their prestige and their fortunes on a gamble for public favor, and nobody pretends for a moment that the public's and the critics' responses are without influence on subsequent production. But nobody in the professional world thinks, either, that there is any advantage to be derived from exposing work to the ultimate rigors of practical usage that is admitted by its makers to be in an experimental state. Design need not be perfect, and execution can be very rough indeed; but art that is tentative in conception, that is uncertain about itself on the inside, is not art at all. It is student work, and its faults can be shown up in the classroom or in private performance without exposing its authors to public embarrassment. Heaven knows there are enough risks involved in any public performance without adding to these the basic insecurity of a let's-see-if-it-works theory of style.

Small art theaters do valuable work when they are committed to a policy of æsthetic advance, particularly if that is limited to one kind of æsthetic advance. They often do good work when devoted to æsthetic stabilization when they conserve traditional techniques against erosion. They are useful also sometimes for demonstrating to parents and others student work in authorship or in elocution. They are not likely to be effective unless there is a clear theory or a strong personality guiding them. And they rarely work well when much music is involved.

The reason for this is that the musical theater is (excepting only the cinema, which is a special form of it) the most complex artistic entertainment known to man. Its production requires routine; it cannot be improvised. And small laboratory theaters are for the most part not organized for this routine. They can produce successfully (and that is difficult enough) classical operatic works of small format. They can produce modern works in a conventionalized manner provided there is plenty of skilled professional advice available. And they can handle the modern dance. They do not do well with operatic first performances, on the whole, because their methods are too tentative to be efficacious in dealing with so recalcitrant a theatrical problem.

Any such theater needs a clear and simple line of policy. Its aim can be the offering of singing and acting experience to students. Or it can be the offering of a modest theatrical outlet for the work of directors and decorators too advanced for the commercial stage. Or it can be the providing of a means of production to living composers and poets. But it cannot be all these things at once. It must specialize. The musical theater is not only too complex a form of collaboration for small institutions to handle without specializing; it is also too little understood among us to make any but the most prudent approach to it profitable. Dramatic composition for poets, musical declamation for composers, the projection of the English language (or of any other) for singers, all those basic trainings are weak in our pedagogy. No musical art theater can expect to be more than tentative till they shall have been built into solid and well-understood techniques.

It is the business of our small art-theater projects to do this. And they must take up the problems one by one. A theater specializing in vocal diction need not be pretentious in its repertory or its visual productions. The training of composers to write correct declamation depends on singers who can project consonants, but it does not require the production of operas based on pageantry or an atmospheric orchestral composition. And the drilling into poets of stage ways, of an ability to create character and to tell a story clearly in words that can be sung, is in no small degree dependent on the existence of composers and singers capable of making these unaccustomed practices worth the effort. In the present chaotic state of our musical theater it does not seem to serve any good purpose that singers none too well trained to the techniques of the stage should be asked, as they were recently at the Brander Matthews Theater, to interpret a text that was trivial, banal, and indelicate set to the music of an otherwise skillful composer who has little feeling for the theater, no experience in writing for it, and only the most elementary acquaintance with the quantities of the English language.

One thing at a time, gentlemen, please! And if you must try

them all at once, just to see what happens, give yourself a break with a serious story. Don't complicate your "experiment" with the exigencies of farce timing!

May 21, 1944

Advice to Opera Singers

MARY GARDEN used to tell her students "Take care of the dramatic line, and the musical line will take care of itself." Sounder words were never spoken about the problems of the singing actor. Nothing is rarer today on the local operatic stage, however, than artists who work on this principle. Some of the Europeans still do, like Pinza and Baccaloni, Petina and Novotná, and some of the singers from elsewhere who have had sound European training and experience, like Brownlee and Sayao and Grace Moore. But the mark of the outsider, of the provincial, is the purely musical performance with a little acting stuck on.

There has been a good deal of this at the Metropolitan Opera in the last few years. It was to be hoped that the New Opera Company would provide a corrective. After two seasons (and I have seen the whole repertory) it is possible to say with assurance that in spite of some excellent conducting and some very good sheer vocalism, in spite also of appropriate-sized theaters and an unhackneyed repertory, circumstances that would have seemed to stimulate a more convincing dramatic approach than usual, the New Opera productions, far from being an improvement over the stodginess of many at the Met, have been a field day of everything that should not be done on an opera stage.

The first thing that should not be done is to treat the opera as an impure musical form, as a sort of concert in which one also pretends to act a little bit and in which the presence of scenery and an orchestra justifies an occasional attempt to bellow beyond one's means. The opera is not a musical form, pure or impure. It is a theatrical form and one of the most intense, most concentrated and most highly stylized of these. Singing is its medium, of course, just as elocution is the medium of the spoken stage. It goes without saying that unless one can sing correctly one has no business appearing in it, any more than one should appear in the "legitimate" theater without being able to read lines. Singing is its medium, its fascination and charm, if you like, too; but singing is not its subject. Its subject is whatever the subject of the play is. To approach any work of art otherwise than with a determination to give a clear and convincing rendition of its subject is to approach it indirectly, impurely, insincerely.

Even concert music goes dead when an artist tries to interpret a piece as if it were a mere vocal or instrumental example. There is no such thing as *the* symphony, *the* fugue, *the* song. An aria is not a piece of singing; it is a piece of music. Current pedagogical methods tend to isolate voice placement from diction, both from interpretation, and all three from dramatic rendering. As a result, the vocalism of our young singers quite regularly breaks down when it moves from studio conditions to the concert hall or to the stage. The overlays act as complications rather than simplifications of the singing process, and an overcomplicated singing process makes it impossible to interpret music.

I recognize that analysis, the isolation of all the component elements, is essential to a proper learning of anything. It is right to practice vowel vocalization and to study languages. But the synthesis of the component elements is where technical practice ends and music-making begins. Now, when music-making begins, a wholly different range of values comes into play. A piece must be approached as an expressive thing; a role must be rendered as character. The artist must avoid vocal error, of course, as the actor must avoid stumbling and mumbling and as the painter must keep his colors clean. But the things to keep the mind on are character and meaning. Character and meaning rendered through correct vocalism are what make style in singing. And style is carrying-power.

Once a singer is sufficiently in command of verbal vocalism to appear on a professional stage at all, his duty to himself and to his public is to reduce his technical preoccupations to a sort of censorship and to put his main mind on positive expression. Also, since detailed expression is likely to lack continuity, he must put his mind on the progress of the play. That is what Miss Garden meant by the "dramatic line." She did not mean that good acting will enable any one to sing who doesn't know how to sing. She meant that attention to the meaning of a role will enable a singer who already knows how to sing to interpret both the *words and music* of that role.

The truth of this may seem obvious, once one says it that way. But it is surprising how many young singers have never envisaged operatic interpretation in terms of any obligation to dramatic sincerity. They think because Tetrazzini and Caruso appeared to be merely singing when they were on the stage that these artists were getting away with murder from a dramatic point of view. This is not true. These artists acted well in the statuesque Italian tradition. They rendered character convincingly, in spite of their monumental physiques; and their diction was not something stuck on, when they thought of it, to vowel vocalization. It was the essence of their execution, the binding substance that made the play clear and the vocalism expressive. They believed in the play. If they hadn't they would have been concert artists like John McCormack, who was marvelous in songs and separate arias but who could never get into a role.

My advice, therefore, to the singers of the New Opera Company and to many at the Metropolitan is the same as Miss Garden's. Get into your roles, sing the words, render character. If your vocal technique won't stand up under this, leave the stage at once and take more lessons. Otherwise you will have a public failure and injure your voice at the same time. Above all, take the opera seriously as a dramatic form. It is certainly the most serious one left since the demise of poetic tragedy.

November 29, 1942

Mugging at the Opera

No serious instrumentalist would dream of accompanying his public musical renditions with a play of facial expression. Something of the sort is occasionally indulged in by gypsy violinists in night clubs, the rapt countenance being supposed conventionally in such locales to indicate nostalgic or erotic transports. Sometimes a swing drummer, too, will bring to his eye an insane gleam as he goes into a cadenza, in order to make it seem as if the compilations of his solo performance were wholly spontaneous and due rather to inspirational seizure than to art. But in spite of such showmanship of this nature as is met with on the lower levels of musical exploitation, it has never been considered good form for serious instrumentalists to make faces. Certainly not Hofmann nor Kreisler nor Rubinstein nor Casals nor any of the great conductors even, for all their graceful wavings of hair and wrist, ever indulged deliberately in anything of the kind. Heifetz's dead pan, indeed, is as complete as that of any reception clerk at the Ritz or of any salesman at an establishment dealing in Old Master paintings. The concert tradition everywhere is a firm one that no serious musician should accompany his instrumental execution with any play of facial expression whatsoever. He should not even smile too much when bowing.

A slightly greater liberty is allowed to vocalists. These may smile all they like when greeting the audience or acknowledging its applause. They can make friends with the house at all times except during the progress of a musical rendition. They may laugh, blow kisses, curtsy, or cavort; but when about to sing, they must compose the visage, take a correct stance, and get to work. For tradition requires that all concert music, even vocal music, be rendered as music and not as theater. Hence the vocalist is not expected to appear either amused or depressed by the substance of what he is singing. He is expected, on the contrary, to make his effects by musical means, not by pantomime. John Charles Thomas and Kirsten Flagstad and Alexander Kipnis and Helen Traubel, for example, all sing with a perfectly straight face, though Thomas does occasionally add a little staging to a cowboy ditty.

In the theater all is different. Opera singers are supposed to act, and almost any tradition of acting allows some facial pantomime. It is just as well not to overdo this at the opera, because it isn't visible very far away. What one must count on chiefly for carrying one's performance to the top rows is vocal expression amplified by movements and attitudes of the whole body. There is a certain range of facial expression that is permissible (when one is not actually singing), but that range is small and must not be counted on to carry. Most of the great singers have always dispensed with it entirely, preferring to use make-up as a tragic or comic mask that portrays the meaning of each role more clearly than facial play ever can.

Even in operatic comedy there is not much face play worth doing beyond eye-rolling à la Baccaloni and occasionally looking stupid. Opera is not realistic enough and our opera houses are not small enough to make it profitable for singing actors to work with the face. It is more like ballet, which is classically and correctly performed with a minimum of mugging.

The purpose of this preamble is to restate the principles of platform behavior that govern serious musical performance. I include comedy because that, too, is serious musical performance in so far as the performers of it wish to be considered seriously as musicians and as musical actors. The reason for restating these well known principles is that I have noticed a tendency on the part of certain singers at the opera this year to disregard them. This disregard may be due to lack of proper theatrical training in some cases and to a mistaken calculation in others, but in all cases it lowers the artist's musical and dramatic tension.

I refer to the tendency to grin constantly that mars the acting of Miss Grace Moore, of Miss Gladys Swarthout, and of Miss Josephine Tumminia. That tendency has been developed of late years in all those activities of our lives that it is considered proper to photograph. It has been encouraged by press photographers particularly, because it is the easiest way to bring into the eye of the subject that tiny sparkle that alone keeps him from looking in any final overlit picture like a corpse. That photographers working under pressure of time and in unpropitious lighting should sacrifice every other facial value to that light in the eye is reasonable enough. In the process of so doing, however, they have filled our periodicals and our daily press with row upon row of biting teeth and with faces that look as if they had lost all muscular control. The discomposed visage has even become a sort of standard mask that people put on before entering a room at a party. It has come to symbolize energy, pleasure, amiability, and goodwill in front of any public whatsoever.

The artist who wishes to use this mask when saluting the public in his own person—when taking curtain calls, for instance—is free to do so. Let him grin to his heart's satisfaction, if not to ours. But in a dramatic role his face should be kept in place. It does nothing at all toward animating a musical performance to smile and show the teeth and turn the head vaguely toward the house as if to indicate what a wonderful time everybody must be having. It deadens the performance rather. It takes the singer half-way out of his assumed character and makes a personal appeal to the audience. It says in effect: "You may not like the show, but you do like me. Don't you!" It is disloyal to the authors of the piece and to the other artists of the cast. It deceives nobody and only tends to make the audience suspicious about the artist's self-confidence.

In the case of Miss Tumminia I fancy the constant smiling is due simply to lack of stage training. In the case of Miss Moore and Miss Swarthout, both of whom have sung in opera for years, it is probably their Hollywood experience that makes them both so conscious of their faces. In all three cases the grinning is unnecessary, because they can all sing very beautifully indeed and do not need to make any special appeal. It is unbecoming, as well, because they are all quite good-looking women when their faces are in repose. But nobody is good-looking with his face in explosion and all his molars exposed.

Flagstad and Novotná and Albanese and Lotte Lehmann let their faces alone for the most part. When they do frown or smile, it is at some other character on the stage. When they need to express something by pantomime they use their bodies. This tradition is the correct one. I am surprised that somebody in authority at the Metropolitan Opera House, if there is anybody there who has any authority over stage deportment, should not have put a stop already to violations of it that mar the whole spectacle whenever they occur.

March 30, 1941

What's Wrong with the Met?

THE METROPOLITAN OPERA HOUSE has been full every night all season, and so has every other Broadway theater. It would be a mistake to consider the box-office reports of this one as meaning anything beyond the fact that all entertainment is doing business. Musicians and other experienced opera-goers have noted a number of excellent opera performances, nevertheless. On the whole, or so it seems to this reviewer, who has been a fairly regular attendant, the taking of a ticket has been perhaps a less hazardous action this season than it has in previous years. But essentially the Metropolitan hasn't changed much. Its policies and administration have long seemed to him a muddle; and a muddle they remain, in spite of good shows now and then.

If the Metropolitan performances were not so unpredictable and so varied in quality there would be no reason for a music critic to comment on the organization that produces them. But being as they are—sublime, ridiculous, and everything in between—and being also the visible reason for existence of a corporation that raises money by public passing of the hat and that is recognized by the state as of cultural utility, they make one wonder willy-nilly whether we, the public, are getting all we are entitled to out of our contributions. Consequently, though I have no intention of recommending specific changes in the personnel, since my interest is only in policies, I do think it my privilege, if not my duty, to point out that some kind of reform is desirable in the running of that enterprise.

My argument is not based on information about interior frictions, though everybody who knows anybody working there has heard about those. It is based on the simple fact, clearly visible to any regular patron, that the quality of the performances is undependable. Now, a business that puts out an undependable product is not a sound business, though it may for a time be a profitable one. Still less is an intellectual or artistic establishment worth its investment unless its work is authoritative. That is what such projects exist for and why they enjoy the financial privileges they do. It is their business to establish real intellectual and artistic standards and to maintain them.

It is not as if the Metropolitan were a young institution of cultural value not yet proved. It is sixty years old and known throughout the forty-eight states to be of tremendous value to culture. The history of the establishment is too full of splendor (and I don't mean diamonds) for anybody to misunderstand what we expect out of it now. And we do not expect the impossible, either. If good singers are scarce, which they are, we can put up with the best available. If public taste is conservative, which it is just now, we can do without novelties. If American artists can't get to Europe, and they can't now, we will take them without previous operatic apprenticeship. But if the standards of everything in a grand old cultural house go erratic, we are entitled to complain, I think, that the house is being badly run.

Continuing establishments have their ups and downs, of course. But they also have their traditions. The Metropolitan's best tradition is one of going on. Its worst tradition is one of not having any very solid musical traditions at all. There is no proper library of annotated scores, for instance. There is literally no way for singers to study there great interpretations from the past of the works they appear in. There are some persons around who remember these things; but it is clear that they seldom get a chance to tell anybody about them, because, although the artists who have sung or learned their roles elsewhere frequently give an authoritative reading, those who have prepared their roles on the spot practically never do. The Metropolitan has a glorious history, but a history is not a tradition. A tradition is precise knowledge about the way something has been done in the past; a rich tradition includes knowledge about a great many of the ways that something has been done in the past. An ancient, conservative house needs to conserve something besides property values. It has no business dealing in improvisation.

The Metropolitan's conducting staff is first class. The singing company is an excellent troupe, a better troupe, indeed, than consistent miscasting often shows it up to be. The orchestra is second class but fair. The chorus is a disgrace. It sings in no recognizable language and habitually off pitch. That is, when it sings at all; one third of it comes in at about the fourth measure, usually. The stage direction is timid and, for new productions, pretty sketchy. There is a vast store of none too fresh costumes and of water-soaked scenery. Lighting is effected by equipment of antediluvian model and largely without rehearsal. All this is obvious to anybody who goes there often. And yet, in spite of it all, some beautiful performances turn up.

There is no reason to suppose that the beautiful performances are planned any more than there is to think the less fortunate ones are. An accident of balanced casting and a little extra care, in consequence, on the conductor's part will do wonders, especially with conductors like Beecham and Walter and Cooper and Szell or with artists like Baum and Castagna and Singher and Albanese, with Peerce and Branzell and Pinza. With brilliant but not wholly dependable singers like Milanov and Roman and Warren, with Traubel and Moore and Harshaw, that little accident makes all the difference in the world. That it is an accident one cannot doubt, since even the best-balanced cast rarely stays together for more than one or two performances. It is my reflected opinion, after four years of pretty steady attendance, that the best performances at the Met are more the result of spontaneous accord among musical artists than they are of office planning or of rehearsal. Such planning as shows up in performance is more likely than not to impress one as reflecting indifference, carelessness, irresponsibility, and boredom.

Either the above observations are sound or they are not. If they are, musicians and other experienced opera-goers will corroborate them. If not, then I don't know a right show from a wrong one. But if I am right, if the one quality manifested consistently in recent years by the Metropolitan Opera performances—underneath all the sincere effort exerted by the various artists and all the real talent, even genius, these have shown for putting over a show in spite of difficulties—is a lack of taste, of judgment, of showmanship, of style, then the institution's directorial and organizational staff is at fault. This does not mean that the staff should or should not be altered. It means that the institution's whole conception of what opera should be needs to be altered, and radically. There is too much inefficiency there and not enough idealism.

April 9, 1944

RECITALISTS

Classical Beauty

JOSEF HOFMANN, pianist, in recital last night at Town Hall, performing Schumann's Sonata, Op. 14, Beethoven's Sonata No. 32 (Op. 111),
and Chopin's Sonata in B minor, Op. 58.

As LONG as one keeps to piano concerts, truly the town is
teeming with delight. Last night it was Josef Hofmann's turn to
feed our auditory nerves and to caress our intelligence.

His playing is less monumental and less streamlined than
that of any of the other pianistic great in my memory, saving
only that of the incomparable de Pachmann. The pillars and
buttresses of its architecture are thin and strong. The rooms
above are high, airy, clean, and eminently habitable. His forms,
to change the figure, grow like trees. No leaf but is attached
to stem and branch; no branch but leads us downward to the
root. All is organic, orderly, straight-grown toward the light.
The word *pedagogic* springs constantly to mind as one listens.
Not pedagogic in any pejorative sense. But pedagogic as if each
execution were an example to be preserved of how incredibly
right piano-playing can be when it is right.

The Schumann sonata could have been taken down by dictation from his playing of it without so much as a sixteenth-note
rest being lost or a doubled inner voice being obscured. The
clarity of his articulation was as complete in every rhythmic
detail as in the piece's main foundations. And heaven knows
that piece is a tangle of finicky rhythms.

The Beethoven opus 111, despite the rival claims of various
bravura compositions, remains, in my opinion, the most difficult
piano piece in the world. Not only because the trills and tremolos and stretches are ungratefully placed and unconscionably
tiring to play, but because the work presents as great a difficulty
to the mind as to the hand. To make anything consistent out of
it is both an intellectual and a technical achievement. Do not
think I am being flippant about a great piece of music, for I am
not. I am merely insisting that the work is hermetic, complex
and knotty from every point of view.

A good deal of this knottiness comes from the fact that Beethoven was experimenting with pianistic dispositions that he could not hear very well, if he could hear them at all. Very few pianists can ever make anybody hear them. Mr. Hofmann did make them heard, and clearly. In addition, the whole gamut of dynamic violence and delicacy and deep song, with its undercurrent of musical meditation, that is the special palette of Beethoven's later works was richly set out before us, as though the piece were as straightforward a sonata as the "Waldstein" or the "Appassionata."

The Chopin B-minor Sonata was my completest enjoyment of the evening. Mr. Hofmann has always put his super-best into Chopin. So it is just as well to mention in that connection certain technical and musical excellences that are the very substance of Mr. Hofmann's piano-playing, because it is in his playing of that composer's works that they are most sumptuously and completely laid before us.

The sustaining force of his Grand Accent is always there, of course, though without any undue heaviness in the bass. His orchestral variety of kinds and heights of touch is large indeed. But instead of orchestrating melodies and figures by using for each a special kind of tone that is unvaried during the progress of the phrase, as is the more common modern practice, he turns and shades each part and phrase within the limits of the special kind of tone that he has chosen for it. The result is less like the sound of many mechanical instruments subject to one man's will, as is the current taste in pianism, than it is like an orchestra of living musicians subject to a conductor only in the main line of the music's interpretation.

This living, non-mechanical quality is achieved by no exploitation of human frailty. His scales are as even as well-matched pearls. No crescendo or diminuendo is ever made because that is the natural or easy way of playing something. All is willed. But it is willed to be shaped in the round. No phrase is ever flat or plane. The result of this rich instrumentation is a musical beauty that is not only noble in its proportions but humane in all its aspects. It is a classical beauty, scaled to the measure of man.

November 7, 1940

Great Music

ARTUR RUBINSTEIN, pianist, in recital last night at Carnegie Hall, performing works by Chopin including Sonata in B minor, Op. 58; *Polonaise Fantaisie*, Op. 61; *Fantaisie Impromptu*, No. 66, and scherzos, études, mazurkas, and nocturnes.

Iᴛ is not easy to define what we mean by great music, but it is very easy to agree that the nineteenth century produced lots of it. It is also easy for musicians to agree that Frédéric Chopin was one of the great composers of that century, quite possibly the very greatest of them all. Last night a whole fistful of Chopin's greatest works were played in Carnegie Hall by one of our greatest living pianists, Artur Rubinstein.

Mr. Rubinstein is a delight to watch as well as to hear. Though he is as fastidious as one could wish in his musical execution, his platform manner is straightforward, well bred, businesslike. His delicacy is delicate, his fortes powerful, his melodic tone rich and deep. He can play loud and soft and fast and slow without interrupting the music's rhythmic progress. He is a master of his instrument and of the music he plays, and he finds no reason for attracting undue attention to anything else. He is authoritative, direct, and courteous, like the captain of a transatlantic liner.

His pianism is of the close-to-the-key school. Hence the good marksmanship. Hence, also, its lack of any bright, pearly brilliance. His arms and torso are of stocky build. Hence the power of his climaxes, the evenness of his pianissimo. He is Polish by birth, if I mistake not. Hence his complete at-homeness in Chopin's music, like a host in his father's house.

He is most at home in straightforward pieces, like the études, and in long, massive works like the sonatas, the ballades, the scherzos, works that call to action his mastery of dramatic line, of architectural sweep. He plays the tricky mazurkas and nocturnes with less ease. They don't give him enough room to move around in, and so he rather streamlines them than builds them.

His rubato is of the Paderewski tradition. I do not know how that tradition got started, but I do not think it comes from Chopin. It sounds Viennese to me.

Chopin's prescription for rubato-playing, which is almost

word for word Mozart's prescription for playing an accompanied melody, is that the right hand should take liberties with the
time values, while the left hand remains rhythmically unaltered.
This is exactly the effect you get when a good blues singer is
accompanied by a good swing band. It is known to the modern
world as *le style hot*. The Paderewski tradition of Chopin-playing
is more like the Viennese waltz style, in which the liberties in
the melody line are followed exactly in the accompaniment, the
two elements keeping always together and performing at the
same time a flexible distortion of strict rhythm that manages by
its very flexibility to keep the procedure from seeming arbitrary
or the continuity from collapsing. Mr. Rubinstein is skillful with
this kind of rubato. He keeps the music surging. But I don't
believe for a moment it resembles anything Frédéric Chopin
ever did or had in mind.

On more than this count does Rubinstein make one think of
Paderewski. Among his encores (he played the C-sharp minor
Waltz and the Étude for the Little Finger also) he did such a
rendition of the A-flat Grande Polonaise as it has not been my
pleasure to hear in many a day. Such speed, such power, such
fury, such truly magnificent transcending both of the pianoforte's limitations and of his own customary accuracy were the
very substance of Paderewski's greatness. They were Mr. Rubinstein's last night, a final jewel in his already laureate crown.

October 26, 1940

Master of Distortion and Exaggeration

VLADIMIR HOROWITZ, pianist, in recital last night at Carnegie
Hall, performing Bach's Toccata in C major, two Bach chorales, two
Brahms intermezzi, Chopin's Sonata in B-flat minor, three Chopin
études, Liszt's *Marche funèbre*, and Liszt's transcription of Saint-Saëns's
Danse Macabre.

IF ONE had never heard before the works of Mr. Horowitz
played last night in Carnegie Hall, or known others by the
same authors, one might easily have been convinced that Sebastian Bach was a musician of the Leopold Stokowski type, that
Brahms was a sort of flippant Gershwin who had worked in a

high-class night club and that Chopin was a gypsy violinist.
One might very well conclude also that Liszt's greatest musical
pleasure was to write vehicles for just such pianists as Vladimir
Horowitz. The last supposition would be correct. Liszt was that
kind of pianist himself, and he turned off concert paraphrases
of anything and everything from the *Faust* waltz to Palestrina
motets. Whether he was quite the master of musical distortion
that Horowitz is, history does not record; but I think there is
little doubt possible that a kinship of spirit exists between the
two pianists. One has only to hear Horowitz play Liszt's music
to recognize that.

Do not think, please, that my use of the word *distortion* implies that Mr. Horowitz's interpretations are wholly false and
reprehensible. Sometimes they are and sometimes they are not.
His Bach is no worse and no better than Stokowski's, on which
I take it to be modeled. His Brahms may be less light-minded
on other occasions than it was last night. His Chopin varied a
good deal during the evening. The sonata was violent, coarsely
conceived, melodramatic. He made the Funeral March sound
like a Russian boat song by accentuating all of the off-beats of
the bass, and he turned its serene middle section into the most
affected of nocturnes. His Études, however, were recognizable
and, of course, quite brilliant, as they should be; and the A-flat
Waltz (an encore) was as normal as his Liszt.

Supernormal would be a better word for the way he renders
the works of the great Hungarian Romantic. He seems to have
a perfectly clear understanding of what they are about and a
thorough respect for them. He exaggerates when exaggeration
is of the essence, but he never tampers with their linear continuity. He makes all the right effects, and he makes them in the
right places. The only distortion is one of aggrandizement. He
plays the Liszt pieces faster and louder and more accurately than
anybody else ever plays them. Sometimes he plays the music of
other composers that way too, and the effect is more tremendous than pleasant. In Liszt it is both tremendous and pleasant,
because Liszt's music was written for that kind of playing and
because Mr. Horowitz really loves and understands that kind of
music. It is the only kind that he approaches without fidgeting,
and last night it was the only kind the audience didn't cough
through.

If I speak chiefly of interpretation, it is not that I am wanting in admiration of Mr. Horowitz's justly acclaimed technical powers. But these powers are exploited by a violent and powerful personality that is, after all, a part of his virtuoso equipment. Paderewski had and Artur Rubinstein has a strength of crescendo comparable. Schmitz has an equal cleanness of articulation and a more even trill. Lhévinne's octaves and general marksmanship are far from despicable by comparison. And almost any of the more poetic virtuosos, Serkin or Casadesus, for example, has a lovelier tone. But none of these pianists is so free from respect for the composer's intentions, as these are currently understood. Horowitz pays no attention to such academic considerations. He is out to wow the public, and wow it he does. He makes a false accent or phrasing anywhere he thinks it will attract attention, and every brilliant or rapid passage is executed with a huge crescendo or with a die-away effect. It is all rather fun and interesting to students of what I like to call the wowing technique. It is a great deal more than that, however, when he gets into his own arrangement of Liszt's arrangement of Saint-Saën's arrangement for two pianos of an orchestral version of a song called *Danse Macabre*. His rendition of that number is in every way the berries.

March 7, 1942

Pianism as a Sport

E. ROBERT SCHMITZ, pianist, in recital last night at Carnegie Hall, performing Franck's Prelude, Chorale, and Fugue, Debussy's Dance in E major, six Debussy Preludes, and works by Scarlatti, Bach, de Falla, Albéniz, Ravel, and Joachín Nin.

AFTER SOME YEARS of absence from these parts E. Robert Schmitz returned last night to play in Carnegie Hall in a recital that can only properly be described as a triumph. It was a triumph from every point of view, musical and technical, as well as in terms of bravos shouted, of encores demanded and executed.

Mr. Schmitz's pianism is and always has been of a transcendant order. It was that twenty years ago when last I heard him play. Since that time it has been elaborated and perfected by practice and by pedagogical experience to such a degree that it resembles now more the work of Tilden or Budge on a tennis court than anything of a merely musico-poetic nature.

Not that his playing is lacking in either musicianship or poetry. On the contrary, his readings of the Bach A-minor organ fugue and of the Franck Prelude, Chorale, and Fugue were of a subtle and refined clarity, an apparent simplicity of architectonics that only the most comprehensive musicianship ever conceives and only the most commanding technique renders possible in execution. No slowing up for difficult changes of hand position, no pounding beyond the instrument's resources. When he wants to play fast octaves with the left hand he plays them. When he wants more volume he gets it. When he wants to let the music fall as lightly on the ear as summer rain, that is the way the music falls. And what he wants is always a clear and sensible exposition, as well as a sensitive one, of the piece's shape and content.

As for poetry, he avoids at all times the personal and the pseudo-emotional. He expounds each piece through its own rhetoric, makes its instrumentation and continuity clear, lets it sing for itself. So that in addition to the intrinsic beauty of the melodic material and of its expressive ornament there is the abstract poetry of a physical act beautifully accomplished. That is what I mean by comparing his work to that of a good tennis-player. It isn't that his motions are merely agreeable to watch. So are those of many a third-rate athlete. It is that the constant accuracy of the results, under the most varied musical circumstances, makes it evident that there is a fine harmony between the muscular effort and what it accomplishes.

Last night's triumph with the audience, though the warmth and the applause grew from the beginning, was crowned by the playing of six Debussy Preludes, plus two more and some other Debussy as encores. Here was the occasion to exploit the gamut of varied timbre and touch that Schmitz is a master of as is no other pianist. He did so exploit it, but withal so musically, so intelligently, with such sweet comprehension of the works themselves, that they were as if viewed under a magnifying glass in high illumination.

There is a poesy of dim lights and fog and faint suggestion, and there are many musicians who think that is what Debussy should sound like. I know no historical evidence to make me believe that such vagueness ever was anything but a trickery

of the not very competent. Debussy was a fanatic for precision and for delicate adjustments of timbre and of volume. To
make these adjustments more than ever precise and elaborate
by slightly magnifying the dynamic proportions is in no way
to diminish the poetry of the final effect. Rather the contrary.

It has been a long time since we have heard Debussy played
like great music. That it may not be so long before we hear it so
played again is the fervent wish of this reviewer. That the next
time Mr. Schmitz deigns to visit these parts he may honor us
with a complete rendition of the Debussy Études, all twelve of
them, is my equally fervent hope. It is absurd that these master
works should be so neglected by pianists and unbelievable that
they should not be in the repertory of a pianist so completely
in sympathy with their content as Mr. Schmitz and so magnificently equipped to treat their difficulties as no more terrifying
than a good serve from a worthy opponent.

March 27, 1941

Equalized Expressivity

ARTUR SCHNABEL, pianist, in recital last night at Carnegie Hall,
performing four Beethoven sonatas: No. 6 (Op. 10, No. 2); No. 17
(Op. 31, No. 2); No. 31 (Op. 110), and No. 32 (Op. 111).

ARTUR SCHNABEL, who played last night in Carnegie Hall the
second of three recitals, presented by the New Friends of Music,
devoted to the piano music of Beethoven, has for some thirty
or forty years made this composer the object of his especial attention. He passes, indeed, and with reason, for an expert on
the subject, by which is usually meant that his knowledge of it
is extensive and that his judgments about it are respected. Any
issue taken with him on details of tempo, of phraseology, of
accent is risky and, at best, of minor import. Minor, too, are
criticisms of his piano technique, which, though not first class,
is quite adequate for the expression of his ideas. His ideas about
Beethoven's piano music in general, whether or not one finds
his readings convincing, are not to be dismissed lightly.

Neither need they, I think, be taken as the voice of authority.
For all the consistency and logic of his musicianship, there is
too large a modicum of late-nineteenth-century Romanticism

in Mr. Schnabel's own personality to make his Beethoven—who was, after all, a child of the late eighteenth—wholly convincing to musicians of the mid-twentieth. No one wishes to deny the Romantic elements in Beethoven. But I do think that they are another kind of Romanticism from Schnabel's, which seems to be based on the Wagnerian theories of expressivity.

Mr. Schnabel does not admit, or plays as if he did not admit, any difference between the expressive functions of melody and of passage work. The neutral material of music—scales, arpeggiated basses, accompanying figures, ostinato chordal backgrounds, formal cadences—he plays as if they were an intense communication, as if they were saying something as important as the main thematic material. They are important to Beethoven's composition, of course; but they are not directly expressive musical elements. They serve as amplification, as underpinning, frequently as mere acoustical brilliance. To execute them all with climactic emphasis is to rob the melodic material, the expressive phrases, of their singing power.

This equalized expressivity ends by making Beethoven sound sometimes a little meretricious as a composer. His large-scale forms include, of necessity, a large amount of material that has a structural rather than a directly expressive function. Emphasizing all this as if it were phrase by phrase of the deepest emotional portent not only reduces the emotional portent of the expressive material; it blows up the commonplaces of musical rhetoric and communication into a form of bombast that makes Beethoven's early sonatas, which have many formal observances in them, sound empty of meaning and the later ones, which sometimes skip formal transitions, sound like the improvisations of a talented youth.

The work that suffered least last night from the disproportionate emphasizing of secondary material was the Sonata opus III. Here Mr. Schnabel achieved in the first movement a more convincing relation than one currently hears between the declamatory and the lyrical subjects. And in the finale he produced for us that beatific tranquillity that was a characteristic part of Beethoven's mature expression and that had been noticeably wanting, though there were plenty of occasions for it, in the earlier part of the evening.

March 28, 1944

Personal and Viennese

RUDOLF SERKIN, pianist, in recital last night at Carnegie Hall, performing Mozart's Fantasia and Fugue in C major and Sonata in G major, Beethoven's Sonata No. 23 (Op. 57, "Appassionata"), and Max Reger's Variations and Fugue on a Theme by Telemann.

RUDOLF SERKIN's pianism is Viennese by schooling, close to the key, unerring in text and weight. He exploits no Parisian gamut of bell and piccolo and trumpet evocation. His tone is the same in all the ranges of its power, rich, smooth, and mat, never tinkling, never forced. It resembles in a most surprising way Fritz Kreisler's diapason-like violin tone, still sounding in the ear from Thursday night.

One is reminded, too, of Josef Hofmann as I first heard him thirty-odd years ago. Like Hofmann, Mr. Serkin is not only a master pianist, firm and possessive with the loved instrument; he is a master of music as well. Without an iota of textual violation, with, on the contrary, a closer observance of Mozart's and Beethoven's indications than one practically ever hears from the concert stage, he transforms each piece into a song of his own, warms it in the palm of his youth and molds it to a living and personal expression of his own Sacred Flame.

Of the works so lovingly presented last night, the Reger is the least interesting musically. It is skillful, superficial, not untuneful, and full of ingenious bravura figuration. The audience loved its finale, a *Grand Valse de Concert* in the form of a double fugue, a typical Reger idea and good fun.

Beethoven's "Appassionata" was built, like the drama of mystery and terror that it is, on an inexorable rhythm against which its dynamic and passional surprise-gamut was thrown into relief without seeming querulous or exasperated. The interpreter understood that Beethoven, as always, was putting into a concert piece a dramatic conception of life. Beethoven never succeeded in making his dramatic conception of life. Beethoven never succeeded in making his dramatic concepts dramatic on a stage. But those who have heard the *Leonore* Overture No. 3 played between two acts of *Fidelio,* as is the custom in some opera houses, usually sense that Beethoven's instrumental music is all of the theater and its drama conceived. The last movement was disappointing. Taken as a *presto possibile*, it lost weight and grandeur; and its coda sounded gay rather than victorious.

It is natural that I should love the Serkin Mozart, because it concords with my own pet theories, though I doubt if it is a product of the reason. Rather, it sounded to me like a creation of taste and instinct. In any case, it was broad without being brutal, refined with no trace of effeminacy.

The G major Sonata was played for what it most certainly is, a symphonic ensemble piece evoked at the pianoforte. The pianist used no rhythmic trickery here, either. He played it with the rhythmic regularity of ensemble music and observed Mozart's accents convincingly. The tempos were those appropriate to ensemble evocation, excepting, as in Beethoven, that of the last movement, which was fast and pianistic. The piece thereby lost body.

November 16, 1940

The Strange Case of Claudio Arrau

CLAUDIO ARRAU, pianist, in recital last night in Carnegie Hall, performing, among other works, four Debussy *Etampes*, Mozart's Rondo in A minor, Chopin's Ballade in F minor, Beethoven's "Eroica" Variations, Op. 35, and Liszt's Mephisto Waltz No. 1 and *Jeaux d'eau à la Villa d'Este*.

To FIND a musical parallel for the pianism of Claudio Arrau, one must look outside the circle of keyboard virtuosos. His particular combination of technical security and musical irresponsibility, which used to be found among singers, today is chiefly limited to violinists. He delights a vast audience (Carnegie Hall had even its stage full last night) and impresses the most serious musicians. (I could have touched five world-famous pianists from where I sat.) His physical mastery of the art of piano-playing is so satisfactory and the charm of his explosive temperament is so acute that one does not always realize right off how shallow is the musical thought behind all the brilliance (and solidity, even) of the execution. Perhaps at the last no one will care about the faults, in view of his overpowering appeal; but just for the present your reviewer is torn between his admiration for skillful hand work and his inveterate prejudice against faulty musical conceptions.

Mr. Arrau's musical conceptions seem scarcely to have been reflected at all. Phraseology, architecture, continuity, all the objective rhetorical devices for conveying the substance of a composition, are replaced by a subjective, instinctive rhetoric that is in itself a mark of high musical gifts. One may even consider that it doesn't make much difference how he reads a piece, since he always makes it sound like music. Well, that is what I mean by musical irresponsibility. Mr. Arrau is no traitor to his own musical feelings. But those feelings seem chiefly to be concentrated on his own act of playing the piano and to have very little to do with his music's author beyond the use of that author's text as a vehicle for improvisation. He doesn't improvise any notes in the music he plays; these he renders with greater power and exactitude than most. He merely improvises its sense.

This divergence from customary readings is chiefly a question of rhythm. That is where all musical texts allow liberty and require discernment. In playing Debussy last night Mr. Arrau seemed wholly unaware that neither Spanish nor Javanese rhythms admit the use of rubato. He played a fragile Mozart rondo in the declamatory style. He read a Chopin ballade as if he were accompanying a film. His Beethoven began beautifully (as did the Liszt *Mephisto Waltz*) and fell to pieces in the middle. Saving the South American works, which I most regrettably was unable to stay for, the only single piece that sounded to me as sensibly as it did beautifully was Liszt's *Fountains at the Villa d'Este*. That was unsurpassable pianism and a clear musical communication.

October 28, 1943

American Rhythm

JOHN KIRKPATRICK, pianist, in recital last night at Times Hall, New York, performing works by American composers including Ives's Sonata No. 2 ("Concord, Mass., 1840–60"), Theodore Chanler's Toccata in E-flat major, Edward MacDowell's *Woodland Sketches,* and Roy Harris's Piano Sonata, Op. 1.

JOHN KIRKPATRICK, who gave a piano recital last night in Times Hall, has a way of making one feel happy about American music. He does this by loving it, understanding it, and playing it very beautifully. He plays, in fact, everything very beautifully that I have ever heard him play. But people who play that beautifully so rarely play American music that Mr. Kirkpatrick's recitals are doubly welcome, once for their repertory and again for his unique understanding of it.

The loveliness of his playing comes from a combination of tonal delicacy with really firm rhythm. Exactitude with flexibility at all the levels of loudness is the characteristic of American pianism that transcends all our local schools of composition and lack of same. It is what makes us a major musical people, and it is exactly the rhythmic quality that escapes our European interpreters. European tonal beauty, of course, more often than not escapes American pianists. Mr. Kirkpatrick's combination of European tonal technique with full understanding of American rhythm makes his playing of American works a profoundly exciting thing and a new thing in music.

Charles Ives's *Concord* Sonata was esteemed by Lawrence Gilman the finest piece of music ever written by an American, and it very well may be just that. Certainly it is a massive hunk of creation; four massive hunks, in fact. Because it is really four symphonic poems, named respectively, "Emerson," "Hawthorne," "The Alcotts," and "Thoreau": four full-length portraits done with breadth, tenderness, and wit. "The Alcotts" is the best integrated formally of these and probably the most original, or indigenous, in its musical material and fancy. I suspect that concert audiences would take eventually to all these portraits if they were performed separately for a time, since the whole work is longer than the ones people are now used to listening to. In any case, here is music, real music; and Americans should have no serious difficulty accepting its subject-matter or understanding its ingenuous grandeurs.

Of the other works performed last night Theodore Chanler's *Toccata* seemed to me the most finely conceived and the most delicately indited. Roy Harris's early Piano Sonata, opus 1, is a coarse work and laborious. The MacDowell pieces seemed charming and poetic, as always, but a little soft in their melodic material.

The encores consisted of two works by Stephen Foster, *The Old Folks' Quadrille* and a flute piece called *Anadolia*; a Prelude by Robert Palmer; Arthur Farwell's *Navajo War Dance*, and a *Trumpet Aire* by James Bremner, a composer of Revolutionary times. All these were good to hear, especially Mr. Palmer's strongly knit Prelude and Farwell's handsome evocation of Indian themes and rhythms. The others were agreeably antiquarian. And everything Kirkpatrick played turned into a poem.

November 24, 1943

A Good Start

WILLIAM KAPELL, pianist, in recital last night at Town Hall, performing Beethoven's Sonata No. 16 (Op. 31, No. 1), and works by Scarlatti, Mozart, Chopin, Liszt, Prokofiev, Persichetti, and Anis Fuleihan.

OPERATING on the principle that one good recital deserves another, the Town Hall chooses each year a debutant musician of noteworthy qualities and awards him an engagement the following year in its endowment series of musical events. Last year's laureate was William Kapell, pianist, nineteen years old at the time of his first Town Hall recital. Last night he gave his award recital; and pretty fine it was, I must say.

It is a mistake to expect of youth any unusual concentration of fire and poetry. This is more normally an attribute of middle age. What youth has, at its best, is a small, hard, real musical gift and a certain freshness of technical training. The latter is likely to be tensely efficient rather than beautiful, the former clearly visible through it rather than wholly expressed. In Mr. Kapell's case the technical proficiency is most impressive. He plays clearly and cleanly and powerfully, with good tone and with an ample range of weights and colors. His natural musicality shows up in the rhythm and in his tonal proportions and balances, which are always interesting, occasionally quite novel. His temperament is evident in the way different pieces come out sounding like different pieces in spite of the fact that they are all approached with the same grandiose preoccupation.

Mr. Kapell was better in the modern works than in the classical ones. Scarlatti, Beethoven, and Mozart might have been three pseudonyms of one man, so little did he appear to feel any necessity for varying his stylistic approach to them. The Beethoven sonata, however, was notable for its final rondo, which was dry and precise, and high in coloristic relief. Everywhere, too, there was a sense of music's continuity, an over-all conception that is characteristic of musicians with more than average mental powers. It was this continuous progress, indeed, that saved Mr. Kapell from superficiality in the pieces of Chopin and Liszt.

Prokofiev, Persichetti, and Fuleihan, however, were the writers who drew from him the completest intellectual understanding. He made them all sound rather alike, I must say, as he had previously done with his classics and his Romantics. But they sounded as if he had chosen them for their resemblance to his own image of the modern world, not as if he were imposing an inappropriate similarity upon them. He gave, thus, a most unusual tone to his recital, namely, that of an unconscious but perfectly real modernism. And here his youth served him well. The middle-aged play old music as if they owned it; but they are mostly pretty inept, in spite of goodwill, at rendering the contemporary. Mr. Kapell walked through the ancients (if so we may refer to our predecessors) like an intelligent somnambulist, making no false steps, but seeming to be aware of nothing beyond the exactitude and grace of his locomotion. But when he played the music of his own time he woke up and made sense.

January 21, 1943

Very Loud and Very Soft

ROBERT CASADESUS, pianist, in recital last night at Carnegie Hall, performing Beethoven's Sonata No. 32 (Op. 111); Fauré's Theme and Variations, Op. 75; twelve Chopin études, and three songs by Isaac Albéniz.

ROBERT CASADESUS, who played a piano recital last night in Carnegie Hall, is an ace technician and a clear-headed man of music. He lays a piece before you without any confusion of its phraseology or any obscurity of its detail. And his pianistic and analytic powers are all the more dramatically exposed because of his constant differentiation between meter and accent. This gives a thrilling steadiness to runs, trills, and passage work and a grand onward sweep to the progress of a piece. It is regrettable that his extraordinary skill and musicianship are not complemented by an instinct for dynamic proportion.

No matter what he plays, the volume range is always extreme; he plays very loud or very soft most of the time. This lack of imagination about the middle sizes of loudness amounts, in the long run, to a lack of poetry in the musical renderings. In the Beethoven Sonata opus 111, for example, he dramatized handsomely the violence of the opening theme against the beatific pathos of the succeeding one, but the less broad expression of the variations escaped him. Similarly, twelve Chopin Études, though handsomely phrased and fingered, were chiefly a contrast of light and dark, of *ppp* and *fff,* which is tiresome.

The Fauré Theme and Variations, though not a great work, is an agreeably lyrical one. But Mr. Casadesus weakened it beyond any real carrying-power by trying to make a "strong" work out of it. The evening's worst example of ineffective proportion was in the three pieces of Albéniz with which the program ended. Here the guitar imitations lost all their color and flamboyance through being played too loud. They might as well have been the evocation of a calliope.

The folly of the "big" tone is one that affects many excellent musicians, especially in this country. Cellists are notably prone to it, though neither fiddlers nor pianists are immune. Mr. Casadesus is the most exaggerated case I have encountered among the last. It is not that there is anything wrong about playing

majestically loud from time to time. The folly consists in distorting music's natural dynamic proportions, in leaning on passages
that should be only medium loud with such persistence that the
only possible contrast is to play the softer passages very, very
soft. The vice starts by neglecting the most sensitive part of the
dynamic range—that between *p* and *f*—and ends by obliterating
all the shades of tone color that exist only in that range, which
means nine tenths of them. The "big" tone is thought to be
box-office, though whether it can last long even there I doubt;
but certainly it is an unfortunate investment musically.

February 17, 1944

Rhythmic Grandeurs

WANDA LANDOWSKA, harpsichordist, in recital last night at Carnegie Hall, performing Bach's "Goldberg Variations."

WANDA LANDOWSKA's return to us after a fourteen-year interval was celebrated yesterday afternoon at the Town Hall in a
ceremony both imposing and heart-warming. She played Bach's
thirty "Goldberg Variations" to a full house that was virtually
a social register of professional musicians; and she received a
welcome and a final ovation from the distinguished assembly
that were tribute equally to her penetrating musicianship and
to her powers of virtuoso execution on that most exacting of
all keyboard instruments, the harpsichord.

I am not going to review the "Goldberg Variations," which
are one of the monuments of musical art, except to note that, as
Madame Landowska played them, there were no dull moments,
though the concert lasted little less than two hours. I should
like rather to cast an analytic eye on the work of this extraordinary performer, whose execution, no matter what she plays, is
one of the richest and grandest experiences available to lovers
of the tonal art. That she should play for two hours without
striking a false note is admirable, of course; that she should play
thirty pieces varying greatly in volume without ever allowing us
to hear any thumping down of the keys proves a mastery of the
harpsichord that is, to my knowledge, unique. That she should
phrase and register the "Goldberg Variations" with such clarity
and freedom that they all sound like new pieces is evidence of

some quality at work besides mere musicianship, though the musicianship does run high in this case.

A performance so complete, so wholly integrated, so prepared, is rarely to be encountered. Most artists, by the time they have worked out that much detail, are heartily sick of any piece and either walk through it half asleep or ham it up. It is part of the harpsichord's curious power that the more one is meticulous and finicky about detail, the livelier the whole effect becomes.

All musicianly and expert qualities are observable at their highest in Madame Landowska's harpsichord-playing. But so are they in the work of many another virtuoso. Her especial and unique grandeur is her rhythm. It is modern quantitative scansion at its purest. Benny Goodman himself can do no better. And it is Bach's rhythm, as that must have been. Writing constantly for instruments of no tonic accent, like the harpsichord and the organ, all Bach's music is made up out of length values. If you want to realize how difficult it is to express a clear rhythm without the aid of tonic stresses, or down-beats, just try it on an electric buzzer. And if you want to realize what elaborate rhythmic complications the eighteenth-century performers did manage to make clear (else these would not have been written) on accentless instruments, just take a look at Bach's music for organ and that for harpsichord, particularly the "Goldberg Variations."

The introduction of the pianoforte and the invention of the orchestral crescendo at the end of the eighteenth century changed the nature of music radically by substituting pulse for measure and punch for complexity. Only in our day, through the dissemination of American and South American popular music, which differs from European in being more dependent on quantitative patterns than on strong pulsations, has a correct understanding of Bach's rhythm been possible and a technique reinvented for rendering it cleanly and forcibly. (Highly dramatic accents can be obtained with no added force, for instance, by delaying ever so slightly the attack on the note it is desired to accent. Also, expressive liberties of rhythm only take on their full expression as liberties when they are liberties taken upon some previously established rhythmic exactitude.)

Of all these matters Landowska is mistress. The pungency and high relief of her playing are the result of such a mastery's being placed at the service of a penetrating intelligence and a passionate Polish temperament. The final achievement is a musical experience that clarifies the past by revealing it to us through the present, through something we all take for granted nowadays, as Bach's century took it for granted, but that for a hundred and fifty years has been neglected, out of style, forgotten. That is the cultivation of rhythmic complexity by an elimination from musical thought of all dependence on rhythmic beat.

February 22, 1942

A Shower of Gold

WANDA LANDOWSKA, harpsichordist, in recital last night at Town Hall, performing Rameau's Suite in E minor, Johan Jakob Froberger's *Lament Composed in London to Dispel Melancholy*, and three works by Bach: Prelude and Fugue in E-flat minor, Partita in B-flat major, and Chromatic Fantasy and Fugue.

WANDA LANDOWSKA's harpsichord recital of last evening at the Town Hall was as stimulating as a needle shower. Indeed, the sound of that princely instrument, when it is played with art and fury, makes one think of golden rain and of how Danaë's flesh must have tingled when she found herself caught out in just such a downpour.

Madame Landowska's program was all Bach and Rameau, with the exception of one short piece by Froberger. She played everything better than anybody else ever does. One might almost say, were not such a comparison foolish, that she plays the harpsichord better than anybody else ever plays anything. That is to say that the way she makes music is so deeply satisfactory that one has the feeling of a fruition, of a completeness at once intellectual and sensuously auditory beyond which it is difficult to imagine anything further.

On examination this amplitude reveals itself as the product of a highly perfected digital technique operating under the direction of a mind which not only knows music in detail and in historical perspective but has an unusual thoroughness about all its operations. There are also present a great gift of theatrical simplicity (she makes all her points clearly and broadly) and a

fiery Slavic temperament. The latter is both concealed and revealed by a unique rhythmic virtuosity that is at the same time
characteristic of our century and convincingly authentic when
applied to the execution of another century's music.

It is when this rhythm is most relentless that I find Madame
Landowska's work most absorbing. Free recitative and the affetuoso style she does with taste, and she spaces her fugal entries
cleanly. But music becomes as grand and as impersonal as an
element when she gets into a sustained rhythmic pattern. It
makes no difference then whether the music is dainty, as in the
Rameau suite, or dancy and vigorously expository, as in both
the Rameau suite and the Bach Partita. It is full of a divine fury
and irresistibly insistent.

There is no need of my reviewing the works played, which are
all great music, save perhaps to pay tribute to Rameau, who got
so much of the sweetness of France, as well as its grace and its
grandeur, into his E-minor Suite. And to mention the romantic
and rhapsodical beauty of the Froberger *Lament.* There is even
less occasion to point out stylistic misconceptions and interpretative errors on the executant's part, because there weren't
any. At least, it seemed to this listener that every work was fully
possessed by her. If the audience was as fully possessed by these
superbly convincing renditions of some of the grandest music
in the world as this auditor was (and certainly it appeared to
be), there really isn't much that any of us can do about it further, except to make sure of not missing this great artist's next
performance. Last night's was as complete as that.

October 22, 1942

Complete Authority

JOSEF LHÉVINNE, pianist, in recital last night at Carnegie Hall,
performing Schumann's Toccata in C major, twelve Chopin études
(Op. 25), and works by Brahms and Balakirev.

MR. LHÉVINNE seems to have replaced the late Leopold Godowsky as the acknowledged master of pianoforte-mastery. A
full house paid him homage last night at Carnegie Hall, as he, in
turn, paid his audience the honor of executing a distinguished

program of the piano's masterworks with authority and no playing down to anybody.

A more satisfactory academicism could scarcely be imagined. Mr. Lhévinne's performance, especially of the Schumann Toccata and the Chopin Études, was both a lesson and an inspiration. He made no effort to charm or to seduce or to preach or to impress. He played as if he were expounding to a graduate seminar: "This is the music, and this is the way to play it."

Any authoritative execution derives as much of its excellence from what the artist does not do as from what he does. If he doesn't do anything off color at all, he is correctly said to have taste. Mr. Lhévinne's taste is as authoritative as his technical method. Not one sectarian interpretation, not one personal fancy, not one stroke below the belt, not a sliver of ham, mars the universal acceptability of his readings. Everything he does is right and clear and complete. Everything he doesn't do is the whole list of all the things that mar the musical executions of lesser men.

This is not to say that tenderness and poetry and personal warmth and fire are faults of musical style, though they frequently do excuse a faulty technique. I am saying that Mr. Lhévinne does not need them. They would mar his style; hence he eschews them. He eschews them because his concept of piano music is an impersonal one. It is norm-centered; it is for all musical men. Any intrusion of the executant's private soul would limit its appeal, diminish its authority.

Thus it is that Mr. Lhévinne's performance is worthy of the honorable word *academic*. And if he seems to some a little distant, let us remind ourselves that remoteness is, after all, inevitable to those who inhabit Olympus.

November 18, 1940

Correct and Beautiful

KIRSTEN FLAGSTAD, soprano, in recital last night at Carnegie Hall, performing Grieg's "Haugtussa" cycle and songs by Brahms, Hugo Wolf, and four contemporary Americans. Accompanist: *Edwin McArthur*, piano.

STRAIGHTFORWARDNESS on the concert platform is something rarely encountered except on the part of children and of the very greatest artists. Straightforwardness in musical execution is met with practically only on the part of great artists. Madame Flagstad is straightforward in her platform manner and in her musical interpretations.

She is not, for that, an unsubtle musician. Nor is her splendidly majestic voice an unsubtle instrument. All the shading is there that one might wish and all the refinement of expression that lieder repertory requires, which is much. But such an assured mistress is she of her voice, and so clear is her comprehension of the songs she sings, that she is not constrained to seek to please her listeners by any trick of willful charm or cuteness or feigned emotion.

In consequence, she can afford the highest luxury of the concert stage, which is to sing the songs of Brahms and Grieg and Hugo Wolf and of our American song-writers as simply and as candidly as Miss Helen Hayes, say, might read Shakespeare's sonnets in a drawing-room. No intonation is false, no word unclear, no sentiment either under- or overstated. By eschewing exploitation of her personality, she warms all hearts to that personality. By not feeling obliged to give her operatic all to every tender melody, she offers us each song as if it were a living and a fragile thing in our hands, like a bird.

Our century has known great mistresses of vocalism and many intelligent interpreters of songs. I doubt if there has existed within the memory of living musicians another singer so gifted as to voice, so satisfying as to taste, and withal such mistress of her vocal instrument as Madame Flagstad. Some singers sing by nature, others take lessons for years. It is scarcely more than once or twice in a century that any vocalist ever masters his voice with the kind of mastery that pianists have of the pianoforte, masters it seriously and completely, while he is still in command of all his vocal resources. Mostly they sing by ear and learn to use the voice correctly only after its best notes are worn out and gone. Madame Flagstad has a great voice now which she handles as if it were a race-horse she had bred and trained.

She can sing loud and she can sing soft. She can sing fast and she can sing slow. She can sing high, low, in strict time, in free time, with clear words, on pitch, swelling or diminishing in volume. This, plus a clear comprehension of the human significance of the music one wishes to sing, is the whole art of singing.

Her voice must not have been an easy one to train, either. Her high, low, and middle registers are noticeably different in timbre. Her scale is as smooth as that of a flute or trumpet; but her ranges, heard separately, are as sharply differentiated as the ranges are of any wind instrument. One of the most satisfying qualities of her singing is the way her chest-voice sounds like chest-voice, her head-voice like head-voice, and her middle-voice like ordinary speech, while at the same time the transition from one range to another is so gentle and so even as to be virtually imperceptible excepting when there is a skip in the melodic line.

Mr. Edwin McArthur accompanied from memory. He gave support, allowed flexibility, was in general straightforward and highly pleasant to hear. He was more like a partner in an adequately rehearsed duet than like the more usual obsequious accompanist.

November 9, 1940

Glamour and Loyalty

MARIAN ANDERSON, contralto, in recital last night at Carnegie Hall, performing four Negro spirituals and songs by Galuppi, da Capua, Marcello, Brahms, Gounod, Saint-Saëns, Fauré, and Ravel. Accompanist: *Franz Rupp*, piano.

MARIAN ANDERSON's recitals (she gave one last night in Carnegie Hall) have more quality than most such events. The beauty of her person, the glamour of her personality, which has something of royalty in its simultaneous graciousness and reserve, the rigid sumptuousness of her costumes, the charm of her voice, the excellence of her vocal command, the high musical distinction of her programs, the careful musicianship of her executions—all these elements make for an occasion of no mean impressiveness. If your reviewer's enthusiasm is a little less intense than what a summation of such glories might normally have produced, that is perhaps because he thought he ought, in view of Miss Anderson's great loyalty to the art of music-making, to put his mind chiefly on the nature of that music-making.

He found it, under the physical appearance of simplicity, to be a little ornate for his taste, ornate and timid. Rarely does she attack a note frankly; she hums her way into them nearly all. Almost never does she end one, either, without tapering it off. This constant crescendo and decrescendo, though most tastefully encrusted upon every phrase, gives to the whole articulation of a song or aria, as well as to its phrases, a carved-in-mahogany quality that is more genteel than authentically stylish, more ladylike than wholly frank.

Miss Anderson's best quality, indeed, as an interpreter is a kind of inwardness that comes from that same timidity. It is lovely in German and French songs, hopelessly out of place in operatic arias. She sings all foreign languages, in fact—and that meant four fifths of last night's program—with her eyes closed. The effect is that of a very, very, very good student being careful not to do anything wrong. When she drops her timidity and inwardness, opens her eyes, and sings English, she is the most straightforward artist in the world and one of the most satisfying. Your reviewer considers it rather a pity that she feels obliged, out of her loyalty to recital conventions, to go through so much Classical and Romantic repertory—all of which others do better—before she gets down to singing in her own language the religious music of her own people. That is where she leaves off being a lovely icicle and becomes a flame.

November 4, 1943

God Bless Ireland

JOHN CHARLES THOMAS, baritone, in recital last night at Carnegie Hall, performing Italian and German songs, new American songs, and American folk and parlor songs including Stephen Foster's "Gentle Annie." Accompanist: *Carroll Hollister*, piano.

JOHN CHARLES THOMAS pleases all. Not necessarily everybody all the time. But at some point or other in each program, everybody. Last night he gave us old Italian songs of finest vintage, poured to perfection. He gave us works from French and German masters who bridged the nineteenth and twentieth centuries. There was a famous operatic aria, "Eri tu," from Verdi's *Ballo in Maschera*. There was a group of recital ballads in the American recital style. And there was a group of highly dramatized American folk-songs that included even a Negro spiritual. All were executed with consummate art, and all were enthusiastically received by some part of the large audience. Most were applauded heartily by the whole house.

Mr. Thomas has a different style of delivery for each kind of thing he does, and each style is appropriate to its kind. What permeates all the styles is his remarkable and instinctive musicality.

This is not to say that his voice and style are untrained. They are very well trained indeed, though I think his voice would gain in beauty if he placed its resonance more squarely in what Americans call, not very clearly, the head and what French vocalists refer to as the *masque*. High baritones sometimes fear to sound like heroic tenors, but the simple truth is that they are heroic tenors and have everything to gain by displaying to the full the beauties of the so-called head resonance. Aside from this reserve, I can find no fault in his schooling. He sings beautifully.

I call his musicality instinctive, because only those with melody in the soul ever sing so easily or pronounce so clearly. He does not pronounce words to a vocal line; he makes a vocal line out of words sung. Naturally they come out clear in any language. And naturally the music comes out as melody.

His is the Irish* gift at his best, which means thoroughly trained. He reminds one at the same time of Chauncey Olcott and of John McCormack. The first because of his combination

---

*Mr. Thomas's racial origins are actually Welsh.

of personal charm with dramatic power; the second because of his high perfection in the kind of easily floated melody-with-ornaments that used to be called, when singers still had enough nervous control to master it, *bel canto*.

If Mr. Thomas were not such a fine musician, it would be difficult to forgive him for making every number a wow. If he were not such a natural musician, his lighter numbers would be ham. Gifted so rarely and schooled so soundly, everything he touches becomes, in a different way and for a different public, beauty.

November 26, 1940

Chestnuts, but Not Roasted

DUSOLINA GIANNINI, soprano, and JAN PEERCE, tenor, in joint recital last night at Carnegie Hall. Miss Giannini performed Italian folk songs and five songs by Brahms, Mr. Peerce performed songs by Handel, Torelli, Durante, Ponchielli, and others. Together they sang "Ah, lo vedi," from Mascagni's *Cavalleria Rusticana*. Accompanists: *Edwin McArthur* and *Fritz Kitzinger,* pianos.

Miss Dusolina Giannini and Mr. Jan Peerce, who sang a joint recital last night in Carnegie Hall, are two of America's finest vocalists. Mr. Peerce (he pinch-hit for Pinza, who was ill) is a tenor of excellent voice and unimpeachable vocalization, though his work leans toward monotony. Miss Giannini has a dramatic soprano voice that resembles no other among the living, though its similarity to that of the late Emma Calvé has often been remarked. She is, moreover, a mistress of vocal art with a dramatic temperament of great power. The program was made up of chestnuts, and all the encores were war-horses. I have rarely had so good a time at a recital of vocalism. The audience was still applauding when I left at eleven.

In a concert of that kind it is always the encores that are the real substance. The printed program is made up chiefly of studio material, songs that everybody has worked on or heard worked on. The encores are the great vocal numbers that students are rarely allowed to work on. Mr. Peerce sang the tenor aria from Halévy's *La Juive* and the *Rigoletto* "La donna è mobile." Miss Giannini did the "Pace, pace" from *La Forza del Destino* and the *Carmen* Habanera. As I left for my office, they had just finished adding to the *Cavalleria Rusticana* duet the one from the first act of *La Tosca*. There had been a half-dozen famous songs added previously. You can see what a display of vocalism was offered and why the whole thing, given by two such excellent vocalists, was invigorating and fun.

Miss Giannini is my favorite of the two. She has more flexibility of style and a wider range of vocal color. Mr. Peerce is an American from New York City who has made his singing into a perfect replica of the Italian tenor style. His production is rather more even than that of most Italian tenors, I must say. But his imitation of their faults of style is complete and just a shade comic. His voice is not really so robust as his vocal manner, and his sliding and scooping à la Caruso is just permissible for the singing of modern Italian works. It is out of place with music more than seventy-five years old, and it is certainly no way to sing anything French. It will do for the English claptrap he rendered, merely because there is no sensible way of singing that kind of thing anyway. The genuine pleasure of Mr. Peerce's work lies in the unvarying placement of his middle and upper tones (though his low register is not sufficiently projected). The unvarying color of these is also the source of a certain monotony.

Miss Giannini's voice is the subject of much dispute in vocal circles. Its admirers are devoted, its detractors rather impatient. Again the Calvé parallel comes to mind. Myself, I love it. Of her vocal mastery there is no question. Her way of singing songs (she did Brahms last night) is intelligent and musical but not wholly satisfactory. They do not give sufficient scope for her dramatic temperament. The sound of them seems to come from no lower than the lungs, the expression from no farther down than the heart. When she sings opera airs she sings from the hips, projects character and feeling with her whole body. I have never at any time in my life heard a rendition of the *Carmen* Habanera that was even faintly comparable to hers for acuity of expression, for controlled variety of vocal color. The Italian folk-songs, arranged by her brother, Vittorio Giannini, were similarly dramatic and vocally masterful. I regret never having had occasion to hear this great vocal artist in the opera, because it is obvious that the musical theater is her home.

Two accompanists were listed. I could have sworn they were the same man, because they looked alike and played alike. My guest assured me they were really two and that Mr. Kitzinger played fewer wrong notes than Mr. McArthur. Both played plenty. And neither seemed to have much care for piano tone or for any of the other musical amenities beyond playing fast and loud and keeping up a general hubbub under the singing. It didn't seem to make much difference, though.

February 4, 1942

Some Beautiful Songs and the Sad Story of Dorothy Maynor

DOROTHY MAYNOR, soprano, in recital last night at Town Hall, performing "Cake and Sack," "Old Shellover," and "Tillie" from Theodore Chanler's *Five Rhymes from "Peacock Pie,"* three Negro spirituals, and songs by, among others, Handel, Fauré, Bizet, and Mussorgsky. Accompanist: *Arpad Sandor*, piano.

THE CHIEF PURPOSE of my visit to Town Hall last night was to hear the *Five Rhymes from "Peacock Pie"* by Theodore Chanler. Three were sung, and very nicely indeed, by Miss Maynor. They were a pleasure in every possible way.

Mr. Chanler's music is French by schooling, though not imitative of any Frenchman's mannerisms. It hasn't any mannerisms of its own, even. It is the expression of a man so gently and so delicately bred that he would consider the conscious injection of his own personality into his music an affectation. He writes, therefore, with conscious sincerity and with unconscious distinction. The vulgar, the careless, the meretricious are as if unthinkable. There is precision in the melodies without any harshness, and amplitude in the musical structure without any boasting. His particular achievement, of abundance in musical expression without extravagance, I can only describe as Gallic. His songs have what is known in French manners as *tenue*.

Miss Dorothy Maynor's recital, which included the three Chanler songs, was on the whole a disappointment, though it did clear up one matter that has bothered all her admirers of late. There can be no further question, I think, that her vocal technique is woefully inadequate and that her voice itself is in danger.

Vocal gift she has in abundance, and good musical instincts, and a platform personality of great power. She has one of those characteristically negroid voices that seem to be three voices at the same time. Trained one way, she might become a female baritone. Trained another, she might sing coloratura. Without any training at all she might have sung as simply and as beautifully in the middle range as she does now. With exactly the amount of training that she has, she sings simply and beautifully in the middle range and nowhere else. Her lower tones are forced and breathy. Above D she is usually flat. She scoops, she spreads, she hoots; and she is not above screaming if she can't get her note any other way.

If she were not such a good comedienne, so assured in her ability to put over virtually any number she likes, her performance last night would have sounded amateurish. Vocally it was. She sang as if she were vocalizing first and pronouncing only incidentally. In consequence she was very difficult to understand. For two thirds of the evening she was tense and highly inaccurate, as if she had no confidence at all in what might be coming out of her throat, as if anything might happen vocally. With the spirituals she started singing words for the first time instead of vocalizing. Having no secure vocal method for doing this, she simply threw all vocal method aside and sang like any enthusiastic untrained colored girl. The human effect was agreeable, but only her youth and strong vocal cords prevented her from cracking. There was betting in my row as to whether she would be able to finish the recital.

Curiously enough, she went right into the Chanler songs without any trouble. Lying chiefly in the middle range, they probably rested her. After that she whooped it up and screamed some more.

How long Miss Maynor can continue to overwork her vocal resources without working them out I could not say. Not long, I imagine. Already her voice has lost its velvet. She has no real power; and there is a very small range, about an octave, where she can sing with ease. Also, a telltale tremolo is developing. It is all very much too bad, for she was gifted with voice, with musical talent, and with a rare personal projection.

January 9, 1941

High-Quality Singing

JENNIE TOUREL, mezzo-soprano, in recital on November 13 at Town Hall, performing songs by, among others, Rameau, Mozart, Debussy, Rossini, Mussorgsky, Alexander Gretchaninov, Leonard Bernstein, David Diamond, and Joachín Nin. Accompanist: *Erich Itor Kahn,* piano.

ALL THROUGH Jennie Tourel's recital on Saturday night at Town Hall one had the impression of being present at the take-off of some new and powerful airplane for a round-the-world flight. One was aware that her previous vocal performances here, her test flights, so to speak, had inspired high confidence. Word had gone round the music world that her work was excellent in a way far beyond that of the average good singer; and a packed-in houseful of that world was present to judge, to describe, and, hopefully, to acclaim it. Miss Tourel's conquest of this well-disposed but critical audience was of a completeness without any local parallel since Kirsten Flagstad's debut at the Metropolitan Opera House some nine seasons ago.

Miss Tourel is of a wholly different musical temperament from Miss Flagstad, the only basis for comparison between the two artists being the degree of their vocal mastery, which places them together in the top category of living vocal musicians —together and virtually alone. Miss Tourel, who is a young woman (not far off thirty, I should guess), is not quite the mistress of her throat and face muscles in big climaxes that Miss Flagstad was (already over forty when she came here). Her fault in this respect comes, I fancy, from a way she has of opening her mouth very wide without compensating at the lips for this excessive relaxation. My explanation may not be physiologically correct, but I do think there is a slight fault in Miss Tourel's jaw position that shows up when she sings high notes loud. I also fancy that that fault is neither grave nor irremediable. With this single reserve, I found her vocal performance, generally speaking, impeccable.

The voice is a mezzo-soprano of wide range, warm in timbre and unbelievably flexible. Miss Tourel is a mistress of a wider range of coloration in all ranges and at all volumes than any other singer I have ever heard. Her pitch is perfect in the most difficult modern music. Her legato skips are the kind of *bel canto* one dreams about. Her enunciation in all languages, even in so introspective a work as Debussy's songs to words by Baudelaire, is cleanly projected at all times. Her musicianship in every domain is so thorough that from the whole technical and intellectual aspect her work belongs clearly with that of the great virtuosos of music.

Her gift for languages is at the bottom of much of her stylistic virtuosity. On Saturday night she sang in Italian, French, Russian, English, Portuguese, and Spanish, making them all sound like themselves, coloring her vowels to the characteristic timbres of those languages, revealing their special music, and cherishing their particular ways of expressing feeling. She moved around in each tongue as if it were a whole landscape and climate, untranslated, untranslatable, and unique. In none of the European ones did I sense any accent. Certainly in her English there was none.

This extreme mental and emotional flexibility, commanding a vocal skill of transcendent nature and commanded by musicianship of the highest order, produced, in a program of diversified works, a variety of musical experiences that is rarely encountered in a soloist's recital. There are singers who have her stylistic knowledge, but they mostly have inferior vocal powers. There are other singers, though few, who sing that well; but they are mostly either inferior as musicians or limited in their expressive scope. Miss Tourel is, I believe, unequaled among living singers for the high concentration in one artist of vocal skill, sound musicianship, and stylistic flexibility.

November 15, 1943

Fine Fiddling

EFREM ZIMBALIST, violin, in recital last night at Carnegie Hall, performing, among other works, Beethoven's Sonata No. 9 (Op. 47, "Kreutzer"), Tchaikovsky's Sonata in D major, Op. 35, and Carl Engel's *Sea-Shell*. Accompanist: *Vladimir Sokoloff*, piano.

THE FULLEST HOUSE I have seen this season (chairs and standers on the stage, too) listened last night with rapt faces to Mr. Zimbalist in Carnegie Hall. I confess to a not great taste for violin recitals myself, because the Baroque instrument has somehow not managed to inspire our best composers to do their best work. At least, not since the invention of the over-sensitive Tourte bow made the playing of it a pure virtuoso job. Nevertheless, virtuoso workmanship has its interest for almost anybody; and last night's concert was a noble display of that.

Mr. Zimbalist, as a musician, is sound and straightforward, seldom strikingly original, never commonplace. He gives himself the trouble to play a long melodic phrase with steady tone, for instance. This means real trouble, because it requires complete control of the bow arm and of its weight. I do not know a more dependable right arm in the violin-playing world. Consequently his phrasing is musical and architectural. There are no inexplicable crescendos due to changes of direction in the bowing. He is not obliged to substitute for clear articulation a simulation of intense personal feeling in the form of heavy vibrato. His vibrato is most discreet, indeed. His right-arm control permits him to use a variety of tonal color that makes for auditory relief and produces a certain lightness in the whole texture of his work that keeps the violin sound from becoming oppressive.

Each of the great violinists has his characteristic fiddle tone. Kreisler, Heifetz, all of them one can recognize blindfolded, as one can a well-known singer's voice. Of all the fiddle tones, Mr. Zimbalist's is the least strained, the most pure. It is also one of the most human. It is not so organlike as Kreisler's nor so suggestive of precious stuffs as that of Heifetz. It is not nearly so sharp and brilliant as Szigeti's nor so discreetly inexpressive as that of Busch. It is nevertheless a more truly musical sound than any of these, because it is round. It is round like the sound a good singer makes when he hums. Its vocal placement is perfect. Also, like a good singer, Mr. Zimbalist never forces.

The program was usual enough. Its reading might have passed for usual, too, if one didn't know from experience what liberties most violinists, even the best of them, are prone to permit themselves. The Beethoven last movement was lacking in rhythmic weight, perhaps; but the slow one profited by this same absence of dynamic insistence. The Tchaikovsky was a dream of graciousness and elegance. The arrangements and the violinistic stuff were exactly as you can imagine them. The only one that seemed to me worth especially noting is Mr. Carl Engel's

Sea-Shell, a songlike piece in the MacDowell taste which, though not thematically very original, is musically sophisticated and instrumentally most gracious.

The evening's great success seems to me to be due to fine technical work and genuine musicianship. It was pleasant to observe a large musical public being completely responsive to these qualities without the artist's having recourse to the sentimental, the violent, or the meretricious.

January 21, 1942

Silk-Underwear Music

JASCHA HEIFETZ, violinist, in recital last night at Carnegie Hall, performing, among other works, Robert Russell Bennett's *Hexapoda: Five Studies in Jitteroptera*, Spohr's Concerto No. 8 ("Gesangscene"), Richard Strauss's Sonata, Op. 18, and Mozart's Sonata No. 10. Accompanist: *Emmanuel Bay*, piano.

ROBERT RUSSELL BENNETT's musical sketches of the jitterbug world are pretty music. Also they are evocative of swing music without being themselves swing music or any imitation of swing music. They manage with skill and integrity to use swing formulas as a décor for the musical depiction of those nerve reflexes and soul states that swing-lovers commonly manifest when exposed to swing music. They are, in addition, expertly written for the violin. They come off, as the phrase has it, like a million dollars.

Mr. Heifetz's whole concert rather reminded one of large sums of money like that. If ever I heard luxury expressed in music it was there. His famous silken tone, his equally famous double-stops, his well-known way of hitting the true pitch squarely in the middle, his justly remunerated mastery of the musical marshmallow, were like so many cushions of damask and down to the musical ear.

He is like Sarah Bernhardt, with her famous "small voice of purest gold" and her mastery of the wow-technique. First-class plays got in her way; she seldom appeared in one after thirty. Heifetz is at his best in short encore pieces (the Bennetts are beautifully that) and in lengthy chestnuts like Spohr's

Gesangscene (an old-time war-horse for violinists), where every device of recitative style, of melodic phrase turning, and of brilliant passage work is laid out, like the best evening clothes and the best jewelry, for Monsieur to put his elegant person into. No destination, no musical or emotional significance, is implied.

The Strauss Sonata, a work of the author's early manhood, lacks none of that composer's characteristic style. The themes could only be his (albeit one was practically straight out of *Carmen*), bombastic, second-rate (I except the one that starts the last movement, which is bombastic and first-rate), inflated, expressing nothing but the composer's fantastic facility, his jubilant gusto at writing music. Mr. Heifetz's execution of this was almost embarrassingly refined.

Of his Mozart, the less said the better. It is of the school that makes a diminuendo on every feminine phrase-ending, that never plays any phrase through with the same weight, that thinks Mozart's whole aim was to charm, that tries so hard to make out of the greatest musician the world has ever known (those are Joseph Haydn's words) something between a sentimental Pierrot and a Dresden china clock that his music ends by sounding affected, frivolous, and picayune. If that is Mozart, I'll buy a hat and eat it.

I realize that my liking or not liking what Mr. Heifetz plays and how he plays it is a matter of no import to the stellar spaces in which he moves. But it happens that I did go to the concert last night and that I did observe pretty carefully his virtuosity. It was admirable and occasionally very, very beautiful. The fellow can fiddle. But he sacrifices everything to polish. He does it knowingly. He is justly admired and handsomely paid for it. To ask anything else of him is like asking tenderness of the ocelot.

Four-starred super-luxury hotels are a legitimate commerce. The fact remains, however, that there is about their machine-tooled finish and empty elegance something more than just a trifle vulgar.

October 31, 1940

In Tune, but Not with the Infinite

ISAAC STERN, violinist, in recital last night at Carnegie Hall, performing, among other works, Beethoven's Sonata No. 7 (Op. 30, No. 2), Bach's Partita in D minor, Vieuxtemps' Concerto No. 5, and Debussy's Sonata in G minor. Accompanist: *Alexander Zakin*, piano.

ISAAC STERN, who played a violin recital last night in Carnegie Hall, is one of the world's master fiddle-players. His tone is large and deep and never forced; his finger and bow control are impeccable, and he plays in tune virtually all the time. His musicianship, moreover, is marked by an astonishing purity of taste; his interpretations are quite without sentimental gimcrackery.

It is difficult to isolate the fault in his work; but there is one, nevertheless. It lies, I think, in a certain absence of poetic continuity. His intellectual penetration is mature, and he has a way of sweeping through a long piece that leaves the whole shape and sonorous substance of it clear in the memory. This ability to build a wide and towering structure out of the most handsome auditory materials is no less a proof of genius for all the care and all the intellection that are involved. The trouble is that nobody seems to live in his houses. Their structure and their style are perfect, but they lack human warmth. Neither the executant of the music nor its designer seems to have any personal involvement with it.

The nearest to a personal rendering among last night's interpretations was that of the Beethoven Sonata opus 30, no. 2. This had, along with its sweeping architectonics, an improvisational fury that suggested a bit Beethoven the man, the young man, who loved nothing better than to improvise with fury grand architectural forms. The least personal but the most satisfactory sonorously was that of the Bach Suite in D minor for violin alone, where no piano was present to falsify the accuracy of Mr. Stern's amazingly correct pitch. True intervals and good tone filled great Carnegie Hall with resonance as only true intervals and a correct tone production can do.

The Vieuxtemps was breath-taking for its brilliance and surety. The Debussy was intoned with delicate understanding of its auditory line. The whole evening was full of competence and of lovely music. It is rare to encounter artistry of this excellence.

Mr. Stern would have transported us all (or *sent* us, as the young people say) if he had not lacked a final commitment to passion and to poetry.

January 12, 1944

Extraordinary Cello-Playing

LUIGI SILVA, cellist, in recital last night at Mannes Music School, New York, performing works by Della Ciaja, Beethoven, Brahms, and Boccherini. Accompanist: *Leopold Mannes*, piano.

LUIGI SILVA is a unique and profoundly original cello-player. His originality lies in certain technical innovations about fingering and bowing. These are a carrying forward of the innovations of Pablo Casals, who revolutionized cello-playing by introducing violin fingerings and violin bowing style to that instrument. The musical advantages of these were many— lightness, speed, accuracy of intonation, greater melodic smoothness, greater facility in the upper positions of all four strings. Mr. Silva's carrying forward of these innovations sets him apart both technically and musically from the rest of the cello-playing world.

For a listener uninitiated to the characteristic difficulties of the instrument and unacquainted with the classical methods of overcoming these, Silva's unique musical performance might well seem to be merely a matter of musicianship. It is not entirely that. He is a musician of great gifts, of broad experience, and of unusual penetration. His knowledge, temperament, and scholarship are of the best. But it is his broadening of the cello's technical resources that has enabled his musicality to flower, that has permitted him to give a greater clarity and amplitude to his renditions of cello literature than one is likely to hear elsewhere these days, excepting perhaps in some of the Casals recordings. That is why I call his work both original and unique.

Last night's program included Mr. Silva's own transcription of a work for cembalo by Azzolino Bernardino della Ciaja, the Beethoven Sonata in A major, opus 69, the Brahms F major, op. 99, and a sonata by Boccherini, the figured-bass realization in this being Mr. Silva's work also. Each of these works was executed in a musical style appropriate to its epoch and authorship. The della Ciaja was neat, clean, and organlike. The Beethoven was broad, its soft passages incredibly poetic and flutelike. The Brahms was more passionately sung, its timbre richer and more reedlike, its bass accents more dramatic, its fingered tremolos mysterious and nearly inaudible. The Boccherini was played in an orchestral gamut of sharp and thin colorations that brought out all the delicacy and the brilliance of that composer's cello-writing. For good measure, and possibly for a bit of a joke, Mr. Silva added a transcription for cello of the Paganini Capriccio for Violin, No. 13, in B-flat major, commonly known as "La Risata," a virtuoso study in double-stops.

I have described so far the singular mastery and unusual breadth of Mr. Silva's work in terms of what he does. Further I cannot go except by saying what he does not do. He does not play off pitch, for example. This exactitude sets him apart from all cellists below the rank of the very great. Neither does he slide or scoop. His changes of hand position are made with such speed and such accuracy that they are virtually unheard. Neither does he attempt to avoid technical difficulties by making expression out of them. He makes crescendos and diminuendos to express the music's long-line phraseology, never to excuse a lack of control over the bow arm. Nor does he allow melodic passages that go from one string to another to sound as if they were being played on different instruments.

This skill at equalizing the tone color of his four strings is perhaps a positive skill rather than a negative virtue. It is, in fact, the complement to his extraordinary repertory of tone colorations. For just as he makes the cello sound at different times like many different instruments or voices, he sounds each of these at all times in an equalized scale from the bottom of the C-string to the top of the A. To hear the cello's finest literature expounded so orchestrally in tone, so pungently in rhythm, so penetratingly as to stylistic comprehension and so broadly as to sustained passion and rhetoric, the whole backed up by such musicianly accompaniments as Mr. Leopold Mannes provided last night, is a musical experience of the first water.

February 24, 1941

A Noble and Lovely Evening

RENÉ LE ROY AND ASSOCIATES in concert last night at Town Hall, presenting Mozart's Concerto for Flute and Orchestra, Mozart's Concerto for Flute, Cello, Harp, and Orchestra, Bernard Wagenaar's Triple Concerto for Flute, Cello, Harp, and Orchestra, and Jean-Marie Le Clair's Concerto for Flute and Orchestra with Harpsichord Obbligato, performed by *René Le Roy*, flutist and conductor, and a twenty-piece chamber orchestra with soloists *Carlos Salzedo*, harp and harpsichord, *Marjorie Call Salzedo*, harp, *Janos Scholz*, cello, and *Mr. Wagenaar*, piano.

THE ELEGANT INFORMALITY of René Le Roy's concert of last night in Town Hall has not been equaled this season (in my experience) at any public gathering. Neither has the musical excellence of it been surpassed. A chamber orchestra of twenty playing impeccably, four distinguished soloists and two composers performing, not a conductor in sight. The program consisted of four concertos, one for flute, one for flute and harp, one for flute, harp, and cello, and a final one for flute again, this time with an imitation harpsichord in the orchestra. Two were by Mozart, one by the great Jean-Marie Le Clair, one by our own Bernard Wagenaar. At the beginning of three, and during an occasional tutti, the beat was given by the flute soloist, Monsieur Le Roy. In the other, the composer, Mr. Wagenaar, indicated basic tempos from the pianoforte. Other needed leadership was supplied unobtrusively and most satisfactorily indeed by the concertmaster, Mr. Bernard Ocko. Everything sounded shipshape and beautiful, lively, intelligent, civilized.

Le Roy is a great artist of the greatest of all schools of flute-playing, which is the French. He is master of an incredible pianissimo in both the high and low ranges of his instrument and of a steady, pale-colored tone that blends most graciously with that of strings and of the harp. During the first two pieces he had some pitch trouble in the lower register that was due, I imagine, to temperature conditions in the crowded hall. The harp did not sound quite exactly, either, in the Mozart; but these maladjustments were alleviated after the intermission. From certain parts of the house, production noises were audible, too, such as a slight breathiness in the lower flute tones and some clatter of the key-mechanism in the trills. There is little to be done about these *bruits parasites*, as the French call them. The best flute-playing in the world is never wholly free from them. I mention them merely because Monsieur Le Roy, who is one of the best flute-players in the world, is not able to eliminate them entirely from the hearing of those close by. Nevertheless, he plays the flute with a lovely silken sound; and his mastery of its style and technique is that of the great virtuosos.

Indeed, what carried the evening to a height of musical distinction far beyond that of ordinary first-class execution was Le Roy's—and Salzedo's, too—power of sustained musical discourse. He shades a musical line without leaning on it. He diminishes his volume on the eighteenth-century feminine phrase-endings without letting the musical sentence fall apart. He plays Mozart on the flute as Beecham conducts it in the orchestra or at the theater. The grand line never breaks, and yet no detail of inflection is sacrificed. The result is a performance at once manly and delicate, noble and gracious, emphatic, sweet, and wholly elegant.

Mr. Wagenaar's Triple Concerto is a handsome work and full of interesting sounds. I suspect the sounds of being a shade more interesting than the thematic substance. However, when Salzedo plays the harp, it is like Landowska playing the harpsichord. The instrument itself takes on such a fascination that I don't always care what the piece is like. I have heard this work before and I have always liked the sound of it. Last night it was a dream of trick sonorities and of graceful expression. I felt no need, any more than I have on previous occasions, of penetrating beneath its shimmering surface.

The Le Clair is a masterpiece of early eighteenth-century French style, vigorous, noble, and squarely gay. Monsieur Le Roy's pacing of it was something all musicians should be able to refer to when they get bothered about what Sebastian Bach meant by the *stile francese*. This was the real article, believe me. The whole evening, indeed, was the McCoy, including the excellent cello-playing of Janos Scholz, but not including the harp work of Marjorie Salzedo, which though pretty enough to look at, sounded fuzzy and vague beside the rhythm and color of her husband's.

March 5, 1942

SACRED AND CHORAL

Styles in Sacred Music

LISTENING last week to a radio half-hour of flamboyant religious music has provoked your commentator to meditate on the world-wide decline of that kind of sacred art. The program, which is a weekly one, takes place on Monday evenings at 9:30, station WOR. Alfred Wallenstein conducts and there are an orchestra, a chorus, and excellent soloists. Last week Rose Dirman, soprano, and William Hain, tenor, were starred. The works rendered, which were all famous ones, might be called chestnuts except that, for all their currency, many accomplished consumers of music have never heard any of them.

There were the Gloria from Mozart's Twelfth Mass; Gounod's cantata (or anthem) *Gallia*; Handel's aria, "Sound an Alarm," from *Judas Maccabæus*; Mendelssohn's "If with All Your Hearts," from *Elijah*; *O bone Jesu*, a sixteenth-century motet incorrectly ascribed (or so the scholars tell me) to Palestrina; and the wonderfully theatrical "Inflammatus" from the *Stabat Mater* of Rossini. Excepting for the so-called Palestrina piece, every one of these works is written in a grandiloquent and ornate style. Any of them would do honor to an operatic score. All presuppose big, beautiful, well-trained voices and mobilize numerous instrumental effectives. All observe a liberty in the treatment of sacred text that the music world of our century considers to be of questionable taste.

The music world of our century does not feel quite at home with religious subjects, any more than the directors of our religious establishments feel confident about contemporary composition. The making of a joyful noise unto the Lord and the praising of Him upon a loud instrument are practiced in our time with more timidity than gusto. A lugubrious respectability overlays nearly all our religious music-making. And our best composers tend more and more to reserve their joyful noises, as well as their really terrifying ones, for secular circumstances.

The basis of this timidity is not so much, I fancy, a lack of religious faith on the part of musicians or any suspicion of music's efficacy on the part of religious administrators as it is an

erroneous conception by both of what constitutes a proper
sacred style. It is thought that profane associations invalidate
stylistic elements for religious usage. And yet the history of
religion, if it proves anything at all about music, proves the contrary. The exchange of material and of device between sacred
and secular usage is the one constant pattern discernible in the
musical history of the last twelve hundred years. And at no
point in that time is it possible to distinguish save by sheer functional criteria, such as instruments or verbal texts employed, the
music of worship from that of sheer entertainment.

Professionals of religion have constantly tried to censor the
music used in their establishments. But whenever the censorship
of tune or of technical device becomes strict, inspiration moves
over to the market-place. The "purification" of church music
that followed the pronouncements of the Council of Trent
provoked in less than fifty years the invention of the opera.
And the real originality of the seventeenth-century operatic
style caused its adoption within twenty-five years by the religious
establishments. The modernized plain-chant of the Benedictine
monks made possible, too, the writing of Debussy's *Pelléas et
Mélisande* and Satie's *Socrate*, although it has not yet produced
one first-class piece of church composition.

Church music in our century, whether Catholic, Protestant,
or Jewish, has been conservative and, compared to the music
of theater and concert, inexpressive. It lacks self-confidence,
liberty, assertion. The reforms of Pope Pius X have strangled it
with the ideal of purity. These reforms, which have influenced
the whole Western world, were no doubt useful as preparation
for the reception of new influences. But in themselves they constitute no positive program. They are at best a housecleaning,
a throwing out of operatic styles that had served well for three
centuries but that had clearly lost, even in the theater, their
expressive power. The recommendation of the Palestrina style
to composers is even more backward-looking than the identical
recommendation made by the Council of Trent nearly three
hundred and fifty years before.

The next step, the only possible step forward today in music
destined for church usage, is the full employment of the modern
techniques. Musical advance is not now a specialty, as it has
been during some epochs, of the religious establishments.

Neither is it of the contemporary stage. The concert hall is where it flourishes. And it is our concert composers who have today the greatest mastery extant of all the composing techniques, ancient and modern, and the most expert acquaintance with their expressive possibilities. To any who may imagine that church music does not need to be expressive, let me point out that if it doesn't there is little besides habit, or some possible magic efficacy, to justify it. If our best modern church music seems, on the whole, less expressive, less moving than that of former centuries and of our own concert literature, that is because churchmen and musicians have been mutually suspicious ever since the encyclical *De Motu Proprio* of 1903 denounced the musical gang then in power.

That old gang is all dead now, and the generations now alive have been brought up with a healthy respect for religious decorum. It would be unfortunate if decorum itself became so stiff that it prevented living composers from writing live music for live worshippers. And if it did, it would just have to be reformed one day, like any other abuse.

Wherever religion is a wide enough house to have room in it for men of spirit, there is likely to be a lot of joyful noise-making, not only on psaltery and harp and timbrel but on quite loud instruments like the crashing cymbals, with high notes and trills and rapid arpeggios for voices and jostling counterpoints and terrifying harmonies. There never has been a Sacred Style; but sacred music, like any other, can have style, which is carrying-power. And it can have that today only on condition that, like all the memorable sacred music of past centuries, it be not afraid of its own time or timorous to employ the art's full resources.

July 23, 1944

Hymns of Tribulation and Rejoicing

BACH CHOIR OF BETHLEHEM, *Ifor Jones*, conductor, with the
MORAVIAN TROMBONE CHOIR and members of the PHILA-
DELPHIA ORCHESTRA, on May 16, the first day of a two-day Bach
Festival, at Packer Memorial Chapel, Lehigh University, Bethlehem,
Pa., performing two programs of music by Bach: *Afternoon*: Cantata
No. 19 ("There Uprose a Great Strife"), Motet "Come, Jesu,
Come," and Cantata No. 180 ("Beautify Thyself, My Spirit"); *Eve-
ning*: *Weinachtsoratorium*, Part IV, Cantata No. 146 ("We Must
Come Through Great Tribulation"), and *Magnificat*. With *T. Edgar
Shields*, organist, *Gretchen Newhart Iobst*, pianist, and soloists *Ruth
Diehl*, soprano, *Saida Knox*, contralto, *Hardesty Johnson*, tenor, and
Mack Harrell, baritone.

THE NOT so little town of Bethlehem, Pennsylvania, permanently the seat of a steel manufactory of the same name, as
well as of Lehigh University, becomes temporarily in May the
center of a musical pilgrimage. Friday the thirty-fifth Bach festival began, and Saturday it was over. The first Friday session
consisted of two choral cantatas with soloists and orchestra and
one unaccompanied motet for eight-part double chorus. The
evening brought Part IV of the *Christmas Oratorio,* another
cantata, and the famous *Magnificat*. The soloists were from
New York and the orchestral musicians, forty or more, from
Philadelphia; only the chorus was strictly local, Mr. Ifor Jones,
the conductor, being a Philadelphian too, I believe.

Under these circumstances there was every reason for the
performances to be excellent. They were. Orchestral balances
and the beauty of the soloists' tone-production, excepting for
some of Mr. Hardesty Johnson's work, were of rare distinction.
The choral work had gusto and some precision. It was rough
in timbre, but handsomely balanced and blended; and the soft
work was beautifully alive. All in all, saving certain inexactitudes
in the rapid passages, it was top-flight choral singing.

The size of the chorus and orchestra, though determined,
no doubt, by the space available for musicians in the Packer
Memorial Chapel of Lehigh University, is a good one for Bach.
Fewer give a good result, too, provided the auditorium is not
too large. More make a messy effect in any size of auditorium.
The chorus at Bethlehem numbers about a hundred. The voices

are mature and resonant. An orchestra of forty provides ample support without crushing the soloists. Really, both as to the manner of execution, the dimensions, style, and professional integrity of it all, and in the spirit that informed the renditions, Friday's Bach was something well out of the ordinary run of festival performances.

Of the works performed, two seemed to stand out as particularly rich and expressive, the lovely cantata No. 180, "Beautify Thyself, My Spirit," and the cantata No. 146, "We Must Come through Great Tribulation." The latter was notable not only for its fine solos and its touching final hymn, but for its lengthy and fanciful instrumental overture. Beyond all of these, of course, towered the superb and impossible *Magnificat*. Superb, also, were the soloists in this, all of them; and equally so were the flutes and oboes of the Philadelphia Orchestra. It was grand to hear so nobly rendered this noble and difficult work.

May 16, 1942

Sacred Swing

LAST SUNDAY I went to Newark to attend the evening services of a Negro congregation known as The Church of God in Christ, where Brother Utah Smith, a traveling evangelist of that denomination, was closing his engagement. Brother Smith is a stocky gentleman in the mid-forties, neither old nor young, whose musical accomplishments had been signaled to me by swing experts. He is known in religious circles as The One-Man Band, was so introduced, in fact, by the local pastor, or rather by his *locum tenens*, the pastor himself having been detained that evening by religious work elsewhere. His whole musical equipment is an electric guitar, his only vestment an ordinary sack suit of dark blue, with a pair of white wings made of feathered paper and attached to his shoulders like a knapsack by crossed bands of white tape.

His religious message is delivered more by music and dancing than by preaching. Only after the preliminary prayers, solos and congregational hymns are over does he take charge of the meeting. Then an open space is cleared between the chancel rail and the first congregational seats. These last are allowed to be wholly occupied, no mourners' bench being reserved at all, since the nature of the service is one rather of general rejoicing than of personal penitence. The Brother makes a few remarks to the congregation and then, without any formal address or other preface, goes straight into his number, if I may so refer without irreverence to his music-making.

He plays the guitar with a high pick-up that fills the auditorium with a rich and booming sonority. He does not sing. He only plays and, like all swingsters, pats his foot. His musical fancy is of the highest order. I have rarely heard such intricate and interesting swing. From time to time he shouts: "I've got wings! Dust my feet!" Persons in the congregation reply with: "Dust my feet!" with "Praise the Lord!" and similar ceremonial phrases, as is customary among many colored religious groups. Practically everybody claps his hands in time to the music, claps on the off-beat, as is also customary in swing circles.

The music goes on for quite a long time, the Brother swinging chorus after chorus with ever increasing fantasy and insistence. Various persons of the congregation who feel so inclined first edge timidly toward the edge of the open space and then one by one start dancing. Each dances alone, some with raised and some with lowered head, all with eyes closed. Some jerk a little; others do rapid and complex footwork. The floor sways with their impact as if about to collapse. When the music stops, the dancers come out of their trancelike absorption and regain their seats as calmly as persons leaving any ballroom floor.

At no time during my stay did I observe any licentious behavior or other evidence that the ceremony was not a bona fide religious manifestation. Brother Smith himself, though full of humor and jollity, and not without a certain naïve showmanship, impressed me as a sincere and probably a consecrated character. And if I was not conscious during my one brief visit to his services of any extraordinary or commanding inspiration in them, neither was I aware of anything that might make me think them phony.

In any case, his musical gift is real and his musical imagination abundant. I am, consequently, taking occasion this Easter Sunday to make a seasonal reference to what struck me as an interesting musical manifestation and to point an example from contemporary life of the truism that in those societies or groups where religion is most vigorous there is no difference whatever between the sacred and the secular musical styles, the consideration of what is sacred and what is profane in music applying only to the moral prestige in society of the ceremonies that it accompanies. As a swing artist Brother Utah Smith is worthy to rank among the best. As a stimulator of choric transports he incites the faithful to movements and behavior not very different from those of any true jitterbug. Myself, I found it distinctly pleasant to hear good swing and to observe its effects in surroundings imbued with the white magic of Protestant Christianity, rather than among the somber diabolisms and the alcoholic stupidities of the night-club world.

April 13, 1941

For Choral Music

NEW YORK has never been a major center of choral singing. Its musical ideals are instrumental, chiefly. Also, it is deeply suspicious of amateur effort. Explanations of all this are not hard to think up, the diversity of our language traditions being one that jumps to mind and the plethora of distracting activities that preempts our leisure being another. But the reasons are less certain than the fact. And the fact is that New York, though a first-class power in the orchestral world, is inferior to London and possibly to Berlin, even, as a producer of choral performance. It is only a little better off than Paris in this regard and far poorer, in the proportion of its choral activities, than secondary musical centers like Zurich and Geneva and Amsterdam and Boston and Barcelona.

For all the complaining that goes on in musical circles and in this column about the limitations of the orchestral repertory available to us here, our instrumental fare is richer and more catholic than our vocal. In the course of a season we get from concert and broadcast a pretty large selection of orchestral music, ancient, Romantic, and modern, most of it admirably rendered. We are lucky if we hear a half-dozen choral works properly presented in the same period. One or two of the Handel oratorios (usually one), a bit of Bach, a revival of something by Mozart or Berlioz, Beethoven's Ninth Symphony or

Missa Solemnis, a concert or two of Renaissance polyphony and maybe a modern work—this would represent an average New York season's choral performances with stylistic pretensions.

Obviously, it is not enough. There are other oratorios of Handel than *Messiah* and *Judas Maccabæus.* There are other Masses by Mozart than the Requiem and the unfinished C minor. There are many Masses by Haydn and two lovely oratorios, *The Seasons* and *The Creation.* There are masterpieces on the *Stabat Mater* text by Dvořák and by Rossini. There are a dozen beautiful works by Purcell for orchestra and chorus with soloists. There are religious pieces of the highest skill and poetry by Heinrich Schütz and by other German predecessors of Bach. There is the whole seventeenth century of Italy and an abundance of French material from Lully to Couperin. Surprisingly enough, there is a large modern repertory, too, twentieth-century masterpieces by twentieth-century masters, that makes a fine effect when properly presented. And then there is the opera.

Operas based on a choral background are hardly appropriate for the Metropolitan in the present state of its choral forces. But many of these could be presented in concert form, or even, with a bit of staging, by the singing societies. Purcell's *King Arthur*, with text by Dryden, Mozart's *Idomeneo* (though the solo roles are difficult), the operas of Monteverdi, Lully, and Rameau, the proud dramatic works of Handel, the whole Russian repertory from Glinka to Shostakovich (though the latter's *Lady Macbeth of Mzensk* is no longer considered *in motu proprio* by the Soviet government), and a dozen modern stage pieces from Debussy's *Le Martyre de Saint Sébastien* to my own *Four Saints in Three Acts* offer musical interest even without stage presentation. All they need is trained vocal effectives and proper conducting.

The conducting is available. Paul Boepple, of the Dessoff Choirs, and Robert Shaw, of the Collegiate Chorale, are choral conductors of the very first quality. J. Finley Williamson, of the Westminster Choir, and Hugh Ross, of the Schola Cantorum and Saint Cecilia Club, are highly accomplished chorus masters, though the latter is a little disappointing in public performance because of his rhythmic indecisiveness. There are other leaders and choir masters, too, of notable abilities and elaborate musical knowledge. Leonard De Paur, of the Hall Johnson Choir, and

Lehman Engel (both at present in military service) have done distinguished work. So has Arthur Mendel, of the Cantata Singers. And various of the orchestral conductors are effective in vocal repertory, though they usually require that somebody else prepare the chorus for them. Toscanini, Beecham, Walter, Rodzinski, and Smallens—opera men, all of them—have vocal understanding and lots of experience with choral works. Koussevitzky and Stokowski communicate inspiration to singers less dependably than to instrumentalists. Ormandy's hand with vocalists is unknown to me: I have never heard him conduct them. Alfred Wallenstein's is excellent.

I suspect that in the long run the finest renderings of choral works are those that have been prepared entirely by the conductor of the performance. A choir never sings so beautifully as for its own leader. The members will sing on pitch and in tune for another; they will obey him with vigor and all promptitude. But their work will not have the poetry, the personality, the expressive variety that it has under the man they are used to, the man with whom they have an accustomed spiritual intimacy. I think it is probably this habit in our big orchestral foundations of having in a choir just from time to time that gives to the best of their choral performances a certain lumpiness, a thickness of choral texture, and a lack of vibrancy in the expression that make these occasions less stimulating musically than the purely instrumental concerts of the same orchestral groups. Certainly the most sensitive renditions I have heard of works for chorus and orchestra have been performances organized by choirs under their own leader, the orchestra being had in for the occasion, or else performances given by orchestral or operatic organizations where a well-trained choir was part of the permanent set-up.

In the former category the annual performances of the Bach Mass at Bethlehem, Pennsylvania, and the recent performance of Bach's *St. John Passion* under Mr. Paul Boepple in Carnegie Hall are memorable. In the latter one belong the celebrated performances of similar works under Mengelberg by the chorus and orchestra of his own Concertgebouw in Amsterdam and an occasional performance of opera by some Russian troupe. Toscanini and Walter have given us massive renditions with the aid of the Westminster Choir, and the latter has recently given us a *St. Matthew Passion* of more than ordinary delicacy. But the best of these have shown a tendency toward the opaque and the monumental that makes for unfavorable comparisons between choral and purely orchestral music. Even the Verdi *Requiem*, which was certainly intended to be monumental, can lose by moments the acuity of its dramatic impact and become a bludgeon, while Bach and Handel and Mozart and Haydn and Beethoven, for all their grandeur, can easily sound (and not seldom do) more than a shade stuffy.

Now, choral music is not a stuffy literature, though the performances of many an oratorio society, including New York's own, may have pretty systematically given out that impression. Nor is the chorus an insensitive instrument. Indeed, it is almost too sensitive. It cannot be manhandled, like an orchestra; and guest conducting does it no good. But choral literature, ancient and modern, is as extensive and as beautiful as instrumental literature. Not to perform it more than we do is a mistake. To perform it the way we usually do is unfortunate. Our major orchestras should have permanent choral establishments. And it is preposterous that the Metropolitan Opera should maintain its own at so low a level of musical efficiency. Lest anyone suppose the loss of male voices to the military services may have created an insoluble crisis in choral circles, I hasten to add that the recent season has been marked by better choral balances and better choral performance all round than either of the previous ones during which I have reviewed concerts.

May 9, 1943

Musical Matriarchate

CHRISTMAS CONCERT BY THE TRAPP FAMILY SINGERS, *Dr. Franz Wasner*, musical director, with *Baroness Maria von Trapp*, yesterday afternoon at Town Hall, presenting the Trapps singing traditional European carols and liturgical songs of the season by Purcell, Bach, John Wilbye, and others.

THE TRAPPS are thirteen, if you count Dr. Wasner, their musical (and presumably religious) director. Papa and the baby, however, are merely exhibited; they do not sing. This leaves a musical matriarchate of eleven. And pretty impressive it is, both artistically and humanly. If it did not perform so well as it does, the charm of the *famille nombreuse* might cloy, as do eventually the Baroness's little speeches. But the ensemble is so neat, the repertory and style so musically high class that one cannot really mind the big play made for additional sympathy on grounds of family solidarity. It is rare enough, after all, that we encounter such excellent music-making in madrigal vein; it is even rarer to meet a family of twelve in which everybody is good-looking, good mannered, cheerful, and, to all appearances, intelligent and well. The spectacle of them would be heart-warming whether they sang or not.

They perform motets, madrigals, and glees in English, in German, and in Tyrolerdialekt. Also Christmas carols of divers origins and instrumental music for spinet, viola da gamba (without gamba), and recorders in all sizes. Their execution is well bred, modest, and thoroughly clear. They sing on pitch and play in time, never very loud, but always with full projection of the words and the notes. They seem to be *at home* with music as well as *en famille*.

They represent the ideal conditions of amateur music-making as well as I have ever seen these displayed. And the fact that they are a professional touring organization (in the business sense) does not diminish, augments rather, the essentially amateur spirit of their performance. Their voices are sweet but not brilliant, and their vocalization competent (in the dynamic range suitable to persons of gentle breeding) without being stylized. Their diction is the speech of intelligent, educated people. And if their expression is never passionate or dramatically exciting, it is none the less animated by good spirits, goodwill and a real tenderness about family relationships.

Maternity and family life are, indeed, the subjects they render with deepest conviction. And since the hallowed nature of these is what Christmas carols are all about, one can scarcely imagine carol-singing more touching than that of the Trapps. They are harmonious, very quiet, straightforward and wholly united at such moments. They don't go in for theatrical pathos or vocal effect. They sing the music and the words as sincerely as they might recite the Lord's Prayer at a breakfast table or build a toy manger for Christmas Eve. And so, in the midst of a gentleness

and a quiet that are dominated ever so lightly (but firmly) by
mother and priest, arises a sort of vibrancy; and the family unit
becomes a humming dynamo energized at once by the god
of domesticity and by the Prince of Peace. At such moments
anything might happen.

December 14, 1942

Harvard Fair but No Warmer

HARVARD GLEE CLUB and RADCLIFFE CHORAL SOCIETY,
G. Wallace Woodworth, conductor, last night at Town Hall, performing,
among other works, Holst's *Dirge for Two Veterans,* Thomas Tallis's
"Lamentations of Jeremiah," Byrd's "Justorum Animae," "Dona Nobis
Pacem" from Bach's Mass in B minor, Constant Lambert's *Rio Grande,*
the opening scene of Verdi's *Otello,* and choruses from Johann Strauss's
Reine Indigo. Soloist: *William W. Austin '39,* piano.

THE CONCERT of Harvard's boys and girls, for Radcliffe College is, indeed, a part of Harvard University, left many questions
in one's mind. Why did they sing six funeral pieces, for instance?
These were set off in the printed program by black lines, as if to
memorialize somebody; but no name was mentioned. Could it
be that these young men, presumably about to be mobilized,
were singing us their own requiescat, that those who imagine
themselves about to die were saluting themselves before us in
valedictory vein? One hesitates to believe Mr. Woodworth, their
leader and program-maker, capable of such a breach in taste.
Could it be that these works were intended to honor the recent
European war dead? If so, why not say so? Or were they thought
merely appropriate to the Lenten season? In that case, the operatic selection from Verdi and the utterly frivolous selections
from Constant Lambert and from Johann Strauss that followed
remain inexplicable.

Another question raised is perhaps more easily answered.
From the straightforward and serious style with which the
naughty French words of Strauss's *Reine Indigo* were rendered,
I wondered for just a moment whether the boys and girls really
knew about harems. Further reflection assured me that they
were most likely pulling Strauss's (and the audience's) leg,
rather in the way Eva Gauthier used to do when she sang *Alexander's Ragtime Band* and Gershwin's *Do It Again* in the best

funereal concert style at Aeolian Hall, back in 1922, holding a little black book as if to remind herself of the words, as was the concert custom of the time.

A third question was brought to mind by a study of the program's word book and program notes. The printing of vocal texts and of ascertainable historical facts about the works to be performed and about their authors is normal procedure at serious musical occasions. The addition to these ascertainable facts of admiring phrases about the works, giving us cues on why we must approve them, is neither good concert manners nor good Harvard tradition. Can it be that since the retirement some years ago of Professor Walter Spalding, formerly head of the Music Division, who opposed them firmly, the Music Appreciation interests have gained entry to the oldest of our university music departments?

These and like matters furnished more material for reflection during the concert than the music itself did. It is difficult to analyze objectively the performance of an organization with which one has been so intimately and so actively associated in the past as I have been with the Harvard Glee Club. I tend to opine that the Radcliffe Choral Society sings better than it did twenty years ago and that the Harvard Glee Club sings less well. Certainly the programs, if last night's was typical, have slipped a little.

Claptraps like Holst's *Dirge for Two Veterans* and Lambert's *Rio Grande* are all right to do, either of them. Both on one program, plus the *Otello* storm scene, in excruciating English text, plus the charming but frivolous *Reine Indigo* choruses, gave to the evening's entertainment an air of eagerness to please at any price, of apology for the high seriousness of the works of Bach and Tallis and Byrd and Dr. Arne and Francis Hutchinson.

Great choral literature needs no such apology. And if young people's passion for musical experience is today like what it was in my day (as there is every reason to suppose it is), college men and women seriously disposed to show us what they are doing up in Cambridge do not need to kid us along with all the folksy "production" numbers in their repertory in order to make us take their better ones. It is possible that musically Harvard is not what she used to be. From last night's concert I couldn't tell. But the program did raise my suspicions.

March 31, 1941

The Collegiate Chorale

COLLEGIATE CHORALE, *Robert Shaw,* conductor, last night at
Town Hall, performing modern British choral works including Harold
Darke's "O Brother Man," Arnold Bax's "Mater Ora Filium," excerpts
from Benjamin Britten's "Hymn to St. Cecilia," three songs by Peter
Warlock, excerpts from Sir William Walton's cantata *Belshazzar's Feast,*
Healey Willan's *Missa Brevis,* and Ralph Vaughan Williams's "Wassail
Song" and "God Save the King."

MODERN ENGLISH MUSIC is at its best in choral form, and
almost any choral music is at its best when rendered by the
Collegiate Chorale under Robert Shaw's direction. We had a
full evening of both on Saturday night at Town Hall, and very
fresh indeed it all was.

Mr. Shaw's full chorus consists of about a hundred and twenty-
five singers, as nearly as I could estimate. A smaller group of
about forty sang certain pieces. The full ensemble sings as precisely as the smaller one; but it has, of course, a fuzzier tone,
as well as a more powerful fortissimo. Music in madrigal vein
and texts of personal sentiment sound rather better from the
smaller group than from the large one, where the strength of
crescendo is out of proportion to such music's expression. In
massive works, like Walton's *Belshazzar's Feast,* the full effect is
most impressive.

Impressive at all times in the work of this chorus is its impeccable pitch. This is maintained by mixing the singers
homogeneously—instead of separating them into soprano, alto,
tenor, and bass sections—and by a discreet use of piano support. When the instrument is concealed behind the singers,
as it was last year in the Museum of Modern Art Serenades, it
is heard by them but remains imperceptible to the audience.
In last night's arrangement, which was determined by space
limitations, the two pianos were frequently audible in *a capella*
music. The effect was not ideal; but, even so, the advantages
to intonation were so great that one cannot regret their use.

The music performed was of high quality, particularly agree-
able to this reviewer being the pieces that followed the Walton
Belshazzar, with the single exception of Darke's *O Brother Man.*
The works of Bax, Britten, and Warlock seemed to me less

clearly composed than those by men not so famous. Walton's cantata, though not without its dramatic accents, sounded to me shallow, flashy, laborious, and, on the whole, less barbaric and sumptuous than its text. Healey Willan's *Missa Brevis* in E flat (performed without the Credo) appeared to me as a skillful and gracious work in the Elizabethan taste that would do honor to any musical or religious occasion. The Vaughan Williams pieces in folk vein for children were of the highest melodic beauty.

One man's preferences among eighteen works, all heard by him for the first time, are, of course, tentative; and they are not here advanced as reflected opinions. What seems fairly clear, however, from Saturday night's concert and from former acquaintances with Mr. Shaw's work is that this conductor is a musician of taste, high temperament, and no mean skill. I do not know his equal in the choral field today, and I have not heard in some years choral renderings at once so musicianly and so vivid as those produced by the smaller group of the Collegiate Chorale.

November 8, 1943

Renaissance Musical Grandeurs

DESSOFF CHOIRS, *Paul Boepple*, conductor, last night at Town Hall performing works by Orlandus Lassus (1532–1594), including *Providebem Dominum, Timor et Tremor, Lamentationes Hieremiae*, three German psalms, three settings of texts by Ronsard, three settings of texts by Petrarch, and three motets for two voices.

ROLAND DELATTRE, of Mons, variously known as Roland de Lasse, Orlando di Lasso, and Orlandus Lassus, was the most internationally famous and accomplished of all the Netherlands masters who ruled European music in the sixteenth century. He worked in Antwerp, traveled and conducted in England, France, Italy, and Germany, Munich being the longest of his residences, where he conducted and wrote for a choral and instrumental band of great virtuosity, got together from all the musical centers. His works, which number more than 2,500, are in both sacred and secular vein. He wrote with perfection in all the known styles of his time and set to music verses by all the most celebrated poets, regardless of their native languages, all of which he prosodized with ease and with freedom.

It is not every day that we hear his music performed. Last night's concert of the Dessoff Choirs in Town Hall, which was devoted entirely to his works, was consequently, by that mere fact, an event of the highest musical interest. It was additionally agreeable by the excellence of the chorus's work and by Paul Boepple's completely intelligible conducting. The singers sang on pitch and in rhythm and pronounced perfectly comprehensible Latin, Italian, and French. The French was especially good; I have not heard such correct vowel sounds sung, even by a soloist, all season. The German, strangely enough, was less well articulated.

The weakness of the Dessoff Choirs is the inevitable one of all amateur and semi-amateur groups. The sound of it lacks character. Its fortes are not brilliant, and its pianissimos lack vibrancy. There is nothing to be done about that, however, in a choral society that does not consist of singers prepared by previous training to sing both brilliantly and vibrantly. Neither is there anything to be done about the insoluble difficulty of rendering works written for male voices (men's and boys') with mixed voices. The mixed chorus is a modern social formula; men and women like to get together and sing. And they have to sing something. So the more cultivated groups of them sing the great choral literature of Renaissance times.

This is musical education for them and for those who listen. But the sound it makes is a far cry from the kind of sound it made when men and boys sang it. There is no possibility of making a dead social custom function; men and boys do not work well together in the modern world. Adults and children, generally, are enemies. Consequently, if we are to have a singing acquaintance with the greatest singing music in the world, the mixed chorus of adults is the only formula we can employ.

Nevertheless, a great deal of fine harshness is lost and most of the syncopation. For women's voices are round and breathy, compared with boys'; and their rhythmic attack is fuzzy. Also, there is no even choral scale from bass to soprano, as there is with males. The sex of each part is always audible, and the sonorities invariably align themselves as two kinds of sonority in rather the same way as a violin and a pianoforte never really blend.

This dichotomy is most evident in the four- and five-part writing, least evident in the massive ten-part scores and in the ten-part double choruses with interlocking chord-distribution. The two most impressive performances of the evening were, consequently, the Biblical *Timor et Tremor* and Petrarch's *Passan vostri triomphi.*

The final echo-song was fun, as all such numbers are, but musically less interesting than the more complex polyphonic textures. The much admired (in script) *Lamentations of Jeremiah* were thin by comparison and less expressive than ritualistic in their content. The Ronsard madrigals, however, were of a tenderness and beauty incredible, solidly fragile and sincere, like all good things French.

A fine evening it was, though a shade on the cultural side, full of good music (the best) and good ensemble singing. A fault of style deserves correction, which is the holding on to final *m*'s, *n*'s, and *l*'s by humming. This is one of those so-called "cathedral effects" dear to Anglican choir-masters, like the Stokowskian closing chordal diminuendos. It is unworthy of so straightforward a musician as Mr. Boepple.

January 28, 1942

Fa Sol La Fa Sol La Mi Fa

THESE are the syllables used by oldsters in rural regions of the South to intone the major scale, exactly as they were used in the British Isles long before Shakespeare. Indeed, the Elizabethan fa la la is no more than a conventional reference to the habit of singing any part-song first with the tonal syllables, so that melodies may be learned before words are attempted. So, still, is the custom in all those parts of America where *The Sacred Harp* and *Southern Harmony* are used as singing-books.

The former is common in Georgia, the Carolinas, Kentucky, Tennessee, Alabama, Arkansas, Louisiana, and Texas. It has been reissued four times since its first appearance in 1844 and has sold upward of five million copies.

Southern Harmony, published in 1835, sold a half-million

copies before the Civil War, then was out of print till the Federal Writers' Project of Kentucky, under the sponsorship of the Young Men's Progress Club of Benton, Marshall County, reprinted it in facsimile in 1939.

By far the most celebrated in musicology circles of all the American song books, since Dr. George Pullen Jackson, of Vanderbilt University, revealed it to the learned world in *White Spirituals in the Southern Uplands,* its usage among the folk is confined today to a very small region in southwest Kentucky. William ("Singing Billy") Walker, its author, considered it so highly that he ever after signed himself, even on his tombstone, A. S. H., meaning "Author of *Southern Harmony.*" Today it is used by about forty old people, who meet every year at the County Court House of Benton and sing from nine till four.

I went to hear the *Southern Harmony* singing this year, lest it cease to exist before another, though most of the ancients looked healthy enough, I must say, and sang with a husky buzz; and a handful of youngsters of forty or more seemed active in perpetuating the style and repertory of it all.

The style is that of all back-country vocalism: a rather nasal intonation, a strict observance of rhythm and note (plus certain traditional ornaments and off tones), and no shadings of an expressive nature at all. Each song is sung first with the Fa Sol La syllables and then with its words. Various persons take turns at leading. The effect of the syllable singing is rather that of a Mozart quintet for oboes; the effect of the verbal singing rather that of a fourteenth- or fifteenth-century motet.

The repertory is all the grand and ancient melodies that our Protestant ancestors brought to America in the seventeenth and eighteenth centuries. Most are pentatonic and hexatonic, many of them Dorian or Phrygian in mode. The part-writing is French fifteenth-century. There are usually three parts: a bass, a tenor (the melody) and a treble. Both of the latter are doubled at the octave by women and men, making of the whole a five-part piece. Since chords of the open fifth are the rule and parallel fifths common, the addition of these constant octaves gives to the whole an effect at once of antiquity and of the most rigorous modernism. Each part is a free melody, constantly crossing above or below the others; no mere harmonic filling attenuates the contrapuntal democracy. There is something of the bagpipe, too, in the sound of it all, as well as in the configuration of many of the tunes.

Though the words are always sacred words (often of high poetic quality), neither the *Southern Harmony* nor *Sacred Harp* singings are, strictly speaking, religious manifestations. The proof of that is the fact that they have never become involved in the sectarian disputes that are under the life of religion. Religion is rather the protective dignity under which a purely musical rite is celebrated. That rite is the repetition year after year of a repertory that is older than America itself, that is the musical basis of almost everything we make, of Negro spirituals, of cowboy songs, of popular ballads, of blues, of hymns, of doggerel ditties, of all our operas and symphonies. It contains our basic conceptions of melody, of rhythm, and of poetic prosody. It contains in addition the conception of freedom in part-writing that has made of our jazz and swing the richest popular instrumental music in the world.

To persons traveling southward I do not recommend the *Southern Harmony* singing as the best introduction to this richness of style and repertory. The ancients are too few in number and too note-bound, and the singing is far too slow for nervous city tastes. Easier to find on any summer Sunday and more lively in tone and rhythm are the devotees of the *Sacred Harp*. The style and repertory are similar, but the vigor of the rendition is greater. If possible, buy a book and learn to sing yourself from the square and triangular notes. It is more fun that way.

May 26, 1941

Wedding Music

WEDDING MUSIC is like children's books; it is usually most successful when it was written for some other purpose. The classic Mendelssohn and Wagner marches are no exceptions, since, though their original subjects are nuptial, their composers' intention in each case was theatrical rather than sacramental. It is probably their lack of specific liturgical meaning that makes them so useful. They express a happiness and a sweet tenderness that are appropriate to the occasion without engaging the

participants of it to any particular dogma or sectarian observance. They are used for Jewish weddings and for Christian
weddings, both Catholic and Protestant, their direct religious
significance being limited to the establishment of a general atmosphere of love and legality. Indeed, their association with
marital benediction is so firmly a part of life among the bourgeoisie of Europe and America that the convention of their
usage in this connection may legitimately be said to constitute
a part of what Mr. Thurman Arnold terms "the folklore of
capitalism."

Note that that usage violates all the most sacred pretenses
of the musical world. It violates the pretense that one does
not use theater music in religious ceremonies, and it violates
the equally sacred pretense that one does not "arrange" and
"adapt" the musical classics indiscriminately. The Mendelssohn
march, which is a part of the incidental music written for Shakespeare's *Midsummer Night's Dream*, was scored by its author
for full symphony orchestra. The Wagner Bridal Chorus from
Lohengrin is a choral piece for mixed voices with orchestral
accompaniment. Neither piece is ever heard at a wedding in
anything like its original version. They are played on pipe organs
and cottage pianos, on Belgian chimes and marimbas, on fiddles,
pantechnicons, harps, and concertinas. All of which proves the
pieces to be a sort of folklore, since no single instrumental investiture is ever considered, for nuptial uses, to be the authentic
one, least of all that which, for theatrical or concert purposes,
bears the signature of the composer.

Every now and then, however, some bride revolts, says she's
tired of the old things and wants a change. French composers
have always found a market for the composition of Marches
Nuptiales, but none of these works has ever achieved the world-
wide usage that the Mendelssohn and Wagner pieces have. In
the days when I was a church organist I used to recommend to
customers desirous of varying the wedding routine the organ
works of Sebastian Bach. Various of these are appropriate, but
two in particular I always found admirably suited to both marital
and funereal occasions. They are the Canzona in D minor and
the E-minor Prelude and Fugue known as "The Judgment
Day." These works are noble and churchly and serious. They
lack the tearful note that is so unwelcome at funerals and the

sentimental note that can so easily make a marriage sound silly, keeping present in the minds of all the sacramental nature of both occasions.

A few weeks ago I went to a church wedding where all the music used was by Mozart. Mark you that Mozart, though he played the organ all his life, never, to my knowledge, wrote a piece for the instrument.* The nearest thing to organ music I know of in his published works is a sort of Toccata for a mechanical clock. This can be played almost note for note on the organ and sounds extremely well. At the wedding I recently attended the organist had added some transcriptions of his own of other Mozart works. A part of one of the sonatas for violin and piano was played by a violin soloist with the organ. The famous *Ave Verum* communion motet was executed in the same manner, and divers Andantes and Larghettos from the instrumental concerted works were played on the organ alone. There was something from *Il Re Pastore*. The bridal procession entered to the March of the Priests from *Idomeneo* and went out to the triumphal Agnus Dei of the Coronation Mass.

I must say that in spite of the far from purist attitude shown by the organist and his clients in their employment of theater music for church usage and in their toleration of "arrangements," an attitude no different, after all, from that which tolerates the Mendelssohn and Wagner marches, the whole thing sounded extraordinarily well. There was a cheerfully festive note about it all that was most appropriate. There were joy and a refreshing loveliness in the music that no other music ever quite has. And if Mozart's ecclesiastical style may seem to some a little ornate for ordinary church services, its flowery grace is, on the other hand, exactly right for a June wedding.

Most curiously, also, the organ seemed to be as advantageous to Mozart's music as Mozart's music was to the occasion. One has long suffered from the nervousness and the general insecurity both of tonal balance and of rhythm that mark the usual renditions of this master's work. Even the greatest among our contemporary interpreters are prone to make it sound impossibly delicate and difficult. On the organ all that disappears.

*Grove's *Dictionary of Music and Musicians* lists, to my dismay, "17 sonatas for organ, usually with violin and bass, intended as graduales."

The instrument's steady tonal volumes give a welcome feeling
of ease and of security against which the characteristic exuberance of the melodic lines and of their ornamentation stands out
to great advantage. Nothing simpers; nothing flirts; nothing
says: "See how cute I am!" The music is as sumptuously florid
as that of old Sebastian Bach himself, and its harmony is every
bit as noble. In addition it has its own kind of matchless grace
and joy. I wish organists would play more Mozart. It might rid
the public mind of the idea that there is something essentially
fragile about this music, something nervously malequilibrated
and ill at ease. On the organ it sounds as solid as Handel; and
its animation, as well as its lyricism, is doubly delicious for the
presence at all times of a mechanically sustained wind pressure.

June 28, 1942

PROCESSED MUSIC

Processed Music

THE GRAMOPHONE, the cinema, and the radio are what make the difference between today's musical life and that of preceding centuries. The concert, the theater, the opera, the social dance, church services, military parades, and musical practice in the home go on much as they have always done, subject to influences no more radical than those that determine fashions in the kinds of music employed. The music that we make up fresh and use on the spot has probably not changed much in amount, either, though there has been some shifting around of the proportions. We support more symphony orchestras, for instance, than our grandfathers did and fewer troupes performing light opera. If there has been any change in the total quantity of music executed each year, that change has probably been an increase. But I know no reason to suppose humanity has altered in any marked degree the musical habits it already had at the beginning of this century, habits that have remained, saving superficial changes, basically unaltered since the year 1600 and maybe since farther back than that. We have, however, added to our lives a new habit: that of consuming music not made on the spot.

This music is never wholly realistic. The electro-mechanical devices by which music is preserved or transmitted all give it a slight flavor as of canned food. The preserved stuff, however, is nourishing and incredibly abundant; and one could neither wish nor imagine its abolishment. Everybody, as a matter of fact, consumes it in some degree; many use it almost exclusively.

This does not mean that processed music is completely interchangeable with fresh. It will sustain life, of course, at least for brief periods; and some of it has a special charm of its own, liked canned peaches, boxed sardines, and filets of anchovy. But for most people of high musical consumption it is a supplement to fresh musical fare rather than a substitute for it. Proof of this lies in the fact that in spite of there being a radio in every home and in nearly every drug store, there are just as many people as ever who earn their living by playing or singing in public. Nor has the sale of pianofortes diminished; it has increased, rather, since 1927.

The easily noticeable differences between fresh and processed music are several. Deformation of instrumental timbres is not the gravest of these, there being very little of it in what comes out of a really good instrument. Diminution of the original dynamic range is a far greater musical distortion. The limits between loud and soft at any given tuning are so much narrower than the dynamic range of a full orchestra, or even of a singer or of a pianoforte, that music which exploits a wide range of dynamic difference—Beethoven's, for instance—loses under any processing most of its build and emphasis. Music of a quiet lyrical character stands up better. Both these matters and their implications for culture are discussed in the published reports of Columbia University's Institute for Social Research. It is no derogation of recording, of radio, or of musical film-strip to repeat them. It is rather to the advantage of these media that their natures should be publicly defined.

It is desirable, I think, to remember that although the cinema is an art, a new narrative form, operating not at all essentially through an auditory medium but very essentially through the visual medium of animated photography, the gramophone and the radio are not art forms. They are merely means of conserving and distributing auditory art. The only device either of them possesses that is new to expression is that close-up of the human voice that makes crooning and soap operas so poignant. The cinema possesses two powerful and novel devices, the realistic depiction of natural scenery and the gigantic enlargement of the human face. No wonder it has become a fully conscious art in so brief a time. The mechanical means for conserving sound have not so far uncovered any comparable expressive possibilities.

Gramophone recording is like printing. Its function is the reproduction and preservation of something. Radio might develop into a new musical form, but so far it has not done so. And I see no new device of musical expression save the crooning technique which could serve as the basis for any musical form that would be specifically a radio thing. Consequently, for the present, we are obliged to consider these two media of communication as exactly that, as an enlargement of music's distribution, not of its expressive powers. Sociologically considered, they are new; but æsthetically they are just more of same.

Nevertheless, they are not quite the same as fresh music; and all the misunderstandings that arise from private or public criticism of them are due to a failure to consider what is different about them. Processed music may occasionally be preferable to fresh; but it does not sound like fresh music, and one's relation to it is not that of a listener to a live executant. It is like a photograph of somebody—that is to say, more or less resembling. But there is no communication between the observer and the subject of the picture. Distance is part of the set-up. And though many concerts are broadcast from places where there are a live audience as well as live performers, the private listener is no part of that audience. For him it is just another element in a far-away show. He cannot applaud with it and whistle with it and talk back to it and ask for an encore. He can only listen to the whole thing or else turn it off, take it or leave it as he would a book.

Now, since most families (and lunch counters and drug stores) leave the radio turned on all the time, another novel situation has come about. Never before has civilized humanity lived in an auditory décor, surrounded from morn till night, from cradle to coffin, by planned sound. It is harder today in the United States to avoid music than to hear it. Commercial music, folk music, art music, all day long they bathe us. Mozart and Schubert and Beethoven and Wagner are known to as many people as *God Bless America*. As cultural opportunity for all, this is a fine thing. As forced consumption of everything by everybody, it is a horrid thing. One used to have to work hard to keep in touch with the cultural tradition. Today educated people are obliged to immure themselves in order to avoid suffocation from constant contact with it.

This means that though a fresh performance of a classical or modern work is still a luxury product costing at least the price of a ticket, a processed performance of the same work is cheap as dirt and costs nothing at the time. There is, hence, a difference in the way we all feel about a processed performance. We may enjoy it either more or less than a fresh one, but we never enjoy it in just the same way as a fresh one. It is the same music, new or old, though it does taste somewhat of the preservative. What is not the same for us about it is its place in our day and in our budget. This is a new one altogether, not a replacement of anything but, for good or ill, an addition to our musical life.

May 16, 1943

Processing for Fidelity

PROCESSED MUSIC, as everybody knows, does not sound exactly like fresh music, though with good engineering at the source and with careful handling of a good receiving instrument, its final reception can be pretty convincing. Fidelity is the word used in radio and gramophone circles to express this convincingness. The highest fidelity in the rendering of processed music is not, however, a literal fidelity like print. It is a fidelity to sense, like that of a good translation. The actual sound that a symphony orchestra makes in Carnegie Hall or in NBC's Studio 8-H, even if it were transmissible intact to the hall bedroom of John Doe, Esq., would not be as convincing a rendition of symphonic sound as what comes out of the most modest radio instrument. Admitting, then, as I think we must, that the processing of music involves as much of translation as it does of literal rendering, let us consider for a moment the nature of the departures from exactitude involved in processing and what they do or do not do to music's sense.

A piece of music makes whatever sense it makes, holds the attention of any hearer, by the way its material, sound, is varied in pitch, volume, timbre, rhythm, and contrapuntal complexity. Processing methods deal imperfectly with every one of these elements. Low pitches, loud volumes, "dark," or non-brilliant, timbres, and ultra-complex rhythmic or tonal textures do not transmit as faithfully as high pitches, medium intensities of volume, bright timbres, and simple tonal textures. The reasons for this need not be expounded here, being largely of a technical nature. Technical progress in diminishing the acoustic limitations of processing has already gone far, however, and will certainly go farther in coming decades. Also, it is not only processed music that knows these limitations. Direct performance has its acoustic problems, too, as every musician knows who has performed the same piece in the same way in enclosures of varying size and different wall materials, not to speak of what happens when he tries it out of doors.

A good orchestra in a good hall produces the maximum today available of variation in all the elements of music named above, with the exception, possibly, of effective contrapuntal complexity. That seems to come off better on instruments of bright color with narrow limits of variation in both timbre and volume, like harpsichords, string quartets, and jazz ensembles not larger than ten. All such instruments and ensembles, incidentally, record and transmit beautifully. Processing reaches its highest fidelity, in fact, both acoustical and artistic, in dealing with them. And the transmission of their sound from studio to home involves no alteration of any æsthetic nature. Their music, recorded or broadcast, remains chamber music, which it does not always do when transported to the concert hall.

Orchestral music requires more translation. Volume variations must be reduced without destroying basic expression. The faithful rendering of high or bright sounds needs often be modified, too, in order to assure a credible rendering of lower or darker ones. And many complexities in the musical texture—of rhythm, of counterpoint, and of chord structure—have to be simplified. This necessity is due to an acoustic phenomenon known as "resultant tones."

Whenever any two tones are sounded at once the resultant, a third tone, lower than either, is heard at the same time. Resultants are less troublesome in direct performances than in processed ones, though their presence in large numbers is what limits always the effective contrapuntal complexity of orchestral writing. In processed renderings of complex music they make a sort of low-lying fog that will obscure the whole passage unless one alters the indicated balance of parts by picking out from emphasis one tune at a time and keeping the rest subdued. Leopold Stokowski, who is both learned and experienced in matters of processing, has told me that he is obliged to use orchestral balances far less delicate, for instance, when conducting Debussy for recording than he customarily employs in concert performances of the same music.

Since the acoustic limitations of radio transmission and of gramophone recording (by whatever process) are very similar, it turns out, therefore, that the most convincing broadcasts of orchestral music are those made from records. Real concerts, when broadcast, have a human quality, a warmth that is appealing and that often makes up to the listener for acoustical inefficiencies. Concerts broadcast from studios where no public is present are second in fidelity only to those broadcast from record, because the adjustments necessary to good transmission can be made without the music's having to sound well in both its processed and its unprocessed state. The least efficient kind of radio concert is the one with an invited audience. This has the acoustical disadvantages of the public concert without any of the warmth of the audience that has paid for the right to manifest its feelings.

This kind of broadcast is known by radio executives to be unsatisfactory. It is a compromise between the acoustical excellence of the pure studio execution and the comfort some conductors and soloists feel at having listeners around them. The invitational formula has been adopted in order to avoid taxes and circumvent municipal regulations governing places of public entertainment where admission is charged. For business reasons it may survive. But from the listener's point of view, orchestral music broadcast under studio conditions, or, better still, from records made at leisure under those conditions, will always be superior. The transmission of real public occasions is the only proper alternative.

October 31, 1943

Fantasia

MR. STOKOWSKI's musical taste has always been questionable, his technical competence never. This is as true of his work in films as it was in flesh-and-blood concert work.

What he does to dead composers' music is nobody's business. Bach's organ music is anybody's to orchestrate, though why not just play it on the organ is a question I find hard to answer. Beethoven's "Pastoral" Symphony will no doubt survive its Walt Disney accompaniment, scenes from life among the centaurs that include the mating of these with young and attractive "centaurettes" in flowered brassières. It will certainly survive Mr.

Stokowski's interpretative cuts and tempos. Tchaikovsky's *Nut-cracker Suite* and Ponchielli's *Dance of the Hours* have already been through worse. And Schubert's *Ave Maria* has long ere now served church organists as a pretext to exploit echo effects from the back of the balcony.

The only live composer represented in *Fantasia* is Igor Stravinsky. Being on the job himself (and with his musical rights well protected in law and equity), he got the best musical deal of the evening. His *Rite of Spring* sounded, in consequence, more like "legitimate" music and less like vaudeville than the other pieces did. Dukas's *Sorcerer's Apprentice* ran it a close second. Both had appropriate pictorial accompaniments, the first a sort of geology lesson, the second a Mickey Mouse on the story the composer wrote his piece to illustrate.

As a spectacle with music, *Fantasia* is no high art job, though certain moments have charm and others humor. Only the geology lesson to Stravinsky's fine score is in any way superior to the famous *Silly Symphony* of several years back in which Donald Duck conducted the *William Tell* Overture.

The novelty of the film, as presented here, is a system of musical photography and its auditive projection called by the Disney promotion department "thrilling Fantasound." (The adjective is apparently inseparable from its noun as in "Holy Church.") The science of reproducing sound through photography will no doubt survive this, we hope, not copyrighted baptism. Stokowskisound, if one must have a trade name, might better honor its godfather. For Leopold Stokowski, whatever one may think of his musical taste, is unquestionably the man who has best watched over the upbringing of Hollywood's step-child, musical recording and reproduction.

Alone among successful symphonic conductors he has given himself the trouble to find out something about musical reproduction techniques and to adapt these to the problems of orchestral execution. Alone among the famous musicians who have worked in films he has forced the spending of money and serious thought by film-producers and their engineers toward the achievement of a result in auditive photography comparable in excellence to the results that the expenditure of money and thought have produced in visual photography.

Musicians will thank him and bless his name. Producers may

have a few headaches ahead. Because once the public has heard a good transmission of music, I doubt if it will ever again be satisfied with poor. On the other hand, a whole new field is opened for musical commentary in films that may very well pay receipts in the future.

Artistic receipts it will certainly pay. And here is where the careful art of Walt Disney begins to show up in *Fantasia*. Not that it is any different essentially from his previous work. It is simply that a whole evening of it, combined with music that really sounds like first-class music, makes it perfectly clear that the integration of music with pantomime produces a far more powerful effect on the beholder than the accompaniment of pantomime by "neutral," or unnoticed, music can do.

The integration, phrase by phrase, of music with naturalistic acting and speech is going to produce lots of directorial headaches; but sooner or later it will have to be done. Thanks to Disney and Stokowski, it will probably have to be done rather sooner than later.

The system of multiple loudspeakers that has been installed in the Broadway Theater, though advantageous to good sound-reproduction and essential to the best, does not oblige composers and conductors to make the same musical uses or abuses of its advantages that Mr. Stokowski makes. On the whole, he was discreet.

It was interesting to note, also, that he has taken some trouble to secure a good fortissimo. This fortissimo does not sound much like the fortissimo of the best symphony orchestras. But the fortissimo of the best symphony orchestras rarely sounds very good, anyway. Its effect is nearly always one of strain rather than of power. Power is not lacking in the Stokowski filmed fortissimos. And if they sound more like an organ than like a real live orchestra, the answer to that is that an organ is exactly what a real live orchestra should spend more time and money trying to sound like.

November 14, 1940

Chaplin Scores

As we know, Charlie Chaplin, though no musician, plans his own musical scores, working through a trained composer. In the case of *The Great Dictator*, the musical direction is credited to Meredith Willson. It is to be presumed that the opening fanfares and such occasional bits as occur throughout the film that are not recognizably quotations are of this musician's composition. They are not very good; they are musically uninteresting.

What is good and extremely interesting is Mr. Chaplin's way of using music in films. His concept of its function has been clear ever since his first sound-film, *City Lights*. He integrates auditive elements with animated photography by admitting them to the rank of co-star with the poetic and visual elements.

He does not try to use music as mere accompaniment, as neutral background. He knows that a well-cut film can get along without that. Nor does he try to drag in lyric appeal by making one of his characters a music student who can go into a song if necessary. Unless he can co-ordinate music with the action in such a way that the two play a duet, each commenting upon and heightening the other, he leaves it out altogether. For the same reason he has hitherto omitted the speaking voice from his own characterizations. He has not needed it. It would have introduced a jarring naturalistic element into his far from naturalistic acting-style.

The Mayor's wordless speech, sounded on a trombone, in *City Lights*, shows one of Chaplin's best procedures. The dictator's speeches in semi-nonsense German are the same trick done with his own voice. His bubble dance (to the *Lohengrin* Prelude) and the shaving scene (to a Brahms *Hungarian Dance*) are a different form of musical integration. The first procedure is a substitution of stylized sound for naturalistic speech. (Note that when he is acting naturalistically he speaks naturalistically.) The second procedure is not a substitution; it is an adding of stylized sound to stylized movement, to pantomime. He has here introduced the straight music-hall turn he was brought up to, as artificial a thing as the classical ballet, into movies, the most naturalistic form of theatre that has ever existed. The result is artistically successful.

Mr. Chaplin has not made a complete musical film. He has made a silent film with interpolated musical numbers. But he has obviously reflected about the auditive problem; and so far as he uses music at all, his use of it is unfailingly advantageous. He uses all the auditive effects correctly. He employs very little naturalistic noise, for instance. He takes as a basic æsthetic principle the fact that movies are pantomime. Anything expressible by pantomime is not expressed otherwise. He introduces speech, music, and sound-effects only when they are needed to do something pantomime can't do. There is a little bombing in the war scenes, a strict minimum. When he belches after having swallowed three coins, he lets the coins jingle. But nowhere does he overlay the film with speech that says nothing, with music that just accompanies, with noises that merely express hubbub.

This is the proper way to integrate auditive elements into any visual spectacle, not to use them at all unless you can use them to heighten the visual effect directly. The Hollywood idea of using background music for its emotional value without anybody ever noticing it is there is nonsense. Because music has to be either neutral or expressive. If it is neutral, it has no expressive value. If it is expressive (in the same way and at the same time as the incidents of the photographic narrative; that is to say, accurately expressive), then it is not neutral. It is very noticeable indeed and must be well written and correctly integrated with the action. Nobody knows how to write neutral music nowadays anyway, as I have explained elsewhere.* Bromides are all that ever result from that effort. And bromides solve no æsthetic difficulty. They merely obfuscate expression.

There are others in the world besides Chaplin who have sound instincts about musical usage with films. The wailing Russian locomotive at the end of *The Road to Life* was a case of what music and sound-effects can do together. René Clair, too, has often used music and sound to advantage as substitutes for complete visual depiction. Chaplin has not included in *The Great Dictator* every device known to film art of incorporated auditive effect. That was not his aim. But in no other film that I have seen are speech and music and sound incorporated into

* *The State of Music* (New York: William Morrow & Co.; 1939), pp. 173–90.

a photographed pantomimic narrative with such unvarying and deadly accuracy, nor omitted from the spectacle so rigorously when no way seems to have presented itself for using them to advantage.

Beethoven in the Home

PHILHARMONIC-SYMPHONY ORCHESTRA, *Bruno Walter*, conductor, yesterday afternoon at Carnegie Hall, performing the following works by Beethoven: Overture to *Leonore* No. 3, Symphony No. 8, and Symphony No. 5.

THE PHILHARMONIC BROADCAST of yesterday afternoon, as listened to in the home, was a pleasantly domestic ceremony. Two Beethoven symphonies, a light one and a heavier one, preceded by a familiar overture and accompanied by those intermittent frying noises that my instrument likes to add to everything, gave the whole a flavor of church-going and of Sunday dinner with the preacher present that was in no wise contradicted by the edifying story about Abraham Lincoln that Mr. Carl Van Doren recounted so lugubriously between courses.

There is nothing banal about Bruno Walter's Beethoven. It is plain, sensible, eloquent, clear. And the tempos are all reasonable ones. I presume it was as a statement of faith and a proof of orthodoxy that he chose to begin the summer broadcasts with a full program of this music, which has been for over a century now the Credo and Gloria of the symphony-orchestra business. It must have been some theoretical consideration, at any rate, that determined his choice since there is no other symphonic music that broadcasts so badly.

If one did not know the pieces and could not evoke from the radio performance memories of what they really sound like, one would have strange ideas indeed about them. In spite of Mr. Walter's lucid exposition and the charming way he has of making solo instruments sing, Beethoven, heard over the radio, sounds disjointed and picayune.

The limited dynamic range that a microphone will carry has something to do with this distortion; and so, I imagine, has the placing of microphones. Yesterday, for instance, the fortes all lacked background, as if the violins were too close; and so the essential majesty of Beethoven, which comes from his constant contrasts of loud and soft, was reduced both by the radio's inability, at best, to transmit a really loud ensemble of musical sounds and by the fact that the bottom was out of these, even in their toned-down state. There was continuity in the rhythmic layout but no real strength in the dynamic pattern or any massiveness in individual chords. The lyrical passages came off prettily, as they always do in broadcast music; but the dramatic eloquence that constitutes such a large part of Beethoven's thought sounded puny.

Mr. Fredric March, who read for Mr. Van Doren Lincoln's farewell speech to his friends and neighbors of Springfield, Illinois, was funereal in the extreme; and his voice lacked resonance. I do not know on what authority he represents that great President, certainly no inexperienced public speaker, as pronouncing the *u*'s in *duty* and *endure* like double *o*'s. I do know that the gentleman who introduced the Beethoven symphonies, when he endeavored to depict the composer as a jolly little man just like you and me, sometimes gay and sometimes sad, did so on no historical authority whatsoever. And, of course, he had to repeat the wheeze about how the first theme of the Fifth Symphony is rhythmically identical with the letter V in Morse code, three dots and a dash. If that long E flat is a dash I'll eat a telegraphic instrument in public.

May 24, 1943

Music-Announcing

FAVORABLE COMMENTS received on a recent discussion here of the state of program-note writing have encouraged me to continue the subject. Particularly do the presentation speeches that accompany radio broadcasts of cultural music seem to me, for the most part, unsatisfactory. Printed notes for house programs present no novel literary problem. All they need is real scholarship and some care in the writing—in other words, a return to the way they have always been done whenever they have been done properly. But a proper formula for radio introductions of music has never been established; it still needs to be built from the ground up. And though such a building up involves, of necessity, a large part of proceeding by trial and error, it appears to me that there is already a tendency in radio circles to accept as standard practice far more error than is necessary.

By error I do not mean merely misstatements of fact, though these are numerous. I mean also every detail of material, style, and attitude that makes the framework in which music is presented appear unworthy beside the music itself and that tends, therefore, to trivialize the music. When an announcer tells us, as I heard one do recently, that François Couperin's *Tic-Toc Choc, ou Les Maillotins,* is a picture of bloodthirsty women knitting as they watch heads roll from the guillotine, that is merely a factual mistake. (It is really two mistakes. One is that the word *maillotin* does not refer to knitting but to the hammering of metal; and the other is that the author of the piece died about fifty years before the good Dr. Guillotin had even invented his famous machine for making decapitation efficient.) But when historical matter, even if true, is presented in an irrelevant context by men of uncouth speech and patronizing tone, it tends, I am sure, rather to offend the cultivated listener (for whom the broadcasts of classical music are, after all, intended) than to instruct him.

It is not desirable, I should think, that American radio speakers attempt BBC pronunciation, though I see no objection to the Boston Symphony Orchestra's being introduced in good Bostonian or to the Philharmonic's being associated in the nation's mind with cultivated New York speech. But certainly such informative matter as is provided with cultural broadcasts should be addressed to persons of the same intellectual attainments as the programs themselves postulate. Cultivated speech need not sound affected. Indeed, the use of anything else in association with distinguished musical executions can easily appear to a cultivated listener as both affected and patronizing.

How much talk really is needed with musical broadcasts is still uncertain. Obviously, the listener needs to be told what is being performed. Sometimes a further identification of work or author is valuable. Also, when the program originates at a public concert the intermission has to be filled up with something. I do not think lengthy explanations heard *before* a rendition are ever very enlightening, except when they recount a plot, as at the opera. Comment and analysis that take place *after* a piece has been played are, on the other hand, capable of being used by the listener as aids both to memory and to the formation of taste. I have always thought it would be valuable to hear the first part of a concert discussed by competent musicians while it was still fresh in everybody's mind. Instead of quiz programs that are nothing more than a game or of historical and patriotic diversions that are mere time-fillers, I should like to hear a real argument about the work just played, with fair statement of opposing points of view. I think some such discussion as goes on in a real intermission among real musicians and music-lovers would help any listener to form his own opinion and remove from the broadcasts of serious art music their present unfortunate air of being handouts from on high. In any case, by whatever formula this is to be operated, radio needs more of free discussion with its music and less of both tomfoolery and pompous exposition. The latter, especially when it precedes the hearing of the music, has a way of turning itself into blurb that is unbecoming to a serious musical presentation.

There is no bad will involved, I think, in the neglect by radio companies to observe the intellectual amenities. There just hasn't been time so far to bother about the framing of art in business establishments where the presence of art at all is still something of a surprise to everybody. But the time has come for framing to be considered. Virtually every first-class musical organization in the United States is now available on the air; and there are special ensembles, in addition, playing rare music ancient and modern all the time. Radio has long since surpassed the concert-giving agencies in the quantity of high-class music furnished weekly to the public. Real concerts, though a fine thing, are no longer what we musically live by. Processed music is nine tenths, at least, of every music-lover's diet; and the radio furnishes a big part of this. It is a matter of universal regret that the verbal presentation of it is almost invariably unworthy and as often as not ignoble. I have never encountered a habitual listener to serious radio music who did not deplore the way it is currently commented on and announced.

If my observation has been correct, if nobody at all likes the way music is being presented on the air, then some change in this may no doubt be anticipated. The purpose of this article is not, however, to encourage my readers in overhopefulness about quick results, but rather to remind the radio people of what we should like, of what most of the radio world itself, in fact, knows to be the next step in radio's amazing musical advance. Experiment all you like, gentlemen, with the dramatic form of your presentations. That is the way to find out a good one. But please couldn't you maybe right now establish some minimum intellectual requirements among the boys that introduce Beethoven and Stravinsky?

October 24, 1943

The Cultural Obligation

Iᴛ is a curious fact that the chief purveyors of processed music—the broadcasting and recording companies—though far from innocent of monopolistic tendencies in business, are less limited in their æsthetic outlook than the purveyors of fresh performance and in effect more public-spirited. Many of these latter are not profit-making institutions at all. The Metropolitan Opera Company, the Philharmonic and other symphonic foundations, the Stadium and similar summer establishments in other cities are, in theory at least, devoted to performing only such music as will raise the cultural standards of their communities and limited in that effort only by the cultural resistance of those communities. And yet the repertory performed by all these organizations over any five-year period, for all the good intentions of their backers and all the struggling of their conductors to enlarge it, is more notable for its standardization than for its comprehensiveness.

The processors, on the other hand, perform everything. They not only have a broader range of musical interest, covering, as they do, popular, folk, and art music. But within the field of art music itself their repertory is larger. They play everything the purveyors of fresh music habitually play and a great deal that these do not. The musical habits are less institutionalized, less bound down to the Classical and Romantic concepts of greatness. Their orchestral musicians are better paid, their conductors (at least in radio) are younger, more expansive, more alert. Compared to the opera-and-symphony world, which is weighted down by all the conservatism of a great tradition and all the stuffiness of its ancient but still very real power, the radio people who deal with art music are a lively crew. They are like an air force to the others' navy. And it is far from certain yet which should command their joint operations.

No box-office neurasthenia of a philanthropic trustee class nor any stylistic conservatism of elderly subscribers acts as a repertory check in recording and broadcasting. The public for these is not a unified group, nor has it any obligations to like everything. Its members are isolated and free. And the processors have themselves no musical prejudices. They give the public everything they can think of; and if any kind of music finds thus a response, they have found a new way of pleasing the clientele. Radio, for instance, doesn't aim to please all its clientele all the time—a narrowing purpose. It aims to interest all the tastes of all the population at some time or other during the week—a broad purpose and a progressive one.

The amount of excellent music excellently performed that is available to radio listeners in the New York region is vast. It is less vast in the middle regions of our country, where the local stations are less elaborately cultural than ours, the musical fare in those parts being chiefly what is available on two of the chain programs. In the western European cities, however, it is enormous. In Paris, with a quite modest instrument, I used to get thirty stations with no trouble at all. A circumference described by London, Athlone, Helsinki, Moscow, Ankara, Cairo, Rabat, and Lisbon, including stations both governmental and commercial, comprises every nationality in Europe and North Africa. Every kind of music—folk, popular, and art—is available in peace times (or used to be) from every tradition within this region, plus lots of American swing.

In the New York region we have the chief American chain programs—Columbia, NBC Red and Blue, and Mutual—plus five local stations of medium wave-length and seven operating on frequency modulation. Two of the local stations, QXR and NYC, are devoted in large part to broadcasting art music of the highest quality from everywhere, using gramophone records as well as performers for this purpose. Alfred Wallenstein's Sinfonietta and Symphonic Strings play year in and year out more music from the eighteenth and twentieth centuries than do any two other organizations in the world that I am acquainted with. Frank Black, of NBC, Howard Barlow and Bernard Herrmann, of Columbia, do a broad repertory and are friendly toward contemporary composition. All winter our Philharmonic, the Boston, Philadelphia, Cleveland, and NBC symphony orchestras are available weekly. So is the Metropolitan Opera.

I am not pretending that all this is equal to fresh performance. Very little processed performance is. Or that all the abundance of musical indulgence in the modern world is going to make better citizens of us. Because I don't think it will. Or that passively listening to music is a proper substitute for actively making it. I do not consider Radio City a nobler institution than Carnegie Hall, though I doubt equally that the contrary is tenable. I yield to no man in my contempt for radio announcers and in my private resistance to cultural paternalism in all its forms. The thesis I hold about processed music is very simply this: That the music available for consumption in any place at any time is the whole of music available for consumption in that place at that time. That at present the purveyors of processed music are supplying a larger repertory of art music to the lovers of same than any single concert-giving foundation is or than all of them together are. That for all their ineluctable ugliness as mere sound and for all the frank commercialism of their purveyors' motives, radio and the gramophone have a musical edge on the symphony orchestras.

Maybe these last are going to turn into just house organs of the radio companies and a pretext to rehearse for recording without paying the full fee. I hope not. For the present their repertory, their ambitions, and their outlook are smaller than those of the processors. Their chief advantage lies in the fact that they sound better. This is not enough. If they are to survive not as vassals of business but as instruments of culture, they will have to have a better program for culture than any of them is offering today. The Philharmonic long ago ceased to be a part of New York's intellectual life. The Chicago and Philadelphia orchestras do not represent to their intellectual communities what they did twenty years ago. Only the Boston Symphony still holds its rightful place between Harvard University and the Museum of Fine Arts.

What the Philharmonic will become between Artur Rodzinski

and the United States Rubber Company nobody knows. The former can be counted on to clean up the execution, at least, and probably to make the repertory make more sense. I fancy the commercial sponsorship won't hurt. It may even act as a reminder of the orchestra's national obligation to be something more than a museum piece. Certainly a similar sponsorship has not hurt the Metropolitan Opera. The nation-wide audience of music-lovers is, after all, both more receptive and more demanding than any merely New York one has ever been in my lifetime.

May 23, 1943

GENERAL IDEAS

Season's Impressions

IN the course of attending musical events this season as a reviewer, it has been a source of considerable enlightenment to me to observe the state of the musical tradition in the metropolis, in so far as that is capable of being observed through its public manifestations. I have in mind a more detailed account of all this than could be exposed convincingly in one Sunday article, one which could be perhaps the thread of several during the vacation season. Today I should like merely to state some general impressions derived from my attendance at musical events and from some scrutinizing of the programs and announcements of those I have not been able to attend.

First of all, the soloists. By far the most interesting musically to me are the pianists. These have, we know, the largest repertory available to any soloists of great music that is still comprehensible to a twentieth-century audience. They have also the largest variety of technical styles. In violin technique there is only good, less good, and bad. There are at least three and maybe five ways of playing the pianoforte, all perfectly legitimate and musical. This richness both of repertory and of executional form gives to the piano-playing world a musical breadth unknown today among any other group of solo musicians. Also, that world is less hermetically sealed against knowledge of other music than it has been in the past. The acquaintance with the conceptions of ensemble music, that of the large orchestra in particular, that is universal in our day has tended to encourage a more penetrating comprehension of the piano works of the great symphonic composers and to eliminate among pianists the merely facile virtuosity that still gets by among the violinists.

Among string-players the cellists seem to me the most vigorous. I think this is due to the fact that the technique of cello-playing is at present in a state of lively expansion. There are not enough solo artists playing the viola or the double bass to give their situation any general significance. The concert halls can be said almost literally, however, to be lousy with violinists. Many of these are superb technicians. Few present an interest as

267

interpreters that is at all comparable in either depth or originality with their technical abilities. As a group they are conservative
about stylistic novelty and mostly preoccupied with slickness of
execution. They are an unhappy group, in spite of their prosperity, and without much confidence in what the century may hold
for them. They seem to have no clear orientation regarding
their instrument's function in it.

Singers vary. The legend that they are mostly musical illiterates
is, of course, utterly false. It comes from the fact that success
in singing is still possible to musical illiterates. It goes on being
repeated, simply because the irony of it is amusing, although
everybody knows a vocalist or two who is a first-class musician
as well. Their public work varies, like their talents and their
education, between the sublime and the ridiculous.

Their recitals are among the most rigidly conventionalized
ceremonies of the modern world. The public is accomplice in
the maintenance of this rigidity. It has opposed itself firmly
to the execution of any vocal music with pianoforte accompaniment excepting short songs. Operatic arias, which used
to grace recital programs, are rarely heard nowadays in Town
Hall, saving a few from Handel operas that might pass for oratorio music. All attempts to introduce long works containing
a great variety of vocal effect have produced only momentary
successes. For some reason, the repertory of voice recitalists is
as limited and as conventional as is that of our major symphony
orchestras.

These last are troubling indeed to the sincere musical conscience. The WPA orchestras, the second- and third-class professional groups, the student bands, the amateur symphony
societies, present their musical results to the public without false
pretense and with a minimum of publicitary chichi. Some play
well, some badly; but on the whole the picture of their efforts
all over the United States is one of healthiness and vigor. Their
contribution to musical culture and its tradition is a real one
and far more important, I suspect, than is currently imagined.
The WPA groups, in particular, are indefatigable at playing and
replaying the music of our own time, especially that composed
in the United States. The major orchestras play comparatively
little of this and a still smaller proportion of the classical and
Romantic repertory that is the main storehouse from which

all their programs are drawn. Like the virtuoso violinists, they seem to be consecrated chiefly to the resurfacing of a few standard numbers. About fifty pieces form the basis of international symphonic repertory among the high-hat organizations. Even the much advertised resurfacing that these pieces are constantly being put through is not always first-class work. The great provincial orchestras are more dependable at this than our local Philharmonic is, which varies from marvelous to awful in a way that can only be explained by its lack during the last thirty years of a constant musical discipline and of a personified responsibility before the public for all of its concerts.

Conductors are a special subject in themselves and not as fascinating a one to this reviewer as to some. Their profound musical knowledge and their ability to bluff have both been overemphasized in print. They are for the most part well-educated musicians. Their job is to discipline and train an orchestra and to lead it in public concerts. Many try to achieve success in the second job without going to the trouble of fulfilling their duties in the first. They fail. Few fail who accomplish the first duty adequately. Because nobody can give good concerts regularly with an orchestra he has not trained (though a certain effect can be made guest-conducting familiar works). Whereas anybody, literally anybody who is capable of training a first-class symphonic band, can give successful concerts with the band he has trained, because public execution is child's play compared to the technical preparation of a hundred musicians to read together both accurately and spontaneously music in all the known styles according to the trainer's understanding of those styles.

The only difference between the operatic picture and the symphonic is that there is no WPA opera, no amateur opera, and very little second- and third-class opera comparable in vitality and excellence to the similar range of symphonic playing in the United States. There is some, but not nearly enough. First-class opera is virtually a monopoly of the Metropolitan at present. This organization is as troublesome to the sincere musician as the luxury orchestras are. Like the Philharmonic, it is sometimes excellent, sometimes perfectly terrible. Considering that the house is usually sold out anyway, amelioration or radical change of any kind seems quite improbable for the present.

Between the oversized Metropolitan opera and the undersized

and mostly amateurish chamber opera troupes, there isn't much opera available, in spite of the success in the last ten years of Gershwin's *Porgy and Bess*, of Blitzstein's *The Cradle Will Rock*, and of my own *Four Saints in Three Acts* at medium-sized theaters. Producers are not averse to the formula, and composers abound capable of doing any musical job successfully. It is libretti that are lacking, sensible dramatic works capable of being heightened by music and worth somebody's taking the trouble about them that such heightening involves. Neither the musical nor the literary world has yet faced squarely in our century the stylistic problems raised by the possibility of their collaboration. So that for the present we must admit that in spite of the existence of three American operas of outstanding originality (four if you count Hall Johnson's dramatic oratorio, *Green Pastures*), there is no local group of serious theater composers in any way comparable to the several groups of symphonic writers that produce annually reams of music that could only have been made in America.

As for composers in the local musical picture, they peer out from every nook and cranny. Neither France nor Italy nor Germany, not to speak of England, could show the world anything like the number the United States can muster of first-quality composers resident on her soil. The number of these who are native-born citizens is about two fifths of the group, I should say. That is a larger proportion of native-born among the quality workmen than France or Austria or Germany has ever been able to show at the periods when the metropolis and capital of each of these countries has been a center of creative activity in music. The American composer is doing very well, thank you; and much pleasant music of domestic origin has been heard in our concert halls this winter.

May 11, 1941

Singing vs. Crooning

EVERYBODY knows that singing is not what it was thirty and forty years ago. The beautiful memories people have of Caruso and Melba and Muratore and Garden might be considered as romanticized if gramophone records were not there to prove them right. It isn't that nobody sings that well any more; it is simply that there aren't so many as there used to be who do. Only recently Kirsten Flagstad was among us, and Elisabeth Rethberg did perfect work well into the 1930's. There is some pretty grand vocalism available on the operatic boards today in Paris, in the Italian cities, in Buenos Aires, and in New York. The art of singing is not lost. Good examples of it have grown scarce, that's all.

Everybody knows, too, that fine vocal organs are not scarce, that musical talent has not ceased to flourish, and that instruction in all musical branches is more easily available throughout the land than formerly. The mystery about the singing business is the fact that with all the talent there is around and all the studying that goes on so few singers nowadays ever arrive at mastery of their art.

It is the opinion of not a few experienced pedagogues that radio is responsible for our vocal decline. The dissemination by this means of symphonic and chamber music has certainly not lowered our standards of instrumental execution; and with equal certainty it has raised our level of musical taste, amplified our experience of skills and repertories hitherto difficult of access. But the microphone has toned our singing down for the simple reason that its own ceiling of dynamic power is a low one. And singing well depends on being able to sing out.

The human voice is a musical instrument (a wind instrument, to be exact); and, like all other instruments, it requires to be played both loud and soft. The pianoforte, the violin, the oboe, the flute, the trombone, the clarinet, and all the rest of them are mastered by constant practice at the extremes of their force ranges. Playing or singing mezzo-forte gets nobody anywhere, because progress in muscular control comes from working close to the limits, without overstepping them, of muscular strength. If one can execute a musical passage very softly with perfect evenness and very strongly with the same evenness, the moderate levels of power will give no trouble.

Formerly singers practiced this way, and when they sang in public they were always eager to show off their ability to sing both loud and soft. Opera singing was the crown of vocalism because it was at the opera that people sang the highest and the lowest, the loudest and (with a special technique of distance projection) the softest. Below this came, in descending order of technical mastery required, the oratorio, light opera, recital, and church. Everybody who sang anywhere sang both loud and soft every day.

Nowadays singers are constantly getting engagements on the radio. Even when they don't have such engagements they dream about them, because these often pay well. But radio singing encourages a different technique. It is of no value to sing loud, because the microphone can't take that. So the singers who work in radio during their formative years and those who practice with the radio in mind use their full power less and less. And since control in soft singing is largely a product of control in loud singing, both ends of the dynamic gamut tend to wither away, leaving only the mezzo-forte intact, since that is what is chiefly used. This is supplemented with a special form of soft singing that carries well over a microphone but that is not part of classic vocal technique. On the lower levels of musical repertory this device, which is a sort of humming with the mouth open, is called crooning. When employed at the opera, as it often is nowadays, it shows up as faulty placement.

It is faulty placement because it works only at a low breath level. It cannot take much crescendo without getting ugly. It is a special effect, extremely limited in musical applicability. It is also an insidious habit that grows on singers before they know it, and it often ends by injuring the voice. The reason why so few singers today can sing out their high notes good and loud without screaming or wobbling is that the crooning technique has crept into all their lives and falsified their production a little bit. This shows up first at the extremes of range and of power. There are various ways of singing prettily in the middle of one's voice mezzo-forte. But there is only one way of singing high or low at a maximum of resonance, and that is the correct way. All the other ways sound ineffectual, just as all singing that is not based on the constant testing of one's placement through singing every day high and low and really loud and soft (making all the transitions smoothly) ends by sounding timid, ineffectual, and amateurish.

I do not propose that opera singers should refuse radio engagements, though it is a curious fact that many of our best ones do not perform much on the air and that most of our great radio vocalists are disappointing in the theater. I merely wish to point out that radio, in this case, is not so much the disseminator of an already existing vocal art as it is the creator of a new vocal manner. It is also the destroyer of an old one exactly in so far as the workers in the new medium think the two singing styles are identical. The only way singing can be preserved as a great art that exploits to the full all the range and power of the human voice is to give to radio singing a place apart in the vocal tradition. It is not only a more limited medium of expression than public singing is; it also tends to exploit a low-breath production that is outside the great tradition of singing and that must be kept outside it.

It is all right to croon to the heart's content, so long as that amuses anybody and so long as there is money in it. But any singer who mistakes crooning for singing and starts mixing up the two techniques does so at the expense of his singing style. The future of classical vocalism depends on the recognition by pedagogues and by practitioners of the fact that microphone singing is another accomplishment. The two may not be mutually exclusive, but it is pretty certain that they are mutually contributory.

January 9, 1944

Tempos

NO ELEMENT of musical execution is more variable from one interpreter to another than tempo. No problem, indeed, is more bothering to any musician, even to the composer, than that of determining the exact metronomic speed at which he wishes or advises that a piece be made to proceed in performance unless it is that of sticking to his tempo once he has decided on it. Many musical authors, beginning with Beethoven, have indicated in time units per minute their desires in this matter. And yet interpreters do not hesitate to alter these indications when conviction, based on reasoning or on feeling or on executional circumstances, impels them to do so.

The truth of the matter is that very few pieces require to be played at a given speed in order to make sense. Serge Koussevitzky last season gave an excellent performance of the Berlioz

Symphonie Fantastique that took a good ten minutes more of actual playing time than Monteux or Beecham or Toscanini ever needs for this piece. Toscanini himself once angered Ravel considerably by sweeping brilliantly through his *Bolero*, which is not a long piece, in four minutes less time than the composer considered legitimate. I have heard the fugues and toccatas of Sebastian Bach played by organists at the cathedral of Notre Dame in Paris, which has some of the most complex echoes and reverberations of any building in the world, at tempos twice, thrice, and even four times as slow as those the same organists employ in churches of drier acoustic properties. They sounded perfectly well, too.

The reason why such variations shock us as little as they do is that speed itself is not nearly so expressive an element in musical communication as clear phraseology and exact rhythmic articulation are. These matters require, in the course of studying a work and preparing its execution, a great deal of thought on the interpreter's part and no small amount of adjustment to instrumental limitations—to practicability, in short. But once set in the artist's understanding, they are not likely to change for many years. They constitute the whole shape and substance of what is correctly called his "interpretation" of any score.

Within this pretty rigid framework he can alter speeds of execution, adapt them to unfavorable acoustic conditions, profit by exceptional abilities, play up or down to audience psychology, follow, even, his own fancy or inspiration about emphasizing certain aspects of a piece's expressive content. The more fixed and firm, in fact, his convictions are about a work's correct rhythmic articulation and phraseology, the greater his facility will be in adapting this interpretation to varying executional circumstances and the greater freedom his own temperament will have for producing an inspired performance.

It is of little value for young singers, soloists, or conductors to try to imitate the exact tempos of Pinza or Lehmann; Rubinstein, Horowitz, or Schmitz; Beecham, Stokowski, Toscanini, Koussevitzky, or Walter. These are not fixed quantities, anyway. What counts is their phraseology and their articulation of each phrase's exact rhythmic content. If one knows or has a conviction about the musical meaning of a rhythm—whether its reference is to a waltz, a minuet or a lullaby, a march, a tango or a jig—and about the specific characteristics of a musical phrase—whether it imitates the inflections of a voice, of a trumpet, or of a music-box, whether it follows the cadence of rhymed poetry or the free accents of prose declamation—tempo will take care of itself; and so will the pacing of the piece as a whole.

The greatness of the great interpreters is only in small part due to any peculiar intensity of their musical feelings. It is far more a product of intellectual thoroughness, of an insatiable curiosity to know what any given group of notes means, should mean, or can mean in terms of sheer sound. The composer himself is often less curious, because he works by more subconscious methods. He hears something in the mind and writes it down; too great an awareness of what he is doing will impede the flow. But the great interpreters are those who, whether they are capable or not of penetrating a work's whole musical substance, are impelled by inner necessity to give sharpness, precision, definition to the shape of each separate phrase.

The composer does not think much about exact speeds or exact volumes while writing down his thought. Whatever indications he may add about these matters—and some are fanatically detailed about them—are the result of later reflection. At this later point he is merely another interpreter. And like any interpreter who is fairly familiar with a work, he is capable of giving invaluable advice about its phraseology and its basic rhythms. Unless, however, he is an experienced conductor or executant, he is likely to imagine his adagios as taking place in an eternalized slow-motion that it is quite without the power of human breath or muscles to sustain and his prestos as being executed at a speed just within the ability of the human ear to follow.

It is not the purpose of this article to encourage interpreters in those violations of an author's clear wish or in those lapses from taste and discretion in general that the best of them are all too prone to commit. Neither is it to encourage composers toward any lazy dumping into the harassed performer's lap of interpretative problems that it is his duty to solve so far as he is able. It is rather my wish to recall to the attention of all musicians and music lovers the fact we all know but sometimes forget, that speeds (and volumes, too) do not offer half the expressive value to performance that a right and reasonable phraseology, a complete rhythmic articulation do. Force is relative; speeds are variable and contingent. But above that mere production of a reasonably good tone on pitch that is the foundation of all music-making, rhythm and breath constitute the fixed and indispensable framework for any inspired performance.

June 11, 1944

Transcriptions

WHETHER the transcribing and arranging of classical pieces for executional conditions different from those conceived by their authors is a legitimate practice or not is a question that frequently bothers music-lovers. Persons of refined taste are likely to disapprove it in principle but to tolerate it when it is carried out with brilliance or with some authoritative reference to the past. Stravinsky's modernization of music by Pergolesi in his ballet *Pulcinella* and the restorations by d'Indy and by Malipiero of the orchestral accompaniments to Monteverdi's operas, though anyone may question a detail or two, are nowhere considered to be improper musical efforts. To evoke the past in contemporary language or to reconstitute it in the closest resemblance we can achieve to what we believe was its original speech is, indeed, a triumph of musicianship.

What chiefly bothers people of taste is ignorance and the indiscriminate exploitation of the past for commercial purposes. Stokowski's enlargements for Wagnerian orchestra of organ pieces by Sebastian Bach and Liszt's reductions to pianoforte proportions of polyphonic church music and even of whole scenes from popular operas have never been considered quite loyal. Schönberg's orchestrations of Bach's organ music, on the other hand, and Mozart's reorchestration of Handel's oratorios, as well as Debussy's orchestral version of Satie's *Gymnopédies*, though they may well involve misconceptions about the character of the original works, are respected in musical circles for the purity of the arrangers' intentions. Each represents a serious homage from one man of genius to another.

Nevertheless, we cannot demand genius as a condition of music's legitimacy. If Beethoven was entitled to write symphonies, so is everybody else. And if Sebastian Bach can make orchestral or pipe-organ arrangements of Vivaldi's violin pieces, altering anything he feels like in the process, there is no reason why the Boston Pops Orchestra should be restrained from blowing up *Tiger Rag* to eighty musicians and tarantella speed. It is just a little comic; that's all. And it is more than a little absurd of Leopold Stokowski to have orchestrated a choral piece called *Adoramus Te*, ascribing it to Palestrina and using a faulty text. He obviously accepted the Harvard Glee Club's published version without question, when a telephone call to the New York Public Library would have informed him that the piece has been known for years to be a fake. (Though inspired from a work by, I believe, Agnielli, it is in that edition largely the work of Dr. Archibald T. Davison.)

Musicians mostly don't hold, either, with the popular practice of swinging the classics, though they constantly do it to amuse one another at social gatherings. And yet every age has forced the music of previous ages to obey the rhythmic customs of its own. I have never been especially amused by Miss Hazel Scott's so-called swinging of Bach Inventions, because it has always seemed to me that these came out less "hot," even by modern standards, in her versions than in the originals; but I have never minded the attempt. And I have found charming entertainment in an evening radio hour during which Miss Sylvia Marlowe at the harpsichord and some excellent jazz musicians improvise in the American rhythmic style on melodies from Haydn and Rameau.

There is so much that is merely habitual about the way we long-hairs treat the classics, anyway, that a skillful violation of all we hold most familiar not only refreshes the old repertory but forces us to renovate a bit our treatment of it. The quotation from a Tchaikovsky piano concerto in a familiar juke-box disk has not injured the popularity of the original work at all, though many young people who have first picked up this melody in a pub are surprised, when they meet it later at the pop concerts, to find that it is in three-four time. Beethoven's "Farewell" Sonata, Schubert's *Serenade*, and Rossini's *William Tell* Overture have, indeed, been transcribed, arranged, and misquoted so often that the correct execution of their original versions has come to have a certain novelty value in the concert hall.

Old music is everybody's property, and one is entitled to do what one likes with it. If anybody wants to play on the mouth-organ a violin transcription of Debussy's *Afternoon of a Faun*, as I once heard done in Town Hall, who is to pretend that this procedure is any different from the adoption in the twentieth century as our national anthem of a song about the War of 1812 that had previously been a drinking glee? Or from the adaptation by Handel and by Beethoven of their own works to different instrumental techniques and to wholly different expressive purposes? Or from the performance by Horowitz of his own version of Liszt's piano transcription of Saint-Saëns's orchestral tone-poem based on a song of the latter called *Danse Macabre*. Or, for that matter, from the playing on a pianoforte of any harpsichord piece by J. S. Bach.

All musical execution entails transformation, and it is not necessarily the part of taste to keep this minimal. Knowledge and skill and authority are valuable. But so is a common-sense approach. The two things most discreditable to any musician in dealing with the past of his own art are a degradation from commercial or ambitious motives of standards to which he has had access by education and the observance of scholastic taste canons at the wrong time and place. It has never accomplished much to have symphony orchestras play Beethoven's string quartets on sixty instruments. But the execution in the home of classical overtures and symphonies transcribed as piano duets is the very fundament of our musical culture.

June 4, 1944

Masterpieces

THE ENJOYMENT and understanding of music are dominated in a most curious way by the prestige of the masterpiece. Neither the theater nor the cinema nor poetry nor narrative fiction pays allegiance to its ideal of excellence in the tyrannical way that music does. They recognize no unbridgeable chasm between "great work" and the rest of production. Even the world of art painting, though it is no less a victim than that of music to Appreciation rackets based on the concept of gilt-edged quality, is more penetrable to reason in this regard, since such values, or the pretenses about them advanced by investing collectors and museums, are more easily unmasked as efforts to influence market prices. But music in our time (and in our country) seems to be committed to the idea that first-class work in composition is separable from the rest of music-writing by a distinction as radical as that recognized in theology between the elect and the damned. Or at the very least as rigorous an exclusion from glory as that which formerly marked the difference between Mrs. Astor's Four Hundred and the rest of the human race.

This snobbish definition of excellence is opposed to the classical concept of a Republic of Letters. It reposes, rather, on the theocratic idea that inspiration is less a privilege of the private citizen than of the ordained prophet. Its weakness lies in the fact that music, though it serves most becomingly as religion's handmaiden, is not a religion. Music does not deal in general ideas or morality or salvation. It is an art. It expresses private sentiments through skill and sincerity, both of which last are a privilege, a duty, indeed, of the private citizen, and no monopoly of the prophetically inclined.

In the centuries when artistic skills were watched over by guilds of workmen, a masterpiece was nothing more than a graduation piece, a work that marked the student's advance from apprenticeship to master status. Later the word was used to mean any artist's most accomplished work, the high point of his production. It came thus to represent no corporate judgment, but any consumer's private one. Nowadays most people understand by it a piece differing from the run of repertory by a degree of concentration in its expressivity that establishes a difference of kind. And certain composers (Beethoven was the first of them) are considered to have worked consciously in that vein. The idea that any composer, however gifted and skillful, is merely a masterpiece factory would have been repellent to Bach or Haydn or Handel or Mozart, though Gluck was prone to advertise himself as just that. But all the successors of Beethoven who aspired to his position of authority—Brahms and Bruckner and Wagner and Mahler and Tchaikovsky—quite consciously imbued their music with the "masterpiece" tone.

This tone is lugubrious, portentous, world-shaking; and length, as well as heavy instrumentation, is essential to it. Its reduction to absurdity is manifest today through the later symphonies of Shostakovich. Advertised frankly and cynically as owing their particular character to a political directive imposed on their author by state disciplinary action, they have been broadcast throughout the United Nations as models of patriotic expression. And yet rarely in the history of music has any composer ever spread his substance so thin. Attention is not even required for their absorption. Only Anton Rubinstein's once popular symphony, "The Ocean," ever went in for so much water. They may have some value as national advertising, though I am not convinced they do; but their passive acceptance by musicians and music-lovers can certainly not be due to their melodic content (inoffensive as this is) or to their workmanship (roughly competent as this is, too).

What imposes about them is their obvious masterpiece-style one-trackness, their implacable concentration on what they are doing. That this quality, which includes also a certain never-knowing-when-to-stop persistence, should be admired by laymen as resembling superficially the Soviet war effort is natural enough. But that what these pieces are up to in any musical sense, chiefly rehashing bits of Borodin and Mahler, is of much intrinsic musical interest I have yet to hear averred by a musician. And that is the whole trouble with the masterpiece cult. It tends to substitute an impressive manner for specific expression, just as oratory does. That music should stoop to the procedures of contemporary political harangue is deplorable indeed.

There are occasions (funerals, for instance) where the tone of a discourse is more important than its content, but the concert is not one of them. The concert is a habitual thing like a meal; ceremonial is only incidental to it. And restricting its menu to what observes the fictitious "masterpiece" tone is like limiting one's nourishment to the heavier party foods. If the idea can be got rid of that a proper concert should consist only of historic "masterpieces" and of contemporary works written in the "masterpiece" tone, our programs will cease to be repetitive and monotonous. Arthur Judson, the manager of the Philharmonic, remarked recently that the orchestral repertory in concert use today is smaller than it was when he went into the business of concert management twenty-five years ago, and this in spite of the fact that orchestras and orchestral concerts are many times more numerous. I am sure that this shrinkage is due to a popular misconception about what constitutes quality in music.

If the Appreciation Racket were worth its salt, if the persons who explain music to laymen would teach it as a language and not as a guessing game, the fallacy of the masterpiece could be exposed in short order. Unfortunately, most of them know only about twenty pieces anyway, and they are merely bluffing when they pretend that these (and certain contemporary works that sort of sound like them) make up all the music in the world worth bothering about.

June 25, 1944

Understanding Modern Music

COMMON BELIEF has it that new music is difficult to understand, while older and more familiar music presents comparatively few problems of comprehension. I do not think this is true. It is certain that in the epochs of rapid æsthetic advance there is always some time lag between the understanding of new work on the part of persons connected with the movement that produces it and the understanding or acceptance of that same work by the general public of music-lovers. Professional musicians and pedagogues, if they happen not to be part of the inner circle where such work is being produced, are sometimes more uncomprehending than the general public, even.

But this age is not one of rapid advance in music. It is one rather of recession. The great frontal attack on musical conservatism that is still known as Modern Music took place between 1885 and 1914. Its salient victories include the works of Richard Strauss, of Debussy, of Ravel, of Schönberg, Stravinsky, and Erik Satie. No composer has made since 1914, if we except the works that some of these same men wrote after that date, any impression on his time comparable to that made by these composers during the great revolutionary years before the other World War.

We have since witnessed the triumphal progress of careers laid down before that war, and we have assisted at the test flights of two minor musical movements. The first of these, characteristic of the 1920's, was known to its adepts as Contemporary Music and included two branches, the Twelve-tone School (seated in Vienna with an outpost in Berlin) and the Neo-Classicists, or School of Paris. A second movement (also seated in Paris) was the characteristic musical movement of the 1930's and is called Neo-Romanticism. It is exactly contemporaneous with the painting movement of the same name.

I call the last two decades and their characteristic movements minor, because they were occupied chiefly with the exploitation of technical devices invented by a previous generation. I may be underestimating the Neo-Romantics. Indeed, I hope I am, because I am one of their founding fathers. But the possibility that the progress of the movement may have been only interrupted by the present war rather than terminated by it cannot obscure the fact that the Neo-Romantics, like the Neo-Classicists before them, represent for the most part a novel usage of syntactical devices perfected long before rather than any notable discoveries in musical technique.

The gamut of musical device that was correctly called Modern, or Revolutionary, before 1914 is now taught in most of our schools and colleges. In any case, it is available to educated composers; and the whole musical public has been exposed to it for twenty-five or more years. Many of the works that exemplify it have enjoyed, indeed, a world-wide success. There is no reason why anybody in the music world, professional or layman, should find himself in the position of not understanding a piece of twentieth-century music, if he is willing to give himself a little trouble.

It is probably the fact that today's music is at least partially comprehensible to all that makes it so amazing to some. The habit of merely enjoying music without attempting to understand it literally is a comfortable one. And it is far easier to indulge that habit in listening to the music of another age and century than it is when music made in our own time is being played. Because, in spite of the worst will in the world, no listener can fail to penetrate, at least partially, a contemporary work.

The art music of the past, most of all that eighteenth- and nineteenth-century repertory known as "classical" music, is, on the other hand, about as incomprehensible as anything could be. Its idiom is comprehensible, because it is familiar. But its significant content is as impenetrable as that of the art work of the Middle Ages. It was made by men whose modes of thought and attitudes of passion were as different from ours as those of Voltaire and Goethe and Rousseau and Casanova and Heine and Lamartine and Victor Hugo were different from those of Bernard Shaw and Marcel Proust and Ronald Firbank and E. E. Cummings and Gertrude Stein and Mickey Mouse and William (if any) Saroyan. Not that these writers are always of the utmost limpidity. On the contrary, they are mostly either deceptively lucid or deceptively obscure, as is the custom of our century. But it is difficult not to find in ourselves, as twentieth-century men and women, some spontaneous identification with the world that they depict. Whereas the travels of Lord Byron, the private lives of John Keats and of Emily Dickinson, are as far from anything we have ever known as is the demise of Richard Wagner's Isolde, who, with nothing wrong organically about her, stands in the middle of a stage and falls dead merely because her lover has just died, who had got himself some real wounds in a fight.

These reflections occurred to me one evening apropos of a gathering that I had attended to hear some musical compositions by Stefan Wolpe. Mr. Wolpe is a skilled and highly original composer whose works have so far been little performed here, on account of what passes in professional circles for their extreme difficulty both of execution and of interpretation. In one corner four musicians were gathered together to glance at the scores of the music played and to discuss its nature and merits. That they all understood it both as to technique and as to substance is proved by the fact that they found themselves in perfect agreement about these. Four musicians who agree on practically nothing else in music not only thought that Mr. Wolpe's work was interesting and excellent (that would have been easy) but thought so for the same reasons.

Those same four musicians are irreconcilably divided about Mozart and about Sibelius. None of them would be capable of explaining in any reasonable manner at all a sonata by Haydn, much less of convincing the others that his explanation was correct. Their divers comprehensions of Schumann's piano music, of the Beethoven quartets, of Schubert, and of Chopin, though they might agree on the excellence of all these, have nothing in common. On controversial figures like Brahms and Berlioz and Wagner they could almost come to blows.

And so I got to thinking about what is called "difficult new music," and I concluded that there is no such thing any more. There used to be, I presume. It certainly must have taken more than goodwill and a mild effort of the mind for persons hitherto unacquainted with Debussy's work to accept and understand *Pelléas et Mélisande* in 1902. In 1941 there is no longer any really novel music. There is only live music and dead music, the music of our time and the music of other times.

Dead music is very beautiful sometimes and always pretty noble, even when it has been painted up and preened by the undertakers who play or conduct it with such funereal solemnity at our concerts. Live music is never quite that beautiful. Neither that beautiful nor that dumb. Because live music speaks to us all. We may not like what it says, but it does speak. Dead music, that whole Baroque, Rococo, and Romantic repertory we call "classical," is as comfortable and as solacing to mental inactivity as a lullaby heard on a pillow made from the down of a defunct swan.

I am not proposing its abolishment from our lives or from our concerts. No sensible person would wish to be without access to the history of culture. I am merely saying to those persons who think the music of today is accessible to the comprehension of only a limited group that it is, on the contrary, much easier to understand than the music of the past. Very few people have any real comprehension at all of the art of preceding generations, of what it is all about and of how the men felt who made it. Those who do have an inkling or two about it, who have made up for their own use a certain way of envisaging the relics of times past by applying to their interpretation facts and principles they have learned from modern life, are, of course, always persons who have a pretty comprehensive acquaintance with the music of the modern world. All modernists are not necessarily musicologists. I have known people who understood Stravinsky or Schönberg pretty thoroughly but whose knowledge of Bach and Beethoven was conventional and unreflected. I have never, however, known a person with any original or penetrating knowledge about the musical past who had not arrived at that understanding by first mastering the elements of the divers musical procedures that lay about him.

There are difficulties about presenting large quantities of new music in our orchestral concerts, but these are chiefly monetary. Live music requires the payment, for one thing, of a performing-rights fee to its author, which most dead music does not. More costly than this modest outlay is the rehearsal time (at the Philharmonic this comes to something like ten dollars a minute) necessary for getting a new piece into shape. These are not, however, unsurmountable difficulties, as has been proved during Mr. Mitropoulos's present visit. This skilled orchestral foreman has managed to prepare novelties for all his programs and to prepare them all, whether one approves or not of each interpretation, with complete thoroughness.

I do not pretend that the new works this conductor has been giving us are all of equal and certifiable excellence. If one wants guaranteed literature one has to stick pretty close to Shakespeare and the Bible. I am merely saying that the interpretation and the understanding reception of new music are not today rare or recondite accomplishments. Naturally, the separation of repertory into works we want to keep and works we want to throw away is a choice we are not obliged to face in dealing with the "classics." But that separation is a very exciting occupation both for producers and for audiences. It is what brings real life and occasionally real profits to the theater, to the movies, to the jazz world. Continuous opportunity for its practice at Carnegie Hall is the only means I have to suggest (and we have all worried about this) for restoring our major orchestra to its rightful place in our intellectual life.

January 4, 1942

Reviewing Modern Music

A MONTH or so ago, having been invited to address a group of students at the High School of Music and Art, and thinking that instead of giving them a speech on some set subject it might be livelier if I simply let these bright young people ask me questions, I found myself having to improvise on all the most fundamental themes of musical philosophy. One little girl asked if composers felt any obligation to "correct" the harmony in their free compositions. Another wanted to know how legitimate it was to arrange or orchestrate pieces by classic authors. The

most breath-taking question of all was: "What criteria of judgment do you employ in reviewing modern music?"

I seem to remember making quite a speech on that subject.
Also being reminded on my way home that I had omitted some
important considerations. Having reflected a little further about
the matter, I decided the best thing to do was to go on with the
subject in this column, since, no matter how many of my readers may disagree with my conclusions, the theme itself, which
is that of the relation of criticism to creation, is of interest to
almost everybody.

One demands of any work, new or old, that it hold the attention. In order for it to do this it must bear some resemblance to
something one has heard before. The obligation in this regard is
upon the listener, not the author. A person who has never heard
any Chinese music or any medieval polyphony or anything like
either cannot easily find a point of reference for following their
progress. Consequently the listener must ask himself what such
music most resembles among familiar music of the past and
among what he knows of contemporary work, if he is to follow
it at all. Such a resemblance may be one of contradiction. Music
that sounds consistently discordant, for example, sounds so only
when compared with music that is consistently harmonious, of
which it is the reverse image. The avoidance of conventional
"melody" implies, likewise, a stricter observance of the melodic
conventions than plain melodiousness itself ever achieves.

This kind of contrariety, or of "contrariness," as some would
consider it, is one of the classical procedures in Western art.
Music, the most traditional of all the Western arts, is by that
very fact the most frequently revolutionized, a constant violation of tradition being its most traditional requirement. Now,
nobody can violate a tradition that doesn't exist or swear off a
habit he hasn't acquired. Therefore the listener may rest assured
that however direct or simple, pleasant or unpleasant, any piece
may sound, its technique invariably constitutes some form of
attack on the kind of thing it most resembles.

The technical comprehension of modern music consists,
therefore, in the unmasking of its technical tradition. One must
find what it most resembles, both by positive and by negative
image, among the music of the past and of the present, before
one can have a very good idea about whether its traditional
observances and violations are major or trivial.

I speak first of the technical understanding of modern music because that is the first aspect of it the mind encounters. We know whether the mere sound of a piece, the kind of noise it makes, is attractive or boring long before we perceive its emotional significance, its message. An interesting texture is one of the most easily recognizable signs of interesting content. There can be no valid meaning in any art work that is expressed in bromides, because bromides have no meaning. That's why they are bromides. When a Tin Pan Alley hit-tune or an academic symphony sounds like all the other Tin Pan Alley hit-tunes or all the other academic symphonies, when they go in one ear and out the other leaving no sediment at all in memory's stream, we can be pretty sure that further acquaintance would bring little nourishment to the soul. The soul doesn't get much nourishment out of first hearings, anyway. But one can get a quite fair indication of music's inner nature from examining with the mind its surface of sound.

I put small faith in the "moving" effect of music as an indication of its quality, because our visceral responses are seldom significant and always capricious. The only rule I observe about my own is to respect their intensity. The force of any spontaneous reaction to music is more interesting than its nature or direction. That force is a product of traditional culture and of sensitivity to its violation. Violent manifestations of disapproval, as observed within oneself or in one's neighbors, are therefore another clinical sign that there is probably good stuff in the work that provoked them. An ovation may be only an expression of factitious excitement. A scandal is almost invariably evidence of quality. In any case, one has to be wary about what one merely likes and very wary indeed about disapproving of what one merely thinks one dislikes. Just as the emotions, being all alike, are only interesting by their intensity, music is, on the contrary, only interesting by its particular nature, its individuality, the differences between one piece of it and another.

The fact of the emotions being brought into play at all is of some importance, though not much. Love at first sight is rather the exception than the rule in music, as it is in human relations. What really counts in music is not attractiveness but style. Style is character, original variations on customary patterns. There is no style without tradition, but style is not tradition. It is a personal comment on tradition. It may be a rude comment, or it may be the gentlest of hints; but it must be corrective in its effect. From the composer's point of view, style is best achieved by forgetting all about it and concentrating on meaning, by saying only what one really means and by being perfectly certain one really means everything one has said. This makes for a functional, a note-by-note integrity of sense with sound that produces automatically a maximum of carrying-power in the whole work.

But though style, like happiness or success, is a by-product of efficiency and hence not a proper objective for a sincere workman, its presence in any completed work is a touchstone of that work's authenticity. Thus it is that the application of style criteria to the judgment of music is a legitimate way of estimating, or of beginning to estimate, the nature and worth of that music. Thus, also, since all real style inevitably contains a good deal that is novel, personal, individual to its author, it is perfectly correct to esteem in an unfamiliar work everything in it that is novel, fresh, original, personal, particular.

Let us not confuse reception with creation. Nothing is more tiresome and stale than work animated by a desire to be original or to play up what the author imagines to be his personality. An author should strive not to be personal; objectivity is the nobler aim. But a music-consumer, during the early stages of his acquaintance with any new work, has every reason to seize upon and to cherish exactly those aspects of it that reveal its indissoluble uniqueness. That a piece should please millions is a social and an economic datum, but it proves nothing either way about artistic worth. That a piece should please or displease any given critic, or all the critics, proves no more. That a piece should be, in even the tiniest way, different from anything one has ever heard before is evidence that it will probably bear further acquaintance. But before one can put one's finger on the elements of that originality, it is necessary to explore a little the range of traditional observances in the same work.

And so I suppose my answer to the question, and my advice to music-lovers bothered by the problem, is that the best procedure I know for sizing up new music in a preliminary way is first to identify it with all the music and all the kinds of music it resembles, and then to note the number and nature of the passages where the writing most radically deviates from its models. All such passages may thereupon be checked up confidently, I think, in the piece's credit column. Nothing goes in the debit column, because there is no such thing as sin or evil in music; there is only a lack of virtue, art being entirely a positive conception.

A procedure like this should enable one to describe a piece to somebody else with a fair degree of objectivity and to communicate something about its quality. In reviewing for print, it is only fair to add some indication of one's own prejudices with regard to the kind of tradition the piece represents. This enables the reader to take account of the critic's personal equation and to have, therefore, a clearer idea of his own possible relation to the work than he might have had if the critic had kept up a pretense of complete neutrality.

January 11, 1942

Getting Used to Modern Music

ON RECENT SUNDAYS I have exposed in this column my conviction that modern music, by which I mean all the music written in our time, is easier to understand spontaneously than the music of another century. By "understand" I mean whatever is meant by that word in anybody's English. I mean recognition, acceptance, and retention. I have also counseled persons wishing to make a preliminary size-up of new work, provided they have a fair knowledge of historical repertory and some experience at musical analysis, not to bother too much trying to understand its meaning but to seek out rather the exterior signs of its originality, as these are manifest in the actual style of the work's writing. It is obvious, I hope, that nobody ever listens to music entirely for its inner substance or entirely for its surface texture. These two aspects of any art work are interpenetrative, the technical and stylistic elements of composition being really explicable only in terms of their animating inspiration and that spirit being only finally visible through, and in terms of, the body specially built for its habitation.

Nevertheless, complete understanding is rarely accomplished all at once. The various elements of anything are usually best encompassed by temporarily abstracting them from their context.

Which of these one takes up first depends on which one is best prepared to take up. We prefer to leave the more difficult things for the last. Hence it is that persons not skilled in musical analysis often go more directly to the heart of modern music than musicians themselves. The musician's road, on the other hand, to a piece's central thought is always by way of its expressive means. Not till these have been encompassed and, as it were, understood does a musician even imagine he has an understanding of the whole work. The painters, the poets, the men of science and the men of prose letters, the philosophers, the political revolutionists, and the world of fashion have long been the bulwark of comprehension for musical advance. Even the general public of low musical literacy has shown less resistance to progressive tendencies in music than musicians have. A little knowledge makes anyone conservative.

Let us take for granted, as I think we may, that art is sometimes progressive and sometimes apparently retrogressive. I think we can agree, too, that there is plenty of pseudo-progressive art work around that is merely reaction *camouflé*. Also that history cites numerous examples of work animated by a strongly conservative spirit that has turned out to be at once a pinnacle added to its own or to some previous age's achievement and a cornerstone of technical objectivity for succeeding epochs. The Parthenon at Athens, the dramatic poetry of Racine, and the fugal style of Sebastian Bach are cases in point. Consequently, when I refer to modern music, I do not mean necessarily "modernistic" music, much of which is a pale afterglow of the great and original modernism of yesteryear, especially in this conservative decade; I mean literally all the music that is being written today or that has been written in our lifetime.

I also think we may assume that the vigor of any musical life is dependent on the constant winnowing out, among the work that is conservative and the work that is revolutionary, all the work that represents retrogressive tendencies, in order that progressive work be encouraged, understood, and accepted into that body of reputable music literature we call our tradition. Also that this process be speeded up by the employment of every natural sensitivity and every intellectual technique. For persons who are acquainted with artistic or intellectual advance in some other domain but who lack familiarity with the technique of music, I recommend non-analytical listening, which is what they mostly do anyway, whether I recommend it or not. And for persons capable of following music in detail, I recommend listening analytically to a piece they haven't heard before. Even though their analytical technique may bog down, I think a failure to attack along that line is intellectually retrogressive.

Now, the first group of persons operates more successfully with regard to modern music than the second group does, for the simple reason that the emotional acceptance of modern art work is much easier than its technical comprehension. Persons quite uneducated musically have accepted Stravinsky's *Rite of Spring*, as that is rendered in Disney's film *Fantasia*, merely because it seemed to them expressive of prehistoric life and landscape (as was, indeed, the composer's intention). And audiences composed of experts in modern musical analysis have been held in rapt attention by the works of Berg, Schönberg and others of the twelve-tone school without being in the least bothered by their essential meaning, simply because the mere following of that music was occupation enough to absorb the mind, and the discrimination of originality from cliché within the frame of that stylization a quite sufficient guide in judging the work's integrity.

From the foregoing it can be deduced that I advocate an attitude of goodwill toward contemporary music on everybody's part and a sincere attempt to digest it by whatever means are available to one's mental powers. I do not pretend, however, that such goodwill is universal. Roughly, its dissemination is something like this:

The ignorant are, on the whole, well disposed in advance toward all music. When they can't follow it, their attention merely wanders. They reproach the composer with nothing, the conductor or performing artist merely with failing to give a pleasing concert.

Persons who are highly educated but not very musical usually prefer modern music to old music. They buy tickets more often to modern than to "classical" concerts.

Managements have a slight prejudice against any novelty, ancient or modern, because they are not sure about its money-making power. Also because modern music requires payment of a performing-rights fee. This last, however, is no deterrant if there is confidence in the work's pleasing. Mostly they don't expect a modern work to please. They count its performance a goodwill gesture. Given a choice among new pieces, they almost invariably prefer the harmless and the insignificant to the incendiary or the in any way memorable. Managements, on the whole, may be said to be ill-disposed toward new music, though only for commercial reasons. If it's good business, they're for it.

Conductors, on the contrary, nearly always adore it. They have constantly been the arrowhead of its flight into the world, the missionaries of its propagation among the heathen. Rare are the leaders of international renown who have refused that responsibility and missed that cue to historical fame.

Pianists, violinists, and singers are well disposed but resistant. They can't afford to have much truck with it if they want to make big money. It is not as profitable to them as it is to a conductor.

Symphony and opera subscribers are very resistant. Their ability to analyze music is not, on the average, sufficient to enable them to get hold of it. They feel incompetent and hence inferior in front of it, hating, naturally enough, the cause of their inferiority feeling.

Critics, like subscribers, vary in their instinctive attitude about it in exact proportion to their ability to analyze its procedures. This does not apply to modern music work by work. One does not love a piece inevitably just because one knows how it is made. No, nor dislike it because its texture escapes one's analysis. I am speaking of a certain attitude of eagerness or of hesitation observable in any critic's approach to a new piece and verifiable by the average of his judgments. By and large, your critic, who is, after all, a form of musician and hence now wholly instinctive about music, if he depends on his instincts and his emotions for sizing up a new piece, is obliged to do so because his knowledge of modern musical procedures is inadequate. He can, therefore, be depended on, unless he hedges, to review unfavorably any new work that employs technical devices he is unable to follow. Your critic who is better equipped in this regard loves to practice his skill. You will find him regularly taking a more active part in the contemporary movement than his more instinctive colleague, who really feels most at home among the certified masterpieces of repertory and the sure-fire virtuosos of execution.

The moral of this piece is that although almost anybody (excepting, maybe, a musician) can get some communication out of modern music without half trying, merely because its author is alive in the world we all live in, any further penetration of its meaning or estimate of its value to the living musical tradition is dependent on one's acquaintance with the whole tradition, including the living part of it. Nevertheless, even without taking too much conscious thought about it, one can learn to swim by swimming; and that is why I advocate for all some regular immersion in the living stream. We can't all be pioneers, but there is profit to be derived from staking out a claim, however small, in those so-called new regions that have been opened up to musical habitation and investment for a good quarter of a century now.

January 18, 1942

Conducting Modern Music

THE PRIME CONSIDERATION in interpreting new musical works is to avoid doing anything that might possibly make these appear to be emulating the music of the past. Such emulation may or may not have been a part of the composer's intention, but playing it up in presentation produces a false relation between a work and its own time that is fatal to the comprehension of the work by its own time. Dressing and directing *Hamlet* as if it were a modern play is a piquant procedure. Treating a modern play as if it were Shakespeare's *Hamlet* can only make for pretentiousness and obscurity.

There is a prestige attached to any art work that has survived the death of its author that no work by a living hand can enjoy. This fact of survival is correctly called immortality, and that immortality surrounds the surviving work with a white light. In that radiance all becomes beautiful. Obscurities disappear, too; or at least they cease to bother. When I refer, as not infrequently I do, to live music and dead music, I mean that there is the same difference between the two that there is between live persons and dead ones. The spirit and influence of the dead are often far more powerful than those of the living. But they are not the same thing, because you can only argue *about* them, never *with*. The dead have glory and a magnificent weight. The living have nothing but life.

The glorification of the dead is a perfectly good thing. Indeed, the greater civilizations have always done it more than the lesser. But a clear separation of the dead from the living is also a mark of the higher cultures. That is the fecundating drama between tradition and spontaneity that keeps peoples and empires alive. Consequently no good is accomplished by pretending, or seeming to pretend, that a work by Igor Stravinsky or Aaron Copland or myself is a museum piece, because it isn't and won't be till we're dead, if then. And framing such a work among museum pieces in such a way that it appears to be subsidiary to them invariably makes the living work seem deader than a doornail. Its lack of white-light immortality makes it appear gravely inferior to the works on the same program that have such an aura and glamour.

The moral of this explanation is that new works must be played alone, in company with other new works, or surrounded by old ones carefully chosen, if one wishes to bring out their resemblances to the traditional past as well as their essential differences from that past. A new work may not be the most important piece on the program; but unless it is the determining item in the choice of the whole program, it will always sound like second-rate music, because it is pretty certain to be placed in unfair glamour competition with the classics of repertory. Modern music indiscriminately programmed, no matter what kind of music it is, is framed to flop.

Neither can it be interpreted in the same style as older music. Insufficient rehearsal often works to a new piece's advantage. When there isn't time to do much but read the notes and observe the author's tempos, it gets a neutral reading that is at least better than a false interpretation. If the conductor has time to work it up into an imitation of all his favorite war-horses or to streamline it into a faint reminder of Beethoven and Tchaikovsky, it is very difficult for the listener to hear anything in it but a memory of these authors, or at most a feeble attempt to dethrone them by being arbitrarily different.

The best international style for playing the classics is one that reduces them to a common denominator of clarity and elegance. That was always Toscanini's force as a conductor of standard repertory. He was never very effective as a conductor of modern music (and he avoided it whenever possible, for that reason, I imagine), because he knew no other way of conducting anything. Characteristic national differences, which are of minor importance in standard repertory but which are the very essence of modern stylistic comprehension, seem to have escaped him. And being a musician of too high temperament to be satisfied with a mere neutral reading of anything, he wisely refrained from taking on a job in which neither he nor the living composer was likely to do much shining.

The conductors who do best by the music of our century are seldom equally good at interpreting all the kinds of it. Koussevitzky does well by anything Russian and fair by the English and the Americans, provided these last are not too local in flavor. He is not bad with German music, adds to it a Slavic elegance that is sometimes advantageous. French music escapes him utterly, in spite of his many years' residence in Paris. Mitropoulos is at his best with the central-European styles. Beecham is fine for English music, for all Slavic, for some German, for anything that has lyric afflatus or rhythmic punch. The Germans are rather messy when they play German music—always were, as Richard Wagner pointed out. Some are excellent with French music, however, Furtwängler, for instance, and Stock, of Chicago. Italians do not always do their best by Italian works, especially those of strong French influence, though they do beautifully by anything Germanic, even Brahms. Only the French (and a few Germans) make sense with French music. Nobody, literally nobody, who has not passed his formative adolescent years in this country ever conducts American music with complete intelligibility.

The basis of American musical thought is a special approach to rhythm. Underneath everything is a continuity of short quantities all equal in length and in percussive articulation. These are not always articulated, but they must always be understood. If for any expressive reason one alters the flow of them temporarily, they must start up again exactly as before, once the expressive alteration is terminated. In order to make the whole thing clear, all instruments, string and wind, must play with a clean, slightly percussive attack. This attack must never be sacrificed for the sake of a beautiful tone or even for pitch accuracy, because it is more important than either. Besides, once a steady rhythm is established, the music plays itself; pitch and sonorities adjust themselves automatically; as in a good jazz band the whole takes on an air of completeness.

French music is the nearest thing in Europe to our music, because French rhythm, like ours, is less accentual than quantitative. Keeping down-beats out of a Debussy rendition, for instance, is virtually impossible to anybody but a Frenchman. Steady quantities, a little longer than ours and requiring no percussive definition at all, are its rhythmic foundation. Definition is achieved by a leisurely breathing between phrases and an almost imperceptible waiting before attacking, with no added force, what in any other music would be played as a down-beat. As with American music, a proper rhythm is cardinal and must be achieved before the pitch and the tone-production can be polished up.

Modern German music is not very interesting rhythmically. It needs no exact quantities, only a thwacking down-beat. Even that can be advanced or held back, as is the Viennese custom, to express sentiment. What is most important is to get the harmony right, for pitch is all-important to the German mind. Get the harmony right and don't go *too* sentimental. Nothing else counts, provided care for the harmony includes a clear plotting out of the key-relations in the whole piece. This means being sure there is always plenty of bass at the piece's joints.

Russian music is an alternation of very free rhythms with rigid and insistent ones. The latter are easy to render. But few conductors ever take enough liberties with the sentimental passages. English formulas are always closely related to the Russian (*vide* the English novel and the English Church). In music, both peoples conceive of rhythm as either non-existent or quite inflexible. Both observe beat-rhythms, too, not quantities. And both alternate speech inflections with footwork, as in a song-and-dance. The chief difference between them is that the Russian mind dramatizes itself with a grandiloquent simplicity, whereas the English tradition values a more intimate and personal kind of forthrightness in the expression of tender thought. The grander passages of both repertories may be rendered with the utmost of pomp and of panache.

Matters like these seem to me more important to restate than international æsthetic principles. All conductors know nowadays what the Neo-Classic style is all about. Also the Neo-Romantic style and the twelve-tone syntax. And certainly the survivals of late Romanticism are not difficult to decipher. But these are the stylistic elements that underlie all modern music; they have been written about *ad infinitum* and *ad nauseam*. What I am pointing out is that underneath these international tendencies and observances there are ethnic differences that must be taken account of. Also to remind my readers that these ethnic differences preclude the possibility that conductors of foreign upbringing now resident among us will play a leading role in our present musical expansion. They render great service by their constant acts of goodwill toward home-made music. But they have only the vaguest idea of what it's all about. And so has that part of our musical public that hears it only through their well-intentioned but unconvincing renditions.

January 25, 1942

Music's Renewal

THE IDEA that theater music—the opera and the ballet—is inferior to the concert forms is a nineteenth-century German heresy that seems to be dying out as the whole German tradition breaks up. It is an idea that never spread far in France or in Russia and that never even penetrated at all into Italy. Indeed, the opposite has always been Italian belief. Verdi referred to Mozart, we are told, with some disdain as a "quartet-writer." Even in Germanic regions the theatrical forms bore a major prestige till well into the last century. It is probably the clear absence of theatrical gift in Beethoven and Schubert and Schumann and Mendelssohn and Brahms that led the central Europeans and their Anglo-Saxon pupils to build up a certain prejudice against music written for dramatic collaboration.

The career of Richard Wagner, instead of contradicting this prejudice, seems to have encouraged its spread. Gifted with as marked a genius for personal propaganda as for music itself, this remarkable man wrote many articles and several books to prove that all theater music since Gluck was inferior to his. He explained his own works away by refusing to admit they were operas. He invented the word *Musikdrama* for them; and he maintained to his dying day that they had nothing to do with anything we know as opera, that, on the contrary, they were a development of the Beethoven symphony. In my own youth there were still serious German musicians around who believed all opera except the Wagnerian to be a sort of light-hearted musical diversion suitable enough for the Latin mind but lacking both in musical interest and in profundity of expression.

This attitude toward the theater has brought German musicians to an impasse. By failing to center their attention on lyrical declamation and bodily gesture they have cut themselves off from the generative sources of melody and of rhythm. By counting on harmonic complexity as a chief means of expression they have sacrificed emphasis and coherence (which it is harmony's first function to support) to a secondary harmonic function and one incapable of sustaining complete interest. As a result the best German music of today—that of Hindemith, of Berg, and of Schönberg—is complex in manner out of all proportion to the meaning expressed.

It is to be hoped that America's present interest in the musical theater will serve to eradicate from our thinking once and for all whatever traces of the Germanic heresy may remain. Composers must write lots of operas and lots of ballets, and these must be performed. Musical authors must learn by lots of practice to express feeling through song alone and bodily motion through rhythm. Complexities for their own sake of harmony and of instrumentation are the bunk; anybody can learn to do them. They chiefly serve nowadays to conceal a lack of precise expression. Let the writers of music give us correct English declamation in cadences that can really be sung and the clear expression of unequivocal sentiments in melodies that mean what the play means; let them give us harmony that makes some kind of acoustical emphasis, and rhythms that can really be danced, or at least moved around to; and the whole art of music will take on new life.

At present the music world is clinging to an immediate past that becomes every year more recondite. There are a thousand refinements in the late Romantic and early modern styles that make no sense at all any more. The writing of music has become everywhere a foolishly complicated business. Among the

Germans it has reached a point of Byzantine elaboration from which it can only fall, as their sonorities fall upon the ear, with a thud. Music's renewal will probably take place on this continent, where the ancient skills are less ingrown than they are in Europe. We listen to lots of elaborate symphonic music, I must say; it has become popular entertainment second only to the cinema in appeal and far more generally enjoyed than the spoken theater. But it is its very popularity that may prevent us eventually from taking symphonic music too seriously. What we need, anyway, is not less of that but more of opera and ballet; and that is what we are apparently going to have after the war. That, too, is what will cure us, if anything will, of our unhealthy attachment to a dying tradition.

Opera and ballet deal with prime elements in human expression—namely, the human voice and the human body. They deal also with precise meaning. Not only are these the broad stream of musical art; they are its fountain head as well. Because way back in the mind, where music gets born, it has a closer concordance with language and with gesture than it can ever possibly have with the obscure movements of the viscera or with states of the soul.

January 16, 1944

The French Style

THE FRENCH STYLE of musical execution, like the French school of composition, is a little bit different from all the others. Central-European artists have been for a century now such a standard article of exportation—the Italian, the Slavic, and the British virtuosos being merely colorful variants of the model— that it is something of a shock to encounter first-class French artistry in phalanx and to realize how far removed it is in basic musical concepts from the rest of Europe. This does not mean that France is in divergence from the main stem of our musical thought. On the contrary, France in our century is closer to the great tradition than the rest of Europe is. The pianism of Robert Casadesus, the flute-playing of René Le Roy, the keyboard execution on both the harpsichord and the pianoforte of Wanda Landowska, the vocal interpretations of Jennie Tourel are not

accidental phenomena. They are the products of a musical tradition more ancient, more sophisticated, and more continuous
than anything available elsewhere in the Western world.

The life of French music has always been its rhythm, just as
that of Italian has always been its cantilena and that of German
its harmonic architecture. This rhythm is of two kinds, verbal
and muscular. The first is derived from declamation and represents a pattern of varied tonal lengths. Accents, or stresses, may
be composed with this; but the quantitative pattern can exist,
and often does, without any pulsation at all, any down-beat,
being present. The second is a pattern of varied stresses within
an unvarying pulsation. Both kinds of rhythm are likely to be
present simultaneously in classical music.

The jerky rhythm that Sebastian Bach cultivated under the
name of the "*stile francese*," a steady alternation of dotted
quarter-notes with sixteenths, is derived from French tragic
declamation and its musical counterpart, the French opera, the
short notes representing a quick movement of the actor's arm
or wrist as he adds a visual accent to the phrasing of his poetic
syllables. To render this jerk as a measured sixteenth-note is
incorrect, because it represents a gesture, not a verbal quantity.
It must be short, like an ornamental drum tap. So rendered,
many of the movements from the Brandenburg concertos and
from Bach's keyboard works lose the unfortunate resemblance
to the chugging of a model-T Ford that we have so long associated with them and take on that grandeur at once statuesque
and animated that was beloved of the Baroque age.

Similarly, the playing of a dotted quarter-note rhythm against
one in triplets, which one finds so frequently in the music of that
time, becomes intelligible to the ear only when the jerky rhythm
is exaggerated and made to stand thus in relief against the rigidity of the other. Madame Landowska's and Mr. Le Roy's correct
renderings of these formulas are not mere refinements of style.
They are simply musical sense. So is Miss Tourel's happy integration of real words with vowel vocalism. These artists do not
evoke the past through a haze of romantic poesy; they give us
the real article, or as much as it is possible to have, authentically
backed up by modern scholarship and by a tradition of rhythmic
discrimination that in France has never died.

It was Beethoven who first among the great masters of music

made a serious effort to introduce rhythmic and dynamic ex-actitude into musical notation. And it was Berlioz who elabo-rated these efforts into the modern French practice of putting everything down in black and white just as one wishes it to be heard. An orchestral score of Chabrier or of Debussy or Ravel or Stravinsky is as accurate a project as any architect's blue-print. If it is still incomplete in certain respects, that is because musical notation is still incompetent to distinguish completely between quantitative and pulsating rhythmic patterns. Never-theless, French musicians, just as they take greater liberties with old music than persons do who are not acquainted with the real meanings behind old notational inexactitudes, are more scrupu-lous than others about reading modern scores literally.

The French conservatory training in *solfège* is the most rigor-ous in the world. It teaches meter as a basic pattern of quantities and analyzes any passage into the smallest time units present in that passage. If there is a conflict among small units, a still smaller one is adopted, until the lowest common multiple is reached. The measure (or bar) is considered to be nothing more than a practical grouping of these values for convenience in en-semble playing. No down-beat is given stress unless the metrical formation of the whole passage seems to suggest a clear refer-ence to one of the pulsating dance rhythms. No dynamic, color-istic, or sentimental expression is added that is not requested by the author or, in the opinion of the executant, logically implied by his indications. A reasonable breath between phrases is con-sidered legitimate and, in most cases, desirable.

This is the sort of impersonal procedure that gives to French solo execution on the lower levels of mastery an air of childish incompetence and on the higher levels a breadth as of the clas-sical humanities. The central-European style, for all its grand afflatus, is elementary in comparison and really only works with music of the Romantic period. It is excellent for revealing the dramas of the lonely soul, but delicate sensuality and high in-tellectual content are beyond the scope of its rhythmic under-standing. Those who have heard the recent performances of old music by Le Roy and by Landowska have recognized in these artists something deeper than a preoccupation with prettiness or with the memory of passion, something broader and cleaner and more humane. And those who heard the playing lately at one of the Modern Museum Serenades of Debussy's Sonata for flute, harp, and viola by Messrs. Le Roy, Salzedo and Brieff witnessed a comparable achievement in modern music. Indeed, the elaboration of that work itself and the equally elaborate perfection of its performance represent not only a triumph of French music-writing and executional technique but a rare manifestation of the higher human faculties.

It is a principle of French thought that analysis and reflection are not inimical to spontaneity, that art, indeed, represents all these collaborating toward a single action. It has long been the practice of American music schools to neglect the training of students in rhythmic analysis, in the exact reading of musical notation, and in the quantities of the English language. As a result our instrumentalists, our vocalists, and our composers are lacking in the basic ability to read music correctly or to write it down as they want it to sound. In former times this defect was remedied (badly and late) by post-graduate European study. For the present there is no European study. I wonder if it would be hoping too much to wish that the directors of our music schools might reflect on the rigorous training in *solfège* and its allied subjects that makes the work of the great French artists now among us so solid an achievement. It is time our students stopped fooling around with beautiful tone and velocity execution and learned some basic musical literacy, without which beautiful tone and velocity execution are incapable of saying anything serious to anybody.

March 14, 1943

THE ART OF JUDGING MUSIC

EXPLANATORY NOTE

The essay from which this book takes its title was delivered as an address in Sanders Theater, Cambridge, Massachusetts, on May 2, 1947, at the Harvard Symposium on Music Criticism. It was later published in the Atlantic Monthly. *The other pieces appeared originally in the* New York Herald Tribune, *most of them between September 1944 and August 1947.*

V. T.

New York, 1947

The Art of Judging Music

THE LAYMAN is under no obligation to exercise judgment with regard to musical works, to describe to himself their characteristics, or to estimate their value for history. He can take them to his heart or let them alone. He does not have to be just or fair, or to reflect about them in any way. He can accept, reject, tolerate, using only caprice as his guide. The professional has no such liberty. Neither has any musical patron or amateur who has chosen to follow in his role of music consumer the standards that govern the music producer.

These standards are not immutable, but they do exist. They exist because being a professional involves, by definition, the assumption of a responsible attitude both toward the material with which the profession deals and toward society in general, which the profession unquestionably serves. Service, indeed, is the price of any profession's toleration by society. And the acceptance of money for professional services rendered is the criterion by which professionalism is determined. This transaction is no guarantee of quality delivered, but it *is* a symbol of responsibility accepted. And once that responsibility is accepted, the workman must be at least morally worthy of his hire, however limited his skill or mental powers may be. He must be willing, in other words, to rise or fall professionally by his sincere opinions, as expressed in his professional actions.

Every musician, therefore, is a music critic. He is obliged to make musical judgments and to act on them. This necessity obtains primarily, of course, with regard to the work of other musicians, living and dead, in so far as his work is at all a comment on theirs or an interpretation of it, which nine tenths, at least, of anybody's musical work is. Even the composer, no less than the scholar, the pedagogue, the executant, and the reviewer, is constantly under the necessity of making a fair estimate, and a decently responsible one, of other people's musical output.

The making of such an estimate, hasty or slow, involves three possible operations. The first operation has nothing to do with deliberate fairness. It consists of listening to a piece, or of reading it, rather in the way that a cook tastes food. This act of cognition, this beginning of acquaintance, is probably a more powerful determinant in our final judgments, the ones on which we act, than the subsequent cerebrations are by which we endeavor to correct them. And one cannot prepare for it by purifying the spirit. One does not need to, as a matter of fact, because curiosity is stronger than prejudice. Any musician, faced with a new piece, will listen. He may not listen long, but he will submit himself to it, if only for a moment. He will listen, in fact, as long as he can, as long as it holds his attention.

The second stage of the first operation, after the initial tasting, is going on listening, the experience of having one's attention held. Not all pieces hold one's attention. One is regretful when they don't, but one must never undervalue the fact of their doing or not doing so. Fatigue here is of no more importance than prejudice. In reasonable health, and awake, any musician will listen to music, to sound of any kind, rather than merely ruminate, just as a painter will observe or a dancer will move around. That is why he is a musician to start with, because listening is his line of least resistance. When a musician can't keep his mind on a piece of music, that fact must be considered when he comes to form his judgment.

The final stage of the first operation is the aftertaste, the image that the whole piece leaves in the mind for the first few moments after it ceases to be heard (I say *heard* because reading a piece is hearing it in the mind, in however attenuated a fashion). This is as significant a part of its gustation as the first taste of it and the following of it through. It is a recalling of the whole while memory is fresh and before correction and reflection have begun to distort it. Never must one forget, never does one forget, hearing for the first time a work that has absorbed one from beginning to end and from which one has returned to ordinary life, as it were, shaken or beatified, as from a trip to the moon or to the Grecian Isles.

All new music does not produce this effect. But the degree to which it does is as valuable a datum for judgment as any that can be found on subsequent analysis. A great deal of subsequent analysis, as a matter of fact, is a search for the reasons why the piece did or did not hold one's attention on first hearing. And the initial taste or distaste for its qualities will constantly return to plague one's researches or to illumine them, to discourage or to inspire one in the process of making fuller acquaintance.

If tasting or savoring a piece is the first operation, the prelude to judgment, making its fuller acquaintance is the second. The latter depends, of course, on the success of the first. If first acquaintance has proved agreeable or interesting, one undertakes the second. The undertaking is a result of first judgment, though not necessarily of reflection. The whole first operation, let me insist, is spontaneous; and so is the initiation of the second. At this point, however, spontaneity ceases to be the main highway to experience, the guide to knowledge. We must now amplify and correct our first impression. If our first impression of a piece was gained from auditory means, from hearing only, we must now see the score. If it was gained from a score, we must hear it in execution. Many pieces look better than they sound, and even more of them sound better on first hearing than their design justifies. Because ordered sound is usually pleasant in itself, whether or not high intrinsic interest of an expressive or of a textural nature is present. In the case of executant musicians there is a constant shifting, during the study of a work, between score reading and execution, each approach to the piece correcting the other till the artist's interpretation is fully formed as a concept and completely clothed in sound. Thorough acquaintance with any piece of music, its mastery for responsible professional purposes, is not possible without this double possession, visual and auditory. At such a point of mastery one has material for a reflected judgment, and one *formulates* that judgment if there is any necessity for doing so. Otherwise one continues to study and to correct until interest lags.

The third operation of judgment, which is revisiting, can be undertaken only after a period of rest, of vacation from the subject. One has to forget the study period and its results, to approach the work all over again from a distance. Here the acquisition of experience and those shifts in the center of emotional interest that come from growing older are capable of lighting up the work in a new way. Sometimes they make it appear nobler; sometimes they show up shoddy material or poor workmanship; sometimes one can't see why one ever bothered with the piece at all. As in reading old love letters, however, or reviving an old quarrel, one's former emotion is still a fact to be dealt with. It involves one in loyalty or ruthlessness, in any case in lots of remembering. The music is no longer new and shining; nor has it been kept bright by continual use. It has acquired a patina that must be rubbed away before one can see the object as anything like its old self. Restudy and more rehearsing are therefore necessary if a new judgment has to be made. And one does have to be made if one is going to use the work again for any purpose whatsoever.

No judgment, of course, is ever final or permanent. At any stage of musical acquaintance action may become necessary; one may have undertaken to perform the work or to explain it to students or to describe it in public. For any of these purposes one must formulate such judgment as one has arrived at to date, if not about its value, at least about its nature. This formulation can take place at any point of experience. Reviewers often describe new music from one hearing, as pedagogues criticize student compositions from one reading. In nine cases out of ten this is sufficient for the purpose, and no injustice is done. Works of standard repertory are more often described after both hearing and study, that is to say, after the second phase of acquaintance, such acquaintance being easily available nowadays to all, though the press is not invariably as well prepared in standard repertory (by score study) as it might be, and many members of the teaching profession have not always as broad a prepared repertory as might be desired for the answering of student questions and for exposing to the young all the kinds of music that there are. The press in general tends to express judgments of new work from hearing only, just as historians, especially those dealing with remote periods, are obliged to describe from score a great deal of music that they have never heard at all.

In order to make a fair judgment from only the first stage of acquaintance, either from hearing or from reading, one is obliged to have recourse to the aid of clues or clinical signs. The clinical signs of quality are three: 1) the ability of a work to hold one's attention, 2) one's ability to remember it vividly, and 3) a certain strangeness in the musical texture, that is to say, the presence of technical invention, such as novelty of rhythm, of contrapuntal, harmonic, melodic, or instrumental device. The pattern that a score makes on a page can be enticing, too, even before one starts to read it. In the matter of attention, it is not germane that one should be either delighted or annoyed. What counts is whether one is impelled to go on listening.

"Can you listen to it?" and "Can you remember it?" are, I think, answerable in the affirmative only when real invention is present. Everybody likes novelty. People's responses to novelty are diversified, however, since the amount of it that anyone can take in is a personal quotient. Some like a little; some like a lot. This is why strong feelings of pleasure or displeasure are likely to accompany its encounter. These feelings, like those of love and hatred, reverse themselves with the greatest of ease. Their value as a clinical indication that one is probably in the presence of strong music lies in their strength, not in their direction.

It is necessary to keep wary, too, and to examine one's mind constantly for possible failure to make the cardinal distinctions. The cardinal distinctions in music are also three: 1) design *vs.* execution, or the piece itself as distinct from its presentation; 2) the expressive power of a work as distinguishable from its formal musical interest; and 3) a convincing emotional effect *vs.* a meretricious one.

One must ask oneself always, therefore: 1) "Have I heard a pretty piece or just some pretty playing?" 2) "Is this just a piece of clockwork, or does it also tell time?" and 3) "In the process of receiving its message, have I been moved or merely impressed?"

Study and reflection will provide answers to all these questions; but when one has to act quickly, one must assume that one's first impression, so far as it goes, is a true view. And it is, in fact, as true a view as any, since most of what is revealed on further acquaintance is of a descriptive nature, a more detailed picture, filling in outlines already sensed. This is not always so; but far more often than not it is so. In the case of successive contradictory impressions, it is the first, I think, that tends to survive.

And so to recapitulate.

First, one votes about a piece, spontaneously, sincerely, and more often than not, permanently; one adopts it or rejects it. Liking is not necessary for adoption, but interest is. If interest is present, one can study the work further with profit. If not, one tends to forget it. After study one can forget it too, but not completely. In this case one can revisit it after a time. But at any time when the formulation of a judgment or opinion is found to be desirable, that formulation must be based on a description of the work. The techniques of musical description are:

1) *Stylistic* identification, recognizing its period or school from internal evidence, from the technical procedures of composition employed. Identifying these procedures will answer the question, "What is it like?"

2) *Expressive* identification is the second technique of musical description. One must decide whether a piece depicts the cadences of speech, bodily movements, or feelings (that whole series of anxiety-and-relief patterns that constitutes our emotional life). This decodifying is a more difficult operation but also a more important one, since one can, if necessary, and the passage of time aiding, neglect stylistic differences or even abstract them from the problem, whereas one cannot perform, communicate, or in any other way *use* a piece of music until one has found an answer, correct or incorrect, to the question, "What is it about?"

3) The third technique of description consists in summoning up the classical aids to memory. These are the known methods of melodic, harmonic, orchestral, and formal analysis. They are of little value without stylistic and expressive identification; but they help one to remember detail, provided one has first understood stylistically and emotionally the whole. By *understand* I mean *accept*, be satisfied with something. George Bernard Shaw once showed the futility of a formal analysis of art without reference to its content in a parody of program notes such as might have been written about the most famous of the five Hamlet soliloquies. He begins (I quote from memory): "The theme is first stated in the infinitive mood, followed immediately by its inversion." Analysis is an indispensable procedure, but the analysis of a given piece is valueless to anyone who does not have some previous knowledge of the piece. That is why one must first, in describing a work verbally, answer the questions, "What is it like?" and "What is it about?" before attempting to answer, "How does it go?"

4) The fourth procedure of musical description is verbal formulation. This is, of course, a literary rather than a musical problem; but no one escapes it, not the teachers, the conductors, nor the string-quartet players, any more than the historians

and the journalists. In some of the musical branches it is easier
than in others. Vocalism is particularly hard to teach otherwise
than by example, or to describe in any circumstance, because
there is no standard vocabulary for the purpose. Instrumental
terminology is richer, though most of this is borrowed from the
language of painting. Composition is chiefly described in metaphor, though the stylistic and expressive identifications do have
a scholastic terminology. That for styles follows the history of
the visual arts except for the years between 1775, say, and 1825,
where the visual artists discern a classic-revival period and the
musicians a Classical one (with a capital C). The classification
of musical phraseology as strophic, choric, or spastic is valuable;
but the last division, which includes so much of our grander
repertory, is incapable of further precision than that available
through poetic allusion. The same is true of musical landscape
painting. Here one must use similes; there is no other way.

You will note that I have said nothing about communicating one's passion with regard to a work. I have not mentioned
it because it presents no problem; it takes place automatically
and inevitably. Insistence on it, moreover, is immodest. What is
most interesting about any musical judgment is the descriptive
analysis on which it is based, or, if you like, since one's judgment
is likely to precede the analysis, by which it is defended. This is
revelatory and stimulating. The fact that one man likes or does
not like the finale of Beethoven's Fifth Symphony will influence
nobody. The fact that I for one consider that piece to be, shall
we say, more like a newspaper editorial about something than
a direct transcript of personal statements is, however right or
wrong, convincing or foolish, possibly worth following up, if
only for refutation.

The public does not have to be right. Musicians do not have
to be right. Nobody has to be right. Any opinion is legitimate
to act on, provided one accepts in advance the responsibilities
of that action. Any opinion is legitimate to express that can be
stated in clear language. And any opinion at all is legitimate
to hold. As I said before, it is not the yes or no of a judgment
that is valuable to other people, though one's original yes or
no about a certain kind of music may have determined a whole
lifetime's activity. What other people get profit from following is
that activity itself, the spectacle of a mind at work. That is why,

just as an emotional reaction is more significant for its force than for its direction, a musical judgment is of value to others less for the conclusions reached than for the methods by which these have been, not even arrived at, but elaborated, defended, and expressed.

ORCHESTRAS, CONDUCTORS, RECITALISTS

The Philharmonic Crisis

Artur Rodzinski has gone and done it. For years the knowledge has been a secret scandal in music circles. Now he has said it out loud. That the trouble with the Philharmonic is nothing more than an unbalance of power. Management has usurped, according to him, certain functions of the musical direction without which no musical director can produce a first-class and durable artistic result. He has implied that no conductor, under present conditions, can keep the orchestra a musical instrument comparable to those of Boston and Philadelphia. He points to Arthur Judson, a powerful business executive who manages the orchestra as a side line, as the person chiefly interested in weakening the musical director's authority. He is right; he is perfectly right; he could not be more right. An orchestra can use one star performer and one only. And such a star's place is the podium, not the executive offices.

The American symphony orchestra, like the American government, is an operation of three powers. Its trustees are the power responsible to the community. They provide (or collect) money and determine how it is to be spent; they hire a manager to handle the business details of concert giving; and they entrust to a conductor the production of music for these. The manager in his office and the conductor before his orchestra both have full authority to run their departments, the trustees preserving a veto power over policies only. The trustees, a self-perpetuating body, are thus the initiators of the orchestra as a project and the court of final appeal about everything regarding it.

The musical director's job is the most responsible post of its kind in the world. He has all the authority of a ship's captain. Hiring and firing of musicians, their training and discipline, the composition of all programs and their public execution are his privilege. Any visiting conductor or soloist is a guest in his house. The manager's job is purely organizational, a routine matter that anyone can handle who has a knowledge of standard business methods and some diplomacy. The latter is essential for him, serving constantly, as he does, as go-between in whatever brush-ups occur between the conductor and the trustees. Since the symphony orchestra is a nonprofit-making institution serving the community in a cultural capacity, its trustees must be men and women of culture and of unquestioned civic responsibility, its conductor a musician with courage and judgment as well as technical skill, its manager a model of integrity and of tact.

The Philharmonic case is simple. Arthur Judson is unsuited by the nature and magnitude of his business interests to manage with the necessary self-effacement a major intellectual institution doing business with his other interests. He is also a man of far too great personal force to serve effectively as a mediator between a proud musician and the equally proud trustees. That is probably why no conductor ever stays long enough with the Philharmonic to accomplish the job that everybody knows should be done, namely, to put the orchestra permanently on an artistic equality with the other American orchestras of comparable financial resources.

Artur Rodzinski has done more for the orchestra in that respect than any other conductor in our century has done. Mahler and Toscanini were greater interpreters, were not such great builders. If Stokowski and Munch, also great interpreters, have been able this winter, as guests, to play upon the orchestra in full freedom and to produce from it sonorous and expressive beauties of the highest quality, that achievement has been made possible by Rodzinski's personnel replacements and his careful training. Such an achievement on the part of guest conductors has not heretofore been possible. Today the Philharmonic, for the first time in this writer's memory, is the equal of the Boston and Philadelphia orchestras and possibly their superior.

Stabilization of these gains is the next step indicated. With that in mind the trustees in December voted Mr. Rodzinski a long-term contract "without strings attached." One gathers that the contract he actually received contained not strings but chains, that his right to decide who besides himself shall conduct his orchestra, to confer with his guests about their programs, even to determine in full freedom his own was seriously jeopardized. It seems doubtful that any conductor would leave so important a post unless the working conditions were about to become intolerable. So far, they have not been that for him, and the orchestra's improvement under his leadership has proved that they were not.

What awaits his successor is anybody's guess. Dramas and heartbreaks probably, unless the trustees decide to hire another such orchestra builder and give him full power to go ahead and build. In that case, it is scarcely worth while to have provoked the present conductor into resigning. (The contention that he resigned merely because a better job was offered him is not credible, because there is no better job.) In any other case, the Philharmonic will decline as an orchestra as inevitably as winter will return. There is only one way to have a first-class orchestra and that is to let the conductor run it. If he fails, he can be replaced. But while he lasts he has to be given full musical authority as that is understood in the major symphonic establishments.

Rodzinski's career will not be gravely interrupted, we hope, by his courageous gesture. New York will miss him and regret his musical benefits bestowed. The last and greatest of these will have been the most valuable of all, if his exposure of what has long been known in music circles as a scandal and a shame shall encourage the trustees to correct it. There is no reason why the Philharmonic should not remain what it is now, the tip-top executant musical organization of the world. All it needs is a competent and energetic musical director and a disinterested management.

February 9, 1947

The "New Friends"

A PROSPECTUS announcing next year's plans for the New Friends of Music concerts arrived recently at this desk accompanied by a letter from Ira Hirschmann, president of the society. "Am I right," he asks, "in saying that very few enterprises of any kind, especially those that deal with the living spirit of music, can show a record of the consistency we were privileged to practice; and do you think it is of sufficient interest to you to justify the republication of these aims?

"I hope," he continues, "that you are not disappointed with our next year's plans."

One cannot deny that the aims stated in the original prospectus of 1936 are excellent and that the New Friends have pursued them assiduously. They are:

1. To offer the best in the literature of chamber music and lieder.

2. To embrace complete cycles of composers' works rather than "little pieces," wherever possible.

3. To conceive the music in the season's programs as a unit divided into sixteen concerts, with a view to offering the subscribers as complete a representation of the literature of individual composers as feasible.

4. To perform neglected music in unusual instrumental and voice combinations along with better known chamber music works.

5. To build the programs first and choose the artists on the basis of the programs.

6. To make this music available at very low prices on a subscription basis; most cases under $1 and student tickets at 25 cents.

7. To eliminate all elements foreign to the music itself, such as exploitation of artists' personality, display pieces, encores, flowers, interruptions between movements, intermissions, etc.

8. To offer no free passes, with a hope of helping to curb this practice, so unfair to artists and managers.

9. To attempt to demonstrate that there is a large public for the best in music and that even at low prices, under careful management, the best music can be self-supporting without patrons or patronesses.

As to whether I am disappointed with next year's plans, yes, Mr. Hirschmann, since you ask, I am. Devoting the season to Bach, Schubert, and Brahms seems to me a retracing of your footsteps. For eight years the society gave nothing but Central European music. In its ninth it began to branch out and spent half its time on French music, ancient and modern, the other half being given over to Mozart. Evidently the Germanically schooled element among the subscribers did not like this admission that chamber music exists beyond the West Wall, since a more timorous retreat could scarcely be imagined than your announced return to the triple fortresses of Bach and Schubert and Brahms.

"To offer the best in the literature of chamber music and lieder" could not have been accomplished without the admission of French repertory. To do the job completely would still require that Italian (at least the madrigal literature) and English and Russian chamber music be included. There are vast repertories of chamber music written outside Central Europe, in fact, that a comprehensive program should have dealt with before going into such minor masters, as the New Friends did a few seasons back, as Mendelssohn and Dvořák. To turn tail on the non-Germanic world after one brief expedition into France I find a little cowardly.

The announced return to Central Europe is no doubt the result of subscriber pressure. Certainly the Germanic-minded are the most faithful element in the New Friends' audience. Dealing with their conservatism and their prejudices is your problem, Mr. Hirschmann, not mine. But since you have asked me for my sentiments about next year's program announcement, I am obliged to express the disappointment that your question foresaw. And I should like to take this occasion to bring out another complaint that has been burning my pocket for a long time. I find not only that the programs are weighted unjustly on the Central European side but that the choice of interpreters is, too. If we must be limited in our repertory by the Rhine, the Danube, and the Curzon line, couldn't we maybe have some of it played more often by French quartets? Turning over French music this year to too many German-school executants was a mistake, I think. But the opposite procedure has long been known to produce excellent results. French and Italian interpreters often do a better job, in fact, on the German classics than the Germans themselves do.

Lest any one imagine that I am trying to drag our present war with the Central Powers over into the field of art, I hasten to add that I have no unfriendly feeling at all toward German music and German musicians, ancient or modern. I merely insist that the German tradition is not the whole story of chamber music. Any attempt to pretend that it is is just ostrich tactics. And I deplore obscurantism in all its forms, especially on the part of a society that furnishes to New York most of the classical chamber music we hear. The New Friends are no longer just a private society, entitled to play what they please. They have assumed a responsible role in our cultural life. And the carrying out of their obligation requires that they continue to give us not only "the best in the literature of chamber music and lieder" but *all* that best, however unfamiliar some of it may be to music lovers of strictly Teutonic upbringing.

March 25, 1945

Pierre Monteux

PIERRE MONTEUX's two-week visit as guest conductor of the Philharmonic-Symphony Orchestra, which ends today, has led music lovers of all schools (the critical press included) to two conclusions: namely, that this conductor has drawn from our orchestra more beautiful sounds and more beautiful mixtures of sound than any other conductor has done in many years, and that his readings of Brahms are highly refreshing.

It has been a long time, a very long time, since our Philharmonic sounded like an orchestra. It has always been an assemblage of good players; and the changes of personnel operated last year by Mr. Rodzinski, on his accession to the conductorship, have improved further its musical potentialities. Sometimes of late the playing has been most agreeable. Sometimes, too, no matter who was conducting, the performances have sounded more like a reading rehearsal than like a prepared execution. This lack of dependability in the ensemble—so noticeable in contrast to the solid teamwork, no matter who conducts them, in the orchestras of Philadelphia, Boston, and Chicago—has long been a trouble. As far back as 1936 Sir Thomas Beecham, who served a half-season that year as guest, annoyed the directors considerably by replying, when asked to diagnose the musical ills of the organization, that though it contained many excellent players it was not an orchestra.

Many conductors, Mr. Rodzinski included, have produced a pretty good balance of timbres and made music, usually unfamiliar music, sound pretty well. Arturo Toscanini has occasionally, without any beauty of sheer sound being involved, made familiar music sound unusually eloquent. It has remained for

Pierre Monteux to achieve what many of us thought was hopeless. He has made the Philharmonic play with real beauty of tone, many kinds of it, and with perfect balance and blending—to sound, in short, like an orchestra, a real, first-class orchestra requiring no apology. And he has also played music as familiar as that of Brahms and Beethoven (not to speak of Debussy) with not only a wonderful beauty of sound but a far from usual eloquence as well. This is the way a real orchestra *should* sound, the way the first-class orchestras of the world all *do* sound. And this is the way many musicians have long wished the music of Johannes Brahms could be made to sound.

It is a strange anomaly that although Brahms's symphonic music is extremely popular (in some years it tops even that of Beethoven for frequency of performance), almost nobody's reading of it is thoroughly satisfactory. How to discern the rhythm that underlies its slow and its energetic passages, to make these sound in any given piece as if they are all parts of the same piece, is one of the unsolved problems in music. Certainly the meditative ones require to be read as inward rather than as extrovert sentiment. And certainly the animated ones and the passages of broad eloquence, such as the codas and finales, tempt any conductor to make oratory out of them. But alternations of introversion with extroversion do not make a unity in the reading of anything, and there is no reason to suppose that so experienced and so consecrated a musician as Brahms was basically incoherent in thought. It is far more likely that his exact poetic temper, being profoundly personal, escapes us.

In my time only the late Frederick Stock of Chicago has been able to envelop the Brahms symphonies with a dreamy lilt that allowed the soft passages to float along and the loud ones to sing out as elements of a single continuity. A rhythmic propulsion that was steady without being rigid was the basis of these readings. Orchestral tone that was light in texture and wholly transparent was its superstructure. Mr. Monteux is less expert than Dr. Stock was at preserving a poetical and rhythmic unity throughout, but he is more expert than anybody at lifting the velvet pall that is accustomed in our concerts to lie over the Brahms instrumentation and allowing everything, middle voices too, to shine forth with translucency. His strings never obscure the woodwinds. His trumpets and trombones never blast away the strings. His horns, when force is indicated, play very loud; but their loudness is bright, not heavy; it is a flash of light rather than a ton of bricks.

Both these conductors have been celebrated for their renderings of French music, especially of Debussy, which requires a similar rhythmic continuity and identical refinements of balance. Sheer weight, like sheer brilliance, must always, in this kind of music, be avoided, because it destroys the translucency that is the music's main means of evoking an atmosphere. And the rhythm must be alive but steady, the cantilena floating on the delicate wavelike motion of this without effort or any insistence. Mr. Monteux, when playing both these composers, sometimes allows the slower passages to go dead. At these moments the rhythm stops supporting the flow of sound, all animation disappears, and the sounds themselves lose their ability to blend. But these moments are never long. As soon as the rhythm reasserts itself, the tonal fabric comes to life again and breathes like a sentient being.

Listening lately to Pierre Monteux conduct Brahms and Debussy on the same program brought to mind how much the music of these two authors is alike, or at least demands like treatment. The secret of their rhythm is very much the same secret. And nonviolation of their rhythm is essential and preliminary to producing among their orchestral sounds luminosity. That and the use of transparent, or nonweighty, orchestral tone. By what occult methods Mr. Monteux produces in our Philharmonic-Symphony Orchestra a real community of rhythmic articulation, not to mention the delights of delicate balance and blending that proceed from this, I cannot even guess. The guest conductors who have failed where he has succeeded would like to know, too, I imagine.

November 12, 1944

The Sanguine Temperament

ROCHESTER PHILHARMONIC ORCHESTRA, *Sir Thomas Beecham*, conductor, on March 17 at Carnegie Hall, performing Haydn's Symphony No. 93, the Handel-Beecham Suite from *The Great Elopement*, Beethoven's Symphony No. 7, and Berlioz's *Marche Troyenne*.

THE CONCERT that Sir Thomas Beecham conducted with the Rochester Philharmonic Orchestra in Carnegie Hall on Saturday night was a personal triumph for the English leader. The massive applause that greeted, in a far from full house, his incomparable readings of Haydn, of Beethoven, of Berlioz, and of his own ballet music (out of Handel) could only have been gratitude for the grandeur and buoyancy of those readings as such, since the orchestral execution of the Rochester society is certainly no marvel for fine finish. When, at the close of the concert, the audience demanded extra numbers (the Andante from Elgar's String Serenade and the March from Sibelius's *Karelia* suite were what they got), it seemed reasonable to suppose that what they wanted was not so much further acquaintance with the pleasant but roughish playing of the Rochester band as more of Sir Thomas's deeply joyous music making.

This reviewer confesses to a similar predilection for the Beecham readings. His Haydn has gusto and sentiment along with its grace. It breathes with ease and steps a real measure. It is no line drawing of antiquity but a full evocation in the round of music that everybody knows to have passion as well as decorum, but that no other conductor seems able to bring to life with quite that ruddy glow.

The new Handel-Beecham suite, which received its first New York hearing on this occasion, is out of a ballet entitled *The Great Elopement*, undertaken, I believe, for the Ballet Theater, but not yet produced on any stage. Here is no sullen expatriate Handel, yearning after the unhappy Germany he grew up in (and never liked) or after the perverse and monumental Italy of his youth. It is the British Handel, as square-toed as a country squire, as witty as a London playwright, as dainty as a beau of Bath, as expansive as the empire itself. One looks forward to a stage performance of the work. Frederick Ashton would probably be its ideal choreographer.

Beethoven's Seventh Symphony received the roughest execution of the evening but the most enlightened reading it has had in my lifetime. Nothing in its whole progress was either long or wrong. And when one remembered the innumerable booby traps for conductors with which that work is sown, it was with amazement and respect that one observed Sir Thomas sidestepping them all and going straight to the heart of the matter. This heart is the funeral-march Allegretto, the saddest, most deeply tragic piece Beethoven ever wrote, surrounded and framed by three of the most exuberant affirmations that exist in musical literature. We have had choleric Beethoven of late and melancholy Beethoven and even some lymphatic. Myself I like it sanguine, because I think that is the kind of man Beethoven was. And Sir Thomas's Seventh Symphony, for all its studied proportions, was abundantly that.

March 10, 1945

The Ormandy Case

PHILADELPHIA ORCHESTRA, *Eugene Ormandy*, conductor, last night at Carnegie Hall, performing, among other works, Kodály's Concerto for Orchestra and two Debussy Nocturnes, *Nuages* and *Fêtes*.

THE PHILADELPHIA ORCHESTRA, which opened our indoor orchestral season last night at Carnegie Hall, has a sound that is pungent and mellow like the smell of fall fruits. No other instrumental assembly has quite the quality of impersonal, almost botanical, beauty that this one possesses; and none of the other conductors who appear regularly before us has quite Eugene Ormandy's way of offering really excellent workmanship without personal insistence.

Persons who cherish star quality in public performers often feel let down by Mr. Ormandy, though it is surprising how satisfactory the work he does with his orchestra turns out to be on accustomed acquaintance. There is, indeed, no final flame of eloquence in it and no categorical authority. But there is always beauty and order and an approach to all kinds of music that, if it does not manifest the ultimate of sensitivity, is nevertheless marked by an understanding of all the musical languages, that is at once sensuous and delicate.

With no preparation, for instance, by early training or by residence, for the playing of French music, and with, to this day, an incurably Viennese irregularity of rhythmic scansion, he manages to expose French music with less distortion of its original sense than almost any of the other interpreters do, saving only those of extended Parisian experience. He does this by cultivating in his orchestra the whole gamut of sounds and colorations of sound—not just the pushing or the throbbing ones—that are the full French orchestral palette. And he keeps these cleanly separate from one another, equilibrating and contrasting, as is the custom of the French conductors, rather than mixing them.

He just misses full identification with the French style in his rhythm. He has neither the instinct nor the training for exact quantities that are characteristic of French musicians and that are necessary above all for the lucid exposition of Debussy. And he does not quite seize the strophic nature of French musical discourse. What is meant for a simple breath, a hesitation, becomes too often a hiatus. His whole rhythmic outline is too flexible for full metrical clarity.

All the same, French works, as he plays them, come out less distorted than is usual here and with far more vibrancy of timbre than is common anywhere. The trumpet passages that start the march section in Debussy's *Fêtes*, for instance, were articulated last night so brightly, and yet so softly, that one might easily have taken them for an off-stage effect. I have never before heard trumpets to be played so quietly and still to sound like trumpets.

The novelty of the evening was a Concerto for Orchestra (it might as well have been called an overture) by Zoltán Kodály, written for the fiftieth anniversary season of Chicago's Symphony Orchestra and performed there in 1941. This is a lively piece, gay and clean and fresh and soundly sonorous. Mr. Ormandy read it straightforwardly and with full appreciation of the special Hungarian savor that characterizes the work of this composer, who was, in fact, Mr. Ormandy's teacher.

October 4, 1944

Wrestling and Shadow Boxing

NEW YORK CITY SYMPHONY, *Leonard Bernstein*, conductor, last night at the New York City Center, performing Bach's Brandenburg Concerto No. 3, Milhaud's *Création du monde*, and Schumann's Symphony No. 2.

THE NEW YORK CITY SYMPHONY gave a concert last night at the City Center of Music and Drama that was in every way vigorous and refreshing. The new conductor, Leonard Bernstein, is on the whole rather too vigorous for the complete enjoyment of this sedate observer. But the freshness of his attack on musical problems both technical and interpretative is a delight to bear witness to. And if his work more resembles to the eye shadowboxing than standard orchestral conducting, there is auditory proof aplenty that this gifted young musician is also wrestling with angels.

He came off best last night, it seemed to me, in his bout with the spirit of Robert Schumann. One so rarely nowadays hears this composer's Second Symphony at all that there was double pleasure in hearing it read with such romantic brio. I have not heard such a warm and spirited rendering of any orchestral piece by Schumann in a long time.

The same warmth was Mr. Bernstein's downfall in the Third Brandenburg Concerto of Sebastian Bach. Like many of his elders, in dealing with this music, he mistakes dynamic exaggeration for fullness of utterance. Fullness in the Baroque style comes from rhythmic exactitude, not from runaway tempos, from the line nobly curved in repose, not from gasping phraseology. Solidity of pace becomes it, and all brilliance of tone, rather than breathless passion and huskiness.

Darius Milhaud's masterpiece, *The Creation of the World*, had brought out a lively audience; and there seemed to be no public disappointment with the work. Myself I was a little disappointed in Mr. Bernstein's reading of it, though hearing at all a piece so famous and so seldom presented was perhaps enough to have asked. All the same I regretted, as I had in the Bach, that overweening dynamism in the beat ended by obscuring somewhat the static and primeval character of this jazz poem.

The music itself alternates so sharply between tranquillity

and syncopation that any reading of it based on whipping it up and then letting it down tends to let the whole piece down. Its continuity requires a steady rhythm and the avoidance of all excitement on the conductor's part. He must traverse it as if it were a massive and sluggish river with whirlpools in it. Having fun in the whirlpools is tempting, I know; but keeping the boat in equilibrium gives the passengers a better view of the stream.

November 20, 1945

You Can Listen to Him

BOSTON SYMPHONY ORCHESTRA, *Leonard Bernstein*, conductor, last night at Carnegie Hall, performing Schubert's Symphony No. 7 and Stravinsky's *Sacre du printemps.*

STRAVINSKY's *Rite of Spring*, which closed last night's concert of the Boston Symphony Orchestra in Carnegie Hall, is probably the most influential work of music composed in our century and the most impressive in performance. Not having heard its execution in November by the Philharmonic under Artur Rodzinski, the present writer has no basis for a comparison of that reading, which was much admired, with last night's by Leonard Bernstein. He has heard many another, however; and none has seemed to him more straightforward or more moving.

The work does not stand much interpretative tinkering, as a matter of fact. The more rigid its beat the greater its expressive power. What it needs is clean rhythm, clean tonal balances, and understanding. Its subject, human sacrifice, is too grand and terrible to permit personal posturing. And Mr. Bernstein, often a sinner in that regard, gave it none. If he did not extract from the score one tenth of the detailed refinement that older hands at it do—conductors like Monteux and Ansermet and Désormière—he nevertheless got the rhythm right and made the meaning more clear than usual. One felt that he loved the music, understood it, and submitted his will in all modesty to its relentless discipline.

The work is not a clear masterpiece, like the same composer's *Petrouchka;* but it is more original. It cuts farther below the surface of musical convention, goes straight to the heart of the whole stylistic problem of Romanticism, comes out both deeply expressive and completely impersonal. Its complex rhythmic interest, its high harmonic tension, and its rigid orchestral textures are justly famous. Its patent of nobility, however, lies in the extreme beauty of its melodic material. Partly Russian folklore and partly inventions in the same manner, its themes are short, diatonic, and narrow. They rarely cover a larger range than the perfect fifth. They are as plain as granite and as resistant to time. If the work did not lose intensity in the early part of its second half, it would be the solidest single monument of musical art our century has erected. Just possibly it is that in spite of everything.

Mr. Bernstein's reading of the Schubert C-major Symphony, which preceded the Stravinsky work, was open-hearted, animated, youthful, and full of life. Texturally it was a little rough, and at no point was it particularly Viennese in lilt. But it was passionate and sweet. Anybody can question another artist's interpretation. What seems to be beyond question in Mr. Bernstein's case is that he is a real interpreter. His orchestral hand is still young and a little heavy, and sometimes his personal projection is overweening. But his is a real temperament for making music. What he conducts rarely sounds beautiful to a sensuous spirit. And his musical culture is far from mature. But you can listen to him. That is the first and the last test of any interpreter.

February 13, 1947

Among the Best

PHILHARMONIC-SYMPHONY ORCHESTRA, *Charles Munch*, conductor, last night at Carnegie Hall, performing Handel's Water Music Suite, Honegger's Symphony No. 3 ("Liturgique"), Debussy's *Ibéria*, and Ravel's Suite No. 2 from *Daphnis et Chloë*.

CHARLES MUNCH, who conducted last night's Philharmonic concert in Carnegie Hall, has been for some fifteen years, till recently, conductor of France's oldest and best-known orchestra, that of the Société des Concerts du Conservatoire. Alsatian by birth and a French citizen by adoption (in 1918), Mr. Munch, who was at one time first violinist of the Cologne Orchestra and long a pupil and protégé of Furtwängler, would seem admirably prepared to bridge, as an interpreter, that ever-widening gap between the German and the French musical styles which is one of the most troublesome musical phenomena of our century.

All the same, and with a vast experience behind him on both sides of the Rhine, he remains Alsatian. You never know quite where his musical sympathies lie. He plays German music, particularly Beethoven, better than most of the French conductors now working in France. And he certainly plays French music better than any of the German conductors now working in Germany, though many a German not now working in Germany, Furtwängler included, has had a sounder understanding of the French Impressionist style.

Last night he played Handel's *Water Music* (arranged by Sir Hamilton Harty), a new symphony by the Franco-Swiss Honegger, and familiar works by Debussy and Ravel. The first was charming and animated, the second, if one could judge in an unfamiliar work, a masterful rendition. The last two readings, though impressive enough as a display of both technics and temperament, missed the musical point of both pieces about as completely as could be imagined.

In the Debussy *Ibéria* Mr. Munch sacrificed color to dynamics, and metrics to accent. He took romantic liberties with the sentiment and with the time and leaned on all the melodic lines. As a result, the piece sounded like an unsuccessful attempt on Debussy's part to write real Spanish music instead of a successful attempt to evoke poetically, as in a dream, the whole sensuous panorama of a Spain he had never seen.

Ravel's second *Daphnis and Chloë* suite was similarly weakened by the imposition on it of a personal romanticism that it was never made to support. By taking its tempos consistently rubato and by exaggerating the climaxes, Mr. Munch managed to make it sound like an inferior *Tristan and Isolde*, which it is not, instead of the superior *Scheherazade* that it is. This was all very disappointing from a conductor who has been both a first-class musician and a Frenchman long enough to know better.

Arthur Honegger's Third (or "Liturgical") Symphony consists of three symphonic odes that express the emotional content of the Dies Irae hymn, of the De Profundis psalm, and of the final phase, "Dona nobis pacem," from the Agnus Dei of the

Mass. They do this most effectively indeed in a turbulent and dissonant style that is not difficult to follow and that is rhythmically far from platitudinous. If the harmonic and orchestral seeming complexity is a little bit, with regard to the thematic, the melodic content, like sauce cooking that conceals the poverty of the basic food materials, the result is tasty all the same. The work is both meritorious and masterful, and it is interesting to listen to. It is also a shade theatrical in the sense of obvious.

The public received both Mr. Munch and the Honegger symphony warmly. All present seemed to recognize, in spite of a certain expressive poverty, the high qualities of skill and temperament that characterize the work of both and place it among the best of our time.

January 21, 1947

Birthday Salute

ARTURO TOSCANINI will be eighty years old on Tuesday, March 25. The occasion is notable not merely for the fact that age has not withered nor custom staled his infinitely satisfactory musicianship, but also for the reminder that he is today, exactly as he has been for twenty years, the first conductor of the world. His primacy in the field of opera has been clear for nearer forty years, since his appearance at the Metropolitan Opera House in 1908, in fact. Since 1926, when he first conducted the New York Philharmonic Orchestra, his mastery of the concert style has been equally unquestionable. From that day till now it has not been possible for any musician or musical observer to list the great living conductors of an age that has been glorious for great conducting without putting Arturo Toscanini's name squarely at the top.

His most remarkable quality as a public performer has always been his dependability. He never lets his audience down nor lets music down. When announced to appear, he appears. When he conducts any work, however familiar, unfamiliar, difficult of execution, facile of sentiment, no matter what kind of work or by whom, he knows the score and gives it as careful, as polished a reading as if his whole musical life depended on that single work. It is this unusual dependability, indeed, that has given rise to the legend of his musical infallibility. Actually he misses the point of a piece, misunderstands a composer's thought as often as any other musician. Where he does not fail is in the ability to call forth on any platform the full resources of his own musical interest and attention. Music, any music, all music stimulates in him as automatically as in the proverbial circus horse the full functioning of his professional capacities.

Those capacities derive not only from a nervous stability superior to that of any of the other great living conductors, but also from a musical instinct as simple and as healthy as that of a gifted child. Toscanini, and let us make no mistake about it, is a natural musician. His culture may be elementary but his ear is true. He makes music out of anything. And the music that he makes is the plainest, the most straightforward music now available in public performance. There is little of historical evocation in it and even less of deliberate emotional appeal. It is purely auditory, just ordered sound and very little else. There is not even much Toscanini in it. For in spite of his high temperament, this musician is strangely lacking in personality.

That is why, I think, he has based his interpretative routine on as literal as possible an adherence to musical texts. A respect for the written note and the adherence to any composer's clearly indicated intent have always been the procedure of first-class conductors of ensemble music. But the composer's expressive intent is more often than not far from clear; and musical notation, particularly as regards phraseology and rhythmic inflection, is extremely imprecise. Imagination and a deep historical culture are the classical approaches to the problem of invigorating the music of the past. Toscanini has no such culture to channelize his imaginative faculties. He is not in any sense an intellectual. He is not ignorant; he has heard, read, and played vast quantities of music; and his mind is as sound as his body. But he has not the humane letters of a Beecham, a Reiner, a Monteux, the refined sensuality of a Stokowski, an Ormandy, the moral fervor and sense of obligation toward contemporary creation of Koussevitzky. He simply sticks as closely to the text as he can and makes music.

Actually, of course, he takes as many liberties with a text as any other executant. He neglects Beethoven's metronome marks, as everybody else does. He corrects a balance for clarity's sake. He speeds up a finale for general excitement. He has gravely falsified, moreover, the musical tradition of our time by speeding up the Mozart minuet movements to a point where all memory of the court dance has disappeared from them. What he does not do is to personalize his interpretations. He adds a great deal of excitement to any piece, but that excitement is of a purely auditory and cerebral, rather than of an expressive character. His appeal is thus deeply contemporary to an epoch which has accepted abstractions in art, in science, and in politics as the source of its most passionate loyalties.

Nobody else in our time has been so simple or so pure toward music as Toscanini. He will not loom large, I imagine, in the history books of the future, because he has mostly remained on the side lines of the creative struggle. And music's history is always the history of its composition. Toscanini has radically simplified the technique of orchestral conducting, and he has given a straightforwardness to all interpretation in our time that cannot fail to facilitate the execution problem for living composers. But his involvement with the formation of our century's musical style, with the encouragement of contemporary expression in music, with the living composers, in short, whose work will one day constitute the story of music in our time, has been less than that of any of today's other orchestral great. He has honor and glory now, but by posterity his work will probably pass unremunerated.

That is why we must enjoy him and be thankful for him and cherish him. For when he leaves there will be little left save a memory and a few gramophone records; and these give hardly any idea of his electric powers as a public performer. By a miracle we have him with us still and, by a greater miracle, in full possession of his powers. That those powers are without peer in our time cannot be denied by anybody. That they may long be preserved to him and to us is the prayer of every living musician and lover of music.

March 23, 1947

The Koussevitzky Case

SERGE (or Sergei) Koussevitzky, conductor of the Boston Symphony Orchestra since 1924, is an aristocrat among American conductors and in Boston music circles something of an autocrat. Born seventy-two years ago in Russia and reared there in poverty (his family, though Orthodox Jews, never lived in a ghetto), he has attained wealth, world-wide fame and the highest distinction in his profession. As a virtuoso on the double-bass viol and as a conductor his ranking, by any standards, has been for many years among that of the very greatest in our time. As a composer he has contributed to the reputable literature of his instrument. As a publisher and a patron of contemporary music he has probably made a more lasting contribution to the art than any other single person living, excepting five or six composers. His place in its history is already assured and glorious.

Just to make assurance doubly sure, the Boston immortality machine has started issuing this winter what looks like a series of books bearing the papal imprimatur of the good doctor (LL.D., *honoris causa*, Harvard, 1929, and elsewhere). M. A. De Wolfe Howe, official biographer to the Bostonian great, has furnished *The Tale of Tanglewood, Scene of the Berkshire Music Festivals* (Vanguard Press, New York, 1946, $2), prefaced by Mr. Koussevitzky himself. And Hugo Leichtentritt, a musicologist of repute and a former Lecturer of Harvard University, has fathered *Serge Koussevitzky, the Boston Symphony Orchestra and the New American Music* (Harvard University Press, Cambridge, Mass., 1946, $3).

Both volumes are slender, and their tone is unctuous. The first sketches ever so lightly the history of the celebrated summer festivals that have now grown into a training school for composers, conductors, and orchestral musicians. The second enumerates the American compositions played by Serge Koussevitzky and the Boston Symphony Orchesta (sometimes under other leaders) since 1924. The list is large and impressive. If Mr. Leichtentritt's critical paragraphs are weakened by the fact that he has neither heard many of the works nor had access to their scores, the tabulation of Mr. Koussevitzky's public encouragements to American composers alone is of value as proving once and for all (if Walter Damrosch, Frederick Stock, Pierre Monteux, and Leopold Stokowski had not proved it before) that a sustained program policy supporting contemporary composition does not keep subscribers away from symphony concerts.

And now to supplement these two books, which are clearly official and more than a little superficial, arrives a full-length biography of the maestro which is neither. It is entitled simply

Koussevitzky, by Moses Smith (Allen, Towne, and Heath, New York, 1947, $4). Announced for sale on February 15, its distribution has been held up for the time being by an injunction that prohibits its publication, sale, and distribution till Justice Shientag of the New York Supreme Court shall have determined whether the book's circulation will do its subject "irreparable harm." If the present writer, who has read an advance copy received before the injunction was issued, is in any way typical of the American reading public, it certainly, in his opinion, will not. The only possible harm he can envisage to so impregnable a reputation as that of Serge Koussevitzky is that already done by his own efforts to suppress the book.

Moses Smith, a trained newspaper man, for many years music critic of the *Boston Evening Transcript* as well as a friend of Mr. Koussevitzky, has produced a far more thorough study, a better work of scholarship than either Mr. Howe or Mr. Leichtentritt, scholars both by trade. There seems little in the book of factual statement that is subject to question. Whether Mr. Koussevitzky, in view of his great devotion to the memory of his second wife, is made unhappy by mention of his first marriage, hitherto not publicized in America, is scarcely germane. Neither is his possible sensitivity to reports of his quarrels with musicians and with blood relatives. These are, as a matter of fact, common knowledge; and they legitimately form part of the whole story of his musical life, just as his first marriage does of any complete biography.

Judgments and opinions, expressed over any writer's signature, are, of course, personal. The conductor's legal complaint objected to Mr. Smith's statement that Koussevitzky had succeeded as a conductor in spite of imperfect early training in musical theory and score reading. This also, if I may make so bold, has long been common knowledge among musicians. Nor is the estimable doctor unique among the conducting great for being in a certain sense self-taught. Leopold Stokowski, Sir Thomas Beecham, and Charles Munch, great interpreters all of them, did not come to conducting through early mastery of the conservatory routines. They bought, muscled, or impressed their way in and then settled down to learn their job. They succeeded gloriously, as Koussevitzky has done. All honor to them. They have all, Koussevitzky included, contributed more of value to the technique of their art than most of the first-prize-in-harmony boys ever have.

But great pedagogues, and the good doctor is one, do hate hearing that their own education has not been conventional, though it rarely was. And all great artists loathe criticism. They do; they really do. What they want, what they need, what they live on, as Gertrude Stein so rightly said, is praise. They can never get enough of it. And sometimes, when they have come to be really powerful in the world, they take the attitude that anything else is libel and should be suppressed. Dr. Koussevitzky's complaint, as I remember, did not use the word "libel." It spoke of possibly "irreparable injury." Well, criticism is often injurious; there is no question about that. Many a recitalist, receiving unfavorable reviews, finds it more difficult to secure further engagements than if the reports had been less critical. Minor careers have been ruined overnight that way. Major careers are rarely harmed by criticism, because major artists can take it. They don't like to; but they have to; so they do. All the same, it is the big boys, the great big boys that nothing could harm, that squawk the loudest. I know, because I have been in the business for several years now.

Mr. Smith's book makes Koussevitzky out to be a very great man indeed, but it also makes him human. Gone is the legend of his infallibility. Renewed is one's faith in his deep sincerity, his consecration, his relentless will to make the world permanently better than he found it. Nobody, I am sure, can read the book through without admiring him more. And the faith of the pious need not be shaken by reading that he has not always been toward his fellow man just and slow to anger. Civilization would be just a racket if we had to learn all we know about the lives of great men from their paid agents.

Mr. Koussevitzky is not the only first-class conductor in the world, though he is one of the best. Nor is he the only first-class conductor the Boston Symphony Orchestra has enjoyed. Nor does he any longer play the double bass in public, though when he did he was, by common consent, world champion. His unique position in a world full of excellent conductors, many of them devoted to contemporary music, is that he has played more of it, launched more of it, published more of it, and paid for more of it than anybody else living. That is the clear message

of Mr. Smith's biography. Everything else, a petulant gesture
here and there, a musical or family quarrel, a pretentious remark, a vainglorious interview, the present court action—all
these things serve the picture; they bring him more vividly to
life. How can anyone mind knowing them? Only he himself, apparently, hasting fearfully toward Parnassus, though his throne
there has long been reserved for him, and involved, no doubt,
in a publicity apotheosis that has already begun, would see any
value in posing before an already worshiping universe without
the customary habiliment of one human weakness. His lawsuit,
of course, adds to the tableau that he has essayed so carefully
to compose just that.

February 23, 1947

The Horowitz Mood

VLADIMIR HOROWITZ, pianist, in recital last night at Carnegie
Hall, performing *Bruyères, General Lavine,* and three études by Debussy, the Mendelssohn-Liszt *Hochzeitsmarsch* and Variations, and
works by Haydn, Schumann, Prokofiev, and Chopin.

VLADIMIR HOROWITZ, who played last night in Carnegie
Hall his second piano recital of the season, is justly famous
as a marksman of the keyboard. To play the piano quite that
loud and quite that fast with accuracy is given to few in any
generation. To project at the same time so strongly a sentiment
of controlled and relentless violence is given to none other in
ours. It is, no doubt, the very intensity of this characteristic
Horowitz mood, or expression, that makes his quieter passages
sound mostly, by comparison, tame. By themselves they are
pretty good music making, though not invariably of the best.
Heard beside his bravura work, it becomes clear that they are
not what one has come to hear, what anybody present would
come a second time to hear.

Just as there is a characteristic Horowitz mood of expression,
there is also, equally characteristic, the Horowitz piano tone.
This is plangent, brassy, and dark in color. It evokes the trombone rather than the trumpet. And it is mostly richly in evidence
in loud passages. At any dynamic level lower than mezzo forte
it fails to vibrate. From mezzo forte to fortissimo and beyond it

is commanding and, because of this artist's unusual finger and arm-weight control, varied and interesting. This is why, I think, Mr. Horowitz's public is likely to be a bit restless in the early part of a program or during the meditative and poetic parts of any long piece. One is waiting for the moment when both the characteristic sound and the characteristic fury will be turned loose, when Horowitz will stop being respectful of the classics and start being his unafraid self.

The Horowitz tone is not varied in color. Debussy shows up that weakness in it. But it is so highly varied in weight and articulation (in staccato playing he uses at least four different shortnesses) that its coloristic monotony is compensated for by its wide gamut of dynamic differentiation. Abstention from excessive use of the sustaining pedal brings out all this variety of percussive attack with a dryness and a clarity unequaled in the work of any other pianist now appearing before the public.

Nevertheless, for all the technical mastery displayed and all the real musical excitement provoked, Horowitz's playing is monotonous and, more often than not, musically false. He never states a simple melody frankly. He teases it by accenting unimportant notes and diminishing his tonal volume on all the climactic ones. The only contrast to brio that he knows is the affettuoso style. Only when handling the objectively pictur-esque, as in Debussy, does he seem at home in soft music. There, though he lacks the lighter, brighter colorations, he tam-pers little with the plain expressivity and gives, in consequence, a reading musically acceptable. But even here he is more con-vincing in the technically elaborate Études than in the poetically more delicate Preludes.

Last night's big show of the evening was a fancied-up ver-sion, by himself, of Liszt's Variations on the Mendelssohn Wed-ding March. Last year it was Sousa's *Stars and Stripes Forever*, complete with piccolo part. Another time it was Saint-Saëns's *Danse Macabre*. There is always something of the kind. Nobody else plays that kind so devastatingly well. Your reviewer always regrets there isn't more of it on any program. When a man can play hard music like that so satisfyingly, one regrets that he should spend so much of the evening worrying standard repertory.

April 9, 1946

Money's Worth

ALEXANDER BRAILOWSKY, pianist, in recital last night at Carnegie Hall, performing the Bach-Busoni Toccata and Fugue in D minor, Hummel's *Rondo Favori*, Liszt's Sonata in B minor, Brahms's Intermezzo in B-flat minor, the Mendelssohn-Rachmaninoff Scherzo from *Midsummer Night's Dream*, Debussy's *Reflets dans l'eau*, Ravel's Toccata, and seven works by Chopin.

ALEXANDER BRAILOWSKY's recital of piano music last night in Carnegie Hall was a model of the "good show" produced by legitimate means. He dramatized the music that he played, and he dramatized the excellence of his excellent execution. He dramatized these as a harmony, too, not as a conflict of opposing elements. Everything he played was consequently a human, as well as a musical, pleasure. Not a very deep pleasure, perhaps, but a real one.

Mr. Brailowsky has a natural gift for making music, untainted by intellectuality, and a masterful hand. His instincts are as gracious as his technique is sound. He exploits sentiment without getting hot around the collar, brilliance and brio with a visible delight. He paces a piece, any piece, as if it were an act of a play, builds it up, tapers it off, without hurry and without lingering. And he plays the right notes.

No audience can fail to respond to such charm, such competence, such courtesy. This member of last night's audience responded most vigorously to the Liszt Sonata, which offered the further delight of an apt stylization. This consisted of executing all its rolling and rumbling figurations with the driest, cleanest, and most exact modern finger mechanics. To the mere power of its climactic moments, which was already considerable, there was added thus an incisiveness that this work rarely enjoys; and its Romantic fury took on, in consequence, a diabolic quality at once terrifying and completely appropriate.

Mr. Brailowsky's Chopin benefited from the same clarity of articulation; and so did his Hummel Rondo, his Mendelssohn, Debussy, and Ravel. A Brahms Intermezzo, though cleanly read, lacked intimacy. And the Bach organ Toccata and Fugue in D minor (in the Busoni transcription) rather missed out all around. This is a clocklike piece, not a storm in the mountains.

Its themes and its figurations are all mechanistic. Its expressive power in performance comes from playing up this mechanical quality rather than from trying to conceal it. Any organ transcription, moreover, must derive on the pianoforte any overpowering effect that is desired from a relentless rhythm rather than from mere pounding.

With these two exceptions, the evening was full of good musical value. No revelations, mind you. Mr. Brailowsky projects little original poetry and almost no novel meanings. But he makes music harmoniously, brilliantly, and quite soundly enough for anybody's price of admission. He is an honest virtuoso.

December 6, 1945

The Noble Style

ALEXANDER BOROVSKY, pianist, in recital last night at Carnegie Hall, performing, among other works, the Bach-Liszt Organ Prelude and Fugue, Beethoven's Thirty-two Variations on an Original Theme, Chopin's Sonata in B-flat minor, two Messiaen preludes, Prokofiev's *Danza* and *Sarcasm*, two Rachmaninoff preludes, and Liszt's *Sonnetto del Petrarcha* No. 104 and *Étude transcendante* No. 10.

ALEXANDER BOROVSKY, who played a piano recital last night in Carnegie Hall, is a technician of the first water and a musician of impeccable taste. He is businesslike, forthright, masterful. Nowhere in his work is there any vulgarity, any obscurity, or any inadequacy. Few pianists give such deep satisfaction and oppress the spirit so little, and only a very few great have his rhythmic solidity. His work is serious, solid, sound, and sober.

It is sober, not from any lack of fire in the temperament, but rather from the nature of Borovsky's piano tone, which is all of one color. This is not at all an ugly tone, but neither is it exactly pretty. It is merely a little lacking in variety. It is hugely varied in weight, or loudness, and most exact about durations. But it lacks on its palette the lighter colorations. Its noble unity at all the levels of loudness has been achieved, apparently, at the sacrifice of brightness, brilliance, and liquidity.

This artist, a very great one and a man of broad musical understanding, is at his best, consequently, in music that calls for little coloristic expression. His Bach and his Beethoven last night were admirable in every way, though the present reviewer could have wished for a less consistent legato in the former, a more pointed evocation of harpsichord sonorities. His Proko-fiev and Rachmaninoff were impressively sonorous too, dark-sounding, clear, and harmonious.

All the music of the Parisian school—Chopin, Messiaen, and Liszt—though thoroughly eloquent and lucid—left one long-ing for a sweeter caress, a gratuitous beauty of sound, a more imaginative orchestration. Color is part of such music's planned expressivity. A black-and-white photograph of it shows the for-mal composition but does not make a complete communica-tion. In all these works Mr. Borovsky achieved effects of no mean grandeur, but the poetry of them all was pale from a lack in their performance of full tonal luminosity. Mr. Borovsky is at his best in the noble, or massive, style.

March 18, 1947

Grace and Power

GEORGE CHAVCHAVADZE, pianist, in recital last night at Carnegie Hall, performing Beethoven's Sonata No. 21 (Op. 53, "Waldstein"), the de Falla-Chavchavadze Suite on Themes from *El Amor Brujo*, the Debussy Suite for Piano, and four works by Chopin.

GEORGE CHAVCHAVADZE, who gave a piano recital last night in Carnegie Hall, his first appearance here in several years, is one of the most delightful pianists of them all. There is variety in his work and spirit and imagination. His are a high color-range and a broad dynamic gamut. There are force and tenderness in him, relentlessness of rhythm and flexibility, wide sweep in any piece's progress, and an incredible luxury of detail. And always he plays with freshness, so that even works as familiar as the Chopin G-minor Ballade or Beethoven's "Waldstein" Sonata become absorbing to listen to, as if one had not heard them in twenty years.

The sources of that freshness are several. One is a natural feel-ing for Romanticism, a gift for moving about with grace among the passions. Another is the kind of alertness that keeps his full musical faculties employed in what he is doing. He never gets bored and begins to pound. Still another is his quite phenomenal finger agility, which enables him to sweep clearly through complexity and right up to a climax without any hesitation. He dramatizes the music, not his technical accomplishments. These last are many, but he does not throw them at you. He is an artist fecund of thought, right in sentiment, and vastly abundant as to means.

His whole program was a delight for the genuine originality of his readings, an originality all the more welcome for being at no point arbitrary. He played the first movement of the "Waldstein" Sonata somewhat faster than we are used to hearing it, gave it by that means a fury that becomes it well. His Debussy suite *Pour le piano* had a breadth all unusual to it, but one that the work sustains without giving at the seams. His Chopin was a dream of supple grace, sweet, full, passionate, and grand. And if, in the great A-flat Polonaise, his finger strength was less impressive in the mounting scales than that, say, of Horowitz, the beauty of his tone at all the levels of loudness, from a whisper to a full military evocation, was more consistent, more varied in all imaginable kinds of loveliness than almost anybody else's ever is.

Mr. Chavchavadze's own Suite on themes from Falla's *El Amor Brujo* is a masterpiece of piano transcription. It evokes the very sound of de Falla's orchestra. Whether the work, as played last night, is perhaps a little long for concert usage remains to be ascertained from further performances. Few theater works are tight enough in structure to support concert exposition at the length of more than fifteen minutes. The present version is nowhere lacking in interest for piano detail, but the original work was not built for concert conditions. It is quite possible that the omission of certain passages that seem musically static in the concert hall would lighten the suite up and give it the full force of its great musical beauty without the loss of pianistic brilliance.

March 24, 1947

In the First Category

MARYLA JONAS, pianist, in recital yesterday afternoon at Carnegie Hall, performing Handel's Passacaglia, Michelangelo Rossi's Andantino in G major, Haydn's Variations in F minor, W. F. Bach's Capriccio, Mozart's Rondo in D, Schubert's Sonata No. 3 and Impromptu No. 3, and six works by Chopin.

MARYLA JONAS, who played the piano yesterday afternoon to a packed Carnegie Hall, is everything the reviewers said of her last spring. One can like or not this-that-or-the-other about her performance, but she is a solo pianist of the first category in any meaning of that term.

Her technique is clean and dry, her tone agreeable and varied in color, her musical understanding sound, her communication straightforward. Straightforwardness, indeed, is the quality of her work that lifts it above mere competence and puts it among that of the great. There is nothing kittenish about it or affected or flamboyant or timid or tentative or ostentatious. Miss Jonas makes her every musical point in the most direct manner imaginable. All is under control: her thought, her feeling, her fiery Polish temperament; and her technical powers respond without hesitancy to every expressive demand.

The basis of this alacrity, the organizing force behind all her skill and knowledge, is a rhythmic instinct unspoiled by bad training or mental cross-purposes, refined, on the contrary, by a far from superficial musical culture. In the classic style, playing Handel and Haydn and Mozart and Beethoven, the metrical march of her readings is as relentless as Landowska's. And when she plays the high Romantics, like Schubert and Chopin, her rubato, at the height of its freedom and fancy, never lets one forget for one instant that rhythmic freedom is a comment on measure, not a violation of it. Only first-class musicians ever work in this way.

Another region in which this artist's work is more sophisticated than that of ordinary good pianists is that of dynamic relief. When she plays plain chord passages she plays them with all voices equal. But when the musical texture is more complex, which is most of the time, she organizes her melody, her accompanying figures, her bass, her countermelody, and her interjected melodic comments at different levels of loudness, using also different kinds of tone, orchestrating the piece, so to speak, for clarity. The variety in dynamic relief that she employs is very great indeed, and the boldness with which she brings forward or almost whispers that which merits such treatment is invariably justified by the lucidity that results. She oversimplifies nothing; she merely amplifies emphasis by composing her dynamics rather elaborately.

Nor does she shy away from sentiment. When she makes a crescendo on a rising melodic curve, she lets it continue to the top of the curve. When passage work is fast and furious she keeps it fast and furious, no matter what technical difficulties it may present. She deals with every kind of emotion frankly and with every executional problem courageously. This frankness and courage are the marks of her individuality as a performer. As for mere mannerisms, technical or expressive, she has fewer, probably, than any other artist of her class now working before the public.

That she is a curious and wonderful Romantic survival, as many thought on hearing her last season, I do not believe. Schooled quality like hers and working methods of that efficiency are not atavistic throwbacks. They imply a musical understanding that can meet more emergencies than those of any particular repertory. That Miss Jonas is at home in all the centuries was proved yesterday by her impeccable renderings of both the early eighteenth century and (in the encores) of our own. She is a modern musician so thoroughly equipped that she can even play the Romantics convincingly. Being Polish, of course, helps.

December 8, 1946

Incomparable Chopin

GUIOMAR NOVAES, pianist, in recital yesterday afternoon at Carnegie Hall, performing Chopin's Sonata in B-flat minor and works by Bach, Scarlatti, Beethoven, Albéniz, Camargo Guarnieri, and Isador Philipp.

GUIOMAR NOVAES gave yesterday afternoon in the Town Hall the most absorbing, as well as the most convincing, rendition of Chopin's B-flat minor Sonata that this reviewer has ever heard. Her whole recital, indeed, was lovely and sensible. Bach, Scarlatti,

Beethoven, and divers light modern pieces were interpreted
with full competence both mental and fingerwise. But the poetry and the grandeur of the Chopin sonata were beyond all
comparison with any reading of the work that this student has
previously encountered. Cheers seemed to indicate that the
audience was impressed, too.

Against all precedent, Miss Novaes dramatized the piece itself
instead of the difficulties of its execution. These she accepted
as incidental, as something never to be allowed to get in the
way of the musical discourse. She took up no time reaching for
notes or hesitating before heavy chords. She played her climaxes
as musicians think them, on the upward sweep of feeling. As a
result, the piece came off with a spontaneity and a conviction
that left one no less swept away by her eloquence than admiring
of her marksmanship.

The climactic section of the work, in Miss Novaes's reading,
was the Funeral March. The passionate earlier movements led
up to the tragic calm of this; and the finale was like a coda to it,
light as the wind, brief, desolate, all passion spent. The March
itself was majestic in rhythm, impersonal in pathos. It was the
evocation of a burial scene, not any artist's display of grief. And
the softly soaring middle section was little but a melody and a
bass, its inner notes as light as a harp or a clarinet heard outdoors with the wind blowing the other way.

It seemed rather a pity that so great a pianist as Miss Novaes
(who is no newcomer to New York, either; she has appeared
here pretty regularly since 1915) should have accepted to play on
such an inferior instrument as the Steinway she used yesterday.
Its tone was brassy throughout and lacking in depth. Its one
virtue was the uniformity of its sound. It was not, like so many
of the pianos heard nowadays in concert halls, all bass and high
treble with no proper resonance at all in the center of the scale.
In a season full of ugly-sounding pianos, however, it was the
least agreeable your announcer has encountered.

October 27, 1946

Warm Welcome

MYRA HESS, pianist, in recital yesterday afternoon at Town Hall, performing Bach's French Suite No. 5, Beethoven's Six Variations on a Theme in F major and Sonata in A-flat, and Brahms's Sonata in F minor.

DAME MYRA HESS, who played a pianoforte recital yesterday afternoon in the Town Hall, has, as a musician, instinct and intelligence. She has the quality which in France is called *musicalité*, the gift for making music sound like music. Also, she is a workman of taste and refinement. She takes convincing tempos, phrases soundly, analyzes a work correctly, executes it with ease and distinction. What she lacks is temperament, the power always to respond in public to her music's own sound and to add, inevitably, communication. She plays intelligently and she has a natural nobility. But she doesn't easily "give," as the young people would say.

Her playing yesterday of a Bach French Suite was pleasant, of two Beethoven works (the Six Variations, Opus 34, and the A-flat Sonata, Opus 110) pretty but distant. It was as if, having known them all her life, she were reminding other musicians of how they went. She did not so much play them as strum them. She exposed them clearly, sounded them out agreeably, but abstained from any personal involvement with their expressive content. The result was hard for a disinterested listener to keep his mind on. And her constant imposition of slight crescendos and decrescendos on every phrase removed from musical design its expressive urgency, reduced all to a restful lullaby.

Halfway through the Brahms F-minor Sonata (Opus 5) a change took place. She got into the scherzo through its rhythm, stopped strumming and really played the piece. From there to the end of the work she made music squarely, forthrightly, convincingly, instead of just dreaming about it in a flowing robe. One realized then that her celebrity is not due merely to her admirable wartime activities. Here her work had a plainness of speech, an impersonal grandeur that was served rather than diminished by refinements of touch and phraseology.

Dame Myra is no devotee of the big tone, though she can play loud enough when she needs to. It is the breadth of her musical thought that gives dignity to her execution. For all the gentleness of her sentiments, the grace of her musical orna-ments, the wit of her dry little scale passages, she is not a finicky musician. She is sensible, straightforward, and noble, when she gets warmed up.

Yesterday she was rather slow warming up, though the mas-sive audience had warmed to her from the beginning, had stood up, indeed, to welcome her. Perhaps the gracious speech she made at the end of the first half of the program, in which she thanked America so prettily and with such sweet sincerity for its moral and financial help in continuing throughout the war daily free concerts at the National Gallery in London, had broken down by verbal means her previous emotional reserve. In any case, she was first-class when she finally got going.

October 13, 1946

Violence and Charm

RUDOLF FIRKUSNY, pianist, in recital last night at Carnegie Hall, performing Mozart's Fantasy in C minor, Haydn's Sonata in C minor, four Chopin études, Beethoven's Sonata No. 21 (Op. 33, "Waldstein"), Martinů's Fantasy and Rondo, and two Czech dances by Smetana.

RUDOLF FIRKUSNY, who played a recital of piano music in Carnegie Hall last night, is a dynamic temperament with lots of punch in his fingers. He plays very loud and very fast most of the time. He plays most of the written notes, too, and often adds extra ones by accident. I once heard him play a concerto with orchestra most prettily. But concerto playing doesn't show up faults of musicianship as a recital does. Last night's concert revealed a pianist with far from negligible (though not com-plete, by any means) keyboard mastery and a musical tempera-ment of such banal violence as it has not often been my lot to encounter among reputable performers.

Excepting for two of the Chopin Études, which were sensibly and agreeably read, everything—literally everything—was so deformed by speed and pounding that it was difficult to tell one piece from another. Under such circumstances it was not pos-sible for one to have any clear impression of Martinů's Fantasy and Rondo beyond recognition of the fact that it is a work of serious intentions and some length. What a listener not familiar with Beethoven's "Waldstein" sonata might have made of the piece is difficult to imagine. It was recognizable to your reviewer only by the notes of it, its expressive content, as rendered, being chiefly reminiscent of the movie pianism of his youth.

The first movement might have been entitled "A Day at the Races," with steeplechase hazards being got over at full speed and ponies constantly coming lickety-split down the home-stretch. The rondo was like the accompaniment to a class-B Western. A young miss of pastoral upbringing had apparently been seized by a band of outlaws on horseback, taken to a lonely spot, and left there. She was very sad about this, and then the outlaws took her to an even lonelier place and tied her hands behind her. A gallant young cowboy, however, came to her rescue and galloped her away. On the ride home the two had a tender moment in which she thanked him for his trouble. And when they got back to town there was general dancing.

If you think I am making fun of either Beethoven or Mr. Firkusny, just try playing the "Waldstein" Sonata at 120 half-notes to the minute. You will see that the effect is somewhat as I have described it, especially if you play all the passages marked *f* as if they were marked *ffff*. The result is both piquant and trite. If you play a whole program through in this way you will discover that only so tough a work as this particular sonata is capable, under the speed-up and the pounding process, of sounding as if it had a subject at all. Music fast and furious is not always fun. If Mr. Firkusny were less charming as a platform personality, it is doubtful whether his kind of music making would be as appealing to music lovers as it clearly was, I must admit, to last night's audience.

December 14, 1944

Too Fast for Brilliance

SIMON BARERE, pianist, in recital last night at Carnegie Hall, performing, among other works, Bach's Chromatic Fantasia and Fugue, Liszt's *Gnomenreigen*, the Gounod-Liszt Waltz from *Faust*, and Chopin's Fantaisie in F minor and Andante Spianato et Grande Polonaise.

SIMON BARERE, who played a piano recital last night in Carnegie Hall, is justly famous for his technical skill. For finger agility and velocity execution he has few equals. But he is also a better musician than one would expect a pianist to be who is celebrated chiefly for technical prowess.

Curiously enough he plays easy pieces more effectively than he does hard ones. In the technical repose of the former his honest and graceful readings are most agreeable. In difficult pieces he almost invariably plays too fast. Not too fast for accuracy; at any speed he plays the right notes, all of them. But too fast to make a really brilliant effect.

Brilliance is the dramatization of speed. It is the throwing of it into relief by the use of great variety in rhythmic articulation and in loudness. Mr. Barere has a steady rhythm but not, in loud fast passages, much variety of accentuation. Here is where his high speeds become ineffective. A harmonious acoustical blur is produced that lacks the final clarity of dramatized emphasis. He proves that almost any piece can be played faster than is customary, but he does not prove that any brilliance or other expressive value is added to it by this fact. On the contrary, he demonstrates rather that pieces have a "critical" speed, as the physicists might say, beyond which added velocity of execution produces diminishing expressive returns.

From an expressive point of view his most powerful execution last night was that of Bach's Chromatic Fantasia and Fugue. Here the rapid swoops of the ornamentation, played without weight, were highly dramatic in contrast to the chordal phrases of the Fantasia and to the clear articulation of the successive thematic entries in the Fugue.

Liszt's *Gnomenreigen*, also played softly, was interesting as a velocity stunt only. In the Chopin works Mr. Barere played the slow soft passages charmingly, missed the grand accent of the loud fast ones. The *Faust* Waltz, in Liszt's transcription, was welcome for its rarity on contemporary programs. It was played too fast for real brilliance; but it has pretty tunes and its acrobatics are no end of fun.

November 19, 1946

Sound without Fury

ALEXANDER UNINSKY, pianist, in recital last night at Carnegie Hall, performing Schumann's *Carnaval*, six pieces by Chopin, and works by Scarlatti, Bach, Debussy, and Stravinsky.

ALEXANDER UNINSKY, who played a piano recital last night in Carnegie Hall, is a sound artist both technically and intellectually. He plays correctly, and he understands the rhetoric of music. He knows about styles, too; and he respects the texts of the historic masters. He is a completely accomplished musician. And that is about the list of his qualities.

It is not quite the list, because there are certain special beauties in his execution that are beyond this stipulation. These consist chiefly in the advantages of a wide dynamic range. He can play softer and louder without sounding ugly than almost anybody else. And from his tiniest pianissimo to his majestic forte the control is perfect, the crescendo constant. One is grateful for such care. And so satisfying an amplitude of sound is not often at the disposition of any soloist.

One is grateful, too, for musicianly readings; and one wishes these were sufficient satisfaction for concertgoing. But they are not. We like personal poetry and passionate clarity and something of the unforeseen. Lightness of hand is not full compensation for the heaviness of a methodical spirit. And a magnificent loudness, though pleasant enough in itself, adds little to the meaning of the music of Robert Schumann. We forgive more easily, I think, an inspired misconception than we do a stodgily reasonable rendering of familiar pieces.

The stodginess in Mr. Uninsky's work is due largely to a not very interesting rhythmic articulation. His beats and quantities are all in place, but they are read rather than felt. His rhythm lacks tension and breath. As a result his piano playing always sounds like piano playing, never like singing or trumpets or harps or wind or quiet rain. It evokes no orchestra, no land-scape, no dancing, no meditation, and no fury. The notes are there, and the sound of them is good. But they carry one no-where save right back to the printed page they came from. Perhaps also a bit to Russia, where Mr. Uninsky originally came from. Because there is a kind of Muscovite crudeness beneath all his studied imitation of flexibility. He has facility, schooling, and knowledge, but no real ease.

In view of the reverberant acoustics of Carnegie Hall, it might be a good idea if pianists playing there would use a mini-mum of pedal instead of the more customary maximum. A dry articulation, especially in the left hand, is always of advantage in rooms where the cessation of sound is not instantaneous. That particular room gives its best result to pianists when all middle and low-lying passages are kept brittle.

January 18, 1945

Young Man, Why So Serious?

WEBSTER AITKEN, pianist, in recital yesterday afternoon at Town Hall, performing Bach's Toccata in C minor, Mozart's Rondo in A minor, and Beethoven's "Diabelli" Variations.

WEBSTER AITKEN, who gave the first of a series of three piano concerts yesterday afternoon in Town Hall, is a master pianist and a master musician. He can play anything and play it right. His tone is beautiful; his execution is dry and clean; his rhythm is impeccable; and everything sings. Really, one doesn't hear piano playing like that every year. Technicians of that order do not commonly toe so strict a line between sweetness and virtuosity, all the while keeping everything intense.

What bothered this writer about yesterday's concert was what seemed to him an excessive seriousness about the whole thing, both program and playing. It is proper enough to begin with a Bach toccata and a Mozart rondo, and certainly both were executed yesterday with admirable clarity and with an amazingly straightforward loveliness. Perhaps it was frivolous to wish for something lighter to follow up these substantial matters. In any case, Beethoven's "Diabelli" Variations seemed to him a heavy dish, handsomely presented though they were.

And they must have had something of the same effect on the pianist himself, because after the fifty-one minutes that they required of continuous and thorough music making, he responded to the warm applause of the house with seven or eight returns to bow, but refused firmly to play any encores. Not a tidbit or sweetmeat did we get, though we all wanted something of the kind and needed it to activate digestion.

There was nothing wrong about the "Diabelli" Variations except the work itself, which is laborious, cumbersome, and long. As read by Mr. Aitken, it was far from boresome, which it can so easily be. But it was tiring, nevertheless. It brought out all the rather heavy seriousness of this pianist's temperament, offered no play at all to his gift for simple song or to his genius for American-style, twentieth-century rhythmic scansion. He plays the Variations too beautifully for one to mind greatly his putting them on the program. But this reviewer kept wishing, all the same, that Mr. Aitken had had the wit to be less ponderous. It was a throwing away, as if deliberately, of his genuine charm and youth for an old-master effect that seemed all the more inappropriate for being so complete.

January 21, 1945

Intensity and Brains

ROSALYN TURECK, pianist, in recital last night at Town Hall, performing Preludes and Fugues from Bach's *Well-Tempered Clavier*, Mozart's Sonata in C major, Beethoven's Sonata No. 23 (Op. 57, "Appassionata"), the Copland Piano Sonata, and Brahms's Variations and Fugue on a Theme by Handel.

ROSALYN TURECK, who played a recital of piano music last night in Town Hall, is an invigorating musician. We are not used to encountering in the same person a passionate temperament and a first-class mind. And we are certainly not used to finding in the same pianist a first-class technique and a correct sense of rhythm.

Nothing Miss Tureck played last night was lacking in stimulation to the musical faculties except the Mozart C-major Sonata (K. 330). Even that was more interesting to listen to than the performances of it that one usually hears, though she misconstrued its sentiments, I think, broke the back of its rhythm, and utterly missed the fact that its slow movement is a minuet. The secret of her work, at its best, seems to be that her passionate nature finds its completest expression in works that demand by their own nature an objective approach.

Her playing of Bach, for instance, was vivid. And her execution of the Brahms-Handel Variations was a triumph of expressive variety. She warmed up these somewhat cold masters and made them stimulating, gave them high relief, projection, carrying power. The Beethoven "Appassionata" she is not quite so fully in command of yet. The shape of it is there and all its healthy violence of expression, but Miss Tureck seems to be not quite willing to let it play itself. She loses its relentless continuity by mooning over the soft passages and whipping up the loud ones.

The Aaron Copland Sonata is not quite her piece, either. It is a meditative, a lyrical, an improvisatory work. She lacks the lightness of touch, the spontaneity it requires. She gets excited by it and pounds. Its beauty is its ease, and Miss Tureck has no ease. She has intensity, both of feeling and of intelligence. But she works best in corseted music. Copland's neo-Romantic elegance of expression is almost as foreign to her temperament as Mozart's urbanity.

Many a contemporary pianist, especially among the younger American ones, is weak in Romantic repertory but completely at home with the moderns. Miss Tureck is quite good in Romantic works, not at all comfortable in modern ones, and amazingly, wonderfully exciting in the music of pre-Classic times. Indeed, the farther away she gets from contemporary life the more sure-footed becomes her command, intellectual, technical, and passional, of the musical terrain.

She is a musician of high gifts, and she is maturing most satisfactorily. It was perfectly clear to last night's audience on the tenth anniversary of her Town Hall debut that she is an artist any country might be proud of. She has gone far in one decade, and she will go farther in another. Miss Tureck is not just an ordinary good pianist. She is invigorating; she is interesting; she is somebody.

November 13, 1945

Young but Not Romantic

SIDNEY FOSTER, pianist, in recital last night at Carnegie Hall, performing the Bach-Liszt Organ Fantasia and Fugue, Brahms's Variations and Fugue on a Theme by Handel, five études by Chopin, Prokofiev's Valse from *War and Peace* and *Suggestion diabolique*, Norman Dello Joio's *Prelude: To a Young Musician*, two Mexican dances by Paul Bowles, and three pieces by Liszt.

SIDNEY FOSTER's piano recital in Carnegie Hall last night was honored by the first performance of a gracefully meditative piece by Norman Dello Joio and of two picturesque Mexican dances by Paul Bowles. Also by the American premiere of a waltz from one of Prokofiev's forthcoming operas, *War and Peace*, which turned out to be good routine Prokofiev of the noisy kind.

It is possible that Mr. Foster's noisy execution may have contributed to the routine effect of this work, as well as to that of the even noisier *Suggestion diabolique*, by the same author. Most pianists seem to think Prokofiev's music needs an iron touch, and this pianist is not one to spare the ends of his fingers.

He rattled quite as noisily and with no small violence through Liszt, Chopin, and Brahms. Only in the Liszt transcription of Bach's Fantasia and Fugue in G minor did he show a consistent nobility of tone and a delicate continuity in the feeling expressed. The works of his fellow Americans also drew from him care for the music's plain sense. In spite, however, of strong fingers and much dexterity, Mr. Foster seems not to perceive very exactly the subject matter of the great Romantics. No matter how different their notes are, the pieces all sound alike.

The phenomenon is one I have observed before among the most brilliantly gifted of our young Americans. They plow through the Romantic repertory because it is expected of them, but their hand is brutal with it. The eighteenth century and the twentieth they understand; they handle these with love and with a care for differences. But the history of music between 1790 and 1890 is their blind spot. They spend nine tenths of their working time practicing it, and it occupies at least that proportion of their concert playing-time. All the same, exactly as most Central Europeans of an older generation have no real understanding of any music but this, lots of our younger American

musicians, in spite of elaborate instruction about it and of inveterate assiduity toward it, find themselves stymied by this very
repertory. It escapes their comprehension; it is alien to their
ways of feeling. And the sooner they find this out the better.
In spite of the conservatism of the concert public, there is no
future for a musician in anything he doesn't like, understand,
take on with ease.

October 19, 1944

Perfect Host

MAXIM SCHAPIRO, pianist, in recital last night at Town Hall, per-
forming Beethoven's Sonata No. 21 (Op. 53, "Waldstein"), Schumann's
Kreisleriana, Nikolai Medtner's *Improvisation (Theme and Variations)*,
Fauré's Barcarolle No. 5, Ravel's Toccata, Villa-Lobos's Chôro No. 5,
Milhaud's *La Libertadora*, and Chopin's Andante Spianato et Grande
Polonaise Brillante.

MAXIM SCHAPIRO, who played his annual piano recital last
night in Town Hall, is a gentlemanly musician in the best
modern sense. Our preceding century knew the "gentleman
musician" in another form, namely, that of the man whose distinguished bearing (and private fortune) gave his lack of professional execution a certain immunity to criticism.

This species of elegant amateur has largely disappeared from
modern life, even in Boston. He has been replaced by thoroughly trained professionals who, nevertheless, approach music
with a certain reserve. This reserve is neither an emotional one
nor wholly intellectual. It is a kind of good manners toward
composers and their works which expresses itself in a style of
execution that, while neglecting no known device of clarity or
of comprehension, still omits any irrevocable personal involvement with the goings on.

Thus it was that Mr. Schapiro, though an expert technician
and an artist of no mean imagination, ended last night by presenting Beethoven and Schumann and Chopin along with the
composers of our century as if they were all guests at a musical
party of which he himself was the host. And, naturally, in such a
gracious and democratic arrangement, it was the younger men
who attracted most of the attention. The ancestral figures had

their proper program precedence. But the host, being a man of our time, could not quite conceal the fact that he was more at ease with his contemporaries than with his elders. And so it turned out to be a young people's party in spite of the fact that the list of composers physically present on the program appeared to the eye as a catholic one.

This is not to say that Mr. Schapiro was in any way negligent in his attentions to the great Romantics. He gave them their due and a smile, handled them with care, and went on to have fun elsewhere. He had fun with Medtner, formerly his teacher, with Fauré and Ravel and Milhaud and Villa-Lobos. He handled them all with skill, with care, and with a perfect knowledge of what they were up to. The results could not have been more charming. Or more entertaining, either. Especially when it turned out that Milhaud's *La Libertadora*, in his own version of the Brazilian style, was, to us foreigners, more convincingly Brazilian in language than a Choros subtitled "The Brazilian Soul" by Villa-Lobos, Brazil's most determinedly nationalistic composer.

Fauré's Fifth Barcarolle was gracefully tossed. And the Ravel Toccata from *Le Tombeau de Couperin* was a joy for sound. Perhaps the fuller pleasure one derived from the modern works was due in part to the fact that they were being played on the instrument they were written for, namely, the modern pianoforte. Even so, they were admirably rendered, as was also the final Chopin Andante Spianato and Polonaise. The Beethoven "Waldstein" and the Schumann *Kreisleriana*, like all good chaperones, seemed at the end of the evening to have called little attention to themselves, to have bored no one, and to have cramped nobody's style.

November 10, 1945

Gershwin Black and Blue

PHILHARMONIC-SYMPHONY ORCHESTRA, *Artur Rodzinski*, conductor, last night at Carnegie Hall, performing Gershwin's *American in Paris*, Piano Concerto in F, excerpts from *Porgy and Bess*, and *Rhapsody in Blue*. Soloists: *Oscar Levant*, piano, *Anne Brown*, soprano, and *Todd Duncan*, baritone.

THE MUSIC was charming; the performance was first-class; and the audience enjoyed itself thoroughly at last night's Pension Fund Concert of the Philharmonic in Carnegie Hall. It is a pleasure to see an audience react so favorably to all the pieces on a program. It is a pleasure to find that audiences are still reacting favorably to Gershwin's music, that they love it and understand it, admire it, respect it, and communicate with it. It is a pleasure to observe how stylishly Artur Rodzinski conducts it, Anne Brown and Todd Duncan sing it, Oscar Levant plays it on the pianoforte. The impeccable Oscar, as a matter of fact, is a pretty fascinating spectacle, no matter what he does.

Miss Brown sings the *Porgy and Bess* airs in standard concert manner. Mr. Duncan sings them in the black-face comedian style. Both manners seemed equally acceptable to the audience as a whole. Your reviewer found more dignity in her performance than in his, however, and more real singing. He has never been wholly comfortable in the presence of Negroes interpreting Negro life through the conventions of the white black-face stage. The whole procedure seems to him unbecoming. Gershwin's music, moreover, is neither Negroid nor in any sense primitive, and it always comes out more humane in a straightforward rendering.

Mr. Levant's renderings of the Concerto in F and the *Rhapsody in Blue* are scholarly, in the sense that they are the product of thorough study. They are authoritative, in the sense that nobody else plays these pieces with quite that air of knowing exactly what they are all about. They are masterful, in the sense that technically they are both powerful and accurate. They are a little dead, too, because though they have every other quality of great musical execution, they lack spontaneity.

The works themselves, of course, especially the *Rhapsody*, are not so fresh to us, nor to him, as they once were. And it is not easy to toss lightly any piece that is so impressive at the box office as the latter one is. Also, Levant is too loyal a musician to traffic in the charm of youth when maturity comes upon him. He is a serious pianist nowadays and one of the most competent. And if he plays Gershwin with all the weight and prestige that the great Europeans lend to their own repertory, plus a natural platform impressiveness such as few possess, that is the beautiful and wise thing for him to have learned to do.

He could not have kept his spontaneity, anyway; nobody can who has such gifts and real ambition. Gershwin's music remains a music of youth and full of youth's sweetness and ease, like Schubert's music. But Levant has grown up and become a master. He rather overpowers Gershwin, in consequence, as all the great mature interpreters do to the music of those who died young.

April 19, 1946

Musical Badminton

VERA APPLETON and MICHAEL FIELD, piano duo, in recital last night at Town Hall, performing works by Mozart, W. F. Bach, Bartók, Debussy, Fuleihan, Khachaturian, Richard Strauss, and Liszt.

VERA APPLETON and Michael Field played a far from banal program of music for two pianos in the Town Hall last night. There were unusual old pieces, brand new ones, and some pretty competent execution. The audience was grateful for all this and most responsive. Your reviewer regrets that attendance at bouts of duo-pianism is not his favorite form of spectator-sport.

Two pianists can play twice as many notes as one, and two pianos can make twice as much noise. They do not ordinarily make half as much music. The modern instrument, which is designed chiefly to hold its own against modern symphony orchestras in concerto playing, is inexpressive at all dynamic levels louder than one *f*. Two of them can increase in volume up to five or six *f*'s. But there is no beauty in the sound and little variety. It is too heavy for real brilliance, and the players are seated too far apart to achieve fine adjustments of balance, delicate give-and-take in rhythm. They take refuge inevitably in speed and in too heavy accents. The whole business is a sort of musical badminton, a game of crude energy rather than of refinement or of studied skill.

Appleton and Field do not perform less charmingly, within the limits of their medium, than most other duo-pianists. The intellectual tone of their programs, if last night's is typical, is higher than common. They have an awareness, evidently, of style, too, of varied approaches to different kinds of music. I suspect they are more interested in style, in fact, than in streamlining, because they did get the style for each piece roughly right and because they did not sacrifice this to the niceties of simultaneous attack.

Their work does not have the commercial polish we are used to in that of more famous teams. Its intentions are musical rather than slick. Unfortunately, unless I am wrong about the nature of the medium, duo-pianism has little to offer in the way of musical returns for musical labor. It is too inflexible a setup. All the teams go slick eventually. A smooth surfacing of the execution does not make their work any more interesting. But it does tend to conceal the paucity of expression.

November 9, 1944

Costume Party

PIERRE LUBOSHUTZ and GENIA NEMENOFF, piano duo, in recital last night at Town Hall, performing works by Bach, Brahms, Schubert, Mendelssohn, Koutzen, Rossini, Gretchaninov, and Riegger.

PIERRE LUBOSHUTZ and Genia Nemenoff, duo-pianists, gave an evening of imitations last night at the Town Hall. Their arrangement of a Bach Chorale-Prelude imitated tastefully the rubato style that was considered appropriate in my youth for rendering the Brahms Chorale-Preludes, and their rendering of the Brahms Variations on a Theme by Haydn imitated the ruinous rigidity with which enlightened provincial music teachers sometimes still play Bach's "Goldberg" Variations. The Prokofiev arrangement of Schubert waltzes, which followed, transported us to a Tyrolean-style beer hall possessing a mechanical pianoforte. And Mr. Luboshutz's arrangement of the Mendels-sohn Allegro Brillante sounded like nothing so much as a well-functioning coffee grinder.

The next masquerade, complete with scores and eyeglasses, represented a world-famous two-piano team being nice about modern music. Boris Koutzen's Sonatina for Two Pianos was the sacrificial offering, a hard and ugly tone being employed throughout so as to make it sound like some forgotten work from back in 1922, and a few (just a few) false notes being thrown in to show that the piece probably wasn't worth learning completely.

After that we had an arrangement of Rossini's baritone aria, "*Largo al factotum*," from *The Barber of Seville*, an artistic equivalent of Leschetizky's once-popular transcription for left hand alone of the sextet from *Lucia di Lammermoor*. Gretchaninov's *Berceuse*, which followed, is itself an imitation of the one by Chopin and of a music box at the same time. While Wallingford Riegger's *New Dance* is the finale of Stravinsky's *Sacre du printemps* with a couple of syncopated tunes added to make it sound American.

Consisting, as it did, almost entirely of transcriptions, the program as a whole was rather in the manner of those made popular in the last century by Liszt and Thalberg. I imagine we were all supposed to enter into the game, too, and applaud like mad. Indeed, many did. And indeed the precision with which Mr. and Mrs. Luboshutz imitated a single executant was no end impressive as a trick. If they had only imitated a rather more poetic executant, and if they had played, for that purpose, music of higher intellectual content, the evening, though it might have seemed less like a game, would have been more fun. It would also have been more worthy of the distinguished audience that it drew out.

January 27, 1945

New High

ARTHUR GOLD and ROBERT FIZDALE, piano duo, in recital last
night at Town Hall, performing J. C. Bach's Duetto in F major, Satie's
Trois Morceaux en forme de poire, the piano sonatas of Paul Bowles,
Igor Stravinsky, and Alexei Haieff, Virgil Thomson's *Five Inventions*,
one of John Cage's *Three Dances for Prepared Piano*, and three waltzes
from Rieti's *Second Avenue Waltzes*.

Duo-pianism reaches heights technical and artistic in the
work of Arthur Gold and Robert Fizdale, who gave a recital
last night in Town Hall, hitherto unknown to the art. Such
consistent beauty of tone and sweetness of sound, even in fortissimo passages, such refined precision of rhythm and grace of
phraseology, such masterful penetration of the nature of music,
of the differences between one piece and another, between one
composer's thought and another's, such a thoroughly musical
approach to music and to concert-giving produced an evening
that left one elated, not tired of ear and mentally worn down,
as is the common effect on this listener of two-piano recitals.

The program, save for a charming duet by Johann Christian
Bach, which got the late comers to their seats, was strictly modern. The novelties were a sonata by Paul Bowles and one by
Alexei Haieff. Mr. Bowles's piece consists of a lively and a slow
movement in his most poetic early-Ravel vein and a finale in imitation of African drum sounds and rhythms. The effect of the
whole is that of a strong musical work that is nowhere lacking
in charm. Mr. Haieff's piece, though longer, is less serious and
less forceful. Its textures are expert; but its thematic material
wears thin under repetition, and its extended conservatory-style
format (à la Anton Rubenstein) is inappropriate to the tight,
modern-music-style angularity of its tune content.

Among the other modern works Satie's *Three Pieces in the
Shape of a Pear* seemed to this observer the most richly packed
with plums. Composed in 1903, these are still an unexhausted
source of pleasure for listening and of lessons in musical composition. Seemingly unpretentious, they contain not one measure
of banality, not a phrase that is not profoundly expressive and
original. Beside their firm and gracious rightness, Stravinsky's
Sonata for Two Pianos, also a work of gentle character, seemed
lacking in concentration, though the latter is, compared to most

contemporary works for that medium, expressively pretty compact. Its musical intention, if I mistake not, is to evoke Bach's "Goldberg" Variations.

John Cage's Dance for two prepared pianos is a rhythmic composition of tiny thudlike sounds that recalls Indonesian gamelang music. It is distinguished and beautiful and makes one feel good. Vittorio Rieti's *Second Avenue Waltzes*, of which three were played, are the original version of his ballet, *Waltz Academy*. They are graceful and melodious and not banal, even when they quote (knowingly) Verdi's *La Traviata* and Ravel's *La Valse*. There was a piece of mine on the program, too.

An audience of New York's best in music and letters applauded all this modernity with delight and discussed everything with vigor at the intermission. Opinions varied, as is natural, about the comparative value of the divers works played. That all were played to perfection was not questioned in my hearing. Nor was anything but gratitude expressed for the universal consideration shown by Messrs. Gold and Fizdale in offering so much music that can be enjoyed as a part of contemporary living.

February 16, 1946

Definitive Renderings

WANDA LANDOWSKA harpsichordist, in recital last night at Town Hall, performing Couperin's Passacaille, Rameau's Gavotte and Doubles in A major, Bach's French Suite in E major, Mozart's Sonata in D major (played on piano), the Vivaldi-Bach Concerto in D major, and Bach's Italian Concerto in F major.

WANDA LANDOWSKA's playing of the harpsichord at Town Hall last night reminded one all over again that there is nothing else in the world like it. There does not exist in the world today, nor has there existed in my lifetime, another soloist of this or of any other instrument whose work is so dependable, so authoritative, and so thoroughly satisfactory. From all the points of view—historical knowledge, style, taste, understanding, and spontaneous musicality—her renderings of harpsichord repertory are, for our epoch, definitive. Criticism is unavailing against them, has been so, indeed, for thirty years.

Her piano playing is another story. She likes to play Mozart in evocation of the way Mozart himself must have, or might have, played on the early fortepiano. To this end she employs, as Mozart certainly employed, a high-fingered technique similar to that which gives the best result in harpsichord playing. She never plays louder than forte, not because she wishes to keep Mozart's music small, but because she wishes to keep it musical. The modern pianoforte gives another kind of sound, in many cases an ugly one, when played with arm weight. In any case, the extension of piano writing into the domain of modern power pianism, an extension that began only with Beethoven, seems inappropriate to her, as it does to many other modern musicians.

And so, limiting her dynamic range to approximately what was available to Mozart on the Stein fortepiano, she plays his solo sonatas for the musical contrasts that they unquestionably possess rather than for those for which they were never planned. As to rhythm, tempo, phrasing, and ornamentation—all the rendering of their basic musical content—her performance is matchless. She makes them large and alive and vivid, just as she does the harpsichord works of Couperin and Scarlatti and Rameau and Bach. Her conceptions and interpretations are a lesson to any musician. Pianistically, all the same, her execution is a little unsatisfactory.

It is not unsatisfactory because of any technical inefficiency. It is unsatisfactory because the modern pianoforte, a less brilliant instrument than Mozart's, does not yield what brilliance it has save by the exploitation of its full dynamic range. And Mozart's piano music, as we know, was of brilliance and virtuosity all compact. It need not glitter but it has to shine. Landowska gives us a photograph of it on the modern piano, very much as other pianists give us a photograph of Bach's harpsichord music.

Our instrument is closer to Mozart's than it is to the plucked instruments. But it is not the same instrument. That is why Mozart's symphonies and operas and chamber music always sound more vivid to us in execution than his piano music does. Fiddles, wind instruments, and voices do not have to walk through Mozart on tiptoes. The pianoforte, no matter how elegant its phrasing, inevitably sounds clumsy and a little meticulous.

I recommend Landowska's pianoforte Mozart, because I recommend any music she touches. It is the best piano Mozart I know. It is a model of understanding musically, as it is a tour de force technically. Nevertheless, by the very fact of being a translation—which her harpsichord playing, of course, is not—it is a slightly less authentic, less vigorous reconstitution.

November 20, 1944

Consort of Viols

SYLVIA MARLOWE, harpsichordist, and the BOSTON SOCIETY OF ANCIENT INSTRUMENTS, *Alfred Zighera*, conductor, yesterday afternoon at Carnegie Chamber Music Hall, performing Couperin's *La Sultana*, Karl F. Abel's Sonata in G, Rameau's Gavotte and Variations in A minor, Buxtehude's Sonata in D major, Orlando Gibbons's Two Fantasias, five Scarlatti sonatas, and Telemann's Suite in C major. Soloists: *Paul Federowsky*, descant viol, *Albert Bernard*, treble viol, *Mr. Zighera*, viola da gamba, and *Gaston Dufresne*, violone.

Sʏʟᴠɪᴀ Mᴀʀʟᴏᴡᴇ, harpsichordist, and the Boston Society of Ancient Instruments gave yesterday afternoon in Carnegie Chamber Music Hall the first of three concerts devoted to the music of pre-Classical times. Miss Marlowe, an artist of the first quality, is well known to New York audiences, both as soloist and as participant in rare chamber music combinations. The Boston group, though certain of its members, such as Alfred Zighera, who plays the viola da gamba with a fine mastery, are familiar to local music lovers, has not previously appeared here manipulating a chest, or consort, of viols.

The program was of the most distinguished, the sweetest of all the works played being perhaps two Fantasias for quartet of viols by Orlando Gibbons. The whole afternoon, however, was rich in musical delights from a bygone age. Buxtehude and Telemann, Couperin and Rameau, Karl Abel, Gibbons, and Domenico Scarlatti were all represented by major works; and the execution of these was in every way handsome.

To Miss Marlowe and Mr. Zighera must go the honors of the occasion for their virtuoso solo renderings of Scarlatti and Abel. The viol quartet, though better equilibrated in the Gibbons work than elsewhere, fell short of perfection through a certain heaviness and some inaccuracies of pitch on the part of the bass violone.

The viols, more limited in expressive scope than instruments of the violin family, have two extremely pleasant kinds of tone. One is a sweet, soft sound not unlike that of violins muted. The other is a nasal quality suggestive of the oboe or the English horn. The bass viol produces also a neutral tone that is ineffective for solo purposes because of its poverty in upper harmonics but that makes, for the same reason, an admirable bass in soft passages. Bowed too heavily, this instrument produces a boom, not unlike the boom of modern electronic instruments, that disrupts smooth ensemble effects.

Together, if the bass is played accurately and with dynamic discretion, viols produce a harmoniously blended tone more easily than a modern string quartet does. Taken separately, only the viola da gamba and the slightly larger viola bastarda, which was not played yesterday, offer sufficient variety in either tone color or volume to make proper solo instruments, though the viola d'amore, with its extra set of strings that add sympathetic vibrations to those produced by direct bowing, offers an inimitable timbre that is delicious in brief phrases.

One cannot be too grateful to Miss Marlowe and the Boston group for giving us great music from the past on instruments closely resembling those for which it was conceived. I say closely resembling because Miss Marlowe plays a modern harpsichord—a Pleyel, the finest in town, I should think—and the Boston viol players do use the modern bow. All the same, a concert like yesterday's gives us a closer idea of what instrumental chamber music by great masters sounded like in the sixteenth, seventeenth, and eighteenth centuries than it is currently our privilege to hear.

February 17, 1947

Variety without Loudness

SUZANNE BLOCH AND ASSOCIATES in concert last night at Times Hall, New York, presenting English and Italian Renaissance songs sung and played by *Miss Bloch* on lute, virginal, and recorders, with *Eugene Morgan*, baritone, *Paul Smith*, recorders, *Betty Martin*, virginal, *Nina Courant*, viola da gamba, and *Monina Távora*, *Margot Ramsay*, and *Joseph Precker*, lutes.

SUZANNE BLOCH gave last night in Times Hall a concert of Renaissance music in strictly prebaroque instrumentation. There were solos for lute, duets for two lutes, music for a quartet of the same, vocal solos and duets accompanied by them, and divers compositions that included a recorder, a viola da gamba, and a pair of virginals, as well. There was also solo music for the virginals, for though the phrase seems self-contradictory (a pair of anything playing a solo), the virginals are, at least linguistically, a plural instrument, like scissors.

Gerald Hayes, an English writer about old music and old instruments, states in one of his books that there is in existence more first-class music for the lute than has ever been written for any other solo instrument. Certainly the music played last night was all first class and thoroughly delightful. And if Miss Bloch undertook none of the monumental Elizabethan fantasies that compare for length and variety with the Viennese piano sonatas of the classical period, she gave us a highly digestible selection of charm numbers from all over Europe.

The lute is a hand-plucked instrument related in sonority both to the mandolin (which is not hand-plucked) and to the Spanish guitar (which is). Like the mandolin, it plays melodies effectively and even counterpoint. Unlike the guitar, it cannot easily play chords across the board. It has too many strings to allow chord playing by any but selective means. Consequently, though the instrument resembles the guitar somewhat in sound, it has none of the latter's romantic abandon. It is a plain and noble instrument that lends itself to the execution of music of the highest complexity, rhythmic, harmonic, and contrapuntal. It sounds rather like a harpsichord without a keyboard mechanism.

Since wide variations of loudness as an expressive (and even rhetorical) device are an invention of the seventeenth century, no music written before that time counts on them for effect. The chamber music of Renaissance times was regularly and systematically quiet. Its interest is melodic, harmonic, contrapuntal, and rhythmic, but never dynamic. It can be played and sung for hours without any strain on the listener's nervous system, because loudness was never a part of its pattern.

The music making that Miss Bloch and her associate artists offered last night was like a cultivated conversation rather than like an exhortation of any kind. It was fanciful, instructive, intimate, gay, delicious, and vast for vistas opened. It was not emotionally portentous, but it was deeply refreshing.

The audience, a large and cultured one, took evident delight in it all; and Miss Bloch herself, an artist of no mean skill, seemed pleased to be communicating the things she has for so long studied to re-create. Let us hope that her clear success will encourage her and others to give us more frequent auditory access to a great musical repertory than has been our privilege of recent years. Contemporary life has need of music based on ingenuity and sentiment, music in which dynamic strain, however noble as mere sound, plays no part.

March 5, 1947

Strings Bowed; Strings Plucked

ALEXANDER SCHNEIDER, violinist, and RALPH KIRKPATRICK, harpsichordist, in joint recital last night at Kaufmann Auditorium of the 92nd Street YMHA, New York, performing two sonatas by Bach (No. 2 and No. 4) and three by Mozart (F major, G major, A major).

HARPSICHORD and violin certainly make a lovely duet. As played last night by Ralph Kirkpatrick and Alexander Schneider in a recital of sonatas by Mozart and Bach at the Y.M.H.A. in Lexington Avenue at Ninety-second Street, they produced one of the happiest musical evenings this critic has spent in a long time. Even when the detailed rendering was not fully to his taste the sound was always attractive to the ear. One could bear to listen to all the music all the time. And since at least two of the works played, the Mozart G and A major sonatas, are in themselves works of rare grandeur, one was grateful to the artists for giving them to us so nearly, so very nearly, intact.

By nearly intact I mean that there were rhythmic irregularities in the harpsichord playing and some imperfect cantilena on the violin. Tempo rubato, for instance, however slight, is scarcely appropriate to syncopated passages, as Mr. Kirkpatrick used it in the slow movement of the Mozart A-major sonata. And haste to get back to the nut of the bow will always produce a bumpy violin phrase. Both Kirkpatrick and Schneider are skilled technicians and experienced players of chamber music. Their work has ease, confidence, understanding, and some brilliance. What it lacks for full distinction and for the brio that it essays is equalized tension. It is clear but not wholly clean, highly presentable as reading but not very deeply thought.

Everything was played a little fast, as if speed were being used to conceal a want of exact rhythmic articulation. This procedure is less objectionable in Mozart than in Bach, because the Mozart last movements, at least, do demand a sort of demonic fury, though velocity is not necessarily the best means for achieving this. In Bach it only produces confusion. The attempt to make a show-off, à la Paganini, out of that most methodical of workmen is false stylistically, psychologically, and musically. The fury in Bach is the fury of complete control, a relentlessness of exactitude rather than of sweep. A too facile approach to his complexities captures no heavenly citadel; it is merely barnstorming.

Rather wonderful barnstorming the whole concert was. The music was recondite but not too much so for comprehension. The playing was adequate and pleasantly superficial. The sound of it all was delicious, spicy, eminently digestible. If nothing was played with penetration, neither was anything gravely violated. The evening was a revelation of how delightful music can be without a thumpy pianoforte or violin E strings of wire. Also, the Mozart A-major violin sonata is worth going some distance for.

November 2, 1944

An Evening of Delight

PHILHARMONIC-SYMPHONY ORCHESTRA, *Leopold Stokowski*, conductor, last night at Carnegie Hall, performing the Stokowski-Victoria Motet ("Jesu, Dulcis Memoria"), Mozart's Overture to *Don Giovanni*, Hindemith's Symphony No. 1, Édouard Lalo's *Symphonie Espagnole*, Milhaud's *Saudades do Brasil*, and Debussy's *L'Après-midi d'un faune*. Soloist: *Jacques Thibaud*, violin.

THE RETURN of Jacques Thibaud, violinist, to the American concert platform after a fifteen-year absence and some high-powered musical magic on the part of Leopold Stokowski, conductor, set apart as memorable last night's concert of the Philharmonic-Symphony Orchestra in Carnegie Hall. The program itself, moreover, was one of no mean distinction, containing, as it did, in addition to a familiar Mozart overture, a familiar violin concerto, and a popular Debussy tone-poem, two of Milhaud's seldom heard *Memories of Brazil* dances and the elegant but little known First (and only) Symphony by Hindemith, not to speak of a transcription by Mr. Stokowski of a ravishing Victoria motet.

Stokowski's transcription of the nineteenth-century *Jesu, Dulcis Memoria* was sonorous and in performance pleasantly atmospheric. But in conception it was less a direct translation of choral sound into orchestral than an organist's version of this turned into an ensemble piece. The Milhaud *Saudades do Brasil*, to dispose of the other small works, are ever a delight, vigorous in rhythm, gaily discordant in harmony, and poignantly nostalgic in their evocation of Brazilian song-and-dance poetry.

The Hindemith Symphony is a modernistic evocation of Brahms's Romantic evocation of Beethoven's middle period. It is not, however, a Romantic work. It is a neo-Classic (or neo-Romantic) work, concise, concentrated, buoyant, cheerful. It is agreeable to listen to rather for its masterful shipshapeness than for any especial eloquence or profundity. Its tonality is clear, if a little crowded, its counterpoint animated, its orchestral texture transparent. Rhythmically it is not very expressive, and its melodic content is far from striking. But it is an accomplished, a civilized work; it says what it says with authority, with dispatch, and with a certain amplitude. As to what it says, anybody's guess is as good as this reviewer's. In his opinion Mr. Hindemith has evoked a certain period in the history of the symphony rather than made up a really original piece.

Jacques Thibaud's performance of the solo part in Lalo's *Symphonie espagnole* was violin playing of the Franco-Belgian school at its most admirable and, for the present, most satisfactory. Accustomed as we are to the heavier-handed and more sentimental Russian style, it is no end refreshing to return to the smaller and finer but musically more ample manner of Ysaÿe and his pupils. Thibaud's tone, though not large, is beautiful; and his technical mastery has not diminished with the years. The ovations he received both before and after playing were witness of New York's loyalty to a great artist all too long missing from our platforms and of the fact that our taste in violin playing has not deteriorated in his absence.

As for Mr. Stokowski's conducting, it was pure miracle from beginning to end. Often in the past, critics, the present one included, have protested at errors of taste on this conductor's part. Last night there was none. Everything was played with a wondrous beauty of sound, with the noblest proportions, with the utmost grandeur of expression. The perfection of tonal rendering for which Stokowski and his Philadelphia Orchestra were so long famous was revived last night with the Philharmonic men in a performance of Debussy's *Afternoon of a Faun* that for both beauty and poetry has been unmatched for many years, if ever, in my experience.

January 3, 1947

Good Goods

ZINO FRANCESCATTI, violinist, in recital last night at Carnegie Hall, performing Fauré's Sonata in A major, Ravel's *Berceuse* and *Tzigane*, Bach's Chaconne, Stravinsky's Duo Concertant, and three pieces by Fritz Kreisler. Accompanist: *Artur Balsam*, piano.

ZINO FRANCESCATTI's violin recital of last night in Carnegie Hall was a display of solid workmanship from beginning to end. By *workmanship* let us understand interpretation as well as technique. He not only played on pitch and correctly, but he gave musical readings of depth, breadth, and lucidity. Everything was powerful and plain to the understanding as well as shipshape to the ear. Nowhere in his work was there anything of bluff, of inadequacy, of vulgarity, of hesitation before any difficulty either of execution or of expression. Everywhere there was beauty, dignity, repose, and the authority of solid worth.

If violin playing is in the way of becoming a noble art again, after a generation of technical brilliancy used all too often for meretricious musical ends, this artist is one of those responsible for the change. So, also, of course, is the fact that the Auer pupils have mostly passed the peak of their powers without reproducing their kind. The classical Franco-Belgian school of string playing remains a lasting glory, while the cometlike Russian school seems about to fade from the sky.

Unique in contemporary music making is Francescatti's performance of Ravel's concert rhapsody, *Tzigane*. Nobody else has ever played the work so thoroughly. He has dug into its difficulties, mastered them, and come up with a repertory piece worthy of placement beside the best on any program. Last night he placed it beside the Bach unaccompanied Chaconne (no less), a juxtaposition dangerous to both works. Mr. Francescatti's thoroughness and sincerity made it of advantage to both and even to the Stravinksy *Duo Concertant*, which followed.

This reviewer does not remember a nobler or more powerfully sustained rendering of the Bach piece. Nor was the violin part of the Stravinsky work anywhere short of satisfying. Unfortunately the piano part was too ugly in tone and too subservient in volume to make of the whole a real duet. It was more like a beautiful and deeply expressive violin solo with a competent routine accompaniment of the kind the violinists don't seem to mind. The same infelicity of piano marred the Fauré Sonata. Mr. Francescatti's own modesty made of the Kreisler pieces at the end slightly dry marshmallows, though their accuracy of execution was far greater than what one is accustomed to hear.

April 9, 1947

Musical Satisfaction

JOSEPH FUCHS, violinist, in recital last night at Carnegie Hall, performing Handel's Sonata No. 5, Beethoven's Romance in F, Fauré's Sonata in A major, Alexei Haieff's Suite for Violin and Piano, three Paganini caprices, Camargo Guarnieri's *Cantica la de Longe*, and Enrique Fernández Arbós's *Tango*. Accompanist: *Artur Balsam*, piano.

JOSEPH FUCHS, who gave a violin recital last night in Carnegie Hall, is ever a musical delight. He makes beautiful sounds, and he knows what the pieces he plays are about. His work never falls short of either beauty or distinction, and at its best it is unequaled by either test among the violin playing of our day.

It was at its best last night in the Fauré Sonata, Opus 13, in the Haieff Suite, and in the Paganini Caprices. The Fauré piece brought out his gift for a lyricism that soars without effort and without arrogance, a sweetness that is nowhere lacking in either grace or power but that seems to know no strain. The Haieff brought forth virility and rhythmic strength, the Paganini pieces a display of accurate acrobatics that left one gasping with admiration. All these works were read with a breadth of over-all planning, an awareness of their shape and progress that gave proof of intellectual powers in no way inferior to Mr. Fuchs's high skill of hand and accomplished musicianship.

Alexei Haieff's Suite, the chief novelty of the evening, is a broadly conceived work with lots of rhythmic drive. By broadly conceived I mean that it is neither short nor hesitant. It states its thought forcibly, amply, completely. It also states it with high finish; it is admirably, even brilliantly, written for the violin. Mr. Haieff has unquestionably a Russian taste for instrumentalism and no mean skill at exploiting it.

The fast movements are the most satisfactory, the slow ones having a certain immobility that seems to reflect an emotional modesty that is becoming enough, heaven knows, but that provides him, at the present time of his life, with a less absorbing subject matter than frank displays of physical energy do. Certainly Haieff is a composer to watch, one of the brightest among our rising stars.

Camargo Guarnieri's *Song from Afar* was also a novelty. Guarnieri represents poetic Brazil, as contrasted with Villa-Lobos's travelogue Brazil and with the salon manner of Francisco Mignone. It is a really pretty piece. Arbós's *Tango*, which closed the concert (save for encores), is a set of variations on a Madrid-style popular song. It reminds one rather of the *Carnival of Venice* and is fun to hear once.

January 26, 1946

New Era

ROMAN TOTENBERG, violinist, in recital last night at Carnegie Hall, performing Bach's Sonata in E minor, Mozart's Concerto in G major, Debussy's Violin Sonata, three new pieces by Lukas Foss ("Early Song," "Dedication," and "Composer's Holiday"), the Szymanowski-Kochanski *Chanson Polanaise*, Paganini's Caprice No. 17, and two pieces by Pablo de Sarasate. Accompanists: *Artur Balsam* and *Mr. Foss*, pianos.

THE ENTHUSIASTIC RECEPTION that Roman Totenberg's violin recital got in Carnegie Hall last night is no doubt a sign of the times. Violin virtuosity has been the intellectual low point of the concert world for a good forty years now and maybe more. As smooth as an overgrown peach and about as tasteless, it has represented a maximum of surface appeal and a minimum of musical content. In just the last year, however, the recitals of Isaac Stern, of Joseph Fuchs, and of Mr. Totenberg have proved that there is a public for contemporary standards of musicianship, as well as of technique, in violin playing.

Technically speaking, Mr. Totenberg can play anything his predecessors could. He is, in fact, more expert than most of them. His is the smoothest bow arm of all and, in consequence, the most evenly sustained legato line. He plays on pitch, in time, and without bumpiness; and he has rhythm. He also has temperament, the ability to put himself inside a piece, which is valuable, and stylistic understanding, the knowledge of how one piece or period differs from another, which is indispensable. He has by gift, moreover, an awareness of music's continuing line that enables him to project a work as a single, whole thing, and to hold thus by sheer musical communication almost any musical person's interest.

If his execution has a major fault, it is a slight unevenness of color control. A shade acid is most of his work on the A and E strings. This does not appear when he plays high or in double stops, and it is quite lacking from his work on the G and D strings. It has to do, I presume, with the imperfect co-ordination of bow pressure with bow speed at a certain height of the arm. The sound produced is not ugly, but it is less beautiful than that produced in other registers. With this reserve, and with all admiration for his solid octaves, his clean harmonics, and his mastery of all the other difficulties usually troublesome to violinists, it seemed to me that Mr. Totenberg made remarkably lovely sounds and rich strong ones, too.

His Bach and his Debussy sonatas were musicianly performances of great breadth. The rhythm was right, as well as the pitch. His Mozart concerto was equally delightful as far as the solo part was concerned. Unfortunately the work as a whole was deformed by an imprecise and sloppy accompaniment that seemed to lack preparation. The Paganini and the Sarasate showpieces were not only brilliantly executed but interesting to listen to as well. Their musical content was exposed with such straightforward dignity that their bravura writing seemed to require no apology and, in consequence, to lower in no way the tone of the evening.

Lukas Foss's three pieces are the work of a skillful musician and a spontaneous one. They sound well; their sentiments are simple; and they are clearly expressed. They are not very original (the first one is an alternation of passages almost straight out of Copland with material that is recognizably imitated from the *Gymnopédies* of Erik Satie). But they are not stale either, and they are never forced. The public's response to this direct and sincere music was as heartening as was its warm reception of Mr. Totenberg's solidly beautiful playing of the violin.

November 19, 1944

King of the Gypsies

TOSSY SPIVAKOVSKY, violinist, in recital last night at Carnegie Hall, performing Viotti's Adagio in E major, Beethoven's Sonata No. 9 (Op. 47, "Kreutzer"), Bartók's *Four Rumanian Folk Dances*, Copland's *Ukulele Serenade*, Paganini's *La Campanella*, three Chopin études in the violinist's own transcriptions, and two works by Bach: Prelude and Fugue in G minor and Adagio and Fugue. Accompanist: *Frank Glazer*, piano.

TOSSY SPIVAKOVSKY, who played a recital last night in Carnegie Hall, is a sensationally effective violinist when he is effective and a major disappointment when he is not. The gypsy style is his meat; there he is forceful, varied, brilliant, and explosive. His classical violin playing has a certain grandeur, too, a hard nobility in slow passages. But it is so lacking in both flexibility of expression and, when he plays fast, accuracy of pitch that one cannot but regret the sacrifice he has made to achieve power in the other style.

The sacrifice has to do with his adoption of a right-hand position that is unique among reputable artists and, so the professionals tell me, heretical. He grasps the bow by bending his thumb clean around the nut and flexing the other fingers over it at the outer joints. In this position he has the full weight of his forearm available for bow pressure with small chance of producing an unsteady sound. Hence the nobility of his sustained cantilena. Hence also the unusual force he can put into off-center tonal effects, such as are produced by playing right on the bridge or way down on the fingerboard.

This strong but insensitive bow position, which lacks the cushion usually provided by a relaxed first finger, deprives him of two major expressive devices, the long light bow and the short light, or bouncing, bow. He is obliged, in legato playing, to alleviate the bad acoustical effects of excessive arm weight by drawing his bow too fast across the strings; and his wrist is too inflexible to allow him much play in the lighter qualities of spiccato and saltando playing. He changes the direction of his bow about twice as often as another good player needs to. He does it most skillfully, but he breaks up a phrase unnecessarily all the same. He also attempts to compensate for diminished phrasing interest by excessive vibrato.

A strong but indelicate bow arm, lots of vibrato, and an unusual mastery of off-center colorations, combined with the agilities and high pitches available to very long fingers, all go to make up the gypsy style of violin playing. Spivakovsky is admirable in works written for this style or in something resembling it. His performance, for instance, of Bartók's Violin Concerto several years back, with Artur Rodzinski and the Philharmonic, was a memorable performance of a memorable work. Last night he played with equal brio the same composer's Four Rumanian Folk Dances and Copland's entertaining *Ukulele Serenade*. Everything else, in spite of occasional moments when slow sound was handsomely sustained, was disappointing.

The disappointment was all the greater from the contrast of the ineffective classical renderings with the extreme brilliance and power of the more fiery and picturesque pieces. Matters were not helped out by a toneless piano, a Baldwin this time, which merits certainly some kind of prize in a season already notable for its bumper crop of inferior instruments.

December 12, 1946

Great Quartet Playing

GUILET STRING QUARTET last night at Times Hall, New York, performing Haydn's String Quartet No. 53 ("The Lark"), Randall Thompson's String Quartet No. 1, and the Debussy String Quartet. *Daniel Guilet* and *Louis Gralitzer*, violins, *Frank Brieff*, viola, and *Lucien K. Laporte*, cello.

THE PRESTIGE of string quartet music is often a mystery to those who have never heard it played in the Great Tradition. But this normally recondite form of expression has never presented difficulties to any music lover when so played. In my lifetime the Kneisel Quartet from Boston, the Flonzaley from Lausanne, the Quatuors Capet of Paris and Pro Arte of Brussels, the Quartetto di Roma, perhaps, and the Kolisch Quartet from Budapest, and that is about all, have done the business right. Daniel Guilet is one of the great quartet leaders; and New York now has, in the Guilet Quartet, which has been playing together some three or four years already, and which played last night in Times Hall, one of the great string quartets of our century.

Believe me, the way they play is the way the great quartets in my time have always played. Such a group either holds the interest completely or puts one to sleep, and the Guilets last night certainly had the latter effect on no one in my neighborhood.

No other quartet now appearing before the American public has either the homogeneity of tone or the brightness of color that the Guilets have. And since sound pitch in ensemble playing is obtainable only when there is homogeneity of color, no similar group plays quite so harmoniously. Further elements of musical expression, such as amplitude of volume variation, coloristic contrast, and, most important of all, rhythmic freedom, are dependent on the same pitch security, which is in turn a function of the tonal blend. Having this last, the Guilets have, consequently, everything. Musical intelligibility goes without saying in such an ensemble, because only the most discerning and enlightened musicians are ever willing to go through the labor of attaining a clear blend of sounds, just as only the really great minds (and not all of them) ever master simple clarity in the art of writing music.

Last night's program contained a Haydn quartet and the now classical Debussy wonder piece in that form, as well as a contemporary work. This was Randall Thompson's gracious and songful Quartet No. 1, which it has been my joy to hear some three or more times in the last year. Each rehearing brings it closer to my heart, not only for its touching Appalachian Mountain Americanism but for its broader musical interest as well. It is one of the lovely pieces our country has produced, that any country, indeed, has produced in our century. And its reading last night by Mr. Guilet and his teammates—Louis Gralitzer, Frank Brieff, and Lucien K. Laporte—was a dream of sweetness and of poetry.

April 18, 1945

Soaring Unit

PASCAL STRING QUARTET last night at Town Hall, performing Mozart's String Quartet No. 17 ("Dissonant"), Brahms's String Quartet in C minor, Op. 51, No. 1, and the Ravel String Quartet. *Jacques Dumont* and *Maurice Crut*, violins, *Léon Pascal*, viola, and *Robert Salles*, cello.

THE PASCAL STRING QUARTET, newly arrived from Paris, is a pleasure and a refreshment. America has many excellent string teams but none that works with quite the technical precision and expressive freedom that this group manifested last night in Town Hall. The Flonzaleys used to work like that, but no other quartet appearing here now does. The Budapest at its best is musically handsome, but its accents are rougher; and the Guilet, for all its perfection of tone and balance, lacks breadth. Mr. Pascal and his colleagues play together, in tune, with thoroughly blended sound and in meter. Moreover, their music soars in both line and volume.

The soaring quality in ensemble playing is obtainable only when measure bars, a typographical device useful chiefly in rehearsals, are forgotten about in performance. I do not mean that simultaneity is not essential to good execution, for it is. I meant that in any final reading the phrase is the minimum unit of communication. Each must go through to its end without hesitation. When music is well written and reasonably well rehearsed, simultaneous articulation in performance is not hard to achieve. It is produced, indeed, most dependably as a by-product of common understanding among the players about the meaning of the expressive line.

Keeping the meaning, the expressive nature of the piece, always in full view of the audience is the chief preoccupation that has made French and Belgian string quartet playing the most musical, as well as the most intelligible, of our century. By this means the music not only comes out saying something; it also takes on beauty, since beauty in music is a by-product, too, a by-product of clarity. Beauty can exist sporadically, in detail, without there being any general clarity at all; but it can only exist throughout a rendering when the rhythmic and phraseological layout of the whole is firm and simple. Otherwise loveliness is mostly crowded out by bad planning.

The Pascal Quartet's work is full of lovely sound and gracious gesture, also of handsome loudnesses and of grand passion. I have never heard any Brahms quartet played with such warm romantic feeling as was the Opus 51, No. 1, last night. The Mozart No. 17 was lovely too, though it is not one of Mozart's most highly concentrated works. The Ravel quartet, though cleanly exposed with no scratching, was not so convincing as I have sometimes heard it. Possibly this piece needs a more luxurious sound than the Pascal instruments, which are not quite first-class, can produce. I had not, at any rate, so vividly missed expensive effects in the earlier works as I did in this. Mozart and Brahms, of course, do not require high coloration.

December 10, 1946

Jeritza's Return

MARIA JERITZA, soprano, in recital last night at Carnegie Hall, performing works by, among others, Wagner, Schubert, Tchaikovsky, Debussy, and Richard Strauss. Accompanist: *Paul Meyer*, piano.

MARIA JERITZA's return to the concert stage was cheered last night at Carnegie Hall by a capacity house that overflowed on the platform. Admirers stood to applaud her before she sang, in the middle of the program, and at the end. And like a schooled prima donna of the great tradition, Miss Jeritza was infallibly gracious of her person and generous with encores. All evening long she seemed to be bowing and singing encores, adding to a program of taxing songs and arias not only divers salon pieces but operatic numbers of the give-all type, such as the "Suicidio!" from *La Gioconda* and Brünnhilde's Cry from *Die Walküre*. When this reporter left, the public was calling for *La Tosca*.

As dramatic expression, nothing seemed last night to tax her. She is a great actress, always was, always will be. And she has the gift of glamour, a styled, a powerful projection elsewhere nonexistent today. She has beauty, too, and dignity and grace and ease. Her rendering of the final scene from Strauss's *Salome*, fully clothed and with only a pianoforte accompaniment, was breathtaking in its expressive intensity. One forgot for a moment the vocal inefficiencies. There was a dramatico-musical creation the like of which we do not witness currently, nor shall, I imagine, till singing actors again find it worth while to master their art.

From a purely vocal point of view Miss Jeritza has lost most of the beauty that once was hers, and all of the accuracy. She can still sing very loud, amazingly loud, and very soft. But loud or soft, she sings flat; and her enunciation has become so obscure that one cannot half the time tell even what language she is singing. Power she has and confidence and a completely authoritative presence, but the beauty of sound is gone.

Neither is there in her work any unusual musical interest, intrinsically speaking. I don't suppose there ever was. In the old days she sang handsomely enough and accurately, but chiefly she was an actress. Nowadays the sounds she makes are neither handsome nor accurate. But she is still an actress. And that is something to stand up and cheer about in a decade of dearth. Miss Jeritza's particular personality, moreover, has long been dear to the New York public; and it was heart warming to see New York turned out in its best clothes and its happiest face to welcome her home with bravos and flowers.

April 30, 1946

France Delivers

MARTIAL SINGHER, baritone, in recital last night at Town Hall, performing early French songs and works by Lully, Rameau, Martini, Mozart, Schubert, Berlioz, Gounod, Mussorgsky, Brahms, Debussy, Chabrier, and Ravel. Accompanist: *Paul Ulanowsky*, piano.

IN VIEW of all the gasping and sighing and good, solid hand clapping that received Martial Singher's recital last night in the Town Hall, it seems hardly necessary to add my humble testimonial. It is, nevertheless, my privilege as well as my pleasure to report that everything went off elegantly, most elegantly, including the music.

Mr. Singher is a musician, a showman, and an artist to his fingertips, a French baritone in the great style. The perfect charm of his platform manner would be a little terrifying if it were not so clearly the buttonhole flower that merely sets off an artistic accoutrement of the solidest stuff and tailoring. His singing and his gestures are neither studied nor natural. Schooled is nearer the word for them, schooled and stylish and free, all at the same time. They are frank, too, but about as spontaneous as the Maison Lanvin, in which establishment I should take a small bet his dress suit was cut and fitted.

One could use the word *taste* with considerable force with regard to Mr. Singher's work if that word really meant what the French word *goût* does. Unfortunately, our English word has chiefly negative connotations; it means mostly restraint, avoidance of the noticeable. Mr. Singher's quality is composed of high skill, sound knowledge, daring, confidence, and authority. He does not hesitate, for instance, to sing once in a while falsetto, provided this resonance is appropriate to the composition and provided also it is approached by a gradual transition of the vocal placement. He does not hesitate, either, to dramatize a song, because he knows how to dramatize music without throwing his personality at you. And he loyally gave his accompanist last night, Paul Ulanowsky, a bow every time the latter executed a piano part requiring especial precision or fluidity.

Mr. Singher's vocal gifts are great, though his voice is not one of unusual natural majesty. His vocal mastery is definitely unusual, especially around here, where baritones are likely either to imitate the barrel tone of a basso profundo or to affect a tearful tenor timbre. He sings squarely in the masque the whole time, in all ranges, at all volumes, and on all vowels. That is why his consonants could be so clearly projected that an English-speaking audience laughed, wept, and obviously understood what he was singing, though he sang only in French and in German (plus once in Italian, which he sings not quite so confidently).

A great singing style and a great musical understanding, assurance, dramatic power, and impeccable taste all go into his interpretations. But beneath everything, animating the grand line and sustaining his delicate phraseology, are a rhythmic tension and flexibility of rapier steel. A brief vocal fault here and there and a suggestion of fatigue toward the end of the concert were of no moment in a performance of such penetrating artistry and of such breath-taking elegance all round.

A spokesman for the artist informs me, for the benefit of many bothered by the problem, that the name is correctly pronounced Sang-gehr.

January 26, 1944

Pretty Singing

MURIEL RAHN, soprano, in recital last night at Town Hall, performing Negro spirituals and works by, among others, Purcell, Gluck, Schumann, Brahms, Franck, Grieg, Amy Beach, and William Grant Still. Accompanist: *William Lawrence*, piano.

MURIEL RAHN, already well known to New York audiences as one of the two Carmens in *Carmen Jones*, gave a formal recital of songs and arias last night in Town Hall. There is no questioning the fact that Miss Rahn has a pretty voice and a charming personality and that she sings well. Whether she is better suited to the operatic or to the concert stage remains unsettled in your reviewer's mind, after having heard her work most effectively indeed in both circumstances.

In addition to excellent natural advantages both of voice and of person, Miss Rahn is a soundly trained singer. Excepting for the failure to bring the notes of her low register frankly forward (she swallows them a little bit), there is no fault in her vocalization. There is, indeed, much beauty and no mean skill in her handling of an organ that is by nature neither unusually wide in range nor of any arresting loudness. Vocal schooling and good musicianship marked all her work last night, and there were the additional graces of a pleasant personality and of easy dramatic projection.

A large part of this dramatic effectiveness, which she displayed in no manner inappropriate to recital conventions but merely as the natural mood of presentation for each song, is due to her verbal articulation. I doubt if one has ever before heard the words of a recital so completely. So clearly does Miss Rahn enunciate, and with so little apparent effort, that she was several songs along in her program before I realized that I was not having to listen for the words. They came at one with no explosive force; but they came infallibly, completely, correctly. If Miss Rahn were not an artist of other and fuller qualities, I should like to salute her for perfection in the rarely mastered art of singing words.

She can sing songs, too. The high point of her recital, according to this listener, was the rendering of six pieces by Negro composers, notable among these being the delicate and poetic *Breath of a Rose*, by William Grant Still. It was the easy projection of modern American songs that made me think Miss Rahn is possibly destined in the long run for a theatrical career. If our theater offered more roles for the dainty soubrette, and if it were not quite so indifferent to good singing, I should welcome such a future for her. Things being as they are, however, she is wise to "keep up her music," so to speak, by singing Town Hall recitals, too.

April 4, 1945

Folklore in Sunday Clothes

OLGA COELHO, soprano and guitarist, in recital last night at Town Hall, performing works by Scarlatti, Pergolesi, de Falla, Segovia, and others; folk songs from Spain, Italy, and South America; and Brazilian songs by Tavares, Guarnieri, and others.

OLGA COELHO, who sang a recital last night in Town Hall, accompanying herself on the guitar, is a folk-song artist of the drawing-room, rather than of the night club, type. Her voice is pretty, light, and clear; and her presentation is in every way refined. Even her repertory, which is extensive enough, including material from all the South American countries, as well as her native Brazil, seems, all the same, to have been chosen with the thought of keeping its subject matter well within the limits of what is appropriate to parlor entertainment before mixed company.

Everything she sings is innocent, virtuous, thoroughly washed behind the ears, combed, dressed up in the most stylish harmony (though never overdressed), and schooled for charm. The pieces she sings are all of the best quality, and their renderings are impeccable for breeding. They were even presented last night, every one, with a pedigree, recited in advance by the artist. These spoken program notes covered their origins, discovery, arrangement, and literary content, including, as well, translations of the words and explanations of all obscure references. If the furnishing of all this useful information was a shade relentless, consuming often more time than the rendering of the song in question, it was enlightening, all the same. One came away edified, instructed, and not without certain pleasant memories, even, of a strictly musical character.

One of the pleasantest of these, to your correspondent, was

the admirable thoroughness with which Miss Coelho plays the guitar. No strummer she. She knows the instrument, plays tunes on it as well as chords, and is master of fifty varieties in tone and touch. This part of her musicianship, in fact, is more interesting to observe in action than her vocal interpretations, because it is more varied. The latter are a little too studied to be wholly convincing. They lack the improvisatory character that lends life to folklore. One feels she has worked them out too thoroughly.

When folk songs are interpreted as scholastically as that (for even charm and the affettuoso style can be scholastic), we are right back to the worst aspects of the lieder recital or caught up on the Wheel of Fate with Frank Sinatra. The whole point of any native idiom, its usefulness to the concert tradition, lies in its freshness. Miss Coelho is nice to look at, and she has the prettiest manners. She is an agreeable singer, too, and a good musician. But she does seem awfully determined that we should take the native music of South America on her terms. There are some who prefer it a shade less genteel.

February 22, 1947

The Concert Song

POVLA FRIJSH, soprano, in recital yesterday afternoon at Town Hall, performing nine new songs by Francis Poulenc; new American songs by John Duke, Paul Sargent, and Emanuel Rosenberg; and works by, among others, Schumann, Schubert, Grieg, and Christian Sinding. Accompanist: *Henri Deering*, piano.

POVLA FRIJSH, who gave a song recital yesterday afternoon in the Town Hall, is a remarkable musician, an interpreter of intelligence and high temperament. The sound of her voice, which is neither fresh nor beautiful, is a little shocking for the first fifteen minutes. After that, one doesn't notice it at all, so skillfully does the artist use it as a means of revealing a song rather than for any intrinsic qualities it may formerly have possessed. She doesn't exactly sing a song, in the concert sense of singing; nor yet does she merely speak it. She shows you how it goes. And she gives a deep musical pleasure. She is mistress of her art.

The meat of yesterday's program was nine songs, all of them new, I think, by Francis Poulenc. This composer, though not always satisfactory in instrumental music, is without rival as world master of the concert song. The mantle, indeed, of Gabriel Fauré may well be said to have fallen upon his shoulders. No other composer, in fact, since Fauré has written for voice and piano so copiously, so authoritatively, with such freedom of musical thought, such variety of expression.

Poulenc is no child of Fauré, however; he is the musical offspring of Chabrier and of Erik Satie. His songs, in particular, derive directly from those of the Sage of Arceuil, from *Daphénéo* and *Le Chapelier* and *La Diva de l'Empire* and the waltz-songs, *Je te veux* and *Poudre d'Or*. They use musical materials objectively, for their customary associations rather than for possible subjective ones. Their romantic ancestor is therefore Schubert rather than Schumann, from whom both Fauré and Debussy stem. And their expressive variety is greater, from the very objectivity of their procedures, than is possible to any composer working by introspective methods.

The wit that points up many of Poulenc songs, just as it does so much of modern poetry, enjoys its newfound ease not because Satie, his master, was fond of fun, but because Satie's music has shown us all a way of admitting humor to musical expression on a basis of equality with sadness. By using all the musical materials, melodic, rhythmic, and harmonic, for their common rather than for their uncommon associations, he has made it possible to use formulas from folklore, from popular commercial music, from the classical masters, and from yesterday's little masters right along side of invented material, and without any vulgarity. The musical vocabulary that results is comparable in origin and in richness to that of Mozart and Haydn and Beethoven. Satie's working methods represent thus a renewal of the classic, the eighteenth-century Viennese tradition and a spectacular showing-up of the poverty of musical Romanticism.

Poulenc's songs are varied and rich and ample in expression because they treat music not as a kind of sorcery or as a form of prayer but as a means of straightforward human communication. They do not plot or yearn; they say things. And they say lots of things. Their vocal lines, their harmonic substructures, their pianoforte accompaniments, have freedom and variety because they are not afraid to be specific about what they mean.

The American songs on yesterday's program said little that was specific or that one had not heard before. John Duke's *Bells in the Rain* was the only one that stood up as workmanship beside the Poulenc pieces. The others were all posey or cute. What stood up beautifully beside Poulenc's and Miss Frijsh's artistry was Henri Deering's piano playing. Twice in ten days now I have heard accompaniments of that intellectual and technical quality. The previous delight was George Reeves's playing for Maggie Teyte.

January 7, 1946

A Miracle and a Monument

MAGGIE TEYTE, soprano, in recital last night at Town Hall, performing five songs by Ravel, three by Fauré, and two by Debussy, as well as works by, among others, Pergolesi, Mozart, John Alden Carpenter, and Émile Paladilhe. Accompanist: *George Reeves*, piano.

MAGGIE TEYTE, who gave her second Town Hall recital of the season last night, is both a miracle and a monument. To have retained both her beautiful singing voice and complete mastery of it over a period of some thirty-five years (I last heard her in 1912 at the Chicago Opera) is the miracle. The monumental nature of her work comes from the fact that she remains virtually alone today as an exponent of the French vocal style of the period that preceded the other war. If you want to hear the Debussy songs and the Ravel songs and Fauré sung by a vocalist who still knows what they sounded like in the epoch that saw their creation, there is no other living artist that can evoke them for you so authentically or so vividly. And if you want to hear the French singing style as Jean de Reszke invented it, as Muratore and Mary Garden practiced it, you will have to elbow your way into Town Hall the next time Miss Teyte gives a recital, though the house is already sold out, I believe.

That style is based technically on being able to sing any vowel in any color and at any degree of loudness or softness on any note of one's voice. It is based interpretatively on reading aloud. It is intoned elocution that uses so large a variety of vocal coloration that in no single piece is the gamut ever exhausted. Each song is a little drama, a slice of life that takes place in its own poetic climate, uses its own special and appropriate palette of sound. This vocal impressionism is of the utmost auditory richness, and also of the most intense poetic clarity. Such musical variety combined with ease of understanding, such apparent naturalism, is a summit of vocal art from which the singing of our epoch has long since declined. Miss Teyte alone has the key to it, the discipline of it, the workmanship and the knowledge to expose it before us.

It is a dramatic art. There is nothing personal or introspective about it, excepting that most of the repertory that shows it at its best is music of highly introspective subject matter. But introspective subject matter requires for its clear projection the most impersonal dramatic technique. Otherwise you get only obscurity. There is nothing inspirational about Miss Teyte's musical procedures. Her renderings are the product of discipline, reflection, and lots of rehearsal. Imagination and exactitude are what make them so dramatic. And naturally, they are not dramatic in any inappropriate sense. She projects poetry without getting theatrical. It is as if somebody were singing very beautifully and reading very beautifully at the same time.

It would be hard to say which among the songs she sang offered the greatest revelation. Her Fauré was marked by a wonderfully unifying rhythm. Her Debussy had the real Debussy immobility, the rocklike reality of emotion that is the essence of Debussy. Her Ravel had a wiry delicacy that I have not heard applied to these songs since Eva Gauthier used to sing them for us with such fine awareness of their essential wit and parody.

Perhaps the grandest dramatic achievement of the evening was the letter scene from *Pelléas et Mélisande*, which Miss Teyte added at the close. This was so simple, so clear, and so relentless, so plain at the same time, that one was reminded of how touching *Pelléas* can be whenever anybody lets us hear the words of it.

In face of such thoroughly conscious workmanship it seems almost unnecessary to mention Miss Teyte's personal charm. But that charm is itself so deeply gracious, and Miss Teyte's schooled temperament as an actress and a musician is so wonderfully warmed by it, that the very sweetness and ease of her woman's personality becomes a valid part of her work as an artist. It is something of the kind, I am sure, that has made possible the miracle by which time has touched her singing so little.

December 29, 1945

THE OPERA

Singing Today

THE TECHNIQUE of singing, as practiced today in our concert halls and at the Metropolitan Opera House, is not the same technique that was employed by the masters and mistresses of vocal art thirty years ago. Many persons now alive, recalling the performances of that time and being able to verify the expert character of these through gramophone recordings, or even through listening to Maggie Teyte, who still sings that way, believe the art to be in decline. Judged by the standards that prevailed in 1910, it certainly is. But the standards of 1910 are not necessarily a unique summit. Singing style has changed several times in recent centuries, and I suspect that it is undergoing right now an evolution of some kind. That, at least, seems a legitimate presumption to make about any art that, being still copiously patronized by the public, in every way prosperous and prized, mysteriously loses contact with its most admired models in a time when these have in no grave way ceased to be accessible.

"Nothing changes from generation to generation," as Gertrude Stein once remarked, "except what people are looking at," which is to say, what they have their minds on. And certainly the human voice is a wind instrument of which the essential structure has not been altered, to my knowledge, within recorded history. Any wind instrument can be made to produce sound in various ways, and any generation defines as "correct" that method of production which produces the largest variety of sounds within the limits of what it finds, for reasons mysterious, "pleasing." Thus it is that the more pinched sounds, what we call commonly "nasal," were cultivated in Europe between 1650 and 1750, because velocity execution and altitudinous pitches, both of which are facilitated by a "nasal" production, were what the musical public had its mind on.

Round tones and chest registers were slow to be admitted as legitimate singing. Rameau and Gluck used basses for representing gods or priests, but their scores call for no baritones or altos. Human beings were supposed to be either high tenors or sopranos, sometimes very high tenors. The baritone came into glory with Mozart; but the female alto was a rarity on the operatic stage till the 1840's, when Bellini, Donizetti, and the young Verdi began using that chesty voice as a normally expressive kind of sound. Even today the lower part of the tenor voice is not expected to carry much weight, though it is perfectly capable of doing so if trained toward that end.

The most striking characteristic of today's vocalism in the field of popular music is the way it centers around the lower female ranges. If you write out what most lady night-club and radio artists really sing, you will find yourself using either the bass clef for it or constantly three, four, and five ledger lines below the staff. Most of them have light voices, but almost none sings soprano. Few sing at all, of course, in the 1910 sense; they mostly croon. Even on the concert stage and at the opera one hears a good deal of crooning these days. It isn't at all effective in those acoustical setups; but singers, particularly young ones, will do it, because it is effective for microphone work; and the well-paying microphone is what they all have their little minds on, what they dream about, think about, and practice toward.

Naturally, they have to pretend to learn to sing, too, because classical concert and operatic repertory, being written for the last century's effective singing range, which was quite a large one, cannot be altogether crooned. And so they partly sing and partly croon. What none of them can do dependably is to sing, really sing, very loud or very soft. When they try to sing loud they either wobble or scream; and when they try to sing softly their voices change color all the time and fail to project. In both cases there is insufficient control of the throat muscles that determine pitch and color (neither of which should ever alter during the utterance of any single note) and of the abdominal muscles that regulate wind pressure.

In classical singing, the throat muscles are held firm during the projection of any note, while the abdominal muscles cause the lungs to supply a steady pressure of air across the vocal cords. The sole musical function of this controlled exhaling is to keep the vocal cords in vibration. In classical singing, projected singing, the wind pressure should be the maximum possible for steady vibration at the desired volume level. Excess pressure will make the sound louder or, if the throat muscles allow it to escape, breathy. Insufficient pressure will fail to produce a complete vibration of the still air in the mouth vault and the sinuses, which constitute the vocal soundbox.

Screaming is another process than singing. It uses excess wind pressure on a pinched throat. It is not "legitimate" singing, because its pitch is uncontrollable and because it is likely to make an irreparable tear in the vocal cords. Crooning, on the other hand, differs from classical singing by using a minimum of wind pressure. It makes a pretty sound; but it does not project well, because it is poor in upper harmonics. It is a limited kind of sound that "takes" well on the microphone (which has limited acoustical vibrations); but it is not very useful in halls, which mostly have unlimited acoustical vibrations. A classical pianissimo carries to the top gallery because it is a "rich" sound, a full harmony of overtones just like a fortissimo. Crooning carries about ten feet only, because it is a "pure" or "poor" sound. It is easier to produce, however, than a classical pianissimo, which requires a maximum of abdominal muscular control, more, even, than a fortissimo does.

If the music of the future and the chief market of the future are to be microphone music, young singers are wise to dabble in the techniques that are appropriate to that acoustical circumstance. Not knowing, or caring much, perhaps, about the future, but faced with the facts that today there is money to be made through both the processed and the nonprocessed musical operations and that for both operations they are obliged to use a repertory that was built entirely for public halls, they are right to compromise, to work on both sides of the fence. The price they pay is being not really first-class in either field. No concert or opera singer now working before the American public, at least none who is under forty, can match the classical workmanship, available on records and through living precept, of Eames or Melba or Nordica, on the one hand (not to mention the even fuller expressive ranges of Mary Garden and of Maggie Teyte), or Frank Sinatra's crooning, on the other. The two vocal techniques are wholly different and probably opposed. Nobody I know of has ever mastered them both. Coming to terms with both, however, whether by synthesis or by exclusion, is the vocal problem of our time. Till it is solved, one way or the other, singing is likely to remain unsatisfactory.

January 13, 1946

Voice Forum

Two weeks ago this column was devoted to a communication on the subject of voice fatigue from an elderly throat specialist who had cared for many singers in the course of his career and who included with his letter a chapter from a medical textbook. The theme of the letter and of the quoted article was that *myasthenia laryngis*, as distinguished from acute laryngitis (a mucosal condition), is a muscular condition due to overstrain and must be treated as such. Like all other conditions of muscular fatigue, said the author, that of the "phonatory muscles" imposes rest. Tired muscles can be restored to use by no other means. Consequently, to all persons who use these muscles professionally, whether they are hog callers or opera singers, "periods of silence" were recommended as a prophylactic measure; and these were prescribed, moreover, as an absolute necessity in cases where such fatigue has produced a vocal disability. The penalty, in the latter case, for laxity about following the silence regimen was stated by Dr. Chevalier M. Jackson to be permanent professional disability.

Whenever the subject of vocalism is brought up in this column readers write lots of letters. Most of them on this occasion express hearty applause. Echoing the doctor, another laryngologist says that he has "never been able to make any headway in saving young voices through 'prophylaxis.'" "Nobody seems to care," he adds, "or, at least, to care enough; hence the vocal cripples keep coming through this office. Anything you can do to help the voice physician will bring you great and deserved praise." He protests further that many managers and teachers "allow vocalization right through an attack of acute laryngitis, some even recommending it because it 'exercises the muscles.'"

Medical men are unanimous that muscular fatigue, however provoked, cannot be relieved without muscular repose. Not a few letters, however, expound the idea that voice fatigue is the product of a faulty singing technique. Most vocal teachers, of course, though convinced that their methods of training are perfectly designed to prevent fatigue, will admit that a great many singing voices are lost through "overstrain." It would be difficult to prove that any bodily action can be performed without the use of some muscle. A standard contention of sing-ing teachers, nevertheless, is that the muscular effort involved in singing is so slight when a "proper," or efficient, use is made of the muscles involved, that serious fatigue can appear only from an "improper" use of these. The physicians reply that all singers, good, bad, or indifferent, are subject to voice fatigue and always have been, and that the more one uses the voice the more likely one is to strain it. The best swimmers do get cramps and the best leg men "Charley horses." "Form," classical medi-cine holds, though valuable to efficiency, is never foolproof; and excess is excess no matter who commits it.

The vocal teachers' argument savors of salesmanship. Cer-tainly it is true that a schooled method of doing anything aids the doer. No one believes that naïve vocalism will get him through an opera, even, much less a career. Voice lessons are a prerequisite for high-class singing. And everybody knows that nowadays high-class singing is rare, though voice lessons can be bought in any block. The teachers maintain correctly that training, if efficiently accomplished, will enable a singer to sing higher, lower, faster, slower, louder, softer, and prettier than he did before. Also longer, both on any one evening and during a lifetime. There is no real argument about this, since all the voice-training methods in Christendom are designed with the same end in view.

Assuming that a given teacher is preferable to another because of his devotion to these aims merely eliminates the wholly unfit, since only the most ignorant and irresponsible have any other aim. Choosing a teacher by the evidence of successful pupils produced is sounder practice, but also risky, since all students do not work equally well with all teachers and vice versa. Besides, many of the best singers have had several teachers; and it is not always easy to judge which among them is responsible for the sound technics. The sense of well-being that many a vocalist experiences with a new teacher is no criterion at all, because it is practically universal. Everybody knows what the purpose of vocal training is; nevertheless, good singing is on the wane. Consequently, before we take any teacher's sales talk at face value in those cases, all too frequent, when he maintains that his teaching alone is capable of reversing the trend, we have to have more evidence in the way of sound singing by his pupils than any vocal teacher alive today can offer.

This article is no attack on singing teachers, for whom I have the highest respect, nor on singing students, toward whom I have the warmest feelings. I pity both, indeed, because neither is achieving what they both so passionately desire, namely, to make the world ring with beautiful song. I also wish to add to this forum my own opinion that when a good voice cracks up prematurely (that is to say, before the middle or late forties) the trainer of that voice is not necessarily at fault. The doctors tell me anybody can strain any muscle, and I believe them. The vocal teachers tell me a good "production" will help anybody to avoid the grosser forms of vocal strain, and I believe them, too. What I don't believe (nor has any doctor asked me to) is that medical care is a substitute for voice lessons. And neither do I believe (though many voice teachers have tried to persuade me of it) that any voice training, however sound, will eliminate the physiological effects of fatigue in the voice-producing apparatus, any more than it will prevent singers from catching cold. Moreover, everybody knows who has ever cheered at a football game that the voice-producing apparatus strains very easily.

There might be a way of getting around the present vocal impasse by pooling all the knowledge there is about the subject. Several of my correspondents have proposed in the past that a congress of singing teachers and throat doctors work out together a standard course of training for singers. If such a project were ever realized the assembly's first job would be, as a recent letter states, to agree on a vocabulary. Here I heartily applaud. No two singing specialists understand the same thing by "focus," "spread tones," "breath control," "breath support," "head resonance," "nasal resonance," "chest resonance," "throatiness," "pinched tone," "white voice," "brilliance," and so on. A standard set of words describing auditory vocal phenomena is necessary before the physiologists can even begin to list the conformations and positions of the vocal apparatus required for their production. A listing of these must precede any establishment of a standard method for eliminating the undesirable ones and for cultivating those considered appropriate to music.

The more I talk with singers and teachers the more I am convinced that words are their main trouble. It is not hard to recognize a faulty tone, but it is virtually impossible in any European language to describe it politely. As for correcting it, three fourths of the best instruction still depends on imitation. The other fourth uses up lots of time in talk, and at the end the pupil can only try everything till he makes some kind of sound his teacher doesn't veto. Neither of these classical systems is working very well today, and those that are advertised as based on "medical and scientific" knowledge are not doing one whit better. Maybe if the best of the old-line teachers and some medical men with a reasonably musical ear got together on the matter as a research job, something useful might be found out. If they merely got the terms defined they would have accomplished more than anybody has since Manuel García invented the laryngoscope.

December 1, 1946

Opera's Next Step

A FIRST-CLASS PERFORMANCE of anything is one in which the major element is first-class. Excellence among the subsidiary elements makes for glamour, but it cannot substitute satisfactorily for excellence in the major domain. A poetic tragedy is primarily poetry, and a good performance of it must consist first of all in elocution. It is nice to have scenery and costumes and incidental music that are appropriate, but first-rate declamation is more important. Sarah Bernhardt and Forbes-Robertson could play Racine and Shakespeare without any scenery at all, but the greatest scene designer in the world or the greatest director cannot make a worthy production of a classic work unless some pretty good readers are available.

The same applies to ballet, of course. Good music is not an essential; good dancing is. Ballet is not very glamorous without rich music and decorations; but it can be ballet and very good ballet indeed, as we have all seen recently in the performances of the Ballet Theater.

The opera, at its best, should please the eye as well as the ear; but when sacrifice is necessary (and some always is) visual beauty can always be sacrificed to the auditory elements without the performance ceasing to be first-class. For though the opera, like poetic tragedy, can be, at its grandest, a complete art form, with a whole universe of entertainment on the stage, it can still be great opera though there be nothing more to look at than a conductor and an orchestra and some singers in street clothes.

Even musically, however, it is pretty rare to find everything perfect. The greatest music, the greatest singers, the greatest conductors, and an impeccable orchestra are not always obtainable cheap. Excepting for the operas of Mozart and Wagner and Strauss and for isolated works like *Fidelio* or *Pelléas et Mélisande*, most operatic repertory has always sounded quite well enough with second-class orchestral support, provided the singing was tops. Even Wagner, in recent years, seems to be acceptable on that basis; and Mozart used to be, though nowadays a good conductor seems to be as necessary to the Mozart operas as good vocalism.

Most musicians agree that there are not available anywhere in the world today enough vocalists to supply the opera houses of the world with singing such as was available in all the great houses in 1900, say, or 1910. Neither has the decay of the bravura style been accompanied by any noticeable improvements in diction or in dramatic interpretation. Mary Gardens are even rarer than Melbas these days. For it is the tradition itself of great singing that is lying fallow. There are plenty of voices, but it seems hardly worth while for the possessors of them to go through a complete vocal discipline in an epoch when the public doesn't care so much about great singing as it used to.

The public cares a lot these days about great conducting. In consequence of this, there are more good conductors available in the world than there ever were before. And there are so many first-class instrumentalists around that it is far from rare to encounter them among the ranks of the unemployed. A goodly number of these fine leaders and players are in the United States. As a consequence of this, our orchestral and chamber music organizations have attained a degree of excellence that leaves little to be desired as far as execution is concerned. And the orchestra of the Metropolitan Opera House is so capable these days that it doesn't seem to make very much difference who conducts it, at least among the second-string conductors.

A first-string conductor makes considerable difference, as we have all noticed since Bruno Walter has been appearing there occasionally as guest, because first-class orchestral interpretation is way ahead of second-class in style and power. Still, any night at the Met is a pretty good night orchestrally.

Most nights are good vocally, too, and some quite fine. Because there are lots of good voices around. There are more good voices than good vocalism, in fact, and more good vocalism than good musical or dramatic style. And there is far more good style than there is star quality. All this is due, I think, to a change that has taken place in the comprehension of music. Singers no longer expect conducting to be subservient to their whims. They want good direction and need it. That is the extraordinary and noticeable difference between the singing stars of our day and those of thirty or more years ago. They have neither the prestige nor the vanity that used to make them so glamorous and musically so hard to handle. Even they have come to understand that musical architectonics are the order of the day and that a firm foundation of these is the prime requisite for the success of serious music. Universal acquaintance by means of records and radio with the symphonic style of musical interpretation has made that style, which is primarily occupied with unity, proportion, and emphasis, more popular than the old-fashioned way of merely producing as often as possible a momentary enthusiasm by the effective rendering of single pieces, single phrases, even single notes.

As I have listened to the Metropolitan performances this winter and fondled over many of them in recollection afterward, I am astonished at the amount of good singing there has been in them in minor as well as in major roles. I am astonished because that singing, except in the Wagner operas, which have become for our time the vehicles of vocalism that the operas of Verdi and Donizetti were for a previous epoch, is somehow not played up in performance by the singers themselves to the extent it would have been thirty and more years ago. There are singers with fine voices and good schooling, all doing excellent vocal work but somehow doing it passively, as if they were waiting for somebody to put their show over for them, as if they were counting on the conductor to animate their conception. I have also noticed that, lacking such directorial domination, the tendency to try animating the performance from the stage itself by taking every occasion that presents itself for sticking in a bit of ham comedy and even for running around in circles is growing and is at present nearing the point where it makes the whole cast look a little silly.

I feel a certain lack of authority in most of the Metropolitan performances, and I've an idea the next move in opera everywhere (for this lack of authority is not merely a local phenomenon) will be to put in star conductors in order to give the performances the authoritative accent that the singers are no longer able to provide by themselves. The public of our century loves conductorial rhetoric and adores good teamwork. It is suspicious of personal display and confused by anything that is not streamlined. Streamlining a theatrical or a musical production is a dictatorial job. Diffuse direction makes for hodgepodge in an epoch when the performers themselves don't really believe in personal display and have not been trained in its traditional techniques. The old-time vocal stars sang handsomely no matter who conducted or how inefficient the orchestra was. They often made their biggest successes with a self-effacing accompaniment. Today they actually sing better under a conductor like Toscanini or Walter or Reiner or Rodzinski than under the modern second-class leader, who is neither wholly authoritative, like the great ones, nor wholly subservient, like his predecessors.

Wagner performances do not follow this rule, because they have become chiefly vehicles to display vocal mastery. For seventy-five years Wagner has been a conductor's fief. Today the *Tristan und Isolde* orchestra is being led (and quite satisfactorily) by Kirsten Flagstad's personal accompanist, while the Verdi operas languish everywhere unless animated by a masterful hand.

Flagstad herself is a unique survival. Singers of that quality are rare, of course, in any epoch, though there has always been the legend that at some former time they were more common. But the prima donna who, with superb assurance and knowing exactly what she wants, can take command of her own performance and put it over to everybody's satisfaction, even that of musicians, does not exist, to my knowledge, elsewhere in the world today.

Singers used to be the gods of the opera house. Today they are mostly at best just good executant musicians like those in the pit. They need direction; they want it; they beg for it. To the conductor they offer the kingdom and the power and glory that once were theirs. It is my prophecy that when our operatic establishments shall have finally placed thus all musical authority in his hands, as the contemporary public has long since placed there its worship and confidence, a new era of operatic grandeur will ensue.

That era may not be of long duration. Indeed, I cannot imagine it as other than brief, because no amount of fancy conducting can ever very long take the place of living music. And what the opera lacks most of all in our century is a satisfactory contemporary repertory. But it will be brilliant while it does last, as Salzburg was. And at the end of it the opera will either have transformed itself into a contemporary medium of expression (as it has always done at about the middle of the century) or have passed over into Valhalla midst the iridescent glories of its own Götterdämmerung.

March 9, 1941

Reconverting Opera

WHETHER an operatic repertory theater like the Metropolitan—and its artistic equivalents in other countries—is engaged in public instruction or in the entertainment business is not always clearly understood, I think, by those directing the enterprise. The public, curiously enough, knows what it wants and what it should be getting. It expects education, culture, contact with beauty and with the history of spiritual values. It demands of its subsidized opera companies exactly what it demands of its symphony orchestras, its art museums, and its universities, namely, a true and disinterested representation of the cultural past. But managements, though they know this, do, in penurious epochs, tend to diminish their spiritual, like their financial, largesse and to drain the excess quality off their performances down to a mere money's-worth level.

Wartime restrictions being now loosened up about raising money for what we may call nonmilitary objectives (restrictions that were none the less firm for being chiefly a matter of taste), it would seem only natural that subsidized opera should be getting back to its normal way of life. That way is to operate as a successful money-spending enterprise rather than as an unsuccessful money-making one. In other words, the dissemination of real culture and education is the proper business of the Metropolitan Opera, no matter what that costs.

A reasonable amount of showmanship is no hindrance to the educational function. On the contrary, gracious, charming, or impressive presentation has long been considered valuable, even

in university circles. Indeed, our national talents for showmanship and for giving one another a good time have often made
American educational methods seem superficial to Europeans
who haven't looked at what really goes on beneath the musical-
comedy exterior. Similarly, our art museums and our symphony
orchestras use every device known to psychology, to business,
and to religion for rendering their programs attractive. One
almost wishes sometimes that our cultural presentations were
less oppressively luxurious, so closely does their high finish—as
at the Museum of Modern Art, for instance, or at a concert of
any of our major orchestras—resemble a merely commercial
patina, a luxury packaging.

But all that is really unimportant when the matter put out
is first-class. It is the excess of a proud and culture-conscious
nation. And it expresses a general will that where culture is concerned no care must be spared. We do not expect culture to
show a profit; we expect of it spiritual and intellectual benefits,
which are without price. As a nation we are intellectually ambitious, devoted to self-improvement of all kinds, insatiable consumers of books, music, and drama. Also we are rich. There is no
reason in the world why we should not have the finest opera
money can buy, and I don't mean just showmanship. I mean
Classical, Romantic, and modern repertory correctly and beautifully sung, thoroughly rehearsed on the stage and luxuriously
accompanied in the pit, stylishly presented all round, with magnificence the standard. The show behind the footlights has got
to live up to the solid values, both financial and cultural, that
the audience itself represents in all parts of the house.

Plenty of living citizens remember this kind of opera in Chicago, in Boston, and in New York, not to speak of memorable
moments in Milan, in Paris, Vienna, London, Munich, St. Petersburg, and Berlin. It can be produced again if anybody wants it,
and I think that America does want it. I think she wants it for
the simple reason that she wants everything she uses, particularly the art she patronizes and most particularly her music, to
be of the best. Not just the best there is around, but the best
that anybody anywhere knows how to make. And there are
certainly lots of people in the world who know how to produce better opera performances than anybody in the world is
producing just now.

The chief thing required for good opera production is the same thing that it takes to make a symphony orchestra: money. Money has to be spent on every detail, the top price paid for every workman. Otherwise one can't have top quality. Grandeur and penury make bad bedfellows. You can't be magnificent and economical at once. And believe me, for what the Metropolitan pays its artists you couldn't cast a Broadway operetta. It takes more than talent to sing Wagner and Verdi or to play the oboe. It takes brains and sacrifice and years of expensive preparation. It takes leisure, too, and rest and good food and a comfortable house and vacations for study and the ability to put one's mind on the problem in hand without having to worry about the years when one won't be able any longer to sing Wagner and Verdi or to play the oboe.

Any community can have a first-class opera company that will spend the money it costs. Artists are available, plenty of them. And you don't have to make prices prohibitive, either. There is always a price level that brings in the maximum of receipts, but in no field of cultural endeavor are box-office receipts sufficient to pay for top quality. Extra money must be found through state subsidy, private philanthropy, or popular subscription. We raise lots of money in these days for colleges, hospitals, scientific research, and symphonic foundations. I know of no reason why it can't be raised for opera. America is a rich country or it isn't, and the war is over or it isn't. I believe America to be a rich country, perfectly capable of having the finest opera anybody ever heard; and I think we all consider anything less to be unworthy of us. Also, I suspect, though none of the victorious countries has admitted the fact yet, that the war is over and that it is time to start getting our cultural institutions back to peacetime standards and to operating them on the only method known to history that has ever produced first-class cultural results, namely, an economy of abundance.

In other words, let's start spending some real money on our opera. It is not important whether the present directors be entrusted with this spending. If our musical and civic leaders have confidence in these directors, let us keep them. If not, let's thank them prettily and get new ones. Or start a new opera project from scratch and let the old one worry along with its real-estate mortgages. Whether to work through the present setup or to walk out on it is a delicate decision, with many cultural advantages to be gained and lost either way. But it is not an impossible decision. What is important is that we start acting toward opera like the rich, cultivated, ambitious, proud people that we are. We have first-class symphony orchestras. There is no reason why we shouldn't have one opera company, or even several, upholding comparable standards.

December 9, 1945

English at the Met

THERE is no doubt that the performance of opera in English to an English-speaking audience brings enormous benefits in the way of general understanding. There is also no question but that such performance presents unusual difficulties to an organization like the Metropolitan Opera Company, which was long ago set up for another purpose. Ideally, and naïvely, viewed, this troupe has usually been considered a polygot repertory theater, prepared to offer a proper performance of almost any known opera in its original tongue. Actually it has rarely been convincing in any languages but the Italian and the German. It still has enough good Italian singers to cast and render Italian opera correctly and enough German-speaking Central Europeans (mostly of Swedish or Hungarian birth) to give a reasonably satisfying performance of Wagner. French opera rarely sounds like French opera at the Met; and English, though the mother tongue of many of the artists, more often than not leaves much to be desired in the way of clarity.

Russian opera, when performed there, is offered in translations more or less fortuitously chosen. Mussorgsky's *Boris Godunov* is currently given in Italian, that being the native language of Ezio Pinza, who sings the title role. Rimsky-Korsakov's *Golden Cockerel*, formerly given in French, has been heard of late years in a language that might be described as Basic Bromide English. Similarly, the Czechish *Bartered Bride*, by Smetana, has been moved from the German in which it used to be given over to our own vernacular, and none too effectively, I may add.

The Metropolitan is lucky to have a chorus capable of singing German, Italian, French, and English and enough soloists to cast any opera with moderate effectiveness in those languages. To offer the Slavic ones as well, though not at all out of the question in New York City, would require firing most of the present Italo-German chorus and hiring a Russo-Polish one with Western language accomplishments. Even the giving of *Boris* in Italian is condonable on the ground that it leaves the excellent Mr. Pinza in the cast, though why this artist should not, in his more than twenty years' American residence, have learned, even accidentally, to speak and sing our language passes my comprehension. One would have thought that simple curiosity might have led him somewhere in that direction.*

The same slow progress that has got all the Slavic operas but *Boris* into English at the Metropolitan has begun now to work on the production in translation, one every two or so years, of operas from the more familiar European repertory, chiefly, so far, from the German. Mozart's *Magic Flute* and *Abduction from the Seraglio* and Humperdinck's *Hansel and Gretel* are now given in an English that, if not exactly of the highest literary distinction, is perfectly clear and for the most part inoffensive. Little by little, if present trends continue, the Met will go on augmenting its in-English list, though the Italian wing of the company, as Italian wings have always done everywhere, will no doubt oppose progress in this direction by every means in its power. Since one of these means is the refusal to co-operate, to sing in English on any stage, the in-English productions will, of course, be deprived of all the best acting talent in the company, which is, to a man, Italian.

Articulating the English language clearly in a house of that size, though this has not always in the past been accomplished impeccably, is not an insoluble problem. The present production of Mozart's *Seraglio* is highly presentable in that regard, and that of Bernard Rogers's *The Warrior* is well nigh perfect. Opera in English for an English-speaking audience requires a good initial fitting of words to music by the composer, if the opera is composed in English; a good literary and prosodic translation, if it is a foreign work; and a clear projection of the verbal text by all the singers on the stage, including the chorus. Without these elements the show is bound to be second-class

*Pinza sings English in concert.

and to disappoint any audience that expects a first-class entertainment for its seven dollars. But both are in the long run,
with patience on everybody's part, obtainable, as current productions prove.

What is going to give trouble from now on is acting. Acting
in English to music has no local tradition; and one must be
formed, in however elementary a fashion, right away. So far the
Metropolitan management has tried to side-step the problem
by giving in English only comedies and fairy-tale fantasies. The
acting in Humperdinck's *Hansel and Gretel* will do. That in
Mozart's *Seraglio* will not. I do not believe, moreover, that a
proper technique of rendering grown-up comedy is available
among the Met's English-singing artists. Neither do I believe
that bad acting is more nearly acceptable in the comic style than
in the tragic. On the contrary, an amateur *Hamlet* or *Macbeth* is
far easier to listen to than an amateur *Twelfth Night* or *Tempest*.
Anybody can act *Il Trovatore*, and the popular Puccini operas—
La Tosca, *La Bohème* and *Madama Butterfly*—are foolproof in
any language. Tears need no timing, only insistence. Farce and
fantasy are a monopoly of the great stage technicians.

Here, I think, is the reason why Mozart's *Seraglio*, for all its
sound musical execution, has not yet caught public favor at the
Metropolitan. It has a silly plot that does not lend itself to easy
rendering. *Figaro*, on the other hand, which makes sense as a
play, is rarely ineffective in any language, played by no matter
whom. Even Debussy's *Pelléas et Mélisande*, for all its intimate
French tone and its thoroughly French vocal line, can be convincing in English, as the Philadelphia Opera Company demonstrated several years back. But silly plots and silly jokes are all the
sillier when one can understand them. Those are the operatic
elements that profit best from being left in a foreign tongue.

To the Metropolitan management, therefore, the writer
suggests that the next time an opera is to be translated and
refurbished, one with a serious story be chosen. If our English-
speaking singing actors and actresses are going to learn to act,
which they must do eventually, they must be given, for their
early efforts in that enterprise, something that is capable of
being acted. *Seraglio*, *The Magic Flute*, and *The Golden Cockerel*
are hard jobs for the most expert and imaginative comedians.
For average singing actors they are hopelessly difficult. We must

give our American singers every facility. Give them young love, irate parenthood, sexy seduction, the royal mien, maternal sentiments, jealousies, noble friendships, priesthoods, vendettas, tears, and tuberculosis. And if the Met must do farce comedy, let some insistence be made that Baccaloni learn to sing English. Or, failing that, how would it do if a stand-by sang the bass solos while somebody like Bobby Clark did some real clowning?

January 26, 1947

Fairy Tale about Music

DIE MEISTERSINGER, opera in three acts by *Richard Wagner*, last night at the Metropolitan Opera House, *George Szell,* conductor, *Herbert Graf,* stage director, with *Charles Kullman* (Walther von Stolzing) and *Eleanor Steber* (Eva).

RICHARD WAGNER's *Die Meistersinger von Nürnberg*, which was given again at the Metropolitan Opera House last night after an interval of five years, is the most enchanting of all the fairy-tale operas. It is about a never-never land where shoemakers give vocal lessons, where presidents of musical societies offer their daughters as prizes in musical contests, and where music critics believe in rules of composition and get mobbed for preferring young girls to young composers.

It is enchanting musically because there is no enchantment, literally speaking, in it. It is all direct and human and warm and sentimental and down to earth. It is unique among Wagner's theatrical works in that none of the characters takes drugs or gets mixed up with magic. And nobody gets redeemed according to the usual Wagnerian pattern, which a German critic once described as "around the mountain and through the woman." There is no metaphysics at all. The hero merely gives a successful debut recital and marries the girl of his heart.

And Wagner without his erotico-metaphysical paraphernalia is a better composer than with it. He pays more attention to holding interest by musical means, wastes less time predicting doom, describing weather, soul states, and ecstatic experiences. He writes better voice leading and orchestrates more transparently, too. *Die Meistersinger* is virtually without the hubbub string-writing that dilutes all his other operas, and the music's pacing is reasonable in terms of the play. The whole score is reasonable. It is also rich and witty and romantic, full of interest and of human expression.

The first of the successful operatic comedies for gigantic orchestra, like Verdi's *Falstaff* and Strauss's *Rosenkavalier*, it is the least elephantine of them all, the sweetest, the cleanest, the most graceful. For the preservation of these qualities in performance George Szell, the conductor, and Herbert Graf, the stage director, are presumably responsible. For the loan of some new scenery, which enhanced the final tableau, the Chicago Civic Opera Company merits our thanks. For careful singing and general musical good behavior all the artists deserve a modest palm.

Charles Kullman, who sang the tenor lead, did the most responsible and satisfactory work, I should say. John Garris, as David; Herbert Janssen, as Hans Sachs, and Gerhard Pechner, as Beckmesser (and he didn't ham this role, either) were highly agreeable. Eleanor Steber's Eva was pretty to look at but vocally satisfactory only at the difficult moments. Elsewhere there was a careless buzz in her voice. Emanuel List, as Pogner, sang well but a little stiffly, keeping his voice down to match the others, who are all small-volume vocalists. Mr. Szell kept the orchestra down, too, so that everybody could be heard. The performance all through was charming, intelligible, and a pleasure to this usually anti-Wagnerian opera fan.

January 13, 1945

Good Singing

NORMA, opera in two acts, libretto by *Felice Romani*, music by *Vincenzo Bellini*, last night at the Metropolitan Opera House, *Cesare Sodero*, conductor, *Lothar Wallerstein*, stage director, with *Zinka Milanov* (Norma) and *Jennie Tourel* (Adalgisa).

BELLINI's *Norma*, as given last night at the Metropolitan Opera House, was a distinguished performance. Jennie Tourel, who made her first appearance of the season in the role of Adalgisa, proved to us all over again that the human voice is a first-class musical instrument. Zinka Milanov, who sang the title role, did some beautiful work in her great "*Casta diva*" air and in the three duets with Miss Tourel. Otherwise she showed us, as she so often does, that the bravura style cannot be produced by mere courage without skill.

Miss Tourel is a great pleasure to hear. She is very short and she doesn't wear quite the right clothes, but every phrase she sings is a musical act. And everybody who sings with her sings better than usual. Miss Milanov, always erratic from lack of technique, reserved vocal risks for her own solos. When the two ladies sang together, she sang securely and right. Their duets contained some of the best singing heard here this winter. I do hope there will be more performances of this opera with the same artists, because, working well together, they are certain to profit by repetition and to give much pleasure to the lovers of song.

I wish Miss Milanov would practice more at home. She has a beautiful voice and a taste for the bravura style. Unfortunately, bravura singing is always a failure unless based on the daily exercise of scales and arpeggios. Overconfident and underexercised, Miss Milanov invariably in moments of temperamental enthusiasm sings off pitch and with ugly tone. This is not only unfortunate but unnecessary. An artist of her abundant natural gifts is foolish not to acquire a mastery over them. She would be a great singer if she could bring herself to accept the necessary routine of perfection and if she could refrain from getting excited. If more sure of her throat muscles and of her breath, she would probably not need to get excited.

The rest of the cast was good, and Cesare Sodero conducted with delicacy and animation. The Metropolitan has given some incredibly bad performances this year, but *Norma* is not among them. It is not among those memorable in any year, either, for dramatic conviction. But it contains a great deal of very beautiful singing, and Bellini's melody is always a delight for its instinctive elegance and its sustained complexity. The artist chiefly responsible for the vocal distinction of the whole thing is Jennie Tourel. May we hear more of her, please, and often!

December 16, 1944

Two New Stars

LA TRAVIATA, opera in four acts, libretto by *Francesco Maria Piave*, music by *Giuseppe Verdi*, last night at the Metropolitan Opera House, *Cesare Sodero*, conductor, *Désiré Defrère*, stage director, with *Dorothy Kirsten* (Violetta), *Robert Merrill* (Germont), and *Armand Tokatyan* (Alfredo).

VERDI's *La Traviata*, as sung last night at the Metropolitan Opera House, presented for the first time in those premises the admirable Dorothy Kirsten as Violetta. Miss Kirsten's handling of the role, already favorably known from last season at the City Center, brought liveliness and beauty in no lesser degree to the grander establishment. Backed up by a first-class orchestra and chorus, with Cesare Sodero conducting, and surrounded by such excellent singers as Robert Merrill and Armand Tokatyan, she appeared to this observer as definitely a singer and a singing actress of the first category.

Miss Kirsten is still young, of course; and her star quality is almost brutally brilliant. But she is not afraid of her voice, which is big, beautiful, and well trained, or of her person, which she projects dramatically with confidence not only in herself, which is common enough these days, but in the reality of her role, which is all too rare on the operatic stage. She seems to have all the material, vocal, personal, and intellectual, for a great operatic career. If she has any vocal disadvantage (and this is not grave), it lies in her singing the closed vowels, the Italian *e* and *i*, less perfectly than she does the darker, open ones, the *a* and *o*. Her range is wide; her scales are clean, her marksmanship impeccable. And whether she is uttering a musical line or crossing the stage, she means it.

Robert Merrill is also a fine singing actor. His noble baritone voice and his intensely dignified bearing gave a pathos to the parental role of Germont that was in no way forced and in no way sentimental. To be as moving as that in a frock coat is evidence of mental power, as well as of vocal skill. For two singers of such well-matched equipment as Mr. Merrill and Miss Kirsten, and of such mutually complementary vocal color, to have had almost a whole act, the third, to themselves is a bit of luck all round. Their work together was not only handsome to hear; it was deeply, wonderfully, quite unexpectedly, expressive.

La Traviata has long been one of the Metropolitan's pleasanter evenings, thanks to Mr. Sodero, who leads it to perfection. There have been some good Violettas, too, in late years,
notably Licia Albanese. With Miss Kirsten and Mr. Merrill in the
cast and Mr. Sodero conducting, it is one of the few genuinely
sweet and animated performances in the repertory. Armand
Tokatyan, who sang Alfredo, adds distinction to the cast,
though last night he was not always vocally at ease.

March 8, 1946

First-Class Thriller

LA GIOCONDA, opera in four acts, libretto by *Arrigo Boïto,* music
by *Amilcare Ponchielli,* last night at the Metropolitan Opera House,
Emil Cooper, conductor, *Désiré Defrère,* stage director, with *Zinka
Milanov* (La Gioconda), *Risë Stevens* (Laura Adorno), *Ezio Pinza* (Al-
vise Badoero), *Richard Tucker* (Enzo Grimaldo), and *Leonard Warren*
(Barnaba).

THERE is no denying that Ponchielli's *La Gioconda* makes a
good show when they really sing it. It is tommyrot from beginning to end, skillfully varied, exciting hokum. But since hokum
is chiefly what makes a good show anyhow, and since the musical part of this particular hokum was written for tiptop show-
off, the piece is capable of producing shivers no end when the
musical execution is a bang-up one. And that is exactly what
Emil Cooper, who conducted, and a brilliant cast of singers
gave us last night at the Metropolitan Opera House.

Lush-throated Zinka Milanov, who sang the title role, has
never been in better voice. Risë Stevens, who sang Laura, has
never in my hearing sung half so well. And her voice, when she
does sing well, is one of rare beauty. Ezio Pinza, as the Doge of
Venice, could not have been more distinguished, both vocally
and dramatically. Richard Tucker did his tenor stuff most handsomely. Leonard Warren articulated his baritone villainies with
all power and elegance, though it did take him an act and a half
to get the meal out of his voice. Margaret Harshaw, as the Blind
Woman, sounded rich in the concerted numbers. And even the
ballet troupe put on a Dance of the Hours that was more than
merely presentable.

Mr. Cooper is the only conductor on the Metropolitan's

present staff for whom the orchestra plays invariably in tune. And since his readings are always intelligent and warm, his work rarely fails to give pleasure all round. Last night the pleasure began a little quietly, as if the musical elements were all in place but as if some final Italian oomph were missing. This tranquility turned out to be just more showmanship on Mr. Cooper's part, because when the third act had got going and built up through the ballet to its choral production-number finale, one realized that saving the excitement had all along been the better part of wisdom.

That excitement was the most prodigious theatrical climax I have ever witnessed in that house. It wasn't about anything, because Victor Hugo's play and Arrigo Boïto's libretto and Amilcare Ponchielli's music are not about anything, unless one counts the provoking of applause sufficient motivation for an opera. But the moment was thrilling and the applause whole-hearted; and we were all, I think, grateful for an experience so rare at the Metropolitan. Besides, hokum properly performed has a purity about it that is refreshing. It makes one feel good, like a shower bath, leaves a clean taste in the mouth the way a good murder story does. From that point of view Ponchielli's opera is one of the best, and last night's brilliant performance was more than worthy of it.

December 22, 1945

Aggressive but Harmonious

OTELLO, opera in four acts, libretto by *Arrigo Boïto*, music by *Giuseppe Verdi*, yesterday afternoon at the Metropolitan Opera House, *George Szell*, conductor, *Herbert Graf*, stage director, with *Torsten Ralf* (Otello), *Leonard Warren* (Iago), and *Stella Roman* (Desdemona).

VERDI's *Otello*, which was revived yesterday afternoon at the Metropolitan Opera House after a four-year interval, is an "effective" musico-theatrical work very much in the vein of Ponchielli's *La Gioconda*. Indeed, the latter piece, which preceded *Otello* in composition and in production by eleven years, is probably responsible, along with the revised (and theatrically successful) version of Boïto's *Mefistofele*, which appeared a year before that, in 1875, for the violent theatricalism of this particular work, of which Boïto himself was the librettist.

The word "violence" comes constantly to tongue in speaking of *Otello*. And yet, as Italian opera plots of the late nineteenth century go, there is not much visible violence in this one. The spectacle is, on the whole, statuesque. But violence is present, nevertheless. It is present in the attitude of the composer toward his audience, which for three acts is allowed no respite from aggression. Every remark is exaggerated, every sentiment blown up into a passion. And since the passions, however they may differ in origin and in social reference, all have exactly the same amount of emotional content (the maximum) and a virtually identical (at that intensity) expressive content, the first three acts of *Otello*, for all their masterful orchestral detail, are as monotonous in their insistence on applause-at-any-price as any Broadway musical or floor show.

The fourth act is less wearing. It takes its time, makes its points one by one, and allows, in consequence, a certain awareness of the actors as characters in a play. It allows one time to feel sorry for them, even. If Verdi, at seventy-four, had not lost the abundance of melodic invention that flowed throughout his early and middle years, the last act of *Otello* might well be as deeply touching as those of *La Traviata* and *Il Trovatore*. The repose and the leisurely timing are there, the whole shape and progress of a noble act; but its "*Ave Maria*" is a far cry from the great "*Miserere*."

Yesterday's performance under George Szell was orchestrally a delight for precision and for variety. Vocally it was a delight for the handsome sounds uttered by Torsten Ralf, as Otello, by Leonard Warren, as Iago, and by Stella Roman, who sang Desdemona. The others sang agreeably, too, even the chorus. And everybody moved about with style. The only serious fault in the vocal rendering was forced sounds that came from the three principals every time an overloud orchestral climax threatened to submerge their efforts. The performance on the whole was one of the most satisfactory to the ear that this announcer has lately had the pleasure of attending.

February 24, 1946

A Happy Return

MADAMA BUTTERFLY, opera in three acts, libretto by *Luigi Illica* and *Giuseppe Giacosa*, music by *Giacomo Puccini*, yesterday afternoon at the Metropolitan Opera House, *Pietro Cimara*, conductor, *Désiré Defrère*, stage director, with *Licia Albanese* (Cio-Cio San) and *James Melton* (B. F. Pinkerton).

PUCCINI's *Madama Butterfly* came back to the Metropolitan yesterday afternoon. The war had caused it to be put in storage, apparently because it shows Japanese behaving more or less properly and a United States naval officer behaving (with consular benediction) improperly. The work seems to have been extremely popular in Italy during our occupation of that country, Italian families loving to point out to their daughters the unfortunate results of becoming seriously attached to members of our armed forces. It will probably be popular here too now, though less for moralistic reasons than for the fact that it is a beautiful and touching opera.

The present production, though not a world-beater, is good. Licia Albanese sings the title role with full vocal beauty and acts it with style. Her power of vocal projection is somewhat weak in the lower passages, but her top voice sails out admirably. James Melton sings Pinkerton most pleasantly, except for the inability to project with resonance any note above A flat. The notes are in his voice; he merely doesn't know how to make them carry. John Brownlee's work, as Sharpless, is distinguished, if a bit tame. Lucielle Browning sings Suzuki with handsome sounds. Osie Hawkins, as the Uncle-Priest, does the most striking bit of acting in the whole show.

Mechanically, too, yesterday's performance was well adjusted and quite reasonably pleasing. Pietro Cimara, who conducted, began nervously and too fast; but after Butterfly's entrance, some ten or fifteen minutes later, he settled down to a normal pacing and got music out of the orchestra. It was regrettable that somebody had not noted in rehearsal the injurious effect on the love duet of a scenic device that might well, in more appropriate circumstances, have been any electrician's pride. The moment was a tender one, and the two principals labored admirably. But a garden background full of fireflies was no help to them. Nobody should be asking to sing a difficult and romantic number against an animated lighting effect that cannot fail to distract the audience's attention.

It was refreshing to discover, after not hearing *Madama Butterfly* for some years, what a fine piece of music it is. Every phrase has meaning, and the texture is admirably economical. It is not padded anywhere. A well-made play with simply drawn characters is explained by music of the most ample clarity. Not once does the composer lose interest in the plot and start writing hubbub. The score is full of apt invention that all serves the play. Since the play, even unaccompanied, is an unfailing tearjerker, with music of pointed expressivity and masterful cut it becomes a work of great power and no inconsiderable charm, in spite of its lack of even the most elementary intellectual content, or thoughtful tone. *Madama Butterfly* is not a work of art in the class with *Pelléas et Mélisande* or *Don Giovanni*, but it is a masterpiece of effective musical theater. It is a pleasure to have it back in repertory, especially with Albanese singing it.

January 20, 1946

Glamorous Evening

LA BOHÈME, opera in four acts, libretto by *Giuseppe Giacosa* and *Luigi Illica*, music by *Giacomo Puccini*, last night at the Metropolitan Opera House, *Cesare Sodero*, conductor, *Désiré Defrère*, stage director, with *Ferruccio Tagliavini* (Rodolfo), *Licia Albanese* (Mimi), and *Francesco Valentino* (Marcello).

FERRUCCIO TAGLIAVINI's debut at the Metropolitan Opera House last night brought out an unusually large and enthusiastic audience. Such unrestrained applause has not been heard in that house for some years. It was heart-warming. It was merited, too, for Mr. Tagliavini has a handsome voice and sings better than merely well. With Licia Albanese, as Mimi, and Francesco Valentino, as Marcello, supporting him in first-class style, Puccini's *La Bohème* took on an animation that was in every way enjoyable. Cesare Sodero and these principal artists gave the work, moreover, a genuinely Italianate reading. It was warm, and it did not drag. I suspect, moreover, that the artists responded to the audience's wideawakeness and gave a better show for solid appreciation shown at the outset.

Mr. Tagliavini has a lyric tenor voice, fresh in timbre and not without power. It is a typical Italian voice, frank and not very subtle, but smooth of scale. His singing style is typically Italian, too, though without the ostentation one is accustomed to associate with Italian tenors of an older generation. Mr. Tagliavini sings high and loud with perfect adequacy and no inconsiderable brilliance, but he does not gulp or gasp or gargle salt tears. He is a competent artist, thoroughly straightforward, quite without airs of genius and a little lacking in variety of coloristic vocal effect. To the eye he is plump but manly and a perfectly good actor. He has a pleasing personality, a temperament of no unusual projection.

The dominating quality of his work, besides its genuine competence, both vocal and dramatic, is its youthfulness. He sings like a young man who enjoys singing and who is neither afraid of high notes nor especially proud of them. He has reserves of energy and a great naturalness. Not in a very long time have we heard tenor singing at once so easy and so adequate. He makes no attempt to sing like a baritone, and neither does he croon. At least he did not last night. He even at one point sang a genuine open-throated pianissimo, the first I have heard in Thirty-ninth Street since I started reviewing opera six years ago. So sound an artist could go far. Without going any farther than he has, he can give great pleasure to anybody who likes singing.

Mimi Benzell's Musetta was good to look at, if a little buzzy to the ear. Mr. Valentino sang well, looked well, acted well. His beautiful baritone voice was nicely matched for size with Mr. Tagliavini's and with that of the ever-lovely Miss Albanese. And last night the wonderful thing took place that happens all too rarely these days. Italian singing actors, working under an Italian conductor before an audience that was pretty largely Mediterranean, gave us real Italian opera. Not ham Italian opera, but the real thing, the kind in which the play and music come alive because the cast knows what the show is all about and is singing, every one of them, the same piece. Genuine enjoyment all round was the note of the evening, the glamorous, incandescent kind of enjoyment that makes audiences listen better and artists work better. The performance, for once, seemed unusually short, in consequence.

January 11, 1947

Charade with Music

THE GOLDEN COCKEREL, opera in three acts, libretto in English by *Tatiana Balkoff Drowne* (after the Russian original by *Vladimir Bielsky*), music by *Nikolai Rimsky-Korsakov,* last night at the Metropolitan Opera House, *Emil Cooper,* conductor, *Désiré Defrère,* stage director, with *Patrice Munsel* (Queen of Shemakha), *Norman Cordon* (King Dodon), and *Margaret Harshaw* (Amelfa).

THE GOLDEN COCKEREL, which was produced last night at the Metropolitan Opera House, is Bielsky's (after Pushkin) *Le Coq d'or* in nursery-rhyme English text and with Donald Duck stage direction. Fortunately it is also Rimsky-Korsakov's lascivious and sparkling score directed by Emil Cooper, who conducted the premières of the work in Moscow in 1909 and later in Paris and in London. Orchestrally the performance is a delight for its animation, clarity, and general authority. Vocally some of it is pretty good, too, especially the work of Patrice Munsel as the Queen of Shemakha. As a piece of sexual and political satire, which I gather its authors intended it to be, the play makes no more sense, as here directed and performed, than a children's performance of *Salomé* might.

Miss Munsel is a little young for Oriental seduction scenes. Her acquaintance with such matters, like that of many another young Miss of today, seems to be derived from the burlesque stage by way of the films. She even did a sort of strip tease in the second act with no end of fetching Hollywood vivacity. But she sang like an angel, like a not quite mature angel, still a very, very gifted one.

Her voice has grown in volume since last year. The middle part of it is louder now and quite beautiful. The very top of it, everything above high C, has always been firm and richly brilliant. There is still a region, most of the octave just below high C, the one where coloraturas spend the best part of their singing time, that is wavery. She is far from being mistress of her instrument; but it is a great instrument, or seems to be growing into one. And she has a natural talent for making music with it.

Norman Cordon and Margaret Harshaw sang their parts pleasantly but acted them absurdly, just bouncing about. Mr. Cordon might have been playing Foxy Grandpa. Both showed up to advantage singing in English, however, because with the vowels of their own language to vocalize on, they were quite free of the hot-potato effect that has marred the work of both recently in foreign languages. They sang right out through the face, instead of through the top of the head; and they projected their consonants. The effect was most agreeable.

Miss Munsel's enunciation was excellent, too. So excellent that she nearly brought down the house when in the last act she came forth in her stentorian middle voice with the following literary gem:

> "That old man has surely push;
> He doesn't beat about the bush!"

March 2, 1945

Lurching and Mugging

SALOMÉ, opera in one act, libretto in German by *Hedwig Lachmann* (after the English original by *Oscar Wilde*), music by *Richard Strauss*, performed last night at the New York City Center by the New York City Opera Company, *Laszlo Halasz*, conductor, *Leopold Sachse*, stage director, with *Brenda Lewis* (Salomé), *Teresa Gerson* (Herodias), *Frederick Jagel* (Herod), *Ralph Herbert* (Jochanaan), and *William Horne* (Narraboth).

RICHARD STRAUSS's *Salomé*, a musical version of Oscar Wilde's play, was produced last night at the City Center of Music and Drama. The orchestral version used is one for slightly reduced forces, reported to have been made by the composer. The musical execution was shipshape and most agreeable to the ear. The visual production, though no more absurd than most, was a hodgepodge of stylistic elements, running from Assyrian architecture to Hollywood kimonos split down the front and gilt leather G-strings. There were pasteboard goblets aplenty, too, and artificial peaches that got thrown about like pincushions, and for once a realistic head of the prophet. That helped, though Brenda Lewis, who sang the title role, didn't seem to know quite what to do with it when she had got it.

Miss Lewis is a skilled vocalist with a pretty voice. Her singing, save for a few forced moments, was excellent. So was that of Teresa Gerson, the Herodias; of Frederick Jagel, the Herod; of Ralph Herbert, the Jochanaan; and of William Horne, as the young Captain who kills himself. The orchestra sounded well, too; and Laszlo Halasz conducted with spirit and an admirable clarity. The whole opera would probably have been a pleasure over the air. But as a stage spectacle it was consistently inept. This is unfortunate, because *Salomé* is a highly dramatic piece, lurid, outrageous and thoroughly gripping.

Somebody should teach opera singers not to lurch. This movement is never graceful and rarely convincing. Mr. Jagel did it oftenest last night, though the others indulged when they couldn't think of anything else to do. He suggested Soglow's Little King played by Mr. Zero Mostel, rather than a figure in an erotic tragedy. Miss Lewis did a good deal of lurching, too, and lots of leaning backwards. The constant projecting forward of the pelvis may be a sexy movement, but it is not a sensuous one. It is a concomitant rather of commercialized vice than of seduction. In a role of this kind it betrays, indeed, a certain innocence, a child's concept of the lascivious. And it can easily be comic.

Miss Lewis's Dance of the Seven Veils was full of good will and not wholly lacking in charm, though real style it had none. Where she failed as an actress most gravely was in the final scene with the head. She might have been singing it a lullaby. And she took her last lines standing and looking upward, as if she were playing Joan of Arc. Her miming of this sensational scene was not in any sense puritanical. It was sexy enough, as I said before; but it gave no suggestion of sensuality. No small part of its ineffectiveness came also from her constant attempt to act with the face, a procedure known commonly as "mugging" and one that has no place in opera. In opera the face is used for singing. One acts with the body. It would be interesting to hear this excellent singer in a role more becoming to her age and temperament.

April 17, 1947

After Thirty Years

ARIADNE AUF NAXOS, opera in a prologue and one act, libretto by *Hugo von Hofmannsthal*, music by *Richard Strauss*, performed last night at the New York City Center by the New York City Opera Company, *Laszlo Halasz*, conductor, *Leopold Sachse*, stage director, with *Ella Flesch* (Ariadne), *Virginia MacWatters* (Zerbinetta), *Polyna Stoska* (Composer), and *James Pease* (Music Master).

RICHARD STRAUSS's *Ariadne on the Isle of Naxos*, which was given its first professional New York performance last night at the City Center of Music and Drama, is considered by many Strauss fanciers to be its composer's masterpiece. That it is the work of a master there is no doubt. If it lacks, perhaps, the lurid vigor of *Elektra* and *Salomé* or the straight sex appeal of *Der Rosenkavalier*, it has a clarity of musical texture that is missing from these earlier works. It is indeed a pleasure to hear Strauss's music pruned of the 10,000 useless notes per act with which he was so long accustomed to clutter up his scores. *Ariadne*, though thin, perhaps, of expressive substance, has great charm, both melodic and harmonic; and its small, clean orchestra is a perpetual delight.

Last night's performance of the work under Laszlo Halasz was a pleasure all round. The orchestra was lovely; the singers sang with style; the staging, if not especially chic, was at the same time neither dull nor clownish. The work was not played for laughs or for easy applause; it was presented as a serious piece of theater. And the audience responded with gratitude to the compliment paid its intelligence.

It responded most of all to Virginia MacWatters, who sang the difficult coloratura aria with a purity of style and an accuracy of pitch unmatched in New York City by any other coloratura soprano during my reviewing years. Second in audience favor was Polyna Stoska, who sang the role of the Composer. Ella Flesch, curiously, did not work at her best as Ariadne. She is a schooled artist, and her voice is a commanding one. But she mostly just stood around looking like the Statue of Liberty and sang flat. The three ladies who waited on her in exile—Lillian Fawcett, Rosalind Nadell, and Lenore Portnoy—sang their trios with skill and beauty. James Pease, as the Music Master, was first class in every way.

The work itself, from both the literary and the musical points of view, is what the Marxians would probably call "decadent capitalist art." It is shallow of substance and utterly sophisticated in style. It is a masterful display of learning, skill, and deliberate charm, all luxury and no meat. It evokes the eighteenth century through the conventions of the Reinhardt baroque. It aims, one learns from the librettist Hofmannsthal's own publicity, at a certain profundity, which this writer finds scant, and at a humor which he finds facile. Musically it is an elaborate joke about how much fun it is to play around with the classical techniques.

From any point of view it is good to listen to, because it is in its own way a completely successful work. About what its place in musical history will be a century from now I have no guess. But for thirty years it has had a unique place in the contemporary world of music, and the City Center has contributed to New York's intellectual life by making us acquainted with it. Whether in all those thirty years the Metropolitan Opera, upon whom the responsibility for our operatic culture has chiefly rested, could ever have produced it I do not know. Their setup is, of course, almost unbelievably inefficient; and the work requires skill and lots of rehearsal. In any case, the fact remains that *Ariadne auf Naxos* is New York news this morning and its City Center performance musically good news.

October 11, 1946

Carolina Carmen

CARMEN JONES, it is agreed by press and public, is a good musical show. But not a few sincere persons, accustomed to hearing Bizet's *Carmen* given by operatic repertory companies in mammoth houses and being a little surprised at the vigor it has when given in the vernacular with a properly rehearsed troupe in a place of reasonable size, are asking themselves, with an excess of scruple, "Is the new version *Carmen*?" and "Is it grand opera?"

This writer's answer to the first question is an enthusiastic yes. The plot is there and the music is there; the whole shape and sequence of the musico-dramatic work are intact. The landscape has been altered from Spain to Carolina, but that is standard operatic procedure. Verdi's *Un Ballo in Maschera* has shuttled back and forth for years between Sweden and Massachusetts. Spain's gypsies have in this case become Carolina's Negro proletariat, and the bull fighter is pugilist. The social parallel is really surprisingly close. And when one considers that the Negroes are here speaking their own language (or at least what passes up North for Negro English) the verisimilitude is even closer than that of Spanish gypsies singing in French. The music is cut some, but that is nothing new in opera. What is new is that the translation has wit, makes sense, and fits the music. It is superior to anything of the kind that I know in English, excepting only the musical translations of Marion Farquhar. All things considered, it seems to me that *Carmen Jones* has at least as much of Bizet's *Carmen* in it, dramatically and musically speaking, as the current production by the Metropolitan Opera Company has, for all that the latter boasts a bigger and better orchestra plus Sir Thomas Beecham to conduct it.

The answer to the other question is no. *Carmen Jones* is not grand opera. Neither is the Bizet work. The transformations that have been operated on the French piece have been mostly in the way of restoring to it its original style and dimensions. *Carmen* is no more grand opera than *The Daughter of the Regiment* is. It is *opéra-comique*, differing from the *opéras-comiques* of Grétry and Boïeldieu and Auber only by the literary genre of its libretto, which is that of realistic proletarian melodrama. This genre had never been used previously with any success in either light opera or grand. There had been romantic melodrama operas of the cape-and-dagger school and proletarian idylls in pastoral vein; but lust and murder among the workers and hijackers was Bizet's revolutionary contribution to the musical theater. Wagner's return to gods and goddesses was reactionary by comparison. The French proletarian operas of Bruneau and Charpentier, the *Lady Macbeth* of Shostakovich, and the whole of Italian *verismo*—the works of Mascagni and Leoncavallo—as well as Gershwin's *Porgy and Bess*, are all Bizet's progeny. The works of Puccini and Montemezzi and Alfano, too, derive from him rather than from Verdi their musical technique of direct dramatic impact, though their subject matter involves a certain return to high Romanticism in the fact that their melodramas mostly take place among persons of some economic substance.

Bizet's *Carmen* is a realistic proletarian melodramatic *opéra-comique* with lots of spoken dialogue, and so is Billy Rose's *Carmen Jones*. The Metropolitan production, though orchestrally and even vocally, for the most part, superior, is less true to the genre of the original piece and far less convincingly presented.

This does not mean that the new production is a masterpiece. I think it suffers a little from New York theater disease, a nervous habit of building up excitement too quickly. Most of our musicals are less interesting after the intermission than before. There is a pretty tasteless Brazilian ballet, too, in the second part, in which Negroes who can really dance well are required to dance badly because somebody thought that would be funny. Or perhaps because it was considered that they couldn't really carry off the Brazilian style, though what Brazilian dancing is if not Negroid I wouldn't know. Some of the solo singing, though no doubt the best available, is less expert than the ensemble work. The show has its disappointments; but taken all round, it is the kind of musical show I wish there were more of and the kind of opera we certainly need lots and lots more of.

The production has two elements of authenticity. One is Oscar Hammerstein's translation, and the other is the Negro company. All the rest is Broadway, good Broadway, but nothing very powerful. The fitting of new words to old music, however, as Mr. Hammerstein has done it, is ingenious, neat, and wholly triumphant. It should serve as a model, or at least as a minimum standard of excellence, for other efforts of the kind. It certainly makes the *Magic Flute* translation used at the Metropolitan sound silly, though this latter is not by current operatic standards a bad piece of work.

The Negro singers, as always, make opera credible. And, as always, they make music shine. They have physical beauty of movement, natural distinction, and grace. Musically they have rhythm, real resonance, excellent pitch, perfect enunciation, and full understanding of the operatic convention. They never look bored or out of place on a stage or seem inappropriately cast for any musical style. I had thought in advance that the Spanish coloring of Bizet's score might prove to be the intractable element in this adaptation of it to American Negro life. Not at all. It swears less with its Negro subject than the Viennese and Broadway elements do in Gershwin's *Porgy*. The people on the stage might very credibly have Caribbean blood in them, so naturally does this Spanish half-caste music (written by a Frenchman) espouse Negro rhythmic firmness and Negro vocal *melisma*. This is not the first Negro opera production Broadway has seen nor the most distinguished. But it is a contribution to the repertory of that permanent Negro opera company that is going to provide the solution one day for all opera problems.

December 5, 1943

Farce and Melodrama

THE TELEPHONE, comic opera in one act, and THE MEDIUM, opera in two acts by *Gian-Carlo Menotti*, performed last night at the Hecksher Theatre, New York, by the Ballet Society, *Leon Barzin*, conductor, *Mr. Menotti*, stage director, with, in the first, *Marilyn Cotlow* (Lucy) and *Paul Kwartin* (Ben), and, in the other, *Marie Powers* (Madame Flora) and *Evelyn Keller* (Monica).

THE BALLET SOCIETY produced last night at the Hecksher Theater two operas by Gian-Carlo Menotti, one of them, *The Telephone*, a world première. The other, *The Medium*, had been given for the first time last May at the Brander Matthews Theater in Columbia University by the Columbia Theater Associates. Both are first-class musico-theatrical works. The first is an opera buffa, light and full of laughter. The second is a tragedy in melodramatic vein that is the most gripping operatic narrative this reviewer has witnessed in many a year.

The Medium is about the private life of a woman who evokes by trickery, for paying customers, visions and voices of the dead. Caught up in her own psychic ambience, and aided by alcohol, she imagines she feels a hand on her throat. Terrified by the experience, she renounces her racket and exposes it to her clients. They refuse to believe that what they had wanted to believe in was false. At this point, the medium goes hysterical and murders a dumb boy who was previously part of her household and an aid in her trickery setup.

No such reduction of the plot can give an idea of how absorbing this work is. I have heard it three times and it never fails to hold me enthralled. Mr. Menotti's libretto, which he wrote himself, and his music form a unit that is deeply touching and terrifying. And if the second act is a little reminiscent as theater (though not as music) of the second act of Puccini's *La Tosca*, the piece in no way suffers by comparison with that infallible piece of stage craft. The play wrings every heart string, and so does the music. I cannot conceive the whole work otherwise than as destined for a long and successful career.

The Telephone, or *L'Amour à Trois*, is a skit about a young man whose girl friend is so busy talking to people on the telephone that the only way he can get her attention for a proposal of marriage is to go out to the corner drugstore and call her up himself. It is gay and funny and completely humane. Both operas, indeed, are infused with a straightforward humanity that is a welcome note of sincerity in contemporary operatic composition. Their librettos are skillfully made, and their music is skillfully composed. But that is not the main point. Their unusual efficacy as operas comes from their frankly Italianate treatment of ordinary human beings as thoroughly interesting.

The visual production of *The Medium* was one of unusual distinction. The casting of both operas was excellent. Particularly notable for both singing and acting were Marie Powers, who sang the title role in *The Medium* (her predecessor, Claramae Turner, was immediately engaged by the Metropolitan Opera), and Evelyn Keller, who sang the part of her daughter. Leo Coleman, who mimed the mute, was admirable also. Both operas were decorated and costumed more than prettily by Horace Armistead. Mr. Menotti, who directed them, in addition to having written both words and music, proved himself no less an expert in this domain than in the others. The musical direction of Leon Barzin was, as usual, impeccable.

Evviva Menotti!

February 19, 1947

Acting to Song

WHEN Americans speak words on a stage they act them out in one way, and when they sing they mostly act them out in another. It seems to be considered normal procedure, especially among our women actors, to play down the dramatic characterization of any singing role and to play up at the same time their personal charms in a way that is not considered proper at all by European stage folk. For these latter tragedy, comedy, farce, realistic drama, the poetic recital, opera, operetta, musical comedy, fantasy, vaudeville, torch singing, and even the cinema, however much the cadence of their verbal articulation and the style of their pantomime may vary (for each has its manner of elocution and its repertory of appropriate gesture), are all branches of the mummer's art, since they all involve impersonation.

Now the first rule of convincing impersonation is that one must not try to impersonate more than one character at a time. American singing actors, however, like American film actors, seem more and more to be dealing in double characterization. This is effective in films, because the films, especially the American films, do not aim much at creating an illusion of reality but rather at creating a dream, with all that that implies of obscurity as to what it is really about. (A film, like a dream, takes place in the dark, and for the most part in black and white, whereas live theater plays in a gamut of light and of color.) Miss Helen Hayes, for instance, does nothing in *Harriet* except to present as clearly and convincingly as she is able (and she is very able) the character of Harriet Beecher Stowe. Miss Gertrude Lawrence, on the other hand, though an able actress, too, of spoken parts, played *Lady in the Dark* as a double role. Only part of the time did she impersonate an editress in need of psychoanalysis; she also played Gertrude Lawrence up to the hilt. Not Gertrude Lawrence as she is in private life, either, but a fictitious Gertrude Lawrence, a personality of pure glamour.

In the course, one evening last week, of a genteel pub crawl, it came into my reflections that double characterization has probably crept into American singing by way of advertising, where everything, from lollipops to laxatives, is described in the language of love. In any case, it is pretty common among American singers and quite rare among the Europeans. At an establishment called "Paris qui Chante," which cultivates the French style, I found the *chanteuses* no less charming from the fact that the songs they sang were the songs they acted. At "The Blue Angel" I found the American style in flower. One young woman sang a straightforward sentimental song while her face and body acted the role of Delilah. Then she sang about a tough gold-digger. But to the deaf she could only have been impersonating somebody pretty hoity-toity, say a suburban hostess bidding good-by to tea guests.

At "Casablanca" the style was frank again. There was a pair of ballroom exhibition dancers that did ballroom exhibition dancing. And Miss Muriel Rahn, from *Carmen Jones*, sang a series of opera solos absolutely straight, very beautifully indeed, and without electrical amplification. She sang the three great airs from *Carmen* in the Hammerstein translation and one from *Martha* in a not dissimilar literary revision. At a later show she sang the *"Vissi d'arte"* from *La Tosca* in Italian and a piece from *Porgy and Bess*. Not only was it a pleasure to hear really expert vocalism (which is rare enough anywhere) in a night club, but it was deeply comforting to encounter a young American actress who does not seem to feel that the musical medium justifies an indirect style of character presentation.

Our singing actresses would do well to observe more carefully the work of the European *chanteuses* and other musical entertainers, as well as of the great European opera singers, of whom we still have several among us. The force of the impersonations that these artists project is due to the fact that, whatever the musical style or the dramatic medium may be, a single, complete characterization is the thing that is being projected. Half the trouble with our younger singers at the Metropolitan Opera, for instance, is that nobody seems to have told them that they do not have to do anything on a stage but the role they are doing. The art of acting is not especially recondite. The chief techniques involved are speaking and singing, and those can be perfected by study. For the rest, a simple understanding of the motives and sentiments implied by the text will do wonders toward creating a convincing impersonation. But any assertion, conscious or otherwise, of one's own personality and still more the attempt to add a fabricated platform charm to dramatic characterization will diminish the force of dramatic impact and destroy the illusion that is the basic reality of the stage.

January 24, 1944

RESPECTING COMPOSERS

Choral Effectives

CHORAL MUSIC almost never sounds well in performance. Chamber music, orchestral music, even the opera, can be produced efficiently and satisfactorily, given experienced workmen and enough rehearsal. That is because everybody involved knows the purpose of the enterprise, which is to produce the music in hand efficiently and satisfactorily. In choruses this purpose is only a part of the business, the other part, probably the more exigent one, being to provide musical exercise for the participants.

Amateurism, in other words, is inherent to the present setup. There are professional choruses, of course, though not many. And they perform less well, for the most part, than the amateur ones. In the instrumental field, in recital repertory, in the theater, though there is much good amateur music making, the standards of execution that prevail are those established by professionals. And by professionals I mean exactly what is meant by professionals in any activity; I mean they receive money. But in choral singing, and this is true all over the world, the highest standards of efficiency are those set by amateurs, by societies in which the members pay for the privilege of participating.

The advantages of amateurism in the choral field are well known. Nothing is so lifeless as a professional chorus. Amateurs put passion into their work; they will rehearse indefinitely; they adore their conductor. They love the whole business. Indeed, there are few greater sources of lasting satisfaction than the practice of communal singing. It is the very richness of the experience that produces both the virtues and the defects of our great choral organizations.

The chief trouble with these is that they have no standard size. The modern world has never arrived at any agreement about what number of choral executants makes for maximum musical efficiency, for the very simple reason that in our best choral societies, all of which are amateur, the privilege of participation is recognized as of such great value, culturally and humanly, that it is not considered loyal to refuse it to anyone who can meet the technical requirements. Since these do not need, for the best execution, to be very high, all our societies tend toward hypertrophy; they get too big for efficiency. They begin small; and as long as they have only fifty or sixty members, they do beautiful work. Then they start growing, overflowing on every stage; and nothing stops that growth but the architecture of Carnegie Hall, the limits of how many can be crowded on the platform behind a symphony orchestra.

By this time they have lost their flexibility and most of their effective repertory. They look very impressive in their robes as they sit there waiting through three movements of Beethoven's Ninth Symphony just to stand up in the last and force their voices. Gone by now are the days when they could sing the great choral literature of pre-Baroque and modern times. They go through a certain amount of it, even reducing their number for an occasional work that just won't let itself be sung by 250 people. But once they have become 250 people, their chief work is serving as an adjunct to symphony orchestras. They cannot deflate. And since at that size nothing sounds well but shouting and whispering, they lose first their beauty of tone, next their variety of tone, next their diction, with which goes all rhythm and preciseness of attack, and finally their ability to sing on pitch, leaving to the orchestral musicians the responsibility of making clear to the audience the harmony of any piece. They just shout and whisper and stand there looking impressive in cassocks or gowns or in dark suits and maidenly white dresses.

These thoughts occurred to me the other evening at a concert in Carnegie Hall of the Collegiate Chorale. This excellent organization is just beginning its downward path. All it has lost so far is tonal beauty. Our next best outfit, the Westminster Choir, a semiprofessional organization made up from students of the Westminster Choir School in Princeton, has gone one step farther; it has had no diction for five years. The New York Oratorio Society, once, I am told, musically high class, has nothing left but a medium pitch average. The Harvard Glee Club, twenty-five years ago a virtuoso group in its own right, is now, so far as musical values are concerned, only an occasional tail to the Boston Symphony Orchestra's kite. The Dessoff Choirs have gone symphonic too. They have not much tone left; but their pitch, rhythm, and diction are still good.

The truth is that almost none of the great choral literature, ancient or modern, will stand blowing up. It is chamber music of personalized expression and high coloristic refinement. This applies to all liturgical music and also to the choral works of J. S. Bach, though we have become so accustomed to hearing these sung by depersonalized armies, like the Schola Cantorum and the Bach Choir of Bethlehem, Pennsylvania, that few living musicians know the brilliance and real power they can have when produced with limited effectives. The only part of great choral literature, as something over and beyond orchestral works with choral interpolations, that can stand numbers is the oratorio. Handel can be blown up both chorally and orchestrally and still sound well. It doesn't have to be, but it can. That is because it is broadly dramatic in conception. It is theater music, the theater's only first-class contribution to choral art.

If music were the only aim in choral singing, we could standardize the procedures and improve the sound of it. Unfortunately the social, the religious, the cultural purposes served are no less valuable. And so we have a whole literature of the most sensitive music in the world shouted at us by a football cheering section. There is nothing to be done about it. One cannot argue with a social custom. Nor would one wish to hamper the functioning of one so rich. But as a reviewer attending concerts regularly and listening, as George Antheil used to say, not so much *to* music as *for* it, I am more often than not, at choral ceremonies, reminded of one of the season's classical sentiments. I salute you with it, choral devotees, even as I wish that we critics might perhaps, just for Christmas, occasionally be greeted so. "God rest you merry, gentlemen! Let nothing you dismay."

December 23, 1945

Majestic but Inefficient

BACH CHOIR OF BETHLEHEM, *Ifor Jones*, conductor, with members of the PHILADELPHIA ORCHESTRA and *E. Power Biggs*, organist, last night at Carnegie Hall, performing Bach's Mass in B minor. Soloists: *Ruth Diehl*, soprano, *Lilian Knowles*, contralto, *Lucius Metz*, tenor, *Calvin Marsh*, bass, and *Edwin Steffe*, bass.

THE BACH CHOIR OF BETHLEHEM, Pennsylvania, which has not visited New York in twenty-five years, brought its full effectives to Carnegie Hall last night. These consist nowadays of about two hundred choristers, trained and directed by Ifor Jones; some sixty members of the Philadelphia Orchestra; E. Power Biggs, organist; and the necessary vocal soloists, these last varying from season to season. The evening's music was the work that music lovers have long traveled in May to Bethlehem for hearing sung by this choir, Bach's Mass in B minor.

Let us praise last night's performance right off as the best of its kind this Bach lover has ever heard. Its kind is that invented by Mendelssohn, namely, a transformation, or distortion, or, if you like, transfiguration of Bach's intricate music for small forces into a massive Romantic oratorio like Mendelssohn's own *Elijah* or *Saint Paul*. The appropriateness of the operation need not be questioned, since for a century now it has been considered acceptable by music lovers all over the world. It has been recognized, however, for forty or more years as a distortion, and a grave one. This writer, for one, considers it unfortunate that so much devotion, sound musical skill, and publicity should be mobilized for the preserving of a tradition that has long been known to be historically and esthetically false.

The falsity lies in the inability of that number of executants to render this particular music, which is full of linear complexity, with a reasonable degree of exactitude. Any chorus of two hundred can make a majestic noise; and Mr. Jones's chorus makes the most agreeable, the most brilliant and bright-sounding choral fortissimo I have ever heard. But when they get to the intricate and rapid passages they go fuzzy, just like any other group of that size. Moreover, the very grandeur and power with which they sing the choral numbers inevitably makes the solos sound puny.

Faced with this prospect, the soloists attempt to sing their arias louder than they can do correctly. Nobody living can sing those solos with power vocalism. They are fluid, florid, and melismatic; the only possible way to make them expressive, to stay on pitch, and to blend the vocal line with the instrumental obbligato that accompanies it is to sing lightly, with a marked nasal resonance. But this produces chamber music and makes the massive choir sound coarse. So the choral conductor cannot let them do it. Thus a full half of the Mass, the solo half, ends by sounding strained, incompetent, and foolish. Since a good half of the choral numbers are already overstuffed and not sounding at their best, this leaves only about one fourth of the work making the kind of musical clarity that we all know Bach's music should make.

Hearing the work at all, of course, is a major musical experience. And hearing even so much as a quarter of it sound forth so frankly and so confidently as the Bethlehem group makes it do is reason for throwing anybody's hat in the air. But how much richer and grander it would be if Mr. Jones would cut his chorus down about eighty per cent and his orchestra by half, spend more time and thought on the soloists, and move the whole thing to Town Hall. The benefit to Bach would be enormous.

February 19, 1946

In the Royal Style

COLLEGIATE CHORALE, *Robert Shaw*, conductor, with a chamber orchestra and *Ernest White*, organist, last night at Hunter College Auditorium, performing Bach's Mass in B minor. Soloists: *Anne McKnight* and *June Gardner*, sopranos, *Lydia Summers*, contralto, *Lucius Metz*, tenor, and *Paul Seymour Matthen*, baritone.

THE COLLEGIATE CHORALE, conducted by Robert Shaw, gave last night in the Hunter College Auditorium an uncut performance of Bach's B-minor Mass. Though this lasted nigh on to three hours, your reporter experienced no fatigue and observed no sleepers. Indeed, it has not previously been his privilege to hear so thoroughly delightful a reading of this majestic work, though he has attended many. How Mr. Shaw worked his miracle on this most recalcitrant of pieces is the subject of this morning's sermon.

He started by organizing his musical effectives in proportions not unlike those available in the German eighteenth-century courts, for one of which the work was originally planned. A chorus of sixty mixed voices (American amateur female sopranos are not as loud as trained German boys), an orchestra of strictly chamber proportions, a harpsichord, an organ used with extreme discretion, and the necessary soloists were quite sufficient for volume and not excessive for the florid style. He further reduced the orchestral effectives in accompanying the solos and duets to single instruments or, in the case of string backgrounds, to two on a part. And then he rehearsed the choruses for lightness and clarity, the vocal soloists for harmonious blending with the instrumental soloists that accompany them.

As a result, the accompanied solos, in reality small chamber ensembles, took their place in the choral framework very much as the concertino group in a concerto grosso is set off against the larger instrumental body. The work became thus a dialogue, an antiphony, each kind of music being beautiful in its own way, the two kinds giving amplitude and perspective to the whole.

That whole turns out to be, as one might have expected, not at all a giant Lutheran cantata, nor yet a liturgical Mass, but a grand and sumptuous court oratorio on the subject of the Mass. Its grandeur lies in its vast proportions and in its completely simple expressivity, its sumptuousness in the extreme and formal floridity of the musical texture. Its layout is huge but perfectly clear; its style is the ultimate in ornateness. It is at once enormous and graceful, like the palace architecture of its time, complete with gardens, ponds, statues, and vistas.

Mr. Shaw preserved these proportions and all their grace by simply limiting his forces to a size capable of achieving grace. He added, moreover, a grace of his own in the firm lilt of his beat. His rhythmic alacrity evoked a court ballet. The "*Cum sancto spiritu*" that ends the Gloria was as gay as a hornpipe; and the bass aria "*Et in spiritum sanctum*," from the Credo, tripped along none the less reverently for being light on its feet. Just as the alto Agnus Dei might easily have rocked a cradle.

Rhythmic courage, tonal exactitude, pretty balances, and sweetness all round allowed the proportions of the work to take on full majesty without any heaviness. If Mr. Shaw and his admirable colleagues will give us such a performance annually, Bach's choral masterpieces will cease in short order to be merely edifying and become humane, as I am sure, from last night's performance of the Mass, they were conceived to be. The sacred music of the great masters is not designed to shake humanity; that is a function of the theater. It is made to please God by fine workmanship. This one was planned, as well, to get its author a job at the Saxon court.

January 29, 1947

Beethoven's Fifth

BEETHOVEN's C-minor Symphony is the most famous piece of orchestral music in the world. Everybody knows it; everybody loves it; everybody admires it. Other pieces have their special charms and their devoted publics, but this one is accepted by all as the world masterpiece of monumental abstract, or "absolute," music. For the grandeur and simplicity of its melodic materials, the nobility of its formal proportions, and the forthrightness of its expression it has been esteemed throughout the Western world for over a century now as a sort of Parthenon among symphonies. Yet what it means nobody really knows. It has been as much argued about as *Hamlet*, and it remains to this day as movingly obscure a work.

The Germans long ago associated its opening phrases with their favorite idea of Fate Knocking at the Door. The French have always taken the work as a whole to be connected in some way with political liberalism. It was so completely appropriated as a theme song, in fact, by French socialists of the Second International that adherents of the Third and Fourth have tended rather to keep quiet about its possible political significance. Of late more conservative politicians have taken it over as the slogan, or symbol, of military victory, specifically the victory of the United Nations.

The Germans were clumsy not to think of this first; the victory idea would have fitted perfectly with their already popular interpretation of the piece as having to do with fate. It could have become thus a forecast of their "manifest destiny." Perhaps they felt its author was not quite the right man to put forward as the advocate of unbridled submission to authority. In any case, their propagandists have pretty much let the work alone. Whether ours would have done well to let it alone, too, was the subject of considerable reflection on your reviewer's part week before last, when George Szell conducted the Philharmonic-Symphony Orchestra through a thoroughly demagogic and militarized version of it.

If thinking of the work as embodying faith and hope has helped conquered nations to resist tyranny, that is all to the good. An energizing moral result is more valuable than any misreading of the composer's specific thought is dangerous. Besides, the piece will recover from its present military service just as easily as it has from its past metaphysical and political associations. But as a musician I was interested to observe the amount of distortion that Mr. Szell was obliged to impose on the work in order to make it seem to be representing military struggle and final victory.

There is no intrinsic reason, in this work or in any other, for considering contrast to mean conflict. The expression of strength, even of rudeness, in one chief theme of a piece and of pathos or tenderness in another does not mean that there is a war going on between the two sentiments. The highly contrasted materials of the Fifth Symphony have always seemed to me as complementary rather than conflicting. They make it whole and humane, the complete picture of a man. And I cannot find in the last movement of it, for all its triumphal trumpets, any representation, thematic or otherwise, of the victory of either sentiment. I find, rather, an apotheosis, in which the two are transformed into a third expression, which is one of optimism and confidence, a glorious but still dynamic serenity. Neither assertiveness nor lyricism wins; they simply decide to co-operate.

This is no picture of military victory. It is the purest Hegelian dialectic, by which thesis and antithesis unite to form a third element, or synthesis. It may be an enlightened way of resolving contrasts, or even of conflicts, this using of them as complementary floodlights toward a general luminosity. And it may be an enlightened way of envisaging postwar problems, including Germany itself, though I am suspicious of the Hegelian dialectic, which lends itself to much trickiness in handling. Like most other philosophic methods, it can be made to give any result the handler desires. But in no case is it involved with anybody's unconditional surrender. It offers exactly the opposite kind of solution to a military victory. It is a peace proposition all round. Nowhere in Beethoven's Fifth Symphony, moreover, is there any suggestion of military operations, though other works of his portray them plentifully.

In order to throw the symphony into a key of direct action, Mr. Szell has been obliged to emphasize the assertiveness of the masculine material and to sort of slip over the significance of its tender and gentle passages. He made the strings play loud and rough, with that fierce impact that the Philharmonic strings achieve so admirably. He managed to keep the horns, with some difficulty, up to a reasonable balance with these for three movements. With the appearance of the trombones, at the beginning of the last movement, the horns appeared as hopelessly outclassed in the weight-throwing contest as the woodwinds had been from the beginning. The whole disequilibrium made Beethoven sound no end authoritative and didactic as a composer, which he certainly was, but hopelessly incompetent as an orchestrator, which he was not. And it is exactly the musical ineffectiveness of the orchestral contrasts that proved, in spite of the moral impressiveness of the rendering, that violence was being done to the spirit of the work, whatever one may consider this to be.

Lots of people don't mind that sort of thing at any time; it rather amuses them. And nobody at all minds when it serves a national emergency. We were all interested, I think, to hear this piece played right up to the hilt as a sword of psychological warfare, as the symbol of military victory that it has come to represent in Allied strategy. I doubt if a more thoroughgoing job of the kind could be done on it; certainly none has. And now that military victory seems to be imminent in the European theater, where the Fifth Symphony has its chief psychological utility, it is hardly to be expected that other conductors will attempt to carry it much farther in this direction. It is always a satisfaction to have visited the ultimate outpost of anything; and it is a pleasure to have viewed once this O, so familiar piece in a new light, however false. But the expedition is about over now, and I imagine that all the conductors, including Mr. Szell, will be getting back to Beethoven's plain markings, or else inventing a new distortion of them to please other times.

March 18, 1945

Brahms without Bathos

PHILADELPHIA ORCHESTRA, *Eugene Ormandy*, conductor, last night at Carnegie Hall, performing three works by Brahms: *Akademische Festouvertüre*, Symphony No. 3, and Symphony No. 2.

"BRAHMS is so dependable," said a musician's wife at last night's concert of the Philadelphia Orchestra. Certainly he filled Carnegie Hall at the beginning with customers and at the end with cheers. For the latter, Eugene Ormandy and his orchestra were, of course, in part responsible, because they read the all-Brahms program with a sweetness and an alacrity all too rare in current performances of this master's work. Nothing was soggy or heavy in their lyricism. Two symphonies, the Second and the Third, had wind in their sails from beginning to end. The *Academic Festival Overture*, which presents no problem of animation, was no less a delight for being by nature a piece easy to infuse with spirit.

The Brahms symphonies do not support becomingly much dalliance. Richly impregnated with sentiment, they are nevertheless works of predominantly rhetorical structure and require a continuous forward movement if they are to be apprehended as whole pieces, and not merely as plum cakes from which one picks out for immediate enjoyment the juicier morsels. Their structure is loose but real. Excessive lingering over the vast outlay of expressive detail that accompanies it is as injurious to their noble proportions as insufficient care for the rounded execution of that detail can be. They need loving care, a light hand, and a dreamlike continuity. Otherwise they bog down and have to be rescued at the climactic moments by an overinsistence that destroys the natural emphasis of their grand but leisurely build-up.

Just such care and such a hand were Mr. Ormandy's last night. Seldom has the length of the Brahms symphonies seemed less insistent to this listener, their present public favor more deserved. The Second and Third were not only beautiful, as they have always been. They were easy to listen to. A just balance between expeditious tempos and expressivity of detail, aided by orchestral balances of perfect transparency, gave them a clarity and a luminosity all unusual to them.

That luminosity was Eugene Ormandy's achievement. It is not in Brahms's scoring, which is neither bright in color nor entirely limpid. Excessive doubling of woodwinds in octaves and insufficient uncovering of expressive clarinet or bassoon phrases are characteristic of Brahms's orchestral style. These habits are not necessarily inefficient, for they have an undeniable charm. But they do make it difficult for a conductor to keep the predominantly grayish texture of Brahms's woodwind writing from going muddy. Mr. Ormandy's success in avoiding this sonorous pitfall was as notable last night as his triumph in

achieving through reasonable tempos and a forward-moving
rhythm eloquence without bathos, song without sobbing, mag-
niloquence and authority without any bluster or bluff.

April 2, 1947

Bruckner

PHILHARMONIC-SYMPHONY ORCHESTRA, *Artur Rodzinski*,
conductor, last night at Carnegie Hall, performing Bruckner's Symphony No. 7 and two works by Beethoven: Overture to *Coriolanus* and
Piano Concerto No. 3.

ANTON BRUCKNER, whose Seventh Symphony was played last
night in Carnegie Hall by the Philharmonic-Symphony Orchestra under Artur Rodzinski, became a cause in his own lifetime
and has remained one ever since. The public has never either
accepted or rejected him. Musicians have always loved or hated
his music; they have never quite classified it. And yet its virtues
and its weaknesses are admitted by all.

A high songfulness in the melody of it is one of its charms.
A great suavity of harmonic figuration (one can scarcely call it
counterpoint) is another. A real seriousness of thought and a
certain amount of purity of spirit it undoubtedly has. There is
nothing vulgar, cheap, or meretricious about it. And it sounds
extremely well; it is graciously written.

On the other hand, the eight symphonies, which constitute
the major body of Bruckner's work, are none of them well integrated formally; they barely hang together. And their unvarying
pattern of four-measure phrases brings them, like Cesar Franck's
two-measure monotony, dangerously close to a doggerel
meter. Also, their melodic material, for all its grace, is derivative.
Schubert, Brahms, and Wagner are never wholly absent from
the memory as one listens. The music is intended, I think, to
feel like Brahms and to sound like Wagner; and unfortunately
it more often than not does just that.

It does another thing, however, which is probably not in-
tentional but which gives it what personal flavor it has. It imitates, by orchestral means, organ registration. Bruckner uses his
brasses exactly as an organist uses the reed stops; and he uses the
woodwind more often than not as a choir-organ, or *positif*. His

masterful cleanliness in the antiphonal deployment of the different kinds of sound is the work of a great organ player, which he was. The looseness of his formal structures is due, no doubt, to the same professional formation, as is certainly his unvarying use of the apocalyptic climax to finish off his longer works.

There is a pious theatricality about all Bruckner's symphonies that, combined with his constant reverence toward his masters, makes them most attractive. They represent esthetically a philosophy of quietism, musically the ultimate of humility. They rest one; they are perfect to daydream to. Of real originality they have, I think, very little to offer.

April 6, 1945

MacDowell's Music

Revisiting the music of Edward MacDowell, through copies found in a borrowed house, was one of the pleasures of your reviewer's late summer vacation. What the larger works would sound like nowadays—the two Suites for Orchestra, the two piano concertos, and the four piano sonatas—he does not know, because he has not for many years handled their scores; and they have almost disappeared from our metropolitan programs. But the shorter piano works—the *Woodland Sketches*, the *New England Sketches,* and the *Sea Pieces*—have kept an extraordinary freshness through the years. Rereading them brought the reflection that although no living American would have written them in just that way (the Wagnerian harmonic texture having passed out of vogue), no living American quite *could* have written them, either.

Let us take them for what they are, not for what they are not. They are landscapes mostly, landscapes with and without figures, literary or historical evocations, *morceaux de genre.* The test of such pieces is their power of evocation. Couperin, Mendelssohn, Schumann, and Debussy are the great masters of genre painting in music, Grieg, Smetana, and possibly Albéniz or Villa-Lobos its lesser luminaries. MacDowell might well rank with these last if he had had access to a body of folklore comparable in extent to theirs, an access that Americans do have, in fact, now. He divined the problems of style that face American composers, but he was not able to solve them singlehanded. So he borrowed more from German sources than he would have liked, I think, and more than anybody has to do today.

Nevertheless, the scenes he describes are vivid. His rhythmic contours evoke the stated subject quickly, accurately. No other American composer has painted a wild rose or an iceberg, a water lily or a deserted farmhouse so neatly. The rendering is concise, the outline definite. No piece is a rewriting of any other. Each is itself, economical, elegant, clearly projected. The impersonality of the procedure is proof of the author's sincerity; its evocative power is proof of his high skill as a craftsman. MacDowell did not leave his mark on music as a stylist; he left us merely a repertory of unforgettable pieces, all different from one another and all charming. And he left to American composers an example of clear thought and objective workmanship that has been an inspiration to us all.

There is a movement on foot toward influencing the American Academy of Arts and Sciences to place his bust in the Hall of Fame at New York University. Stephen Foster is the only writer of music there honored at present. MacDowell could not be in better company, because his music, like that of Foster, is part of every American's culture who has any musical culture. Everybody has played it, loved it, remembered it. Just as no student who ever attended MacDowell's classes at Columbia University ever forgot the master's penetrating observations about music, no musician or no music lover has ever forgotten the delicate firmness of MacDowell's melody, the exactitude with which his rhythm (and his piano figuration, too) depicts the picturesque. To have become, whether by sheer genius for music making, as in Foster's case, or, as in MacDowell's, by the professional exercise of a fully trained gift and by an integrity of attitude unequaled in our musical history, part and parcel of every musical American's musical thought is, in any meaning of the term, it seems to me, immortality.

November 5, 1944

The American Song

ENGLISH-SPEAKING SINGERS are trained and grow to maturity on one of the most curious musical literatures in the world. German vocalists cut their professional teeth on the lieder of

Romantic masters and, if the voice is strong, on airs from Weber and Wagner. The Italians, to a man (or woman), sing Puccini and Verdi and very little else. The French have their Fauré, their Gounod, and their fragments from Massenet. All this is perfectly reputable music. The Continent has its popular religious pieces, too, like Fauré's *The Palms*, Adam's *Minuit Chrétien*, and Bach's *My Heart Ever Faithful*, and its glorified folklore like Irish mother songs and Italian boat pieces.

But just cross the Channel, and you find that the basic vocal repertory is not either the classics or the indigenous folk lyric. It is a commercial product known variously as "ballads" or "art songs" or just "songs," though it is not in a proper sense any of these things. You hear it in homes, at banquets, in recitals, and over the BBC. In its manlier forms it is a hearty baritone number about how "when we were young and I went down to Rio." Its tender mood deals with gardens and somebody referred to as "YOUUU." For a light touch children are introduced who resist medicine or dislike the cook, though they never go so far as to refuse spinach. The American version of this vast Anglo-Saxon musical literature admires trees and sunsets, believes that marriages are made in heaven, faces the future with confidence, and enjoys playing cowboy.

There is nothing wrong, of course, about any of these ideas. They represent ethnic aspirations and touch infallibly the English-speaking heart. What is curious about the musical literature in which they are embodied is its stylistic vulgarity, its technical and esthetic ineptitude. The literary aspect of it, though often banal in verbiage, is as to sentiment perfectly sound and humane. But take a look, I ask you, at the musical settings; or listen to them at recitals. A sunrise is described in the idiom of *Tristan und Isolde*, trout fishing in that of *Pelléas et Mélisande*. A nursery incident may be blown up till it suggests *The Sorcerer's Apprentice*. As for mating, you would imagine the whole population sex-starved if you believed in the amorous intensity of our "art-song" harmonizations. The musical vulgarity of the literature I am describing is due, as a matter of fact, not only to its exaggerated passional make-believe but to its practice of describing everything, literally everything, in the musical language of love.

The stuff needs only comparison with the Continental equivalent for the technical ineptitude to be patent. The rhythmic inflections of the English language are more often than not correctly observed and neatly dramatized. But vowel quantities are handled with as complete disregard for their exigence as could well be imagined. An otherwise skillful song by the late Carl Engel asks that three beats of slowish time, plus a retard, be occupied to pronounce the word *stop*. And one by Bainbridge Crist, quoted in this composer's far from uninteresting brochure, *The Art of Setting Words to Music*, asks that the word *kiss* be held on a high F for something like five seconds. If you think my criticism finicky, just try this trick out; and you will discover that the result is neither English nor music.

The esthetic fault most commonly committed in American vocal music is the confusion of genres. Setting a simple love lyric as if it were an operatic aria removes all poignancy from the poem. Dramatic expression in music requires a dramatic situation in the text. The Continental song literature from Mozart through the German Romantics to Fauré, Debussy, Ravel, Sauguet, and Poulenc deals, in any one piece, with a single person in an unequivocal mood. No event, inner or outer, takes place; and no logical conclusion is arrived at, though the sense of the whole may be summed up in a final couplet. These are the classical limits of lyric poetry. The ballad form, as in *Der Erlkönig*, is equally set and stylized by its stanza construction. Epic recitation and dramatic narrative demand still another musical form. I accuse the English and American composers (especially the Americans) of having hopelessly confused one kind of poetic expression with another in their vocal concert music. I am not naming any names, because they are practically all guilty. Just listen, if you want examples, to the American group of any singer's recital program. Or take a look at what your kid sister is given by her vocal teacher.

Is it any wonder that our American singers are not masters and mistresses of their art, when the repertory they all learn music through is so incompetently composed? They don't know that English vowel lengths, like Continental ones, are immutable. They don't know that poetic expression, no matter what its subject, falls into four or five styles, or genres rather, and no more. They don't know that lyric poetry does not permit an aggressive mood, that impersonation of the poet by the interpreter is unbecoming to it, that it can be recited or sung but never acted, though the ballad style can, on the contrary, be dramatized up to the hilt.

How can they know these things when the composers of the music that is virtually their whole fare write as if they didn't know them either, and when singing teachers, for lack of a better repertory, give them for study year after year pieces that nobody can vocalize correctly or interpret convincingly because they are incorrectly composed? They are incorrect as to vowel quantities, false to the known esthetics of poetry, and irresponsible in their misapplication of a climactic and passionate musical style to virtually any subject, even the sacred. America is full of beautiful young voices and high musical temperaments. The singing teachers are not bad either, on the whole. Students often learn from them to vocalize the long vowels quite prettily. After that they commit every fault. What about our composers' sitting down and writing them something that can be sung without fault? Our playwrights write plays that can be acted. Our painters paint pictures that can be hung, looked at, lived with. Our better composers write fair symphonies and thrilling ballets. But the human voice they have left in second-rate hands. There are probably not twenty American "art songs" that can be sung in Town Hall with dignity or listened to there without shame. Nor are there five American "art composers" who can be compared, as song writers, for either technical skill or artistic responsibility with Irving Berlin.

February 16, 1947

American Conservatives

PHILHARMONIC-SYMPHONY ORCHESTRA, *Howard Hanson*, conductor, last night at Carnegie Hall, performing new American music: Walter Piston's Suite from *The Incredible Flutist*, Charles T. Griffes's *White Peacock*, C. M. Loeffler's *Pagan Poem*, William Bergsma's *Music on a Quiet Theme*, and Mr. Hanson's Symphony No. 2 ("Romantic").

HOWARD HANSON, who conducted the Philharmonic-Symphony Orchestra last night in Carnegie Hall, is a thoroughly competent conductor, particularly of American music. The program of American music that he played was more than a shade on the conservative side, but the fact that it was played at all leads one to hope that the Philharmonic Society may be finally, in its own conservative way, taking up America. If this is true, and one American program is not just a brush-off to the whole problem (or to Mr. Hanson), it is equally to be hoped that so adequate a protagonist of the struggle will be asked again to lead the home-front forces.

The conservatism of last night's problem might be taken for reactionary if one did not know the passive resistance to American composition that exists among subscription audiences, long duped on this subject by unfavorable propaganda of German origin. It was sagacious of Mr. Hanson to select works of known audience appeal. Piston's *Incredible Flutist*, Griffes's *White Peacock*, Loeffler's *Pagan Poem*, and Hanson's own "Romantic" Symphony are pieces of tested popularity; they will carry anything, cushion the fall of anything.

They carried last night, or cushioned, a short work by William Bergsma entitled, *Music on a Quiet Theme*. Still far from mature as a writing personality, Mr. Bergsma has not yet shaken off the vices of his teacher, Mr. Hanson. These are chiefly a tendency to belabor his thematic material and a habit of working anything, literally anything, up to a feverlike climax and then letting it fall with a gasp. This procedure turns any short piece into a *Liebestraum* and any long one into a series of *Liebesträume*. Let us hope that Mr. Bergsma, who is clearly a musician of high natural gifts, will start now to forget about his schooling and to write music in his own way. His schooling is no worse than anybody else's, better, indeed, than most. But all schoolings have to be got round. That is the way one becomes a real creator.

Mr. Hanson, though long a successful pedagogue, has never been, in my judgment, a very real creator. He has written lots of music that lots of people have enjoyed listening to, and that makes him a real composer. But I have never yet found in any work of his a single phrase or turn of harmony that did not sound familiar. His "Romantic" Symphony is no exception; it is as standardized in expression as it is eclectic in style. Not a surprise from beginning to end, nor any adventure. Unless the attempt to construct melodies by the constant repetition, or "riffing," of short motives and the attempt to substitute ostinato accompaniment for inner contrapuntal life in symphonic writing be considered a noble experiment. Riffing procedures have the advantage of making musical composition easy, but no amount of bombastic orchestration can conceal their expressive poverty. Their abuse by Mr. Hanson limits, I am convinced, his possible achievement as a musical creator.

January 18, 1946

Annual Gesture

NBC SYMPHONY ORCHESTRA, *Arturo Toscanini*, conductor, yesterday afternoon in Studio 8-H, Radio City, performing music by living composers: Mario Castelnuovo-Tedesco's *Overture to a Fairy Tale*, Vittorio Rieti's *Sinfonìa Tripartita,* Paul Creston's *Frontiers*, and Elie Siegmeister's *Western Suite.*

ARTURO TOSCANINI paid his annual compliment to living composers yesterday afternoon at the weekly concert of the NBC Symphony Orchestra in Studio 8-H at Radio City. Of the four works played three were fairly negligible in substance, though one was not without style. The fourth was more robust.

The Castelnuovo-Tedesco *Overture to a Fairy Tale* is an inoffensive repetition of an inoffensive theme lightly, though not very fancifully, orchestrated. Vittorio Rieti's *Sinfonìa Tripartita* is a neoclassic work, diatonic in material and straightforward of manner. It could be made into a ballet, perhaps. As a concert work it has more style than intensity. It is modest and a little empty, but it is well made.

Paul Creston's *Frontiers* is unclear to me in subject. I could not tell whether it referred to the kind of frontiers that get pushed back or to the kind one crosses. Its musical material, which was as varied in origin as what collects in any customs warehouse, rather suggested the latter. Its chief interest to this listener was its successful handling of the problem of keeping opposed masses of orchestral sound opposed.

Elie Siegmeister's *Western Suite* is livelier stuff. Its material, cowboy folklore, is of the highest beauty; and its treatment is full of sound sense, as well as skill. Its moods run from the tenderest sentiment to the roughest roughhouse, and all are convincing. It is outdoor music with air in it and horses around.

It is written with love and with gusto. Also with an experienced folklorist's judgment. The tunes are put through their paces without any timidity but equally without any misunderstanding of their nature and habits. Mr. Siegmeister's suite is a real rodeo.

The orchestral execution of all these works was of the utmost clarity under the maestro's impeccable (and even prudent) hand. It has long been a matter of regret to this concertgoer that Mr. Toscanini does not oftener put his admirable lucidity at the disposal of contemporary music.

November 26, 1945

Melodious and Skillful

CONCERT OF MUSIC BY ERNST BACON last night at Times Hall, New York, with the MADRIGAL SINGERS OF SYRACUSE UNIVERSITY and other musicians including *Claire Harper,* violinist, and *Elizabeth Mulfinger, Elena Irish,* and *Mr. Bacon,* pianists, performing *Four Songs from Emily Dickinson,* three pieces for violin, *From Emily's Diary* (cantata for women's voices), *From the Appalachians* (suite for violin), and three pieces for two pianos. Soloists: *Priscilla Gillette,* soprano, and *Raymond di Giacomo,* baritone. Presented by Syracuse University.

A PROGRAM of music all by one composer, such as that of works by Ernst Bacon which was given last night in Times Hall, is a good way to exhibit any good composer's music. A mood is established, a temperament made clear, mastery demonstrated through a variety of subjects. Since Mr. Bacon is a very good composer indeed, one of America's best, last night's concert was both an interesting and a pleasant experience.

The mood and temper of Mr. Bacon's work are chiefly a meditation on nineteenth-century rural America. He is full of our Scotch-Irish folklore, knows it from the inside, speaks and writes it as his own musical language. Mr. Bacon also has a modern musician's knowledge of American speech cadences. Few living composers prosodize to music so accurately. His piano accompaniments, too, carefully plain of harmony and never note-heavy, are most ingeniously evocative of our back-country musical style. They do not imitate ignorance or assume a naïve air; but they are poetical and reflective in an atavistic direction.

The violin pieces played last night showed a less original approach to than instrument, a less confident mastery of its expressive possibilities than the writing for voices or for the piano. A two-piano piece called *The River Queen,* all about President Lincoln's stern-wheel yacht, was in every way charming and picturesque. All the works performed, with the exception of a *Coal-Scuttle Blues,* jointly composed with Otto Luening, eschewed effects of dynamism for its own sake. The music was mostly soft and pretty in sound, deriving its interest from melodic, rhythmic and prosodic design rather than from oratory or from any kind of punch.

Mr. Bacon's work is remarkably pure in its expressive intent. It communicates its meaning with a straightforward and touching humanity. It is not got up with chromium-plated cadenzas or lace-curtainlike instrumental figurations, and it poses in no passionate attitude. But it is full of melody and variety; it makes, so far as it goes, complete sense. If it doesn't go very far forward, in the way of technical or expressive originality, it at least looks backward toward an ideal and primitive America without snobbery, self-deception, or truculence. It is honest and skillful and beautiful. One is grateful to Syracuse University, where Mr. Bacon professes his art, for presenting us with a whole evening of it, executed under the composer's direction by a bevy of personable young women.

March 4, 1946

New and Good

LEAGUE OF COMPOSERS presenting a concert of new music last night at the Museum of Modern Art, New York, including Roger Sessions's Piano Sonata No. 2 and works by Jacob Avshalomoff, Yves Baudrier, Kurt List, Theodore Chanler, Elliott Carter, and David Diamond performed by musicians including *Andor Foldes* and *Alvin Bauman,* pianists, *Emanuel Vardi,* violist, and *Carolyn Blakeslee* and *Helen Boatwright,* sopranos.

THE LEAGUE OF COMPOSERS, which has been giving unusually agreeable concerts this winter, presented a charmingly varied and admirably executed program last night at the Museum of Modern Art. There were works in all the modern styles—the neo-Classic, the neo-Romantic, the twelve-tone technique, and the new French neo-Impressionism. All were interesting and many were lovely, but the nugget of the evening was a brand-new piano sonata by Roger Sessions.

Roger Sessions, in spite of considerable renown as a talked-about composer and a long history of success as a pedagogue, is little known through his music. His production is small; and the few works available are seldom performed, because they are difficult to play and not easy to listen to. They are learned, laborious, complex, and withal not strikingly original. They pass for professor's music, and the term is not wholly unjustified. Because the complexity and elaboration of their manner is out of all proportion to the matter expressed. Nevertheless, they are impressive both for the seriousness of their thought and for the ingenuity of their workmanship. They are hard to take and even harder to reject. They represent the most embarrassing problem in American music, because though they have unquestionably quality, they have just as certainly almost no charm at all. And we have no place in our vast system of musical distribution for music without charm.

The piano sonata played last night by Andor Foldes (and dedicated to him) is Mr. Sessions' second. The first dates from nearly twenty years back. Like the first, it is composed in a consistently dissonant but tonal style. Unlike the first, it is in melodic style largely chromatic. Like all of this composer's music, it bears no clear marks of its national or local origins. It could have been written anywhere in the world—in Leningrad, Shanghai, Paris, Buenos Aires, Vienna, Rome, or Melbourne —as easily as in Berkeley, California, where it actually was composed, and by a man of any race and clime as easily as by a one-hundred-per-cent New Englander. Its speech represents the international neo-Classic style at its most complete and eclectic, though the feelings expressed in the work are derived from the violence-and-meditation contrast beloved of the German Late Romantics.

It is not music of direct melodic or harmonic appeal for the uninitiated; nor yet has it great stimulus value for modernists, who have already heard elsewhere practically everything in it. All the same, it is interesting to listen to, because it is wonderfully, thoroughly sophisticated. The slow movement, moreover, is almost atmospheric. Operating in a small range of pitch, with little variety of rhythm and, for once, no great variety of musical device employed, Sessions has achieved here a completely absorbing tranquility. The work is not likely to be popular, I should think, either soon or ever. But it is not a negligible composition, and Roger Sessions has reminded us through it that his very existence as a musician is a far from negligible contribution to the history of America.

Space forbids my reviewing in detail, as I should like to do, the other works presented. Notable, however, were the half-Jewish, half-Chinese, Sonatina for Viola and Piano, by Jacob Avshalomoff, a sweet and lyrical piece; some luminous French recitative songs by Yves Baudrier; the far from banal twelve-tone *Isthmus Tonalis* for string quartet, by Kurt List; and a pretty *Flight Into Egypt*, by Theodore Chanler. Elliott Carter's long songs on texts by Whitman and Hart Crane were weakened in impact by the composer's insistence in treating short vowels as if they were long ones. David Diamond's Third String Quartet, which closed the concert, though a shade facile in sentiment and far too easygoing about length, is string writing of the first quality, varied, precise, graceful, and free.

March 17, 1947

Schuman's Undertow

WILLIAM SCHUMAN's ballet, *Undertow*, which will be played again tonight at Ballet Theater's closing performance of the season, has enlarged our acquaintance with this composer's personality; and I suspect it may be about to add something to the repertory of his concert works. It is the first narrative instrumental piece by him that many have had occasion to hear, possibly the first he has composed, though he has worked successfully in most of the other musical forms both vocal and instrumental. Whatever may be the future of Antony Tudor's ballet, there is probably an effective concert piece to be derived from this score.

There is no question, I think, that American composers by and large, at least those of the presently mature and maturing generation, have done their most striking work in the theater.

Also that the best training available for serious musico-theatrical work is practice in the concert forms. Interestingness of texture and soundness of continuity are the minimal requirements of concert music, and a composer cannot hold the attention of concert audiences without mastery of these qualities. On the other hand, concentration on a specific subject, the depicting of it without expansion or digression, which is the minimal requirement of any music destined for theatrical collaboration, is exactly where American concert composition tends to fall down. It is weak in specific expressivity, partly because our American training in composition is formalistic, seeking abstract perfection, even at the expense of direct speech, and partly because our concert audiences are not sufficiently accomplished at seizing the meanings in music to require of musical composition the kind of coherence that they demand, for instance, of literature.

Formed entirely by American teachers and American audiences, William Schuman is a product of the American musical scene. He has written symphonies, string quartets, overtures, band pieces, and lots of choral works; and they have all been performed by major musical organizations. His workmanship is skillful, individual, striking. His expressivity has always been tenuous, timid, conventional. His serious works have shown a respectable seriousness of attitude without much private or particular passion, while his gayer ones have expressed either a standard American cheerfulness or the comforting bumptiousness of middle-quality comic-strip humor. He has written easily, abundantly, and, in a technical sense, well; but his music has been, on the whole, reticent, has communicated to the public little about himself or about anything else.

Undertow has a sounder proportion of matter to means. The story of this particular ballet has required, to begin with, vivid rather than formalistic treatment. That story, or plot, for all its inefficiencies as dramatic literature (it has a realistic but nonessential beginning and a nonrealistic, quite unbelievable ending; with all that public opinion around, the young man would certainly have been arrested for murder if he had committed one), has a serious subject, namely, the pathos of sexual initiation. The music is full of frustration and violence. It has a static intensity in the passages of pure feeling and a spastic muscular energy in the passages that depict physical action that are completely appropriate to the subject and completely interesting. The climactic *pas de deux* is the most realistic piece about sexual intercourse we have had since Shostakovich's *Lady Macbeth of Mzensk*. And the contrapuntal accompaniment to the scene of ganged-up love-making between one girl and four men is both exciting and convincing.

Whether Schuman has a real theatrical gift or merely certain qualities that are useful in the theater, I am not sure. The whole score does not accompany the ballet as consistently as certain passages underline it strikingly. If Schuman were a born man of the theater, he ought to have given to the choreographer, or secured from him, a closer communion. But Tudor, who likes to work from ready-made music, may not be easy to do a duo with. Further dramatic works from Schuman will no doubt reveal further his qualities. For the present he has shown a gift for expressing the lurid; and the lurid has afforded him a more ample field for exploiting his full powers as an artist than the formalistic, middle-ground modernism of his concert style and the boisterous-but-not-much-else Americanism of his assumed concert personality have done. Also, his gift for massive orchestration, which lends so easily a merely demagogic air to his concert works, becomes an element of magnificent emphasis when applied to a melodramatic subject in a theater.

And so, viewed freshly through his new-found medium, Schuman turns out to be not at all the composer of small expressive range and assumed monumental proportions that his concert music has long led one to consider him, but a man of high, of spectacular expressive gifts who has been constricted by the elegant abstractions of the American concert style—and a little bit, too, perhaps, by his youth. The concert forms have been good schooling for him, but he has never expressed himself in them with any freedom. The theater gives him elbow room. His mind can move around in it. And his feeling-content, his compassion, as well as his inveterate love for depicting physical movement, take on an unexpected strength under the theater's channelization of them to purposes of specific meaning. *Undertow* is not a masterpiece of music, any more than it is of choreography. But it is full of music that says something. It speaks. It can even be listened to. I think it will be remembered. And the man who wrote it, whether he cares to exploit the achievement further or not, has become visible to us through it as a stronger, a bigger, and a more generous personality than he had appeared before.

April 29, 1945

Good Music, Poor Literature

NEW YORK CITY SYMPHONY, *Leonard Bernstein*, conductor, with the COLLEGIATE CHORALE, *Robert Shaw*, conductor, last night at the New York City Center, performing Mozart's Overture to *The Abduction from the Seraglio* and Violin Concerto in D major, and Marc Blitzstein's *Airborne Symphony*. Soloists: *Werner Lywen*, violin, *Charles Holland*, tenor, and *Walter Scheff*, baritone. With *Orson Welles*, speaker.

MARC BLITZSTEIN's *The Airborne*, which was heard last night for the first time anywhere at a concert of the City Symphony in the City Center of Music and Drama, is an ingenious piece of musical work and far from uninspired. Its ingenuity consists in the composer's having managed to inject a high degree of musical interest into an entertainment formula that has hitherto been musically pretty sterile. I refer to the kind of broadcast perfected at the Columbia Workshop and made famous by Norman Corwin, the patriotic poem about current events that mobilizes for its recitation actors, vocal soloists, a chorus or two, a symphony orchestra, and any number of microphones. The inspiration of the present piece consists in the more than merely ingenious use of contrasted musical styles for purposes of specific expression. There is detailed invention in it, a real musico-dramatic texture that is communicative.

Whether there is much real communication in Mr. Blitzstein's poem I doubt. It is a pæan of praise to aviation in general, and to military aviation in particular, that smacks more of directed publicity than of original thought. Actually it says little that is not already a commonplace of the sentimental press, and its folksy language is both facile and affected. With such a text it was inevitable that any musical setting designed to throw the words into relief should have difficulty rising above the banality of these. For that reason the most distinguished music in the work is that of the purely instrumental interludes, which are less earthbound than the choral and recitative passages. Only two of these last seemed to this listener musically adequate at all, a piece for speaker and chorus called *The Enemy* and a sentimental song in which a young bombardier writes a letter to his girl back home. These have continuity and musical progress, just as the orchestral intermezzi do.

They do not, however, have quite the originality and the forceful musical texture of the instrumental sections. Mr. Blitzstein's musical style in these is diatonic, dissonant without the use of chromatics, and highly melodious. His tunes are both distinguished and singable. His whole invention, melodic, contrapuntal, and orchestral, has a higher degree of specific expressivity, a clearer way of saying what it means, than we are accustomed to encounter in the work of American composers.

He sets stylistic formulas against one another in much the same way that a stage director will turn on his scene spotlights, floodlights, footlights, and borders, composing these for specific expressivity rather than for any mere display of his equipment. That is why, beyond its straightforward diatonicism, there is little in the Blitzstein musical style that is strikingly personal or consciously characteristic. Blitzstein has, however, the more valuable power to call on a large repertory of varied stylistic conventions and to use these as a musical vocabulary, making thus, as scene designers do, a language out of the history of styles and an expressive syntax out of constant stylistic cross reference.

The execution of this masterful but not entirely satisfactory work under the direction of Leonard Bernstein was a triumph of efficiency. Orson Welles, who spoke; Charles Holland and Walter Scheff, who sang; and a male chorus from the Collegiate Chorale were impeccable. And the City Symphony played its orchestral passages, which are not easy, with full clarity. Previously Mr. Bernstein and the orchestra had given a lively and careful reading of Mozart's *Seraglio* overture and, with Werner Lywen, the concertmaster, as soloist, as sweet and sensible a performance of Mozart's Violin Concerto in D major (K. 218) as any of us is likely to hear in many a day. Mr. Blitzstein's *The Airborne*, I may add, was more than warmly received by the audience both for its handsome execution and for the unquestioned merits of its composition.

April 2, 1946

Two Ballets

THE POSTSEASONAL WEEK of ballet, if that is the proper term for it, that Martha Graham and her dance company have been offering at the National Theater has given New York finally a hearing of Aaron Copland's *Appalachian Spring* and of Paul Hindemith's *Hérodiade*. Crowning a season that had already offered (through the Monte Carlo company) Stravinsky's *Danses Concertantes* and Richard Strauss's *Le Bourgeois Gentilhomme*, (through Billy Rose) Stravinsky's *Scènes de Ballet*, (through Ballet International) Paul Bowles's *Colloques Sentimentales* and Menotti's *Sebastian*, and (through Ballet Theater) Rieti's *Waltz Academy* and William Schuman's *Undertow*, not to speak of John Cage's strange and delicate scores for altered pianoforte which Merce Cunningham presented in recital, one of which, *Strange Adventure*, was heard again at Miss Graham's recent festivities, these two latest musical works have made it clear to all, even, we hope, to dancing's "modern" wing, that terpsichoric entertainment can be something more than cavorting to a scenario with sound effects.

   Miss Graham has given us in the past music by reputable living composers, notably Paul Nordoff and Hunter Johnson; but none of this has ever been strong or memorable. It has all been little music, well meaning but agitated and unsure. And Charles Mills's *John Brown*, heard twice last week, is of the same subservient tweedle-dee-bang-bang school that has long been cultivated by nonclassical dance troupes. The Copland and Hindemith scores are another line of musical country, I assure you, higher and more commanding and incredibly more adequate both to the support of a choreographic line and to the evocation of their stated subjects.

   The Copland subject is marriage preliminaries in nineteenth-century rural America. The style is pastoral, the tone, as is appropriate to the pastoral style, blythe and beatific. The material is folklore, some of it vocal, some violinistic. The harmonic treatment, based chiefly on open fourths and fifths, evokes our sparse and dissonant rural tradition rather than the thick suavities of our urban manner. The instrumentation is plain, clean-colored, deeply imaginative. It is designed not only to express the moods of the story but to amplify the characteristics of the dramatis personae. It is both poetically effective and theatrically functional. It is also musically interesting; it has style.

Every aspect of the work is musically interesting, though all of it is not equally intense as expression. If there is by moments, even in energetic passages, a static quality that does not seem to be advancing the story, that same immobility, when it comes off right, gives us both the very particular Copland miracle and that blythe Elysian-Fields note that is ideally the pastoral manner. Specifically, this effect seemed to me on first hearing to be more intense at the beginning and at the end of the work than in its middle sections. A second hearing revealed it at somewhere near its best in the second, as well as in the first, number and in the central (country-fiddle style) *pas de deux*. Elsewhere the expressivity seemed less powerful, though the musical texture was always interesting and the adequacy of the poetic and theatrical treatment, even at its least intense, of great help to those on the stage.

Aided as little, in the past, by her musical as by her pictorial collaborators, and devoted, by temperament and by preconception, to the rendering of emotion (specifically, feminist emotion) rather than of character, Miss Graham's work has long leaned toward the introspective and the psychologically lurid. Copland, in *Appalachian Spring*, has, by the inflexibility of his pastoral landscape mood, kept her away from the violence of solitary meditation and drawn her toward awareness of persons and the sweetness of manners. Paul Hindemith, long acquainted with the traps that Miss Graham's Germanic approach to the theater presents, has led her away from them by another means. He has given her a subject that is lurid enough for any taste but that is objectively rather than subjectively so. By this simple device he has forced her to represent a real and visible person rather than a state of mind about one. And, of course, in such a situation, she turns out to be, as one has long suspected, not only an expressive dancer but a great actress, one of the very great among living actresses, in fact.

The piece, called *Hérodiade* (though the English form *Herodias* would have been preferable), is derived from Mallarmé's French poem of that title. It represents the boudoir afternoon of a woman who is beautiful, sensual, intellectual, proud, passionate, rich, and middle-aged. She consults her mirror and converses with her maid, frankly, without illusion and without despair. And then she dresses for the evening. The music is sumptuously evocative, rich, complex, and civilized. Also solidly sustained architecturally. If it is reminiscent, in the central portion, of Strauss's *Salomé*, with its characteristic jumping-all-about-the-place melodic line, who is to say that the hyper-trophied and decadent manner is inappropriate to the Herod family? Mallarmé's conception is stiffer and more concentratedly sumptuous, and so is Miss Graham's. But the Hindemith score, though not completely distinguished, is a fine piece of music. And it has inspired Miss Graham to the creation, for once, of a character that is real enough, I should think, for other dancers to undertake.

The music has more ease in it than Copland's and a higher level of picturesque and dramatic fulfillment. At no time, how-ever, does it touch the poignancy of certain moments in the other, those special Copland moments when the whole musical texture reaches an ultimate of thinness and of translucency. It is not my purpose here to weigh the works against each other, but rather to show how they set each other off. Both are sound theater and beautiful music. And both can be heard, along with *Letter to the World*, the well-known ballet about Emily Dick-inson, at tonight's final performance of Miss Graham's all too brief New York season.

May 20, 1945

Expressive Percussion

JOHN CAGE, pianist-composer, with ARTHUR GOLD and ROBERT FIZDALE, piano duo, in recital yesterday afternoon at the New School for Social Research, New York, performing the following works for prepared pianos: *The Perilous Night* (six solos), *A Book of Music for Two Pianos*, and *Three Dances*.

JOHN CAGE, whose recent compositions made up the program of a concert given yesterday afternoon at the New School for Social Research, is already famous as a specialist in the use of percussive sounds. Two years ago the Museum of Modern Art presented pieces by him for a large group of players, using flow-erpots, brake bands, electric buzzers, drums, and similar objects not primarily musical but capable of producing a wide variety of interesting sounds all the same. The works offered yester-day included an even greater variety of sounds, all prepared by inserting bits of metal, wood, rubber, or leather at carefully studied points and distances between the strings of an ordinary pianoforte.

The effect in general is slightly reminiscent, on first hearing, of the Balinese gamelang orchestras, though the interior struc-ture of Mr. Cage's music is not Oriental at all. His work attaches itself, in fact, to two different traditions of Western modernism. One is the percussive experiments begun by Marinetti's Futurist Noise-makers and continued in the music by Edgard Varèse, Henry Cowell, and George Antheil, all of which, though made in full awareness of Oriental methods, is thoroughly Western in its expression. The other is, curiously enough, the atonal music of Arnold Schönberg and his school.

Mr. Cage has carried Schönberg's twelve-tone harmonic ma-neuvers to their logical conclusion. He has produced atonal music not by causing the twelve tones of the chromatic scale to contradict one another consistently, but by eliminating, to start with, all sounds of precise pitch. He substitutes for the classical chromatic scale a gamut of pings, plucks, and delicate thuds that is both varied and expressive and that is different in each piece. By thus getting rid, at the beginning, of the con-stricting element in atonal writing—which is the necessity of taking constant care to avoid making classical harmony with a standardized palette of instrumental sounds and pitches that ex-ists primarily for the purpose of producing such harmony—Mr. Cage has been free to develop the rhythmic element of compo-sition, which is the weakest element in the Schönbergian style, to a point of sophistication unmatched in the technique of any other living composer.

His continuity devices are chiefly those of the Schönberg school. There are themes and sometimes melodies, even, though these are limited, when they have real pitch, to the range of a fourth, thus avoiding the tonal effect of dominant and tonic. All these appear in augmentation, diminution, inversion, fragmen-tation, and the various kinds of canon. That these procedures do not take over a piece and become its subject, or game, is due to Cage's genius as a musician. He writes music for expressive purposes; and the novelty of his timbres, the logic of his discourse, are used to intensify communication, not as ends in themselves. His work represents, in consequence, not only the most advanced methods now in use anywhere but original musical expression of the very highest poetic quality. And this has been proved now through all the classical occasions—theater, ballet, song, orchestral composition, and chamber music.

One of the works was played yesterday by the composer, the other two by Arthur Gold and Robert Fizdale, duo-pianists. The perfect execution of these young men, their rhythm, lightness, and absolutely equality of scale and the singing sounds they derived from their instruments, in spite of the fact that the strings were all damped in various ways, made one wish to hear them operate on music less special, as well. The concert was a delight from every point of view.

January 22, 1945

Swiss Festival

NICOLAS DE FLUE, dramatic legend with French text by *Denis de Rougemont*, music by *Arthur Honegger*, performed last night at Carnegie Hall by the Dessoff Choirs, *Paul Boepple*, conductor, with the Orchestra of the New Friends of Music and a children's chorus directed by *Warren Foley*. With *Fernand Auberjonois*, speaker.

DENIS DE ROUGEMONT's text deals with politics. It is about how the Swiss Federation foolishly got itself into a war, surprisingly won, quarreled among itself about the peace terms almost to the point of civil war, and finally came to its senses at the exhortation of a hermit named Nicolas de Flue. It was intended, with music by Arthur Honegger, to be performed as an outdoor spectacle of the sort not uncommon in Switzerland, where a thousand or more executants sometimes participate in festival pageants celebrating local history or legend.

Last night's performance mobilized no such army of amateurs, but it did fill the stage of Carnegie Hall with three choirs, an orchestra, and three gentlemen "speakers," one of whom, as a matter of fact, never spoke. It filled the hall with good, loud musical noises, too, a fine specialty of Mr. Honegger's, and with bad, loud, and thoroughly unmusical noises during those moments, all too frequent, when music and a speaker, transmitted through a public-address system, were both going full blast. Speech with instrumental accompaniment ("melodrama" is the musical word for this) is, heaven knows, silly enough most of the time. Speech with choral accompaniment is not even silly; it is just unfortunate, since no listener can possibly follow one set of sung words and another set of spoken ones at the same time.

Aside from these moments, which one gathers were no part of the composer's intention (the original pageant and its subsequent abbreviation for concert purposes requiring no such makeshift as last night's amplified narrator), Honegger's score is pointed and dramatic. If it is musically not very original or intensely inspired, it is still a resonant and workmanlike job. It reminds one of his twenty-year-old *King David*, which it resembles without excelling. Indeed it is far less fresh and spontaneous. It is essentially the same piece rewritten twenty years later by a man who has learned from long practice in the films how to write minutes and minutes and minutes of adequate music in the shortest possible time. He has not written cheap music, at least not often; but he has repeated all his best formulas over and over, ever more confidently and more economically and ever less and less convincingly as to their original sincerity.

Honegger is really a curious case. Gifted and skillful like few. Industrious like almost none. More insistent than most at producing works that aim to storm Parnassus by sheer weight (the French call this kind of thing *le genre chef-d'oeuvre*). Constantly subjected to the public failure of these (*vide Rugby* and *Horace Victorieux*). Constantly signing movie scores, even writing many of them himself, I imagine. His musical texture is never below a respectable level in quality, rarely up to that of his early works.

He does two pieces admirably, a pastoral and a battle scene, puts them everywhere. I have never heard his opera *Judith*, said to be excellent. I have often heard and enjoyed *King David* and the famous *Pacific 231*, a mechanization of the battle piece. He can produce effective and dignified work when he is moved by the subject of it, which isn't always. He can make the most uninteresting and ineffective "machines" of any well-known living musical author when he isn't. I shall never forget *L'Impératrice aux Rochers* at the Paris Opéra, which fell as flat as anything could fall in spite of the presence on the stage at one and the same time of the Pope, the Emperor, the Virgin Mary, Madame Ida Rubinstein, and twenty live horses.

Nicolas de Flue did not fall flat last night, was a success with the public, in fact. Part of this I credit to the utter and rather charming Swissness of the whole thing, part of it to the admirable execution of the Dessoff Choirs and part of it to Honegger's neat and businesslike way of writing music. I cannot imagine any of it as due to Denis de Rougemont's poem, which is inflated, bromidic, in every way lacking in distinction.

May 9, 1941

Democracy and Style

PHILHARMONIC-SYMPHONY ORCHESTRA, *Artur Rodzinski* and *Darius Milhaud*, conductors, last night at Carnegie Hall, performing selections from Mendelssohn's *Midsummer Night's Dream*, Beethoven's Violin Concerto in D major, and two works by Mr. Milhaud: *Suite francçaise* and *Le Bal martiniquais*. Soloist: *Yehudi Menuhin*, violin.

GUSTO and poetry, tenderness and strength and no fear of anything or anybody, these are the elements that make the music of Darius Milhaud inspiring to composers and heartwarming to audiences. And they are the qualities that made his *Suite française* and *Bal martiniquais*, which the composer conducted at last night's concert of the Philharmonic in Carnegie Hall, a unanimous delight.

There is humanity in the very texture of Milhaud's writing. Tunes and countertunes and chords and percussive accents jostle one another with such friendliness, such tolerance, and such ease that the whole comes to represent what almost anybody might mean by a democratic way of life. Popular gaiety does not prevent the utterance of noble sentiments, and the presence of noble sentiments puts no damper at all on popular gaieties. The scenes have air in them and many different kinds of light, every brightness and every transparency, and no gloom or heaviness at all.

The *French Suite* is in five parts, all based on folk material. Normandy is represented by a cocky march, Brittany by an ethereal revery interrupted here and there by tiny gusts of discord, by little drafts, as it were, on the back of the neck. The Ile-de-France is a cancan, not a floor-show cancan, but a real one, such as young women might dance in a public square on the night of a victory celebration. Alsace-Lorraine is a sustained song with faith in it and a constancy half amorous, half religious. The finale, Provence, is a carnival of songs and dances from Mr. Milhaud's native region. The whole suite is a model of how to treat folk material, a little masterpiece of musical landscape-with-figures.

Le Bal martiniquais consists of a Creole song and a beguine. The treatment is similar to the French scenes, and the material is even gayer. This beguine is a sort of Calypso-style hoe-down of the most colorful orchestral texture imaginable. It should serve well as a dessert piece to end orchestral programs. I wish that Mr. Milhaud might always be available to conduct it, because he has a firmly delicate hand that knows how to make music sound loud but not rude.

His delightful executions were framed by performances of Mendelssohn and Beethoven that were in different ways not quite satisfactory. No sooner had the *Midsummer Night's Dream* got under way than your reporter was awakened by a drizzle of rain that continued to fall for some thirty or forty minutes in the region where he was seated and that somewhat disturbed, in consequence, his concentration on the music.

The Beethoven Violin Concerto, which ended the evening, took place in dry weather, but Mr. Menuhin, the soloist, seemed to be having atmospheric trouble with his instrument, for he played off pitch, mostly flat, in a way that is not his habit. Parts of the second movement were harmonious, but mostly the performance was a disaster.

December 7, 1945

Musical Gastronomy

THE MENU of Manuel Rosenthal's *Musique de table*, which the Philharmonic-Symphony Orchestra played at its second pair of subscription concerts, October 10 and 11, and on its broadcast concert of Sunday the 13th, is perhaps a trifle copious for American digestions. We have lost, since Victorian days, the ability to consume at one sitting an hors d'oeuvre, a fish, an entrée, a roast, a vegetable, game, salad, cheese, ice cream, coffee, and a liqueur and then go on joyfully to cigars and conversation. An American composer, designing for musical depiction his ideal dinner, would certainly either have left out half of this abundance or topped it off with a finale about bicarbonate. A Frenchman, writing before the war, would probably have extended it even further to include soup.

The program of Mr. Rosenthal's *Dinner in Music*, to render the title freely, contains another curious omission, that of wines. I understand his leaving out the soup. Even before the last war, diners among the Paris international set had shown a tendency to skip this traditional observance. Lady Mendl (an American by birth and consequently only a mild soup addict) invented in the 1930's the slogan, "You can't build a good meal on a lake." And during the Occupation, watery brews with very little nourishment in them were so nearly everybody's whole diet in France that today nobody there, preparing a feast for guests at home or ordering one in a public place, would think of including a *potage* in the menu. With all such greaseless nourishment the French are quite literally fed up.

Wine, on the other hand, which they have lacked since 1940 and which even now is neither overabundant nor cheap, is essential to the ingestion of any reasonably good French meal, not to mention the majestic menu dreamed up in 1942 by Mr. Rosenthal. Perhaps its omission from the program notes provided with his score is merely a device for circumventing the wine snobs, for no subject in gastronomy is so riddled with pretentiousness and vanity.

In any case, no wine is mentioned; but this listener was convinced that he heard in the luscious and delicious scoring of this memorable work plenty of appropriate grape. The characteristic blood flavor of the roast beef and the darkly outdoor taste of venison, rendered in the scoring by trumpets and trombones in the one case and by hunting-horn sounds in the other, were so aptly set off by contrasting instrumental timbres that the richness of the whole effect could only have been conceived with something more on the imaginary palate than meat alone. The salad, on the other hand, with which one does not drink wine, because it tastes already of vinegar, had no such third dimension. It was all light and high and clear and clean and pale, fresh and quite without perspective to the taste.

It is unfortunate that the Philharmonic's program notes did not include a translation of the menu, that they did not even give it complete, as it appears in the musical score. Let us try our hand at it, though with all hesitation, since the rendering of cookery terms in English is beset with pitfalls. The meal begins with *salade russe*, a dish for which the term *Russian salad* is a far from precise description. Precisely, this is a mixture of diced vegetables in mayonnaise, somewhat meager, in fact, as an hors d'oeuvre unless accompanied by cold ham, which Mr. Rosenthal does not offer. (A musical prelude, entitled *Entrée des convives*, or "The Guests Enter the Dining Room," has previously introduced us to the party.) This slender hors d'oeuvre is followed by a *matelote d'anguilles*, eels in red wine. The entrée, untranslatable by this writer, is *quenelles lyonnaise*. *Quenelles* are a paste of chicken or of pike fish mixed with cream, a little flour, and the beaten whites of egg. Shaped like small sausages, they are poached and served with a sauce. As presented in the *lyonnaise*, or Lyons, manner, this is a fresh cream sauce with a chicken-broth base. In classical gastronomy, pike *quenelles* are served with a fish sauce, usually one made of fresh-water crayfish, and chicken *quenelles* with the chicken-stock-and-cream sauce.

The roast is a simple tenderloin of beef, followed (in the French manner, rather than accompanied) by a dish of mixed fresh vegetables. The game is *cuissot de chevreuil*, or loin of venison. *Salade de saison* is whatever the market offers. *Fromage de montagne* I take to mean goat cheese, admirable for the gustation of red wines. Ice cream, liqueurs, cigars, and conversation end the ceremony. Coffee is not mentioned in the text.

The musical rendering of all these delights is most suggestive, though the piece about *quenelles lyonnaise*, a bland dish and a luxurious one, contained an allusion to spicy street songs that I did not understand. As a piece of musical design the work is solid and skillful. As orchestration it is masterful in a manner not at present to be matched in the work of any other living composer. Its finale, representing animated general conversation, is one of the liveliest pieces I know. Its whole effect is a triumph of orchestral cuisine, as delicious as its stated subject. And if it represents, as so much of contemporary French music does—the works of Messiaen, of Jolivet, of Barraud, of Poulenc, and even Honegger—a return to the Debussian, or Berlioz, esthetic, in which color is as important an element of composition as linear drawing, it carries the technique of coloristic design into realms of brightness, especially through the use of high, thin sounds, that the Impressionists, who worked most originally in the bass ranges, had left untouched. *Musique de table* is an utterly charming piece and an utterly French one. Like many other good things French, it combines skill of hand with the frank assumption that living is a pleasure. Thank you, Mr. Rosenthal, for a delightful party!

October 20, 1946

Children's Day

PHILHARMONIC-SYMPHONY ORCHESTRA, *Artur Rodzinski* and *Heitor Villa-Lobos*, conductors, last night at Carnegie Hall, performing Haydn's "Toy" Symphony, Paganini's Violin Concerto in D major, Liszt's *Mephisto Waltz*, and two works by Mr. Villa-Lobos: Chôro No. 8 and Chôro No. 9. Soloist: *Zino Francescatti*, violin.

HEITOR VILLA-LOBOS, who conducted two of his Chôros for orchestra, Numbers 8 and 9, last night with the Philharmonic in Carnegie Hall, is one of the world's most prolific composers. Also one of the most gifted. His works are innumerable and full of bright ideas. Their excellent tunes, their multicolored instrumentation, their abundance of fancy in general, and their easy but perfectly real modernity of thought have made them universally acceptable as valid musical creations of this century. For all the French influence on their harmonic texture (chiefly that of Milhaud), they are also valid musical creations of this hemisphere. They sound, as is, indeed, their composer's intention, most convincingly like Brazil.

Chôro Number 8, last heard here at the World's Fair, sounds to me like rural Brazil, like rivers and plains and mountains and Indian villages and jungles. The jungles seem to have lots of trees in them, big ones and small ones, also some snakes and wild animals. Certainly there are birds around of all sizes. And I thought I spotted, as the civilized note, a sturdy stock of European canned nourishment and a few reels of the best Hollywood sentiment.

Chôro Number 9, which was a North American première, is more urban. It has dance music and crowds and general gaiety and some wit and quite a lot more of Hollywood sentiment. It is all very pleasant, and it is loosely enough constructed so that one doesn't have to pay attention all the time. The composer conducted one through both pieces with courtesy, making everything clear and keeping us interested at every moment. If one felt at the end like a tourist who has seen much but taken part in little, one was grateful for the trip, all the same. One could almost hear the voice of the travelogue saying, "Now we are leaving beau-u-u-tiful Brazil."

We left it for the comfortably suburban Violin Concerto of Paganini and some astonishingly accurate violin playing by Zino Francescatti. And thus safely returned to Europe and the nineteenth century, we paid ourselves an old-style treat in the form of Liszt's great orchestral Mephisto Waltz, which was certainly the original of Ravel's *La Valse*. A wonderfully beautiful piece this, and not a bit devilish, just sweet and romantic and full of an inward light. Our thanks to Artur Rodzinski, who thought of playing it, and who played it enchantingly.

Mr. Rodzinski's little treat for himself, which he shared, of course, with us all, was the playing, to start the evening off, of Haydn's charming and absurd "Toy" Symphony, a publicity tribute to his newborn son. Perhaps it was all this preparation —the toy trumpet and the cuckoo and the whistles and all, then the educational trip through picturesque Brazil, then the dressing-up-in-grandpa's-clothes effect of the Paganini concerto— that made the Mephisto Waltz sound like adult music. In any case it did. And it was most welcome.

February 9, 1945

Revueltas Evening

ANNA SOKOLOW AND DANCE GROUP in performance last night at the Mansfield Theatre, New York, with *Alex North*, pianist and musical director, and a chamber orchestra conducted by *Alex Saron*, presenting seven dances: *Opening Dance, Slaughter of the Innocents,* and *Exile,* to music by Mr. North; *Visión Fantástica,* to music by Padre Antonio Soler and Mr. North, and *Homenaje a García Lorca, Canciones para Niñas,* and *El Renacuajo Paseador,* to music by Silvestre Revueltas. Soloists: *Estelle Hoffman,* soprano, and *Arno Tanney,* baritone.

EUROPE has often produced composers like the late Silvestre Revueltas, the Americas rarely. Our music writers are most likely to do the light touch with a heavy hand. Revueltas's music reminds one of Erik Satie's and of Emmanuel Chabrier's. It is both racy and distinguished. Familiar in style and full of references to Hispanic musical formulas, it seeks not to impress folklorists nor to please audiences by salting up a work with nationalist material. Neither does it make any pretense of going native. He wrote Mexican music that sounds like Spanish Mexico, and he wrote it in the best Parisian syntax. No Indians around and no illiteracy.

The model is a familiar one of the nationalist composer whose compositional procedures are conservative and unoriginal but whose musical material consists of all the rarest and most beautiful melodies that grow in his land. Villa-Lobos is like that and Percy Grainger; so was Dvořák. The contraries of that model are Joseph Haydn and Satie and a little bit Georges Auric, certainly Darius Milhaud. These writers use the vernacular for its expressivity. But their musical structure and syntax are of the most elegant. Their music, in consequence, has an international carrying power among all who love truly imaginative musical construction.

Revueltas's music could never be mistaken for French music. It is none the less made with French post-Impressionist technique, amplified and adapted to his own clime. It is static harmonically, generously flowing melodically, piquant and dainty in instrumentation, daring as to rhythm. He loves ostinato accompanying figures and carries them on longer than a more timid writer would. He orchestrates à la Satie, without doubling. He fears neither unexpected rhythmic contrasts nor familiar melodic turns. His music has grace, grandeur, delicacy, charm, and enormous distinction. It was a pleasing gesture on Miss Sokolow's part to give us three meaty works last night from a composer so excellent and so little played.

Of the three works the *Homage to García Lorca* was the richest musically, though the *Songs for Little Girls* (if I may correct the program's translation of *Canciones para Niñas*) are indeed worthy to rank beside the best child-inspired music we know, including that of Schumann and of Maurice Ravel. *The Fable of the Wandering Frog* sounded less convincing to me. Was it unexpectedly given us in pianoforte reduction, I wonder? The program mentioned a conductor, not a pianist.

The rest of Miss Sokolow's recital was consecrated to Mr. Alex North and to a ballet (after Goya) called *Visión Fantástica*, by Padre Antonio Soler, a capable and skillful eighteenth-century Spanish composer. Mr. North's best work of the evening, *Slaughter of the Innocents*, was of Spanish inspiration too. It sounded, in spite of good musical ideas, as if it had been written to fit a dance number already conceived. This is not good procedure. It invariably makes the music sound timid and the orchestra like a projection (by means of slave labor) of the chief dancer's will, instead of making the chief dancer seem like the personification of the collective imagination of the instrumentalists. Neither did it seem very good taste to insert in the middle of the Soler work a section written by Mr. North in another style, particularly since that section was not the equal in either elegance or expressive power of the Soler music that surrounded it.

March 4, 1941

A Master in Our Time

CONCERT IN MEMORY OF BÉLA BARTÓK last night at the New York Public Library, presenting the following works by the late composer: five new songs and three selections from *Twenty Hungarian Folk Songs*, performed by *Enid Szantho*, contralto, accompanied by *Paul Ulanowsky*, pianist; five selections from *Mikrokosmos*, arranged by Tibor Serly and performed by the Léner String Quartet (*Jenö Léner* and *Michael Kuttner*, violins, *Nicholas Harsanyi*, viola, and *Otto Deri*, cello); and *Dance Suite*, performed by *Gyorgy Sandor*, pianist. With a tribute by *Curt Sachs*, musicologist.

BÉLA BARTÓK, by virtually any criterion Hungary's top-ranking composer of our century, died in New York City on September 26 of last year. The New York Public Library's music division held a memorial concert to his memory last night in the Main Library, at which works of the late master were sung by Enid Szantho and played by Gyorgy Sandor, pianist, and the Léner String Quartet. Paul Ulanowsky accompanied Miss Szantho. The executions were admirable, and the occasion was wholly devotional and touching. It would have been more impressive musically than it was, however, if Bartók had been represented by at least one major work.

Dr. Curt Sachs, of New York University, in an opening tribute, remarked that Bartók had never used Hungarian folklore as an exotic element for spicing up his own musical language, in the manner of Brahms or of Liszt, but that he wrote it as the very substance of his musical thought. The idea, as expressed, sounded convincing. But when one remembers that Bartók treated the folk music of Rumania, Bulgaria, Yugoslavia, and French North Africa with equal aptness and by not dissimilar musical procedures, one wonders if it was altogether the Hungarian turns of folklore that constituted his musical mother tongue, if he did not envisage all the folklores of the Mediterranean regions as a sort of lingua franca.

Certainly Bartók's public for music of Hungarian (and points south) material was an international one. His musical procedures, no matter what kind of melodic material he used, were so widely imitated in the 1920's that they became the standard formula for producing, with no matter what melodic material, a piece of "modern music" that could be played on any modernistic program anywhere in the world. He thought of himself, I am sure, as always and predominantly a Hungarian; but he was in effect an internationalist and the inventor of one of the most widely practiced international styles of the period between the two wars.

Today that style seems as old-fashioned to us as the flat-chested girls in Chanel dresses one fox trotted with in 1926. But let us not be hasty to condemn it, or them. The twenty-year armistice that lasted from 1918 to 1938, from Versailles to Munich, was a brilliant and fecund period of musical creation. If few of its masterworks are current in repertory today, many are remembered and will be revived in a later decade. Bartók was one of the masters of that period, the third in stylistic carrying power, I should say, of all the musicians who represented to the rest of the world modernistic *Mittel Europa*. Schönberg and Hindemith have survived him. His influence on the young was even in his lifetime less than theirs.

Nevertheless, it was a wide influence. And any musician can see, from the mere skill of his musical textures, that he was a master. The prestige of the Bartók style is today less than the respect and admiration in which the man himself is held. His music will probably pass through a period of decline in currency and then be rediscovered. He never touched the musical masses of the world very deeply, but he wrote well. In another decade or so we shall be able to estimate his stylistic power and to understand his communication better, I think, than any of us can do just now. He has been a master in our time. That we can be sure about.

January 12, 1946

Going Contemporary

BOSTON SYMPHONY ORCHESTRA, *Serge Koussevitzky,* conductor, last night at Carnegie Hall, performing Prokofiev's Symphony No. 5 and Beethoven's Overture to *Coriolanus* and Symphony No. 6 ("Pastoral").

Prokofiev's Fifth Symphony, which the Boston Symphony Orchestra played here for the second time this season at last night's concert in Carnegie Hall, remains on second hearing chiefly interesting to his listener as a neo-Romantic work by a formerly neo-Classic-and-Impressionist composer. Its more picturesque sections, which are the second and fourth movements, present no novelty of any kind, though they are good Prokofiev, the first of these being a sort of Soviet-style blues, or Muscovite one-step, and the other standard finale in the composer's best calisthenic vein. Both are brightly, if a little weightily orchestrated. The last has even more reminders than mere coloration of Strauss's *Till Eulenspiegel*.

The first and third movements, which are less striking, deal with a more difficult problem, namely, making a piece of some length out of pliable material. The third movement, a lament, or elegy, is less successfully developed than the first. Slow movements have never been Prokofiev's forte, and of late years he has taken more and more to concealing their lack of expressivity (and of rhythmic variety) with an overlay of cinema sentiment.

The first movement, however, is as neat a piece of symphonic workmanship as has been exposed to us locally in many a day. The rounded, graceful theme of it is no theme at all in a classical sense. It is a motif that generates a flow of music. This is not made up of themes or of formal melodies; it is rather a constant outpouring, an oratorical discourse that never repeats itself but that springs always from the original motif, or source, and that returns constantly to it for refreshment.

The movement is a neo-Romantic work because it faces the central problem of neo-Romanticism, which is the making of sustained music out of non-angular material. This is a technical statement of the neo-Romantic meaning-problem, which is that of sustained personal lyricism. But the two problems are one. The neo-Classicists of the 1920's used angular or motionless material. Any neo-Classicist who, knowingly or unawares, has got involved with rounded or flowing material has found himself up to his neck in personal lyricism, the most treacherous of contemporary esthetic currents. That Prokofiev has not, in this work, found himself out beyond his depth either technically or emotionally is proof that he is not an old man yet. That he has walked out after one movement on all the serious difficulties presented proves also that he is not quite at home in contemporary waters.

The concert began with Beethoven's *Coriolanus* Overture and "Pastoral" Symphony. Both sounded to perfection instrumentally; but as meaning, they were poor and thin. The first was overdramatized till it resembled Dargomizhsky. The second was overcorseted rhythmically till all the jollity went out of it. The slow movement, scored in twelve-eight time, was conducted in six-eight. And quantitative meter was consistently mistaken for accentual. As a result, two hundred years' evolution of the German pastoral style, of which this work is the apex and flower, came to nothing but beautiful tone.

February 14, 1946

Brilliant Farewell

NEW YORK CITY SYMPHONY, *Leonard Bernstein*, conductor, with a men's chorus directed by *Robert Shaw*, last night at the New York City Center, performing the following works by Igor Stravinsky: *Oedipus Rex* (oratorio, with text by Jean Cocteau), Pastorale for Five Instruments, *Ragtime* (for piano), Elegy for Two Violas, Royal March from *L'Histoire d'un soldat*, and Suite from *The Firebird*. Soloists: *Leo Smit*, piano, and *Beatrice Brown* and *Walter Trampler*, violas. With *Norman Corwin*, speaker.

THE FINAL CONCERT of our City Symphony's all too brief season took place last night at the City Center of Music and Drama. The program, devoted to Stravinsky, was anything but a stale one, the *Firebird* suite being the only number on it that is current in repertory. Leonard Bernstein, the conductor, made a pretty speech. Divers soloists from the orchestra played expertly chamber works by the White Russian master. And Mr. Bernstein led a handsome and (for once) thoroughly prepared performance of the rarely heard dramatic oratorio, *Oedipus Rex*.

The latter, which your scribe had not encountered since its first performance in Paris nearly twenty years ago, is the same troublesome work it was then. It has not aged becomingly, as *L'Histoire d'un soldat*, from 1917, has, nor lost its savor altogether, like the *Ragtime*, of 1919, both of which were represented on the program. It is a great big lump of wonderful music, some of which never did come off right and still doesn't.

It is noble, grandiose, complex, massive, stony. Only a master could have written it; and only a master with purely instrumental turn of thought, like Stravinsky or Sebastian Bach, could have written it so ungratefully for the human voice. A linguistic problem is somewhat responsible for the vocal ineptitudes; but so is the composer's imperfect acquaintance with vocal ranges; and so is a certain stylistic willfulness on his part that he hoped, I presume, would conceal the faults of the original literary conception.

The text, believe it or not, is a translation into modern Sorbonne Latin of a French adaptation of an English literal translation of Sophocles. It is no wonder that all literary quality got lost in the process. There was not much Stravinsky could do with such a text but what he did is to make it sound as much as possible like Russian. Last night Mr. Norman Corwin went further and, using a public address system, recited between the numbers a sort of explanation, translated, I imagine, from Jean Cocteau's French, which is quite elegant, into radio American, a far from distinguished literary idiom.

For all its final ineffectualness, and forgetting Mr. Corwin, the work has considerable expressive power and a musical seriousness of the grandest kind. It is full of real invention, also of outmoded stylistic affectations. The latter, imitated mostly from Verdi and from Handel, just barely, in some cases, escape the comical. The former, plus its strong dramatic plan, saves the work from silliness.

Neither saves the singers from giving an effect of swimming in molasses, because their solos are all conceived as if the human wind instrument were a trumpet or a keyed trombone. Linear shape and ornament are expected to produce all the expressivity, verbal color and vocal sweetness being omitted wholly from the requirements. Even the male chorus, save for a few really terrifying percussive moments, did not sound as if the music they were singing was their music, though Robert Shaw had obviously prepared them thoroughly. The work is not well written vocally, simply that. But it is nobly conceived.

Hearing it occasionally is a privilege, and Mr. Bernstein is to be thanked for giving it to us. Also for so thoroughly efficient a rendering. He knew the score, and so did his executants. The final *Firebird*, though far more familiar to all, was less clearly read.

Mr. Bernstein, along with tantrums and occasionally immodesty, has given us lots of good music, especially in the domain of modern revivals otherwise not available. One will miss the concerts of his orchestra. Their programs have been more distinguished intellectually than those of any similar group, in spite of the brilliant season the Philharmonic has lately been offering. And the relation of all this to the City Center audience has been a vivacity unique in the orchestral world. Also, Bernstein conducts like a master when he knows and really likes a score.

November 26, 1946

The Poetry of Precision

PHILHARMONIC-SYMPHONY ORCHESTRA, *Igor Stravinsky*, conductor, last night at Carnegie Hall, performing Glinka's Overture to *Russian and Ludmilla*, Tchaikovsky's Symphony No. 2, and four works by Mr. Stravinsky: *Ode*, Concerto for Piano and Wind Orchestra, *Four Norwegian Moods*, and *Circus Polka*. Soloist: *Beveridge Webster*, piano.

IGOR STRAVINSKY, who conducted the Philharmonic-Symphony Orchestra last night in Carnegie Hall, prefaced a delightful little concert of his own works with a spirited reading of Glinka's *Russian and Ludmilla* overture and a correct but on the whole pedestrian excursion through Tchaikovsky's rarely explored Second Symphony. Whether this work is worthy of the respect that the greatest living Russian composer has long borne it is not a matter on which this reviewer has any opinion. It is obviously a well-written work, full of original fancy and clearly expressed. Whatever feelings anybody may have about it (and feelings are all most people have about Tchaikovsky) are his own business. Myself, I was not enthralled; but I am not a Tchaikovsky fan.

Having long been a Stravinsky fan and long an admirer of the Piano Concerto that Beveridge Webster played so brilliantly last night, your reviewer spent one of the pleasanter moments of the season rehearing it under the composer's direction. Noble of thematic invention, ingenious of texture, and eloquently, grandiloquently sustained, this brilliant evocation of Baroque musical sentiments and attitudes has too long been left on the shelf. It was last played here, if the files in my office are correct, exactly twenty years ago. If patrons walked out on it in scores then, as they did last night, one can understand the hesitancy of conductors to revive it. But if the ovation it received last night from those who stayed (and they were a vast majority) means anything prophetically, the concerto will one day be as popular as Tchaikovsky's in B flat.

The *Ode* retains its elegance on rehearing and gains in intellectual interest, but it remains for this observer a little distant in sentiment. The *Norwegian Moods* are not distant at all. They are warm and picturesque and cheerful, wonderfully melodious and impeccably tailored. At present a sort of *Peer Gynt* suite for the musically sophisticated, they will shortly, I am sure, find themselves at home in the "pop" concerts. The *Circus Polka* has already done so. And indeed a lively picture it is of the sawdust ring. Apparently, the only music lovers who haven't enjoyed it are the elephants for whose dancing it was written. I am told that they scented satire in it, a bit of joking about their proportions (which they are extremely sensitive about) and didn't like working to it. They did not, however, walk out on it.

Mr. Stravinsky's conducting of his own work was, as always, a delight to those who take his works seriously. His rhythm was precise, his tonal texture dry, the expressivity complete. It was complete because only through the most precise rhythm and the driest tonal textures can the Stravinskian pathos be made to vibrate or the Stravinskian tenderness to glow. His is a poetry of exactitude, a theater of delicate adjustments and relentless march. Conductors who sweep through his works as if they were personal oratory of some kind inevitably find these going weak on them. Stravinsky admires Tchaikovsky but he doesn't write or feel like Tchaikovsky. How much added juiciness the latter can stand is an unsettled problem of interpretation. Stravinsky can bear none. It is all written in. His scores are correctly indited, and the composer's reading of them is the way to go. It is also the way they go best.

February 2, 1945

Viennese Lament

NBC SYMPHONY ORCHESTRA, *Dimitri Mitropoulos*, conductor, yesterday afternoon in Studio 8-H, Radio City, performing the Couperin-Milhaud Overture and Allegro from *La Sultane*, Berg's Concerto for Violin and Orchestra, and Berlioz's Overture to *Le roi Lear*. Soloist: *Joseph Szigeti*, violin.

DIMITRI MITROPOULOS, who conducted, and Joseph Szigeti, who played the violin solo, lent an unaccustomed distinction to yesterday afternoon's program of the N.B.C. Symphony Orchestra at Studio 8-H, Radio City, by giving us Alban Berg's Concerto for Violin and Orchestra. They lent to the work itself their inimitable comprehension and care of execution, as well. One may understand or not, "like" or not Berg's music; but one can scarcely fail to be grateful for the rare occasions when one is allowed to hear it.

This music is largely atonal in texture; and this particular piece of it is elegiac in character, introspective and deeply sentimental. It is concentrated Vienna, the Vienna of this century, between the two wars. It could not have been conceived, expressively or technically, at any other place or in any other time. It is as Viennese as the music of Erik Satie is Parisian. For the initiates, therefore, it is full of a heart-rending nostalgia. For the profane it is inevitably something of a bore. Either one melts before its especial expressivity or one stiffens at the seeming exaggeration of both its content and its texture. But whatever way one takes it, it is sincere and skillful music.

Myself, I do not care for it with passion, but I enjoy hearing it. It is full of lovely moments. I am not sure, however, that its beauty is entirely transparent. I suspect that its technical procedures are not wholly at the service of this work's generative emotion, that part of the time they limit the free flow of the expressed feeling and part of the time give it a lachrymose and lugubrious tone that overstates it. I may be wrong; I have only heard the piece once. Clearly it is a work of more than ordinary intensity and, if you respond to it, charm.

Mr. Mitropoulos had framed it between Darius Milhaud's arrangement of selections from Couperin and the Berlioz *King Lear* overture, both of them works that are rarely played here and both of them brilliant theatrical evocations. Milhaud has not forgotten in orchestrating Couperin that the latter was an organist. He has imitated organ registration with many octave doublings and with marked contrasts in volume and color. The Allegro, in which orchestral brasses play rapidly, like the bright and brilliant reed stops of Couperin's own instrument (which is in excellent condition at the Church of St. Gervais in Paris), has a dazzling alacrity.

The orchestra's rendering of the Berlioz overture had been elegantly drilled; but the sound of it suffered somewhat from the dark and weighty character of American trombone and double-bass tone, which was no part of its composer's calculation.

December 31, 1945

Schönberg's Music

On September 13 Arnold Schönberg, the dean of the modernists, will be seventy years old. And yet his music for all its author's love of traditional sonorous materials and all the charm of late nineteenth-century Vienna that envelops its expression, is still the modernest modern music that exists. No other Western music sounds so strange, so consistently different from the music of the immediately preceding centuries. And none, save that of Erik Satie, has proved so tough a nut for the public to crack. Only the early *Verklärte Nacht* has attained to currency in our concerts. The rest remains to this day musicians' music.

Musicians do not always know what they think of Schönberg's music, but they often like to listen to it. And they invariably respect it. Whether one likes it or not is, indeed, rather a foolish question to raise in face of its monumental logic. To share or to reject the sentiments that it expresses seems, somehow, a minor consideration compared with following the amplitude of the reasoning that underlies their exposition. As in much of modern philosophical writing, the conclusions reached are not the meat of the matter; it is the methods by which these are arrived at.

This preponderance of methodology over objective is what gives to Schönberg's work, in fact, its irreducible modernity. It is the orientation that permits us to qualify it as, also, in the good sense of the word, academic. For it is a model of procedure. And if the consistency of the procedure seems often closer to the composer's mind than the expressive aim, that fact allows us further to describe the work as academic in an unfavorable sense. It means that the emotional nourishment in the music is not quite worth the trouble required to extract it. This is a legitimate and not uncommon layman's opinion. But if one admits, as I think one is obliged to do with regard to Schönberg, that the vigor and thoroughness of the procedure are, in very fact, the music's chief objective, then no musician can deny that it presents a very high degree of musical interest.

This is not to say that Schönberg's music is without feeling expressed. Quite to the contrary, it positively drips with emotivity. But still the approach is, in both senses of the word, academic. Emotions are examined rather than declared. As in the workings of his distinguished fellow citizen Dr. Sigmund Freud, though the subject matter is touching, even lurid, the author's detachment about it is complete. Sentiments are considered as case histories rather than as pretexts for personal poetry or subjects for showmanship. *Die glückliche Hand*, *Gurre-Lieder*, and *Pierrot Lunaire*, as well as the string sextet, *Verklärte Nacht*, have deeply sentimental subjects; but their treatment is always by detailed exposition, never by sermonizing. Pierrot's little feelings, therefore, though they seem enormous and are unquestionably fascinating when studied through the Schönberg microscope for forty-five minutes of concert time, often appear in retrospect as less interesting than the mechanism through which they have been viewed.

The designing and perfecting of this mechanism, rather than the creation of unique works, would seem to have been the guiding preoccupation of Schönberg's career; certainly it is the chief source of his enormous prestige among musicians. The works themselves, charming as they are and frequently impressive, are never quite as fascinating when considered separately as they are when viewed as comments on a method of composition or as illustrations of its expressive possibilities. They are all secondary to a theory; they do not lead independent lives. The theory, however, leads an independent life. It is taught and practiced all over the world. It is the lingua franca of contemporary modernism. It is even used expertly by composers who have never heard any of the works by Schönberg, by Webern, and by Alban Berg that constitute its major literature.

If that major literature is wholly Viennese by birth and its sentimental preoccupations largely Germanic, the syntax of its expression embodies also both the strongest and the weakest elements of the German musical tradition. Its strong element is its simplification of tonal relations; its weak element is its chaotic rhythm. The apparent complexity of the whole literature and the certain obscurity of much of it are due, in the present writer's opinion, to the lack of a rhythmic organization comparable in comprehensiveness and in simplicity to the tonal one.

It is probably the insufficiencies of Schönberg's own rhythmic theory that prevent his music from crystallizing into great, hard, beautiful, indissoluble works. Instrumentally they are delicious. Tonally they are the most exciting, the most original, the most modern-sounding music there is. What limits their intelligibility, hamstrings their expressive power, makes them often literally halt in their tracks, is the naïve organization of their pulses, taps, and quantities. Until a rhythmic syntax comparable in sophistication to Schönberg's tonal one shall have been added to this, his whole method of composition, for all the high intellection and sheer musical genius that have gone into its making, will probably remain a fecund but insupportable heresy, a strict counterpoint valuable to pedagogy but stiff, opaque, unmalleable, and inexpressive for free composition.

There is no satisfactory name for the thing Schönberg has made. The twelve-tone technique, though its commonest denomination, does not cover all of it. But he has made a thing, a new thing, a thing to be used and to be improved. Its novelty in 1944 is still fresh; and that means it has strength, not merely charm. Its usage by composers of all nations means that it is no instrument of local or limited applicability. Such limitations as it has are due, I believe, to the fact that it is not yet a complete system. So far as it goes it is admirable; and it can go far, as the operas of Alban Berg show. It is to the highest credit of Schönberg as a creator that his method of creation should be so valuable a thing as to merit still, even require, the collaboration of those who shall come after him.

September 10, 1944

FROM OUT OF TOWN

Overtrained

BOSTON SYMPHONY ORCHESTRA, *Serge Koussevitzky*, conductor, last night at Carnegie Hall, performing Beethoven's Symphony No. 3 ("Eroica") and Berlioz's *Harold en Italie*. Soloist: *William Primrose*, viola.

THE BOSTON SYMPHONY ORCHESTRA's first concert of the season, which took place last night in Carnegie Hall, consisted of two works and lasted two hours. They were beautiful works and handsomely executed. With the exception of the impossible horn passage in the trio of Beethoven's "Eroica" scherzo, your commentator could find no fault in the playing. And yet he was aware of the passage of time.

Serge Koussevitzky's tempos were not slow. In the Beethoven symphony they were, in fact, most gratefully animated. And the mechanism of orchestral articulation was, as always with this group, delightful to observe. Everything was right, including William Primrose, who played the viola solo of Berlioz's *Harold in Italy*. It was the old story, I am afraid, of familiar pieces so elegantly turned out that one scarcely recognized them. They were not deformed. Their clear spirit was not violated. They were simply so completely groomed that one was not aware of any spirit present. The slickness of their surfacing made them seem hollow and laborious underneath, which they are not.

The truth of the matter, in my opinion, is simply that the Boston Symphony Orchestra is overtrained and has been for several years. Its form is perfect, but it does not communicate. The music it plays never seems to be about anything, except how beautifully the Boston Symphony Orchestra can play. Perfection of execution that oversteps its purpose is a familiar phenomenon in art. That way lies superficiality and monotony. And music has no business sounding monotonous, since no two pieces of it are alike. Wherever a series of pieces or of programs starts sounding that way you may be sure that the execution is at fault, is obtruding itself.

One longs, in listening to this orchestra's work, for a little ease. It is of no use for all the sonorous elements to be so neatly in place unless some illusion is present that their being so is spontaneous. Music is not the result of rehearsal. It is an auditory miracle that can take place anywhere. When it occurs among disciplined musicians its miraculous quality is merely heightened. When the frequency of its occurrence in any given group starts diminishing, there are only two possible remedies. Either the members must play together more often, or they must get some new pieces.

Obviously, this group does not need more rehearsing. And it knows now all the pieces there are in standard repertory; it even knows all the kinds of pieces there are for large orchestra. There is nothing to be done about it. It has passed the peak of useful executional skill, and executional hypertrophy has set in. The pattern is a familiar one, and regrettable. But there is no use trying to deceive one's self about it.

November 16, 1944

Chicago's Orchestra

AMONG America's symphony orchestras that of Chicago stands third in seniority (only Boston and the New York Philharmonic being older) and among the first four in quality (its standards of execution being comparable to those of New York, Boston, and Philadelphia). For fifty-one years it had only two permanent conductors, Theodore Thomas and Frederick Stock, though Eric DeLamarter took it over for two seasons during the other World War, when Dr. Stock, at that time a German citizen, was in retirement from public life. On Dr. Stock's death, two years ago, the post fell vacant, his assistant Hans Lange being asked to carry on for the rest of the season.

From an artistic point of view the post is a plum, since the orchestra is first-class, the Chicago musical public both large and enlightened, and the tradition of long tenure for conductors one inspiring of any man's best efforts. Among many distinguished applicants, the appointment fell a year ago to the Belgian conductor Désiré Defauw, previously known on this continent chiefly through his work with the Montreal Symphony Orchestra and from a few guest appearances in Boston. Chicago has been a battle ground ever since.

The front of the opposition has been Claudia Cassidy, music critic of the *Chicago Tribune*, who has carried on a press campaign of no small vigor to expose what she considers to be Mr. Defauw's musical unworthiness for a post so rich in tradition and so high in responsibility. Being curious to taste the qualities of a workman who has been the object of so sustained a discussion, your reviewer took occasion last week to attend the opening concert of the Tuesday afternoon series in Orchestra Hall. With no wish in the world to insert himself into a Chicago dispute and one which shows signs of quieting down this season, anyway, he offers here no reflected opinion of Mr. Defauw's work (nor could he from one hearing) but simply a review of a musical occasion that he happened to attend.

The program was one well designed to show off any conductor's gifts and weaknesses; it might have been set as an examination. There was a Berlioz overture (the *Benvenuto Cellini*), a Brahms symphony (No. 2), Prokofiev's *Scythian Suite* and (of all things) the Scriabin *Poème d'Extase*. The Berlioz is an easy piece, though few play it well; they mostly let it go rackety. The Scriabin is not at all an easy piece either for the players or for the conductor. Its rhythm has a tendency to go spineless and its instrumentation to get blurred. It requires eight horns, moreover, an outlay of brasses difficult to produce in wartime. Their presence is required also for the *Scythian Suite*. As for Brahms and Prokofiev, the conductor does not live who can interpret both writers equally well, so utterly opposed are they in their understanding of rhythm.

Brahms, as you may well imagine, came off least well among the composers represented. I say you may well imagine, because Mr. Defauw is a musican of French rather than of German training and because, as a youngish man (turned fifty, I should guess), he is a child of the twentieth century rather than of the nineteenth. His Brahms was handsomely phrased and cleanly articulated, but it didn't seem to be about anything. It was not careless or mushy or overweening. It was just too neatly sculptured to make any of the kind of sense Brahms's music must make if it is to avoid being pompous. Certainly it had none of the dreamy quality that made Stock's playing of this same music so lovely and so enveloping.

The Gallicism of Mr. Defauw's musical mind was exemplified constantly in the clarity of his orchestral textures. Loud or soft, you could always hear what was being played. That orchestra in that hall can make the most resonant fortissimo in America. Terribly, wonderfully loud, these were always beautiful and always clean. The modernity of his rhythmic understanding was exemplified in the Prokofiev and Scriabin works, where quantitative scansion and tonic stresses must be kept separate. Defauw is a clear-minded musician, a master of equilibrium, of rhythm, and of phraseology; and he has a taste for brightness of sound. For these qualities I can forgive him much. He makes good programs, too, if the four or five printed in the program book are typical, mixing the nineteenth century constantly with our own and not forgetting the eighteenth.

It is not for what musicians play badly that we remember them but for what they play well. And this listener will long remember the performance he heard in Chicago of Prokofiev's *Scythian Suite* and of Scriabin's melodically outmoded but orchestrally still sumptuous *Poem of Ecstasy*. He has heard many pretentious and vain renderings of both. Neither is it the first time he has slept through somebody's Brahms. He has never heard the two Russian works rendered with so high a degree of luminosity. That luminosity was the result of precise orchestral balances and correct rhythmic scansion. One is grateful for these qualities in a world where overworked orchestras and overadvertised conductors are becoming increasingly careless about both.

October 29, 1944

Orchestrally News

DETROIT SYMPHONY ORCHESTRA, *Karl Krueger*, conductor, last night at Carnegie Hall, performing Rachmaninoff's Symphony No. 2, "Dido's Lament" from Purcell's *Dido and Aeneas*, Oscar Lorenzo Fernández's *Batuque*, Charles T. Griffes's *White Peacock*, and "Dance of the Seven Veils" from Richard Strauss's *Salomé*. Soloist: *Marjorie Lawrence,* soprano.

EVEN through the mud and sugar of Rachmaninoff's Second Symphony, it was clear in Carnegie Hall last night that Karl Krueger is a virtuoso conductor and that the Detroit Symphony Orchestra is one of our top professional outfits. The string work in particular is the sort of thing one hears only from first-class workmen, trained by a musician who knows about workmanship and cares. Deep, rich, and suave, or light as transparent silk, the tone of it has that sumptuous sound that Leopold Stokowski used to produce from the Philadelphia strings twenty years ago. Whether this opulence might cloy under sustained acquaintance, as that of the old Philadelphia group was likely to do, remains to be learned from experience. One evening of it was luxurious and one would like more.

Mr. Krueger's program would have been better suited to an outdoor "pop" concert than it was to a New York winter occasion. Excepting for the short air from Purcell's *Dido and Aeneas*, which Marjorie Lawrence sang (I think in English) without any stylistic restraint, there was not one piece on it that could be considered classical symphonic music, ancient or modern. The final scene from Strauss's *Salomé*, which Miss Lawrence sang with a fine dramatic gusto, and which Mr. Krueger conducted with full exploitation of all its grand theatrical violence, was the only piece that had even any serious entertainment value for this listener. The rest of the time he observed the sound orchestral work and admired the courtly elegance of the conductor's deportment.

For the record, let it be put down that Mr. Krueger was born in Atchison, Kansas, that he learned his art in Vienna, and that he perfected it during a decade's tenure at the Kansas City Philharmonic. He has been in Detroit for two years now. I have heard him work in both cities and found him excellent, if a little heavy-spirited, perhaps, by temperament. He is a virtuoso performer, however, and, for all his Viennese dignity, a born showman. His repertory has been notable for breadth and for its high percentage of novelty.

Just why so skillful an operator should have offered us the program he did last night escapes me. It was successful enough in terms of a full house and massive acclaim. I put the latter down to the sad fact that a New York audience will applaud with abandon anything that is handsomely enough executed, which last night's program certainly was. It may be, of course, that I overestimate our musical needs. More likely I am underestimating Mr. Krueger's sagacity. In any case, and giving him and his men full credit for a show pulled off, the calculation behind it all may well have been the advertising maxim: "Tell it to Sweeney; the Stuyvesants will understand."

January 31, 1945

From Hollywood via Indianapolis

INDIANAPOLIS SYMPHONY ORCHESTRA, *Fabien Sevitzky*, conductor, last night at Carnegie Hall, performing Berlioz's "*Carnaval Romain*" Overture, Haydn's Symphony No. 73 ("La Chasse"), Lionel Barrymore's *Praeludium and Fugue*, and Shostakovich's Symphony No. 5.

THE INDIANAPOLIS SYMPHONY ORCHESTRA, of which Fabien Sevitzky is the conductor, made its first appearance in New York last night at Carnegie Hall before a large and warmer than warm audience. Though scarcely ten years old as a major orchestra ("major" means that the annual budget exceeds $200,000), it has already made itself known in the Middle West for high standards of execution and throughout the country for advanced program making. Only Boston tops Indianapolis in the proportion of annual playing time consecrated to the works of either living composers or American composers.

Last night's bouquet of works, I must say, was far from novel, its one fresh flower being a work by, of all people, Lionel Barrymore. For the rest, there were a Berlioz overture, a Haydn symphony and one of those interminable Shostakovich numbers.

The orchestral execution and the conducting throughout were excellent. Mr. Sevitzky is a sound musician, a leader of force and refinement. It seems a shame to waste him and his men on a program that might have been heard at almost any time during the last five years at the Stadium or other "pop" concerts.

Mr. Barrymore's *Praeludium and Fugue* (sic) is an eclectic work of not much interior tension; but it is painstakingly, rather elaborately, indeed, composed. Orchestrated, though the program did not say so, by a Hollywood expert, its surface overlay contains just about everything, including a storm, some "Chinese" effects and, of course, chimes at the end. It evokes Ronald Colman getting out of an airplane in a snowstorm or Miss Lana Turner in trouble or about anything one might care to select along that line, simply because it has been dressed up to sound that way. A pianoforte reduction of the piece would show, I am certain, a very different expressive content.

The prelude is a wandering improvisation such as any church organist might make who had been brought up on Bach but who admired Richard Strauss more. The fugue has a Straussian subject derived from *Also Sprach Zarathustra*. This is treated successively in ironic, atmospheric, pathetic, and oratorical vein. Put through such a workout, it ceases, long before the end, to mean anything at all. Mr. Barrymore's good will in all this seems impeccable; but his instructors should have told him that the purpose of fugal device is to magnify the subject's characteristic expression, not to obliterate it.

The curiosity interest of this little work and the excellent playing of the orchestra were not, unfortunately, quite enough to hold the interest of the concert up to where one felt all the time it should be. Perhaps Mr. Sevitzky's tempos are a shade slow, too. In any case, this listener found the music all evening, though clear and in every way shipshape, not completely absorbing.

December 7, 1944

Music in Pittsburgh

Fritz Reiner's excellence as a conductor, though we do not hear him here as often as lovers of fine musical workmanship could wish, is well known to New Yorkers. And the Pittsburgh

(Pennsylvania) Symphony Orchestra, his regular charge, has of late become more and more agreeably familiar to collectors of gramophone records. Hearing the two together and *in situ* was the privilege of your reporter on a recent week end spent in the city of smoke and steel, birthplace of Stephen Foster and of Oscar Levant.

The orchestra's habitat, a building in the arabesque taste called Syria Mosque, is not ideal acoustically. Its auditorium, which is at least twice as wide as it is deep, has no proper focus of sound. All the same, the orchestra makes good music in it, Mr. Reiner's impeccable clarity of texture replacing most effectively auditory advantages that the architect's proportions fail to provide. His program was a pretty one, lively, modernistic, and not banal. It contained, in reversed chronological order of their composition: Milhaud's *Suite française*, a novelty of this season; Stravinsky's suite from *Pulcinella*, a masterpiece of twenty-six years ago that is more familiar to audiences as a violin or a cello solo piece than in its orchestral version, and Debussy's *Ibéria*, now in its thirty-ninth year. There was also a conservative work, Wieniawski's Violin Concerto, No. 2, the chief attraction it presented being the more than merely beautiful violin playing of Isaac Stern.

To a New Yorker the evening was a delight. We do not often hear in Carnegie Hall a program so fresh, so light of texture, so still alive. The Milhaud piece we have heard just once. We almost never hear *Pulcinella*. And we are not overaccustomed to *Ibéria*. I don't think I have ever heard, even from Pierre Monteux, so eloquent, so absorbing a performance of this beautiful and troublesome work, so difficult to project because of its evanescent continuity. In Reiner's hands it made both music and sense; and the rhythm, for once, as Debussy must have intended, sustained its supple strength like a spinal column.

On another evening there was a concert of modern sonatas, presented at the Carnegie Institute of Technology by the newly formed local chapter of the International Society for Contemporary Music. The program included piano sonatas by Aaron Copland, by Stravinsky, and by the present writer; a sonata for cello alone by Jerzy Fitelberg, a world première; and one for violin and piano by Hindemith. The executant artists were Webster Aitken, pianist; Stefan Auber, first cellist of the symphony orchestra; Isaac Stern, violinist; and his admirable accompanist, Alexander Zakin. It is not often that one hears modern works, either standard or new, performed with such technical brilliance and such conviction. Their stimulating effect on the audience present was proved by the vigor of the discussion that took place for over an hour in the forum that followed. The composer Nikolai Lopatnikoff, professor of composition at the Carnegie Institute, presided over this, the other composers present, as well as the evening's executant artists, participating from the platform. It was a lively evening.

A performance by the local opera company of Puccini's *La Bohème* proved less rewarding. Musical *verismo* is not for amateurs, because dramatic continuity, rather than musical, is its sustaining element. With this missing (and it is normally missing from amateur operatic performance) Puccini's music, which has little sustained rhetoric, however great its moment-to-moment expressivity, tends to fall apart, to lack concentration and trajectory. Even the presence of experienced soloists (mostly imported) like Dorothy Kirsten, Hugh Thompson, and Giulio Gari (a soundly resonant Rodolfo) and of an unusually well-prepared local artist, Mary Martha Briney, who sang Musetta, could not keep the evening alert.

The week end, as a whole, however, was more than satisfactory to one who, in spite of season's-end saturation, can still take musical nourishment. And spring in Pittsburgh, with trees and grass picked out in baby-leaf green against the blackened violet that is the city's tone, is not without a certain poetry.

April 14, 1946

A Touching Occasion

BALTIMORE SYMPHONY ORCHESTRA, *Reginald Stewart*, conductor, last night at Carnegie Hall, performing Bach's Fugue in C major and "*Kom süsser Tod*," Lukas Foss's *Pantomime for Orchestra*, and Brahms's Symphony No. 3 and Concerto for Violin and Orchestra, Op. 77. Soloist: *Georges Enesco*, violin.

THE BALTIMORE SYMPHONY ORCHESTRA played last night in Carnegie Hall under the leadership of Reginald Stewart its first New York concert. The program was conservative, the execution clean but not very communicative. The evening would have been, on the whole, uneventful had not Georges Enesco, as soloist in the Brahms Violin Concerto, brought fire to the program and tears to all our eyes.

The great Rumanian composer, conductor, and violinist has not previously appeared in downtown Manhattan since before the war. Wartime privation and suffering, which have left their mark of arthritic distortion on a once noble figure, seem to have affected hardly at all Enesco's mastery of his instrument. His tone is full and sweet, his pitch impeccable, his style in every way serious and grand. Not only was his playing a musical pleasure, but his return to Carnegie Hall physically bowed but spiritually indomitable was the occasion for cheers and solid applause. I think all hearts were deeply touched.

Lukas Foss's *Pantomime for Orchestra*, which received its first New York hearing last night, is a spotty and discontinuous composition, not at all lacking in fancy but insufficiently sequential for concert listening. It sounded as if it had been composed to accompany an acrobatic comedy number and as if the composer had followed in his score, step by step, the stage routine. Lacking program notes, I cannot be sure that I am right about the work's origins. With or without notes the piece lacks continuity. One has faith in Mr. Foss's very real talent as a composer, in his skill, his fancy, his dedication. But he does mature more slowly than most. Perhaps that is a favorable sign.

Mr. Stewart's orchestra is not one of America's finest, but it is a reasonably efficient machine for making music. Its sound lacks cohesion, as Mr. Stewart's conducting lacks the ultimate in urgency. All is sane and civilized but not, to surfeited New York ears, completely absorbing. The readings are clean, but they are only readings. They are not in any sense interpretations. That is why, especially in the familiar works, last night's concert was somewhat short of compelling. In music making it is always better to be wrong than reserved.

February 6, 1947

Landscape Music

DALLAS SYMPHONY ORCHESTRA, *Antal Doráti*, conductor, yesterday afternoon in an NBC radio broadcast from Fair Park Auditorium, Dallas, Texas, performing Mozart's Symphony No. 27, Hindemith's *Symphonia Serena*, and Copland's Three Dance Episodes from *Rodeo*.

THE DALLAS SYMPHONY ORCHESTRA, Antal Doráti, conductor, gave yesterday afternoon in a program broadcast by NBC the first performance of a work in four movements by Paul Hindemith entitled *Symphonia Serena*. At today's concert of the same orchestra in Fair Park Auditorium, Dallas, Texas, the first public performance will take place. Yesterday's broadcast was one of a series called "The Orchestras of the Nation," which occupy the three o'clock hour, locally speaking, on Saturday afternoons over WNBC. The work in question, a commission of the Dallas Symphony Orchestra, was composed during November and December 1946. On yesterday's program it was preceded by Mozart's jolly G-major Symphony, No. 27, and followed by Three Dance Episodes from Aaron Copland's ballet, *Rodeo*, a concert suite not yet heard in New York. (One of these dances was conducted by Leonard Bernstein at a Stadium concert on July 8, 1945.)

The Hindemith symphony, this composer's second, is a large essay in pastoral vein. Eschewing voluntarily the pathetic style, the composer has aimed, I think, at a direct rendering of landscape. No land or seascape so specific as that of Debussy's *Ibéria* or *La Mer* is invoked; but the piece is a pastoral symphony all the same, a formal communion with nature not dissimilar in approach to Mendelssohn's "Italian" and "Scottish" symphonies. Whether the landscape is one with or without figures is hard to say, though there is certainly an echo present in the slow movement. All the same, there is no such broad humanity included as that which joins in the village dancing of Beethoven's Sixth Symphony.

The first movement seems to be about the countryside, perhaps a walk through this in spring or summer; at one point water, possibly a rivulet or cascade, is suggested. The second, a scherzo for wind instruments based on a quickstep theme by Beethoven, is light in texture and extremely animated. Possibly insect life may be its subject. The third is a dialogue for two string orchestras, two solo strings (a violin and a viola), and two more of the same playing off-stage right and left. The sentiment is tender, sweet, and not without a deliberate nobility. Echo effects evoke a décor with some distance in it. A certain pathos of expression indicates a spectator. The last movement, which is one of considerable thematic complexity, is certainly dominated by the sound of birds.

The entire piece is contrapuntally complex in the sense that almost no theme is ever stated without a countertheme in contrasting rhythmic values being present. This procedure gives objectivity to the expression, impersonality and reserve. The work is distinguished of texture and most agreeable in sound (the dissonant diatonic is its syntax). It will take its place in the repertory of evocation rather than in that of symphonic sermonizing. Exactly what that place will be is difficult to predict; but if manliness of spirit and sound workmanship have any carrying power in our land and century, that place will be one of honor. Hindemith's *Symphonia Serena* is a solid, conservative work from the studio of one of the solidest and most conservative workmen alive.

Copland's *Rodeo* dances are outdoor music, too, and with lots of humanity in them. They are gay and sweet, jolly and heartbreakingly sentimental. Their reading by Mr. Doráti and the Dallas orchestra was vivid, clear, animated. So was that of the Hindemith symphony. The Mozart reading was admirable for clarity and cleanliness, but its rhythmic layout was perhaps a shade foursquare.

February 2, 1947

Modernistic Piety

SAN FRANCISCO SYMPHONY ORCHESTRA, *Pierre Monteux*, conductor, last night at Carnegie Hall, performing, among other works, Messiaen's *L'Ascension: quatre meditations pour l'orchestre*, and Richard Strauss's *Tod und Verklärung*.

PIERRE MONTEUX, who conducted his own orchestra, the San Francisco Symphony, last night in Carnegie Hall, is one of the greatest among living conductors. His orchestra, unfortunately, on account of budgetary limitations, is not so perfect an instrument as he is a musician. Its imperfections were somewhat exaggerated, moreover, last night by the unfamiliarity of the players with Carnegie Hall's rather special acoustics. It is hard for any group to strike a balance on a stage which projects sound so fully that not enough resonance is left on that stage to enable the men to hear one another. Also, it is very easy, with the present soundboard, for any conductor to overencourage the brasses.

Both the brasses and the woodwinds of this orchestra are of good quality. It is the strings that are weak. Not weak in sound, because they do make quite a racket, but not entirely transparent, because of incomplete unanimity both of pitch and of rhythm. Their tone is live but scratchy. In fast passages or under heavy bow-arm pressures it explodes, goes brittle and overbrilliant, loses tonal focus. All the animated passages sounded last night, in consequence, in spite of Mr. Monteux's admirable tempos and careful phrasing, a little rowdy.

The novelty of the evening was Olivier Messiaen's four "symphonic meditations," entitled *The Ascension*. This work, though not by any means its author's masterpiece, is pleasant music, easy to listen to and, with or without footnotes, easy to understand. I shall not use up my space today repeating its footnotes and subtitles. Suffice it to remark that Messiaen alone among the composers of our day has achieved a convincing synthesis of musical modernism with devotional piety. He has thus enlarged not only his art's technique but also its expressive range. His music is vibrant and fresh in sound, deeply affecting also as emotion communicated. Its faults of both technique and taste, and it has many, are as nothing compared to its originality and its force. It is new, powerful, and good.

So, I presume, was Richard Strauss's *Death and Transfiguration* fifty years ago. Today it seems labored and obvious, but it still has a kind of life in it. The juxtaposition of this work to Messiaen's piece on a similar subject was a happy thought on Mr. Monteux's part. It brought out more similarities, indeed, than basic differences. Strauss pulls at the heartstrings with a violin solo accompanied by harp, a procedure no doubt infallible in the nineties. Messiaen uses a trumpet solo accompanied by other brass to achieve a similar result. Once the contemporary charm of the latter procedure has worn off, the effect may be about that of Strauss's violin solo today.

Neither composer's reputation rests or is going to rest on one work. Both are abundant and masterful writers, and I should hazard the guess that Messiaen presents right now the spectacle of a musical genius in almost full-blown flower not dissimilar in either contemporary appeal or prospects of permanent value to that offered fifty years ago by Richard Strauss. Though neither composer, as I said before, was represented last night by his best piece, their treatments of a certain subject (the shaking off of mortality) at almost the same age (when in their thirties) give a basis for comparison. Both pieces played last night came off well in that comparison. One, perhaps, is overglamorous with up-to-dateness, but thrilling nevertheless, the other more than a little faded, but still good for jerking a tear.

April 12, 1947

University Festival

FISK UNIVERSITY in Nashville, Tennessee, is one of America's major institutions of learning. Its high academic standards and elevated cultural tone, as well as its seniority, have long justified its familiar appellation, "the Negro Harvard." Not the least of its titles to distinction is its possession of one of the largest and best music departments to be found in our whole Southern region. During the course of a recent visit to the campus it was your reviewer's privilege to be present at the annual Festival of Music and Art, a three-day series of concerts and similar ceremonies, and at the formal inauguration of an important addition to the musical resources of the Fisk Library, namely the George Gershwin Memorial Collection of Music and Musical Literature.

The latter, a gift to the university from Carl Van Vechten, is housed in a special room that the library authorities have provided and for which the heirs of the late Lee J. Loventhal, long a benefactor of the university, have provided the furnishings. Mr. Van Vechten, one of our best-documented writers on both musical and Negro subjects, has here disposed of his large musical collection in a manner well designed to enhance its usefulness. He had already founded at Yale a collection of material by and about Negroes which bears the name of a former professor of Fisk University, the poet James Weldon Johnson. His musical offering bears the equally appropriate name of America's most celebrated composer, George Gershwin, and is deposited at the library of an institution where music is a major subject of study. The fact that this library is situated in a region only too scantily supplied with music libraries makes the choice of the depository all the more a happy one.

The collection, which is large, contains the vocal and piano scores of "almost every opera in the world," to use Mr. Van Vechten's words, an unusual number of composers' manuscripts and of letters from both composers and executants, and several thousand photographs of well-known musicians. There are, in addition, standard historical works and copies of practically all the books on musical subjects that have appeared in the United States in recent years. A great many composers and other musicians have already given priceless items to the collection, and Mr. Van Vechten himself has undertaken to continue supplying contemporary books about music for the period of his lifetime. The present collection is thus not only a valuable library but also a nucleus about which an even larger and more valuable one has begun already to grow. And Fisk University, long a pioneer in the South both for musical studies and for sound race relations in matters scholarly, is the perfect location for such a library.

The festival ceremonies of which the Gershwin Collection's inauguration was a part consisted of an opera performance, a piano recital, and two concerts of contemporary music. The opera produced was Puccini's *Madama Butterfly*. I missed the performance itself; but I saw photographs of the production, which was visually most stylish; and I heard sing on another occasion the leading soprano, Lenora Lafayette, an artist of unusual vocal gifts and professional qualifications. I missed also the final concert of choral music sung by the Fisk University Choir (a student organization not to be confused with the Fisk Jubilee Singers, who are a professional group having no connection with the Music Department). On this occasion the program consisted of Gustav Holst's celebrated but seldom performed *Hymn of Jesus*, William Schuman's *Requiescat*, Aaron Copland's *Lark* and Igor Stravinsky's *Symphony of Psalms*, the latter helped out by members of the Nashville Symphony Orchestra.

The two musical occasions that I did attend were a concert of contemporary American music and a piano recital played by Philippa Duke Schuyler. This talented young artist has long been popular as a child prodigy. At the age of fifteen she is no longer a child, but her musical performance is no less prodigious. It is prodigious not from a technical point of view, since technical mastery among young musicians of that age, though far from common, is a musical phenomenon less rare than among children. What remains prodigious about Miss Schuyler's work is the sincerity of her musical approach and the infallibility of her musical instincts. Though thoroughly accustomed to platform appearance, and with every other circumstance lending itself to personal exploitation, she makes no personal play whatsoever. She plays music, not Philippa Schuyler, even when she performs her own compositions. And she gets inside any piece with conviction. Her emotional understanding of longer works is about what one would expect from a young person of considerable musical experience. That is to say that it is immature. But her understanding of music as a language and the confidence with which she speaks it are complete. Her work has a straightforwardness comparable to that of the great interpreters; and the clarity of her execution, no less than the absorption of her musical thought, is proof that Miss Schuyler is a musical personality of the first water.

The contemporary concert began with my own *Medea* choruses and ended with a goodly chunk of Marc Blitzstein's *The Airborne*. Between these choral works came a violin sonata by

Piston, songs by Diamond, Ames, Naginsky, Strickland, and Still, an organ piece by Sowerby, and divers piano versions. Among the latter, only Copland's *Danzon Cubano*, for two pianos, is originally a piano work. Excerpts from Miss Schuyler's *Fairy Tale Symphony* were played by the composer in pianoforte transcription; and two movements of John W. Work's *Yenvalou* suite (originally for strings) were played in a two-piano arrangement that might well have passed for an original, so idiomatic was the piano writing.

Miss Schuyler's symphony, composed several years ago, is the work of a gifted child. It is harmonically plain, melodically broad, brilliant but not original as figuration. Like her piano playing, it shows a thoroughly musical nature and a real gift for expression, for saying things with music. It is in every way as interesting as the symphonies Mozart wrote at the same age, thirteen. Mr. Work's suite is the finest piece on a Haitian subject I have yet heard. If it sounds as well for string orchestra as it does on two pianos, it is one of the finest pieces of contemporary music in the whole American repertory. First performed at Saratoga in 1946, it has not yet been played elsewhere. One looks forward to its introduction into symphonic repertory with eagerness and with confidence about its success. It is a charming work and thoroughly interesting to listen to. The high points of the festival in this reporter's experience of it came from making the acquaintance of Mr. Work's composition, of Miss Schuyler's piano playing and general musicianship, and also that of one of the university's non-Negro instructors, Elmer Schoettle, a pianist of the highest attainments both technical and musical.

May 4, 1947

FROM OVERSEAS

Paris Items: Oratorios and Organs

THE NEWS of things musical in Paris, as that reaches me from military correspondents and from press clippings, indicates that concert repertory there has virtually settled down to normal, normal meaning, in that enlightened capital, that constant performance of new works, as well as the revival of old.

The recent winter season has offered repeatedly homage to Gabriel Fauré, 1945 being the centenary of his birth. Festivals devoted to the works of other standard modern composers have honored Ravel, Stravinsky, and Milhaud. Hindemith and Schönberg have reappeared in repertory, too, the latter calling forth the usual French opinion about it that although one may not like it much, it is remarkable music, all the same. Come to think of it, that is about the standard opinion of it everywhere among persons who have been brought up to respect contemporary creative effort. Some English music has been played, too, and a teensy weensy bit of American, William Grant Still's "Afro-American" Symphony, when played at the Concerts Pasdeloup, provoking the comment from a press critic that "it was not disagreeable to hear, *certes*; but we would rather have had Louis Armstrong."

Among the new French works in large form, Manuel Rosenthal's oratorio, *Saint Francis of Assisi*, seems to have been liked by almost everyone. A Requiem of Tomasi, the Fifty-sixth Psalm (or Fifty-fifth by our count) of Jean Rivier, and the *Benedictiones* of Roland-Manuel were also given for the first time. These works, all for large chorus and orchestra, are significant of two trends in present-day French music. One is the revival of choral singing that dates back to the time of the Popular Front of the mid-1930's. The other is the funeral note, the memorializing of those killed in military action and of those who have lost their lives as hostages or as active resisters to tyranny. All the non-collaborating dead are considered martyrs to the cause of freedom. And artists who have survived trying times seem eager to honor those whose personal sacrifice and courage have recreated, at least temporarily, the dignity of man.

490

The high position that Olivier Messiaen holds among the young in France, and even among his elders, is an expression of the same spirit. Leader of *La Jeune France*, a group formed in the 1930's of young composers who admitted openly to a religious orientation of thought, professor at the Paris Conservatory and organist at the Church of the Holy Trinity, this brilliant executant and abundant composer has become, in Darius Milhaud's absence, the chief rallying point of the younger creative spirits in French music. His recent emergence as a national figure corresponds to that preoccupation with spiritual grandeurs that has seemed more appropriate to many, during the last decade's visible decline of France's temporal power, than the cultivation of sensual delicacies and poetic refinements that was characteristic of French music in the preceding epoch.

He represents thus the serious-minded intellectual tradition of the Church and of the universities rather than the more witty and worldly one of the literary salons, the poet-and-picture-dealers' conspiracy, and the luxury trades. He is not even involved with Marxism. He is a sort of cultural fundamentalist. And whether this position represents in the France of today a reactionary influence remains to be seen. In any case, it is the position of the Conservatory and of the universities. The Marxists, who run the radio, are frankly demagogic, the operatic establishments and the orchestras maintaining a respectable, if not very exciting, policy of detached bourgeois liberalism.

Two brochures sent me by Pvt. Lincoln Kirstein deal with one of the noblest of all French musical traditions, namely, that of organ building. *Les Clicquot, facteurs d'orgues du Roy*, by Norbert Dufourcq (Librairie Floury, 1942), is the history of a family of organ builders that, from around 1670 to 1785, designed, executed, and curated some of the finest organs in France. Several of these are still in use, those of Saint-Nicholas-des-Champs and of Saint-Merry in Paris having been restored in our time from the original specifications, those of the Abbey of Souvigny and of the Cathedral of Poitiers having survived intact. Others, like that of the Palace chapel at Versailles, have been reconstructed. All form part of that unique heritage that has enabled the organ to survive into our time as a major musical instrument in the one country where the tradition of its design as a serious musical instrument was never really lost.

The other brochure, also by Dufourcq, deals with the most recently built of France's great instruments, the organ at the Palais de Chaillot. This largest and newest of the Paris concert halls was completed in 1937, replacing the unlamented Trocadéro of 1878 in a new architectural layout of the whole hill that dominates from the Right Bank of the Seine the Eiffel Tower and the Champ de Mars. The new organ, an eighty-stop instrument, employs many pipes from the one that Aristide Cavaillé-Coll had installed in the original Trocadéro. Completed in 1938 and fully adjusted only in the following year, it was not till after the armistice of 1940 that it began the brilliant career as a solo instrument that has revealed to French music lovers in a time of national mourning a vast repertory of great music and that has drawn to an instrument formerly considered to be the prize among musical bores the enthusiasm of a whole youthful generation.

The most novel element of this instrument's design consists in the placement of the whole organ, which weighs seventy tons, in a metal cage that can be closed away from public view at the back of the stage by a metal curtain or moved forward on tracks a distance of some forty feet. The work of Cavaillé-Coll, soundest of the nineteenth-century organ builders, and of V. and F. Gonzalez, expert among modern restorers of ancient instruments, this organ represents, like the new organ at the Church of Saint Mary the Virgin in New York, the maximum available today of classical scholarship and of modern convenience. And just as the cases and façades of the historic organs of France are more often than not examples of the finest decorative art from their respective periods, this one presents to the eye, with its row upon row of exposed pipes in functional geometric arrangement, a matchless piece of contemporary design.

April 1, 1945

Olivier Messiaen

"Atomic bomb of contemporary music" is the current epithet for Olivier Messiaen. Whether France's thirty-seven-year-old boy wonder is capable of quite so vast a work of destruction as that unhappy engine I could not say. But certainly he has made a big noise in the world. And the particular kind of noise that his music makes does, I must say, make that of his chief contemporaries sound a bit old-fashioned.

What strikes one right off on hearing almost any of his pieces is the power these have of commanding attention. They do not sound familiar; their textures—rhythmic, harmonic, and instrumental—are fresh and strong. And though a certain melodic banality may put one off no less than the pretentious mysticism of his titles may offend, it is not possible to come in contact with any of his major productions without being aware that one is in the presence of a major musical talent. Liking it or not is of no matter; Messiaen's music has a vibrancy that anybody can be aware of, that the French music world is completely aware of, that has been accepted in France, indeed, for the postwar period as, take it or leave it, one of the facts of life.

Messiaen's pieces are mostly quite long; and their textures, rhythmic and harmonic, are complex. In spite of their length and their complexity their sounds are perfectly clear. They are nowhere muddy in color but always sonorous. Their shining brightness takes one back to Berlioz. So also does their subject matter. "Dance of Fury for the Seven Trumpets," "The Rainbow of Innocence," "Angel with Perfumes," "The Crystal Liturgy," "Subtlety of the Body in Glory," "Strength and Agility of the Body in Glory," "God with Us," and "Vocal Exercise for the Angel Who Announces the End of Time" are some of the simpler subtitles. And the renderings of these are no less picturesque than Berlioz's descriptions of doomsday (in the Dies Iræ of his Requiem Mass) for chorus and full orchestra plus twenty-eight trumpets and trombones and fourteen kettledrums.

Messiaen is a full-fledged romantic. Form is nothing to him, content everything. And the kind of content that he likes is the convulsive, the ecstatic, the cataclysmic, the terrifying, the unreal. That the imagery of this should be derived almost exclusively from religion is not surprising in a church organist and the son of a mystical poetess, Cécile Sauvage. What is a little surprising in so scholarly a modernist (he is organist at the cultivated parish of La Trinité and a professor of harmony at the Paris Conservatory) is the literalness of his religious imagination. But there is no possibility of suspecting insincerity. His pictorial concept of religion, though a rare one among educated

men, is too intense to be anything but real. Messiaen is simply
a theologian with a taste for the theatrical. And he dramatizes
theological events with all the *sang-froid* and all the elaborateness of a man who is completely at home in the backstage of
religious establishments.

The elaborateness of Messiaen's procedures is exposed in
detail in a two-volume treatise by him called *The Technique
of My Musical Language* (*Technique de mon langage musical*;
Alphonse Leduc, Paris, 1944). The rhythmic devices employed,
many of them derived from Hindu practice, are most sophisticated. The harmonic language is massively dissonant but not
especially novel. It resembles rather the piling of Ossa on Pelion
that formerly characterized the work of Florent Schmitt. There
are layer cakes of rhythms and of harmonies but there is little
linear counterpoint. The instrumentation is admirably designed
to contrast these simultaneities and to pick them out. Derived
from organ registration, it exploits the higher brilliancies (as of
mixture stops) to great advantage. The weaker elements of
Messiaen's style are his continuity, which, like that of many
another organist-composer, is improvisational rather than structural, and his melodic material, which is low in expressivity. The
themes are lacking in the tensile strength necessary to sustain
long developments because of his predilection for weak intervals, especially the major sixth and the augmented fourth, and
for contradictory chromatics.

Among the works which one hopes will soon be heard in
New York are *Forgotten Offerings* (*Les Offrandes oubliées*) for
orchestra, by which Messiaen became known way back in 1935,
I think it was, as a major talent, and *The Nativity of Our Lord*,
nine meditations for organ, published in 1936. These pieces
have charm and youth in them and a striking virtuosity of texture. Among the more recent works of some length are *Seven
Visions of the Amen*, for two pianos; *Twenty Admirations of the
Infant Jesus* (unless I mistranslate *Vingt Regards sur l'enfant
Jésus*), for solo piano; *Three Short Liturgies of the Divine Presence*
(they last a good half-hour, all the same), for women's voices
and orchestra; and a *Quartet for the End of Time*, which was
composed during his German captivity.

The most satisfactory of these works to me is the two-piano

work. The most impressive to the general public, however, is the orchestral one, which was first presented last April at a concert of *La Pléiade* in the Salle du Conservatoire. I have heard a recording of these liturgies, made from a subsequent broadcast under the direction of Roger Désormière; and though certainly they have a spasmodic flow (and no little monotony) they do make a wonderful noise.

The instrumentation, though top-heavy, is utterly glittering. It consists of vibraphone, celesta, maracas, gong, tam-tam, nine sopranos singing in unison, piano, *les ondes Martenot* (a form of theremin), and strings. The three sections are entitled: "Antiphon of Interior Conversation (God present in us . . .)," "Sequence of The Word, Divine Canticle (God present in Himself . . .)," and "Psalm of the Ubiquity of Love (God present in all things . . .)." The text employed by the singers is of Messiaen's composition, as were also program notes printed on the occasion of the first performance. Of the "Antiphon" he writes:

"Dedicated to God present within us through Grace and the Holy Communion. After a most tender beginning ('My Jesus, My Silence, Abide with Me'), accompanied by the songs of distant birds (on the piano), there follows a contrapuntal middle section of great polyrhythmic and polymodal refinement. ('The Yes which sings like an echo of light.' 'Red and lavender melody in praise of The Father.' 'Your hand is out of the picture by one kiss.' 'Divine landscape, reverse your image in water.')"

All these are clearly a believing organist's ideas. César Franck and Anton Bruckner, though neither had Messiaen's humor, worked from just such preoccupations. I once described this religio-musical style as the determination to produce somewhere in every piece an apotheosis destined to open up the heavens and to bring down the house. Certainly the latter action is easier to accomplish in modern life than the first. And certainly Messiaen has accomplished it several times in the *Liturgies.* The success of his accomplishment is due to a natural instinct for making music plus the simplicity and sincerity of his feelings. These are expressed, moreover, through a musical technique of great complexity and considerable originality. The faults of his taste are obvious; and the traps of mystical program music, though less so, are well known to musicians, possibly even to himself. Nevertheless the man is a great composer. One has only to hear his music beside that of any of the standard eclectic modernists to know that. Because his really vibrates and theirs doesn't.

September 23, 1945

Lively St. Francis

MANUEL ROSENTHAL's oratorio *Saint Francis of Assisi*, which I have been listening to of late through gramophone recordings of its original broadcast of France's National Radio under the composer's direction, is one of the most striking and picturesque musical works of our time. Composed in 1937, 1938, and 1939, it was first performed in November of last year; and though its repercussion in musical circles, both lay and professional, has been considerable, the slowness of publication procedures and the difficulties of international traffic in general have retarded the propagation of a work that in more normal times would certainly have begun already to be heard around the world. Indeed, since Arthur Honegger's piece of twenty-five years back about a type of railway locomotive, *Pacific 231*, I have not encountered a musical *grande machine* so obviously built to travel.

The biography of the Saint is recounted in speech and through choral recitative. His major moments are described by orchestral set pieces. The program of these runs as follows: "Prayer," "Youth," "The Kiss to the Leper," "Saint Clara," "Sermon to the Birds," "Hymn to the Sun," "The Angelic Kithara," "The Grand Miracle" (of the stigmata), "Death," and "The Choiring Angels" (or "Chorus Angelicus"). Certain of these numbers are more vividly picturesque than others, but all are displays of orchestral workmanship of the highest virtuosity and of the most ingenious fancy. And though Mr. Rosenthal's use of the vibraphone and of an electronic instrument somewhat like our theremin known as "*les ondes Martenot*" (rather a favorite with the contemporary French) is not without a certain vulgarity of effect, his musical textures are notable for the purity of their design.

By purity I mean honesty and straightforwardness. Basing his pictorial descriptions on orchestral device alone, he has chosen at all times melodic material, harmonic filling, and contrapuntal device of the plainest nature, formed his musical phrases, as Berlioz did, for what he wishes the whole to imitate or evoke rather than for the expression of personal lyricism or for the striking of any classic poetical attitude. The sounds he uses, like the colors of an impressionist's palette, determine the nature of his drawing, which in itself on the score page is about as neutral, as subservient to the coloristic effect as could be imagined.

The piece that depicts the Saint in his roistering youth is a serenade of plucked instruments interrupted by street fighting and by dancing. "The Kiss to the Leper" imitates the sound of ancient church organs, with all the strings divided into four, five, and six parts to recall composite organ stops, and woodwinds playing in hollow double octaves, while three trumpets, played very softly with the Ball mute, give a lifelike effect of the higher mixtures. "Saint Clara" is a bell piece, with big bells, little bells, loud bells, every kind of bell in the world, all sounding at once by means of musical suggestion and acoustic imitation.

The "Sermon to the Birds" is perhaps the most astonishing auditory evocation of all. Certainly the twittering of our feathered neighbors is not a new subject in music any more than bells are. But no such deafening bird noise as Rosenthal's have I ever heard outside a zoo. The "Hymn to the Sun," which I take for a representation of sunlight, is less striking than the auditory evocations. But the sound of the angelic popular music that Saint Francis once heard in a dream (after Brother Pacificus had refused to play the kithara for him out of scruples about light-mindedness) is a delicious concert of mandolins and lutes. "The Miracle of the Stigmata" and the "Saint's Death," sober pieces not unlike the opening "Prayer," lead up to a final "Chorus Angelicus," which represents a jostling of hallelujahs rather like what one hears when several military bands are parading all within hearing distance.

The work should not be difficult to give in New York, because the purely orchestral sections, though requiring exact rehearsal, are not beyond the powers of a good American orchestra; and the choral parts, partly in Latin and partly in French, are not difficult at all, save in the "Chorus Angelicus," which lies a bit high. The French choral recitatives could even be translated with little alteration of their rhythm patterns; and I think on the whole such a procedure would be of advantage to the full understanding of a work that seems destined to enjoy a season or two, at least, of real popularity. Make no mistake about it; Rosenthal's *Saint Francis* has not one drop of mystical content. It is a realistic picture, both touching and vivid, of real events. At least they seem real as one listens. And though the work lasts in performance some fifty minutes, at no point did your hardened reporter find his interest in it less than complete.

September 16, 1945

The Vacant Chair

VIEWING the French musical scene in close-up, one is impressed with the cardinal importance to it of him who is absent; of the central position in the picture that is being reserved for the return of Darius Milhaud. Just as Ravel before him, and Debussy before that, was in the eyes of all beholders clearly the first composer of his country, Milhaud's primacy is no less obvious than theirs in a landscape that is no less copiously adorned by figures of considerable brilliance.

These figures are of three functions—the academic, the impressive, and the poetical. The academics, the standard masters of the borrowing procedure, are Jacques Ibert and Jean Rivier. The work of such men is never very commanding and rarely wholly offensive. It usually passes for well written, and indeed its presence is a mark of the higher musical civilizations. It has to be there if only as an example to the young of the ultimate futility of knowledge as a point of departure toward style.

The composers whose chief aim is impressiveness, the hit-'em-between-the-eyes-and-knock-'em-over boys, are in descending order of seniority Arthur Honegger, Manuel Rosenthal, and Olivier Messaien. Masters of the picturesque and of the obviously striking, these authors are at their best in the sort of oratoriolike number for complex musical forces that was Berlioz's invention and that has always been dear to the heart of the Paris (as also the London) musical public.

Jeanne au búcher (*Joan at the Stake*) and *La Danse des morts* (*The Dance of the Dead*), both written to texts by Paul Claudel, are Honegger's latest creations in the genre. We heard another in New York a few years back called *Nicolas de Flue*, on a nationalistic Swiss poem by Denis de Rougemont. *Jeanne au bûcher*, first given in Brussels and in Paris before the war, with Ida Rubinstein speaking the lead, is still a successful work. And *La Danse des morts*, of more recent composition, has been recorded commercially.

Rosenthal's *St. Francis of Assisi* and Messaien's *Three Short Liturgies of the Divine Presence* have been described recently in this column. Rosenthal's equally sensational *Musique de table*, which describes such succulent dishes as stewed eels and venison, I have not yet had occasion to hear. All these works are examples of program music pushed to its, for the present at least, ultimate assertion. Their authors are specialists of the objectively grandiose and of the striking. None of them has ever shown himself apt at personal lyricism.

The poetical writers in France are still Francis Poulenc, whose songs and choral pieces are tops in our time; Georges Auric, whose film music is the most apt in the world (he is doing Shaw's *Caesar and Cleopatra*, for England at the moment); and Henri Sauguet, whose short opera *La Gageure imprévue* (after an eighteenth-century comedy by Sedaine) and ballet *Les Forains*, both produced last season, are his latest and most impeccable gifts to the theater of delicacy. His string quartet and piano concerto, both begun before the war, have since been completed. The latter is recorded, I believe. Sauguet's full length opera *La Chartreuse de Parme*, which was produced during the season of 1938–9 and removed from the repertory during the German occupation because of its librettist's religion, has not yet been restored to production.

Among the newer composers in a lyrical and poetic vein the most skillful is Henry Barraud, whose chamber music is delightfully embroidered and who seems from the ballet I have heard, *Le Diable à la kermesse* (*The Devil at the Fair*), to have considerable theatrical force. Of grander pathos (and indeed rather wonderfully lugubrious) are the works of André Jolivet, a member of Messaien's original *La Jeune France* group. His *Trois Complaintes du soldat* for baritone, text by himself, are deeply touching as expression and original. There is also an evocative and ghostly work after Poe's *Eleonora* for four woodwinds, trumpets, harp, *les ondes Martenot* and strings, by Yves Baudrier, another member of *La Jeune France*. The fourth of these gifted and highly serious young men is Daniel-Lesur, whose *Pastorale variée* (from 1937) for a similar though not identical combination of instruments, is delicately conceived but a little jerkily paced and whose *Suite française* for piano is a lovely piece.

Darius Milhaud fits into this picture as the great man who dominates all the categories. His is no limited palette; he works in all the styles save that which is forbidden to genius, the eclectic one. His *grandes machines, Les Choréophores* (after Æschylus), *Maximilien*, and *Christophe Colomb* (both after Claudel), are no less impressive than Honegger's and far more humane. His ballets are both bright and sensitive. His religious works are deeply serious. His light operas are completely gay. His orchestral works are comparable with the noblest of our century. His twelve string quartets are models of the intimate poetic style. And his opera *Bolívar* (on a play by Jules Supervielle), as yet unproduced, will probably, if my acquaintance with its score entitles me to place a bet, constitute the crowning glory of a great career.

Milhaud has written music in all the kinds and for all the occasions. Some of it, as is inevitable with so fecund a workman, is inferior in quality. But the amount of it in all the kinds that is of the first quality is sufficient alone to denominate him as a master. And the variety alone of the occasions for which he has produced work of the first quality places him as the most ample among living masters. No amount of professional intrigue can conceal a matter of patent fact. That is why, in spite of all the brilliant figures now occupying the musical scene in France, there is a vacancy in the center of the stage. Neither Honegger nor Rosenthal nor Messaien, for all their spectacular qualities, can fill it. Nor can Sauguet, for all his delicacy and tenderness, be quite sufficient for the place. And so everybody is working busily and beautifully at writing music for the repertory adorning, to change the metaphor, France's musical house—already and by far the richest of our century—in view of what all musical France hopes will not be too long delayed, the return of its master—Darius Milhaud.

September 30, 1945

Pelléas *and* Pénélope

O$_N$ Election Day in the afternoon, October 21, the Opéra-Comique gave a perfect performance of what all musical France esteems its most perfect operatic monument, Debussy's *Pelléas et Mélisande*. On the following day it was my pleasure to hear at the Opéra an excellent performance of a far from perfect work, but one that is nevertheless inspired by such a deep instinct for rectitude of expression that it nobly merits honor as a lost cause, Fauré's *Pénélope*.

The latter is all wrong from a theatrical point of view, but it is musically beautiful. Its poem, by René Fauchois, nowadays an experienced and successful playwright (New York admired ten years ago his *Prenez garde à la Peinture* under the title of *The Late Christopher Bean*), is not striking as either literature or drama. Its music, moreover, by a master of the recital song, is intimately expressive but without breadth of line. It creates no ambiance, no atmosphere, no excitement, delineates no character, paints no scene. It is recital music orchestrated, and not by its own composer at that. For Fauré, who was not a master of orchestration, customarily farmed out this privilege to friends and commercial hacks.

Its timing is all wrong, too. The action, thin enough at best, is stretched out for musical purposes to such lengths, though the opera itself is not a long one, that the actors are left for most of the time standing around with nothing to do but sing. Or worse, waiting for it to be their turn to sing. Moreover, in all three acts a chorus is almost constantly present on the stage without singing at all. It murmurs here and there a chord, but it never plays any musical role commensurate with its dramatic function. The vocalized conversation that makes up the opera is impeccably prosodied and of the utmost musical beauty. But the whole is essentially a *pasticcio* of Fauré songs, without contrast or dramatic progression. And the orchestral accompaniment, though far from ugly, fails wholly to support or to create a dramatic line.

The performance I heard was conducted with real sensitivity by François Ruhlmann. Suzanne Juyol, in the title role, displayed a dramatic soprano voice of rich color. Her musical artistry might well have appeared as equally striking if it had not been overshadowed by the literally perfect style and emission of the tenor Georges Jouatte, who sang Ulysses. Such beauty of voice, of diction, and of phraseology, such refinement of musical utterance at all the levels of pitch and of power, is unique, to my knowledge, on the contemporary musical stage. One wishes that all vocalists, all musicians, all music lovers could know this impeccable workmanship and cherish in their memories forever the proof that singing in public is an art and not a stunt.

Debussy's *Pelléas et Mélisande* has, as music, every beauty that *Pénélope* has, with none of its faults. It has atmosphere, continuity, shape, style, and progress. It delineates character and tells a story. That story, moreover, the play itself, by Maurice Maeterlinck, is literature. It, too, has atmosphere, continuity, shape, style, and progress. The marriage of the literary and musical elements in Debussy's opera is one of the miracles of the modern world. There has been nothing like it since Mozart. And it is indeed touching that a state theater should celebrate France's first national election day in more than nine years and the anticipated birth of her Fourth Republic by the perfect performance of a work that may well go down in history as the chief artistic monument of her Third.

The perfection of that performance was due to the precise and loving care of the conductor, Roger Désormière. The vocal rendering under his direction was no less notable than the instrumental for its respect toward both the letter and the spirit of the work and for the observance of the musical amenities in general. The cast consisted of, on this occasion: Janine Micheau, as Mélisande; Renée Gilly, as Geneviève; Christiane Gaudel, as Yniold; Willy Clément, as Pelléas; Henri Etcheverry, as Golaud, and Henri Médus, as Arkel, with Jean Vieuille and Maurane singing the minor roles of the Doctor and of the Shepherd. Both the leading singers were appearing in this work for the first time.

Miss Micheau was impeccable both vocally and stylistically, though a little more statuesque in action than one might have wished. Mr. Clément, a very young man, revealed a warm tenor voice of great beauty and sound schooling. Miss Gilly and Miss Gaudel, Messrs. Etcheverry and Médus were all that one could wish for musically; and certainly in this work one wishes for a great deal. As dramatic action the performance had little warmth; it was almost oratoriolike, in fact, by its dignity and by its employment of minimum gesture. I suppose this is what happens to works that become national monuments. The concept is a legitimate one of a *Pelléas* all stylized and medieval and far away. But the *Pelléas* of Garden and Dufranne and certain tenors who really acted, including our own Edward Johnson, was warmer and more vigorously dramatic.

As for the auditory performance, I have never heard a lovelier one. I have never heard the work read with such clear rhythm and such sure progress and at the same time such complete orchestral transparency. The string sounds were like nothing in this world that has substance. Even the wind harmonies floated in the air like veils, the simplest phrase of bassoon or clarinet like an almost imperceptible sigh. Nothing was muffled. The instrumental timbres, in fact, as they should be in a proper Debussy rendering, even when the composer's coloration is somber, were light and clean. What gave them their ideal consistency is the fact that under Désormière's firmly delicate stick they were without weight, as without obscurity. To have achieved so luminous a texture without any softening up of Debussy's rapier-steel rhythm or any clouding of the vocal enunciation places Roger Désormière, long known as a precision workman, among the very great musicians of our time and among the great French conductors of all time.

He recorded three years ago, during the German occupation (but with no political collaboration involved), the entire opera. When shipping becomes available for cultural exchanges, American collectors will no doubt be acquiring these albums, though they are already hard to get here. I have not heard the disks myself; but if they approach in quality his rendering of the opera in the pit, they must long provide a model to musicians of what *Pelléas* should and can be made to sound like, namely, the most beautiful and the most monumental work for the musical theater in all the modern world.

November 4, 1945

Méhul's Joseph

Etienne-Henri Méhul's *Joseph*, which was revived at the Opéra on Friday, June 7, is one of the most famous stage works in the world and one of the least familiar to present-day audiences. Composed in 1806 and first presented to the Parisian public in February 1807, it enjoyed a wide popularity in Germany for several years before the French discovered that they had a classic on their hands. Its last Paris revival in dramatic form took place in 1896. There were two concert performances in 1935 at the Salle du Conservatoire. It was for these last that Henri Rabaud composed the recitatives used in the present production. The work in its original form was not a grand opera at all, but an *opéra-comique*, with spoken dialogue.

Alexandre Duval's poem is not, however, at any point comic. Nor does it tell a love story. It simply narrates, in somewhat pastoral vein, the story of Joseph and his brethren. The music of Méhul's score is straightforward in style, quite without displays of local color, noble but not pompous, varied in expression, and remarkably touching. The characters, when they sing, have life in them; and they express themselves with an astonishing simplicity. There is not a vocal high note or arpeggio in the whole opera. But its musical composition is not, for all that, unsophisticated. There is, indeed, in Méhul's music a contrapuntal life that is lacking in that of Gluck, his master, and that gives to his simplest hymn or romanza an intrinsic musical interest that supports the expressivity of the whole without thickening the texture.

The unobtrusiveness of Méhul's musical mastery is particularly advantageous to the ensemble pieces, where the individuality of the different characters is preserved at no sacrifice to apparent simplicity. The chorus of Joseph's brothers, for example, is a notable piece of contrapuntal writing without any of the baroque or rococo ornateness that we are used to associate with the contrapuntal style. The whole opera, in fact, like many another triumph of fine French workmanship, is deceptively plain. And it achieves by a masterful but abstemious use of the more elaborate musical procedures a humanity of expression that is as sweet today as it was nearly a century and a half ago.

Méhul's career as a composer, which covered the years 1787 to 1817, comprised the Revolution, the Directory, the First Empire, and Napoleon's fall. His style, which was formed in the Revolutionary years, is comparable to the neoclassic manner in architecture and decoration that was practiced contemporaneously in France and that we call in America the "Federal style." A republican simplicity was its ideal; clean, light colors were its taste; the Rights of Man was its Bible. Méhul, Gossec, and Cherubini perfected the style together. Though they all left handsome works behind them, the style itself did not survive the Bourbon Restoration. The dynamism of Beethoven and the violence of Berlioz made it seem, by comparison, picayune to the Romantic age. It is a noble style, all the same, and one that has left its ideals of personal modesty and of professional perfection on the tradition of the Paris Conservatory, where all three masters worked, and where they left their perhaps most lasting mark on music.

Méhul's *Joseph* is not passionate and grand, like Beethoven's *Fidelio*, nor fun, like Rossini's *Barber of Seville*, though as a professional job it is probably superior to either. It is a quiet piece and a well-nigh perfect one. It remains after a hundred and forty years one of the sweetest in all dramatic literature. Its revival just now, in a period of musical, as well as of political, unrest, was a more than merely bright idea on the part of the Opéra's directors. It seems to point a moral to the effect that art, at least, can be efficient without having recourse to sensational measures. The appropriateness of its subject matter, too, which treats of displaced persons and Jewish resettlement, is inescapable.

The performance is a sweet one. Reynaldo Hahn conducts it in that restrained manner, virtually without dynamic accent, that the French call the "classical style." Edmond Rambaud, replacing on the opening night the indisposed Georges Jouatte, sang the tenor role of Joseph with the utmost of vocal grace and musical dignity. Charles Cambon, baritone, as the confidant Utobal, sang, as always, like a master. And the American Arthur Endrèze, though lacking nowadays ideal vocal resources, was a model of both vocal and dramatic elegance. Huguette St. Arnaud, who sang Benjamin, was a delight to eye and ear. And the decorations of Pierre Chéreau, though not unusual or striking, were pleasant to look at.

The opera was paired on the opening night with a ballet divertissement called *Suite in White* (*Suite en Blanc*), danced to music from Edouard Lalo's *Namouna*. The execution of the girls, particularly that of Miss Bardin and of Miss Vaussard, was pretty high-class, that of the men disappointing. Lalo's music is utterly delightful; and its musical performance, directed by

Roger Désormière, was the finest piece of musical work, bar none, that I have heard this trip. Indeed, to match it for precision, clarity, inner animation, and beauty of tone, all the qualities that make the difference between conducting and mere reading, I am obliged to go back to a performance heard at the Opéra-Comique last fall of Debussy's *Pelléas et Mélisande*, also led by Désormière. No other opera company with which I am acquainted has conducting to offer that is comparable in either beauty or efficiency to Désormière's. As for what most ballet troupes give us nowadays as orchestral accompaniment, especially in America, the best that can be said is that it seems to presuppose a public wholly visual-minded.

June 23, 1946

Thaïs *with Géori-Boué*

GÉORI-BOUÉ's return to the Paris Opéra in Massenet's *Thaïs* on Monday evening, June 3, after eight months' absence, was greeted by an impressive audience demonstration. Indeed, few French lyric artists have Miss Boué's natural gift for provoking displays of audience gratitude. She is young, well under thirty, beautiful, and a great actress; and although her vocal resources are by no means under control, these are enormous and in their ensemble most striking.

Training in the provinces, without benefit of the Paris Conservatory or of the great private studios, this remarkable Miss made her operatic debut less than five years ago at Toulouse, from which city she came directly to the capital. As wife of the tenor Roger Bourdin, with whom she frequently appears in recital, she has had access to the subtleties of French vocal style. Actually, save for the lack of that assured vocal perfection that almost nobody ever achieves nowadays under forty, she is a more absorbing operatic performer both to watch and to listen to than almost any other now appearing before the public.

Her voice is a strong lyric one with the range and agility of a coloratura. Its timbre is bright, in loud passages almost trumpetlike. Loud passages are not, however, what Miss Boué does best. It is in these that she sings off pitch occasionally and is often unpleasantly brilliant. She does not force; she does not need to do that with a voice that is naturally penetrating and that attains without effort heights that for another might be precarious. She simply is not yet firmly schooled in the classical, the proper way to sing both high and loud.

In all the kinds of singing that lie below the ultimate of loudness she is most skillful. Her mezza voce in all ranges is sweet and quite without the banality that characterizes the middle intensities of most operatic singing. And her pianissimo is unique. It has been many years since one has heard anyone sing so softly, so clearly, and withal so easily. The sound is objective, no crooning involved; and her words are heard in every part of the house. Indeed, Miss Boué's diction is of the kind one dreams about but hasn't heard in a theater practically since Mary Garden.

There is, in fact, a great deal about the work of this pint-size redhead that recalls that of Garden, as the Scottish beauty must have looked and sounded in the earliest years of her career. Whether Garden ever had such a natural glory of voice, I do not know; certainly she did not have it in 1911, when I first heard her. And whether she ever sang so badly in public as Miss Boué, on any evening, is likely to do, I doubt. But the two artists are of a type, musically gifted, physically beautiful, and with an instinct for the musical stage that is not only infallible as taste but in every way sensational in its effect upon the public.

So far Boué's chief roles have been Thaïs, Juliette (in Gounod's *Roméo et Juliette*) and the name part in Gounod's *Mireille*, all of them roles requiring dramatic skill, high notes, and a luminous personality. On the one occasion when I heard her it was the high notes that came off least well. Not because she doesn't possess them, but simply because she is young and courageous and sings a little wild.

All that is easily enough corrected by experience and a good trainer. Miss Boué shocks the devotees of sheer vocal opulence, just as Garden always did. She has a lovely voice, just as Garden did, too, perhaps a bigger and better one than Garden ever had, though it is less thoroughly schooled than Garden's. She uses it, moreover, to the same end, as an instrument of dramatic projection, not, for all its extraordinary qualities, as the subject of the evening's entertainment. One cannot avoid the conclusion, observing her work, that her faults are of no gravity at all beside the splendor of her qualities and that one is in the presence of a real star.

Paul Cabanel, who sang the baritone role of Athanael to

Miss Boué's Thaïs, has a fine, big voice, perfect diction, a noble singing style, and distinguished qualities as an actor. He will be heard, I understand, in America next season. The rest of the cast was most agreeable and the scenery excellent. As pacing, the musical direction was a shade pedestrian. The conductor, François Ruhlmann, observed tempos as close as is humanly possible to those prescribed in 1894 by the composer and carefully preserved since in the establishment. But in spite of the fervor of the two chief singers and all their ingenuity, the music never quite got going. And it is not stupid music, either. For all its thinness of texture, it is cleanly composed, melodically charming, and expressive.

The house itself has, of course, an architectural disadvantage in the great breadth of its orchestral pit that tends to slow up the effective speed of any musical execution. The singers are removed not only from the audience by a chasm too wide to bridge with personal warmth but from the conductor, as well, by a distance that diminishes his visibility to a point where the prompter is obliged to replace him for effective vocal leadership in delicate passages. This double direction tends to stiffen any performance, and long waits between scenes add nothing to dramatic animation.

Strict observance of traditional tempos, too, though preferable to our Metropolitan's irresponsibility in this matter, gives nowadays to all performances at the Paris Opéra a pedagogical flavor, as of classics read rather than played. There is considerable misunderstanding these days on both sides of the ocean about the nature and value of musical traditions. The Paris Opéra has a whole library of recorded traditions; our Metropolitan has no library at all, even of scores. The advantages are probably in favor of Paris, in the long run, though not for the reason obvious. Because what is important about traditions and their preservation is not only that a given conductor should observe such of the recorded ones as please his fancy, since he cannot observe them all, but also that his deviations should be recorded, as evidence of his contribution to the history of the work. Mr. Ruhlmann seemed the other night to be making little contribution to such a record.

June 16, 1946

Purging the "Collabos"

Who collaborated with the enemy and what sanctions are being meted out to those who did are the subject of constant queries to reporters working in those European countries that were occupied during the war by German troops. A full answer is impossible, because no complete documentation exists or can exist till the purgings shall have been completed. These are being operated differently in each country and differently by various trades, professions, and social groups. They are being applied in France to the musical confraternity in the following manner:

Let us distinguish, to begin with, collaboration from treason. Any citizen who betrayed state secrets to the enemy, who denounced Communists, Jews, Allied agents, or members of local resistance movements or who by maladministration allowed works of art or other national wealth to fall into enemy hands is a traitor to his country and must be punished. Collaboration is more difficult to define and consequently to judge. It is doubtful, indeed, whether there is any basis in law for judging it at all. Certainly the facts are so confusing—because everybody has at some point or other made some compromise, and because even the most cynical among the "collabos" have all concealed Jews in their houses or helped French young people to avoid deportation —that no clear division is possible of sheep from goats.

Nevertheless, every social group and professional body feels the need of expressing its disapproval of those members whose conduct toward the enemy has been lacking in moral dignity, and of imposing some kind of punishment for this. Consequently, in those cases where the law does not apply (which means in the majority of cases), sanctions have been left to the social groups and professional bodies whose moral prestige has been lowered by such conduct. At the beginning a good deal of spontaneous direct action by the Resistance troops took place; but most of that has ceased now, and purging is orderly. It is not, however, a state action except in treason cases. The French have avoided, as far as possible, defining collaboration as a political crime, because that would have involved them in the very abuse of power that they hated most in the German and Vichy administrations, namely, political arrest.

There is today no legal hindrance to the public appearance of musicians who collaborated, excepting of those who are under provisional arrest. They can accept any engagement offered and they can organize any concert they wish, short of hiring for it state-owned premises, like the Théatre de l'Opéra. Even here the hindrance is one of administrative discretion, not of legality. There are certain things that are hard to do, however, such as to work for the state radio or for the state theaters. All the state theaters were purged a year ago by committees of their own members. Singers and instrumentalists formerly working at the Opéra, for instance, whose conduct has been judged unpatriotic by their own Musicians' Resistance Committee are not being allowed to work in that house for the present. The committee has not been oversevere. Every group, in fact, has tended toward tolerance in the judgment of its own members.

Every group has tended equally toward intolerance in judging the conduct of others. It is not the musicians and dancers, for instance, who are preventing the return to the Opéra ballet of Solange Schwartz and Jean Peretti and Serge Lifar. It is the stagehands' union, which threatens to strike every time the subject is broached. Since nobody wants a public controversy with so powerful a union on any subject (and particularly not on that one), the stagehands remain masters in fact of the situation, though purging musicians is properly no right of theirs, any more than purging the backstage is any right of the orchestra. The Soviet Embassy is at the moment, for reasons unknown, being kind to Lifar (a White Russian); and it seems likely that pressure from that source on the Communist cell within the stagehands' union may eventually bring about his return to the Opéra, for which there is considerable public demand. The orchestra of the Opéra-Comique has recently refused to perform a work by Marcel Delannoy which the management had planned to revive this fall, though the composer is under no formal ban of any kind, official or unofficial.

The musical profession and the musical public, at least in Paris, are eager to forget the whole collaboration story, if not to forgive, and to get back the use of music's full effectives, throwing just a few of its more outrageous sinners to the wolves of superpatriotic opinion. Already the cultural department of the Foreign Office is sending to England as propagandists for

French music many artists it does not dare yet to bless at home. And the composer Henry Barraud, musical director of the state radio, has on several occasions used artists who are on the radio's black list. He has used them because he needed them and because he considers the present procedure of radio black-listing to be unjust.

The radio purges have been the strictest of all, because they have been made not by musicians but by Resistance politicians, and because they follow a logical method. Playing publicly in the symphony orchestras involved no trading (technically) with the enemy, because these are co-operative associations. Neither did working at the state opera houses, because there one was employed by one's own government. (The stagehands are forgetting, however, in their present moralistic fervor that they accepted tips from Germans at the German-organized gala performances.) Performing at Radio-Paris, however, which was German-run, entailed open acceptance of money from the enemy, of working directly for him.

Now it happens that the bookkeeping of Radio-Paris is intact. So, instead of allowing the musicians' union or some similar professional body to make up the black lists, the government office in charge of the radio (I think it is the Ministry of Information) simply black-listed everybody who had ever received a check from Radio-Paris. The time an artist has to remain in Coventry is two weeks for each broadcast he made under the Germans. In some cases the period is brief; in others it mounts as high as seven years. In the case of choirs, quartets, dance bands, and other name groups only the leader is black-listed, because he is the one who received the money. There is no way of punishing the associates who broadcast with him, because their names are not on the Radio-Paris books.

The system, as you can see, is both logical and completely unfair. It is unfair because judgment has been imposed on artists by nonartists in a matter where no crime, but only professional misconduct, is charged. It is unfair also because it has chosen its scapegoats from lists that are not complete. And it is unfair because it has condemned, on a mere technicality, a very large part of the profession with a severity that neither the profession itself nor public opinion condones. The poor musician or entertainer who, in order to eat, occasionally performed French music (he was not allowed to perform German) at Radio-Paris may not be the noblest form of man. But to penalize him financially and morally, while not punishing at all the workers at state theaters who performed occasionally, under orders, German music that the French state paid for is one of the injustices that is bringing the whole operation of purging musician collaborators into disrepute. If the discussions of it that I have heard (and during my recent two months in Paris I heard many) indicate a general trend in French public opinion, I think that the purging of the artistic professions is likely to be dropped within another year and that practically everybody will be glad.

November 18, 1945

Orchestral Standards

AMERICAN SYMPHONY ORCHESTRAS differ from those of Europe chiefly by the high finish of their execution. Whether they offer many deeper perfections has long been a disputed question. Renewed contact with our Big Three of the Eastern seaboard, after a recent visit abroad during which I had occasion to work with several of the Paris associations, has brought to my mind certain further comparisons that are not wholly to our advantage.

Notable as a characteristic of contemporary American orchestral style is the systematic employment of forced tone, of overbowing and overblowing. Alone among our Eastern orchestras, that of Philadelphia has resisted this heresy. Western Europe, excepting, a little bit, Italy, has never subscribed to it. Paris, London, Vienna, and Berlin have always operated on the assumption that auditory beauty (and, indeed, expression) diminishes where forced tone begins. Brilliance rather than mere weight of sound has always been their ideal for loud passages, exaggerated dynamic impact being considered as a sort of bluff, a playing to the audience's grosser nervous and emotional reactions in lieu of making specific sense—what the theatrical world calls *ham*.

The French orchestras do not have our power of crescendo, even within the range of legitimate tone. At its best and still unforced, our loud playing is louder than theirs. This added power is due partly to the instruments employed. The fine Cremona fiddles that our players are able to afford are capable of a wider dynamic range, both loud and soft, than mediocre instruments can give. The B-flat trumpet, which we commonly employ, is also more powerful than the C and D trumpets beloved of the French. Another source of power is our indifference about exact balances of sound. We allow our first flute, first oboe, first trumpet, horn, or trombone to dominate his colleagues simply because he is usually a more accomplished player and able to produce by legitimate means a larger tone. All this adds to the decibel count, though not necessarily to richness of effect.

Our habit of constantly showing off the wind instrument soloists makes for an impoverishment of sound that is peculiarly American. A passage for three clarinets, oboes, or bassoons, for instance, always sounds here like a solo for the first desk, the other parts constituting merely his more or less harmonious shadow. And we almost never achieve the equilibrium in trumpet, horn, or trombone chords that is characteristic of even the most routine French playing. Identical training is partly responsible for the French superiority in this regard. Because musicians who produce the same kind of tone are able to blend, and consequently to harmonize, far more effectively than players who, however excellent individually, have been trained in different schools.

Thus it is that the French orchestras, like the singers of the French opera, make a more in-tune, a more harmonious music than ours do. In spite of the inferior conditions under which they work, their equilibration of complexities is more subtle, more clear, and more varied of texture. The finished product they present to the public is, however, not nearly so expensive sounding as ours. There are likely to be bad spots in any rendering, places where the whole thing goes higglety-pigglety for a moment, because low standards of living, undernourishment, and fatigue are unquestionably productive of inattention.

Many American soldiers have spoken to me about what they consider the low general standard of execution at the French orchestral concerts. Accustomed to a high polish in performance, they are shocked at its absence. The younger ones, of course, don't know that French taste has never considered a high polish essential to first-class workmanship. The French work from another premise. They work from the inside out, believing that correct phraseology, appropriately varied coloration, and exact balances, particularly among instruments of the same family, will produce live music and that live music needs no make-up. Its natural bloom is considered to be sufficient.

Europe should hear our Philadelphia Orchestra. Our still admirable Boston and our improved Philharmonic have also many delights to offer. And I do hope that the Paris Conservatory and London Philharmonic orchestras will come over and play for us. Europe has much to learn from us now, particularly the advantages to music of high economic standards. But we need to be reminded again about the relative importance of interior equilibrium in music as against luxury surfacing. Also of the increased expressivity that comes from eschewal of all passional camouflage, particularly that of forced tone. Indeed, a multiplicity of cultural visits, of which orchestral exchanges would be only one, seems to me the correct basis for rebuilding international artistic standards, which have suffered everywhere during the war far more, I think, than we like to admit.

November 25, 1945

Atonality in France

FRENCH MUSIC today presents a novel, and to many surprising, development, namely, the successful implantation on Gallic soil of Schönbergian atonality. By successful I do not mean that the public likes it. This kind of music is genuinely popular nowhere. I merely mean that it is being written in France by French composers, written skillfully and, within the composing fraternity, taken seriously.

Twelve-tone row atonality, invented in Austria during the first decade of this century and perfected there during the succeeding two, has since spread all over the world. A sort of musical Esperanto, it is current practically everywhere now except in Russia, where state policy discourages the recondite. In our hemisphere from Iceland to the Tierra del Fuego and in the western European enclave from Norway to Jerusalem and to Gibraltar, no country, no musical region now lacks its twelve-tone school. And if the cult seems to be dying out in the Austro-German regions that nurtured its beginnings, its adoption by France and

Italy, following on earlier successes in South America, means that this new language of Germanic origin has conquered the most unfriendly of all possible terrains, has taken root, indeed, at the very center and stronghold of the Latin tradition.

Schönberg's music has long been known in Paris to a few initiates, of course; and his *Pierrot Lunaire*, which Darius Milhaud gave there as early as 1922, has several times produced a striking effect at public concerts. So has Alban Berg's *Lyrische Suite*, for string quartet. But the other music of these masters has made slow progress in general acceptance by musical Paris. Its sincerity has long been acknowledged, but its acquaintance and real understanding have been postponed for some eventual rainy day.

That day seems now to have arrived, and the brighter young, reacting against an outmoded nationalism, are passionately involved with the new international style. Some embrace it, and some resist with vehemence. But all are having to deal with it, and many are practicing it with assiduity. It has ceased to be a curiosity and become a cause. And the principal persons available who actually learned its technical procedures in Vienna—Max Deutsch, a pupil of Schönberg, and the young René Leibowitz, who once had some lessons from Anton Webern—are enjoying a prestige as mentors that their somewhat literal and stiff adherence to the system's rules of composition would probably not have gained for them as composers.

The most pretentious of the young atonalists is Serge Nigg, a former pupil of Messiaen. He has written in the strict technique of the twelve-tone row a piano concerto that is far from easy to listen to but that is also a work of far from negligible ponderousness. No less ingenious and learned but more digestible as a musical dish is a Sonata for Flute and Piano by Pierre Boulez. This young man is the most brilliant, in my opinion, of all the Parisian under-twenty-fives. Whether he remains attached forever to "*la musique sérielle et dodécaphonique*," as the French term precise adherence to the twelve-tone-row syntax, he is bound to write interesting and lively music, because he has a talent for that. And the practice during formative years of the strictest counterpoint available to the modern world cannot fail to liberate by discipline the creative faculties of any genuinely gifted musician.

The attractions of the system are, I think, two. Its first delight is its seriousness. No composer primarily occupied with merely pleasing or with getting on in the world ever takes it up. It is not easy to listen to; no public likes it. Its adoption is proof that one wishes to write music for music's own sake and that one is willing to sacrifice money and quick fame to that end. One can accuse the twelve-toners of scholasticism, but no one can say they are not consecrated. Its practice has literally no meretricious success to offer anybody.

Its second fascination is its dangerousness. It presents all the charms and all the perils of logic, of complete consistency. Consistency can lead artists to high triumphs of style, but it can also lead them into sterility of expression. Nobody knows yet whether consistent atonality is a new road to expressivity or an impasse of noncommunication. With the Austrians it has been a fair medium for the communication of limited sentiments. Outside of Austria it has so far remained pretty closely involved with the sort of psychoanalytic depiction of intimate sentiments that was its chief expressive achievement in Vienna. If any nation in the world can enlarge this music's scope, that is the French. They should be able to give it sweetness, lightness, charm, ease, and to adapt it even more successfully to the theater than Alban Berg has done in *Lulu*. (His *Wozzeck*, though highly chromatic, is not a twelve-tone work.)

The discipline should have a good effect on French music, too, which is in danger right now of falling into eclecticism of style. French music needs tightening up both in thought and in technique. And the international atonal style needs loosening up. Its expressivity is too tenuous, too introspective, too hopelessly standardized; and its technical practice lacks freedom. The French are good about freedom and good about objectivity. The Italian atonalists are already adding to standard practice that gracious and soaring lyric line that has long been the joy of Italian music. If the French can add to the new idiom precision of thought, taste, drama, and the power of evocation, the twelve-tone world will seem less oppressive to music lovers than it does just now.

Atonality is the last of the modernisms remaining unacceptable to the general public. Straussian expressionismus, Debussyan impressionism, the dissonant neoclassic style, and the neoromantic rounded contours are all a part of standard musical language. Even the symphony-orchestra public, the last bastion of lay conservatism, takes them as normal. If the French can't make an airplane that will fly with the twelve-tone syntax, nobody can. But if they succeed in doing so, then the last battle of modernism will have been won; and our century can enter on its second half with no regrets. A modern classic period will no doubt then ensue, with everybody writing in an amalgamated modern style. A very few years more should suffice to determine whether the twelve-tone manner is to be part of this or not.

October 27, 1946

State and Private Radio

RADIO-LUXEMBOURG is the only major broadcasting station in Europe that is privately owned. Before the war, there were a number of such stations, the most successful in western Europe, besides Luxembourg, being one in Athlone, Eire, and Radio-Normandie at Fécamp.

The chief *raison d'être* of these stations was the broadcasting of advertising matter in English, though accounts involving German and French were not refused. Today there is a certain amount of advertising, largely local, to be heard over the European air; but it comes from government-owned stations reduced to this expedient in order to keep alive. There is advertising with the programs of the largely French-government-owned stations in Monaco and in Andorra and with a few of those that come from Toulouse. Italian state broadcasting is supported almost wholly by this means.

Outside these exceptions, however, all radio in Europe is state radio, whether operated directly by a government, as in France and Belgium, where it is a function of the Information Ministry; by a special agency virtually indistinguishable from the government, like the British Broadcasting Corporation; or by a private corporation working under government directives, as in Sweden.

Before the war, France permitted the existence of commercial stations, along with government-owned ones, and granted them wave lengths; but nowadays in that country broadcasting is a state monopoly, exactly as it is in Britain, Ireland, Spain, Portugal, the Low Countries, Finland, Czechoslovakia, Poland, the Balkan states, and the Soviet Union. In occupied regions it is run by the occupying power. The British and the American armies also operate continental networks that serve their troops.

Luxembourg remains unique. Here a private company, chiefly owned in France, runs the station as a concession, annually paying the Duchy a part of its profits from advertising. At the moment the profits are not large, the most impressive account being Coca-Cola, which offers during the winter a weekly program by the Luxembourg Radio Symphony Orchestra; the concert is performed publicly at the same time. The station has been running for the last year chiefly on money paid during the previous year for its loan to the United States Army.

Nevertheless, the station is considered in business circles to be a good investment; and an Anglo-American group is thought to be trying to buy the plant and its broadcasting concession from the French owners. Winston Churchill's visit to the Duchy in July was explained to your reporter as having to do with this attempt. But regardless whether the ownership changes in the next few years, there is supposed to be money for somebody in Europe's one station that is devoted to the art of making friends for commercial products and influencing people to buy them. And this in spite of the fact that the station, formerly known as "the pirate of the air," has never had an official wave length assigned it by the international commission that regulates such matters.

Operating for the present on a limited budget, the musical director, Henri Pensis, back from the United States to his prewar post, has assembled a symphony orchestra that is surprisingly efficient and that plays programs of musical distinction equal to any in Europe. The city of Luxembourg offers, too, a string quartet that is usable for chamber-music broadcasts. Otherwise the programs are much like those of any other commercial station. There are news reports, light opera, dance music, and folklore of the Stephen Foster school arranged after the manner of André Kostelanetz or of Morton Gould. It is hoped soon to introduce a European version of the soap opera. Through polling procedures similar to those employed in America, the management keeps itself informed of the approximate number of listeners in France, Britain, and elsewhere.

State broadcasting operates on a quite different premise. Its purpose is not the mass sale of inexpensive products but the spreading of information and education. At its worst, state radio goes in for mendacious political propaganda. The German stations were notorious sinners in this regard, and the Yugoslav station in Belgrade, the radio world in Trieste tells me, is becoming one. At its best, however, state radio is a cultural arm of great power and complete responsibility. In all cases it is a form of public instruction, an autonomous enterprise responsible only to the intellectual world and to its representatives in the government. Henry Barraud, musical director of the French radio, says he is not interested in the number of his listeners or overfearful of diminishing this by the performance of recondite music. The duty of the state radio is, in his opinion, to produce everything, at every level of intellectual difficulty, that is in itself excellent, offering a sufficient variety of programs simultaneously so that every listener will have always a choice among several kinds of fare.

These include, as music, on any well-run station, opera, orchestral music, classic and modern chamber music, operetta, musical comedy, folklore, popular songs, dance music, and jazz. All together these make up a balanced musical diet; and it has seemed to me that the French, the Belgian, and the British broadcasts are admirably designed in this regard. Holland and the Swiss lean unduly, perhaps, toward the serious side; Spain, Hungary, and Ireland go in for nationalistic sentimentalities somewhat too stereotyped to be convincing. All provide a more varied musical fare than does Luxembourg or any single American station. One of the happiest virtues of state broadcasting is its abstention from song plugging, as well as from all those procedures by which the listener's mind is subjected to a third degree, preliminary to extracting from him a vow to change, or not to change, his habitual brand of something or other.

All the Big Three state radios (France, Belgium, and the BBC) give lots of modern music. So much, in fact, that those radio systems have largely replaced private subsidy and the mobilizing of chic society for the launching of new works. Nowadays these are given directly to the whole public, and the time lag of their general acceptance has been thus considerably speeded up. The most extreme in its modernism among Europe musical programs is the Belgian Flemish radio. Its director,

Paul Collaer, searches the world over for novelties of the most unaccustomed kinds. Nothing delights him so much as to feed his faithful Flemings atonality, harmonic complexity, and the newer percussive schools. Schönberg, Ives, and John Cage are his oyster. Varèse, Webern, and Henry Cowell jostle one another on his programs, which remind one of the heroic days of the BBC, before the political purges of 1934, when British radio was musically afraid of nothing.

Beside the abundance that European radio offers in music of every kind, every period, every style, our American programs seem falsely weighted. We overdo the plugging of both standard symphonies and commercial songs. Our preoccupation with large numbers of listeners makes us unfair toward modern music and toward all those members of our public who are capable of taking part in its evolution. There is no government agency in America now that is prepared to assume any part of the responsibility of supplying information and culture to our people, and it is far from proved that such an undertaking would be desirable. Certainly it would be fought. Nevertheless, the cultural broadcasts that the better state radios put out in Europe make a reflective visitor wonder whether there isn't some way, with all our financial and intellectual resources, of achieving programs comparably unhackneyed and broad.

September 8, 1946

Musical Belgium

THE MUSICAL LIFE of Belgium, as this reporter has observed it recently, is marked by dependable standards of execution and by an efficiency of organization rarely to be met with in Europe during these postwar days. Indeed, save for the visible ravages of bombing, which in Antwerp alone amount to the gutting of every third house or building, the whole country is nearer like its prewar self than almost any other in Europe. There is an abundance of food and clothing; and the gap between price levels and wages is not the abysm that one encounters in Italy, say, or even in metropolitan France. In Brussels, moreover, there are taxis; and the restaurants and cafés for which that rich and cultivated city has long been justly celebrated are full of decently dressed people eating a large variety of foods, drinking good beer, and even ordering French or Rhenish wines.

Richest of all the Belgian musical institutions, the National Radio, which receives from the government 250,000,000 francs a year (nearly eight million dollars at official rates), enjoys in addition the convenience of a modern plant, built just before the war, and achieves the kind of efficiency that only special concentration can offer. All the Belgian programs, including those in Flemish, originate within its walls and are broadcast from its studios. (In Paris the National Radio works in thirty-eight converted houses and office buildings scattered all over town.) These studios represent the last word in acoustical luxury; and the establishment's three concert halls are, if not acoustically ideal, admirably laid out for the comfort of executant musicians and no end handsome to the eye.

The station possesses a symphony orchestra of first quality, also chamber-music resources that are seemingly inexhaustible, and a chorus. The conductor, Franz André, leans in his programs toward a modernism and a receptivity to foreign works similar to the practice, in these regards, of the French radio. Paul Collaer, who directs the music of the Flemish broadcasts, is even more devoted to the rare and the advanced. His programs represent an extreme of modernism that is without parallel in contemporary broadcasting. They read like a festival of the International Society for Contemporary Music.

The Belgian radio emits two simultaneous broadcasts, one known as the French program and the other as the Flemish. All programs are announced in both languages, since the country is officially, as well as really, bilingual. But the Flemings, who make up some sixty per cent of the population, are proud of their language and disdainful of the Walloons with their Frenchified ways. The Flemish programs are designed, consequently, by Flemings for Flemish tastes. And since Flemish taste has long been more courageous and more catholic than that of the Gallic contingent, the Flemish radio programs, like those of the National Flemish Opera in Antwerp, express a policy of giving to the dissident majority (for the ruling group is still Walloon), if not the separate administration that it demands, at least the kind of art it likes.

In Antwerp, the Flemish metropolis, the Opera has already

produced in the Flemish tongue Benjamin Britten's *Peter Grimes*, which the Théatre de la Monnaie in Brussels, though an advanced establishment by our standards, or even by Parisian, has not yet got round to. Your correspondent witnessed at the Antwerp Opera an off-season performance in Flemish of Offenbach's *Tales from Hoffmann* that was remarkable for musical solidity and general satisfactoriness, in spite of the absence of star casting and other costly production circumstances. La Monnaie, in Brussels, which is one of the great opera houses of Europe by anybody's standards, leans, regarding repertory, toward the conservatism of its kind. But Antwerp gives everything. And the more new horizons music opens to the mind the more the Flemings enjoy it and take pride in it.

As characteristically Belgian as is the Flemish love of musical advance are the country's famous "singing towers," carillons, or musical chimes. Your correspondent, visiting one Sunday those of the cathedral at Malines, was surprised at the delicacy of their sound. This resembles far less the genteel orotundity of the chimes at New York's Riverside Church or at St. Thomas's in Fifth Avenue than it does the tinkling of a trayful of glasses. Indeed, its climactic moments are not unlike the sound of that same tray dropped.

As readers of Dorothy Sayers's *The Nine Tailors* all know, English chime playing is numerological and nonexpressive. To "ring the changes" is simply to toll the bells in all the sequences arithmetically possible. The Belgian school, on the other hand, plays tunes and even harmonies; and Belgian chimes are designed with this end in view. The carillon of Malines contains a full chromatic scale in three sizes or pitches of sound. There is a range of high tinkling bells, another of medium-pitched bells and a third of lowish ones. The booming bass range is omitted, probably because it might overpower and would certainly confuse the lighter sounds in *tutti* passages.

The prettiest music these keyed, hand-played instruments offer is a kind of three-part counterpoint, abstract in design and lacy in effect. The least effective is music of personal expressivity. Hymn tunes and carols make excellent matter for bell composition if appropriately treated. Transcriptions of well-known vocal airs, however great their sentimental appeal, risk being found comic. Delightfully so, indeed, your reporter found an execution, complete with *tempo rubato* and *tremolando* effects, of Saint-Saëns's "My heart at thy sweet voice," from *Samson and Delilah*. The musical chimes in general he found to be a limited but not wholly ineffective instrument. What they seem to him to need is music by John Cage, especially composed to bring out their percussive character.

The present musical travelogue would not be complete without reference to an admirable Belgian institution known as the Palace of Fine Arts. This is a building in Brussels, paid for by the government and free of taxes, in which some fifteen or twenty diversified cultural activities, all self-supporting, present themselves to the public. There are a symphony orchestra, a chamber-music series, lectures galore, recitals, a film library with public showings, an auction room for works of art, a theater, a restaurant, the handsomest modern concert hall your announcer has ever seen, and about a mile of gallery for loan exhibits. Whatever needs doing in culture, whatever is not being done by business or government initiative, gets done by the Palais des Beaux Arts.

Its latest success is a combined music-appreciation and youth movement known as Musical Youth, or *Les Jeunesses Musicales*. This international society, formed in 1940, has at present 15,000 members in Belgium alone and some 300,000 in France. It holds meetings, conventions, classes, competitions, and concerts. And the young people choose their own programs. This writer is notoriously suspicious of all such movements, both on musical grounds and on political. But he is also aware that laymen with musical predilections profit by access to what we call "good" music and that in most of western Europe guidance toward the understanding of this has hitherto been denied to all but professional students. *Les Jeunesses Musicales* is but one of many projects aimed to remedy this state of affair. The French school system plans a systematic alteration of it as soon as the necessary army of teachers can be trained in the conservatories. Meanwhile, French-speaking young people have sort of taken the matter in hand themselves; and the Palais des Beaux Arts has encouraged them.

September 1, 1946

Trieste's Music and Radio Setup

TRIESTE is a clean, modern seaport of some 300,000 inhabitants with little of the picturesque about it save for the mountains at its back and the vast blue bay in front. Like any other Italian city of its size, it has two lyric theaters, one for winter and one for summer.

The Allied Military Government, as sole administrative authority in the province of Julian Venetia, has taken on, along with the other municipal services, the direction of these, as well as of the local radio station and of the Trieste Philharmonic Orchestra. Virtually the entire musical life of the city is thus in the hands of British and American army officers who, if they lack in most cases experience of the routines involved, are equally without the cynicism of the professional impresario.

Summer music takes place in the square courtyard of the Castello San Giusto, a medieval hilltop fortification entered by a drawbridge. Arranged in 1938 for outdoor opera and concerts but ruined for this purpose by bombings during the war, the theater has been restored and put to use under the direction of the British officer in charge, Major the Hon. J. H. St. Clair-Erskine. The stage is in one corner of the square, with dressing rooms and wardrobe space below it. The seats, accommodating 6,000 spectators comfortably or 10,000 in a pinch, are aligned diagonally across the square. Scenery is stored behind a false stone parapet at stage left that matches the real one at stage right. There are lighting towers but no flies and no curtain, bright projectors turned toward the audience replacing the more usual velvet or canvas. Décors are painted on the spot, costumes hired from rental houses in Milan. Similarly, the orchestra and chorus employed are local, soloists being imported for the season.

The present season, which runs through July and part of August, has a repertory of four operas—Boïto's *Mefistofele*, Ponchielli's *La Gioconda*, Bizet's *Carmen*, and Verdi's *La Forza del Destino*. Each of these works receives three or four performances, operatic evenings being interspersed with symphony concerts and with cinema.

The concerts employ guest conductors and visiting soloists.

Lawrence Tibbett and Robert Lawrence appeared earlier this summer. George Chavchavadze, playing with orchestra a program of piano concertos, is billed for later. The Austrian conductor Herbert von Karajan seems to have impressed all with his dynamism and clarity. He had led four concerts last winter before the purging commission decided that he was not yet acceptable politically.

The performance of *La Gioconda* that your correspondent attended would have done honor to any operatic establishment in the world. The cast, excellent all through, contained three artists of such outstanding quality that they seem worth writing to New York about. The first of these, in rising order of impressiveness, is a young tenor, Nino Scattolini. Powerful of voice, skilled in its use, and handsome of figure in a way not common among tenors of any age, this modest youth (somewhat too modest, indeed, to be a really good actor) held the stage without effort beside two of the most accomplished divas in Italy, Maria Grandi and Cloe Elmo.

Miss Grandi, Irish by birth, has sung in all the best Italian opera houses. A dramatic soprano of wide range and perfect mastery, she gave the other evening a vocal performance impeccable for style and beauty. Unfortunately she is not a young woman. The decline of her vocal powers, though as yet barely evident, cannot fail to appear as grave before many years. At present she is a distinguished dramatic soprano.

Cloe Elmo, mezzo-soprano or contralto, as you will (for she sings both kinds of role), is the most brilliant bravura singer that the writer knows of anywhere. He first heard her in 1940 as Azucena in *Il Trovatore*, in a performance broadcast from La Scala at Milan. It seemed to him at the time that he had never heard a vocal display at once so brilliant pyrotechnically and so terrifying dramatically. Seen on the stage, as Laura in *La Gioconda*, she turns out to have a personal projection of the first magnitude in addition to her unique vocal strength. In her middle thirties, she is now at the height of her powers, with a possible twenty years of great work ahead of her. I cannot imagine her not being engaged for American appearance; and once engaged, I cannot imagine her not having a durable success. Her trumpetlike alto voice is both strong and agile; her personality is warm; and she is mistress of her art.

The Allied Information Service has two radio stations in the region, one in Trieste, at the very center of the present political storm, and another near Udine, which is some forty miles away, in the undisputed Italian provice of Friuli. Both stations operate musically on records and on what live music the city of Trieste provides, chiefly opera and the symphony concerts, though there is also a first-class chamber-music organization known as the Trio di Trieste. Announcements are made in both Italian and Slovene, sometimes in Serbo-Croat as well. But the Trieste station is aimed at an Italian-speaking audience. It is the station at Udine, safely installed in Italian territory, that broadcasts to Yugoslavia.

This is a field station, complete in nine trucks, that was captured from the Germans. Compact, efficient, powerful, it projects a signal twenty kilowatts strong, twice that of the permanent installation in Trieste. It is an extremely complex mechanism, however, and one that the Allied engineers have proved unable, without plans, to make function. It was got into operation by German prisoner-of-war technicians who had worked with it before its capture; and these are the men at present in charge of its technical maintenance. The German major in command of their detail was actually one of the original designers, I believe, of the equipment, or at least connected with its manufacture.

He and some eight or nine assistants live in tents on a hilltop five miles from Udine, commanded by a British officer and guarded by American soldiers. Programs in Slovene and Serbo-Croat are received by wire from Trieste and broadcast directionally to Yugoslavia. The German prisoner-engineers work twelve hours a day, and their life is not gay. But they are proud of their complex and powerful machine and of their ability to make it work. A more responsible or dependable team of technicians could scarcely be imagined; and they are not anti-Nazis, either. Either they or their chief, a strong pro-Nazi, could sabotage the machinery at any moment without our knowing what had gone wrong. It is from sheer pride of workmanship that these men do for the Allied Information Service a job that they may or may not favor politically.

In addition to the radio's nine trucks and the men's living tents, the barbed-wire hilltop enclosure contains a tar-paper shack arranged as a broadcasting studio. This is not in use now, all programs being received by underground cable from the Trieste studios. But the day that the "Jugs" (as U.S. soldiers call our Yugoslavian allies) attempt, if they do, to capture Trieste, the news will be broadcast to the world from Italian territory over German equipment operated by German technicians for an Anglo-American joint operation known as Allied Information Service.

August 18, 1946

Venice Unvanquished

VISIBLE VENICE has not been touched by the war. Its historic stones are all in place, their meringue textures and ice-cream colorings intact. Walking among them and looking in the shops, calculating one's expenditures in dollars, one might easily imagine that the city's life, like its aspect, were little altered, save for the temporary general inconvenience of a strike among waiters and hotel help. For the citizenry, of course, monetary inflation, run-away prices, and rising tuberculosis rate make a life picture not wholly composed in appetizing tints. An increased tourist trade, moreover, sovereign remedy for most of the city's monetary ills, cannot be expected till state railways and civil aviation shall have been got into a running order capable of transporting foreign gold bearers.

Auditory Venice, on the other hand, bears on its surface the signs of poverty, while the inner structure of the musical life is scarcely damaged at all. The city's chief summer holiday, the Feast of the Holy Redeemer (or Redentore), which your correspondent witnessed on July 20th, was notable for the absence of brass bands and of other paid musical ensembles on the decorated floats and barges that crowded the lagoon. There is no music nowadays at any time in the Piazza San Marco save that of occasional itinerant singers or accordion players. Even gondola parties seem less vocal than formerly, probably because there are fewer Venetians on any evening just riding around, at the present price of water taxis.

There are excellent concerts, however, of a Sunday, in the sculptured courtyard of the Doge's Palace or, in case of rain, in the color-of-peaches-and-roses-and-ivory opera house, La

Fenice. Sometimes these are symphonic, executed under visiting conductors by the opera's own orchestra, which is a quite good one. (It enjoys an especially fine first horn player and the best oboe soloist, by general admission, in all Italy.) On other evenings the concerts are choral or mixed. A singing society from Vicenza performed, on one evening of your reporter's stay, madrigals and sacred set pieces by Monteverdi, ending up with Carissimi's oratorio, *Jephtha's Daughter*.

The local conservatory, the Liceo Benedetto Marcello, long one of the most highly reputed in Italy, has been directed since 1938 by Italy's number-one composer (estimating him by both his national influence and his foreign prestige), Gian Francesco Malipiero. Surrounding him is a group of his maturing pupils who might almost be said to constitute a Venetian school. Esthetically these writers do not represent either of the chief trends now dominant in Italian composition, namely, the neo-Classic and the atonal. They follow rather the neo-Romantic humanism of their master, an esthetic that seems to offer more freedom to the Italian mind than does direct adherence to the tenets of either Paris or Vienna.

These last are represented elsewhere in Italy by Petrassi, who derives from the later works of Stravinsky, and by Dallapiccola, a former Malipiero pupil lately turned Schönbergian, or dodeca-phonic, as the Italians term the twelve-tone syntax. That Italian composers should practice to some extent the major modes of international thought is to be expected. Indeed no country today, not even France, is without its twelve-tone school. But that beside such observances there should exist music making based on an indigenous intellectual tradition, itself one of no mean prestige, is a sign of vigor most agreeable to encounter in a time of general international conformism.

It was a privilege to inspect the scores of certain young Venetians and to hear them performed, if only under studio conditions. The most impressive of these in expressive content, as well as in technical complexity, is a Requiem Mass for double chorus, soloists, strings, three pianos, and thirteen brasses, by Bruno Maderna. A short concerto for eleven instruments, by the same author, scheduled for performance at the September Festival of Contemporary Music, is gay and ingenious, but less handsomely planned than the Requiem. This last, for all its attachment to contrapuntal textures, achieves an intensity of expression that places its young author in the high company of Berlioz and Verdi. It is not every day that one encounters religious music at once so noble of tone and so striking in effect. One wonders if this boy of twenty-six might not perhaps be destined to make that rejuvenating contribution to the Italian opera that his master has long essayed and never quite pulled off.

Even more notable for instrumental effectiveness, though thinner as expression, is a quintet for piano and strings by Gino Gorini which recalls by its instrumental aptness the string quartets of Malipiero himself, which are among the most individual contributions of our century to string repertory. Previews of the master's own recent work included a choral "*sinfonia eroica*," entitled *Vergilii Aeneis*, and the purely instrumental Third Symphony. Both will be heard next season in the United States.

The Festival of Contemporary Music, formerly held every autumn at the Lido, is being resumed this year during the week of September 15–22. Guest conductors include Hermann Scherchen, Gregor Fitelberg, Fernando Previtali, Ildebrando Pizzetti, and several younger, less famous musicians. There will be six concerts, four of them orchestral. American composition is represented by George Antheil's Fourth Symphony and Leonard Bernstein's *Jeremiah*, France by Milhaud's *Death of a Tyrant* and songs of Messiaen. Heard for the first time in Italy will be Schönberg's second Chamber Symphony, Bartók's Third Piano Concerto, and Stravinsky's Sonata for Two Pianos. The twelve-tone faith is represented by Schönberg, Webern, Dallapiccola, and Nielsen, who is Italian in spite of his name; up-to-dateness in general by England's Benjamin Britten, Belgium's Chevreuille, Italy's own Petrassi, and some half-dozen of her genuinely young. Nor are the indispensable festival modernists— Martinů, Malipiero, Szymanowski, and Pizzetti—omitted. The programs are not designed this year to attract foreign novelty fanciers so much as to inform the Italian public. The several festivals of this kind held in Rome, Florence, and elsewhere since the liberation of the peninsula have all received high public favor and the most considered critical attention.

Among the young Venetian executants whom this writer had occasion to hear during his recent visit, the most notable are the composer Gino Gorini, an excellent pianist, and the Nuovo Quartetto Italiano. The latter is one of the most charming string quartets I have ever heard. Their work is not always traditional, but it is invariably beautiful. They play without notes, as is the contemporary Italian fashion, and with a lyrical warmth that is juvenile, poetic, inspired. Like the equally juvenile Trio di Trieste, they combine technical precision with musical freshness in the most touching way imaginable. Indeed, financial circumstances permitting, they may well, and in very few years, become one of the great quartets of Europe. They are already one of the lovely ones. Their present quality, I may add, like so much else that is valuable in the music life of Italy, is largely the result of Gian Francesco Malipiero's encouragement and counsel.

August 25, 1946

Salzburg Festival

THE SALZBURG FESTIVAL of last year, according to the reports of those present, was but a shadow of its prewar self. That of 1946, which this reporter attended, was a first-rate show, both socially and musically. To be sure, there was no Toscanini, no Walter to conduct, no Flagstad on the stage; and few of the old international smart set were out front. But there was the Vienna Philharmonic Orchestra; there was Charles Munch from Paris, conducting; there was some definitely first-class singing; there was the best-prepared performance of Mozart's *Figaro* I have ever heard; and the audience was starred liberally with dignitaries from our military and civil administrations. Indeed, the neighboring estates, occupied in many cases by high-ranking American officers, offer nowadays week-end parties at which visiting generals, judges from Nürnberg, ambassadors, handsome aides-de-camp, well-dressed wives and daughters, and cavalcades of Packard cars present a spectacle of no mean brilliance. In the city itself there are Austrian music lovers and the French from Innsbruck. Every seat is always full at every festival performance. And the Oesterreichische Hof is still a hotbed of political and musical, if no longer of amorous, intrigue.

The opera repertory consists this year of Mozart's *Don*

Giovanni and *Marriage of Figaro* and Strauss's *Rosenkavalier*. The spoken plays are Goldoni's *Servant of Two Masters* and the old morality, *Everyman*, both in their prewar Reinhardt staging. The conductors of the Vienna Philharmonic concerts have been Alceo Galliera, Carl Schuricht (an excellent classical musician whom I heard earlier this summer in Venice), Bernhard Paumgartner, John Barbirolli, Ernest Ansermet, and Charles Munch, the latter paired with the only orchestral soloist of the festival, the excellent French pianist, Nicole Henriot. There were four serenade concerts, recitals by Grace Moore, by Yehudi Menuhin, and by the Swiss pianist Edwin Fischer, and quartet evenings by the Philharmonia, Winterthur, and Calvet Quartets. Religious music was furnished by the Vienna Choir Boys and by performances with the Cathedral Choir and the Mozarteum Orchestra of Masses by Schubert, Bruckner, and Mozart.

Rosenkavalier and *Figaro*, a Philharmonic concert with Munch and Miss Henriot, the Philharmonia Quartet, and a performance of the Mozart Requiem were the fare during your correspondent's three-day visit. The Strauss opera, ill cast and sloppily played, was the performance among these least worthy by Salzburg standards, though Hilde Konetzni, who sang the Feldmarschallin, is both a singer and an actress of quality. The Requiem was no better given than choral works are anywhere, which means it was pretty rough. It did have, however, the kind of ease that comes from devotion and familiarity, the quality that the Bach Mass has in Bethlehem, Pennsylvania, as if performing it and listening to it were a perfectly natural thing for everybody to be doing. Equally easy and natural, but more refined, were executions by the Philharmonia Quartet, from Vienna, of works by Haydn and Dvořák and Schubert. At the head of the writer's memories of the whole will long remain a reading by Munch of Berlioz's *Fantastic Symphony*, unique for its lyric grace and for its fiery white light, and a performance of Mozart's *Figaro* that was not only well sung in the solo numbers but wholly delicate and precise in the concerted work.

Maria Cebotari, who sang the Countess, has a beautiful voice and grace of phraseology. Though eight months with child, she sang the difficult-to-breathe "*Dove Sono*" with a sustained line and a nobility of expression rarely to be met with in these days of the vocal art's decline. Irmgard Seefried, the Susanna, has a fine voice, too, and is clearly a good musician. Both artists are worth watching. The conductor who prepared the performance, Herbert von Karajan, is Austria's coming man, an original and a powerful musician. Temporarily under political ban (his is a "mild," or borderline case), he did not conduct the performance. But through a connivance between the Festival directors and the American political authorities, he was enabled to rehearse for another conductor a production that everyone present, I think, will long be happy to have heard. Delicate without being bloodless, exact without being mechanical, quiet in the ensemble passages almost to the point of being conversational, this interpretation is nevertheless one of high dramatic intensity and wide dynamic range. It is also, as expression, humane and sweet. There may be here the model for a new approach to the musical execution of Mozart's operas.

The Austrian style of playing Mozart, as prewar visitors to Salzburg knew it, is no ancient tradition. It was invented in Vienna about fifty years ago by Gustav Mahler and transmitted to our own time by Bruno Walter. Noble in proportion but careless of detail, at least in the Walter version, it resembles more the whipped-cream-in-stone aspect of Austrian baroque architecture than it does the firm workmanship of Mozart's music. As a reaction against the outmoded romantic style of playing Mozart, it was more than welcome after the last war; and it brought to a great master new public favor. But there is nothing eternal about it. A new kind of Mozart would not now be unwelcome to musicians. It could, as well, if properly exploited, bring much-needed money into Austria's coffers.

September 15, 1946

Germany's Music Life

OUR CONTROL OFFICERS in Germany for theater and music, virtually all of whom this reporter has talked with and observed in action, are devoted men and miracle workers. All four military governments, moreover, favor the reconstruction of Germany's artistic and intellectual life. The framework of this reconstruction, thanks to everybody's indefatigable effort, is already well above ground. There is music, for instance, lots of it, all over the land, some of it quite first-class. What differs from zone to zone is chiefly the flexibility with which the different high commands implement an identical policy. The Russians and the French are politically quite lenient toward artists. The British are more interested in getting on with their job than in hamstringing themselves on categorical regulations. The American generals seem to consider that the progress of intellectual reconstruction is less important than the preservation of the "hard peace" attitude that public opinion at home has so far favored.

In the American jurisdiction, which includes the provinces of Bavaria, of Württemburg-Baden, and of Greater Hesse, the Bremen Enclave, and our Berlin sector, there were on August 28 of this year 412 licensed theaters, theater troupes, and concert halls. This in addition to 705 film houses. The number of musical and dramatic artists cleared of Nazi party membership and permitted to work before the public amounted to 24,494. Among these the dramatic artists represent a much larger number than the musicians do. Thanks to the particular organization of the German spoken theater, which consisted chiefly of repertory troupes closely bound together and animated by a strong *esprit de corps*, the pressure toward Nazi party membership had made fewer inroads on Germany's dramatic personnel than on the musical profession, where many a free-lance singer or instrumentalist had found himself obliged to join up in order to earn a living. As a result, about half the actors in our zone have been cleared and can work, whereas less than one per cent of the musicians, according to an estimate of the American Control Officer for Music and Theater, are available for engagement.

Nevertheless, both music and drama flourish vigorously in all the zones; and the German population, with not much to do of an evening but sit around in its overcoat, if it owns one, is assiduous in attendance at musical and dramatic entertainment. The citizens of Munich can choose among fifteen legitimate theaters, ten variety halls, a political cabaret, a circus, a puppet show, and twenty-nine movies. In addition to these events there are nightly opera at the Prinzregenten Theater and an average of ten to twelve concerts a week, including three or four by the local Philharmonic Orchestra, plus innumerable occasions for indulgence in choral singing. If no other city in our zone offers quite such bounty, that is because no other German city in any zone is at present quite so well equipped with halls. It is housing, not money, that is scarce. There is lots of money in circulation; and subsidies, both state and municipal, are generous.

But, somehow, though Munich looks like a complete wreck, like a construction in pink sugar that has been rained on, more of it is usable than one might imagine. The opera house, the assembly halls of the University and of the Deutsches Museum are in good shape. The Bavarian State Theater, or *Staatsschauspielhaus*, has been rebuilt. The Philharmonic is building itself a new hall; so are various theatrical groups. The other usable locales employed are chiefly beer halls and converted gymnasiums. Nymphenburg Palace, untouched by bombing, provided in July a perfect Baroque setting for a three-weeks' festival of eighteenth-century music, including an opera by the little known von Seckendorff on a text of Goethe, *Lila, oder Phantasie und Wirklichkeit*. There is a municipal conservatory with seven hundred students, too; and the state conservatory, or *Bayerische Akademie der Tonkunst*, will open this fall under the direction of Josef Haas with two hundred pupils.

Stuttgart, though less bombed out than Munich, has fewer halls and theaters available for use. The opera house, which is intact, has been requisitioned by the Army for movies, USO shows, and a Red Cross club, complete with barber shop and shoe shines. It can be used for opera only at those moments that do not inconvenience our military. The situation in Nuremberg and Wiesbaden, where opera houses are also still usable, is even graver, because the military will not even lend them to the local opera company. In the latter city our Air Force continues to give movies in the opera house, while the opera company performs in a movie theater. The Army movies are not well attended anywhere. I counted in Stuttgart's opera house about one hundred people, though the place seats 1,400. Our military is fearful of releasing all such properties, lest the G.I. newspapers editorialize unfavorably. The pampering of our soldiers is considered everywhere to take precedence over the reconstruction of German cultural life, even when this has been thoroughly denazified.

All programs for re-educating the German people count heavily on the rebuilding of their intellectual life. As I mentioned in a previous article, overdenazification and undernourishment are a hindrance to the carrying out of the United States program. But these policies follow formal decisions of our military government and can be altered. Indeed, our severity toward minor collaborators is being relaxed already. Our general disdain, however, for honest German citizens (and a German had to be either pretty honest or *non compos mentis* to avoid Nazi party membership) is in every way deplorable. We treat them very much as we do Negroes in the United States. We expect them to work hard and to be very grateful to us. But we refer to them as "krauts" and do not eat with them in public.

Hard as it has been to liberate and to reconstruct the theaters and concert halls in the Württemberg-Baden area, it has been even more difficult to house German entertainment in Greater Hesse. Frankfurt's opera and state spoken theater are in ruins. All utilizable large halls are used for the necessary purposes of our central military administration, USFET. A year ago Frankfurt's first postwar musical event took place on the floor of the Stock Exchange, which still had three walls standing and half a roof. Today this same space has been remodeled and a small stage added. That is where the opera company plays. A gymnasium, or *Turnhalle*, in the suburbs is used for spoken plays. Recitals take place in the assembly hall of the university. There are in divers basements and beer halls a cabaret, a variety show, and a circus. The former stock exchange now offers almost any week two grand operas, two recitals, and four plays. The conservatory has about a hundred students. The Cæcilian Verein, a famous choral organization, gives two concerts a year.

Wiesbaden, a smaller city, has about the same number of halls available and a similar number of musical events per week. Both the opera house and the thermal casino, or *Kurhaus*, where a small theater is still in good shape, are used to entertain American soldiers. Darmstadt offers the public a reduced symphony orchestra that plays once a week at the Polytechnic Institute, a few musical lectures at the Palace and about two operetta or opera performances. That is all there is room for. Kassel, which is flat, has virtually no music at all. Neither Wiesbaden nor Darmstadt nor Kassel has a working conservatory.

The Bremen Enclave has eight theaters, 1025 licensed musical and dramatic artists. Our Berlin sector has fourteen licensed theaters and concert halls, 6870 artists registered and cleared of Nazi taint. The most important musical organization in this jurisdiction is the Berlin Philharmonic Orchestra. This distinguished musical body, which lives, except for the first-desk men, on No. 2 ration, is suffering from hunger. It has been a great orchestra; it has a place in the history of music. With a little more food and a little loosening of the denazification rules, it could take up its merited place again. Both the Russians and the British are more careful of the opera companies that work in their zones than we are of the Philharmonic.

Our denazification policy is slowly being altered, but our feeding policy is not. An American orchestra, or some related organization that has at heart the interests of music and of its faithful servants, could render both no more valuable service than to send food packages regularly to this orchestra. There are no Nazis in it; many of its members have done time in concentration camps. All of them are hungry and tired and discouraged. If our government will not pamper them a little, perhaps American musicians will. Last spring they played for a party given by an American Army officer, himself a professional musician in private life. Whether they were paid for their evening's work or not I do not know; but I do know that they were allowed to pass through a supper room in which buffet tables groaned with food, without being offered so much as a sandwich. It is illegal, I believe, to give away commissary merchandise to citizens of an enemy country.

September 29, 1946

Music in Berlin

BERLIN still enjoys two opera companies and one symphony orchestra. The State Opera Company (or *Staatsoper*) plays in the Russian sector. The municipal troupe (or *Städtische Oper*) plays in the British sector. The Philharmonic Orchestra is seated in the American sector and mostly plays there, though once a fortnight it gives a concert in the British sector for Allied troops. It also plays from time to time for the powerful Berlin radio station, which, though located in the British sector, is controlled by the Russian Military Government. All radio in Germany comes under the direction of the occupying armies.

Music, theater, and film showings, excepting such entertainments as are provided for the troops themselves, are produced by Germans for the general public. In every case, the hall, the management, and the executant artists are licensed by the occupying military power. The strictness of the screening varies in Berlin, as it does in the whole German territory, according to the divers policies of the Big Four governments about previous relations of individual Germans with the Nazi party.

The Russians, the most liberal toward artists in their denazification policy, were the first to get their major Berlin musical enterprise, the State Opera, into successful operation. The British opened the Municipal Opera somewhat later. The Americans, who are so strict that more than ninety-nine per cent of the German musicians in their zone and sector are still blacklisted, have not yet been able to bring the Berlin Philharmonic Orchestra back to anything like its former musical efficiency. It has given concerts from the beginning of the occupation, but its work bears little relation to the standards for which it was famous before the war.

Its present conductor, Sergiu Celibidache, a Rumanian by birth, is a musician of broad culture but not as sound a technician of the baton as one might wish. The program that your correspondent heard in the Titania-Palast, a former film house, consisted of Berlioz's *Benvenuto Cellini* overture, the second suite from Prokofiev's *Romeo and Juliet*, and Brahms's First Symphony. All were read clearly, but the sound of them had little charm. Neither the woodwind, the brass, nor the percussion of the orchestra is quite first-class. The strings are all those of a major symphonic ensemble, and the discipline in general still bears a resemblance to that for which this group has long been famous. But the ensemble is not invariably harmonious. The orchestra is a victim, in fact, of two American administrative tendencies, indifference about the fate of artists and over-denazification. Musicians cannot work properly on No. 2 ration, which represents barely a thousand calories. It is hoped that our recently adopted policy of handing over denazification to German tribunals, which have so far shown considerable leniency toward minor political peccadilloes while maintaining severity toward major fascist action, will permit the re-engagement of certain valuable musicians. Whether Furtwängler, the former conductor, is to be allowed to return to his post will probably be decided in the near future.*

The State Opera, which falls under Russian jurisdiction, is in better shape. The orchestra is excellent, the stage direction first-class, the singing favorably comparable with that offered by any other house in the world. All the artists, moreover, receive special food packages from the Soviet government and a workers' ration of 1,350 calories, which enables them to rehearse and to perform with a minimum of fatigue and to conserve thus a reasonable artistic efficiency. A performance heard at the Admiralspalast, a former operetta theater, was, by anybody's present-day standards, first-class. And the public was entitled to consume food and drink during the intermission without ration points. There were available at the bar open sandwiches, thin soup, beer, vodka, and German cognac.

The musical offerings that your reporter heard were Puccini's *Il Tabarro* (*The Cloak*) and Busoni's *Arlecchino*. The Puccini work was presented in a charming set that really looked like Paris and that was architecturally interesting to play in. It is about the prettiest and most satisfactory realistic stage setting this reviewer has encountered in some years. Like that of *Arlecchino* (and the costuming of both operas), it was the work of the well-known painter Paul Strecker. The direction of the piece, both musically and visually, was a pleasure. The cast contained no celebrated stars; but the voices were warm, and the vocalism was schooled. Sigrid Ekkehard, Karola Goerlich, Jaro Prohaska, and Erich Witte sang the major roles with beauty and no little distinction. Both production and performance were superior in every way to those of *Il Tabarro* offered in New York last season at the Metropolitan Opera House.

Ferruccio Busoni's *Arlecchino*, based on a libretto by himself and subtitled "a theatrical capriccio," is cast in the mold of the *commedia dell'arte*. Which is to say that it tells its tale through the standardized masquerades of Harlequin, Pantaloon, and Columbine, with a few more characters added. Its full significance escaped your reviewer, though he was aware of both satirical and philosophical overtones. There was clearly a literary take-off on Goethe's *Faust*, and the music made open references

---

*He was allowed to conduct slightly less than a year later.

to Mozart, to Richard Strauss, and to Wagner's *Lohengrin*. He gathered that the whole was supposed to be both witty and profound and greatly regrets his inability to find the work funny, even, not to speak of deep or moving.

Its musical texture, however, is, like all of this composer's work, utterly distinguished. Busoni's music is always skillful and civilized, even, by moments, original. It contains no bluff, no stupidity, no whiff of insincerity; and it evolves on the highest plain of competence, both esthetic and technical. What it lacks is plain feeling. Its manner is grand and thoroughly elegant, but its emotional content is weak. One is always glad to hear it, which happens seldom enough; but one tends to prefer for steady consumption the meatier simplicities of a Verdi or of a Puccini, on the one hand, the more incisive modernities in both thought and texture, on the other, of a Debussy, a Stravinsky, a Schönberg.

The production was a stylish one and carefully rehearsed. Mr. Strecker's set and costumes, like the choreography (for the work was played in strictly regulated pantomime), were well designed to situate the work in the period of its composition. Black-and-white post-World-War-I Expressionismus was the style, one long since outmoded, even in Germany, the land where it flourished most abundantly. What model its arrogance and ugliness can offer to today's postwar Berlin I cannot imagine, where Germans are, for once, being really humble and where the city itself, more than ever monumental in its ruined state, is for the first time really beautiful.

It is possible that the German mind, scraping history for whatever might possibly serve as lamp or guide in German culture's present state of anarchy and desolation, has seized on Germany's last original theater style that anybody had liked at all and revived it just to see if it still meant anything.

The Soviet cultural officers do not appear very enthusiastic about the work or about its production. The German public seems to like the show. For your reporter it represented an effort at artistic presentation unparalleled today in the musical repertory theaters of Paris or Milan or New York, but one scarcely justified, even if it were stylistically more congenial, by the slender content, literary and musical, of Busoni's opera.

September 23, 1946

German Composers

MUSICAL COMPOSITION in Germany and Austria, relieved from Nazi censorship by the Allied invasion, has gone back to where it left off when Hitler came in. This is not to say that nobody in those countries wrote any good music during the Nazi years. I mean rather that the newer music now available there by print or performance bears a closer relation to that current in pre-Nazi times than most of the music honored by the Third Reich did. In other words, the break with the modernist tradition that accompanied the triumph of National Socialism is being repaired under the esthetically less dictatorial Allied Military Occupation.

The mending job will not, however, be complete, with no seams visible, because certain powerful influences on central Europe's music life that were exiled in the mid-1930's will never, can never return. The principal of these is that of the twelve-tone trinity—Schönberg, Berg, and Webern. The first of these masters, now resident in California, is seventy-two years old and not in perfect health; the other two are dead. And though their influence might be expected to go on through their published works and through the teaching of their pupils, the curious fact is that in Germany it does not. There is a little of it left in Austria, where the pre-Schönbergian atonalist, Josef Matthias Hauer, survives, along with two or three Webern pupils. The younger Austrians mostly follow other leaders, other styles. In Germany this reporter inquired diligently without encountering one twelve-tone writer or finding any German musician who knew of the existence of one in the land.

The influences of Paul Hindemith and of Kurt Weill, on the other hand, both resident in the United States, are considerable. That of the former is less notable on musical composition, curiously, than on pedagogy. Musicians who write like Hindemith are not so plentiful as those who teach his theory. In the process of getting the conservatories started again, a revision of German music teaching seems to be desired. And since personnel is lacking for the teaching of atonal theory, this school of composition is not represented on the faculties. But the Hindemith textbooks are held in high respect and seem likely to form the basis of the most advanced pedagogy. Hindemith's works are held in honor, too, but rather as proof of their author's personal gift than as models being followed. In any case, though Hindemith is a burning subject of discussion in music circles, it is his undeniable influence on music teaching that is chiefly defended and attacked rather than his direct influence on musical composition. Evidences of the latter are, though not wholly lacking, more rare. In Germany, as here, he has formed more good teachers than he has successful composers.

Kurt Weill, though not a theorist at all, seems to have left a strong mark on German music. At least, there is an influence around that is not easily explainable through any of the existing pedagogical traditions and that this detective strongly suspects to come out of *Mahagonny* and *Der Dreigroschenoper*. The academic German styles today are two, the Hindemith style and the Reger style, both contrapuntal. Like all contrapuntal styles, these are more entertaining to write in than to listen to; they lack expressivity. The rival style, which leans more on melodic and rhythmic device, is lighter of texture, more varied in expression, less pompous, and more easily digestible.

The most successful writer in this vein is Carl Orff, who lives near Munich. His works are chiefly dramatic oratorios, which is to say, choral works with orchestral accompaniment that require (or at least are enhanced by) staging. Their texts are elaborately cultural, their musical textures almost willfully plain. One, called *Carmine Catulli*, consists of odes by Catullus, in Latin, interspersed with modern recitatives, also in Latin, by the composer. Another, *Carmine Burana*, uses student songs in medieval Latin mixed with Old German. An opera entitled *Die Klüge* has a rhymed text by the composer. Another now nearing completion, *Die Bernauerin*, is in Bavarian dialect. The direct musical model of all these works is Stravinsky's *Les Noces*. They employ lots of rhythmic chanting, and the orchestral accompaniment is percussive. The music is simplified, however, to a point where the basic musical elements—melody, harmony, and counterpoint—are almost nonexistent. The rhythm itself, even, has not much intrinsic interest. What holds these works together is first-class handling of words and their excellent orchestration. Otherwise they are monotonous. Surprisingly enough, they have considerable success in performance, even on the radio, where stage spectacle is not there to help out.

More interesting musically, though also an example of the

simplification for expressive purposes that I credit to Kurt Weill (radio work is also, no doubt, an influence), is the music of Boris Blacher and of his pupils. Blacher is Russian by birth, a child refugee of the Revolutionary years. He is musical director at present of the Russian-run Berlin radio station. His music, though aware of both Stravinsky and Satie, is gayer than that of either. At its simplest it is full of musical interest; at its most complex it is still full of life, clear and expressive. His suite, *Concertante Musik* (Bote and Bock, Berlin, 1938), would be an ornament to anybody's orchestral program. His pupil Gottfried von Einem, an Austrian, writes operas in which rumba rhythms turn up at the most tragic moments, unexpectedly but not always inappropriately. Blacher's work and von Einem's have a touch of wit that is welcome in German music. Blacher himself is the most vigorous single musical influence now present in the country.

Another composer that we shall all be hearing from is Kurt Hessenberg, of Frankfurt. This young man in his early thirties is the author of neo-Romantic songs, cantatas, and piano pieces that evoke directly and without detours the spirit of Schumann. His Symphony No. 2 is melodious and completely successful. Unfortunately it received a Nazi prize award in 1942, an honor that makes it something of a hot potato anywhere just now. It is a beautiful work, all the same, and will no doubt come later into its own. Everybody, literally everybody, I am sure, will love it. It is quite without the turgidity of the German contrapuntalists and equally void of those vulgarities in sentiment and in style that make the works of the more official Third Reich composers (Werner von Egk, for instance) not worth worrying about at present. Hessenberg is a schooled workman and a composer of very real, if somewhat obvious, poetic feeling.

Blacher and Orff are the most original composers whose work this reporter encountered in Germany. Whether Orff can remain long acceptable to musicians I cannot say, though I doubt that he will. Blacher is growing in interest and influence, but I do not believe he will remain long in Germany. After twenty-five years, he seems to have had enough. Hindemith, whether he ever returns or not to the land of his birth and major successes, will certainly continue to occupy there for many years the central musical position.

October 13, 1946

Visit to Dresden

THE SOVIET UNION's control over cultural activities in the Russian zone of Germany is organized in imitation of ours. Ours, like the British, is an offspring of the Anglo-American Psychological Warfare Branch, the overseas equivalent of OWI. Our head information control officer, Brigadier General Robert McClure, was previously in charge of PWB. The French setup is slightly different, education and the fine arts being directed, as in France itself, by other persons than those controlling cinema, press, and similar media of direct information. In all zones the specialized field workers, whose job it is to help the Germans get theaters, opera houses, art schools, newspapers, the whole intellectual machinery, into operation, depend from central offices in Berlin. Their labors are necessarily somewhat decentralized, however, since the subsidies that support German cultural activities must come out of German taxes, which are at present collected only by the separate German state administrations and by municipalities, since no central German government exists.

The degree to which Allied control officers use Germany as an outlet for their divers national art products varies partly with the amounts of such art available. Theaters in our zone, for example, give a great many American plays, but the concert programs include only such American works as happen to be in the music library of the Quadripartite Control Commission in Berlin. These are chiefly photographed scores and parts inherited from PWB. The British and Russian shelves are somewhat fuller than ours; there is no French music there at all. So far, American publishers have not been willing to ship additional material, though the War Department has offered facilities. Performing rights fees are collected by STAGMA, the German equivalent of ASCAP, and held for the present in blocked marks.

In spite, however, of the large repertory of Russian works available (there is a Soviet book and music shop open to all in the ruined Unter den Linden), the Russian control officers do not overly encourage their performance. Major Sergei Barsky, music control officer for the Soviet military government in Germany, explained to your reporter in the following terms his government's present cultural policy as regards Germany. The concept of Russia as an exotic land with special ways of life and a morality of its own, a fairy-tale Russia, colorful, grand, and cruel, is to be slowly eradicated, if possible, from the Western mind. The Soviet Union hopes eventually to be considered as a part of the world, which is one world, rather than as a special case among countries, which people feel obliged to love or to hate. The choice of Russian operas and plays to be performed in German theaters, therefore, is encouraged in the direction of their classical-humanities content. The too picturesque and the violent are tactfully avoided, as are historical subjects showing the Russian nation as unfriendly to the German people.

Re-educating Germany through music, according to Major Barsky, who is a grandnephew of Anton Rubinstein, is less a matter of censoring repertory, however, than of building up a new style of execution. The works played, unless openly anti-Russian, are of less import than the manner in which they are played. Militarism, for two centuries, has been ground into the German mind and ground so deeply that it has come to permeate every detail of living, every German way of doing anything. It must be removed because Russia's peace and prosperity are at stake. And the removal will be a long and tedious operation, "like picking out splinters one by one from a hand or foot." The Soviet military government would like, or at least Major Barsky would like, to reform German musical education with a view to inculcating eventually in German musicians a less narrow and vainglorious attitude toward music and a set of working methods that will oppose a deeper resistance to military tyranny than the existing German musical tradition has, in our century, proved capable of doing.

During the course of a recent visit to the Russian zone, your correspondent received similar declarations on this subject from Major Auslander, Soviet culture control chief for the State of Saxony. This officer also brought to a vodka-and-champagne breakfast in Dresden *Ministerialdirektor* Pappe, German Communist organizer of Union No. 17, the union of free-lance artists and intellectuals in the Russian zone, which was holding that day its first birthday celebration and annual congress.

This is an industrial union comprising musical soloists and stage artists, film and radio workers, vaudeville and circus performers, orchestral musicians, theater technicians, authors, composers, painters, architects, and journalists. The admission of medical men, scholars, and scientists is envisaged but not yet a fact. It is thought probable that these may be more efficiently served by the teachers' union. The locals of Union 17 are attached, so far as is possible, to producing units, each theater, newspaper, radio station, etc., being a separate grouping. "One shop one local" is the aim. Exception made for former adherents of the Nazi party, who cannot work anyway, membership is open to all intellectual workers without professional examination. It is also, with minor leniencies, obligatory, after the classical principle of "open unions and closed shops." The right to strike is admitted; but there have been no strikes so far. Frozen wages and frozen prices have not provoked any need for economic adjustment, and the observances by management of contractual engagements is enforced by the Saxon state.

The chief faults of union organization under the Weimar Republic, according to Mr. Pappe, were the multiplicity of unions claiming jurisdiction in a given shop or industry, and a tendency of the arbitration courts to side with management. The present union structure of the Soviet zone, though not in theory monopolistic, is designed to discourage rival jurisdictions; and arbitration courts have been abolished. They have been replaced by a chamber of commerce and industry, of which the membership is one third representatives of management, one third union delegates, and one third state officials, experts on labor and production questions. All contracts have to be passed on by this board; and when they have been accepted, the state police enforces them. The board is thus automatically stacked in favor of whichever group is more powerful in the state government, management or labor. Whether Soviet influence will in the long run exert itself on the side of labor or of capital remains to be seen.

Working regulations for musicians in the Soviet zone demand a forty-eight-hour availability week, with a maximum of around thirty hours' actual work before overtime pay begins. This last figure is thought by most musicians to be excessive, and they are hoping to get it diminished to the twenty-four-hour norm effective in Berlin, a norm comparable to our American week of nine services, where any normal performance or one two-and-a-half-hour rehearsal constitutes a service. Musicians' wages in Saxony are about the same as in Berlin. They vary, according to the skill of the artist and the importance of his post, from a minimum of 300 marks a month ($30 in American money) up to twice that. Opera stars and guest conductors sometimes receive as high as 1,800 marks ($180) a month. The provincial governments in all zones reduce a man's income by nearly half through taxation. Life for all, under these circumstances, is difficult, but not more so in the Russian zone than elsewhere. Artists there receive a higher food ration than they do in the other zones, and political bans are less rigidly enforced than in ours. But interzonal travel is virtually impossible for them. Working in the Russian zone is thus tempting to many, but all know that settling there is an irrevocable act as long as the iron curtain remains closed.

The musical events which this visitor attended in Dresden consisted of two operettas, *Die Czardasfürstin*, by Emmerich Kálmán, and a Tyrolean piece called *Monika*, by one Dostal, standard repertory works both. The performances were musically quite adequate but visually primitive, since an improvised stage in a beer hall and a half-bombed-out suburban summer theater imposed limitations on stage display. The major opera company, directed by Joseph Keilberth, who also conducts the Dresden Philharmonic Orchestra, had not yet opened its winter season. It has performed up till now in a Christian Science church. The physical state of Dresden, where the whole center of the city, including its priceless Baroque monuments and noble opera house, was destroyed in one bombardment, is unfavorable to music and drama. Nevertheless music and drama go on, and the conservatory has 180 students. A large theater, the former Schauspielhaus, is being restored.

Space forbids, even if my competency permitted, reporting on the art treasures of the former State Museum, now hung at the eighteenth-century Pillnitz Palace in the suburbs, on the curious absence from this collection of certain famous works, including Raphael's *Sistine Madonna*, and on the fact that the Russians don't seem to be looking very hard for these. Also on the large retrospective show of German modern painting now open at the former military academy. On the 28th of September there is to be held in Dresden a congress of German artists from all the zones.

The United States Information Control Division seemed to

this observer both more enlightened and more efficient than the Russian in the fields of journalism and of drama, less so with regard to education, the visual arts (excepting old masters), and trade-union organization. On all the latter subjects our policy is obscure and our action, in consequence, slow. Musically one zone is very much like another, though we have not yet produced with our Berlin Philharmonic as good performances as the Russians do with their Staatsoper or as the British are said to do at the Hamburg Opera House. All field workers everywhere pray for the abolition of interzonal barriers. The Russian field workers in music appeared to me as no less devoted and self-sacrificing than ours and as possibly better supported in detail by their higher officers and by their government at home. The Soviet hierarchy, in any case, has certainly a clearer understanding of what it is up to culturally than ours has. The avowed aim of all the occupying powers is to put an end, and quickly, to Germany's present state of moral, intellectual, and economic anarchy, which risks infecting the whole European continent and sowing destruction broadcast.

October 6, 1946

THOUGHTS IN SEASON

Repertory

IT is a commonplace of contemporary esthetics that music of marked originality is likely to be found shocking by the epoch that gives it birth. The inability is notorious not only of the lay public but of trained musicians to perceive beauty in any work of which the style is unfamiliar. And program makers are aware that this blindness obtains not only with regard to contemporary composition but with regard to the past as well. When one considers the vast amount of music written since 1600 that is perfectly well known, published, and available for performance and that is never given by our operatic or orchestral establishments, in spite of the eagerness of conductors to vary their monotonous routine, one is obliged to conclude, I think, that the tininess of our effective repertory is due to psychological factors that are beyond anyone's power to control.

Epochs, styles, and authors all have a way of becoming invisible, of passing in and out of focus, rather, that is not easy to explain. The facts of this matter constitute the history of taste. Our inability to cope with the unfamiliar is equaled only by our inability to maintain interest in the too familiar, in that which is no longer in any way strange. The vogue of our popular songs is typical. Within a few years, sometimes within one year, it is possible to observe in succession the enthusiasm, the indifference, and the ridicule with which one of these is treated; and we have all experienced the renewed charm of some old song that has been left in limbo long enough to be all but forgotten. There is no way of preventing it; the things we get used to tend to become invisible. They are there all the time, and we know they are there, and we think we love them dearly; but if they were taken away we should half the time not remark any difference.

Schumann's music, for example, is in a decline of favor just now; nobody has a lively feeling for it any more. Interpreters find it more and more difficult to render, audiences more and more difficult to listen to. It is passing out of our focus. Debussy is in an even more curious phase. He is listened to increasingly, understood less and less. Haydn seems to be emerging from

548

his recent obscurity and taking on contours again. Bach, after having been genuinely popular among the *cognoscenti* for thirty years, is losing a bit his appeal for intellectuals. Mozart has, in fact, taken Bach's place of late as the master most admired among connoisseurs. Wagner and Brahms have still a broadly based popularity but a markedly diminishing attraction for musicians. Verdi, though he has lost much of his former power over the masses, has acquired in the last twenty years a prestige in university circles that would have shocked profoundly the scholastic musicians of fifty years ago.

Always, in the case of such revivals, there is imposed a certain falsification upon the original. No matter how much we pretend we are restoring old works at their pristine state, we are obliged at the same time to modernize them somewhat if we expect our contemporaries to take them seriously. Returns to popularity of past styles in architecture and decoration have usually been accompanied, therefore, by complete resurfacing. The nineteenth century unpainted its Gothic monuments and left them a unified gray. It covered up the bare wood of its Louis XVI furniture with a bluish color known as Trianon gray. It built Greco-Roman houses everywhere and painted them white, which is still considered, indeed, to be the appropriate color for classical antiquity. In recent decades flamboyant Victorian interiors, also, have regained their charm through the use of white paint, which was practically never used on them originally but which our age finds cheerful and associates with asepsis.

The Bach revival of the 1830's, which Mendelssohn and Schumann fathered, translated this music into all the idioms of contemporary executant style, using Tourte bows for the orchestral suites and violin pieces, gigantic organs and choruses for the religious works, pianos for the domestic keyboard music, and employing a constant crescendo and diminuendo within all phrases, as was considered necessary at that time for true expression. Bach was modernized all over again in the early years of this century. His rhythm was made to sound more mechanical, dynamism was everywhere diminished, phraseology streamlined, the harpsichord revived, the old, small, bright-sounding organs restored to use.

A healthy traffic goes on nowadays in the reinstrumentation of eighteenth-century music of all kinds, but we have not yet done over the Romantics very much. Though the nineteenth century is dying slowly, there is vigor in its traditions still. Not for some time will they be forgotten so thoroughly that a resurfacing of the Romantic masters will be possible to envisage. When this does take place, they will lose, of course, the somber patina that a century of daily handling has laid upon them and appear as bright again to us as cleaned and revarnished masterpieces from the past do in a gallery of painting.

Meanwhile, we must put up with our own age, because, whether we like it or not, its habits are for us the facts of life. That age listens to a great deal of new music, likes practically none of it, but would not for the world forgo hearing it. It respects a vast repertory of old music, complains no end at the infrequency with which most of this is heard, discourages firmly the introduction of any of it into the major programs. Exception is made for pre-Romantic works when wholly reinstrumented. It holds to its Romantics with determination, will no more allow them to be restyled than it would consent to having its grandmother's face lifted. Grandma is not kept dressed in the style of her 1880 coming out, however; a seemly adaptation to the mode is encouraged. She is constantly told how young she looks. She is given the place of honor at every ceremony and treated generally with the consideration that we observe toward those whom we know will not be with us forever. Her frequentation is considered to be a privilege for all and of inestimable value to the young.

Whether all this is as it should be I do not know, but certainly that is the way it is. And the concert season just now beginning will, I am sure, hold to its conservative path as relentlessly as all the other seasons have done. These do not vary noticeably from one year to the next or very much from decade to decade. From close up, from a reviewer's seat, their details are clearly always different. But from a little way off, from a summer vacational vantage point, say, they appear as comfortingly alike as successive Harvard graduating classes. Mei Lan-fang, the Chinese actor, confessed to a friend when visiting New York some years ago that he found it hard to tell one Occidental from another.

October 8, 1944

Program Notes

PROGRAM NOTES used to be a form of belles-lettres. As composed by Donald Tovey in Edinburgh, Philip Hale in Boston, Lawrence Gilman in New York, and Felix Borowski in Chicago, they were charming to read, informative, and often penetrating. At their least so, they were accurate, and their language was genteel. Their purpose was to supplement the listener's spontaneous musical understanding with detailed analyses of the works played and with such appropriate selection of historical data and classic comment as would tend to clarify the music for him, both its style and its content. Of recent years a tendency has been noticeable in program notes toward hastily gathered and often incorrect information, toward the omission of the analysis of form and the quotation of themes, and toward a substitution for the quoting of diversified critical opinion about works of the past, of sales talk about how beautiful they are. Even when notes are couched in good English (which is far from always), they are likely to resemble less a scholarly discourse than a publisher's blurb.

The sort of introductions that precede radio broadcasts of high-class music is even more offensive, on the whole, than what the symphony orchestras print in their house programs. The salesmanship note is nearly always dominant. The selection about to be played is praised as something especially picked out for the listener's private delight and brought to him through the benevolence of a loving radio company or some other equally affectionate lessee of that company's time. Since the purpose of all broadcasts is to create good will toward somebody's business, it is almost impossible for the executives of that business to think up a disinterested presentation. Radio disseminates huge quantities of cultural music of the highest quality, but it also disseminates simple entertainment. And so far the kind of honorific introduction it has been putting out with its cultural offerings is uncomfortably close to ballyhoo, or the advertising style of the entertainment industries.

It is quite probable that the decline of the concert program note in both scholarship and charm is due to the increased influence of radio's financial prestige on our symphonic organizations. It has not been my observation, however, that this influence is a direct one. Radio companies and the sponsors of cultural broadcasts are likely to show more respect for the radio public's intelligence than managers and conductors do. The conservatism of the Philharmonic's Sunday-afternoon programs is due to no pressure from either the Columbia Broadcasting System or the United States Rubber Company, so far as I can find out. There is every reason to believe, on the other hand, that the Philharmonic management is the timid one. Convinced by long experience in concert organization that the larger any audience is the safer the program must be, that management (and practically every conductor) is equally convinced that a nationwide broadcast is no place to do experimental or unfamiliar music.

The error in this calculation is to suppose that private listeners respond to music in the same way they would if they were gathered together in a hall. Group responses to anything tend to approximate those of the least intelligent persons present. The bed or fireside listener, like the reader of books, responds to art with his full intellectual equipment, no matter how elaborate this may be. He may get bored and turn the music off, or he may wander into another room. But if he listens at all he is not influenced by crowd psychology. The music itself must interest him. The radio people know that a considerable variety in programs is necessary in order to keep up this interest. Their advertisers know, too, that cultural broadcasts and mass entertainment are not the same. When they buy culture for prestige purposes they want the real thing.

It is my suspicion that the writers of concert program notes are reacting, as intellectuals so often do, to the presence of radio in everybody's musical life in an excessive and contradictory fashion. They imagine that because the radio announcing of high-class music is mostly a pretty low-class literary performance the radio public for that music must be ignorant and indiscriminating. This reasoning, which is, no doubt, largely unconscious, carries them to conclude further that the whole music public, since it certainly takes that sort of presentation, probably likes it. In any case, their notes tend to imitate the worst features of radio introductions—inaccuracy, inelegance, and blurb. They are not only debasing in this way a once respectable species of belles-lettres, they are removing from the symphony concert itself that aspect of serious instruction that is no less responsible than their fine musical executions are for the esteem in which our orchestras are held.

To print no program notes at all would be better, if that were practical. Such is the Continental habit. But it is not ours. We have always had them; we like them; we are entitled to proper ones. (We are also entitled to enough light in concert halls to read them by.) Proper ones consist of:

a. Historical information about composers and their intentions that is up to date and verifiable.

b. Analysis, with musical quotations, of the works to be played.

c. Fair statement, with quotations from other commentators and critics, of controversies previously raised by these works.

d. If a work is being performed for the first time, whatever preface the composer wishes to add.

There still are program annotators in the United States who attempt to furnish this information and who do so in graceful language. They are rare, though. What we mostly get is both incorrect and unreadable. This protest is not made out of any wish to delay the ultimate commercialization of our major orchestras. I am inclined, rather, to hasten that consummation if I can, because I believe that radio executives will take care eventually of our conductors' present conservatism about programs. They may even come to the rescue, too, of the program note, though that will be more difficult. I think it would be a good idea for the orchestras to improve their program notes right now, if only for business reasons. Because those notes are a cardinal element in the creation and the maintenance of any American orchestra's intellectual prestige. And its whole intellectual prestige (of which the orchestra's playing ability is only a part) is exactly what any orchestra has to sell to the broadcasters. The chief budget buckler, moreover, of our orchestras in the next ten years is going to be the money that is paid in by broadcasting companies, by lessees of broadcasting time, and by the corporations, mostly subsidiaries of broadcasting, that manufacture gramophone records. This support will be forthcoming exactly as long as the orchestras maintain their nationwide intellectual prestige. And they will maintain that only so long as they are clearly instruments of public instruction.

October 3, 1944

The Piano

THE MODERN PIANOFORTE, though the sound it makes is quite different from anything Mozart or Beethoven knew, is an invention of the late eighteenth century. Its characteristic quality, that which distinguishes it from all the preceding keyboard instruments of domestic usage, is expressed in its name; it can play both loud and soft. Like the modern orchestra, moreover, it can produce the effect that is the specific, the differential characteristic of musical Romanticism; namely, the quick, or expressive, crescendo. Mozart discovered both on his way to Paris in 1777, the modern orchestra at Mannheim and the piano (or fortepiano, as it was then called) at Augsburg.

The first of Mozart's real piano sonatas—the No. 7, in A minor—which was written the following year in Paris, not only makes use (in the slow movement) of expressive crescendo and diminuendo, but (at the end of the first) of an architectural crescendo that is the keyboard transcription of an orchestral effect. The three dynamic levels—soft, medium, and loud—that were never blended in Baroque and Rococo music but merely contrasted are here still used (and Beethoven also so used them throughout his life) for their effects of contrast. But these contrasts are no longer a merely architectural or rhetorical device; they are exploited freely (as in the development section of the first movement) for their value as expression. This is the first of all those romantic and modern piano sonatas, at once intimate and grandiose, that imitate at the keyboard the symphonic style. The scored crescendos of the Mannheim orchestra and the possibility that the fortepiano offered of imitating these on a solo instrumental determined in Mozart's lifetime the characteristics of a cycle in musical history that has not yet come to an end.

The evolution of the pianoforte from Mozart's time to ours has been continuous. The instrument Beethoven and Weber knew was already a more powerful one. That of Chopin marked a return to the clear articulation of the earliest ones without any loss of power. Liszt knew at the end of his life something that we should recognize by its loudness as a modern instrument, though he still played it with his fingers and very little arm weight, the keyboard action being lighter than that in use now. Even Debussy knew a lighter piano than we have here, the French

Pleyel being a more flexible and less emphatic instrument than our American Steinways, Knabes, and Baldwins.

The twentieth-century piano, nevertheless, as manufactured anywhere, is darker in tone than its eighteenth- and nineteenth-century ancestors. Also, it can play a great deal louder, especially in the bass. The chief motive of its designers has been to provide soloists with an instrument capable of holding its own in concertos against an orchestra of a hundred musicians. Modern piano technique is also designed to make possible, at all degrees of speed, a high degree of loudness. A wide dynamic range is now available to all properly trained pianists. Whether they wish to use it or not, it has been drilled into their hands, as it has been built into the pianos under them. It is less trouble to use it constantly than to refrain from doing so.

As a result, they blow up the piano music of the past to dynamic proportions that are not always an advantage to it. The works of Beethoven, Brahms, Liszt, and, curiously enough, Chopin are not as gravely obscured by the procedure as those of Mozart, Weber, Schubert, and Schumann are. If the solo piano music of the latter composers tends downward nowadays in popularity, that is due, I think, to the fact that overemphasis in the rendering of it has destroyed that mood of ease and of spontaneity through which alone it can be understood.

Wanda Landowska has restored the Mozart piano sonatas to life by removing from their execution all undue exercise of force. And she has not, as is the habit of lesser musicians, allowed them to fall thereupon into dimness and low relief. Her Mozart is as large in thought as it is reasonable in volume. Listening last Sunday night at Town Hall to her vivid evocation on the modern instrument of what these sonatas must have sounded something like (if our knowledge of the past means anything at all) when played by the composer on his own forte-piano made me wish that some pianist with a real understanding of Romanticism (rather than merely an atavistic feeling for it) would give us Schumann's music again, make it clear to us and friendly and direct. We know it is beautiful, but nobody plays it beautifully any more. It needs, I think, a smaller range of loudness and a more precise rhythm, more song, more syncopation, more breath, and a less agonized cantilena than we are accustomed to associate with it.

If much of the great piano music of the past has lost its savor for us, that is not the fault, I think, of pianists, who, as a class, are enlightened musicians, so much as of the modern piano it-self. The instrument has evolved so gradually toward its present dynamic range that we are likely to forget we are not dealing with the favorite instrument of the Romantics in the form in which the Romantics knew it. The best pianistic result obtains when a different dynamic gamut and a different kind of touch is employed for each composer. The pianists are certainly at fault who consider loudness a proof of sincerity or a substitute for sound rhythm. But there are many intelligent and consecrated musicians among them who need only to be shown the way of discrimination. Landowska's Mozart is a signpost pointing al-ready to happy hunting grounds. It shows us what delights can be derived from using the piano as a means toward the inter-pretation of music. That way lies infinite variety. Using all music as a vehicle to demonstrate modern power pianism is not even good showmanship. That way lies monotony and the limitation of repertory.

The violinists have brought their art to something of an im-passe by doing a similar thing. With the best intentions in the world, they are mostly unable any longer to conceive music as anything but a vehicle for personal display. If the pianists are to avoid this dead end they must start by limiting their dynamic palette. They must limit it in each piece to what is appropriate to that piece, reserving the full range of it for modern works written with an awareness of their instrument's power gamut. Organists do not turn on the full organ every time they see the sign *ff*. Gradations of loudness are the piano's chief source of variety. Using them all up in one piece is both stylistically and psychologically indiscreet. The painter Inna Garsoian recently remarked that a pianist at a grand piano always made her think of Jonah and the whale. Certainly, courage in the face of im-minent disaster marks the approach to his instrument of many a pianistic virtuoso. I like, however, to think of that powerful and sensitive mechanism rather as a serpent, deadly if approached with rough gestures, but capable of being charmed by music.

November 26, 1944

The Violin

THE FOLLOWING LETTER from a pedagogue of the violin expresses the despair that many music lovers have felt about the state to which that noble instrument has come down.

Nov. 1, 1944

My Dear Mr. Thomson:

I am increasingly concerned with a problem confronting my own profession and have decided to ask you, as a critic of long standing and one who is undoubtedly aware of the situation, what you think of it. I have been playing and teaching the violin for more than thirty years; and I am convinced that the days of great violin playing are numbered, that the time is coming when we shall have to be satisfied with inferior artistry unless something is done about it.

Each season high-lights the situation more, as brilliant new talent and new blood is introduced in all the arts. But for many years we haven't had one outstanding new violinist, and there are no sure indications of any on the way. We have only to count our few remaining artists, who must serve the entire world, to see how very serious it is. Why should this static and lifeless condition exist regarding one of our most important and beloved solo instruments?

If we had no talent there would be an excuse for it. But that is not so. Take, for example, the army of brilliant violin prodigies of ten or twelve years ago. They thrilled audiences throughout the country, amazed artists and critics alike. Whether or not we approve of prodigies, they were at least a substantial indication of talent. We were all sure, and justifiably so, that some of them, at least, would mature into fine artists. Unfortunately, however, they disappointed us. I think, Mr. Thomson, that if we could discover our mistakes with them we might find the key to the whole situation.

That brings us to the point of teachers. In piano we still have great pianists teaching. And we have always a new crop of finished pianists. In dancing, all of the great dancers teach. In violin, then, we need the same thing. More so, perhaps, for the violin is not an easy instrument, and not a profession for self-development at all. Since the birth of the violin all the magic performers have combined their performing gifts with the equally great and necessary profession of teaching; but now not one assumes the responsibility of making artists. It is indeed

unfortunate. If we could have more performing artists teaching
again, so that there would be a secure means of reaching the
top, and if the need for this could be explained, I am sure violin
playing would be healthy again.

If you feel for this as I do, your voice, through the press,
could help to bring some light and hope to the situation. I am
sure it would be very much appreciated. Thank you very much.
Sincerely,

Joseph Osborne.

It is not only the wonder children of ten years back that are
a disappointment to us. I am afraid the ones of thirty years
ago are just as unsatisfactory. They play the violin with high
skill, and they have made money. But they have remained wonder children, even into middle age. They still go by their baby
names, in fact, of Toscha and Jascha and Mischa and Sacha and
the like. Can you imagine what would happen to piano playing
if a whole generation of the best started calling itself "Artie"
Rubinstein, "Bobbie" Casadesus, "Rudy" Serkin and "Laddie"
Horowitz? It is all right to be a wonder child; many of the great
have been such. But the status should be scrapped at eighteen if
one wishes to take part as an adult in the adult life of one's time.

Technically, the violin is well taught and well played today
all over the world. Esthetically, our century has not come to
terms with the instrument. The last to be invented among our
common types of instruments, it is, nevertheless, the oldest of
them, because it has not been altered, to speak of, since the
seventeenth century. Scarcely a measurement or a procedure of
construction has changed. It is a survival intact of the Baroque
age. Only the bow with which it is played has evolved since the
days of the Cremona designers, and that attained its present
form more than 150 years ago.

The violin has the largest expressive gamut of any instrument
in the world. Sweetness, passion, terror, mystery, and grandeur are equally its province. And no other agency of music,
even the pipe organ or the lordly harpsichord, can approach its
unique fusion of nobility with grace, that particular intensity
among opposites that expressed to the century of Louis XIV
majesty. Well, our century is not much interested in majesty.
Grace in firmness and nuances of nobility are not our preoccupation. We like better displays of power and exhibits of intricate

mechanism. The pianoforte is our favorite solo instrument, as it was of the nineteenth century. From there we move to the complex assembly line that is the modern orchestra.

Against these superior efficiencies the solo violinists have taken refuge in sentiment; they have become purveyors of tenderness, of heart throbs, of musical small change. They have presented these minor comforts to us in a packaging of pseudo-modernity, silken-surfaced and utterly inconsequential. Their work has been neat in detail but lacking in simplicity, in grandeur of line. They have sacrificed, to be technical about it, steadiness of the bow arm to finicky fingering. Their right arm is so far inferior to the other that many of us have sympathized with the late Leonard Liebling's crack that what the modern world needs is a good violin concerto for the left hand alone.

All this is changing. Mr. Osborne is wrong, I think, in finding the violinists of today lacking in mature musical artistry. The wonder children of ten, twenty, and thirty years ago were. Today violinists like Isaac Stern, Joseph Fuchs, Roman Totenberg (and there are more) can interpret both old music and new with the full breadth of adult thought—straightforwardly, clean, steadily—without shocking their public. Violinists of this water have heretofore been confined to chamber music and to playing in the symphony orchestras as outlet for their musicianship. Technically they are as competent as the preceding generation of virtuosos. Musically they are superior. If their handling of audience psychology is less suave than the streamlined approach of the wonder boys, it is, nevertheless, more attractive to the musically literate. It may be that the solo violin is about to return to its rightful place as an instrument of major music making. I hope so.

November 19, 1944

The Organ

THE MODERN PIPE ORGAN and its repertory make a strange dichotomy. The instrument itself is the most elaborate, the most ingenious, the most complex, and the most expensive of all instruments. Also one of the most common. Hamlets that never saw a bassoon or a French horn or an Australian marimba or even a concert grand pianoforte will occasionally house a quite decent one. City people give them away like drinking fountains and stained-glass windows. And yet, in two centuries scarcely twenty pieces have been written for the organ that could be called first-class music. The learning, the taste, the engineering knowledge, and the skilled handicraft that go into the manufacture of even a reasonably satisfactory instrument are enormous. Nevertheless, not one major composer, since Sebastian Bach died in 1750, has written for the organ with any notable freedom or authority. Very few have written for it at all.

César Franck, perhaps, did the best, though none of his half-dozen best organ pieces is as commanding a work as any of his half-dozen best chamber and orchestral works. Also, Franck's position as a major composer in any medium is doubtful. The organ got much of their best work out of Frescobaldi and Couperin and Handel and Bach, not to mention a hundred other composers of the Baroque age. Since that time it is chiefly the second-rate that have written for it. Mozart, though a skillful organist himself, never wrote a solo piece for the instrument (though Grove's *Dictionary of Music and Musicians* lists seventeen sonatas for organ, "usually with violin and bass, intended to be used as graduales" in the Church service). Mendelssohn wrote six solo sonatas for it that are sound music, if a little stuffy. Brahms wrote eleven chorale-preludes, his last opus number, of which two are genuinely inspired, though neither of these is particularly well conceived for the instrument. And there are twelve organ pieces by Franck that are respectable as music. The rest of the post-Baroque repertory has been written by the Gounods, the Saint-Saënses, the Regers, the Viernes, the Widors, and their like—at its best, second-rate stuff by second-rate composers. Among the modern masters, only Schönberg, and that just once, has produced a work of any grandeur for the organ.

The cause of this neglect lies, I think, in the nature of the instrument itself, which has nowadays little but a glorious moment of history to offer. For the organ, like many another instrument of ancient lineage, did have its hour of glory. This hour, which lasted a good century and a half, say from roughly the year 1600 to quite precisely 1750, covers the whole of that period commonly known to the fine arts as the Baroque. And though in the visual techniques the high Baroque style is associated chiefly with the Counter Reformation of the Catholic Church, the musical Baroque penetrated, both in Germany and in England, to the heart of Protestantism itself.

That was the age that created the fugue, the aria, the free fantasia, the opera, the oratorio. It invented the violin, too, and carried to an apogee of musical refinement the keyed instruments, notably the organ and the harpsichord. It was the age of oratory in music, of the grandiose, the impersonal, the abstract. When it gave way in the middle of the eighteenth century to the beginnings of a more personalized romanticism, certain of its favorite media ceased to have effective power. The oratorio, for instance, has never recovered from that change in taste; nor have the fugue and its running mate, the free fantasia, ever since had quite the authority they enjoyed before. The opera survived by going in for personal sentiment in the arias and by giving up all that was merely grandiose in the set pieces. The violin also, played with the new Tourte bow (an invention of the 1770's), took on an appropriate sensitivity of expression. But the harpsichord fell wholly out of use, a new keyed instrument, the fortepiano, offering possibilities of voluntary accent and of crescendo that were far more attractive to the Romantic mind than the equalized articulation and terraced dynamics of its predecessor.

The organ survived the Romantic revolution, but it lost its primacy among musical instruments. It remained (and remains still) firmly intrenched in its privileges as a handmaiden of religion; but it has never since dared venture far, as the rest of music has done, from the protecting walls of the Church. It plays today the tiniest of roles in the concert hall and in the theater, while attempts to give it a new (and secular) prestige through its exploitation in department stores and cinemas have merely ended by robbing it of what little secular dignity was left to it after a century and a half of cloistered servitude.

Nevertheless, the instrument went on growing. It hypertrophied, to be exact. All through the nineteenth and early twentieth centuries it got bigger and bigger. It grew row after row of additional pipes, which included every possible reminder of other instruments, including the human voice; and the manufacturers imperiled its very existence by weighing it down with

every imaginable useless labor-saving device. It went to leaf
and flower, grew very little musical fresh fruit. In our time a
movement to restore to use the surviving organs of the Baroque
age, which are fairly numerous in Europe, and the construction
of new instruments modeled after these, have given us a new
enlightenment, just as a similar revival in harpsichord-building
has, about Baroque keyboard music. This revival, for all its antiquarian nature, has played a role in the drama of modernism.
Whether it is capable of reinvigorating the organ as an instrument of contemporary expression I do not know. But certainly
the communion it has provided with the Baroque keyboard
repertory, which is one of the world's very greatest musical literatures, is a closer one than was previously available. And that
has brought fresh ideas into modern writing, just as the studies
of medieval chant which the Benedictines of Solesmes carried
out in the late nineteenth century had given a new life both to
harmony and to the French vocal line, and just as the Greek
studies of the late Renaissance in Italy had rendered possible in
the year 1600 the invention of the opera.

And so the organ, in terms of its once central position in
musical advance, is today, as it has been for nearly two centuries
(and in spite of its continuing to be manufactured in ever more
and more pretentious format), as dead as the harpsichord. But,
as in the case of the harpsichord, an inspired resuscitation has
given today's world of music a source of knowledge, of real
acquaintance with the auditory past, that has brought the instrument back to a worthy and possibly to a proud position in
our creative life. Not that there is anything intrinsically unfortunate about having worked so long for religious establishments.
But religious establishments have for so long dallied on the
sidelines of musical advance that sacred organ composition,
like any other musical enterprise limited to Church patronage,
has usually found itself outclassed intellectually in the world of
free artistic enterprise. And thus it is that antiquarianism and
scholarship, for all their supposed sterility, have, by enabling us
to hear Bach fugues as Bach himself heard them, made to music
a gift that no other agency could have done, would have done,
or, to stick to the simple fact, did do.

August 5, 1945

The Great Tradition

FINDING himself, the other evening, alone and with an open mind, in, of all places, a night club, your reviewer took occasion to reflect upon, of all subjects, the problem of sincerity in musical interpretation. The artists who stimulated these reflections were, in the order of their appearance, Pearl Bailey, Claude Alphand, and Maxine Sullivan, the latter two of whom he has long admired. The other, Miss Bailey, turned out to be no end potent as a personality. But for all the personality, plus high skill in its projection (and, indeed, because of both), her work seemed to lie somewhere without the special interest of his department, in the domain, shall we say, of entertainment rather than of straight musical art.

There are few vocal artists now appearing in either opera or concert whose musical style is so straightforward as that of Miss Sullivan and Mrs. Alphand. Straightforwardness in musical interpretation has become, in fact, so rare a quality that the public does not always quite know what to make of it; and managements tend, in consequence, to discourage it. It is, nevertheless, the gauge of any artist's responsibility toward his art and the hallmark of the Great Tradition.

The Great Tradition in music, either of composition or of rendering, is not the history of techniques, their perfection and transmission. Still less is it the history of styles, of manners, of conventions. It is not the history of anything, in fact. It is a continuity, a thread that runs through all the histories, an attitude of certain artists toward their work that is in concord with a similar tradition in painting, in humane letters, and in scholarship. Its basic concept is that art is an image of reality, a telling of the truth about something. There is no class difference between the high-brow and low-brow music, between the "classical" and "popular" styles. Both are exploitable as entertainment, and both are appropriate media for expression. Expression, however, which involves objectivity and hence sincerity, is the grander usage, as we all know.

Straightforwardness in the rendering of music presupposes a respect on the interpreter's part for the authenticity, or truth, of the composition to be rendered. It admits the piece to be intrinsically worth doing. And since the doing well of anything that is in itself interesting gives the nature of that thing precedence over the manner of doing it (that nature being the determinant, after all, of the manner), a straightforward rendition, therefore, is one in which fifty-one per cent, at least, of the emphasis is not centered on either the interpreter's person or his means of operation. It shows us a piece of music that, in turn, shows us a piece of life. It does not offer us anybody on a platter; it merely transports us mentally to a place different from the one we are in.

All musical performance is a kind of acting. And the more completely the performer gets inside the role of each piece he plays or sings the more vividly does each piece impress us with its content. The more completely does he convince us, too, of his artistry. The use of music, or of any other technique, for the enhancement of the personality is an ancient practice and perfectly legitimate. The displaying for their own sakes of personality and of skill is ancient and legitimate, too; and musical performers, even composers, have often enough indulged in it. But it is not the Great Tradition either of music or of acting, which has always been one of keeping the script the center of interest.

In an objective operation like this, skill and charm get used to the full. No one wishes any artist to sacrifice his personal advantages. All we ask is that these chiefly serve the representation of something else. When women as beautiful as Claude Alphand and Maxine Sullivan (and musical executants of high finish they are, too) wear their charms and their accomplishments with so little of ostentation, they operate artistically with an effectiveness that is all the greater for their performance's being about something beyond the mere exhibition of those advantages. I only wish that more musicians worked in that loyal manner.

December 31, 1944

Radio Is Chamber Music

CHAMBER MUSIC is a natural for radio, and radio is exactly what chamber music has long needed. Bringing the symphony orchestra or the opera into the home is an adventurous operation involving, at best, so many distortions of both sound and sense that constant advertisements of the wonder of it all have to be added in order to make everybody feel right about it. But chamber music gets broadcast all the time and listened to without any alibis having to be furnished by the Appreciation slaves. Chamber music, in other words, is completely at home in anybody's home. And the radio, which exists in nearly every home, is, along with its elder sister, the gramophone, the universal chamber instrument of our time.

By chamber music let us not mean merely string quartets and the like. Chamber music is any music designed to be executed by a small number of musicians and to be listened to informally. Any instrument or any voice is appropriate to it; and any listener can enjoy it in his own way, so long as he listens in his own person and not as a member of an audience. It includes all the music in the world except that which deals in masses—masses of instruments or of voices in the execution and masses of listeners in the audience, which it is aimed to move as a unit, usually in the direction of applause. It is, in fact, the absence of applause as a mass reaction that distinguishes the opera and the concert from private music, from the music of the home.

Chamber music in public halls, though common enough, is really a recondite exercise. So are symphony concerts in the home. Both require, for full comprehension, a previous acquaintance with the works executed and a large effort of the imagination, to compensate for the acoustic and psychological distortions involved. People do not have to study in advance an opera they are about to hear, unless this is to be given in a foreign language (as is unfortunately the custom here). Neither is it of much value to prepare oneself for direct symphonic listening. Studying concert works *after* the performance, when the sound of them is already familiar, is by far the more rapid method of absorption. The same is true of chamber music, whether this is string quartets or madrigals or jazz. As long as the circumstances of listening are not too public, anybody who likes music at all can understand without ex-cathedra assistance any piece of any of the kinds of chamber music that he happens to like. At least he can begin to understand it; he can make its acquaintance, which is all that even the most musically expert ever does anyway at a first hearing.

And so, for all the charm of translations and of popular simplifications, it is just as well to remind oneself from time to time that opera is heard at its best in the opera house, symphonic music in the concert hall, and chamber music in some kind of semiprivacy. Now it just so happens that the radio and the gramophone—all the instruments, in fact, of processed music—operate most effectively in the very limitations that are chamber music's characteristic advantages. Individualized instrumentation, complexity of linear design and of rhythm they transmit beautifully. The things they do not transmit well— mass instrumentation, harmonic complexity, and variations of dynamic impact—are exactly the things that, though specific to the large orchestra, are unbecoming, if not downright impossible, to small groups. Not only, therefore, has the radio, by the convenience of its use in the home, become our principal chamber instrument. By the very virtues and limitations themselves of electrical transmission it has enlarged the usage of chamber music as chamber music many thousand times, and with a minimum of falsification.

As a disseminator of chamber music of all kinds, the radio is an organ of unquestionable value to culture. Its services to culture as a disseminator of operatic and symphonic music, though undeniable, are less clear, from the fact that it does not distribute these in anything like so true a reproduction. Listening by radio to music of mass execution is a convenient way of supplementing visits to its public manifestations. But as a substitute for these, though it enriches the lives of many a country dweller and shut-in, it is definitely unsatisfactory, just as reading plays is not a satisfactory substitute for going to the theater. I must say that the music of individualized instrumentation—chamber music—sounds, on the whole, better to me in the chamber, even though electrically transmitted, than it does in a public hall. There is no major change of proportion; and the loss of the living tone is slight compared with the advantages of privacy and of proximity which are gained.

Chamber music needs to be heard close by. Distance lends it no enchantment. The radio gives it to us in close-up. One can hear what goes on. Playing music with friends is a pleasure reserved for few and one that is even less generally available than formerly, since the professional standards of gramophone and radio execution have made everybody a little intolerant of amateur effort. The regular engagement of musicians for making music in the home is a still rarer indulgence nowadays; even the rich don't do it any more. But everybody has a radio and that means that everybody now has chamber music. Some of what the radio emits is massive music reduced to the possibilities of a chamber instrument; and a good deal of what it puts out is, of course, not music at all. There are speeches and soap operas and news. But a quite large part of the music broadcast is chamber music of all categories. It is right that this should be so and highly satisfactory. None of the legitimate reserves, indeed, that everybody has about radio in general applies at all to the broadcasting for private and semiprivate consumption of the music of individualized instrumentation.

January 7, 1945

Symphonic Broadcasts

LAST SUNDAY this column considered the radio as a chamber instrument, the universal chamber instrument of our time, and commented on the satisfactoriness in general of chamber music heard by that means. Chamber music, we repeat, does not mean merely European music in sonata form; it includes, of course, all the music of individualized instrumentation; and that means madrigals, string quartets, female trios, hillbilly songs, and most of our jazz—all of it, in fact, that is describable as hot. But let us consider today the radio as a purveyor of more massive music, of orchestral and operatic literature. There is no generic term for this, for the music that uses instruments or voices in phalanx. If we contrast its texture with that of individualized instrumentation, it is clearly the music of massive, or massed, instrumentation. If we contrast its acoustical layout and social function with those of chamber music, it becomes simply theater or hall music; and perhaps that is as descriptive a name for it as any.

The transmitting of chamber music from studio to home is a simple matter, a matter of sending it from one room to another. No distortions are involved save those inherent to any transmission; and nowadays these are almost imperceptible, especially if frequency modulation is employed. That is why radio music is naturally and normally chamber music. The transmitting of

theater or hall music, however, necessitates two major alterations, an acoustic one and a social or psychological one.

The acoustic distortion involved is the minimization of the
specific virtue of massed instruments or voices, namely, the
power range. There is very little advantage, excepting that of
added volume, in the employment of any body of string players,
for instance, or of singers more numerous than the independent lines of the music. I do not mean that sixteen first violins
sound like one violin, only louder; I merely mean that sixteen
violins have very little expressive advantage over one violin,
save that they can play louder. A wide dynamic range is an
advantage to expression, however; and the whole flowering
of orchestral composition that has made music so glorious in
the last 150 years has come about through the invention of the
scored crescendo, which makes of this whole range a unified
and enormous dynamic palette. The color palette has been enlarged, too; but a large color palette is not basic to orchestral
composition. Brahms, for instance, holds one's interest with
very little exploiting of it. But nobody ever writes an orchestral
work of any length that does not exploit as a major means of
expression the full range of orchestral loudnesses.

Orchestral literature is all built to sound clearly both soft
and loud, and the maximum spread of clear sonority between
these two extremes is attained in halls. In the open air it does
not balance properly or carry far, and in small rooms it creates
a confused reverberation. Importing this literature into the
home, whether by pianoforte transcription, music box, gramophone, or radio, is a matter of reducing it to room size. Neither
the instrument nor the room can take it in its original intensity,
in its original range of intensities, to be exact. And since this
range is almost its whole reason for existence—its specific difference from chamber music, in any case—hearing it in the
home, though a pleasure and a privilege, is not at all the same
thing as hearing it in a hall. Chamber music is like easel painting. It can be brought into the home intact or in the form of
amazingly faithful original-size reproductions. Orchestral and
operatic music is like architecture. It can be studied in the home
but not fully experienced there. Its broadcasts and its gramophone records bear about the same relation to their originals
that photographs of a cathedral do.

The psychological distortion is somewhat the same, too, because neither cathedrals nor symphonies were ever built for private use. Chamber music and easel painting, yes. But hall music and public edifices are intended for ceremonial usage—mass usage, emotional or intellectual unity, observances in common. Without the presence of a participant public (though the gesture of participation may be limited to applause only) these structures do not have the same quality, the same meaning to offer us. We can study them better in privacy, but we can really know them only in the exercise of their intended functions. Opera music and symphonic music are not different from each other save in the clarity of their literary programs. Both are public statements made to public gatherings. In both cases there is a good deal of musical execution in unison, and the whole thing is heard by rows and rows of citizens sitting elbow to elbow, observing toward one another and toward the performing artists the courtesy of silence, voting their degree of gratitude or approval at the end by the agreed-upon gesture of applause.

Do not think that Beethoven's, or anybody else's, symphonies are not meant to be applauded. They are mass music aimed at mass effect, and this is in no way to their discredit. Applause is not an aim, on the other hand, in string quartets; and this is not to their discredit. It is not an aim in jam sessions, either, or in any of the hotter forms of jazz. It is an aim in musical comedies. It is an aim in all the kinds of music that use massed musicians, excepting only the music of church services, where applause is replaced by the equally communal manifestation of common prayer. Make no mistake about it. Symphonies and operas are formal harangues, not fireside chats.

Chamber music on the radio needs no blurb. But broadcasts of orchestral music and opera have to be sold to the consumer. Every device of cajolery and impressiveness is employed in the introductory publicity to make him feel he is part of an audience, to create the illusion of participation in a ceremony. This is a legitimate procedure on the part of the broadcasters and a necessary one. Indeed, what we need is more explanation rather than less. That is why it has occurred to me as possibly of interest to point out to radio music consumers what I think is the true nature of the material they are dealing with.

Radio can amplify the usage of chamber music, has already

done so. It can broaden our acquaintance with symphonic music and opera, too. But in the one case the image of reality is resembling. In the other it is distorted. There is misunderstanding of a whole literature if the transmission of an orchestral concert or opera to a private room is taken to be anything but a rudimentary representation of the real thing. Broadcast chamber music comes very close to the real thing, and sometimes it is an improvement over it. Broadcast mass music gives only a part of the real thing and not its most characteristic enjoyments, which are the expressivity of volume variation and participation in a public event. That is why so much explaining on the part of the broadcasters and so much sales-resistant discrimination on the part of the consumers are necessary for obtaining a cultural result.

January 14, 1945

Surrealism and Music

THE SPRING NUMBER of *Modern Music* opens with four articles of homage to Arnold Schönberg on the occasion of his seventieth birthday, of which those by Ernst Křenek and by Lou Harrison are both penetrating and informative. It closes, as usual, with a fireworks display of critical articles that illumines the contemporary music front all across the United States. But the real novelty of the issue is a reflective article on the place of music in modernist esthetics by a man who has admittedly little taste for the art and no precise knowledge about it. The author of this far from undiscerning essay is no less a writer than André Breton, founder, defender of the faith, and for twenty years pope of the surrealist movement in French poetry, at present head of the surrealist government-in-exile in New York City.

Mr. Breton defends his own antagonistic attitude toward music on the grounds that it is identical with that of most of the nineteenth- and twentieth-century French poets. He admits, however, the desirability of some fusion between it and his own art. And he recommends to musicians a "return to principles" comparable to that which has made surrealism for two decades now the chief movement of renovation in European poetry.

The first observation needs no rebuttal. It is, alas, only too true that since the divorce of poetry from music (Thomas Campion was the last in England to practice both with distinction) the poets have manifested consistently a certain bitterness toward the rival auditory art. They have indited odes to it aplenty, I know, and spoken of it on many occasions most feelingly; but their homage has rarely been without guile. Shakespeare very nearly gave the plot away when he referred to music as a "concourse of sweet sounds." (Imagine the explosion that would have occurred had any one dared in Shakespeare's London to call poetry a "running together of pretty words.") The great one eventually carried his campaign for the discrediting of music as a major art to the point of proclaiming it frankly "the food of love." His disinterestedness in this matter has not hitherto been questioned. But music died in England shortly after him.

What Mr. Breton, a poet, fails to consider here is the propaganda for the dignity and the grandeur and, most important of all, the meaning of music that was operated so successfully by the nineteenth-century philosophers. It is not the exceptional suffrages of Baudelaire and Mallarmé that have given to music its prestige in contemporary society but the systematic and relentless praise of its expressive powers by Hegel, by Schopenhauer, and by Nietzsche.

On the fusion, or re-fusion, of the two great auditory arts Mr. Breton adopts without argument the Wagnerian thesis that this is desirable. As a good Marxian he refuses the "reformist" program of closer collaboration between poets and composers, maintaining with some justice that poems "set to music" serve no valid artistic purpose and that opera librettos are and always have been a pretty silly form of literature. He seems to think that the fusion might be operated by some one man working at a high emotional temperature, and he suggests the passion of love as possibly useful to this end. What such a fusion would accomplish beyond a regression to primitive esthetics is not proposed to us. One wonders if Mr. Breton envisages as desirable a similar fusion of the visual arts, the reunion of painting and sculpture, for instance, with or without a framework of architecture, the event to take place by no collaborative procedure. One wouldn't wish that dish on his dearest enemy. The musical theater is only now recovering from Wagner's megalomaniac seizure of all its creative privileges, and convalescence is still far from complete.

That music should take a lesson from contemporary French poetry and go back to principled operations is not a bad idea. That the functioning of the auditory invention to be studied in its divergent manifestations of poetry and of music is an even better one. It is probable that persons of strong auditory memory vary in the relation that their auditory function bears to specific bodily regions. Audito-cerebral types are likely to make poets, orators, preachers, and even statesmen. Audito-visceral types, persons whose reactions to sound and to the memory of it are organic (which means emotional) rather than visual or muscular, make musicians. The audito-kinetic make dancers, acrobats, and the like. Persons for whom noise is merely a sexual stimulant, as it is for rats, may reasonably call music "the food of love"; and their type, though common, is a low one in the biological scale.

The fusion of divers artistic techniques through personal collaboration is an ancient procedure. Their simultaneous exercise by one person is an even more ancient procedure, a primitive one, to be exact. The desirability of reestablishing this in custom depends on the feasibility of trying to develop in human beings a generalized bodily reaction to sound in place of the specifically varied ones that seem to be at present a mark of the higher human types. The matter is worth investigating; but so far as anybody knows now, music is better off without its former legal and virtually indissoluble union to the word.

What Mr. Breton does not seem to have grasped about music is that, instead of being behind poetry in its evolution, it is in many ways more advanced. The dissociative process, which has made possible Mr. Breton's whole career and that of the poetic movement he presides over, has long since lost its novelty for composers. The composer who doesn't use it freely is simply not a very interesting composer; his work lacks fancy, surprise, richness, originality, depth. The right of poets to express themselves by means of spontaneous, subconsciously ordered sequences of material has seemed to many in our century a revolutionary proposition. It is, however, the normal and accepted way of writing music. Any imposition of logic upon this, whether in the form of allusions to classical rhetoric or in the observance of the only rigorous syntax known to our time, the twelve-tone system, is considered in some circles as dangerous radicalism.

The Romantic revolution, in short, was successful in music. It won real freedom for the composer. That it was not successful in literature is proved by the fact that Mr. Breton and his friends are still fighting for it. Haydn, Mozart, and Beethoven, sometimes foolishly spoken of as classicists, were the most radical of libertarians; and sonata form, their favorite continuity convention, was, as is well known, no strict formula at all but the slenderest possible framework for the display of musical fancy and for the expansive expression of spontaneous, non-verbalized feeling.

Music's modern movement is another thing from poetry's. The verbal art is still demanding liberty from arbitrary intellectual restraints. The tonal art, that freedom long since gained and the things it was gained for saying long since said, has fallen, through the progressive lowering of its intellectual standards, into demagogic and commercial hands. Its modern movement is based on the demand that music be allowed to make some kind of plain sense again. We seek no loosening of our intellectual clothes; they are so loose now we can barely walk. What we want is readmission to intellectual society, to the world of free thought and clear expression.

It is more than probable that some of the surrealists' psychological devices for provoking and for sustaining inspiration can be used to advantage by composers, since they are largely of musical origin anyway. They cannot fail, certainly, to encourage spontaneity of auditory invention, because they represent a return to the best Romantic practice in this regard. What they do not represent is any kind of novelty for the musical world. They are, in fact, what the post-Baroque musical world is all about. Musicians are only too delighted, I am sure, to lend them for a while to poetry, with all good wishes for their continued success.

April 2, 1944

French Rhythm

WHAT makes French music so French? Basically, I should say, it is the rhythm. German musicians and Italian musicians tend to consider rhythm as a series of pulsations. French musicians consider pulsations as a special effect appropriate only to dance music, and they train their musical young most carefully to avoid them in other connections. In the Italo-German tradition, as practiced nowadays, the written measure is likely to be considered as a rhythmic unit and the first count of that measure as a dynamic impulse that sets the whole thing in motion. In French musical thought the measure has nothing to do with motion; it is a metrical unit purely. The bar line is a visual device of notation for the convenience of executants, but the French consider that it should never be perceptible to the listener.

The French conceive rhythm as a duality of meter and accent. Meter is a pattern of quantities, of note lengths. Its minimum unit in execution is the phrase. Accent is a stress that may occur either regularly or irregularly; but in any case, it is always written in. It may occur on the first note of a measure; but in well-written music it will usually appear more frequently in other positions, since any regular marking off of metrical units tends to produce a hypnotic effect. French music, unless it is written for the dance or unless it aims to evoke the dance, has no dynamic propulsion at all. It proceeds at an even rate, unrolls itself phrase by phrase rather like Gregorian chant.

It is more than probable that the classical Viennese symphonists were accustomed to this kind of rhythmic articulation and took it for granted. That pulsation came into Viennese symphonic execution somewhere around 1830, after the waltz had come to dominate Vienna's musical thought. At any rate, discerning Germans have frequently pointed out the superiority of French renderings of their own classics. Wagner found the Beethoven symphonies far better played by the Paris Conservatory Orchestra than anywhere in Germany, and he based his own later readings on those of the French conductor Habeneck. Alfred Einstein, German Mozart specialist of our own day, has avowed in his book, *Greatness in Music*, his preference for French renditions of that composer. And certainly German organists have not in our century played Bach with any authority comparable to that of Saint-Saëns, Widor, Vierne, Guilmant, and Schweitzer.

This acknowledged superiority of the French approach to classical German music is due, I believe, to the survival in French musical practice of classical observances about rhythm, elsewhere fallen into disuse. Those same observances are responsible, I believe, for the vigorous flowering of music in France that is the most noteworthy event in the musical history of the last seventy-five years. French harmonic innovations have been striking, but so were those of Richard Strauss and of Arnold Schönberg, of Gustav Mahler, even. Everybody has played around at inventing a new harmony. Scriabin in Russia, Ives in Danbury, Connecticut, were not less original harmonically than Claude Debussy. What their music lacks is true rhythmic life. The only music of our time that can compare in this respect with that of the school of Paris is American hot jazz. And this is based on the same duality of meter versus accent that underlies French music.

The French rhythmic tradition is at once more ancient and more modern than any other. It includes the medieval plain song and the Benedictine restoration of this, in which a wholly quantitative syllabic execution without any regular stresses whatsoever turns out to be expressive and interesting. It includes the French medieval and Renaissance music that grew out of plain song, the schools of Champagne and of Burgundy. It remembers its own Baroque and Rococo styles. It is least aware, perhaps, of the domain that is the very center and pivot of German musical understanding, the world of nineteenth-century Romanticism, though Chopin, Liszt, and, curiously, Schumann it considers as its own. All these it thinks of, along with Mussorgsky and Stravinsky and Spanish dance music and the popular music of Java and Bali and Morocco and the United States, as in no way foreign to itself.

The binding element, the thread that runs through all these different kinds of music is an absence of pulsating rhythm. In Greek theory quantities are one element of rhythm; stress is another; cadence (or phraseology) is the third. Pulsation has no place in this analysis. It is a special effect, derived from round dancing, only to be added to musical execution when round dancing is clearly implied as the subject of a musical passage. Its introduction elsewhere brings in a sing-song element that tends to trivialize musical rhetoric. Bach played by Schweitzer or Landowska, Mozart and Haydn played by Beecham (who is no Frenchman but who remembers the eighteenth century as it was) and modern French music conducted by Monteux or played on the piano by Schmitz are anything but trivial.

Other artists in other repertories have their charms and their especial powers, like Horowitz's Liszt, Toscanini's Wagner, Walter's Brahms. These always seem to me like cases of pure genius, supported (excepting possibly for Walter) by no major tradition. But the others not only are supported by a major tradition; they support it, too. They are constantly tending it, pruning it, watering it, grafting new shoots on it, gathering from it new fruits. The parent stem of that tradition is, I think, a certain approach to rhythm. That approach is as ancient as Hellas, as far-flung as China, Marrakech, and New Orleans, as up-to-date as boogie-woogie or the percussion music of John Cage. I take this occasion to speak about it because there is better access to it right now in New York City than there has been in some years and because I hope some of our young musicians, both composing and executant, may be induced here and now to profit by the occasion. I believe this view of rhythm to be the open sesame of musical advance today exactly as it has been all through history.

November 14, 1943

Expressive Content

EXPRESSIVITY in music is its power of communication. All the music that is any good says something. A great deal of music says things that are clear to all. This is particularly true of music that has words to it—songs, oratorios, and operas. Also of music that has fanciful titles or footnotes—such as *Lullaby*, *Rustle of Spring*, *Turkish March*, *A Faust Overture*, *Cowboy Rhapsody*, *Kitten on the Keys*, or *The Sea*. But even music that bears on its title page no such revelation does have meaning all the same. For the passive listener it may be sufficient that a Beethoven or Tchaikovsky symphony seems pregnant with meaning in general, the imprecision of that meaning being part, indeed, of its power. The interpreter can afford no such vagueness. He must make a guess at the music's specific meaning. Otherwise he has no test for determining tempos, rhythmic inflections, and climactic emphases beyond the notes and markings of the score. And these are never enough, musical notation being as inefficient as it is.

Nor can the composer avoid deciding about the character of his work. He may have created it in a fine fury or in a semi-euphoric state of automatism; but if he wants anybody to use his creation he has to provide some clues to its meaning. He must indicate the speed, the loudness, the kind of lilt he wants. If he wishes orchestral performance he must clothe his creation in unalterable colors and accents. No composer can orchestrate a piece without deciding on the expression that he wishes given to every phrase. A theme conceived for flute has quite another character when played in unison by thirty-two violins. Though both versions may appear in the same composition, only the composer can determine which appears first; and that determination involves a decision about the kind of feeling that he wishes his music to communicate, both as a whole and in detail.

Any performance is correctly called an interpretation. The creator creates and then adds, somewhat later, as many aids as he can think of toward a clear interpretation. The final, or public, interpreter thereupon translates the whole into sound, making his own decisions in every measure about the exact inflection that will best transmit what he esteems to be the composer's meaning. If he thinks the composer's specific indication requires violation in order to attain what he believes to be the work's larger sense, he makes that violation and takes responsibility for it before the musical world. He is right to do so, though he should not do so without reflection. The composer's specific indications are themselves not always a part of his original creation but rather one musician's message to another about it, a hint about how to secure in performance a convincing transmission of the work's feeling content without destroying its emotion and intellectual continuity. The latter continuity, of course, is not an end in itself; it is merely the composer's means of achieving, of not interrupting, emotional continuity.

There is no such thing as an abstract, or meaningless, musical work. There are brief musical phrases and formulas so common that they are in themselves neutral, but these are not neutral when placed in a context. They take on meaning, or they underline by a merely apparent neutrality the meaning of something else. The materials of art are all, taken separately, expressively neutral—colors, words, grammar, sounds, and seams no less than metal and stone. The most valuable are those capable of taking on in a variety of contexts a large number of meanings. That is why the oboe is superior as art material to the saxophone. The latter is powerfully affecting but limited in its gamut of expressivity, notably in the direction of self-effacement.

The creation of meaning by the use of musical lines and formulas, familiar and unfamiliar, is the art of composition. Nothing else is involved. Classical and structural observances have no other value, nor has novelty. In themselves they are without significance, and no employment of them in composition has any value beyond the immediate context. Nor are they capable of acquiring any value in a specific context other than that which the meaning of the whole lends to them for that occasion.

A composer's education involves acquiring a vocabulary of useful turns and formulas. The employment of these and the invention of others in musical works with a unique expressive content is the operation that determines a composer's quality as an artist. The techniques of musical composition are many. The purpose of it is single. That purpose is the creation of art. Art is an infinitive multiplicity of unique objects known as works of art. Their materials are limited; consequently they bear to one another a great material resemblance. Where they differ notably is in meaning, or expressivity; and their survival is determined by that meaning, provided their structure is not just too stupid to bear repetition. If that meaning is unique it can be remembered, and reconsulting it is a pleasure. If not, remembering it is scarcely worth while. The original of which it is an imitation is good enough for us.

And so, to recapitulate my theme, expressivity is what a piece of music says. That communication, as is appropriate to music, is chiefly emotional; and its form in memory is auditory, because sound is its medium. The communication can vary somewhat from interpreter to interpreter, from age to age and even from place to place; but such variation is not large. It cannot be, because any piece of written music, to be performable at all, has to have implied expressive content and some kind of supplementary indication as to the specific character of that content. Otherwise it is sound without sense, and musicians just won't go on with it. Even paid or commanded they won't.

The determination of music's sense is the privilege, in any group, of the leader, though there is always some communal contribution to this. The definition of this expressivity in words is the hardest thing any critic or historian ever has to undertake, though the recognition of its presence, and even the degree of its presence, in any composer's work is not difficult. Most musicians and most habitual concertgoers are able to recognize strength when they encounter it. Sometimes their recognition takes the form of anger, sometimes not. But it is likely to be fairly dependable. Audiences are easily bored by nonentities but not easily angered by them. Active audience resistance to anything is one of the clinical signs by which we recognize quality. Because it is not the direction of an audience reaction that is critical; what is significant is its strength. And that strength, believe me, is not determined by the mere sounds made. It comes from the character, the individuality of the music's expressive content. Audiences have always complained about what they call dissonance in one piece, while accepting the exact same tonal relations in another. Here is proof aplenty, if more is needed, that what they really mind is something in the expression.

April 13, 1947

Intellectual Content

MUSIC, a creation of the human mind, has its appeal for all the faculties of the mind. Its message, its direct communication, is to the feelings, of course. But the methods by which continuity is sustained and interest held are a result of thought taken. And though it is desirable that this thought be not too evident, that it not interfere with the transmission of feeling that is music's both immediate and final aim, it does have a listener interest over and above its functional efficiency, because any construction of the human mind is fascinating to the human mind. This is the workmanship aspect of music, the quality that adds beauty to expression. And so if the power of provoking specific emotional effects can be referred to as music's expressive content, the power of provoking cerebration, of interesting the mind, may legitimately be called, I think, its intellectual content.

The intellectual content of anything—of music, painting, poetry, oratory, or acting—consists of references to tradition, to the history of its own technique as an art, of a wealth of allusions, indeed, to many things under the sun. Expressive content is personal, individual, specific, unique. It cannot be borrowed. If it is not spontaneous it is not sincere, hence not, in the long run, convincing. But intellectual content is all borrowed; it is only the choice and the appropriate usage of allusions and devices that give them validity in any work. Exhibited overostentatiously, they merely prove vanity. Aptly applied they enrich the texture and delight all.

The richness of music's intellectual substance varies from composer to composer. It is greater in Bach, for instance, than in Handel, though the latter, predominantly a man of the theater, has a plainer and more direct emotional appeal. Mozart's frame of reference, likewise, is more ample than that of Haydn. It is characteristic of both Bach and Mozart to use dance meters without the idea of dancing being the only thought communicated. Bach writes between an organ toccata and its fugue a siciliana which is at the same time a religious meditation. And Mozart writes in a piano sonata (O, how often) a slow movement which is both a minuet and a love duet, as well as a piano solo.

The best opera composers have usually avoided, in writing for the lyric stage, any duality of allusion that might weaken the impact of the expressive content. The best concert composers, on the other hand, are those who employ the techniques of multiple meaning, adding thus to simple expressivity contrapuntal interest and the perspective effect of contradictory evocations. It is Beethoven's gift for working opposites in together that gives to his concert music its phenomenal power of suggesting drama, which is struggle. Beethoven has for this reason intellectual content to a high degree. He did not refer much, except in his later works, where he employed constantly the deliberate archaism of fugal style, to the history of composing techniques; but he did manage by careful handling of the contemporary techniques, to make one thing mean many things (as in the variation form) and to make many things mean one (as in the ten-theme symphony form). He holds attention to this day, in consequence. He keeps the listener occupied.

Wagner's operas have the highest intellectual content of any. I don't mean the philosophical tomfoolery of his librettos, either, though this was necessary to him as a pretext for elaborateness of musical texture and for the whole psychological refinement that was his chief legacy to the stage. Puccini's operas have probably the lowest intellectual content of any, though their plots are far from stupid. Their expressive content, which is chiefly self-pity, is powerful by its simplicity. But the emotional composition of this has little depth or perspective, and the musical textures employed are of small interest as workmanship.

Tchaikovsky, Sibelius, and Shostakovich are demagogic symphonists because the expressive power of their work is greater than its interest as music; it does not fully or long occupy an adult mind. Debussy and Stravinsky are fascinating to the adult mind. They stimulate feelings and provoke thought. Schönberg and Hindemith are overrich of intellectual interest in proportion to their feeling content; they are a little dry, in consequence. Bartók, Milhaud, and Copland strike a sound balance between mental and emotional appeal, even though their intensity in both kinds is less than one could wish it were. Roy Harris oscillates between extreme intellectuality, for which he has little gift, and a banal, a borrowed emotionalism, which he cultivates out of a yearning for quick-and-easy success. At his best, however, he is both moving and interesting. Olivier Messiaen is a similar case, though his musical gift is greater and his mind more ingenious.

The music of the great masters is always good both ways. So is that of the little masters; they merely produce less of it. One could go on for columns describing the music of past and present masters in terms of its vital equilibrium, its balance of heart and head. And one could get into some pretty arguments. Brahms, Bruckner, Mahler, César Franck, Ravel, and Liszt are tough cases to judge. So are the great men of jazz. Schubert, Schumann, Verdi, Mussorgsky, and Fauré are more clear. They were truly great artists, though all suffered from technical deficiencies.

What makes possible the writing of good music, beyond that talent for handling sound that is required for being a musician at all, is emotional sincerity and intellectual honesty. Both can be cultivated, of course; but no man can quite lift himself by his boot straps. Unless he has a good heart (the psychiatrists nowadays call this affectivity) and a strong, vigorous mind, he will not write any music capable at once of touching the human heart and interesting the human mind. Art that does not do both dies quickly. And longevity is the glory, perhaps even the definition, of civilization's major achievements.

April 20, 1947

Ethical Content

JUST as we require of music, in order that it be acceptable as "serious," not only that it move our hearts but also that it be interesting to the mind, there is yet a third qualification about which we are no less exigent. We insist that it be edifying. This demand is as old as time. Every civilization and every primitive community have recognized a music of common or vulgar usage and another music, grander of expressive content and more traditional in style, a music worthy of association with the highest celebrations of religion, of patriotism, and of culture. This latter kind of music is known to our time as "classical" music (as distinguished from "popular"). Whether its intrinsic content, expressive and intellectual, is all that determines its position of prestige among us I am not sure. The case of jazz, a highly civilized but persecuted music, leads one to think that other factors may be involved. In any case, all the music that our time accepts as noble is endowed by that very acceptance with an ethical content. This means that dealing with it in any way is believed to be good for one.

Saint Clement of Alexandria was convinced that goodness is intrinsic to certain kinds of music and wickedness to others. He encouraged the faithful in the usage of diatonic melodies and regular meters, exhorted them to avoid "chromatics and syncopation," which he believed led to "drunkenness and debauchery." This belief is still widespread. Indeed, the proposition has never been disproved. And though Sebastian Bach employed both devices consistently and convincingly (at least to posterity, though his congregation did complain) in the praise of God, and though Beethoven employed them no less to celebrate the brotherhood of man, the fact remains that when any composer wishes to depict heaven in contrast to hell or the serenities of virtue versus the excitements of sin, he is virtually obliged to use for the one a plainer, stiffer melodic and rhythmical vocabulary than for the other.

Olivier Messiaen has devoted his whole musical career to the purging, so to speak, or conversion to devotional uses, of all the most dangerous musical devices. The augmented fourth (or *diabolus in musica*), the major sixth, the false relation (or use of contradictory chromatics in two voices), the exaggerated employment of chromatics in melodic and harmony, the ornamental dissonance, the integral dissonance, the highest elaborations of syncopated and other broken rhythms, and an almost sinfully coloristic orchestration are the very substance of his musical style, though piety is certainly its subject. And yet even he is obliged, for the depiction of evil, to go farther in the same direction and to insert additional violations of custom and of symmetry. I suspect, indeed, that it is not so much the employment in music of all the known picturesque effects that is valuable for suggesting the dark forces as it is a certain absence of symmetry in their employment. There is no reason why the music of the higher spheres should not be represented by the higher complexities and that of man's lower tendencies by all that is banal, bromidic, and puny, though so far no major composer has, to my knowledge, essayed to represent beatitude by interest and fantasy, in contrast to a damnation (as in Sartre's *No Exit*) of boredom by monotony.

The endowing of music with an edifying ethical content is a problem every composer has to face. He may face it by avoiding it. This is the romantic procedure, to assume that art's only connections with morals lie in the sincerity of the artist's personal sentiments and in the honesty of his workmanship. Or he may face it by the more classical method of associating his work with ideas, institutions, ceremonies, and events of an edifying character. Drama with a moralistic ending, poetry of known cultural value, the court symphony, the patriotic occasion, anything whatever having to do with religion, ancestors, or anthropology—all these are sure-fire associations; and there is no composer, living or dead, of major repute who has not employed one or another of them.

A major problem of our time is the concert symphony. The court guest of Haydn's and Mozart's day was less exigent than we are about moral impressiveness. What he liked was liberty. The nineteenth-century music lover, a bourgeois, loved literary, nationalistic, and travelogue content. In our time many composers have endeavored to satisfy the public's taste for news commentary by using current events and international relations as a subject of musical reflection, but so far the results have not been very satisfactory. No contemporary composer has yet matched Beethoven's mastery of the editorial vein, though they can draw circles around him at literary and exotic evocation. And though a great deal of the supposed editorial content in Beethoven is an invention of later times (that which associated his Fifth Symphony, for instance, with the ultimate victory of our side in the last war), it is perfectly certain that his "Battle of Vittoria" does represent a comment on a news event (over and above its delightful straight reporting) and that his Third (or "Heroic") Symphony is the ancestor of the modern editorial symphony.

But if Beethoven invented the editorial symphony, he also furnished, in my opinion, the earliest precedent for its misuse. The precedent is the final movement in his Fifth Symphony. In this piece, I am convinced after much reflection, the form is determined not by any inner necessity or logic derived from its musical material, nor yet from any expressive necessity that grows out of the preceding movements. I think it is a skillful piece of pure theater, a playing upon audience psychology that has for its final effect, along with the expression of some perfectly real content, the provoking of applause for its own sake. If I am right, here is the first successful precedent and model (the finale of Brahms's First Symphony being the second) for that application to symphonic composition of the demagogic devices that are characteristic of so much symphonic music in our time.

Whether the technique of this demagogy is derived from Beethoven, who fell into it, if at all, only that once, or whether it is an invention of smaller men, there it is, in any case. The similar vulgarization that overcame Italian opera about fifty years ago, a concentration on applause at the expense of communication, is nowhere suggested in the work of the great Verdi, though it is in that of Boïto and of Ponchielli. A tolerance of such procedures gives us that cult of "pure" theater which finds any Broadway melodrama or Hollywood sex trifle a model of dramatic procedure. There is no such model to be found where expressive, intellectual, or ethical content is low. And the modern symphony-about-current-events has somewhere along the line accepted expressive and intellectual standards (chiefly the latter) unworthy of its ethical aspirations.

The symphony, after all, is a romantic form. It is subjective and must therefore be sincere. And though any man can have sincere sentiments about a political matter, I have yet to hear a political symphony, excepting Beethoven's Third, that convinced me that the sentiments expressed were entirely spontaneous. There is a hortatory tone about all such work nowadays that is unbecoming to a form with so grand a history of deeply personal expression. Perhaps the political symphony is eloquent only when inspired by protest or revolt. Perhaps, too, the political passions of our time are less grandiose than we like to think. Certainly they are less impressive than the vast variety of human suffering that has been provoked by their translation into political, economic, and military action.

Somewhere in the modern world or in the history of music there may be available an attitude that would enable composers to view today's political events in a manner at once intelligent, ethical, and compassionate. I sincerely hope such an attitude can be found. Until it is, however, a great deal of contemporary composition, operatic as well as symphonic, is bound to appear to us as animated by either a banal escapism or by an assumption of ethical rightness, of a moral nobility that is not justified by either the intellectual or the expressive context offered in support. On the whole, modern composers have done better work when they have treated history, travel, anthropology, autobiography, sex, and abnormal psychology than they have done with current events. Simple patriotism they handle well, too. Even religion they can be convincing about, though few of them are pious men. Their political ideas, however sound from a voting point of view, have not yet proved adequate for the graver responsibilities involved in concert exposition.

April 27, 1947

Americanisms

For all the vaunted virtuosity of the American symphony orchestras, your correspondent has long wondered what, if any, has been, or is likely to be, their contribution to art. American ensemble playing on the popular level has given to the world two, perhaps three, expressive devices of absolute originality. One is a new form of tempo rubato, a way of articulating a melody so loosely that its metrical scansion concords at almost no point with that of its accompaniment, the former enjoying the greatest rhythmic freedom while the latter continues in strictly measured time. Another characteristically American device is playing "blue," using for melodic expression constant departures from conventionally correct pitch in such a way that these do not obscure or contradict the basic harmony, which keeps to normal tuning. Simultaneous observance of these two dichotomies, one metrical and one tonal, constitutes a style of playing known as "hot." And although precedents for this are not unknown in folklore and even in European art custom, our systematization of it is a gift to music.

Another device by which our popular ensembles depart from European habits is the execution of a volume crescendo without any acceleration of tempo. It is possible that Sebastian Bach may have played the organ without speeding up the louder passages, but Bach did not know the volume crescendo as we conceive it. He only knew platforms of loudness. The smooth and rapid increase of sound from very soft to very loud and back again is a Romantic invention. It is possible, even today, only with a fairly numerous orchestra or chorus, on a pianoforte, or on the accordion. It is the basic novelty of musical Romanticism; and the nineteenth century invented a fluid rhythmic style, in which pulsations were substituted for strict metrics, to give to the planned crescendo a semblance of spontaneity.

It was the conductor Maurice Abravanel who first called my attention to the rarity of the nonaccelerating crescendo in European musical execution. It has long been used to suggest armies approaching and then going off into the distance, its rhythmic regularity being easily evocative of marching. But aside from this special employment it is foreign to Romantic thought. If you want to get a laugh out of yourself, just try applying it to Wagner or Chopin or Liszt or Brahms or Beethoven or even Debussy. These authors require a fluid rhythmic articulation. And though one may for rhetorical purposes, as when approaching a peroration, get slower instead of faster as the volume mounts, it is obviously inappropriate in Romantic music to execute a subjectively expressive crescendo or decrescendo without speeding up or slowing down.

The modern world, even in Europe, has long recognized the rhythmically steady crescendo as, in theory, a possible addition to the terraced dynamics of the eighteenth-century symphony. In fact, however, European composers have never, to my knowledge, used it without a specifically evocative purpose. Of the three most famous crescendos in modern music not one is both tonally continuous and rhythmically steady. Strauss's *Elektra* is tonally continuous, rising in waves from beginning to end; but it presupposes no exact metrics. Stravinsky's "Dance of the Adolescents" (from *The Rite of Spring*) and Ravel's *Bolero* do presuppose a metrically exact rendering, but they are not tonally steady crescendos. They are as neatly terraced as any Bach organ fugue.

The completely steady crescendo is natural to American musical thought. Our theater orchestras execute it without hesitation or embarrassment. Our popular orchestrators call for it constantly and get it. Our symphonic composers call for it constantly and rarely get it. The conductors of European formation, who lead most of our symphonic ensembles, simply do not understand it. Very few of them understand metrical exactitude in any form. American music, nevertheless, requires a high degree of metrical exactitude, emphasized by merely momentary metrical liberties. Also lots of crescendo, which is our passion. The music of Barber and Schuman and Piston and Hanson and Copland and Harris and Bernstein and Gershwin and Cowell and Sowerby and Randall Thompson and William Grant Still is full of crescendos. It is also full of rhythmic and metrical irregularities. But none of it is romantic music in the European sense, because the crescendos and the rhythmic irregularities are not two aspects of the same device. The separation of these devices is as characteristic of American musical thought as is our simultaneous use of free meter with strict meter and free with strict pitch. These three dichotomies are basic to our musical speech.

Hearing Howard Hanson or Leonard Bernstein conduct American music is a pleasure comparable to hearing Pierre Monteux conduct French music or Bruno Walter interpret Mahler and Bruckner. The reading is at one with the writing. Our foreign-born conductors have given the American composer a chance to hear his own work. Also, they have built up among the public a certain toleration of American music, or encouraged, rather, a toleration that has always existed. But they have built up also a certain resistance to it which did not exist here previous to the post-Civil-War German musical invasion. This resistance comes from a complete lack of adaptation on the part of the European-trained to American musical speech. They understand its international grammar, but they have not acquired its idiom and accent.

In so far as they are aware that there are an idiom and an accent (as several of them are), they are likely to mistake these for localisms of some kind. They are nothing of the sort; they are a contribution to the world's musical language, as many postwar Europeans are beginning to suspect. American popular music has long been admired abroad, but American art music is just beginning to be discovered. It would probably be a good idea for us here to keep one step ahead of the foreign market by building up a record library of American works in authoritative renderings by American-trained artists. Also to accustom our own public to this kind of authoritative collaboration. We shall need both a professional tradition and broad public support for it if we are to accept with any confidence the world-wide distribution of American music that seems to be imminent, in view of the world-wide demand.

Actually we are producing very nearly the best music in the world. Only France, of all the other music-exporting countries, operates by stricter standards both of workmanship and of originality. Not Germany nor Italy nor Russia nor England nor Mexico nor Brazil is producing music in steady quantity that is comparable in quality to that of the American school. And we are a school. Not because I say so, but because we have a vocabulary that anybody can recognize, I think, once it is pointed out, as particular to us.

January 27, 1946

Modernism Today

MUSICAL MODERNISM, as this has been understood for fifty years, is nowadays a pretty dead issue. Its masters are all famous and their works are known to the public. Its libertarian attitude toward dissonance, rhythmic and metrical irregularities, and unconventional sonorities is no longer revolutionary. Children are brought up on these liberties; and even symphony subscribers, a notoriously conservative group, accept them as normal. The only form of modernism that remains to be imposed (or finally refused) is atonality.

In such a situation, with little left to fight for, what future is there for the composing young beyond a prospect of inevitable conformity? How can they avoid being placed in the public's present scheme of things as mere competitors of their elders? How can they be fresh and original and interesting in their own right? Having observed them pretty carefully during the last ten years both here and abroad, I have come to the conclusion that they are doing exactly what anybody could have figured out by pure logic that they would do. They have taken up the only battle left, namely, that of atonality and its allied techniques.

Not all the young, I grant you, are atonalists. There are neoclassicists and neoromantics and even a few retarded impressionists among them. But a generation takes its tone from those who branch out, not from those who follow in footsteps. And today's adventurous young, believe me, are mostly atonal. This position has more to offer them in artistic discovery and less in immediate royalties than any other available, excepting only the tradition of pure percussion. The latter is for the present so limited in scope and so completely occupied by John Cage that there is not much room left in it for anybody else.

The atonal techniques, however, are more ample. One can move around in them. And the young of England, France, Italy, and the Americas have recognized that fact. Germany and Russia, on account of their lack of expressive freedom in the last ten and more years, are slower in taking up the new manner. There are still too many older ones that have not been accepted there yet. But in the countries where intellectual freedom is the norm, young composers are busy with nontonal counterpoint.

Nontonal music, any music of which the key and mode are

consistently obscure, has so far always turned out to be contrapuntal. It cannot be harmonic in the conventional sense, because chords pull everything back into a tonal syntax. And if harmonic in an unconventional way, through dependence on percussive and other pitchless noises, it becomes contrapuntal through the necessity of writing for these in varied simultaneous rhythmic patterns, these being its only source of formal coherence.

Counterpoint within the conventional scales can be of three kinds. That practiced in Europe from the twelfth through the fifteenth century is known as quintal, which means that, read vertically at the metrical accents, the music will be found to contain chiefly intervals of the fourth and fifth. Tertial counterpoint, which was the official style from the sixteenth through the nineteenth century, exhibits principally thirds and sixths when read this way. Secundal counterpoint, which is characteristic of our time, stacks up on the down beats as mostly seconds and sevenths.

Any of these styles can be used with either a diatonic or a chromatic melodic texture. The twelve-tone syntax, the strictest form of chromatic writing, can even be made to come out harmonically as tertial counterpoint. The music of the chief living neoclassicists—Stravinsky, Milhaud, and Hindemith—is diatonic secundal counterpoint. That of Schönberg is mostly chromatic secundal counterpoint. On account of this music's lack of a full acceptance by the general public such as that of the neoclassicists enjoys, it remains, with regard to the latter, though it was conceived, in point of time, earlier, in an "advanced" position. The more vigorous movements among today's young are, in consequence, all more closely related to Schönberg than to the others.

The newer music offers a divergence, however, from Schönberg's practice in its consistent preoccupation with nondifferentiated counterpoint, a style of writing in which all the voices have equal obligations of expressivity and identical rights in rhetoric. The dramatizing of counterpoint into melody, bass, countermelody, and accompaniment is abolished in this style for an equalized texture that recalls the music of the pre-Renaissance period. There are advantages here to intimacy of expression, since the composer can speak in this technique as personally through a vocal or string ensemble as through a solo instrument. The disadvantage of it is that it is not easily applicable to diversified ensembles, where variety of timbre and technique imposes a certain differentiation of melodic style from one voice to another.

The new music, therefore, is mostly homophonic in sound, or instrumentation. It is personal in expression, too, and contrapuntal in texture. Its counterpoint is secundal and generally chromatic. If it were not the latter, it would resemble more closely than it does official, or neoclassic, modernism. It can appear tonal or nontonal when examined closely; and it can follow or not Schönberg's strict twelve-tone syntax, which this composer himself does not always follow. But its chromaticism invariably approaches atonality. This last, let us remember, is not a precise or easily attainable end. It is rather an ultimate state toward which chromaticism has always tended. Its attractiveness to our century comes, I think, from its equalization of harmonic tensions. We like equalized tensions. They are the basis of streamlining and of all those other surface unifications that in art, as in engineering, make a work recognizable as belonging to our time and to no other.

February 2, 1947

"*Theory*" *at Juilliard*

REVISING THE CURRICULUM is a major American sport. Everybody enjoys it. Students and faculties alike find it invigorating. For presidents of educational institutions it is the *sine qua non* of tenure. It is the perfect mechanism for getting rid of one's predecessor's aides-de-camp and putting in one's own. And it is proof both to students and to the intellectual world that the job is no sinecure but a full-time occupation. It offers to all the comforting conviction of progress. And it is intrinsically good for educational institutions, for without it they do go to seed.

The Juilliard School of Music has just announced such a revision of its "theory" department, "theory" meaning all the branches of musical instruction that have to do with understanding the texture, structure, and composition of music, as distinguished from its performance. The announcement is welcome, not so much because of any notorious inefficiency in the present instruction as because of its fittingness in the general pattern of William Schuman's presidency of the institution, a reign, or regime, that has begun brilliantly and that offers every prospect of continuance with high benefit to American music.

Mr. Schuman is young, vigorous, sincere, passionate, and competent. To follow in his predecessor's footsteps would be neither appropriate nor interesting though these footsteps have marked out trails of no mean value. Nor is there any question of backtracking and of calling those trails an error. It is simply that Mr. Schuman must go on from there. And the way any first-class American educator goes on from where he took over is to remake the institution into the kind of household where he can live and work with comfort. He must re-form it into his own image.

It is a characteristic of American life that many of our greatest teachers, from Mark Hopkins to Frank Lloyd Wright, have been less the product of schools than of self-education. Now when these men take over the instruction of others, they tend not to destroy the systematic or formal elements of education. They value, rather, the formalities that their own youth was deprived of. But they do tend to alter the content of those formalities. They revise the curriculum with an eye to making it a systematized version of their own nonsystematic education.

William Schuman is a composer and teacher whose preparation has been, in any scholastic sense, of the sketchiest, but whose practical experience in both composition and pedagogy has been marked by continued success. He is a practical man, an autodidact, an eclectic. He has learned his business the easy way (for any American of talent and character), that is to say, by doing it. He now proposes to offer his students a systematized version of his own training; and if all our grandest American precedents hold, he will be successful. He will be successful not because his system is any better than another, but because he is a good teacher and because, like any other good teacher, he must teach his subject the way he learned it.

That way is the way of personal initiative. Schuman proposes to let the students learn methods rather than rules and to derive these from the study of classical and modern music rather than of rule books. The procedure is similar to the famous "case system" of the Harvard Law School, where the principles of law are arrived at through the study of many court cases rather than learned in advance and applied to the interpretation of court cases. It works beautifully if the instructors see to it that the proper principles are arrived at. It works badly unless the student acquires a repertory of principles, in one way or another, along with his repertory of cases.

In musical "theory" instruction the abandonment of textbooks for case books is a normal accompaniment to that revision of the curriculum that takes place in any case about every twenty or twenty-five years. When the old books lose their savor and the older instructors their understanding, the old books have to be thrown out and the instructors changed. The young instructors, when this happens, are likely to teach for a year or so right out of Palestrina's and Bach's and Schönberg's own works. Then gradually they systematize, too, their teaching, settle on certain examples that they have found more useful than others for exposition purposes, and codify the principles of composition, as they understand them, with these tested examples as illustrations. Next, to simplify transmission of their now codified thought, they print, first a syllabus of their course, and then a whole textbook of it. And everything is right back where it was twenty years before. So a new president takes over and throws out the old textbooks and gets some new blood into the teaching staff.

It is the opinion of this writer that one system of instruction is about as good as another, exception made for whichever one has just been in use. Teachers vary in effectiveness, however, and so do students. The ungifted will always blame their failures on the setup. A good teacher and a good student can always come to terms, no matter what system of instruction is in vogue. A good president can rarely come to terms with the system and personnel he has inherited from his predecessor. It is a proof of William Schuman's devotion to his job at the Juilliard School that he has undertaken a thorough revision of its teaching. A busy man and a successful composer, he could so easily have kept the status quo and let his institution quietly run down. But he has accepted the responsibility of keeping a great institution at least as effective as it has been before. He would even like to make it more so. Consequently, he has undertaken a massive curricular revision. This involves lots of work, but there is no other way. There is nothing in the whole intellectual domain so elaborate to install and, once installed, so fragile and so impermanent as any of the pedagogical methods by which civilization is preserved and transmitted.

May 18, 1947

Second-Rate Season

LOOKING BACK at the music season now approaching its end, this reviewer finds he can remember very little that took place. Discussing it with friends and colleagues, he finds that in the opinion of these very little that was out of the ordinary, in fact, did take place. There were lots of concerts and recitals and the usual number of operatic performances, but unusual departures from routine repertory or from average standards of competence in execution have been almost nonexistent.

The New York Music Critics' Circle will have to make its annual awards on a basis of very few available works, since the new American pieces given here for the first time can almost be counted on five fingers. And our New York situation is not unique. The Pulitzer Prize Committee has been worried all spring lest the number of new American works performed anywhere in America be insufficient to justify the giving of that prize at all. Our City Symphony has been fairly assiduous about novelties; our Philharmonic has been skimpy about them. Philadelphia, not of late a very novelty-minded orchestra, has furnished about its usual quota. Boston, formerly our chief source of fresh musical material, would seem to have gone ultraconventional all of a sudden. In any case, all of the orchestras that play here regularly, excepting the City Symphony, which has kept a lively repertory, have played hardly enough new music, American or other, for anyone but their conductors to shake a stick at.

The local opera companies at the Metropolitan and City Center, as well as the Salmaggi and San Carlo troupes, have long disaccustomed us to novel repertory. Of that they offer us literally and exactly nothing, and they do not pretend otherwise. Their policy is identical with that of the New Friends of

Music, conservatism for the box office's sake. And the regular run of recitalists follow the same slogan. A few here and there play something new and get applauded for it. But mostly they stick to the conventions. And the conventions would have one believe that the music-consuming public only wants, and will buy, chestnuts.

The falsity of the supposition is proved by the devotion of certain small groups among the public to musical advance and to quality. Nobody pretends that these small groups are capable of supporting large institutions. But they are capable of supporting a great deal more modern music and quality music than they are nowadays being given a chance to do. They flock to hear Maggie Teyte and Landowska and the Cantata Singers. They turn out for Povla Frijsh and for the two-piano playing of Gold and Fizdale. They even mobilize, on occasion, the literary world. They are a devoted public. To throw away their special custom by lumping them with the mass public is to act like a book publisher who would refuse to publish a manuscript not clearly destined to sell a hundred thousand copies.

This latter seems to be the calculation of the recording companies. Their output of anything beyond the Fifty Pieces is pathetically small. They are commercial institutions and may possibly be excused from the cultural obligation, though their virtual monopoly of materials and distribution facilities will one day force a raising of the cultural question. But the orchestras and the Metropolitan are, in theory, intellectual foundations. They are committing intellectual suicide by not appealing to the intellectual public. Let them give standard repertory for the young people and for the musically retarded who are not yet familiar with it. The reciting of sacred texts has no doubt a place in art, as in religion; let it by all means go on. But not to give special concerts for the musically active (concerts that they are perfectly willing to pay attention to) is like making adults take all their meals at the children's table. This is faulty cultural policy and, in the long run, bad business policy, though it is defended at present as a business economy.

Just how much opera companies and symphony orchestras contribute to real musical life is questionable, anyway. They go through a routine about this; and some of their customers certainly get pleasure, even profit. Whether these benefits are worth what the whole thing costs is hard to say. Certainly expensive orchestras are a more important part of music's business setup, which could not do without them, than of our cultural setup, which could. They are the branches of a vast international chain store of music, with interchangeable managements, musicians, conductors, soloists, and repertory. They supply to the public only a very small part of the repertory that is properly their stock in trade.

The performance of this repertory is a public service. Wherever business does not supply it, governments do. Where business does supply it, the circulation is larger; but the number of pieces supplied gets smaller and smaller every year. I have no proposal for remedying the stalemate beyond elaborating the scheme. I do think that supplying all the kinds of music for all the kinds of musical taste in separate concerts and separate series of concerts would serve the public better and that it would, in the long run, be more profitable. Beyond this innocent suggestion, I can only comment, as a regular concertgoer, that giving the same kind of thing to everybody does not seem to me a satisfactory system of cultural operation. I find less and less memorable difference, as any season goes on, between one concert and another; and I do not believe this standardization to be culturally advantageous. Paternalism in cultural matters is always oppressive, even when practiced by enlightened governments. When practiced by business under the guise of philanthropy, it amounts to forcing the consumption of an inferior product. Because art that is not full of variety and surprise is, by definition, second-rate.

May 5, 1946

A War's End

MODERN MUSIC, distinguished quarterly review edited by Minna Lederman and published by the League of Composers, has ceased publication after twenty-three years. Musicians and laymen who are part of the contemporary musical movement will of necessity be deeply moved by this announcement, because *Modern Music* has been for them all a Bible and a news organ, a forum, a source of world information, and the defender of their faith. It is hard to think of it as not existing, and trying to imagine what life will be without it is a most depressing enterprise. Nevertheless, we shall be living without it, whether we like that or not. Some other magazine or group of magazines may substitute their charms for its uses and delights; but none can replace it ever, for none was ever like it.

No other magazine with which I am acquainted has taken for its exclusive subject the act of musical composition in our time or sustained with regard to that subject so comprehensive a coverage. This one reported on France and Germany and Italy and England and Russia and Mexico and the South American republics, as well as on its own United States. It covered musical modernism in concerts, in the theater, in films, radios, records, and publication. Jazz and swing procedures were analyzed and Calypso discovered in its pages. Books dealing with contemporary musical esthetics were reviewed. The only aspects of music excluded from it were those that make up the ordinary layman's idea of music, namely, its composition before 1900, its interpretation, and its exploitation as a business.

Modern Music was a magazine about contemporary composition written chiefly by composers and addressed to them. It even went into their politics on occasion. When our entry into the recent war brought to certain composers' minds the possibility that perhaps our government might be persuaded not to draft all the younger ones, thus husbanding, after the Soviet example, a major cultural resource, Roger Sessions disposed of the proposal firmly by identifying it with the previous war's slogan "business as usual." And when, on the liberation of Europe, consciences were worried about musical collaborators, a whole symposium was published, exposing all possible ways of envisaging the problem. Darius Milhaud, as I remember, said that traitors should be shot, regardless of talent or profession. Ernst Křenek pointed out that Shostakovich, who had accepted from his own government artistic correction and directives regarding the subject matter of his music, was the prince of collaborators. While Arnold Schönberg opined that composers were all children politically and mostly fools and should be forgiven.

In the atmosphere of sharp esthetic controversy that pervaded the magazine and with its constant confrontation of authoritative statement and analysis (for there is practically no living composer of any prestige at all whose works have not been discussed in it and who has not written for it himself), wits became more keen and critical powers came to maturity. It is not the least of many debts that America owes Minna Lederman that she discovered, formed, and trained such distinguished contributors to musical letters as Edwin Denby, Aaron Copland, Roger Sessions, Theodore Chanler, Paul Bowles, Marc Blitzstein, Samuel Barlow, Henry Cowell, Colin McPhee, Arthur Berger, and Lou Harrison. My own debt to her is enormous. Her magazine was a forum of all the most distinguished world figures of creation and of criticism; and the unknown bright young were given their right to speak up among these, trained to do so without stammering and without fear.

The magazine's "cessation of hostilities," as one of its European admirers refers to the demise, is explained by its editor as due to "rising costs of production." Considering previous difficulties surmounted, I should be inclined to derive the fact from a deeper cause. After all, the war about modern music is over. Now comes division of the spoils. Miss Lederman's magazine proved to the whole world that our century's first half is one of the great creative periods in music. No student in a library, no radio program maker, dallying with her priceless back issues, can avoid recognizing the vast fertility, the originality, ingenuity, and invention that music has manifested in our time.

This is all admitted now, and modern music is played everywhere.* There is no war about it any more. Our century's second half, like any other century's second half, will certainly witness the fusion of all the major modern devices into a new classical style. That fusion, in fact, has already begun; invention is on the wane, comprehensibility within the modern techniques on the increase. And the public has ceased resisting them as such. The stabilization of modernism's gains is the order of the next few decades. Other organs of musical opinion will no doubt take over *Modern Music*'s leadership. But what has been done well and finished off cleanly will remain as history.

*An encyclical of Pope Pius XII, entitled "*Mediator Dei*," dated November 20, 1947, recommends its use in the services of the Catholic Church. This lifts the ban on contemporary musical styles that the encyclical of Pius X, "*De Motu Proprio*," had imposed in 1903.

No other musical magazine of our century can possibly have the place in history, either as monument or as source material, that *Modern Music* already occupies, because no other magazine and no book has told the musical story of its time so completely, so authoritatively, so straight from the creative laboratory and from the field of battle. Its twenty-three volumes are history written by the men who made it. For the history of music in any epoch is the story of its composers and of their compositions. Nobody ever tells that story right but the composers themselves. What Haydn thought of Mozart and Beethoven, however wrong as opinion, is true as musical history. What Heine thought of Beethoven, however right, is literature and belongs to the history of another art. The subsequent recounting of musical history from documents of the period belongs, of course, to still another. Thanks to *Modern Music* the last quarter-century has probably a better chance of being written up convincingly than any other, save possibly those years between 1820 and 1845, when Schumann, Berlioz, Wagner, Liszt, Weber, and Jean-Paul Richter (himself a composer) all wrote voluminously about their contemporaries.

January 12, 1947

MUSIC RIGHT AND LEFT

Prelude

TEN YEARS AGO, as this book goes to the printer, I made my bow to the New York musical scene in a role I had not previously undertaken, that of a reviewer of music in the daily press. Misgivings were in my mind about my appropriateness for the task. As a composer of definite orientation about schools and styles, I had some fear lest inevitable offense to vested musical interests bring on battles that my employers might find inimical to a newspaper's duty, which is informing the public.

Such battles did not fail to burst. But considerably to my surprise, the editors of the *New York Herald Tribune*, far more used than I to public controversy, seemed less to be worried than interested. They found it only natural that differences of opinion should exist between their critical columns and their organizers of musical events. Their own aim, indeed, was early revealed to me as identical with my own. We were not interested in either backing or attacking, on principle, the Philharmonic-Symphony Society or the Metropolitan Opera Association or the commercial associations engaged in concert management. We were simply informing the public, to the best of our ability, about the products offered by these groups, as well as by all others.

In my first years on the paper I laid about me a good deal, and the paper took the brunt of the counterattacks. With punctilious consideration for my inexperience, my employers actually kept from my knowledge the troubles I had caused them. Ogden Reid, the editor, Geoffrey Parsons, the chief editorial writer, Mrs. Reid, the whole editorial and business staff stood behind me. So did my music staff, headed by the devoted and impeccably informed music editor, Francis Perkins. At no time, in fact, during my ten-year association with the *Herald Tribune* have the editors interfered once with the statement of my musical opinions or offered me a directive along that line. Counsel I have received, and mostly I have had to ask for that, about the ethics of controversy and the amenities of public statement. But from the beginning it is I, not those who fancied themselves my opponents, who have had the paper's support.

Also from the beginning I have held to my line. That line

assumes that a musician's account of a musical event has legitimate interest for readers. Personal tastes I consider it fair to state, because by admitting one's prejudices and predilections one helps the reader to discount these. I do not consider them otherwise interesting nor ask for agreement regarding them. Description and analysis, however, I have tried to make convincing and, as far as possible, objective, even when sympathy is present. My own sympathies, frankly, are normally with the artist. I try to explain him, not to protect the public against him, though preserving a status quo or protecting anybody's career is not my intention either. Neither do I think myself entitled to make out report cards. I do not give an examination; I take one. I write a theme about an occasion. If my remarks are not found apt, that is no fault of the subject.

Over the years, I do find, however, that my coverage has altered. At the beginning it was more catholic. I reviewed the big names and the little names, the old music and the new. Nowadays I pay less attention to standard repertory and standard soloists, to what one might call the nationally advertised brands. They get covered, of course; but I tend to leave these more familiar assignments to my ever-patient colleagues of the staff. I like to examine the newer trends, the nonstandardized musical life of outlying cities, experiments in the universities, everything that might be preparing the second half of our century for being different from the first. That is why the present volume has so much to do with the problems of modernism and so little with Marian Anderson or Toscanini.

With all the battles of modernism now long since won excepting that of the atonal style, the twelve-tone-row composition of Schönberg and his school has been of late a constant subject of my awareness. It is my firm hope that the latter part of our century will see the amalgamation of all the modernist musical techniques into a twentieth-century classic style. Such an evolution, indeed, has been in progress ever since the First World War. Whether any of the atonal ways, the most resistant of all to absorption, can be saved for posterity or whether, as many atonalists believe, this style must either kill off all others or wholly die is a matter of passionate preoccupation to musicians. A large part of the youth in America, in France, in Italy, in England, in South America has already placed its faith in the twelve-tone syntax. The question of its future, nevertheless, still burns. That is why I cannot keep from coming back to the subject again and again and why I hold by sharing my interest in it with readers.

Another subject that has been constantly in my thoughts, and in those of many another reviewer, is the future of opera in America. I have searched out novelty with hope, and I have watched with anxiety repeated efforts of the Metropolitan establishment to lift itself out of a stagnancy. Just now a new general manager, Rudolf Bing, is taking over that establishment. His intentions are certainly of the best, but nobody knows what he will be able to do with an impoverished and seemingly moribund institution. His mere presence, however, has rendered obsolete all preachments about the ineffectiveness of previous policies. I have omitted, therefore, most of my general articles about the Metropolitan and left merely some reviews of specific performances. If the coverage seems skimpy here, it has not been so, believe me, in my column.

My ten years on the *New York Herald Tribune* have been lively for all concerned and for me a happy decade. I have had some good fights, heard lots of beautiful music, made a few enemies and hundreds of friends. Earlier volumes of my collected reviews give a broader view, show more of the whole musical scene. This one, which includes reviews and Sunday articles published between October, 1947, and June, 1950, falls short, I realize, of being a full panorama of music at the half-century. It is rather a peep into certain forces at work, in my opinion, toward the realization of our century's identity. Those forces are abundantly present in our concert halls and opera houses these days; listening to and for them is a delight. They are not the only delight of musical attendance, but they are the chief source of that "strangeness in the proportion" that is ever the foretaste of beauty. The rest appears more and more to me, after ten years' press service, as not quite news.

V. T.

October, 1950
New York City

ORCHESTRAS AND CONDUCTORS

Conservative Institution

THE SYMPHONY ORCHESTRA, among all our musical institutions, is the most firmly established, the most widely respected and, musically speaking, the most efficient. It is not, however, either the oldest or the most beloved. The opera and the singing society, I should think, have better right to the latter titles. Nevertheless, the orchestra is what all music, its prestige, its exploitation, and its teaching, turns round. It is the central luminary of our contemporary musical system.

Someone, I cannot remember who, suggested several years ago that the strength of the institution comes from the fact that the concert orchestra is a representation in art, a symbol, of democratic assembly. Certainly it is so conceivable. And certainly its rise is contemporaneous historically with the rise of parliamentary government. The fact that its most glorious period, as regards composition, the working years in Vienna of Haydn, Mozart, and Beethoven, was a time when, in that place, there was no parliamentary government at all, does not disprove the identification. It merely suggests that the parliamentary ideal, as represented then by England, was strong enough to influence democratic-minded men everywhere and that its picturing through music, an art too difficult to censor, is more than probable in a country which would not have tolerated at the time any such representation through the less hermetic techniques of painting and literature.

In any case, these men in Austria, not the composers of liberal England or of revolutionary France, transformed the court symphony into the popular symphony. Never again, after they had lived, was the symphony an elegant or decorative form. It was larger, louder, more insistent, more humane, broader of scope, and definitely monumental. Its performance ceased to be a private entertainment and became a public rite. Also, there has remained with the symphony ever since an inalienable trend toward, in the broad sense, political content.

Professional symphony orchestras today remain associated with the political unit, the city. They are a privilege and symbol of civic pride. States and central governments rarely support them. Even municipalities do not like contributing taxpayers' money to them, though in a few American cities—Baltimore, Indianapolis, and San Francisco—there is a budgetary provision for such aid. Normally they are a civic proposition, and their deficits are met by public-spirited citizens. Rarely are great orchestras associated with our religious or scholastic foundations (as our finest choruses are more often than not) or directly with the world of big business and finance and fashion (as our best opera companies have always been). They are wedded to our great cities. They are monuments of civic pride and symbols not only of musical achievement but of their communities' whole cultural life.

There are really two kinds of orchestras, the monumental and the directly functional. The latter kind exists in large numbers connected with educational institutions and with the amateur musical life of neighborhoods and of semirural communities. In 1937 there were about 30,000 of these in the United States alone. Their chief purpose is the musical training or musical enjoyment of the players, though they also provide in increasing numbers nowadays professional players to what I call the monumental orchestras. The latter are strictly professional and perform only for the edification of the listener.

The functional orchestras, being educational in purpose, play a larger repertory than the others do. And their style of execution is less standardized. The monumental orchestras, being more ceremonial by nature, are highly standardized in both repertory and execution, internationally standardized, in fact. The players, the conductors, the pieces played (save for a very small number that represents local taste only) can be removed from one orchestra and inserted in another anywhere in the world. Even language is no barrier to rehearsal efficiency. Indeed, it is exactly their international standardization that enables our orchestras to represent localities, to symbolize to the whole world the cultural level—by internationally recognized standards—of the particular city that supports any one of them.

The civically supported symphony orchestra is the most conservative institution in the Western world. Churches, even banks, are more open to experiment. The universities are daring by comparison. This does not mean that new music does not get played by the orchestras. The rendering of contemporary works along with familiar classics is one of their firmest traditions. No orchestra can live that plays only the music of dead composers. As a matter of fact, no orchestra ever essays so radical a policy. The public objects to modern music, naturally, because modern music, however great intrinsic musical interest it may present, simply can never compete as edification with the hallowed past. But the same public that objects to hearing modern music objects far more vigorously to being deprived of the privilege. Just as the music execution of our symphony orchestras is the most conservative and correct that money can buy, so also is the repertory they play, a certain appearance of musical progressiveness being required by tradition itself.

The encouragement of musical advance, however, is not the chief purpose of symphony orchestras. The first-line trenches of that lie elsewhere. They lie in many places, but always the rapidest progress of musical invention takes place where the attention of so large and so pious a public is not present to discourage the inventor. Small groups of musicians working under private or university patronage can produce more novelty in a year than will be heard at the subscription concerts in twenty. Invention takes place sometimes, even under the very eye of a large public, provided that public is looking at something else.

If theatrical entertainment is there to give novelty a *raison d'être*, as at the ballet or at the opera, or if the occasion is not too respectable socially, as in jazz dives, then the circumstances for musical invention are at their most favorable. The symphony orchestra favors musical advance officially, but it dare not offer much of it at a time. It must advance slowly, because it deals with a large public, which necessarily is slow of comprehension, and because the basis of its whole operation is the conserving of tradition anyway. Stability rather than variety is what the faithful chiefly demand of it.

Our symphony orchestras, historically viewed, are solider than our banks. They are always getting born; they rarely die. Constantly threatened with financial disaster (a talking point during campaigns to raise money or in union negotiations), they almost never cease operations. Nor will they, so long as civic pride exists and so long as democratic government through parliamentary procedure shall seem to us a beautiful ideal worthy of representation in art.

December 28, 1947

The Delights of Autumn

PHILADELPHIA ORCHESTRA, *Eugene Ormandy*, conductor, last night at Carnegie Hall, performing Mr. Ormandy's orchestration of the Bach Toccata and Fugue in D minor, Sibelius's Symphony No. 2, three fragments from Berg's *Wozzeck*, and Ravel's Suite No. 2 from *Daphnis et Chloë*. Soloist: *Gertrude Ribla*, soprano.

THE PHILADELPHIA ORCHESTRA opened its New York season last night in Carnegie Hall with a showpiece for the group's justly famous string section, a third-rate symphony correctly supposed to be popular, some excerpts from one of the great dramatic works of our century that is incorrectly supposed to be unpopular simply because our Metropolitan Opera has never produced it, and a standard dessert-piece that is both popular and first-class music. The execution of all these works under the leadership of Eugene Ormandy was a dream of beauty.

Mr. Ormandy's transcription, heard here for the first time, of the Bach Toccata and Fugue in D minor for organ is not limited in its orchestration to the string choir; but it is a showpiece for strings all the same. This arrangement employs only brief moments of woodwind relief and of brass re-enforcement at the climaxes. It makes the strings work practically all the time and mostly alone, displays to advantage all the delicacy and all the power of a string body matchless, to my knowledge, anywhere in the world. With a group of more modest equipment in this regard, the present version might sound poor. For the Philadelphia Orchestra it is just right.

Alban Berg's *Wozzeck*, though familiar in Central European opera houses before the war and celebrated all over the world, has been little given in this country. Whenever it has been produced, even in the form of brief concert excerpts, it has made a profound impression. Last spring Bernard Herrmann played bits of it on the C.B.S. "Invitation to Music" program. Werner Janssen has recorded four sides of it. Publicly, however, the work has not been heard in New York since Leopold Stokowski gave the whole opera here in 1937 for the League of Composers.

That timidity is no longer justified in presenting so simply expressive a work to the public was proved last night by its warm reception. The Sibelius Second Symphony received, along with sustained applause, some boos. The Berg work received only applause, in my hearing, and lots of it. Its instrumental performance, which was a marvel of clarity, was perfectly clear, I think, to all in its direct emotional communication. Vocally Gertrude Ribla got through it, but she could not be said to have done so by the exclusive use of agreeable sounds. It lies a little high for her, as a matter of fact. Also, the work itself is less expressive vocally than instrumentally. But in every way it is deeply moving music and should be heard oftener.

Somehow the idea has got round that this is twelve-tone music and hence hard to understand. It is neither. It is chromatic music of straightforward romantic feeling that should cause no real confusion today, twenty-seven years after its completion. Even if it did, it would still merit more frequent performance than it receives. What are symphony orchestras and opera companies for, after all? Aren't they supposed to educate us, to give us, along with the classics, the best that our time has produced?

The evening ended with a reminder, in the form of Ravel's second *Daphnis et Chloë* suite, that the sound of the Philadelphia Orchestra, indoors, heard again after some months, is one of the dependable delights of autumn.

October 8, 1947

Luminous

PHILADELPHIA ORCHESTRA, *Pierre Monteux*, conductor, last night at Carnegie Hall, performing Beethoven's Symphony No. 7, Willem Pijper's Symphony No. 3, and Ernest Chausson's Symphony in B-flat major.

PIERRE MONTEUX, conducting the Philadelphia Orchestra last night in Carnegie Hall, produced, I think, the most beautiful orchestral sounds I have ever heard. Throughout the whole dynamic range of which that delicate and powerful group is capable there was not one note of heaviness. All was pure glow and luminosity, loveliness, brightness, and sheer auditory incandescence.

The musical readings of the great San Franciscan were no

less passionately lucid than the sounds in which they were embodied. Beethoven's Seventh was ever reposed and alert. The Chausson Symphony was warm of color and rich of contour. Willem Pijper's Third Symphony, played in memory of the composer, who died on March 19 of this year, was a vigorous evocation of a strong spirit and a master workman.

This work, written in 1926, is a period piece from the time when modern music was still uncompromising. Prefaced as an attempt to "move the powers of hell," it exploits the monotony of ostinato, the banality of commercialized dance rhythms, and a general contrariness of harmony and counterpoint with a master's mastery of dissonant effect and with genuinely original invention of surprising sound combinations. Its expressive message, which leans a shade heavily on the tenderness-and-irony of Ravel, is perhaps less original than its instrumentation. That is no doubt the reason for the modesty of Pijper's successes outside his native Holland. The work nevertheless has character and force. It sounds like all the other advanced music of its time, but no other music of the time sounds quite like it. It is arbitrary but not sectarian, harsh but not ugly, minor poetry, if you wish, but far from negligible.

Any work thoroughly characteristic of the 1920's is hard to sell these days. Like yesterday's modernistic furniture made of chromium and pigskin, of rubber, glass, and oriental woods, upholstered in velvets of violet, dark gray, and black, or even in red fur, it seems as outlandish today, as willfully absurd, as late Victorian furnishings, now so fashionable, appeared to the bright spirits of twenty years ago. Time has gone by it, but not yet far enough for the preoccupations of its decade to become for us poetry. They will become so, of course. And when they do, the epoch's works of art that embody them characteristically will take on a new value. Naturally, those that are strongest of construction will survive best our present day's neglect and misunderstanding. A work so solidly, so handsomely built as Willem Pijper's Third Symphony cannot fail, it seems to me, to be highly considered by some later age, perhaps more highly than some of those works of its period that we now consider cardinal. You never can tell, of course; but workmanship and strong materials are a mighty bulwark against moth and rust.

The Chausson Symphony, composed in the 1890's, has

occasionally appeared to me a trifle moth-eaten. Not so last night. It, too, is a period piece, out of Schubert and Wagner's *Parsifal* by a pupil of César Franck. But it is warm, deeply sincere, and not at all badly put together, in spite of its school-of-Franck clichés. It has survived the modernist critics of the 1920's, who couldn't see it at all, and has become beautiful again. At least it was wondrously so last night in Pierre Monteux's luminous transfiguration of it. It is too bad that we have access here to Mr. Monteux's transfigurations only once or twice a year. This listener could do with lots more of Mr. Monteux than that.

October 29, 1947

Prince of Impressionism

PHILADELPHIA ORCHESTRA, *Ernest Ansermet*, conductor, last night at Carnegie Hall, performing Mozart's Symphony No. 38 ("Prague"), Stravinsky's *Chant du rossignol*, Fauré's Orchestral Suite from *Pelléas et Mélisande*, and Debussy's *La Mer*.

CRIES of "Bravo!" sounded in Carnegie Hall last night as Ernest Ansermet, conducting the Philadelphia Orchestra, brought to a close the final dazzling pages of Debussy's *La Mer*. The whole concert had been dazzling, indeed, and not through any playing of tricks on audience psychology or any of the grosser forms of auditory tonal appeal. The great Swiss conductor had held us all enthralled, as he had the orchestra itself, by sheer musicianship, by knowledge, by understanding, by a care for aural beauty and for exactitude.

In appearance a simple professor, touched up perhaps toward both Agamemnon and the King of Clubs, he is at once a sage, a captain, and a prince. With wisdom, firmness, and grace he rules his domain; and that domain is the music of Impressionism. For other leaders the center of the world may be Beethoven or Brahms or Wagner. For him it is the music of Debussy and all that borders thereon. No one living, not even Monteux, can command him in that repertory. Smooth as a seashell, iridescent as fine rain, bright as the taste of a peach are the blends and balances of orchestral sound with which he renders, remembering the lines, the backgrounds, and the tonal images of the great tonal painters who worked in France round the turn of our century.

Mozart he plays with love and with light, too; and he began last night with the *Prague* Symphony, just to show us how a classical rendering can be clean and thoroughly musical without being dry or overcrisp. The Philadelphia players found his company on that ground a privilege and gave of their best, which is the world's best. But it was only royalty on a visit. With Stravinsky, Fauré, and Debussy the king was back in his land, in his own house reigning, informed, understanding, understood, obeyed from a glance.

Stravinsky's *Song of the Nightingale*, arranged from an opera score and reorchestrated into a symphonic poem in 1919, may well represent this composer at his highest mastery of instrumental evocation. Musically, nevertheless, the work is weak from lack of thematic integration and harmonic structure. It gives pleasure as sound, page by page, palls as musical continuity in the concert room. It needs to be played from time to time because it is a work of the highest and most striking fancy, but heaven preserve us from it as a repertory piece.

Fauré's *Pelléas et Mélisande* suite, on the other hand, is a work of deep loveliness that could stand more usage in repertory than it gets these days. When played with such sweet harmoniousness and such grace of line as it was last night, one wonders why one had forgotten how touching it can be.

Debussy's *The Sea* brought the wonders of the evening to a radiant close. It is a piece this reviewer has always found a shade disappointing; but it is a popular repertory work; and if one has to hear it, Ansermet's reading of it is more welcome than most. Actually, while listening to it, this unfriendly witness forgot all about his prejudices and enjoyed himself thoroughly, almost as thoroughly as during the Mozart and the Fauré.

January 19, 1949

Koussevitzky

SERGE KOUSSEVITZKY, in devoting recently to American works two whole programs out of the Boston Symphony Orchestra's ten New York concerts of the season, has rendered a service to music and to the public. He has also reminded us of his own assiduous care for living music and for public instruction. Ten years ago, at the end of the fifteenth year of his tenure with that orchestra, he played a comparable series of works, the cream, in his judgment, of those by American authors that he had previously played. This time he has selected from the last ten years of his activity works and authors that mark a decade and that taken together make up another arch in that vast monument to the creative spirit of his time that is this conductor's whole public career.

It is of no importance to note, save in passing, that Mr. Koussevitzky's list of new works and authors is not the complete list of America's distinguished music. Moore, Luening, Wagenaar, and others are conspicuously absent. Sessions appears but once, and not among the revivals. At no time has Ruggles or Varèse, historical figures both, been represented. It is far more valuable to remember that his complete recent lists are more ample than anybody else's (save possibly Manuel Rosenthal's with the French Orchestre National). It is also useful to recall that though he came to this country with a long history of living works played and of composers encouraged, his collaboration with the musical life of his time in America had been facilitated by the similar activities of his predecessor, Pierre Monteux, in Boston, of his younger contemporary, Leopold Stokowski, in Philadelphia, and of the forerunners of them all, Walter Damrosch, in New York, and Frederick Stock, in Chicago. If Serge Koussevitzky has played more new America music than these others, that is largely because in his time there has been more of it to play. Our enlightened leaders have always given us what there was.

Even so, and placing him in the company of all those responsible to history, Mr. Koussevitzky merits an award in this last year of his Boston tenure, an award that history will certainly bestow upon him but that we still living could do honor to ourselves by offering earlier. For no other musical interpreter living has done so much for so many all over the world. As conductor, as publisher, as commissioner of works, he has assumed the music of his time (and it has been a long time) to be worthy of his support, financial, musical, and moral. He has published, played, taught, and paid, spent of his fortune, his earnings, his time, and his vigor without stint. In Russia, in Germany, in France, and in the United States, wherever his life has been led, even for short periods, he has left his mark on music and helped other men of music to leave theirs. His huge personal talent has been devoted to a cause, that cause the inclusion of the living creator, along with the listener, in the life of art.

Had his talent not been so vast, his achievement would have been less remarkable. But even with gifts so grand, the danger of personal aggrandizement is always present. He could so easily, with a lesser consecration, have come to fame without all that labor and expense. He chose otherwise, because he is a man of moral, as well as artistic, responsibility. He could not devote less than all his resources to the art that is his spiritual life. A man of humble origins, he has known that people, the people, means all the people there are and that art must belong to all the people and draw its strength from all the people. Common folk, aristocrats, intellectuals, the moneyed, the musical—it takes them all nowadays to make music make sense. And being a leader, if one's talent imposes such a responsibility, requires a full man's full time.

Koussevitzky has been a full man and given full-time service during a long lifetime. That service, we hope, is far from ended; but his twenty-five years as conductor of the world's most celebrated orchestra are drawing to a close. It is only just that at this time the whole world of music make him aware of its gratitude for services rendered, pay him some outward sign of the deep honor it owes him. Let these words stand as evidence of one musician's appreciation.

January 23, 1949

Wondrous Musical Beauties

CLEVELAND ORCHESTRA, *George Szell*, conductor, last night at Carnegie Hall, performing Mozart's Symphony No. 41 ("Jupiter"), Bartók's Concerto for Orchestra, and Beethoven's Piano Concerto No. 4. Soloist: *Clifford Curzon*, piano.

THE CLEVELAND ORCHESTRA, playing last night in Carnegie Hall under the direction of its regular conductor George Szell, gave distinguished execution to a distinguished program. Mozart's *Jupiter*, Bartók's Concerto for Orchestra and Beethoven's Fourth Piano Concerto, masterworks all, made no appeal to what we may call the "lower element" in a listener's mind. The latter piece, indeed, as played by Clifford Curzon, brought all our minds, I think, to higher ground than is our concert habitat. The soloist received also, as did Mr. Szell after the Bartók, an ovation hugely larger than it is our New York custom to award.

The beauties of this particular execution came no less from the orchestra than from the solo instrument. Mr. Curzon's vast variety of kinds of tone, his unfailing beauty of sound, his tender grace and grand perspectives of expression all made his rendering both a message and a monument. But Mr. Szell's sensitivity in drawing from his excellent orchestra sounds and curves no less noble, no less constantly fresh and surprising, completed, filled out one of the loveliest musical executions it has been my pleasure to hear in some time.

The other works were read with cleanliness and solid proportions; but a certain foursquareness in the first and last movements of the Mozart symphony and a shade of brutality in the dramatic accents of the Bartók Concerto caused them both to fall short, at least for this listener, of the ultimate elegance. When a leader of lesser refinement progresses as steadily through a Mozart symphony as if he were swimming the Channel, one is grateful for lack of distortion. But when a musician whose musical mind and skill are of the first quality fails to take advantage of every occasion for bringing out metrical contrasts and irregular stresses, one is a little disappointed. One had hoped the streamlining taste in symphonic interpretation had passed from fashion. Certainly no such obviousness marred the performance of the Beethoven Concerto.

The Cleveland Orchestra, long an excellent one, seems to have taken on added musical quality under this conductor. The string section is homogeneous as to color, plays with a mat tone that is dark but never heavy. The vibrato is warm but discreet. The fortissimo is as musical a sound as the pianissimo. The bowing is long, flexible, and subtle. The wind sections are in every way satisfactory, but the strings made a deeper impression on this listener. The Cleveland Orchestra, in fact, seems to him one that bears comparison with the best we know. Certainly its concert last night was full of wondrous musical beauties.

February 15, 1950

Expert and Original

ST. LOUIS SYMPHONY ORCHESTRA, *Vladimir Golschmann*, conductor, last night at Carnegie Hall, performing the Milhaud orchestration of the Overture and Allegro from Couperin's *La Sultane*, Mozart's Symphony No. 40, Manuel Rosenthal's *Magic Manhattan*, Schönberg's *Verklärte Nacht*, and dances from de Falla's *Sombrero de tres picos*.

THE ST. LOUIS SYMPHONY ORCHESTRA, second oldest organization of the kind in the country, now in its seventieth year, gave its first New York concert last night in Carnegie Hall. A brilliant concert it was, too, both as to program and to playing. Vladimir Golschmann, now in his twentieth year as conductor of the St. Louis body, directed with verve and all musical elegance. His orchestra is not quite the equal of our Eastern Big Three nor, perhaps, even of Cleveland now nor of Chicago in its best days; but it is an accomplished and well-trained group, sensitive as to nuance and rich of tone; and Mr. Golschmann is a conductor with life in him as well as musicianship. His concert was for this reviewer one of the most delightful of the season.

An Overture and Allegro from the quartet by Couperin known as *La Sultane*, orchestrated with style and spirit by Darius Milhaud (and similarly executed), began it. Mozart's G-minor Symphony continued its classical portion, played with a manly directness and also a greater attention to shading and phraseology than is nowadays the custom. Schönberg's *Verklärte Nacht*, rendered with all the passionate romanticism of its author's youth, and three dances from de Falla's ballet *The Three-Cornered Hat*, played to the hilt for their Spanish as well as for their theatrical content, closed it with tenderness and brilliance. The center of it was a brand-new piece by Manuel Rosenthal.

This work written in 1948 and entitled *Magic Manhattan*, is a companion piece to Gershwin's *American in Paris*. It represents a Frenchman's visit to New York. Beginning with a train departure from the Gare Saint-Lazare, it continues through a first view of our skyscrapers, the landing pier, a quiet side street or two, Times Square in full blast, Chinatown, the Bowery, the lower East Side, the upper West Side with its majestic Hudson

River, to a spectacle of dawn over the city. It is a panorama with breadth in it, astonishment, and (in the slum scenes) compassion. It is witty, picturesque, entertaining; but it catches also the violence and the power of the world's metropolis. Every now and then a passing elevated train makes its sudden racket and disappears.

As always in the work of this composer, the orchestral score is of an originality, an accuracy of effect, a virtuosity incomparable. The note textures, the tunes, and the harmony, though by no means undistinguished, are perhaps less strikingly inventive than the instrumental sounds and combinations. Their quality, and it is an unusual one in music so clearly pictorial, comes from the fact that they are musical at all. Other writers engaging in what might well be taken for pure orchestration make their pieces just that. They produce the right sounds; but their music, as music, is mostly doodling. Mr. Rosenthal's, for all its predominance of color over shape, bears examination and re-hearing. It is interesting as well as fun, sincerely felt, cleanly thought, wholly void of vulgarity.

Magic Manhattan is not easy to situate among today's music. It has a hard core of originality and a purity of communicative intention that remove it from the Hollywood kind. Its lack of multiple meaning, of perspective in the sentiment, keeps it for the present out of official art-music categories. Its closest mate, though the subject of one is humane and of the other spiritual, is Messiaen's *Liturgies of the Divine Presence*, or possibly his *Turangalila*. In both cases an expert engineer has designed a complex musical machine for specific expressivity. In both cases the machine is efficient, the expression clear. In Messiaen's case the aim is more pretentious; in Rosenthal's the result is more fun. In both, France has produced a new kind of music, beautiful, wonderfully expert, and, as always when there is novelty, a little shocking.

March 9, 1950

Musical Horse Show

PHILHARMONIC-SYMPHONY ORCHESTRA, *Victor De Sabata*, conductor, last night at Carnegie Hall, performing Rossini's Overture to *La Gazza Ladra*, Berlioz's *Symphonie Fantastique*, Vito Frazzi's *Preludio Magico*, Morton Gould's Spirituals for String Choir and Orchestra, and "Ride of the Valkyries" from Wagner's *Die Walküre*.

VICTOR DE SABATA, if one may believe last night's concert of the Philharmonic, which he conducted, is what used to be called in horsy circles a great whip. Certainly he rode the orchestra hard and well, made it play soft and slow, loud and fast, stop dead in its tracks, change gaits, do everything but spell. He himself spelled out the scores for us clearly, unmistakably. If occasionally, as in the Berlioz *Symphonie Fantastique*, he seemed doubtful of our ability to catch the meaning, or, as in the Morton Gould Spirituals, to have missed it himself, there is no question but that he knew their notes backwards. Surely he is a skilled technician of the *haute école*.

His program, consisting entirely of showpieces, offered as its only rarity a *Preludio Magico* by Vito Frazzi, an Italian professor now in his sixties. This work, composed in the Impressionistic taste and suavely orchestrated, is a civilized piece. It lacks a striking thematic content; but it is agreeable to listen to, with its spicy string-and-wind mixtures of sounds, its clean rhetoric and accomplished workmanship. It would have been even more a pleasure had the conductor not overplayed his brasses in the climax.

He overplayed everything, in fact, to such a degree that what with huge accents, imperceptible pianissimos, interminable pauses, and static slow passages, everything lost cohesion, came out void of line or progress. This kind of musical eagerness-to-hit-us-between-the-eyes could not wholly conceal from us the familiar thought content of Rossini and Berlioz, though it did occasionally bury the sound of the full string body under a brassy canopy. But Mr. De Sabata's incessant tampering with tempos caused him to miss every trick in playing with Mr. Gould's seemingly simple but far from unsophisticated American metrics. This composer's Spirituals for String Choir and Orchestra, overdressed as it is orchestrally and harmonically, has its own rhythmic life, supports no imposition of any merely theatrical animation. Itself all trickiness, the addition of jugglery from another school plain breaks its back.

Thankfully, deadline considerations made joining Wagner's Valkyries in their Ride inadvisable for the reviewer. One had been carried along by that time on quite enough battle horses. One had admired the skill of the rider but lost confidence in his sense of destination. He had put the orchestra through its paces over and over but not convinced one of a single thing. So much musical skill combined with so little musical taste would surely be of more brilliant effect in the theater than in the concert hall.

March 3, 1950

A Knack for Landscape

PHILHARMONIC-SYMPHONY ORCHESTRA, *Victor De Sabata*, conductor, last night at Carnegie Hall, performing Verdi's Overture to *I Vespri Siciliani*, Mozart's Piano Concerto in A major, Dvořák's Symphony No. 5 ("From the New World"), and Rachmaninoff's *Rhaposody on a Theme of Paganini*. Soloist: *Artur Rubinstein*, piano.

Victor De Sabata, conducting the Philharmonic last night, revealed an aspect of his mind that had not been strongly in evidence on the previous occasion of this reporter's attendance. I refer to his subtlety in the handling of landscape music. The program opened with a skillful but on the whole claptrap reading of Verdi's overture to *The Sicilian Vespers*. Whether a similar dynamic exaggeration at the expense of line marred his reading at the end, with Artur Rubinstein as piano soloist, of Rachmaninoff's Paganini Variations the lateness of the hour forbade my knowing, though the work is surely temptation to that for a conductor bent toward that. Nothing of the kind, however, marred the Mozart Piano Concerto in A major the Dvořák *New World* Symphony.

The former was played straightforwardly and neatly by both soloist and conductor. If it lacked brilliance in the piano part, delicacy was nowhere absent from the accompaniment. Mr. Rubinstein did not make ugly sounds, but he used weight crescendos that are more expressive in the Romantic repertory than in classical works. On the whole, the concerto sounded gray and a shade ineffectual; and I think the soloist is more to be blamed for that effect than the conductor. Mr. Rubinstein was respectful of shape and detail; but he made the work sound small, very small.

Dvořák's *New World* Symphony received from Mr. De Sabata a reading thoroughly live and fresh. Making no effort to confound this with the music of oratory and personal passion, as so many do, he gave it to us very simply as the work of a European landscape painter charmed by American subjects. He even restrained the lyric outpouring of woodwind soloists, kept the whole a picture. It was rich in color, vibrant, full of light in the climaxes, everywhere atmospheric, pastoral, an outdoor piece. Hearing so hackneyed a work sound fresh and new was a pleasure, because the work is intrinsically tender and imaginative. It kept its distance, spoke in poetry, penetrated the spirit in spite of familiarity.

The technical methods by which this effect was achieved were the whole gamut of orchestral fine adjustments and balances that mark the work of skilled conductors. But the poetic idea behind the interpretation was proof of other qualities in Mr. De Sabata, of an intellectual distinction, a refined musical imagination far more in keeping with his European repute than any reading had indicated at his first concert in this city.

March 24, 1950

France at Its Best

FRENCH ORCHESTRAS are the best in the world when they are good and the worst when they are not. Last Sunday's concert of the Orchestre National gave us France's (and probably Europe's) best orchestra playing in a way the present writer has rarely heard the same group do at home. The result was an ultimate in musical delight. But lest any (and they are many) who have been shocked and disappointed, visiting Paris, at run-of-the-mill French orchestral execution, let me explain a little of what really goes on.

Paris has at present five major orchestras besides those of the two chief opera houses. Four of these—the Conservatory, the

Colonne, the Lamoureux, and the Pasdeloup—are musicians' co-operatives. They hire their own manager and conductor and share receipts. The two opera orchestras and the fifth symphonic group, l'Orchestre National de la Radiodiffusion Française, are employed by the government; and their members are civil servants. They are paid a modest wage the year round and work eleven months. Since a steady wage is preferable to problematic profits, appointments to these orchestras are sought after. The only group that approaches them in breadwinning power is the Conservatory Orchestra, which gets considerable outside work recording for films. Vacancies in the personnel of all orchestras are filled by open competitive auditions. Conductors' and soloists' fees are not high.

On account of the low salaries paid and low profits shared, French orchestral players have long been accustomed to accept outside engagements and sent their substitutes to any concert or rehearsal. This substitution privilege makes for undependability in performance. When the National was reorganized after the Liberation by two composers—Henry Barraud, musical director of the French Radio, and Manuel Rosenthal, conductor—the substitute system was abolished in the National Radio Orchestra. Top salaries as French salaries go, and the assured presence of the true personnel at all rehearsals and concerts enabled Barraud and Rosenthal to make of the National an absolutely first-class orchestra. Also, responsibility only to the government and to the judgment of the musical world (since the National, like our N.B.C. group, charges no admission) enabled these enlightened directors to pursue a progressive program policy. The National offers a repertory of all that is most rare, special, and advanced and a galaxy of conducting talent and soloists, all chosen for quality rather than for box-office value. Since 1944 five American conductors, not counting the French-born Vladimir Golschmann, have appeared with the National; and about fifteen living American composers have been represented on its programs (more than all the orchestras of America have played of living French composers in that time).

Why this orchestra, in spite of its freedom from the substitute system and from the brutalizing effects of having to plug box-office repertory, does not always at home play as perfectly as it did here last Sunday is hard to explain, but not hard to

understand if you know something of the crushing fatigue involved in all French living just now and something of the independence of the French musical workman. No French orchestra
will do its best for a conductor it does not like or respect. Any
French orchestra will play beautifully for Charles Munch, whom
all musicians genuinely like and respect. This is not Munch's
orchestra. His was the Conservatory till he resigned last year.
This was Rosenthal's orchestra till he also resigned last year. At
present, like our own Philharmonic, it has no regular conductor. But, also like our Philharmonic, it can and does play handsomely when the circumstances are favorable to good work.
It is a compliment both to Mr. Munch and to the prestige of
New York's musical judgment that last Sunday the National
played as I have rarely heard any such group play in France or
anywhere else.

Do not imagine, however, that mere inspiration can produce
the kind of work we heard. The ability of the French orchestras
to play the way they can when they get around to it is based on
the following purely French professional factors:

1. French instrumentalists are the best-schooled players in
the world.

2. They are all schooled in the same school, which is that of
the Paris Conservatory and of the provincial conservatories,
which all take their standards and working methods from Paris.

3. The French conception of orchestral sound is that of a
large chamber-music group. This means that a harmoniousness
of blending and balancing is considered essential at all times.
Blending is a musical effect never to be sacrificed for emphasis
or weight.

4. In order to make blending and balancing possible, a certain kind of tone is cultivated by the different instruments. That
tone is a transparent one, forward-placed (in terms of vocal
analogy) and, by American tastes, a trifle thin. The sacrifice of all
weight and thickness makes clarity, however, and true balances
possible. It is not a perversity of the French mind that makes
French tone diaphanous. A decision has been made, an artistic
compromise, to achieve beauty.

5. The basic procedures for obtaining equilibrium among
sounds of diversified origin are considered to be, and correctly
so, the blending of timbres and extreme care for true pitch. These

qualities can be maintained only by using vibrato with discretion and by eschewing at all time the forced tone. The reward for their achievement is double, a greater suavity of sound in mixed chords and a clearer rendering of the elements that compose those mixtures. A good French orchestra keeps its colors clean, achieves luminosity by their equilibrated juxtaposition, not by mixing them up in a gravy of forced string-tone and parade-ground brass.

6. Rhythm is correctly judged in every bar as a counterpoint of stresses and quantities. Alone among Europeans, the French do not confound the rhythmic elements. They also play *on* the beat the exact written notes and stop cleanly when a note has reached its written end. Their percussion players are better musicians than ours.

7. French orchestras tolerate no star system, no highly paid first-desk wind players who invariably, as ours do, play a little louder than their team-mates. Three oboes playing do-mi-sol play with absolutely equal loudness, with the same kind of tone, without vibrato, and on pitch. The resultant harmoniousness is utterly delightful.

October 24, 1948

Beecham's 70th Birthday

On the 29th of April, 1949, Sir Thomas Beecham was seventy years old. The British Broadcasting Corporation, in honor of the event, put on a week of concerts, operas, and divers other events dedicated to the great man. Naturally he took part in most of them, for the doughty knight (and baronet) is no passive recipient. If this writer knows that joyful energy, he was all over the place, conducting everything, making all the speeches, cracking jokes, delighting everybody, terrifying everybody, horrifying the thin-skinned, and solemnly alerting his country to the dangers of musical negligence and irresponsibility.

A glorious festival it has been, I am sure, and one absolutely impossible to imagine taking place here. Toscanini's eightieth birthday, the seventieth of Koussevitzky, Walter, and Monteux, all were passed off with a few editorials in the press and a sanctimonious mention or two on the radio. Even Koussevitzky's retirement from the Boston Symphony Orchestra after twenty-five years of tenure netted him in New York one platinum watch and one public dinner. The truth is, of course, that no musician means to America what Beecham means to Britain. The music life of America has come to maturity through the efforts of many. Today's vigorous music life in England is traceable in virtually every branch to Beecham's indefatigable activity.

His taste and his talents, aided in the beginning by his father's wise benefactions, made Covent Garden for thirty years a synonym for the highest quality in operatic production that our century has known. His insistence on playing them brought British composers from Delius to Vaughan Williams a world public. His loving attention to Handel, Haydn, and Mozart has revolutionized the contemporary attitude toward these composers and changed them, as Albert Schweitzer did with Bach, from formal classics into a living force. He was at the heart of the movement, too, that revivified the Elizabethan and pre-Elizabethan music of England, restored England's glorious musical past to her living tradition.

Wherever a musical job needed doing, there was Sir Thomas, sleeves rolled up, doing it. Folklore studies, the Renaissance revival, the masters of the Classical period, neglected Romantics like Berlioz, scandalous moderns from Strauss to Stravinsky, the discovery of Sibelius, the importation of new French masters and of the Russian ballet, the successful encouragement of British composition. British soloists, British ballet, opera in English, modern music concerts, touring opera companies, everything sound in music from the most scholarly research to the most radical experimentation has benefited by his intelligent backing and his enlightened assiduity.

To build a musical new Jerusalem in England's green and pleasant land has from youth been his aim; or, failing this, to make of that country, which has for a century and more borne music an unrequited love, a fit place for musicians to live. He has attacked the problem from all sides; and if England is not today quite yet a musical Garden of Eden (and what country in Europe is?) the erosion of her once rich musical resources has been arrested. From now on she can take a place among the world's music-producing countries comparable to that she has long occupied among the consumers. I am not saying that the whole British revival is Sir Thomas's work, for some of it began before he was grown. I merely wish to point out that he has been the greatest single animator, living or dead, in that whole astonishing movement. It is no wonder that his country gives him honor, pays him thanks.

A part of those thanks are his, of course, not only for merely doing what he has done but also for doing it well. In the course of giving to England all the music there is in all the kinds, this man of impeccable taste, voracious talent and energy became not only a great impresario but also a great conductor. As the former (and being able to do so as a philanthropist), he provided survival for Britain's four chief orchestras during World War I. As the latter, he has toured the world ever since, offering to the astonished continents the spectacle of a British artist comparable in every way to the best from any land and superior to most. Germany found his Mozart a revelation. France has considered his renderings of French opera, from Berlioz to Debussy, as exemplifying perfection and authority. Russians have taken his Mussorgsky and his Korsakov, Italians his Verdi and his Rossini right into the body of their tradition. The present writer is witness that when he plays American music he plays it right.

Beecham's interpretative and technical skills are available at their highest in that most modern branch of the executant's art, gramophone recording. To tell the truth, Sir Thomas is not always at his best in the concert hall. When he is in form, there is nobody so live, so loving, so gracious, so powerful, so perfect. But sometimes he gets overexcited, falls short by his own standards of grandeur and refinement. Not so in the recording studio. There he works in calm, rehearsing, playing back, retaking each record side over and over till every sound in it is a musical sound and contributes to the whole piece's meaningful design. The result is a body of recorded music unequaled by that of any other conductor for either size or quality. The Beecham records have become known round the world both as authoritative musical renderings and as the very definition of good recording.

Four years ago, at the age of sixty-six, Sir Thomas organized a new orchestra, the Royal Philharmonic, trained it, perfected it in the concert hall, began making disks with it for the H.M.V.

company ("His Master's Voice"), under the new full frequency recording range ("ffrr") now employed in England. America has received his *Messiah*, *Electra*, and divers symphonic releases, all excellent. The R.C.A.-Victor Company is now releasing here, as part of the birthday honors, his version (complete) of Gounod's *Faust*, made in London two years ago with the assistance of an all-French cast from the Paris Opera. I heard the test-pressings of this set last year and recommend the album highly. Indeed, my impression from one hearing is that Sir Thomas has again made both musical and recording history, as he did back in 1936 with his recording of Mozart's *Magic Flute* with the Berlin Philharmonic Orchestra and singers from the Berlin Opera.

Considering his excellent health and undiminished vigor, we may hope (d.v.) for a great many more fine concerts and recordings from Sir Thomas, as his enemies may also look for lots more trouble from him, and for a long time. His quarrels, his lawsuits, his indiscreet public addresses are signs of that vigor, its overflow. But the vigor itself is in the music he makes, in the deep humane culture of his mind, in the warmth of his sentiments, in the liveliness of his wit and spirits, in the huge and undaunted devotion of a great man and a great seigneur to all that music means, ever did, ever will, or ever could mean in the life of a great people.

The English aristocracy, notoriously unmusical, is afraid of him, disapproves of him, calls him "Beecham." America, suspicious and a little resentful of harsh words but respectful all the same, calls him "Sir Thomas." In Britain the plain, common people, who have followed his career for fifty years and know him for a friend, speak of him as "Tommie." But whether in love, respect, healthy fear, or all three sentiments, the English-speaking world has reason to honor and to thank this great man for restoring us all to music's great tradition.

May 8, 1949

Children's Voices

LITTLE SINGERS OF PARIS, *Fernand Maillet*, conductor, on October 11 at Carnegie Hall, performing songs, mostly French, including Poulenc's *Tenebrae factae sunt*, Milhaud's *Deux Cités*, works by Lully, Rameau, Mozart, d'Indy, and Grieg, and traditional children's songs.

"THE LITTLE SINGERS OF PARIS" (or "La Manécanterie des Petits Chanteurs à la Croix de Bois") gave a concert of unaccompanied vocal music, sacred and secular, last Saturday night at Carnegie Hall. Founded some twenty years ago by their present conductor, the Abbé Maillet, the group is made up of underprivileged slum children, the Parisian equivalent of what we call here "dead-end kids." From a social point of view the enterprise, which is self-supporting, is in every way admirable. From a purely musical one it has, too, many excellences; and its faults, which are few, are only those inherent to the set-up.

The gravest of these is a lack of tonal balance. The basses and tenors are too few, and these are all young adults only recently boy singers in the choir. Their voices are neither strong enough nor resonant enough to support adequately the penetrating brilliance of the sopranos. Even the altos, as is common in boy choirs, are weak compared to the higher voices. As a result, the whole tonal fabric, though piercingly beautiful at times, is top-heavy.

Another disadvantage lies the in musical personality of the choir's founder and director. The Abbé Maillet, though a first-class technician in the training of child voices, a schooled musician, an incomparable animator and executive, is not an interpreter invariably of the highest taste. His program the other evening was overweighted with choral arrangements of familiar melodies and disappointingly skimpy in its attention to the grander reaches of liturgical repertory. His renderings of the lighter numbers, moreover, were marred by overdone comic effects and a lack of sustained rhythm more appropriate to the vaudeville stage than to the concert hall.

On the other hand, he did give us two first-class modern works in serious vein, both written for the Little Singers, a *Tenebrae factae sunt* of Francis Poulenc and Darius Milhaud's cantata in three movements, *Les Deux Cités*. The latter was last sung here, I believe, by the Collegiate Chorale in 1942 at a Serenade Concert in the Museum of Modern Art. Both are noble works, and both might well prove difficult of execution by an adult professional choir. Well-nigh perfectly intoned by the Little Singers, they gave proof of the choir's sound musical training, of that mastery of rhythm and interval that is the glory of French choral singing today. Throughout the evening, indeed, the boys took in their stride vocal and harmonic difficulties that our own boy choirs are rarely required to hurdle, much less to consider as normal.

A sheer delight were certain soprano voices in solo passages and all the altos singing together. These last had the coppery tinge of violins. The soprano soloists came out like hitherto unheard woodwinds, sailing up to high C with the utmost of naturalness and ease. The whole choir humming gave out a sound as of the most velvet-toned string orchestra. At no point did the boys try to sing like women. They sang in the masque, or upper part of the face, as trained singers should; and their sound was that of true child voices, reedy, rich, sweet, inhuman, disembodied. The experience of this sound, made further nasal and oboelike by a frank intoning of the French vowels, is only to be met with in French child-singing. Heard at its best, as in the work of the Abbé Maillet's Little Singers, it is an experience unforgettable, literally out of this world. It is too bad that the Abbé does not have available to him some mature French tenors and basses and perhaps one adult male alto, singing falsetto, to give body to the lower child voices. The result would certainly be, in the great classic religious repertory, as deeply satisfying as the sound of his present choir is thrilling.

I have dwelt on the sound of the Little Singers because that is unique. It would not be fair to close, however, without mention of their appearance, which is indeed an attractive one. Whether in dark blue street suits with white socks or in their religious robes of white cotton ornamented by a plain wooden cross, they are in every way straightforward and charming. The Abbé is something of a comedian and an inveterate between-courses speaker, but the children are as unpretentious as their singing is beautiful.

October 13, 1947

RECITALISTS

King of Pianists

ARTUR RUBINSTEIN, pianist, in recital last night at Carnegie Hall, performing Chopin's Sonata in B minor, Schumann's *Fantasiestücke*, Albéniz's "Albaicin" and "Triana," four mazurkas by Szymanowski, and Liszt's *Valse Oubliée* and Rhapsody No. 12.

ARTUR RUBINSTEIN, who played a recital of piano music last night in Carnegie Hall, made his first American appearance more than forty years ago. He has long been a great musician and a grand executant; and now, approaching sixty, he is king of his profession. Others may be regularly more flashy, though few can dazzle so dependably; and none can match him for power and refinement. He plays very loudly and very beautifully, very softly and thoroughly clean, straightforwardly, elegantly, and with a care for both the amenities of musical discourse and the clear transmission of musical thought. He is a master pianist and a master musician. There has not been his like since Busoni.

The program last night was standard but choice. There were a Chopin sonata (the opus 58), all eight of Schumann's *Fantasiestücke*, two Spanish evocations by Albéniz, four Szymanowski mazurkas, Liszt's exquisite *Valse Oubliée* and Twelfth Rhapsody. There is no point in searching especial excellences of interpretation, for all the works were read, as they were executed, to perfection. Perhaps the Liszt Rhapsody was most striking to this listener for the way Rubinstein made a modern pianoforte sound like a Hungarian zembalom and even like a whole orchestra of them. Perhaps the simplicity of Schumann's *Warum?* merits note, too, the way poetry was here achieved by not insisting on it.

As a matter of fact, Rubinstein builds his huge climactic effects, the most impressive that exist today in piano playing, by "throwing away," as theater people put it, nine-tenths, at least, of his lines. He does not obscure a minor turn or cadence, but neither does he lean on it. He treats it casually and gets on to the main thing. I should not be willing to call his manner of moving through a piece streamlined. It is too deeply aware for that. But the longest and loosest works, under his fingers, do get themselves organized and move forward.

A major device to this end is the lack of all technical hesitancy in sweeping through difficult passages, in keeping their speed, however fast, a function of the whole melodic line and harmonic rhythm. In this respect he is not unique; there are a few other masters who do the same thing. In his handling of transitions, however, in getting from a fast passage into a slow one, in moving from one expressive range to another, he is alone. It is hard to know just how he does it so gracefully, because the new theme has always begun before one has quite noticed. I think, though, that his transitions are operated a little more quickly than is customary. They are not brusque, but he does not hold them back. He moves through them as smoothly as a Diesel locomotive moves in and out of a railway station.

The Szymanowski mazurkas, dedicated to the pianist, are melodious, lacy, charming, and, to this reviewer, disappointing. I suspect that after Chopin, the concert mazurka could benefit more from a return to naturalistic treatment than from efforts at further fanciness. Szymanowski's examples seem to me finicky and overembroidered as folklore evocations.

February 14, 1949

Dramatizing the Structure

CLIFFORD CURZON, pianist, in recital yesterday afternoon at Town Hall, performing Chopin's Sonata in C minor, Schubert's Sonata in D major, and Schumann's Fantasie in C major.

CLIFFORD CURZON, who played yesterday afternoon in the Town Hall, is far and away the most satisfactory interpreter I know of the pianoforte's Romantic repertory. Horowitz may play Liszt with a more diabolic incandescence, and anybody can fancy himself a specialist of Chopin. But Schubert and Schumann are composers whom almost nobody plays convincingly any more. Certainly no one brings them to life with quite the delicacy and the grandeur of Mr. Curzon.

He prefaced them yesterday afternoon with a Mozart sonata, as if to show us how his special treatment of the Romantics had been arrived at. If I understand correctly, he has approached them not so much with a romantic feeling about them as with a taste for classic rhythmic and dynamic layouts. His Mozart sonata (the G minor K. 457) was treated as a symphony. Huge varieties of shortness in the articulation of notes, of color in the sound, of loudness levels sharply differentiated gave it the variety and the proportions of an orchestral score. Metrical steadiness without the imposition of any regular downbeat gave freedom to the Mozart stresses (as written), gave rhythmic perspective and objectivity to the musical shape. He exposed the work as a wide and solid building, made no effort to use it for personal meditation.

The Schubert Sonata in D, opus 53, a far wider and more personally conceived structure, he walked around in. He did not get lost in it or allow us to forget its plan, but he did take us with him to the windows and show us all its sweet and dreaming views of the Austrian countryside, some of them filled with dancing folk. The terraced dynamics and the abstention from downbeat pulsations, just as in the Mozart piece, kept the rendering impersonal at no loss to expressivity. On the contrary, indeed, the dramatization of it as a form, the scaling of its musical elements gave it evocative power as well as grandeur of proportion. And its enormous variety in the kinds of sound employed, its solid basses, and a dry clarity in the materials of its structural filling prevented monotony from becoming a concomitant of its vastness.

With the Schumann Fantasy in C, a work of intense personal lyricism and very little shape at all, Mr. Curzon's objective, orchestral approach turned out, surprisingly, to be just what was needed. It interfered at no point with eloquence or poetry. It merely held the piece together, gave it a color gamut, provided a solid setting and a rich frame for the passionate feelings that are its subject. Again the impersonal, the dramatic approach gave power to the work and breadth to its communication. By sacrificing all improvisatory, all minor-poetry attitudes, he gave us the piece as a large composition and as great poetry. Surely Schumann himself, in composing his personal intensities into a large form, however loosely this is held together, must have had something comparable in mind.

January 8, 1950

Modern Piano Playing

YVONNE LÉFÉBURE, pianist, in recital yesterday afternoon at Town Hall, performing Mozart's Fantasia in D minor, the Bach-Liszt Prelude and Fugue in A minor, Beethoven's Sonata No. 31 (Op. 110), Debussy's *Trois Images*, Fauré's Nocturne No. 13 and Barcarolle No. 6, and Ravel's *Tombeau de Couperin*.

YVONNE LÉFÉBURE, who played a piano recital yesterday in the Town Hall, is France's top-ranking pianist among those hitherto unheard in this country. At once a technical and a musical master, she belongs in the glorious company of Pierre Fournier, Francis Poulenc, Pierre Bernac, the musicians of the Quatuor Loewenguth and those of the Orchestre National, all of whom have given to our fall season examples of the very best contemporary musical workmanship.

In a program marked throughout its execution by intelligence, musicianship, sensitivity, and solid brilliance, Miss Léfébure's playing of Liszt's transcription of Bach's great A minor organ fugue and of Debussy's rarely played *Images* stood out as unusual experiences for this listener. Her Mozart was sound; her *Tombeau de Couperin* of Ravel was distinguished, her Beethoven Sonata (opus 110) first-class; and her Fauré was perfect. Her Bach and her Debussy seemed to your reviewer a sort of ultimate in both sense and sensibility. Also in the evocation by pianistic means of the quality and color of other instruments.

This orchestrating, so to speak, of the literature of the piano is the specific approach to piano playing that differentiates our century's practice of the art from that of its immediate predecessor; and modern piano music, of course, has mostly been composed with that approach in mind. Debussy, Ravel, and their followers are of orchestral evocation wholly conceived. So also, I am convinced, is Mozart's piano writing; and so certainly, in terms of the organ, are Liszt's arrangements of Bach.

Modern piano technique exploits, for the purpose of suggesting a great variety of kinds of sound, a great variety of kinds and heights of touch. One of Miss Léfébure's most impressive achievements as a technician is the accuracy with which she can strike whole chords from a height of fifteen inches above the keyboard, strike them with perfect note-balance and agreeable tone at any speed and at any degree of loudness or softness.

Her differentiations between time and accent also aid orchestral evocation, because melodic passages, as on the *bel canto* instruments, are played without downbeat stresses, the accentual pattern being rendered, as in real orchestral playing, by sharp pings, deep bell strokes, and articulations recalling those of harp, bow-heel, and the orchestra's percussion group.

This kind of piano playing is far from unfamiliar to us, though our own pianists do not do it so well, on the whole, as the French do. What makes Miss Léfébure's work so thoroughly exciting and fresh are the soundness and the penetrating nature of her musical mind, the rightness of her rhythmic instincts, and the breadth of her musical conceptions. There is fecund drama, too, between the strength of her temperament and the discipline of her preparation. She catches flame but does not burn up. She is at all times spontaneous, but she never improvises a reading. She is a first-class pianist, a first-class musician, and an artist. She is of our time, moreover, even playing Bach.

November 15, 1948

Fulfillment Experienced

WEBSTER AITKEN, pianist, in recital last night at Town Hall, performing two Scarlatti sonatas, Ives's Four Transcriptions from *Emerson*, the Elliot Carter Piano Sonata, Menotti's Ricercare and Toccata, and Beethoven's Sonata No. 32 (Op. 111).

WEBSTER AITKEN played last night in the Town Hall one of his most rewarding recitals of piano music. The program, as is so often the case with this artist, was a severe one. A lesser technical and musical master could hardly have got through it, much less held the absorbed attention of his audience. But Mr. Aitken left us all, I think, with a feeling of fulfillment. It is not often in the concert hall that one experiences so deep a satisfaction.

Save for the Scarlatti sonatas, that served for little more than to warm up the pianist's hands and to quiet the audience, everything was thoroughly rendered and thoroughly communicated. Charles Ives's Four Transcriptions from *Emerson*, dated 1920, is a normal-length piano sonata fashioned by its author out of the first movement of his vaster *Concord* Sonata. Like all of Ives's music, it is fascinating harmonically but not very personal in expression; and rhythmically it is a little dead. It is a polyharmonic evocation of German Late Romanticism rather than, to my perception, a portrait of its subject. It can scarcely be a portrait of Mr. Ives's feelings about his subject, either, since its emotional content is all too familiar in other, and many other, contexts. Its chief originality is its chord structure, which is both consistent and interesting. I doubt if it will ever be a very useful repertory piece, for all its airs of grandeur. It is, as expression, too banal.

Elliott Carter's Piano Sonata, written in 1945 and '46, might just possibly be a work for the repertory. This is a sustained piece full of power and brilliance. Its relatively quiet moments, though a shade reminiscent of both Copland and Stravinsky, are not entirely, in feeling, derivative; and as figuration they are quite personal. The brilliant toccatalike passages, of which there are many, are to my ear completely original. I have never heard the sound of them or felt the feeling of them before. They are most impressive indeed. The whole work is serious and not superficial. It would be a pleasure to hear it again, and soon.

Gian-Carlo Menotti's Ricercare and Toccata, composed in 1942 but not previously heard in New York, is perhaps a bit superficial, compared to the Carter sonata. But it is so brilliant, so cheerful and generally pleasant that one was grateful for its presence, along with the Scarlatti pieces, on a program of more weighty works. The chromatic Ricercare, in fact, was melodically most graceful. This listener would have liked it to go on a little longer.

The evening ended not with light fare but with Beethoven's Sonata, Opus III, no less. Here Mr. Aitken gave a reading not at all traditional but one restudied in the light of tradition. He did not moon over the easy slow passages or slow up for the hard fast ones, as is customary. He gave the whole a rhythmic structure and an emotional progress. If one regretted slightly at moments its relentlessly metallic coloration, one was grateful at all times for the clarity and the force of his transcendent execution. Also for his real Beethoven culture. The piece sounded a little hard, but we are told Beethoven played like that. And its hardness was of crystal and granite, not that of stale Christmas cookies. Mr. Aitken is the most masterful of all our American pianists, and his musical culture is the equal of anybody's from anywhere.

March 13, 1948

Thoroughly Contemporary

EUGENE ISTOMIN, pianist, in recital last night at Carnegie Hall, performing Beethoven's Sonata No. 14 (Op. 27, No. 2, "Moonlight"), eleven Chopin Preludes, two Rachmaninoff preludes, Debussy's "La Fille aux cheveux de lin," Schumann's Variations on the Name *Abegg*, and Ravel's *Gaspard de la Nuit*.

EUGENE ISTOMIN, who played a recital of piano music last night in Carnegie Hall, is a schooled technician, a natural musician, and a very young man. The first two advantages keep his work interesting and alive. The other state gives it a certain immaturity that weakens from time to time its expressive tension.

Like many another young person of today, he is not at his best in Romantic repertory. He respects it, plays it with what grace and sentiment he can muster; but he cannot really keep his mind on it. Only the music of his own century draws forth his full mental powers. Just as most of the other pianists, especially those brought up away from the centers of contemporary creation, fake their moderns, when they play them at all, so Mr. Istomin is obliged to fake his Romantics—his Schumann, his Chopin, and his Beethoven. The former's *Abegg* Variations he got through on sheer virtuosity. But his Chopin Preludes and his *Moonlight* Sonata were the work of a skillful and gifted child, nothing more.

Even two Preludes of Rachmaninoff and one by Debussy were read with more plain animal warmth than imaginative penetration. It was Ravel who brought out the young man's full expressive powers. The latter's triptych, *Gaspard de la Nuit*, which has tripped up both technically and expressively many a mature master, was just homework to this gifted youth. He played this intricate and difficult work so cleanly, so delicately, so powerfully, with such variety and beauty of touch, such easy understanding of its sense and motivations, with such command and such sincerity that it is impossible, on the basis of that rendering alone, to deny him recognition as an artist of the highest possibilities.

It is not fair to ask the young people of today, simply because they are in accord with their time, to drop the Romantic repertory and the Classical sonatas. The whole of music is their province, and they must get to know it as best they can. All the same, the modern world is where they live and feel at home. Their dealings with Romanticism are a child's version of an old wives' tale, or a city boy's dream of the Far West. They are Romanticism's drugstore cowboys, or at best college students who know the heroic days out of books and photographs. But they do know their time, love it, and take it for eternal, just as the Romantics did theirs. That is why they can make beauty of its masterpieces. That part of their work is real and thoroughly grand. The rest is just culture. And it is on the whole healthier for art that the contemporary in spirit should be authentic and the revivals of past time a product of intellectual ingenuity than that the reverse should obtain. Mr. Istomin is, in this sense, a healthy spirit as well as a good musican.

February 21, 1948

Beauty, Distinction, Mastery

NATHAN MILSTEIN, violinist, in recital last night at Carnegie Hall, performing, among other works, Anton Stamitz's Adagio and Rondo, Bach's Partita in D minor, Beethoven's Sonata No. 8 (Op. 30, No. 3), and Nicolas Nabokov's Introduction and Allegro. Accompanist: *Artur Balsam*, piano.

NATHAN MILSTEIN gave last night in Carnegie Hall one of the most delightful evenings of violin music that your announcer has experienced in some time. Long suspicious of nationally advertised brands in violin playing, this writer had never before attended a recital by Mr. Milstein, though occasional concertos heard in orchestral concerts had prepared him for full technical satisfaction and pretty sounds. But you can never tell from a concerto what an artist's personality is like and whether he has a banal or an interesting communication to make with his technical skill.

Mr. Milstein, in the opinion of this reporter, is one of the most distinguished musicians now playing the violin in public. He has a cool mat tone, and he does not force it. He has an impeccable left hand technique and a bow arm that never takes anything the easy way if another is more beautiful. His phrase is long, sustained without heaviness, turned with a natural grace.

His musical understanding is broad, his personal presentation both authoritative and modest.

The most notable musical achievement of the evening was his performance of the Bach D minor Partita, for violin alone, that lasted nigh on to a half hour and that was sheer heaven from beginning to end for beauty of tone and all round musical lucidity. A work ordinarily considered difficult for audiences was projected with full clarity and a consistent loveliness that provoked the kind of applause that the press used to call an ovation and that last night caused Mr. Milstein to interrupt his program by the insertion of an encore (a Bach Gigue, I think it was).

Beethoven's G major Sonata, Opus 30, No. 3, was played, with Artur Balsam at the piano, no less lavishly. The rapid passages were light as wind, airy and dry and insubstantial. The cantilena was poetic without insistence, the whole a triumph of taste and of delicate understanding. Mr. Balsam's work throughout was a musical contribution not to be dismissed with the term accompaniment.

The novelties of the evening were an Adagio and Rondo of Stamitz, played at the beginning, and an Introduction and Allegro by Nicolas Nabokov (first performance), played at the end. The first was melodious and graceful enough to explain Mozart's admiration of this composer. The second had a quality of personal poetry all too rare in these days of knock-'em-out neo-Classicism. It is a neo-Romantic piece rather than a neo-Classic one, because it is about its subject, not its form, and because that subject is personal feelings. These seem, from the melodic conformation, to be connected with Russia—a wistful sadness, a moment of exuberance, and a return to the wistful note. It is thin writing, widely spaced by moments and always conceived as a blend of piano and violin sound. It is brilliant, too, an original and effective piece of music. Coming at the end of the program, it crowned charmingly an evening of serious and sincere music making, left no taste of condescension or of that relaxing of the musical standards so common at the end of recital programs.

November 18, 1947

Violence and Virtuosity

ERICA MORINI, violinist, in recital last night at Carnegie Hall, performing Handel's Larghetto, the Vivaldi-Respighi Sonata in D major, Bach's Chaconne, Henryk Wieniawski's Concerto No. 5, Hindemith's Sonata in D, Shostakovich's Three Fantastic Dances, and Leo Nadelmann's Invocation and Dance. Accompanist: *Leon Pommers*, piano.

ERICA MORINI, if one can judge from her last night's recital in Carnegie Hall, is a violinist of transcendent technical equipment with an especial gift for brio. She plays so handsomely as to pitch and sound and with such dramatic impact as to rhythm that one is tempted, at the beginning, to throw the metaphorical hat in the air and shout to oneself, "This is it!" Nevertheless, after a bit, the mind begins to wander. By intermission time it is saying to itself, "What's wrong with this?" By the end of the evening one knows that the musical conceptions of this otherwise deeply impressive artist have all been superficial.

They were superficial last night because they were all based on violent contrasts of volume from one phrase to another, even, occasionally, within a single phrase. This kind of expression is appropriate to some music. The Wieniawski Concerto and Shostakovich's Fantastic Dances take it admirably, especially if the technique of the executant, as in Miss Morini's case, is solid enough not to explode under its stress. It does not do much, though, for Handel and Bach and Vivaldi. And it is the last thing in the world for plumbing the rich depths of Hindemith's Sonata in D, Op. 11, No. 2.

This last, a work of its author's romantic youth, is both melodious and massive. It stems architecturally from Brahms and soars like Fauré. It is a grand piece and a difficult one. Miss Morini, not fazed in the least by its technical difficulties, gave it a serious and certainly a reflected reading. But her preoccupation seemed to be chiefly one of making it sweep along, rather than of allowing it a full expressive articulation in its progress. The work is a pleasure to hear, because one hears it seldom. But one regretted that Miss Morini, for all her good will toward it and serious intentions, did not seem to feel as comfortable with it as she obviously did with the Wieniawski.

Perhaps the Wieniawski Concerto is her piece, or her kind of piece. Perhaps, also, on other occasions she can be convincing in other kinds of pieces. Last night your reporter suspected that she would always be at her best in works that it is legitimate to conceive as vehicles for violence and virtuosity. Certainly she was handsome in those.

November 29, 1947

Virtuoso Makes Music

PIERRE FOURNIER, cellist, in recital yesterday afternoon at Town Hall, performing Bach's "*Nun kommt der Heiden Heiland*" and Suite No. 6, Brahms's Sonata No. 2, Debussy's Sonata for Cello and Piano, Pietro Locatelli's Cello Sonata in D, and Paganini's Variations for One String. Accompanist: *George Reeves*, piano.

PIERRE FOURNIER, who played a cello recital yesterday afternoon in the Town Hall, is at the top of a profession in which skill runs high these days, especially in France. I do not know his superior among living cellists, and there are few who can equal him either for technical mastery or for musical taste. Some play louder, many exploit a more obvious sentiment. I do not know any who give one more profoundly the feeling of having been present at music making.

Excellence in the technical handling of the cello is always primarily a matter of avoiding pitfalls. Mr. Fournier does not let his instrument groan or scratch or squeak or buzz, and yesterday he did not miss exact pitch on more than just a very few notes. Neither did he at any time force his tone beyond the volume of optimum sonority. His sound, in consequence, was always pleasant and, thanks to Mr. Fournier's fine musical sensitivity, extremely varied.

That sensitivity was present in positive form, moreover, as liveliness of rhythm and in the wonderful shaping and shading of each line and phrase. Many cellists can play with dignity and style, as Mr. Fournier did, an unaccompanied Bach suite; but few can play a Brahms sonata, as he did yesterday the F major, with such buoyancy and spontaneity, such grace of feeling and no heaviness at all. I know of none who can match him in the Debussy Sonata.

This work is rather a rhapsody than a sonata in the classical sense, and yet it needs in execution a sonata's continuous flow and long-line planning. It needs also the utmost of delicacy and of variety in coloration and a feeling of freedom in its rhythmic progress. Its performance yesterday by Mr. Fournier and his accompanist, George Reeves, was a high point in a season already notable for good ensemble work and a summit capable of dominating many, as regards the rendering of this particular piece.

A master's program such as Mr. Fournier gave us would have been incomplete without a work from the cello's classical period; and there was one, a sonata by Locatelli, noble, charming, and brilliant. The closing piece was a transcription from Paganini, originally written, I think, for the violin's G string, in this version played on the A string of the cello. It is a set of variations on a tender theme of Victorian cast, not a work of marked musical invention but one rich of fancy as regards technical figuration. Its well-nigh impeccable execution brought forth applause of a kind every artist loves to hear. In this case I am sure it was a tribute not only to a virtuoso's prowess but also to his taste and musicianship.

November 14, 1948

Brilliant and Diffuse

GREGOR PIATIGORSKY, cellist, in recital last night at Carnegie Hall, performing Boccherini's Sonata in C major, Bach's Prelude and Fugue in C minor (from Cello Suite No. 5, "Discordable"), Chopin's Sonata in G minor, Debussy's Sonata for Cello and Piano, Fauré's Élégie, Stravinsky's Aria, and Mr. Piatigorsky's Variations on a Theme by Paganini. Accompanist: *Ralph Berkowitz*, piano.

GREGOR PIATIGORSKY, our most popular touring cellist, played to a large audience last night in Carnegie Hall. He played a distinguished program and was more than warmly received. The soloist's execution was brilliant and his accompanist, when audible, excellent. And yet somehow the evening was not quite a first-class musical occasion.

The trouble seems to be that Mr. Piatigorsky is more expert than imaginative. He is a virtuoso in the old style. He has a huge sound, huge hands to reach the cello's fingerboard with, and a vast variety of tone color. His musical sense is a cultivated one, too. He would seem to have everything. Everything, at least, but concentrated thought. He rarely keeps to the same mood for fifteen seconds. In the midst of a smooth cantilena like that of the Fauré *Élégie* he suddenly introduces the biting-bow declamatory style. To the sustained and interior poetry of the Debussy Sonata he adds an oratorical crescendo, returns to the poetry, then pushes his bow into more crescendo, plays handsomely in duet with the piano in the pizzicato passages, then utters a phrase of interlocked harmony with the pianoforte as if he were all alone on the stage. He plays one phrase like an angel and then scratches the next as only a six-footer with a long bow-arm can scratch. He makes beautiful sounds and ugly sounds, complete sense and no sense, fine music and common-place music all in one piece, in any piece. His talent and mastery are tops; but he does not seem always to have his mind, though it apparently is a good one, on what he is doing.

From the Boccherini Sonata in C major through the Prelude and Fugue of the Bach C minor ("Discordable") Suite (played in normal tuning), the Chopin Sonata, and the Debussy Sonata to the final oddments, not one piece was read with sustained expressive power; and yet not one reading was without its com-manding traits. An enormous competence and a certain indif-ference marked them all. In spite of a receptive audience, the artist seemed unable to call forth that concentrated attention on his own work that is, if not the whole state of inspired artistry, its sine qua non.

Perhaps your reporter is lending his own incomplete attention to the proceedings to a sincere and hard-working soloist. He hopes not. And he thinks not, since he is ascribing to the artist not lethargy so much as a nervous, almost a mercurial discon-tinuity of thought. If that were of a continuous intensity, Piati-gorsky would be continuously fascinating. As it is, or as it was last night, this listener found him both fascinating and tedious, impressive and banal all at once.

March 20, 1948

A Major Experience

MARTIAL SINGHER, baritone, in recital yesterday afternoon at Town Hall, performing, among other works, three Reynaldo Hahn *Etudes Latines*, de Falla's "Jota" and finale from *El Retablo de Maese Pedro*, Ravel's *Chansons Madécasses*, and Mussorgsky's *Chantes et danses de la mort*. Accompanists: *Paul Ulanowsky*, piano, with *Mildred Hunt-Wummer*, flute, and *Hermann Busch*, cello.

MARTIAL SINGHER was in voice yesterday afternoon. He made the Town Hall ring and vibrate. He also, at the end of his program, made this wearied intelligencer sit up and listen. For his rendering of Mussorgsky's tragic *Songs and Dances of Death* was a vocal reading (in French) of such dramatic intensity as has not been experienced by your reviewer previously this season, or often in any.

The program was a good one and the whole afternoon a delight, from the spacious eighteenth-century arias of Bach and Gluck and Rameau to Ravel's picturesque and acidulous evocations of Madagascar, sung on this occasion to their proper accompaniment of cello, piano, and flute. There were also five tasteful, if somewhat thin, songs by Reynaldo Hahn and two sturdy bits from de Falla. The latter of these, the finale from *Master Peter's Puppet Show*, even when accompanied by only a pianoforte, is a handsome number indeed. Mr. Singher's rousing rendition of it (in Spanish) made one regret that nobody ever gives us any more the full dramatic version of *El Retablo*.

The Hahn songs gave us Mr. Singher at his most charming. A concert version of the salon style is not an easy note to achieve, but Mr. Singher observed it with all the grace (and some of the unction) of a French restaurateur. If Hahn's songs are not quite first-class provender, they are none the less delicate cuisine; and no public's taste for them can be reproached. They are hot-house Parnassian poetry blended to suave melodies and set off by delicate accompaniments, bland nourishment, a little monotonous each. Sung in anything but half-tints and perfect French, they are unendurable. Impeccably presented, they become, if not works of art, a luxury product of distinction.

Mussorgsky's four vast pieces (cantatas really) called *The Songs and Dances of Death* are as real as war and very nearly as terrifying.

They are hugely varied, dramatic, intense, and musically of the highest beauty. Few singers attempt them, and fewer make of them anything but a tedious proof of devotion. In Mr. Singher's hands they came to life so vividly and with such grandeur that the whole house, as well as your critic, sat enthralled, immobilized by their terror and their beauty.

For this work, as for the others, Paul Ulanowsky provided accompaniments for any singer to dream about and audiences to pray for. Mildred Hunt-Wummer, flutist, and Hermann Busch, cellist, played with him not at all ungracefully in Ravel's *Chansons Madécasses*.

January 19, 1948

The Accents of Passion

ELENA NIKOLAIDI, contralto, in recital last night at Town Hall, performing Greek folk songs and works by Domenico Cimarosa, Schubert, Wolf, Weber, Mahler, de Falla, and Fernando Obradors. Accompanist: *Jan Behr*, piano.

ELENA NIKOLAIDI, who sang last night in the Town Hall, is Greek by birth and German trained. Her voice, an alto by its weight and dark color, is wide of range and spectacularly powerful at the top. Her personal beauty is of the Juno type, with facial expressions and bodily attitudes of the highest dramatic expressivity. She is clearly an artist, a musician, and an actress.

Last night her program, mostly German, ran from Weber and Schubert through Wolf and Mahler. The language of these composers she projected impeccably, and she sang their tunes on pitch. She added drama, too, to their communication, staged everything, so to speak, and that most impressively.

Her dramatic accents, indeed, were more impressive than appropriate. Filling the house with sound and with large, plain emotional meaning is an operatic procedure not necessarily advantageous to the intimacies of lieder. Miss Nikolaidi sounded well and looked striking while doing this, but stylistically her work was exaggerated.

Vocally it was also excessive by moments, as if she felt sheer loudness were a virtue. Loudness does give an intrinsic pleasure, of course, when the voice is rich, vibrant, and handsomely colored. But the ultimate in loudness is rarely becoming to settings of lyric poetry, and it does tire the voice. Last night the artist had used her powers vocal and dramatic with such freedom that when she came to sing Eglantine's aria from Weber's *Euryanthe*—the only piece on the program that justified such emphasis—she found herself screaming, if ever so little, on the high notes and unable to articulate clearly the rapid scales.

It is possible that Miss Nikolaidi, an extrovert Mediterranean talent, has missed as much as she has gained from her Central European schooling. I am sure she believes deeply in German lieder. But I could not help wishing last night that she would stop worrying this repertory and sing more Verdi, for which she appears to be gifted like few. The minutiae of sentiment and poesy are not for her. She belongs, I believe, to the accents of passion and to the bravura style.

October 11, 1949

Lovely Voice, Perfect Taste

HELEN THIGPEN, soprano, in recital last night in Town Hall, performing four songs by Howard Swanson ("The Valley," "The Negro Speaks of Rivers," "Night Song," "Joy"), three songs by Berlioz ("La Mort d'Ophélie," "Villanelle," "Le Spectre de la rose"), a Mozart aria with violin obbligato, and songs by Purcell, Mozart, and Wolf. Accompanists: *Hellmut Baerwald*, piano, with *Frank Kneisel*, violin.

HELEN THIGPEN sang last night in the Town Hall, giving great joy. The joy came from her lovely voice, from her program of rare and handsome works, and from her distinguished musicianship. Not often of a winter does one hear a vocal evening of song so high-class all round.

Three works by Berlioz and four by Howard Swanson were an especial delight, being both unfamiliar as recital fare and in themselves *grande cuisine*. The Berlioz *Death of Ophelia* is one of the great French long songs, perhaps the model of them all. *The Ghost of a Rose* and the *Villanelle* are no less perfect, no less musically imaginative; but the Ophelia piece is longer, grander, evocative of a more spacious picture. Miss Thigpen gave them all to us with clarity and breadth.

Howard Swanson is a composer whose work singers (and

pianists, too) should look into. It is refined in sentiment, sophisticated of line and harmony in a way not at all common among American music writers. His songs have a delicate elaboration of thought and an intensity of feeling that recall Fauré. Of the four sung last night only one, *The Negro Speaks of Rivers*, overstated its subject; and here the fault, I think, was largely that of the poet, Langston Hughes. The other three are a contribution to song repertory. One is grateful to Miss Thigpen for singing them, doubly for interpreting them so sensitively.

Sensitivity, as a matter of fact, is this artist's most imposing quality. That and her high standards of musical taste. She phrases; she pronounces; she floats a musical line; she keeps a rhythm; she makes beautiful sounds; she stays on pitch. All the musical amenities are hers. If occasionally she croons a bit, she is also mistress of the finest spun, the most penetrating true pianissimo now available, to my knowledge, on the American concert stage. She is an artist and a musician through and through.

Her voice, one of great natural beauty, is a lyric soprano of no extraordinary range or volume; yet it sails high with comfort and is not wanting in dramatic accents or in vibrancy. Its greatest warmth is in the lower and middle ranges. Its greatest natural appeal, however, its special quality of sweetness, lies at the top. Here it is an impersonal vibration, utterly true acoustically, a little disembodied, as resonant as an E string or a flute. Concert experience will give it, I imagine, more body. It is not a weak voice, but it does tend to dissociate itself now and then from the producing artist. At such moments it loses no beauty; the music sung merely ceases to be a human communication and becomes a sort of angelic sound-effect. Miss Thigpen's whole vocal production is that of one who cares for loveliness. With more stage experience, and with her already great musical authority, she should be a recitalist of the first class.

November 17, 1949

La Môme *Piaf*

THE PRESENCE among us of Edith ("la Môme") Piaf, currently singing at the Playhouse, is a reminder, and a very pleasant one, that the French *chanson* is an art form as traditional as the

concert song. It has a glorious history and a vast repertory. Its
dead authors and composers have streets named after them.
Its living ones, just like the writers of operas, symphonies, and
oratorios, enjoy a prestige that is not expressed in their income
level. Its interpreters are artists in the highest sense of the term,
easily distinguishable in this regard from the stars of commercialized entertainment.

If the official art music of our time expresses largely the life
and ideals of the bourgeoisie and penetrates to the basic strata
of society *from above*, the *chanson* is almost wholly occupied
with depicting contemporary life from the viewpoint of the
underprivileged and comes to us *from below*. The habitats of
the official style are dressy places with a sanctimonious air about
them. The *chanson* lives in the neighborhood "music halls," as
the French call them, or what we refer to, using a French term,
as "vaudeville" houses. The *chanson* has nothing to do with
farm life, either. Farm workers, unless they are itinerants who
spend their winters in town, sing, when they sing at all, an older
repertory, that which we denominate folklore. The *chanson* is a
musical art form of the urban proletariat.

Its social origins and preoccupations are expressed not only
in the words of the songs but also, in performance, by a vocal
style opposed in method to that of the vocal studios. The latter
consider high notes their greatest glory and make every effort,
in training the voice, to spread the quality of these downward
through the middle and chest ranges. The *chansonniers* use
principally chest resonances, carrying these as high in the vocal
range as possible and avoiding pure head tone as rigorously
as singers of the official school avoid an unmixed chest tone.
Head tone is used, if at all, for comic or character effects, to
represent the voices of children, of the not very bright, and of
the socially hoity-toity.

Miss Piaf represents the art of the *chansonnière* at its most
classical. The vocalism is styled and powerful; her diction is
clarity itself; her phrasing and gestures are of the simplest. Save
for a slight tendency to overuse the full arm swing with index
finger pointed, she has literally no personal mannerisms. She
stands in the middle of a bare stage in the classic black dress of
medium length, her hair tinted red and tousled, as is equally
classical (Yvette Guilbert, Polaire, and Damia all wore it so), her

feet planted about six inches apart; and she never moves, except for the arms. Even with these her gestures are sparing, and she uses them as much for abstractly rhetorical as for directly expressive purposes.

There is apparently not a nerve in her body. Neither is there any pretense of relaxation. She is not tense but intense, in no way spontaneous, just thoroughly concentrated and impersonal. Her power of dramatic projection is tremendous. She is a great technician because her methods are of the simplest. She is a great artist because she gives you a clear vision of the scene or subject she is depicting with a minimum injection of personality. Such a concentration at once of professional authority and of personal modesty is both delightful and no end impressive.

If Miss Piaf had not impressed me so deeply with the authenticity of her repertory and her convictions about its rendering, I should have used my column today for praising Les Compagnons de la Chanson, a male chorus of nine singers who precede her on the program. They sing folksongs to the accompaniment of athletic pantomime with a perfection of drill, vocal and muscular, that is both sidesplitting and utterly charming. If anybody wants to find a political reference in their song about a bear that terrified the village but became, when legally elected, as good a mayor as his predecessor, I presume such an interpretation could be discovered without too much effort, since otherwise the number has little point. Their imitation of an American radio quartet accompanied by a swing band, however, needs no further point than its excellent satire. Their work in every number is funny and unusually imaginative. "La Môme," or "Pal" Piaf, to translate her cognomen, may be strong meat, artistically speaking, for American theater audiences, though I hope our public will long go on loving and applauding her. But Les Compagnons are more the sort of act we can take without effort. I must say they are easy to enjoy.

November 9, 1947

Personal Distinction

MARGARET TRUMAN, soprano, with the ROBERT SHAW CHO-RUS and the FRANK BLACK ORCHESTRA, presenting a concert of seasonal music last night in an ABC radio broadcast from Carnegie Hall. The orchestra performed Tchaikovsky's Waltz from *The Sleeping Beauty*, Humperdinck's Overture to *Hansel and Gretel*, and "Dance of the Chinese Dolls" from Rebikoff's *Christmas Tree Suite*. The chorus performed "Adeste Fideles," Hugo Junst's "Christmas Echo Song," and Leontowitch's "Carol of the Bells." Miss Truman sang "O mio Babbino Caro" from Puccini's *Gianni Schicchi* (with the orchestra), and "Little Town of Bethlehem" and "Silent Night" (with the chorus).

MARGARET TRUMAN made her first appearance as a concert artist in New York at a short broadcast of semipopular music that took place last night before an invited public in Carnegie Hall. She sang one brief aria from Puccini's *Gianni Schicchi* and two familiar Christmas carols. The rest of the program was of negligible interest to a reviewer.

Miss Truman herself presents surely a greater personal than musical distinction. One was prepared for the grace, warmth, and refinement of her presence; but this reporter, having seen only the grinning photographs that present-day publicity sanctions, was not at all prepared for the beauty of her face in repose. Few artists now appearing before the public have Miss Truman's physical advantages, and almost none other has her dignity.

Her vocal advantages are far less impressive. The voice is small in size and range and not at all beautiful. The lower notes of it do not project, and the upper ones are hollow. Nowhere is there any vibrancy or richness. She seems to sing carefully, is obliged to, indeed, by the poverty of her resources. Her English enunciation in one of the carols was remarkably clear. Of temperament, of the quality that enables a musician to bring music to life, she seems to have none at all. Her singing did not communicate last night as powerfully as her personality did. Only at the end of each piece, when she stopped singing and smiled and became the lovely Miss Truman again, did she make real contact with the guests of the evening.

December 21, 1949

OPERAS

Perfect and Powerful

SALOMÉ, opera in one act, libretto in German by *Hedwig Lachmann* (from the English original by *Oscar Wilde*), music by *Richard Strauss*, performed last night at the Metropolitan Opera House, *Fritz Reiner*, conductor, *Herbert Graf*, stage director, with *Ljuba Welitsch* (Salomé), *Kerstin Thorborg* (Herodias), *Max Lorenz* (Herod), *Joel Berglund* (Jochanaan), and *Brian Sullivan* (Narraboth).

STRAUSS's *Salomé*, restudied, refurbished, and rehearsed, was the vehicle for two debuts last night at the Metropolitan Opera House—that of Fritz Reiner, who conducted, and that of Ljuba Welitsch, who sang the name part. The occasion was instrumentally perfect, vocally well-nigh so, and dramatically sensational. Never before in the hearing of this listener has the work been led so suavely, so powerfully, or with so luxurious a sound. Rarely has it been sung so well. And only in the memory of those older opera goers who remember Fremstad, Garden, or Vix, has it ever been acted so thoroughly.

A blueprint for acting is clear in the score; but not often have we had offered us the full realization, in all its fascinating horror, of that perverse and sensual story. Miss Welitsch could not have given it to us last night without the understanding aid of Mr. Reiner, and he would have been impotent to communicate the work's full expressive sense without the detailed and courageous collaboration of a major singing actress. The whole staggering effect, moreover, had to be made possible by a solid supporting cast, clear stage direction, and plenty of rehearsal both with and without the orchestra. Under such circumstances and with such artists, the Metropolitan can produce today, did last night produce one of the great musico-dramatic performances of our century.

The score itself, like the play on which it is built, makes its effect by accumulation. When played for momentum and trajectory, without haste and without respite, it leaves one shaken. It does this by the expressive power of its orchestral textures and the elaborate organization of its expressive devices, rather than by any especial beauty or aptness in its melodic material.

It is like a modernistic sculpture made of cheap wood, glass, rocks, cinders, papier-mâché, sandpaper, and bits of old fur. The material elements of it are without nobility; but the whole makes a composition, and the composition speaks. Even poorly led, sung, or acted, it speaks. Led, sung, and acted with detailed and cumulative emphasis, it is staggering both musically and emotionally.

The cast which helped Miss Welitsch and Mr. Reiner to such an effect last night was notable in the supporting roles. Max Lorenz, as Herod; Brian Sullivan, as the Young Captain; Dezso Ernster, as the First Nazarene; even Kerstin Thorborg, whose Herodias was less than striking vocally; and, above all, Joel Berglund, whose Prophet was in every way handsome—all were part of a team and a first-class team. Everybody on the stage, down to the last slave and soldier, was playing in a play; and they were all playing in the same play, just as the musicians in the pit were all playing the same piece. The result, at that level of talent and skill and with a script of that strength, was overpowering, though nobody screamed or blasted.

Detailed examination of the leading soprano's vocal qualities must await further appearances. So must any recounting of the excellent *Gianni Schicchi* performance, full of fine Italian singing and stage work, which started off the evening. It will certainly be a pleasure, too, to follow Fritz Reiner's work in the theater, long a delight in the concert hall and now fully revealed as great opera conducting, the greatest, I should think, that we have heard here in several decades.

February 5, 1949

Musically Authentic

PELLÉAS ET MÉLISANDE, opera in five acts, libretto by *Maurice Maeterlinck*, music by *Claude Debussy*, performed last night at the New York City Center by the New York City Opera Company, *Jean Morel*, conductor, *Theodore Komisarjevsky*, stage director, with *Maggie Teyte* (Mélisande) and *Fernand Martel* (Pelléas).

DEBUSSY's *Pelléas et Mélisande*, as produced last night by the New York City Opera Company at the City Center of Music and Drama, marked another advance in the achievements of both institutions. Musically it was a delight, and verbally it was clear. If the visual aspect of the performance was in general unsatisfactory, that was a not ineradicable blot on a distinguished piece of work.

Credit for that distinction goes first to Jean Morel, who conducted a reading at once beautiful and authentic. His cast, headed by Maggie Teyte, did beautiful work musically. Their movements may be more convincing at later performances. At present these are tentative, because a unit set of unbelievable ugliness and ineptitude keeps everybody climbing up and down stairs and over curbstones. Full freedom of action on such a cluttered stage is not to be expected ever.

Miss Teyte sang beautifully. So did Mary Kreste, as Geneviève. Carlton Gauld, as Golaud, was the best of all, though the role lies a shade high for him. Virginia Haskins, as Yniold, was excellent. Norman Scott, as Arkel, was a pleasure, too. Fernand Martel, a Canadian, who sang Pelléas, got better as the evening went on. He is not yet at home, I think, on stages and does not project completely. His voice, though pretty, is neither large nor expressive; and he mouths a bit, singing the while in his throat. But he has musical taste and sings a lovely French.

Everybody, in fact, sang good French, pronounced it clearly, made that, rather than mere vocalization, the object of the evening. Consequently the singing all had color in it and variety. Diction, expressivity of timbre, and a care for the musical amenities made of the whole performance a pleasure. And it was not, surprisingly enough, very much more Miss Teyte's show than anybody else's, though, of course, her experience with the whole repertory of Debussy's vocal works did give her an edge on the others for interpretation.

Miss Teyte was grand, if also a bit stiff. But the real hero of the occasion was Jean Morel. If we heard more French works prepared with his care and his understanding, we might all go oftener to the opera. Because French opera is the one repertory that makes today dramatic as well as musical sense. Unfortunately it was only the musical (and the verbal) sense that came over last night. I recommend listening to this show with the eyes closed.

March 26, 1948

In Fairy Tale Vein

DAS RHEINGOLD, opera in four scenes by *Richard Wagner*, yesterday afternoon at the Metropolitan Opera House, *Fritz Stiedry*, conductor, *Herbert Graf*, stage director, with *Joel Berglund* (Wotan), *Max Lorenz* (Loge), *Gerhard Pechner* (Alberich), *Jerome Hines* (Fasolt), *Polyna Stoska* (Freia), and *Blanche Thebom* (Erda).

THE CAST, as you can verify above, was a distinguished one at yesterday afternoon's performance of *Das Rheingold*. The musical audition, too, was far more polished than most of those one hears these days at the Metropolitan Opera House. And the new scenery proved to be in every way worthy of the grandiose style that Wagner's *Ring of the Nibelungs* tetralogy demands. Particularly satisfactory was the shipshapeness with which lighting, stage movements, and scene changes were operated. It assured us that the Met can still put on a show in professional style, even when the scenic set-up is complex, and that any other kind of presentation at that establishment is attributable either to carelessness or to an attempt to make outworn material do.

Lee Simonson's sets follow in spirit and general plan the Kautsky designs with which we have long been familiar and which once bore the blessing of Bayreuth itself. Their chief departure from these is a translation of Romantic detail into modernistic detail. Mr. Simonson's rocks are more simplified, more angular than what a nineteenth-century artist would have conceived; and his Valhalla bears such a clear resemblance to the Cornell Medical Center (amplified to Radio City proportions) that it suggests some massive real estate development entitled, perhaps, "The Valhalla Apartments."

This last detail is not entirely happy, and the cubistic rocks are a bit brutal in outline. Also, the latter budge when clutched. One hopes they are better built than their present instability suggests. But everything else is tasteful and solid. Even the Worm is impressive. Particularly delightful are the giants and the dwarves. The former, shod on stilts and clothed in fur, are hugely effective; and the latter are terrifyingly true to fairy-tale life. The child of any age who did not respond to both these creations would be poor indeed of spirit. The Rhine maidens appear about as usual, since their visual shape is largely determined by that of the chairs concealed beneath their trailing

best playing, the best singing, the best scenery, the best direction and lighting, the most impressive effects of every kind. It is
as if only he were worthy the deployment of so vast a machine.
The contrast between these works and the rest of opera, as
given year after year in that house, is striking and revelatory.
Not of Wagner's musical primacy, however. Mozart and Bizet
remain greater composers and more expert men of the theater,
and Verdi is at least his equal. But it does show us what the
Met, its whole set-up and management, are good for. Good *for*
because good *at*.

January 21, 1949

Louise as a Wan Blonde

LOUISE, opera in four acts by *Gustave Charpentier*, last night at the
Metropolitan Opera House, *Louis Fourestier*, conductor, *Désiré Defrère*,
stage director, with *Dorothy Kirsten* (Louise), *Raoul Jobin* (Julien),
Margaret Harshaw (Mother), *John Brownlee* (Father), and *Emily Sachs*
(Street Sweeper; Chair Mender).

CHARPENTIER's *Louise*, which was heard again last night at the
Metropolitan Opera House after nearly a five-year interval, is
a good play and a good score. The play, incidentally, is not by
Charpentier, as the printed program states and as the printed
score would lead one to believe, but by the poet Saint-Pol-Roux
and is so registered at the Société des Auteurs Dramatiques,
in the rue Ballu. The present Metropolitan production of this
sound and charming work is still visually evocative of the turn of
this century and auditively agreeable in the small roles. It lacks
force and brilliance at the key positions, all of them, including
that of the conductor. Consequently the show is pale and cold.

Dorothy Kirsten, in the title role, would seem deliberately
to have affected pallor. She wears the palest of yellow hair, the
wishy-washiest of pinks in her dresses, and an almost dead-white
make-up. Her voice seems light for the role, too; and though
she sings almost prettily and pronounces clearly, she does not
come over vocally as a character of much emotional weight.
Even her acting is puny. She represents Louise as constantly
clutching at things and people, constantly weeping and constantly pitying herself. The absence of physical alacrity from
Miss Kirsten's movements, the insistence on an extreme and

obviously artificial blondness (if she expects to pass for a Paris working girl) in her get-up, and an almost crooned song-speech end by giving to her whole interpretation a suggestion of Mae West. She has worked hard and prepared her reading carefully, but I think she has missed the point of Louise.

The latter is no tender bourgeoisie wrapped up in pink silk shirtwaists all for love. She is a working girl brought up on socialism, adding thus to the normal revolt of youth a certain political and philosophic education. She would leave home shortly in any case. Her mother knows this only too well and hopes to keep her under guard till an offer of legitimate marriage in her own class turns up. Louise, however, is more interested in emancipation than in working; and when Julien offers her, along with socialist conversation and the independence of the artist's life, the full doctrine and practice of free love, it is perfectly clear that the family is not going to see much more of her. Even if Julien should not pan out, her decision is made. Home and mother have lost.

Here I am telling what the opera *Louise* ought to be like instead of what it was like last night. It was a clean performance but a lifeless one, save for the small roles. One of these was charmingly sung by a newcomer to the house, Evelyn Sachs. The most disappointing of the principals were Miss Kirsten, Mr. Brownlee, and the conductor Mr. Fourestier. Mr. Jobin and Miss Harshaw were not always convincing dramatically, but at least they made some noise. The performance was lifeless at the top.

December 13, 1947

Toscanini's Aïda

AÏDA, opera in four acts, libretto by *Antonio Ghislanzoni*, music by *Giuseppe Verdi*, performed in part last night in Studio 8-H, Radio City, by the NBC Symphony Orchestra, *Arturo Toscanini*, conductor, with *Herva Nelli* (Aïda), *Eva Gustavson* (Amneris), *Teresa Stich Randall* (Priestess), *Richard Tucker* (Radames), and a chorus of sixty voices, *Robert Shaw*, director.

ONCE A YEAR Arturo Toscanini, who conducts operas better than almost anybody else but who will not work with the Metropolitan, gives us the music of one by means of radio. Yesterday afternoon the first half of Verdi's *Aïda* was our fare, and next week the other half will be coming along. The N.B.C. Symphony Orchestra provides the instrumental support. Singers are listed above. The real star, of course, is the Maestro himself, showing us by means of music alone what dramatic animation means and how it need not at any point make war on clarity.

The Maestro, broadcasting, takes advantage of the fact that no distracting visual element or stage necessity is present to act as a brake. His music flows like running water, hasting o'er pebble and sand; and the sound of it is every bit as refreshing. His opera performances are limpid, lucid, expeditious. You hear the whole texture of the score better than you ever could in an opera house or from the broadcast of a full theatrical execution. They are a privilege, a pleasure, and, for all their distortion through speed, a model of pacing.

The faults of yesterday's *Aïda* lay on the vocal side. The singers were not poor singers, but neither was any one of them quite up to the occasion. They kept up with the Maestro's pace all right and mostly sang on (or near) the pitch. They had pleasant voices. They mostly wabbled a little, and they did not seem to have invariably a sure placement. What effect they gave in the hall I cannot imagine, since I could get no hint from the broadcast about the real volume of any of them. It sounded to me as if the soloists were too close to the microphone and the choral singers too far away.

Some engineering fault, moreover, either at the studio or in my machine (which is supposed to be a good one) made the voices seem to spread and blare and buzz. The Priestess, for instance, as sung by Teresa Stich Randall, might easily have been two Teresa Stich Randalls singing together. A double auditory image was present whenever she sang, also a huge and barnlike reverberation. This effect was engineering trickery, I am sure, because it came on and off with the temple music. It was not entirely pleasant to the ear or resembling, for Mrs. Randall's voice is in real life remarkable for its clarity and focus.

Engineering also played tricks on the scene between Amneris and Aïda by varying the volume in such a way (or possibly by not correctly adjusting it) that they seemed to be yards apart, though their conversation at this point is intimate. Who was responsible (engineers or artists) for the lack of vocal glamour in the two big arias, the tenor and soprano ones, I should not care to guess. Nor why the choral ensembles, all of them, lacked penetration in the soprano element. Perhaps it is thought not important, when the Maestro conducts, what the voices sound like. It is his show, not theirs. Well, his instruments sounded well yesterday and balanced brightly. I suspect that a change of acoustical set-up is needed for his opera broadcasts, if their vocal effects are to be a match for their instrumental perfection and for the brilliance of the Maestro's rocketlike readings.

March 27, 1949

Give the Singers a Break

Every time a reviewer describes a musical performance that happens also to have been broadcast, differing evidence comes to him from listeners who were not present. In the hall, opinions differ widely about the artistic value of a musical action; but those accustomed to musical audition are not likely to be far apart in their estimate of just and unjust musical balances and of whether a given singer sang predominantly on pitch. It is like tasting lemonade; almost anybody can identify the mixture correctly as sweet or sour. One's preference in either direction remains a personal factor, a legitimate one, of course, but merely personal. Transmission by radio gives a different musical mixture from the original one and brings forth, in consequence, differing testimony. Radio listeners do not vary among themselves about the facts any more than those present at the performance do; but what they hear has small relation, as acoustical balance, to what was heard in the house. Microphone placement and the dial adjustments of the engineer in charge can either destroy an equilibrium or, in some cases, produce one.

Strauss's *Der Rosenkavalier*, as heard at the Metropolitan Opera House on the opening night of the season and as heard in some five or six American cities by television broadcast, would seem, if one pools the evidence, to have been two different performances. Only when one separates those present from those not present does the testimony make sense. In the house the singers were hard to hear, especially during the first act. There is pretty general agreement about that. The television broadcast, whether heard here or in Detroit, seems to have caused no such discomfort. The only witness who has told me otherwise turns out to have been listening in a saloon, where distractions may have made concentration incomplete. The second act, in the opera house, brought better stage-and-pit cooperation but was still, to this listener, a bit loud from the pit. The third act he did not hear.

This sifting of evidence is merely preliminary to a further discussion of the work and its performance. I must insist that whatever I say about the Metropolitan Opera performances is based on what I hear at the Metropolitan Opera House. The broadcasts are another story. And what I heard on opening night seems to have been just about what everybody else heard who was present. The overbalance of sonorities in the orchestra's favor was, moreover, the work of the great Fritz Reiner—an impeccable ear, an impeccable musician, and a specialist of Richard Strauss. I am not presuming, therefore, any accident or inefficiency. I take it that a performance so handsomely cast and so thoroughly rehearsed could only have been the one he wished us to hear. And it is with full respect for so experienced an operatic director and in full awareness of the hazard that my own opinion of the work may be an isolated one, that I venture to differ with Mr. Reiner's conception.

Some fifteen years ago I heard this conductor give the same work at the Academy of Music in Philadelphia. The soloists were of top quality; the Philadelphia Orchestra was in the pit; rehearsals had been plentiful. The musical effect was much the same as that heard recently at the Metropolitan. It was that of an orchestral piece with vocal accompaniment. Now here is where I presume to differ with Mr. Reiner. I do not find such a conception of *Der Rosenkavalier* either theatrically effective or musically satisfactory. Such an approach to Wagner's *Götterdämmerung* is far more convincing, though there is some question about its being the composer's own. It works beautifully with Strauss's *Salomé*, as we heard it last under this same conductor. But *Götterdämmerung* and *Salomé* are slow-moving tragic stories; emotional expansion is appropriate to them, gives them power. *Der Rosenkavalier*, a comedy of sentiment, needs lightness of hand, a mercurial wit, and all the charm possible on the stage.

It does not seem proper to me that the singing actors in this work should be treated like bellowing statues. I think they should be given their ease, encouraged to pronounce, and allowed to both sing their lines and play the play. Such a treatment need require no violation of Strauss's score. It would merely mean asking the orchestra for transparent sounds. Mr. Reiner, fully aware the other evening that certain of his singers were not being heard, held the accompaniment for pages on end to a low dynamic level. But he never got the opacity out of it. A single clarinet, using the round tone, was sufficient to eat up Eleanor Steber's voice. Now Miss Steber's voice is a beautiful one and not weak, but its projection was subject to orchestral interference. I believe that interference to have been largely an acoustical effect due to the use of excessive instrumental vibrato and similar devices for achieving a rich tonal color. I know, further, that a rich tonal color in the orchestra, especially when the scoring is elaborate, is very hard to sing against. Only the most powerful voices can compete with it. And throwing this particular opera, or any other comedy, indeed, into a key of vocal strain removes a great deal of its playing quality as drama and almost all its possibilities for vocal charm.

The above observations apply equally to Verdi's *Falstaff* and to Wagner's *Die Meistersinger*. All three of these operatic comedies, over and above their complex orchestral commentary, need clarity of stage speech and ease of stage movement. Neither can be obtained from singers who are preoccupied constantly with giving their sonorous all. I am convinced that these works would make their dramatic points better and lose no musical interest if the musicians who conduct them would let the dramatic line dominate. The musical line, in that case, would suffer, I am sure, no injury; and the musico-dramatic spectacle would be stronger. Such a change in Metropolitan habits would require, of course, a good deal more stage rehearsal than is customary or convenient; but the result, if tastefully operated, might well delight both the music-minded and the play-minded. Certainly it would put the singers into a more graceful position than the one they now occupy, in which only the microphone public can hear what they are doing.

December 4, 1949

Success Tactics

PETER GRIMES, opera in a prologue and three acts, libretto by *Montagu Slater*, music by *Benjamin Britten*, last night at the Metropolitan Opera House, *Emil Cooper*, conductor, *Dino Yannopoulos*, stage director, with *Frederick Jagel* (Peter Grimes) and *Regina Resnik* (Ellen Orford).

BENJAMIN BRITTEN's *Peter Grimes*, which was added last night to the repertory of our Metropolitan Opera, is a success. It always is. Given in any language in a house of no matter what size, it always holds the attention of an audience. As given last night "the works," so to speak, which is to say, the full mechanism, musical and scenic, of a mammoth production establishment, it still held the attention.

This is not to minimize the excellences of the present production, which are many, or the care that has gone into it, which is considerable. It is merely to point out that the steam-roller processing that our beloved Met, geared to Wagner, puts any new work through is one of the severest known tests for the strength of theatrical materials. If Mr. Britten's work came out scarcely in English, vocally loud from beginning to end, and decorated in a manner both ugly and hopelessy anachronistic, it also came through the ordeal with its music still alive and its human drama still touching.

Make no mistake about *Peter Grimes*. It is varied, interesting, and solidly put together. It works. It is not a piece of any unusual flavor or distinction. It adds nothing to the history of the stage or to the history of music. But it is a rattling good repertory melodrama. And if the executant artists, beginning with Emil Cooper, who conducted, going on through Frederick Jagel and Regina Resnik, who sang the tenor and soprano leads, to the smallest role in a large cast and even including the chorus, treated the work with no consideration for its special or poetic subject matter, but rather as disembodied, or "pure," theater, just "wow" material, that is exactly what the composer himself has done, what his score invites and asks for.

There is everything in it to make an opera pleasing and effective. There is a trial scene, a boat, a church (with organ music), a pub (with drinking song for the full ensemble), a storm, a night club seen through a window (with boogie-woogie music off stage and shadow play), a scene of flagellation, a mad scene, and a death. There are set-pieces galore, all different, all musically imaginative, and mostly fun. And there are a good half-dozen intermezzos, most of which are musically pretty weak but expressive all the same.

The musical structure of the opera is simple and efficient. Everything and everybody has a motif, a tune or turn of phrase that identifies. The entire orchestral structure, and most of the vocal, is pieced together out of these in the manner of Italian *verismo*. The harmony is a series of pedal-points broadly laid out to hold together the bits-and-pieces motif continuity. There is no pretense of musical development through these motifs, as in Wagner. They are pure identification tags, as in Dwight Fiske. The music is wholly objective and calculated for easy effect. That is why it works.

It works even in spite of its none too happy handling of English vowel quantities. It sacrifices these systematically, in fact, to characteristic melodic turns, as if the composer had counted from the beginning on translation. A good part of the obscurity that was characteristic of last night's diction, in spite of the singers' visible efforts to project sung speech, was due to the deliberate falsity of the prosodic line. Mr. Britten is apparently no more bothered about such niceties than he is by the anachronisms of an almost popishly High Church service in an English fishing village of 1830 and an American jazz band in the same time and place. He has gone out for theatrical effects, got them, got his success. So did the Metropolitan. And still *Peter Grimes* is not a bore.

February 13, 1948

Lively Revival

THE CRADLE WILL ROCK, opera in two acts by *Marc Blitzstein*, performed last night at the New York City Center by the New York City Symphony, *Leonard Bernstein*, conductor and stage director, with a chorus of eleven voices and a cast of twenty-seven singers and actors including *Will Geer* (Mr. Mister), *Shirley Booth* (Mrs. Mister), *Howard da Silva* (Larry Foreman), *Muriel Smith* (Ella Hammer), and *Estelle Loring* (Moll).

MARC BLITZSTEIN's *The Cradle Will Rock*, which was performed last night at the City Center under Leonard Bernstein's direction, remains, ten years after its first New York success, one of the most charming creations of the American musical theater. It has sweetness, a cutting wit, inexhaustible fancy, and faith. One would have to be untouchable (and who is?) by the aspirations of union labor to resist it. Last night's audience did not. No audience I have ever seen, in fact, and I have heard the work many times, ever has.

It was inevitable that the piece (call it, if you will, an opera, a musical comedy, or a play with music) should be revived; and it is a sound idea on Mr. Bernstein's part to revive it just now. In a year when the Left in general, and the labor movement in particular, is under attack, it is important that the Left should put its best foot forward. There is no question, moreover, but that the Left's best foot is its Left foot. In the opinion of this reviewer, Mr. Blitzstein's *Cradle* is the gayest and the most absorbing piece of musical theater that America's Left has inspired. Long may it prosper, long may it remind us that union cards are as touchy a point of honor as marriage certificates.

The Cradle is a fairy tale, with villains and a hero. Like all fairy tales, it is perfectly true. It is true because it makes you believe it. If the standard Broadway "musical" plugs what Thurman Arnold called "the folklore of capitalism," this play with (or "in") music recites with passion and piety the mythology of the labor movement. It is not a reflective or a realistic work. There is not one original thought or actual observation in it. Everybody is a type, symbolizes something; and the whole is a morality play. Its power is due in large part to the freshness, in terms of current entertainment repertory, of the morality that it expounds. That morality is a prophetic and confident faith in trade unionism as a dignifying force morally, as well as economically.

An equally large part of its power comes from its author's talent for musical caricature. He makes fun of his characters from beginning to end by musical means. Sometimes his fun is tender, as in the love duet of the Polish couple; and sometimes it is mean, as in the songs of Junior and Sister Mister. But always there is a particular musical style to characterize each person or scene; and always that style is aptly chosen, pungently taken off. The work has literary imperfections but musically not one fault of style.

Its presentation last night followed the style of its 1937 production, save for the substitution of Mr. Bernstein at a small orchestra in place of Mr. Blitzstein at a small piano. As before, there were costumes but no props or scenery. As before, the system of presentation was completely effective, though the orchestra added little musically. The cast was fair, some of it excellent, notably Will Geer and Howard da Silva, who had sung Mr. Mister and Larry Foreman in the original performances. Muriel Smith, as Ella Hammer, sang her scenes charmingly; Shirley Booth, as Mrs. Mister, got constant laughs; and Estelle Loring, as the Moll, did a professional job. The others were less than ideal, but that made little difference. The work is a tough one and hard to spoil. It was not spoiled. It was played with love and received a rousing welcome home.

November 25, 1947

Little Musical Foxes

REGINA, opera in a prologue and three acts by *Marc Blitzstein*, performed last night at the Forty-sixth Street Theatre, New York, by a small orchestra (*Maurice Abravanel*, conductor) and a cast of twenty-one actors, musicians, singers, and dancers (*Robert Lewis*, stage director, and *Anna Sokolow*, choreographer) including *Jane Pickens* (Regina Giddens), *Priscilla Gillette* (Alexandra Giddens), *Brenda Lewis* (Birdie Hubbard), and *William Wilderman* (Cal).

WHETHER Marc Blitzstein's *Regina* is an improvement on Lillian Hellman's original play is not for this reviewer to judge. His only concern is with its intrinsic quality as musical theater; and that is none too easy to perceive through the presentation at the

Forty-sixth Street Theater. The latter, unfortunately for the music-eared, is not very musical, though it is unquestionably very, very, very, very theater. The play, the spectacle, has certainly a high degree of sustained dramatic tension; it is no bore. There are also moments of musical delight. But by and large the tonal habiliment of the script, as performed, is raucous in sound, coarse in texture, explosive, obstreperous, and strident.

Exceptions to the generally unmusical quality of the rendering are the excellent voices of Brenda Lewis and Priscilla Gillette. William Wilderman, too, is vocally adequate. And Jane Pickens has a clarity of singing speech that is in every way admirable. The rest of the cast is without musical distinction. Even the orchestra, directed by no less a musician than Maurice Abravanel, has a splintery sound. It doesn't blend, and it doesn't support. It either drowns the singers or disappears.

The musical composition is that of an incomplete opera, of one that hands over the expressive obligation to mere speech whenever the composer feels inadequate to handle the dramatic line. It contains many tuneful and well-conceived set-pieces and also a great deal of carefully composed recitative. The transitions from speech to singing are ever so skillfully handled. The recitative itself, however, covers in most cases so wide a vocal range and is so heavily accompanied that it has to be sung fortissimo. It takes on, hence, a melodramatic quality not always appropriate to the verbal text, which is mostly quite simple conversation; and it also loses, of necessity, that verbal clarity that is recitative's chief beauty.

The music's most sophisticated aspect is its characterization of persons. Also, the elaboration of its musical ironies and cross-references is evidence of Mr. Blitzstein's penetrating mind. This is no banal love-me-love-my-tune music. It is dramatic comment of a high order. However, as usually happens with scores of predominantly ironical character, it tends to go a little bland when simple sentiment is its subject.

Rhythmically it did not seem to me structurally adequate, though this weakness may have come partly from the conducting. Time after time, energizing the metrics of a vocal line became the responsibility of the singing actor, the orchestra merely following him instead of carrying forward the composition.

In general, I should say, an undue dramatic obligation is placed on the singers. They are made to shout for minutes on end in the chest register of the speaking voice just before singing an aria. And since the music stops for quite long intervals, the pacing of the work cannot be controlled from the pit and falls to the singers, too. It is no wonder that the performance takes on early a hectic, a hysterical quality, loses musical tone, and fails to achieve musical shape. The piece has power, and some of this comes from the musical setting; but it remains in your reporter's mind a work of incomplete musical responsibility.

November 1, 1949

Pathos and the Macabre

THE CONSUL, opera in three acts by *Gian-Carlo Menotti*, performed last night at the Ethel Barrymore Theatre, New York, by a small orchestra (*Lehman Engel*, conductor) and fourteen actors (*Mr. Menotti*, stage director) including *Patricia Neway* (Magda Sorel), *Cornell MacNeil* (John Sorel), Marie Powers (Mother), *Leon Lishner* (Police Chief), and *Gloria Lane* (Secretary).

THE CONSUL is all Gian-Carlo Menotti's—the play, the music, the casting, the stage direction—a one-man music drama concentrated and powerful. To report on it as merely a piece of music would give no idea of its real nature. To recount it as drama would not explain its intensity. It is a play of horror and deep pathos, but these qualities in it are as much a result of musical stylization as they are of dramatic exposition.

It is musical investiture, with all the stiffness of stage movement that this involves, that has allowed the author to point up the story with irony and with a comic relief that in any realistic presentation would have been offensive to taste. Also, the story might have come out weak, from the very concentration of its appeal to pity, in a more straightforward telling. All the theater conventions, indeed—prose speech, rhyme, instrumental music, song, recitative, and choreography—have combined to give that story breadth of appeal and emotional perspective.

The musical score is apt and ever illustrative. Also, it is valuable to the narrative through its sustained emotional plan. Harmonically it is a bit chromatic and fussy, melodically a shade undistinguished. Constant undecisive modulation and the insistent repetition of melodic fragments tantalize the listener more than they satisfy musically. Recitative passages, however, are so skillfully set as to be almost unnoticeable, to provoke no listener resistance to this most perilous of all opera conventions. And the music of orchestral commentary is everywhere inventive and a help. The two big solos, a lullaby and a denunciation scene, are valuable to the play's progress and emphasis, but musically not very memorable.

The most striking and original musico-dramatic effect in the whole spectacle is the final scene, a fifteen-minute suicide by gas. Here the orchestra and choreographer take over, though there is some singing, too. A vision of death beyond the threshold, set to a waltz in coffin clothes, brings the play to a moving end by exploiting in the most daring manner Mr. Menotti's gift for combining the macabre with the pathetic. A nightmare scene in the second act and a hypnotist's trick on the customers waiting in the office of the consulate had prepared stylistically this finale. All the same, it is as surprising as it is brilliant and vigorous, the most hair-raising among the many virtuoso theatrical effects that the author's fancy has conceived.

In a cast notable for musical excellence Patricia Neway, as the wife of a Resistance hero, stands out as a singing actress of unusual power. Marie Powers, the Mother, though satisfactory, is less impressive. Gloria Lane, the consulate secretary, is thoroughly pleasing in every way. All the men are good, and so are the singers of secondary roles. Lehman Engel, at the conductor's desk, produces sound orchestral balances, impeccable pacing of the whole, and unfailing dramatic animation. *The Consul* is a music drama of great power in a production remarkably efficient. I doubt if it makes musical history, but the musical elements contribute in a major way to a spectacle that may well have its place in our century's history of the stage. Mr. Menotti, though not quite a first-class composer, is surely a bold, an original dramatic author. And music is the language that he writes his dramas in.

March 17, 1950

The Met and the City Center

THE SEASONAL CLOSING of our two chief operatic establishments has left pleasant memories of both. There has been, indeed, a goodly number of uncommonly good opera performances at both houses. And if certain off nights have seemed lacking in spark or in the ultimate refinements, others have been thoroughly musical, animated, communicative.

The Metropolitan has given us a revived *Simon Boccanegra* by Verdi and a new production of Mussorgsky's *Khovantchina*. Both were musically sumptuous and careful. Both are works of the highest musical value; and both are, relatively speaking, novelties. The former, we are told, will stay in repertory next year. The latter, it seems, will not, though surely it is to be hoped that so noble a piece will not go to storage for long. The Metropolitan's glory is its ability to perform difficult and complex works. *Khovantchina* is one of the grander monuments of music's history. It needs the kind of grandiose production that only the Met can give; and we, the public, need to hear it more frequently than has been formerly our privilege.

The City Center Opera Company has kept in the spring repertory its excellent production of last fall, Prokofiev's *The Love for Three Oranges*, and given us a new one, Puccini's *Turandot*. Both have delighted the public. Both are distinguished works. And both are a welcome refreshment to repertory. Both works, of course, are over twenty-five years old. Both houses have been reluctant to offer operas, either foreign or domestic, of recent composition.

Opera at the City Center is a genuinely charming entertainment. The price is not high; tickets, with a little forethought, can be had; the productions are agreeable; the audience is lively. Almost any evening spent there is a rewarding one. The Metropolitan is expensive, difficult to get into, and not much fun except for the music. One is exigent about a show under those conditions. When something costs all that money and trouble (including often scalpers' prices, too), we expect of the performance nothing less than perfection. Musical inefficiencies that we condone at the City Center are not forgiven to the Met. When a Metropolitan performance is really good it is unforgettable. Perfection attained is no end impressive. But perfection missed is never a lively spectacle.

The City Center, with no such high-flown role to play, has no such disappointment to offer. Its excellences, ever a welcome surprise, provoke feelings of gratitude and warmth. Warmth, indeed, is felt constantly at this house. It is the tone of the audience.

No such public, with its eagerness, liveness, cultural awareness, and quick-to-applaud friendliness, is elsewhere available in New York. It is as delightful a part of the show as the show itself. The City Center public is aware of quality and grateful for it. Since quality is abundant in the musical productions, the house is ever alert, happy, full of excitement. Any failure to achieve quality is quickly forgotten in the joy that accompanies its recognition in some other element of the performance.

It must be a pleasure for artists to work before such an audience. Certainly it is a pleasure to be part of that audience. The present writer finds at the City Center, moreover, a kind of opera production that he has always held in deep affection, a kind represented in Europe by the municipal establishments of Nice, Marseille, Strasbourg, Bordeaux, and some of the north Italian cities. The aim is quality and taste at the highest level attainable under the circumstances, and the amount of quality offered is invariably a money's worth.

Operas presented in this way often tell their story more vividly than when treated as vehicles for great vocalism and star conducting. These latter elements, when perfect, are a show in themselves. Occasionally, just occasionally, they light up the score. When this miracle occurs, all the establishments pretending to absolute excellence are for one evening justified. The rest of the time they are pretty oppressive.

The municipal establishments do not fly so high or fall so dismally. They hedge-hop happily. The City Center has proved, moreover, with its ballet company, that its audience is thoroughly receptive to contemporary music and contemporary æsthetic conceptions. It can succeed with many an advanced work that might be risky for the Met. The latter can produce complex and difficult works with dignity and high musical power, but ever the success of the operation is precarious. The City Center gives operas at a price available to all and in a manner eminently acceptable, charming, graceful. Also, its performances seem always to have as their theme the work performed rather than the cast performing it. It makes no money, loses no money, asks no contribution, gives a wonderful show. No competitor to the Met at all, it is one of the most valued and valuable cultural institutions in a city rich in cultural offerings of every kind.

May 7, 1950

STRICTLY OF THIS CENTURY

Glorious Loudness

PHILHARMONIC-SYMPHONY ORCHESTRA, *Leopold Stokowski*, conductor, with SCHOLA CANTORUM, the WESTMINSTER CHOIR, and the boys' chorus from P.S. 12, Manhattan, last night at Carnegie Hall, performing Mahler's Symphony No. 8. Soloists: *Frances Yeend*, *Uta Graf*, and *Camilla Williams*, sopranos; *Martha Lipton* and *Louise Bernhardt*, contraltos; *Eugene Conley*, tenor, *Carlos Alexander*, baritone, and *George London*, bass.

GUSTAV MAHLER's Eighth Symphony, as directed last night by Leopold Stokowski in Carnegie Hall, was a glorious experience to one who had not heard it before. Its sculpture of vast tonal masses at the end of each of the two movements was handled by the conductor in so noble a manner that the sound achieved monumentality while remaining musical. The effect was unquestionably grand.

The whole work, indeed, has grandeur and humility. In its eighty minutes of execution time no touch of the meretricious mars its devotional concentration on the meaning of its texts. These are two, the Latin hymn *Veni Creator Spiritus* and the last scene (in German) from Goethe's *Faust*. The symphony holds together as a musical piece and expresses its author's deepest religious impulses, as well as cultured convictions. A master workman, he gave to this work his utmost of seriousness and inspiration. It is a statue to his memory, if not his finest music.

Both as music and as a monument it is weakened by its melodic material, which is banal. Also by its harmony, which, though structurally adequate, is timid, unoriginal, unexpressive. The orchestral writing is ingenious, as always, though lacking somewhat in color for so long a piece; and the handling of the huge choral masses is both firm and delicate. The solo parts are lovely, too, as vocal writing. What the work lacks is melodic point, sharpness of outline. Weak thematic material, developed beyond its natural strength, becomes repetitive, loses communicative power. The last five minutes contain a real tune. The rest, for all the thought and skill involved in its composition, is pretty amorphous.

Some of this amorphousness comes from the composer's basic æsthetic assumption. This assumption, derived from the Finale of Beethoven's Ninth Symphony, seems to be that it is possible to make an artistically perfect work of music that will combine in equal proportions the symphony and the oratorio (or cantata). No such work has yet been produced. Even the Beethoven movement has never been universally voted by musicians to be successful. I do not think Mahler's Eighth is successful, either. It is not, in my estimate of it, a pure crystal. It is ambitious and sincere, and it has character. But its grandeur lies in certain skillful handlings and in the conception. It does not permeate the piece, which is soft inside.

One is grateful to Mr. Stokowski and to his assembled forces for letting us hear it. Also for giving it to us with such great care for musical decorum. Such handsome loudnesses as took place in both perorations one does not encounter often in a lifetime. The soloists were excellent, too. It was a glorious performance of a noble but not wholly satisfactory work.

April 7, 1950

In Waltz Time

PHILHARMONIC-SYMPHONY ORCHESTRA, *Dimitri Mitropoulos*, conductor, last night at Carnegie Hall, performing Schönberg's Five Orchestral Pieces and works by Mozart, Schumann, and Brahms.

ARNOLD SCHÖNBERG's Five Orchestral Pieces, which Dimitri Mitropoulos conducted at last night's concert of the Philharmonic-Symphony Orchestra in Carnegie Hall, were written in 1909, nearly forty years ago. Previously they have been played in New York, I believe, one and three-fifths times. They are among the more celebrated works of our century, and yet few musicians or music lovers have heard them. The present writer, though the owner of a printed orchestral score for twenty-five years, listened to them last night with a virgin ear. Having followed the performance score in hand, he is able to certify that Mr. Mitropoulos and the Philharmonic boys read them to perfection and faithfully. His opinion of the work is that it deserves every bit of its world-wide prestige and none of its world-wide neglect.

The orchestral sound of the work is derived from French Impressionism in general and from the music of Debussy in particular. The orchestra is delicate, coloristic, and clean, at no point emphatic or demagogic. There is not in it one doubling of a note for purposes of weight. Harmonically the work is dissonant and atonal, though there is no twelve-tone row in it. Contrapuntally and rhythmically its texture resembles that of the Brahms Intermezzi, though it offers a more advanced state of the technique.

That technique tends toward fragmentation of the musical material through rhythmic and contrapuntal device. Schönberg here carries it close to the state of ultimate pulverization that his pupil Anton Webern achieved fifteen years later. Rhythmic contradictions, the gasping, almost fainting utterance of intense emotion in short phrases conventional of curve, the chromatic character of these phrases—all this is out of Brahms, though the harmony is far harsher and the sound of it all, orchestrally, is French.

The expressive character of the Five Pieces is deeply sentimental, in spite of a touch (and more) of irony. Four of the five are in triple time. Composed, as they are, almost wholly of phrases consecrated by Vienna to waltz usage, your reviewer is inclined to consider them a sort of apotheosis of the waltz. He realizes that their waltz structure is no obvious or perhaps even consciously intended communication. All the same, except for the one called "The Changing Chord" (in reality an unchanging one), which is an essay in pure orchestration, he finds them evocative of waltz moods and waltz textures, an etherealization of a theme that is at bottom just good old Vienna. He also suspects that in another decade they may be understood by all as something like that.

The rest of the program was carefully executed, a little dry, perhaps, but very neat, very pretty as workmanship and only occasionally a bit loud.

October 22, 1948

Star Dust and Spun Steel

PHILHARMONIC-SYMPHONY ORCHESTRA, *Dimitri Mitropoulos*, conductor, last night at Carnegie Hall, performing Cherubini's Overture to *Anacreon*, Beethoven's Piano Concerto No. 5 ("Emperor"), the Anton Webern Symphony, and Rachmaninoff's Symphonic Dances. Soloist: *Robert Casadesus*, piano.

ANTON WEBERN's Symphony for chamber orchestra, the novelty of last night's Philharmonic concert in Carnegie Hall, was "advanced" music when first played here twenty years ago; and it still is. For all the world-wide spread of the twelve-tone technique that has taken place since then, it would be hard to find today five living adepts of it whose writing is so firm and so sophisticated as Webern's was. The audience effect of this work attested also to its vitality. Not only were repeated bows taken by the conductor, Dimitri Mitropoulos, and his excellent musicians. There was actually booing in the hall, a phenomenon almost unknown at the Philharmonic.

The piece itself offends, as it delights, by its delicacy, transparency, and concentration. The first movement, for all its canonic rigor, is something of an ultimate in pulverization—star dust at the service of sentiment. Each instrument plays just one note, at most two; then another carries on the theme. The theme itself is a row of tones isolated from one another by scale skips. The texture is thin, too. One note at a time, just occasionally two or three, is the rule of its instrumental utterance. And yet the piece has a melodic and an expressive consistency. It is clearly about something and under no temptation to fidget. Its form, I may add, is roughly that of a binary, or Scarlatti-type sonata; and its rhythmic pulse, save for a few retards in the second movement, is steady.

This movement (there are only two) is a set of variations on the work's whole twelve-tone row, first stated completely at this point. Rhythm is broken up into asymmetrical fragments. The melodic pulverization is less fine, however, than that of the first movement. Occasionally an instrument will articulate as many as eight or ten notes at a stretch. Some of these are even repeated notes. Metrical fragmentation has taken the place of melodic. The sonorous texture becomes even thinner at the end than anything one has heard previously. A tiny sprinkle of sounds; two widely spaced ones on the harp; and vaporization is complete.

There is every reason to believe the Philharmonic's reading of this tiny but ever so tough work to have been correct. Musicians following the score could question only the size, here and there, of some minute crescendo. The rendering was clear, clean, tonally agreeable, and expressive. Expressive of exactly what, would be difficult to say, as it is of any work. Nevertheless, consistency and self-containment, ever the signs of expressive concentration, were present to the ear, just as they are to the eye reading the score. Once again there was cause to be grateful to Mr. Mitropoulos for his assiduity toward neglected distinction and for his enormous loyalty to the text of a work rare, complex, and in every way difficult.

The rest of the program, standard stuff, sounded gross beside Webern's spun steel. Robert Casadesus played a Beethoven concerto in businesslike fashion, with dispatch and efficiency. A Rachmaninoff piece gave the conductor the conventional odds. Only the Cherubini overture, *Anacreon*, long absent from programs, reminded us that ancient springs can still run fresh when overuse ceases to pollute them. It also reminded us that Rossini's much-admired lively spirits were not so much a personal gift as a heritage from predecessors and fellow countrymen, from this one in particular. A jolly piece and a shapely one by the founder of French musical pedagogy.

January 27, 1950

Gloomy Masterpiece

PHILHARMONIC-SYMPHONY ORCHESTRA, *Dimitri Mitropoulos*, conductor, last night at Carnegie Hall, performing Weber's Overture to *Der Freischütz*, Bach's Violin Concerto in G minor, the Alban Berg Violin Concerto, and Vaughan Williams's Symphony No. 4. Soloist: *Joseph Szigeti*, violin.

THE STAR of last night's Philharmonic program was the late Alban Berg, author of the violin concerto played by Joseph Szigeti. Mr. Szigeti himself, who also played a Bach concerto (the G minor), and the other composers represented all fitted modestly into a background for this striking work. Only Dimitri Mitropoulos, who conducted, stuck out a bit. Apparently in one of his febrile moods, he kept getting between each work and its rendering, standing out against it, till closing the eyes, with all the risks of somnolence entailed, became the only escape. Even then one could not avoid an awareness that everything was being overplayed, overpushed, overdramatized, overexpressed. Everything, at least, but the Berg Concerto, itself so powerful, so lucid an introspection that even a tortured and twisting conductor could not overshadow its gloom.

Expressionismus at its most intense and visceral is the work's æsthetic. The twelve-tone-row technique is the method beneath its coherence. Pure genius is the source of its strength. Somber of coloration, its sound is dominated ever by the soloist, the string section, and the horns. Based on a row that begins with a circle of fifths, the constant recurrence of this easily noticed progression brings some monotony to the texture. Expressive chiefly of basic pleasure-pain and tension-relief patterns (the reason for my calling its expression visceral), its few cerebral references (to a Viennese waltz in the first movement and to a Bach chorale in the last) stand out like broken memories in a delirium.

The piece is too continuous, of course, too consistent to represent mind-wandering. It is a work of art, not a madman's dream, though its gloom is almost too consistent to be real. Nevertheless, it would not be fair to suspect a piece clearly so inspired in musical detail of essential second-rateness. One must, I think, take it or leave it as a whole. Your reviewer has long been willing to take it, to enjoy its musical fancy and to admire its coloristic intensities, without, however, at any time finding his emotions transported. Such an experience often accompanies the hearing of works removed from one's personal sensibilities by space and time. It does not prove a thing against a masterpiece.

Alban Berg is dead; he has joined the classic masters. One does not have to vote about his work, to love it or to hate it. It exists in perfection, for whatever use we may care to make of it. I suspect that the world will be making more and more use of this particular piece. And I believe strongly that Mr.

Mitropoulos has rendered the music world a service by providing on this occasion (as on a previous one back in 1945, when he led it in a broadcast N.B.C. concert) auditory access to it. So has Mr. Szigeti by playing the solo part so manfully on both occasions. I suspect that the trouble with the rest of the evening came from the conductor's devotion to the Berg Concerto. He seemed to have got by means of it into a state of intensity, almost of sanctification, that rubbed off on everything else. It did the other works little good, as you may imagine.

December 16, 1949

The Ultimate of Lucidity

NBC SYMPHONY ORCHESTRA, *Ernest Ansermet*, conductor, on January 24 in Studio 8-H, Radio City, performing Templeton Strong's Paraphrase on a Chorale by Hans Leo Hassler, Debussy's *Jeux*, and Martinů's Symphony No. 5.

ERNEST ANSERMET, conducting last Saturday afternoon's concert of the N.B.C. Symphony Orchestra in Studio 8-H, Radio City, gave us two works virtually unknown to New York listeners and one brand-new one. He also showed us the conductor's art at a degree of mastery rarely to be encountered, even in these days. The works were beautiful and their readings perfection. The orchestra itself, which varies in efficiency from week to week, like any other guest-conducted ensemble, gave out on this occasion sounds to remind us all that its executant personnel is that of a great orchestra.

The string section was shown us in glory by means of a Paraphrase on a Chorale by Leo Hassler. The chorale is the Good Friday one, *O Sacred Head Now Wounded*. The composer of the work is the aged Templeton Strong, an American long resident in Switzerland. The style of the paraphrase is derived from Bach's chorale-preludes by way of Romantic modulation. It is tasteful, touching, and skillfully written, if not unusually original. The pleasure of hearing it was double, because it is intrinsically a far from stupid piece and because the N.B.C. strings are among the finest in America.

Bohuslav Martinů's Fifth Symphony, which ended the program, an American première, shows this living master at his highest point, for the present, of originality and freedom. Martinů is clearly, as of today, a symphonist. He moves in the form with ease, makes it speak for him. This symphony speaks in double-talk, says always two things at once. Almost nowhere else in the music of our time is antiphony, both of sound and of sense, so constantly present. The tunes, the counterpoint, the harmony of this work are personal and expressive. Its shape is plain and free, without any looseness. Its speech is noble, without any demagoguery or any pretentiousness. Others have used the symphony for its prestige, for its box-office power, or for private musical ends. To Martinů alone among contemporary masters has it been given to elevate the symphonic tone.

Debussy's ballet *Jeux* (or *Games*), written in 1912 and produced by Diaghilev in 1913 (the scenarist and choreographer, Nijinsky, also dancing the male role), has long been neglected by conductors, even in France. The last orchestral work to be fully orchestrated by Debussy himself, it represents at its ultimate that tendency toward the attenuation of musical materials into a luminous and golden dust, of which *La Mer* and *Images* are earlier examples. It glows like mercury vapor or a sunset in Texas and is as immaterial to the touch. Sonorously it is a piece for two harps, four flutes, and subdivided strings, in which the rest of its large orchestra merely amplifies climactically the basic coloration. Expressively it is an apotheosis of the waltz. Formally it is a masterpiece of continuity that employs no classical continuity device for its own sake but that holds together in the most surprising way. Its musical language, starting out with twelve-tone chords and continuing to the end in polyharmony and polyrhythm, achieves an effect close to atonality and remains today advanced.

Jeux is a unique work, an ultimate work, an end, and maybe a beginning. Executed with Mr. Ansermet's equally unique and ultimate lucidity, it is also one of the most ravishing pieces imaginable. In hands less loving it might easily take on weight and fall apart. In his it is a lesson in how French music at its summit of achievement should, could, and must be made to sound. Mr. Ansermet himself, in case you haven't heard about him, is

conductor of l'Orchestre de la Suisse Romande in Geneva and
one of the half-dozen greatest living orchestral workmen and
interpreters. He has two more Saturday concerts at N.B.C.

January 26, 1948

The Style Is the Subject

CHAMBER ART SOCIETY, *Igor Stravinsky* and *Robert Craft*, con-
ductors, last night at Town Hall, performing the following works by
Mr. Stravinsky: *Symphonies d'instrument à vent, Danses Concertantes*,
Capriccio for Piano and Orchestra, and Symphony in C. Soloist: *Elly
Kassman*, piano.

THE MUSICO-INTELLECTUAL WORLD turned out in considerable numbers for last night's concert in Town Hall of the Chamber Art Society. Igor Stravinsky's music and presence were the
attraction. The program gave us four works rarely heard, covering a period of twenty years in the composer's middle and later
middle life, from 1920 to 1941. Two of these, the *Symphonies
of Wind Instruments*, from 1920, and the *Danses Concertantes*,
of 1941, were conducted by himself. The Symphony in C, of
1940, and the Capriccio for Piano and Orchestra, of 1929, were
led by Robert Craft. Elly Kassman played the solo part in the
latter work. Execution throughout was excellent.

The wind piece, dedicated to the memory of Claude Debussy,
was given in a recently made revision. Though it remains a
striking piece chiefly for its dissonant and almost motionless
chorale at the end, throughout it is a deeply expressive work in
mortuary vein. The other pieces, neoclassic in character, are less
directly expressive, being chiefly evocative of scenes, periods,
and circumstances from the history of musical composition.

The Capriccio, derived from Weber's Konzertstück, is a brilliant
potpourri of Schumann, Chopin, Liszt, Delibes, and probably
some others. The *Danses Concertantes* evoke the ballet music
of Adam in particular and of the mid-nineteenth century in
general. The Symphony in C is modeled after the Viennese
classical works in that form, after Haydn, Mozart, and the early
Beethoven.

The Symphony is the noblest of the three works, by its grandly simple material, its shapeliness, and its elevated tone. The others are a bit frivolous, though plenty of fun, and more than a little discontinuous. Even the Symphony falls apart a bit in the last movement. All the same, it is a handsome piece, as the Capriccio is a jolly and brilliant one and the *Danses Concertantes* an attractive one for anybody who likes to get sentimental about the ballet.

Stravinsky's neoclassic music having never had a real audience success, as his Impressionistic early theater works have had, his friends and disciples tend to defend it as a cause rather than to discriminate one piece of it from another. Last night's concert gave us a chance, however, to do just that by providing three celebrated and varied examples of it in a row. My choice among these, if I must make one, is the Symphony in C. Another's will be the Capriccio or the *Danses*. The attractiveness of Stravinsky's whole neoclassic production lies, however, less in the expressive power of a given work than in the musical language in which they are all written.

This is a compound of grace and of brusqueness thoroughly Russian in its charm and its rudeness and so utterly sophisticated intellectually that few musicians of intellectual bent can resist it. The general public has never cared much about modern neoclassicism, but does listen to it more easily than it used to. I don't think musical ticket buyers are overfond of indirectness, and certainly most of anybody's neoclassic works are indirect. Every now and then, however, one of them forgets its game of reminding you about the history of music and starts saying things of its own. To me the Symphony in C does that, just as the wind instrument *Symphonies,* on the whole an inferior work but not an eclectic or derivative one, have always done.

April 12, 1948

Joan of Arc in Close-Up

PHILHARMONIC-SYMPHONY ORCHESTRA, *Charles Munch*, conductor, with the WESTMINSTER CHOIR, last night at Carnegie Hall, performing *Jeanne d'Arc au Bûcher*, dramatic oratorio for speakers, singers, and chorus, text by *Paul Claudel*, music by *Arthur Honegger*, with *Vera Zorina* (Jeanne) and *Raymond Gérôme* (Frère Dominique), speakers. Soloists: *Nadine Conner* (Virgin Mary), *Jarmila Novotna* (Marguerite), *Enid Szantho* (Catherine), and *Joseph Laderoute* and *Lorenzo Alvary* in multiple roles.

THE PERFORMANCE itself was perfection, that of Honegger's *Joan of Arc at the Stake*, as given at last night's Philharmonic concert in Carnegie Hall under the direction of Charles Munch. Orchestra, chorus, and soloists (as listed above) did everything convincingly, musically just right. And everybody's French was excellent.

The piece itself is what the French call a "big machine"—a work of some musical and literary pretensions set for orchestra, chorus, soloists, and speaking voice. The inventor of the formula, so far as I know, is Berlioz. Its local version is the Norman-Corwin-style radio number. Its most successful European practitioners, among the living, are Arthur Honegger, who composed the present score, and Paul Claudel, author of the present text.

Joan at the Stake aims to please all, save possibly the Marxian Left, by exploiting religious and patriotic sentiments without doctrinal precision. It appeals to the theater instinct in us all by the realistic evocation of horror scenes. It appeases the lover of modern music with bits of polytonal composition. It impresses all by its elaborate mobilization of musical effectives. It offers, in short, virtually everything a concert can offer but bets on nothing.

The weakness of the work lies exactly in its failure to bet, to make clear whether we are listening to a musical work on a literary text or to a literary work with musical commentary. The fact that the title role is a speaking role, not a singing one, is the chief source of this ambiguity. Another is the lack of musical shape in the set-pieces.

These are full of expressive variety and abundant of apt musical invention, but they are tied tightly to a text that has itself little of formal shape or progress. The music illustrates the text in running commentary but does not take it in hand, add unity and emphasis. As a result, the work makes rather the same effect that a film of the same length (seventy-five minutes) might. It is picturesque at all moments, varied, and vastly detailed; but it lacks the monumentality that its oratorio layout would seem to impose. It is all in close-ups. At no point do we get a panoramic view, an epic breadth in the narrative.

This is why, for all the fine fancy in Honegger's music, *Joan at the Stake* remains somewhat trivial. It is closer in feeling to devotional than to dramatic literature. It is like some garrulous meditation on the Stations of the Cross. Its convulsive tone is striking, but there is not the dignity in the whole conception that one might expect from a musician of world-wide prestige dealing with a subject so familiar, so touching, and so grand. The effort to please everybody possible in every possible way has left the whole effort touched with a flavor of insincerity, that same flavor we all know so well from our own "big machines" of radio and the films.

January 2, 1948

Handsome Period Pieces

JUILLIARD FESTIVAL OF CONTEMPORARY FRENCH MUSIC, second of four programs last night at Juilliard Concert Hall, presenting *Entr'acte* (1924), silent film by *René Clair*, with a score by *Erik Satie* adapted for two pianos by *Darius Milhaud* and *Harry Brant* and performed by *Frederic Cohen* and *Frederic Waldman*; Francis Poulenc's *Le Bal Masqué*, a setting of six poems by Max Jacob, performed by the Juilliard Chamber Orchestra, *Mr. Waldman*, conductor, with *Warren Galjour*, baritone; and *Le Pauvre Matelot*, opera in three acts, libretto by *Jean Cocteau*, music by *Darius Milhaud*, presented by the Juilliard Opera Theatre, *Mr. Waldman*, conductor, *Mr. Cohen*, stage director.

ERIK SATIE's *Entr'acte*, which opened last night's program at the Juilliard School (the second in a series devoted to contemporary French music), is, in the judgment of this reviewer, the finest film score ever composed. The film itself, made by René Clair after a scenario of Francis Picabia, is a brilliant piece of work but completely nowadays (if also delightfully) a period piece. Produced in 1924 as a divertissement joining two scenes of a ballet, *Relâche* (composed by Satie and decorated by Picabia), it takes us back to the still innocent last days of Dada, before Surrealism had turned our fantasies sour, sexy, and mean. It is not about anything at all but being young and in Paris and loving to laugh, even at funerals. In those days there was still comic cinema, too.

The excellence of the musical score composed to accompany this otherwise silent film with real orchestral sounds (these were played last night by two pianists) is due to Satie's having understood correctly the limitations and possibilities of a photographic narrative as subject matter for music. Also to the durable nature of his musical invention. The whole is made out of short musical bits like building-blocks. These are neutral enough in character to accompany appropriately many different scenes and images, but also interesting enough as music to bear repetition without fatigue to the listener. These musical blocks are organized into a rondo form as squarely terraced as a New York skyscraper and every bit as practical in function.

Satie's music for *Entr'acte*, consequently, is not only beautiful in itself. It is also efficient as expression; it is appropriate to the film. It avoids banality of sentiment by avoiding sentiment altogether, by keeping its expressivity objective, by never identifying itself with any person on the screen. By remaining ever as cool and clear as René Clair's photography itself, it remains also as clear in meaning and as satisfying intrinsically. I do not know another film score so durable, so distinguished.

Francis Poulenc's secular cantata *Le Bal Masqué*, on poems of the late Max Jacob, a piece in six sections for baritone and chamber orchestra, shows us a master of musical exuberance at the climax of his youthful period. It was composed in 1932, about the last year anybody in Europe was really carefree, and it is musical highjinks from beginning to end. Its *pasticcio* of urban banalities, melodic and rhythmic, is rendered personal and interesting by the extreme elegance of the vocal lines and instrumental textures. Thin, clean, brilliant, frank, and delicate, its charm, its good humor, its wit and poetry, like those of Satie himself (though the invention of it is less jewel-like and original than Satie's) are as fresh as the day the piece was written.

The Poulenc piece and Darius Milhaud's short opera *Le Pauvre*

Matelot, to a text of Jean Cocteau, were conducted with taste and understanding by Frederic Waldman. The latter work, which I shall not review, because time presses and because it has been given before in New York, was decorated imaginatively by Frederick Kiesler. Neither work was as well projected vocally by the Juilliard students as they were instrumentally. The Poulenc cantata, from the latter point of view, was an impeccable execution. All three works were a pleasure to hear. Perhaps the Milhaud opera has aged a little; and certainly it always was, though largely composed of gay sailor chanteys like "Blow the Man Down," a shade lugubrious. Also a bit heavy in orchestral texture for its vocal line.

December 2, 1948

Religious Corn

PHILHARMONIC-SYMPHONY ORCHESTRA, *Leopold Stokowski*, conductor, on November 17 at Carnegie Hall, performing Louis Aubert's *Offrande*, Poulenc's *Concert Champêtre*, Messiaen's *Trois Petites Liturgies de la Présence Divine*, Handel's Harpsichord Concerto in B flat, and Mozart's Symphony No. 35 ("Haffner"). Soloist: *Wanda Landowska*, harpsichord.

OLIVIER MESSIAEN's *Three Short Liturgies of the Divine Presence*, which received their first American hearing Thursday night under the direction of Leopold Stokowski at a regular subscription concert of the Philharmonic-Symphony Orchestra in Carnegie Hall, were composed in 1944. The program notes of the occasion give their première date as 1946, and that is probably correct for public performance in a hall. Nevertheless, I reviewed them in this newspaper on September 23 of the previous year, my acquaintance being based on a recording made by the French National Radio from a broadcast performance that had taken place even earlier. The work has been known to musicians here and in Europe for some five years as its composer's most generally successful work in large form. By successful I mean both typical of his procedures and having a direct audience appeal.

Somehow a good deal of that appeal got lost Thursday night in the broad spaces of Carnegie Hall. Though small of instrumentation, the piece needs to sound loud and full and penetrating. Heard that way, its rhythmic and instrumental variety holds immediate attention. Heard at a distance, its trite melodic content and static structure dominate the effect. There is no question that this work is the product of a delicate ear and an ingenious musical mind. Its æsthetic value has not been entirely convincing to the purely musical world, though laymen have usually cast their vote in its favor. My own opinion is that its author is a case not unlike that of Scriabin. That is to say that he is a skilled harmonist and orchestrator, full of theories and animated by no small afflatus, but that there is a sticky syrup in his product which hinders its flow at concert temperatures.

The two composers have an identical preoccupation with ecstasy and an identical inability to keep a piece moving along. Their religious inspiration has no energizing force; it is druglike, pretty-pretty, hypnotic. In Messiaen's case all the paraphernalia of commercial glamour are mobilized to depict the soul in communion with God—a ladies' chorus, divided strings, piano, harp, celesta, vibraphone, Chinese cymbal, tamtam, and an electronic instrument playing vibrato (in this case the Ondes Martenot). The sounds of such an ensemble, however intelligently composed, cannot transport this listener much farther than the Hollywood cornfields. Placing them at the service of religion does not, in his experience, ennoble them; it merely reduces a pietistic conception of some grandeur to the level of the late Aimee Semple McPherson.

Framing this novelty, which for all its silliness is musically highly original, one heard twice the impeccable and ever wondrous Wanda Landowska. She gave us Poulenc's *Concert Champêtre* in its original form (for harpsichord with orchestra) and a Handel organ (or harpsichord) concerto too. Nothing banal, nothing unlovely marred her readings; and the seemingly frail instrument sounded forth with a lordly clang through the fine textures of both composers. Earlier there had been an *Offrande* by Louis Aubert, a short memorial work pleasingly sonorous but not in itself, I should think, memorable. Afterward came the Mozart *Haffner* Symphony. This last your reporter regretfully passed up, the hour being already past 10:30.

November 19, 1949

Thanksgiving Turkey

PHILHARMONIC-SYMPHONY ORCHESTRA, *Dimitri Mitro-poulos*, conductor, last night at Carnegie Hall, performing Franck's *Chasseur Maudit*, Ernst Krenek's Symphony No. 4, and Tchaikovsky's Violin Concerto in D major. Soloist: *Mischa Elman*, violin.

DIMITRI MITROPOULOS conducted the Philharmonic last night at the regular subscription concert in Carnegie Hall in a way to make the heart rejoice. His work was the only unalloyed pleasure, however, that can be testified from this mourner's bench. César Franck's *Le Chasseur Maudit* is a harmless enough piece, all about what happens to people who go hunting on Sunday. And Mischa Elman, a ripe but still sound violinist, playing the Tchaikovsky Concerto, an overripe but still not wholly withered comestible, offers quiet entertainment for a Thanksgiving night.

Ernst Krenek's Symphony No. 4, a first performance, was the really indigestible dish. The style of this work, pan-diatonic neoclassicism, and the subject matter of it, an emulation of Beethoven's middle period, are familiar to all nowadays. They are the veriest routine of the conservatories. Mr. Krenek's high musical skill and serious aims are far from offensive, either. They are perhaps the leavening element, indeed, if any is present, in that sad cake. It is troublesome to encounter a work so seemingly serious in thought, so certainly ambitious, and so thoroughly well composed, in a practical sense, and yet to be utterly unable at any point to be convinced by it.

Perhaps the overweening ambition of it is what sinks it. The idea of making a symphony that shall be monumental, impressive, forcible, easy to understand, and at the same time of an impeccable modernism is not a new idea; but neither is it a very good one. It is not a good one because it starts with an effect that it is desired to achieve rather than with a real musical idea that it has become urgent to communicate. Sometimes, starting from such a program, a composer gets his ideas to flowing; and real music comes out after all. The depressing quality about Mr. Krenek's new symphony is that the author has carried out his admitted intention to the letter. He has produced, in consequence, a pseudo-masterpiece with about as much savor to it as a pasteboard turkey.

The presentation by Mr. Mitropoulos and the Philharmonic boys of this (in the Broadway sense) turkey lacked nothing as a professional performance. All was clear, smoothly turned out, equilibrated. The work itself, in no way difficult of comprehension, confused nobody. Anybody could see that it was as empty as it was handsome. Anybody could hear, too, that Mr. Mitropoulos, playing no matter what, is a musician of quality so distinguished that one scarcely minds his playing, as he so often does, no matter what. He rather enjoys, I think, animating dead turkeys.

November 28, 1947

Masterpieces Revived

NATIONAL ASSOCIATION FOR AMERICAN COMPOSERS AND CONDUCTORS, concert of new and early twentieth-century works for wind instruments, last night at Times Hall, New York, including Henry Cowell's Suite for Wind Quartet, Vincent Persichetti's Pastorale for Wind Quintet, Elliott Carter's Quintet for Winds, Ingolf Dahl's Music for Five Brass Instruments, Richard Franko Goldman's Duo for Tubas, and Carl Ruggles's *Angels*, performed by students of the Juilliard School of Music, *Mr. Goldman* and *Lou Harrison*, conductors; also songs by David Diamond, Eunice Lea Kettering, Mary Howe, and Everett Helm, performed by *Sara Carter*, soprano, accompanied by *David Garvey*, pianist.

CARL RUGGLES's *Angels* was the high point of the concert presented last night in Times Hall by the National Association for American Composers and Conductors. Other works had elegance or musical distinction, and all were handsomely executed. But Ruggles's piece is a masterpiece and one almost wholly unknown today. Its revival after more than twenty years was accompanied by the kind of intellectual excitement that has ever attended its performance, plus the deep joy of the young just making its discovery.

Angels is part of a longer work entitled *Men and Angels*, composed in 1921. This section, as rescored in 1938, is a sustained and tranquil motet for four trumpets and three trombones, all muted. The texture of it is chromatic secundal counterpoint. Its voices, nondifferentiated as to expressive function, are woven together by thematic imitation. The dissonance-tension is uniform throughout, hence, in the long run, harmonious, though that tension carries the maximum of dissonance possible to seven voices. Complete avoidance of the dramatic and the picturesque gives to the work a simplicity and a nobility rare in the music of our time. Its plain nobility of expression and the utter perfection of its workmanship place Ruggles as one of our century's masters, perhaps the one among all from whom the young have most to learn just now.

Preceding this extraordinary and secretly powerful work, there had taken place a concert of music for wind instruments, including the human voice, the only exception being a pianoforte, played ever so beautifully by David Garvey to accompany the singer. Most impressive among these works, to your reporter, was a Quintet for Winds by Elliott Carter, a solid work with musical interest in it and weight in the expression. A Duo in three movements for two bass tubas, by Richard Franko Goldman, had naturally a certain comic charm and surprisingly both musical grace and sweetness of sound. It was soft, velvet-footed, and in every way delicately pleasing.

The rest of the program was agreeable but not particularly fresh, excepting for one delicious Chorale movement in Henry Cowell's Suite for Wind Quintet. Vincent Persichetti's Pastorale for the same group showed fancy but was loosely held together. Ingolf Dahl's Music for Five Brass Instruments, an ambitious work in three extended movements, is more worthy than original of thought. Among the songs, all had quality but none, I think, a completely sustained inspiration.

The wind players, all Juilliard students, had been trained by Richard Franko Goldman; and genuinely fine they were for technical excellence and musical understanding. Sara Carter, soprano, did well by the songs. Lou Harrison conducted Ruggles's *Angels* reverently, admirably. It was a lovely concert, in every way out of the ordinary; and Ruggles's piece is great music.

February 28, 1949

Yesterday's Modernism

LEAGUE OF COMPOSERS, concert dedicated to Paul Rosenfeld, last night at the Museum of Modern Art, New York, presenting works by composers championed by the late music critic, including Charles Mills's Sonata for Oboe and Piano, performed by *Melvin Kaplan* and *Sylvan Fox*; Leo Ornstein's *Three Moods*, performed by *Grant Johannesen*, pianist; Roger Sessions's Duo for Violin and Piano, performed by *Nicolai Berezowsky* and *Donald Kemp*; Stefan Wolpe's *Six Palestinian Songs*, performed by *Arline Carmen*, mezzo-soprano, and *Leon Lishner*, baritone, accompanied by *Irma Wolpe*, pianist; Roy Harris's Concerto for String Quartet, Piano, and Clarinet, performed by *Richard Adams* and *Emma Jo McCracken*, violinists, *Gabriel Gruber*, violist, *Charles McCracken*, cellist, *Herbert Tichman*, clarinetist, and *Joseph Bloch*, pianist; and Edgard Varèse's *Hyperprism*, performed by an ensemble of twenty-four, *Frederic Waldman*, conductor.

THE LEAGUE OF COMPOSERS concert, which took place last night in the Museum of Modern Art, lasted till eleven o' clock; and your reviewer, the night being rainy, did not reach his desk till fifteen minutes later. Consequently, in order to cover a concert of some intellectual importance, he is going to take the liberty of stating his judgments in summary, stenographic fashion. But first it must be listed that all the executions were excellent, unusually distinguished being the piano playing of Grant Johannesen, the violin playing of Nicolai Berezowsky, and the singing of Arline Carmen. Especial thanks are due also to Frederic Waldman, who conducted the Varèse piece perfectly, at least to these ears.

The Varèse work, entitled *Hyperprism*, is real "modern music" of twenty years back; and it still makes its point. That point is that beauty does not require cantilena, harmony, contrapuntal imitation, or deliberate pathos. It can be made with elements commonly considered to be noise, and it does not even have to confine its sound sources to the conventionally ignoble. Trumpets, trombones, flutes, horns, piccolos, and the classical instruments of percussion give out purer sounds than flower pots and brakebands. Consequently they are useful. But out with their sentimental connotations! They are there as sound sources, not as poetic references.

The sounds that Varèse makes in this piece are handsome

in the abstract. Their composition is rhythmically interesting, moreover; and with no cue as to the work's particular meaning, your listener found it absorbing, convincing, beautiful, and in every way grand. That the League of Composers, which fought this composer bitterly and all too successfully twenty years back, should revive him now is poetic justice. Let no one think, however, that they have just made his acquaintance or that they are recalling any historical benefaction of theirs.

As recalling former successes of the modern-music movement, the League gave us last night three jolly pieces by Leo Ornstein, from 1916, rhythmically thoroughly alive, if harmonically nothing difficult. Three piano pieces by Roger Sessions, though harmonically sophisticated, were as dead as the day of their birth. Roy Harris's Concerto for String Quartet, Clarinet and Piano, is still, twenty years later, real chamber music, with no more faults than are to be found in Brahms and with all the virtues. And Stefan Wolpe's songs, the evening's only first performance, are knockouts in the vein of yesterday's modernism and up to date in their use of Hebraic texts, references to Israel being the last word today in successful public relations. They are really quite good songs, but so are Ornstein's pieces good piano music. It was hard to know, indeed, among all these period-style compositions, exactly where real quality lay, excepting for the Varèse work, which, by any standards I know, is great music.

January 24, 1949

Five Symphonies

ONE of the striking characteristics of contemporary musical modernism is a tendency on the part of composers to write symphonies. The heroes and founding fathers did no such thing. Not Richard Strauss or Satie or Debussy or Ravel ever touched the form for its own sake, and Stravinsky's early student piece of that title was long viewed by his friends as a youthful indiscretion. The pupils of César Franck, conservative modernists, did write them—d'Indy and Chausson and Dukas and d'Indy's pupil Albert Roussel. But the composers who really forged the modern language stuck pretty consistently to objective expression and avoided the formally introspective. Even Debussy, who invented in the last decade of his life our century's characteristic form of neoclassicism, carried its æsthetic no farther in his three sonatas than an evocation of historic textures. Expansion of the ego, à la Beethoven, was generally considered in the advanced music world that preceded World War I as an unworthy source of inspiration and reactionary.

After 1918 the whole advanced world went a little reactionary, however, and began to work at the abstract forms that for two centuries had provided vessels for musical private thoughts. First the fugue was restored to favor and then the symphony. Milhaud, Honegger, Hindemith, and Prokofiev approached the latter with circumspection through the concerto, the string quartet, and the sonata. So did Stravinsky and Ravel and Schönberg. The last two never wrote an orchestral work of that title; but Stravinsky has followed his younger colleagues in their dangerous path; and nowadays every child in a conservatory, or just out of one, will write you a symphony with no more sense of sin than he would have in taking a highball.

There remains, however, a marked difference among modern composers in the way they approach the form. The Soviet Russians use it for impersonal editorial ends (à la Brahms). The Central Europeans impersonate oratory with it, also à la Brahms. The French stick close to landscape, as Berlioz did. The Americans, and this includes Europeans long resident here, Stravinsky and Milhaud and Hindemith and Krenek and Tansman, mostly follow the Viennese masters. So do the English, excepting Vaughan Williams, a pupil of Ravel, who preserves an almost Impressionistic, or at least Mendelssohnian, relation to landscape painting.

When I say that Stravinsky and Milhaud, for all their training in landscape and the picturesque, follow a Viennese model when composing symphonies, I mean simply that, like Beethoven, they are preoccupied with making a familiar form expressive. The French of France, on the other hand, are more likely to start from an expressive concept and to use familiar form as merely an expedient for sustaining length and emphasis, much as Richard Strauss did long ago in his Sinfonia Domestica. Even their titles betray this difference. Our local writers give their symphonies numbers. Honegger calls his also *Liturgical* or *The Delights of Basel*. Rosenthal calls his most recent *Christmas*

Symphonies and adds a precise description of each movement's pictorial content. Antheil, Cowell, Copland, Piston, Schuman, Harris, Ives—the Americans in general—offer no explanation. When they do, in program notes, they make a strictly formal analysis and insist that any resemblance to real persons or places is accidental.

Five notable new symphonies have come to my ears this season in New York and its environs. Locally we have heard Honegger's Fourth (*Deliciae Baslerienses*) and Antheil's Fifth. I heard Rosenthal's *Christmas Symphonies* in Philadelphia. Cowell's Fifth was played in Washington. Honegger's work is the portrait of a city, how it looks, how it feels, what it sounds like. Rosenthal's is not a formal symphony at all (hence the plural of the title) but a series of picture postcards, extraordinarily vivid in color, of scenes from the Nativity story. Antheil's piece, on the other hand, is about other symphonies in the same way that Stravinsky's and Hindemith's symphonies are. It is chiefly about Beethoven's Eighth and Prokofiev's *Classical*, I should say. And although it is a well written, vigorous, and thoroughly viable work, it represents an observance of some kind, the ceremony of writing a symphony, perhaps, more than a direct statement about anything beyond its references to the history of symphonic expression. The same applies to William Schuman's and to Harris's symphonies and to Piston's and to Copland's Third, all heard or reheard here in recent seasons. Also to both of Stravinsky's late works in that form and to both of Hindemith's, though the second of these latter has a mood title, *Symphonia Serena*. If it does not quite apply to Milhaud's Second and Third, that is because Milhaud has succeeded, in this listener's judgment, in filling the form with content, not with oratory or with theater but with a deeply personal expression of private feeling, just as Schubert and Mendelssohn and Schumann did a century and more ago.

Cowell's Fifth I have not heard, but the composer's notes make it clear that it embodies researches in both form and expression. It aims at an international communication based not on the cross-reference methods of neoclassicism nor yet on the twelve-tone canonic technique but on the universal applicability of primitive and folklore patterns. This æsthetic is not very different from that of Bartók, though the dominant localism is

Celtic-American rather than Balkan. The work's achievement I cannot judge, but certainly its aim is to move us all out of the dead end that the neoclassic symphony appears more and more to be.

The neoclassic symphony is the least successful of all contemporary musical forms, judged by any standard. The picture or landscape symphony is thoroughly successful, but it is not a contemporary form. It is just Mendelssohn's *Scottish* and Debussy's *La Mer*. What the modern world needs is symphonies of private and personal lyricism couched in the language of the modern world. Unfortunately the spiritual resources of the modern world are low for that. The depths of fresh and intense personal feeling that made possible the symphony from Mozart through Schumann are not available anywhere in music today. They exist among Central and East European Jews; but the Jews are using that energy to build a republic, not for supplying repertory to Western concerts. All the new symphonies I have mentioned are good works; but not one, saving possibly the Cowell Fifth, which I do not know, and the Milhaud Second and Third, which have a personal life in them comparable to that of Milhaud's best music of an impersonal character, shows a clear way out of the impasse. Personal lyricism, I am sure, is the ideal way; but in an age characterized by low resources of personal lyricism, depending on them is like making up one's budget to include income that there is no reason whatever for counting on. There might be some chance of an improved result from switching roles, from encouraging the French to write introspectively and the others picturesquely. But Elsa Barraine's Second Symphony, which is French abstractionism, might as well be by a pupil of César Franck. And few of the Americans have anything like the orchestral mastery that it takes to depict the visual. That, of course, they could learn from Manuel Rosenthal.

February 20, 1949

English Landscape

PHILHARMONIC-SYMPHONY ORCHESTRA, *Leopold Stokowski*, conductor, last night at Carnegie Hall, performing Ernest Moeran's *In the Mountain Country*, Vaughan Williams's Symphony No. 6, Gershwin's Piano Concerto in F major, and Liszt's Hungarian Rhapsody No. 2. Soloist: *Byron Janis*, pianist.

RALPH VAUGHAN WILLIAMS's Sixth Symphony, composed last year at the age of seventy-five, was the star novelty on last night's Philharmonic program. Whether Leopold Stokowski conducted it with understanding I cannot say, since I had not heard the work before nor seen a score. But it sounded mighty beautiful to me.

Like the rest of this composer's music, it is at once personal and objective, an expression of private feelings and a depiction of English landscape. A neighbor who knows Mr. Williams and his music well tells me the reflective subject matter is war and peace. Also that a good deal of the thematic material and orchestral color of the first movement is quoted or paraphrased from the same composer's ballet *Job*. There is some jigging on the village green, too, an old custom in Mr. Williams's music. Never mind. The piece has power and depth and a very personal, very English beauty. It resembles more the English Romantic poets than it does English art work of our century, though its texture and idiom are modern—modern and medieval, rather. A lovely piece and one I should like to have heard right over again.

In the Mountain Country, a "symphonic impression" by Ernest Moeran, is a youthful work, some twenty-five years old, by a British composer now turned fifty. Pleasantly sweeping but not strikingly original, the material of this is developed in sequence patterns that weaken its impact as a landscape piece. I doubt that it is his most characteristic work, but its color and tunes are not ugly.

George Gershwin's Concerto in F is not an ugly piece, either; but it is a pretty empty one. Even treated to so loud and so irregularly metered a reading as was given it last night by Byron Janis and Mr. Stokowski, it failed to fill with afflatus, though the last movement did move along. All the sweet rapture and ease of the Gershwin style got lost, of course; but virtuosity of another kind came through. That kind, Mr. Janis's kind, is hard and bell-like, clear, dark, steely-fingered. This twenty-year-old boy from Pittsburgh is a whopping piano player both by technique and by temperament. What his musical nature is like one could not tell from one concerto, and that a minor one.

The final novelty of the evening was Liszt's Second Rhapsody, conducted by Mr. Stokowski in the old barnstorming manner one thought he had long since out-grown. It would have been more effective if the orchestra had followed him better. The rendering came off higglety-pigglety, but this reviewer cannot reproach him for having spent his rehearsal time on the Vaughan Williams symphony instead. That was worth pains taken.

January 28, 1949

A String Octet and a Temple Service

THE SAN FRANCISCO BAY REGION'S summer music season differs notably from that of most other urban centers in the high seriousness of the programs offered. Not led by climatic intensities to center itself about outdoor circumstances and the intellectually easy-to-take, its repertory regularly includes material that would do honor to any community at any time. Among the new works presented this year, two by Darius Milhaud have had a striking effect on listeners. Unusually impressive both by weight and by volume, their presentation, as well as their composition, represents musical achievement of a high order. It was your correspondent's privilege recently both to hear and to examine the French master's String Octet and his Sacred Service for the Jewish Liturgy.

Milhaud's String Octet is really two String Quartets, numbered in this composer's production Fourteenth and Fifteenth. Intended to be played both separately and together, they were recently so presented in first performance by the Budapest and Paganini Quartets at the University of California in Berkeley. Your correspondent was not present on that occasion; but he listened later, score in hand, to a tape recording of the execution. He also heard the two Quartets played, both separately and simultaneously, by students of Roman Totenberg at the Music Academy of the West in Carpinteria. Their sound, let it be said right off, is an uncommonly tonic musical experience.

Any composer's main problem in writing such a double-barreled work is to differentiate the musical expression of the separate units, to make of them two communications which, when combined, offer a third. The degree to which Milhaud has solved this problem your correspondent would not like to be hasty about estimating. The mere hearing of the double piece, the following of it in sound, is so complex an exercise that judgments of an æsthetic nature must wait upon really learning the piece. Nevertheless, it is clear already that the degree of successful meaning-projection is high.

Quartet No. 14 is a more straightforward lyrical expression than No. 15. The latter has, I think, poetry of a deeper meditation. Both are composed, as is Milhaud's custom, with the freest use of double harmonies. Even heard alone, they sound pretty dissonant. Heard together, they make a bumping and a jostling that is full of vigor but not at all easy to analyze with the ear. Double harmonies become triple and quadruple to produce a kind of sound that might easily, in the hands of a less skilled polytonalist, have turned into a colorless or muddy gray. It is unquestionably a technical achievement on Milhaud's part to have kept so complex a texture full of light and brightness to the ear.

The first movement of Quartet No. 14 is flowing in character, moderate in animation. That of No. 15, though the tempo of execution is necessarily the same as that of the other, is a light and lively scherzo. In simultaneous performance, the first of these movements tends, I think, to dominate the expression, the second to make commentary on it. The harmony of the two pieces is not always, measure by measure, the same harmony. Consequently, when played as an octet, their sound is fresh.

The two middle movements are even more different. That of No. 14 is a sort of lullaby, that of No. 15 a mystical landscape or pastoral that hardly progresses at all, so intense is its inner dream life. Technically, No. 15 is a four-part reversible canon that after completion turns round on itself and proceeds crab-wise back to its beginning. During this latter operation No. 14 performs a thoroughly developed fugue. The effect of the whole, surprisingly, is one of intense luminosity. I am inclined to consider this movement, in all of its forms, the most striking of the three.

The last movement is a jolly rondo in both Quartets; and though no thematic material is ever passed from one to the other, the expressive content in the two is roughly similar. Hearing them together offers a new experience chiefly from the huge fun involved in the way the eight parts elbow one another around. The whole Octet, indeed, is fun to listen to, fun to follow in score, fun to practice swimming around in. Its ultimate value to repertory I have no prescience about, but it seems clear even now that here is a unique composition by a master and that its gustation can offer to music lovers a kind of auditory delight not at all common these days.

Milhaud's Sacred Service, also a double-barreled work, though not one involving superposition, consists of settings for cantor, chorus, and orchestra of both the Friday Evening and the Sabbath Morning Services from the Jewish liturgy. About half the musical matter is common to the two, the rest separately composed. No melodies of traditional origin are employed (save for one briefly), and no evocation of Near East orientalism is allowed to sentimentalize or to localize a musical conception of universal applicability. The style, though personal to Milhaud, is easily comprehensible anywhere. The service is occasionally bitonal in harmony, often a flowing counterpoint of two or three parts freely juxtaposed, now and then noisily evocative of jostling crowds and alleluias. But for all its occasional brilliance, the service is marked throughout by a tone of intimacy wholly appropriate to the Jewish temple and deeply touching. Its grandeur and its plainness impressed this listener as being somehow related in spirit to those of Purcell and his Elizabethan forebears in their settings of Anglican worship forms.

As performed in Berkeley, the composer conducting, or in San Francisco's Temple Emanu-El to organ accompaniment, under the direction of Professor Edward Lawton, with members of the University Chorus, the service seemed to this listener a profoundly reverent offering both to music and to religion. Not in many a moon has he encountered liturgical music so convincing, so natural, so humane in its utterance. May New York not long delay knowing it!

September 18, 1949

The New Germany and the New Italy

LEAGUE OF COMPOSERS, concert of new European works, last night at Times Hall, New York, presenting Guido Turchi's Concerto Breve, performed by the La Salle String Quartet (*Walter Levin* and *Henry Meyer*, violins, *Max Felde*, viola, and *Jackson Wiley*, cello); Luigi Dallapiccola's *Sex Carmina Alcaei*, performed by an instrumental ensemble, *Reginald Stewart*, conductor, with *Patricia Neway*, soprano; and *Romeo und Juliet*, opera for radio in three acts, music by *Boris Blacher*, libretto adapted by *Mr. Blacher* from *August Wilhelm Schlegel's* German translation of Shakespeare's play, performed by an instrumental ensemble and chorus, *Mr. Stewart*, conductor, with *Robert Harmon* (Romeo), *Eileen Schauler* (Juliet), *Stanley Kines* (Capulet), and *Cleo Fry* (Lady Capulet).

NEW MUSICAL STYLES from Italy and Germany were the subject of last night's League of Composers concert in Times Hall. A string quartet by Guido Turchi, a set of six monodies with instrumental accompaniment by Luigi Dallapiccola, and a radio opera by Boris Blacher were the examples exposed. The La Salle String Quartet, divers excellent musicians and choral singers from the Juilliard School, and certain admirable vocalists listed above were the executant artists. Reginald Stewart conducted to perfection the works by Dallapiccola and Blacher. Real novelties handsomely performed had brought out a full house of musical personalities.

Blacher's *Romeo and Juliet*, the freshest among the novelties, the most different from standard modern models, is a radio opera based on a cutting of Shakespeare's tragedy in Schlegel's German translation. It was given last night in an adaptation, made partly by the composer, to the original English version. These fit their musical setting surprisingly well.

The choral and solo parts are everywhere in this opera the point of attention. These are musically most expressive and always rhythmically animated. The instrumental accompaniment is expressive, too, though sparse. With sagacity and skill, Mr. Blacher has reduced this to a skeleton that is functionally no less complete for its extreme thinness. Everything contributes toward throwing the text into high relief. The result is moving and genuinely distinguished.

Blacher represents the new Germany in music. He turns his back on harmonic and contrapuntal complexity and on the romantic afflatus in expression, on all heaviness, obscurity, and introversion of sentiment. He cultivates the elements that have long been absent from German composition, namely, rhythmic life, instrumental wit, harmonic and contrapuntal succinctness, naturalistic declamation. With the simplest of means, he makes a straightforward and meaningful communication.

His influences are chiefly Satie, Kurt Weill, and Stravinsky, though he has neither the commercial folksiness of Weill nor the intellectual ambitions of Stravinsky. The sophisticated plainness of his music is close to that of Satie, though his does not shine with the French master's pure white light. It is invigorating like milk and apples, clean, sensible, healthy, and just what German music needs after a century of overeating.

Whether the twelve-tone style is what Italy needs just now I am not so certain. Perhaps the truth is opposite. Possibly the twelve-tone style can profit from an Italian trip. Certainly Dallapiccola gives to its characteristic broken melodic line a grand lyric quality.

His *Sex Carmina Alcaei* are a group of poems from the Greek, set for soprano voice and about ten instruments. They are vocally ornate, instrumentally delicate, and warm of expression. They evoke antiquity much as Debussy and Ravel did, by the use of semistatic rhythms, bright instrumental colors, and an impersonal intensity of expression. They are lovely, elegant, sweet, and just the right amount recondite.

Turchi's String Quartet, written two years ago at the age of thirty-one, is the work of an unusually gifted and skillful young man. Dedicated to the memory of Béla Bartók, it imitates the Hungarian master chiefly in its use of spooky sonorities. These are applied with imagination and a light hand. The last movement has rhythmic life in it, too. The whole piece is graceful, sensitive, serious. It will be a pleasure to hear more from this composer.

April 11, 1949

Ragtime Revived

Bᴀᴄᴋ in the 1890's and around the turn of the century, ragtime was new, popular, sinful. By 1910 it had lost both its novelty and its sinful quality to jazz, but it was still popular. In 1920 it was out of style; jazz ruled the roost. In the 1930's swing came along and did to jazz what jazz had done two decades earlier to ragtime. Nowadays jazz, swing, and ragtime are all old-fashioned; bebop has the new and shocking quality. The earlier styles are just chamber music.

It is not the privilege of this observer to choose among them; but it has amused him to notice that the scholarly enthusiasts, the æsthetic polemicists, and the record collectors who admire American popular music intensely behave toward it very much as the longhairs do toward European classical music. Their respect is in proportion to its age in the modern world. Victorian popular music is obviously prehistoric, just as the music written before Bach is to the ear of an average classical music lover. In spite of research and revivals, Bach remains the beginning for us of everything that is really ours. And just so, ragtime is basic American to all who hold dear the national vernacular of our time. Out of that has come all the rest, even the bebop that is so despised, as swing was before it, by the defenders of tradition.

It was the pleasure of your reporter on Saturday a week ago to hear devoted to ragtime, at the Carl Fischer Auditorium on West Fifty-seventh Street, a whole concert, "the first ever given in New York history," according to Mr. Rudi Blesh, who introduced it. A trio known as The Ragpickers consisted on this occasion of Tony Parenti, clarinetist, Ralph Sutton, pianist, and Tony Spargo, drummer. (The latter, a veteran of the Original Dixieland Jazz Band, used to be known as Toni Sbarbaro.) All three are technical masters and musicians of refined style, as becomes the exponents of a classical repertory. If any of them seemed to this listener more remarkable than the others, it was the pianist. Perhaps we are more used to fine clarinet and drum playing than to pianism of Mr. Sutton's solid standards. In any case, I found the latter most satisfying. The program was as follows:

I

Maple Leaf Rag	SCOTT JOPLIN
That Eccentric Rag	J. RUSSEL ROBINSON
Clarinet Marmalade	SHIELDS-SBARBARO
Sensation	EDDIE EDWARDS

II

Hysterics	BRESE-KLICKMAN
Grace and Beauty	JAMES SCOTT
Praline	TONY PARENTI
Swipesy Cake Walk	JOPLIN-MARSHALL
Hiawatha	NEIL MORET
Sunflower Slow Drag	JOPLIN-HAYDEN

III

Whitewash Man	JEAN SCHWARTZ
Twelfth Street Rag	EUDAY L. BOWMAN
Dill Pickles	CHARLES L. JOHNSON
St. Louis Blues Fantasy	W. C. HANDY

IV

Cataract Rag	ROBERT HAMPTON
Crawfish Crawl	TONY PARENTI
Nonsense Rag	R. G. BRADY
Red Head Rag	IRENE FRANKLIN-GREEN
The Lily Rag	CHARLES THOMPSON
The Entertainers Rag	JAY ROBERTS

Group III consisted of piano solos. The rest was ensemble play-ing, enlivened by frequent solos. Historic pieces like *Hiawatha* and the *Maple Leaf Rag*, *Dill Pickles*, the *Twelfth Street Rag*, and many another ditty famed in story gave it a remembrance-of-things-past appeal. *The St. Louis Blues*, that Fifth Symphony of the jazz world, made it legal.

Your announcer has no intention of criticizing the concert in detail. He is not one of ragtime's detail men. He found the whole thing thoroughly distinguished and delightful. He also enjoyed the audience, which consisted largely of quiet, well-behaved young people. It was no house of transported "alliga-tors" or jittering "cats" from the swing days and still less of holy-rolling beboppers. It was like college boys and girls listen-ing to Mozart. They were wide awake, respectful, thoroughly interested but not taking part in the show. I wish you all could have shared, as I did, their lively attention. I wish, too, that a great many more concerts of this kind were given in New York. This one's excellence was comparable to that of the best offered here in "standard" music.

April 24, 1949

Hollywood's Best

Aaron Copland's musical accompaniments to a film called *The Red Pony* (by Milestone, out of Steinbeck) are the most elegant, in my opinion, yet composed and executed under "industry conditions," as Hollywood nowadays calls itself. Other films shown this winter have had ambitious scoring or talented sonorous detail, but those this writer has seen have not offered any consistently distinguished music. Mr. Copland himself, Hollywood's most accomplished composer, has not in his earlier films—*Of Mice and Men*, *The North Star*, and *Our Town*—produced for cinematic drama a musical background so neatly cut and fitted.

It is the perfection of the musical tailoring in this picture that has made clear to me in a way I had not understood before just where the artistic error lies in the industry's whole manner of treating musical backgrounds. Hollywood has often engaged high-class composers, but Hollywood has also been notoriously unable to use these in any high-class way. European films have made better use of the big musical talents than we have. Honegger, Auric, Milhaud, and Sauguet in France, William Walton in England, Kurt Weill in Germany, Prokofiev and Shostakovich in Soviet Russia have all made film music that was more than a worthy contribution to film drama. Here privately produced or government-produced documentaries have occasionally made film and music history, but our industry-produced fiction films have not included in their whole lifetime five musico-dramatic productions worthy to rank beside the fifty or more European films that as musico-dramatic compositions merit the name "work of art."

It is not talent or skill that is lacking here. It is not intelligence, either, or general enlightenment on the part of directors and producers. The trouble goes deep and has, I think, to do with our distribution rather than with our production system. But first let me talk a bit about *The Red Pony*.

The film itself, as a visual narrative, is far from perfect. It is diffuse; it tries to tell more stories than it can integrate with the main one or bring to a conclusion. Also, it has too many stars in it. It is about a boy and a pony, both admirably played. What the child star and the animal need is acting support, not glamour support. What they got, however, is not acting support at all but the glamour competition of Robert Mitchum and Myrna Loy. As a result, the composer has been obliged to hold the show together with music. There are some sixty minutes of this; and Mr. Copland has made it all interesting, various, expressive. If he has not made it all equally pointed, that is not his fault. He has met beautifully and effectively all the possible kinds of musical demand but one. That one is the weak spot in all American fiction films. It is a result of our particular treatment of the female star.

Wherever Copland has provided landscape music, action music, or a general atmosphere of drama he has worked impeccably. Here his music sets a scene, illustrates action, advances the story. Wherever he has essayed to interpret the personal and private feelings of Miss Loy, he has obscured the décor, stopped the action, killed the story, exactly as Miss Loy herself has done at those moments. His music at such times goes static and introspective, becomes, for dramatic purposes, futile. In a landscape picture, which this is, interpreting emotion directly in the music destroys the pastoral unity of tone. Miss Loy's sadness about her marital maladjustment might have been touching against a kind of music that suggested the soil, the land, the farm, the country life—all those attachments which, not shared by her husband, are the causes of her sadness. But the sadness itself, when blown up to concert size and deprived of specific musical allusion, loses point. The composer here may have helped to build up the glamour of the actress; but he has, by doing so, allowed the author's narrative to collapse.

American films have occasionally omitted all such fake *Tristan und Isolde* music, using simply dialogue or sound effects to support the stars' close-ups. It is much easier, moreover, to handle musically a male star in emotional crisis than a female one, since our mythology allows character and even picturesqueness to the hero. Our heroines, on the other hand, are supposed to be nymphs—all grooming, all loveliness, all abstract desirability, though capable of an intense despair when crossed in love. It is not easy to make a successful picture about one of these goddesses unless the contributing elements—music, costumes, furniture, housing, male adoration, effects of weather, and triumphs of technology—are made to contribute to the myth. Our industry, our whole design, manufacture, and distribution of fiction films, is the commerce of this goddess's image. She is what Hollywood makes and sells. It is easy for a classically trained composer, one for whom art means reality, to enhance the reality of scenic backgrounds, to animate passages of action, to emphasize dramatic values, to give shape and pacing to any narrative's progress. But it is quite impossible for him to be a salesman of soul states in which he does not believe.

No composer working in Hollywood, not even the great Copland himself, has ever made me believe that he believed in the reality of our female stars' emotions. That is the spot where American films go phony, where they fail of truth to life. In so far as this spot is a box-office necessity (and with million-dollar budgets it may well be a necessity), it is impossible for the film industry to make a musico-dramatic work of art. The film, as Europe has proved, is an art form capable of using to advantage the collaboration of the best composers. The film as produced by the American industry has never been able to show any composer at his best. *The Red Pony*, in spite of its mediocrity as a film drama, comes nearer to doing this than other American fiction films I have seen. It is the nearness of its miss, indeed, that has made me realize where the fault in our Hollywood musical credo lies. It lies in the simple truth that it is not possible to write real music about an unreal emotion. An actress can communicate an unreal emotion, because tears, any tears, are contagious. But no composer can transform a feeling into beauty unless he knows in his heart that that feeling is the inevitable response of a sane human being to unalterable events.

April 10, 1949

IN MEMORY OF . . .

Claude Debussy

THIRTY YEARS AGO last Friday, on March 26, 1918, Claude Debussy died in his fifty-sixth year. Though his three decades of artistic productivity lie on both sides of the century-mark, just as Beethoven's did a hundred years earlier, musically he is as clearly a founding father of the twentieth century as Beethoven was of the nineteenth. The history of music in our time, like any other history, is fully to be reviewed only in the light of all its origins and all its roots. Nevertheless, modern music, the full flower of it, the achievement rather than the hope, stems from Debussy. Everybody who wrote before him is just an ancestor and belongs to another time. Debussy belongs to ours.

It is doubtful, indeed, whether Western music has made any notable progress at all since his death. Neoclassicism, the evoking of ancient styles in general and of the early eighteenth-century styles in particular, he invented. Even atonality, the consistent employment of contradictory chromatics, is present in his later works, notably in the ballet *Jeux*. No succeeding composer has augmented his dissonant intensity, though some have made a louder noise. Stravinsky's early picturesque works and his later formalistic ones are no more radical in either sound or structure than Debussy's landscape pieces and his sonatas. Schönberg's twelve-tone row, though Debussy never knew it, is merely a systematization, a rule of thumb to make atonal writing easy. Expressively it has added nothing to the gamut of sensibility that Debussy created and Schönberg adopted. If, as Busoni believed, one could reconstruct the whole German classic and Romantic repertory out of Sebastian Bach alone, certainly modern music, all of it, could be rebuilt from the works of Debussy.

What music has lost since Debussy's death is sensitivity of expression and expressivity of instrumentation. Our feelings are more brutal and our statements about them less precise. Similarly, our language of chord dispositions and musical sounds is less competent, less richly evocative than his. We have all gone in for broader, cruder effects. We have had to, because his way of writing was at the end of his life almost unbearably delicate. Refinement could be pushed no further, though Anton Webern tried and succeeded at least in not falling far short of Debussy's mark. But the others could not face going on in that way. Sensibly they turned to easier paths. The fact remains, nevertheless, that Debussy's work is more radical than theirs and, in the ways both of expression and of the use of musical materials to this end, more powerful.

Curiously enough, Debussy's employment of orchestral sound, though commonly described as "colorful," was not so envisaged by him. Variety of coloration is certainly present, and knowingly, in his piano writing. Like that of Schumann and that of Mozart, it is full of the imitation of both orchestral and naturalistic sound-effects. But he avowed the aim of *Fêtes*, for instance, to be monochromatic, "a musical equivalent of the *grisaille*," which is a watercolor or ink brush-drawing done entirely in grays. The secret here is that Debussy did not, in this piece or in any other, ever, save for purposes of avoiding them, seriously respect the gamut of orchestral weights. He used the orchestral palette as the Impressionist painters used theirs, not for the accenting of particular passages but for the creation of a general luminosity. And the surface tension of his scores in performance is no less equalized than that of a Renoir, a Pissarro, a Monet canvas. Something like this must have been what he meant by comparing them to a *grisaille*.

Debussy's instrumentation, though it is an advance over Berlioz, is derived from the latter's practice, from the use of sound as a purely acoustical phenomenon. He depersonalizes all instruments. His piano writing, too, though an advance over Chopin's, is derived from that of the Great One. It is not designed, like that of Liszt, for ease of execution but all for delighting the ear and for making music mean things. His melody is Massenet purified, plainsong, and memories of popular song. His counterpoint, though rarefied almost to the point of nonexistence, is straight out of Mozart by way of the Paris Conservatory. Every line communicates. Even his harmony, for all its imaginative quality and its freedom, is made up out of Satie plus a taste for the archaic. Maybe there is just a touch of Mussorgsky, too. But his profound originality lies in his concept of formal structure. Where he got it I do not know. It may come out of Impressionist painting or Symbolist poetry. Certainly there is small precedent for it in music. It remains, nevertheless, his most radical gift to the art.

This formal pattern is a mosaic texture made up of tiny bits and pieces all fitted in together so tightly that they create a continuity. The structural lines of the composition are not harmonic, not in the bass, but rhythmic and melodic. Debussy freed harmony from its rhetorical function, released it wholly to expression. He gave everything to expression, even structure. He did not sculpt in music or build architectural monuments. He only painted. And no two canvases are alike. They are all different and all intensely communicative. The range of their effective expression is the largest our century has known, the largest that music has known since Mozart. Piano music, the song, the violin sonata, the cello, chamber music, the opera, the oratorio, the orchestral concert piece all receive from his hand a new liberty, say things and mean things they had never said or tried to mean before. His power over all the musical usages and occasions comes from his complete disrespect for the musical forms and from his ability to replace these by a genuinely satisfactory free continuity.

That France, classically the land of freedom, should have produced a model of musical freedom is only natural. All the same, Debussy, even for France, is something of a miracle. No composer ever wrote with such absence of cliché, detailed or formal. And few have achieved such precision, such intensity, such wide range of expression. His music is not only an ultimate, for our century, of sheer beauty. It is a lesson to us all in how to make use of our liberty.

Isidor Philipp, the great piano pedagogue, now in his middle eighties, tells of a visit received in Paris from Béla Bartók, then a young man. He offered to introduce the young Hungarian composer to Camille Saint-Saëns, at that time a terrific celebrity. Bartók declined. Philipp then offered him Charles-Marie Widor. Bartók again declined: "Well, if you won't meet Saint-Saëns and Widor, who is there that you would like to know?" "Debussy," said Bartók. "But he is a horrid man," said Philipp. "He hates everybody and will certainly be rude to you. Do you want to be insulted by Debussy?" "Yes," said Bartók.

March 28, 1948

Maurice Ravel

TEN YEARS AGO next month, December 28, 1937, Maurice Ravel died. He was not old, only sixty-two. Many people living knew him well. I knew him myself a little. He was cultivated, charming, companionable, neither timid nor bold, in no way difficult. That is why he is not today, nor was he during his lifetime, a misunderstood man or a misunderstood composer. For all its complexity of texture, wealth of invention, and profound technical originality, his work presents fewer difficulties of comprehension than that of any of the other great figures of the modern movement. Satie, Debussy, Schönberg, Webern, Stravinsky all remain, in many facets of their expression, hermetic. Ravel has never been obscure, even to the plain public. His early work produced a shock, but only the shock of complete clarity. Anybody could dislike it or turn his back, still can. Nobody could fail, nobody ever has failed to perceive at first sight what it is all about.

What it is all about is a nonromantic view of life. Not an antiromantic view, simply a nonromantic one, as if the nineteenth century had never, save for its technical discoveries, existed. All the other modernists were children of Romanticism—worshipful children, like Schönberg, or children in revolt, like Stravinsky, or children torn, like Debussy, between atavism and an imperious passion for independence. Even Satie felt obliged to poke fun at the Romantics from time to time. But for Ravel there was no such temptation, no Romantic problem. When twentieth-century models failed him he had recourse to eighteenth-century ones. And he used these not at all to prove any point against the nineteenth century, but simply because they were the most natural thing in the world for him to be using. Couperin, Rameau, and Haydn were as close to him as Chabrier and Fauré, his immediate masters.

Maurice Ravel was not interested in posing as a prophet, as a poet, or as a writer of editorials. He was no sybil, no saint, no oracle nor sacred pythoness. He was simply a skilled workman who enjoyed his work. In religion a skeptic, in love a bachelor, in social life a semirecluse, a suburbanite, he was not in any of these aspects a disappointed man. He was jolly, generous, a wit, a devoted friend, and as much of a *viveur* as his none too solid health and his temperate tastes permitted. His was an adult mind and a good mind, tender, ironic, cultivated, sharply observant. He was kind but not foolish, humane but not sentimental, easygoing but neither self-indulgent nor lazy. There was acid in him but no bile; and he used his acid as a workman does, for etching.

He considered art, and said so, to be, at its best, artifice, and the artist an artisan. For all the clarity that his music embodies, its crystalline lucidity in every phrase, it probably expresses less of personal sentiment than any of the other major music of our century. He worked in the free Impressionistic style, in the straight dance forms, in the classic molds of chamber music, and for the lyric stage. His masterpiece is a ballet. Always he worked objectively, with the modesty of an architect or a jeweler, but with the assurance of a good architect or a good jeweler. He was equally master of the miniature and of the grander lay-outs. At no necessary point does his expression lack either subtlety or magnitude. It lacks nothing, as a matter of fact, except those qualities that are equally lacking, for instance, in La Fontaine and in Montaigne, namely, animal warmth, mysticism, and the darker aspects of spirituality.

Ravel was a classical composer, because his music presents a straightforward view of life in clear and durable form. The straightforwardness and the clarity are, I think, obvious. The durability will be no less so if you consider the hard usage that *La Valse*, *Daphnis et Chloë* (at least the Second Suite from it), the Bolero, the *Pavane for a Dead Princess*, the Piano Sonatina, and *Scarbo*, a pianists' war horse, have been put through already. I call them durable because they stand up under usage. And they stand up under usage because they are well made. They are well made because they are clearly conceived and executed by an objective and responsible hand. The hand is objective and responsible in the way that it is because it is a French hand, one that inherits the oldest unbroken tradition in Europe of objective and responsible artisanry.

Ravel's music represents, even more than does that of Debussy, who was more deeply touched than he by both the Slavic and the Germanic impulses toward a spiritualization of the emotional life, the classic ideal that is every Frenchman's dream and every foreigner's dream of France. It is the dream of an equilibrium in which sentiment, sensuality, and the intelligence are united at their highest intensity through the operations of a moral quality. That moral quality, in Ravel's case, and indeed in the case of any first-class artist, is loyalty, a loyalty to classic standards of workmanship, though such loyalty obliges its holder to no observance whatsoever of classical methods. It is an assumption of the twin privileges, freedom and responsibility. The success that Ravel's music has known round the world is based, I am convinced, on its moral integrity. It has charm, wit, and no little malice. It also has a sweetness and a plain humanity about it that are deeply touching. Add to these qualities the honesty of precise workmanship; and you have a product, an artifact, as Bernard Berenson would call it, that is irresistible.

France has for centuries produced this kind of art work and, for all the trials of the flesh and of the spirit that she is suffering just now, is continuing to produce it. Rosenthal, Sauguet, Poulenc, Jolivet, Barraud, Rivier, and the dodecaphonic young, these and dozens more have vowed their lives to sincerity of expression and to high standards of workmanship. The music of Milhaud and Messiaen has even grander aspirations. But all French composers, whether they care to admit it or not, are in debt to Ravel. It was he, not Gounod nor Bizet nor Saint-Saëns nor Massenet, nor yet César Franck nor Debussy, who gave to France its contemporary model of the composer. That model is the man of simple life who is at once an intellectual by his tastes and an artisan by his training and by his practice. He is not a bourgeois nor a white-collar proletarian nor a columnist nor a priest nor a publicized celebrity nor a jobholder nor a political propagandist—but simply and plainly, proudly and responsibly, a skilled workman. Long may the model survive!

November 30, 1947

Kurt Weill

KURT WEILL, who died last Monday at the age of fifty, was a composer who will be missed. Nothing he touched came out banal. Everything he wrote became in one way or another historic. He was probably the most original single workman in the whole musical theater, internationally considered, during the last quarter century.

His originality consisted in an ability to handle all the forms of the musical theater with freedom, to make them expressive, to build structures with them that serve a story and sustain a play. He was not a natural melodist like Richard Rodgers or George Gershwin, though he turned out some memorable tunes. Nor was he a master of thematic development, though he could hold a long scene together impeccably. He was an architect, a master of musico-dramatic design, whose structures, built for function and solidity, constitute a repertory of models that have not only served well their original purpose but also had wide influence as examples of procedure.

Weill came to the light musical theater, for which most of his American works were conceived, from a classical training (he was the pupil of Humperdinck and of Busoni) and long experience of the artistic, the experimental theater. His literary collaborators were consistently writers of distinction. Georg Kaiser, Yvan Goll, Bertolt Brecht, Arnold Sundgaard, and Maxwell Anderson were among them. Brecht was the librettist of the epoch-marking works of his German period—*Der Jasager*, *Der Dreigroschenoper* and *Aufstieg und Fall der Stadt Mahagonny*. Also of a ballet with words, composed in Paris, *Les Sept Péchés Capitaux*, played in England as *Anna-Anna*.

These works have transformed the German opera. Their simplicity of style and flexibility of form have given, indeed, to present-day Germany its only progressive movement in music. Without them the work of Boris Blacher and Carl Orff would be inconceivable. Without their example also we would not have had in America Marc Blitzstein's powerful *The Cradle Will Rock* and *No for an Answer*. Whether Weill's American works will carry as far as his German ones I cannot say. They lack the mordant and touching humanity of Brecht's poetry. They also lack a certain acidity in the musical characterization that gave cutting edge to Weill's musical style when he worked in the German language.

Nevertheless, they are important to history. His last musical play, *Lost in the Stars*, for all that it lacks the melodic appeal of *Mahagonny* and even of *Lady in the Dark*, is a masterpiece of musical application to dramatic narrative; and its score, composed for twelve players, is Weill's finest work of orchestral craft. His so-called "folk-opera," *Down in the Valley*, is not without strength either. Easy to perform and dramatically perfect, it speaks an American musical dialect that Americans can accept. Its artfulness is so concealed that the whole comes off as naturally as a song by Stephen Foster, though it lasts a good half hour.

Weill was the last of our local light theater musicians to orchestrate his own scores and the last to have full mastery of composition. He could make music move in and out of a play with no effect of shock. He could write a ballet, a song, a complex finale with equal ease. (A successful Broadway composer once asked me, "What is a finale?") These skills may turn up again in our light theater, but for the present they are gone. Or they may be replaced by the ability of Menotti, Blitzstein, and other classically trained composers to hold public attention through constructed tragic music dramas. Just at present the American musical theater is rising in power. But its lighter wing has lost in Kurt Weill a workman who might have bridged for us the gap, as he did in Germany, between grand opera and the *singspiel*. The loss to music and to the theater is real. Both will go on, and so will Weill's influence. But his output of new models—and every new work was a new model, a new shape, a new solution of dramatic problems—will not continue. Music has lost a creative mind and a master's hand.

April 9, 1950

Béla Bartók

BÉLA BARTÓK's music, always respected by musicians, seems now, some three years after his death, to be coming into its reward of love. Not only is the number of musicians who are attached to it increasing; laymen are beginning to bear it affection. Every orchestra plays a Bartók piece now once a year, and his string quartets appear regularly on the chamber music programs. The Juilliard String Quartet played three of these last month, will complete the cycle of six at Times Hall on Monday evening, the 28th of this month.

This examiner has never been deeply impressed with the technical originality of Bartók. His major virtues, in my view, lie in the expressive domain. He was a master, of course. He had a good ear and abundant fancy. He knew the technical innovations of our century, used most of them, invented innumerable small adaptations of variants of them. But there is very little of textural ingenuity in his music that could have been derived by any active musical mind from the works of Debussy and Stravinsky. Exactly such a mind, that of Manuel de Falla, did derive a comparable rhetoric from these sources, employing Spanish local color as Bartók did Hungarian and achieving a musical result not essentially different, a nationalistically oriented Impressionism admirably suited to evoking the dance.

Bartók, however, though he began as a picturesque composer, had another string to his harp. He wrote chamber music of a reflective character. Impressionism was paralleled in his practice not by neoclassic constructions, as was the practice of Western composers (even de Falla, in his harpsichord concerto, essayed the formal), but by Expressionism, by an outpouring of private feelings that is related as an æsthetic method both to the loose formal observances of nineteenth-century Central European chamber music and to that extreme subjectivity of expression that is characteristic of Arnold Schönberg's early works.

The formal preoccupations of Western neoclassicism do not lend themselves easily to emotional effusion, and neither do the techniques of picturesque sound. Emotional outpourings work best with loose structures and a gray palette. So Bartók kept his continuity loose, abbreviating it more and more into a semblance of tight form, and neutralized his color. At heart, however, he loved bright colors; and in his concertos he continued to employ them. In his later quartets he replaced surface color with emotional vividness. And if this last is less lurid and private than it is in Schönberg's chamber works, it is no less tonic.

Hans Heinsheimer, visiting a Boston performance of Bartók's Concerto for Orchestra, has recounted how at the end of the piece a neighbor turned to her husband and said, "Conditions must be terrible in Europe." She was right, of course. They were, especially in Central Europe, where Bartók lived. And she was right in sensing their relation to the expressive content of Bartók's music. It is here, I think, that his nobility of soul is most impressive. The despair in his quartets is no personal maladjustment. It is a realistic facing, through the medium of pure feeling, of the human condition, the state of man as a moral animal, as this was perceptible to a musician of high moral sensibilities living in Hungary.

No other musician of our century has faced its horrors quite so frankly. The quartets of Bartók have a sincerity, indeed, and a natural elevation that are well-nigh unique in the history of music. I think it is this lofty quality, their intense purity of feeling that gives them warmth and that makes their often rude and certainly deliberate discordance of sound acceptable to so many music lovers of otherwise conservative tastes. Nobody, as we know, ever minds expressive discord. The "modern music" war was a contest over the right to enjoy discord for its own sake, for its spicy tang and for the joy it used to give by upsetting applecarts. Bartók himself, as a young man, was a spice lover but not at all an upsetter. He was a consolidator of advance rather than a pioneer. As a mature composer he came to lose his taste for paprika but not for humanity. His music approached more and more a state of systematic discord, rendered more and more truly and convincingly the state of European man in his time. His six string quartets are the cream of Bartók's repertory, the essence of his deepest thought and feeling, his most powerful and humane communication. They are also, in a century that has produced richly in that medium, a handful of chamber music nuggets that are pure gold by any standards.

March 20, 1949

FROM OUT OF TOWN

The Berkshire Music Center

THE FESTIVAL CONCERTS of the Berkshire Music Center at Tanglewood, near Lenox, Massachusetts, long nationally famous, are attended by a large and demonstrative audience. The scholastic activities of the center, though they serve a much smaller number of persons, are internationally held in high repute; and entry either to the faculty or to the student body of these is considered an honor among musicians of Europe and South America, as well as among those of this continent. Indeed, the school shows its director, Serge Koussevitzky, in a most becoming new role, that of pedagogue. As interpreter, publisher, and patron of living composers, he has a half-century of loyal service behind him. Last Tuesday his seventy-fifth birthday found him in a fourth position, that of educator, and with nearly a decade of achievement to his credit in that capacity.

The Berkshire Music Center is not, as many of its good neighbors imagine, mainly a concert-giving organization. As such it would be of only local interest. Its international prestige comes from the fact that it is a top-standard professional music school. The Festival concerts, in this conception of Tanglewood, are a peripheral activity, an icing on the cake. Artistically, of course, they need no apology. But economically, too, they are of value, since their profits (and they do make profits) go toward the upkeep of the school. Also, the personnel of the orchestra provides a faculty for professional instruction that would be hard to match anywhere in the world. The school is built about the orchestra and depends on the orchestra. It offers to the orchestra, in return, an outlet for the orchestra's individual and collective abilities that tends in this particular time to outrank as a cultural influence even the orchestra's known value as a concert instrument.

The school has five departments—conducting, orchestral playing, musical composition, operatic performance, and choral singing. All lie under the general direction of Dr. Koussevitzky and of his assistant, Aaron Copland, both of whom direct departments and teach classes as well, the former assuming responsibility for the students of conducting and the latter for those of composition. In the conducting department Dr. Koussevitzky is assisted orchestrally by Richard Burgin, Leonard Bernstein, and Eleazar de Carvalho, chorally by Hugh Ross and Christopher Honaas. Every Friday there is an orchestral concert of which the conducting is shared between one of these professionals and one of the more advanced conducting students.

The orchestra at these concerts is a group of 110 players, all students in the department of orchestral performance. The faculty of the latter is made up of first-desk players from the Boston Symphony Orchestra and known chamber music specialists. These last, this year, are Gregor Piatigorsky, William Kroll, and the members of the Juilliard Quartet. Students in this department play both in orchestral and in chamber-music groups.

The composition students are shared between Aaron Copland and a distinguished foreign composer. This year Olivier Messiaen is the guest, succeeding Darius Milhaud, Arthur Honegger, and comparable masters. There is both class and private instruction. Every Sunday night there is a concert at which works by the young composers are performed by singers and instrumentalists from the other departments.

Opera is the province of Boris Goldowsky. His students consist of thirty singers (chosen by audition), of forty auditors, and of divers technical aspirants. These learn not only the art of singing in opera but also conducting, stage direction, scenery and costume design, lighting, and all such contributory techniques. There are four students vowed to the rare, special, and deplorably misunderstood art of libretto writing. The opera department has its own theater and its own student orchestra, produces every year whole acts or scenes from standard operas and two rare lyric stage works entire, an old and a new one. This year the complete productions will be Gluck's *Iphigenia in Tauris*, in English, and Benjamin Britten's *Albert Herring*. The former is a classic work seldom heard in the United States. The latter, a comic piece based on de Maupassant's *Le Rosier de Madame Husson*, has never been heard here at all, though it has had considerable success in England.

The fifth department, that of choral singing, formerly the charge of Robert Shaw, is at present in the equally capable hands of Hugh Ross and Christopher Honaas. The students sing in three groupings, the largest being that of the Festival

Chorus, employed for choral works in the Festival concerts. The others are a Madrigal Chorus, which sings historic works from medieval, Renaissance, and modern times, and a Bach Choir, which gives cantatas and like masterpieces from the period of the Lutheran Baroque. This department has also its own student orchestra.

What with the big Festival concerts, the smaller Bach-Mozart series, the opera productions, the weekly concerts of the No. 1 student orchestra, the chamber-music concerts, choral concerts, composers' concerts, and I don't know what all else, there is constantly available to the students music old and new in executions of the highest quality and in a repertory remarkable for its breadth. Selected students (465 of them at present) from all over the world, a faculty of first-class practicing artists, and a wide-range cultural program of the best music impeccably performed all go to make a pedagogic institution of great value. Though this chiefly serves professional aspirants, the layman also has a place in the scheme through the classes in choral singing, which, by offering real musical exercise, are of value toward raising cultural standards in general.

The weakness in so nearly ideal an institution is the fact that it is merely a summer school. Limited to six weeks' time, any course tends to become just a glimpse. Mr. Copland told your reporter during a recent visit to Tanglewood that he considered the major value of the school to be the stimulation it offers to students and instructors from their brief but intense encounters. Many young professional musicians do, in fact, go back year after year for just that stimulation. It is to be wished that eventually musical schools of comparable standards, working on a full-time schedule, can be formed around other great symphonic foundations. Serge Koussevitzky and the Berkshire Music Center have given us a model of procedure. Tanglewood is what all our musical pedagogy *must* look toward for professional standards and what our symphony orchestras *should* look toward for the fulfilling of their cultural possibilities. Also, I suspect, for solving their budget problems in the second part of this century. Because education is always clearly worth its price, whereas mere concerts, however cultural, may not always be found so.

July 31, 1949

The Delights of Denver

DENVER in the summer offers to the visitor more of music and theatrical entertainment than most cities can provide at any time of year. Not to speak of a hospitality that is unique for abundance and charm. There are two stock companies, an excellent symphony orchestra, student plays and operatic productions at the university, and, at nearby Central City, opera of the first class in a setting that is both stylish and of historical interest. The symphony orchestra itself plays both popular-type and intellectual programs. The former are given once a week at Elitch's Gardens, a large amusement park which incloses also a theater, the seat of one of the oldest summer stock companies in America, founded in 1890, at present directed by Norris Houghton. The intellectual programs are presented at Red Rocks Theater, an outdoor auditorium in the mountains, some seventeen miles from the city, a site of the highest natural beauty and architectural distinction.

Saul Caston, formerly first trumpet of the Philadelphia Orchestra and assistant to both Leopold Stokowski and Eugene Ormandy, is musical director of the Denver Symphony Orchestra. In three years, under his leadership, the group has become one of the major orchestras of America, estimated by either artistic or budgetary standards. Your correspondent heard a "pop" concert at Elitch's and a Red Rocks program. Both were marked by a fine solo in the wind sections, by delicacy and precision of string playing and by impeccable musicianship in conducting. The first was led by Mr. Caston himself. The second, largely prepared by Mr. Caston in preliminary rehearsals, was conducted by Igor Stravinsky. No other summer orchestra enjoys, to my knowledge, quite the rehearsal luxury of this one. Mr. Caston has a full rehearsal (three times the preparation of the Boston Pops) for each popular concert and five for each concert at Red Rocks (ten times that of our Lewisohn Stadium programs), a figure approached, though still not equaled, only by the Boston Symphony Orchestra playing in Tanglewood. All this care shows up, of course, in the quality of the execution.

The Red Rocks concert that your correspondent heard was marked by the American debut of the pianist Soulima Stravinsky and by a work unfamiliar, in its present form, to New Yorkers, a Divertimento, or Suite, from Igor Stravinsky's ballet *Le Baiser de la Fée*. The latter was preceded by Igor's Capriccio for Piano and Orchestra, Soulima playing the solo part, by Tchaikovsky's Second Symphony, and by Glinka's *Russlan and Ludmilla* overture. The Divertimento, melodious music no less charming in concert than in theatrical presentation, will probably achieve a merited currency. Its performance at Red Rocks was gravely marred by the presence on the stage throughout its duration of three photographers, employees of a nationally circulated magazine, who walked around and rattled flash bulbs in seeming unawareness that the occasion had any other purpose than providing them with a subject. That the piece could be attended to at all against such visual and even auditory distraction is evidence of its solid qualities and also of Igor Stravinsky's iron-willed power as a conductor. The audience, in gratitude, gave him a long ovation with cries of "More, Igor!" and "Encore, Igor!"

Soulima Stravinsky had previously been acclaimed at length and had played, after the Capriccio, three encores. The demonstration had seemed, to this listener, fully merited, though he would not like to pronounce, from one performance in a concerted work and three short pieces, all heard outdoors, on the full quality of Soulima Stravinsky as a piano virtuoso. That he is a musician of refinement and sound taste was clear from his renderings of a Stravinsky Etude and two works by Scarlatti. That he has a better than average technical equipment was also clear, though transcendent virtuosity was nowhere in evidence. His work throughout was clean and musicianly, his tone and passage work dry, in the best contemporary taste. The most impressive element of the performance was the authoritative, the definitive character of the Capriccio's interpretation. Igor and Soulima Stravinsky understand the piece in the same way, play it as a real duet, with the greatest freedom and firmness. There should be no questioning henceforth of the work's essential character. The way the Stravinskys play it is the way it goes and the way it should, within any artist's temperamental limitations, be made to go.

The performances of my own opera *The Mother of Us All* at Denver University, being student work, are not properly a subject for public criticism, though I should like to commend the ingeniousness and imagination of their staging, which was the work of Roi White. Neither shall I go farther in reporting performances of the summer theater troupes than to attest that I enjoyed the one I saw. Let me give what space I have to the big-time theatrical executions, those given at the Central City Opera House. I shall also skip briefly over the architectural and other delights of that locale, a gold mining town of the 1870's with a theater and hotel of noble design and two of the best bars in America. Of the physical advantages let me only remark, because of its determining influence on the brilliance of the opera performances, that the Central City Opera House, seating some 700, has an acoustical liveness, a fullness of resonance without any echo, that is not equaled by more than a half dozen houses of its kind in the world. It is completely advantageous to music, makes everything sound bright and warm.

That the performances were worthy of their enhancement is due to the producer, Frank St. Leger, and to the chief conductor, Emil Cooper. These musicians assembled this year two casts of first-line singers and an excellent orchestra and with the aid of Herbert Graf, stage director, and of Donald Oenslager, designer, produced two operas, which were given on alternate nights for twenty-five performances in July. The season's works were Mozart's *Così fan tutte* and Offenbach's *Contes d'Hoffmann*, both sung in English. For general musical excellence the performances were the equal of any opera performances available anywhere today and far, far better than many produced in more pretentious circumstances. For specific excellence, vocal and histrionic, I should like to mention the work of Jerome Hines as both Coppelius and Miracle in *Hoffmann* and of Graciela Silvain, who sang Olympia in the same opera. This admirable singer, an Argentinian, not yet heard in New York, may well be our first coloratura for the next decade or two. Her voice has brightness and body, and she is obviously both a musician and an artist. Surrounding these exceptional performances were the handsome vocalism of Igor Gorin, who sang Lindorff and Dappertutto, of Philip Kinsman as Schlemil, and of a fine dramatic soprano hitherto unknown to this reviewer, Mariquita Moll, who sang Giulietta. The rest of the cast, which was good, if vocally less striking, contained many famous and about-to-be-famous names. Mario Berini, who sang Hoffmann the night I was there, bawled a bit. His alternate, Thomas Hayward, I did not hear.

The cast of *Così fan tutte*, as is proper for this work, was equilibrated for volume, beauty of sound, and musicianship, Anne Bollinger, Jane Hobson, and Marilyn Cotlow were the ladies. Joseph Laderoute, Clifford Harvuot, and Lorenzo Alvary were the men. All sang with grace and style, and their concerted numbers were perfection save for being maybe a little louder than that house requires. There were some loud moments in *Hoffmann*, too, but this opera can support an occasional knock-'em-out-of-their-seats effect. Hearing *Così* in English, a not at all bad translation by Phyllis and George Mead, gave your prognosticator the idea that a modern-dress production of this lovely and touching work might, if directed with taste, add a certain poignancy to it without the loss of any sparkle. Inconstancy among soldiers' fiancées, after all, is not wholly funny; nor is it, historically speaking, any monopoly of the eighteenth century.

August 1, 1948

Convention in Cleveland

THE MUSIC TEACHERS NATIONAL ASSOCIATION, meeting in Cleveland during the week of February 24, was the center around which had gathered no less than fifteen other musical organizations. These included the National Association of Schools of Music, the teachers of singing, the choir directors, the string associations, the piano teachers, the Matthay Association, the College Music Association, the Accordion Teachers Guild, the Hymn Society of America, the Ohio music teachers, and five musical sororities and fraternities.

The corridors of the Statler Hotel were full of brilliant figures from professional music life—scholars, composers, professors, administrators, executant artists. The publishers were there, too, since these meetings are always accompanied by an exhibit of stocks. No direct sales are made; but musicians constantly pore over the printed music, inspecting, taking notes, listening to everything they would like to use later. There is lots of fraternizing all round; teaching jobs change hands; performances are arranged; contacts, finagling, and a real exchange of ideas are all part of the intense activity.

Lecture and panel-discussion subjects at these meetings ran from the recondite and technical to such broad but also worrisome matters as how to teach music appreciation in the high schools. All day long in general and in special sessions, theories and experiences were exposed regarding college opera production, ensembles of archaic instruments, the music of ancient Mexico, the psychology of the bow-arm, the performance of Baroque church music, and how many languages should be required of debutant vocalists. A great deal of attention was paid to American composition, to examining the American orchestral, vocal, and pianistic repertory. And numerous short recitals by top American pianists and singers gave evidence of its variety and distinction.

Among the artists performing were Beryl Rubinstein, John Kirkpatrick, Eunice Podis, Denoe Leedy, and the excellent Stanley Quartet. Among the composers played were practically everybody. Particularly impressive to this reporter was a piano recital in which John Kirkpatrick played with love, with poetry, and with a musicianship both impeccable and penetrating American piano works from MacDowell's time to ours. Both pleasing and a shade disappointing was a suave performance of John Verrall's Fourth String Quartet. This work was disappointing for lack of salient profile in the melodic development but infinitely delightful for delicacy of harmonic texture and general workmanship.

Outside the hotel, Cleveland musical establishments offered to the visitors special programs of unusual quality. The Cleveland Orchestra played them a private concert in Severance Hall, including the thirty-year-old *Overture to a Drama* by Arthur Shepherd, still a vigorous and buoyant piece. Edwin Arthur Kraft played them an organ recital at Trinity Episcopal Church, where the Kent State University A Cappella Choir also sang contrapuntals from the sixteenth century and modern Russian motets. The music and drama departments of Western Reserve University presented two operas, *Il Maestro di Musica* by Pergolesi and Ralph Vaughan Williams's *Riders to the Sea*. A concert by the visiting St. Louis Symphony Orchestra added to the general brilliance.

Extra special and quite unique were the performances of Cleveland's Negro opera company at the Karamu Theater. Established by a settlement house thirty-five years ago, this oldest among America's Negro theaters has recently turned musical. Its director is Benno D. Frank. The repertory, so far, is completely contemporary. Its present program consists of Menotti's *The Medium* and a brand-new German work. The latter is *The Wise Maiden*, a translation of *Die Kluge* by Carl Orff. This work, commented on by your reporter in 1946 from a German radio performance, is one of the most striking examples of the new German declamatory style and of a form which Orff and Boris Blacher have been bringing to perfection in recent years, the radio opera that also makes a theater-piece. The Karamu Theater's performance is the first in this country of any work by Orff.

Hearing everything and seeing everybody at such a gathering of gatherings was not possible to your reviewer. He did not even hear all the music mentioned in this report. But the whole convention, with its fine offerings of music and talk, its assemblage of bright minds, of intellectual, artistic, and administrative personalities, was so rich an experience that he thought it only fair to readers that he should report to them, however summarily, on the high standards of the American musical profession, creative, executant, and pedagogical, as viewed through a cross-section of its leadership.

March 12, 1950

Pittsburgh Week End

FINDING himself in the city of Pittsburgh, Pennsylvania, last Sunday on other business, your correspondent took a busman's holiday by attending two concerts. He heard the Pittsburgh Symphony Orchestra, conducted by Paul Paray, in the afternoon. And in the evening he went to a concert of the International Society for Contemporary Music, Pittsburgh chapter, at the Carnegie Institute of Technology. The first, a program without any soloist's interference, gave opportunity to hear the distinguished French conductor work in varied styles with an excellent orchestra. The second presented four modern works for violin and piano through the powerful and impeccable hands of Joseph Fuchs and Leo Smit.

The Pittsburgh orchestra has been without a permanent conductor ever since Fritz Reiner left two years ago, but it has not lacked a caretaker. Vladimir Bakaleinikoff, formerly assistant to Mr. Reiner and now listed as Musical Adviser to the orchestra, has gone right on conducting a great many of the concerts. He it is also who makes the necessary replacements every season in personnel, and he it is who keeps the group in training. Guest conductors move in and out, but Mr. Bakaleinikoff goes on. The effectiveness of his regular ministrations is proved but the fact that in spite of having been put through many different kinds of paces for two years by many different star interpreters, the orchestra still plays like an orchestra. It has not fallen, at least not yet, into the splintery string sonorities and faulty general balances that mark the work of habitually guest-conducted groups.

Actually the string body is highly unified in sound and disciplined in technique, the cello and bass sections being particularly notable for power and suavity and the first violins being unusually unanimous of articulation. The woodwinds are excellent, too, and the horns. Trombones and trumpets are a little coarse; the percussion lacks refinement; and I think the brilliant acoustics of the Syria Mosque are not entirely responsible for the stridency of these groups. But otherwise the orchestra impressed your reviewer as being in good shape, surprisingly good shape.

Paul Paray's program contained, as novelty, Two Dances by Maurice Duruflé, a Parisian organist whose orchestral works, few in number, have not, to my knowledge, been previously played in America. These dances are skillful in harmony, if a shade conservative for France, and ever so charmingly orchestrated. If their expressive content is not strikingly original and their melodic line a bit overthematic in structure, they are nevertheless Kapellmeistermusik of a delicacy and sophistication that compel the ear.

In Beethoven's *Fidelio* overture Mr. Paray proved once again that the French can play Beethoven without bombast and yet nobly. Similar treatment applied to Brahms has occasionally, as in the readings of this composer by Pierre Monteux, seemed to this reviewer highly valuable as a detergent, or grease remover. Mr. Paray, interpreting Brahms's Third Symphony, gave to its rhythm a lilt and steadiness most advantageous to the architectural line. The expressive line would have been equally enhanced (and was, for the most part) if the conductor had allowed a little more time for those cadences and phrase-endings in which rapidity of harmonic change, or chord-incidence, requires for clarity of hearing a stretching out of the melodic line. Overstretching in such passages has produced the rubbery rhythm and sticky pathos that mar so many contemporary readings of the Brahms symphonies. Mr. Paray's steady progress restores to them serenity and a classic poise; but I do think, now he has got them to moving along again, that a bit more flexibility would give added grace to their lyrical passages. Finesse and delicacy marked his reading of Chabrier's *España*, a work that has regrettably tended to disappear from our programs after long war-horse treatment.

Joseph Fuchs and Leo Smit played that same evening Duos for Violin and Piano by Arthur Berger and Igor Stravinsky and Sonatas for the same combination by Nikolai Lopatnikoff and your reporter. All four works were performed with a technical mastery and a musical authority incomparable. Three of them are relatively familiar and need no comment at this time. The fourth, Lopatnikoff's Sonata No. 2, was new to your reporter and merits, in his judgment, proclamation. A dissonant neoclassic composition of extended format and high eloquence, it is difficult to play, brilliant, original of sonority, and in every way powerful. What effect it would make when played by artists of lesser skill and understanding I do not know. As played by Mr. Fuchs and Mr. Smit it provoked a favorable audience demonstration rarely accorded to contemporary works. Both the piece and its reception impressed your reviewer as promising a future of some brilliance for this sonata in the repertory of our more courageous recitalists.

It is not hard to understand, mind you. I do not think it would provoke listener resistance unless poorly performed. But virtuosity is of its essence, and any reading of it that was less than perfect technically might fail to communicate its especial delights. On the other hand, a really handsome performance of it gives the double delights of skillful writing and skillful execution. Last Sunday its effect on your reporter was that of a heady mixture. Since the morrow brought no disillusion or bad aftertaste, he would like, if only out of curiosity, to enjoy the experience again, and soon.

April 2, 1950

Modernism in Los Angeles

THE LOS ANGELES REGION, visited last week end by your correspondent, is an outpost of musical advance on several fronts. Its Philharmonic Orchestra, of which Alfred Wallenstein is conductor, ranked first last season among all the American orchestras in performance of contemporary music. The radio station KFWB has for over a year now offered the local public one of the very few distinguished modern music programs available on the American air. And both the local universities have first-class opera workshops.

Hearing the Los Angeles Philharmonic Orchestra in rehearsal only, since a public concert was not available during his brief stay, your correspondent was particularly impressed by the work of the string section. Woodwinds and brasses, which are likely to be good in all American orchestras, are no less excellent here than elsewhere; but a string section at once so live in sound and so homogeneous in color, so sensitive, so silken, so handsomely drilled and blended for beauty is not to be encountered in more than five or six of our cities. Such a string section, I hardly need add, is where really first-class orchestral work begins.

The radio program mentioned above is called "Music of Today." Its director is Julius Toldi. Its coverage is advanced contemporary composition. It lasts a half hour, beginning at 3 o'clock, Western time, on Sunday afternoons. Its programs consist of all the rarest modern chamber music, and its executions are tops. An interview with the composer of the afternoon is usually offered along with his music, even when this had to be recorded in some other part of the world and shipped to Los Angeles. I do not know so consistently high-class a program of modern music elsewhere on the American air. "Music of Today" is in the class with the Flemish broadcasts of the Belgian National Radio, directed by Paul Collaer, with the B.B.C. Third

Program, with the best sent out over the French and Italian national systems.

My attendance at the rehearsal and broadcast of some extremely difficult works of my own, including the ultra-dissonant Sonata da Chiesa, for five disparate instruments, left me gasping with admiration for the executant musicians, for Ingolf Dahl, who conducted, and for, of all people, the Warner Brothers, who own KFWB and who tolerate as a station activity a program of that modernity in presentations of that elegance.

A series of chamber music programs called "Evenings on the Roof," not broadcast, offers at the Wilshire-Ebell Theater conservative modernism and rarish classics in performances of a standard only a shade less high than those of Mr. Toldi's radio program. I heard on one of these one of Reger's sonatas for cello alone and some works of mine, all adequately performed.

Both opera workshops were showing that week end. That of U.C.L.A. (the University of California in Los Angeles) had run up as the main number in a concert devoted to my works a scene of some length from *The Mother of Us All*. Presented with piano accompaniment and with only the sketchiest attempt at costuming, it was nevertheless admirably sung and proved again that Jan Popper, the workshop's director, formerly of Stanford University, can make the musical theater communicate under any circumstances.

The University of Southern California happened to be giving a full-dress production of Benjamin Britten's *Albert Herring*. This was professionally led, staged, and framed and would have been acceptable in any professional theater, save for the singing; and even that was merely a little green. The conductor was Wolfgang Martin, formerly of the Metropolitan. The producer and stage director was Carl Ebert, formerly of the Städtische Oper in Berlin and of Glyndebourne. The sets were by Benjamin Grosche. The orchestra was composed of top students and faculty members.

The singers, though not quite ready yet for professional work, were with one exception good singers. Their diction, moreover, their projection of words, a matter of special coaching by William Vennard, was genuinely professional. No Broadway theater offers better; the Metropolitan does not invariably offer as good. If Mr. Martin has not, as a conductor, the infallible dramatic animation of his U.C.L.A. colleague Mr. Popper, he is a thoroughly competent and experienced musical man of the theater. And Carl Ebert is one of the great opera directors of all time. With men like this available and with students of good voice as well as good will, both opera workshops in Los Angeles are capable of offering work that is limited in its carrying power only by the essential weaknesses of student singers. A certain rivalry between the two establishments, moreover, seems to help along both. Certainly both are doing distinguished work right now in a field where surely an important part of America's musical future lies. The whole Los Angeles musical scene, I repeat, is full of an awareness of present trends and future opportunities.

Only the film industry lives in and on its own inglorious musical past. That industry, which never has taken a part, any part at all, save perhaps on the trade union front, in either California's or America's intellectual life, has no place in a picture of California's musical life. It has brought musicians to the southern counties, true; but so has the climate. It has given them little work to do worthy of their abilities.

December 18, 1949

Texas's Major Orchestras

THE STATE OF TEXAS, long a center of intercity rivalries, has in recent years added symphonic execution to the fields in which civic emulation is played out before the public. Southern Methodist University, in Dallas, has just staged a music festival, the first in an annual series, between March 15 and 22, in which the Big Three among the Texas symphony orchestras all played for the Dallas public. San Antonio, Houston, and Dallas itself showed off their wares and prowess in Dallas's best auditorium; and critical discussion has been statewide.

There was no jury, no award, no settling of anything. Final opinion seems to have left the orchestras, like the cities themselves, as each unique, each vigorous and full of its own character. It was lately the pleasure of your correspondent to hear all three groups, and not under Dallas conditions but playing in their own ball parks.

The term is not reproachful but almost literally true, since all three orchestras play regularly in convention halls, two of which are commonly used also for sports events. They fill these, too, more often than not. Even without a name soloist for drawing power, any of them is likely to play to an audience of 5,000 or more. Such support is particularly striking in San Antonio, a city of barely 450,000 people, many of whom are Spanish-speaking poor and virtually excluded by this fact from the city's intellectual life. For symphonic attendance, under these conditions, to exceed one per cent of the population is impressive indeed. I do not know the city that can match this devotion to musical art.

To take them in alphabetical order, the Dallas Symphony Orchestra, conducted by Walter Hendl, appeared to this listener as less firmly characterized in its work than the others of the Texas Big Three. This is Mr. Hendl's first year in command of it, and his personnel is not yet firmly set. The group is predominantly first-class; but there are a few spots where changes are indicated and, I believe, planned. The conductor, still in his early thirties, is a musician of unusual preparation, technically and intellectually speaking. He plays the most difficult scores, classic and modern, with clarity and accuracy. He is still learning the repertory, however; and his interpretative powers in the region of the Romantic symphony, which is the center of orchestral repertory, remain a little immature. Also, his ability as a trainer of orchestral musicians has yet to be proved, and probably to be developed, by experience. He makes enlightened programs and plays them cleanly. In modern works he has brilliance and fire. His youth and Americanism endear him to the community. His orchestra, just now, is not quite a homogeneous instrument.

The Houston Symphony Orchestra, conducted by Efrem Kurtz, is a virtuoso group comparable to the northern orchestras. A powerful and solidly blended string body, completed by excellent woodwinds and brasses and topped off by impeccable soloists in all the sections, gives the color range completeness and flexibility. Mr. Kurtz himself, a musician of temperament and culture, is an interpreter, too. His work is brilliant and bright, refined, elegant, and nowhere lacking, either, in that warmth of feeling that gives inner life to classical and Romantic symphonies. His repertory is broad, his style that of a master workman of long experience just now approaching the height of his powers. Having conducted two of his orchestras, in

Houston and in Kansas City, this writer can attest to the solidity of their musical training, their discipline, their ability to play anything at any time in any way the conductor sees fit to ask. Houston today is a major orchestra and among the better ones.

The San Antonio Symphony Orchestra is a maverick; there is nothing else quite like it. Founded only ten years ago by Max Reiter, a German-Italian from Trieste, the group has frequently come to national notice through the freshness and distinction of its program policy. What your reporter had not been prepared for is the liveness and loveliness of its playing. The group is young, on the average, and animated by an esprit de corps that reminds one of a football team or a college glee club. It is not a virtuoso orchestra like Houston or Dallas; but it is good throughout, homogeneous, live, lovely and shining. The percussion section is the finest this observer has encountered in any American orchestra. The sound of the whole is silken, suave, translucent. Its recent visit to Dallas produced not only press criticisms and public demonstrations of the highest praise but the honor of an editorial in the Dallas *Morning News.*

All the Texas orchestras play a good deal of American music and encourage Texas composers. San Antonio has also introduced to America a series of postwar works by Richard Strauss, including the *Rosenkavalier* Waltzes and the concert version of *The Legend of Josef,* not yet heard in New York. Next season this composer's last composition, Four Songs for Soprano and Orchestra, will have its American première in San Antonio with Kirsten Flagstad as soloist.

Mr. Reiter and San Antonio have also shown American cities the way to solve their opera problem. An experienced opera conductor both in Germany and in Italy, this director has simply used his own orchestra and an excellent local chorus as the basis of his opera troupe and engaged first-class soloists to complete the cast. He has given operas of Wagner and Strauss not usually possible to regional forces, and he has filled his vast hall at every performance. Two week ends in February constitute at present the season. Four operas, different each year, make up the season's repertory. Air-conditioning of the auditorium will eventually make possible a summer opera season, as well as summer concerts. Skillful financing and the goodwill co-operation of trade unions keep deficits down. A similar operation, I am sure, would provide to many another city opera performances of an artistic quality comparable to that now the standard in orchestral concerts. Everybody interested in giving opera to America should take a look at what San Antonio, a Southwestern city not among our largest or richest, has done.

March 26, 1950

FROM THE U.S.S.R.

Composers in Trouble

THE RUSSIANS are at it again. First there appears in the left-hand column of *Pravda*'s front page a criticism of the nation's leading composers. They are charged with "formalistic" tendencies, with being influenced by the "decadent" West, with neglect of Russia's "classical" tradition, with failure to maintain the ideals of "socialist realism" and to ennoble as they ought the Russian people. Next the Central Committee of the Communist Party issues a formal denunciation by name and in detail. Next the offending works are removed from the theaters, the symphony concerts, and the radio. Then the composers under attack write open letters to *Pravda* and to the Central Committee thanking them for the spanking, confessing all, and expressing full intention, with the kind advice of the Committee, to reform. After that there is nothing for them to do but "purify" their music, to write new works that will hopefully be in accord with that "new look" that has been the stated ideal of Soviet musicians (and their political leaders) for the last twenty years. Then in a reasonable time they will mostly be back in favor.

For a Soviet composer there is no other solution. Publication and performance being a monopoly of the state, he cannot, nor can any group of composers, operate as a minority appealing to public opinion for justification. Never forget that in Soviet art there is no underground, no unofficial movement, nor, for the present, any possibility of one. This being so, and all observers agree that it is, let us examine, from previous occasions, what is likely to happen to Prokofiev, Shostakovich, Khachaturian, and company while they remain out of favor.

While Shostakovich was being disciplined in 1936 and 1937 for the "bourgeois" tendencies that Stalin himself had noticed in *Lady Macbeth of Mzensk*, his works intended for wide consumption were not performed or sold. His chamber music, however, continued to be played and printed; he continued to write it with no alteration of style; and he went on receiving a salary from the Composers' Union. He lived in Moscow, as

before, got married, went on working. He was poor and unhappy, drank heavily, we are told by people who visited him; but
he was not destitute. He also wrote during this time two symphonies, both of which were rehearsed and performed privately,
the last of them only, however, his Fifth, being accepted for
public audition. That he had lost no popularity in the meantime
was proved by the enormous lines that for three weeks before it
was given stood to get seats for the new symphony.

In the case of the literary purge that has been going on since
1936, the majority of those being disciplined have lived in about
the same circumstances as Shostakovich had ten years earlier.
Graver cases, however, especially those involving political disaf-
fection or extreme and recalcitrant individualism, have received
graver sanctions. Zoschenko, Pasternak, and Akhmatova, for
example, were expelled from the Writers' Union. This meant a
cutting off of their income and the loss of priority on a Moscow
apartment. Until ration cards were abolished it meant also
the loss of access to a reasonably nourishing diet. I have not
heard of a verified case of a mere writer being sent recently to
the Siberian salt mines, as was done with political offenders
in the mid-1930's. Expulsion from the Writers' Union (or the
Composers' Union) remains, however, a grave form of excom-
munication, not only for its moral stigma and for the virtual
exile from intellectual company but also for the great physical
dangers entailed. It has not yet been employed against any of
the composers recently denounced.

Whether Shostakovich and Shebalin, professors at the Moscow Conservatory, will be temporarily retired from their posts I
cannot say, though it is rumored that they have already left. Certainly Kharapchenko, the director, has lately been discharged.
And it seems likely that Khachaturian, president of the Composers' Union, may find it difficult to remain at that post while
under a disciplinary cloud.

What have they done, these composers, to provoke denunciation and disciplinary action? And what moral right has the Central Committee to order their even temporary disgrace? Well,
what they have done is to fail, in the judgment of the Party leaders, to conform to the æsthetic of Soviet music in its relation to
the whole public, as this was laid down by the musicians themselves back in 1929. That conception is, in our terms, certainly a

false one; but it is already an old one, and it is certainly nothing imposed from above. The Russian Association of Proletarian Musicians worked on it for five years before they got it stated the way they wanted it. And though the Association itself was dissolved in 1932, the declaration of 1929 remains to this day the basic æsthetic of Soviet music, of the proper relation of any Soviet composer to decadent "bourgeois" Western culture and to the rising masses of Russia.

In this conception, a composer is an editorial writer. He is supposed to elevate, edify, explain, and instruct. He is to speak a language both comprehensible to all and worthy by its dignity of a nation-wide public. He is to avoid in technique the over-contrapuntal and the overharmonic, in expression the abstract, the tricky, the mystical, the mechanical, the erotic. He is to turn his back on the West and make Russian music for Russia, for all of Russia, and for nothing beyond. His consecration to this aim is to be aided and reinforced by public criticism, as well as by the private counsels of his colleagues. Judgment as to the ac-complishment of the aim is not, however, his privilege nor that of his critics. That belongs to the Communist Party, which has the responsibility for leadership and guidance in artistic as in all other matters. The composers, in other words, have determined their own ideal and accepted, along with the ideals and forms of the society in which they live and work and which they have helped toward the achievement of its present internal solidity, the principle that the professional body alone, and still less the listening public, is not the final judge of music's right to survive.

This idea is not in accord with our Western concept of the integrity of the professions. Nevertheless, it is that of the Soviet government and of all, so far as we know, Soviet musicians. The hasty *mea culpa* of the Soviet artist in trouble with the Central Committee shocks the Western mind, but I see no reason to doubt its sincerity. Seven of the boys are in a jam right now, and I suspect most of them will get out of it. I sincerely hope they will, because they are good composers and because I like to see good composers writing and getting played and published. Myself I have never taken much stock in Soviet music. I am too individualistic to like the idea of an artist's being always a ser-vant of the same set-up, even of so grand a one as a great people organized into a monolithic state. I don't like monolithic states anyway; they remind me of the great slave-owning empires of antiquity.

But my tastes are not involved in the matter. Soviet music is the kind of music that it is because the Soviet composers have formally and long ago decided to write it that way, because the Communist Party accepts it that way, and because the people apparently take it. When the Party clamps down on it for "deviation," who am I to complain if the composers of it themselves don't? Whether they could do so with any hope of success, of course, is doubtful. All we know from previous occasions is that he who confesses and reforms quickest gets off the lightest. I do not find, given the whole of Russian political and æsthetic theory, that the procedure is undignified; and apparently the composers do not find it so, however much they may regret having to submit to the sanctions. It seems likely that they would feel far worse, even if they could survive, excommunicated from the intellectual life and deprived of their forum.

Russians mostly, I imagine, believe in their government and country. Certainly these great, official public figures do. They could not, in so severe and censored a period, have become national composers by mere chicanery. That is not what bothers me about them. Nor yet that they are always getting into trouble from excess of musical fancy. What worries me, and has for twenty years, is that, for all their devotion, noble precepts, faith in their fatherland, and extraordinary privileges, their music, judged by any standard, is no better than it is. I only hope, against all reason and probability, that a similar preoccupation on the part of the Central Committee is at least a little bit responsible for the present disciplinary action. Russian music may or may not need ideological "purification." But it certainly needs improvement.

February 22, 1948

Soviet Aesthetics

THE FORMAL CENSURING of Russia's eight top composers by the Central Committee of the Communist Party, an action that seems to have caused no less excitement in the Soviet Union than in the West, continues to be explained, defended, and insisted upon by dignitaries of Soviet musical life. At the recently held Congress of Soviet Composers there were innumerable speeches of apology and exhortation, confessions of backsliding, further denunciations, preachments, protests, and ukases from on high. The whole effect, to an outsider at some distance, is reminiscent at once of those interminable conversations about the state of somebody's soul that abound in Dostoevsky and of a revivalist camp meeting. Certainly the boys are worried about themselves and about one another.

The present outsider is under no illusion that æsthetic matters would be handled any more convincingly in his own country by a committee made up of either Democratic or Republican party chiefs or by a consortium of concert managers and publicity agents or by any other group among us that might be animated by an itch to use music and the public's enjoyment of it for its own purposes. It is probable, even, that a congress of American composers, held under a similar emergency, would show a not inconsiderable amount of conformist sentiment and also that some of the resistant spirits would remain shamefully (if sagaciously) silent. All the same, the Russian spectacle is entertaining, more so, indeed, to this observer than a great deal of the music that it is all about. And little by little one gets an inkling of what it is the Party in Russia has on its mind, musically speaking.

The magazine *Sovietskoye Iskusstvo* (*Soviet Art*) published on February 28 of this year articles by Tikhon Khrennikov and Marion Koval that, for all the carefully routined phrasing of their indignation, here and there let the cat out of the bag. The former, moderately well known here as a symphonist, has lately replaced Aram Khachaturian as president of the Society of Soviet Composers. The latter is music editor of *Soviet Art* and president of the State Music Publishing Committee for the selection of works to be printed. Both use the word *formalist* (or, rather, its Russian equivalent) as a term of intense reproach and join it regularly for emphasis with the adjectives *Western* and *decadent*. Both have some difficulty defining formalist tendencies, but both insist that when a work's subject matter is not clear to all formalism is present. Wherever the subject matter is frivolous, pessimistic, or "unhealthy" it is also assumed to exist, though its running mate, the word *decadence*, is more easily comprehensible to us in that connection.*

In Soviet æsthetics, however, undesirable subjects and sentiments are assumed to be inseparable from "formalistic" expression. And "formalistic" expression (also equiatable with "individualistic") is recognizable in music by excessive dissonance, harsh instrumentation, unusual instrumentations (of a kind not available in provincial orchestras), percussive instrumentation, too much counterpoint, "linearity" in general, slow tempos, failure to employ folklore themes, the distortion of folklore themes, failure to follow "classic" models, distortion of classic models, and the use of any device or texture for its intrinsic interest rather than for directly expressive purposes. For critics unskilled in musical analysis, subject matter, where clear, is apparently sufficient basis for judgment, since sound subjects are assumed to make for sound musical expression, just as "decadent" subjects make for "decadent-formalistic" (add "Western" and "bourgeois") expression. The work which set off the recent troubles, however—Muradeli's opera *The Great Friendship*—is one in which the subject, Stalin's years with Lenin, is obviously both a noble one, in Russia, and one extremely touchy to handle. Composing it, or even reviewing it, is a major hazard.

Miss Koval attacks the music critics for not having, since 1936, kept Shostakovich in line and utters a clarion call for the reorganization of musical science, musicology, and music criticism, that these may all be turned "without losing a single day" "to the fulfillment of tasks laid down by the historical decision of the Party." All this is plain enough as an order, though the constant testing of music for "formalist-decadent" tendencies seems a delicate operation and one for which the intellectual instruments available are far from exact. Perhaps musical science, musicology, and criticism are supposed to set about perfecting these. In any case, Miss Koval warns the critics who used to admire Shostakovich, but recently haven't dared, that they have done a U-turn once too often. They should have anticipated the

---

*The Russian word translated as "formalism" seems to mean something like "form*u*lism," that is to say, composition by means of stock formulas, technical or expressive.

Party's decision instead of being caught by it riding on a wrong bandwagon. The critic is thus conceived not as a reporter but as a mentor "expressing the opinion of the Soviet public," an instrument of the Party actually, a beacon light and a fog horn, warning everybody constantly against writing for the intellectual group. Beauty without distinction, a nonsensical concept to the Western mind, is apparently the present ideal in Russia.

Mr. Khrennikov purports to give, in his article on *Formalism and Its Roots*, the story of how modern music went wrong. This he traces, in Russia, back to the period of political reaction that followed the unsuccessful revolutionary uprisings of 1905. Serge de Diaghilev is an agent of evil in this picture, Stravinsky and Prokofiev being his tools. But perhaps I had better quote the composer's own words (in a translation which I owe to the courtesy of our State Department).

"Diaghilev openly called on Russian artists to serve an apprenticeship with the modern West. The modernist movement in Russian music is thus closely linked with frank servility before the Western musical market."

"The basic aim pursued by authors of these works [Stravinsky's *Petrouchka*, *Rite of Spring*, and *Les Noces*, Prokofiev's *Scythian Suite* and *Chout*] is to withdraw from the contemporary human world into the world of abstraction."

"In *Petrouchka* and *Les Noces* Stravinsky, with Diaghilev's blessing, uses Russian folk customs in order to mock at them in the interest of European audiences, which he does by emphasizing Asiatic primitivism, coarseness, and animal instincts and by deliberately introducing sexual motives."

"In Hindemith's *Saint Susan* religious eroticism is shown in revoltingly naturalistic detail. Similarly pathological are the neuropathic operas of Alban Berg and, in recent times, especially *The Medium* by Gian-Carlo Menotti, which has scored a great success with the bourgeois public of America. The central character of this opera is a woman who is a professional spiritist and faker, a dipsomaniac, and a murderer to boot."

"The operas of . . . Hindemith, Krenek, Alban Berg . . . Britten . . . and Menotti are mere concatenations of hideous sounds marked by complete disregard of natural human singing. This music openly harks back to the primitive barbaric cultures of prehistoric society and extols the eroticism, psychopathic mentality, sexual perversion, amorality, and shamelessness of the twentieth-century bourgeois hero."

"Olivier Messiaen, according to his own statement, draws his creative inspiration from ecclesiastical books and from the works of medieval Catholic scholastics such as Thomas Aquinas."

"Igor Stravinsky, apostle of the reactionary forces in bourgeois music, creates a Catholic Mass in conventional-decadent style [a work Mr. Khrennikov cannot have heard, since it is still unpublished and unperformed] or circus jazz pieces, with equal indifference."

"Among the works of Soviet composers of the twenties and thirties that offer numerous instances of formalistic tendencies are: Shostakovich's opera *The Nose*, his 2d and 3d Symphonies; Prokofiev's ballets *The Prodigal Son*, *On the Dnieper*, *Steel Leap*, his opera *Fiery Angel*, 3d and 4th Symphonies, 5th Piano Concerto, and 5th Sonata for Piano; Mossolov's *Iron Foundry* and *Newspaper Advertisements*; Knipper's operas *North Wind* and *Tales of a Plaster Buddha*; Deshevov's opera *Ice and Steel*; Miaskovsky's 10th and 13th Symphonies, 3d and 4th Piano Sonatas; S. Feinberg's piano sonatas and 1st Piano Concerto; Shebalin's *Lenin* Symphony and 2d Symphony; G. Popov's 1st Symphony; B. Lyatoshinsky's 2d Symphony and songs; I. Belza's 1st and 2d Symphonies, also his songs; L. Polovinkin's *Telescope* for orchestra and *Incidents* for piano; G. Litinsky's quartets and sonatas; V. Shcherbachov's 3d Symphony; and so forth."

"Formalist tendencies received their most striking expression in the opera *Lady Macbeth of Mzensk*, by Shostakovich, and in his ballet *The Luminous Brook*, both of which were flatly condemned in the articles of *Pravda*, published in 1936, when *Pravda* acting on instructions of the Central Committee of the Communist Party, exposed the harm and danger of the formalist school for the future of Soviet music."

As I said before, the maneuvers are not wholly clear, but it would seem that the Russians are trying to do two things. One is to limit music to its possible uses as an arm of the state's social policy. Many governments have tried this at one time or another. The idea is not a new one, but the history of its success is meager. The other effort is to create a nonexplosive, a foolproof kind of art, a beauty with no "strangeness in the proportion."

This is not a new idea either, although precedent for its success is, to my knowledge, nonexistent. On both counts the talented boys have reason to be worried.

May 2, 1948

Russians Recover

DMITRI SHOSTAKOVICH, the most popular of living Russian composers, inside the Soviet Union or out, has apparently been reinstated in the favor of the Politburo. A year ago he had been removed from that favor, along with five other well known composers—Prokofiev, Khachaturian, Miaskovsky, Shebalin, and Popov. He had also been removed, along with some of these others, from public office. Shostakovich and Miaskovsky ceased to teach composition at the Moscow Conservatory. Shebalin was replaced as head of that institution by A. Sveshnikov, a choral conductor. Khachaturian lost to Tikhon Khrennikov the position of Secretary General of the Union of Soviet Composers. He also ceased to be head of its Orgkomitet, or organizing committee. This group, working in close collaboration with the Committee on Arts of the Ministry of Education, has huge power, since it decides what works will be printed and recommends works for performance to opera houses, symphony orchestras, and touring virtuosos.

Prokofiev, who did not teach or hold any official post, was ostracized by the simple means of removing nearly all his works from the opera and concert repertories. The same measure was applied, of course, to the other purged composers, but less drastically. Shostakovich's First and Fifth symphonies, Miaskovsky's Symphony on White-Russian Themes, Khachaturian's Cello Concerto, and divers other pieces by the denounced "formalists" have gone right on being played, at least occasionally, since the purge.

Last year's offense, let us recall, was not the first for Shostakovich. Back in 1936 he had been subjected to disciplinary measures of a similar nature lasting a year and a half. His chief offense had been the opera *Lady Macbeth of Mzensk* and his work of restitution the Fifth Symphony. This time the troublesome piece was his Ninth Symphony; and his comeback has been accomplished through two film scores, *The Young Guard* and *Michurin*. The first of these is a heroic and optimistic melodrama about the exploits of the Komsomol during the defense of the Don Basin. The other is a biography in color of a Soviet hero, I. V. Michurin, founder of Soviet anti-Mendelian biology. Though neither film has yet reached the Stanky Theater, they have passed the musical judges; and two musical excerpts from *The Young Guard* have been printed in *Sovietskaya Muzyka* of October, 1948.

The cases of Khachaturian and Shostakovich are simpler than that of Prokofiev. The former's "illness," as the Russians like to refer to any artistic deviation, is only recently contracted and is 50 per cent non-musical, anyway. This half is a result of his political position. As a Party member, president of the Orgkomitet, and Secretary General of the Composers' Union, he was naturally held responsible for whatever protection the "formalists" had enjoyed prior to their denunciation. A first offender, a man of charming personality, and a convinced Bolshevik from the periphery of the Union (Armenia), he represents to the Politburo the achievements of a national-culture policy dear to its initiator Stalin. Of all the purged six, he has been the most played since his purge. As a Party member, he has continued, moreover, to serve on Union subcommittees. Professor T. Livanova (sole woman member of the Presidium of the Composers' Union) dealt with him indulgently in the July, 1948, number of *Sovietskaya Muzyka*. His successor as Secretary General of the Composers' Union, T. Khrennikov, also patted him on the back (for effort) in his "state of the Union" message of January 1, 1949.

If Khachaturian appears now as on his way out of trouble, Prokofiev seems to be in no such position. Not a product of Soviet culture but of the pre-revolutionary Czarist regime, a traveled man long resident in such centers of "bourgeois corruption" as Paris and the U.S.A., an associate of the Russian émigré enterprise, Serge de Diaghilev's Ballet Russe, and a resident of the Soviet Union only since 1933, this composer is being referred to more and more in the Soviet press as an incorrigible case. The recently deceased Boris Asafiev, Acting President of the Composers' Union (Stalin being Honorary President), also

Khrennikov and Marion Koval, editor of *Sovietskaya Muzyka* and a party-line whip, have all denounced him. Consistently and, one surmises, deliberately nowadays, his name is linked with such "servile and corrupt musical businessmen" as Stravinsky, such "degenerate, blackguard, anti-Russian lackeys of the Western bourgeoisie" as Diaghilev. His latest opera, moreover, composed under the purge, has been found unacceptable.

The latter, based on a story by Boris Polyevoi and entitled *The Life of a Real Person* (libretto by the composer's second wife, Mira Mendelssohn), deals with a Soviet flier and hero who lost both legs in the war. In December of last year the conductor Khaikin, who seems to admire Prokofiev deeply, organized in Leningrad a public reading of the opera. He apparently overstepped in this case his prerogatives, for the Leningrad papers scolded him severely; and Khrennikov called the incident "a fatal one for Prokofiev." Khrennikov specified further that "this opera shows that the traditions of Western modernism have captivated his consciousness." Moreover, "To him an acute dramatic situation is an end in itself; and the overplay of naturalistic details seems more important than the creation of musically truthful and convincing images of a Soviet hero with his life-asserting, ebullient will and his bold outlook into the future." Khrennikov also regrets that Prokofiev did not submit the work to his comrade-composers for criticism before its unfortunate concert hearing. The critic of *Izvestya*, Mr. Kukharski, dismisses the piece as "impractical, ivory-tower workmanship" and the composer as "an artist who has severed all connections with real Soviet life." *Pravda* thinks it "doubtful" whether one "can expect anything to satisfy the needs of the great Soviet people" from a "composer whose work is penetrated to the core" by "Western formalist decay."

In contrast to the apparently incurable maladjustments of Prokofiev (who is physically ill, as well, for he seems to have had last spring another stroke like the one he suffered in 1946), Shostakovich is clearly on the road to recovery. Not only is he being sent to us on a mission; he has also been praised by the head of his union for his " successful" film music. His position last year was grave. As a second offender he might easily have lost his apartment. Koval actually suggested at a Composers' Union meeting as late as last October that those afflicted with "decadent, bourgeois tendencies . . . could very profitably move out of Moscow to the periphery of the vast Soviet land and get their inspiration from a close contact with the life of the people in the provinces, in collective farms and factories." Happily, however, Mr. Shostakovich encountered nothing so drastic as forced residence on the "periphery" of the Soviet Union.* His case was argued in the magazines; his confession was accepted at face value; his penitential work has been judged good. And so (the United States willing) he is going to be sent to visit us.

Koval has analyzed his chronic "illness" as follows. Shostakovich's great natural gift has been perverted by:

1. Discordant German counterpoint (presumably the Hindemith style).

2. Introducing into the "sacred soil of the pure classic Russian tradition jazz neurosis and Stravinskyan rhythmical paroxysms."

3. Inability to write "singable" melodic lines.

4. Naturalistic approach to subject matter. (The love scene in *Lady Macbeth* shocked some here, too.)

5. "Limitless adulation of a chorus of sycophants" (in other words, success).

He can, however, be cured by the following regimen:

1. Avoiding "dissonance."

2. Avoiding any harmonic syntax more advanced than that of the late Sergei Rachmaninov.

3. Learning to write "easy" tunes.

4. Avoiding dependence on "abstract" instrumental and symphonic forms.

5. Writing more songs.

6. Strictly abstaining from jazz rhythms, paroxystic syncopation, "fake" (meaning dissonant) polyphony, and atonality.

7. Writing operas about Soviet life.

8. Turning his attention in general to the song of the great Soviet people and forgetting about the West.

Whether sending him to visit the West is the best way to make him forget about it is not for a mere Westerner to judge. Certainly his Western admirers will give him an unforgettable welcome. But before we submit him to the temptations of a bourgeois publicity-apotheosis, let us remember him as last

---

*By "periphery of the Soviet Union" many Russians understand Siberia.

described from home sources, piously glorifying Soviet science. In *Pravda*'s art magazine of January 1, 1949, he is mentioned as having written successful music for a charming episode in the film *Michurin*. The biologist is therein described as "standing high above a blooming apple tree and in total self-oblivion conducting a rapturous, wordless chorus of the Voices of Nature." "These Voices," it is added, "have been clearly heard and well expressed by the composer." Hollywood itself could not, I am sure, provide a musician with a more glorious opportunity than the scene here described; nor could any composer wish for a more auspicious way to salute the U.S., hereditary home of "formalistic decadence," than by indulgence in such unashamed hamming.

The above, or, rather, the information contained in it, is derived from a report of some length on the Russian musical press, furnished me, with translations, by the composer Nicolas Nabokov. I regret that space restrictions forbid more extensive quotations from this entertaining material, but I think I have incorporated faithfully the gist of it.

February 27, 1949

REFLECTIONS

The Intellectual Audience (I)

ANYONE who attends musical and other artistic events eclectically must notice that certain of these bring out an audience thickly sprinkled with what are called "intellectuals" and that others do not. It is managements and box offices that call these people intellectuals; persons belonging to that group rarely use the term. They are a numerous body in New York, however, and can be counted on to patronize certain entertainments. Their word-of-mouth communication has an influence, moreover, on public opinion. Their favor does not necessarily provoke mass patronage, but it does bring to the box office a considerable number of their own kind, and it does give to any show or artist receiving it some free advertising. The intellectual audience in any large city is fairly numerous, well organized, and vocal.

This group, that grants or withholds its favor without respect to paid advertising and that launches its ukases with no apparent motivation, consists of people from many social conditions. Its binding force is the book. It is a reading audience. Its members may have a musical ear or an eye for visual art, and they may have neither. What they all have is some acquaintance with ideas. The intellectual world does not judge a work of art from the talent and skill embodied in it; only professionals judge that way. It seeks in art a clear connection with contemporary æsthetic and philosophic trends, as these are known through books and magazines. The intellectual audience is not a professional body; it is not a professors' conspiracy, either, nor a publishers' conspiracy. Neither is it quite a readers' anarchy. Though it has no visible organization, it forms its own opinions and awards its own prizes in the form of free advertising. It is a very difficult group to maneuver or to push around.

In New York it is a white-collar audience containing stenographers, saleswomen, union employees of all kinds, many persons from the comfortable city middle-aged middle class, and others from the suburban young parents. There are snappy dressers, too, men and women of thirty who follow the mode, and artists' wives from downtown who wear peasant blouses and do their own hair. Some are lawyers, doctors, novelists, painters, musicians, professors. Even the carriage trade is represented, and all the age levels above twenty-five. A great variety of costume is always present, of faces and figures with character in them. Many persons of known professional distinction give it seasoning and tone.

The presence of such an audience at a musical event is no result of paid advertising or of standard publicity. Its representation is small at the Metropolitan Opera, the Philharmonic, and the concerts of the N.B.C. Symphony Orchestra, though it will go to all these places for special works. Dimitri Mitropoulos, for example, drew a brilliant audience for his recent performance at the Philharmonic of Strauss's *Elektra*. The smaller symphonic ensembles, the City Center opera, the New Friends of Music, and the League of Composers bring out lots of intellectuals. So do certain ballet performances and the spectacles of Martha Graham, though not, on the whole, for musical reasons. The International Society for Contemporary Music, the Composers' Forum, concerts and opera productions at the Juilliard School and at Columbia University, and certain recitalists are definitely favored. Wanda Landowska, harpsichord players in general, Jennie Tourel, Maggie Teyte, Martial Singher, Gold and Fizdale, sometimes Joseph Szigeti are all notable for the interest they offer to persons of high mental attainments.

The conductors chiefly favored by this group are Reiner, Monteux, and Ansermet. The intellectuals often come in a body to hear them. They come individually from time to time to hear Toscanini, Koussevitzky, Bernstein. They have shown no consistent interest in Rodzinski, Mitropoulos, Munch, Ormandy, or in recent years Stokowski. Beecham's audience appeal, for all his high cultural equipment, remains strictly musical, though his recordings are collected by many persons from other professions.

Flagstad, too, is a purely musical phenomenon; and so is Horowitz. The latter, indeed, no longer pleases wholly even the musical world, if I read his public right. One sees fewer and fewer known musicians at his recitals, more and more a public clearly not familiar with standard piano repertory. The music world attends en masse Landowska, Schnabel, and Curzon. The last two, however, have never made full contact with the world called intellectual, the world of verbalized ideas and general æsthetic awareness.

Management's aim is to mobilize the ticket-buying and propaganda power of this world without alienating the mass public. The latter is respectful of intellectual opinion, which it learns about through the magazines of women's wear, but resistant to the physical presence of the intellectual audience. The varieties of fancy dress and interesting faces, the pride of opinion expressed in overheard conversations, the clannish behavior of these strange and often monstrous personalities are profoundly shocking to simpler people. Their behavior expresses both a freedom of thought and a degree of ostentation that are not available to the standardized consumer. Much as he would like to enjoy everything that is of good report, he is really most comfortable among his own kind listening to Marian Anderson. This is why the Philharmonic and the Metropolitan managements make little or no play for the intellectual trade and discourage efforts in that direction from the musical wing. They have a mass public of sorts already, do not need intellectual promotion. They seem to fear, moreover, that intellectual influence, bearing always toward the left in program-making, may keep away more paying customers than it brings in.

Beneath all of management's dealings with the intellectual group lie two assumptions. One is that intellectuals like novelty and modernity. The other is that the mass public dislikes both. I think the first is true. I doubt the second. I am more inclined to believe, from long acquaintance with all sorts of musical publics, that it is management which dislikes the novelty and everything else that interferes with standardization. I suspect that management's design is toward conditioning the mass public to believe that it dislikes novelty. Some success has already been achieved in this direction. If intellectual opinion has any carrying power beyond the centers of its origin, there is a job to be done, a war to be fought across the nation. The intellectuals' own survival, even, may depend on winning it. For unless these bright ones carry some weight in the forming of everybody's opinions and tastes, they are a useless body and can be by-passed by any power-group that wants to use art for its own ends.

January 15, 1950

The Intellectual Audience (II)

MUSICAL PROGRAMS of a standard character, no matter how polished their execution, appeal chiefly to an audience of musicians and music lovers, in other words, of persons capable of emotional satisfaction through the ear. Musical programs of an unusual character often bring into the concert hall another public. This public, liberally salted, as I mentioned last Sunday, with persons distinguished in other arts and professions, is commonly referred to as the intellectual audience. The term is accurate, because intellectual curiosity rather than an appetite for auditory experience is the reason for its being there. This audience is the element that gives to New York, Paris, Vienna, and London their power as centers of musical influence. There is nothing provincial, musically speaking, about any city where the intellectual audience is large.

Many artists and most managements, certainly those whose aim is the standardization of repertory and execution, would like to dispense with this audience, to trade entirely in musical skill and prestige. It is not possible to do so, because the musical press, which no artist or institution can do without, speaks at least half the time from an intellectual, an æsthetic, a trends-and-general-ideas point of view. Individuals can avoid contact with this kind of criticism, or at least minimize the injurious effects of it on their careers, only by keeping away from the musical centers. Nelson Eddy, Jeanette MacDonald, and formerly Oscar Levant have long followed a provincial career. Others have risked occasional criticism from the New York press for the sake of acquiring institutional prestige, since for radio appearances and some of the touring trade, singing occasionally at the Metropolitan Opera in leading roles provides a substitute for intellectual prestige. Risë Stevens, Gladys Swarthout, Lily Pons, Robert Merrill, and James Melton have followed this line, appearing occasionally in opera here but avoiding as frequently as possible the risks of the midtown solo recital.

Institutions cannot so easily by-pass the press and its power of dispensing intellectual prestige. The nonprofit-making ones need such prestige to raise money. The others—the radio, television, and gramophone companies—need it for public good will, for silencing criticism of their business operations. They all need it for advertising, because the musical press of New York is one of the chief channels of communication between the intellectual world of music, which forms opinion, and the mass public, which buys tickets. This does not mean that all the New York critics are spokesmen for the intellectual world. Some are and some are not. Only that part of the press which defends intellectual opinion against management's conservatism and the inertia of mass receptivity is an intellectual press. The rest is either a low-brow press or an agent of the music business. There is no such thing as a purely musical press, one which reviews only from an auditory point of view, because it is not possible to write about music without thinking about it, or to think about it without taking some position with regard to contemporary æsthetics.

The professional music world itself has little interest in intellectual criticism. It makes up its mind on technical grounds, is suspicious of æsthetics, of all talk about trends and general ideas. Political and religious agencies that patronize music are interested only in trends and general ideas. That is why patronage from these sources always involves either institutional propaganda or something clearly denominable as education. All criticism in such cases, unless favorable, is definitely unwelcome. The intellectual world, on the other hand, the free association of all those who read books, loves to read criticism. It finds the critical columns a battle ground of ideas, a track meet of polemical skills, a festival of intellectual exercise in every way stimulating. Indeed, it follows music far more consistently through reading music reviews than through attendance at musical events.

The intellectual audience wants culture with its music, wants information, historical perspectives, enlarged horizons. It demands of program makers constant experiment and a huge variety. It is far more interested in repertory, as a matter of fact, than in execution. It tends to envisage the whole of music as a vast library in which everything is available, or should be. The strictly musical audience and the mass public are more easily satisfied. They think of the concert life as a sort of boarding house where you take what is offered and don't reach. Their good nature is easily abused by managements and other organizing agencies. The intellectuals are more demanding and refuse to be spoon fed. That is why, as a musician, I value the intellectual element in audiences.

The intellectual world needs us musicians, of course, too. Without some acquaintance of the allied arts, the book-reading public is just a part of the book trade, as the music world, by itself, is only a branch of the entertainment industry. Or worse, a herd of sheep being fattened on propaganda. Propaganda is all right if it is your own. Otherwise it has no place in culture, any more than industrialized entertainment has. There will always be plenty of those around, anyway. What the world needs most just now, beyond food and clothing, is art in the classical sense of the term. In that meaning it is neither propaganda nor entertainment, though it can use both for its own purpose, which is the representation of an inner or outer reality.

I think we need not fear communicating realities to the mass public. I also believe that musicians have reason to welcome, in the process of perfecting for this purpose their communicative powers, not only the criticism of other musicians and music lovers but also the more intellectual response of all those who, without being specifically music-minded, are in their own practice occupied with reality and find pleasure in the constant search for convincing transcripts of it.

January 22, 1950

The Problem of Sincerity

IF ART is a form of communication, and music the form of art best suited to the communication of sentiments, feelings, emotions, it does seem strange that the clear communication of these should be beset with so many difficulties. Perfection of the technical amenities, or at least an approach to it, is more commonly to be met with in the concert hall than is a convincing interpretation of anything. They play and sing so prettily, these recitalists, work so hard and so loyally to get the notes of the music right that it is a matter of constant astonishment to me how few of them can make it speak.

Composers, too, have trouble communicating, especially American composers. They make you great, big, beautiful, shapely structures; but it is not always clear what purpose, with regard to living, these are intended to fulfill. One has a strange feeling sometimes, right in the middle of a concert season, that the music world, both the composers and their executants, are just a swarm of busy ants, accomplishing nothing to human eyes but carrying grains of sand back and forth. How much useful work anybody is doing, of course, is hard to know. But seldom, O, so seldom, does a musical action of any kind speak clearly, simply, without detours.

Part of this inefficiency comes, I am sure, from the prestige of Romantic attitudes in a nonromantic age. From the violinist in a Russian restaurant who hopes to be tipped for pushing his violin into your shashlik to the concert pianist who moons over the keys or slaps at them in a seeming fury, all are faking. They are counterfeiting transports that they do not have and that in nine cases out of ten are not even the subject of the music. For music of passionate and personal expressivity is a small part indeed of standard repertory. There is a little of it, though very little, in Mozart, a bit more in Beethoven, some in Mendelssohn, a great deal in Schumann and Chopin, less in Brahms, and then practically no more at all till you get to Bartók. Its presence in Bruckner and Mahler, though certain, is obscured by monumental preoccupations. Berlioz, Liszt and Wagner, Strauss and Schönberg, even Debussy and the modernists operate mostly on a level of complexity that prevents an efficient interpreter from going too wild and the meaning from getting too private. It is not that technical difficulties prevent introversion. But the simple fact that the subject of most music is evocation obliges both composer and executant to objective procedures.

Music of personal lyricism, Schumann, for instance, can be played or sung without antics and often is. But it cannot be rendered convincingly without personal involvement. This poses the problem of sincerity. You can write or execute music of the most striking evocative power by objective methods, provided you have an active imagination. You can represent other people's emotions, as in the theater, by the same means, plus decorum. But you cannot project a personal sentiment that you do not have. If you fake it knowingly, you are dramatizing that which should be transmitted directly; and if you fake it unknowingly, you are merely, by deceiving yourself, attempting to deceive your audience.

Sincerity is not a requisite for theatrical work, for evocative work, for any music that is, however poetic, objective in character. Taste, intelligence, and temperament are the only requirements. These will enable you to get into any role and out of it again, to perform it perfectly, to communicate through it. They are not sufficient for a proper rendering of Schumann's songs or of the Bartók quartets. These you must feel. What gives to lieder recitals and string quartet concerts their funereal quality, when they don't come off, and their miraculous excitement, when they do, is the absence or presence of authentic feeling in the interpretation.

Any sincerely felt reading must be a personal one. Objective music has, more often than not, traditional readings that are correct. All traditional readings of the music of personalized sentiment are, by definition, incorrect. Because sentiments, feelings, private patterns of anxiety and relief are not subject to standardization. They must be spontaneous to have any existence at all, spontaneous and unique. Naturally, experienced persons can teach the young many things about the personalized repertory. But there is no set way it must be rendered, and any attempt to impose one on it takes the life out of it. The exactly opposite condition obtains regarding objective music. This benefits enormously from exact procedures and standardized renderings, from every thoughtful observance and precision. Personal involvement with it, the injection of sentiment, is a great foolishness.

The whole question of sincerity hangs on a difference between those feelings with which one can become temporarily identified by imagination and those which are one's own and relatively permanent. The former, which make for drama, constitute nine-tenths of the whole musical repertory and nine-tenths of any mature composer's available subject matter. Mixing the two kinds gets nobody anywhere. Treating personal music objectively gives a pedantic effect. Treating objective music personally gives a futile effect. Nevertheless, on account of the prestige that historical Romanticism enjoys, the latter procedure dominates our concert halls. All over America artists are endeavoring to treat the repertory, the vast body of which is objective music, and composers are treating the monumental forms, too, as if their personal fantasies about these were a form of communication. On the other hand, more often than not they treat personal music to a routine and traditional stream-lining that prevents it altogether from speaking that language of the heart that is speech at all only when it comes from the heart. They should leave the stuff alone unless they are capable of spontaneity. Once rid of their romantic pretenses, too, they would certainly do better with the rest of the repertory. For composers the urgency is even greater. Let them do theater and evocations to their hearts' content. But in the domain of private feelings, fooling around with those one does not have is suicidal.

February 8, 1948

Tradition Today

AN IDEAL ORCHESTRAL CONDUCTOR, in the last century, was one who pleased first the musical public and second those persons in the audience whose musical attainments were of a modest character. In those days the aim was public instruction. Hence it was of prime importance that the music be played right. If in addition it could be made attractive, that was luck. Nowadays, with philanthropic subsidies diminished and man-agement, for box-office reasons, firmly in the saddle, the aim of our orchestras is first to please a large ticket-buying public and only second to preserve the traditions of interpretation as these have been handed down and to renew them in full knowledge of their existing state.

We have, as a result, two kinds of conductors, the tradition-als and the independents, the former representing a knowl-edgeable approach, the latter a highly personalized ability to hold attention. The former group is dominated in the United States by Fritz Reiner and Pierre Monteux. The leaders of the other tendency are Leopold Stokowski and Serge Koussevitzky. The enormous prestige of Toscanini is due, I think, not to any gift for combining the personal with the impersonal but to the mercurial speed with which, from work to work and even from phrase to phrase, he can oscillate between them. His application of a theaterlike objectivity to the concert stage is in no sense a preservation of tradition. He has, in fact, blithely broken with as many sound survivals as he has of outworn usages. His concert readings are neither strictly personal nor strictly impersonal, though they are aimed, I think, at impersonality. In the theater, however, he is impersonal and at all times aware of tradition, its nature and necessary reinvigoration.

Managements often refer to tradition-minded conductors as "technicians" and to the independents as "interpreters." As a matter of fact, the Stokowskis and the Koussevitzkys of this world are no less skillful at attaining their musical ends than are the others. They are first-class disciplinarians and justly renowned as trainers of the young. Technicians they certainly are. Interpretation, indeed, is their weaker side. What they rarely do, in any clear meaning of the term, is to interpret, or translate, the known sense of a piece. They improvise it, rather. Their appeal, for musicians and for nonmusicians, is one of sheer technique, of pure beauty in sound. They give offense, when they do, only on grounds of taste. They do not always know, or greatly care, about the exact character, so far as this is known to musicians, of a given work in repertory. The traditionalists do know this, are aware, at least, that the interpretation of music is not entirely a matter of personal fancy and of skill in manipulating crowd psychology.

This is not to say that tempos, accents, and rhythmic inflections are easily ascertainable. If they were, any musician could be a great interpreter. They demand both thought and study. They demand above all, if they are to be convincing to other people who have put thought and study on matters musical, to be arrived at in full knowledge of what these have been in the memory of living lovers of music. One does not expect, moreover, that executants should follow a model precisely. One expects them to preserve tradition by violating it, to clarify it by weeding out the merely habitual, to correct it, to add to it their own enlightenment. Copying one's predecessors is as fruitless as ignoring them. Great interpretation is an offspring of courage, as well as of an awareness of what the music of the past has meant to the musicians of the relatively recent past. Farther than the memory of living men tradition cannot go, because even the written record (take Beethoven's own metronome marks, for instance, or Mozart's precepts of how to play the piano) makes no sense when the effect described has been forgotten.

Second-class French conductors, especially opera conductors, have often a thorough knowledge of how everything ought to go but lack the temperament for infusing their readings with animation. The more powerful conducting personalities in the France of today, Paray and Munch, for instance, often achieve animation by throwing overboard respect for even the composer's expressed intention, for all the world like any second-class Italian opera leader. Our own specialists of animation and beautiful sound are only a little more thoughtful. And they have at least the excuse of having passed their youth out of contact with a major musical tradition, of not having known the classics early enough to feel at home with them. The same is true of them with regard to the modern classics. Monteux and Ansermet remember the sense in Debussy and in the early Stravinsky ballets, the sense as well as the sound, because they were themselves, as young men, part of the modern movement. Most of the others either have forgotten what it was all about or never knew.

Leonard Bernstein knows what American music is all about, but the western European repertory he is obliged to improvise. When he follows a master with regard to it, he follows, moreover, a Russian, Koussevitzky, for whom it has always been foreign matter. That is why, I think, he goes into such chorybantic ecstasies in front of it. He needs to mime, for himself and for others, a conviction that he does not have. He does no such act before American works of his own time. He takes them naturally, reads them with authority. Whether Bernstein will become in time a traditional conductor or a highly personal one is not easy to prophesy. He is a consecrated character, and his culture is considerable. It just might come about, though, that, having to learn classic repertory the hard way, which is after fifteen, and in a hurry, he would throw his cultural beginnings away and build toward success on a sheer talent for animation and personal projection. I must say he worries us all a little bit.

It would be disappointing if our brightest young leader should turn out to be just a star conductor in an age when bluff, temperament, and show-off are no longer effective on the concert stage. They have become, indeed, the privilege of management. Success, today and tomorrow, even financial success, depends on any artist's keeping his ego down to reasonable size. One of the best ways of accomplishing this is to keep one's mind on both the sound and the sense of the music one is playing. All the available knowledge there is about these matters constitutes the tradition. Neglecting to buttress his rising eminence with the full support of tradition is about the biggest mistake an American conductor in this generation could make.

October 19, 1947

Atonality Today (I)

MUSIC that avoids classic scales and interval relations is now the chief region of organized advance. Ten years ago it might have been thought that this music was moribund, that its major achievements lay in the past, that its surviving practitioners and their progeny were a minor sectarian group, rigid, stalemated, immobilized by the complexity of their own syntax. Today it is clear that immobility is a danger facing rather the other schools of modernism than that which derives from Schönberg and that the young, far from being imprisoned by the twelve-tone syntax, are finding a new freedom through its discipline. More than that, they are engaged in research and experiment. Twelve-tone writing is not at all nowadays, if it ever was, a closed technique or a closed æsthetic. On the contrary, it is the main field of musical composition where progress is taking place.

This progress is now operating on an intercontinental, though not a world-wide, scale. Its adepts are numerous in the United States, in France, in Italy, in England, in Switzerland, in Argentina, and in Chile, but not, curiously enough, in Austria, the country of its origin, or in Germany, where its early expansion took place. These countries appear to be relatively quiescent just now with regard to the movement; and Soviet Russia, lately followed by the Iron Curtain countries, is quite out of the picture, technical research there in composition being at present under political ban. Los Angeles, where Arnold Schönberg lives, the founding father of it all, is a sort of Mount Athos to which pilgrimages are made. New York, London, and Venice (also Los Angeles and various European regional capitals) offer their concert privileges to atonal music. Paris, however, is the world center of its creation, analysis, criticism, publication, and propaganda.

Its most authoritative analyst and most widely read propagandist is René Leibowitz. Its chief Parisian creators are mostly the pupils of Olivier Messiaen, himself no twelve-toner at all. Its most intelligent critic, in my judgment, is Pierre Boulez, also a composer of phenomenal gifts. The publication most open to its exposition in detail is the quarterly magazine *Polyphonie*. This review, though only in its fifth issue, has already devoted a whole number to the tonal aspects of dodecaphony and another to musical rhythm in general, with especial attention to the rhythmic opportunities of twelve-tone composition. It is in the rhythmic domain, as a matter of fact, that music's chief advances are being made today; and the primacy of Paris right now in atonal music is due largely, I am sure, to its already affirmed position as the world center of rhythmic research. It is French rhythmic awareness, applied to the writing of twelve-tone music, that has lately initiated a second period in the development of the atonal, or to speak more correctly, the asymmetrical style.

The first period of this development, led by Arnold Schönberg and two of his pupils, Alban Berg and Anton Webern, saw the perfecting of a technique for avoiding classic tonal relations, for keeping the harmonic, the interval content of a piece fluid and of a uniform viscosity. In that technique rhythm is a free, a purely expressive element. The interval relations are very strict, however, homogeneity and the avoiding of all key systems requiring the almost constant presence, or at least the frequent restatement, of all twelve chromatic tones. The device of arranging these twelve tones in a special order, particular to each piece and consistent throughout it, is not an added complication of twelve-tone writing but a simplification, a rule of thumb that speeds up composition. The uses of such a "row," as it is called, are not necessarily intended for listeners to be aware of any more than the devices of fugal imitation are. They show up under analysis, of course, but they are mainly a composer's way of achieving thematic coherence with a minimum of effort.

No such row was present in atonal composition before the

early 1920's, and it was Schönberg's invention. After that practically all atonal composers employed it, though with varying degrees of rigor. Nowadays some twelve-tone writers, like Boulez, will occasionally dispense with a fixed row altogether, or else, like the American Milton Babbitt, conceal it so thoroughly that only a skilled analyst can unmask it. All such music, however, retains the thematic coherence of the more straightforward row music. It is a sophisticated form of atonality, not a primitive one.

The other chief simplifying device of the Schönbergian atonalists is the canon. Since atonal music, to be atonal, of necessity lacks the architectural strength provided by harmony, some system needed to be found for holding it together, for assuring at least a textural continuity. The only classical device of this kind not dependent on tonality is the canon. Consequently Schönberg adopted it and specified it in his simplification rules as the necessary concomitant in composition of any twelve-tone row. Such a row can be repeated canonically in four different orders—forward, backward, upsidedown, and upsidedown backward. However, in the Schönberg system, since rhythm is always free, canonic strictness applies merely to the order in which the tones of the row appear, not to their length values. They can also appear vertically in chords, the row proceeding upward, downward, or both ways, but not in any tonal order other than its predetermined one.

Twelve-tone writing, at its simplest, consists therefore of the chromatic scale arranged in any nonrepeating order one wishes, that order, or row, being exposed in a series of canons. Classical rhythm and metrics are not forbidden. Neither is the imitation of classical harmonic and contrapuntal textures, though the absence of graded interval relations gives to these observances a purely rhythmic character. Twelve-tone music tends, in consequence, toward a rhythmically independent polyphony of equal voices.

According to Mr. Boulez, writing in *Polyphonie*, the twelve-tone-row technique is now perfected. Any composer can master it and can write by means of it in virtually complete avoidance of classical tone-relations. A new thing has been brought to completion. Or rather, let us say, to the first stage of completion. The next stage belongs to rhythm and to the working out of a technique for avoiding classical metrics. This second stage is the preoccupation of young twelve-tone composers everywhere. Its advanced front, however, is the Paris group, because the Paris composing tradition has a backlog of researches in asymmetrical rhythm extending from Stravinsky's early ballets through Messiaen's recent innovations imported from India. An account of these will be our theme next Sunday.

January 29, 1950

Atonality Today (II)

EVERY CENTURY, as Lou Harrison once pointed out, has its chromatic and its diatonic style. Atonality is our chromatic style. Indeed, now that we have it in so highly evolved a form as twelve-tone composition, it seems to be the ultimate condition toward which chromatic harmony has always aspired. That condition is one of extreme fluidity, and its attraction for the pioneer-minded is that of the open sea. Classical scales and harmonic relations, in this conception, constitute reefs and treacherous currents and are hence to be avoided. Arnold Schönberg's twelve-tone-row syntax is a device for avoiding them. It is not the only one in existence, but it is the easiest to handle. Its simplicity and general practicability have caused its adoption by such a large majority among atonal writers that it may now be considered, I think, as the official, the orthodox method of composing in tones without composing in tonalities. Other methods, however excellent or even superior, constitute deviations from standard practice.

That practice is common to most of the mature music of atonality's Big Three—Schönberg, Berg, and Webern. Now two of these three are dead, and the other is seventy-five years old. Their favorite syntactical device, moreover, now available to all, is widely employed. Hence there is every reason to consider the epoch of advance that they represent to be a closed one. Certainly those of their musical progeny who work by identical or nearly identical methods bear the mark of the epigonous. Others, however, who accept the twelve-tone row and its canonic application as their basic method are not satisfied with this as a complete method. For them it is satisfactory only as a way of arranging tones with regard to their pitch. They wish a method

equally convenient for ordering their length. Present-day efforts
by twelve-tone composers to build a rhythmic technique comparable to their tonal system have initiated a second period in
atonal research and composition.

If the first problem in atonality is to avoid familiar tonal relations, its second is surely to avoid familiar metrical ones. Complete renewal of the musical language and not a mere abandonment of its decayed portions, still less a spicing up of spoiled
material, let us remember, is the aim of the atonal group. Also
we must not forget that the Big Three, with slight exceptions
in the work of Webern, made virtually no effort at originality
in the rhythmic direction. Here they remained conservative,
though less by principle, I should think, than from the fact that
all advance needs to proceed in an orderly fashion, one thing at
a time. The rhythmic achievements that now form the backlog
of the second-period atonalists, the knowledge they start from,
came almost wholly from outside the atonal tradition.

These are many. The exactly written-out rubato of Mahler,
the fragmentated developments of Debussy, studies of Chinese,
Javanese, East Indian, and other exotic musical systems, acquaintance with American ragtime and jazz, the epoch-marking
Danse Sacrale from Stravinsky's *Rite of Spring* with its long,
rhythmic phrases developed from tiny cells or rhythmic motifs,
the experiments of Varèse and others in pure percussion, the
introduction into Western music by Messiaen of a Hindu device
for varying a meter's minimum note-length—all have prepared
the way for the new atonalists. Since the new rhythmic efforts
have not yet brought about any standardization of rhythmic
procedures, the field of rhythm is still full of sectarian dispute.
Anybody with a new trick can imagine himself as in possession
of the golden key. So far, however, there is no golden key. The
period is a lively one, and all doors are still open, even to tonal
writers.

The ideal of nonmetrical rhythm, like that of atonality, is
asymmetry. Pierre Boulez states it as *d'éviter la carrure*, that
is to say, the avoidance of everything square. This means that
metrical repeating patterns are out and that even the rhythmic
canon by inversion, the hardest to hear of all rhythmic imitations, requires violation of its exactitude by means of the Hindu
added-dot. There are problems of rhythmic construction, too,

that require solution, though conservative twelve-tone composers like René Leibowitz consider them subsidiary to tonal relations and not soluble independently. John Cage employs a numerical ratio in any piece between the phrase, the period, and the whole, the phrase occupying a time-measure which is the square root of the whole time and the periods occupying times proportional to those of the different rhythmic motifs within the phrase. This procedure, though it allows for asymmetry within the phrase and period, produces a tight symmetry in the whole composition and is not therefore quite the rendering of spontaneous emotion that the European atonalists hope to achieve.

The expressive aim of the atonalists has always been a romantic one, the depiction and provocation of intense, introverted feelings. Berg's music, in this respect, is closely related to that of Hugo Wolf and Mahler. Schönberg oscillates in his feeling allegiance between Wagner and Brahms. Both go into a waltz at the slightest pretext or even with none. Webern is more personal, more fastidious in his expression, as he is more original, more reflective in his applications of the twelve-tone technique. In both respects, and also through his pulverization of sound into a kind of luminous dust, he is an Austrian cousin of Debussy. He it is, in fact, and not Schönberg or Berg, whom the French atonalists tend most to revere and to stem from. He it is, too, who will probably remain most loved among the founding fathers when the atonal world shall have got round to doing over the art of instrumentation. But that will not be for another decade, at least. Just now a new rule of rhythm is the instrument lacking for traveling the trackless ocean of atonality, where the brave adventurer has, by the very nature of his renunciation, no harmony to guide him. The twelve-tone-row technique is a radar for avoiding shoreline hazards, but it has not yet taken any composer beyond the sight of Europe's historic monuments. For that a motor source will have to be found.

February 5, 1950

On Being American

W$_{HAT}$ is an American composer? The Music Critics' Circle of
New York City says it is any musical author of American citizenship. This group, however, and also the Pulitzer Prize Committee, as well as many other award-giving bodies, finds itself troubled in conscience about people like Stravinsky, Schönberg, and
Hindemith. Can these composers be called American, whose
styles were formed in Europe and whose most recent work, if
it shows any influence of American ways and feeling, shows this
certainly in no direction that could possibly be called nationalistic? Any award committee would think a second time before
handing these men a certificate, as Americans, for musical excellence. The American section of the International Society for
Contemporary Music has more than once been reproached
in Europe for allowing the United States to be represented at
international festivals of the society by composers of wholly
European style and formation, such as Ernest Bloch and Ernst
Krenek. And yet a transfer of citizenship cannot with justice
be held to exclude any artist from the intellectual privileges of
the country that has, both parties consenting, adopted him, no
matter what kind of music he writes.

Neither can obvious localisms of style be demanded of any
composer, native born or naturalized. If Schönberg, who writes
in an ultra-chromatic and even atonal syntax and who practically
never uses folk material, even that of his native Austria, is to be
excluded by that fact from the ranks of American composers,
then we must exclude along with him that stalwart Vermonter,
Carl Ruggles, who speaks a not dissimilar musical language.
And among the native-born young, Harold Shapero and Arthur
Berger are no more American for writing in the international
neoclassic manner (fountainhead Stravinsky) than Lou Harrison
and Merton Brown are, who employ the international chromatic techniques (fountainhead Schönberg). All these gifted
young writers of music are American composers, though none
employs a nationalistic trademark or finds his best inspiration
in our local folklore.

The fact is, of course, that citizens of the United States write
music in every known style. There is no such thing, consequently,
as an American style. There is not even a dominant style in

American art music, as there is in our popular music. From the post-Romantic eclecticism of Howard Hanson and the post-Romantic expressionism of Bernard Rogers through the neo-classicized (if I may invent the word) impressionism of Edward Burlingame Hill and John Alden Carpenter, the strictly Parisian neoclassicism of Walter Piston, the romanticized neoclassicism of Roy Harris and William Schuman, the elegant neo-Romanticism of Samuel Barber, the sentimental neo-Romanticism of David Diamond, the folksy neo-Romanticism of Douglas Moore, Randall Thompson, and Henry Cowell, the Germano-eclectic modernism of Roger Sessions, the neo-primitive poly-tonalism of Charles Ives, and the ecstatic chromaticism of Carl Ruggles, to the percussive and rhythmic research fellows Edgard Varèse and John Cage, we have everything. We have also the world famous European atonalists Schönberg and Krenek, the neoclassic masters Stravinsky and Hindemith. We have, more-over, a national glory in the form of Aaron Copland, who so skillfully combines, in the Bartók manner, folk feeling with neoclassic techniques that foreigners often fail to recognize his music as American at all.

All this music is American, nevertheless, because it is made by Americans. If it has characteristic traits that can be identified as belonging to this continent only, our composers are largely un-conscious of them. These are shared, moreover, by composers of all the schools and probably by our South American neigh-bors. Two devices typical of American practice (I have written about these before) are the nonaccelerating crescendo and a steady ground-rhythm of equalized eighth notes (expressed or not). Neither of these devices is known to Europeans, though practically all Americans take them for granted. Further study of American music may reveal other characteristics. But there can never be any justice in demanding their presence as a proof of musical Americanism. Any American has the right to write music in any way he wishes or is able to do. If the American school is beginning to be visible to Europeans as something not entirely provincial with regard to Vienna and Paris, something new, fresh, real, and a little strange, none of this novel quality is a monopoly, or even a specialty, of any group among us. It is not limited to the native-born or to the German-trained or to the French-influenced or to the self-taught or to the

New-York-resident or to the California-bred. It is in the air and belongs to us all. It is a set of basic assumptions so common that everybody takes them for granted. This is why, though there is no dominant style in American music, there is, viewed from afar (say from Europe), an American school.

National feelings and local patriotisms are as sound sources of inspiration as any other. They are not, however, any nobler than any other. At best they are merely the stated or obvious subject of a piece. Music that has life in it always goes deeper than its stated subject or than what its author thought about while writing it. Nobody becomes an American composer by thinking about America while composing. If that were true Georges Auric's charming fox trot *Adieu New-York* would be American music and not French music, and *The Road to Mandalay* would be Burmese. The way to write American music is simple. All you have to do is to be an American and then write any kind of music you wish. There is precedent and model here for all the kinds. And any Americanism worth bothering about is everybody's property anyway. Leave it in the unconscious; let nature speak.

Nevertheless, the award-giving committees do have a problem on their hands. I suggest they just hedge and compromise for a while. That, after all, is a way of being American, too.

January 25, 1948

Too Many Languages

THE KIND OF PROGRAM that vocalists, particularly the younger ones, feel obliged to offer in their recitals is a formula that has long seemed to this reviewer ill suited to advancing either musical or technical excellence. Its fault can be stated in three words—*too many languages.* Not long ago, speaking before a meeting of voice teachers, he reproached them with responsibility for its continued observance and asked why so stupid a violation of all sense, pedagogical and artistic, had ever become established in custom. They answered in unanimity, "We do not know, and we do not approve it." Nevertheless, every aspiring singer in our midst feels obliged to offer in recital an Italian, a German, a French, and an English group of songs.

Naturally, they sing all these languages badly, even, in many cases, English. Often, having merely learned their foreign songs phonetically, they have only an approximate idea of the texts' meaning. The communication of poetry under such circumstances is quite impossible. It is not easy, either, to sing agreeably when the full content of the composer's feelings, as embodied in verbal values, is not clear to the interpreter. Moreover, nobody demands this monkey-like behavior. The public does not like it; the press does not like it; and managements care only for what the audience and the press like. Singing teachers, who are responsible for the tradition and its preservation, all know it is opposed to good artistic standards. And yet they hesitate to do away with it. Several of them have suggested that since music schools in America require of singers three languages besides English, if a degree is to be awarded, they themselves are the victims of a circumstance. But it is the singing teachers who determine, finally, degree requirements for singers. Surely they could demand revision of a faulty curriculum.

Such a curriculum is faulty because it is not a preparation for professional life. Few professional vocalists of the first class ever sing four languages in public. The best usually sing two, their own and one other. Knowing one foreign language gives depth and discrimination to an artist's handling of his own. Helen Traubel, by specializing in German repertory, has had a great career. Mary Garden did the same with French, Jan Peerce and Richard Tucker with Italian. A language means something in the mouths of these artists. They know its feel, its style, its nature, its relation to life and to music. A few singers have the gift of tongues; but for every Jennie Tourel in the world, there are a dozen Lotte Lehmanns, Pinzas, and Carusos, for whom a new language has to be approached slowly, circumspectly, once in a lifetime.

A young singer needs to know, for studio purposes, the Italian vowels, because they are pure. He needs also to sing (and translation will do) enough French, German, and Italian songs to acquire an acquaintance with these musical literatures. Then he should choose one for his own. He should adopt a country, speak its language, read its books, live among its people, eat its food. In this way he may learn to interpret its music with understanding. As he advances in professional life, travels, and reads, he may find it useful to pick up a smattering of other languages, including Spanish and Russian. But he does not have to sing them, and he should not sing them until he feels thoroughly at home with their sound and with their sense. An occasional compliment to local audiences will be enough exception to prove the value of this rule.

All this time he should be singing his own language, learning it, loving it, making its sounds behave, and making the farthest ticket-holder hear what he says. This is the way singers work abroad, and it is the right way. Any other is injurious and silly. Requiring young vocalists to sing four languages is like asking string players to be equally proficient on the violin, the viola, and the cello. Such acrobatics should be discouraged.

If any person reading this column knows any reason why the four-language formula should be further tolerated by teachers or by concert-goers, I hope he will correct my impatience. In my view, and the voice teachers met in convention did seem to agree with me, it is unmusical, unintelligent, inartistic, and pedagogically unsound.

April 23, 1950

High Costs

THE DEPRESSION has hit the music business and no doubt about it. Records, books, and concert tickets are getting harder and harder to sell; and the money for giving prestige recitals in New York is far less plentiful than it was during the war and just after. The cost of such recitals, moreover, has about doubled in the last three years. A Town Hall event, professionally managed and publicized modestly, used to cost the artist about a thousand dollars. It now comes to nearer two thousand. Costs are higher all round; but no management, aware of the public's diminished purchasing power, dares ask us to pay higher prices for admission. Buyer resistance is already formidable. Only a few nationally-advertised artists and organizations can today fill any New York hall without resorting to "paper."

Even rich organizations like the Philadelphia Orchestra and the Metropolitan Opera Association have threatened suicide. I must say they have brought their troubles on themselves.

Not that any group in the country is solely responsible for the rise in prices, not even Congress. But it has long been evident that artistic enterprises which conduct their operations on the models of business must accept the unhappy consequences of a business depression. If our symphony orchestras were more clearly a part of our real cultural life, like the universities, and less a mere front for the music industries, for radio, recording, and concert management, they would be in a better position than they are today to face deficits. Their intellectual function would be worth more as capital. As I remarked several years ago about the Metropolitan Opera, such groups do best when they conduct themselves and think of themselves as successful money-spending enterprises, not as unsuccessful money-making ones.

Neither should they get mixed up in class warfare. It is unfortunate that supposedly philanthropic and cultural foundations serving art and public instruction should appear in the role of labor's enemy. They should economize where and when they can, naturally; and they should negotiate the most favorable contracts they can. They should not waste their funds. But neither should they assume before the whole public any attitude that renders the motivation of their trustees and administrators suspect to a large part of that public, namely, to all those citizens, many of them music consumers, who make up the trade union movement or who believe in its value to our economy.

I mean by this that the negotiation of labor contracts between unions and nonprofit-making institutions should be carried on without recourse to the major arms of the labor-capital struggle. Symphony orchestras have gone on strike in the past, but rarely successfully; and the action has usually, as in the case of the Boston Symphony Orchestra's strike back in 1920, been costly to unionism in terms of public opinion. The Metropolitan Opera's threat of last August to suspend operations and the Philadelphia Orchestra's announcement of last Monday, canceling its whole concert season, risk a similar unfavorable result for management, since both are dangerously close to what is called in industry a lockout. (In neither case was complete liquidation of the enterprise proposed.) That Philadelphia's Local 77 of the Musicians' Union so understood the move was clear from their reply that they were "unwilling and unable" to accept the orchestra board's decision. Both sides left the door open to further negotiations.

The present writer is holding no brief for either contestant. He is simply pointing out that two philanthropic musical enterprises have recently risked unfavorable public opinion by behaving as if they were businesses, as if no obligation to the public had ever been assumed, as if their governing boards were free to discontinue a valued cultural operation on no other provocation than that of a threatened deficit. It is such a board's duty to negotiate contracts, accept the results, and meet deficits. It is also their privilege to call for public support in meeting deficits. It is their duty, moreover, to ask for such support, to give the public its chance to pay up, before cavalierly announcing the interruption of a public service.

The Philadelphia management has long complained that the Musicians' Union local takes to itself an unfair negotiating advantage by delaying each year to propose its terms until just before the season opens. The union, too, may well at present consider the orchestra's directors to have acted unfairly in threatening the public with a stoppage of the concerts merely to avoid the trouble of raising the money for a wage increase. Wage increases are everywhere in discussion; in a time of high prices their demand need surprise no one. Whether granted or not, they have to be considered. I know nothing of the horse trading that must certainly have gone on between management and the union in Philadelphia, or what exasperation provoked the orchestra board to cancel, at least in announcement, its whole concert season. I merely repeat that I find the gesture unbecoming, as was certainly that of the Metropolitan Opera board in threatening last summer to omit a season from its history.

I find the gesture unbecoming because it uses us, the public, as a pawn in the game of costs. We do not care what symphony orchestras cost; our interest is in what and how they play. If an administration is efficient (and one has every reason to believe that Philadelphia's is), then the proper price of musicians, like that of railway fares, hall rent, musical scores, trucking, and publicity, is simply whatever such a management can get the best for, no more and no less. If prices all around are more than we, the public, are able to cope with, then we do without an orchestra or put up with a cheaper one. But we do not like having trustees tell us they are stopping our concerts simply because they find some necessary element of the enterprise, in their opinion, overpriced. What have they in mind as their trust, one wonders, when they assume what is, after all, our privilege? Are they acting as trustees of all our interests and of music's place in the intellectual tradition, or are they merely playing trustees of private capital in capital's age-old war with labor?

October 3, 1948

The Oratorio Style

SPRING always brings forth choral festivities. Many of these involve soloists. Most of the latter are less effective than one would wish. The circumstances that war against musical efficiency on the part of soloists are many. Chief among them is the fact that standing on the same level with an accompanying orchestra puts vocalists at a disadvantage. Even so skillful a conductor as Toscanini cannot prevent a platform orchestra from occasionally overpowering the voice. If the choral "big machines" could be given in an opera house, with the orchestra in a pit, the solos would be easier to project.

Another trouble is the inability of middle-sized orchestras to play softly (there rarely being room either on the platform or in the budget for a full contingent of strings). A very small group, chamber-music size, can play pianissimo; and so can a full symphony orchestra with thirty-two or more violins. But a middle-sized orchestra cannot do it. Acoustical facts are involved, and so is a certain auditory illusion; the matter merits study before a true explanation of the phenomenon can be advanced. But conductors are acquainted with it. Stated roughly it amounts to this, that a large orchestra can play softer than a small one. Oratorio orchestras are rarely big enough to play a real pianissimo. And soloists, especially when standing right beside an orchestra, have need often of a really pianissimo accompaniment.

A third offender is the "oratorio style" itself. This is a faulty conception of how soloists should interpret a sacred text to orchestral accompaniment in a large hall. There is no one style suitable to all such works. The idea that something halfway between a broad operatic manner and an intimate recital refinement will do merely makes for a style that is neither one thing nor the other. What you get mostly is a manner of execution lacking the vocal refinements of recital art and the expressivity of the theater. The only valid part of the so-called "oratorio style" is the maxim that personal expressivity, impersonation, is inappropriate to texts, sacred or secular, that involve no impersonation.

Now there is such a thing, and very beautiful it is, as the Handelian style. It works for Handel's operas as well as for his oratorios. It also works, with tenderness added, for the Mendelssohn oratorios, which are designed after those of Handel. It does not work for Bach or Haydn or Mozart or Beethoven or Brahms and still less for Rossini, Berlioz, Verdi, Honegger, or Stravinsky. A good rule of thumb is to approach any composer's concert works of large format (works for chorus, vocal soloists, and orchestra) in the same manner as one would approach his stage works. When, as in the case of Bach and Brahms, there are no stage works to give the cue, other criteria must be found. But roughly speaking, any composer's stage style is the touchstone to his works for similar musical forces.

Thus it comes about that Beethoven's Missa Solemnis gives a better effect when read as a version of his *Fidelio*, impersonation omitted, than when read as an emulation of Handel's *Messiah* or of Mendelssohn's *Elijah*. Haydn's *Creation* and *The Seasons* should be evocative and pastoral, like most of his operas. Berlioz's Requiem is not very different from *The Trojans* or from his *Romeo and Juliet* or *The Damnation of Faust*. Verdi's Requiem is certainly not far from *La Forza del Destino* or Mozart's Requiem from *The Magic Flute*. Debussy's *Prodigal Son* and *Blessed Damozel* (the latter not a sacred text at all) are of the family of *Pelléas*, not of *Judas Maccabeus*. Stravinsky's *Oedipus Rex* is by the author of *Les Noces* and *L'Histoire d'un Soldat*; and though the Handelian style is certainly here evoked, it is evoked only, not at any point directly employed.

Brahms has given us no stage clew to his choral works, but he has left a huge body of songs greatly resembling them. My recommendation to conductors is to read the *German Requiem* as sensitively and as intimately as if it were *Mainacht* or the *Sapphische Ode*. And the Bach Passions, Christmas Oratorio, and Mass in B-minor were unquestionably composed, like the same author's church cantatas, for small choral bodies and with chamber-style instrumentation. Their dominating quality is less the massiveness of certain choral effects than their extreme floridity everywhere or, in the case of the Passions, their tenderness and intimacy.

A grander and more elegant Handelian style than is currently available would be welcome in our concert halls. It would not be difficult to achieve, either, if our singers and conductors would try a little harder, because its characteristics are nowhere in dispute. I should even like to see the Handelian style used as the bedrock of vocal training, since Handel offers the best-written body of vocal music available to English-speaking singers. But this does not mean that the Handelian style should be applied willy-nilly to the whole chorus-with-soloists repertory. Its indiscriminate application in England is, indeed, the origin of that false concept "the oratorio style." The continentals make no such error. That is why Walter and Monteux and occasionally Koussevitzky give us regularly such delightful readings of the choral classics, while our own conductors, influenced by the false concept of an "oratorio style" that excuses every fault but lack of loudness, give us year after year performances of the chorus-with-soloists repertory that are styleless, inaccurate, and inexpressive. The soloists are somewhat at fault, too, though not entirely. They can do better work than they generally do; what they chiefly need is conductors who know what they want to hear and how to ask for it. You cannot, of course, produce an oratorio properly, any more than you can an opera, by rehearsing only the choral passages.

May 9, 1948

The Catholic Church Accepts Modern Music

POPE PIUS X's encyclical of November 22, 1903, entitled *Motu Proprio*, which dealt with church music and the proper manner of its performance, was a revolutionary document. Its radical pronouncements were three: (1) Gregorian chant was declared the official and true music of the Roman Catholic liturgy; (2) the sixteenth-century "Roman school" of polyphony (or Palestrina

style), ordained as appropriate for the grander ceremonies of
the church in connection with certain texts of the liturgy, was
so nominated for its derivation from Gregorian chant and its
adherence to the spirit of this; and (3) musical styles associated
with the opera, which means, in practice, all musical styles developed after 1600, were condemned as non-liturgical, irrespec-
tive of their intrinsic musical merits. Masses composed by such
sound Catholics as Mozart, Rossini, Schubert, Bruckner, and
César Franck were thus removed from Church usage, along with
sacred settings of the Sextet from *Lucia di Lammermoor*, the
Drinking Song from *Lucrezia Borgia*, and Liszt's *Liebestraum,
No. 1*, all of which, believe it or not, were in those days both
current and popular.

From that time to our own, Catholic church music has been
marked by a sobriety, a seemliness, and a decorum that have gradually come to give the tone, the acceptable tone, to all the church
music of Western Christendom, wherever this follows reflected
procedures rather than folk patterns. Nevertheless, that whole
revision of musical syntax that has been our century's most impressive contribution to the art has begun to creep into Catholic services and to add to the mystic medievalism of Gregorian
chant and to the Counter-Reformation-style humanism of
Palestrinian polyphony a definitely contemporary, a twentieth-
century note. This came earliest in France, through the Parisian
organists, whose improvisations, from Vierne to Messiaen,
have long followed, with archiepiscopal toleration, the most
advanced procedures of composition.

Contemporary church architecture and decoration, moreover,
have tended everywhere, save perhaps in the United States,
toward liberation from the antimodernist papal influence of the
last fifty years, which, if it gave to the plastic side of devotion,
as to liturgical music, an incomparable criterion of taste, limited
the living creators of ecclesiastical art to imitating the antique.
Certain bishops have been more lenient than others, however,
in the application of the law; and little by little churches of
reinforced concrete, on the cheap scale, and churches designed
and decorated by celebrated modern artists, on the expensive scale, have been rearing their modernistic heads over the
landscape. The French Dominicans, who have been for some
time the spearhead of a movement within the Church toward

proselytizing twentieth-century intellectuals through friendliness toward twentieth-century intellectual manifestations, have probably been no less influential of late on papal thought than has the exigency of rebuilding ruined ecclesiastical edifices all over Europe at the lowest possible cost.

In any case, Pope Pius XII has come out for modernism in the arts. The encyclical of November 20, 1947, entitled *Mediator Dei*, in which his acceptance of modernism is incorporated, is no such revolutionary document as the *Motu Proprio* of 1903, which condemned, for church usage, most of the music written since 1585. Its subject is the liturgy as a whole; and it reasserts, as regards music, two of the basic precepts of the earlier pronouncement. The Gregorian chant is to remain the "true music" of the service, and congregational participation in this is to be encouraged. On the other hand, where the *Motu Proprio* allowed the congregational use of regional-style hymns only on condition that these seem not irreverent to persons from other regions, the *Mediator Dei* recommends them with no such reserve. And the Palestrina (or "Roman") style is not mentioned.

The blessing of modern music reads as follows (I translate from the Italian version of the Pope's Latin text, as published in *L'Oservatore Romano*, Vatican City, December 1, 1947, since no official complete English version of the encyclical has yet arrived in this country): "It cannot be asserted . . . that modern music, instrumental and vocal (*la musica e il canto moderno*), should be excluded altogether from Catholic worship. Therefore, unless this is profane in character or unseemly of expression with respect to holy places and sacred service, or derived from a vain research for unusual and outlandish effects, it is necessary surely to open to it the doors of our churches, since both kinds of it [instrumental and vocal] can contribute in no small way to the splendor of the holy rites, to the elevation of the mind, and . . . to true devotion." A similar blessing follows of modern architecture, painting, sculpture, and decoration, with regard to their use in churches.

There is little more to be said. Modern music is now official to the Roman Church, the very fount and center of musical conservatism. Long ago it was received in the schools, by the theater, at the subscription concerts. No major musical power is today vowed to musical reaction save the Soviet government and possibly the American films. Either might do a U-turn tomorrow. And the contemporary musical world has long since learned to get on without both. Not, however, without the Church. Her reserve we have always regretted. There are still minor points to be decided, of course. How far, for instance, can twelve-tone-row music be called "a vain research"? And may not, perhaps, repetitions of the text and instruments of percussion, if tastefully introduced, be returned discreetly to liturgical custom? All such matters will be decided in the Church by papal counsel and by conferences, in other institutions by custom. But the schism is healed. Not in our lifetime will modern music ever again be seriously a problem to anyone living between the Iron Curtain and Los Angeles.

For church practice, I gather that the Pope wishes the Gregorian chant, its study and practice, to remain the Church's musical main foundation, and that the monotony and somewhat recondite character of this be relieved on the simpler religious occasions by hymn singing, on the grander ones by set-pieces of contemporary composition. Palestrina and his school are not to be ejected, nor is the florid music of Mozart and other composers whose manner has theatrical or profane associations yet to be taken back. What any music director can get by with, as modernism, will continue to depend on the culture of his local pastor and the enlightenment of his bishop. But an order from Rome is an order. Little by little you will be hearing, along with the plainsong, a new kind of music in Catholic churches. And the world-wideness with which the Catholic Church operates in liturgical matters cannot fail to lend to its new repertory an influence on Protestant music. It is probable, indeed, that in opening the doors of his Church to musical advance the Pope has spoken, how consciously I could not say, for the whole Judeo-Christian world, at least for the intellectual confraternity within it that holds the children of the twentieth century entitled to speak their own language without shame. To speak it, moreover, not only among themselves but also to God.

February 1, 1948

from

MUSIC REVIEWED
1940–1954

Preface

Once in the dear dead days beyond recall I worked for a newspaper. It was called the New York *Herald Tribune*, and its owner-editor was Ogden Reid. Its editorial page was liberal Republican, its readership reasonably cultured and well-to-do. With a circulation of only 450,000 (the weekly book section went to 750,000), it was in no sense a mass medium. On the contrary, it sought direct political influence, largely through family acquaintances, and aspired to intellectual distinction, the latter chiefly through its columnists—including in my day Walter Lippmann, Dorothy Thompson, Joseph Alsop—and its critical writers—Percy Hammond and Richard Watts for drama (later Walter Kerr), Royal Cortissoz (later Emily Genauer), for art, and my predecessors for music Henry Edward Krehbiel and Lawrence Gilman.

On that paper a writer's distinction was judged less by his leadership of public taste—high, low, or middlebrow—than by his skill in handling words, sentences, and paragraphs. Neither Ogden Reid nor Geoffrey Parsons, his chief aide in matters cultural, could be shocked by radical opinions on art, nor by the reactionary. Their attitude was that any informed statement *could* be published if it observed the amenities and was expressed in clear English.

My engagement as music critic of the *Herald Tribune*, which took place in October, 1940, was determined less, I think, by my musical accomplishments, though these were known, than by my particular way of writing about music (at once sassy and classy), which had earlier come to notice through *Vanity Fair* and the quarterly *Modern Music*, and just the year before in my book *The State of Music*. For only such an assumption can explain why a musician so little schooled in daily journalism, a composer so committed to the modern, and a polemicist so contemptuous as myself of music's power structure should have been offered a post of that prestige. Still more, why the paper kept me on for fourteen years. No other would have done so, I am sure. My editors, during the first two stormy seasons, I know were not wholly happy about their choice. But after that

779

they relaxed and began to purr. My column carried professional prestige; it even, they believed, sold papers.

The present assemblage of reviews and Sunday articles from that column paints a picture of music during World War II as reviewed from New York and points west, of music during the succeeding decade as observed from Europe as well. Many of the pieces in this omnibus volume have already appeared in books now out of print. Those written after 1950 are from the files. A chronological arrangement of them all has been adopted for narrative interest. And the publisher has encouraged me to cover the period copiously.

How wholly of the past that period can seem today only young people know. For them the world did not begin till 1950, or at whatever date around that time television became universal and obligatory. They still read books, I know; they certainly buy them. But there is little time for talking with their elders any more and small way except through reading to imagine what people's lives could possibly have been like before theirs began. This personal account of a prehistoric time—World War II and the ten years that followed—is offered therefore not only as information, but also for whatever shiver of strangeness it may provoke. And should some be surprised at what I got away with on a serious and responsible paper, if only in terms of uncustomary views and coverages, that very fact may help to bring the 1940s back as a golden time. Which they were, of course, as all decades tend in memory to become.

New York, 1966

1940s

French Loveliness

ORCHESTRE NATIONAL DE FRANCE, *Charles Munch*, conductor, last night at Carnegie Hall, performing music by French composers including Berlioz's Overture to *Le Corsair*, Honegger's Symphony No. 2 for Strings and Trumpet, and Ravel's *Tombeau de Couperin*. Presented by Henri Bonnet, the French Ambassador to the United States, and American Aid to France, Inc.

FEW MUSICAL DELIGHTS are so deeply satisfying, both sensuously and intellectually, as a good French orchestra, in form, playing French music under a good French conductor; and the Orchestre National, playing last night in Carnegie Hall under Charles Munch, was exactly that. From beginning to end the concert was both electrifying and delicious. For any who might have had doubts about the ability of this, or of any other European orchestra, to bear comparison with our million-dollar-a-year groups, such hesitations were relieved after the opening overture (Berlioz's *Corsaire*) and not at any time again brought to mind.

In certain ways, this orchestra, playing at its best, does better work than we are accustomed to hear. The clean unanimity of its string playing, the exactitude of its string and woodwind balances, the shading and stability of its percussion section and, of course, the matchless phrasings and other tonal refinements of the French woodwind soloists are standards of comparison that our orchestras, preoccupied in many cases by the appeals of emphasis and warmth, do not always try to meet. On the question of brass, America follows the German taste for heavy round sounds. The French thinner brasses, which operate as woodwinds in soft passages and in loud ones as a stronger counterpart to the nasal timbre of strings, oboes, and bassoons, are consciously avoided in this country, even in the performance of French music.

How brilliant, how tender and how poetic French music can sound when played in the French way is a rare experience for us. The French orchestral style is one of equilibration, of clear balances and clean colors, of poetic luminosity rather than of animal warmth. And the whole repertory of French music composed since Berlioz has been designed to profit by this delicate performing style. When French orchestras are not in form or well led, which is all too often, they are without vitality. When they are really playing well under a good leader, and playing French music, they offer orchestral sound at its maximum of sophistication.

October 18, 1948

A Brilliant Assumption

JAZZ: *A People's Music*, by Sidney Finkelstein (Citadel Press, New York, 1948. $3), has one distinguishing feature among books on jazz. It attempts to explain the nature of this music, its development and its vigor under persecution in terms of Marxist sociology. The idea that jazz is a music of revolt and of America's economically submerged is perspicacious and merits a more elaborate documentation than the author has provided for its defense. The use of the word "people" to define the lower economic levels of our society is a Stalinist obscurantism that prevents by moral intimidation detailed investigation of the field it pretends to delimit. Nevertheless, there is certainly some relation between jazz and the class structure of American society, a relation not at all to the discredit either of this music or of the people who make it, though the circumstances in which their lives are led are often, from any bourgeois or social-worker point of view, appalling.

Aside from its class-angle approach, Mr. Finkelstein's book is not very original or acute. As another volume on the subject, it can be read by the pious and placed on the sacred shelf; but I do not think there is much in it not elsewhere available, beyond its brilliant basic assumption. And certainly there is far more reviewing of famous recorded performers and performances in it than proves anything. That aspect makes it just another Appreciation book. I do wish the author had developed further his social view of a major musical phenomenon.

January 9, 1949

Stiffly Conducted

BOSTON SYMPHONY ORCHESTRA, *Igor Stravinsky*, conductor, last night at Carnegie Hall, performing four works by Mr. Stravinsky: Ode, Concerto for Piano and Wind Instruments, Concerto in D for String Orchestra, and Suite from *Orpheus*. Soloist: *Soulima Stravinsky*, piano.

STRAVINSKY's ballet *Orpheus* had not been heard here as a concert piece till the composer conducted it last night in Carnegie Hall. When Ballet Society produced the work last season the score made a deep impression. At last night's performance of the Boston Symphony Orchestra it struck this observer again as an unusually rewarding work.

Though dominated at all times by the strings of the orchestra, its sonorous variety runs high. Constantly static of harmony and rhythm, it evokes action, all the same, as well as feeling. Wholly diatonic in style, it has a harmonic plainness and melodious grace that are just right for a subject out of classical mythology. Mostly the music is slow, too; but from beginning to end it is all so interesting, so full of expressive life, that monotony is at no point present. A magical sort of work it is, because it creates a spell. That spell resembles a little the mood of Satie's *Socrate*, as if the whole air were become suddenly motionless and vibrant.

The Concerto in D for String Orchestra, usually considered a minor work, delighted all by its jollity and animation. Indeed, it was the only piece that Mr. Stravinsky led last night with any ease. Perhaps his lively way with it explains its happy reception. In any case, it was the one moment of the evening when fun got loose. The other works were all tragic of theme; and they were tightly, laboriously led.

Soulima Stravinsky, playing the twenty-five-year-old Piano Concerto, read it correctly, gave us the notes. Igor Stravinsky, conducting it, somehow squeezed all the life out of it with his stubborn and hesitant beat. The same was true in the Ode, which began the program. Granted that three sad pieces and one jolly one do not make an ideal menu, I think the great man was not in his best form. He let his sonorities thicken unblended and his phrases bog down from lack of afflatus. Nothing moved along except the String Concerto. Many, discouraged, left the hall.

February 17, 1949

Brilliant Conducting

JUILLIARD ORCHESTRA, *Eleazar de Carvalho*, conductor, last night at Juilliard Concert Hall, performing Shapero's Overture to *The Travellers*, Schönberg's Chamber Symphony No. 1, and Berlioz's *Symphonie Fantastique*.

ELEAZAR DE CARVALHO, conducting the Juilliard School Orchestra, gave a sensationally successful performance of the Berlioz *Symphonie Fantastique*. Earlier in the evening he had thoroughly muffed Schönberg's Kammersymphonie, and before that, your informant had messed up his own coverage by arriving late (what with wet streets and a concert that really began on time) for Harold Shapero's *The Travellers* overture. Carvalho's New York début, nevertheless, offered compensations.

Exasperated by his own miscalculation, your investigator was inclined toward sympathy with that of the young Brazilian conductor in the Schönberg work. The fact remains, however, that Mr. Carvalho failed to induce his fifteen instrumentalists to make any kind of balance that sounded like chamber music. He forced them to force their tone, strove for effects of dynamism unattainable with single strings and woodwinds and in general threw his weight around pretty carelessly. The Kammersymphonie, all tenderness, formality, and meditation, resisted such treatment. Neither the work nor the interpreter came out of the match to advantage.

Both shone in the *Fantastique*. Note that almost any conductor makes a fine effect with the last two movements of this piece, which are foolproof. But few, very few, ever get much life into the first three. Mr. Carvalho, I must say, let the first go static on him by arbitrarily holding back the beat every few measures, but in the waltz he found a trajectory and kept to it. His balances everywhere were clear, moreover; and his orchestral tone was consistently agreeable, in spite of a certain violence in expression that is essential to a live reading of this work. The *Fantastique* is not an easy work to conduct at all, much less to interpret convincingly. Mr. Carvalho proved himself a leader of unusual skill and unusual platform power in a performance memorable for clarity and pacing.

Faults the young conductor has aplenty. Like many another Koussevitzky pupil he swims in molasses, chews the air, and in general pleads for personal attention. He puts on a ballet of hands, moreover, that is affected and of questionable value to the players. Like many another barehanded leader, too, he throws an overheavy and over-detailed beat. All this is of no gravity whatsoever to a musician of his brains and temperament. What is cardinal to conducting is an ability to make other musicians make music. That Mr. Carvalho has. He can even prevent them from doing so, as he proved in the Schönberg work, when he misconstrues a piece and miscalculates sonorous limits. A conductor with a future, I say, and already worth listening to.

March 26, 1949

Piano-Playing as Music

MIECZYSLAW HORSZOWSKI, pianist, in recital last night at Town Hall, performing, among other works, Haydn's Andante and Variations in F minor, Beethoven's Sonata No. 29 (Op. 106, "Hammerklavier"), Villa-Lobos's *Hommage à Chopin*, and Chopin's Scherzo in B-flat minor.

MIECZYSLAW HORSZOWSKI played the piano last night in Town Hall, and that is news. This extraordinarily sensitive and powerful musician, though he lives no further away than Philadelphia (where he teaches at the Curtis Institute), seldom crosses the Delaware for our benefit. When he does, it is a good day for us, for few pianists play with such beauty, such distinction, such unfailing seriousness of thought.

The first quality one notices in his work is the beauty of the sound that it makes, the genuinely musical character of all that strikes the ear. The second is grace, the airy way he treats a melody and its ornaments, throwing up the latter like spray round the coastal contours of the former, using two kinds of tone, one resonant and weighty, the other light as bubbles, the presence of both making depth, perspective, roundness.

Then little by little one grows aware of the man's strength, physical, emotional, intellectual. He does not let the composer down. He goes straight to the meaning of a piece and gives it to you. His ways are subtle but never devious, his readings at once elaborate and straightforward. For all his preoccupation with detail, which is great, he indulges no personal or outlandish fancy. The whole complex variation of tonal color, accent, and phraseology that goes to make up great piano playing is dominated by a grand line that sweeps through a piece, holds it firm and clear, makes it meaningful, keeps it a composition.

Two works were particularly happy under this breadth of conception last night; Beethoven's Sonata in B flat major, opus 106, a far from easy piece to keep in motion, and the Chopin B-flat minor Scherzo, which regularly falls apart in lesser hands. Everything played had shape, as well as beauty of sound, depth and clarity of communication.

Least communicative—and that through no fault of Horszowski—was Villa-Lobos's *Homage to Chopin*, a seasonal offering that seems little likely to survive the frost. Surprisingly full of drama was Haydn's hackneyed Andante (with variations) in F minor. Utterly welcome at this time, when everybody rattles off Chopin in his own version of the standard international touring style, was a certain Polishness in the pianist's understanding of that composer. National origins here, instead of presenting a difficulty to surmount, offered occasion for added picturesqueness of style, especially in the mazurkas, without intruding on their period elegance.

October 20, 1949

1950

The First Fifty Years

THE FIRST DECADE AND A HALF of this century were a glorious time for music. Creative originality has rarely run so high. In the flowering of modernism that took place during that time, the prize blooms were from three gardens. France gave us Debussy and Ravel, the impressionist technique of detailed musical description. Austria produced Schönberg and his school, the expressionist æsthetic, the use of atonal harmony as a psychological microscope. Russia's cultural ambitions also received international blessing through the ballet successes of Serge de Diaghilev, whose original offering was the nationalistic primitivism of Igor Stravinsky. When the first World War interrupted for four years artistic expansions in all forms, the garden of musical modernism was already laid out.

During the two decades that followed, the structure rose. The modern techniques got disseminated rapidly, in part through the aid of mechanical media such as the gramophone and the radio. They were popularized, vulgarized, generalized, taught in the schools. Neoclassicism was the official æsthetic everywhere. Originally a romantic invention and tainted for the modernists by its associations with Mendelssohn and Brahms, this had been rediscovered by Debussy and the Impressionists, who used it not for faking the past, as the Romantics had done, but for evoking it, for making hand-colored picture-books out of it.

The atonal school during this time was not very successful. Its practitioners did not get the good teaching jobs, and their works rarely made the big concerts. The first upturn of their fortunes would seem to date from the late 1920's, when Alban Berg's opera *Wozzeck* began making the big opera houses, at least in Central Europe. The racial and political persecutions that began in Germany shortly after this retarded, I think, the rising movement, though they hastened its dissemination throughout the Western world. The Schönberg school at this time became a sort of musical underground. When the smoke of World War II blew away in 1945, that underground turned out to have been an aid in what we may call, to carry out a metaphor, the musical liberation of France.

Today atonalism is on the rise again, and the neoclassic school wanes. In the final edifice of our century's music, it seems probable now that atonal harmony, completed by the new researches in asymmetrical rhythm, will have a place in the upper structure comparable to that already assigned to it in the ground plan. Impressionism and expressionism, in other words, are approaching integration. It is not yet predictable whether that integration will be a European achievement, like their invention, because both movements have today a world-wide practice. The French, the Italians, the Americans, and the Argentines are equally adept at their handling.

The most remarkable changes in the musical scene that have become visible since World War II are the removal of the world center of music's distribution from Europe to America and the emergence of an American school of composition. In 1900 everything good in music came out of Europe—works, even of popular music, executants, styles, ideas, teachers, publications. Today we own the world market in light music and export as much of the rest as anybody. New York has not yet monopolized contemporary "serious" publication, but it determines the world price of executants and pedagogues. It has become the musical stock exchange, the center of stabilization for musical opinion. It establishes reputations and fees, crowns careers with the ultimate honor just as Paris did in 1900, as Vienna did in 1800, and as Venice had done a century before that.

The 1950 picture, by nations, reads something like this. Three countries produce new music abundantly in good quality—France, Russia and the United States. The Russian production, on account of political interference, is lacking in scope just now, in elbow room both technical and expressive. The other two countries produce in all the kinds and keep up experimental effort. They lead the world, in fact, for " advance" in all directions. Italy, Argentina and Chile are also among the advanced; but none of these countries is doing much in the vein of public-pleasing serious music. That is Russia's specialty and a little bit England's, with Benjamin Britten a local Shostakovich. Neither country, however, produces this kind of work at as high a level

of sincerity and refinement as France's Poulenc and Messiaen
(the latter also an innovator).

Germany, Austria, Central Europe in general form a small
part of 1950's musical scene. Greece, Spain and Mexico have the
beginnings of a musical movement and an avid public; but their
social institutions are unfavorable. Brazil and Canada are good
public. The former has excellent composers but no school, no
style, no source save indigenous folklore. The republic of Israel
is music-mad from top to bottom. It offers, however, chiefly
executants and a warm audience. Its composing time is far from
ripe.

I do not think musical execution has improved in fifty years,
but the number of skilled executants available today is much
larger than it was. The number of symphony orchestras is also
larger, hugely. The number of opera houses is smaller. Neither
do I believe that musical pedagogy has improved at the top,
though there is far more good instruction available in provincial
centers than there used to be. Opera—its singing, its production, its composition—has declined spectacularly. So has ballet
since Diaghilev's first five years in France, 1909–14. The films,
which scarcely existed in 1900, have, on account of their higher
cost and the consequent necessity of appealing to a very large
public, made a virtually negligible contribution to the history
of music.

Radio's services and those of the gramophone have been
rather to distribute than to create. They have helped the spread
of knowledge, hastened the using up of works, activated composition very little. In Europe, however, the state radio, aware
of its cultural privileges, has by-passed the small audiences of
metropolitan *élites* that used to serve as opinion formers for advanced movements. Broadcasters now speak straight to the nation. In America radio plays no such cultural rôle, being wholly
in the hands of salesmen.

In conclusion, one may say that nothing has improved since
1900 save the size of the musical machine. The world situation
of music has altered in every detail, and in most cases there has
been a loss of distinction. Even the audience, though much
larger and, in the provinces, better informed than it was, is less
subtle, less intelligent, less sure of itself. As for Sunday articles,

they are written nowadays by people like me. In the early years of this century the critical fraternity contained Ernest Newman, a better historian, and Claude Debussy, a better composer.

January 8, 1950

A Poulenc Cantata

SCHOLA CANTORUM, *Hugh Ross,* conductor, last night at Carnegie Hall, performing, among other works, Poulenc's *Figure Humaine*, a choral setting of the poem by Paul Éluard.

FIGURE HUMAINE (or *The Face of Man*) is a poem of 160 lines by Paul Éluard celebrating clandestine French resistance to the German conquerors. It is plain in meaning, lilting of meter, and both fanciful and familiar as to imagery. Irresistibly touching in sentiment, it is also a work of no mean literary sophistication, a devotional and patriotic text. Francis Poulenc's music, no less straightforward in melodious contours and dramatic accents, is its match for both simplicity and inventive workmanship. The former quality keeps the verbal prosody clear without phraseo-logical distortions or undue extension of vowel sounds. The latter underlies a loose but ingenious linear construction in twelve-part counterpoint for unaccompanied double chorus. It has also added many delicate refinements to the harmony.

This harmony, like so much contemporary French writing, has an acoustical freedom that is more easily rendered by keyed instruments than by voices. Its progression from relatively con-sonant chords to highly dissonant ones and back again is not at all systematic. There is an accidental quality in the sound of it that resembles the seeming messiness of a great deal of the best French draughtsmanship. It looks careless, but it reads with utter clarity. This kind of vocal music is not easy to sing, but it can be sung. And when well sung, it has charm and a great freshness. *Figure Humaine* is a sweet, vigorous and lovely work; and the Schola Cantorum, led by Hugh Ross, gave it to us just that way.

February 18, 1950

On the Whole, Derivative

PHILHARMONIC-SYMPHONY ORCHESTRA, *Leonard Bernstein*, conductor, last night at Carnegie Hall, performing, among other works, Mr. Bernstein's Symphony No. 2 (*The Age of Anxiety*). Soloist: *Lukas Foss*, piano.

LEONARD BERNSTEIN's *The Age of Anxiety*, for pianoforte and orchestra, conducted by himself in a Philharmonic concert with Lukas Foss at the solo instrument, is a meditation on the poem of that title by W. H. Auden. Scored with a sure and ingenious hand, its chief interest for this observer lay in its orchestral timbres and their disposition. These are dominated, colored everywhere by the percussion choir and related sonorities of harp, piano, plucked strings. The textures are transparent, easy to hear, picturesque, expressive. The rhythm is lively, too, in the animated passages. Otherwise the work does not hold inevitably the musical attention. Its form is improvisatory, its melodic content casual, its harmony stiff, its counterpuntal tension weak. The piano writing is excellent; the figuration shines; the whole sounds out beautifully; but the expressive content seems to me (and I have read the score as well as heard it) banal, derivative in feeling.

A lugubrious beginning and some desultory variations on no theme are replaced half way through the piece by an active section for the solo instrument and percussion in the jazz style known as "Harlem party piano." This makes a most brilliant effect in the Gershwin taste. Then comes a finale out of Strauss's *Death and Transfiguration*. Over the whole floats an intangible shadow of Mahler. As a study in orchestration the work has interest for musicians. As a ballet it may support choreographic fantasy. As a concert piece it is lacking in the chief elements, or so it appears to me, that make for survival in repertory.

February 24, 1950

Unique and Unforgettable

NBC SYMPHONY ORCHESTRA, *Arturo Toscanini*, conductor, on the afternoon of April 1 in Studio 8-H, Radio City, performing the first half of Verdi's *Falstaff*, with *Giuseppe Valdengo* (Falstaff), *Frank Guarrera* (The Ford), and *Cloe Elmo* (Dame Quickly).

Arturo Toscanini directed in concert performance last Saturday afternoon the first half of Verdi's *Falstaff*. Next Saturday at the same hour—6:30 E.S.T.—the other half will be given. This reporter would like to add to the above bare announcement his feeling that those who miss hearing these performances (or their broadcast) will have passed over a unique and probably irreplaceable musical experience.

It is not that this opera does not here and there get given. It is simply that Verdi's great farce, for divers and complex reasons, almost never comes off in the theater. As instrumental music, as vocal music, and as pantomime, it is powerful like a bulldozer, elaborate like an electronic calculator, and yet simple and broad in its humor like a comic strip. It is the busiest opera in the world and the most exigent as to timing. It asks the singers to behave like clowns while singing with animation and precision. What they sing, moreover, is vocally difficult without being, in terms of audience effect, grateful. It is a conductor's opera, a virtuoso piece for the musical director. One might almost imagine it as having been especially designed for Mr. Toscanini.

The N.B.C. opera broadcasts in general are conceived as starring-machines for this conductor. Timing, the trajectory of an overall musical line comes first, orchestral refinement second, vocal charm last in their hierarchy of values. As correctives to a music world that more commonly cherishes these values in reverse order the N.B.C. operas have been tonic. They have also given us an opportunity to hear the most admired opera conductor of our century in the repertory that first brought him fame. Save for these broadcasts, Toscanini has not directed opera here in many years and seems determined not ever again to work in the American theater.

Falstaff, moreover, among all the works of standard repertory, is the one that profits most by the Toscanini treatment. No other conductor, in my experience, has ever made it sound so light and fast, filed its delicacies and its accents to so sharp an edge. He gives us, too, along with the music of it, an evocation of the stage, an essence of the theater, a concentration of comedy speeds and farce timings, a zest, an outline incomparable. His reading is a lesson to all who think that the theatrical circumstance profits by coarseness in texture or of appeal. Its steely elegance, like that of the score itself, is a far more powerful mover of audiences than any concession to vulgarity could possibly be.

The vocal execution on Saturday, though less brilliant, on the whole, than the orchestral, was clean and generally agreeable. This observation, I hasten to add, applies strictly to the center balcony seats of Studio 8-H. What the singers sounded like elsewhere in that tricky hall, or when heard through engineering adjustments, I cannot report. Listeners to these broadcasts have given highly divergent testimonies about vocal effectiveness.

April 3, 1950

For Teaching and for the Mind

CONCERT OF MUSIC BY JULIA SMITH AND LOU HARRISON, in the Composers' Forum series, on April 15 at McMillan Theater, Columbia University, featuring performances of, among other works, Miss Smith's *Folkways Symphony*, excerpts from her opera *The Gooseherd and the Goblin*, and Mr. Harrison's *Two Little Pastorals.*

THE COMPOSERS' FORUM gave us last Saturday night in the McMillan Theater of Columbia University one of its more entertaining contrasts. Music by Julia Smith and Lou Harrison made up the program. The easy-going jollity of the former set off perfectly the quiet poetry and intense auditory expertness of the latter without placing either at an unnecessary disadvantage.

Miss Smith had mobilized two pianists, three singers, two conductors (including herself) and an orchestra of some forty players. She produced with these forces extended selections from a fairy-tale opera, a five-piece twelve-tone piano suite, and a symphony on American folk airs. All were marked by animation, clear expressive intent and a preoccupation with the school trade.

Mr. Harrison, with a quartet of string players, a solo cellist, a harpist, and three works of the most unassuming dimensions, produced memorable music. His Suite for Cello and Harp is, I think, not really a suite, but rather a group of four pieces united technically by their use of scales as thematic material. The whole is delicate of sound, thoroughly alive rhythmically and melodically, evocative of some tranquil and vibrant scene. Few composers now alive can fascinate the ear, as Mr. Harrison does, with simple procedures. At once plain and sophisticated, his music reflects a concentration on music's basic elements that is as expressive, surprisingly, as it is intrinsically interesting.

His Suite for Strings, No. 2, consists of two movements in secundal diatonic counterpoint framing a chromatic duet for violin and viola. All three are canonic in structure. The whole work, lyrically conceived, is a meditation on Sebastian Bach's contrapuntal style-sources. It could not be more delightful to listen to, more musical, more graciously songful. Like the cello and harp suite, it communicates a beatitude as of Elysian Fields.

The evening's final delight (preceding the forum discussion) was a pair of Pastorals for strings that imitate the sound of a vielle, or medieval hurdy-gurdy. Sophisticated, picturesque, and exquisitely melodious, these pieces use Mr. Harrison's elaborate skill in composition toward the service of an utterly simple expressive purpose. And they, too, transport us to a dream world where all is music, really music, really interesting musically, really sensitive and elaborate and lovely and not about anything in the world but how beautiful the materials of music can be when handled with tenderness and with intelligence.

April 17, 1950

Joan of Arc to Music

THE TRIUMPH OF JOAN, opera in three acts, libretto by *Norman Dello Joio* and *Joseph Machilis*, music by *Mr. Dello Joio*, performed by students and faculty of Sarah Lawrence College, *Hugh Ross*, choral conductor, on May 9 at Bates Hall, Sarah Lawrence College, Bronxville, New York, with *Gisela Fischer* (Joan), *Jerome Swinford* (Bishop Cauchon), and *John Druary* (The Dauphin).

NORMAN DELLO JOIO's lyric drama *The Triumph of Joan* was recently produced at Sarah Lawrence College. The music of the spectacle seems to me more vigorous than its dramatic composition. The latter contains no element of plot or character not familiar to contemporary audiences, and the tension of the narrative is low. The device of presenting this through memories recalled during the Maid's imprisonment gives the story a static quality, and the fact that all but one of the episodes (her acceptance as a military leader by the Dauphin) show her as unsuccessful in some immediate objective gives a depressive tone to the recital. The Maid's own meditations, moreover, which bind the remembered scenes together, consist largely of self-pity. The whole libretto lacks animation and lift.

The music is more inspired. This is at its most distinguished in the set-pieces. The coronation choruses, a lonesome soldier's song about a girl, Bishop Cauchon's prayer before the courtroom scene, the music accompanying Joan's march to the stake— all these have imagination, character, force. The recitative passages are vocally a bit wooden and instrumentally static. Their melismatic line and note-heavy harmonies do not easily move along. The purely instrumental passages are all delicious. They evoke the late medieval world with poignancy and grandeur. So does the choral writing. But the solo voice more often than not, and particularly when it is that of Joan herself, seems to deprive the composer of that boldness and freedom that are elsewhere his. The background of the story he has described with abundance of fancy. The saint, one suspects, he found a slight bore. Certainly her monotonous insistence, in this text, on how she is always right and everybody else is wrong might well provoke impatience.

The recitative line is derived from Gregorian chant. It moved diatonically for the most part and in skips of the minor third. Larger skips, which give such force to dramatic declamation, are few in number. The vocal line, as a result, is more atmospheric than communicative. The references to fourteenth-century musical styles that give to the ballet and to the church scenes power and picturesqueness have a weakening effect on the solo passages. Here they depersonalize the text, give it a ritual tone, retard its movement, diminish the possibilities of characterization. A spectacle that is full of fine music comes off, as a result, a bit heavily for audience comfort. Normally, recitative should speed the play and set-pieces hold it back where emotion needs time for expansion. In *The Triumph of Joan* it is the set-pieces that give whatever movement there is. The verbal text is somewhat at fault in this matter, but I think the musical text is too. Both harmonically and melodically it is a little stiff in dealing with persons. The music of the soldier and that of Cauchon are exceptions and welcome. The work, indeed, is full of handsome music; but as a theater piece it lacks variety of pace.

May 11, 1950

A Specialty of Our City

STADIUM SYMPHONY ORCHESTRA, *Alexander Smallens,* conductor, last night at Lewisohn Stadium, City College of New York, presenting the twentieth annual George Gershwin Night program. Soloist: *Oscar Levant,* piano.

GERSHWIN NIGHT at the Stadium, complete with Alexander Smallens and Oscar Levant, was attended last night by some twenty-three thousand persons. This estimate by the box-office people, who ought to know, is larger by three thousand than the seating capacity of the place. Neighboring rooftops were not untenanted either. Whether the music's sound was also audible in the passing airplanes I cannot say. We heard theirs, as usual.

We also heard a great deal of lovely music. For George Gershwin was a maker of tunes. There is life in them and grace and a wonderful sweet tenderness. They are sewn together no matter how in the symphonic works and orchestrated by no matter whom. And still they speak and are moving. They are music, our music, everybody's music. Their annual performance, moreover, is one of New York's specialties.

Not that other cities do not have their annual Gershwin Night, and often with Oscar Levant playing the *Rhapsody in Blue* and the Piano Concerto. But the New York population (you can't call 23,000 people by any lesser noun) has an especial love for this composer. He was one of them. And Alexander Smallens, also a New Yorker, has an especial knack for playing him.

No other conductor reads Gershwin with quite the ease that Smallens does, or half the seriousness. The commercial leaders play this music without depth, and the symphonic conductors play it mostly without feeling. Smallens allows its melodic line to speak in the vernacular without vulgarity and without pomposity. He actually gives you real Gershwin and a real symphonic sound at the same time. The achievement is unique, delightful and utterly distinguished.

Nothing of the above applies to the Concerto in F, as played last night. Not that either straightforward Smallens or the impeccable Oscar was lacking in observance of the musical amenities. It is simply a piece so poorly conceived, with its overweening Tchaikovskian intent, and so weakly inspired, with its derivative themes and mechanical developments, that it rarely sails before the wind. It asks, moreover, on every orchestral page, for an oratorical rendering, though without offering matter for oratory. There is no choice but to give it the "wow" treatment, to simulate in performance the Tchaikovsky-like passions and climaxes that the composer has simulated in his composition.

So treated last night, the Concerto in F came out as a nervous piece and very loud. Levant produced huge sounds, and not at all ugly ones, from the pianoforte. Smallens drew massive sonorities, and occasionally quite ugly ones, from the orchestra. Every phrase, every turn, every grace-note was blown up to Holy Scripture authority and stentorian volume. The result was as portentous as a radio commercial, and about as convincing.

July 7, 1950

Taste Survey

THE INDIANAPOLIS SYMPHONY ORCHESTRA has recently tab-
ulated the results of a musical preference poll carried out last
spring among season-ticket holders. The survey was conducted
by Dr. Dennison Nash, of Washington University, St. Louis,
Missouri, and seems to have observed all the devices of fairness
required by the statistical profession. Answers were sought to
the following questions:

1. What types of music does the Indianapolis audience prefer?
2. What specific composers?
3. Does the symphony audience approve of Dr. Sevitzky's
   [the conductor's] policy of fostering American music?
4. What is its attitude toward "modern" music?
5. Do men and women differ in their music tastes?
6. What types of music are preferred by listeners of different
   ages?

The answers to questions 1 and 2 will astonish no one. By
dividing the symphonic repertory into five style-periods—
classic (meaning before Beethoven), classic-romantic (meaning
Beethoven), romantic (centering around Brahms and Tchaikovsky), modern (including Debussy, Sibelius and Gershwin)
and extreme modern—the result obtained was that symphony
subscribers prefer the romantic style. This taste tends to diminish, however, after forty in favor of the classic-romantic style,
which is that of Beethoven. Music written before Beethoven
has its highest preference among the very young and the very
old. Those in middle life care least for it. Ten composers are
preferred by the whole audience in the following order—
Beethoven, Tchaikovsky, Brahms, Bach, Mozart, Wagner, Debussy, Chopin, Sibelius, and Haydn.

American music and its performance are resoundingly encouraged by the poll. One-fourth of the audience would accept
as much as half the playing-time from this category. Another
fourth would limit American works to five per cent of the repertory. Forty-five per cent of the listeners would settle for a ten
per cent Americanism in the programs, which has long been the
proportion observed in Indianapolis. No particular American
composer seems to be favored. It is American work in general

that the audience enjoys, very much as Italian and French and Russian audiences have long been known to respond favorably to a musical diet rich in home-grown products.

This preference contradicts the conviction of many orchestral managements that American music is not popular. The truth is probably that it is not comparable with name soloists for attracting single-concert ticket purchasers to the box office, but that it is highly approved by season subscribers. Boston's experience corroborates this judgment. Its sold-out subscription houses have never raised any serious complaints against American music. Indeed, these have ever taken pride in the high interest and toleration they have been able to show toward the large amounts of American music long characteristic of Boston programs.

Modernism also comes in for an accolade. The Indianapolis audience (and this surprises even me) expresses a willingness to hear as much "extreme modern" music as it does of Beethoven, its favorite composer. Beethoven's present percentage of the playing time is probably around twelve. Thirty-one per cent of the subscribers would even accept as much as half the programs devoted to modern music.

Sex, you may be pleased to learn, plays no role in musical taste. Men and women at all ages, according to Dr. Nash's survey, appear to like exactly the same works, authors and styles.

Age, on the other hand, is a huge determinant. Those really receptive to modernism are almost all under forty and mostly under thirty. These ages want lots of modern music, including all the "extreme," or "dissonant" types; and they constitute an audience for this by no means negligible in numbers. Our orchestras should ideally, in order to serve the whole public, play two series of programs, one for the elderly and another for those under forty. Their present efforts to please everybody at once derive from a paucity of rehearsal time, no doubt; but I am sure that somewhere behind them is an assumption that mature taste is the best taste and that it should dominate. The present survey has surely rendered culture a service in calling attention to the fact that those under forty have tastes of their own, that these are not the same as those of their elders and that there will be a long period after forty when they will be older persons themselves and can listen to all the Beethoven there is.

Another service of this survey (although a shocking one) is contained in a study of the influence of regular symphony-concert attendance on anybody's taste. For the first year romantic preferences run high, and so do those for modern composers. After one year of attendance, however, there is a sharp drop in both tastes and a strong move toward the classic-romantic, or Beethoven-dominated repertory. After that there is little change save for a slowly increasing interest in the classic, or pre-Beethoven, masters and a decreasing toleration of the contemporary. This evolution runs parallel, of course, to the changes in taste that accompany maturity. The striking data for education are those that show the active influence of regular orchestra-concert attendance on any subscriber's taste to be limited to the first year. That is the time when the whole educational benefit is operated. Afterwards very little takes place. Dr. Nash concludes his report with the statement that "an increasing length of concert attendance is associated with a narrower and narrower preference range, i.e., a greater preference for fewer [and fewer] composers."

September 17, 1950

Golden Throat

VICTORIA DE LOS ANGELES, soprano, in recital last night at Carnegie Hall, performing songs in Italian, German, Italian, and English. Accompanist: *Paul Berl*, piano.

VICTORIA DE LOS ANGELES, singing last night in Carnegie Hall, won the votes of a large audience with her very first piece. By the last one, these had turned into a general acclaim. Success was hers and by no narrow margin. Speaking purely as a musician, your reviewer finds himself wholly in accord with that success. The voice is one of rare natural beauty, the schooling impeccable, the artistry first class. Miss de los Angeles is a real singer. Make no mistake about it.

She is also a young singer. Her interpretations of German lieder are still a little mannered. And she withholds her high notes. She takes them commandingly but she diminishes usually before they have given their full delight. Only a few times during the evening did she omit to tease the searcher after effects of obvious vocalism. Indeed, so careful was she not to insist on bravura utterance that it is a little hard to know just how high and how loud she can sing. A perfect vowel projection, whether in pianissimo or in forte singing, filled the hall at all times with vibrancy, beauty, warmth of tone. Nothing was ever forced and nothing failed to carry. She is a true lyric soprano, does not need to falcon.

Her most striking gifts are a natural cantilena, or sense of melody, and a complete ease in florid passages. She tossed these in the Handel aria as lightly and as accurately as a pianist might play them in a piece by Mozart or Chopin. Indeed, an unhesitating precision about pitches marked all her work. She sang not only beautifully but true. Her kind of ear and training are rare these days, and one could not be more grateful to be reminded that they have not been lost to music. To find them guiding a voice that is sweet, young, and fresh is more than surprising. Here is vocal delight unique in our time. I must say that this delight, being attained wholly through vowel vocalism, was not accompanied by much clarity of enunciation. At least, not in the Italian and German works, plus one English piece, that made up more than half her program. In Spanish she really pronounced. Consonants clicked like castanets, and the bright Spanish vowels glowed like copper and shining brass. Perhaps she does not have the gift of tongues. But she does relish her own. And whatever the tongue, she has a golden throat.

October 25, 1950

Milhaud Compared

PHILHARMONIC-SYMPHONY ORCHESTRA, *Dimitri Mitropoulos*, conductor, with the WESTMINSTER CHOIR, last night at Carnegie Hall, performing, among other works, Milhaud's music for *Les Choéphores*, a drama from Aeschylus by Paul Claudel, with *Mack Harrell* (Orestes), *Eileen Farrell* (Elektra), and *Madeleine Milhaud* (Narrator).

DIMITRI MITROPOULOS, conducting the Philharmonic-Symphony Orchestra, the Westminster Choir, seven vocal soloists, and Madeleine Milhaud, who spoke, gave in Carnegie Hall last night Darius Milhaud's music composed for Paul Claudel's French translation of *Choephoroi* (The Libation-Bearers) by Aeschylus.

The story of this work, recited, is plain, its music broadly conceived. Its climax, a passage for speaking voice and shouting chorus accompanied only by percussion, is as terrifying on a platform as on a stage. Rarely, indeed, in any presentation does the fury of Aeschylus communicate itself so powerfully as in this French version.

The work invites comparison with Strauss's *Elektra*. The Austrian composer's music-drama is all of a piece, violent and sensual. Also, it is a musical structure throughout. Milhaud's tragedy is statuesque, monumental, objective, sculptured in granite till the speaking begins. Here tonal music ends; words and rhythms take over; and the dramatic impact becomes direct, immediate. Then there is music again, and at the end a brief return to speech and percussion. Whatever disunity may be felt by some spectators between the differing dramatic tensions of the speech passages and the singing passages is probably compensated by the composer's obvious determination to give you a Greek tragedy with all the ritualistic tension and all the horror of mood that the text implies. He has not written an opera, nor attempted one. He has brought an ancient work of poetry to life. The achievement is as impressive as *The Libation-Bearers* itself is. *Les Choéphores* probes the mind, plows deep in the feelings, shakes foundations. It has the power of great poetry. *Elektra*, for all its musical concentration, does not quite, in your reporter's experience of it, have that.

November 17, 1950

1951

Israel in America

ISRAEL PHILHARMONIC ORCHESTRA, *Serge Koussevitzky*, conductor, on January 13 at Carnegie Hall, performing *Psalm*, from Paul Ben-Haim's Symphony No. 1, Prokofiev's Symphony No. 5, and Tchaikovsky's Symphony No. 4.

THE ISRAEL PHILHARMONIC ORCHESTRA, conducted by Serge Koussevitzky, played its second New York concert last Saturday night in Carnegie Hall. Its first had taken place last Monday night at the Hotel Waldorf-Astoria, following a $100-a-plate dinner. A second Carnegie Hall concert was conducted last night by Leonard Bernstein.

Mr. Koussevitzky's program, for reasons impenetrable by this reviewer, turned out to be a Russian program. One brief compliment to Israel itself preceded the Slavic devotions. That compliment was a slow movement, entitled *Psalm*, from the Symphony No. 1 by Ben-Haim, an Israeli citizen of German birth formerly named Paul Frankenburger. This is a lyrical work, near-Eastern by its melodic allegiance to chants from the Hebrew liturgy but wholly West-European in its climactic structure. The central climax, indeed, of this sustained pastoral movement is an outpouring of song that carries high conviction. This listener would have preferred hearing the rest of the symphony to sitting through Prokofiev's Fifth, which followed it. Tchaikovsky's Fourth, which concluded the program, also told us more about Mr. Koussevitzky's hand with familiar repertory than about the musical temper of Israel.

The orchestra has a string body of unusual skill and power. Wind solos were played with grace, but nowhere in the wind ensemble was there brightness, brilliance, or any fullness of sound comparable to that of the strings. These played with the impeccable flexibility and with the unanimity of sound that mark the string playing of great orchestras. Volume, delicacy, finesse, and all the varieties of handsome tone are available to them. If the strings have any fault, that would lie in a tendency of the first violins to dominate all the other sections and to render thus some of the balances a little top-heavy.

Hearing Koussevitzky (or Bernstein, either) can be a pleasure, even when the pieces played have little to offer that is fresh to the ear. But bringing a whole orchestra from Tel Aviv just to offer these artists in familiar repertory is surely carrying perfume to Paris. Has Israel no confidence in its own conductors? Or in its own music? Or in America's thirst for that which is new as well as of good report?

Israel is news, and Israel is popular. Its orchestra, moreover, has the major element of a fine orchestra. It must have also a musical orientation, as any region or country does. When a French or British or Italian orchestra is heard in New York, its programs and its playing reflect musical attitudes different from ours. That is its chief contribution. The Israel Philharmonic, as here presented, offers nothing of the kind. Even its admirable strings, for all their warmth and sweetness, are not very different from those of our own best orchestras. When we are given at the same time two of our own best conductors playing their own best pieces, we learn nothing about Israel save that its orchestra is a link in the international guest-conducting chain.

January 15, 1951

Supercilious and Arty

CAVALLERIA RUSTICANA, opera in one act, music by *Pietro Mascagni*, staged by *Hans Busch*, and I PAGLIACCI, opera in two acts, music by Ruggero Leoncavalo, staged by *Max Leavitt*, last night at the Metropolitan Opera House, *Alberto Erede*, conductor.

CAV AND PAG, done over from scratch (and it was about time), drew a demonstrative audience to the Metropolitan Opera House last night. The conductor, Alberto Erede, did not play up much their Italianate vividness, their urgency. He seemed rather to be seeking in them grace and transparency, for all the world as if they were oratorios by Saint-Saëns.

Neither had the mounters and stagers of these new productions made much effort to keep that essential Italianness. Horace Armistead's set for *Cavalleria Rusticana* was a Sicilian village of today, and the singers all wore the kind of clothes modern Sicilians wear. But their gestures were straight out of Victorian English melodrama. Laundry on the line hit a trivial note. A statue of the Madonna, carried in an Easter procession, gave a false one. A large chorus walked into church and never came out again. There was a great deal of running around and crossing of bridges. Indeed, the whole tragic story came out slightly humorous, as if it were being observed by tourists. A supercilious note was present in the scenery, the costumes, and the staging; and as a result this ever so plain and touching drama wavered, from being poked fun at, between a tasteless joke and plain bathos.

Pagliacci, though more tasteful in conception, was even farther removed from Italian melodrama. It seemed to be taking place in the ruins of a recently bombed building, though the costumes were of no period recognizable to this reporter. Stylizations derived from contemporary ballet were also present in Max Leavitt's stage direction. The spectacle had color and fancy, but it was more an artistic evocation of *Pagliacci* than a direct rendering. If the music had not been there to reassure one that the piece, for all its universality of appeal, is utterly and completely Italian, one could have easily imagined it as taking place in the ruins of Berlin among the homeless members of some modern-dance troupe.

Modernizing operas like these is not a rewarding effort. They do not lend themselves to indirection, to added poetry, or to intellectual embellishment. All evening I was reminded of the French chef who in serving a New England boiled dinner had carved the beets like roses and turned turnips into lilies. *Cav* and *Pag* are spaghetti alla Napolitana. They can be done poorly or well. But their classical presentation cannot be altered to advantage.

January 18, 1951

Flagstad and Reiner

TRISTAN UND ISOLDE, opera in three acts by *Richard Wagner*, last night at the Metropolitan Opera House, *Fritz Reiner*, conductor, with *Kirsten Flagstad* (Isolde), *Ramon Vinay* (Tristan), and *Blanche Thebom* (Brangaene).

STANDING APPLAUSE and lengthy cheers (nineteen curtain calls) were the reward of Kirsten Flagstad last night after the first act of Wagner's *Tristan und Isolde* at the Metropolitan Opera

House. Absent from that stage for ten years, she has returned with her vocal powers intact and her dramatic projection more imperious than ever. In a house that has long given the Wagner operas better, on the whole, than anything else, Miss Flagstad still set the place afire. Vocally vast and impeccable, and dramatically as convincing as this statuesque work allows, she held the attention and drew the gratitude of even so seasoned an anti-Wagnerian as this reporter. She also, and quite literally, held the center of the stage throughout the first act by working in a circle not much larger than twelve feet across, right in the middle down front.

This maneuver kept Blanche Thebom, her Brangaene, constantly up stage or off side. As a result, though she sang richly she could not match for volume the sounds that Miss Flagstad projected from downstage center. In the second act, however, she got that spot herself for a short moment and rang out handsomely. Ramon Vinay, as Tristan, came nearer being a match for the soprano.

Besides Miss Flagstad, the other star of the evening was Fritz Reiner. Transparency in the sound, flexibility and firmness in the beat, meaning and incandescence in the whole made the work what it really is, a symphonic poem with vocal *obbligato*. Mr. Reiner was respectful of that *obbligato* and gave it acoustical elbow room. But his orchestra, where all the real characterization and the continuity take place in this piece, was the source of musical line and substance. Save for the delights of the Flagstad voice, which are huge, the musical pleasure of the evening lay for this listener in an instrumental reading by Fritz Reiner that was no less impeccable than Flagstad's vocal one and far more intricate musically. That, after all, is the nature of the composition.

January 23, 1951

Reactionary Critic

EDUARD HANSLICK, a Bohemian born in 1825 in Prague, came to Vienna in 1846 as a law student. He had already received a musical education, had met Schumann and Wagner, corresponded with Berlioz, and written music criticism. While preparing his doctorate in law, which he took in 1849, he continued to write music criticism, for most of which he was not paid. His first Viennese contribution was an analysis of Wagner's *Tannheuser*, published by the *Wiener Musikzeitung* in eleven installments. Hanslick was at this time a deep admirer of Wagner's genius and music. Till his death he continued to admire the genius; but from *Lohengrin* on, which he reviewed from the Vienna production of 1858, he did not approve the music.

Meanwhile, by easy stages, he had given up law (or rather the civil service career for which it had prepared him) and become a salaried reviewer of music in the daily press. From 1855 to 1864 he wrote for *Die Presse* and from 1864 to his retirement in 1895 for *Die Neue Freie Presse*. From 1861 he was Extra-ordinary Professor of the History and Aesthetics of Music at the University of Vienna. In the middle 1850's he had written a book on *Beauty in Music*. Thereafter, at the university and in print, he posed as world-expert and final authority on the subject. A classical education and a facile pen enabled him to defend his assumed position with ingenuity and wit. His determination to uphold the cause of classicism in music involved him in systematic denial of the artistic validity of Liszt, Berlioz, Wagner, Bruckner, Hugo Wolf, Verdi, and Richard Strauss. He barely tolerated Tchaikovsky and Dvořák, ignored wholly the rising movement in Russia and France. Henselt, Lachner, and Johann Strauss he always mentioned benevolently. The dead—Schumann, Schubert, Mendelssohn, Weber, Beethoven, Mozart, Handel, Bach—he treated with respect. The only living composer of class that he deigned to defend was Brahms. His banner Hanslick carried aloft as the banner of counter-revolution till his own death in 1904.

Except for his early brochure on *Beauty in Music* Hanslick's work has not till now been available in English. Henry Pleasants III, formerly music critic of the *Philadelphia Evening Bulletin*, has recently edited and translated admirably a selection of Hanslick's reviews, complete with notes and biographical preface, under the title of *Vienna's Golden Years of Music: 1850–1900* (Simon and Schuster, N.Y., 1950, 31 illustrations, 341 pp., $3.75). One is grateful for even this brief acquaintance with the man Wagner pilloried as Beckmesser in *Die Meistersinger*. One is pleased to learn that he was not, as Wagner gave him to us, a bad composer, a lecher, and a boor, but a skilled belles-lettrist and a master reporter. One is charmed, too, by his literary culture, his musical penetration and smooth easy man-of-the-world ways. Reading him lightly, one might almost take him for the perfect music critic, if perfection is conceivable in so invidious a genre.

But no, three times no! Once because there was no real warmth in the man. Twice because the truth was not in him. And thrice because he never stuck his neck out.

To those who may think a twenty-five-year war with Richard Wagner enough bravery to ask of any man, I recall that Wagner did not live in Vienna and that Hanslick's readers, who did, were middle-aged, well-to-do, bourgeois. He wrote for a conservative paper. His readers asked no better than to see a man of novel genius reduced to the level of an incompetent entertainer. Critics writing all over Europe on conservative papers—Chorley in London, Fétis in Paris, not to speak of the German reviewers—had given Wagner the same treatment; and in 1856 *The New York Times* had denied to *Lohengrin* "a dozen bars that could be called real melody." Anybody knows it is easier to defend the public against novelty in art than it is to defend an original artist against the public's comfortable conservatism.

Actually there is not a point in Hanslick's attacks on Wagner that had not been made before. Berlioz, Meyerbeer, Rossini, and the young Bizet had long since put their finger on the inequalities in his talent. These were common knowledge in music circles. Time has not altered, moreover, their reality. Wagner's contemporaries, including Hanslick, denied him no excellence for which he is still cherished. Nor were even his closest friends, save a few, unaware of his imperfections. Even Hanslick's main theme about how for all its beauties this music is not "the music of the future," not a beginning but a glorious and dangerous end, that too was a familiar idea. That is what the famous Wagner "case" has always been about, and Hanslick did not invent it. As a matter of fact, his reviews spent far more space unmasking Wagner's literary weaknesses, which he was capable of doing quite well, than analyzing the musical structure which he could not always follow, even with a score. He knew that Wagner could orchestrate, paint tremendous musical landscape scenes, and prosodize in German; but he had not the musical technique to understand Wagner's complex chromatic harmony and asymmetrical rhythm. So he complained about the "lack of melody," made fun of the librettos, and refuted the advertising. Compared with Nietzsche on Wagner, he was thoroughly superficial.

To protect himself against the possible charge of not patronizing home industry, Hanslick had sagaciously picked on Brahms as his "side" in the Brahms-Wagner war. He was sold this position by a surgeon named Billroth, who was a close friend of Brahms, and who, according to Dr. Max Graf, Hanslick's successor on the *Neue Freie Presse*, furnished the critic with analyses of Brahms's works. Hanslick cared little for Brahms; what he really liked was waltzes, light airs, and Offenbach. But Brahms was useful to him, and he to Brahms. The pair of them, if stories of the time and Bruckner's letters are to be believed, carried on a relentless intrigue, aided by two other critics who were also friends of Brahms, to prevent Bruckner's rise in popularity from endangering the carefully constructed celebrity of the older man. Brahms's ironic gesture of gratitude was the dedication to Hanslick of his *Love Waltzes*. To Billroth, who understood depth and complexity, he dedicated two of his grander quartets.

Hanslick could describe a performer to perfection—Liszt, von Bülow, Clara Schumann, Lilli Lehmann, Adelina Patti. He tells you what they looked like, the kind of sounds they made, the nature of their technique, and the character of their temperaments. His musical analysis of any composition was elementary and timid, reads like a quoted program note. Also he was a dirty fighter. He was a dirty fighter because his extraordinary intellectual and literary powers were used solely to convince people that he alone was right and all the living composers, except for a few minor melodists and for Brahms, were wrong. A mere reviewer, a belles-lettrist, a reporter, and a professor of Music Appreciation (the first, I believe), he pitted himself in his own column against the creative forces of the age. Anywhere but in his own column, or surrounded by its glamour in a Viennese salon, he was just another irate customer complaining about modern music. In his column, and in private intrigues, he was formidable.

Having gone through my two provable indictments in reverse order, I am now back to the first, which is a matter of feeling.

For me there is no warmth in the man, no juice, no passion for music. Sensuality, grace, some sparkle, a gift for ridicule, and a colossal vanity shine through his selected reviews. So does the insincerity of his pretended love for Brahms's music. He states it over and over, but he cannot make it glow. What comes through everything is an ever-so-careful conformism to the bourgeois tastes of his time, which, I am very sorry to say, are still the tastes of bourgeois Vienna at home and abroad. But he did not invent even these. He invented nothing but the style and attitude of the modern newspaper review. That, with all its false profundity and absurd pretensions to "sound" judgment, he will probably have to defend at everybody's Last Judgment. He was second-rate clean through, and he had no heart. Max Graf thinks highly of Hanslick's literary gift. "His essays and articles," says Dr. Graf in his excellent book, *Composer and Critic*, "have been published in twelve volumes, in which his intelligence, charm, clarity, and wit are preserved, like drugs and poisons in cut-glass vessels on the shelves of a pharmacy." "Venom from contented rattlesnakes" was the late Percy Hammond's term for similar critical contributions.

February 4, 1951

From the Heart

PHILHARMONIC-SYMPHONY ORCHESTRA, *Leonard Bernstein*, conductor, last night at Carnegie Hall, performing, among other works, Ives's Symphony No. 2.

LEONARD BERNSTEIN, conducting the Philharmonic-Symphony Orchestra last night in Carnegie Hall, gave us Charles Ives's Second Symphony, a work composed in the late 1890s but never before performed in its entirety. This is a five-movement rhapsodic meditation on American hymns of the nineteenth century, American dance ditties, and football songs. It is essentially a landscape piece with people in it.

The first movement gives us the lush Connecticut valley through a musical technique derived from the Bach chorale-preludes. It is sustained, songful, organ-like, graciously contrapuntal, predominantly a piece for strings, with at the end a

quotation from "Columbia, the Gem of the Ocean" to make
the note of faith specific.

From here on, song and dance material dominate. There
is an ecstatic slow movement based on the hymns "Bringing
in the Sheaves" and "Beulah Land." There are two animated
movements involving dance music and the Yale "Boola Boola"
song, with a restatement in the last one of the initial landscape
material and an apotheosis in which "Columbia, the Gem of
the Ocean" sails out complete over a busy texture containing
dances and gay songs in contradictory keys. A Fourth of July
picnic might well be the scene here evoked. Orchestrally, harmonically, and melodically the symphony is both noble and
plain. It speaks of American life with love and humor and faith.
It is unquestionably an authentic work of art, both as structure
and as communication.

February 23, 1951

Successful Modernism

PHILHARMONIC-SYMPHONY ORCHESTRA, *Dimitri Mitropou-
los*, conductor, with SCHOLA CANTORUM, last night at Carnegie
Hall, performing music from *Wozzeck*, opera in three acts, libretto by
George Büchner and *Alban Berg*, music by *Mr. Berg*, with *Mack Harrell*
(Wozzeck) and *Eileen Farrell* (Marie).

WOZZECK, the atonal opera that brought fame and financial security to its composer Alban Berg way back in the middle twenties, brought a full house to Carnegie Hall last night. Played
and sung as a concert piece by the Philharmonic-Symphony
Orchestra and a cast of admirable vocalists under the direction
of Dimitri Mitropoulos, it attracted an audience of music lovers,
opera lovers, atonality fans, and German literature devotees that
should reduce to folly anybody's idea that modern music is not
box-office. The occasion also disproved for all time, I imagine,
any belief that anybody might have retained that Alban Berg's
music is in any way recondite.

The music of this opera and its plot, as told by the music, are
easier to follow than *Madama Butterfly*. The tragic story about a
soldier who kills his girl is plain and deeply touching. The music

that points this up, blows it up, one might say, to epic pathos, is constantly on the job, alert, abundant, imaginative, and far easier to follow in its meaning than Wagner. The vocal line imitates, in large exaggeration, the cadences of speech. The orchestral composition gives in detail both the setting of every scene and its full emotional implications. Persons and locales that the composer disapproves are caricatured in broad strokes. Those for which he feels tenderness are caressed with a love no one could mistake. The whole is a theater piece that has never failed to move its hearers and that should certainly be in the repertory of our resident opera troupes.

There is charm in the music, moreover. For those unaccustomed to off-key harmonic textures it is a little surprising right off. But after fifteen minutes all sounds normal. The waltzes, the military references, the devotional music, the satire, the eerie landscapes, the scene of soldiers snoring, all the picturesque paraphernalia of it come forward in their off-center tonal garb even more sharply than if they were wrapped up in classroom chords and counterpoints. The dissonant interval-syntax actually serves the communication as no other idiom could do. It floodlights the meaning of everything until all that is left of the high dissonance content is a thin veil of dazzle, like that from a neon or fluorescent bulb. It does not get in the way. On the contrary, it becomes early in the opera an element of pleasure all the more welcome from its services to comprehensibility.

April 13, 1951

Pretentious and Unclear

PHILHARMONIC-SYMPHONY ORCHESTRA, *Dimitri Mitropoulos*, conductor, last night at Carnegie Hall, performing, among other works, music from *Arlecchino*, opera in one act by *Ferruccio Busoni*, with *John Brownlee* (Arlecchino).

BUSONI's *Arlecchino* (*The Harlequin*) was the novelty of last night's Philharmonic program. Though the Busoni comic opera is subtitled a "theatrical capriccio," your informant has long found himself resistant to the idea that there is either fun or funniness in this work. At this point his objections end. It is skillfully composed, intellectually and musically sophisticated to the last degree, a major effort of a major musician. Also, its execution, though a bit loud throughout, was a triumph of loving care on the part of Dimitri Mitropoulos, who conducted.

Reviewing this opera from a Berlin performance in 1946, your correspondent found that its music contained everything but "plain feeling." Having recently read it in score and last night heard it again, he remains of that opinion. It represents a hopeless effort to combine Italian animation with the heaviest sort of German satire and an equally impossible desire to eliminate schmalz from the German operatic style without renovating the late Romantic and early Modernist harmonic vocabulary of Germany, in which that schmalz is firmly embedded. The composer had, besides, no talent at all for writing tunes. The result is a mess all the more pitiful from its author's accomplished musicianship, high motivation, and, let's say it, overweaning ambition.

October 12, 1951

Essentially Frivolous

JASCHA HEIFETZ, violinist, in recital last night at Carnegie Hall, performing, among other works, Schubert's Sonatina No. 3, Bruch's Concerto in C minor, and the Richard Strauss Violin Sonata. Accompanist: *Emmanuel Bay*, piano.

JASCHA HEIFETZ, playing a violin recital last night in Carnegie Hall, proved himself still a king among violin operators. In the opinion of many this king can do no wrong. Certainly the dictum holds if you define as "right" whatever the king does. But if you admit in advance that he might, just might be guilty of something, then you do not have to look very far to find something for him to be guilty of.

What Heifetz is guilty of (always supposing, just supposing, that he might be less than perfect) has always been the same thing, a certain lightness of mind commonly known as bad taste. Technically, he plays the violin better than anybody else living. He makes unusually pretty sounds, too. It was the appropriateness of the kind of sounds he used last night to the pieces he used them on that could be called in question as taste. So was the choice of pieces that he played, since the Strauss Sonata and the Bruch C-minor Concerto, entertaining as they are for demonstrating instrumental mastery, are not really serious repertory for a serious artist of his fame to play in a New York recital. The Schubert Sonatina No. 3 might have been, had he played it more graciously, made one feel less than he did that one had somehow got on the *Queen Mary* to go to Brooklyn.

The faults of taste that occur within an interpretation by Heifetz, almost any interpretation, have to do with irregularities in the application of right-arm weight. His bow-stroke is likely to be so emphatic that it produces, even on an up-bow in a soft passage, accents that are no proper part of the music's line. He makes crescendos, too, in the middle of notes that have no rhetorical importance, simply, one imagines, because he finds it interesting to vary the tonal weight. As a result, his melodic line, for all its perfection of pitch and sweetness of sound, has no continuing emotional tension and makes no sustained musical sense. Not, at any rate, in the way that I understand emotional tension and musical sense.

It is this teasing way of treating musical sounds and musical structures that led me long ago to consider Mr. Heifetz as essentially a frivolous artist, in spite of his incomparable mastery of violinistic operations. There is no weakness in him; he can do anything he wants to do with the instrument. There is merely, for the listener, a vast banality about what he seems to want, or at any rate to be satisfied with, as musical communication. I am not inclined, even, to grant him the word "communication." "Effects," rather, are what he produces for me.

November 22, 1951

Spokesman for the Met

DURING an intermission of the Metropolitan Opera broadcast of December 15 the General Manager of that esteemed institution said, "Now you might say that only by trying out these new operas, even if they are not too exciting, can an opera house hope to find the great work that no doubt one day will appear. This frankly is a moot question."

Will you say that again, Mr. Bing? What is it you consider a moot question? If I read you right (and I have before me a copy of the manuscript you spoke from), you consider that there are other methods of adding great works to the opera repertory than by putting new operas into production. I have never heard of any such method. Reading scores will, of course, enable your musical directors to eliminate many works. But it cannot pick out the "great" ones of any decade or epoch. That is done by the public. And if there is any way the public can be led to consecrate with its favor the greatness of a *Carmen* or *Lohengrin* or *Aïda* or *Figaro* without some opera house having actually produced that work first, then I am sure we should all like to know what it is.

Perhaps Mr. Bing means that the Metropolitan does not need to give world premieres, that it can let the subsidized European houses do our try-outs for us. By skimming thus the cream off the world's production we might indeed procure a quite good contemporary repertory at small risk. But such a policy does not seem to be this manager's idea. In referring to Alban Berg's *Wozzeck*, a famous opera now thirty years old and consecrated by some quite impressive box-offices, he admits it to be an "extremely important opera" that "has been played in many European opera houses." But he also remarks that it has become part of the standard repertory in very few theaters.

Just a minute, Mr. Bing. You know perfectly well that it was removed from the German and Austrian theaters in the 1930s both for its political content and for its composer's religion. You also know that both its political content and its musical style place it out of bounds today everywhere behind the Iron Curtain. Also, that last summer's production in Salzburg, which you mention as selling less well than Verdi's *Otello* (hardly surprising) had to run against the opposition of the powerful Austrian clergy, determined to remove it from the repertory on theological grounds. You know, too, that Switzerland and Italy have seen the work revived since the war and that Paris will see the Vienna Opera Company's production next spring. Nobody ever suggested to you that *Wozzeck* would be a draw at the Metropolitan like *Cav* and *Pag*, though it would probably do as well in any season as *Parsifal*. It has merely been pointed out that if the Met is looking for twentieth-century works of unquestioned musical "importance" and tested appeal, *Wozzeck* is up near the top of the list. And if the Met is afraid of attempts at political or religious censorship, then I am ashamed of it.

Mr. Bing later in his speech denied acquaintance with any recommendable modern works and suggested "that anybody should send [him] a list of those new works performed in recent years that live to see a second season." I should not care to offer such a list myself lest it be thought I were proposing that the Met mount all the operas on it. But just for fun I might mention Prokofiev's *The Love of Three Oranges* from the City Center, Poulenc's *Les Mamelles de Tirésias* from the Paris Opéra-Comique, Milhaud's *Bolívar* from the Paris Opéra, Britten's *Peter Grimes*, not so long ago of the Met itself. All these have seen second seasons in one house, two of them even more. As for modern operas that have survived in the repertory of many houses and even in some cases enjoyed runs in the commercial theater, there are Hindemith's *Mathis der Maler* and the late operas by Richard Strauss, all of them current in Germany and Switzerland these days, Menotti's *The Medium* and *The Consul*, worldwide successes both, and Gershwin's beloved *Porgy and Bess*.

Opera writing is, by actual count, not at all a dead art. And neither, by actual count, is opera production. It may be at the Met but not in the world picture. And when Mr. Bing states it as "a highly regrettable fact that so few new operas of real musical consequence are being offered" one wonders what he means by "real musical consequence." But one does not wonder long. He means and I think I read his thoughts correctly, pure box-office. He "regrets" that Beethoven "receives greater support" than Schönberg from symphony audiences, though why he should regret it I do not know. He ought to be happy that our symphony audiences have access to Schönberg as well as to Beethoven. We opera audiences get no such heady diet.

But the slip about Beethoven is minor. Here is the evidence on which I accuse him of a box-office view of music. He says: "No one in the world of the theater puts on any show unless he is convinced that it will either be a 'hit success' or at least attract sufficient public acclaim to justify the effort. I cannot see why this sound principle, which is commonly accepted in the theater, should become a criminal offense when applied to opera."

Some member of the Metropolitan board should explain to the General Manager that the Metropolitan Opera Association is not engaged in show business, that it is a nonprofit society vowed to the advancement of musical art and of public taste, that this purpose has been recognized by the State of New York as justifying an exemption from real estate taxation and recently by the Federal government as justifying exemption from the amusements tax. Gifts to the Metropolitan, moreover, can be deducted from anybody's taxable income up to fifteen per cent. Such privileges are not granted to the amusement trades.

It is not a "criminal offense" to play so conservative a repertory as Mr. Bing has laid out for this season, and nobody ever said it was. It is merely a neglect of duty. I have long found his program regrettable; and I found his radio speech of two weeks back acceptable only for the frankness of his admissions, shocking as they were. He admitted his lack of faith both in the music of his own time and in the public's aspirations regarding this. He does not believe, apparently, that good operas are being written now or are likely to be written in the near future; and he considers that it would be a waste of the Met's money to produce the contemporary stuff that *is* written. He does not think the Met audience wants to hear new things anyway, says he did not get one letter all last year asking for them.

All the same, he plans to take a flyer next season with the new Stravinsky opera. "We shall then see what the public reaction will be," he added. Does this mean that he is giving contemporary music just one chance to compete with *Carmen*? Really, one has heard double-talk before from Metropolitan spokesmen but nothing quite so cynical as this.

December 30, 1951

1952

A Great Temperament

PHILHARMONIC-SYMPHONY ORCHESTRA, *Guido Cantelli*, conductor, with the WESTMINSTER CHOIR, last night at Carnegie Hall, performing Beethoven's Symphony No. 5, Monteverdi's *Magnificat*, and Ghedini's orchestration of four organ pieces by Frescobaldi.

GUIDO CANTELLI, conducting the Philharmonic-Symphony Orchestra last night in Carnegie Hall, risked everything, program-wise, and lost nothing. Indeed, if applause is the measure, his winnings were large. Even Monteverdi, which is far from a sure thing, payed off. On Beethoven, at the end of the concert, he really cashed in.

A young man making his first bow before a great orchestra risks a great deal by filling half his program with arrangements of music by seventeenth-century organists. He risks even more—all, in fact—by essaying Beethoven's Fifth Symphony, the hardest piece in the repertory with which to show originality or to compete with the interpretations of older men. Mr. Cantelli held his audience firmly, triumphantly in both halves. Here is obviously a great music-making temperament.

The four organ pieces by Frescobaldi, in Ghedini's instrumentation, were noble and rigid, evocative of a primitive instrument and of pre-Bach church services. The Monteverdi *Magnificat*, orchestrated also by Ghedini, seemed even more archaic in its contrapuntal textures, though its lengthy pedal-points (or long held notes against which other voices move) were really a modernism in 1610. They gave architecture to a piece, and poignant expressivity could take place against them. Equally a modernism then (and still surprising) is the intense emotional expression which this composer achieved. The emotional resources of the time both for composing and for receiving music must have been vast. Certainly Monteverdi's music, like that of Schütz in Germany, is vibrant with feelings more powerful than anything that preceded or followed it by nearly a century. And its rendering of verbal texts is heartbreakingly meaningful.

Mr. Cantelli, though a protégé of Toscanini, gave us no streamlined Beethoven. He gave us a young man's Beethoven, all passion and lyricism. His reading was not at all times orchestrally elegant. Once or twice roughnesses were heard that were certainly not his intention. But they mattered little beside the grace of his line, the warmth of his assertions. We are used to a colder violence in this piece and a more calculated showmanship. Mr. Cantelli was not occupied with either. He made it sing; he made it dance; he even made it rejoice. Let us be thankful for the presence among us of so pure a spirit.

January 4, 1952

Dramatically Expressive

DESSOFF CHOIRS, *Paul Boepple*, conductor, with *Claude Frank*, pianist, and *George W. Volkel*, organist, last night at Carnegie Hall, performing Frank Martin's *Golgotha*, an oratorio in two parts.

FRANK MARTIN is a Swiss composer whose work has long impressed your reviewer with its deep seriousness of aim and high skill. His oratorio *Golgotha*, heard last night in Carnegie Hall, added to these solid quantities a grandeur of dramatic expression rarely encountered in our century's compositions for massed choral and orchestral effectives. As sung by the Dessoff Choirs and conducted by Paul Boepple, it was wanting in the highest polish of execution. The musical sense of it was there, however, and the meaningful impact. It was an unusual experience and, to this listener, absorbing throughout.

Not quite throughout, perhaps. The beginning was a bit stodgy, as if the composer's thought had not yet found its ease. About half way through the first half of the Passion (for such is the oratorio's text and subject) your listener became aware that music was taking place which he had not heard before. From there to the end, its varied musical invention and expressive content seemed inexhaustible, unendingly powerful and fresh.

Sometimes he would listen libretto in hand. And Martin's elegant prosodizing of the French text seemed to him the main matter. At other moments, following the concert with no attention for the verbal content, he was struck by how completely interesting every number was sheerly as music. The melodic lines, their harmonizations and contrapuntal additions, their rhythmic life and orchestral colorations, their vocal variety and invariable beauty all seemed to him infinitely satisfactory. The musical complexities, too, for Martin is a learned man, were welcome evidence of mastery, of fecund labors, of trouble taken toward the covering of a grand gamut.

Surely religious sincerity has gone into the making of this work too. Such fine pictorial vividness combined with delicate feelings and a sweet taste is not achieved by dramatic talent alone. One number, as a matter of fact, that which recounts the trial before Pontius Pilate, is a dramatic scene of the most exciting immediacy. That is no mere meditation on a sacred story. That is real theater with a real presence.

Here is the vein where I shall look in future for Martin's most forceful work. He is a skilled and serious-minded musician with a gift for the voice, for words, for specific meaning, and for (which is the real test) dramatic animation. Such composers are not plentiful these days. The opera, as well as the oratorio, can use another good one.

January 19, 1952

The Abstract Composers

WHEN John Cage came to New York some ten years ago out of California (by way of Chicago), he brought with him a sizable baggage of compositions. These were scored for divers groups of what are usually called "percussion instruments," orthodox and unorthodox.

Orthodox percussion instruments, let me explain, are those manufactured with musical intent, such as tom-toms, temple bells, and the like. The unorthodox are those whose adoption by the music profession is not yet general. These include, in Mr. Cage's case, flower pots, automobile brake drums, electric buzzers, tubs of water, and many other sources of interesting and characteristic sounds. Cage's first New York concerts were given with ensembles of players using all these instruments and many more, himself conducting.

A few years later he simplified the execution of his music by devising an instrument on which it could be composed for one man. This instrument, an orthodox one with unorthodox attachments, was none other than the familiar grand pianoforte muted with screws, bits of rubber, copper pennies and the like to give a large gamut of pings, thuds, and other delicate aural stimuli. As my colleague Arthur Berger has pointed out, the Cage "prepared piano" is a conception not dissimilar to that of the one-man bands common in the jazz world. Nor has the Cage method of composition been radically altered for the solo circumstance.

This method is Cage's most original contribution to music. Designed specifically for making extended and shapely patterns out of non-tonal sounds, it is the most sophisticated method available in the Western world for composing with purely rhythmic elements and without the aid of tonal scales. To quote Lou Harrison, long an associate of Cage in percussive studies and rhythmic research, Cage has substituted "chronological" for "psychological" time as the continuing element of his music. Any composer who has ever worked with percussion has discovered that all our traditional composing methods deal with the psychological, or "expressive," relations among tones which have among themselves differing and *unavoidable*, acoustical relations. To make musical forms or constructions without these relations requires a substitute for them. Cage has substituted an arithmetical relation among the durations of sounds for the traditional arithmetical relation among their pitches. He has isolated rhythm as a musical element and given it an independence it did not have before.

In the last year or so he has added a further element to composition, which is chance. So secure does he feel in the solidity of his composition method that he has essayed to prove its worth under conditions the most hazardous. Last year we heard, in a concert of the New Music Society, a piece by Cage for twelve radio receiving-sets. The use of fortuitously chosen material in composition has long been familiar to the visual arts. The collage, the spatter, the blot, the accidental texture have been exploited by painters for forty years. From Duchamp and Picasso to the latest American abstractionists, the history is continuous. Music itself accepts a high part of hazard in execution, and perhaps it is from this fact that composers have not exploited its possibilities much in actual scoring.

Mozart did play around with composing machines, as well as with performing machines (like the mechanical organ, for which he wrote some very pretty music); but he did not go far with them. How far Cage will go with his Chinese dice-game (for this is the game of chance by which he at present chooses the next sound and its loudness) remains to be seen. One presumes that he will renounce it if and when it ceases to be valuable, as he, the composer, judges value. But let no one think his *Music of Changes* is wholly a matter of hazard. The sounds of it, many of them quite complex, are carefully chosen, invented by him. And their composition in time is no less carefully worked out. Chance is involved only in their succession. And that chance is regulated by a game of such complexity that the laws of probability make continued variation virtually inevitable.

Thus, in Cage's hands, the use of chance in composition gives a result not unlike that of a kaleidoscope. With a large gamut of sounds and a complex system for assembling them into patterns, all the patterns turn out to be interesting; an arabesque is achieved. In the hands of his pupils and protégés the result is not always so distinguished, simply because the musical materials employed are less carefully chosen. The method of their assembling, however, remains valid and will remain so until a better approach to rhythmic construction is discovered.

What kaleidoscopes and arabesques lack is urgency. They can hold the attention but they do not do it consistently. The most dependable device for holding attention is a "theme" or story, the clear attachment of art patterns to such common human bonds as sex and sentiment. How far an artist goes in this direction, or in the opposite, is up to him. "Abstraction" in art is nothing more than the avoidance of a *clear* and *necessary* attachment to subject matter. It is ever a salutary element in art, because it clears the mind of sex and sentiment. Only briefly, however. Because the human mind can always find ways of getting these back into any picture. And since the civilized mind likes to share its intensities of feeling, and since all the feelings provokable by abstract art are individual, abstract movements invariably end by attaching to themselves an intense feeling about the one thing that is consistent throughout their works, namely, a method of composition. The composition, or the method of composition, becomes the "subject," in the long run, of all abstract art.

This has happened to the music of Cage and his followers. Its admirers, who are many (and include your commentator), tend ever to defend it as a species rather than to attach themselves to any particular piece. This has happened before. Stravinsky's neoclassic production was long a similar cause. Whether it happened just this way in the 1890's to Debussy's impressionistic works I am not sure. We do know that something not dissimilar took place around Beethoven in Vienna, though the attendant polemics were not an attack upon intellectuality in music but rather upon an unusual degree of expressivity.

In any case, Cage and his associates, through their recent concerts at the Cherry Lane Theatre, have got the town to quarreling again. Many find the climate of the new downtown group invigorating. Others are bothered by the casual quality of their music. They find it hard to keep the mind on. This has always been one reaction to abstract art. I am sure that Cage's work *is* abstract, in any contemporary meaning of the term. I am also convinced that the workmanship is of the best. The fact that younger men are adopting its methods, as Cage long ago took on the influence of Cowell and Varèse, means that it has become something of a movement. Myself I find it only natural that music, usually, in our time, a good quarter century behind the visual arts, should have finally acquired its own "abstractionist" pressure group.

February 3, 1952

Good Chorus from Upstate

CRANE CHORUS, *Helen Hosmer* and *Robert Shaw*, conductors, with the ORCHESTRA OF THE TEACHERS COLLEGE OF POTSDAM, last night at Carnegie Hall, performing, among other works, Josquin des Prez's *Miserere mei Deus* and Norman Dello Joio's *Psalm of David*.

SINGING under their regular director, Helen Hosmer, the Crane Chorus from the State University Teachers College at Potsdam, New York, proved themselves to be one of the great singing societies. Directed last night in Carnegie Hall during half their program by the celebrated Robert Shaw, they sounded not nearly so well. Guest conductors do not usually, as a matter of fact, bring out the best powers of choral groups.

I sometimes wonder whether Robert Shaw, who has such an inspiring hand with choral singers and who seems to feel music profoundly with his body, really hears it at all with his ears. Last night he forced the choral tone, obscured the diction, and got no harmony at all out of the orchestra. Yet all the while he was executing a pantomime of personal transports, as if the music were somehow being just too beautiful to bear. If he had really been listening, he must have known, as we all did out front, that nothing of the kind was going on.

Then Miss Hosmer conducted a group of some forty unaccompanied singers in the *Miserere* (Psalm 50) of Josquin des Prez, and suddenly the voices were sweeter. This subtle music may have lacked the ultimate in expressivity under her delicate fingers, but Norman Dello Joio's work on the same text did not. Scored for large chorus, strings, brasses and percussion, this tender and powerful piece received from Miss Hosmer and her choir of 250 voices a performance in every way moving and beautiful.

During a large part of this psalm the orchestra plays antiphonally to the unaccompanied chorus. Its voice is like that of liturgical response and its tunes and harmonies follow those of the singing body. When the orchestra plays with the choir its music has less character. But at all times its work is pleasingly composed. So is the choir's, too, though I was not entirely convinced about the appropriateness of an almost cheerfully energetic finale. None the less, this Psalm of David is a distinguished work and an expressive one. Said to be constructed in emulation of the des Prez *Miserere* that preceded it, it seemed to me to be modeled, in spirit at least, much more after Monteverdi. This composer's passionate immediacy is surely closer to Dello Joio's than are the stylistic elaborations and mystical vibrancies of Josquin. In any case, the Psalm of David, though a very simple piece and not at all complex in texture, is constantly interesting because it is at once sensitive and straightforward.

February 4, 1952

Harmonious Powers

GRANT JOHANNESEN, pianist, in recital last night at Town Hall, performing, among other works, Beethoven's Sonata No. 5 (Op. 10, No. 1), Schumann's Fantasie in C major, Copland's Piano Variations, Stravinsky's *Tango*, and Albéniz's "Eritagna."

GRANT JOHANNESEN's piano recital last night in Town Hall was, for this listener, an unusually satisfying experience. Seldom does one hear solo playing so clean, so elegant, so thoroughly competent, and at the same time so completely informed with all the qualities that are called "musical."

Grant Johannesen seems to be the rare artist who can both hear and play, understand and render. Listening to him, consequently, is ever a "musical" experience. It is also a distinguished experience, because there is no vulgarity in him and no weakness. For all the power of expression that is his, one encounters in a whole evening of his work no affectation, no clumsiness, no willful distortion. He renders straightforwardly music's emotional content, without exaggeration and without timidity. He also plays the written notes without fear, without self-assertion, without ugliness, and virtually without error.

An early and rather stiff Beethoven sonata (opus 10, No. 1), a set of graceful and slender pieces by Grieg, the great Schumann Fantasy, formless but full of wonderful thoughts, Aaron Copland's stylish and hieratic Piano Variations, a delicious (and rare) Impromptu by Chabrier, Stravinsky's night-clubbish evocation of a Tango, even Albéniz's repetitive but technically impressive *Eritagna*, all came to life at his hands. This life was a matter of rhythm, of tonal beauty and of phraseological grace. It also had to do with emotional warmth and with the intellectual ability to plan a shape without destroying that warmth.

Mr. Johannesen worked all evening at the center of music's problems. Technically, expressively, and "musically," he skirted no edges. Talent, training, a mature mind, and mature feelings were everywhere evident in harmonious operation. I cannot tell you how rarely a music reviewer meets this harmony in the concert hall, or how satisfying is the encounter.

March 17, 1952

Don Carlo *and the Pickets*

JUST FOR PLEASURE, and also to impress a visitor from Europe, your announcer dropped in last Monday night at the Metropolitan Opera for a performance of Verdi's *Don Carlo*. He had not seen or heard the production since it opened the house last season and inaugurated the managerial regime of Rudolf Bing; but he knew it for a distinguished one and thought it a good example of New York opera presentation at its best, all the more worth showing off since the work itself is not anywhere a common repertory item.

It was something of a surprise to learn that the performance was being picketed. Investigation revealed the following facts. The Archdiocesan Union of the Holy Name Society of New York, the American Society for the Preservation of Sacred, Patriotic, and Operatic Music, and the Children's Drama Guild have all made protests to the Metropolitan management. The latter group had already asked the Manhattan Supreme Court, back in 1950, for a declaratory judgment enjoining the Metropolitan Opera Association from disseminating subversive anti-religious propaganda. This suit is still awaiting action. A spokesman for the Holy Name Society has declared that he is informed that the script of the opera has been changed in such a way as "to have appear on the stage a character in the garb of a clergyman who points out Don Rodrigo to an assassin, directs the assassination, and then shields the assassin by taking him away from the scene."

This spokesman has been misinformed. The script calls for a man "dressed in the uniform of the Holy Office," and he is so represented at the Metropolitan. The uniform, moreover, is not historically exact but of fanciful design. It bears no resemblance to the clothing of a priest. And the Holy Office, or Inquisition, did not consist wholly of priests. It was a large organization employing many laymen as administrators, office workers, guards, and other functionaries, all of whom were distinguished by their uniform from members of the clergy. Verdi's stage direction has been scrupulously observed at the Metropolitan. And Franco Colombo, managing director of G. Ricordi and Co., has assured Mr. Bing by letter that he has "never heard that this opera has ever incurred any form of censorship on the part of the Catholic Church since the time of its first performance in Paris in 1867 or on occasion of any later performances, including those which have recently taken place in Italy, Austria, France, and Spain."

Further evidence of hasty judgment on the part of the picketers is provided by the fact that they first arrived at the Metropolitan on a night when *Die Fledermaus* was the opera. They had not even got their dates right. They seemed to be in some confusion, moreover, about their exact complaint. The signs carried by the picketers, who are about thirty in number, bore the following legends:

"The opera *Don Carlo* is a mockery of religion."

"The opera *Don Carlo* is anti-state and anti-religious."

"Stop Sovietizing operas."

"Moscow termites invade the 'Met.'"

"Don't support 'Met' Opera as long as they hire subversives."

"Who gets the money that the 'Met' loses?"

"Planned deficit financing is anti-American."

The main charges, therefore, are: That the "Met" has changed Verdi's script (which is not true); that this change (still not true) is the work of Stalinists within the organization; that these subversive characters should be fired; that they may well be tapping the till for the benefit of the Communist Party. All these charges are grave; and till evidence supporting them is offered, we must consider all attempts at "proof by picketing" as utterly irresponsible. There may be some commies around the Met; they turn up everywhere. But there is no evidence that they have made propaganda for their faith through the distorting of any opera text or opera presentation. As for the hint that the Met's annual deficit is a kickback to Communism, the idea is really the funniest I have encountered this season, especially if you stop to remember how completely the Metropolitan is controlled by political conservatives. One would have to look far for an institution more thoroughly in the hands of capitalists, their sons and daughters, their wives, their widows, and their lawyers.

March 31, 1952

Recital Songs

Singers' recital programs come up for attack about once a year from this reviewer. In past times he has complained vigorously against the multilingual convention which leads vocal debutants to expose their ignorances of German, French and Italian all in one evening, along with, more often than not, their lack of a cultivated English diction. He has also lamented the musical poverty of the English-language song repertory.

Not much can be done to change the multilingual convention as long as our music schools enforce it for degrees and credits. Young artists have to sing what they have studied. And what they have studied is the standard scholastic requirements of selections from German lieder, French art-songs, Italian airs and arias, and English verse settings. Fine programs can be assembled from these sources. And if few singers are prepared to shine in so grand a galaxy, they can usually do pretty well in one of the groups. Also, their program's musical offering is far richer in such a layout than would be possible in a program devoted to English vocal literature alone. The only way out of the difficult situation is to specialize, to really sing well German lieder or French songs and to stick fairly close to that specialty.

For these two repertories are the great vocal repertories. Neither the English nor the Italian communicates so urgently. You have only to hear a whole evening of music from England's, or from Italy's, finest vocal period, which in both cases is the seventeenth century, to realize that for all that music's noble proportion and infinite grace of line, it does not work in depth like those fusions of music and poetry that are the particular glory of Germany's nineteenth-century and of France's early twentieth.

Not Dowland, not Purcell, not Handel nor Blow, not Cesti, Carissimi, nor even Monteverdi has the psychological power in short songs of Schubert, Schumann, Brahms, Wolf, Mahler, Fauré, Ravel, and Debussy. Neither were they able to extend their inspirations into long vocal forms without some cost to their expressive intensity. The Romantics and the moderns in Germany, Austria, and France have worked far closer to poetry's meaning than did their predecessors; and they have worked with poetry of greater complexity. The classical and pre-classical masters, though they often set the best poets of their time, never faced—such things were not there to be faced—the emotional elaboration and verbal subtleties of Goethe, Heine, Baudelaire, Verlaine, Mallarmé, Apollinaire, and Max Jacob.

The modern Italian and modern English vocal repertories do not come up to the French and German either. The poetic texts used are less substantial, the musical settings less detailed. The Italians have written in the last century and a half lots of fine arias for the theater. In English we have Sir Arthur Sullivan, also of the theater, and Stephen Foster, strictly for the home. The Russians have a handful of wonderful songs by Mussorgsky that are appropriate for recital use and some by Rachmaninoff that are far from negligible. Grieg wrote some in Norwegian, and Sibelius has composed well in both Finnish and Swedish. De Falla, in Spanish, and Villa-Lobos, in Portuguese, have written charmingly for the solo voice; but their work is closer to folk-lore evocation than to those psychologically powerful fusions of music and poetry that stem from Schubert. It is all a little objective, impersonal, does best in any program's final group.

German and French songs of the last century and a half are to the song recital what Haydn, Mozart, Beethoven, Brahms, and Debussy are to the orchestral concert. They are the center of the repertory, its real weight and grandeur. All the rest is contributory. And only in France, in the work of Francis Poulenc and Henri Sauguet, is that great tradition being carried on today. The English, the American composer has not seized, not understood the fusing of music and poetry into an alloy stronger than either alone. He has realized, I think, the nature of lyric poetry. But he has underestimated the need, in this kind of expression, for a personal intensity, the kind that can come only from sincerity, emotional concentration, and self-containment.

The great composers of art songs have all identified themselves with the poet's feeling or with some aspect of it. They have got inside the poetry. The rewards of doing this are Franz Schubert's great and original contribution to music, and his 600 songs are a corpus of achievement now basic to the art. The composers who have not built on this foundation have built weakly. Their songs do not stand up under usage. It is a matter of regret to us all that the English-speaking composer has not achieved that inward-turned concentration that is the sine qua non of great song-writing since Schubert.

Consequently our recital singers are obliged, like those of many another country, to work mostly in foreign languages. I have heard rumors ever since I was a child that a few English and American composers were about to change all that. Certainly most of our composers have tried their hand at the recital song, many of them assiduously. But if the usable American repertory is any larger or more distinguished today than it was in the time of Edward MacDowell and George B. Nevin, I am unaware of the fact. Neither is Benjamin Britten, in England, one whit more significant as a song writer, for my money, than the late (and thoroughly charming) Liza Lehmann.

It is pathetic to hear our artists, especially the younger ones, mouthing French and German that they scarcely understand. But it is even more painful to see them struggle with poorly conceived and amateurishly written English songs. There is nothing to be done about the matter. Only a great repertory of English songs can change it. And for that we must wait till our composers acquire the knack of working closer to poetry than they are accustomed to do just now. A good melody is not just a poem's new suit. It must be a new skin, inseparable.

April 27, 1952

Copland Songs

PATRICIA NEWAY, soprano, and AARON COPLAND, piano, in recital yesterday afternoon at Town Hall, performing Mr. Copland's *Twelve Poems of Emily Dickinson*.

Aaron Copland's *Twelve Poems of Emily Dickinson* are Copland at his most characteristic and most reflective. The broken rhythms, the pandiatonic harmony, the subtle spacing of notes in a chord, the open piano writing, the melodic lines that seek wide skips, all color the work with this composer's personality. So do the seriousness and the poetic penetration with which the texts have been studied, and the frank search for charm (equally characteristic of Emily Dickinson) with which their thought has been expressed.

If this admirer of Copland has a reserve about the present song cycle, otherwise so appealing, that reserve comes from a certain ineptitude in the vocal writing. The range is extreme (a half-tone over two octaves) and the tessitura, or "lie" of the vocal line, is cruel. For a light voice the cruelty would come in the low notes, the Bs, B-flats, and the A. For Patricia Neway, whose low voice is warm, the cruelty comes at the top, from F sharp to B-flat.

This cruelty is less a result of the wide melodic skips, which are in themselves effective in a declamatory sense and strikingly expressive, as in the vowel sounds to which the high and the low-lying notes are set. Certain extensions of the short vowels also oblige the singer to deform these. And occasionally a lengthening out, syllable by syllable, of a word group that for comprehensibility requires being pronounced as if it were a single word ("the breaking of the day," for instance) makes it hard for the singer to communicate the sense of the poems.

These poems, more than a little arch sometimes in sentiment ("Dear March, come in!"), are nevertheless compact in phraseology and require time to understand. Spacing their ideas would have helped them more than stretching out their syllables does. Actually their sense is more picturesquely illustrated in the piano part (birds twittering, horses trotting, an organist improvising) than it is projected through their vocal declamation. The accompaniments are perfect, and they "sound." The vocal line, though full of expressive intentions, really comes off only part of the time. In three cases—*Nature, the gentlest mother, Heart, we will forget him* and *I've heard an organ talk sometimes*—the songs seem to me completely successful. In the rest, for all their tenderness and vibrancy, something experimental in the vocal writing, something not quite mastered in Copland's technique of handling words and singers, tones down their power to touch the heart, though this clearly is what they aim to do.

November 3, 1952

Metropolitan Opera Not Yet a Part of New York's Intellectual Life

TWELVE YEARS AGO this commentator observed that the Philharmonic was "not a part of New York's intellectual life." Today that remark would not be true. It is still true, however, of the Metropolitan Opera.

By "New York's intellectual life" I mean everything that

inspires, even briefly, the interest of our powerful "intellectual audience." This audience is not wholly musical; nor does it represent any social class. It is made up of book-readers and book-writers, civic leaders and stenographers, artists of all kinds, and all the art consumers who have faith in the future. It is a critical audience, but a warm one; and it can make or break the prestige of any institution dealing in products of the mind.

Its dynamic character, its faith in tomorrow, is backed up by a better knowledge of the past than the non-intellectual audience has. You can't fool it by talking about "tradition," as you can often do with the less knowledgeable. It demands that the past be treated as a living thing and that today be considered as an honorable heir of the past and a gateway, the only gateway, to the future.

Typical of the intellectual operation I am describing is the recent performance at the Philharmonic concerts of Darius Milhaud's celebrated opera *Christopher Columbus*. This work has been in existence for over twenty years. It has been performed in Germany, France, and Belgium. It has never been a popular success, and it has never been agreed to be an artistic failure. It is a monumental work by a world-famous master, and New York also has a right to judge it. If recent judgments have not been wholly favorable, neither have they considered the Philharmonic to have done a foolish thing in giving it. Indeed, the Philharmonic's intellectual prestige has risen with the event.

The Metropolitan Opera production on Feb. 14 of the Stravinsky-Auden opera *The Rake's Progress* will certainly bring similar prestige to that establishment. But one event does not define a policy, and it is surely to be hoped that a policy of producing each season a certain number of contemporary and other works of intellectual distinction will one day put the Metropolitan into a higher intellectual neighborhood than it has dwelt in of late years. *Salomé* and *Elektra*, as conducted there by Fritz Reiner, have been "musts" for the musical public that leads taste. And Alfred Lunt's staging of *Così Fan Tutte* enjoys attention from this audience. *La Forza del Destino*, for its scenery by Eugene Berman, and *Don Carlo*, for its scenery by Rolf Gerard and staging by Margaret Webster, have attracted similar interest; but musically neither work has inspired much public gratitude, though the singing in them has been excellent. The

Met's other recent revivals, though necessary as refurbishments, have added nothing remarkable to our musical or to our theater experience.

The City Center has given us in one calendar year a contemporary opera, *The Dybbuk*, and four famous works of this century—Wolf-Ferrari's *I Quattro Rusteghi*, Alban Berg's *Wozzeck*, Bartók's *Bluebeard's Castle* and Ravel's *L'Heure Espagnole*. Earlier, Prokofiev's *Love of Three Oranges* and Debussy's *Pelléas et Mélisande* made history for popular prices. As for the ballet companies, they all do new works constantly. Their relation to their own time is perfect, and a huge audience of young people is their reward.

Philharmonic spokesmen used to maintain, and Metropolitan spokesmen still do, that their institution cannot afford at present a policy of intellectual distinction but that if and when more money became available they would be delighted to spend some of it pleasing the intellectual minority. All such statements assume that a directorship which has for years abstained from any such effort has the taste and its subscribers the experience to take part in the life of their time by merely changing their minds. We have no evidence that this is true. At the Philharmonic it took a new conductor to make the change, and that change is not yet complete. But the change has brought into the house for the more advanced programs a public not previously served by the Philharmonic, and it seems not to have caused any grave defection among the subscribers.

Money does not produce intellectual distinction, nor does poverty prevent its exercise. Actually, in any given house one opera production costs about the same as another. The ones that make history are the ones that show choice, taste, and solid imagination. And it does seem to me that making history is the only criterion that we can accept in judging the activities of our cultural institutions.

November 16, 1952

Contemporary Festival in Pittsburgh

PITTSBURGH INTERNATIONAL MUSIC FESTIVAL, a series of ten concerts of new music, November 24–30, at Carnegie Music Hall and Syria Mosque Auditorium, Pittsburgh, Pennsylvania, featuring the PITTSBURGH SYMPHONY ORCHESTRA, *William Steinberg*, conductor, other regional music organizations, and an international list of soloists. The festival was organized by Roy Harris and sponsored by Carnegie Institute and the Pennsylvania College for Women, Pittsburgh.

THE FIRST Pittsburgh International Music Festival took place the week of November 24–30. From the works heard by this reviewer, here are some of the impressions retained.

A Concerto, Opus 56, for piano, four hands unaccompanied, by Vincent Persichetti seemed to me extraordinarily expert in its piano writing. It is difficult; but it sounds, and its figurational ingenuity is vast. Musically the work is prolix and its expressivity diffuse; but the sound of it, moment by moment, is unusually brilliant. Its performance by the composer and Dorothea Persichetti was perfection, the ringing quality of their piano tone being especially noticeable beside the deadness of tone in the otherwise highly musical performances of Johana Harris, who played on the same program.

Quaderna Musicale di Annalibera ("*Annalibera's Musical Notebook*") by Luigi Dallapiccola, most poetically played by Mrs. Harris, is a homage to childhood composed in the twelve-tone technique. It is a series of short pieces, ever songful and sweet, and might easily become a popular number on recital programs.

Arnold Schönberg's Trio for Violin, Viola, and Violoncello, Opus 45, composed for the Harvard Symposium on Music Criticism in 1947 and seldom performed since, is not much loved, even in twelve-tone circles. Myself I found it, as played by three members of the New Music String Quartet, delicious for sound. I do not pretend to know its emotional content, and I insist that persons who seek to recognize Schönberg's emotional content by sheer intuition are in general slated for disappointment. His microscopic examination of emotion precludes easy recognition, and the value of it comes far more from the surprising details revealed than from any resemblance his study may bear to any possible common-sense view or large-scale perspective rendering of a similar subject.

Vaughan Williams's *Tudor Portraits*, five very long pieces for chorus and orchestra on texts by the fifteenth-century satirist John Skelton, is the least subtle work I have ever heard by this composer. It must have been written for some provincial English singing society, and a none too sophisticated one at that. It is brash and brassy, noisy, bustling, as if the available executant forces were all vigor and no refinement. As a college glee-club-and-orchestra romp it might be fun for five minutes. At a length of somewhere near forty I found it bearable only by the beauty of Nell Rankin's lovely singing in the solos. As a matter of fact, it was the only large piece heard all week that seemed to me undistinguished.

Especially grateful to these ears was Roy Harris's Fifth Symphony, composed in 1942. In one sense Harris's large works are all the same work. He seems to approach a single problem of expression in varying ways rather than to use a perfected and personal instrument of expression for depicting a variety of subjects. His central problem of expression is by now familiar to us all, and the solution offered in his Third Symphony has become America's most popular (and most explorable) single expression in symphonic form. That offered in the Fifth, though less compact, seems to me to have a greater intrinsic beauty. Whether its expressive force is as great I cannot say. Only time and the box office can tell that.

What it does have is Harris's two best advantages handsomely embodied, his extended thematic line and his skill in treating the orchestra as an antiphony of strings and brass. His tendency to write as if the work he is writing has already been judged a masterpiece (at least by himself) even before it has been composed is not one of Mr. Harris's most winning traits. But I must say that it bothered me less in his Fifth Symphony than it has ever done before in an orchestral piece. And I strongly suspect that this circumstance was produced by Harris's having composed and orchestrated the piece with a high degree of perfectly real mastery. In the American repertory it is a far from negligible work.

December 7, 1952

1953

Musically Enchanting

THE RAKE'S PROGRESS, opera in three acts and an epilogue, libretto by *W. H. Auden* and *Chester Kallman*, music by *Igor Stravinsky*, yesterday afternoon at the Metropolitan Opera House, *Fritz Reiner*, conductor, with *Hilde Gueden* (Anne Truelove), *Eugene Conley* (The Rake), and *Mack Harrell* (Nick Shadow).

THE RAKE'S PROGRESS brought yesterday afternoon to the Metropolitan Opera House the brilliance of a great premiere. The cast, headed by Hilde Gueden, Eugene Conley, and Mack Harrell, sang impeccably. The orchestral accompaniments, after forty hours of rehearsal under Fritz Reiner, were perfect. The scenery of Horace Armistead was adequate, the stage direction of George Balanchine brilliantly unobtrusive. As for the opera itself, it has a fine libretto by W. H. Auden and Chester Kallman; and its music by Igor Stravinsky is enchanting.

The subject is a young man's downfall through money, drink, gambling, sex, and speculation. He ends up in Bedlam, imagining himself Adonis in the arms of Venus, but really being rocked to sleep by his hometown sweetheart. He is abetted in self-destruction, I may add, by a Mephistophelian servant named Nick Shadow. The story is thus a morality play touched up with Goethe's *Faust*. Setting it in eighteenth-century England has allowed the authors to lean on the prestige of Hogarth's engravings of the same title and also to stylize their poetic language. Very pretty is that language, too. Few composers in our time have been served by an English libretto so high-class all through.

Dealing with a poem made all out of references to a period of literature, it was appropriate (indeed inevitable) that the composer should derive his inspiration from the same period in music. Mr. Stravinsky has clearly used as his model the operas of Mozart and Pergolesi, adding touches of thematic material and devices of musical syntax from classical composers as closely related to the Mozart tradition as Bach, Gluck, and Donizetti. There is even here and there a memory of Beethoven's *Fidelio*.

But *The Rake's Progress* is no eclectic score. Its style is power-fully Stravinskian. I should say that it sounds throughout more like Stravinsky than any other single piece we have heard from this master in twenty or more years, since *Oedipus Rex* and the Symphony of Psalms, to be exact.

Its difference from those earlier vocal works lies in the greater freedom, variety, and expressive power of the vocal line. The opera is full of fine airs, set-pieces, and recitatives, all hand-somely designed to show off both the human voice and the English text. Its similarities lie in the harmonic texture, a dis-sonant diatonic idiom of almost arbitrary simplicity, and in the complexity of the musical metrics. Stravinsky's inspiration, let us remember, has always been rhythm, dancing, gesture. Song is secondary with him. And although the present work is chock-full of good tunes, many of them more or less familiar, it is the rhythmic structure of the instrumental accompaniments—elaborate, subtle and tense—that gives to the whole work its electric potential. This tension, characteristic of all Stravinsky's music, is in his stronger works the most powerful musical in-dividuality of our time. Its permeating pressure in *The Rake's Progress* is grounds for suspicion that this work is probably among his finest.

If so, it will stay in the repertory. If not, it will still have de-lighted us all with its musical fancy. Certainly there is no weak-ness in the poem or in the possibilities of its dramatic mounting that would tend to make the work, like *Les Noces* and *The Rite of Spring*, fall out of the theater into the concert hall. If there were any such weakness, it would lie, I think, in the passages having to do with the Bearded Lady, a character drawn from female impersonation and not easy to make convincing. All the rest works perfectly, in my opinion, and should continue to do so for quite a time. In the Metropolitan's admirable produc-tion, the artists will probably (unless the cast begins to shift) little by little add characterization to a spectacle that so far has been drilled primarily for musical excellence. *The Rake* is a fine opera in an extraordinarily perfect musical production. It is no tear-jerker nor much of a melodrama. It is simply a quite good poem on a moralistic theme, and the music is enchanting.

February 15, 1953

Germany's Funeral Song

PHILHARMONIC-SYMPHONY ORCHESTRA, *Bruno Walter*, conductor, last night at Carnegie Hall, performing Mahler's *Das Lied von der Erde*. Soloists: *Elena Nikolaidi*, contralto, and *Set Svanholm*, tenor.

BRUNO WALTER, conducting the Philharmonic-Symphony Orchestra last night, gave a burningly clear and moving performance of Gustav Mahler's *Das Lied von der Erde*. The excellent soloists were Elena Nikolaidi and Set Svanholm.

This *Song of the Earth* is really six songs, plus a short orchestral interlude, set alternately for tenor and alto voice to German translations of Chinese poems. The sadness of wine, of the seasons, and of growing older is their theme. And if a certain self-pity is not absent from the composer's treatment, neither is the objective enjoyment of nature. The amplitude of the work's expressive content comes, indeed, from the placement of a personal sadness in a landscape that sets it off by every device of contrast.

This sumptuous orchestral landscape is no attempt to reconstruct an authentic China. It is rather a wish, a yearning toward a China picturesque and exotic in detail but filled to the brim with Germanic pathos. The permanence of the East is there only as décor for the decline of the West. And make no mistake about it; Mahler's sadness at the approach of his fiftieth year was no private vanity. He thought of himself as the end of German music, just as Brahms had done. Brahms in spite of Wagner, Mahler in spite of Strauss, and later, Alban Berg in spite of Schönberg and Webern, all considered their music to be the closing off of a great epoch.

All were right in the sense that German music was experiencing in their time a sumptuous and deliquescent decay. It had lost all sense of form, all reserve, all ethical distinctions among the sources of emotion; and the aging giant had no strength to revive him. He could only die in grandeur. And each of these introspectives, bound to pessimism by clarity of mind as well as by temperament, wished that the whole great fireworks could expire with him in one final bursting.

It did not happen that way. German music still goes on, running weaker and thinner, but alive. It is all a very sad story; and Mahler was right to be sad. But he did leave, in *The Song of the Earth*, at least one lovely burst, an opulent and ornate poetic address to the musical decline of the great tradition of which he was so proud to be a part. All this somehow came through last night in the reading of it, tender, eloquent, and grand, by Bruno Walter and the two soloists.

February 20, 1953

Glorious Organ-Playing

JEANNE DEMESSIEUX, organist, in recital last night at Central Presbyterian Church, New York, performing two of her own compositions and works by Bach, Handel, Liszt, and Dupré.

FRENCH ORGAN-PLAYING has been one of the musical glories of our century; and Jeanne Demessieux, who played an organ recital last night in the Central Presbyterian Church, is clearly a light in that glory. All evening long your reviewer, who has known most of the great organ playing of our time, from that of Widor and Bonnet and Vierne through Dupré to Messiaen, could only think of those masters as company for this extraordinary musician and virtuoso.

Miss Demessieux's program contained from the Baroque period (which is the organ's classical period) a Bach overture from a cantata and a Handel concerto. From Romantic times came the Liszt Fantasy on *Ad Nos, Ad Salutarem*. Two works by the organist herself and a movement from Marcel Dupré's *Symphonie-Passion* brought us into the modern world. And for dessert the artist improvised on a theme presented her on the spot. None of the works was a hackneyed piece. Indeed, the Liszt Fantasy is so little played that many organists have never heard it at all. It is a wondrous work all the same, abundant of musical invention, brilliant in technical display, richly imaginative as to harmony, and utterly grand in its moments of apotheosis, diabolic and celestial. When one remembers that the great Romantics wrote so little for the organ, and for the most part without any boldness, this work stands almost as a solitary beacon in the deep fog that surrounded this noble instrument throughout the nineteenth century.

Miss Demessieux's work as a composer appeared, from the two selections offered (a chorale-prelude on *Ubi Caritas* and a Study in Thirds), to be skillful and musically sophisticated. It was not possible to gather from them any characteristic profile of individuality. Neither was anything of the kind manifest in her improvisation beyond perhaps an assurance of taste, intelligence, and technical skill of the highest order. She improvised, as is the French custom, in the Baroque forms, including a dazzling Toccata. Since the theme composed for her by Seth Bingham did not lend itself easily to fugal treatment, she omitted the customary fugal finale and finished her series of improvisations quietly with a poetic variation based on thematic alterations.

Notable throughout the evening were the soloist's elaborate and subtle treatment of registration and her powerful rhythm. No less subtle and no less powerful were her phraseology and her acoustical articulation. Accustomed, no doubt, to compensating for the acoustical lags and other echoing characteristics of France's vast cruciform churches, all stone and glass, she employed to great advantage in the smaller but similarly reverberant walls of the Central Presbyterian a staccato touch for all rapid passage work involving bright or loud registration. This device kept the brilliance clean; and its contrast with the more sustained utterance of broader themes gave a welcome variety, a contrapuntal dimension. We are not used here to so dry an articulation, to so striking a clarity in organ-playing. I must say that the fine brightness of the registration possibilities in the organ she was playing on aided the artist, as a good French organ also does, to avoid the muddy noises that so often pass for serious organ execution.

Last night there was no mud anywhere, only music making of the most crystalline and dazzling clarity. Every piece had style, beauty, gesture, the grand line. And perhaps the grandest line of all, the richest color and the most dramatic form were those of Liszt's magniloquent Fantasy. I wonder why organists play this work so rarely. Is it too hard to learn? Surely not. Miss Demessieux swept through it, as she did everything else, from memory.

March 23, 1953

Loud and Grand

NBC SYMPHONY ORCHESTRA, *Arturo Toscanini*, conductor, with the ROBERT SHAW CHORALE, yesterday afternoon at Carnegie Hall, performing Beethoven's *Missa Solemnis*.

BEETHOVEN'S MISSA SOLEMNIS is a work which this reviewer has long preferred reading or thinking about to actually hearing. The grandeur of its conception cannot be questioned, but much of its detail is weak and does not carry. Nor does a great deal of the choral writing really "sound"; it is too loud and too high too much of the time. Orchestrally also the work has little to offer of charm or variety. The scoring lacks color, as does also the harmony, which is limited almost entirely to its architectural function. The work is of an extraordinary plainness, in spite of its length and seeming complexity. Its glory lies in its straightforwardness, its insistence, its triumphal assertion, as if the whole Mass were one dauntless, relentless Hallelujah.

Naturally the execution by mere musicians of so grand a concept is limited by human possibilities. And Mr. Toscanini resolved none of the work's well known practical difficulties save only that of giving us whole and straight its noble simplicity of mood. The N.B.C. Orchestra did not play throughout with an agreeable sound, nor did the Robert Shaw Chorale so sing. The soloists were lovely, especially the soprano Lois Marshall; but the conductor left them little leeway for singing other than at the top of their power all the time.

The whole reading seemed to me weighted on the loud side, and there derived from this loudness a certain monotony. Excitement there was, yes, a tension of rhythmic insistence and a tension of strain. Also that fullness of affirmation that is the glory of Beethoven. A not dissimilar affirmation on the interpreter's level, of course, is the glory of Toscanini, just turned eighty-six. For these gifts let us be thankful. All the same, I do repeat, every time I hear the *Missa Solemnis*, that there seems to be no satisfactory way of making this work sound less like a tempest over the Atlantic and more like a piece of music comparable in intrinsic interest to any of the same composer's symphonies.

March 30, 1953

Singing English

THE INCREASING USE of English on our operatic stages has begun to make evident the inefficiencies of many an opera singer's diction in that language. Also the fine verbal projection of certain others, of Mack Harrell's, for instance. Several times lately, in reviewing such occasions, this reporter has mentioned the tendency, encouraged by many vocal studios, to mute, to neutralize all unstressed English vowels into a sound such as might be represented in spelling by the letters *uh*. This sound exists in many modern languages; and it has a sign in the international phonetic alphabet, which is a lower-case *e* printed upside down. It is also recognized by all students of pronunciation that English vowels, unless they bear the stress accent of a word or word-group, tend toward neutral sound. The first and last syllables of *potato* and *tomato* are partially neutralized vowels; but they remain *o*'s never the less, especially in speech destined for large-hall projection. The last syllable of *sofa*, on the other hand, is completely worn down to the neutral state of *uh*; and no speaker can say it otherwise without seeming affected.

Several letters from phonetic students have seemed to invite discussion of these matters, and almost all of them have assumed as axiomatic that musical declamation should imitate as closely as possible the customs of spoken speech. I find the assumption hasty, if only in view of the fact that conversational speech and shouted speech do not observe the same vowel qualities. Nowadays that public speaking is done more and more through electrical amplification, it tends more and more also toward the conversational tone. But the great orators and the great actors, when working without a microphone, still project their phrases through vowel observances that at a lower level of loudness would be considered frank distortion.

Singing requires even greater distortion of speech customs, since tonal resonance must be preserved at all times. It is most curious, once you think about it, that while no one would ever mistake a British actor's speech for that of an American, and vice versa, there is practically no difference at all in the way that British and American artists articulate their common language in song. This means that some dominant consideration wipes out in their singing all localisms of speech. What is that consideration? It is the essential difference between speech and song, the simple fact that singing permits an extension of the vowel sounds that is outside the convention of speech.

It is unfortunate that most of the phonetic studies available in print deal only with speech. They are all right so far as they go; but they do not, as a rule, deal at all with the tonal problem that is cardinal to musical declamation. They are like qualitative analysis in chemistry. The next step will have to be a quantitative analysis of English vowels and diphthongs. Because our vowels are not equally extensible. Those of *pit*, *pat*, *pet* and *put* allow of hardly any holding time at all. Whereas the *o* of *home* can be sustained to the farthest limit of breath, though the identical *o* in *pope* resists extension.

All these matters need study. And for singers a great refinement in vowel intonations is needed if the unaccented ones are not to be hastened pell-mell into that limbo of similarity where popular radio and movie artists tend to throw them. Singing is by its nature conservative in this regard, because neutralized vowels are neither beautiful nor sonorous. And composers can be ever so cruel in asking for extension of these weak sounds. The word *garden* is correctly spoken as *gahdn*, but it cannot be sung that way if the second syllable has a long note. A vowel must be invented for it by each singer, a sound at once becoming to his voice and not too absurdly inappropriate to the speech-sound of the word. *Jerusalem* is another tricky word, at least the first syllable of it. *Jee* and *Jay* are clearly absurd, though I've heard both in New York City. On the whole, American artists prefer *Jeh*, though the British have long maintained that only *Juh* is correct.

Gradations of vowel color are necessary even for long accented syllables, because vocal beauty demands some darkening of the bright *ay*'s and *ee*'s, some brightening of the dark *oh* and *ou*, especially if the notes involved are high or loud. Further gradations are needed for the vocalization of unaccented vowels. The *er* of *river* in "Swanee River" comes out best, for instance, if sung as something very like the French sound *eu*. The *y* in *melody*, though it may seem to ask for an *ee* sound, admits tempering in some cases. The word *little* is a headache all round, and so is *bottle*. The last syllable of *Saviour* is clearly neither *yrrr* nor *yaw*; as in *river*, something approaching the French *eu* is probably the best solution.

A cultivated singing-speech does not fear to exaggerate, to color, to alter English vowel sounds (as these are used in speech) for clarity, for resonance, for carrying power. What it must avoid like sin, for it is one linguistically, is the undue neutralization of vowels, which can endanger clarity, resonance, and carrying power. Studios teach the correct declamation of Italian, German, and French. Some teach good singing English, too. Many do not. And many English-speaking singers sing a corrupt and vulgar English. This fault should be corrected in the studios. Indeed, it *must* be corrected if English-language opera is to be successful. The music public will accept an occasional folksy touch, but by and large it wants a classical style in its musical executions. And declamation, diction, are a part of musical execution. They are in need right here and now of serious attention.

April 12, 1953

Great Man in Decline

PHILADELPHIA ORCHESTRA, *Eugene Ormandy*, conductor, last night at Carnegie Hall, performing, among other works, Prokofiev's Symphony No. 7.

SERGEI PROKOFIEV's last symphony, No. 7, composed only last year, was the novelty nugget of last night's concert of the Philadelphia Orchestra in Carnegie Hall. Eugene Ormandy conducted it with perfect clarity; and since the work itself is both simple and frank, there need be little hesitation about anyone's attitude toward it. That of the audience, as expressed in applause, was warm. The piece seems to have been designed, indeed, for appealing easily. How long this charm will last leaves many a reserve in this listener's mind, since it failed for him to survive through even the first hearing.

In his judgment the work shows the influence of the composer's long illness. He would not care to credit any of its faults to government pressure, because Prokofiev has long composed better music under identical pressures. I must admit, however, that it bears a striking resemblance to what the Party leaders say they want. It is flowing, facile, open, and filled with reminiscences, both melodic and harmonic, of the kind of tune and sentiment that all of us associate with films manufactured for wide distribution.

It is not impossible that the symphony may have been derived or assembled from a film accompaniment, though I know no evidence to prove this. It is ever so loosely built; and its melodic content, though broad and songful, is quite without dignity. It is both casual and, artistically considered, corrupt. It does not sound in any way like Prokofiev, who, though he had a streak in him of vulgarity, a very little one, was also a distinguished musical mind. The commonplaceness in this work is not that of basic music materials nor of universal human communications. It is the banality of commercial art and commercialized sentiments. It is sticky and sweet and, in its lighter moments, just plain silly. Were it not so signed, I should not believe that Prokofiev wrote it. And surely the Prokofiev that did is not the same Prokofiev that the music world has so long loved for his vast vitality, his pungent skill and acid sarcasms, his insistent and delirious powers of sustaining an ecstasy. Even more than from the news of his death we shall miss him terribly now.

April 22, 1953

A Powerful Work

WALDEN STRING QUARTET last night at McMillan Theatre, Columbia University, performing, among other works, Elliott Carter's String Quartet. *Homer Schmitt, Bernard Goodman*, violins; *John Garvey*, viola; *Robert Swenson*, cello.

ELLIOTT CARTER's String Quartet is a sumptuous and elaborate structure that lasted forty-five minutes without losing at any point its hold on this listener's attention. The piece is complex of texture, delicious in sound, richly expressive, and in every way grand. Its specific charm is the way in which it sounds less like a classical string quartet than like four intricately integrated solos all going on at the same time. Each instrument plays music which is at any given moment melodically and rhythmically complete. It could be played alone. But it also serves as contrasted thematic matter against which three other seemingly independent parts all stand out as if in relief. As in fugal writing, the tunes, rhythms, figurations, and placements as regards pitch are mutually contrasted and mutually contributory. Their relation to one another lies in their studied differences.

They are all in the same key; but often, by the use of double-stops, each instrument makes its own harmony. They also swap their tunes and counter-tunes about, too, as in the fugal style. Only toward the very end do they actually cooperate in the production of a communal, a blended harmony. And this passage seemed less interesting than the rest of the piece, simply because the rhythmic contrasts of the work's contrapuntal texture were no longer present to animate its flow—again a phenomenon not uncommon in fugal writing.

The work is not a fugue; it is a free composition deriving equally from the improvisational toccata-style and the constructed sonata. It is a summation of many composing methods, though its source lies in neoclassicism. Richness and variety are its glory, freedom and mastery its most impressive message on first hearing. It is difficult to play; it was beautifully played by the Walden String Quartet of the University of Illinois. It is an original and powerful piece, and the audience loved it.

May 5, 1953

Henri Sauguet

CONCERT OF MUSIC BY HENRI SAUGUET last night at the Museum of Modern Art, New York, with musicians including the JUILLIARD STRING QUARTET, *Leontyne Price*, soprano, and *Martial Singher*, baritone, performing Sauguet's String Quartet No. 2; *Le Voyant*, cantata; *La Nuit*, ballet; *Le Chevre-feuille*, song cycle, and *Bocages*, a work for ten instruments.

THE MUSIC of Henri Sauguet, as presented in the Museum of Modern Art under the auspices of the International Society for Contemporary Music and of the Juilliard School, came to many as a surprise as well as a delight. The warmth and the spontaneity with which New York responded both to the music and to the person of the composer was a match, indeed, for the same warmth and the spontaneity that are his music's most powerful qualities. And the rarity of these qualities in contemporary music makes them all the more welcome in a time when music lovers have grown used to hearing from composers every imaginable idiom save the language of the heart.

Sauguet has been speaking his heart in music for nigh on to thirty years, and he has long been loved in Europe for doing so. But America has had little chance to love his work. His operas, of which there are four, have not been produced here, presumably because our troupes are not staffed for producing French opera. And his ballets, of which there are upwards of twenty, have mostly been composed for organizations that do not visit our shores. Even his chamber music and his songs, which constitute a large repertory, have scarcely been touched; and when isolated works of any kind have been given, they have usually passed almost unperceived. It took a whole concert of Sauguet's work to make clear that it is the expression of a remarkable personality, one of the strongest personalities, in fact, now alive and working.

Perhaps the time has not been ripe till now for America to love and understand a music at once so elegant and so humane, so void of insistence and so deeply felt. We have had to work our way through all the fashionable forms of stridency to arrive at the point of being able to hear again that which is not strident and to exhaust our delight in violence, frigidity, and the obsessions of abnormal psychology before we could notice again the dignity of the more nourishing sentiments, the ones we live on. Perhaps also a few vested interests have discouraged up to now any venturings of the contemporary music societies into paths not clearly marked as leading to the further success of already successful movements.

The quickest musicians to take up Sauguet may well be the recital vocalists. His production of songs has been large and ever distinctive. Admirably composed for singing and perfectly prosodized, these comprise settings of some of the finest French lyric poetry by Paul Éluard, by Georges Hugnet, by Max Jacob, by Mallarmé, Laforgue, and Baudelaire, as well as French translations of Rilke and Schiller. These are French songs in the tradition of Poulenc and Fauré, the lyrical tradition, rather than the more declamatory vein of Debussy and Berlioz. They have not Poulenc's bounce nor Ravel's irony; they simply have a lovely tenderness and a tragedy all their own. Like all fine songs, they are a distilled poetic essence, different each from each yet all full of the composer's own flavor.

It is surprising that a composer so gifted for the theater and so versed in the dramatic forms should indulge so little in rhythmic surprise or weighty emphasis. It is Sauguet's sharp sense of character differences and of distinctions among the sentiments that make violence no temptation to him. Everything in his music is made up out of contrasts and oppositions; but these elements are composed into a harmony, not set at war. The result is a vibrant equilibrium rather than a tension. Sauguet does not purge the emotions; he feeds them, makes them flower, give off perfume. The drama in his stage works is as intimate as in his chamber music, just as his chamber music is capable of evoking vast scenes and lofty laments worthy of the opera.

This primacy of expression makes him a romantic; and the consistent shapeliness of his work unmasks him as a neo-Romantic. He is, indeed, one of the founding fathers of the musical movement so denominated, as he was the close friend and frequent theatrical collaborator of Christian Bérard, its leader in painting. Whether this movement has run its course or scarcely begun, I shall not argue here, though my faith is in the latter outcome. But whatever the future may decide, Henri Sauguet has already brought us a sweetness, a beauty, a sincerity, and a savor that contemporary music has long lacked and that are dew and strawberries to us just now.

May 9, 1953

Choral Conference

THE AMERICAN COMPOSER AND CHORAL MUSIC was the subject of a two-day conference held last Monday and Tuesday at Harvard University.

The ceremonies included also two evening concerts held in Harvard's thoroughly ugly, nearly a century old, and acoustically

perfect Sanders Theater. The second of these was a choral concert conducted by Harold C. Schmidt, of Stanford University,
director of this year's Summer School Chorus, and by myself.
This group, numbering about forty, sang everything brilliantly
and beautifully.

Randall Thompson's *Last Words of David* is notable for its
ending, a softly floating Alleluia. Elliott Carter's *Musicians
Wrestle Everywhere* partly displays and partly conceals its fanciful
Emily Dickinson text in a deliciously complex contrapuntal texture modeled, if I guess rightly, after the madrigals of Orlandus
Lassus. It is a gay and busy piece, at once airy and compact in
sound, and marked by the very great precision of workmanship
that is characteristic of Carter. Irving Fine's *Have You Seen the
White Lily Grow* and *O Do Not Wanton With Those Eyes* have
all the tender poetry and very unusual melodic grace that are
Fine's especial gifts. The first of these in particular struck me as
one of the really lovely contemporary works in madrigal style.

Contradicting the musical distinction of these selected works,
the forum discussions of the two-day meeting had returned
again and again to the American composer's lack of interest in
writing for chorus and his poor mastery of the medium. It had
been pointed out frequently that American choral works have
been, on the whole, neither inspired nor expert, as compared
to those that have come out of Europe in our century. Debussy,
Ravel, Roussel, Stravinsky, Milhaud, Honegger, Poulenc, Malipiero, Hindemith, Orff, Blacher, Frank Martin, Holst, Vaughan
Williams, Walton, and Britten have all composed as pungently
for grouped voices as for grouped instruments. But our American choral work seems, on the whole, to compare less well with
our country's contributions to orchestral and to chamber music.

The choral conductors present were all for changing this situation by a program of commissioning choral works and of collaborating technically with composers. The composers showed
small enthusiasm for the prospect, harped continually on the
musical and textual limits of the choral medium, on its compromising associations with musical amateurism, and its hopeless
involvement with all that is most basic in American life. Far
too basic, indeed, for much freedom of feeling about them are
religion and patriotism as subject-matter for art nowadays. And

far too basic also for comfort in artistic execution is all that close ambience of the church, the school, and the home that binds the choral circumstance to respectability, to impersonality, and to emotional common denominators.

No artist is opposed to these firm foundations. Nor are they here, as they have long been in Europe, in any grave danger of collapse. We accept, approve, take them for granted, build our lives on them. But as artists, we try to get away from their power over us. This is why, I think, the American composer has rarely embraced choral composition with any warmth. And it is the reason choral singing in America, for all its wide practice and frequent high standards of execution, remains after three centuries of undiminished vigor more striking as a sociological phenomenon than as a musical gold mine.

At the same time, educators, conductors, and choral singers are yearning for a contemporary American repertory comparable to the European. How to get it out of our composers was the subject of a symposium lasting nearly two hours. Nobody seemed to think that money could not be found, if necessary, for commissioning works. What everybody wanted to know was how to choose the composers, how to inspire them and how to cooperate with them on the technical level. The composers tried to tell them. Nevertheless, to the end the composers remained coy, engaged themselves to no program. And the educators remained determined. I suspect that that determination, backed up by commission money and here and there by an understanding of the composer's essentially childlike mentality, may end by creating an American choral repertory and a tradition, a style. This, at least, plus the excellent performance of some pleasing choral works, was as near to a hopeful note as the Harvard Summer School Conference on *The American Composer and Choral Music* could find to end on.

August 16, 1953

In Spite of Conducting

PHILHARMONIC-SYMPHONY ORCHESTRA, *Dimitri Mitropou-los*, conductor, last night at Carnegie Hall, performing Stamitz's *Symphonie Konzertante* for seven instruments and orchestra, Schumann's Symphony No. 3 ("Rhenish"), and Berlioz's *Harold en Italie*.

WILLIAM LINCER, playing viola solo last night in the Philhar-monic's opening concert of the season at Carnegie Hall, was a delight for his dark tone and the grace of his phraseology. If he did not project dramatically the solo part of Berlioz's *Harold in Italy* as one sometimes hears it done and did not attempt to make a concerto out of a work that is nothing of the kind, that reluctance was welcome, too. It enabled one to hear the piece as what it is, an orchestral landscape "featuring," as show business would put it, the viola.

Dimitri Mitropoulos, conducting, was less discreet. He did not cover the viola with noise when it was playing. But he crowded it, when it was not, with sudden loudnesses and brassy balances. Indeed, our Philharmonic's celebrated conductor overplayed his brasses most of the evening. And in the *Symphonie Konzertante* of Karl Stamitz, which "featured" seven other of the orchestra's first-desk musicians, he pushed his soloists for time as well as for volume.

The conductor's personal excitement, bordering on hysteria, was least under control in the Schumann Third, or *Rhenish* Symphony. Here the rhythm was often unclear, the counter-points lost, the shape of the lovely work distorted by a nervous passion. If its reading nowhere lacked eloquence, it was every-where lacking in elegance, in sweetness, in proportion, and in that spontaneity that is the heaven-sent grace, the unique gift of Robert Schumann.

Actually, when the conductor, in moments of calm, con-ducted straightforwardly and with a minimum of motion, his orchestra followed with a maximum of beauty and with the authority of style that is our Philharmonic's way. But for the most part he did everything to the orchestra but conduct it. He whipped it up as if it were a cake, kneaded it like bread, shuffled and riffled an imaginary deck of cards, wound up a clock, shook a recalcitrant umbrella, rubbed something on a washboard and wrung it out. Really, there were very few moments when a film taken of the conductor alone, without sound, would have given any clue to the fact that he was directing a musical composition.

October 9, 1953

Scientists Get Curious

THE SCIENTIFIC SCHOOLS, long a fortress of pure reason and practicality, have lately been encouraging in their students a curiosity about the arts. The Massachusetts Institute of Technology and other technical centers have introduced music to the elective parts of their curricula with notable success. Even on the philosophic plane the scientific world, classically disciplined to a positivistic attitude, has begun to wonder if perhaps there is not something to be learned from the more spontaneous working methods of the musician, the painter, the poet.

Last week at a convention held in this city the Engineering College Research Council of the American Society for Engineering Education devoted a whole morning to "creativeness." The painter John Ferren, the novelist Ralph Bates, and the present writer, as composer, were asked to explain "creativeness" and answer questions about it. The assignment was a tough one, partly because artists and scientists do not use the same vocabulary, and also because the very word "creativeness" assumes a good deal.

For scientists it seems to imply that something has been invented out of nothing, or at least that some object or principle has been arrived at without its discoverer having followed the deductive procedures. For artists it implies nothing at all about method; it means originality rather, the bringing into existence of something different from everything else. This difference may be vast or very small, but it must be there. If it is, something has been created. If not, we have merely a copy.

Copies are legitimate, of course. The world lives on them. Their production and distribution are a province of engineering, as witness the printing press and the gramophone. But music recognizes two kinds of copies, the multiple and the unique. Multiple copies, all pretty much alike, are an industrial product. Single copies made by hand are an art product. A painter's copy of another painter's picture has a personal expression in spite of all attempts to keep it out. And an executant musician's rendering of a composition is as individual an achievement as what a builder erects from an architect's design. This duet of design and execution, thoroughly familiar to engineers, is characteristic of music. Painting is a one-man job and does not, in its high-art aspects, envisage reproduction. Poetry is a one-man job which envisages (or hopes for) multiple reproduction by print. Music, like architecture, envisages from the beginning collaboration. It is a design for execution.

Now considering the design as "creative" and its execution merely an "interpretation" is customary among musicians. But it applies better to the execution of scores from the past than to contemporary music. Co-operation between the living composer and his executants is an essential part of musical creation, of bringing a work into real existence. Because music's real existence is auditory; it is sound, not notes on a page. Actually, music and architecture, music and engineering, are similar in their dependence on execution. Who am I to say that the executant's contribution to my work is not a "creative" act? It is certainly part of one.

What scientists want to know, of course, is how a composer arrives at his design. Well, sometimes an expressive, a communicable idea is arrived at by reasoning. Sometimes it bursts up from the unconscious. And its organization into a piece of music comes in the same two ways. Often a practical workman will write it all down quite rapidly, as if he were taking dictation. At other times it comes more slowly. And if he hits a snag he has to reason his way around it. The simplest parallel I know for what a composer does is what anybody does when he writes a letter. He wants or needs to make a communication. He thinks about it a little. He writes it. Then he reads it back to find out whether he has said what he meant to say and, most important of all, whether he is willing to mean what he has actually said.

Music, all art for that matter, depends on meaning. The prestige of non-Euclidean geometry has all through this century caused artists to insist that their work at its best and most "advanced" is theoretical, an abstraction comparable to the higher equations. At the same time they have hoped that within twenty years its acceptance as communication would make them loved and famous. Actually music does not work like that. The most novel modern music has always had a public that understood and accepted it. The battle has been one of obtaining access for it to the existing mechanisms of distribution. All music is about something, just as all music that can stand up under concert usage has a sound technical structure. There is no abstract music. There is only expressive music. This expression may depict an inner or an outer reality. But it always depicts something. And unless both the reality depicted and its manner of depiction have an essential uniqueness, a personality strongly different from that of all other existing artifacts, there is no work of art. "Creation" has not taken place.

Science deals with a unified universe governed by laws universally applicable. Art deals with a multiple universe in which no two apples or carburetors or love affairs are alike. Revealing the common properties of apples and carburetors and love affairs is the business of science. To individualize them is the province of art. As to what is "creative" and what not, I suppose that the defining of all that is the critic's job. But critics can be terribly presumptuous. Who is to say that Stravinsky is more creative than Einstein? As Gertrude Stein used to say, there is the "human mind" and there is "human nature." There is also the visible or knowable universe. The human mind, like the rest of the knowable universe, follows patterns. That is its strength. Human nature, which is essentially unknowable, is at its most interesting when least predictable. And art, poetry, music are similarly most powerful when from work to work, school to school, age to age, and decade to decade they show the widest imaginable diversity from their own standard patterns of style, of subject-matter, of communicative effect.

October 18, 1953

Chunky and Palatable

LITTLE ORCHESTRA SOCIETY, *Thomas Scherman*, conductor, last night at Town Hall, performing Pergolesi's *Stabat Mater*, Creston's Symphony No. 2, and a concert version of *Mavra*, opera in one act, libretto by *Mr. Scherman* (from the Russian original by *Boris Kochno*), music by Igor Stravinsky, with *Ann Ayars* (Parasha), *John Druary* (Vassili/"Mavra"), *Sandra Warfield* (Mother), and *David Randolph* (Narrator).

THOMAS SCHERMAN, conducting the Little Orchestra Society's first concert of the season last night in Town Hall, gave us three chunky and highly palatable works, two of them contemporary. The other, Pergolesi's *Stabat Mater*, is a characteristic eighteenth-century piece whose popularity I have never quite understood. Gracefully written and melodious enough, this setting of the liturgical hymn for soprano, alto and orchestra has long been a favorite with audiences. Myself, I have never been able to keep my mind on it; and I had the same trouble last night, though Ann Ayars and Sandra Warfield seemed to be singing ever so nicely.

Paul Creston's Second Symphony, which Mr. Scherman conducted lovingly, is an easy-to-listen-to work, melodious and orchestrally rich. A certain self-indulgence on the harmonic plane makes for lushness, and constant use of ostinato figures in the structure gives a semblance of emotional intensity. All the same, though the work is seriously conceived and skillfully scored, it did not impress me on last night's hearing of it (my third in eight years) as quite first-class. It is a work that stands some rehearing, and it has dignity. But I do not find its expressive content very personal. And its ending up with a wholly objective dance number denies the validity of the meditative mood in all the rest of it. That dance does not come out of the symphony's premise.

Stravinsky's comic opera *Mavra*, which closed the evening, is a delicious piece of musical fooling and of real dramatico-sentimental expression under all the fooling. Playing it for low farce, as was done (although in evening clothes and with no scenery), is, I think, a mistake. The characterization needs to be taken seriously, leaving all comic comment to the orchestra and to the music's own exuberance. Perhaps a puppet show would be the work's ideal presentation. Either that or a wholly stylized choreography that would evoke the pathos of puppets. Its irony, a double-take, gets lost in comic-strip clowning.

The singers sang it straight, and Mr. Scherman played the music straight. That was as it should be. Only the acting, far too easy-going for so intense a work, a piece at once bitter, biting, hilarious, and tender, was out of key. That and also an explainer who addressed us at the beginning through a microphone, reading a script that recounted the plot (though program-notes were provided, and the opera was sung in English anyway) and told us what to think of the music, for all the world like a radio announcer. I never figured out what he was supposed to serve for. Maybe he had been left over from an earlier children's concert. Especially pleasing on the other hand, was the singing of Ann Ayars and of John Druary in this difficult and ever-so-Russian florid-aria skit on a *Charley's Aunt* theme out of Pushkin.

October 20, 1953

Interpretation

WHAT does a composer of music need from his interpreters? What are the living composer's rights about the interpretation of his work? And what are an interpreter's obligations? All these matters have been disputed for centuries, because music is a collaborative art like architecture or engineering. A piece of music on a page is only an idea. Its real existence is in performance.

By performance I mean live performance. The transmission or recording of live performance has great value, like photography or print. But unlike print, it does not replace the original. Even when adjustments are made to compensate for accidents of performance and for the inefficiencies of recording, the result is still an imitation. A recording is not even a performance; it has to be itself performed on a machine operated by a live man or woman or child. And don't think such performances do not vary enormously in sound quality, in their volume patterns, even in speed. A recording played or a live performance broadcast under an engineer's control (plus the receiver's control) is an interpretation of an interpretation, a performance of a performance.

But let us get back to performance itself, as this takes place with live musicians and no microphones. And let us further suppose that the composer of the work has been present at rehearsals. Is the performance merely a rendering of the composer's plan? Or do the executants add something valuable of their own? The answer is that they do. Even if they try to do nothing but reflect the composer's thought and feeling, that effort at neutrality gives its own emotional tone, its own expressivity. It is a style like any other and comparable to what happens when you read aloud a piece of literature as if it were a contract. (Over-expressivity in performing Stravinsky can be like reading a contract as if it were literature.)

The truth is, of course, that a musical score is not a contract. It is much more like a cooking recipe, an indication (in many details quite precise and in others wholly approximate) that presupposes familiarity with traditional techniques and current tastes. For musical notation is highly inexact at best. It is a text that requires in the most literal sense "interpretation." And even when the author of it is present to guide that interpretation into the channels of his own desire, he must work through live people, accept their inefficiencies and take advantage of their particular temperaments in order to arrive at a result that will have life in it.

As a matter of fact, the composer in such a case is the interpreter of his own work. And the performance that he gives or guides is as much that of an experienced performing artist as it is that of an author. For it is a mistake to think the composer always knows what he wants. At certain points in the piece he knows precisely, has a vivid auditory image of a particular sound or a particular expressive effect. At others he is mostly aware of what he does not want.

If a piece of music depicts some scene or other exterior view, such as landscape or hell-fire or dancing, its score is likely to contain many indications of what is and is not wanted; and its tempo requirements can be quite exact. Even many years after its first performance this kind of music tends to preserve a standard interpretation. The landscapes of Debussy and Ravel, the ballets of Stravinsky do not vary enormously from performance to performance in tempo or in tonal balance. The symphonies of Sibelius, on the other hand, which are roughly contemporary with these, have no standard reading, cannot have, indeed, because their theme is not objective. They are depictions of the composer's emotional life.

The music of introspection, the music of the heart, requires of its interpreter that which is specific to the heart, spontaneity. If the music of Schumann or Schubert or Brahms or Fauré or Richard Wagner, for that matter, and certainly that of Arnold Schönberg is to be read convincingly, it must be read also with conviction. The composer can and should make an effort to get over to his interpreter how he wants the music to sound and to feel. But the artist must then take the music for his own, adopt it, feel it, and perform it as if it were an expression of his own deepest needs. If he does not treat it so, it will not communicate. If he overtreats it so, it will also not communicate; the interpretation will seem false. But in performing the music of anxiety and relief, of private tensions and their resolution—the music, in other words, of pure feeling—there is no substitute for feeling.

The music of the last three centuries, our practicable repertory back through Monteverdi and Schütz, includes depictions of both outer and inner realities. Both require interpretation. But the depictions of outer reality require an objective reading, while the others demand subjectivity. The musical depictions of outer reality are likely to be quite precisely scored also and to acquire early in their life-course a standard reading which is the correct one. The depictions of the inner world are of necessity less precisely set down, since spontaneity of expression is essential to their existence. Such music varies vastly in tempo, in rhythmic flow, in rhetorical emphasis from one interpreter to another, from one age or country to another. And no reading is ever definitive. The symphonies of Beethoven, for example, exist in the mind only. Their reality is a memory of many versions, not of one.

Interpreters vary, too. Some are better with objective music, and some specialize in the introspective. The great ones imagine themselves as masters of both, just as great composers do. But it is not true in either case. What is true is that all music requires interpretation. Even when a composer conducts his own music, his reading is not quite definitive. It is merely one version, perhaps the most authoritative and perhaps not, depending on how skillful a performer he is and how precise his original idea was. In all cases it is a privileged communication. The professional performer must consult it if he can and consult the composer if he can. But the best final result obtains, even in objective music and in the theater, when the interpreter, in full knowledge and in full acceptance of responsibility, takes over the show and plays Hamlet not as if he himself were Shakespeare, but as if he were Hamlet.

October 25, 1953

Bigger Than Baseball

AMONG all of America's leisure activities, the most widely indulged, believe it or not, is the art of music. I am not talking about radio music, the universal background of home life, or the various forms of transmitted music that are the steady accompaniment to public eating and drinking, to bus-riding, automobile trips, and shopping. "Canned" music has become an auditory décor so constantly present in American life that virtually nobody can escape from it.

But music in this sense cannot be called a leisure activity any more than sleeping in a bed or wearing shoes can. An activity is something one is active about. Well, the latest bulletin of the National Music Council, a very serious documentary publication, reports over the signature of Mrs. Helen M. Thompson, executive secretary of the American Symphony Orchestra League, that thirty million people in this country are "actively interested in concert music." This does not mean jazz or popular ditties, or hillbilly dance-bands, or shows and films employing music, or hymn singing, or wedding marches. It means the classical music of the last three centuries, including the one we live in. And thirty million people are one-fifth of our population.

The statement is even more difficult to believe when one realizes that only half that number, fifteen million, watched major league baseball games last year, that only thirteen million ordinarily engage in hunting, and that a mere five million, according to the same report, play golf. Considering classical music as a spectator sport, its total cost in a recent year, says Mrs. Thompson, was $45,000,000 compared to the following gross revenues of organized sports:

> Baseball $40,000,000
> Horse and dog tracks 38,000,000
> Professional football 9,000,000

In addition to the $45,000,000 paid at the gate for public performances of classical music, which represents 30,000,000 separate paid admissions, last year's sales of classical recordings totaled $60,000,000. This amounts to 24 per cent of all record sales. And among the ten best sellers were two full-length classical symphonies.

Let me give you some more details about our professional music life. America has eighty opera companies operating in nineteen states. We have 150 music periodicals, 750 music critics, 1,196 writers on musical subjects. We have 938 symphony orchestras, all or in part professionally staffed. One of our large booking organizations reports that last year three times as many concerts were given in the United States as in all the rest of the world put together. Music in general—its teaching, performance, manufacture of equipment, and distribution—has for some years now ranked sixth among America's industries in volume of business, being somewhat smaller than food or motor cars but a much bigger affair than steel.

As for music on the non-professional level, let us begin by noting the existence, again according to the National Music Council, of 20,000,000 music students. More than one-tenth of our population is taking lessons of some kind toward the acquisition of musical skill. Seventy-five lay organizations comprising over 600,000 members aid in disseminating international standards of workmanship. Fifteen thousand school orchestras actually perform symphonic repertory. For adults who enjoy playing string quartets and the like there is a society of more than 3,000 members called Amateur Chamber Music Players. They have a national directory, too, where they are graded A, B, C, D for skill, and they can phone one another anywhere, just like Alcoholics Anonymous. As for choruses, choirs, glee clubs, and singing societies, they number surely upward of a million. There are very few citizens among those able to carry a tune at all whose lives have not at one time been permanently enriched by participation in this most rewarding of all forms of musical exercise.

Now with a large part of our nation involved in some way with music, nobody has to worry right now about the state of the art. It is in every way a going concern. But it might help to understand how deeply music is honeycombed into American life if I sketch, even superficially, music's organization. For with the possible exception of medicine, music is the most highly organized activity in the Western world. Religion has its sects, literature its language barriers. Sports have different rules in different countries. Love and war, as we know, have no rules at all. But the symphony orchestra is a machine so standardized that any conductor, any player, any piece in its repertory can be replaced overnight by a conductor, player, or composition from any other orchestra in the world of similar skill-category. And the skill-categories are only about three. All this without language difficulties. The instruments used, the manner of sounding them, and the compositions performed do not differ in any notable way from Tel-Aviv to Valparaiso.

And since the symphony orchestra is the kingpin of our whole musical system, the conservatories of music from Tel-Aviv to Valparaiso and from Cape Town to Murmansk, by way of Seattle and Tokyo, are devoted to the production of players, conductors, and composers who will be ready at a moment's notice to step into any symphonic operation. Also, since a standardized art needs a standardized public, our schools, colleges, and universities have set themselves the task of teaching to future orchestral subscribers an accepted history of music (with orchestral composition at the top), a standard method of musical analysis (for the understanding of orchestral music), and a standard hierarchy of values for the admiration of orchestral works.

Contributory to this effort of our educational system is a network of music clubs, laymen's auxiliary aid societies, technical guilds, and trade groups. National associations of music teachers, of instrument manufacturers, of piano tuners, of flute players, societies for the pooling of copyrights and the collection of royalties, groups opposed to the performance of contemporary music, others who agitate for it, a managers' association, a union of soloists (in addition to the great Musicians' Union itself), a half dozen sororities devoted to general do-gooding, musical therapists, music publishers, collectors of recorded music, youth organizations of music lovers world-wide in membership, statisticians devoted to the collecting and pooling of information about how symphony orchestras are financed—everybody, literally everybody connected with the music world belongs to something, has a part in its complex organization.

This organization has no hierarchy or center. It is not a professional clan, a business monopoly, or an exercise in amateur philanthropy, though it is something of all these. It is basically a vast network of spontaneous co-operation that happens to work efficiently because the modern world loves music and because musicians themselves are, among all workers in the intellectual branches, the most given to effective organization. Their talent for this is probably associated with their private feeling of consecration. In this they are like the clergy, which is also good at organizing everybody. In any case, the music world is a maze of power-lines in which the professional, the amateur, the educator, the student, the man of business, and the woman of society are equally involved.

Some years ago the late Louis Kirstein, at that time president of Filene's department store in Boston, received a visit from some trustees of the Boston Symphony Orchestra. The orchestra needed $75,000 quickly; could Mr. Kirstein help? Mr. Kirstein, aware of the suburban business which the concerts brought to his store every Friday afternoon, though he himself rarely attended, recognized his responsibility, gave $25,000 and telephoned two other retail merchants, who gave the same. The orchestra's emergency was closed.

Another case of business tie-up came to attention recently in the decision of the General Electric Company to build a subsidiary plant in Louisville.

The cultural advantages of that city, of which the symphony orchestra is one, had determined its being chosen. Culture works as follows in the decentralization of industry. You cannot establish a branch factory without moving executives and technicians. And your executives and technicians cannot move their families without their wives' consent. And their wives will not consent unless the city proposed can offer educational advantages in the form of (and prized in this order) good schools, a near-by college, a symphony orchestra, a public library, and an art museum.

Mayor Charles Farnsley of Louisville demonstrated some years ago in a doctoral thesis that municipal prosperity follows from city to city a curve parallel to the availability in these cities of (in this order) music, theater, and art. In those cities department store business is good, restaurant business is good, hotel business is good; and there is a traffic problem, infallible index of prosperity.

It has long been known from history that culture follows commerce. Today it is clear also that commerce follows culture. And it is also clear to any one who deals with the world of classical, or "serious," music that music is purely a cultural and educational manifestation and forms no part of the entertainment trades, of show business. On the contrary, it is esteemed beneficial like religion; and people give money to it. Musical exercise is well known to be good for the body, the feelings, and the mind. A further presumption that it can also lift up the soul, though rarely stated, is ever present in the American view of life.

To occupy the young, to ennoble adulthood, to train the hand, elevate the mood, lift up the spirits, and at the same time make business boom—all these are what America expects out of music and, surprisingly enough, gets. No country before us, not Germany nor Austria nor Italy nor the England of Tudor times, ever quite so gleefully turned itself over to the tonal art. What will come of it all there is no way of knowing. But for this century at least, music is our hobby and our habit; and the chiefest, after breadwinning, among all our avowable preoccupations.

October 25, 1953

Kapell

THE PIANIST William Kapell, who died in an airplane accident near San Francisco on Oct. 29, was a fine artist. So were Grace Moore, soprano, Ginette Neveu and Jacques Thibaud, violinists, who have died in similar fashion in recent years. Every time an airplane falls persons distinguished in professional, political, business, or military life are among the dead. Because it is exactly such persons to whom the speed of air travel offers an irresistible convenience. A musician who moves about the globe in this way can play twice to three times as many engagements a season as the one who is earthbound. Also it is known that aviation fatalities per passenger-mile traveled are far fewer than those due to the deadly automobile. Still, the number of famous names that appears in the aviation accident lists is impressive. And still the advantages, economic and artistic, that come from being able to move quickly from one date to another will keep a large number of our most valued musicians among the inveterate air travelers.

Among musicians of his generation William Kapell, just thirty-one on Sept. 20, was one of the great ones. His career, like that of Ginette Neveu, was at the point where he was no longer considered just a young genius but was recognized by his colleagues as a mature artist. At nineteen he was winning big prizes. At twenty he began his career as a touring recitalist and a much-in-demand orchestral soloist. But for a decade his repertory had remained heavily weighted with the easy-to-put-over works of Rachmaninoff, Tchaikovsky, and Khachaturian. It was only in the last two years that he had gained real access to the grand repertory of the piano, to the concertos of Mozart and Beethoven and Brahms and Chopin and to the suites of Bach and Debussy, and that he had been genuinely successful with that repertory.

Kapell had fought hard for this access and for this success. He had fought with his management and with the press. And he had wrestled with the repertory itself, not only alone but also with the counsel and the detailed cooperation of musicians who knew that repertory. He had studied, labored, consulted, digested, ripened. Kapell had become a grown man and a mature artist, a master. He could play great music with authority; his readings of it were at once sound and individual. He had a piano technique of the first class, a powerful mind, a consecration and a working ability such as are granted to few, and the highest aspirations toward artistic achievement.

Kapell was conquering the world. In one decade he had won a world-wide audience. At the beginning of a second he was recognized as a master to be taken seriously in the great repertory. He was already laying plans (and operating, too) toward the renewal of this repertory through the application of his great technical interpretative powers to contemporary piano music and through devoted co-operation with contemporary composers. And his conquests were not easy. Few artists have ever battled so manfully with management or so unhesitatingly sassed the press. He was afraid of nobody, because his heart was pure.

It is not germane that as a man he was a good son and brother, a good husband and father, and a loyal friend, though he was all these. What is important to music is that he was a musician and a fighter. He did not fight for himself or for just any music. He fought to play well and to play the best music. Also to take part in the creative life of his time. And he was winning, would have gone on winning, for he had a star.

He had also an unlucky star, else he would not have been taken from us. And our loss, music's loss, is irreparable. Other men of comparable genius and sincerity may arise; but none will ever take his place, because that place was unique. Kapell had built it to fit his own great talents. And built it so that his talents could serve the whole world of music in their own particular and powerful way. Past services will remain and be of use to others. But Kapell himself, that huge life-force, is dead; and his continuing musical presence will not be with us any more. Since he was buried last Monday it has been a week of mourning for musicians.

November 8, 1953

Rich Resources

PHILHARMONIC CHAMBER ENSEMBLE, *Dimitri Mitropoulos*, conductor, on November 21 at Buttenweiser Hall of the 92nd Street YMHA, New York, performing, among other works, Schönberg's *Kammersymphonie*, Beethoven's Quintet for Woodwinds and Piano, Mozart's Duo for Violin and Viola, Manuel Rosenthal's Sonatine for Two Violins and Piano, and Milton Babbitt's Woodwind Quartet. Soloists: *Abba Bogin*, piano; *Leon Temerson* and *Bjoern Andreasson*, violins.

THE PHILHARMONIC CHAMBER ENSEMBLE, which opened its third annual series of concerts on Saturday night at the Y.M.H.A., is the richest among all our chamber music groups in instrumental resources. Drawing its players from the whole

Philharmonic-Symphony Orchestra, and organized as a co-operative society, this group offers regularly in its programs works for a great variety of instrumental combinations; and the great expertness of the players permits them also to offer works of unusual stylistic and technical difficulty.

The star number of last Saturday's program was Arnold Schönberg's early *Kammersymphonie*, Opus 9, for fifteen solo instruments, conducted by Dimitri Mitropoulos. Rarely performed at all, on account of its great technical difficulty, this deeply passionate and eloquent piece is at once a monument of late Romanticism and a picture window turned toward twentieth-century chromatic experiment. It is a powerful work that seems to invite (like its predecessor *Verklärte Nacht*) choreography by Antony Tudor.

No less expert and stylish (in the best sense) was the performance of Beethoven's Quintet for Woodwinds and Piano, with Abba Bogin at the keyboard. Mozart's Duo for Violin and Viola (No. 2, in B-flat Major) came off less well. The string players of the Philharmonic, many of them at least, seem less accustomed to the refinements of chamber music execution than the wind players are, used, these latter, to the constant playing of solo passages. Nevertheless Leon Temerson and Bjoern Andreasson, accompanied by Mr. Bogin, gave a delicious and even brilliant performance of Manuel Rosenthal's *Sonatine* for Two Violins and Piano. This lively work, composed in 1923 at the age of nineteen, is musically inspired by Milhaud and Poulenc, rather than by Ravel, who was Rosenthal's teacher. It is an outgoing work, frank, vigorous and entertaining. Thirty years later, one can still find it valid. It is not only skillful but, for all its youthful enthusiasms, strongly personal.

Milton Babbitt's Woodwind Quartet, an Alma Morgenthau-Locust Valley Festival commission which received its first performance on this occasion, is also a strongly personal work. Music composed in the twelve-tone-row syntax has long tended in its finer examples toward a supercharged emotional expression and in its more commonplace ones toward a sterile academicism. It is Mr. Babbitt's distinction to have produced in a twelve-tone technique derived, like that of the contemporary Parisian school, from Webern rather than from Schönberg or Berg, music of an airy elegance wholly his own. It is not crabbed like the French stuff, nor does it seek pathos at any point. It is lacy, good-humored, disinvolved, water-clear. At its least concentrated it goes a bit abstract. At its most intense it has a studied relaxation that is very American, very Princetonian, and utterly distinguished.

November 23, 1953

Irresistible

NATHAN MILSTEIN, violinist, in recital last night at Carnegie Hall, performing Bach's Sonata in A minor, Beethoven's Sonata No. 9 (Op. 47, "Kreutzer"), Mr. Milstein's "Paganiniana," and works by Brahms, Pizzetti, Vitali, and Josef Suk. Accompanist: *Artur Balsam*, piano.

THE PROGRAM that Nathan Milstein played last night in Carnegie Hall, accompanied at the piano by the impeccable Artur Balsam, was a serious one. Three great chunks of uncompromising music for the violin made up its first three quarters—a Vitali chaconne, a Bach unaccompanied sonata and the Beethoven "Kreutzer." Even the final plate of tidbits offered pieces by Schumann and Brahms. And nothing is more serious than Paganini, especially when it is a set of variations of the utmost difficulty composed on a theme from one of the Caprices by Mr. Milstein himself and executed with the utmost brilliance.

Everything seemed, indeed, to be executed with brilliance, even the severest of the classical selections. For it is the gift of this artist to make music shine. His tone is bright, his rhythm is alive and compelling. His music-making glows not with a surface lustre but with an inner light and a warmth all its own, an animal warmth. Soul is not his specialty; nor are tears. For emotional satisfaction he gives us a clean reading of the text and a boyish humility before the great masters. He gives us too a boyish delight in fine technical workmanship, in controlled muscular activity exercised in his powers' limit.

And that limit is a far one, for nobody plays the violin more expertly. But along with the expertness there is a love of the violin and of playing it well that are irresistible. Mr. Milstein is no great or original interpreter. Nor is he any authoritative spokesman for masters of musical thought. There is no vulgarity in him, but neither is there any deep penetration or especial sensitivity. There is simply a personal vibrancy that makes his work at all times completely alive.

In the "Kreutzer" Sonata of Beethoven the dramatized emphases and strong accents were almost over-live, but they were not rough or ugly. They were simply an interpretation and a legitimate one. And they were matched by fine delicacies and many a full-singing line. Fullness of sound at all the levels of softness and loudness is one of this artist's grander gifts. It gives his playing an equalized surface tension, a power of complete projection, that holds the attention in a way that the work of few artists is capable of doing. And so his exact interpretative conception of a piece is never a very important matter.

It is by sheer efficiency and charm, by modesty, enthusiasm, and an utter loyalty to what he is doing that Milstein makes his mark. After twenty and more years on the concert stage he is still the perfect pupil, reasonable, master of his trade, devoted to the sound of his instrument, and not afraid of it. Neither is he afraid of the great classics nor of approaching them with passion and with common sense. The latter quality, of course, is as rare among musicians of any age as is technical mastery. The combination is irresistible.

December 15, 1953

1954

Remembering Mahler

PHILHARMONIC-SYMPHONY ORCHESTRA, *Bruno Walter*, conductor, yesterday afternoon at Carnegie Hall, performing Haydn's Symphony No. 88 and Mahler's Symphony No. 1.

A VERY GREAT PLEASURE was yesterday afternoon's Philharmonic concert, with Bruno Walter conducting. The program was two symphonies, a Haydn and a Mahler, both evidently beloved of the conductor. And the orchestra played perfectly, sweetly, beautifully. One didn't have to worry about what one thought of the symphonies as musical scripts. It was enough that they were being played, understood, rendered into loveliness.

Mr. Walter's reading of the Haydn G-major commonly known as No. 88 was robust, straightforward, an ultimate in rightness and ease. The kind of sophistication that avoids super-refinement is the ultimate sophistication in the reading of this work. And this kind of sophistication is Walter's gift with the German classics. He can make them seem as natural as breathing. And he can make the Philharmonic, which can do everything, sound as if playing a classical symphony were the most natural thing in the world. All the care for beauty and exactitude that goes into such a reading is great workmanship, of course, on his part and on that of the orchestral players. But the result is not any awareness of workmanship at all; it merely brings a piece to life, makes it real. At least that was your reviewer's experience yesterday.

The experience was no less intense in Mahler's First Symphony than in the Haydn. The Mahler is a young man's work, written at thirty, ambitious as to length, abundant in musical ideas. Most of these ideas are orchestral, the ingenuities of a conductor. Expressively the symphony is a patchwork of contrasts. It begins as a pastoral scene with bird calls and hunting horns but turns military by the end of the first movement. The second is a waltz, something between a real country waltz and the urban kind. One might call it suburban if the term were not derogatory. In any case, it bounces along with good spirits and also turns military at the end.

The third movement, the most original of the four, is a joke about a funeral march, beginning with a solo passage for one bass viol and going on to a ravishing orchestral imitation of the Hungarian night-club style before returning to the funeral, at which point it adds a French children's ditty, *Frère Jacques*, to its comical allusions. The last movement starts apocalyptically, imitates a Viennese sentimental song, adds trumpets, and ends with a brassy coda. Everywhere the tunes are good and the orchestral treatments picturesque. There is a young man's fascination with rhetorical structure elements—with introductions, transitions, and perorations. It is charmingly immodest and delightful for the outrageousness of its satire. I think it is the loving hand beneath it all that gives the work its reality. Mahler loved writing music and loved dramatizing the relation between the composer and his material. This drama, I think, is his music's most intense expression and its most original.

The vigor with which this drama came forth yesterday was Mr. Walter's contribution. Among all living conductors he has the freshest remembrance, I suspect, of exactly how Mahler's music felt in Mahler's time. Certainly it all felt fresh at that time, and certainly the First Symphony felt like a striking and somewhat scandalous piece by a young conductor of genius. Walter did not underline the scandalousness; he leant rather on its sweetness. And by doing so he made it seem youthful and aspiring, which it also is. He could have given it the portentous treatment. Some do. Instead, he read it as if remembering his youth, which was not far, after all, from Mahler's, only a decade and a half.

January 25, 1954

Composer and Critic

MUSIC in the twentieth century is the subject of a congress to be held in Rome this spring from April 4 through 15. Composers, critics, and interpreters from everywhere will be present as the guests of the inviting organizations, which are the European Culture Center (Geneva, Switzerland), the Congress for Cultural Freedom (Paris and New York), and the Italian State Radio. Twelve composers, including the Americans Ben Weber and Lou Harrison, have been commissioned to write works which will compete for three large cash prizes (plus other benefits). There will be lots of twentieth-century music performed by the visiting soloists and conductors. And there will be forum discussions of subjects especially interesting to composers, critics, and interpreters.

This writer has been asked to lead a discussion entitled *The Composer and the Critic*. The choice was an obvious one, I suppose, since he has long been active in both roles. But that very fact may have led him to lack consistency. When another composer's music is unfavorably reviewed, for example, he knows that, just or unjust, the reviewer has done his best. But when his own or that of one of his close colleagues receives such a review he tries to convince himself, just as any other artist does in that circumstance, that the reviewer is ignorant, stupid, and very probably in the pay of some enemy.

The truth is, at least in America, that music critics do not take graft. They are not even offered it on any scale that might be tempting. Neither do they fight very vigorously against the survival of new techniques, new talents, new æsthetic positions. They inform the public as well as they can about these; that is what they are hired for. They cover the musical front, report on it as knowingly and as sympathetically as they are individually capable of doing.

Actually critics, composers, and performing artists have at least one motivation in common, namely the advancement of music, which is the art they live by. They are also busy advancing their own careers. Now any workman in the arts is entitled to consider his own career important. Every career is, as a matter of fact. The music of this our time, indeed, is simply the music composed by the present writer and his colleagues, nothing else. And this goes for music criticism in our time too. All living musicians—and no critic is respected by his readers unless he has some skill in the technique of music and some responsibility to it as an art—all living musicians, I say, are part of one great band (or conspiracy, if you will) vowed to the defense of the musical faith and to its propagation.

Their methods of going about this differ widely, and they are always treading on one another's toes. Treading on the toes of composers and performers is, indeed, considered by many as the main business of critics. This is not so. Their main business, really their only business, is explaining the creative or executant artist to the public. Explaining the public to the artist is management's business and that of older artists. Defending the public against the artist is nobody's business, not the impresario's nor the politician's, nor the clergy's, still less that of the critic, whose living depends on the survival of the art he speaks for. Civic and religious leaders are permitted in free countries to alert the public to the danger of circulating seditious or immoral ideas; but their power to stop such circulation is based in really free countries wholly on an agreement among the adult population about what actions are to be considered seditious or immoral. Critics have a different role; they are commentators, not censors. And artists are producers, not traitors or charlatans. Neither is the public a fool.

A newspaper man once advised me, "Never underestimate the public's intelligence; never overestimate its information." The moral of this for the critic is that he does his duty best by his readers when he describes and explains to the public what the artist is doing. If he adds a paragraph of personal opinion, that is his privilege as a musician. It is also his duty as a reporter, since the confessing of his personal prejudices and predilections helps the reader to discount them. But the description of music is his business, as the performance of music is the performer's business and the designing of it for possible execution the composer's. Consuming it is the public's business and, to this end, judging it. We all judge it. That is a human right granted even to the reviewer. But if the reviewer is not to be mistaken by artists and managements for just a cog in their publicity machine, neither should he set himself up as a Bureau of Standards. We still live in a Republic of Art, thank God. And I, as a member of that republic, as a plain consumer, want access to all the music there is. I also want all the description and information about it I can get, as a consumer's guide. I even enjoy knowing, as a consumer's guide, who likes it and who doesn't. But as an artist, I do not enjoy being disapproved or misinterpreted.

A climate of receptivity is what the artist most desires. It is also a thing that even the most experienced reviewer cannot always offer. Individuality and originality are the bedrock of musical achievement, not ease of learning or technique, which anybody can have. And individuality, originality are no end shocking. The reviewer sometimes takes the shock of them harder than the public. At other times he acts as a buffer, transmits the shock gently to his public. At still other times he serves for nothing at all.

Haydn, Mozart, and Beethoven came to maturity as artists without benefit of the press and without any hindrance from it either. The artist can perfectly well do without criticism, prefers to, in fact. But he loves praise, flourishes on it. And his publisher, his manager help him to live by publicizing the praise that he receives. So any artist tends to consider that praising him is the critic's business, or at the very least giving him lots of space. The critic, on the other hand, is an essayist who knows that he can write a more interesting article about something he knows than he can do about a work or personality that he has only recently encountered. There is the further fact, too, that a vigorous attack is more entertaining than any defense. (As William Blake said, "Damn braces; bless relaxes.") And so any critic, faced with the even faintly unfamiliar, will tend, like any knight-errant, to attack it, or at the very least to dismiss it with a snort.

To the critic every producing composer is a challenge. To the composer every critic is a danger. All this makes tonic the musical air. But there are fools in both camps. The composing fool thinks the press is out to get him, does not realize that he is merely grist for its mill and that as long as he gives it grist the mill will grind for him. The reviewing fool thinks he can make his fame by praising successful performers and dead composers, not knowing at all that critical championships have always been won and are only won still in bouts with a living composer.

The audience for all this is one audience, for the same people read about music that listen to it. Toscanini's public, Stravinsky's public, and Olin Downes's public are drawn from the same pool of music consumers. And all three men are workers before that public and are not, except as individual consumers, members of it. What they have in common is membership in the professional world of music. Their quarrels about music are family quarrels. A critic is therefore a musician who offers to the public as his contribution to the art an inside view of loves and hatreds and mechanics and methodological warfares that were never intended to be exposed, but of which the public exposure is considered to be good for business. Your critic seldom kisses, but he always tells.

February 14, 1954

Critic and Performer

Reviewing performances of familiar music takes up the largest part of a critic's week. It is also the easiest part. Reviewing new pieces is the hardest and the most important, for that is where criticism touches history. The history of music, we know, is the history of its composition, not of its performance. But musical performance, by mere abundance, occupies the foreground of the contemporary scene. Consequently the reviewer is largely occupied with reporting it.

He is usually, moreover, fairly well prepared to report on it, because his musical education has surely given him some experience of a musical instrument. Rare is the reviewer who is not able to identify himself with a man at a pianoforte. Others play a stringed instrument. Many have a vocal history. And if they know before they start reviewing music something of performing techniques, they also, through going to concerts, become soon familiar with the repertory and with current standards of interpretation. It is not hard to spot an ugly tone, an off-pitch phrase, a messy jumble of notes, a lovely sound, a transparent texture, an authoritative personality. One critic can make a mistake, hear wrong; but the ensemble of the press in any musical center rarely misjudges gravely a performing artist.

Misjudgments in this field occur most frequently with regard to advanced styles of interpretation. Reviewers tend to accept the customary approach to any piece as an inherent characteristic of that piece. A radical change based on the most advanced musicological research they not infrequently mistake for clumsiness. They imagine a norm of interpretation to exist for any works or school of work and consider the artist to have failed who deviates from that norm. The opposite is true, however. No such norm exists; there are merely habits imitated from successful artists. The true version of a work is not to be found in the most admired contemporary interpretation but rather in its printed notes and in such historical information as is available about what these notes meant to the composer and to other musicians of his time. Styles of interpretation change about every quarter of a century, and the great interpreters are the ones who change them, not those who copy yesterday's changes.

It is this constant restudy of the classics that gives life to our musical tradition. Attempts to discourage such restudy whenever it does not originate in Vienna, which it seldom does, are characteristic of that large segment of our music world that stems from Vienna. Berlin was never so reactionary and Paris never so powerful. Our musical press in America owes some of its finest qualities (its consecration, for instance) to the influence of Vienna, but also its tendency to reject without examination any restudy of the great classical and Romantic repertories.

But if our musical press lacks (and sometimes willfully) an intellectual background for the judging of new interpretations, interpreters themselves have for the most part no clear conception at all of the reviewer's assignment. They think every review is written to them, is a personal communication. It is no such thing, of course. It is not a free lesson offered the artist; it is a description *for the public* of how the artist works. And if it involves, as it must, some analysis of technical faults and virtues, that analysis has as its only purpose answering the question, "How did he get that way?"

I admit a tendency among reviewers to give vocal lessons in public, and I deplore it. No critic ever complains that a pianist used too little arm weight or that a violinist's bow lacked control from the forefinger. They do not correct the soloist's fingering of octaves or the conductor's beat. But they do say that Miss So-and-So failed to "support her tones." This phrase does not describe an auditory effect but a state of muscular control. Bad pitch, gasping breath, false notes, wavering tone, these things can be heard; and it is legitimate to mention them. It is not legitimate to tell an artist in public how to correct them. Our business is to describe the symptom, not to diagnose its cause or prescribe a cure.

Another common fault of the reviewer, and one which causes the greatest bitterness among artists, is carelessness of statement.

The reviewer all too frequently fails to meet the performer on the performer's own level of workmanship. When an artist has devoted large sums of money and years of his life to acquiring a skill, however imperfect the result may be, the reviewer owes him the courtesy, the proof of integrity, of exercising a comparable care in his report to the public about the artist's work. He does not have to be right; nobody does. But if he wishes the public to believe him and musicians to respect him, he must arrive at his opinion by fair methods; and he must state it in clear English.

The reviewer gets tired toward the season's end of hearing music, all too often the same music, and of sitting through third-class performances. The music world is incredibly full of third-class artists, many of them in first-class posts. It takes some self-control to keep one's patience with them. But they are doing their best; and they have a great deal to lose, even the most famous ones, from a review which lowers their dignity. And the kind that lowers their dignity most is the kind that is badly written.

An artist's privilege is to make music as beautifully as he can, and a critic's privilege is to write about the artists as truly as he can. This involves some thought and some care. Also some humility. The artist works best when his ego is big, when he feels confident. The reviewer works best when his ego is small, when he feels respect for the artist's integrity, however minor may be his interest in the artist's work. The poorest performance does not justify a poorly written review or any assumption of the right to grant or withhold degrees. Writing a review is not giving an examination; it is taking one. The subject is whatever musical occasion one has attended. One has, as in any examination, a limited time in which to produce an essay on some theme suggested by the occasion, preferably one which permits the reviewer to include in his essay a clear report and a fair estimate. It has been my experience that the public is invariably grateful for an informative and well written review and that the artist rarely resents it. It is my conviction that he has every reason, however, to resent from the reviewer inaccurate reporting and slovenly writing.

February 21, 1954

Casals and the Matterhorn

SWITZERLAND contains forty-three big climbs, thirty-nine of which start from Zermatt. The most celebrated of these are the Monte Rossa and the Matterhorn. To this diamond necklace of summits which surround the village, itself as charmingly intimate, and about as inaccessible, as Aspen, Colorado, has lately been added that gem and pinnacle of music-making in our time, Pablo Casals. For three weeks, from August 18 to September 8, the great cellist presided over a summer academy, small but ever so distinguished, and gave for the first time in many years public master-classes in the interpretation of cello literature. He says that he cannot remember exactly when he gave his last course of the kind at the École Normale de Musique in Paris but that surely it was not later than the 1920's. I remember his course on the Bach suites, given there in 1922; but I do not know whether it was the last.

In any case he has been giving such classes again; and this season their subject was the cello works of Beethoven. The Zermatt Summer Academy of Music, let me add, bears little resemblance to its famous elder brother the Prades Festival. The latter is a recording deal, and its concerts are largely concerned with some of our younger pianists, violinists, and conductors. It does not cater to cellists or attract them much, save for a few former Casals pupils who turn up now and then for a private lesson.

Zermatt, on the other hand, is chiefly for cellists. A string quartet in residence (the Végh) illustrated this year a course in quartet playing. A trio (Arpad Gerecz, Madeline Foley, and Karl Engel) did the same for a course in the Beethoven trios given by Paul Grümmer, who also gave, under Casals, a cello class. Sándor Végh (of the quartet) handled the Beethoven violin sonatas and played them with Engel. Vocal coaching, not limited to the works of Beethoven, was offered by Hans Willi Haeusslein. Mieczyslaw Horszowski played a recital of Beethoven piano sonatas but did not teach. He also played (but perfectly) with Casals in two private concerts, limited to the students of the Academy and a few invited guests, all five of the Beethoven sonatas for cello and piano, including the horn sonata, opus 17, which has been played as a cello piece for over a century and which was probably familiar to Beethoven in this form. Casals's own class included sixteen cellists, four pianists who came as members of cello-and-piano teams, two pianists who came independently to study the Beethoven cello-and-piano works (twenty-two working students in all), and nine auditors.

This listener climbed the steep mountain valley (by car and electric train) to hear the master play with Horszowski Beethoven's chief cello works. (The three sets of variations were omitted.) And the experience was both memorable and revelatory. He discovered for himself that Casals is not only a fine musician, which everybody knows, but also a great technician of the cello still, a fact which has been little played up in the Prades publicity and a fact of cardinal importance to music today. Because, though there are fifty, at least, living musicians of the cello literature who are comparably enlightened about it, there is none other, to my knowledge, who knows so well the limitations and possibilities of the cello as an instrument of music and who can demonstrate them so convincingly in their application to the cello's classical repertory. If this is true, as I believe it to be, then the cellists of the world should remain in contact for as long as Casals himself remains in the world, with their instrument's chief present source of artistry and excellence.

There is no doubt that the cello's present period of technical expansion derives from the playing of Pablo Casals. Anybody in the cello world will tell you that. And, though many of the devices involving the so-called "thumb positions" (for playing higher passages, for instance) were invented by the nineteenth-century Belgian virtuoso Franz Popper, their application to music-making in a first-class musical way was made by Pablo Casals alone more than forty years ago. His technique has always excited musicians profoundly because of his musical penetration. And his musicianship has always stirred them because of his technical superiority. He has viewed music through the technician's lens and studied technical problems through the microscope of musical analysis. As a result he makes Beethoven sound better than it ever did before, and he makes the cello sound better too. He has done this for many years; he still does it. And if other cellists are doing it more and more of late, that is because he is the father of them all.

His technical mastery (and musical too, for with him they

cannot be separated; in that way his mind is as Spanish as a bull-fighter's)—his mastery in general, let us say, has always been remarkable for three qualities. These are, still are, his ability to play on pitch, his ability to move his left hand up and down the finger-board without sliding, and the studied character of his vibrato. The first two are technical skills; the other is a matter of musical analysis. All apply to the left hand. It was easily observable the other day in Zermatt that for simple harmony notes that were not part of the thematic discourse he used no vibrato at all. But as soon as melody spoke vibrato began. If a melody note diminished in volume, his vibrato diminished in speed and width, coming completely to rest just before the end of the note. For a crescendo on the bass strings he used a very wide vibrato, produced by means of it a tone of great power. At other times, especially playing without vibrato, his tone was so soft that only its penetrating and stringy character seemed to give it any presence at all.

Great presence it had, nevertheless; and this presence all came from the right arm, from the bow. The evenness of his bow from heel to tip, moving very slowly and playing ever so softly, betrayed a muscular control that few cellists of any age have at their command. In fact, the bow was so wholly under his command, at all times in optimum contact with the strings and moving at exactly the necessary speed, that not once in either of the sessions did the cello's tone whistle, grunt, growl, or scratch. Neither did it weep, I may add, though tears on the cello are a matter of deliberate musical taste rather than of technical abandon. If Casals does not indulge in them, that is because his expression has ever been impersonal, objective, a little distant. His Catalan reserve has no place for self-pity, for what the Spaniards call *patetismo*.

His personal expressivity nowadays is toward a straightforward vigor in vigorous passages, a healthy muscular vigor quite void of emotional urgency, toward a meditative quality in all those misterioso passages that were so dear to Beethoven, and in the songful ones toward an intense sweetness that is less an outpouring than it is an evocation of the memory of song. At the peak of his senescent years, for he is only seventy-two, it was with Beethoven's last cello sonata that the Casals qualities of sensitivity, of sadness, and of resignation seemed most perfectly paired. One understood both in the work and in its performance, the meaning of the poet's phrase "all passion spent." And the whole presence of both was the more vibrant since every other vigor had remained intact.

Vibrancy in resignation is what makes of Casals today a sort of musical saint. But the miracle that he performs, and a true saint must do miracles, is to make familiar music flower and a familiar instrument sing. For doing this he has, like any saint, both inspiration and method. And if the result seems at times almost supernatural, that effect comes from an interpenetration of ends and means so complete that we wonder however it could have been achieved. One can name the elements of it, but not explain their fusion.

Cellists have a great deal to gain from studying that result and consulting the author of it. As does any other musician, too. But let no one ever forget that when Casals plays the classical masters he is also playing the cello, an older and possibly more miraculous creation than any piece ever written for it. I suspect, indeed, that the instrument itself, even more than Bach or Beethoven, is his true love. There is something almost marital about Casals's matter-of-fact command, as if the way he plays the cello were the true way finally found, the way it always should have been played, the way it finally now can be played, and surely the way it will henceforth always demand to be made to sound.

September 14, 1954

OTHER WRITINGS

UNCOLLECTED ARTICLES
AND REVIEWS

Of Diamond and Pearls

ORCHESTRETTE CLASSIQUE, *Frederique Petrides*, conductor, last
night at Carnegie Chamber Music Hall, performing David Diamond's
Concerto for Chamber Orchestra, Brunetti's Sinfonia in C minor, Mozart's Piano Concerto in E flat, Boccherini's Five Dances for Strings,
and Beethoven's Symphony No. 1. Soloist: *Lonny Epstein*, piano.

COMPOSERS, like pearls, are of three chief sorts, real, artificial
and cultured. David Diamond is unquestionably of the first
sort; his talent and his sincerity have never been doubted by his
hearers, by his critics or by his composer colleagues. His fault,
if fault must be found, is in a certain inability to hit his public
straight between the eyes.

His concerto for chamber orchestra, performed last night at
a concert of the Orchestrette Classique, is made of the finest
musical materials; it is neatly put together; it is orchestrated
with a passionate sensitivity to instrumental differences. The
general effect is one of richness, an abundance of fine things.
But its breath is a little gasping, its thought far from continuous. Like most of today's young composers, Diamond is at his
best in slow movements of a meditative character. (The moderns of twenty and forty years ago did most of their best work
in the veins of frenzy or of fun fast and furious.) Explain that as
you will, the fact itself is to be noted. And the fact that David
Diamond, whatever his size may turn out to be when he gets
polished up, is a fine jewel in music's crown is a fact that this
department considers also to be worthy of record.

An etymological conjecture is here proposed that the word
orchestrette, otherwise inexplicable, may belong to the group of
nouns that includes *snark* and *brunch*, that it might just possibly
be a telescoping of *orchestra* with *suffragette*. For it is a women's
orchestra (saving two). And the ladies don't play badly, either.
Neither badly nor really well. They play like a good student
group. Their technique is fair, their intentions of the most honorable. Their faults are mostly the vices of their betters.

Last night's program was all gems: Brunetti, Mozart, Boccherini, Beethoven and a good American. The size of the ensemble, thirty players, is one that gives a good strong noise in Carnegie Chamber Music Hall. That hall seats 362 persons. One musician to twelve listeners is a good eighteenth-century proportion. Our modern proportion, which is more nearly a hundred musicians to a house seating 5,000 people, is definitely on the cheap side. Our full sonorities are likely to be on the skimpy side as well, effortful and brassy, even at their best. The problem of making Mozart and Haydn and Beethoven, not to speak of Boccherini, sound brilliant in big Carnegie Hall is something of a stumper. Playing them with an orchestra the size they were written for in a hall the size of those they were written to be played in, gives a result of brilliance and of complex opulence in the string-sounds that makes our modern opulence of orchestral dissonance sound thin and poor, makes the horn and trumpet themselves sound like solid, manly supports in a tutti, rather than like the buzzards and the isolated but screaming eagles they so resemble in a modern orchestral forte.

We have made money on our orchestras, or, at any rate, cut down our money losses from what such splendors used to cost an eighteenth-century patron or municipality. But we have certainly impoverished our ears in so doing. No major symphony orchestra in the world, playing in a house the size of big Carnegie, can produce the orchestral brilliance that Madame Petrides's thirty young women produced in the Carnegie Chamber Music Hall. To hear the music of the great eighteenth century masters, particularly that of Mozart and of the early Beethoven, played by a group even as modestly expert as this, in such an appropriate acoustical frame is to begin to know something of what that music really sounded like in the ears of its makers and of its contemporary listeners. The experience is likely to provoke one to readjust radically quite a lot of his musical values, particularly, by comparison, the nineteenth-century ones.

October 15, 1940

Undue Modesty

JAN SMETERLIN, pianist, in recital last night at Town Hall, performing, among other works, Schumann's Fantasie in C major, Brahms's Variations on a Theme by Paganini, Mr. Smeterlin's transcription of an Intermezzo from Bizet's *Carmen*, Godowsky's transcription of Johann Strauss's *Küntzlerleben*, and six works by Chopin: three mazurkas (Op. 50, No. 3; Op. 6, No. 3, Op. 17, No. 4), two études (Op. 10, No. 2; Op. 25, No. 2), and Scherzo in E major, Op. 54.

EVERY PIECE a masterpiece and each one fresh as a flower dripping with dew. Not dripping with goo; Smeterlin is not that kind of a pianist. But starry, pearly, iridescent, brightly varied from deepest black through all the colors known to modern pianism, roots deep in the fertile loam of Franco-Polish Romanticism.

I went to hear the Chopin, because none toss it so lightly and so rhythmically as he. Light and rhythmical it was, too, and digestible as sponge cake. The mazurkas, in particular, are a specialty of his. Not somber meditations of a tubercular expatriate but kaleidoscopic pictures of Polish peasant life they come out, with real dance rhythms and flippantly tender sentiments. They seemed last night a little weak on the left-hand side. Not weak from left-hand weakness, but as if the pianist took for granted we all knew the bass and chord parts.

The Schumann Fantasy was a little spotty, unsewn, in the first movement. Partly Schumann's fault that: but still, it needn't be quite so discontinuous. The other two movements were solid and right, full of the singing gayety and manly pathos that make Schumann's music unique.

Brahms's Paganini Variations were a revelation to me. I have always considered them a monumental but on the whole rather dull work, not very idiomatically written for the pianoforte. On the contrary, as Mr. Smeterlin expounds them they become what one might have expected all the time, considering that the theme is a fragment of violin music by a virtuoso violinist. They become an elaborate exploitation of violinistic sonorities in terms of pianoforte writing. So interpreted, and once one sees the pattern it is not possible to believe Brahms's intention to have been otherwise, they take on light and air, sonorous altitude as well as musical depths.

Mr. Smeterlin's own transcription of the *Carmen* third act intermezzo is a charming and tasteful piece. His rendition of Godowsky's fantastically difficult Strauss *Artists' Life* was of a brilliance, a clarity, a sustained sweep such as only a master pianist and a master musician ever achieves.

What is wrong with Smeterlin, if anything is? Something like this: His technique is phenomenal, his musical penetration profound, his taste both solid and exquisite. But there is something a little bit gentlemanly about the way he shrinks from taking authority.

He seems to say about each piece, "This is the way I like it," rather than, "This is the way it is." He puts an elaborate perfection into the execution of middle and upper voices, into the sharp delineation of rhythmic contrasts, especially of free rhythms versus strict rhythms. He gives the grand line of the long pieces by rhythm chiefly. His exposition of a work's basic harmonic structure is a little skimpy, as if he took for granted we all knew that.

The truth is, of course, that we don't. Even if we know a piece by heart, we don't want to have to add the underpinning from memory when we are listening to a supposedly complete rendition. If his rhythm were less varied, if his range of tone-color, his repertory of finger heights and wrist positions were less extensive, if he did not orchestrate, so to speak, the works he plays with such penetration, there would be no complaint to make about the bass. But when an artist gives you as elaborate a superstructure as he does, it is necessary that he articulate the simple lines of the harmonic foundation with massive emphasis.

He sacrifices the bass continually, lest any pedal besmear the upper figurations and middle melodies. This is a mistake. I do not think it is a mistake in his musical thinking. I think it is a spontaneous, an unconscious, an unjustified modesty. For a man to master a major instrument and its repertory as he has and then to shrink from assuming the final obligation to play them with complete and categorical authority may be gentlemanly of him; but it is rather a shame, none the less. Neither Chopin nor Schumann nor Brahms ever dreamed of such reticence.

November 2, 1940

More on Fantasia

CONTROVERSY still goes on about Walt Disney's *Fantasia*. The most interesting thing about this controversy is that it is all over esthetics, nothing else. No question of politics is involved, nor of public morals, only taste. This fact alone gives to the discussion a certain tone of seriousness that is welcome in American artistic life; and it pays the work discussed the honor that is due to a film which, whether one considers it to be artistically successful or not, has motives of the highest seriousness behind it.

As a motive of the highest seriousness, I am not referring to whatever financial exigencies may make it desirable for Walt Disney to produce full-length pictures. *Fantasia* is not, artistically speaking, a full-length picture anyway. It is a series of eight shorts strung together by Mr. Deems Taylor's pastor-like benediction of each piece and by some more or less charming funny business about orchestras. The film could easily be cut up into its component numbers and each of these left to live or die as a short in the neighborhood houses. And I rather imagine this result was envisaged by Mr. Disney, in case the full film as we see it here should turn out to be not easily distributable.

What I call serious motivations are Mr. Disney's desire to raise the standards of musical repertory and interpretation in his work to something comparable to what ten million people hear by radio every Sunday in the concerts of the New York Philharmonic-Symphony Orchestra, his desire, that is, to make the animated cartoon worthy in every way of distinguished musical collaboration, and Mr. Stokowski's desire to make film reproduction of symphonic music sound as well as possible.

There can be no objection to the introduction of standard concert repertory, ancient and modern, into visual entertainment. Chopin, Schumann, Debussy and Bach have been so used ere now by ballet companies, and so have Beethoven's symphonies. The only questions involved are ones of taste, and these must be judged finally for each piece separately. On the whole, and this applies to the ballet as well as to the animated cartoon and to the naturalistic film, musical works that follow a story or paint a picture in themselves are likely to give a better result when tied up to a visual spectacle than musical works do which are constructed according to a purely auditory logic. Even so, Isadora Duncan danced to Romantic symphonies and got away with it, as touring troupes of so-called "Russian" ballet have given for some years now Massine's elaborately choreographed versions of symphonies by Tchaikovsky, Brahms, Beethoven and Berlioz. There are persons who do not care much for these ballets, this writer among them; but it is not because they "degrade" classical music. It is simply because visualization is not as often well fitted to "abstract" music as it is to "program" music. Berlioz's *Fantastic Symphony* and Debussy's *Afternoon of a Faun* make better ballets, because they imply in their compositional plan both a setting and a scenario, than Beethoven's Seventh Symphony and Brahms's Fourth.

In *Fantasia*, all agree, Dukas's *Sorcerer's Apprentice* shocks none. Bach's minor Toccata and Fugue shocks few, because the semi-abstract screen pictures that accompany it are too meager and trifling to bother anybody. Marcel Duchamp, of "Nude Descending a Staircase" fame, once made a film out of moving circles, disks, spirals, angles and similar mathematical elements that was a work of the deepest fascination both visually and intellectually. This writer regrets that Mr. Disney didn't think of doing a similar thing for the Bach piece.

There is not a great deal of disagreement about the suitability of the animated drawings that illustrate Tchaikovsky's *Nutcracker Suite* and Ponchielli's "Dance of the Hours." Some like them more than others do, but few care much one way or the other. The same indifference exists with regard to Mussorgsky's "Night on Bald Mountain." Some found the *Rite of Spring* boring visually. It always has been, incidentally. Nobody has ever made a satisfactory choreography for that superb ballet score, though many, including Nijinsky himself and Martha Graham, have tried. So far no visualization of it has ever survived repeated performance in repertory. Many persons are shocked also by the pseudo-religiosity of the Schubert "Ave Maria" in Disney's film. I admit to being not much edified by what I took to be a procession of Japanese ladies carrying lighted lanterns (or were they parasols?) as they hobbled and minced across a high Japanese garden bridge that was supported by thin pillars and an arch of purest nineteenth-century Gothic.

The real storm center of the esthetic discussion, however, has been Beethoven's Sixth Symphony. Certainly it is for that work that Disney has succeeded the least well in constructing visual images and a thread of story that might seem adequate and appropriate. I fancy that his basic error consists in having scrapped the original landscape and scenario. If it is risky business making up a story for music that was written to have none, it is riskier business inventing a totally new scenario for music that already has a perfectly good one. The "Pastorale" of Beethoven is the plainest depiction of an Austrian countryside, complete with *schnitzel* and beer and a storm and dancing peasants. There is even a rustic band and a bassoonist that can only play three notes.

One can understand the Disney hesitation to employ so sympathetic yet without so Germanic a scene as subject matter of his longest and most monumental number. It is scarcely the moment just now, perhaps, to play around with that. And so he didn't. But he should really have given up the piece too. Keeping it, he felt obliged to scrap the locale, but to make it a pastoral scene all the same. So he went mythological and got into trouble. Mark you, the trouble he got into is not the debasing of classic music, in spite of what Miss Dorothy Thompson says. I have even heard professional musicians complain about that number; and professional musicians don't care what you do to Beethoven, as long as you play the notes with a fair degree of correctness. The trouble is with the story itself, which would probably cause trouble, even if the music were cut out altogether.

Averaging up the complaints I hear, they seem to come out about as follows. Nobody really likes much the Disney Sixth Symphony. Women sometimes hate it. Miss Thompson's now celebrated cry of pain is not an isolated reaction. I have heard the same from a woman musician, who insists she doesn't mind on account of the Sixth Symphony, which she has never cared much for anyway; and from a woman painter who, although not tone deaf, is so visual-minded that she scarcely hears music at all unless she makes an effort to pay auditory attention. Both these ladies, like Miss Thompson, are professional women, proud and independent. There is something about the Disney Pastoral that offends their womanhood. It glorifies mating and breeding, ignores all other aspects of their existence, consecrates the picture with the prestige of a composer traditionally associated with ideas of social liberation. It is not surprising that such ladies should be shocked and horrified or that Miss Thompson, the most vocal of them, should cry "Nazism," crying "Nazism" being rather her specialty, as indeed mating and maternity are, in Nazi theory, supposed to be the unique destiny of womanhood.

Men object, too, to the "Pastoral," though nothing like so violently. That part of the Disney film has raised what is commonly known as a stink. To such a point that the Disney office has thought it wise to circularize the screen and music press with material tending to prove that Beethoven didn't have anything very precise in mind anyway when he wrote that symphony.

My latest communication from that office about the film is an article by Leopold Stokowski on the system of musical reproduction employed. The latter is not controversial matter, so far as I am concerned. I think a good job was done and only want to see half as good a one made standard practice in Hollywood. Since Mr. Stokowski's explanations, however, sales talk though they be, have the interest anything of the kind must inevitably have that comes from a man who knows his trade technically, I am closing herewith my business year by quoting them in part:

"The aim of all of us who worked with Disney for nearly three years to make *Fantasia* was to make use of all the most recent scientific developments in recording and reproducing music, methods that seemed to us helpful in making music more eloquent, and so be of greater service to all those who enjoy music—all men and women and children who go to the 'movies' for recreation.

"We have tried to make the music sound intimate, friendly, close—so that as we sit in the 'movie' house the music surrounds us, we are part of it—we vibrate to it as it envelops us. It does not come from one direction, as formerly in the concert hall or opera house, but is vibrating in the air all around us and is coming from every direction.

"Another thing we have aimed to do is to give true balance to the sound of the modern orchestra. If we listen to an orchestra in a concert hall the deep sounds of the bass instruments, such as the double basses, Kontrafaggot, tuba, do not have the same richness and fullness as the middle and high sounds, such as the violins, clarinets and flutes. This is true of all orchestras. There are acoustical and technical reasons for this which I shall be happy to describe another time when there is more space. This unbalance of the orchestra, especially when all the instruments are playing with full tone, can easily be appreciated by us all if we listen to a good organ. Here the deep sounds played by the pedals are in true balance and relation with the medium and high sounds. But the organ has other limitations, so that the orchestra surpasses the organ as an expressive instrument. In recording and reproducing the music of *Fantasia* we have tried to create a better balance between the low, medium and high sounds so that they will be more equal.

"Another thing we have aimed to do is to make certain parts of the music sound as was probably intended by the composer, but is not possible in concert. Perhaps this can be made clearer by giving one or two examples. In the *Rite of Spring* of Stravinsky on pages 62, 63, 64 and 65 of the orchestral score, there is an upward glissando, or rushing up of quick sounds, for the fourth, sixth and eighth horns, which I have never heard sound as it should in the concert hall or theater. By the use of modern technical methods we have been able to overcome the otherwise apparently insuperable difficulties and make this part of the music sound with full eloquence.

"Another example of something that is impossible in the concert hall and yet has been accomplished in *Fantasia* is the storm part of the 'Pastoral' Symphony of Beethoven. On pages 59 and 60 of the orchestral score there are agitated passages for bassoon, clarinet and oboe which have a clarion-like character, but which are almost inaudible in the concert hall no matter how loudly they are played. In *Fantasia* we have been able to give these woodwind passages their true prominence and importance in relation to the rest of the orchestra, so that for the first time I have heard this part of the music sound with all the instruments in the optimum degree of relief.

"Like every other work of art, *Fantasia* will live or disappear according to the intensity of its appeal to the heart of every one."

December 29, 1940

High-Powered and High-Class

ELSIE HOUSTON, soprano, and YELLA PESSL, harpsichord, in joint recital last night at Town Hall with a program of French and Spanish songs of the fifteenth through eighteenth centuries. Miss Houston also sang Brazilian folk songs with her own percussion accompaniment, and Miss Pessl performed works by Handel, Bach, and Scarlatti.

Two such handsome ladies as Miss Houston and Miss Pessl, both of them thoroughly schooled in the techniques of their respective arts and both animated by ardor of temperament, could scarcely fail to produce a musical evening of the highest artistic quality.

Miss Houston is mistress of a greater range of tonal and verbal coloration than any singer I know. She can sing loud and soft and fast and slow and do all the other things that conventional vocalists do, and she can also sing "native." She can sing from the chest in the richest way imaginable and from the head in the softest way imaginable without ever losing control of her placement or abusing her vocal cords. She enunciates with equal clarity in French, in Spanish and in Portuguese. She knows the differences stylistically between one composer, one country, one epoch and another. Her voice, moreover, in all its ranges and colors is resonant and beautiful.

She is at her best in Brazilian folklore. That repertory shows off to the greatest advantage her enormous temperamental and technical range. It seems also to draw from her the greatest depth of personal identification with the musical material. Her old French repertory is pretty fine too, but she sings it more from the head than from the heart. Her Spanish work is handsomely executed; but it sounds to me less Spanish than Portuguese in vocal style. It is delicate in sentiment and vocal turn like Portuguese *fado* singing. It has not the continuous brilliance, the sustained harshness, as of oboe and trumpet, without which there is no Spain.

The lack of any sustained tonal outpouring is a little disappointing in all Miss Houston's work, excepting in her Brazilian folk-lore. She has no real need of any such timidity, for her placement is correct and she seems to have plenty of breath. Her constant shading of the volume is charming at first, because it is accomplished with intelligence and taste. By the end of a program it gets to be quite exasperating. One feels like calling out to her, as a Venetian song-lover once called out from the gallery to Mme. Claire Croiza, as she was articulating her most delicate and virtually voiceless Debussy, "Meno parlare e più cantare!" Which is to say, "Talk less and sing more!"

Miss Pessl has no such reticence about making "big" musical effects. She performs dramatically indeed on the least dramatic of musical instruments, the harpsichord. Eschewing the tempting tonal volume of the metal-framed Pleyel instrument, she uses the much fainter-sounding all-wooden kind, presumably because of its greater variety of coloristic resource. A microphone and a public address system were employed last night to help out the carrying power. The result was not a happy one in those parts of the hall where the loud speaker could be heard at all. From the center of the house the harpsichord alone sounded richly sufficient.

W. S. Gilbert, in a famous Bab ballad, refers to "the piano's martial blast." If he had said "the harpsichord's military ping" or "war-like twang," he would have been more exact, though less funny. There is no instrument in the world so richly brilliant, not even the pipe-organ or the accordion. And none is so exigently, so satisfactorily, so martially rhythmic when correctly played.

Miss Pessl's rhythm, even among harpsichordists, is remarkable for its precision and its dramatic power. Her speed is at least double that of the fastest piano-playing. Her accentual force (on an instrument that allows almost no accentuation by means of mere stress) is so great that she often makes more noise striking down a key than the key's corresponding quill makes plucking the string. When she gets to crossing her hands and throwing them from one manual to another with the most terrifying speed and accuracy, she reminds one of nothing so much as of a really first-class swing drummer. Well might she be called the Gene Krupa of the harpsichord.

The two ladies performed together last night with the neatest possible collaboration, Miss Pessl even managing some skillful guitar imitation for the Spanish songs. The audience was enthusiastic; there were lots of flowers; and there was even a well-known composer, Mr. Samuel L. M. Barlow, to turn Miss Pessl's pages. The whole occasion was that high-class.

February 2, 1941

Afternoon with Beethoven

EMANUEL FEUERMANN, cellist, and ALBERT HIRSH, pianist, in joint recital yesterday afternoon at Town Hall, performing the following works by Beethoven: Cello Sonata No. 1 (Op. 5, No. 1); Twelve Variations on Mozart's "Ein Mädchen oder Weibchen"; Seven Variations on Mozart's "Bei Männern, welche Liebe fühlen," and Cello Sonata No. 5 (Op. 102, No. 2). Presented by the New Friends of Music.

BEETHOVEN's sonatas for violoncello and piano are not the best Beethoven nor the best cello music. Neither is the combination of cello and pianoforte a particularly satisfactory one. Nevertheless, yesterday's concert of the New Friends of Music, at which Mr. Feuermann and Mr. Hirsh played two of these sonatas, a very early one and a very late one, was a highly agreeable occasion.

Mr. Feuermann plays the cello as few do. He never lets it groan nor encourages it to wail. He restricts his vibrato to the minimum considered respectable by modern string-players, though I must say I could do with even less. His bowing is incredibly smooth. His pitch is well-nigh faultless. His musicianship is of the highest. His modesty and his forthrightness are equally sufficient.

His playing yesterday was at all times subservient to the exposition of Beethoven's not so frequently heard sonatas and of his quite rarely heard variations on Mozart themes. No attempt was made to conceal the episodic character of the early sonata. In consequence none of its youthful, singing quality was lost. In the later sonata every resource of a great player's skill was employed to mark with accent and tonal plenitude the more dramatic musical content of the work.

In the two sets of variations his playing was so transparent as to give one the feeling one gets when reading a score and that one almost never gets from hearing a piece played. It was a feeling of looking over the composer's shoulder, of observing him unbeknownst at work and at play.

The variation formula was one dear to Beethoven's heart. He did not do his greatest work in that field, as Brahms did. He did his spade-work there. All the devices of musical exposition that Beethoven used in his larger works, and many that he never got around to using again, are to be found fresh and full of savor in his innumerable sets of variations for various instruments. Reading them or hearing them read is like walking through Washington Market on a spring morning.

To give us such a feeling of proximity to music in the making, as if no interpreter or intermediary were present at all, is the privilege of only the greatest musical executants. Only they can render technique transparent, and only a very few among them can completely dominate their desire to impose some degree of personal reaction or comment on their rendition of a composer's work. Mr. Feuermann would seem to be one of those rare artists.

Young Mr. Hirsh, at the pianoforte, was no less adequate and respectful, though he did add to the execution of Beethoven's brilliant and far from easy piano parts a loveliness of tone, as of little bells hit with felt hammers, that is entirely his own. This singing brightness was welcome, too, because at best the cello tends to get lost in any duet with piano. Its lower notes are easy for the piano bass to absorb. Only the lightest and most bell-like sort of piano playing can make it clear to the ear at all times which instrument in these sonatas is playing what notes.

This department proffers its sincere compliments to Mr. Hirsh for doing a beautiful job. That the job was not without its additional difficulties was to be seen in the frequent necessity both musicians experienced for turning clear around to look at each other from the rather unaccountable back-to-back position in which they were seated on the stage.

February 10, 1941

Academism with Charm

PHILADELPHIA ORCHESTRA, *Eugene Ormandy*, conductor, last night at Carnegie Hall, performing Samuel Barber's Concerto for Violin and Orchestra and works by Haydn, Mozart, and Richard Strauss. Soloist: *Albert Spalding*, violin.

SAMUEL BARBER's Violin Concerto is tenderly poetic in melody and disarmingly straightforward in its general make-up. Its finale has even a certain brilliance in the violin writing. It cannot fail to charm by its gracious lyrical plenitude and its complete absence of tawdry swank. It did not fail last night. Rarely has one seen in an American concert hall such a warm ovation granted to any composer living and present. If the work were not at the same time a bit superficial in its musical structure, it would have been as satisfactory as it was easy to listen to.

By superficiality of musical structure I mean that all three movements might as well have been written for violin solo with pianoforte accompaniment, so little personality does he allow either the orchestral ensemble or its individual instruments. The most they ever get to do expressively is to echo by contrapuntal imitation fragments of the soloist's phrases. The oboe has a long and eloquent passage all to itself at the opening of the second movement. The violin enters with a counter-melody, and all seems to be going fine. Thirty seconds later the violin is playing the long oboe tune, has appropriated its every characteristic turn; and we know the oboe was just dressing up in the master's clothes before the master came home. This unwillingness to let an ensemble be an ensemble of contrasting and complementary characters proves a lack of comprehension on Mr. Barber's part of what is an ensemble and of what are the possible rôles it can play in accompanying a soloist. This humility about allowing the ensemble any musical autonomy is advantageous neither to the ensemble nor to the soloist.

Further timidity was manifest in the orchestration. Eight wood-winds were used, two horns, two trumpets, percussion, pianoforte, and a full symphonic string choir. This is either too much or too little. An effective scoring might possibly have been made for less than ten instruments. That would have placed the subservient accompaniment within reasonable human proportions. Something brilliant might also have been done for full Straussian set-up that would have picked out the solo violin by surrounding it with piquant and contrasting timbres. Mr. Barber apparently shrunk from viewing the true paucity of his accompanying material, as the adoption of either of these procedures would have obliged him to do. He sought, on the contrary, concealment of it in the small but compact crowd of a heavy string orchestra only momentarily enlivened by wind sounds and from time to time completely neutralized and coarsened by the thumpy pianoforte.

Equally superficial is Mr. Barber's musical syntax. He likes flowing melodies but does not dare to write these in the modern way without any harmonic bass progression at all. Neither does he quite wish to make the bass part fully melodic and active, as Bach and Mozart used to do. So he employs what French musicians call a "goose-egg bass," whole notes that move slowly from one harmonic bass note to another while a melody at the top wiggles and writhes to its heart's content and violas or cellos in the middle range do something shimmery that alters only when the bass moves.

The only reason Barber gets away with such elementary musical methods is that his heart is pure. He writes lovely melodies and doesn't try to sell them to you for anything they are not. I have wondered for some years whether Barber could legitimately be considered a neo-Romantic composer, as that term has been understood to represent the dominant Parisian school of the past ten years. I think not. His abstention from ostentatious dissonance and his cult of the poetic are based on no such penetrative esthetic reflection as are the similar abstention and cult of Henri Sauguet. I think he is simply an academic, but a new kind of academic. Not the storming, dissonance-mongering, fancily orchestrating academic we have been used to for some years. But the gentle sweet-singing sort of academic we used to have in Edward MacDowell and the brothers Nevin.

February 12, 1941

Parisian Cantilena

ALBERT SPALDING, violinist, in recital last night at Carnegie Hall, performing the Corelli-Spalding Sonata in A major, Beethoven's Sonata No. 7 (Op. 30, No. 2), Villa-Lobos's Sonata-Fantasy No. 1 ("Désespérance"), Joachim's Variations for Violin, and works by Chopin, Debussy, Chabrier, and Saint-Saëns. Accompanist: *André Benoist*, piano.

THE CHARM of Albert Spalding's violin playing is slender but perfectly real. Listening to him last night in Carnegie Hall brought no new vistas to mind. It merely left a smooth and pleasant taste in the ear. Yes, and a certain respect for serious work and gratitude for observance of the musical amenities.

The Corelli and Beethoven sonatas were read through in good tone and with professional observance of their musical shapes. Both were lacking in the rough grandeur of thought that is their essential beauty. The Beethoven tempos were better taken than those of the Corelli, varying little from the standard ones that have been observed for nearly a century. There being no standard speeds for the other work, Mr. Spalding's tendency to play fast movements too fast for good rhythmic effect led him to race and rattle through both of the allegros.

The Villa-Lobos Sonata-Fantasy gave more occasion for the refinement of melodic style that is Mr. Spalding's most personal gift as a musician. And the Joachim Variations allowed him to show off his solid technical mastery. The ensuing short pieces with which violin recitals are prone to end were, for once, the nicest part of the evening. These he did with all lovely sonority and with no mush at all. I have rarely heard the French salon style of violin playing more charmingly exposed.

As I said before, his charm is slender but real. It is slender because any charm is a slender quality, being wholly useless for the execution of grand, strong music. His is real, nevertheless, and most welcome, because Mr. Spalding plays like a scholar and a gentleman. He has a wholly Parisian way of spinning out a sustained cantilena without leaning on it. He makes it gracious and gesturelike. At such moments his fine musical ear and solid, technical training come into their own because they have a function to perform that is congenial to Mr. Spalding's temperament. At other times one wonders why he ever bothered to master the most difficult and ungrateful of solo instruments; what inner fire sustained him through the learning pains. Certainly little enough is perceptible now of flame or passion in his businesslike interpretations, or ever was, for that matter, in my memory. Yet, withal, the grace he has is sort of lovely when it gets a small enough piece to flower in.

November 9, 1942

America's Musical Autonomy

WHITE AND NEGRO SPIRITUALS by George Pullen Jackson (J. J. Augustin, New York, 1944) is the fourth, and presumably final, volume of a study in United States musical folklore that has been full of sensational discoveries. Dr. Jackson has had the rare luck to come upon one of those keystones to the understanding of a subject such as scholars dream about. He has uncovered a vast body of religious folksong still in print and in current usage among the white population of this country. His penetrating analysis of this material has clarified the whole question of America's musical resources and made it possible henceforth to classify these with some completeness. It has also rendered it impossible for any informed person ever to take the United States, with our ethnic musical resources and our instinct for preserving them alive, for a second-class musical power.

Dr. Jackson's findings include the following:

All the early settlers brought songs with them.

Most of the latter, excepting those of British Isles origin, passed out of use as the languages in which they were sung gave way to English.

British folksongs of jiggy rhythm were the musical carriers of the religious Revival that started around 1800 in Kentucky and spread rapidly over the English-speaking world.

At about the same time books of traditional tunes with sacred words began to appear, as if a more conservative element among our rural population were desirous of preserving a precious heritage of modal melody from, on the one hand, being wiped out of existence through the spread of the "modern," or major-and-minor, harmonic style, and, on the other, being literally "sung to pieces" in camp meetings.

The publication of such collections, in the shape-notes of the fa-sol-la system, has continued to this day, though it has remained for Dr. Jackson to identify their contents as authentic and ancient folksong. "White spirituals" is the name he gives to these melodies. He has analyzed and catalogued in two of his previous volumes 550 of them.

Negro spirituals, of which some 900 different ones are already collected, are similar in style and construction to their white models and subsequent to these in appearance. One-third of these have already been identified as copies, or slight transformations, of white originals. The present volume contains a comparative catalogue (with words and music) of 116 spiritual songs, the Negro versions being collated on opposite pages along with their previously known and published white originals from the British Isles.

A singing practice of many Negro congregations, especially of the Primitive Baptist faith, that is known among these as "long meter"—a vague and ultra-florid melopoeia with no rhythm in it at all, long thought to be an African survival of some kind—has been identified by Dr. Jackson as nothing less than a continuation into our time of the old Presbyterian psalmody, elsewhere completely lost since the late eighteenth century, at which time it seems to have been replaced by a simpler, livelier, and more rhythmic style of congregational singing.

The ethnic integrity of American folk music will be surprising news to many who have long held to the melting-pot theory of American life. There are probably a few French and a few Spanish tunes that have attained currency here beyond the confines of the regions where those languages are still spoken, but they are very few. Even German songs are rare among our non-German-speaking folk.

Secular origins for religious melody are, of course, as common here as anywhere else. The American dissenters did exactly what medieval Catholics and the Lutheran Reformationists had done. In Dr. Jackson's story, "the religious folk did not confine themselves in their tune selection to any particular type of secular song . . . The pioneer songsters borrowed indiscriminately from the English, Irish, Manx, Welsh, and Scotch. They took over everything they liked whether its song text had been of love, war, homesickness, piracy, robbery, murder, or lament for the dead. They adapted even large numbers of fiddle and pipe tunes—marches, reels, jigs, and hornpipes. But even though the American religious folk were not concerned as to the type of worldliness their favorite tunes had been steeped in, those airs had to be dyed-in-the-wool British . . . *All the known tunes adopted by American religious folk from sources other than British throughout the two-hundred-year period under consideration could be counted on the fingers of one hand.*"

The carriers of this great folksong movement from the British Isles to America and from New England to the South and the Middle West were not, as is commonly believed, the Methodists but chiefly the Baptists, though everybody eventually took part in it under the influences, first, of the Spiritual Revival of the early nineteenth century and later of the millennialist wave that flourished in the 1840s. John Wesley, the founder of Methodism, was opposed to it.

Of the latter, Dr. Jackson says, "No powerful religious movement, he knew, could do without a suitable body of song." So he set himself to provide this after the Lutheran model. But instead of picking up melodies from the "great body of English and Gaelic folk tunes still echoing in the British Isles as they had echoed since the time of the ancient bards, . . . he resolved to ignore what was at hand and borrow from afar—to provide the religious awakening with German tunes. These he found notably among the new-come Moravians who were just then taking root in English soil. To selections of German Moravian tunes Wesley added airs by Handel, Giardini, Lampe, and other composers of the imported elite London musical circle, and it was this hodgepodge of everything but good old English song that made up his first tune book for the Methodists. *A Collection of Tunes, set to music, as they are commonly sung at the Foundery*, London, 1742, set the pace for that upsurging group in its early stages of growth."

White and Negro Spirituals tells one of the most fascinating stories in the world, that of the secret, or nonofficial, musical life of this country. It would seem that this is all bound up with religious dissent. It includes as much dissent from official America as from official Europe. It is based on the privilege of every man to praise God, as well as to court a damsel, with songs of his own choosing. For two hundred years it has refused institutional mediation in culture, as it has denied the necessity of institutional mediation for salvation. As a result, we have a body of British song that has survived the efforts of churches, of states, and of schools—for all have tried—to kill it. As a further result, we have a musical life of high creative energy. It is characteristic of our history that that life should be still today more vigorous and more authentic in rural regions and among the economically submerged than among those of us who are constantly subjected to the standardizing influences of radio, of the public-school system, and of socialized religion.

March 12, 1944

The Dook

DUKE ELLINGTON AND HIS ORCHESTRA, third annual concert last night at Carnegie Hall, performing "Caravan," "In a Mellow Tone," "Take the A Train," and other Orchestra standards, with excerpts from Mr. Ellington's jazz symphony *Black, Brown and Beige.*

DUKE ELLINGTON and his orchestra gave a concert last night in Carnegie Hall. The house having been sold out early, including seats on the stage, overflow customers were offered places upstairs in the Carnegie Chamber Music Hall, where the music could be listened to by means of a wired transmission. Announced to begin at 8:45, the concert actually started at 9:20. By intermission it was time for your reviewer to go to work. Up to that moment nothing of unusual interest had taken place except some pretty skillful off-pitch trumpet and saxophone solo playing. There had been a good deal of that, however.

The chief virtue of Mr. Ellington's ensemble at present resides in the individual skills of the members. Unless one has purist tastes in jazz, the careful solo work that these boys do is bound to give pleasure. Even if one resists the prepared artistry of it, one can scarcely refuse to admire it as display. And Ellington himself, of course, is a pianist of no mean charm.

The group-playing is less impressive to this listener. Like that of the Boston Symphony Orchestra, it is over-rehearsed. Nothing unexpected ever happens; no miracle takes place. It is about as spontaneous as a silk-stocking advertisement. Also, the scorings used, though less banal than most, are rarely nowadays very original. They were far more striking twenty years ago, when the Duke was more assiduous in his search for far-away and covered timbres than he has been of late.

Ellington's qualities as a composer have never excited universal admiration. He has some hits to his credit and a long list of errors. Among the latter must be included an ambitious effort at symphonic continuity known as *Black, Brown and Beige*. All of his work, as played by his own band, is over-elaborate in texture. Its melodic substance is overpowered by the presentation. The expression, in consequence, being falsified by overstatement, comes out either as triviality felt or as convulsive and gasping, in any case overlaid with a partial insincerity.

This constant striving for effect gives to his present work a nervous quality that reaches its climax of unconvincingness in that abuse of sequences and repetitions that the jazz world calls riffing and that is merely the same substitution of nervous excitement for communication that was the plague of the Romantics and the particular vice of Richard Wagner. The best Ellington is other. It is calm and relaxed and straightforwardly lyrical. There wasn't much of that in the first half of last night's concert.

January 5, 1946

Delicious and Fresh

CONCERT OF NEW FRENCH MUSIC last night at Hunter College Playhouse, New York, with *Maggie Teyte*, soprano, accompanied by *Maurice Faure*, pianist, singing Poulenc's *Tel jour, telle nuit*, a setting of nine poems by Paul Éluard; *E. R. Schmitz*, piano, *Daniel Guilet*, violin, *Augustin Duques*, clarinet, and *Lucien K. Laporte*, cello, performing Olivier Messiaen's *Quartuor pour le fin du temps*; *Mr. Schmitz* performing piano works by Barraud, Daniel-Lesur, and Messiaen, and *The Guilet Quartet* performing Milhaud's String Quartet No. 12. Presented by France Forever, the Fighting French Relief Committee of America.

THE CONCERT of new French music that was presented last night at the Hunter College Playhouse by France Forever offered not only a series of novel and interesting works but a display of musical execution far above the current average. What with Maggie Teyte singing the best of Poulenc to Maurice Faure's perfect accompaniment; with E. Robert Schmitz playing piano pieces by Henry Barraud, Jean-Yves Daniel-Lesur, and Olivier Messiaen with his impeccable execution and understanding; with the Guilet Quartet playing Darius Milhaud's Twelfth String Quartet (dedicated to the memory of Gabriel Fauré), and a group consisting of Daniel Guilet, violin; Augustin Duques, clarinet; Lucien Laporte, cello, and Mr. Schmitz, at the piano playing Messiaen's difficult *Quartet for the End of Time* as smoothly as if it were something by Haydn, one was more than agreeably lifted above the level of ordinary chamber-music routines.

Poulenc's *Tel jour, telle nuit,* which has been reviewed earlier this season, is probably the top song cycle by today's top song composer. Milhaud's Twelfth Quartet, which was reviewed by this writer last summer from a San Francisco performance, is probably Milhaud's masterpiece in that medium. The piano works that Mr. Schmitz played are good pieces, all of them, and perfectly useful in repertory. If none is quite a masterpiece, then Messiaen's Seventh and Eighth Preludes are original work, and Barraud's Sixth Impromptu is skillful piano writing and music of great personal charm.

Messiaen's *Quartet for the End of Time,* composed in a German prison camp and first performed there in 1943, consists of eight sections, considerably varied in style and in instrumentation. The first is a "Crystal Liturgy" in which the piano plays an elaborate rhythmic and harmonic ostinato of pale, glassy chords while the clarinet, cello, and violin twitter softly and dissonantly in the "bird style." The second, "Vocalise for the Angel Who Announces the End of Time," is a disjointed piece with some novel far-away effects in it. "Abyss of Time," for clarinet alone, also in the "bird style," Mr. Duques played for the angels. "Intermezzo" is a short piece for cello, violin, and clarinet, full of charming harmonies and pretty sounds. "Praise to the Eternity of Jesus" is a cello solo accompanied by the piano.

So far the work was notable for the harmonic ingenuity of the first movement, the deep sadness of the clarinet piece, and the general sweetness of the intermezzo. "Dance of Fury for the Seven Trumpets," for the full quartet, is the most brilliant and original section of all. Written in unison from beginning to end, it is nevertheless completely complex and fascinating rhythmically from beginning to end. "Conglomeration of Rainbows, for the Angel Who Announces the End of Time," also for quartet, is complex and not so interesting. The final "Praise to the Immortality of Jesus" is an ecstatic violin solo with piano accompaniment. It could not be prettier, nor could one imagine a more impressive rendering than Messrs. Guilet and Schmitz gave it.

The work as a whole, if it is a whole, is marked by great harmonic and some rhythmic originality. It has lots of evocative fancy and considerable expressive power of a contemplative character. Melodically it is rather weak, and it has no shape at all. Messiaen has a fine musical ear and the gift of invention. Of composition, in the sense of interpreting rhetorically one's moments of inspiration, he has not an inkling. Neither has he any fear of the Taste Boys. He writes because he loves Jesus and musical sounds. At its worst his music sounds like Massenet; at its best it is the freshest music now being written and sounds like nothing you ever heard before. As a harmonic colorist he is probably unequaled among living composers.

January 31, 1946

Bruckner and Walter

PHILHARMONIC-SYMPHONY ORCHESTRA, *Bruno Walter*, conductor, last night at Carnegie Hall, performing Vaughan Williams's Fantasia on a Theme by Thomas Tallis, Pfitzner's Three Preludes from *Palestrina*, and Bruckner's Symphony No. 9.

BRUCKNER's Ninth Symphony, which Bruno Walter, conducting the Philharmonic last night in Carnegie Hall, played for its first time here since 1934, is a noble work of music. It is big of sound, long of structure, utterly without vulgarity of thought and deeply expressive. What it is expressive of seems chiefly to be a pure-in-heart devotion to the Viennese symphony. The symphonies of Haydn, Mozart, Beethoven and Brahms are evoked in it as deliberately as are the Handelian aria and the C. P. E. Bach sonata in any neo-classic work of twenty years ago. As in all historical evocations, a refracting mirror is employed,

Bruckner's personal glass being the melodic style of Schumann, the modulatory devices of Wagner and his own way of using the orchestral brasses (augmented for that purpose) like the reed stops of a church organ.

The continuity of the work is loose-hung, though somewhat less so (or so it seemed in Mr. Walter's eloquent reading of it) than that of other Bruckner symphonies, and perfectly clear. Everything about it last night was clear, straightforward, confident; and this listener, though the three surviving movements of the unfinished piece are long, was not aware, as one is so frequently at performances of this author's work, of being present at a devotional act. Mr. Walter played it as live music, and its effect on the audience seemed to be that of live music. Bruckner's very particular approach to musical composition became thus a fact of life and ceased, at least for the evening, to represent any kind of lost cause.

Whether Bruckner is in the long run a losing cause depends on whether Brahms, who was aiming at the same goal, is a losing cause. Both hoped to continue the Beethoven-style symphony in a worthy and resembling manner. This meant basing structure on thematic development. And thematic development, as a continuity device, had already been pretty thoroughly exhausted by Beethoven. Wagner had also applied it to the opera, with spectacularly beneficial results; but that was about the end of it as a major method. Modernism, as we know it, has prospered most when it has used other methods. The fact that Brahms and Bruckner did not choose to search for a replacement to this exhausted device, but blindly, devotedly sought to make it still more expressive, puts them, with regard to all the music written since 1860, in a technically reactionary position. So be it. Reaction of that high intellectual quality and perfect professional integrity is not easy to laugh off. They used a cumbersome and outmoded system of composition, but they were masters. And Bruckner's Ninth Symphony, incomplete, is a master's masterpiece.

A letter received at this office today protested on political grounds against the playing of three preludes from Hans Pfitzner's opera *Palestrina*, written back in 1917. Last night's audience showed no such sensitivity. This citizen has no objection to hearing any music he has not heard before, even though it were written by Hitler himself. Pfitzner's work, which is far more reactionary than Bruckner's and less gifted, is something to hear once; but there is not much life in it today.

Vaughan Williams's Fantasia on a Theme by Thomas Tallis, which opened the evening, was a delight for sweet string-playing under Mr. Walter's string-loving hand.

March 15, 1946

Nobility and Hysteria

PHILHARMONIC-SYMPHONY ORCHESTRA, *Charles Munch*, conductor, last night at Carnegie Hall, performing, among other works, Brahms's Violin Concerto in D major and Franck's Symphony in D minor. Soloist: *Ginette Neveu*, violin.

GINETTE NEVEU, who made her New York debut last night at Carnegie Hall, playing the solo part in Brahms's Violin Concerto with the Philharmonic under Charles Munch, is the finest, from every point of view, of the younger European artists whom we have had the pleasure of hearing here since the war. We have not heard them all, of course, those masterful and strangely concentrated young people who came to maturity midst bloodshed and treason. But in any company (and American competition runs high these days) Miss Neveu is a great artist.

She is a great artist because she has tone, technique and temperament. And she is an interesting artist because she has rhythm and a special intensity of communication all her own. It is not often that we hear the Brahms Violin Concerto read with such depth and nobility and withal so graciously. If the slow movement was somewhat over-refined and lacked, in consequence, its full serenity, the fault, I think, was that of the conductor, who seemed to be seeking in it a sensuality that it does not possess. Uncertain as is the hazard of estimating an artist's value from one hearing, and that in a concerto, I for one could not withhold my fullest admiration and confidence from Miss Neveu after last night's performance of the Brahms Concerto.

The César Franck Symphony, which ended the evening in hysteria and glory, is one of the pieces in which Mr. Munch is most entertaining. I use the word advisedly, because though his reading of the work is tonally handsome and in every other way absorbing, I do not find it especially convincing. He plays it as Toscanini does the Verdi Requiem, as pure theater.

He plays it very slow and very fast, very soft and very loud, reins it in and whips it up, gives it (and us) a huge workout. The result is clean fun at the expense of a piece that is tough enough to take it. The symphony came out of the match last night in no way shorn of dignity and in one way enhanced. Mr. Munch had at least spared it those last indignities of moony sentiment and of sickness long drawn out that so many artists consider obligatory in conducting this work. He handled it as objectively as if it were the overture to *Tannhäuser* or *William Tell*, and ended by making it sound as exciting. As you may gather, I did not quite approve; but neither could I find any reason to imagine that the composer would have seriously minded.

I am sure Brahms would have been delighted with Miss Neveu.

November 14, 1947

Best in Its Kind

IOLANTHE, comic opera in two acts, libretto by *W. S. Gilbert*, music by *Sir Arthur Sullivan*, performed on January 12 at the New Century Theater, New York, by the D'Oyly Carte Opera Company, *Isidore Godfrey*, conductor, *Anna Bethell*, stage director.

IF the D'Oyly Carte Opera Company, now playing at the New Century Theater, presents the operettas of W. S. Gilbert and Sir Arthur Sullivan at their best, so does *Iolanthe*, which was given by this company Monday night, give us both authors at their surest and most inventive. The subject, which is a satirical view of the House of Lords, may have less universal appeal than life in the navy or ministerial government as viewed from the comic angle of a Japanese royal household; but the work itself is well nigh perfect from every angle and in every number. And the D'Oyly Carte presentation of it, if not perfect in every rôle, is impeccable for style and as charming a conception of His Majesty's loyal subjects as has come out of Britain in any art form during this reporter's lifetime.

The secret of operetta is multiplicity of satire. Not only must the subject be treated with humor, but the poetry must make fun of all poetry and the music of all music. The more styles and forms you can debunk the richer the whole work becomes. In *Iolanthe* Gilbert has kidded the history of English poetry from Dryden to Tennyson, and Sullivan has taken off English music from Purcell to the Victorian anthem, including the royal march and the circus waltz, the pastorale, the foreign-style love duet and the manly ballad. All these are framed by finales and set-pieces of the utmost vivacity and set off by patter songs and choruses that leave one breathless with laughter and admiration. Martyn Green, as the Lord High Chancellor, gave Monday night the evening's most breath-taking execution in the famous Insomnia Song. When any actor's diction permits him the utmost in speed along with the utmost in clarity, he has at his disposal a technique of virtuosity that renders mere singing unnecessary.

Not the least of the delights of this company's performances is their possession (a monopoly, I believe) of Sullivan's original orchestra scores. Other troupes are obliged to fake the orchestration. The D'Oyly Carte group gives you the music, instrumental as well as vocal, in its true version. And Sullivan had a lovely hand with the orchestra, light, expressive and infinitely varied. If the present performances are a bit lop-sided tonally, the disequilibrium is due to economy in the string section (only nine strings all told were used last night to six brasses and six woodwinds) and to consequent overplaying of the trumpets in tutti passages. Otherwise the orchestral performance was, for a first night, not at all unpleasant. If it was not exactly symphonic, neither was it at any time coarse or unmusical.

Nothing in the show was unmusical. It was spoken and sung trippingly upon the tongue. Its lightness all round was a refreshment for Americans, oppressed as we are in our musical theater by heavy sounds and sexual insistences. Really there is nothing more delightful for young and old than Gilbert and Sullivan, the best Gilbert and Sullivan, performed by the D'Oyly Carte, unquestionably the ideal performers of Gilbert and Sullivan in our time.

January 14, 1948

Fancy Disembodied

CONCERT OF MUSIC BY HANNS EISLER on February 28 at
Town Hall, with *Tossy Spivakovsky*, violinist, *Leo Smit*, pianist, *Chloe
Owen*, soprano, and other musicians under the general direction of
Frank Brieff, violist and conductor, performing Eisler's String Quartet,
Sonata for Violin and Piano, eight songs, seven piano pieces for chil-
dren, Suite No. 2 for Septet (excerpts from the score for Charlie Chap-
lin's *The Circus*), and the score for *Fourteen Ways to Describe Rain*
(short documentary film by Joris Ivens). Presented by the Friends of
Hanns Eisler.

HANNS EISLER, who has been ordered to leave the United
States by the Immigration Department, was the subject of a
testimonial and benefit concert given Saturday night at Town
Hall. Composers of the highest distinction—Bernstein, Copland, Diamond, Harris, Piston, Sessions and Randall Thompson
—sponsored the evening. Executant musicians of the first
quality—including, among many others, Tossy Spivakovsky,
Frank Brieff and Leo Smit—performed. The program gave us
works by Mr. Eisler covering his entire career, from the String
Quartet, opus 1, through his latest film scores. *Alien Cantata*,
planned for the occasion, was not given, since the composer
had not been able to complete it. The text of this, by Mr. Eisler
himself, was read at the end of the evening by Samuel L. M.
Barlow, who charged that an unfavorable reference to this work
had already appeared in *Time* magazine, though the staff of that
weekly had had no access to the manuscript. The public was
large, attentive and warmly disposed.

A composer's one-man show is a concert formula as definitive as an omnibus book. It shows you all the chief facets of an
author's mind and his whole repertory of techniques. Such a
view of Hanns Eisler's work was particularly welcome to your
announcer, and to many others among those present, since the
composer has never been represented copiously on New York
concert programs. This hiatus is due chiefly, of course, to the
fact that his mature work, both his European and his American
production, has largely been consecrated to the theater and its
allied occasions. Even as a dramatic composer, he has not always
been easy to come upon, since his music has usually been offered

with productions of such advanced or recondite nature that a music reviewer cannot always get around to hearing before they go off the boards. This reviewer had heard, however, and with pleasure, Mr. Eisler's distinguished musical contribution to Experimental Theater's recent production of Bertolt Brecht's *Galileo*. Viewed through this, as well as through last night's concert, Eisler's whole work becomes genuinely impressive.

The impressiveness is due less to any profound originality, as in the case of his master, Arnold Schoenberg, or in that of his sometime model, the German-language works of Kurt Weill, than to his graceful fancy and to his delicate taste. Eisler's music, whether the style of it is chromatic and emotional, diatonic and formalist, or strictly atonal in the dodecaphonic manner, always has charm. It has charm because the tunes are pretty, the textures bright and light, the expressive intentions thoroughly straightforward and clear. Eisler is that rare specimen, a German composer without weight. He uses no heaviness, makes no insistence. Alone among the works played last night, his Violin Sonata indulged, in its final movement, in climactic expansion and frank virtuosity. Everything else was gossamer, elf-like. Also, his rhythm was invariably alive; and this is perhaps his rarest virtue among German composers of our century, so notably lacking in metrical variety and rhythmic ease.

Two essays in film accompaniment were the evening's real novelty. Six excerpts composed to accompany Chaplin's *The Circus*, scored for string and wind septet, offer chamber sonorities in place of the symphonic sounds usually employed to accompany photographic narration. The sounds are delicious, and the musical fancy is exquisite. Whether the expression is apt and whether the absence of volume variety is monotonous in a theater one could not tell. Confrontation with the film itself would be the test. Such a test was provided in a short subject called *Fourteen Ways of Describing Rain*, photographs of Amsterdam under precipitation. The music, strictly twelve-tone, is scored for flute, violin, clarinet, cello and piano. Violin and piano are played to perfection in this recording by Rudolf Kolisch and Eduard Steuerman. The music sounds enough like rain, but the absence of narrative in the film prevents it from adding to this merely atmospheric effect a full emotional account of what rain can mean. As in the *Circus* excerpts, the music was delightful for itself; but dramatic applicability remained uncertain. Dramatic subjects offer Eisler certainly a stimulus. But I suspect the interest of his film music is largely intrinsic. Its fancy and its taste, at any rate, are more convincing to me than its expressive accuracy. This was not true of his music for the spoken play *Galileo*, which performed a variety of dramatic functions more than satisfactorily.

It is a matter of regret to this reviewer that the American theater is to lose a workman so gifted, so skillful, so imaginative. Let us hope that, pending revision of his case that might permit him to return to this country, his musical works may come to us regularly from Europe, where professional engagements galore, it would seem, await him.

March 1, 1948

Substantial Novelties

CONCERT OF NEW AMERICAN CHAMBER MUSIC last night at McMillan Theater, Columbia University, with the GREENWICH HOUSE MUSIC SCHOOL ORCHESTRA, *Fritz Rikko*, conductor, and the NEW MUSIC QUARTET performing Wallingford Riegger's String Quartet No. 2, Ruth Crawford's String Quartet, Lou Harrison's Suite for Strings No. 2, and Alan Hovhaness's *Lousadzak*, a concerto for piano and orchestra. Soloist: *Maro Ajemian*, piano.

NEW MUSIC of advanced design was the subject of last night's concert in the Alice M. Ditson chamber series at Columbia University. Stringed instruments, including the piano, were its medium of execution. Maro Ajemian, pianist, and the New Music Quartet offered admirable executions. An orchestra from the chamber music class of the Greenwich House Music School, conducted by Fritz Rikko, provided tolerable ones. The music itself was of the highest quality.

Wallingford Riegger's String Quartet No. 2 was the weightiest piece on the program, if this composer's transparent textures can be referred to at all as having ponderable mass. By weighty, however, I merely mean full of meaning. The meaning here is slightly less full of Riegger's habitual poltergeist than that of his First Quartet, but it is Puckish all the same. It is serene, too, and beautifully, wonderfully embodied in string sounds exactly calculated. The language is chromatic, approaching the atonal; but no twelve-tone row is present. This work represents the mature thought of a master workman. It is shapely, clear, varied, free and eminently sensible. If it is not deeply moving in any emotional way, such appeal is nowhere in the author's intention. It is no light work, all the same. It has, as I said before, weight and meaning.

A slow movement from a quartet by Ruth Crawford, composed in 1934, was striking for intensity and elevation. Consisting entirely of long notes closely juxtaposed in slowly changing chords of high dissonance content, the piece seemed scarcely to move at all. And yet it was to this listener and, I am sure, many others thoroughly absorbing. It is in every way a distinguished, a noble piece of work. It is also a daring one and completely successful.

Lou Harrison's Suite for Strings No. 2 is a three-movement work composed principally in pandiatonic imitative counterpoint. The movements are not long; the material is firmly Baroque, though derived rather from the simple grace of Purcell than from the sharp gestures and calculated convolutions dear to Bach and Handel. It is sweet music, sincere music; it sounds well. The end of it is original, ingenious and strong. A chromatic interlude for viola and violin solo lends variety to a work that might otherwise appear insistent by its diatonicism.

Alan Hovhaness's *Lousadzak* (or "Coming of Light") is another of this composer's essays in the ancient Armenian style, evoking, I presume, a scene from Armenian mythology. Like the others I know from his pen, it is pretty of sound, charmingly ornate as to figuration, in every way high-class. Also interminable. It seems to need a travelogue to give some reason why it ever should or should not end. Mr. Hovhaness's exoticism is neither facile nor meretricious; but the continuity of his works lacks in the concert hall necessity, proportion and scale.

March 16, 1949

Bel Canto Pianism

ARTURO BENEDETTI MICHELANGELI, pianist, in recital last
night at Carnegie Hall, performing Ravel's *Valses nobles et sentimentales*, Chopin's Sonata in B-flat minor, and works by Clementi, Galuppi, and Scarlatti.

ARTURO MICHELANGELI, who played a piano recital last night
in Carnegie Hall, is clearly a consecrated man of music and a
perfect technician. No shadow of thoughtlessness or vulgarity
mars his careful readings. No ugly sound or unclean phrase
obscures the elegance of his execution. He plays with all power
and with the utmost delicacy, with a huge variety of kinds and
strengths of sound. And always the sounds he makes are musical sounds; always the structure and the text of every piece are
clear; always the ear is delighted and the mind's interest held.

A certain failure, though slight, to hold completely the feeling
attention, to sustain an emotional line, makes his work cerebral,
in the unfavorable sense of the term. He played his harpsichord
masters last night just a shade fast, and lost by this fault the
maximum of meaning variation from one to another. He played
the Ravel *Noble and Sentimental Waltzes* to perfection and then
failed in the dreamy Epilogue to sum up their feeling content.
Mr. Michelangeli is master of the pianoforte and unfailingly
musical, but his communicative power is still, at thirty, a little
underdeveloped.

The B-flat minor Sonata of Chopin showed him at his best
but also revealed his present weakness. For best there was, in
the Funeral March, a *bel canto* line matchless, incomparable; it
might have been Melba singing. There was also the perfect evocation in the finale of a desolate and windy landscape. Smoothly
articulated and quite without accent, this was a triumph of finger work at the service of musical understanding. It could not
have been more lovely or more moving. The weakness of his
reading had come earlier in the failure to bring out inner counterpoints, in an excess of grace about the insistence of leaving
melody all alone with its bass to bear the musical message. Some
richness of thought got lost in the process and the soaring line
of the Funeral March's middle section became, for all its singing
quality, a shade insistent.

This artist's gifts for making beautiful sounds and for shading a melodic line are unique. I have rarely, if ever, heard the pianoforte sound so lovely or piano music chant in so sophisticated a fashion. If his wonderful ability for making music comes, in maturity, to be enriched by a deeper feeling from music's inner structure, he will be a great artist. Just now he is a wonderful accomplished one, intelligent and honest and genuinely preoccupied with beauty. He is also, as I said before, a technical master. But he falls short of full warmth in his caress of the expressive content.

January 21, 1950

A Solid Debut

GERARD SOUZAY, baritone, in recital last night at Town Hall, performing songs by Handel, Scarlatti, Durante, Schubert, Debussy, Fauré, Caplet, and de Falla. Accompanist: *James Shomate*, piano.

GERARD SOUZAY, who sang last night in Town Hall, is a thirty-year-old version of his master, Pierre Bernac. The baritone voice is of modest proportions but fresh. The vocalism is schooled but skillful. The diction, in Italian, French, German and Spanish, is impeccable. The musicianship and taste are miles above that of today's standard vocalists. The awareness of style is complete, the dramatic projection powerful.

Mr. Souzay's program, drawn chiefly from his gramophone recordings, was made up of vocal works of the highest musical distinction. Handel, Scarlatti, Schubert, Debussy, Fauré, and de Falla were represented in their most celebrated numbers. Three songs by André Caplet, though less intensely absorbing as music than the rest of the repertory, offered novelty to New York. Everything was of the best, including the artistry and good sense of Mr. Souzay's interpretations. And a packed house liberally studded with stars from the professional world of vocalism, both executants and teachers, gave the young French singer a knowing and a warm reception.

There is no question, I think, but that the artist made a deep impression on all by his firm mastery of techniques and his authority of style. Your reporter, however, experienced a slight sense of frustration as the evening went on. This was not due to any essential fault in the singer's voice, which is most agreeable. It came, I think, from a certain discontinuity in his melodic line. This, in turn, seems to be the product of his constant preoccupation, for purposes of clear enunciation, with the consonants. More often than not his consonants interrupted the flow of a melodic line and gave to each vowel the purity but also the isolation of a single jewel. The effect was delicious for a time but eventually exasperating, at least to this listener. Even those less bothered by the mannerism came to express reserves based upon it, for by intermission time the word was running around that Mr. Souzay is a perfect *diseur*.

I regret this, because he has a voice and knows how to sing. I should not wish him to essay the outpourings of the vocally powerful, but I did miss last night sustained cantilena. Vocal music, even the best vocal music, such as Mr. Souzay seems always to sing, does have tunes in it; and these are just as important as the words. An artist of his abilities, with a voice still young and flexible, can be asked to give us both as long as he is able. There may come a time, perhaps, twenty and more years from now, when he will be limited to the verbal operations, and he is prepared already for that eventuality. I regret that he seems to feel its presence now, and suspect that a bit of straight legato singing would do him no harm. I am sure it would add the last perfection to an art that in its present vigorous maturity lacks only that.

November 27, 1950

Voices from the Past

No fewer than fifteen long-playing records and albums consecrated to singers and singing have come to this desk in recent weeks. A few of these deal with singers of today, a few more with singers whose careers are just now closed or closing. But the bulk of them is dedicated to the golden throats of twenty and more years back. And a pleasure it is to study their work. For these records permit that. Orchestrally they are primitive, but the voice "takes" are genuinely resembling. I am not sure but that the vocal "presence" is superior in these old recordings to that provided by our own engineers. Present methods of eliminating scratch-noises have helped, and so have our play-back mechanisms. But the real sound of Caruso and Rosa Pon-selle, of John McCormack and Louise Homer is vivid in these recordings, more vivid, in fact, than it was in the pressings and through the horns of any former decade.

Rosa Ponselle sings again on a 10-inch record (RCA-Victor) arias for Spontini's *La Vestale* and Verdi's *Otello*, along with the Schubert "Ave Maria" and Bishop's "Home, Sweet Home." Warmth and power are the qualities of this voice. It is a real dramatic soprano, strong in the low notes and commanding at the top. Its rich warmth is present throughout the range, which is large; and so is an almost contralto-like darkness of hue. So also is its power. This power is a power of great loudness and of great softness. Also of steadily increasing or diminishing the sound through its decibel gamut. It is a voice with unusual pow-ers of expression, too. It colors, projects, pronounces, vibrates, advances or retreats with ease. Its legato is almost a portamento, so smooth is the melodic utterance; and its declamatory attack is like Caruso's. Miss Ponselle is most impressive artistically (on this record) in the operatic airs. Her Schubert "Ave Maria" is a little mechanical and her "Home, Sweet Home" pedestrian. But the "Salce! Salce!" from *Otello* is grand in every way. The voice is the most beautiful female voice I have ever heard, and its expressive power is gigantic in the broad theater style.

Enrico Caruso had probably the finest male voice of our cen-tury. He could sing loud and soft, high and low, slow and fast. Power he had and warmth and a great urgency in the utterance. He attacked like a bull. He could sing sweetly, too, though he rarely did it for long. His style was essentially declamatory. His vowels were vague and usually preceded by an H. He could color his voice at will but seldom willed subtle shading. The sound of him was unique, unforgettable and more than a little monotonous. He invented the "Italian tenor" style of our cen-tury and practiced it without bathos or absurdity. So, in his younger days, did his successor, Gigli. Their influence on the whole, however, has been injurious both to Italian singing and to public taste. Everybody should hear Caruso once. Thanks to the excellent recordings lately re-issued by RCA-Victor, every-body can.

We still hear, too, his more lyrical contemporary John Mc-
Cormack (also on RCA-Victor). This artist had a sweeter voice
than Caruso's and no declamatory story at all. His were the
songful *bel canto*, the perfect speech (in English, Italian, German), the graceful musicianship. His power to touch the Irish
heart was the equal of Caruso's way with Italians. But McCormack had the wider repertory. Italian opera, German lieder,
English song all came to life under his skilled and gentle hand.
He was no actor, though he sang twenty-one roles. His singing
was not really very expressive, either, though he could make
you weep. That it was very beautiful any one can hear. It was so
beautiful that he never had to hurry it along. Every tempo on
the present record is leisurely, and advantageously so. It contains two pieces by Wagner (one from *Tristan*), two by Donizetti (one the great *Elisir d'Amore* air), two English songs (one
of them Irish), the "Jocelyn" Berceuse (with Fritz Kreisler) and
a rendering of the "Adeste Fidelis" (with the Trinity Choir) that
will make you sorry Christmas comes but once a year.

Leo Slezak is the subject of another record (Eterna). Its program is airs from Halévy's *La Juive*, Massenet's *Manon*, Boiel-
dieu's *La Dame Blanche* and Flotow's *Stradella*. The voice is a
tenor of the utmost brilliance, somewhat lacking in color variety
but strong and trumpet-like. Slezak sang scales beautifully, and
his light work had musical distinction. His loud singing was
impressive, too, but not very expressive. His Massenet airs, sung
in German, are more pushed than floated. One misses German
repertory in this recording of a great German-language artist.
He, not McCormack, was the one to hear as Tristan.

A whole covey of great songbirds has been ensnared in the
re-recording of selections from Verdi's *Aïda* (RCA-Victor) and
Meyerbeer's *Les Huguenots* (Eterna). The first contains (not
systematically cast, but all there) Gadski, Ponselle, Rethberg
and Homer, Caruso, Gigli, Amato, Martinelli and Pinza. Every
voice is beautiful, every singer an artist. The opera itself takes
on under their care a musical power I had long since forgot was
in it. Of especial interest to me was the voice of Louise Homer,
more warm and richly vibrant than I had remembered it from
her later days. And that of Johanna Gadski, a super-Traubel.
Gigli in the "Celeste Aïda" is smoother than Caruso, not at all

teary, very stylish indeed. Elisabeth Rethberg in "Ritorna Vincitor" has a wonderful way of keeping the music moving along with ease. Nobody in any of the selections seems to be afraid of the music or its difficulties. They really sing it, interpret it, bring life to it.

Les Huguenots is no less sensational. Here Slezak has color variety. José Mardones's sumptuous bass, singing in the bravura style, is something we have not heard in many a year. Selma Kurz's light coloratura is delicious too. But wholly out of this present-day world is the coloratura work of Frieda Hempel, replete with high F-sharps and with a mastery of execution, both legato and staccato, that simply must be heard to be believed.

Two more records from RCA-Victor are called *Stars from the Golden Age* and *Famous Duets.* On the first of these you can hear Melba (aging), Battistini (at fifty-one), Tetrazzini, Galli-Curci, Destinn, Bori, Scotti, Caruso and Titta Ruffo. Destinn has power and color, Homer a lovely brilliance, Tetrazzini something girlish in the sound and excellent low notes (as well, of course, as the high). Battistini's voice has a rough surface but is utterly flexible. Melba sounds hollow, though the low notes are good. She sings Italian with an English accent. Galli-Curci has surprising speed in her scales and a lovely pianissimo. Ruffo is a baritone Caruso, as Caruso was a tenor Ruffo. Their styles are identical. The Ruffo voice is richly metallic, the legato technique a portamento in which the singer slides all around the true note, settles on it eventually, leaves it, slides back, slides to the next, then jumps a wide leap and lands with the Caruso flourish. It is all most impressive and probably deliberate. The bronze-like voice itself is matchless.

The duet volume adds to these glorious recalls Farrar, Scotti, Schipa, Bori and Journet. None is here extraordinary. Caruso always sings louder than his partner. So does Scotti (with Farrar) in the *Hoffmann* Barcarolle. Farrar herself sounds warm and lovely in the middle range, a bit hollow at the top. Alma Gluck's voice is pretty too, and strong, but also a little hollow at the top. Both ladies are more neutral of sound than the Europeans. Something about them is, for us, affecting. At the same time, they are not remarkable for dramatic expressivity. This quality was not always present in the "golden age," any more than it is now. But fine voices there were. And technical mastery was part of their set-up. At the salaries paid in those days, expertness was worth acquiring.

January 20, 1952

Female Impersonation

LA BOHÈME, opera in four acts, libretto by *Giuseppe Giacosa* and *Luigi Illica*, music by *Giacomo Puccini*, performed last night at the Metropolitan Opera House, *Alberto Erede*, conductor, *Désiré Defrère*, stage director, with *Ljuba Welitsch* (Musetta), *Ferrucio Tagliavini* (Rodolfo), and *Dorothy Kirsten* (Mimi).

THE FRENCH FARCE WRITER Jacques Feydeau, being asked by a famous actor whether he had seen that actor in his latest role, is said to have replied, "Yes, and I apologize." Your reviewer is tempted to pass over Ljuba Welitsch's Musetta, as seen last night in a performance of Puccini's *La Bohème* at the Metropolitan Opera House. But the event cannot be dismissed. A: Miss Welitsch's vocal performance was impeccable. B: The audience loved her. C: The rest of the performance was musically the most convincing and dramatically the most cogent that this reviewer has ever seen of that opera in that house.

If the Metropolitan goes through with its present plan of redecorating and restaging this opera next year, it will be a scandalous waste of money. The sets are handsome, appropriate and in good condition. The stage movement, a bit restudied and rehearsed, as it apparently had been for last night's presentation, wants nothing but the kind of care in performance that it received last night. It is rare in that house to witness the vivid and sensitive narration of a touching story that Dorothy Kirsten and Ferruccio Tagliavini gave us. They acted and they did not overact; they sang and they did not oversing. One could have imagined oneself at the Paris Opéra-Comique in the days when that house was the model to the world of the lyric theater. Every gesture, every note was serious and lovely.

Every note that Miss Welitsch sang was lovely. For the rest, one has not seen such a hilarious piece of female impersonation since the days of the late (and immortal) Bert Savoy. Naturally, the standees went wild. And not only at the phrase ends did they applaud. At her every move they roared with laughter. Staged in a review, Miss Welitsch's number would have brought down the house, as Marie Dressler's travesty of *La Traviata* always did. ("I love the great scene where the huge Tetrazzini coughs up a cadenza and dies"—and Tetrazzini loved it too.) At the Metropolitan itself, with a perfectly serious performance of *La Bohème* going on, one was obliged to pinch oneself from line to line to remember that one was at the Metropolitan (a non-profit-making) Opera House and that a perfectly serious, indeed far more serious than usual, performance of *La Bohème* was also going on.

That performance was so serious and so excellent in every other way that Miss Welitsch's powerful interference offered no more than temporary interruption. She is not in the first act. The last half of the second act is Musetta's anyway. Her upsetting of the snow scene in the third act was thankfully brief. What she did to Mimi's death scene I do not know, though post-performance reports, as I write, bear witness to some restraint. For me the news of the evening was the high degree of musical and dramatic delicacy shown by Tagliavini and Kirsten, artists whom I have previously known as a bit on the hard-boiled side, the brutal side. Maybe it was by contrast with Welitsch that they seemed so tender and so real. But far more likely it was Miss Welitsch's preoccupation with show business on its lowest level that had brought out in them, way back in the rehearsal days, a care for both sense and sensibility.

January 31, 1952

Elektra

ELEKTRA, opera in one act, libretto by *Hugo von Hofmannsthal,* music by *Richard Strauss,* performed on February 18 at the Metropolitan Opera House, *Fritz Reiner,* conductor, *Herbert Graf,* stage director, with *Astrid Varnay* (Elektra), *Walburga Wegner* (Chrysothemis), *Elisabeth Höngen* (Klytaemnestra), *Set Svanholm* (Aegisth), and *Paul Schöffler* (Orestes).

RICHARD STRAUSS's *Elektra,* as presented last Monday night at the Metropolitan Opera House, was the finest musical performance of any opera that I have ever heard. And I have heard some memorable ones. The singing shone, and the orchestra glowed. The sound of it all was rich, sombre, complex and at the same time utterly plain and meaningful. Performances of comparable vocal elegance have been heard in that house, though rarely. Orchestral executions so wondrously balanced and intoned are rarely encountered anywhere. Even our Philharmonic, in its striking concert reading of this opera two years back, was less suavely perfect. As a matter of fact, Fritz Reiner, last Monday's conductor, has assured me that no other orchestra, not even the Philadelphia, with which he gave the work twenty-odd years ago, has ever played it so beautifully for him. And Reiner is not an easy musician to please.

The occasion offered no actor or actress of unusual personality. There was no Flagstad on the stage, no Chaliapin, no Geraldine Farrar. There were simply fine voices; fine musicianship; and teamwork. That opera does not need star acting anyway. What it needs is vocal power and subservience to the conductor. It is a one-act piece lasting an hour and forty minutes; an extended crescendo of horror that can achieve its cumulative effect only by ensemble work both musical and visual. It has to make a composition. Otherwise it does not come off. Last Monday it did come off.

It would have come off even more impressively from the visual point of view if the stage direction had been composed out of a real vocabulary of movement, a dancer's vocabulary. It would not have been necessary to ask of the singing actors a virtuoso dancing technique, but they might have been taught some more meaningful gestures and then limited to these.

In that way improvisation, always a liability, could have been avoided and a certain rigidity achieved that would have set off by contrast the violence of the story.

That story, which is about a series of axe murders in ancient Greece, combines blood-letting with family hatreds in a complex holocaust that is supposed to leave one shaken. And it does. It achieves this end not by arousing our sympathy with any of the characters but rather by carrying us along with all of them in their madness. Every one of them is obsessed, and insanity is contagious. The story of Agamemnon's widow and children is brutal enough in the Greek versions. But von Hofmannsthal has added to it a psychopathic note from Dr. Freud's Vienna that gives it a hidden force all unexpected. It is Cinderella without any fairy intervention and Buchenwald without an Allied victory. Indeed, so intense is its atmosphere of hatred and its preoccupation with torture that the relatively sane Chrysothemis seems like a half-wit retreating from real life when she refuses to be persuaded by her sister Elektra that her one clear duty is to murder their mother. (Brother Orestes, more reasonable, kills the mother and then his stepfather, a drunk who has wandered into the room out of curiosity.)

The situation and its outcome, the people and all they do, could not be more lurid. And the music that describes it all is a masterpiece of the convulsive, the cataclysmic. It is as exaggerated as the characters of the play and just as obsessed. Its most persistent obsession is waltzes, one of which turns up in each of Elektra's big scenes. Its most surprising is a passion for tubas, of which the score requires no less than four. (Very beautifully they were played, too.) The whole conception, literary and musical, is a combination of *Expressionismus* (a German æsthetic of the 1900s which sought out the lurid in art), of a *Golden Bough* view of early Grecian times as a society where the most extreme violence reigned along with women's rights (a view that was new and deeply exciting forty years ago), and of abnormal psychology (which was just then being discovered).

In 1909, Isadora Duncan was an influence, too. And her concept of Greek movement ran parallel (though not quite contiguous) to the scholarly one of Greek drama as a ritual dance. Now this concept, as applied to Strauss and von Hofmannsthal's *Elektra*, is no stage-director's imposition. It is embodied in the script and in the score, which decrees for its principal character a final solo that is not sung at all; a triumphal dance of hatred gratified (by the assassination of her mother, who had previously killed her father), from which she goes really crazy and falls dead. This is the apotheosis of the play, the terminus of its trajectory. Obviously it must be brought about by treating the whole play as a dance composition. The dance in *Salomé* is merely a requested number, Salomé's payment to Herod for the Baptist's head. Elektra's dance is spontaneous; and to seem so, it must be preceded and surrounded by nothing but categorical and stylized movements. Its power, if it is to have any, must be built.

Josef Urban's setting, a heavy and primitive palace courtyard of hot, dark stone-color, and his draped costumes of the strangest red, violet, green, are handsomely designed to facilitate a staging that accents the obsessive, the cruel and the hieratic. The Metropolitan has essayed such a production, too. It is only partially successful as stage-direction, because it does not carry its hieratic theme far enough. The singers don't really dance; they half dance and half act. The indeterminate character of their motions establishes a convention of semi-naturalism that kills any possibility of Astrid Varnay's moving us deeply in her danced finale. I regret this fault in an otherwise perfect production. Even with the visual aspect falling short (just short) of distinction, the musical performance remains the finest I have ever heard of any opera.

February 24, 1952

The Trouble with Billy Budd

BILLY BUDD, opera in four acts, libretto by *E. M. Forster* and *Eric Crozier*, music by *Benjamin Britten*, the original Royal Opera House production, conducted by *Mr. Britten*, performed last May at the Théatre des Champs-Elysées, Paris, with *Peter Pears* (Captain Vere) and *Theodor Uppman* (Billy Budd).

BENJAMIN BRITTEN's *Billy Budd* is another in the series of this composer's recent operas that is full of musical wealth but that does not seem to work quite right dramatically. One is always ready to revise a first impression; but for the present your correspondent's view of *Billy Budd*, heard in Paris at the Théâtre des Champs-Elysées, as part of the month-of-May festival entitled "Masterpieces of the Twentieth Century," is that of a noble work of music not wholly successful on the stage.

The production had been brought over intact from London, complete with orchestra. The scenery, all semi-realistic boat-building and very pretty indeed, was by the excellent English painter, William Piper. The cast, headed by Peter Pears and Theodor Uppman, was letter perfect. Britten himself conducted the two performances. Covent Garden was showing off to the Continent. And its show was excellent, production-wise. If there were no great voices in the cast, neither were there any unpleasing. This writer's only disappointment in presentation came from a certain obscurity in the enunciation of the text. Part of this was the fault of the composer, who has accompanied his recitative a bit heavily; and part was due to British vocalism, always a shade mealy about its vowels. But except for this weakness on the verbal side, the performance bore every sign of musical and dramatic loyalty to its text.

That text, as we know, comes out of Herman Melville by way of E. M. Forster and Eric Crozier. Like *Peter Grimes*, it tells the story of a misunderstood man. Billy Budd, victim of a personal hatred, goes to his death because he cannot verbalize, argue, defend himself. And Captain Vere, commander of the ship, who understands the victim's innocence, cannot prevent the tragedy, because naval regulations are what they are, and because it is war time. Recited in this brief manner, the tale is merely an incident. As told by Melville it is a metaphysical fable with the villain representing pure evil and the hero pure good. But metaphysics are not easy to make clear on a stage. So the librettists and the composer have omitted Melville's rather grand moral conception. And they have not replaced it by any equally impressive general idea, though Captain Vere's hesitancy to interfere with the inefficiencies of martial justice might easily have been rendered in terms of class loyalties and of a fear lest his sympathy for the condemned seaman be misconstrued by his fellow officers as a personal weakness. Actually this last possibility is the work's dominant note, though it is nowhere clearly stated. As a result, homosexuality, never quite overt in the novel, becomes the whole theme of the opera's pathos. In spite of the plot's many melodramatic occasions, the work is thus essentially sentimental. It contains a scene of dancing below decks, a fist fight, a naval battle, a murder, a trial, a dungeon visit and a full-dress execution. The musical treatment of all these is varied and vigorous. Nevertheless, the musical drama does not move forward with any anxiety, any suspense. It mostly just feels very sorry about the sad fate of its hero. It is not so much a play as a series of devotional meditations about a story that is taken for granted as familiar and as void of general significance. "Stations of the Cross" is my term for this kind of dramatic narrative.

Note that many of the scenes, taken alone, have a real dramatic animation, though the spectacle as a whole has none. The execution, in particular, is fine theater; and the dancing below decks, the scene of the quartermaster's first quarrel with Billy Budd, is picturesque and vigorous. Britten has a gift for the musical theater, and moment by moment he exploits it. It is the over-all dramatic impact that is weak in *Billy Budd*, as it was also in *The Rape of Lucretia* and in *Albert Herring*. And this weakness makes of a work that needs to move forward with the sweep of *La Tosca* one that does not move forward at all. For all its detailed excellences dramatic and musical, *Billy Budd* became for this listener, in consequence, as indeed it did also for the festival audiences, an interminable, an unconscionable bore. And it need not have done so.

There may be something in the idea expressed to me by a British writer that success has constricted Britten's dramatic expression. The opera in our time is a popular form and needs a strong social theme. *Peter Grimes*, the story of an individual murdered by mass misunderstanding, had such a theme. But that was written when the composer was still in the orbit of Auden and the social philosophers. As England's official success boy, adopted by the B.B.C. and blest by the Crown, he has never since enjoyed quite the same freedom of protest, nor written for the theater with the same conviction. More and more he becomes, as I suggested several years ago, a sort of English Shostakovich.

The parallel carries even into the technical mannerisms. There is the same dependence on an easy-going, sequence-structured, two-part counterpoint, the same gift for bold and effective orchestration, the same unimaginative harmony and hastily improvised melodic structure, the same clear ticketing by the simplest, plainest themes of the story's most obvious recurrent motives, even the same unfortunate tendency toward accompanying recitative with instrumental counter-melody. Both composers write an effective, if undistinguished, musical journalese. And both have tended in recent years to limit their bent toward unequivocal communication.

In any case, *Billy Budd*, though musically the most sophisticated, the most accomplished of the Britten operas, did seem in Paris to lack dramatic composition, communicative urgency. Part of its tedium, of course, came from the monotony of the male voice, unrelieved for four hours. But mostly it was due to the composer's (and presumably the librettists') unwillingness to give the story a point. All pathos and no moral makes a very dull opera.

June 22, 1952

Irresponsible Music-Making

Erik Satie's *Socrate*, as recorded in Paris under the direction of René Leibowitz and issued here under the label of Esoteric Records, is irresponsible music-making. Not only are the instrumental execution rough and the singing unprofessional, but the composer's clearly marked tempos and dynamics have neither been observed with care nor altered with sensitivity. One wonders whether Mr. Leibowitz or any of his interpreters has ever heard the work performed correctly, so little does their reading concord with the text or with the still living tradition of the composer's wishes. It is an irony of fate, moreover, that at the very moment when this record was being made *Socrate* was being performed in the same city at a concert of the Twentieth-Century Festival by Suzanne Danco and an orchestra conducted by Darius Milhaud. It is infinitely regrettable that this definitive performance was not recorded in place of the present one.

These dialogues from Plato, in the French translation of Victor Cousin, have usually been sung in France by a single woman's voice, though the American tradition (not negligible in regard to Satie) admits also the male. The first complete performance of *Socrate* in the United States was sung in Cambridge, Massachusetts, in 1923 by the tenor Joseph Lautner; and its first orchestral performance was sung in Hartford, Connecticut, in 1935 by Eva Gauthier, soprano, and Colin O'Moore, tenor. Mr. Leibowitz's decision to give the dialogues to five voices is a reasonable one, since five characters actually speak during their course. Unfortunately the fact that all these are in the present disc women's voices tends to obliterate the possibilities of contrast, and the fact that they are poorly schooled voices makes one wish that one really good singer had been engaged rather than five ineffective ones.

How ineffective they are must be heard to be believed. They mouth their French; they run out of breath; their high notes are all loud and a little flat; they sing in many cases notes not those written in the score; their rhythm is literal and lifeless; their tone is lacking in expressive coloration; their work is marked throughout by amateurishness and by what seems like a willful indifference to either musical or verbal meaning. The tenderness of the sentiment, the grace of melodic line, the subtleties of accent and phraseology that make this work vibrate with beauty and penetrate the heart are as absent as in a child's rendition of Mozart.

On the instrumental plane the performance is similarly opaque. Satie's striking harmonies are obscured by poor intonation; his rhythmic solidity is lost through imprecise attacks; his grand and complex musical structure is reduced to a mere paper plan through non-respect for his indicating pacing.

The first movement, for instance, the *Portrait de Socrate* from *The Banquet*, though marked in the first edition of the piano score as ♩=60 and in the second as ♩=66, has been slowed down to ♩=48. And the second, *The Banks of the Ilyssus*, marked at ♩=60, is taken at about ♩=54. *The Death of Socrates* is correctly paced at ♩=72, but virtually none of the indicated retards, pauses, or accelerations is observed. It marches with a relentlessness as monotonous as it is inexpressive. To give an idea of the length to which simplification has been carried, I here cite a few of the pages of the piano score on which indicated speed changes of an expressive character have been neglected—pages 5, 8, 24, 26, 32, 42, 44, 46, 49, 50, 53, 54, and 59. On page 57, on the other hand, a speed-up has been added. A passage on page 67 marked *pp* is sung and played *ff*. In general the work is played loud throughout and very close to the microphone. The final chord of the first movement contains an A-natural in place of the written A-sharp.

Socrate is a unique work in the musical literature. Though seldom performed and never before recorded, it is known by name to thousands of musicians. Its admirers are utterly devoted, and many who do not know it would like to know it. It is too bad that its first recording issued should be so little faithful to the text, so crude as musical execution, and so indifferent to the projection of the work's expressive content.

The Musical Quarterly, January 1953

Pure Horsemanship

PHILADELPHIA ORCHESTRA, *Eugene Ormandy*, conductor, with the UNIVERSITY OF PENNSYLVANIA CHORAL SOCIETY, last night at Carnegie Hall performing Mahler's Symphony No. 2. Soloists: *Rita Kolacz*, soprano, and *Janice Moudry*, contralto.

ANYONE who feels slightly impatient with American or Soviet symphonists who pose in program notes representing editorially the voices of their respective peoples should take a look at what went on in Vienna back in the 1890s. There Gustav Mahler, a gifted conductor just turned thirty, was declaring himself the voice of the universe, no less, and The Artist in person. It is all put down in his own memoirs and further expanded in those of his pupil Bruno Walter, the attitudes of this certainly consecrated artist about his own music, in particular about the Second Symphony, which the Philadelphia Orchestra played last night at Carnegie Hall.

Mahler pretends that he "literally ransacked the literature of the world up to the Bible to find the releasing 'word,'" by which he means that he had some trouble finding a text for the chorus to sing in his last movement, in imitation of Beethoven's Ninth Symphony. Naturally enough, he eventually found what he was looking for right under his nose in a familiar ode by Klopstock and in *Des Knaben Wunderhorn*, a collection known to every

German schoolboy. Then in a "flash of lightning" "everything was revealed clear and plain to [his] soul," and all he had to do was "create in tones" what he had experienced. "And yet," he adds, "if I had not had this work already in me, how could I have had this experience?"

All this pretentiousness could be passed over if the work itself bore an intrinsic musical interest. Alas, though it has a beautiful plot, the dialogue has no vitality. It depicts in five movements the death and funeral of a "hero" (twenty-five minutes), a "friendly incident" from the hero's life, Saint Anthony of Padua's Sermon to the Fishes, "Primal Light," with alto solo, and a Last Judgment, with alto, soprano, chorus and a large off-stage orchestra. (Eugene Ormandy, the conductor, cheated a little here on the ten horns required.) As you can see, the subject is sure-fire, or was in 1893. Indeed, the work's reception last night, after an unbroken reading lasting ninety minutes, made one think that maybe it still is. But the composer's treatment of it is so respectfully derivative from all the Germanic clichés of its time that one wonders what, beyond the obvious technical proficiency of its scoring (though this is quite without imagination), impels a musical director to resurrect this heirloom, which, among its other immodesties, bears the subtitle "Resurrection."

Well, let it be a lesson to us all. Let any composer, tempted by expansive spirits to write another editorial or philosophic or, still worse, mystical symphony, remember that Mahler, long before Scriabin or Roy Harris or Shostakovich or Messiaen, had already run this fox to ground with trumpet and horn and tambour and tally-ho. And let us leave the fox in his hole, save for an occasional display, like last night's, of world's-record horsemanship. That, I suppose and truly hope, was what drew the applause. For no one fell in a creek or even stumbled. The show was perfect. Even the finale crescendo, which rose to what I suspect may have been the loudest sound ever heard in Carnegie Hall, did not upset the balances that are musical beauty. All that was fine, and the soloist too. But the piece itself! Really, how pretentious can you be about a thoroughly conventional harmony-and-counterpoint exercise on the C-minor chord?

February 25, 1953

Technique and Taste

CHARLES ROSEN, pianist, in recital last night at Town Hall, performing two Bach fugues, Beethoven's Sonata No. 32 (Op. III), Ravel's *Menuet sur le nom d'Haydn*, Debussy's *Hommage à Haydn*, one of Babbitt's *Three Compositions*, Stravinsky's Russian Dance from *Petrouchka*, Dallapiccola's Sonatina Canonica, and three mazurkas and two études by Chopin.

CHARLES ROSEN, who played last night his third Town Hall recital, is at twenty-six one of the great piano technicians. He is also a Ph.D. and an assistant professor of French at the Massachusetts Institute of Technology. If you look while you listen, you have an impression of Harold Teen turned Horowitz. If you listen while you look, you become aware that under all the precocity lies a musical mind of great strength and modesty. Also an exquisitely trained taste of no modesty whatsoever. It is that confident and in virtually any musical circumstance utterly right.

Still further below the precocity, the brains and the disciplined musicianship lies a personality not nearly so mature as the musical mastery had led one to hope for. In Bach, in Debussy, in the elegant atonalism of Milton Babbitt, in the Dellapiccola Sonata Canonica, after Caprices of Paganini, Mr. Rosen's objectivity was complete, his understanding impeccable. Indeed, judging from his performance last night of Debussy's Hommage à Haydn, of "La Puerta del Vino" and of the Etude for Eight Fingers (the last two played as encores) and remembering his extraordinary recording several years ago of all twelve Debussy Etudes, one is inclined to rank him as one of the great Debussy interpreters.

But in the Romantic repertory his interpretative powers are not yet fully ripe. Three Chopin mazurkas were like dried flowers. And the Beethoven Sonata, Opus III, though technically a triumph and even intellectually a masterful reading, communicated little warmth. He played the loud notes without ugliness, the rapid bass passages without obscurity and the fiendish trills with no unevenness whatsoever and seemingly no effort. Everywhere the tone was beautiful, the rhythm powerful, the singing line plangent and commanding. But it was all architecture and execution. The heart of the piece (and it has one) he will have to grow to.

There is time for that at twenty-six. And thank heaven technique and musicianship are already there. What Rosen needs now, I believe, is simply to play a great deal, to appear constantly before the public and to learn the great Romantic repertory, which is still the central repertory of the pianoforte, in the only way that it is ever learned, which is by working with it as one grows up to it.

His perfection in French music and in virtuoso display will be an advantage to him in recital giving. But they will not, can not take the place of Beethoven, Chopin and Schumann in a pianist's career. Last night Mr. Rosen showed us, by placing some of the grander nineteenth-century works on his program, that he is not afraid of them. On the day that he gets inside them as he does those from the eighteenth and twentieth centuries, he will be the pianist of all our dreams. His gift and mastery are that good. But his preparatory years are over. For the next ten he must play, play, play, use his talent as one would a muscle, develop it the hard way, the only way musical muscles ever grow after youth is over, by wrestling with angels in public.

November 4, 1953

The Music World Stands Still

THE MUSIC WORLD changes very slowly. And when it seems to change, more often than not it is the persons rather than the programs that are different. Your reviewer, thinking about such things this morning, wondered if perhaps a column of comparisons between today and a decade ago might not possibly be of interest to others.

The two fields in which the least change has taken place since the early 1940s are piano playing and conducting. When this reporter came to work in New York in 1940, the five top pianists were Rubinstein, Horowitz, Casadesus, Arrau and Serkin. They still are. E. Robert Schmitz, expert of French piano music and of modern music in general, is dead; and William Kapell, then just beginning his career, has grown into a most impressive maturity. Other unknowns from at home and abroad have appeared among us, though none has taken so firm a position as Kapell. But the big dates still belong to the big five.

In 1940 the top conductors working in America were Toscanini, Koussevitzky, Stokowski, Walter, Reiner, Monteux, Ormandy and Mitropoulos. With the exception of Serge Koussevitzky, now deceased, all these are still working here and at the top of their form. Beecham and Ansermet and de Sabata have visited us extensively and will no doubt continue to do so, but they have not taken us on as their responsibility. Paul Paray and Charles Munch from France have dug in, the one in Detroit and the other in Boston. Two brilliant young men have appeared, Guido Cantelli from Italy and our own Leonard Bernstein; but neither has yet accepted a permanent orchestral post, though both have been offered them. The most striking change in the orchestral picture has been the installation of American conductors in three major cities. Alfred Wallenstein in Los Angeles, Thor Johnson in Cincinnati and Walter Hendl in Dallas have proved technically and artistically capable of competing with imported conductors and more than a match for their European colleagues in the handling of boards and trustees. Their loyalty to the American composer has also been notable.

Among the singers everything has changed. Or perhaps one should say everybody. In 1940 the great opera stars were Pinza, Pons, Flagstad, Melchior, Swarthout, Traubel, Grace Moore and Rethberg. Martinelli, Schipa and Lotte Lehman still appeared too. Today among all these, only Pons and Traubel still sing in opera, and that more and more rarely. New artists, some from here and some from abroad, are now singing most of their roles. But nobody has taken their place. We have no substitute in coloratura parts for Lily Pons nor in Wagnerian dramatic soprano roles for Flagstad. Neither have we any operatic glamour-and-sex queen to replace the sometimes awful but always wonderful Grace Moore. Jan Peerce has inherited from Schipa the place of elder statesman among tenors. There is a possibility, and a hopeful one, that George London may turn out to be another Pinza. Standard opera repertory has not changed at all. Neither has the lieder repertory. But Lotte Lehmann and Povla Frijsh have left the recital platform. To replace them we have Jennie Tourel, Suzanne Danco, Irmgard Seefried, Pierre Bernac and Gerard Souzay. The domain of lieder singing is richly furnished.

Violin playing is extremely good these days but not glamorous. Yesteryear there were Kreisler, Heifetz, Zimbalist, Elman, Szigeti, Menuhin, Morini, all of them shining personalities. Some of these survive in diminished splendor; but most musicians, if asked to name today's top violin figures, would mention Francescatti and Milstein first. Heifetz would still be listed, of course; and so would Szigeti and Erica Morini. But Kreisler and Zimbalist are retired; Elman and Menuhin are shadows of their great selves. No one who knows the field would omit two American artists of the highest distinction, Isaac Stern and Joseph Fuchs. Europe is not sending us many violinists, because the great teachers of the instrument, it would seem, are mostly working here.

Ten years ago the touring cello stars were two, Feuermann and Piatigorsky. Today one is dead and the other more or less retired into pedagogy. Pierre Fournier and Leonard Rose, both excellent, are the present chiefs of staff. But the technique of the cello is in a vigorous period of evolution everywhere. We may expect, I think, further contributions from Europe. And America has some fine artists of the instrument, including Joseph Schuster. We would hear all of these more often if the cello repertory were not so limited that audiences tend to find cello recitals monotonous. Composers please note.

The chief American composers, just before World War II, were Aaron Copland, Roy Harris, Walter Piston, Roger Sessions and myself, though Sessions was little played and I was best known for my stage works—for one opera, one ballet and two films. Douglas Moore and Marc Blitzstein were known for one opera each. Today Samuel Barber has been added to our list and ranks high, and I am far better known than before to concert audiences. William Schuman, then a brilliant youth, is now a mature composer with six symphonies to his credit; and Roy Harris has somewhat diminished in concert popularity, though he remains a vigorous and far from negligible composer. The most striking career in America during the last decade and a half has been that of Gian-Carlo Menotti as a composer of operas. Nobody, I may add, has taken the place in world popularity of the late George Gershwin.

Among the European composers transplanted to American soil by world events, nothing has changed except for the death of Arnold Schoenberg, world president and last surviving founder of the twelve-tone school. Stravinsky is now our chief master in the over-seventy group, indeed our only one; and certainly he is the most played all over the Western world among living "serious" composers. I doubt whether even Sibelius occurs so frequently in the classical concerts, and he is not in the theater at all any more, nor in the ballets. Hindemith and Milhaud are about where they were a decade ago, and so is Martinů. Among European composers, Honegger is a stayer; another is Poulenc. Britten and Dallapiccola are comers. Prokofiev is still played here and much loved. The Western star of Shostakovich is declining. The death of Richard Strauss and Rachmaninoff has removed from the contemporary scene figures who, like the still surviving Sibelius and the till recently surviving Gustave Charpentier, had little, if any, contact with that scene.

There is no moral to the above save perhaps that there is a high mortality among singers. And that the music world, though choppy on the surface, does not, in its deeper currents, move fast. But I did get to thinking about these things and decided to share my thoughts. Possibly there is a newspeg for them in the announcement of the Metropolitan Opera that next year's novelties, productionwise, are to consist of *Faust*, *Tannhäuser* and *The Barber of Seville*.

March 8, 1953

THE MUSIC REVIEWER AND
HIS ASSIGNMENT

Music Coverage

A NEWSPAPER can no more report all the musical events that take place in the city of its publication than it can report all the political changes proposed or the crimes committed. News coverage of any kind is selective. Indeed, what constitutes news in the musical domain is far from being a settled convention. Most newspapers review merely concerts and operatic performances of the better class. Operettas and musical comedies are left to the drama department, which is jealous of its rights in this matter. Films, no matter how much music is involved, fall similarly to the film department. Ballet, unless there is a dance critic, usually falls to the music writers, simply because the theater writers do not know how to approach it. They are afraid of it, for some reason, though pantomime they can take in their stride and even a certain amount of ballet, provided this is surrounded by musical comedy.

Of late years it has become the custom for metropolitan papers to review band concerts at which new works by reputable composers are played. Almost no paper criticizes church music, though most papers notify the public beforehand of elaborate musical services that are about to take place. Student recitals are not reviewed either, it being considered unfair to criticize by professional standards work that is not offered as ripe for professional exploitation. Books on musical subjects are pretty fully reviewed, sometimes on the book page, sometimes on the music page, sometimes on both. Gramophone records are even more fully reviewed as they appear. Published music is reviewed only in specialized journals and magazines. Radio broadcasts of classical music pass virtually uncriticized unless they take place also as public concerts. No musical occasion, of course, is considered a subject of report which is not open to the public.

Music reviewers tend, I don't know why, to avoid free concerts. They also tend to avoid certain locales. In New York they do not like going very far uptown or downtown, and they almost never go to Brooklyn. They don't mind too much going to the Museum of Modern Art, which is in Fifty-third Street; they rather avoid the Hunter College auditorium, which is in Sixty-eighth. They even resist Carnegie Chamber Music Hall and Times Hall, which are right on their beat, though they do put in an appearance if the occasion is a strictly professional one and recognizable in advance as high-class. In the theater it is the public which does not like going south of Fortieth Street or north of Fifty-ninth; the reviewers rather enjoy an expedition uptown or down. But the music public will go anywhere, while the music critics continue to act as if musical art were an adjunct to real estate, Carnegie Hall, Town Hall and the Metropolitan Opera House being the privileged premises that entitle the lessee of any evening to professional consideration.

Even so, the first critic on any paper's staff does not invariably choose to visit those places. He will sometimes go to Columbia University or the Y.M.H.A. or Washington Irving High School or the New School for Social Research, but he will do this only if Carnegie and the Town Hall are being covered by other members of his staff. Critical coverage, in other words, begins not with any known-in-advance distinction of any musical event but in certain customary halls. Everything beyond that is luxury coverage, the privilege of the rich and elegant papers that maintain a fairly numerous musical staff.

The case of the début recital is a typical one. If it takes place anywhere but in Town Hall, it may or may not be covered. In Town Hall it is invariably covered. That is why the Town Hall recital has become the customary consecration of all young artists' careers; since it is only there that they can be sure of getting reviewed, of acquiring press notices that can (hopefully) be quoted in the quest for provincial and other engagements. Nevertheless, the head critic of any staff will avoid début recitals whenever possible.

One reason for this avoidance is that a début is the most difficult of all musical events to review competently. A début is a bid for the future. And who can tell how a young artist is likely to mature? Who can know from one hearing the state of his talent and technique? Mature artists are striking; their faults and qualities are visible, pronounced, emphatic. Beginning artists have no such assurance, no comparable simplification of style. They merit, for that reason, more severity and more tolerance than older workmen do. And the dosage of these with justice is an impossible calculation. No critic whose mere job itself carries a certain weight with the public likes to risk giving undue encouragement or discouragement to a young career.

And so he sends, if he has one, an assistant. The assistant is in a better position than the head critic, as a matter of fact, to make his comment fit the merit. His readers do not expect an article of given length or elaborateness. If the recital is particularly good, he can write a longer piece than he had planned. If it is only fair, which is what most of them are, he can give it five to eight inches. If it is unusually incompetent, he can write an unsigned news item saying merely that it took place. This is kindness. The head critic can do any of these things, too; but he will have lost an evening's work, because his regular readers still expect an article of some length from him several times a week.

That is why he stays away, if he can, from début recitals. Reviewing them briefly is a waste of his time, and reviewing them as if they were major events is unfair to the artist. An ensemble of short opinions, as these appear in the whole New York press, is likely to give the reader a pretty good idea of the young artist's present ability. If these improve in length and degree of admiration over two or three years, the head critic can no longer avoid reviewing the artist in question, no longer needs or wishes to do so. But by that time the artist is more nearly mature, more sharply characterized, more personal. Describing his work is easier: praising it is more useful to him; criticizing it unfavorably is less injurious to his career. And I assure you that reviewers don't enjoy injuring artists' careers.

January 6, 1946

The Music Reviewer and His Assignment*

MANY PERSONS, particularly young persons, hold the romantic idea about music reviewing that it offers a virtually unlimited field for self-expression. They believe it is any critic's delight and

---

*Talk delivered at the dinner meeting of the National Institute of Arts and Letters, November 17, 1953.

privilege to share daily with a vast body of readers his personal tastes and opinions in matters of art. This is not true, of course. No responsible newspaper owner would consider offering the use of his valuable columns for a private pulpit. A newspaper is published for the benefit of its readers, not of its writers.

The sole justifiable purpose of reviewing, in my opinion, is to inform the public; any other is an abuse of confidence. A critic is paid by a periodical to tell the truth about music as he believes that to be; and if he is not expected to advertise himself, neither is he engaged to encourage particular artists toward success, or to discourage them, or to grade them from zero to one hundred, or to help trustees raise money, or to advertise standard repertory, or to form public opinion in any given way, or to uphold standards of execution—how could he?—or to advertise certain schools of composition, or to defend the public against them, or to teach music appreciation in general, or to spread enlightenment. All these things he may do occasionally or incidentally, but his main business is to report the music life of his community truthfully.

This reporting need not be and cannot be entirely factual. It is the reviewer's duty and his privilege to analyze music and its execution, to examine their nature, and to describe them in words. He is a man of letters whose subject is music. Practical knowledge of music gives penetration to his judgment; literary skill may enable him to express it courageously. A certain involvement with music as an art, a personal engagement to it, if he has any such consecration, will prevent him from making irresponsible statements. But he is under no necessity to edify anybody or to improve taste. Musical edification and enlightenment come from music itself, not from descriptions of it; and public taste in music is raised by sound performances of music, not by literary essays on the subject.

A music review, I insist, is a service of information and little else. It is not even a shopping service, like drama or book criticism, because a musical event usually takes place only once and is unavailable by the time the public reads about it. A music review is paid for by a newspaper and addressed to the whole reading public. It is written by an expert and signed with his name or initials. Any reporter is temporarily an expert if the managing

editor says he is. If the reading public is not convinced of his
knowledge, that is the paper's misfortune. The reporter himself
can always go back to the shipping page.

A metropolitan newspaper should trust on the job only writers of sound musical education. They don't have to be right, but
they do have to penetrate surfaces. In the criticism of anything,
you do not have to be right in your judgment; you have only to
use a legitimate means of arriving at it. If there is such a thing
as a talent for criticism, it is a talent for judgment. Your loyalty
and your workmanship are shown not merely in the way you
write but in the intellectual methods by which you defend your
intuitive judgment. But any opinion about art is legitimate if
it is based on some knowledge and can be expressed in clear
language.

I insist upon the informative character of music reviewing, but
please note that I hold no brief for informing the public about
things that are none of its business, nor do we presume to
offer judgment in matters that do not involve us. We do not
review musical events which take place in private houses or in
clubs, because they are not offered to the public for its judgment. Among matters that are none of our business, let me list
student recitals and church services. Student recitals are none
of our business because we are not competent to estimate anything that does not take place under professional circumstances
or which is not offered to the professional world of music, of
which we are members, for professional consideration. It is difficult enough to estimate the qualities of a professional artist; it
is even more difficult to estimate those of a student. We leave
that to parents and teachers.

As for church services, any religious establishment would
welcome reviewing, on condition that all the comments were
favorable. Churches love advertising, but they resent criticism.
And they have an impregnable position, because the music of
religious worship is not offered to the public for its judgment.
It is actually not offered to the public at all; it is offered to God.
And God does not necessarily judge by professional standards,
since sincerity, in His eyes, may make up for many an incompetence. This does not mean that a great deal of excellent music
is not performed under religious auspices; of course it is. But

judging it is not our business. Besides which, from a purely organizational point of view, it would require a whole separate staff, because most religious music is performed all on the same day and at the same hour.

In offering news and commentary about professional musical events that are open to the public and submitted for its favor, our standards of news coverage are slightly different from those of the city desk. On the news pages, news is classically considered to consist of an extraordinary event happening to anybody, or any kind of an event happening to a famous person. That is to say that if I take a train, it is not news; if Mr. Toscanini takes a train, it is news. If I fall under a train, it is news; if Toscanini falls under a train, then you have a streamer across the front page.

But if we judged the importance of musical events by those standards, we would find ourselves constantly reviewing Toscanini and Marian Anderson. We would be the victims of publicity machinery, because the fame of these artists is not merely a matter of spontaneous public favor; it is also a thing that is worked at by press agents.

We have taken a different attitude on the music pages of the *Herald Tribune*—and this attitude is, I think, shared by most responsible newspapers who give serious attention to music— that intellectual distinction itself is news. It is news on the same basis that my falling under a train might be news, because it is rare. That a famous artist plays a famous piece in public is not news, because it takes place constantly.

The music staffs, if they are musicians—which is largely true in New York City—also find this system of judging the value of news events useful for their private purposes. It makes their work easier, because the performance of a new work, the debut of a new and valid artist, the performance of an old work which is not often heard, or a change in the repertory line of a famous artist—all these things give us a more interesting theme than we could find in constantly reviewing famous people and famous pieces.

All these things we describe for all our readers. We do not write for the artist or for the management or for the backers of concerts or for the trustees of the Metropolitan Opera, and certainly not for our advertisers or their friends. Anybody can understand why you don't write for the advertisers or for trustees. But people do not always remember that your review is not addressed to the artist that you are reviewing. I recall saying to a very experienced singer some years ago, "We don't write for you; we explain you."

She said, "I never thought of that."

I said, "I do not have to mobilize a newspaper in order to make you a personal communication. Besides, correcting you in public would be the kind of rudeness that husbands and wives engage in when they take advantage of a gathering to say things to each other that they haven't dared say in private." Personal criticism is an abuse of the public, and the larger the public the greater the abuse.

In writing about an artist's work, I consider the description more important than the estimate of value. The estimate of value has its use, of course, because it enables the reviewer to confess his prejudices and predilections. No reviewer is a perfectly clear glass between the reader and the subject he is writing about; and if he pretends he is, then he is a very dark one indeed. So that an expression of opinion is a perfectly legitimate thing, and it also makes the reviewer feel good; but it is not a very important matter. Whereas the description of what took place, or of the nature of something, can be a quite broad communication. We try to tell the truth as well as we can, and a part of telling the truth is the admission of our prejudice for or against things. Our aim is to describe a musical event truly, as well as we are able.

In order to tell the strict truth, we must observe, of course, strict courtesy. Because if you observe the amenities, you can say much more unfavorable things than if you express them angrily. Actually, musicians do not differ very much about truth of fact; they only differ about opinion. If a vocalist sings off pitch, every musical ear in the house will know it. And any reviewer who states that she did can defend himself by the evidence of other persons present. The analysis of a musical work is subject to similar correction from other expert persons present; and within several months, or sometimes several years, a fairly definitive agreement is usually reached in the musical world about the structural nature of a piece of music.

At the very beginning, of course, many a highly complex work is taken by the naïve reviewer for pure spontaneity. That happened to the work of Arnold Schoenberg; it happened to Debussy; it happened to Beethoven. The ignorant reviewer likes to think that since he is judging hastily, the work was hastily created. And when his lack of preparation makes him unable to understand, he thinks that the work was written as casually as it is being listened to, which is not necessarily the truth at all.

Let me come back to the matter of courtesy in the statement. It enables you to make the really deadly attack, because the specific adjective is practically never actionable, either in court or in public opinion. The noun, yes. Gertrude Stein was right when she said that nouns are the bane of the language, because if you use nouns in talking about somebody, before you know what you have done you have called him a name. But the specific adjective is merely descriptive. Verbs are dangerous, too, because the verbs of motion and the verbs of action all have overtones of approval and disapproval, as the nouns have. But the adjective, the specific adjective, is virtually neutral.

There are adjectives of approval and disapproval, and we try to avoid using them. If you try to make a hierarchy out of "wonderful," "sublime," "splendid," "magnificent" and "outstanding," you weaken your communication, because you are not using those words in any specific meaning. You have turned them into advertising slogans. I tell the boys who work for me and the young people who come to learn the trade that they may use "splendid" only in its correct meaning, which is "shining," and "magnificent" only in the sense of "grandiose." "Splendid" and "magnificent," unless they mean in English what they mean in Latin, are not specific; and they will always sound foolish.

So far I have been talking about a standard operation, which is the reviewing of an artist performing standard repertory. Music reviewing becomes a part of the intellectual life of its time only when it deals with the composition of its time, that is to say, with new music. Now let us observe a little how you make up your mind about a new work.

You can often make up your mind very well from one hearing,

from first acquaintance. As a matter of fact, that is what most teachers do with their students' works. And the musical historians, I may say, often make up their minds, or at least express an opinion about a musical work from the far past without any other acquaintance than that of the page.

Similarly, from a first performance, professionally presented in public, one can more often than not form an honest opinion and make an honest description. It is not very many times a year, especially in these days, when there is so little music of an advanced nature in existence at all, that one runs into a work of such complexity as requires preparation ahead of time. When those do come up in the programs we know about them in advance; we provide ourselves with scores; we go to rehearsals. There is no question about it—you always write a better article about something you know something about than about something you are not prepared about.

Let us look a little further into that matter of first acquaintance and what really happens. The very first moment of cognition is extremely important, the way the piece begins and how the first few measures or pages of it taste to the auditory tongue. That tasting is not a final judgment, but it is material for judgment. And as soon as you have got the work's taste, the question arises of whether you go on listening. If your mind wanders, you try to pull it back; but it will not always go; the mind is a very strong organ. The beginning of listening and the going on of listening should last you through the piece, but there will be some drama about it. The tendency of the mind to wander does not come about because the mind is lazy, but rather because the mind has its own way of judging, the instinctive mind, over and above your intention and your will.

Now as soon as the piece is over, there is another thing that happens comparable to that very first taste when it began, which is an auditory after-image that will last five, sometimes ten and sometimes fifteen seconds, when you can still hear the whole thing—not necessarily as a shape, but as a sound and almost as a shape, in any case as an experience that you are still having. And in that moment of the after-image, of the after-experience, before the applause of the audience or your own fidgeting with your hat, there is a moment of what the French call *recueillement*, for which I do not know the English word, in which one is still absorbed by the work, still tasting it, still feeling it. The intensity of this third experience is important for your final judgment.

Five minutes later, particularly if it is the work of a rival composer, you will find every reason to disapprove of it. If it is the work of a pupil or of a close friend who is not a rival, you will have found reasons for saying you like it. But to find out what you really think you must remember very hard. Your memory of what the piece tasted like when it started to sound, of how vigorously it made you listen to it while it went on, and of what it tasted like after it stopped sounding—these are the data that you have to deal with. You can verify them, test them, prove them, but they are the only reality that you can bear witness to; and you are a fool and a dishonest man if you do not consider them your major evidence.

On the basis of that evidence, you now have to make up your mind. This consists of putting your evidence through the classical procedures of judgment, of testing your reactions for error. You have already asked yourself, "Does it hold my attention?" "Does it remain in my memory?" "Is the taste of it strange and interesting upon the tongue?" You must now try to distinguish between its design and its execution. "Have I heard a good piece or just a very slick performance which deceived me into thinking it a good piece?" "Have I heard a bad piece, or was I so sales-resistant about an over-slick performance that I resisted the piece itself as vigorously as I did the salesmanship of the performance?"

You must also try to separate the expressive power of the work from its formal or structural or textural interest. The world is full of people who think that Sebastian Bach is an extremely expressive composer. All musicians will admit that he is a fascinating composer, because the intrinsic interest of his musical textures is very great. But only heaven knows what they mean! Choose among the whole series of the forty-eight preludes and fugues in *The Well-Tempered Clavichord* and describe to me what any of them is about; and I will give you fifty cents. They must be about external things, because they are too varied to be about the composer's interior emotional life. As painters know, no two arms look alike. But the emotional life tends to fall into repeating patterns. So wherever you find a composer whose work is varied in melodic invention, texture and form, you can safely bet that the inspiration for each invention of melody and form was of an exterior nature, because that much variety does not exist inside any one human being. And so you must distinguish, in making up your mind about any piece, whether you are dealing with expression or whether you are dealing with an intrinsic musical interest of form and texture.

If you opine that the expressive power of the work is very great, you must further distinguish between a convincing emotional effect and a meretricious one. I cannot tell you exactly what a meretricious one is; but we all know that composers do have ways, just as theater people do, of making us think pleasurably about our mothers or about sex. Such easy effects are at the disposal of any advertiser, of anybody in show business; but a work of art is something different. It needs to have an objective life, a shape of its own. And if expression is its specialty, it needs to have an expressive power of a much more ample nature than that which merely provokes us to applause or tears.

Let us say that by this time you have heard the piece and that you have taken account of your own spontaneous reactions while hearing the piece, and that you have tested these for errors of judgment and errors of reaction, so far as you are able, and that you are back at your office and about to write your review. You can go farther, if you have time. You can identify the style of the work, answer the question, "What is it like?" You can even sometimes identify its expression, answer "What is it about?" For this you must decide whether it is predominantly a strophic work, imitating speech cadences, or a choric work, imitating body movements, or a spastic one, imitating those anxiety-and-relief patterns that make up our interior life. The great monuments of symphonic music, I may add, are mostly of this latter character.

Now you must start writing. As I said before, you use specific words and try to explain them all. A newspaper man once told me, "Never underestimate the public's intelligence, and never overestimate its information." As evidence of good faith toward the reader, you express your personal opinion of the work. But you mostly try to describe the work by the methods of musical description that are available to you. Never bother about trying to express your enthusiasm or lack of it; that will come through automatically in your choice of words. Just keep your mind on the music and describe it loyally.

When your piece is done, you read it over three times: once for grammar, a second time to see if you have said a little bit of what you meant to say, and a third time—this is the most important of all—to see whether you are willing to mean what you have said. If you are not, you cut out that paragraph of opinion. If you are, you send it down to the printers just as it is.

Proceedings of the American Academy of Arts and Letters
and the National Institute of Arts and Letters, 1954

THE COMPOSER AND
HIS CONCERNS

Answers to Questions from Eight Composers

I.

Today, values are continuously shifting in the direction of the practical needs of the moment due to the complexity of the struggle in our social organization. How can we, who wish to express in a high state of organization the most positive and sensitive aspects of life, justify the function of our music?

STEFAN WOLPE

The functions of music in any society are many. The social ones are like folklore patterns and not under our control. The expressive ones need no justification, either, though we sometimes have to fight for the dignity of our sentiments.

2.

Do you consider present-day music as deriving more logically from the pre-classical period or from the 19th century?

WALLINGFORD RIEGGER

Everything we have in music, I should think, comes from the nineteenth century, either by reaction or by direct inheritance. Pre-classical revivalism is itself a nineteenth century formula. I need only cite Mendelssohn, who copied Bach, Brahms, who aped Handel and edited Couperin, and Wagner, who rewrote Gluck. Beethoven revived the fugal style, too. And the Benedictine monks brought medieval plainsong back to life.

3.

Which of the three do you consider most vital to civilization today: painting, music, or literature? Why?
and
To what extent do you believe the subconscious should be allowed free rein during the process of musical composition? Why?

PAUL BOWLES

I can't get anywhere with the first question. It sounds artificial to me.

The subconscious is our wellspring of inspiration. Some need to use a pump. Others have only to cap a gusher.

4.

To be simple, unadorned, natural, to use the humblest musical devices in a new way has been the valuable lesson your music has taught us. Coupled with this is a tendency toward automatic writing which probably comes from a very understandable love of the spontaneous. It is about automatic musical writing that I would like to question you. For I remember you used to advise composers to write, as you sometimes may have done, whatever came into their heads and to stop when inspiration ran out even if it were in the middle of a phrase. You advised them not to torture their ideas with invented developments and continuations but to start afresh every time a new idea arose from the subconscious, from a "semi-euphoric state of automatism" as you phrased it in one of your recent columns.

But the puzzle is this: How can you expect the active listener to keep his mind on his work if the composer didn't keep his mind on his? Attention seems to parallel attention in ascending degrees until you get to the extreme case where the listener is worn down before the music gets very far. But at the other end of the scale, in automatic writing doesn't everybody's mind wander? (Except, of course, for the fellow-composer always on the lookout for surprises to remember.) Or doesn't this make any difference?

ELLIOTT CARTER

Don't confuse a disciplined spontaneity with the laziness of a loose tongue. Of course, music that bores the author will bore everybody. So will lots of music that interests the author. I do think that most of our best work, by anybody's judgment, is the product of a concentrated mental state in which one lets things happen. When concentration leaves and won't come back, it is better to knock off for the day. You save time that way. Concentrated work can always be polished up later, if there is time. Half-hearted work is the very devil to revise.

5.
Explain your conception of the overtone theory of orchestration.

CARTER HARMAN

I am not aware of holding any such theory. Obviously, a well-written orchestral *tutti*, like a well-designed pipe-organ, respects acoustical phenomena. One uses everywhere acoustical compensation, doubling at the octave for brilliancy, adding plucked sounds for rhythmic definition, and so forth. But I am not aware that any good orchestrator uses mathematical acoustics in his calculations. So far, composers seem to be satisfied with ancient rules of thumb and with a trial-and-error procedure based on the instinctive or "musical" ear. Anyway, we write for halls and studios, no two of which are acoustically identical.

6.
What is the present status and character of the French movement that passes under the slogan, neo-Romanticism? I do not recall your having used the term more recently. In any case, you seem to use it less frequently than you once did. What significance, if any, attaches to this? Where do you, as one of the founders of the movement, now stand with regard to it? How has it been affected, if at all, by the war-time reversion of Jeune France to a kind of mysticism which, it seems to me, is a "post-" rather than "neo-" Romanticism—a Romanticism almost without alloy? What prognosis is there for neo-Romanticism?

ARTHUR BERGER

Neo-Romanticism remains the esthetic of Poulenc and Sauguet, to name two successful French composers now in their middle forties. It has also tempered the formerly more ironic and severe neo-Classicism of Milhaud, Honegger and Barraud. La Jeune France I should call neo-Impressionist; and I include Rosenthal under that heading. An addiction to religious subject matter, common all over post-war Europe, is no more significant in Messiaen than is orientalism with Jolivet or the classical humanism of Rosenthal (and Malipiero).

Neo-Romanticism involves rounded melodic material (the neo-Classicists affected angular themes) and the frank expression of personal sentiments. I remain its most easily-labeled

APPENDIX

EARLY ARTICLES AND REVIEWS
1922–1938

Kusevitsky, Conductor

I N THE DESERT of routine concerts in Paris there sprang up recently a tree bearing fruit—six "orchestral evenings" at the Opéra with Serge Kusevitsky conducting. Kusevitsky, known on the continent for many years as a virtuoso of the double-bass, founded in 1910 the Concerts Kusevitsky at Moscow and Petrograd, which brought him immediate recognition for able performances and catholic taste. Last spring he gave a series in London and Paris, and the Concerts Kusevitsky are presumably a semi-annual event now in Continental music, unless some enterprising American should induce the conductor to come over from Macedonia and let us help him make his fortune.

The orchestra was composed of musicians selected from the established orchestras of Paris, individually excellent players. Without limited rehearsals no orchestra can play unanimously. However, Kusevitsky in a few weeks' time prepared six pro-grammes containing not a little novel music, and gave them a performance unequalled anywhere in Paris for precision and commanding force. When the soft chords of flutes and clarinets which introduce Weber's *Oberon* overture opened the first con-cert, we knew that the evening was to contain not only playing, but music. The threadbare old piece was something we had not heard before. The subtle arrangement of the woodwind chords, the mysterious horn notes, were Debussyan: we were in the shining dark greens of a German forest. When the strings played alone the balance was so perfect that each line disengaged itself and became audible by a difference in quality as slight as that between a violin and a viola. And the great swinging movement toward the close showed itself as something quite different from the operetta finale it sometimes resembles. With a longer rhyth-mic sweep, it was dignified and noble, almost grand.

One would like to dwell on the aliveness of the old pieces as Kusevitsky played them—pieces, many of them that we had grown to loathe, as children loathe the Bible through much

clerical mouthing of it, and some of them pieces so lacking in
romantic sensationalism that few conductors dare to play them
at all nowadays. Bach's Brandenburg Concerto in G for string
orchestra, as played by Kusevitsky, was so clear in outline and so
lively in rhythm that the orchestral embellishments of modern
music seemed effeminate and silly. The Symphony in E minor
of Carl Philipp Emanuel Bach was even more moving, particularly the second movement, with long lines of melancholy, a
restrained and tender sadness. Haydn's Symphony in G was as
honest and jovial as old papa Haydn himself and as fresh as a
blooming cheek. Beethoven's overture to *Egmont* seemed more
symphonic in sweep than many of his symphonies, and the great
Fifth became a sheer contrast in forces—the repeated chords
at the end falling like blows from a pugilistic Prometheus, who
cries to Fate, "Take that! And that! And that!"

Wagner, too, came in for a resurrection at Kusevitsky's hands.
Before the Prelude to *Parsifal* and the Funeral Music from
Götterdämmerung, to mention only two pieces, the sheer simplicity of the music and the grandeur of its effect made any
quarreling about theories ridiculous. Modern French classics,
like Debussy's Nocturnes and Ravel's songs of Scheherazade,
received an equally clairvoyant reading. Everywhere, by expressing music in terms of rhythmic periods rather than of measures,
Kusevitsky gave us the music instead of the notes.

Modern novelties included *Le Rêve* of Florent Schmitt, an
extraordinary *mêlée* of color and line with a free canon that is
not far from polytonia. Malipiero's *Pauses of Silence* had their
first hearing in Paris and were not too enthusiastically received.
It is not that they are too cacophonous. It is simply that they are
not too well made. A series of interrupted phrases which, nevertheless, moves on, is a form which probably no one since Bach
has really handled well. The progress is likely to be jerky. Moreover, the melodic contours of the *Pauses* are not seldom a little
crude. But the work has virtues. The debt which Malipiero
owes to the orchestration of Ravel and the counterpoint of
Stravinsky should not conceal the Italian character of his music.
Its intensity, its subtle violence, its cold and assertive brilliance
are exactly what one would expect. They are modern Italy.

The only really important French novelty was a "mimed symphony" of Arthur Honegger called *Horace Victorieux*, designed

for a ballet of Fauconnet after the story of Horatius out of Livy via Corneille. One cannot speak of the music in terms of expressiveness without having seen the action. But as sheer music, *Horace* is impressive. There are eight episodes, depicting love scenes, parades, battles, triumphs, curses and executions. The musical structure is a many-voiced contrapuntal edifice of such truly independent parts that it is about the most cacophonous composition yet heard. It has no harmonic or even a polyharmonic plan. It is sheer counterpoint from beginning to end, without any harmonic implication whatever. It is ponderous and learned. Obviously, coloristic or decorative orchestration is out of place with such architecture. Consequently, there is almost incessant use of strings, subdivided ad infinitum, to carry the many voices in equal power. Is it beautiful or affecting? It seems so. The love scene was such, and so was some of the battle music. There is rather an excess of pompous fugal writing, though setting and action might moisten this dryness. Contrapuntal music of this character can be movingly beautiful. Schoenberg has made it so, and Stravinsky is often not far away. *Horace* is probably the music of the immediate future. And not before has such an elaborate structure been made with it. The musicians of another generation who still believe there is no God but Debussy, and that Ravel is his prophet, consider it dull—all line and no color. The younger French, while remaining faithful to Honegger as a comrade and defending him from a public that wants Saint-Saëns for its money, mostly feel in their hearts that it is a little German, at least un-French. It has so little élan, so little improvisation, so little delicacy or wit. It rolls over the story of battle like an armored tractor. I suspect it of being a not entirely successful attempt at a style which deserves more wit and less labor. But certainly it is the best polytonic piece yet written in the grand style.

Kusevitsky devoted one whole evening to Russian music, most of it unheard before, including the Prelude to Moussorgsky's *Khovanshchina* and his *Defeat of Sennacherib*, a piece with chorus, neither of them too thrilling; a war mass by Kastalasky called *Commémoration Fraternelle*, effective choral writing in modal harmony but rather sugary like most Russian church music; several bits of fascinating orchestral virtuosity by Rimsky-Korsakov from his opera *The Legend of the Invisible City of*

Kitezh and the Virgin Fevronyia, the infernally clever "Flight of the Drone Bee," and some delicate arrangements of Russian folk-tunes under the title of *Dubinushka*. Skriabin's "Poem of Ecstasy" was superbly played and delighted the highbrows. And a piece in four movements, about death, by Prokofiev, written at the age of twenty-three, surprised by the subtlety and daring of its color and by the sheer ecstasy of the final passage, in which three trumpets, very high, flash and conflict until the ear can scarcely bear it, as if blinding sunlight were become audible.

Brahms's "Song of Destiny," heard for the first time in Paris from Kusevitsky, fell perfectly flat. It was badly sung. It was not first-rate Brahms anyway, and these conditions were not likely to make friends in France for a composer whose whole musical mind is as antagonistic to the French as that of Brahms. The Concerts Kusevitsky closed with a performance of Beethoven's Ninth Symphony. The Andante was taken slowly enough and the double-basses in the Finale were soft as a whisper. Even the sopranos of the chorus seemed to sustain their dangerous altitude without great difficulty. But criticism, either detailed or general, is of no avail before such music. As one musician said: "I never have an opinion about the Ninth Symphony, because I always forget myself before the introduction is over."

Boston Evening Transcript, February 8, 1922

Jazz

Jazz, in brief, is a compound of (a) the fox-trot rhythm, a four-four measure (*alla breve*) with a double accent, and (b) a syncopated melody over this rhythm. Neither alone will make jazz. The monotonous fox-trot rhythm, by itself, will either put you to sleep or drive you mad. And a highly syncopated line like the second subject of the Franck Symphony in D minor or the principal theme of Beethoven's third *Leonore* overture is merely syncopation until you add to it the heavy bump-bump of the fox-trot beat. The combination is jazz. Try it on your piano. Apply the recipe to any tune you know. In case you are not satisfied with the result, play the right hand a little before the left.

The fox-trot, which appeared about 1914, is the culmination of a tendency in American dancing that has been active ever since ragtime was invented in the early years of the century. The Viennese waltz and its brother, the two-step, died about 1912. For two years following, fancy steps like the tango, the maxixe, and the hesitation, with their infinite and amazing variations, made anarchy in the ballroom. This was resolved by a return to the utmost simplicity, and the common language of legs became a sort of straight-away walk. Any man could teach his partner in ten steps his peculiar form of it, whether he called it the Castle walk, the lame duck, or what not.

Soon after this primitive step became established ballroom dancing began to show the disturbance that shook all of polite society when the lid of segregation was taken off of vice and the bordello erupted into the drawing-room. Ragging, a style of dancing with slight footwork, but with much shoulder-throwing, came home from the bawdy house bearing the mark of the earlier hoochie-coochie, a monotonous beat without accentuation. It infected the walk-steps, had a convulsion called the turkey-trot, which proved too difficult to keep up, and finally, calling itself both the one-step and the fox-trot, became national and endemic. The former name, which merely indicated a tempo, is no longer used. The tempo of the latter has been expanded to include it.

At present the fox-trot is our only common dance rhythm. Its speed varies from 66 to 108 half-notes to the minute. It will bear any amount of muscular embroidery, from the shimmy to the halt, because its rhythm is in the simplest possible terms. The Viennese waltz is practically extinct in America. What is now called a waltz is simply a three-four fox-trot, as the two-step was a four-four waltz. The rhythm of the Viennese waltz is | ♩ ♩ ♩ | or | ♩. ♪ ♩ | and that of the hesitation | ♩ ♩ 𝄽 | or | ♩ ♩. ♪ |. There is one accent to a measure, as indicated. The two-step also had one accent, | ♩. ♪ ♩ ♩ | or | ♩. ♪ ♩ |. But the fox-trot has two, | ♩ 𝄽 ♩ 𝄽 | , and the jazz waltz has three, | ♪ 𝄾 ♪ 𝄾 ♪ 𝄾 |. The waltz, however, is not at home in jazz. After a century of Europeans, from Schubert to Ravel, had played with it, there was small possibility for further rhythmic variation. It is not comfortable now, for the true waltz-step is almost impossible to do unless the music has a flowing rhythm to tempt a flowing motion of the body.

We learned syncopation from three different teachers—the Indians, the Negroes, and our neighbors in Mexico. It had become firmly established before the Civil War. It is the characteristic twist of nearly every familiar old tune. The dance craze of the last twenty-five years has simply exaggerated it. Because the way to make a strong pulse on 3 is by tying it to 2, thus, | ♩ ♩ ♩ ♩ |. A silent accent is the strongest of all accents. It forces the body to replace it with a motion. But a syncopated tune is not jazz unless it is supported by a monotonous, accentless rhythm underneath. Alone it may only confuse the listener. But with the rhythm definitely expressed, syncopation intensifies the anticipated beat into an imperative bodily motion. The shorter the anticipation the stronger the effect. The systematic striking of melodic notes an instant before the beat is the most powerful device of motor music yet discovered. But a fluent melody with a syncopated accompaniment is an inversion of the fundamental jazz process, and its effect is sedative.

If certain formulas of beat produce motion, probably certain motions have suggested these formulas. But I have no stake in the hen-and-egg controversy. I wish merely to show that the peculiar character of jazz is a rhythm, and that that rhythm is one which provokes jerky motions of the body. Instead of the following "normal" rhythms, | ♩ ♩ ♩ ♫ | and | ♩ ♫ ♩ ♫ | and | ♩ ♩ ♬ |, we have | ♫ ♩ ♩ ♩ | and | ♬ ♩ ♩ | and | ♪ ♩ ♪ ♬ |

and | ♪ ♩.♫♩ |—in brief, all the divisions which the masters of music-not-meant-for-dancing have used sparingly or with special antidotes, for the very reason that they make the body move instead of keeping it quiet so that the music can go forward.

Instrumentation is not an essential element in jazz, as anyone knows who has heard a good performer play it on the piano. It is possible to practically any group of instruments, because, above the rhythmic accompaniment, which also sets the harmony, it is contrapuntal rather than homophonic and does not require balanced timbres. Certain instruments and effects, however, are characteristic, especially the use of the saxophone, which, in pairs or in quartets, makes a rich and penetrating diapason, and the monotonous banjo accompaniment, giving out the ground-rhythm—a rhythm so sonorous that it would be unendurable were not its hypnotic effect turned into motor stimuli by cross-accents.

Another characteristic of jazz is its constant use of glissando. This has long been common on the trombone. It is also possible on the clarinet and the saxophone for about a major third. A descending succession of little glissandi makes the "laughing saxophone." The Frisco whistle plays a continuous glissando; and the glissando on a plucked string, introduced from Hawaii, has been applied to almost every stringed instrument except the banjo. It is difficult there because of the frets and because the banjo, having no sound-box, gives a tone which, though powerful, is of short duration.

With the growth of the contrapuntal style, necessary to disparate combinations, the varieties of wind tone have been considerably extended. Passionate or startling expression has been found in all sorts of vibrati and flutter-tonguing and in the covered tones of the muted trumpet and trombone, the muted clarinet, and the trombone played through a megaphone. Most of these devices, of course, are not new. Rimsky-Korsakov knew all the tricks on the trumpet that you now hear in the dance hall, and more. Berlioz employed the muted clarinet. Richard Strauss and Vincent d'Indy wrote years ago for quartets of saxophones. Stravinsky has even written glissandi for the horn! But the megaphone trick, which takes the blare out of the trombone and makes it sound like a euphonium, is probably new.

Certainly the use of a free-hanging mute is new, though when it takes the form of a tin can or a silk hat it is no great addition to orchestral elegance.

In the current jazz one hears piano figures that are ingenious, counter-melodies that are far from timid, and experiments in instrumental balance that are of interest to any composer. The harmony itself is at times varied and delicate. The blues formula—subdominant modulation with alternations of tonic major and minor—is simple and effective. The chromatic (or diatonic) succession of dominant ninths so dear to Franck and Chabrier has become popular, and the mediant or sub-mediant tonality for modulation offers a pleasing relief from the more obvious dominant. The Neapolitan sixth is quite common and even the "barbershop" chord—the augmented six-five-three, or German sixth—is sometimes used in a manner that is not at all crude.

These characteristics of jazz are partially supported by serious music and partially contributory to it. Classical composers snap up quickly any novelty that the makers of jazz invent. Union musicians often play one night at the movies, and the next night with the local symphony orchestra. They bring a few tricks to the latter, and they take home many more. Orchestral and harmonic styles in jazz are still experimental and shifting. But the essence of the thing remains free melody with a fox-trot rhythm underneath. That rhythm shakes, but it won't flow. There is no climax. It never gets anywhere emotionally. In the symphony, it would either lose its character or wreck the structure. In that respect it is analogous to the hoochie-coochie beat.

The American Mercury, August 1924

The New Musical Mountebankery

ORCHESTRAL CONDUCTING would seem to have attained to the prestige of a national sport. But the game is in need of rules. There is no means at present of yanking Koussevitzky after one inning of Schubert's "Unfinished" or of putting him in the box to lead a Brandenburg Concerto when Sebastian Bach, that seasoned batsman, is about to knock a homer off Bodanzky. There is no regulation stating the maximum number of players allowed to take part in a Mozart symphony or the maximum number of performances any work may receive in one season, and there is no umpire at all. The grandstands are filled with ladies who easily mistake the gesture for the deed and who applaud chiefly their private thrills, while the press box is occupied by busy gentlemen who, torn between their own sportsmanship and the ladies' applause, can never decide whether the performance should be analyzed as a match, reported as news or disputed about as if it were a work of art.

Art, of course, is held in high superstition among us. It is the unknown god to whom every town and hamlet rears a temple. With such a faith, one need not be surprised that critics sometimes seek it in the concert hall. Mr. Downes of *The New York Times* and Mr. Taylor of the *World* grow quite regularly lyrical for the Sunday edition over the thrill that comes once in a lifetime when a new piece is played in their city. They avow that the search for such is the only real delight their profession affords them.

Such pious protestation need not be held against sincerity. Art is all right as an ideal, but these sound critics know that they must not neglect a national sport for it. In January last, such a triumph of works over faith occurred when the New York Symphony offered, all in one performance, the only New York appearance of a French woman famous for her skill in the rare art of playing the organ with orchestras, the first local hearing of a modern piece long celebrated in Paris, and the only local hearing of a brand-new symphony by an unknown American. Messrs. Downes and Taylor were probably tempted. But they stuck to the conductor's press box. They went to Furtwängler's second concert and heard him conduct Brahms.

Leopold Stokowski is the Babe Ruth of the orchestral world. Or perhaps, to relinquish the athletic comparison for an æsthetic one, the Jackie Coogan. This Apollo with the golden curls is a spoiled pretty child to whom anything is allowed. He can play soldier with his men and drill them till the music has exactly as much expression as a military parade. He can play at being grown-up, and mimic, *molto espressivo*, all the gestures of true love. He brings clowns to the stage at a children's concert to imitate Charlie Chaplin. Of late he has taken to making speeches reproving his elders for their manners. And the proud, sweet mammas of Philadelphia (glowing perhaps with something more than pride) smile to themselves and sigh not utterly in vain, "Isn't he too adorable?" The newspapers report that he has a trainer named Bill Morris to rub him down after every performance and that he wears reading glasses at rehearsals. When he figures in a divorce case, he is news of the very first class, like Henry Ford's vacations and the Prince of Wales's hats.

The first requirement in conducting is a figure. The second is impressive ability. The successful leader must depict in his own person at least the spirit of the pieces played. Josef Stránský, an admittedly incompetent leader, delighted the ladies of the Philharmonic for seven years by putting symphonies to gesture, quite regardless of sound or rhythm. Van Hoogstraten, on the other hand, in spite of performances which are quite satisfactory to the ear, has alienated a large part of his public because his jumping-jack motions are not thought to accord always in feeling with the music they accompany. And yet I wonder if interpretive dancing is profitable in the long term. Of all New York's conductors, only Walter Damrosch has kept his job season after season, in spite of an impersonal demeanor, and in spite of having conducted varied programs with a dignified and sympathetic objectivity.

Personality plus, however, has its advantages, even musically. There are usually two or three pieces or composers that each leader can play very well. If an efficient management, instead of stuffing our pockets full of season tickets, would hire the proper conductor for each piece on the program, "cast" them for their parts, as they do actresses, and then open the box office to the general public, we could go to hear music we like conducted by a leader who also likes it, and we could avoid the rest.

Tentatively, I should suggest this cast:

Beethoven and Bach . . . . Serge Koussevitzky
Mahler and Liszt . . . . Willem Mengelberg
Tchaikovsky and Schumann . . . . . Leopold Stokowski
Brahms . . . . Wilhelm Furtwängler
Mozart and the classical style . . . . Arturo Toscanini
Accompaniments to concertos . . . Arthur Bodanzky
                    (L. Stokowski, assistant)
Berlioz, Wagner and
   Rimsky-Korsakov . . . . Anybody at all
French and all other music
   written since 1900 . . . . Pierre Monteux

Many important composers and worthy leaders have been omitted. We should probably have to import somebody to play Schubert, just as we should have to re-import Monteux to play Stravinsky and Debussy and our own new pieces. Mr. Damrosch and the very able Mr. Stock of Chicago have been omitted, too, because they are, after all, occupied simply with the art of performing orchestral music and have no place in a list of professional virtuosi.

Not that their performances are more musical than others. They are often less so and they are almost always less exciting. I only mean that they are animated by a different spirit. Their purpose is to exhibit pieces in as clear a light as possible. Mr. Stokowski, on the other hand, panting in a frock-coat over the love-music from *Tristan*, is giving his own show, just as if the director of the Louvre were to exhibit himself to visitors, posed and breathing through his nostrils, before a Rubens Venus.

My suggestion about casting simply means the establishment of a star-system at Carnegie Hall not unlike the one now operating on Broadway. The repertory conducted would probably survive for a few years in the provinces, to be replaced later by gramophone records of the great and visits from traveling organizations. Evidence is not lacking that such a development is already in progress. There is even a counter-reformation in the form of a Little Orchestra movement flourishing profitably in places like Kansas City and Los Angeles.

Now there is virtue in the star-system as long as the star's name is an assurance of merit, like Chaliapin's. When it is only the guarantee-label for sure-fire mannerisms, like Mary Pickford's, it means that the art has acquired a vice. The theatre has by that means reached such a stage of decay (or is it transmutation?) that the art of the drama is not spoken of seriously anywhere except among professors, women's clubs and college æsthetes; and even they are learning from the metropolitan critics that Al Jolson is more fun than the Manchester playwrights and that Lillian Gish is the great American Something-or-Other.

There is no use fighting progress, even the progress of disorder. And the newer critics all aver that the nonsense arts are more vital or more profound or something than the old arts which had forms and intellectual conventions. Certainly that is true just now as regards the stage. If public acclaim means anything, it is true in the concert hall. Conducting is not really a professional sport, as I pretended above. It is a popular nonsense art. Whether carried out in the New York, Philadelphia, or Boston style, it is a sort of Russian *pas seul* in which the military decorum of a Viennese *Orchesterdirigent* is toned up with as much of the Italian bandmaster as the audience will stand.

And the audience will stand a good deal.

Composers come to us to lead their own works—Strauss, d'Indy, Stravinsky. Their renditions are too impersonal for our taste. We call them tame. Lotsa pep! That's what we want! Straight music is all right for the provinces or for backward civilizations like Munich and Paris. But not for an up-to-date artistic community like New York City. We have Orchestral Conducting.

We have, indeed! Along with jazz, it is America's contribution (with foreign stars, of course, but we provide the public) to modern music. It is the eighth Lively Art.

The New Republic, October 21, 1925

Aaron Copland

AARON COPLAND's music is American in rhythm, Jewish in melody, eclectic in all the rest.

The subject matter is limited but deeply felt. Its emotional origin is seldom gay, rarely amorous, almost invariably religious. Occasionally excitation of a purely nervous and cerebral kind is the origin of a scherzo. This tendency gave him a year or two of jazz-experiment. That has been his one wild oat. It was not a fertile one.

He liked the stridency of high saxophones, and his nerves were pleasantly violated by displaced accents. But he never understood that sensuality of sentiment which is the force of American popular music nor accepted the simple heartbeat that is the pulse of its rhythm, though it is the pulse of his own rhythm whenever his music is at ease.

His religious feeling is serious and sustained. He is a prophet calling out her sins to Israel. He is filled with the fear of God. His music is an evocation of the fury of God. His God is the god of battle, the Lord of Hosts, the jealous, the angry, the avenging god who rides upon the storm. Far from Copland's thoughts are the Lord as shepherd in green pastures, the Lord as patriarch, the God of Jacob, the bridegroom of the Shulamite, the lover, the father, the guide-philosopher-and-friend. The gentler movements of his music are more like an oriental contemplation of infinity than like any tender depiction of the gentler aspects of Jehovah.

Hence the absence of intimacy. And the tension. Because his music has tension. His brass plays high. His rhythm is strained. There is also weight; five trumpets and eight horns are his common orchestral practice. They give the tension and weight of battle. The screaming of piccolos and pianos evokes the glitter of armaments and swords. His instrumentation is designed to impress, to overpower, to terrify, not to sing.

All this I write is overstated. But I put it down because it seems to me to provide as good an evocative scheme as any for fitting together various observations about the way his music is made.

I note the following:

His melodic material is of a markedly Hebrew cast. Its tendency to return on itself is penitential. It is predominantly minor. Its chromaticism is ornamental and expressive rather than modulatory. When he sings, it is as wailing before the Wall. More commonly his material is used as a framework for a purely coloristic compilation.

By coloristic I mean it is made out of harmonic and instrumental rather than melodic devices. This compilation is picturesque and cumulative. It tends to augment its excitement, to add to weight and tension. His dominant idea of form is crescendo. This is Russian, because it is a crescendo of excitement. Of development in the classic German sense, the free development of Haydn and Beethoven, there is none.

His conception of harmony is not form but texture. Hence the absence of marked tonal modulation. His conception of instrumentation is not variety but mass. He has no polyphonic conception at all, because he is alone in his music. His commonest contrapuntal device is a form of canon, usually at the octave or unison, everybody doing the same thing at a different moment. This is counterpoint but not polyphony. He is not walking with God or talking with men or seducing housemaids or tickling duchesses. He is crying aloud to Israel. And very much as if no one could hear him.

The *Piano Variations* have not even this canonic counterpoint. They are a monody, one line repeated, not developed, lengthened out from time to time by oriental flourishes, accented and made sharp, orchestrated, as it were, by slightly dissonant octaves, by grace-notes and arpeggios.

I find the music of them very beautiful, only I wish he wouldn't play it so loud. One hears it better unforced. I miss in his playing of it the singing of a certain still, small voice that seems to me to be clearly implied on the written page.

I also note this:

There is a certain resemblance of procedure between Copland, Antheil, Varèse, Chávez. This in spite of antipodal differences in their personalities and sentiments. Their common homage to Stravinsky honors the White Russian master more than it profits them. It creates a false community and obliterates distinctions. It also smothers quality.

The quality that distinguishes American writing from all other is a very particular and special approach to rhythm. It is in these composers when they forget Stravinsky; it is in all American music whatever its school or origins. It is a quiet, vibratory shimmer, a play of light and movement over a well-felt but not expressed basic pulsation, as regular and as varied as a heart-beat, and as unconscious. It is lively but at ease, quiet, assured, lascivious.

Stravinsky knocked us all over when we first heard him, because he had invented a new rhythmic notation, and we all thought we could use it. We cannot. It is the notation of the jerks that muscles give to escape the grip of taut nerves. It has nothing to do with blood flow. It is spectacularly effective when used to express the movements it was invented to express. It is the contrary when imposed upon our radically different ones. How infinitely superior in simple effectiveness are our popular composers over our tonier ones. They have no technical drama of composition. They are at ease in their notation.

Our highbrow music, on the other hand, is notoriously ineffective. It is the bane of audiences at home and abroad, in spite of the very best will on everybody's part.

I deny that it is really as dull as it sounds. I think our gift, our especial gift, is the particular rhythmic feeling I have described. That is enough to make an epoch. It takes very little. The rest is framing. Our weakness is timidity, hence snobbishness and eclecticism.

Today we ape Stravinsky. Yesterday it was Debussy. Before, it was Wagner. Copland's best recommendation is that he is less eclectic than his confreres. I reproach him with eclecticism all the same.

There is real music in his pieces, true invention, and a high nobility of feeling. He is not banal. He has truth, force, and elegance. He has not quite style. There remain too many irrelevant memories of Nadia Boulanger's lessons, of the scores of Stravinsky and Mahler and perhaps Richard Strauss.

I wish they were plain thefts. Theft is refreshing and legitimate. Copland is like certain American poets (very distinguished ones; supply your own examples), who cannot quite forget their collegiate loyalty to Keats and Browning and who are more occupied with the continuation of some foreign tradition than with style, which is personal integrity.

This may explain a little why Aaron Copland is at the same

time an inspired composer and only a comparatively effective one. Comparatively, because most American music is less effective in performance than his. In fact, his music is often so near to a real knockout that I am sometimes left wondering whether it is a case of a knockout not quite achieved or of an unwise application of the knockout technic to a case where persuasion were more to the point.

In any case, there is a problem of rhetoric for the American composer. The problem of adjusted emphasis, the appropriate stating and effective underlining of personal invention. This means selection and variety. Forcing every idea into the key of the grandiose and the sublime is obviously false and in the long run monotonous.

I fancy there is more of use to us in the example of Verdi than in that of Wagner, Puccini even than Hindemith, certainly Bizet than Debussy, Schubert than Brahms. Simple clarity is what we need, and we will get it only by a radical simplification of our methods of composition. If Copland's simplifications are perhaps not radical enough for my taste, they are important simplifications all the same.

Because he is good, terribly good. A European composer of his intrinsic quality would have today worldwide celebrity and influence. It is a source of continual annoyance to me that his usefulness and his beauty are not fully achieved because he has not yet done the merciless weeding out of his garden that any European composer would have done after his first orchestral hearing.

The music is all right, but the man is not clearly enough visible through it. An American certainly, a Hebrew certainly. But his more precise and personal outline is still blurred by the shadows of those who formed his youth.

Modern Music, January 1932

George Gershwin

GERSHWIN, Cole Porter, and Kern are America's Big Three in the light musical theater. Their qualities are evident and untroubling. Mr. Gershwin has, however, for some time been leading a double musical life. This is the story of his adventures among the highbrows.

His efforts in the symphonic field cover a period of about twelve years and include, so far as I am acquainted with them:

A Rhapsody in Blue, for piano and orchestra

Harlem Night, a ballet

Two concertos for piano and orchestra

An American in Paris, symphonic poem

to which has now been added an opera on a tragicomic subject, *Porgy and Bess*.

The *Rhapsody in Blue*, written about 1923 or 1924, was the first of these and is the most successful from every point of view. It is the most successful orchestral piece ever launched by any American composer. It is by now standard orchestral repertory all over the world, just like Rimsky-Korsakov's *Scheherazade* and Ravel's *Bolero*.

I am not acquainted with *Harlem Night* or the second Piano Concerto. I am not even certain that a second one exists, although I have been told so. I can only speak, therefore, of the Concerto in F and of *An American in Paris*. Both of these show a rather lesser mastery of their materials than the *Rhapsody* does. They have not, however, altered Mr. Gershwin's prestige. He has remained through everything America's official White Hope, and he has continued to be admired in music circles both for his real talent and for his obviously well-meant efforts at mastery of the larger forms. Talent, in fact, is rather easier to admire when the intentions of a composer are more noble than his execution is competent.

Just why the execution is not so competent as in the *Rhapsody* is not clear to me. I used to think that perhaps he was cultivating certain amateurishness because he had been promised that if he was a good little boy and didn't upset any apple carts he might maybe when he grew up be president of American music, just like Daniel Gregory Mason or somebody. Either that, or else that the air of timid and respectable charm which those pieces play up was simply a blind to cover a period of apprenticeship and that one day he would burst out with some more pieces like the *Rhapsody in Blue*, grander. It seemed that such a gift as his, with ten years of symphonic experience, couldn't but turn out eventually something pretty powerful.

It has now turned out *Porgy and Bess*. When a man of Gershwin's gift, experience, and earning capacity devotes in his middle or late thirties three years of his expensive time to the composition of a continuous theatrical work on a serious subject, there is no reason to suppose that it represents anything but his mature musical thought and his musical powers at near their peak. The music, however, is not very different from his previous output of serious intent, except insofar as staging helps cover up the lack of musical construction. Hence it is no longer possible to take very seriously any alibi for his earlier works.

The *Rhapsody in Blue* remains a quite satisfactory piece. Rhapsodies, however, are not very difficult to write, if one can think up enough tunes. The efforts at a more sustained symphonic development, which the later pieces represent, appear now to be just as tenuous as they have always sounded. One can see through *Porgy* that Gershwin has not and never did have the power of sustained musical development. His invention is abundant, his melodic quality high, although it is inextricably involved with an oversophisticated commercial background.

That background is commonly known as Tin Pan Alley. By oversophisticated I mean that the harmonic and orchestral ingenuity of Tin Pan Alley, its knowledge of the arts of presentation, is developed out of all proportion to what is justified by the expressive possibilities of its musical material. That material is straight from the melting pot. At best it is a piquant but highly unsavory stirring-up-together of Israel, Africa, and the Gaelic Isles. In Gershwin's music the predominance of charm in presentation over expressive substance makes the result always a sort of *vers de société*, or *musique de salon*; and his lack of understanding of all the major problems of form, of continuity, and of straightforward musical expression, is not surprising in view of the impurity of his musical sources and his frank acceptance of them.

Such frankness is admirable. At twenty-five it was also charming. *Gaminerie* of any kind at thirty-five is more difficult to like. So that quite often *Porgy and Bess*, instead of being pretty, is a little hoydenish, like a sort of *musique de la pas très bonne société*. Leaving aside the slips, even, and counting him at his best, that best which is equally well exemplified by *Lady, Be Good* or *I've Got Rhythm* or the opening of the *Rhapsody in Blue*, he is still not a very serious composer.

I do not wish to indicate that it is in any way reprehensible of him not to be a serious composer. I only want to define something that we have all been wondering about for some years. It was certain that he was a gifted composer, a charming composer, an exciting and sympathetic composer. His gift and his charm are greater than the gifts or the charms of almost any of the other American composers. And a great gift or great charm is an exciting thing. And a gifted and charming composer who sets himself seriously to learn his business is a sympathetic one. I think, however, it is clear by now that Gershwin hasn't learned his business. At least he hasn't learned the business of being a serious composer, which one has long gathered to be the business he wanted to learn.

Porgy is nonetheless an interesting example of what can be done by talent in spite of a bad setup. With a libretto that should never have been accepted on a subject that should never have been chosen, a man who should never have attempted it has written a work that has considerable power.

The more conventionally educated composers have been writing operas and getting them produced at the Metropolitan for twenty or thirty years. Some of them, Deems Taylor in particular, know quite well how to write in the larger formats. Year after year they write them, perfectly real operas on perfectly good subjects. And yet nothing ever happens in them. No significant musical misdemeanor ever seems to have been perpetrated. Gershwin does not even know what an opera is; and yet *Porgy and Bess* is an opera, and it has power and vigor. Hence it is a more important event in America's artistic life than anything American the Met has ever done.

But before I finally get around to saying all the nice things I have to say about it, let me be a little more specific about its faults and get all the resentments off my chest. Because I do resent Gershwin's shortcomings. I don't mind his being a light composer, and I don't mind his trying to be a serious one. But I do mind his falling between two stools. I mind any major fault he commits, because he is to me an exciting and sympathetic composer.

First of all, the opera is vitiated from the beginning by a confusion as to how much fake it is desirable or even possible to get away with in a work of that weight. The play, for instance, and the libretto derived from it, are certainly not without a good part of hokum. That can be excused if necessary. *La Traviata* and *Tosca* are not free of hokum either. Hokum is just theatrical technic got a little out of hand, tear-jerking for its own sake, an error of proportion rather than a lack of sentiment. The artificiality of its folklore is graver. I must hasten to add that Mr. Gershwin is here a greater sinner than Mr. Heyward, because his work was executed later. Folklore subjects recounted by an outsider are only valid as long as the folk in question is unable to speak for itself, which is certainly not true of the American Negro in 1935.

Let me be clear about folk opera. *Lucia di Lammermoor* and *Madama Butterfly* are not Scottish or Japanese folk operas; they are simply Italian operas on exotic subjects. *Carmen* comes nearer because of its systematic use of Spanish popular musical styles. It is nonetheless a fake. Smetana's *Bartered Bride* is a folk opera and it is not a fake, because it is Bohemian music written by a Bohemian. It is not so fine a theater work as *Carmen*, but it is better folklore. Hall Johnson's music for *Green Pastures* and the last act of his *Run, Little Chillun* are real folklore and also folk opera of quite high quality. *Porgy and Bess*, on the other hand, has about the same relation to Negro life as it is really lived and sung as have *Swanee River* and *Mighty Lak' a Rose*.

The most authentic thing about it all is George Gershwin's sincere desire to write an opera, a real opera that somebody might remember. I rather fancy he has succeeded in that, which is pretty incredible of him too, seeing how little he knew of how to go about it. His efforts at recitativo are as ineffective as anything I have heard since Antheil's *Helen Retires*, where a not dissimilar effect was got by first translating the play into German, then composing music for the German text, and finally translating this back into English. The numbers which have rhymed or jingled lyrics are slick enough in the Gershwin Broadway manner. But his prose declamation is full of exaggerated leaps and unimportant accents. It is vocally uneasy and dramatically cumbersome. Whenever he has to get on with the play he uses spoken dialogue. It would have been better if he had stuck to that all the time.

As for the development, or musical build-up, there simply isn't any. When he gets hold of a good number he plugs it. The rest of the time he just makes up what music he needs as he goes along. Nothing of much interest, little exercises in the jazzo-modernistic style, quite pleasant for the most part but leading nowhere. The scoring is heavy, overrich, and ineffective. Throughout the opera there is, however, a constant stream of lyrical invention and a wealth of harmonic ingenuity.

There is little drama in the orchestra and little expression in the melodies, prettily Negroid though they be. The real drama of the piece is the spectacle of Gershwin wrestling with his medium, and the exciting thing is that after all those years the writing of music is still not a routine thing to him. Such freshness is the hallmark of *les grandes natures*. Every measure of music has to be wrought as a separate thing. The stream of music must be channelized, molded, twisted, formed, ornamented, all while it is pouring out molten hot from that volcano of musical activity, Mr. Gershwin's brain. Never is the flow inadequate. Never does his vigilance fail to leave its print on the shape of every detail. *Porgy* is falsely conceived and rather clumsily executed, but it is an important work because it is abundantly conceived and executed entirely by hand.

There are many things about it that are not to my personal taste. I don't like fake folklore, nor fidgety accompaniments, nor bittersweet harmony, nor six-part choruses, nor gefiltefish orchestration. I do, however, like being able to listen to a work for three hours and being fascinated at every moment. I also like its lack of respectability, the way it can be popular and vulgar and go its way as a professional piece without bothering about the taste-boys. I like to think of Gershwin as having presented his astonished public with a real live baby, all warm and dripping and friendly.

In a way, he has justified himself as a White Hope. He has

written a work that can be performed quite a number of times, that can be listened to with pleasure by quite different kinds of people, and that can be remembered by many. If its eminence, as Shaw once said of John Stuart Mill, is due largely to the flatness of the surrounding country, that eminence is nonetheless real.

Modern Music, November 1935

The Official Stravinsky

Igor Stravinsky's *Chroniques de ma Vie* (Volume II, Paris, Denoël et Steel, 1935) is brief and smug. Smug is perhaps too strong a word to describe the neat aplomb of it, but there is something in the work somewhere, or in the author's attitude toward it, that gives one the feeling that Mr. Stravinsky has just swallowed the canary and doesn't mind our knowing it.

It is all surprisingly like his post-war music. I say surprisingly, because although composers have often written voluminously and well, almost none has ever carried quite the same conviction on foolscap as on music-paper. Stravinsky does. He writes French with the same tension, the same lack of ease with which he writes music. It is a tight little package, like the *Sonate pour Piano*. It is as neatly filled up, too. It may be stiff and *guindé*, but it is not empty.

It seems strange he should continually pose himself such limited problems, that he should never for once really want to do something large and easy. But restriction is apparently of his nature. It certainly is in his later music, much as I admire many of the works. They have tension and quality but no *envergure*, no flight. He seems for some years to have been quite content to say small things in a neat way and to depend on instrumental incisiveness to turn his little statements into concert- or theatre-pieces. He is objective and impersonal like the notices in railway carriages, and not without the same authority.

Objectivity is fine. But how can a man of his vigor be so dry? Reticence about one's family life and feeling is only genteel. But when he stops his narrative to write a formal cadenza in honor of Diaghilev, why do I feel at the end of it that his affection for his life-long friend and patron has been exactly measured out to cover the qualities he discerned in him, just that much and no more. Completeness there is, but never any abundance. There is no evidence of his ever having had a musical idea he didn't develop into a piece. An exact adjustment between inspiration and labor seems to be back of all this ant-like neatness.

He apportions out paragraphs of praise to musicians past and present very much like a college president conferring honorary degrees. Glinka, Tchaikovsky and Beethoven, Weber, Gounod.

Satie and Chabrier receive certificates of merit for having existed and for having been of some service to the art of Mr. Stravinsky. Debussy, Ravel, and Prokofiev come in for honorable mention. The megalomania of orchestral conductors is reproved, but most of the orchestral celebrities get nevertheless a button for having performed some work of the author in a satisfactory manner.

Scattered throughout the book at appropriate intervals are clearly-stated maxims about music. There is nothing in these to quarrel with. They are the truisms of the modern world. They could be framed and exposed (they *should* be indeed) in every conservatory and college. None of these principles are, so far as I know, original with Stravinsky. None of them are at all shocking any more either, though they might be inspiring to the young.

And yet the book is interesting. Because a good workman writing about his trade is always interesting. Also because it convinces one by making it evident all over again through a different medium that the stiff little man we have had to deal with these last fifteen or so years is exactly what he seems to be, a stiff little man, and that we shall probably have to deal with him as that for the next fifteen or so years if we care to deal with him at all.

Modern Music, May 1936

Swing Music

SWING MUSIC is for the layman just a new name for what another generation called jazz. It serves not infrequently, even among its intellectual amateurs, to distinguish jazz of some artistic value from the commercial product. Among professionals, however, it means a certain kind of rhythm. In defining the nature of that rhythm I am going to write a brief history of popular dance steps and their music from the beginning of jazz, around 1912, to the present day.

Primitive, or pre-swing, jazz is definable as an ostinato of equally accented percussive quarter-note chords (these take care of rhythm and harmony) supporting a syncopated melodic line.

I am defining here dance-jazz as it was to be heard almost anywhere between 1912 and 1932. The introduction into popular dance music of the jazz formula, or unvarying accent, was a basic simplification that made possible an added complexity in the ornamental and expressive structure.*

Elsewhere in print are lists of musical means and devices commonly employed in jazz performance. All I care to recall here is that an ostinato of percussive quarter-note chords was their basic support both rhythmically and harmonically.

Swing music is based on a different kind of ostinato. Its rhythm (to use the language of versification) is a rhythm of quantities, not a rhythm of stresses.

Let us examine dance rhythms a little and see how they got that way.

Pre-jazz Ragtime Two-step. | ♩ ♩ ♩ ♩ | ♩ ♩ ♩ ♩ |

Jazz Fox-trot. Basic simplification. | ♩ ♩ ♩ ♩ | ♩ ♩ ♩ ♩ |

*Stravinsky's *Sacre du Printemps*, written in 1912, exploits an identical procedure. (It opens, by the way, with a "hot" solo for bassoon beginning on high C.) The *Danse des Adolescents* begins with equally accented percussive chords to which are added irregularly placed *sfz* stresses and, later, hot solos in nonvertical counterpoint. The contrast between control and spontaneity is the most striking thing of its kind in classical music.

I mention the parallel to show that the dissociation of rhythm from beat took place in different kinds of music and on two continents at the same time. It was nobody's invention.

Tango. Enter the Latin influence. | ♩. ♪ ♩ ♩ | ♩. ♪ ♩ ♩ |

Parisian Tango. Takes on jazz accent. | ♩. ♪ ♩ ♩ | ♩. ♪ ♩ ♩ |

Charleston. Jazz takes a tango accent. | ♩. ♪ ♩ | ♩. ♪ ♩ |

Rumba. Spanish America goes Negroid.

| ♪ ♩ ♪ ♫♫ | ♪ ♩ ♪ ♫♫ |

Beguine. Spain is buried in the jungle.

| ♫♫ ♫♫ | ♫♫ ♫♫ |

Lindy Hop. Swing approaches. | ♩ ♩ ♩ ♩ | or | ♩ ♩ ♩ ♩ |

Continental. Swing is here. | ♪ ♪ ♪ ♪ | ♪ ♪ ♪ ♪ |
                                (tr)   (tr)   (tr)   (tr)
                                        without accent

Spain is back on the dance floor and Africa at her drums, while the richest fancies of melody and harmony frolic in uncontrolled improvisation through the agency of our old friend the two-step.

Let us examine this tabulation more closely. All these dances are of New World origin. The tango is a modern name for an Argentine version of the nineteenth-century habanera (from Havana). The two-step is a 4/4 (*alla breve*) version of the Boston, as distinguished from the Viennese, or whirling waltz. Hesitations, maxixes, barn dances, turkey trots, lame ducks, the superb and buoyant Castle walk, were all New World steps. The fusion of the Hispanic, Anglo-Celtic, and Negroid elements of all these into a single formula was a twenty-years' dance war. It was fought out in Paris mostly, where the Hispanic and the Anglo-Celtic elements could meet on neutral ground. Each side, as we shall see, had its Negro troops.

By 1918 Anglo-America had stripped herself down to the fox-trot and the one-step, Latin America to the tango. In the mid-twenties the battle was still a stalemate. Since French tax laws obliged all nightclubs to have both kinds of orchestras, American trumpet players were fraternizing at the bar with Argentine accordion players. The two sides didn't mix musical efforts much, but the tango unconsciously equalized its accents.

The folks back home were getting bored with all this undramatic trench war. The United States went wild first, and when the dust died down, it was evident that their new wildness, the Charleston, had somewhere or other acquired a suspiciously Hispanic accent. (It had long been the custom of W. C. Handy and the Mississippi Valley school to use a tango-bass in the middle section of a Blues number.)

Then Latin America got jittery too. She went Negroid in the form of rumbas and beguines. The original habanera downbeat reappeared along with floor-length dresses and the Boston waltz. The United States countered with the even fancier Lindy hop and a return to the prewar two-step (off the beat).

With swing music approaching, Latin America held out for a strong downbeat, Anglo America for a strong offbeat. Latin America offered a percussive shimmer on its other beats, Anglo America a rest. Swing rhythm was the solution. The shimmer was kept, but on the offbeats only, and accents were sacrificed by both sides. The percussive shimmer would stop where a beat was expected to occur, only the beat didn't occur. The treaty was signed in the form of an international ballroom accomplishment named appropriately for the chief battleground and popularized from Hollywood, the Continental.

All the characters of our little history are now happily united. The 4/4 Boston waltz, or two-step, is the new basis of operations. Body positions and some footwork are added from the Lindy hop and the tango (all passion restrained, however).

The percussive basis of the new music is now the West Indian shimmer. Downbeats are expressed only by a cessation of that shimmer. Here, therefore, is the special characteristic of swing music. It is founded on a purely quantitative (rather than an accentual) rhythm.*

Melody, harmony, and all thumpy percussion are henceforth liberated from formal rhythmic observances. The melodic instruments are not obliged even to syncopate, either by delay or by anticipation. They are free to improvise (it is more often the harmony that remains fixed than the tune) in that sort of spontaneous lyrical effusion mixed with vocal imitation and

---

*Quantitative rhythm is not new in musical art. The merry-go-round, the hurdy-gurdy, and the pipe organ have no accents at all, only quantitative rhythm.

instrumental virtuosities that the French call so charmingly "le style hot." *

They are not really free not to play "hot"; that is to vary and to contradict at every possible point the underlying measure, because quantitative rhythm is a very powerful thing, as impressive and as boring over any length of time as organ music. Its emotional impassivity incites to emotional wildness, to irregular pattern, to strange timbres, to mysterious outbursts and inexplicable tensions.

It also liberates for free expressive use all the short or thumpy sounds of the percussion section. And few things in music are as expressive as a thump. One cymbal or snare drum being sufficient to keep up the swing, regularly placed *sfz* stresses become in themselves a form of hot solo exactly as they do in the *Sacre du Printemps.*

Liberating the percussive banjo, guitar, and piano also liberates the harmony section from rhythmic control. Hence we have all the emotional elements of the orchestra disengaged from point-counterpoint and released for free polyphony. Steady support underneath by a nonemotional quantitative rhythm both stimulates and accentuates the superposed emotional expression. The result at its best is sumptuous.

I shall not here go into detailed recounting of the higher points of contemporary swing art. They are discussed vigorously in Monsieur Hugues Panassié's fine volume, *Le Jazz Hot.†* You will find there a wealth of fact about "le style Chicago" and "le style New Orléans." About the instrumental innovations of Bix Beiderbecke and Muggsy Spanier (good jazz and swing music have never been Negro monopolies). Of what distinguishes "le style hot" from "le style straight." Of the art of five-part improvisation. Of the diverse merits of the divers famed "solistes hot." Of the difference between real and merely commercial jazz. You will be inducted into an orderly study of the historical and stylistic development of the whole business from Handy to Ellington, with special attention to the Chicago school, where

---

* The technic of this improvisation was developed from the free two-measure "breaks" of the early Blues.
† Hugues Panassié, *Le Jazz Hot*, Paris, 1934. (*Hot Jazz: The Guide to Swing Music*, 1936 American edition reprinted by Negro Universities Press.)

the categorical German and the spontaneous Negro musicalities united to produce in Louis Armstrong (originally from New Orleans) a master of musical art comparable only (and this is my comparison, not M. Panassié's) to the great castrati of the eighteenth century. His style of improvisation would seem to have combined the highest reaches of instrumental virtuosity with the most tensely disciplined melodic structure and the most spontaneous emotional expression, all of which in one man you must admit to be pretty rare. You will also learn something (though not really enough) of the fascinating lingo the swing people use. You will weep tears over the author's efforts to define the word in French, its musical significance being hardly covered by *balancement* and matters being in no way helped by the already accepted French usage of *swing* as a term in pugilism. You will find all this and many more matters of both historical and esthetic importance discussed in *Le Jazz Hot*, the whole topped off by photographs of great men, indexes, and a bibliography of records.

I cannot compete with M. Panassié in either learning or enthusiasm. I can only come back to what I started out to do, which is to state in these pages (being asked) a definition of swing music (the estheticians of swing having neglected that point) which I believe to be correct. That definition, to sum up, is this. Swing music is a form of two-step in which the rhythm is expressed quantitatively by instruments of no fixed intonation, the melodic, harmonic, and purely accentual elements being freed thereby to improvise in polyphonic style.

POSTSCRIPT: I haven't stated, I find, just why swing music swings and beat music doesn't. Remember the Viennese waltz? Well, the whole story is there. It isn't the strong downbeat that makes a dancer swing. A strong downbeat only makes him whirl. A strong offbeat makes him jerk. A percussive roll or trill is what makes him swing. Give him the roll and no beat and he can neither whirl nor jerk. He can only swing and that lightly, because there is no place for the swing to take him. He can also sit still and listen.

Modern Music, May 1936

Swing Again

Iɴ Mᴀʏ 1936 I stated that "swing music is a form of two-step in which the rhythm is expressed quantitatively by instruments of no fixed intonation, the melodic, harmonic, and purely accentual elements being freed thereby to improvise in polyphonic style."

That definition is pretty pompous, but I think it still holds. However, since quantitative rhythm is a concept that a great many people do not understand, my definition has remained not only undisputed but also unaccepted. I am therefore taking this occasion, which arose from an invitation to review Benny Goodman's concert in Carnegie Hall (a quite uninteresting concert on the whole), to talk some more about quantitative rhythm and its function in swing music, in the hope of further clarifying a little the bothersome question, What is swing music anyway?

The melodic matter of swing, though frequently charming, I have never found especially novel or significant. The easygoing *fioritura* of the New Orleans school and the tighter contrapuntal textures of Chicago are equally mannerisms of style; they are not of the essence. They are only significant as indicating, by their presence at such a high degree of elaboration, that there must be some pretty solid underpinning to make such elaboration possible. The constant use of the air-and-variations form is of no significance either, a string of variations being the loosest of all musical forms and at its best only a shape, never a structural system. Similarly as regards contrapuntal freedom, harmonic and instrumental variety. That is all superstructure too. It certainly astonishes no one acquainted with modern musical resources. The existence of such a practical superstructure makes it certain, however, that there is also method. The important place that improvisation has in swing-playing is conclusive. Nobody improvises publicly without a method. Communal improvisation without it is a clear impossibility.

Now the sleuths, amateur and professional, who have looked for this basic method have mostly been taken in by the lingo. Let me remind them that *hot* does not mean passionate. It means rhythmically free, and it applies only, in consequence, to melody or to percussion. More important than that, that swing music rarely has any literal swing in it. Certainly nothing like the swing Viennese waltz music has. At most it sort of quivers or oscillates rapidly like a French clock. At its best it has no motor effects at all. Good jam invariably sounds not unlike a Brandenburg concerto, where every voice wiggles around as rapidly as you please, the rhythmic basis or center remaining completely static and without progression or development of any kind.

If dance music doesn't swing, is it dance music? Answer, no. Motor impulses in dance music are a *sine qua non*. But nobody dances to jam anyway. What kind of metrical routine, then, has replaced the rhythmic beat? That there is a metrical routine of some kind is obvious. Otherwise the rhythmically free (or nonmetrical) "hot licks" would not be free. They would be just a vague melopoeia without tension. Their freedom is real and exciting only because it exists by contrast to a fixed measure of some kind. Also, collective improvisation is not possible without a metrical basis. There is only one answer, because there is only one known form of meter besides the meter of beats. That is the meter of quantities.

Here is the root of the matter. Beat music is accentual music; its rhythmic measure-unit is a succession of blows of varying force. Its effect on the listener is muscular. It is the music of the march, the dance, the religious or sexual orgy. Quantitative music has no accent; it is serene. Its rhythmic measure-unit is a unit of length. Its effect on the listener is likely to be hypnotic. When practiced with sufficient subtlety it becomes not only the lullaby, but also the ballad, the music of prose declamation, of religious rite, of contemplation, of the imaginative intellect.

The piano, the drums, all the stick-and-hammer family, are primarily accentual instruments, although the length, or vibrating time, of the tone produced is usually controllable. The bowed instruments are primarily quantitative, though they can play a fairly presentable accent too. The wind instruments, both brass and wood, are almost completely quantitative, their bravest attacks being always more vocal than percussive, and their diminuendos having always a very audible stopping place. The organ (reed or pipe) is one hundred percent quantitative, no accent of any kind being possible at any time and all tones being completely sustainable. Likewise for the modern electronic

instruments, though a fairly successful imitation of string piz-
zicati is often added to their organlike range of sounds. The
plucked instruments are equivocal. Banjo, guitar, and harp are
chiefly accentual. The lute less so. The harpsichord not at all,
because it has no accents. Harpsichord music therefore is always
quantitative, in spite of the nonsustaining tone of the instrument. It resembles organ music far more than it resembles piano
or harp music. I am now going to explain how in swing music
a similar phenomenon takes place, whereby the foundational
underpinning, its basic rhythm, although quantitative in character, gets expressed by nonquantitative instruments, by drums,
guitars, cymbals, pianos, and hand-plucked string basses.

The basic routines of the rhythm section in a swing band are
as follows:

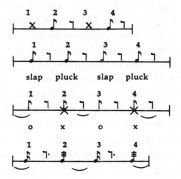

Tom-tom, bass drum,
   snare drum, or string bass

String bass

Cymbal (with hard stick)
   x represents the stroke,
   o the damping.

Snare drum (with sticks,
   brushes, or dragging brush)

There are some variations on the above, such as the double
cymbal-stroke on counts 2 and 4 (with damping on 1 and 3) and
the double brush-tap on the snare drum (also used on counts
2 and 4). Also the combinations of all these. The hot drum
solo is not a basic routine but a cadenza. It is made to sound
as different as possible from the basic routines by the use of *sfz*
stresses in unexpected places and the temporary introduction
of new patterns, sometimes in a variant meter and sometimes
in free prose. It is only a cadenza, however, a little spurt of very
exciting freedom in the midst of the grind.

Notice in the routine exposed above the consistent placing
of what looks like a strong accent on counts 2 and 4. This

cannot be what it looks like, because a musical structure of any length cannot be made on a routine of strong offbeats, since the tendency of any regular strong beat is to become itself the downbeat of the measure. Robert Schumann was fond of playing around with offbeats and frequently got his interpreters into a lot of trouble on their account. No. 1 of the *Phantasiestücke* is a celebrated example, a clear rendition of its rhythmic content (as written by the composer) being one of the more difficult feats in piano-playing.

By what agency is the tonic measure-accent expressed then in swing music if not by the rhythm section of the band? Certainly not by the melody instruments, the saxes, trumpets, clarinets, et cetera. These play with the greatest rhythmic freedom, varying continually both their accents and their quantities to exploit the rich fancy of the arranger and the tonal resources of the instruments. The harmony section, that is, piano, guitar, and the like, seems to string its chords on a rhythmic routine not unlike that of the rhythm section itself. I repeat that there is no tonic measure-accent, that the measure-unit in swing music is a measure of quantities and not of accents at all.

Let me represent the quantities in a measure of four-four time by the following pictures. I presume an instrument of unvarying pitch.

The numbers represent the four counts of the measure. They are theoretically of equal length. In musical performance, number 4 is usually a shade longer than the others. This imperceptible hold (familiar to all organists and harpsichordists) serves to define the measure's limit and to produce a tiny semblance of downbeat at the beginning of the following measure. The horizontal lines represent the duration of the unvarying sound, the blanks between them its absence. There are no stresses. You could play it on an electric buzzer. These two patterns are for theoretical purposes identical, because, unless there is in any measure of repeating pattern a tonic accent on 1 and 3, there is no tonic accent at all (or any measure either, except of two counts), and nobody can ever know which came first, the sound or the silence.

Now superpose on these theoretical, quantitative designs the formulas given above for basic swing rhythm and you will see what happens in a swing band. Remember that the instrumental strokes cannot be considered as marking tonic measure-accents, because they are all offbeat strokes. Yet they must mark something, or they wouldn't be there. They must therefore mark the quantities. The taps and plucks do coincide, as a matter of fact, with the beginning and ending of the units of the quantitative pattern. The cymbal and the snare-drum roll, having a sound of some duration, can actually express these quantities. More often than not, however, in good swing-playing, the continuing, or exactly quantitative, sounds are dispensed with on account of their insistent character, the taps and plucks being left to play the perverse role of indicating and defining a kind of rhythmic pattern that they are by nature incapable of stating in all its plenitude.

Now the two quantitative measure-patterns drawn above, although identical when expressed in quantitative sound, are not identical when expressed by dry taps. Such taps, if placed on counts one and three, would create a tonic measure-beat. Consequently they are placed on two and four in order to make it clear that there is no tonic measure-beat. The cymbal and snare drum occasionally add their precise statement of quantitative pattern number 2 to reinforce the same point.

The result of this elaborate procedure is an amplification of the expressive range. The listener, like the improvising player, is not whipped back and forth by any muscular reactions to regular beats. So marked, in fact, is the absence of regular beats that most players are obliged to keep themselves aware of musical time by rapid foot-patting. Neither is the listener lulled to sleep by an expressed quantitative routine (which can be very monotonous indeed). The pluck-and-tap rhythm is equal and delicate. It never becomes a beat. But it reminds one at all times of that underlying measure of length which is the structural unit of the whole music, reminds one so gently but so continuously that both the invention and the comprehension of musical structures is greatly facilitated.

Notice the high degree of intellectual and nervous excitement present in any swing audience. The listeners do not close their eyes and sink into emotional or subjective states. They sit up straight, their eyes flash, they applaud the licks. They occasionally jerk on the absent downbeat, but on the whole they seem to be enjoying one of those states of nervous and muscular equilibrium that make possible rapid intellection.

Quantitative rhythm in music has long been known to have special characteristics, not the least noticeable being a tendency to develop complex textures for nonemotional purposes, the organ works of Sebastian Bach and his predecessors being pretty spectacular in that way. Beat music, on the other hand, is always emotional and tends to hide rather than parade its complexities. The whole matter, however, has been very little discussed. Even the term "quantitative rhythm" is unknown to many musicians, although the musical notation we all use is as strictly a quantitative conception as though accents didn't exist. Musicians all know there is something rather special about the pipe organ, but they mostly consider the unvarying nature of an organ tone to be a defect rather than a characteristic. I don't want to go into all that any further just now. But I do want to note that quantitative music is having a renaissance under our very noses and that the plucked or tapped instruments are occupying an important place in that renaissance, a place not unlike that occupied by the harpsichord in the equally quantitative music of the seventeenth and early eighteenth centuries.

Modern Music, March 1938

Chronology

1896   Born Virgil Garnett Gaines Thomson, November 25, in an
        apartment at East Tenth Street and Virginia Avenue, Kansas
        City, Missouri, the third child and only son of Quincy Alfred
        Thomson and Clara May (Gaines) Thomson. (Father, the
        son of a Confederate soldier who had died during the Civil
        War, was born in 1862 in rural Saline County, Missouri, and
        had struggled there as a farmer, and then as the owner of
        a hardware store. He had recently moved to Kansas City
        with the financial help of his brother-in-law, Virgil's name-
        sake Charlie Garnett, and found work operating a cable car.
        Mother, born in 1865 in Boone County, Kentucky, was the
        city-loving, socially ambitious daughter of a retired land in-
        vestor. The couple, whose families were neighbors in Slater,
        Missouri, met in 1879 and were married in 1883. Their first
        child, Ruby Elizabeth Richerson Thomson, was born in
        1885. Their second, Hazel Louise Thomson, was born in
        1890 and died of diphtheria at the age of two.) Thom-
        son's family is Lowland Scottish on his father's side and
        mostly English and Welsh on his mother's. His parents are
        staunchly Southern Baptist, and, from infancy, Thomson is
        exposed to Sunday hymns at Calvary Baptist Church, where
        his father is a deacon.

1899   Father passes civil service exams and finds better-paying
        work as a post office administrator. With backing from
        Charlie Garnett, secures a loan to purchase a lot at 2629
        Wabash Avenue, where contractors build a two-story frame
        house of his own design.

1901   When Charlie Garnett moves his family to Colorado, his
        daughter, Lela—who, like Thomson's sister, Ruby, is fifteen
        years old—stays behind to continue her education at Kansas
        City's Central High School. She moves into the Thomson
        house, bringing with her an upright piano. Young Thom-
        son is fascinated by the instrument and, he will later recall,
        begins to improvise on it "with flat hands and the full arm,
        always with the pedal down and always loud, bathing in
        musical sound at its most intense. . . . It was Lela who
        taught me, at five, how to play from notes."

993

1902   Enters first grade at the Irving School (grades 1–6), on
        Prospect Avenue at Twenty-fourth Street, and is immedi-
        ately designated by fellow schoolboys as a victim. "On my
        second day at school I got into a fight," Thomson later re-
        called, "and found myself losing the match. . . . My surprise
        was definitive." His strategy for avoiding future beatings is
        to refuse to fight. "If [this] often brought me the taunt of
        'sissy,' it caused me to grow strong in other ways of defense
        and attack, psychological ways, and in the development of
        independence."

1906   When Lela marries and moves out of the house, taking the
        piano with her, sister Ruby, a talented potter who earns her
        own money by selling her work, buys Virgil a used upright
        of his own. She also pays for lessons from local teachers,
        and shows him off at her evening parties, at which he plays
        waltzes, two-steps, and German polkas.

1908   Graduates from sixth grade with class's highest marks and, as
        a reward, father buys him a ticket to a piano recital by Ignace
        Jan Paderewski. A lover of Sousa marches, attends the many
        free summer band concerts in Kansas City's public parks.
        In fall enrolls at Central High School (grades 7–12). Father
        buys new, bigger house at 2613 Wabash Avenue, on the
        same block as the previous residence.

1909   Meets Robert Leigh Murray, a thirty-eight-year-old tenor
        soloist at Calvary Baptist Church, who for the next ten
        years will be his musical mentor. A talented singer who had
        once toured nationally with various male quartets, Murray
        is employed as a salesman for the Olney Company, dis-
        tributor of Knabe pianos in the Kansas City area. Thomson
        is Murray's frequent guest at Knabe-sponsored recitals by
        singers such as John McCormack, Johanna Gadski, and
        Mary Garden, and pianists such as Vladimir de Pachmann
        and Ferruccio Busoni.

1910–11 Through Murray's connections, family hires piano teach-
        ers appropriate to Virgil's talents, Moses Boguslawski (a
        Russian interpreter of Liszt) and, later, Gustav Schoettle (a
        German exponent of Bach), both affiliated with the newly
        founded Kansas City Conservatory of Music. Learns how to
        accompany a singer, and earns professional wages as Mur-
        ray's recital pianist.

1912   Works with Rudolf King, a former student of Polish pianist
        Theodor Leschetizky, on technique and solo performance.
        Practices two hours a day during the school year, four hours
        a day in the summer. Also pursues organ studies with Clar-
        ence D. Sears of Grace Episcopal Church, and plays organ
        at Grace every Sunday morning at eleven, immediately fol-
        lowing his nine o'clock Bible class at Calvary Baptist.

1914   Graduates from Central High School with honors in En-
        glish literature and composition, shorthand, and public
        speaking. In summer becomes a student of E. Geneve Lich-
        tenwalter, whom he will always consider his most important
        teacher. A midwestern native who had lived in New York,
        France, and Germany, a reader of history and philosophy,
        and a lover of poetry that she set to her own music, she is
        more than a pedagogue to Thomson; she is an intellectual
        role model and a window into the "good life." Under her
        auspices, he makes his recital debut in downtown Kansas
        City, performing works by Franz Schubert and Edward
        MacDowell. "The boy is not quite 18 years old," reports the
        Kansas City Star, "but in last night's exacting programme
        showed a broad musical understanding. His execution . . .
        is smooth, rhythmic, and interesting." Takes postgraduate
        classes at Central High School and works as a page at the
        Kansas City Public Library.

1915   In September enters the two-year program at the newly
        opened Kansas City Polytechnic Institute, a junior college
        where he will study English composition, French, Spanish,
        math, and science. Forms an all-male arts club he calls the
        "Pansophists" and edits its little magazine, *Pans*.

1916   Nearly expelled from the Polytechnic for reading aloud
        to a mixed audience of Pansophists and coeds from Edgar
        Lee Masters's *Spoon River Anthology*, a book the school's
        administration considers deeply shocking. His reputation
        is saved by classmate Alice Smith, who testifies before an
        investigative committee that Thomson had advised all
        young women who might be offended to avoid the read-
        ing. Alice, the Stanford-educated great-granddaughter of
        Joseph Smith, founder of the Mormon Church, becomes
        Thomson's lifelong friend and correspondent.

1917   On March 5, as the United States prepares to enter World
        War I, Thomson—five foot five and 130 pounds—enlists

in the National Guard field artillery. Upon completing the spring semester at the Polytechnic, joins his unit in Independence, Missouri, for basic training. In August transfers to the Kansas City headquarters of the Medical Corps Detachment of the 129th Artillery, where he administers vaccinations and does paperwork. Spends fall at Camp Doniphan, in Fort Sill, Oklahoma, where he is "shaped up, drilled, and disciplined" with the rest of the 129th.

1918   In January accepted by the Aviation Section, Signal Corps, and studies radio technology at the School of Military Aeronautics, in Austin, Texas. In April sent to the Signal Corps's technical school for radio officers at Columbia University, New York City, and in July is made second lieutenant. Transferred first to Fort Sill, and then to Gerstner Field, in Lake Charles, Louisiana, for flight training. In September is ordered overseas, but before he can be deployed, the war ends, on November 11. Thomson, almost twenty-two, returns to his parents' house in Kansas City.

1919   Takes further classes at the Polytechnic, applies to various eastern colleges, and in the spring, with the help of a $2,000 loan secured by Alice Smith's father, enrolls at Harvard College. "Harvard had been chosen," Thomson will later recall, "for my especial needs, which were three—good keyboard lessons, available in Boston; training in harmony, counterpoint, and composition, said to be excellent at this university; and full access to its arts and letters. My ultimate aim at this time was to become an organist and choir-director in some well-paying city church." Upon arriving in Cambridge in August, purchases a brand-new Stieff mahogany grand ($875) and, to the delight of his landlady, installs it in her boardinghouse just north of Harvard Yard. Studies privately in Boston with German-born pianist Heinrich Gebhard, another former student of Leschetizky. Takes lessons from American organist Wallace Goodrich, dean of the New England Conservatory, and rents organ time (25¢ an hour) at Harvard's Appleton Chapel. At Harvard his faculty advisor (and advocate) is the American composer Edward Burlingame Hill, who urges him to take his class on modern French music and to write music criticism. His harmony teacher (and antagonist) is department chairman Walter R. Spalding, who forces him to take Music I in an effort to cure him of his "uppishness." But it is Archibald T. Davison, a pioneer of early music studies and the director of the Harvard Glee Club, who has the greatest influence on his musical development. Davison, by teaching undergraduates to sing seldom performed early church music rather than pep songs, has for seven years been making the Glee Club a force in Boston's musical life while also expanding America's concert choir repertoire. Thomson joins the sixty-member Glee Club as a tenor, and reports to sister Ruby that "the choir is wonderful. We sing medieval things in Latin without accompaniment, and sing them beautifully."

1920   In spring takes paid position as part-time organist and choir director at a Unitarian church in North Easton, Massachusetts, twenty-five miles south of Boston. Meets Harvard English instructor S. Foster Damon, a proponent of the avant-garde who introduces him to the works of Erik Satie and Gertrude Stein, both of whom will become shaping artistic influences. At end of term is named teaching assistant to Professors Hill and Davison. In Kansas City for the summer, composes his first pieces, two songs set to texts by Amy Lowell and William Blake (favorites of Damon) and a choral setting of Psalm 130 ("De profundis"). In fall becomes assistant director of the Glee Club, for which Davison plans an eight-week concert tour of Europe the following summer.

1921   Meets H. T. Parker, music editor of the *Boston Evening Transcript*, who while reporting an article on the Glee Club is impressed with Thomson's quick wit and knowledge of music history. In spring, Hill and Davison arrange to award Thomson the music department's John Knowles Paine Traveling Fellowship for 1921–22. Their plan is for Thomson to tour Europe with the Glee Club and then stay on in Paris for a paid year of study at the newly founded American Conservatory in Fontainebleau. On June 11, the Glee Club leaves New York for Le Havre on the French steamer *La Touraine*, and en route rehearses its program: the French and American national anthems; Palestrina, Praetorius, Hassler; Gregorian chants; English part-songs; folk songs arranged by Brahms and Dvořák; and recent works by Borodin and Sibelius. The concert itinerary includes Paris, Dijon, Nancy, and Strasbourg; Koblenz and Wiesbaden; Milan, Rome, Naples, Venice, and Ravenna. After the tour, Thomson spends two weeks in Switzerland and four in England before beginning his studies in Paris.

His principal teacher at the American Conservatory is the French organist and composer Nadia Boulanger, whose other students include the twenty-one-year-old Aaron Copland. Thomson's acquaintance with the Glee Club's French liaison, the Harvard-educated Bernard Faÿ, leads to encounters with Jean Cocteau, Picasso, Darius Milhaud, Francis Poulenc, and, most important to Thomson, Erik Satie.

1922   At the invitation of H. T. Parker, writes pieces about Paris musical events for the *Boston Evening Transcript*, including an article on a conductor as yet unheard-of in America, the Russian phenomenon Serge Koussevitzky. (Thomson always maintained that this article "set in motion a train of events" that culminated in Koussevitzky's appointment as music director of the Boston Symphony Orchestra in 1924.) Continues his studies with Boulanger, spends hours every day at the piano and the organ, and composes a few more short pieces. In late August he reluctantly leaves Paris, promising himself to return soon. Again takes up residence in the boardinghouse near Harvard Yard, resumes organ lessons with Wallace Goodrich, and takes a demanding but prestigious one-year job as the choir director and noon-service organist at Boston's historic King's Chapel (Episcopal). Joins the Liberal Club, an undergraduate dining club whose members include the poet and polymath Lincoln Kirstein, the aspiring painter Maurice Grosser, and a handsome, pensive junior named Briggs Buchanan.

1923   Overcommitted at King's Chapel, nostalgic for Paris, and troubled by his strong attraction to Briggs Buchanan, Thomson struggles through his final semester at Harvard. Passes the music department's general examinations, but is denied a "degree with distinction" for what Professor Spalding terms his "mediocrity" in harmony, counterpoint, and fugue. ("We wish you to know," Spalding writes on behalf of the faculty, "that we have a high opinion of your general musical ability . . . but we regret that your grammatical knowledge of the subject is so deficient that this distinct deficiency is apparent in your writing of music.") Nevertheless, when the Juilliard Trust gives Spalding $1,500 to award to a deserving senior, he gives the prize to Thomson. Uses the money to move not to Paris but to New York City, where he takes an apartment at 55 East Thirty-fourth Street. Joins the American Orchestral Society, a training orchestra recommended by Professor Hill, and there studies conducting with Chalmers Clifton, director of the Society, and composition with Rosario Scalero, a teacher of music theory at the Mannes School of Music. Begins an intense correspondence with Briggs Buchanan, in which he explores, explicitly, his artistic interests and ambitions, and, allusively, his sexual longings.

1924   In September returns to Harvard as a salaried teaching assistant to Hill and Davison just as Buchanan, to Thomson's surprise and distress, leaves Cambridge for a job on Wall Street. Accepts post as Sunday organist at Village Congregational Church, in Whitinsville (near Worcester), Massachusetts, and becomes the regular weekend guest of the Lasell family, the wealthy patrons of Worcester's musical life. Writes concert reviews for the *Boston Evening Transcript* and, at the suggestion of H. L. Mencken, a musical analysis of jazz for *The American Mercury*, his first article for a national magazine. Realizing that his feelings for Buchanan are keeping him in the States and hindering his professional progress, resolves to go to Paris. Sets sail in September, having found a traveling companion in John Joseph Sherry Mangan, a friend from the Liberal Club who will help him fight loneliness during his first months in France. Rents a student flat on the rue de Berne and frequents Shakespeare and Company, Sylvia Beach's Left Bank bookstore, where he meets James Joyce, Ernest Hemingway, Ford Madox Ford, Ezra Pound, and the young American composer George Antheil, who will become a friend. Resumes studies with Nadia Boulanger and brings Antheil into her American Conservatory circle, which now includes Copland, Walter Piston, and Theodore Chanler. In September is surprised to encounter his Liberal Club acquaintance Maurice Grosser, just arrived in Paris on a Harvard painting fellowship. When, at Christmastime, Thomson is offered use of a two-room flat in the Paris suburb of Saint-Cloud, he asks Grosser, seven years his junior, to move in and share expenses. Their friendship will soon deepen into the most enduring attachment of both their lives. Although after 1934 they do not always live together, they will remain devoted to each other until Grosser's death in 1986.

1925   Writes a series of what Thomson calls "sassy and classy" pieces on musical topics for the American monthly *Vanity Fair*, a bible of the Jazz Age. In July is shocked by the

sudden death of Erik Satie, age fifty-nine. Introduced by
George Antheil to Gertrude Stein, whom Thomson impresses with informed and sincere enthusiasm for her work.
In Thomson's phrase, he and Stein "get on like Harvard
men."

1926   Under the tutelage of Boulanger, completes his first major
            concert work, a three-movement *Sonata da Chiesa* (Church
            Sonata) for five instruments. In May the piece receives its
            premiere at a well-attended concert of new American music
            sponsored by the Fontainebleau conservatory. Secretly ex-
            periments with setting texts by Stein, hoping, as he later
            writes, "to break, crack open, and solve anything still wait-
            ing to be solved, which was almost everything, about En-
            glish musical declamation. My theory was that if a text is
            set correctly for the sound of it, the meaning will take care
            of itself. And the Stein texts, for prosodizing in this way,
            were manna." The first text he sets is "Susie Asado," a prose
            poem from 1913, collected in Stein's *Geography and Plays*
            (1922).

1927   On New Year's Day, plays and sings the music for "Susie
            Asado" for Stein, who is deeply moved and impressed.
            Immediately follows up with settings of her prose poems
            "Capital Capitals" and "Preciosilla," with results so satisfac-
            tory to Stein that she proposes she and Thomson write an
            opera together. After toying with subjects drawn from *Bul-
            finch's Mythology* and Parson Weems's *Life of Washington*,
            they agree to treat the lives of the saints, especially Teresa of
            Ávila and Ignatius Loyola. By June, Stein has finished the
            libretto, which she calls *Four Saints in Three Acts*. Thomson
            will devote most of the next thirteen months to writing
            the music. In the fall, with the benefit of patronage from
            the Lasell family, Thomson secures an eighteenth-century
            studio at 17 quai Voltaire, his Paris residence for the next
            fifty years.

1928   By New Year's Day he is fully engaged with the text of *Four
            Saints*. Seated at his piano, he reads the words aloud, re-
            peatedly, until musical rhythms, contours, and shapes sug-
            gest themselves. Taking no liberties with Stein's libretto,
            he sets every word—including the stage directions—to
            melodies born of American hymn tunes, Negro spirituals,
            and band music, and of the cadences of plain midwestern
            speech. Finishes the piano-vocal version in July, and then

begins scoring the work, which, he tells the Lasells, "will be the longest task of all, certainly the dirtiest, and there is a ballet and an intermezzo and a personal appearance by the Holy Ghost. . . ." Also returns to work and completes a symphony on the Baptist hymn "Jesus Loves Me" and four sets of organ pieces called *Variations on Sunday School Tunes*. After receiving from Stein the gift of an abstract verbal portrait—the short prose work "Virgil Thomson," later collected in her book *Portraits and Prayers* (1934)—Thomson becomes fascinated with the idea of making abstract "musical portraits" of persons of his acquaintance. Begins to write short "sketches from life"—musical ideas jotted on staff paper while his subject sits five or six feet before him—with the aim of evoking some aspect of the sitter's character. Stein's methods encourage him to "try to write automatically, cultivate the discipline of spontaneity, let it flow." The portraits are sketched in silence, usually in about an hour. Thomson does not pause to try out what he has written on the piano, "to hear, correct, or criticize"—such adjustments are left for later. "My effort while at work is to write down whatever comes to me in the sitter's presence, hoping as I transcribe my experience that it will, as the painters say, 'make a composition.'" He will make seven such portraits in 1928, and about 130 more over the next five decades, most of them short works for solo piano.

1929   Spends winter in America, trying to find a producer for *Four Saints* and to arrange performances of his recent concert pieces. In Boston plays his *Symphony on a Hymn Tune* for Koussevitzky, who, happily follows the score, until at last throws up his hands in the middle of the final movement: "I could never play my audience *that!*" (The symphony will not have its premiere until 1945.) In February, plays and sings a one-man piano version of *Four Saints* to an invited audience at the New York apartment of critic Carl Van Vechten, an advocate of Stein's work. Returns to Paris and writes several chamber works, including a piano sonata that will become the basis for his second symphony.

1930   Friendship with Stein becomes strained by petty misunderstandings within their shared social, literary, and publishing circles. From Stein's perspective, Thomson is guilty of repeatedly siding with her rivals, detractors, and "glory-grabbing" French translators, which leads to fewer invitations to her home.

1931   In January, "Miss Gertrude Stein," in a one-sentence letter, "declines further acquaintance with Mr. Virgil Thomson." Thomson, hurt and angry, continues to search for a producer for *Four Saints*. Writes his second symphony, which will not be performed until ten years later, and his first string quartet.

1932   Becomes a regular contributor of articles to *Modern Music*, the journal of the League of Composers, a New York-based organization dedicated to nurturing the American audience for twentieth-century music. For the next fourteen years, until the journal's folding in 1946, he will write on topics ranging from Copland and Gershwin to swing band syncopation and Charlie Chaplin's film scores. Completes String Quartet No. 2 and a *Stabat Mater*, with French text by Max Jacob, for soprano and string quartet.

1933   In the spring, visits America to help lay foundation for the first production of *Four Saints*. Through the efforts of Van Vechten and his friends—including architect Philip Johnson and art dealer Kirk Askew—a group of backers has formed. A. Everett "Chick" Austin Jr., director of the Wadsworth Atheneum, in Hartford, Connecticut, schedules the premiere for the following winter in the Atheneum's new Avery Memorial Theater. Thomson energetically handles all artistic aspects of the production, hiring a conductor, Alexander Smallens, and a designer, the faux-naïf modernist Florine Stettheimer. Retires to the French countryside to finish the score, and gingerly renews contact with Stein to discuss contractual matters. In October, returns to New York, where he hires a young, untried John Houseman as director and Frederick Ashton as choreographer. Through Van Vechten's contacts in the Harlem music world, hires choral director Eva Jessye and an all-black cast—six soloists and thirty-two choristers. Rehearsals start in early December.

1934   *Four Saints* receives its premiere at the Wadsworth Atheneum on February 8. Described by *The New York Times* as a combination "opera, stage cantata, farce, [and] Hasty Pudding show" whose text "is a superb vehicle for [Thomson's] melodic virtuosity [and] cunning," it is an immediate *succès de scandale*, selling out its two-week Hartford run before moving to Broadway for forty-eight further performances.

Stein, at home in Paris, receives a vivid firsthand report from her collaborator: "In every way it was very, very beautiful and of course there were some who didn't like the music and some who didn't like the words . . . but there wasn't anybody who didn't see that the ensemble was a new kind of collaboration and that it was unique and powerful." Upon his return to Paris, Thomson is asked by James Joyce to set to music the guessing game episode of his "Work-in-Progress" (*Finnegans Wake*), but Thomson declines, in part because Stein considers Joyce a "rival." In October, Thomson travels to Chicago to oversee a one-week run of *Four Saints*. There he reunites with Stein, then on the first leg of a six-month American publicity tour. On opening night, Thomson later recalls, the estranged collaborators "kiss but do not quite make up."

1935   Temporarily based in New York City, Thomson organizes a series of concerts for the Wadsworth Atheneum. In the fall, at the invitation of producer John Houseman, composes incidental music and creates sound effects for the Orson Welles/Federal Theatre Project's all-black production of *Macbeth*, to be mounted the following spring.

1936   In January, introduced by Houseman to Pare Lorentz, film-maker for the U.S. Resettlement Administration, a New Deal agency tasked with relocating Oklahoma farm families displaced by drought, wind, and soil erosion. Lorentz, editing a twenty-five-minute documentary on the man-made causes of the Dust Bowl, is facing a tight government deadline and needs music for the film immediately. Thomson delivers the score—a fluid stream of cowboy tunes and mood music—in less than a month. *The Plow That Broke the Plains* is released in May to excellent reviews.

1937   Writes the score for *The River* (1938), a second documentary short by Pare Lorentz, on the man-made causes of floods and the need for dams in the Mississippi delta. (In 1942 Thomson will make concert suites from his scores to *The River* and *The Plow That Broke the Plains*. For his admirer Aaron Copland "they are a lesson in how to treat Americana.") Lincoln Kirstein, Thomson's friend from the Harvard Liberal Club, now the founder-director of the Ballet Caravan dance company, commissions music for *Filling Station* (1938), a comic dance designed "to evoke roadside America as pop art." Thomson's score, a cartoon soundtrack for the antics of a mock-heroic gas station attendant, is the first ballet written by an American composer on an indigenous American theme.

1938   *Filling Station*, choreographed by Lew Christenson, receives its premiere at the Wadsworth Atheneum on January 6. In the spring, Thomson accepts a thousand-dollar advance from Thayer Hobson, the publisher of William Morrow & Co., for a book of linked essays on music and contemporary culture. In June moves back to Paris, and begins work on a second opera—a musical setting of John Webster's *Duchess of Malfi*—but abandons the project by the end of the summer. Renews acquaintance with his friend Sherry Mangan, who, in a series of late-night conversations, asks Thomson basic questions about music, musicianship, and economics that sharpen his thoughts about the book he has promised Hobson. In October he begins to write and, forgoing his piano and his social life, completes the book within six months.

1939   Thomson's book *The State of Music* is published by Morrow in November. In it he describes the modern musician's lot in relation to those of his fellow artists and to the workings of American society. He writes about how musicians are and should be educated, how and why modern music gets made, and, in matters of employment, commissions, awards, and patronage, "who does what to whom, and who gets paid." He argues that music is a profession and that its makers, especially its composers, must take control of its creation, performance, and distribution lest it become "a mere consumer commodity." Reviews are widespread but sales are dismal—only two thousand copies in the first year. Still, the book is a sensation within the world of criticism—and a scandal within the world of philanthropy—and makes Thomson's reputation as a wit, a critic, and American music's strongest advocate.

1940   In June Germany invades France, and Thomson leaves Paris only a few days before the city is occupied. Sails from Lisbon to the United States on August 12, and takes a furnished apartment on the second floor of New York's Hotel Chelsea, at 222 West Twenty-third Street. (Thomson will move into a ninth-floor suite in 1943, and he will keep the

Chelsea as his American residence for the rest of his life.)
In mid-September spends a weekend at the Connecticut
home of conductor Alexander Smallens, and there is introduced to Geoffrey Parsons, lead editorial writer and the
man in charge of cultural coverage at the *New York Herald
Tribune*. Impressed by *The State of Music*, Parsons invites
Thomson to succeed the late Lawrence Gilman as the paper's chief music critic and head of the music department.
Later, in an interview with the paper's publisher, Thomson
will be candid about his reasons for accepting Parsons's
offer: "The general standard of music reviewing in New
York had sunk so far that almost any change might bring
improvement. Also I thought perhaps my presence in a post
so prominent might stimulate performance of my works."
He joins the staff on October 10, and his first review, a
withering appraisal of that evening's concert by the New
York Philharmonic, runs the following morning.

1941   Settles into his *Herald Tribune* assignment, and quickly
        establishes a routine. "During seven months of the year
        I wrote a Sunday article every week and averaged two re-
        views," he will later recall. "During the summer months
        I did no reviewing; I also skipped seven or eight Sunday
        articles. Since these could be sent from anywhere, I toured
        on musical errands of my own or stayed in some country
        place writing music. I also wrote music in town [and] went
        in and out on lectures and conducting dates. The paper
        liked all this activity, because it kept my name before the
        public." Builds a department that within four years includes
        columnists Rudi Blesh (jazz), Edwin Denby (dance), and
        B. H. Haggin (radio and recordings). Solicits pieces from
        such critic-composers as Arthur Berger, Paul Bowles, John
        Cage, Elliott Carter, Peggy Glanville-Hicks, and Lou Har-
        rison. ("I used no one not trained in music," he wrote,
        "for my aim was to explain the artist, not to encourage
        misunderstanding of his work.") His mission, as writer and
        editor, is "to expose the philanthropic persons in control of
        our institutions for the amateurs they mostly are, to reveal
        the manipulators of our musical distribution for the cultur-
        ally retarded profit-makers that indeed they are, and to sup-
        port with all the power of my praise every artist, composer,
        group, or impresario whose relation to music is straightfor-
        ward, by which I mean based only on music and the sound

it makes." On November 17, Thomson's Symphony No. 2 (1931) is given its premiere by the Seattle Symphony, Sir Thomas Beecham, conductor.

1942   On March 14, arrested in an F.B.I. raid on a gay bordello near the Brooklyn Naval Yard. He is bailed out by Geoffrey Parsons, who successfully keeps the incident out of the papers. The arrest report remains on the record, but no charges are ever filed. (All his life, Thomson—haunted since youth by a sense of shame, and by the public humiliation and imprisonment of Oscar Wilde—strove to keep his homosexuality an entirely private matter. He never mentioned his sexual orientation in print, and vocally disapproved of those who did. In the last year of his life he told his biographer, "I didn't want to be queer. No! No! No! That was another hurdle I didn't want to have to jump over. . . . Nowadays it's much easier [but in my youth] you didn't mention it . . . you didn't tell anything.")

1943   Father dies, age eighty-one, on April 6. "My personal regret," Thomson later writes, "was that now I could not let him know my shame for the harsh things said in adolescent years. But he must have known and forgiven me long ago, for he was a Christian . . . and had always understood me and spared reproach."

1944   At the invitation of conductor Eugene Ormandy, orchestrates eight of his musical portraits, which, on November 17, are given their premiere in Philadelphia. Meets Ned Rorem, a twenty-year-old composition student at the Curtis Institute of Music, who leaves school to become his copyist. Thomson pays him twenty dollars a week, and gives him free lessons in orchestration. ("In the eighteen months I worked with Virgil," Rorem will later write, "I was to learn more than during the long years, before and after, spent in the world's major conservatories.") In the fall receives a letter from Gertrude Stein asking him to collaborate with her on a second opera. He tells her that, musically, he would like to treat a theme from nineteenth-century America, "but, please, let's not have any foolishness about Abraham Lincoln. That can't be done!"

1945   On February 22, at Carnegie Hall, Thomson's *Symphony on a Hymn Tune* (Symphony No. 1, 1928) is given its premiere by the New York Philharmonic, in a performance conducted by the composer. In March *The Musical Scene*, a collection of Thomson's articles and reviews from the *Herald Tribune*, is published by Alfred A. Knopf. ("As a literary craftsman, the author is probably unsurpassed in his field," says *The New York Times Book Review*. "His unfavorable opinions are disarmingly sincere—and utterly venomous. His praises are sung with the joy of a child about to receive a second helping of ice cream.") In April, Eugene Ormandy produces a Columbia Masterworks recording of Thomson conducting the Philadelphia Orchestra in a performance of five of the orchestrated musical portraits. (*Five Portraits*, released as a set of two 78-rpm discs, is the first commercial recording of Thomson's work.) In early summer, representatives from Columbia University's Brander Matthews Theater inform Thomson that the late Alice M. Ditson, a wealthy opera-lover with ties to the university, has left them a sum of money with which to commission and mount new works. In August, just weeks after the end of World War II, Thomson visits Paris to meet with Gertrude Stein and discuss the opportunity that Columbia has laid before them: a Broadway budget production of a new Stein-Thomson opera for the spring of 1947. After a week of brainstorming, they agree to write a pageant on the life of the early feminist Susan B. Anthony.

1946   On March 16, Stein sends Thomson the text of her libretto, *The Mother of Us All*. Thomson, writing from New York on April 15, tells her that "it is sensationally handsome and Susan B. is a fine role." The libretto will be the last major work that Stein completes; that spring her health deteriorates suddenly, and she dies of stomach cancer, age seventy-two, on July 27. After a trip to Paris to consult with Stein's companion and literary executor, Alice B. Toklas, Thomson clears his schedule and begins work on the music for the opera. He has a piano-vocal version by December 10, which he auditions for his closest composer friends and his receptive Columbia patrons.

1947   Thomson scores the opera throughout the spring, and *The Mother of Us All* receives its premiere at Brander Matthews Theater on May 7. Otto Luening, professor of music at Columbia and Barnard, conducts an orchestra of student and faculty musicians, and American soprano Dorothy Dow sings the title role. Reviews are mostly favorable:

Olin Downes of *The New York Times* calls it "adroit, entertaining, expressive" and "a piece of admirable métier and
integrated style. . . . It is to be seen." A truncated version
of *Four Saints*, abridged and conducted by Thomson, is
released on disc by RCA Victor to good reviews and strong
sales. "I am sorry now that I did not write an opera with
[Stein] every year," Thomson remarks in his liner notes. "It
had not occurred to me that both of us would not always
be living." Receives order of merit from the French Légion
d'honneur.

1948   In March *The Art of Judging Music*, a second collection of
Thomson's articles and reviews from the *Herald Tribune*, is
published by Alfred A. Knopf. ("Paste-up collections of old
reviews usually make for very dreary reading," says *The New
Yorker*. "Mr. Thomson's book is an exception, because he
can discuss even the most ephemeral musical event in relation to the whole art. He is also, of course, a very witty and
astringent writer.") In May elected a member of the National Institute of Arts and Letters. Completes the score to
Louisiana Story, a feature-length documentary by Robert J.
Flaherty. For this film—a nearly wordless study in the effect
of the oil industry on the environment and the folkways of
Cajun Louisiana, told from the point of view of a twelve-
year-old boy—Thomson writes over sixty minutes of music,
his longest composition outside his operas. When it opens
in New York on September 18, the film and its score receive
uniformly excellent reviews.

1949   On May 2 the music for *Louisiana Story* is awarded a Pulitzer Prize—a first for a motion-picture score. Thomson will
fashion two suites from the soundtrack, *Suite from "Louisiana Story*," conducted by Eugene Ormandy in New York
and Philadelphia that fall, and *Acadian Songs and Dances*,
used by George Balanchine as music for his ballet *Bayou*
(1952). Composes two works for band, *At the Beach* and *A
Solemn Music*, the latter in memory of Gertrude Stein.

1950   Concerto for Cello and Orchestra (1949), a great favorite
of Thomson's among his compositions, is given its premiere by Ormandy and the Philadelphia Orchestra, with
Paul Olefsky, soloist.

1951   In March *Music Right and Left*, a third collection of
Thomson's articles and reviews from the *Herald Tribune*,
is published by Henry Holt & Co. ("Together with the

two previous collections," writes Roger Sessions in *The New York Times Book Review*, "it reflects in a striking way the seriousness, the directness, and the basic simplicity of Thomson's critical approach," which is built on "principles difficult to improve on.") Composes incidental music for the Broadway adaptation of Truman Capote's novella *The Grass Harp*, which will run for thirty-six performances in the spring of 1952.

1952   In April a revival of *Four Saints*, with an all-black cast including Leontyne Price and Betty Allen, mounted at New York's Broadway Theater by the American National Theater and Academy. Thomson is artistic director, publicity consultant, and conductor of the pickup orchestra. After a two-week run, the production travels to Paris where it is presented at the Théâtre des Champs-Elysées. In October completes *Three Pictures for Orchestra*, comprising the "musical landscapes" *The Seine at Night* (1947), *Wheatfield at Noon* (1948), and a new work, *Sea Piece with Birds*. Writes music for Agnes de Mille's ballet *The Harvest According*, which receives its premiere at the Opera House, Chicago, on December 29.

1953   As music consultant to the Rockefeller Foundation, is crucial to the development of the "Louisville project," through which the Louisville Orchestra, under the direction of conductor Robert Whitney, makes the commissioning, performance, and recording of new works for orchestra a centerpiece of its mission for the next quarter-century. Also helps develop Louisville's First Edition Records, the first orchestra-owned record label and a vital producer of recordings of twentieth-century music. Writes incidental music for the Orson Welles–Peter Brook production of *King Lear*, broadcast live on October 18 as part of CBS television's *Omnibus* series. Begins a four-year romance with Roger Baker, an American painter twenty-nine years his junior.

1954   Increasingly in demand as a guest conductor and lecturer, eager to write more books and better music, and convinced that, after fourteen years, he has little left to learn about writing music journalism, resigns from his position at the *New York Herald Tribune*, effective October 1.

1955–58   Various attempts to begin a third opera—on *The Bacchae* of Euripides, on Robert Lowell's *The Old Glory*, on Truman

Capote's "A Christmas Memory"—all come to nothing. "Relieved from deadline pressures and with nothing I had to do, I seemed to write less music than before," Thomson later remarked of this difficult period, which he termed his "reconstruction time." "I wrote songs to old English poetry [Thomas Campion, John Donne, John Woodcock Graves, William Blake] and to Shakespeare, also songs in Spanish [Reyna Rives]. I did [incidental music for] six Shakespeare plays [and] three films . . . I traveled too, to South America, lecturing in Spanish and conducting, to Venice for two festivals, to Berlin for another, eventually to Japan. But I was not content with just moving about, nor with merely composing films, plays, and short recital pieces . . ." Mother dies, age ninety-two, on October 27, 1957.

1959   Begins what will be a two-year collaboration with thirty-four-year-old poet Kenneth Koch, who brings him into a circle of young acquaintances including Frank O'Hara, John Ashbery, and James Schuyler. Sets two groups of Koch's previously published poems (*Collected Poems* and *Mostly about Love*) and urges the poet to write an original libretto on a subject of shared interest: Haussmann, Napoleon III, and the rebuilding of Paris. Meets frequently with Koch, commenting incisively on his libretto as it develops. In May, elected to membership in the American Academy of Arts and Letters. In June the critical-biographical book *Virgil Thomson: His Life and Music* is published by Thomas Yoseloff, New York. Ostensibly the disinterested work of two writers, Kathleen Hoover (the "Life") and John Cage (the "Music"), it was in fact commissioned, edited, and—to the authors' abiding dismay—extensively rewritten by Thomson himself.

1960   Completes a major commission from the State College of Education at Potsdam, New York: *Missa pro defunctis*, a Requiem Mass for double chorus and orchestra. It receives its premiere in Potsdam on May 12, with Thomson conducting. With this creative success, Thomson will recall, "I knew my 'reconstruction time' was over." In December, after more than a year of intense collaboration, Thomson abruptly abandons work on Koch's libretto, cryptically declaring it "a soft egg." (Koch is hurt but resilient. "How could you stay mad at Virgil?" he later said. "I had a good ride even though I wound up back in the garage.")

1961   At the suggestion of Jason Epstein, publisher of Vintage Books, revises the text of *The State of Music* for a new generation of readers. Writes new introduction and afterword to the book, and, in footnotes to the 1939 text, adds comments on the current music scene. ("Autonomy, intellectual and financial, is unquestionably the ideal state for any profession, both for its own well being and for its contributions to culture," he writes. "[Music must] take care of the professional line, and the artistic line will take care of itself. That was my message in 1939. It still is.") Blanche Knopf, who with her husband, Alfred, had published him in the 1940s, invites Thomson to write his memoirs. He signs a contract in August that promises delivery in 1964.

1962   In April, *The State of Music* (second edition) is published in Vintage paperback. Visits Los Angeles and is introduced by Ned Rorem to the poet and actor Jack Larson. Reads Larson's poems, some of which had been set to song by Rorem, and is much taken with "The Candied House," a verse play on the theme of Hansel and Gretel—not what he expected from the young man who, for six years in the 1950s, had played Jimmy Olsen in the Superman television series.

1963   Thomson proposes that Larson try his hand at a libretto. He suggests a subject that he had once proposed to Gertrude Stein, and, more recently, to Gore Vidal: scenes from the life of Lord Byron. Byron was "a genius, a millionaire, a hero, a lover, and a beauty," Thomson explained—the very epitome of the artist as self-made man. "He simply would not be told how to behave, or how not to behave," and would make a wonderful hero for "a poetic drama with music."

1964   Composes the score for *Journey to America*, a twenty-minute documentary about immigration written and produced by John Houseman for the United States Pavilion at the New York World's Fair. (Thomson's concert suite adapted from the score is titled *Pilgrims and Pioneers*.) Delivers his memoirs to Knopf, and, under editor Herbert Weinsock, spends much of the next year revising and enlarging them, transforming a sometimes technical account of his life in music into a warm and gossipy personal history of his Kansas City boyhood, Paris youth, and New York maturity. Larson completes a draft of his *Lord Byron*, which he has conceived as a modest work in two acts. (One admirer characterizes it as "a literate, conversational piece ideally suited to productions in smaller companies"—and, more important, to Thomson's methods of prosody.) Presents the libretto to Thomson and, with the composer's permission, to their friend in common John Houseman. Houseman is enthusiastic about it as a work for the stage, and Thomson says, "It sings."

1965   In January writes a long article on the life and works of Wanda Landowska for the recently founded *New York Review of Books*, a journal that will welcome his essays and criticism for the rest of his creative life. (Subjects he will treat include Boulez, Stravinsky, Janet Flanner, Paul Bowles, Alice B. Toklas, and jazz.) In May is presented the Gold Medal for Music from the American Academy of Arts and Letters. On November 28, Allen Hughes, a cultural reporter for *The New York Times*, publishes an interview-cum-press-release by Thomson and Larson announcing their collaboration.

1966   In the wake of the *Times* piece, Thomson receives inquiries about *Lord Byron* from several opera companies. In the spring accepts a generous preemptive commission from the Metropolitan Opera, made possible by emergency grants to the Met by the Ford and Koussevitzky foundations. The production, according to general manager Rudolf Bing, will be sumptuous—a "grand opera" appropriate to the Met's brand-new hall at Lincoln Center. Larson is distressed by having to reconceive his modest "conversational piece" as a work that will satisfy the Met: "Their audience needed two intermissions, so Virgil needed a three-act libretto. The huge stage would require larger scenes with a bigger cast . . . and a large chorus . . . and a ballet." Larson, in consultation with John Houseman, expands the work accordingly, and delivers a new libretto in July. Thomson, delighted, spends much of the summer at the MacDowell Colony, in Peterborough, New Hampshire, working on the vocal lines. In October his memoirs, *Virgil Thomson*, are published by Knopf to strong sales and favorable reviews. (Alfred Frankenstein, in *The New York Times Book Review*, calls the book "an invaluable contribution to the history of music, theater, film, literature, and painting in the twentieth century . . . crammed with short, brilliant character sketches of Thomson's friends . . . a cast of characters which is unbelievably immense.") In the fall is Visiting Professor of Music at Carnegie Institute of Technology, in Philadelphia.

1967   To capitalize on the success of the memoirs, as well as on nostalgia for the recently shuttered *New York Herald Tribune*, Thomson edits a selection of his music journalism from the 1940s and '50s. Published in June by Vintage Books, *Music Reviewed* contains the author's choice of pieces from his three previous collections and fifty-five uncollected items from the last five years of his *Herald Tribune* tenure.

1968   As the Met becomes more involved in the creation of *Lord Byron*, work on the opera is, in Thomson's words, "beset by disputes, misunderstandings, deceptions, concealments, delays, wrong decisions, and plain stupidities." Bing is determined that the opera be a highlight of the Met's 1971–72 season, his last as general manager. Larson continually rewrites the libretto to meet Thomson's and the Met's everchanging demands for something "grand."

1969   On April 9, a tryout of key scenes from *Lord Byron* is presented by Thomson in a rehearsal room at the Metropolitan Opera, with two soloists and a chorus of nine, accompanied by a staff pianist. Though the performers are well prepared and take a sincere delight in the music, by the end of the audition Rudolf Bing turns markedly cold toward the composer. Five days later, in a letter to Thomson, Bing confesses that he has "grave doubts whether this is a piece suitable for a 4000-seat house." He declines to put *Lord Byron* on the Met's schedule, and suggests it might "first be done somewhere else"—perhaps Dallas—"to see what effect the work has in a large opera house." Thomson is not entirely surprised—Bing's conservatism was legendary—but he is devastated.

1970   At the invitation of WNCN-FM, hosts *Virgil Thomson at the Chelsea*, a partly scripted radio program recorded in his hotel apartment and broadcast Monday nights at 10. This limited series, which runs all year through September 28, features Thomson playing and discussing recordings of his work, interviewing friends and fellow-composers, and commenting on the music world past and present. Writes

American Music Since 1910, the inaugural volume in Nicolas Nabokov's "Twentieth-Century Composers" series. This brief study—Thomson's text runs to ninety pages—recounts "American music's discovery of its own distinct national idiom" through chapters on Ives, Ruggles, Varèse, Copland, and Cage, with glances toward dozens of other composers. The book concludes with an appendix, "The Operas of Virgil Thomson," commissioned by the author from critic Victor Fell Yellin, and a set of biographical notes on 106 American composers, each of which concludes with a tart summing-up by Thomson. (Milton Babbitt: "[His] music has the clarity of distilled water and just possibly the sterility." Christian Wolff: "A Cage disciple so devoted to musical purity that throughout his educative years he avoided all musical education." Eric Salzman: "The best critic in America for contemporary and far-out music, his own work, as can happen with critics, is in danger of neglect.")

1971   In January, *American Music Since 1910* published by Holt, Rinehart & Winston. Receives the Handel Medallion of the City of New York, the city's highest prize for achievement in the arts. In the spring Peter Mennin, president of the Juilliard School, proposes that the Juilliard American Opera Center produce the premiere of *Lord Byron*. Mennin suggests, for director, John Houseman, since 1966 the head of Juilliard's drama department, and, for conductor, Gerhard Samuel, associate conductor of the Los Angeles Philharmonic. Thomson then enlists Alvin Ailey as choreographer and David Mitchell as production designer. In August completes the score and begins to audition Juilliard singers for the twenty-eight-member cast. Rehearsals, preparations, and adjustments by Thomson and Larson will continue throughout Juilliard's 1971–72 academic year.

1972   On April 20, *Lord Byron* receives its premiere at the Juilliard American Opera Center. The reviews are mixed: Harold C. Schonberg of *The New York Times* judges the score "very bland," "distressingly banal," and "frequently gaggingly cutesy," but Patrick J. Smith of *High Fidelity/Musical America* calls it "a masterpiece . . . a genuine musical entity of great beauty. Whatever its final standing in relation to the Stein operas, *Lord Byron* is a credit to our premier opera composer." (When, in January 1977, WNYC-TV broadcasts a video recording of the Juilliard production, the work again divides the critics, but Andrew Porter, in *The New Yorker*, writes that it is "an elegant and cultivated piece," "[its] simplicity that of a master," and it "does not deserve neglect." In a personal letter, Thomson thanks Porter sincerely: "To be treated as a serious composer of operas, just imagine! And not as the operator of some shell game, or some talented amateur who had once met Gertrude Stein in Paris.")

1973   Writes *Cantata on Poems of Edward Lear*. Problems with hearing, which had begun during the writing of *Lord Byron*, make it difficult for Thomson to compose further works: "My own pitches are so completely falsified by now," he tells an old friend, "that I cannot listen to music . . . and get a reliable report of it from my ears." Prepares two series of talks, one on the function of music criticism, the other on prosody, that will earn him several short-term academic residencies, first at the University of Bridgeport and Trinity College, Connecticut, then at Dominican College and Otterbein College (1974), California State University at Fullerton (1975), and UCLA (1976).

1974   Hires Victor Cardell, his former student at Trinity College, as the first of many personal assistants who will answer his phone, type his letters, buy his groceries, and help him face the challenges of growing older. Cardell also helps him catalogue his personal and professional papers—including twenty-five thousand letters—for eventual sale to an academic library, an enormous and painstaking five-year task.

1975   Accepts final large-scale commission, the music and scenario for a comic ballet for the Erick Hawkins Dance Company. *Parson Weems and the Cherry Tree*, based on songs from the Federal period and written for seven instruments, animates episodes from the life of George Washington, a theme long dear to Thomson. After it is given its premiere at the University of Massachusetts, Amherst, on November 1, the piece is toured extensively by the Hawkins troupe throughout America's bicentennial year.

1976   In the spring Thomson teaches a class in music journalism at the Yale School of Music, and there renews acquaintance with Donald Gallup, a soldier friend of Stein's during the war years, now curator of the Yale Collection of American Literature. In celebration of both the U.S. bicentennial and

Thomson's eightieth birthday, *The Mother of Us All* is revived by the Santa Fe Opera, Raymond Leppard, conductor, in a lavish production starring Mignon Dunn as Susan
B. Anthony and with sets and costumes by painter Robert
Indiana.

1977   Receives the Edward MacDowell Medal, a lifetime-achieve-
ment award presented annually by the MacDowell Colony.
Sells his flat at 17 quai Voltaire. Interviewed at length by
John Rockwell, music critic for *The New York Times*, for
a Virgil Thomson tribute number of *Parnassus: Poetry in
Review* (Spring/Summer 1977).

1979   Sister Ruby, age ninety-three, dies June 5. Through Donald
Gallup's initiative, the Yale School of Music Library agrees
to purchase most of Thomson's personal and professional
papers for $100,000. As a condition of the sale, Yale librar-
ians make photocopies of all of Thomson's correspondence,
which are delivered to the Chelsea in 154 archival boxes.

1980   As a present to himself for his forthcoming eighty-fifth
birthday, instigates the publication of *A Virgil Thomson
Reader*, a six-hundred-page omnibus collecting excerpts
from his seven published books, most of them long out of
print, and some twenty previously uncollected pieces, early
and late. Enlists John Rockwell to help make the selection and to write an introduction. Makes a gift of his book
manuscripts to the Rare Books and Manuscripts Library of
Columbia University.

1981   *A Virgil Thomson Reader*, published in November by
Houghton Mifflin Company, receives the year's National
Book Critics Circle Award for Criticism. Is flattered when
Anthony Tommasini, an acquaintance pursuing his doctorate in music at Boston University, chooses Thomson's
musical portraits as his dissertation topic. ("How nice to
be a subject, not a source!") Grants Tommasini many personal interviews and full access to his scores, and provides
introductions to dozens of his "sitters."

1982   In May receives honorary doctorate in music from Harvard.

1983   In December is a recipient of the Kennedy Center Honors, a lifetime-achievement award presented annually by the
John F. Kennedy Center for the Performing Arts, Washington, D.C.

1984   Bitterly disappointed when the fiftieth anniversary of *Four Saints* passes without a revival by a major opera company. A production by the Stuttgart Opera, designed and directed by the American theater artist Robert Wilson, is delayed and then postponed indefinitely.

1985   On December 7, a semistaged production of *Lord Byron*, scaled back to two acts by composer and librettist, is presented at Alice Tully Hall, Lincoln Center, by the short-lived New York Opera Repertory Theatre, Nancy Rhodes, director. Thomson is frustrated by both the stiffness of the performance and the mixed reviews. (The critic and pianist Samuel Lipman, writing in *Grand Street*, finds little fault with the Thomson-Larson opera as a work of art, and argues that its "perceived failure" stems mainly from the fact that "the courage to produce a work such as *Lord Byron* is not to be found anywhere in the land.")

1986   Impressed by the substance and style of Tommasini's dissertation and with the quality of his music reviews for the *Boston Globe*, Thomson invites him to be his authorized biographer. (*Virgil Thomson: Composer on the Aisle*, will be published by W. W. Norton eleven years later, in 1997.) Thomson grants Tommasini unlimited access to his papers and sits for countless hours of recorded interviews. When Ileene Smith of Summit Books, an imprint of Simon & Schuster, asks Thomson for a volume of selected letters, he enlists the music critic Tim Page to make the selection and do the annotation. Though Page and his wife, Vanessa Weeks Page, are credited as editors of the volume, it is very much Thomson's book: he insists on full approval over the volume's contents. Over the Pages' objections, he rewrites their annotations; he also revises the texts of his letters, sometimes altering their meaning. In November, PBS broadcasts *Virgil Thomson at 90*, a one-hour documentary by John Huszar. Maurice Grosser dies, age eighty-three, on December 22.

1987   Invited by John G. Ryden, director of Yale University Press, to write a handbook on prosody. Spends the year working on this brief book, which codifies, in twelve straightforward chapters, all that he knows about setting words to music.

1988   In June *Selected Letters of Virgil Thomson* is published by Summit Books. ("In his long life, Mr. Thomson has waged a subtle yet merciless campaign against pomposity," writes Bernard Holland in *The New York Times*. "His main virtue [as composer, critic, and correspondent] is simplicity without simplemindedness. . . . Good Americans refresh us not with profundity but with directness. Virgil Thomson is one of them.") On August 9, at a ceremony in the White House, is presented the National Medal of Arts by President Ronald Reagan. In November, upon finishing his book on prosody, his body suddenly begins to fail him.

1989   Receives constant care and attention from his personal assistant, three aides, and a night nurse. Takes up residence on his couch, and there corrects proofs of his final book, tape-records memories for Tommasini's biography, and puts his affairs in order. On September 10, *Music with Words: A Composer's View* is published by Yale University Press. Shortly thereafter Thomson retires to his bed and, calmly but firmly, begins refusing food. On the morning of September 30, dies at home, in Suite 920 of the Hotel Chelsea, at the age of ninety-two. On November 25, a memorial service partly planned by Thomson is held at the Cathedral of St. John the Divine in New York City. At his request, no eulogies are delivered; instead, his musical intimates and champions perform a program of his compositions for an audience of nearly two thousand admirers. "In between the performances," reports the *Times*, "came pithy bits of Mr. Thomson's recorded voice from documentaries made in recent years—touching, yet proudly free of the slightest hint of sentimentality." Thomson's ashes are buried in the family plot, near the bodies of his parents, in Rehoboth Cemetery, Slater, Missouri.

Note on the Texts

This volume presents a selection from the writings that Virgil Thomson published during his tenure as chief music critic and head of the music department at the *New York Herald Tribune*, a position he assumed on Thursday, October 10, 1940, when he was forty-three years old, and held through Friday, October 1, 1954, when he was fifty-seven. It contains the texts of three books—*The Musical Scene* (1945), *The Art of Judging Music* (1948), and *Music Right and Left* (1951)—that Thomson assembled mostly, though not exclusively, from his reviews and Sunday articles for the paper. It also contains those *Herald Tribune* pieces printed in the paperback omnibus *Music Reviewed 1940–1954* (1967) that Thomson had not previously collected in book form. The section titled "Other Writings" presents twenty-eight items that Thomson published between 1940 and 1954 but did not reprint in his four collections. The appendix presents, under the heading "Early Articles and Reviews," eight items that Thomson published between 1922 and 1938.

Thomson was hired at the *Herald Tribune* by Ogden Mills Reid, the paper's owner and publisher, after being recruited by Geoffrey Parsons, its lead editorial writer and the man in charge of its cultural coverage. Early in his tenure, he negotiated a regular writing routine with Reid and Parsons. During seven months of the year, October through April, he wrote two or three reviews every week. These reviews were, as a rule, written at night in his office, on the fifth floor of the Herald Tribune Building, 230 West 41st Street, between Seventh and Eighth avenues. He also wrote a longer Sunday article, usually published under the heading "Music and Musicians," which appeared weekly from September through May but only occasionally during the summer. Sunday pieces were written on Tuesdays, at home, in his apartment in the Hotel Chelsea. Summer pieces were frequently phoned in from the road to Julia Haines, his *Herald Tribune* secretary and personal typist.

Geoffrey Parsons was Thomson's boss and mentor but not his editor. After the first month, he seldom read Thomson's copy until it appeared in the paper, but then he read every word closely. Parsons drafted detailed memos to Thomson, praising the "peaches and cream" in his pieces but also detailing the "blunders." "In the early days of my reviewing," Thomson wrote in his memoirs of 1966, "Geoffrey was like a guardian angel, an athletic coach, and a parent all in one, hoping, praying, and probably believing that with constant correction and copious praise I could be kept at top form. . . . I was cautioned to watch my language, use no slang, explain everything, be persuasive. . . . 'Always attack head-on,' he said. 'Never make sideswipes and never use innuendo. As long as you observe the amenities of controversy, the very first of which is straightforward language, the paper will stand behind you.'" (For a sampling of Parsons's memos to Thomson from 1940 to 1943, see "The Art of Gentlemanly Discourse," in John Vinton, *Essays After a Dictionary: Music and Culture at the Close of Western Civilization*, Lewisburg, PA: Bucknell University Press, 1977.)

During page makeup, Thomson claimed, his copy was never cut. "Neither did it ever make the front page. I wrote in pencil [on a yellow legal pad], proofread the manuscript before sending it down [to the typesetters, on the fourth floor], preferring, should errors occur, that they be my own." After his first year, he seldom visited the fourth floor after finishing a review; instead, music editor Francis D. Perkins, who frequently worked through the night, checked proofs for him. Proofs of Sunday pieces were checked by Thomson at home, and were carried to and fro by *Herald Tribune* messenger.

During the whole of Thomson's employment by the paper, Perkins, who had joined the paper in 1919, was his closest editorial colleague and ally. With a great record of accuracy, he culled press releases for those musical events that might especially interest Thomson. He was also a prolific source of ideas for Thomson's Sunday articles. He was, above all else, an exacting researcher, fact-checker, copyeditor, and proofreader: "He allowed himself no weakness or neglect, nursemaiding and housemaiding us all, lest some misstatement or a skimpy coverage make the paper inglorious." Since 1922 Perkins had kept a catalogue, with dates and places, of all the orchestral and operatic works performed in New York City; he had kept well-indexed clipping books containing all the reviews and news relating to music that had appeared in all the New York papers during his tenure; he had also built for the music department an extensive library of reference works, largely at his own expense. He and his library were, for Thomson's purposes, the institutional memory of the New York music world. Perkins's contribution to Thomson's work at the paper, and to the pieces collected here, was significant.

The most thorough account that Thomson left of his fourteen years at the *Herald Tribune* is "The Paper," chapter 27 of his memoirs, *Virgil Thomson* (New York: Knopf, 1966). The quotations above are drawn from that chapter, which can also be found excerpted in *A Virgil Thomson Reader* (Boston: Houghton Mifflin, 1981). For personal and professional letters written during the years 1940–54, many of them occasioned by reviews and articles collected here, see Tim Page and Vanessa Weeks Page, editors, *Selected Letters of Virgil Thomson* (New York: Summit Books, 1988), pages 145–278.

The Musical Scene was compiled and edited by Virgil Thomson during the summer of 1944 and was published in hardcover by Alfred

A. Knopf, Inc., New York, in March 1945. Of the 129 articles and reviews collected there, all but one appeared in the *New York Herald Tribune* between October 11, 1940, and July 23, 1944. The exception is "Chaplin Scores," which appeared in the November 1940 number of *Modern Music*, the journal of the League of Composers. Like the Introduction, the prefatory essay, "Taste in Music," was written specially for the book, in late 1944. The Knopf rights department placed "Taste in Music" in *Town and Country* magazine, where it appeared, as "About Taste in Music There Should Be Dispute," in the number for February 1945. The first Knopf printing of *The Musical Scene* is the source of the text used here.

The Art of Judging Music was compiled and edited by Virgil Thomson during the summer of 1947 and was published in hardcover by Knopf in March 1948. All 136 of the articles and reviews collected there first appeared in the *New York Herald Tribune*, three of them in 1941, the others between November 14, 1943, and May 18, 1947. The title essay was delivered as an address in Sanders Theater, Cambridge, Massachusetts, on May 2, 1947, at the Harvard Symposium on Music Criticism. Before it was printed in *The Art of Judging Music* it appeared in *The Atlantic Monthly*, December 1947, and in Richard F. French, editor, *Music and Criticism: A Symposium* (Cambridge, MA: Harvard University Press, 1948). The first Knopf printing of *The Art of Judging Music* is the source of the text used here.

Music Right and Left was compiled and edited by Virgil Thomson during the summer of 1950 and was published in hardcover by Henry Holt & Company, New York, in March 1951. All eighty of the articles and reviews collected there first appeared in the *New York Herald Tribune* between October 8, 1947, and May 7, 1950. The Prelude was written specially for the book, in October 1950. The first Holt printing of *Music Right and Left* is the source of the text used here.

Music Reviewed 1940–1954 was compiled and edited by Virgil Thomson during the fall of 1966 and was published as a paperback original by Vintage Books, New York, in June 1967. Of the 193 articles and reviews collected in this omnibus volume, 138 had previously appeared in *The Musical Scene*, *The Art of Judging Music*, and *Music Right and Left*. The other 55, which are reprinted here, were published in the *New York Herald Tribune* between October 18, 1948, and September 14, 1954. "Bigger Than Baseball" was originally delivered as an address in the Grand Ballroom of the Waldorf-Astoria Hotel, New York, on October 18, 1953, as part of "New Patterns for Mid-Century Living," the second session of the twenty-second annual New York Herald Tribune Forum on World Affairs. The Preface was written specially for the volume, in late 1966. The second Vintage printing of *Music Reviewed*, released in November 1968 and incorporating a few corrections by the author, is the source of the text used here.

The setting texts of the four volumes listed above were part of a 1980 gift of literary manuscripts and audiotapes from Thomson to the Rare Book and Manuscript Library of Columbia University, New York. The setting texts of *The Musical Scene*, *The Art of Judging Music*, and *Music Right and Left* were created by pasting up *Herald Tribune* columns and other previously printed material. The setting text of *Music Reviewed* was created by pasting up printed pages from *The Musical Scene*, *The Art of Judging Music*, and *Music Right and Left* and previously uncollected *Herald Tribune* columns. Page proofs of all four books, with related material including some editorial correspondence, are also in the Columbia collection.

The section titled "Other Writings" presents twenty-eight items that Thomson published between 1940 and 1954 but did not reprint in his four collections of writings from that period. These items have been organized under three headings, "Uncollected Articles and Reviews," "The Music Reviewer and His Assignment," and "The Composer and His Concerns."

Under the heading "Uncollected Articles and Reviews" are printed twenty-five pieces that, with one exception, appeared in the *New York Herald Tribune* between October 15, 1940, and March 8, 1953. The exception is "Irresponsible Music-Making," which appeared as an untitled item in the "Reviews of Records" column of *The Musical Quarterly* for January 1953. "Undue Modesty" appeared in the *Herald Tribune* under the title "Modern Piano-Playing"; the title has been changed to avoid confusion with the review called "Modern Piano Playing" printed on page 634 of the present volume. Two other titles have been slightly revised for their appearance here: "High-Powered and High-Class" first appeared as "High-Powered Musical Ladies"; "The Music World Stands Still" first appeared as "The Music World Stands Still When Viewed in Perspective." With one exception, the texts are those of the original printings. The exception is "America's Musical Autonomy," which Thomson collected in *A Virgil Thomson Reader* (Boston: Houghton Mifflin, 1981), the source of the text used here.

Under the heading "The Music Reviewer and His Assignment" are printed two of several articles that Thomson wrote on this subject. "Music Coverage" appeared in the *New York Herald Tribune* of Sunday, January 6, 1946, the source of the text used here. "The Music Reviewer and His Assignment" was a talk delivered at the dinner meeting of the National Institute of Arts and Letters, New York City, on Tuesday, November 17, 1953. It was published in the annual *Proceedings of the American Academy of Arts and Letters and the National Institute of Arts and Letters* for the year 1954, the source of the text used here.

Under the heading "The Composer and His Concerns" is printed a symposium-style feature that appeared, as "Virgil Thomson Questioned by 8 Composers," in the journal *Possibilities* (New York: Wittenborn, Schultz, Inc., 1947). John Cage, the music editor of *Possibilities*, was the instigator of this interview feature: he solicited and edited the questions, and then sent them to Thomson for his written response. *Possibilities*, founded and edited by Robert Motherwell, published only one number, dated Winter 1947–48, the source of the text used here.

The appendix presents, under the heading "Early Articles and Reviews 1922–1938," eight pieces that Thomson published before he began his tenure at the *New York Herald Tribune*.

"Kusevitsky, Conductor" appeared in the *Boston Evening Transcript* on Wednesday, February 8, 1922, above the byline "Virgil Garnett Gaines Thomson." Among his earliest published works of criticism, it was one of several "letters from Paris" that Thomson wrote at the invitation of his acquaintance H. T. Parker, music editor of the *Evening Transcript*, during the academic year 1921–22, when, at the age of twenty-five, he was a student at the American Conservatory in Fontainebleau. The *Boston Evening Transcript* of February 8, 1922, is the source of the text used here.

"Jazz," which appeared in *The American Mercury* for August 1924, was Thomson's first piece written for a national magazine. Thomson collected the essay in *A Virgil Thomson Reader* (Boston: Houghton Mifflin, 1981), the source of the text used here.

"The New Musical Mountebankery" appeared in *The New Republic*, October 21, 1925, the source of the text used here. (Thomson regretted the title that *The New Republic* gave this piece. He had submitted it as "Conducting: New York's National Sport.")

"Aaron Copland" appeared in *Modern Music*, January 1932. Thomson collected the essay in *A Virgil Thomson Reader* (Boston: Houghton Mifflin, 1981), the source of the text used here.

"George Gershwin" appeared in *Modern Music*, November 1935. When Thomson collected the essay in *A Virgil Thomson Reader* (Boston: Houghton Mifflin, 1981), he significantly cut the final paragraph. (For the original *Modern Music* version of this paragraph, see the note to 976.3–6 on page 1135 of the present volume.) *A Virgil Thomson Reader* is the source of the text used here.

"The Official Stravinsky" appeared in *Modern Music*, May 1936, the source of the text used here.

"Swing Music" appeared in *Modern Music*, May 1936. Thomson collected the essay in *A Virgil Thomson Reader* (Boston: Houghton Mifflin, 1981), the source of the text used here.

"Swing Again" appeared in *Modern Music*, March 1938. Thomson collected the essay in *A Virgil Thomson Reader* (Boston: Houghton Mifflin, 1981), the source of the text used here.

This volume presents the texts of the original printings chosen for inclusion but does not attempt to reproduce nontextual features of their typographical design. Headnotes to the reviews—which, in the original printings of *The Musical Scene*, *The Art of Judging Music*, *Music Right and Left*, and the uncollected pieces gathered in "Uncollected Articles and Reviews," varied greatly in format, detail, diction, and completeness, and which, in *Music Reviewed*, were omitted altogether—have been standardized for this volume. Otherwise, the texts are presented without change, save for the correction of typographical errors. Spelling, punctuation, and capitalization are not altered, even when inconsistent or irregular. The following is a list of typographical errors corrected, cited by page and line number: 26.26, *Animal's*; 52.33, *Leonora*; 76.20, title:; 83.37, Brahms *Harold*; 88.19, Bjoerling,; 134.3, palid; 142.13 (and *passim*), Kullmann.; 147.32, fors è; 149.27, resources is; 155.1, Lehman; 155.8, Valkyrie's; 157.5, dead pan; 172.16, Mathews,; 183.14 (and *passim*), Tuminia.; 216.24, chords; 234.34, Finley J.; 241.4, Healy; 279.12, that of; 283.20 and 30, Volpe; 314.25 (and *passim*), Muench,; 325.6, whirpools; 347.3, end fun.; 357.16, *Berceuse* which; 377.36, accouterment; 386.12, leger; 386.36 (and *passim*), chords; 405.7, Alfred,; 413.1, Terese; 418.20, Mathews; 433.5, apocalypatic; 451.13 (and *passim*), Edgar; 459.21 and 35, Paginini; 460.26, Josef; 474.26, Delamarter; 474.36, Defauw previously; 483.10, entitled,; 494.8, *Language, (Technique*; 502.29, Pelléas; Etcheverry,; 502. 30, Henry; 505.24, Edouard Rambaud,; 505.28–29, American Endrèze,; 505.30, Hélène St.; 516.23, *Wozzek*,; 522.18, oratundity; 528.37, Maderno.; 534.26, Nuremburg; 541.19 (and *passim*), Hans Orff,; 546.16, Dorstal,; 546.21, Hans Keilbert,; 550.35, classes,; 551.16, past of; 581.14 (and *passim*), Shostakovitch; 583.15, colistic; 586.16, constitute; 599.2–3, material that; 603.23, layed; 613.36, remembering, the; 615.14, have; 618.22, executed) began; 627.19 (and *passim*), Moussorgsky; 639.21 (and *passim*), Nicholas; 645.8, Hunter,; 659.29 (and *passim*), Stitch; 661.10, opera; 682.17, pretentions; 685.34, precedures; 686.9 (and *passim*), Scriabine; 691.17, Stephan; 702.37, bebopers.; 708.30, Isidore; 717.4 and 39, Honass; 717.16–17, Honneger,; 723.38, William's; 735.33, jamb; 795.28, passage; 797.2, of the New; 811.32, Alban's Berg's; 824.11–12 and 28, des Près; 829.3, Appolinaire,; 840.6, Thirds) to; 855.18 (and *passim*), Ayers; 855.37, scenery) is,; 864.20, Khatchaturian.; 866.17, Aba; 885.23, Phanatasia; 890.31, envelopes; 893.4, Venitian; 895.1, composers'; 895.29, Hirsch; 901.5, died-in-the-wool; 906.9. moments; 906.38, Pfitzer's; 907.4, Vaughn; 909.26, Cartes,; 910.17, Spivakosky,; 913.22, lend; 920. 14 (and *passim*), Welitch; 924.21, Varney's; 925.35, in a terms; 933.27, Lehman; 933.39, Siefried,; 944.25, listening,; 950.28, Honneger; 951.38, out of; 951.2, Moore,.

Notes on Musicians

Composers, conductors, soloists, and their associates, 1940–1954. Comments by Virgil Thomson are from his biographical notes to American Music Since 1910 *(1971).*

Maurice Abravanel (1903–1993), Greek-born conductor. Raised and educated in Germany, he emigrated to New York to conduct French repertory for the Metropolitan Opera (1936–38). He was music director of the Utah Symphony Orchestra from 1947 to 1979.

Webster Aitken (1908–1981), American pianist. Born in Los Angeles and educated in Germany and Austria, he had his New York debut at Town Hall in 1935. He was a leading American interpreter of Schubert and Beethoven.

Maro Ajemian (1921–1978), American pianist of Armenian heritage. She was a proponent of the music of Aram Khachaturian and Alan Hovhaness and a frequent collaborator with John Cage.

Licia Albanese (b. 1913), Italian-born soprano. After six years at the Teatro Lirico, Milan, she made her American debut in 1940 as Cio-Cio San in a Metropolitan Opera production of *Madama Butterfly.* She remained with the Met for twenty-six seasons, through 1966.

Franco Alfano (1875–1954), Italian composer of orchestral music, ballets, and operas. In 1926 he completed *Turandot* at the request of the Puccini estate.

Claude Alphand (b. 1918), née Claude Raynaud, French chanteuse and guitarist. She was the wife of Hervé Alphand, French ambassador to the U.S. in the 1940s and '50s.

Louis Alter (1902–1980), American pianist, composer, and popular songwriter. In 1929 he wrote *Moonlight Serenade* for the Paul Whiteman Orchestra.

Lorenzo Alvary (1909–1996), Hungarian-born bass. He sang character roles for the Metropolitan Opera for thirty-six seasons (1942–78).

Marian Anderson (1897–1993), American contralto. When her entrance application was refused by the Philadelphia Music Academy, the Union Baptist Church of South Philadelphia underwrote private voice lessons with a good local teacher. At age twenty-eight she won a singing competition sponsored by the New York Philharmonic and made her debut with the orchestra on August 24, 1925. After a decade touring Europe and the U.S.S.R., she returned to the

U.S. in 1935. When in February 1939 the Daughters of the American Revolution refused Anderson permission to sing at Washington's Constitution Hall, Eleanor Roosevelt publicly resigned from the D.A.R. and helped arrange an Easter Sunday concert at the Lincoln Memorial that was attended by seventy thousand persons and broadcast nationally. In 1955, Anderson sang Ulrica in *Un ballo in maschera* with the Metropolitan Opera, the first African American soloist in the company's history. She gave her farewell recital at Carnegie Hall on April 18, 1965.

Bjoern Andreasson (1922–2001), German-born violinist of Swedish heritage. He performed with the New York Philharmonic from 1949 to 1987.

Ernest Ansermet (1883–1969), Swiss conductor. In 1914 he met Stravinsky, who enlisted him as a conductor for the Ballets Russes (1915–23). He was cofounder and for fifty years guiding spirit of Geneva's Orchestre de la Suisse Romande (1918–67). A frequent guest conductor with American orchestras, he was devoted to modern Russian and French composers.

George Antheil (1900–1959), American composer, pianist, engineer, and author of the memoir *Bad Boy of Music* (1945). A student of Ernest Bloch and Constantin von Sternberg, he lived and worked in Paris from 1923 to 1933. His percussive *Ballet mécanique* (1924), for six player pianos, airplane propellers, electric buzzers, and mechanical instruments of his own design, scandalized Paris in 1926. After 1936, he composed mainly for Hollywood but also wrote six symphonies and numerous chamber works. Thomson said that every Antheil piece "has delicious moments as well as pompous ones," and so the music "will not die."

Vera Appleton (b. 1918), American pianist. In 1943 she formed a piano duo with her Juilliard classmate Michael Field, a partnership that ended with Field's retirement from music in 1964.

José Ardévol (1911–1981), Spanish-born Cuban composer and conductor. A favorite of Fidel Castro, he was Cuba's national music director in 1959–65 and a composer of music for state occasions.

Claudio Arrau (1903–1991), Chilean-born pianist. A child prodigy, he was educated by the Chilean government in Berlin, where he lived from 1910 to 1940. In 1941 he immigrated to New York, where he performed and recorded Mozart's complete piano sonatas and Beethoven's piano sonatas and concertos. He was also known as an interpreter of Bach, Schumann, Schubert, Chopin, Debussy, and Liszt.

Boris Asafiev (1884–1949), Russian composer and, under the name Igor Glebov, a prolific writer of music history and criticism.

Stefan Auber (1903–1986), Austrian-born cellist. After emigrating to

America in 1938, he was a member of the Kolisch Quartet (1939–42) and then principal cellist of the Pittsburgh Symphony Orchestra (1942–65).

Louis Aubert (1877–1968), French composer, pianist, and singer. A composition student of Gabriel Fauré, he wrote ballets, symphonic poems, chamber works, and songs.

Georges Auric (1899–1983), French composer. A protégé of Erik Satie and Jean Cocteau, he was one of a group of young French composers known as Les Six. He wrote several ballets for Diaghilev's Ballets Russes, and, after 1930, scores for dozens of distinguished motion pictures, including Cocteau's *Beauty and the Beast* (1946) and *Orpheus* (1950) and John Huston's *Moulin Rouge* (1952).

Jacob Avshalomoff (1919–2013), American composer and conductor. The son of a Russian musician and his American wife, he lived in China until age eighteen. His work is informed by both Western and Oriental music.

Ann Ayars (1918–1995), American soprano and Hollywood actress. She sang with the New York City Opera in the early 1950s.

Milton Babbitt (1916–2011), American composer, mathematician, and music theorist. A student of Roger Sessions at Princeton, he joined the university's music faculty in 1938 and taught there until 1984. He took a meticulously ordered approach to twelve-tone music and serialism and was one of the first to write concert pieces for synthesizers, tape loops, and other electronica.

Salvatore Baccaloni (1900–1969), Italian bass. Excelling in comic roles, he sang with the Metropolitan Opera for twenty-two seasons (1940–62).

Ernst Bacon (1898–1990), Chicago-born composer, pianist, and conductor. A largely self-taught musician, he drew heavily on American folk songs for his chamber works and on American poetry, especially Dickinson and Whitman, for texts for his art songs. He was a professor of music at Converse College (1938–45) and Syracuse University (1945–64).

Pearl Bailey (1918–1990), American singer and entertainer. She won a Tony Award for her role as Dolly Levi in David Merrick's all-black production of *Hello, Dolly!* (1967).

Vladimir Bakaleinikoff (1885–1953), Russian-born conductor. A protégé of Fritz Reiner, he was assistant conductor of the Cincinnati Symphony (1927–37) and the Pittsburgh Symphony (1938–48) during Reiner's tenure with those orchestras. He was principal conductor of the Pittsburgh Symphony from 1948 to 1954.

Artur Balsam (1906–1994), Polish-born pianist. After studies with Artur Schnabel in Berlin, he immigrated to New York in 1932.

Although he sometimes gave solo recitals, he was chiefly an accompanist to violinists, including Yehudi Menuhin, Isaac Stern, Joseph Fuchs, and Nathan Milstein.

Carl Bamberger (1902–1987), Austrian-born conductor. A teacher at the Mannes School of Music, he was a frequent guest conductor of the New York Philharmonic, the Brooklyn Orchestra, and the New York City Opera.

Samuel Barber (1910–1981), neo-Romantic American composer. Born and raised in Pennsylvania, he entered the Curtis Institute of Music at age fourteen as a student of piano, voice, and composition. His more frequently performed concert works include two symphonies, three "Essays for Orchestra," the Adagio for Strings (1936), and *Knoxville: Summer of 1915* (1948). He also wrote ballets for Martha Graham and two operas to libretti by his lifelong companion, Gian-Carlo Menotti. Thomson said that "Barber's aesthetic position may be reactionary, but his melodic line sings and the harmony supports it."

John Barbirolli (1899–1970), English-born conductor of Italian heritage. From 1936 to 1943 he was music director of the New York Philharmonic. He then returned to England to direct the Hallé Orchestra, in Manchester, his home for the rest of his life.

Simon Barere (1896–1951), Russian pianist. After concert careers in Russia and in Europe, he became a soloist and a teacher in New York City. Known for his speed and dexterity, he was a virtuoso interpreter of Liszt, Rachmaninoff, and Balakirev. He died, aged fifty-five, after suffering a stroke while performing Grieg's Piano Concerto at Carnegie Hall.

Howard Barlow (1892–1972), American conductor and pioneer of broadcast music. He was music director of the CBS radio network (1927–43), frequent guest conductor of the New York Philharmonic (a CBS client), and conductor of NBC's *Voice of Firestone* concert music program (1943–59).

Samuel L. M. Barlow (1892–1982), American composer, pianist, and critic. Educated at Harvard and the Paris Conservatory, he wrote mainly conservative chamber pieces, none of which, in his own phrase, "would shock Papa Brahms."

Elsa Barraine (1910–1999), French composer and political activist. A student of Paul Dukas, she wrote three symphonies and the antifascist symphonic poem *Pogromes* (1939).

Henry Barraud (1900–1997), largely self-taught French composer of operas and oratorios. He was also music director of French state radio (1944–65) and a writer of books on Berlioz and the history of opera.

Lionel Barrymore (1878–1954), American actor, director, and composer. He wrote a symphony (*Partita*, 1944), several symphonic poems, many works for solo piano, and incidental music for stage, film, and radio.

Béla Bartók (1881–1945), Hungarian composer, pianist, and pioneer of ethnomusicology. While a student and teacher at the Royal Academy of Budapest he became fascinated by Hungarian and Slavic folk songs, which he spent a lifetime collecting, often in collaboration with his close friend Zoltán Kodály. Among his most important compositions are the *Mikrokosmos* for piano (1926–36), three piano concertos, six string quartets, and the popular Concerto for Orchestra (1943) commissioned by Koussevitzky. In 1940 he emigrated from Budapest to New York, where he taught at Columbia University until his death five years later.

Bob Barton (fl. 1940s?) According to Thomson, he was a jazz trombonist associated with Willie "Bunk" Johnson during Johnson's year of residence in San Francisco (1943–44). Thomson may have confused him with session player Turk Murphy (1915–1987), a navy youth who jammed with Johnson during this period.

Leon Barzin (1900–1999), Belgian-born conductor and educator. After eight years as first violist of the New York Philharmonic he founded and directed the National Orchestral Association (1930–58, 1970–76), a training orchestra for American musicians. He was also cofounder, and from 1948 to 1958 music director, of the New York City Ballet.

Yves Baudrier (1906–1988), French composer. Cofounder of a group of composers known as La Jeune France, he was a prolific writer of art songs and film scores and, from 1944, chairman of the music department of the Institute for Advanced Cinematographic Studies, Paris.

Kurt Baum (1908–1989), Czech-born tenor. For twenty-five seasons he sang German and Italian repertory with the Metropolitan Opera (1941–66). His leads included Don Alvaro in *La forzo del destino* and Radames in *Aida*.

Arnold Bax (1883–1953), English composer, poet, and writer. His work, much of it influenced by British and Irish folklore and traditional music, includes seven symphonies and a great many songs and choral works.

Thomas Beecham (1879–1961), English conductor and impresario. Born to great wealth, he studied music privately and learned the crafts of conducting and opera production with semiprofessional organizations, some of them of his own founding. In 1910–13 he conducted operas by Richard Strauss and Frederick Delius at Covent Garden and in Drury Lane, and in 1932 cofounded the London Symphony Orchestra, which he directed until 1940. During World War II he lived in the United States, first in Seattle, where he directed the symphony orchestra (1941–43), and then in New York

City, where he was guest conductor at the Philharmonic and the Metropolitan Opera. In 1946 he returned to London to found the Royal Philharmonic Orchestra, which he directed until his death. He was knighted in 1916 for his services to British music during World War I.

Bix Beiderbecke (1903–1931), American jazz cornet player. He was a star of Paul Whiteman's orchestra from 1927 until his death, at age twenty-eight, from alcohol poisoning.

Igor Belza (1904–1994), Soviet Russian composer and music historian.

Paul Ben-Haim (1897–1984), German-born composer and conductor. Born Paul Frankenburger, he was for eleven years music director of the Augsburg Symphony Orchestra. In 1932 he moved to Tel Aviv, adopted his Hebrew name, and began to write orchestral music infused with themes from Middle Eastern folk songs.

Robert Russell Bennett (1894–1981), American composer and arranger. Born in Kansas City, he wrote jazz-inflected orchestral and chamber music. He adapted the music of George Bizet's *Carmen* for Oscar Hammerstein's musical *Carmen Jones* (1943).

Mimi Benzell (1924–1970), American soprano and entertainer. She sang for four seasons with the Metropolitan Opera (1945–49) before pursuing a successful second career as Broadway actress, cabaret artist, and television quiz-show panelist.

Nicolai Berezowsky (1900–1953), Russian-born violinist and composer. He wrote four symphonies, several concertos for string instruments, and a popular children's opera based on the *Babar* books.

Arthur Berger (1912–2003), American composer, music writer, and educator. He composed chamber music, most of it modeled on Stravinsky's neoclassicism and, later, on Schoenberg's serialism. He wrote music reviews for the *Boston Evening Transcript* and the New York *Sun* before joining Thomson's music staff at the *Herald Tribune* (1946–53). He later taught music at Brandeis University and the New England Conservatory.

Joel Berglund (1903–1985), Swedish bass-baritone and longtime star of the Royal Opera, Stockholm. During World War II he lived in Chicago and then for three seasons sang German repertory with the Metropolitan Opera (1946–49).

William Bergsma (1921–1994), American composer and educator. After studies at Juilliard he taught composition at the school (1946–63) and at the University of Washington–Seattle (1963–94). His works include two symphonies, five string quartets, and an opera, *The Wife of Martin Guerre* (1955). Thomson praised his "striking melodic gift," "understatement in harmony and orchestration," and "cool mastery of the conventional techniques."

Mario Berini (1913–1993), Russian-born tenor. He sang for two seasons with the Metropolitan Opera (1946–48) and, later, with the New York City Opera.

Irving Berlin (1888–1989), Russian-born composer for Tin Pan Alley, Broadway, and Hollywood. Among his many famous popular songs are "Alexander's Ragtime Band" (1911), "God Bless America" (1918), "Blue Skies" (1927), and "White Christmas" (1942).

Pierre Bernac (1899–1979), French baritone. From 1926 he was a close associate of Francis Poulenc, who wrote many songs for him and who often accompanied him as pianist on his European and American recital tours.

Leonard Bernstein (1918–1990), American composer, conductor, and educator. Born in Lawrence, Massachusetts, he studied at Harvard and the Curtis Institute of Music. At the age of twenty-five he was appointed assistant conductor of the New York Philharmonic, making a sensational debut—as a last-minute substitute for an indisposed Bruno Walter—on November 14, 1943. In 1958 he became the first American-born music director of the Philharmonic, a position he resigned in 1969 to devote more time to composition. His immensely popular works for stage include *On the Town* (1944), *Wonderful Town* (1953), *Candide* (1956), and *West Side Story* (1957). Among his other works are a film score (*On the Waterfront*, 1954), three symphonies, and many chamber pieces and songs. Thomson found his orchestral music "derivative" but his conducting "top-flight for both concert and opera." He also found him, in his broadcast *Young People's Concerts* and his popular books, "the ideal explainer of music—past and present."

E. Power Biggs (1906–1977), British-born organist, long resident in Boston. His weekly half-hour radio concerts, broadcast by CBS from 1942 to 1958, helped popularize the modern and Baroque organ repertoires.

Rudolf Bing (1902–1997), Austrian-born opera impresario. Trained as a singer and a music historian at the University of Vienna, he worked in the business office of various Austrian music institutions. He moved to the U.K. in 1934, became a British subject in 1946, and distinguished himself as administrator of the Glyndebourne and Edinburgh festivals. In 1950 he succeeded Edward Johnson as general manager of the Metropolitan Opera, a position he held until 1972. In 1971 he was created Knight Commander of the Order of the British Empire.

Seth Bingham (1882–1972), American organist and composer. He was choirmaster at Madison Avenue Presbyterian Church, New York, from 1913 to 1951.

Jussi Björling (1911–1960), Swedish tenor. He sang Italian and French repertory with the Royal Opera, Stockholm (1930–38), and then, for fifteen nonconsecutive seasons, with the Metropolitan Opera (1938–59).

Boris Blacher (1903–1975), German composer. Born into a Russian-speaking family in China, he was educated in Berlin, which became his home for the rest of his life. A prolific writer in both classical and avant-garde forms, he composed music for traditional ensembles but also for electronic instruments and tape loops. After World War II he was director of the Music Academy of Berlin and of Berliner Rundfunk, East Germany's state radio station.

Frank Black (1894–1964), American conductor, pianist, and arranger. He was assistant music director of Toscanini's NBC Symphony Orchestra and director of its "pops" incarnation, the Frank Black Orchestra.

Marc Blitzstein (1905–1964), American composer and pianist. Born in Philadelphia, he was educated at the Curtis Institute of Music and the American Conservatory, Fontainebleau. Profoundly influenced by Brecht and Weill (whose *Threepenny Opera* he adapted for Broadway in 1954), he wrote "politically committed" operas—music, book, and lyrics—including *The Cradle Will Rock* (1937), *No for an Answer* (1941), and *Regina* (1949). He also wrote a symphony, a piano concerto, a string quartet, and many works for solo piano. Thomson praised his "strong *sens du théâtre*" and "gift for clear prosodic declamation, especially of colloquial American."

Ernest Bloch (1880–1959), Swiss-born composer and pedagogue. Educated in Brussels, Frankfurt, and Paris, he came to the United States in 1916. He held successive teaching posts in New York, Cleveland, San Francisco, and Berkeley, and his students included George Antheil, Roger Sessions, Bernard Rogers, and his daughter Suzanne Bloch. Thomson characterized his orchestral and chamber music as "romantic in feeling, classical in form."

Joseph Bloch (1917–2009), American pianist, musicologist, and educator. A teacher of piano literature at Juilliard from 1948 to 1996, his students included Van Cliburn, Emanuel Ax, Garrick Ohlsson, and Mischa Dichter.

Suzanne Bloch (1907–2002), Swiss-born lutenist, educator, and impresario. The daughter of Ernest Bloch, she was a pioneer of the early music revival. Her career was cut short in the 1950s by repetitive-stress injuries to her hands.

Paul Boepple (1896–1970), Swiss-born music historian, educator, and choral conductor. An instructor at Geneva's innovative Dalcroze School for very young musicians, he immigrated to America in 1926 to open the Dalcroze School of New York. Five years later he became assistant music director of the Dessoff Choirs, an a cappella choir founded in 1924 by the Frankfurt-born musicologist

Margarete Dessoff (1894–1944). Under his direction (1938–69) the group became not only New York's foremost proponent of early church music but also of twentieth-century choral works. The Dessoff Choirs (a core group of sixty-five choristers for the concert hall and an elite subgroup for chamber settings) presented their own programs at Town Hall and Carnegie Hall and collaborated on concerts with other New York City musical institutions.

Abba Bogin (1925–2011), American pianist, conductor, and arranger. A graduate of the Curtis Institute of Music and a protégé of Pierre Monteux, he was the longtime accompanist to cellist Janos Starker and music assistant to Frank Loesser.

Anne Bollinger (1922–1962), American soprano. A student of Rosalie Miller and Lotte Lehmann, she sang supporting roles with the Metropolitan Opera (1949–53) and the Hamburg State Opera (1956–61). She died of cancer at the age of thirty-nine.

Alexander Borovsky (1889–1968), Russian-born pianist. Winner of the Anton Rubinstein Prize (1912), he for thirty years toured America and Europe as a soloist, returning to Russia only in 1915–20. He made his U.S. debut at Carnegie Hall in 1923, and became an American citizen in 1941.

Georgette Boué. *See* Géori-Boué.

Nadia Boulanger (1887–1979), French composer, pianist, organist, and pedagogue. A teacher of composition at the American Conservatory, Fontainebleau, her students included Marc Blitzstein, Elliott Carter, Aaron Copland, David Diamond, Philip Glass, Roy Harris, Quincy Jones, Walter Piston, and Virgil Thomson.

Pierre Boulez (b. 1925), French composer, conductor, pianist, and writer. A composition student of Olivier Messiaen and René Leibowitz, he was a pioneer of serialism and electronic music. As a conductor he has specialized in interpretations of twentieth-century classics—Berg, Debussy, Schoenberg, Stravinsky—but has surprised critics with his faithful readings of Beethoven, Berlioz, Schumann, and Wagner. His American career has included tenures as guest conductor with the Cleveland Orchestra (1970–72), music director of the New York Philharmonic (1971–77), and principal guest conductor of the Chicago Symphony Orchestra (1995–present).

Roger Bourdin (1900–1973), French baritone. At the opera he excelled in comic roles, and in concert specialized in modern French songs. He often performed in joint recital with his wife, soprano Géori-Boué.

Paul Bowles (1910–1999), American composer, critic, writer, and translator. He studied composition with Aaron Copland in New York and with Nadia Boulanger in Paris. In the 1930s and '40s he wrote chamber pieces, opera scores, and incidental music for film and theater; he also wrote music criticism for Virgil Thomson at the *New York Herald Tribune*. After he moved to Tangier in 1947, his focus turned from music to literature. His dozens of books include the novel *The Sheltering Sky* (1949) and the memoir *Without Stopping* (1972).

Euday L. Bowman (1887–1949), American composer and ragtime pianist. His compositions include *Twelfth Street Rag*, named after the Kansas City red-light district where, in his twenties, he played piano in bordellos.

Alexander Brailowsky (1896–1976), Russian-born pianist who was a significant twentieth-century interpreter of Chopin.

Karin Branzell (1891–1974), Swedish contralto. After a twelve-year career in Stockholm, Berlin, and London, she sang German repertory with the Metropolitan Opera for twenty seasons (1924–44).

Frank Brieff (1912–2005), American violist and conductor. He was a member of the Guilet String Quartet (1942–50), assistant conductor of the NBC Symphony Orchestra (1940–52), and music director of the New Haven Symphony (1952–74).

Mary Martha Briney (1918–2004), American soprano, cabaret singer, and radio personality who flourished in Pittsburgh in the 1940s and '50s.

Benjamin Britten (1913–1976), English composer, conductor, and pianist. A precocious and largely self-taught musician, he was accepted at age thirteen as a pupil by composer Frank Bridge. Upon graduating from the Royal College of Music he found work at the BBC, where he wrote music for documentary films. In 1934 he met tenor Peter Pears, who became his muse, collaborator, and lifelong partner. His many operas, most of them conceived with Pears in the lead role, include *Peter Grimes* (1945), *Albert Herring* (1947), *Billy Budd* (1951), and *The Turn of the Screw* (1954). He also wrote art songs, cantatas, and orchestral works, including the *War Requiem* (1962) and *The Young Person's Guide to the Orchestra* (1946).

Anne Brown (1912–2009), American soprano. Born in Baltimore, she was the first African American singer to be admitted to Juilliard (1932). She created the role of Bess for George Gershwin's *Porgy and Bess* (1935) but had difficulty finding traditional operatic roles. In 1948 she moved to Oslo, and retired from the stage in 1955.

Merton Brown (1913–2000), American composer. A student of Carl Ruggles and Wallingford Riegger, he wrote avant-garde chamber works and music for dances by Merce Cunningham.

Lucielle Browning (1913–2011), American mezzo-soprano. Educated at Juilliard, she sang supporting roles with the Metropolitan Opera from 1936 to 1951.

John Brownlee (1900–1969), Australian-born baritone. A protégé of

Dame Nellie Melba, he enjoyed a decade-long career in Paris and London before joining the Metropolitan Opera, where he sang French and Italian repertory for nineteen seasons (1937–56). He was president of the Manhattan School of Music from 1956 until his death.

Jean Bryan (fl. 1940s), Canadian concert contralto.

John W. Bubbles (1902–1986), American vaudeville entertainer. He created the role of Sportin' Life for George Gershwin's *Porgy and Bess* (1935).

Richard Burgin (1892–1981), Polish-born violinist and conductor. He emigrated from Helsinki to Boston in 1920 at the invitation of Pierre Monteux, who appointed him concertmaster of the Boston Symphony Orchestra. In 1927, Koussevitzky named him assistant conductor of the orchestra, a position he enjoyed through 1962.

Adolf Busch (1891–1952), German-born violinist, composer, and teacher. Educated in Cologne, Bonn, and Vienna, he emigrated in 1939 from Basel to New York City, where he continued a career as a soloist and as leader of the Busch String Quartet (1919–51). In 1950 he cofounded the Marlboro School and Summer Music Festival, in Marlboro, Vermont.

Fritz Busch (1890–1951), German-born conductor and older brother of Adolf and Hermann Busch. From 1922 to 1933 he directed the Dresden State Opera. After the Nazi Party removed him from his post, he based his professional life in London. In 1945–49 he was a conductor of German repertory for the Metropolitan Opera.

Hermann Busch (1897–1975), German-born cellist. Educated in Cologne and Vienna, he emigrated in 1939 from Basel to New York City, where he had a career as a soloist and chamber musician. In 1950 he cofounded the Marlboro School and Summer Music Festival, in Marlboro, Vermont.

Paul Cabanel (1891–1958), Algerian-born bass-baritone. In 1932, after nearly two decades with provincial French companies, he became, at age forty-one, a sudden star of both the Opéra-Comique and the Paris Opéra. After his retirement from the stage in 1942, he taught voice at the Paris Conservatory.

Charles Wakefield Cadman (1881–1946), Pittsburgh-born composer and ethnomusicologist. Fascinated by the American West, he lived among the Omaha and Winnebago, collecting their songs on wax cylinders and drawing on their melodies for chamber works and art songs. In 1930 he settled in Hollywood, where he wrote music for dozens of films.

John Cage (1912–1992), American pianist, composer, writer, artist, and iconoclast. Born and raised in Los Angeles, he studied there with Schoenberg and in New York with Henry Cowell. Inspired by Cowell's technique of playing directly on the piano strings, he initiated the practice of placing objects made of metal, wood, or rubber atop the strings, thus altering their tone and pitch ("prepared piano"). In all of his work Cage's chief pursuit was to break down distinctions between "music" and "noise," "composition" and "accident," "prescription" and "indeterminacy" in service of an argument that all sound, whether composed and performed or not, is of aesthetic interest. Perhaps his most famous concert piece, *4′33″* (1952), consists of four minutes and thirty-three seconds of silence—a work that invites the listener to experience not a musical performance by a skilled executant but the ambient sounds of the performance environment, including his own breathing, coughing, and fidgeting. As music adviser to choreographer Merce Cunningham from the early 1950s until his death, Cage wrote and commissioned a remarkable catalogue of music for modern dance. Among his many books are *Silence* (1961), *Notations* (1969), and *Cage I–VI* (1990), all of which articulate his musical ideas. He also wrote "The Music," in *Virgil Thomson: His Life and Music* (1959), a monograph coauthored by Kathleen Hoover.

Charles Cambon (1892–1965), French baritone who sang lead roles at the Paris Opéra from 1930 to 1953.

Guido Cantelli (1920–1956), Italian conductor. An open critic of fascism, he narrowly survived internment in a Nazi labor camp. When Toscanini saw him on the podium at La Scala he hired him as guest conductor of the NBC Symphony Orchestra (1949–54). In 1956 he was named music director of La Scala but he died, aged thirty-six, in a plane crash en route from New York to Milan.

Arline Carmen (1920?–2012), American mezzo-soprano and associate of John Cage and Merce Cunningham.

John Alden Carpenter (1876–1951), American composer. Born and raised in Chicago, he was an executive in his father's shipping supply company until the age of fifty, his musical life lived in parallel to his professional career. His impressionistic works, informed by Satie, Debussy, and American jazz, include the ballet *Krazy Kat* (1922) and the orchestral suite *Skyscrapers* (1926).

Jack Carr (1900–1951), American singer and actor. He created the role of Jim for George Gershwin's *Porgy and Bess* (1935) and sang the role of Crown in the 1941 revival.

Elliott Carter (1908–2012), American composer. A native New Yorker, he was educated at Harvard by E. B. Hill, Walter Piston, and Gustav Holst and in Paris by Nadia Boulanger. Thomson thought his chamber music, beginning with his Piano Sonata (1945), "the most interesting being composed today by anyone anywhere. I mean intrinsically interesting, not just attractive to the ear." Carter wrote five string quartets, of which the second (1960) and third (1973) were awarded Pulitzer prizes. He wrote an opera, *What Next?* (1997), in his late eighties, and continued to compose even after his hundredth birthday.

Sara Carter (fl. 1945–60), American concert soprano.

Eleazar de Carvalho (1912–1996), Brazilian conductor and composer. Educated in Rio de Janeiro, he came to the U.S. in 1946 to study conducting with Koussevitzky at Tanglewood. After a successful debut with the Boston Symphony Orchestra, he was in demand as a guest conductor in America and in Europe. He was music director of the St. Louis Symphony (1963–68) and a teacher of music at Juilliard, Hofstra, and Yale.

Robert Casadesus (1899–1972), French pianist and composer. A protégé of Maurice Ravel, he began an international career at the age of twenty-two. From 1940 to 1945, he lived in Princeton, New Jersey, and after the war returned to Paris to direct the American Conservatory, Fontainebleau. He frequently played in joint recital with violinist Zino Francescatti or in a piano duo with his wife, Gaby Casadesus.

Pablo Casals (1876–1973), Catalan cellist and conductor. A child prodigy, he gave his first recital in Barcelona at age fourteen. He made his New York debut in 1904, the same year he formed a long-lived trio (1904–37) with pianist Alfred Cortot and violinist Jacques Thibaud. With his own earnings he founded, staffed, and directed the Orquesta Pau Casals (1919–36), Barcelona's first symphony orchestra. In 1938, in protest against the Franco regime, he moved to Prades, France, and there established the annual Prades Music Festival (1939–66). From 1950 to 1967 he made his summer home in Zermatt, Switzerland, where he conducted master classes for young musicians. His achievement as a cellist is perhaps epitomized by his interpretation of the six unaccompanied Bach cello suites, which he recorded in 1936–39.

Bruna Castagna (1905–1983), Italian mezzo-soprano. After seven years at La Scala, she joined the Metropolitan Opera, where from 1936 to 1945 she sang French and Italian repertory.

Mario Castelnuovo-Tedesco (1895–1968), Italian-born composer. A prolific writer of operas, choral music, songs, and music for guitar, he was a leading Italian composer of the interwar period. In 1939 he was called to Hollywood to write film scores for M-G-M.

Saul Caston (1901–1970), American conductor of Russian heritage. A protégé of Leopold Stokowski, he was associate conductor of the Philadelphia Orchestra (1923–45) before being named music director of the Denver Symphony Orchestra (1945–64).

Maria Cebotari (1910–1949), Romanian-born soprano. A favorite of Adolf Hitler, she sang with the Berlin State Opera (1936–46) and the Vienna State Opera (1946–48). She died, at age thirty-nine, of pancreatic cancer.

George Cehanovsky (1892–1986), Russian-born baritone. He sang German and Russian repertory with the Metropolitan Opera for forty seasons (1926–66) and then served as the Met's Russian-language coach for nine more (1975–84).

Sergiu Celibidache (1912–1996), Romanian conductor and composer. He was music director of the Berlin Philharmonic from 1945 to 1952. After short-term engagements in Stockholm, Stuttgart, and Paris, he led the Munich Philharmonic from 1979 until his death.

Theodore Chanler (1902–1961), American composer. Born in Newport, Rhode Island, he studied with Ernest Bloch and Nadia Boulanger. Thomson favorably compared his chamber music to Fauré's and called his art songs "among the finest of our time in English."

Charlie Chaplin (1889–1977), English comic actor, filmmaker, and composer. From boyhood he could improvise on piano and violin and play popular songs by ear. Later, in his music hall act, he effectively mixed music with pantomimed comedy. When silent films transitioned into talkies, he intuitively grasped the possibilities of a musical soundtrack. Beginning with *City Lights* (1931) he acted as music director of his motion pictures; for that film he improvised ideas vocally and at the piano for composer Arthur Johnston (1898–1954) and arranger Alfred Newman (1900–1970), who, under Chaplin's close supervision, executed a score in six weeks. He worked in similar fashion with other musicians on such movies as *Modern Times* (1936), *The Great Dictator* (1940), and the re-release of his 1925 film *The Gold Rush* (1942). He also cowrote several songs used in his films, including "Smile" (*Modern Times*) and "Eternally" (*Limelight*, 1952).

George Chavchavadze (1904–1962), Russian-born pianist. The son of Prince Alexander Chavchavadze, he was a student of Theodor Leschetizky from age six. Forced to leave St. Petersburg during the Revolution, the family found refuge in London, where Prince George had his debut in 1927. He died, aged fifty-seven, in an automobile accident in the French Alps.

Carlos Chávez (1899–1978), Mexican conductor and composer. As founding conductor of Mexico's National Symphony Orchestra (1928–49) and director of the National Conservatory of Music (1928–34), he had a shaping influence on modern Mexican musical life.

Raymond Chevreuille (1901–1976), Belgian composer. He wrote orchestral and chamber music in traditional forms, but as an engineer for Radio Belgium (1936–76) also experimented with electronic music and recorded tape effects.

Pietro Cimara (1887–1967), Italian conductor, pianist, and composer of art songs. A protégé of Ottorino Respighi, he worked with opera companies in Rome, Florence, Bologna, and San Francisco before joining the staff of the Metropolitan Opera, where he conducted Italian repertory from 1928 to 1957.

Willy Clément (1918–1965), French baritone. He performed throughout Europe, usually in comic roles, and sang popular songs on French national radio and television.

Olga Coelho (1909–2008), Brazilian singer, guitarist, and arranger of folk songs. Educated at the conservatory in Rio de Janeiro, she was steeped in both the European classical and South American folk traditions. A cultural ambassador of the Brazilian government, she performed extensively in the U.S. and Europe during the Cold War decades. From 1944 to 1954 she lived in Manhattan with Spanish guitarist Andrés Segovia.

Paul Collaer (1891–1989), Belgian pianist, conductor, and ethnomusicologist. Director of Flemish music for Belgian state radio (1937–53), he was the founder, in 1955, of the Center for Ethnomusicology in Tervuren, Belgium.

Eugene Conley (1908–1981), American tenor. As a contract singer for NBC, he became well-known as a soloist with the NBC Symphony Orchestra. He later sang lead roles at the New York City Opera (1945–50) and the Metropolitan Opera (1950–56).

Emil Cooper (1877–1960), Russian-born violinist and conductor. Born in Odessa, he enjoyed a twenty-year career as soloist and opera conductor throughout Russia before emigrating to America in 1924. He was a longtime member of the orchestra of the Metropolitan Opera and, from 1944 to 1950, a conductor of its French, Italian, and Russian repertory.

Aaron Copland (1900–1990), American composer, conductor, and author. A student of Rubin Goldmark and Nadia Boulanger, he was a European-style modernist in his Piano Variations (1930), Piano Sonata (1941), Piano Fantasy (1955), and *Connotations* (1962), a twelve-tone work commissioned as the first piece to be played in the Lincoln Center for the Performing Arts. He is much better known as a composer of "Americana," including the ballets *Billy the Kid* (1938), *Rodeo* (1942), and *Appalachian Spring* (1944); his *Fanfare for the Common Man* (1942); and his film scores for *Of Mice and Men* (1939), *Our Town* (1940), and *The Red Pony* (1948). His books include *What to Listen for in Music* (1939) and *The New Music: 1900–1960* (1968). His life as a composer diminished in the late 1960s with the onset of Alzheimer's disease.

Norman Cordon (1904–1964), American bass-baritone. After three years with the Chicago Opera, he sang for nine seasons with the Metropolitan Opera (1936–45).

Marilyn Cotlow (b. 1924), American soprano. Raised in Los Angeles, she sang with West Coast opera companies before moving to New York in 1946. She created the role of Lucy for Menotti's *The Telephone* (1947) and sang Philene in the Metropolitan Opera's *Mignon* (1948). After a brief European career she taught voice at the Peabody Conservatory, Baltimore.

Henry Cowell (1897–1965), American pianist, composer, writer, and ethnomusicologist. A largely self-taught musician, he is best known for his pioneering work with tone clusters, sounded on the keyboard with the forearm or fist, and with playing directly on the piano strings. In his later work he incorporated the music of Japan, Iran, India, Iceland, and other cultures into his compositions. He wrote nineteen symphonies, eighteen orchestral "Hymns and Fuguing Tunes," and dozens of chamber works, choral works, and pieces for piano. "No other composer of our time has produced a body of works so radical and so normal, so penetrating and so comprehensive," said Thomson. "To be both fecund and right is given to few." He was coauthor, with his wife, Sidney Robertson Cowell, of the pioneering study *Charles Ives and His Music* (1955).

Robert Craft (b. 1923), American conductor, writer, and close associate of Igor Stravinsky. Craft met Stravinsky in 1948, collaborating with him on several musical projects and encouraging his exploration of the twelve-tone method. From 1959 to 1969 he coauthored six discursive books with and about Stravinsky, and later edited three volumes of Stravinsky's letters.

Ruth Crawford (1901–1953), American composer and ethnomusicologist. After a nomadic childhood in the upper Midwest and Florida, she settled in Washington, D.C., where she married the musicologist Charles Seeger, father of Pete Seeger, whom she helped to raise. Her books include *Our Singing Country* (with John and Alan Lomax) and *American Folk Songs for Children*. Her "imaginative and inspired" chamber music was highly valued by Thomson, who called her string quartet "a masterpiece [of] sustained expressivity."

Paul Creston (1906–1985), New York–born composer of Sicilian heritage. Completely self-taught, he wrote six symphonies, a dozen concertos for jazz instruments, and many works for band and for solo piano. He earned his living by composing incidental music for radio, television, and film and by writing textbooks on rhythm and harmony.

Bainbridge Crist (1883–1969), American composer of art songs. Born in Indiana, he received lessons in piano, flute, voice, and composition in Boston, Paris, and London before settling in Washington,

D.C. He set texts by English and American poets, including Robert Herrick, Walter de la Mare, Rupert Brooke, and Conrad Aiken.

Clifford Curzon (1907–1982), English pianist. A student of Artur Schnabel, Wanda Landowska, and Nadia Boulanger, he made his American debut at Town Hall in 1939 and quickly established himself as a leading interpreter of Schubert, Schumann, and Brahms. He was created a Commander of the Order of the British Empire in 1977.

Ingolf Dahl (1912–1970), German-born pianist, composer, arranger, and conductor. In 1933 he emigrated from Zurich to Los Angeles, where he found work in radio, film, television, and the recording industry. He also held a long-term teaching position at the University of Southern California.

Luigi Dallapiccola (1904–1975), Italian composer. A disciple of Berg and Webern, he was the chief Italian exponent of the twelve-tone method.

Walter Damrosch (1862–1950), German-born conductor. He was conductor of German repertory for the Metropolitan Opera (1884–85, 1900–1902), music director of the New York Symphony Orchestra (1886–1900, 1902–28), and music advisor to the NBC radio network (1928–50). His personal influence with Andrew Carnegie was instrumental to the founding and building of Carnegie Hall (1891).

Suzanne Danco (1911–2000), Belgian soprano and mezzo-soprano. Educated at the Royal Conservatory, Brussels, she enjoyed a thirty-year career in opera (1940–70) with most of the major European companies. As a recitalist she was one of her century's leading interpreters of French song.

Louis D'Angelo (1888–1958), Italian-born bass-baritone. He sang supporting roles with the Metropolitan Opera for twenty-nine seasons (1917–46).

Jean-Yves Daniel-Lesur (1908–2002), French organist and composer. A cofounder of the composers' group La Jeune France, he wrote operas and ballets, orchestral and chamber music, and, most significantly, choral works, including *Le Cantique des cantiques* (*Song of Songs*, for twelve voices, 1953).

Harold Darke (1888–1976), English organist and composer. Among his works is the well-known Christmas carol "In the Bleak Midwinter" (1909), a setting of the poem by Christina Rossetti.

Howard Da Silva (1909–1986), American singer and actor. He created the roles of Larry Foreman for Marc Blitzstein's *The Cradle Will Rock* (1937) and Jud Fry for Rodgers and Hammerstein's *Oklahoma!* (1943).

Archibald T. Davison (1883–1961), American composer, conductor, musicologist, and pedagogue. Educated at Harvard, he worked for the university all his adult life, as organist and choirmaster (1910–40), director of the Harvard Glee Club (1912–33) and the Radcliffe Choral Society (1913–28), and professor of music and musicology (1917–60). A collector and champion of early music, he was co-editor of the two-volume *Historical Anthology of Music* (1946, 1950) and, from 1922, general editor of Schirmer's Concord Series of teaching scores.

Henri Deering (1895–1973), American pianist. Educated at the Paris Conservatory, he made his debut in Berlin (1922) under the auspices of his teacher Artur Schnabel. He enjoyed an international career as a solo recitalist and an accompanist to singers and string players.

Désiré Defauw (1885–1960), Belgian conductor and violinist. Educated from age seven at the Royal Conservatory, Brussels, he was a soloist and guest conductor with major European orchestras. He was founding conductor of the National Orchestra of Belgium (1937–40) and music director of the Montreal Symphony Orchestra (1941–52), the Chicago Symphony Orchestra (1943–47), and the Gary (Indiana) Symphony Orchestra (1952–58).

Eric DeLamarter (1880–1953), Chicago-based organist, conductor, critic, and teacher. He was organist of the city's Fourth Presbyterian Church (1914–36) and assistant conductor of the Chicago Symphony Orchestra (1918–36).

Marcel Delannoy (1898–1962), French composer and critic. A protégé and biographer of Arthur Honegger, his most enduring work is the opera *Le Poirier de Misère* (1927), an absurd political comedy much admired by Ravel.

Norman Dello Joio (1913–2008), American composer. The son of a church organist, he studied composition at Juilliard with Bernard Wagenaar and at Yale with Paul Hindemith. While teaching at Sarah Lawrence College (1944–50), the school, with a grant from the Whitney Foundation, produced his opera *The Triumph of Joan* (1950). In 1957 his *Meditations on Ecclesiastes*, scored for string orchestra, received the Pulitzer Prize for Music.

Jeanne Demessieux (1921–1968), French organist, pianist, and composer. At age twelve she entered the Paris Conservatory, where her teachers included Paul Dupré. She composed a small but distinguished body of chamber music, most of it for solo organ or piano, and recorded the complete organ music of César Franck.

Leonard De Paur (1914–1998), American composer and choral director. A graduate of Columbia and Juilliard, he was a composer and conductor for the Hall Johnson Choir before founding both the WPA's Federal Negro Theater Project (1936–39) and the all-black De Paur Chorus (1944–57). From 1968 he was administrator of the choral music and community outreach programs at Lincoln Center.

Vladimir Deshevov (1889–1955), Soviet composer of orchestral music and film scores. His opera *Ice and Steel* (1929) concerns the 1921 Kronstadt rebellion against the Bolsheviks.

Roger Désormière (1898–1963), French conductor. Educated at the Paris Conservatory, he was a conductor of the Swedish Ballets Suédois, Diaghilev's Ballets Russes, and the Opéra-Comique as well as music director of dozens of French films. As a guest conductor throughout Europe and America he was both a popularizer of early music and a fierce advocate for the music of his time.

Max Deutsch (1892–1982), Austrian-French composer, conductor, and impresario. A student of Schoenberg, he opened a theater, Der Jüdische Spiegel ("The Jewish Mirror"), that brought German modernism and atonal music to Paris.

David Diamond (1915–2005), American composer. Born in Rochester, New York, he studied in Cleveland, New York, and Paris with Bernard Rogers, Roger Sessions, and Nadia Boulanger. His many significant compositions include eleven symphonies, concertos for piano and for violin, ten string quartets, and dozens of other chamber works. Thomson said that "for all its seeming emotional self-indulgence, this is music of artistic integrity and real thought."

Annamary Dickey (1911–1999), American soprano and Broadway and television actress. She sang with the Metropolitan Opera for five seasons (1939–44).

Rose Dirman (1900–1975), American soprano. She was a recitalist and a frequent soloist with both the Dessoff Choirs and the Cantata Singers.

Doris Doe (1899–1985), American mezzo-soprano. She sang with the Metropolitan Opera for fifteen seasons (1932–47).

Antal Doráti (1906–1988), Hungarian-born conductor. Educated at the Academy Franz Liszt, Budapest, he was a student of Béla Bartók and Zoltán Kodály. He was a conductor of the orchestras of the Ballets Russes (1936–41) and the Ballet Theater (1941–45), founding director of the Dallas Symphony Orchestra (1945–48), and music director of the Minneapolis Symphony Orchestra (1949–60). In the 1960s he conducted abroad before returning to the U.S. to lead Washington's National Symphony Orchestra (1970–77) and the Detroit Symphony Orchestra (1977–81).

Ania Dorfmann (1899–1984), Ukranian-born pianist and pedagogue. Educated in France, she remained there after the Revolution and enjoyed a European career as recitalist and accompanist. Upon emigrating to New York in 1938, she quickly became a favorite of Toscanini, with whom she performed Beethoven's Choral Fantasy and Piano Concerto No. 1. After 1956 she taught piano at Juilliard.

Nico Dostal (1895–1981), prolific Austrian composer of church music, operettas, and film scores.

Celius Dougherty (1902–1986), American pianist and composer of art songs. A protégé of Josef Lhévinne, he was accompanist to a roster of singers including Povla Frijsh, Eva Gauthier, and Alexander Kipnis. In 1939 he formed a piano duo with Vincenz Ruzicka, a partnership that lasted until 1955.

Helen Dowdy (fl. 1930s–60s), American mezzo-soprano and actress. She created the roles of Lily and the Strawberry Woman for George Gershwin's *Porgy and Bess* (1935).

John Druary (1920–2008), American tenor. Educated at Juilliard, where he studied under Mack Harrell, he sang with the New York City Opera (1950–58). He later taught voice at the University of Houston (1959–87).

John Duke (1899–1994), American pianist and composer of art songs. A student of Artur Schnabel and Nadia Boulanger, he taught music at Smith College from 1923 to 1967.

Todd Duncan (1903–1998), American baritone. After hearing him sing with New York's all-black Aeolian Opera Company, George Gershwin invited him to create the role of Porgy in *Porgy and Bess* (1935). In 1945 he played Tonio in the City Opera's *Pagliacci*, the first integrated opera on a New York stage.

Marcel Dupré (1886–1971), French organist, pianist, and composer. He entered the Paris Conservatory at the age of eight, and toured internationally until the 1920s. He was a teacher of organ and improvisation at the Paris Conservatory (1926–54), director of the American Conservatory, Fontainebleau (1947–54), and, from 1934, organist of the Church of Saint-Sulpice, Paris.

Augustin Duques (1899–1972), French-born clarinetist. Educated at the Paris Conservatory, he moved to New York in 1921. He was first clarinetist for the New York Symphony (1922–30) and then the NBC Symphony Orchestra (1936–49). He was also, for fifty years, a member of the Goldman Band.

Maurice Duruflé (1902–1986), French organist and composer. Educated at the Paris Conservatory, he was organist at the Church of Saint-Étienne-du-Mont for more than fifty years (1929–85). His small body of distinguished compositions includes a frequently performed Requiem.

Samuel Dushkin (1891–1976), Polish-born violinist. A child prodigy, he studied in Paris with Fritz Kreisler and Leopold Auer before emigrating to the U.S. with his family in 1899. A prolific transcriber of modern music for his instrument, he was an inspiration to Igor Stravinsky, who wrote a violin concerto (1931) and the Duo Concertant (1932) for him.

Nelson Eddy (1901–1967), American baritone and film actor. A protégé of Alexander Smallens, he sang with the Philadelphia Civic

Opera from 1927 to 1931. In 1932 he signed a contract with M-G-M, for which he made eight immensely popular musicals costarring soprano Jeanette MacDonald (1935–42).

Werner von Egk (1901–1983), German conductor and composer for opera, theater, and radio. Although he accepted commissions from the Third Reich, he was not a member of the Nazi Party and in 1947 was acquitted of wartime crimes by an international tribunal. After the war he was director of the Berlin Academy of Music (1950–52) and a conductor for the Bavarian State Opera (1954–74).

Gottfried von Einem (1918–1996), Swiss-born Austrian composer for opera, ballet, and theater. He was influenced by Stravinsky, Prokofiev, and American jazz.

Hanns Eisler (1898–1962), German composer. After private studies with Schoenberg and Webern he settled in Berlin, wrote theater music for Bertolt Brecht, and joined the German Communist Party. Exiled by the Nazi Party, he lived in New York and Los Angeles for fifteen years, but in 1948 was investigated by HUAC due to his Communist allegiances. He was deported by the U.S. government to East Berlin, where he helped to found the local conservatory (now called the Hochschule für Musik Hanns Eisler) and wrote the music for the East German national anthem.

Sigrid Ekkehard (1920–1996), Swedish-born soprano. She sang with the Berlin State Opera from 1946 to 1961.

Duke Ellington (1899–1974), American pianist, composer, and bandleader. After an apprenticeship with jazz bands in Washington, D.C., he came to New York in 1923 to build, in his own words, "a large ensemble capable of bridging the musical worlds of the Cotton Club and Carnegie Hall." For fifty years he led a collective of composers, arrangers, singers, and players in the creation of what he termed not jazz or classical but "American" music. Thomson listed among Ellington's innovations "the wordless use of voice [scat singing] as a musical instrument in orchestration" and "the use of miniature concerto form in building jazz arrangements around an [improvising] soloist." His more than a thousand published compositions include *Black and Tan Fantasy* (1927), *Mood Indigo* (1930), *Black, Brown and Beige* (1943), and three "Sacred Concerts" (1965, 1968, 1973).

Mischa Elman (1891–1967), Russian-born violinist. A student of Leopold Auer at the St. Petersburg Conservatory, he emigrated from Berlin to New York in 1923. His international career as recitalist, soloist, and recording artist spanned fifty years.

Cloë Elmo (1910–1962), Italian contralto who for twenty years sang supporting roles at La Scala. She also sang for two seasons with the Metropolitan Opera (1947–49).

Ruby Elzy (1908–1943), American soprano and actress. She created the role of Serena for George Gershwin's *Porgy and Bess* (1935) and was a supporting actress in films, including *The Emperor Jones* (1933) and *Birth of the Blues* (1941).

Arthur Endrèze (1893–1975), American baritone. Born in Chicago and educated at the American Conservatory, Fontainebleau, he enjoyed a fifty-year career with the Paris Opéra and the Opéra-Comique.

Georges Enesco (1881–1955), Paris-based Romanian pianist, violinist, composer, and conductor. He entered the Vienna Conservatory at age seven and the Paris Conservatory at age fourteen. Equally adept at piano and violin, he enjoyed a long career in Europe as a solo-ist and then an international career as both soloist and conductor. His compositions, many based on Romanian folk tunes, include an opera (*Oedipe*, 1936), two Romanian Rhapsodies (1901), three symphonies, and a great deal of music for piano and strings.

Carl Engel (1883–1944), French-born music publisher and sometime composer of art songs. He immigrated to America in 1905, where, dividing his time between Boston and Washington, he held posi-tions as head music librarian of the Library of Congress (1922–34), editor of *The Musical Quarterly* (1929–42), and publisher of G. Schirmer, Inc. (1934–44).

Karl Engel (1923–2006), Swiss pianist. He was one of his generation's leading interpreters of Mozart, Beethoven, and Schumann and a favorite accompanist of German and Austrian recital singers.

Lehman Engel (1910–1982), American composer and conductor. He worked primarily with Broadway and television orchestras, and was the founder, in 1961, of the BMI/Lehman Engel Musical Theater Workshop for composers, librettists, and lyricists.

Wilfred Engelman (1905–1978), American baritone. After an appren-ticeship with the Detroit Civic Opera he sang for seven seasons with the Metropolitan Opera (1936–43).

Alberto Erede (1909–2001), Italian conductor. He enjoyed a long career in European opera and was on the music staff of the Metro-politan Opera from 1950 to 1955.

Dezso Ernster (1898–1981), Hungarian-born bass. He sang lead roles with the Metropolitan Opera for seventeen seasons (1946–63).

Henri Etcheverry (1900–1960), French bass-baritone. He sang with the Paris Opéra from 1932 to 1958.

C. Warwick Evans (1885–1974), British cellist and founder of the long-lived London String Quartet (1908–32, 1941–52).

Lillian Evanti (1890–1967), American soprano. Educated at Howard University, she sang in France and Italy throughout the 1920s and '30s and with the National Negro Opera Company (Pittsburgh, Pa.) in 1942–45.

Harry Farbman (1905–1985), American violinist. Concertmaster of the St. Louis Symphony Orchestra (1936–61), he was also founder, in 1940, of a twenty-member string orchestra, the Farber Symphonietta, that toured America for twelve summer seasons.

Marita Farell (fl. 1930–50), Czech-American soprano. She sang lead roles with the Metropolitan Opera from 1937 to 1947.

Arthur Farwell (1872–1952), idiosyncratic American composer, conductor, mathematician, and ethnomusicologist who was the mentor and champion of Roy Harris. He was fascinated with the American West, and much of his music is based on Indian chants and cowboy ballads. "The rest," said Thomson, "is French impressionism diluted."

Maurice Faure (fl. 1940s–50s), French pianist. He was accompanist to a roster of French singers and string players, including Maggie Teyte, Georges Thill, and Maurice Maréchal.

Lillian Fawcett (1912–1999), Belgian-born soprano. Long associated with the Paris and Vienna State operas, she sang with the New York City Opera in 1945–47.

Samuel Feinberg (1890–1962), Soviet pianist and composer.

Emanuel Feuermann (1902–1942), Austrian-born cellist. Educated from childhood at the Gürzenich Conservatory, Cologne, at age sixteen joined both the school's faculty and the Gürzenich Orchestra. He immigrated to New York in 1932, where he enjoyed a ten-year career as soloist and recitalist until his death, from complications following minor surgery, at age forty.

Arthur Fiedler (1894–1979), American conductor of Austrian heritage. He was principal violist of the Boston Symphony Orchestra when, in 1930, he assumed directorship of the Boston Pops. For nearly fifty summers he turned Symphony Hall into a Boston beer garden alive with Strauss waltzes and American band music. He also initiated the popular weekend Pops concerts on the Charles River Esplanade as well as a Fourth of July spectacular that has since become a national broadcast institution.

Michael Field (1915–1971), a lifelong New Yorker who, in 1943, formed a piano duo with his Juilliard classmate Vera Appleton. He abandoned music in 1964 for a successful second career as a food writer and cookbook author.

Irving Fine (1914–1962), Boston-based American composer. His career in concert music spanned neo-Romanticism, neoclassicism, and serialism.

Rudolf Firkusny (1912–1994), Czech-born pianist. Educated in Germany and Paris, his teachers included Leoš Janáček, Artur Schnabel, and Alfred Cortot. He immigrated to New York in 1939, and distinguished himself as an interpreter of Czech composers, especially Janáček, Dvořák, Smetana, and Martinů.

Edwin Fischer (1886–1960), Swiss pianist, conductor, and teacher. Based in Lucerne, he was an exemplar of the German tradition in piano literature and pedagogy.

Dwight Fiske (1892–1959), American pianist and raconteur. He recorded "party records" and worked blue on the nightclub circuit.

Gregor Fitelberg (1879–1953), Polish violinist, conductor, and composer. He was a pillar of the Warsaw Philharmonic Orchestra (1908–34) and founder of the Polish Radio Orchestra (1934–39). He lived in America during World War II, and in 1947 returned to Poland.

Jerzy Fitelberg (1903–1951), Polish-born composer. His neoclassical chamber works, especially his string quartets and violin sonatas, were widely played in postwar Europe.

Robert Fizdale (1920–1995), American pianist. While a student at Juilliard he met his life partner, Arthur Gold, with whom he formed a piano duo (1944–74) extraordinary in its devotion to contemporary composers.

Kirsten Flagstad (1895–1962), Norwegian soprano. Raised in Oslo, she sang for twenty years with Scandinavian opera companies, slowly maturing into the foremost Wagnerian soprano of her time. In 1935, at the age of forty, she made a sensational American debut at the Metropolitan Opera House and for the next six years was the company's biggest box-office draw. In 1941 she returned to Nazi-occupied Oslo at the request of her husband, a Norwegian industrialist who, after the war, was tried and posthumously convicted as a war profiteer. She returned to the European stage in 1947, and in 1951–52, amid much political controversy, again sang with the Metropolitan. In 1958 she sang Fricka in *Das Rheingold*, the first installment in Georges Solti's landmark LP series of the complete Ring Cycle.

Ella Flesch (1902–1957), Hungarian-born soprano. A distinguished singer with the Vienna and Munich opera companies, she emigrated to New York in 1939. She sang German repertory with both the Metropolitan Opera and the New York City Opera from 1944 until 1948, when an automobile accident ended her stage career.

Andor Foldes (1913–1992), Hungarian-born pianist. Educated at the Academy Franz Liszt, where his teachers included Béla Bartók and Erno Dohnányi, he toured Europe throughout the 1930s. In 1939 he immigrated to the U.S., where he became well known for his interpretations of Bartók's solo piano pieces.

Madeline Foley (1923–1982), American cellist. A protégée of Pablo Casals, she was a member of the Schneider String Quartet (1949–56) and, in 1950, a cofounder of the Marlboro School and Summer Music Festival, in Marlboro, Vermont.

Lukas Foss (1922–2009), German-born pianist, composer, and conductor. When he was fifteen his family emigrated from Paris to Philadelphia, where he attended the Curtis Institute of Music. He studied composition with Paul Hindemith at Yale and conducting with Koussevitzky and Reiner at Tanglewood. Thomson called him "a musician of perfect gifts and training, a first-class conductor, as a composer perhaps more accomplished than convincing, but highly ingenious and venturesome all the same."

Sidney Foster (1917–1977), American pianist and teacher. Known in elite piano circles as a virtuoso interpreter of Bach, Liszt, and Godowsky, he performed and recorded only rarely. He taught piano at Indiana University for nearly forty years.

Louis Fourestier (1892–1976), French conductor. A protégé of Vincent d'Indy, he was founding conductor of the Orchestre Symphonique de Paris (1928–38) and principal conductor of the Paris Opéra (1938–65). In 1946–48 he conducted French repertory for the Metropolitan Opera.

Pierre Fournier (1906–1986), French cellist. He enjoyed a robust European career as a teacher, soloist, and recitalist before touring the United States in 1948. The following year it was revealed that during the Vichy period he had taken payments from the Nazi Party and so he was banned from performing in France for a year. He relocated permanently to Switzerland though he remained a French citizen all his life.

Zino Francescatti (1902–1991), French violinist of Italian heritage. He made his American debut in 1939 and quickly established himself as a leading interpreter of the Romantic repertoire. He frequently performed and recorded with pianist Robert Casadesus.

Benno Frank (1908–1980), German-born opera impresario. He resigned as director of the Hamburg Opera House in 1933 to found an opera company in Palestine. He immigrated to New York in 1939, and was chief of the U.S. Army's music and theater operations in Europe from 1943 to 1948. For the next twenty years he was both president of the Cleveland Playhouse and director of the opera program at Karamu House, Cleveland's African American theater and arts center.

William Franklin (1906–?), American baritone. Born in Mississippi, he sang with Negro opera companies in Chicago and Pittsburgh and in recital in New York.

Vito Frazzi (1888–1975), Italian composer. A professor of music at the Florence Conservatory (1912–58), he wrote academic chamber music and, under the influence of his former student Luigi Dallapicolla, experimented with the twelve-tone method.

Povla Frijsh (1881–1960), Danish soprano. Although she sang a few operatic roles at the Danish Royal Theater, she was chiefly an interpreter of the French and English art song of her time.

Joseph Fuchs (1899–1997), American violinist. A native New Yorker, he was concertmaster of the Cleveland Orchestra for fourteen years (1926–40) before returning to Manhattan to begin a career as a soloist. With fellow-violinist William Kroll he formed the Musicians' Guild (1947–56), a chamber music ensemble that championed and commissioned new American music. He taught violin at Juilliard from 1946 to 1995.

Anis Fuleihan (1900–1970), Cypriot-born pianist, composer, and conductor. When he was fifteen his family immigrated to New York, where he made his concert debut in 1919. From 1920 to 1928 he lived in the Middle East and in Cairo, returning to America to write quantities of chamber music, most of it for piano, and to teach at Indiana University. After 1953 he conducted orchestras in Lebanon and Tunisia.

Wilhelm Furtwängler (1886–1954), German conductor and composer. For twenty-four years, from 1920 to 1944, he was at the forefront of the German concert tradition as conductor of the Berlin Philharmonic and Leipzig Gewandhus orchestras and a frequent guest conductor of the Vienna Philharmonic. Only in the last year of World War II did he flee to Switzerland, where he composed the second of three symphonies, the most enduring of his many concert works. After the war, he returned to Berlin, where an international tribunal acquitted him of collaborating with the Third Reich. In 1949 he accepted the directorship of the Chicago Symphony Orchestra, but Chicago rescinded when American public opinion proved hostile. During the postwar period he took both the Vienna and Berlin orchestras on tours throughout Western Europe. He died near Baden-Baden in 1954 at the age of sixty-seven.

Alceo Galliera (1910–1996), Italian conductor. He was resident conductor at Teatro Carlo Felice, Genoa (1957–60), music director of the Strasbourg Philharmonic (1964–72), and a frequent guest conductor of the EMI London Philharmonia and the Vienna Philharmonic.

Giulio Gari (1909–1994), Hungarian-born baritone. He performed with the New York City Opera from 1945 to 1952 and with the Metropolitan Opera from 1953 to 1961.

John Garris (1913–1949), German-born tenor. A talented pianist, he began his career in music as an accompanist to recital singers. After emigrating to New York in 1941, he sang with the Metropolitan Opera for seven seasons (1942–49). He was murdered, at age thirty-six, while touring with the Met in Atlanta.

David Garvey (1923–1995), American pianist. He was accompanist to many singers and violinists, and for forty years (1953–93) the recital partner of Leontyne Price.

Christiane Gaudel (fl. 1933–50s), French soprano. She sang with the Opéra-Comique and the Paris Opéra.

Carlton Gauld (1900–1968?), American bass-baritone. After a debut season with the Metropolitan Opera (1931–32) he sang for three years with the Opéra-Comique, Paris. He later returned to the Met (1938–39) and then sang with the New York City Opera (1944–57). After 1950 he enjoyed a successful second career as a freelance stage director.

Livingston Gearhart (1916–1996), American pianist, composer, and arranger. While a student at the American Conservatory, Fontainebleau, he formed a piano duo with his fellow-student (and, later, wife) Virginia Morley, which toured widely in 1941–54.

Géori-Boué (b. 1918), stage name of Georgette Boué, French soprano. She made her debut at the Opéra-Comique in 1939, first appeared at the Paris Opéra in 1942, and sang with both companies through the 1960s.

Arpad Gerecz (1925–1992), Hungarian-born violinist, long resident in Paris.

Teresa Gerson (1897–?), American contralto and mezzo-soprano.

Giorgio Ghedini (1892–1965), Italian composer. He was the mentor of conductor Guido Cantelli, who championed his compositions.

Dusolina Giannini (1902–1986), American soprano of Italian heritage. Her voice was trained by her father, tenor Ferruccio Giannini, founder of Philadelphia's Verdi Concert Hall (1905–29). She sang Italian repertory with the Metropolitan Opera (1935–42) and the New York City Opera (1942–43). After World War II she lived in Zurich and appeared with most of the major European companies.

Vittorio Giannini (1903–1966), American composer of Italian heritage. He wrote an opera based on Hawthorne's *Scarlet Letter* (Hamburg, 1938), for which his sister, Dusolina Giannini, created the role of Hester Prynne. He also wrote songs, choral works, and chamber music for violin.

Renée Gilly (1906–1977), French mezzo-soprano. The daughter of the Algerian tenor Dinh Gilly (Metropolitan Opera, 1909–14), she sang with the Paris Opéra in the 1930s and '40s.

Arthur Gold (1917–1990), American pianist. While a student at Juilliard he met his life partner, Robert Fizdale, with whom he formed a piano duo (1944–74) extraordinary in its devotion to contemporary composers.

Edwin Franko Goldman (1878–1956), American bandleader and composer. He was the founder, in 1911, of the Goldman Band of

New York City and composer of some 150 Sousa-style military marches, including *Chimes of Liberty* (1922) and *On the Mall* (1923).

Richard Franko Goldman (1910–1980), American bandleader and composer. Associate conductor of the Goldman Band from 1937 to 1956, he succeeded his father, Edwin Franko Goldman, as band director, a position he held until 1979.

Boris Goldowsky (1908–2001), Russian-born conductor, educator, and opera impresario. In 1930 he immigrated to the United States, where he was personal assistant to conductors Fritz Reiner (1931–36) and Artur Rodzinski (1936–42). As a teacher at the New England Conservatory, he founded the opera training school known first as the New England Opera Theater (Boston, 1945–54) and then as the Goldowsky Opera Theater (New York, 1954–84). For nearly fifty years (1943–90) he was the host of the Texaco Opera Quiz, an intermission feature of the weekly Metropolitan Opera broadcast.

Vladimir Golschmann (1893–1972), French conductor of Russian heritage. From 1919 to 1930 he organized the Concerts Golschmann, a Paris-based concert series in which a small orchestra presented new music by Prokofiev, Milhaud, Les Six, and others. In 1931 he moved to America, where he was music director of the St. Louis Symphony Orchestra for twenty-four years (1932–56).

Benny Goodman (1909–1986), American jazz clarinetist, bandleader, and composer. Born and raised in Chicago, he came to New York City in 1926 and quickly established himself as a session musician. By 1936 he had formed an interracial quartet with Teddy Wilson (piano), Gene Krupa (drums), and Lionel Hampton (vibes) that became a template for later small jazz ensembles. He also led a popular dance orchestra with arranger Fletcher Henderson. In 1938 he became the first jazz musician to play Carnegie Hall. As swing yielded to bebop, he turned away from jazz and toward the concert hall. He commissioned music for clarinet from Béla Bartók, Aaron Copland, Ingolf Dahl, Morton Gould, and others, and recorded clarinet concertos by Mozart, Weber, and Nielsen.

Eugene Goossens (1893–1962), English violinist, conductor, and composer. A protégé of Thomas Beecham, he followed Beecham to America and, through his influence, became music director of the Rochester Philharmonic Orchestra (1923–31). He later directed the Cincinnati Symphony Orchestra (1931–46) and the Sydney Symphony Orchestra (1947–56).

Igor Gorin (1904–1982), Austrian-born baritone. He immigrated to New York in 1931 and sang operetta and light classical fare for the NBC radio network. Fascinated by the American West, he moved to California to sing for television and with regional orchestras and opera companies.

Gino Gorini (1914–1989), Italian composer and pianist. A protégé of composer Gian Francesco Malipiero and pianist Vladimir Horowitz, he performed his own compositions and the Italian piano music of his time both in solo recital and in a piano duo with Sergio Lorenzi.

Morton Gould (1913–1996), American composer, conductor, and pianist. His work spanned the worlds of the symphony orchestra, the Broadway musical, and the novelty record. Thomson commented that among composers of "pop-concert" fare, "Gould is probably the one most often played by high-prestige conductors. At the same time his *American Salute* and *Cowboy Rhapsody* are virtually classical for bands and high-school orchestras, his *Interplay* and *Fall River Legend* are repertory dance works."

Percy Grainger (1882–1961), Australian-born composer, arranger, and pianist. He was a champion of the music of Edvard Grieg and a composer of songs and choral music based on traditional English folk songs.

Louis Gralitzer (1893–1977), American violinist. He was second violinist of the Galimir String Quartet and, briefly, the Guilet String Quartet.

Maria Grandi (1894–1972), Australian-born soprano who performed under a number of names, including Djemma Vécla and Margherita Grandi. She made her debut in London in 1918 and sang internationally through 1922. After a ten-year hiatus devoted to further voice training, she performed with many of the major European companies through 1952.

Martyn Green (1899–1975), English actor and singer. He was a star of the D'Oyly Carte Opera Company from 1922 to 1951.

Ferde Grofé (1892–1972), American pianist and composer. He was chief arranger for the Paul Whiteman Orchestra (1920–32) but is best remembered as composer of the pops standard *Grand Canyon Suite* (1931) and as orchestrator of Gershwin's *Rhapsody in Blue* (1924).

Paul Grümmer (1879–1965), German-born cellist. A lifelong associate of Adolf Busch, he was a founding member of the Busch String Quartet (1919–51).

Camargo Guarnieri (1907–1993), Brazilian composer and conductor. Steeped in his country's pop and folk music as well as in the European classical tradition, he was the most prolific and most characteristically Brazilian composer of the generation after Villa-Lobos. He is best known for his more than two hundred songs.

Hilde Gueden (1917–1988), Austrian soprano. She sang with most of the major companies in Europe, and was long associated with the Vienna State Opera (1947–73). Her American career included 138 appearances with the Metropolitan Opera (1951–59).

Daniel Guilet (1899–1990), Russian-born Franco-American violinist. A student of Georges Enesco and Maurice Ravel, he enjoyed a twenty-year career in Paris before emigrating to the U.S. in 1941. He was first violinist of the NBC Symphony Orchestra (1944–69) and the founder of two long-lived chamber groups, the Guilet String Quartet (1942–55) and the Beaux Arts Trio (1955–69).

Josef Haas (1879–1960), German composer and educator. A protégé of Max Reger and a devout Catholic, he excelled as a modernist composer of sacred music. After World War II he devoted himself to rebuilding the Munich Hochschule für Musik, of which he was president from 1945 until his death.

Hans Willi Haeusslein (1909–?), German pianist and vocal coach. He was accompanist to a roster of recital singers, including Heinz Rehfuss, Wilhelm Streinz, and, on occasion, Kirsten Flagstad.

Reynaldo Hahn (1874–1947), Venezuelan-born French composer, conductor, and wit. As conductor he was acclaimed for his interpretations of Mozart at the Paris Opéra. As composer he is remembered for his settings of texts by Hugo, Verlaine, and other French poets.

Alexei Haieff (1914–1994), Russian-born American composer. His orchestral and solo piano works were inspired by Stravinsky and American jazz.

William Hain (fl. 1940s), American tenor. He specialized in sacred music and was a soloist with Hugh Ross's Schola Cantorum.

Laszlo Halasz (1905–2001), Hungarian-born conductor who was founder and guiding spirit of the New York City Opera from 1943 to 1951. He was also principal conductor of the St. Louis Opera Company (1937–41) and, from 1952, a successful producer of classical recordings.

Laurent Halleux (fl. 1910s–50s), Belgian violinist and violist. He was second violinist of the Pro Arte Quartet (1912–40) and the London String Quartet (1941–52). He was also the frequent substitute for violist Denes Koromzay of the Hungarian String Quartet.

Howard Hanson (1896–1981), Nebraska-born composer and conductor of Swedish Lutheran heritage. In 1921 he won the prize in musical composition awarded by the American Academy in Rome, granting him three years of study there. In 1923 he conducted Rome's Augusteo Orchestra in the debut of his Symphony No. 1 ("Nordic"); when Kodak founder George Eastman heard this work, he appointed Hanson director of the Eastman School of Music, in Rochester, New York, a position he would hold for forty years (1924–64). "Hanson is a Romantic composer of warm heart," said Thomson, "and a master conductor." His Symphony No. 4 ("Requiem") won the Pulitzer Prize for Music in 1944.

Carter Harman (1918–2007), American composer. A student of Roger Sessions and Otto Leuning, he wrote an opera, a ballet, a symphony, and a small body of songs and electronic music before abandoning composition for a dual career as jazz critic and record producer.

Mack Harrell (1909–1960), American baritone. He sang lead roles with the Metropolitan Opera for fourteen nonconsecutive seasons (1938–58) and in the '50s also worked with the New York City Opera. As a recitalist he was perhaps the foremost American interpreter of lieder.

Johana Harris (1912–1995), Canadian pianist, composer, and collector of American folklore and folk songs. In 1936 she married composer Roy Harris, with whom she often performed in a piano duo.

Roy Harris (1898–1979), American pianist and composer. Educated in California by Arthur Farwell and in Paris by Nadia Boulanger, he was a prolific composer of orchestral and chamber music. His Symphony No. 3 (1939), commissioned by Koussevitzky, has entered the American repertory. "Harris's best works have a deeply meditative quality combined with exuberance," said Thomson, "with frequently great beauty in the texture. . . . Even without citation of folklore they breathe an American air."

Lou Harrison (1917–2003), American composer, dancer, playwright, critic, and maker of musical instruments. A student of Henry Cowell and Arnold Schoenberg, he created a list of works that is, in Thomson's description, "long and highly varied as to instrumentation and musical format." He built a "prepared clavichord" and composed music for it; he wrote pieces for all-percussion orchestra; he traveled to Indonesia to master the gamelan. "One might be tempted to consider his finest works those of East Asian inspiration (Indian, Indonesian, Korean) were it not for the works inspired by the sweetness of Elizabethan England (the Masses, the string suites) and for the warmly eloquent *Symphony on G*." Harrison edited the score and conducted the premiere of Charles Ives's Symphony No. 3 ("The Camp Meeting," 1908–10), which won for Ives the 1947 Pulitzer Prize for Music.

Margaret Harshaw (1909–1997), American mezzo-soprano. Educated in Philadelphia church choirs and at Juilliard, she sang for twenty-two seasons with the Metropolitan Opera (1942–64).

Georgette Harvey (1882–1952), American singer and actress. She created the role of Maria for George Gershwin's *Porgy and Bess* (1935).

Clifford Harvuot (1913–1990), American baritone. Taught music by school choir directors in his native Ohio, he sang supporting roles with the Metropolitan Opera for twenty-eight seasons (1947–75).

Virginia Haskins (fl. 1939–60), American soprano. After nearly a decade with the Chicago Civic Opera, she sang with the New York City Opera (1947–58) and on NBC television's *Opera Theatre* (1949–54).

Josef Matthias Hauer (1883–1953), German composer, mathematician, and music theorist. In 1940 he developed what he called "twelve-tone games" with music—this innovation independent of, and two years before, Schoenberg's first experiments with dodecaphony.

Osie Hawkins (1913–1993), American tenor. Taught music by small-city choir directors in Alabama and Georgia, he sang supporting roles with the Metropolitan Opera for twenty-five seasons (1942–67).

Thomas Hayward (1917–1995), American tenor. Taught to sing in the public schools of Kansas City, Missouri, he apprenticed with the New York City Opera (1944–46) before singing lead roles with the Metropolitan Opera (1946–60).

Jascha Heifetz (1901–1987), Russian-born violinist. A child prodigy, he was a pupil of Leopold Auer at age nine and made his Russian debut at age ten. He immigrated to America in 1917 and made his debut at Carnegie Hall in October of that year. An accomplished arranger, he made numerous transcriptions of Bach, Vivaldi, and contemporary Russian composers. As a patron of the music of his time, he commissioned violin concertos from Walton, Korngold, Castelnuovo-Tedesco, and others. He retired as a soloist in 1972.

Walter Hendl (1917–2007), American conductor, pianist, and composer. A protégé of Fritz Reiner, he was associate conductor of the New York Philharmonic (1945–49), music director of the Dallas Symphony Orchestra (1949–58), and associate conductor of the Chicago Symphony (1958–63). In 1964 he succeeded Howard Hanson as director of the Eastman School of Music.

Nicole Henriot (1925–2001), French pianist, known after 1958 as Nicole Henriot-Schweitzer. She was educated at the Paris Conservatory from the age of seven, and was a leading interpreter of the French composers for her generation. The niece of Charles Munch, she was a frequent soloist with the Boston Symphony Orchestra from 1949 to 1962.

Ralph Herbert (1909–1995), Austrian-born bass-baritone. Educated as a lawyer, he pursued music seriously only after emigrating to New York in 1940 and within ten years was a member of the New York City Opera (1951–54). He sang supporting roles with the Metropolitan Opera from 1955 to 1963.

Bernard Herrmann (1911–1975), American composer and conductor. Educated at Juilliard, he joined the music staff of CBS radio in 1934 and within five years was conductor of the CBS Symphony Orchestra. He was music director of Orson Welles's Mercury Theatre and provided the music for *Citizen Kane* and *The Magnificent Ambersons*. He later wrote scores for other distinguished films, including *The Day the Earth Stood Still*, *Vertigo*, *Psycho*, and *Taxi Driver*.

Myra Hess (1890–1965), British pianist. She made her London debut in 1907 and her New York debut in 1922. During the Blitz she organized immensely popular lunchtime recitals at the National Gallery, London, and in honor of her war efforts was created Dame Commander of the Order of the British Empire.

Kurt Hessenberg (1908–1994), German composer. He wrote neo-Romantic orchestral and chamber works and, in his cantatas, oratorios, and songs, made a significant contribution to modern Protestant sacred music.

Edward Burlingame Hill (1872–1960), Boston-based composer and educator. Thomson, who was his composition student at Harvard, called him "a sound impressionist composer, a master of orchestration, and a valued pedagogue." He wrote mainly orchestral works, including four symphonies and several suites.

Paul Hindemith (1895–1963), German-born composer and educator. He was a teacher of viola and composition at the Berlin Hochschule für Musik (1927–37) until his idiomatic music came under attack by the Nazi Party. He then taught at Yale (1940–53) and became an American citizen, but in 1953 returned to Zurich, his home for the rest of his life. Among his most frequently performed works are the symphony *Mathis der Maler* ("Matthias the Painter," 1934), the opera *Mathis der Maler* that grew out of this symphony (1938), and the *Symphonic Metamorphosis of Themes by Carl Maria von Weber* (1943). He also wrote a large body of *Gebrauchmusik*, or music to be used in a classroom setting. His influential textbooks include *Elementary Training for Musicians* (1946) and technical works on composition and harmony.

Jerome Hines (1921–2003), American bass. He sang lead roles with the Metropolitan Opera for forty-one seasons (1946–87).

Ira Hirschmann (1901–1989), American businessman and music impresario. He held executive positions at several Manhattan department stores and was vice president of marketing for Bloomingdale's during the 1940s and '50s. A talented amateur pianist who had studied with Artur Schnabel, he was founder of the New Friends of Music (1936–52) and of the pioneering classical music station WABF-FM (1946–53).

Albert Hirsh (1915–2003), American pianist. Although he made his solo recital debut at Town Hall at the age of eighteen, he usually performed as accompanist to string players, notably Emanuel Feuermann, Nathan Milstein, and Yehudi Menuhin.

Jane Hobson (1918–1984), American mezzo-soprano. Educated at

Juilliard, she made her Town Hall debut in 1946 and soon retired from the New York scene. Long resident in West Virginia, she was a frequent soloist with the Cleveland Orchestra in the 1950s and '60s.

Josef Hofmann (1876–1957), Polish-born pianist, composer, and inventor. A child prodigy, he made his European debut at age six and played a concert at the Metropolitan Opera House at age nine. He was the first faculty member hired by the Curtis Institute of Music (1924) and two years later became the school's director (1926–38). He published piano compositions under the name Michel Dvorsky, some of which became part of his recital repertoire. He left the concert stage in 1946, partly due to alcoholism, partly to focus on his second career as an inventor. He held over seventy patents for devices ranging from player-piano rolls to oil burners and windshield wipers.

Charles Holland (1910–1987), American tenor. In the 1930s and '40s he sang with the Benny Carter and Fletcher Henderson bands but found few opportunities for a black tenor on the New York concert stage. He worked in Europe in 1949–69 and resumed an American career in 1970.

Christopher Honaas (1900–1967), director of the Rollins College School of Music, Winter Park, Florida (1933–60).

Arthur Honegger (1892–1955), prolific French composer of Swiss heritage. After studies at the Paris and Zurich conservatories, he was one of a group of young French composers known as Les Six. He found notoriety with his orchestral piece *Pacific 231* (1923), an homage to the American steam locomotive. Other major works include five symphonies, the orchestral score for Abel Gance's silent film *Napoléon* (1927), and several dramatic oratorios, including *Jeanne d'Arc au Bûcher* (1934–35) and *Nicolas de Flue* (1939). A devout Catholic, he made a significant contribution to the sacred music of his time.

Willem van Hoogstraten (1884–1965), Dutch violinist and conductor. After a twenty-year career in Europe, he was music director of the New York Philharmonic's summer season at Lewisohn Stadium (1922–39) and the principal conductor of the Portland (Ore.) Symphony Orchestra (1925–38).

Ellis Horne (1909–?), American clarinetist. A pillar of the 1940s New Orleans jazz revival, he played with "Bunk" Johnson and with Lu Watters and the Yerba Buena Jazz Band.

William Horne (1914–1983), American tenor. A recitalist and soloist who worked closely with Kurt Weill, he sang with the New York City Opera in 1944–48.

Vladimir Horowitz (1903–1989), Russian-born pianist. Educated at the Kiev Conservatory, he made his Russian debut in 1921 and his

New York debut in 1928. In 1933 he married Wanda Toscanini, the daughter of Arturo Toscanini, and made New York his permanent home. He was noted for his interpretations of his fellow Russians, especially Tchaikovsky, Rachmaninoff, and Scriabin, as well as for his Chopin, Liszt, and Schumann. After a recital at Carnegie Hall on February 25, 1953, he canceled all future appearances and announced his retirement from the concert stage. He returned twelve years later, on May 9, 1965, and gave his final U.S. recital at Carnegie Hall on December 15, 1985. He then returned to Russia for a career-capping series of concerts in April 1986.

Mieczysław Horszowski (1892–1993), Polish-born pianist. In 1901, as a nine-year-old pupil of Theodor Leschetizky, he toured Europe as a child prodigy. He briefly abandoned music to study the humanities at the Sorbonne (1911–13) and then, at the urging of his frequent collaborator Pablo Casals, resumed touring Europe through 1939. In 1940 he immigrated to America, and two years later joined the staff of the Curtis Institute of Music, where he taught into his nineties. He gave his last recital on October 31, 1991, at the age of ninety-nine, at the Field Concert Hall in Philadelphia.

Helen Hosmer (1898–1989), American pianist, choral director, and music educator. She joined the staff of the Crane School of Music, Potsdam, New York, in 1922, and within eight years was the school's director. In 1931 she founded the Crane Chorus, which, until her retirement in 1966, she developed into one of America's premier collegiate choral groups.

Elsie Houston (1902–1943), Brazilian singer. In the 1920s she studied with Ninon Vallin in Buenos Aires and Paris, and in Vienna with Lotte Lehmann. In 1940 she emigrated from Rio de Janeiro to New York, where she gave recitals of European art songs, Brazilian folk songs, and Afro-Brazilian "voodoo" chants. She died at age forty, an apparent suicide.

Alan Hovhaness (1911–2000), American composer of Armenian heritage. Born in Somerville, Massachusetts, he was educated at the New England Conservatory, Boston. His spare and simple music, said Thomson, creates interest "through sheer continuity and lovely sound . . . Its variety from piece to piece is infinite."

Julius Huehn (1904–1971), American bass-baritone. Educated at the Eastman School of Music, he made his debut with the Metropolitan Opera in 1935 and later sang with the company for eleven seasons (1942–53).

Mildred Hunt-Wummer (fl. 1940s–60s), American flutist and pianist. She was one of the circle of chamber musicians who gathered around Adolf Busch, the Bach Aria Group, and the New Friends of Music.

Jacques Ibert (1890–1962), French composer and director of the French Academy in Rome (1937–60). Educated at the Paris Conservatory, he was a conservative and highly formal composer of operas and of incidental music for film and stage.

Andrew Imbrie (1921–2007), American composer of avant-garde orchestral and chamber works. He was a protégé of Roger Sessions, with whom he studied at Princeton and at the University of California–Berkeley. Thomson thought his work, like Sessions's, was "a shade hermetic [but] always well constructed."

Eugene Istomin (1925–2003), American pianist of Russian heritage. He was admitted to the Curtis Institute of Music at the age of twelve and later studied privately with Rudolf Serkin and Mieczysław Horszowski. He performed and recorded as a soloist and as a member of a long-lived trio (1961–84) with violinist Isaac Stern and cellist Leonard Rose.

Charles Ives (1874–1954), American composer. Born and raised in Danbury, Connecticut, he received lessons in piano, drums, and composition from his father, a former Union Army bandleader. Educated at Yale by Dudley Buck (organ) and Horatio Parker (composition), he wrote two symphonies while still an undergraduate. He worked for the Mutual Life Insurance Co., New York (1898–1906), before cofounding his own insurance firm, Ives & Myrick (1906–30). While pursuing a business career he composed music during evenings and weekends. Among his works, most of which were not published or performed until after 1930, the best known include the orchestral suite *Three Places in New England* (1903–29, perf. 1930), Symphony No. 3 ("The Camp Meeting," 1911, Pulitzer Prize for Music, 1947), and Piano Sonata No. 2 ("Concord, Massachusetts, 1840–60," 1911–15, perf. 1939). Thomson said that "[Ives] presents in music, as he did in life, two faces; on one side a man of noble thoughts, a brave and original genius, and on the other a homespun Yankee tinkerer. [His] vast production [is] impressive for both size and quality."

Harriet Jackson (fl. 1930s–40s), American singer and actress. A member of the chorus in the original production of Gershwin's *Porgy and Bess* (1935), she sang the role of Clara in the 1941 revival.

Frederick Jagel (1897–1982), American tenor. After an education and apprenticeship in Milan, he sang Italian repertory with the Metropolitan Opera for twenty-three seasons (1927–50).

Byron Janis (b. 1928), American pianist and composer of Russian heritage. A student of Josef Lhévinne and a protégé of Vladimir Horowitz, he has been a leading contemporary interpreter of Chopin and Rachmaninoff.

Herbert Janssen (1892–1965), German baritone. He was for fifteen years associated with the Berlin State Opera before emigrating to the United States in 1939. He then sang German repertory with the Metropolitan Opera for thirteen seasons (1939–52).

Werner Janssen (1899–1990), American conductor and composer. He established himself as a guest conductor in New York and Baltimore before founding, in Los Angeles, the Janssen Symphony Orchestra (1940–54), which recorded music for Hollywood films and for Columbia Records.

Maria Jeritza (1887–1982), Czech-born soprano. An accomplished actress as well as a singer, equally adept in German, French, and Italian repertory, she was prima donna at the Vienna State Opera (1910–21) and sang lead roles with the Metropolitan Opera (1921–32).

Raoul Jobin (1906–1974), French-Canadian tenor. After a decade on the Paris stage he joined the Metropolitan Opera, with which he sang French repertory for ten seasons (1940–50). He later performed and taught in both Paris and Montreal.

Grant Johannesen (1921–2005), American pianist. A student of Roger Sessions and Nadia Boulanger and a protégé of Robert Casadesus, he was devoted to the twentieth-century French repertory and to music by contemporary American composers.

Edward Johnson (1878–1959), Canadian-born tenor and opera impresario. Trained in Florence, he enjoyed a European career (1909–19) under the name Edorado di Giovanni. He then returned to North America, joining first the Chicago Opera (1919–22) and then the Metropolitan Opera (1922–35). In 1935 he was appointed general manager of the Met, a position he held until 1950.

Hall Johnson (1888–1970), American composer and choral director. In 1925 he founded the Hall Johnson Negro Choir, which supplied the chorus and many of the actors for Marc Connolly's Broadway hit *The Green Pastures* (1930). He also wrote the Broadway folk opera *Run, Little Chillun* (1933), the Easter cantata *Son of Man* (1946), and many standard arrangements of Negro spirituals.

Hardesty Johnson (1899–1952), American tenor. He was a frequent soloist with the New York Philharmonic and the Bach Choir of Bethlehem, and often performed in joint recital with his wife, the pianist and soprano Beverley Peck Johnson. He taught voice at Juilliard from 1940 until his death twelve years later, at age fifty-two.

Hunter Johnson (1906–1998), American composer. Educated at the Eastman School of Music, he wrote a piano concerto (Rome Prize, 1935) and several ballets for Martha Graham, including *Letter to the World* (1940) and *Deaths and Entrances* (1943).

Thor Johnson (1913–1975), American conductor. A student of Bruno

Walter and Serge Koussevitzky, he was music director of the Cincinnati Symphony Orchestra from 1947 to 1958.

Willie "Bunk" Johnson (1870?–1949), American jazz trumpeter. He played with several of the leading New Orleans bands of 1890–1915, but after years of poverty and heavy drinking gave up music for the steady life of a manual laborer. In 1942 he was lured out of retirement by independent record producer Bill Russell and for seven years toured America with his New Orleans Band.

André Jolivet (1905–1974), French composer. A student of Edgard Varèse, he was cofounder of the composers' group La Jeune France. A prolific composer in almost every musical genre, he was also music director of the Comédie Française (1943–59) and professor of composition at the Paris Conservatory (1965–70).

Maryla Jonas (1911–1959), Polish pianist. A student of Ignace Jan Paderewski, she made her concert debut at age nine. She toured Europe until, in 1939, she was detained in occupied Warsaw by a German officer who offered her "personal protection." When she refused him, he suggested she seek passage to Rio de Janeiro via the Brazilian Embassy in Berlin. This encounter, and her subsequent Brazilian exile, so unnerved her that she did not perform again until resettling in New York in 1946. Her health deteriorated throughout the 1950s and she died, at age forty-seven, in 1959.

Ifor Jones (1900–1988), Welsh conductor and organist. Educated at the Royal Academy of Music, London, he taught organ and choral music at Rutgers University and Union Theological Seminary before becoming the director of the Bach Choir of Bethlehem (1939–69).

Georges Jouatte (1892–1969), French tenor. After a youthful career as a film actor and entertainer, he sang with both the Paris Opéra and the Opéra-Comique (1932–46).

Arthur Judson (1881–1975), American music impresario. Trained as a violinist and a conductor, he was dean of music at Dennison University (1900–1907) and an editor of *Musical America* magazine (1907–15) before becoming business manager of both the Philadelphia Orchestra (1915–35) and the New York Philharmonic (1922–56). In 1916 he founded artists' management firms in Philadelphia and New York that quickly attracted many of the leading musicians of the period. In 1926 he launched Judson Radio Programs Inc. with the intention of providing live broadcasts by the New York Philharmonic for NBC. When the NBC deal faltered, he purchased New York's WOR and, with fifteen affiliated stations, launched United Independent Broadcasters, which in 1927, with investment from William Paley, became the Columbia Broadcasting System (CBS), NBC's chief rival. In 1930 he and Paley founded Columbia Concerts Inc. (now Columbia Artists Management Inc.), which by 1940 handled bookings for the majority of America's classical music talent.

Suzanne Juyol (1920–1994), French soprano. Educated at the Paris Conservatory, she made her operatic debut in 1942. She was a leading soprano at the Opéra-Comique from 1946 to 1960, and retired from the stage at age forty.

Emmerich Kálmán (1882–1953), Hungarian-born composer for the Austrian stage. Among his twenty operettas are *The Gay Hussars* (1908), *The Czardas Queen* (1915), and *The Empress Josephine* (1936).

William Kapell (1922–1953), American pianist of Russian heritage. A native New Yorker, he studied at the Philadelphia Conservatory and at Juilliard. He made his Town Hall debut in 1941 and excelled as an interpreter of modern Russian and American music. He died, aged thirty-one, in the crash of a commercial airliner just outside of San Francisco.

Herbert von Karajan (1908–1989), Austrian conductor. Educated in Vienna, he made his debut in 1927 as conductor of the Vienna Conservatory Orchestra. He joined the Nazi Party in 1933 and during World War II led the orchestras of the Aachen Theater (1935–41) and the Berlin State Opera (1938–45). The Austrian de-Nazification process banned him from the podium in 1946–47 but afterward he made a spectacular return as music director of the Vienna Symphony Orchestra (1948–55) and then the Berlin Philharmonic (1955–89). By the time he made his U.S. debut in 1955,—amid loud political protests—he had built a large American listenership through his many recordings with German orchestras on Deutsche Grammophon and with the London Philharmonia on EMI. Later American appearances included stints as guest conductor with the New York Philharmonic (1958) and the Metropolitan Opera (1967–69) and several multicity tours with the Berlin Philharmonic (1956–82).

Elly Kassman (1915–1960), Finnish-born pianist. A distinctive interpreter of modern Russian and French music, she was the daughter of the violinist Nicholas Kassman (Boston Symphony Orchestra, 1921–47) and the mother of the writer Nicholas Meyer.

Joseph Keilberth (1908–1968), German conductor, mainly of Wagnerian opera. He enjoyed a long European career and directed both the Dresden State Opera and the Dresden Philharmonic Orchestra from 1945 to 1949.

Evelyn Keller (fl. 1940s–50s), American soprano. She created the role of Monica for Menotti's *The Medium* (1946) and sang with the New York City Opera (1947–49).

Aram Khachaturian (1903–1978), Russian composer of Armenian heritage. His "Sabre Dance," from the final movement of the ballet

Gayane (1942), is one of the most popular pieces in the modern repertory.

Boris Khaikin (1904–1978), Russian conductor and opera impresario. He directed operas in Leningrad, St. Petersburg, and Moscow, and produced the premiere of Prokofiev's *Betrothal in a Monastery* at the Kirov Theater in 1946.

Tikhon Khrennikov (1913–2007), Russian pianist, composer, and, from 1948 to 1991, General Secretary of the Union of Soviet Composers.

William Kincaid (1895–1967), principal flutist of the Philadelphia Orchestra from 1921 to 1960.

Philip Kinsman (1922–?), American bass. After four seasons with the Metropolitan Opera (1946–50) he returned to his native Chicago to found a chain of inexpensive restaurants.

Alexander Kipnis (1891–1978), Russian-born bass. He enjoyed a career with several German and Austrian opera companies, and nine seasons with the Chicago Opera (1923–32), before emigrating to America in 1938. He was a lead Wagnerian bass with the Metropolitan for six seasons (1940–46) and retired from the stage in 1951.

John Kirkpatrick (1905–1991), American pianist. After studies in Paris with Nadia Boulanger, he devoted himself to the work of American composers, especially such contemporaries as Copland, Ruggles, and, most significantly, Charles Ives. In 1939 he gave Ives's "Concord" Sonata its premiere at Town Hall, making both his and the composer's reputation. In 1954 he became curator of the Charles Ives Archives at Yale, where he catalogued, edited, and published Ives's posthumous writings and scores.

Ralph Kirkpatrick (1911–1984), American harpsichordist and musicologist. Educated at Harvard, he was a student of Wanda Landowska and Nadia Boulanger. As a recitalist and soloist he did much to increase American appreciation of the Baroque harpsichord repertoire. As a scholar, especially during his years at the Yale School of Music (1940–76), he published new editions of Bach's "Goldberg Variations" and the sonatas of Domenico Scarlatti. He was also an advocate of modern music and gave premieres of pieces by Stravinsky, Cowell, and Elliott Carter.

Dorothy Kirsten (1910–1992), American soprano. She began as a singer of pop and light classical standards, but in 1938, with encouragement and guidance from Met soprano Grace Moore, she began to sing opera. For three seasons she was a member of the Philadelphia La Scala Opera Company, and then she joined the Metropolitan Opera, her home for the next thirty-four years (1945–79).

Fritz Kitzinger (1891–1947), German-born pianist and voice teacher. He accompanied a roster of recital singers, including Ezio Pinza and Grace Moore, and, after 1940, often perfomed in a piano duo with his wife, Adele Marcus (1906–1975).

Lev Knipper (1898–1974), prolific Soviet composer of operas, including *Tales of a Plaster Buddha* (1924) and *North Wind* (1930). His most widely known work is the Soviet marching song *Polyuska Polye* ("Meadowlands," 1933).

Zoltán Kodály (1882–1967), Hungarian composer and music educator. While a teacher at Budapest's Hochschule für Musik he became fascinated with Hungarian and Slavic folk songs, which he spent a lifetime collecting, often in collaboration with his close friend Béla Bartók. He did much to improve childhood music education in Hungary, developing with his Hochschule staff an eclectic set of pedagogical techniques now known as the Kodály Method. His compositions include the folk opera *Háry János* (1926) and a *Missa Brevis* (1945) for chorus and orchestra.

Rudolf Kolisch (1896–1978), Austrian-born violinist. The brother-in-law of Arnold Schoenberg, he founded the Kolisch String Quartet (1926–40) expressly to play his music and that of other contemporary composers. During World War II he went to the United States, where, in 1944, he founded the Pro Arte String Quartet of the University of Wisconsin–Madison.

Hilde Konetzni (1905–1980), Viennese soprano. Long a member of the Vienna State Opera, she sang the German repertory, and especially Wagner and Richard Strauss, throughout Europe from 1929 through the 1970s.

André Kostelanetz (1901–1980) Russian-born conductor and arranger. He immigrated to the U.S. in 1922 and by the early 1930s was leading the CBS Symphony Orchestra in his own "easy-listening" arrangements of classical and pop standards. From 1939 to 1979 he frequently conducted the New York Philharmonic in its summer series.

Serge Koussevitzky (1874–1951), Russian-born conductor, composer, and double bassist. The child of musicians, he received most of his musical education at home. By age twenty he was principal bassist for the Bolshoi Theater Orchestra, Moscow, and by thirty had moved to Berlin to study conducting with Arthur Nikisch of the Berlin Philharmonic. By 1910, he and his wealthy second wife had founded an orchestra (1910–19) and a summer concert series, the Concerts Koussevitzky, which was based first in Moscow and Petrograd (1910–19) and then in Berlin and Paris (1920–29). In 1924 he was appointed music director of the Boston Symphony Orchestra, a position he held for twenty-five years, until 1949. In the late 1930s he helped found the BSO's Tanglewood summer concerts and music center in western Massachusetts, and in 1942 created the Koussevitzky Music Foundation, which commissions new works by American composers.

Boris Koutzen (1901–1966), Russian-born violinist and composer. He was a member of the Moscow Symphony Orchestra (c. 1920–22), the Philadelphia Orchestra (1923–37), and the NBC Symphony Orchestra (1937–45). He wrote concertos and chamber works for pianos and strings, including two string quartets and a popular Sonatina for Two Pianos (1944).

Marion Koval (1907–1971), Soviet composer of operas and oratorios and, in 1948–52, editor of the journal *Sovietskaya Muzyka.*

Edwin Arthur Kraft (1883–1962), American organist and choral director. From 1907 to 1959 he was organist of Trinity Cathedral (Episcopal), Cleveland, Ohio.

Fritz Kreisler (1875–1962), Austrian-born violinist. A child prodigy, he made his professional debut at age nine and his American debut at age fourteen. After studies in Vienna and Paris, he enjoyed an international career as a soloist until the beginning of World War II, when he emigrated from Paris to New York, becoming a U.S. citizen in 1943. His compositions include the operettas *Apple Blossoms* (1919) and *Sissy* (1933) and several pieces for violin and piano that are now part of the standard recital repertory.

Ernst Křenek (1900–1991), Austrian-born composer of Czech heritage. He had a great success at age twenty-five with *Jonny Spielt Auf* ("Johnny Strikes Up the Band," 1925), an expressionistic opera whose protagonist is a black jazz violinist. In 1938 he moved to the U.S., where he moved with ease from one compositional style to the next: late Romanticism, atonality, neoclassicism, electronic music, and Cage-like experiments with the aleatory.

Mary Kreste (1911–1995), American contralto and mezzo-soprano. She sang with the New York City Opera from 1947 to 1953.

William Kroll (1901–1980), American violinist and composer. With fellow-violinist Joseph Fuchs he formed the Musicians' Guild (1947–56), a chamber music ensemble that commissioned and championed music of their time.

Boris Kroyt (1897–1969), Russian-born violist. After a long association with the Berlin Philharmonic, he fled Nazi Germany to join the New York–based Budapest String Quartet (1936–67).

Karl Krueger (1894–1979), American conductor of German heritage. After four years at the New England Conservatory, he, at his father's insistence, studied law and economics in Vienna. He abandoned his studies there to become a pupil of conductor Arthur Nikisch, who later placed him as an assistant conductor of both the Vienna State Opera and the Vienna Philharmonic. In 1926 he moved back to the U.S., where he led the Seattle Symphony Orchestra (1926–32), the fledgling Kansas City Philharmonic (1932–43), and the Detroit Symphony Orchestra (1943–49). He later founded the label New Records Inc., which produced recordings of American music.

Gene Krupa (1909–1973), Chicago-born jazz drummer. In 1934 he joined Benny Goodman's band and became a national celebrity, noted for his extroverted personality and powerfully athletic playing.

Charles Kullman (1903–1983), American tenor of German heritage. Educated at Yale and Juilliard, he sang for four years with the Berlin State Opera before becoming a lead tenor with the Metropolitan Opera (1935–60).

Meyer Kupferman (1926–2003), American composer and clarinetist. A self-taught musician, he wrote neoclassical chamber pieces and idiosyncratic "atonal jazz." He was a professor of music at Sarah Lawrence College from 1951 to 1994.

Efrem Kurtz (1900–1995), Russian-born conductor. Educated in St. Petersburg, he conducted orchestras in Berlin, Stuttgart, and Monte Carlo before emigrating to the U.S. in 1942. He was music director of the Kansas City Philharmonic (1943–48) and the Houston Symphony (1948–54).

Andzia Kuzak (b. 1921), Polish-born soprano. A native of Chicago, she sang with the city's Civic Opera and on WGN radio's *Chicago Theatre of the Air* (1942–48). She then moved to New York, where she worked mainly as a recitalist and soloist through the late 1950s.

Joseph Laderoute (1913–1979), French-Canadian tenor. A devout Catholic, he sang opera with regional companies throughout North America but preferred to work as a soloist in sacred settings. In 1952 he abandoned music for life in a Benedictine monastery.

Lenora Lafayette (1926–1975), American soprano. After studies at Fisk University and Juilliard, she enjoyed an operatic career in Europe. In 1958 she sang Verdi's Aida at the Royal Opera House, Covent Garden.

Hugh Lamb (1890–1959), American organist, composer, and clergyman, who, after 1951, was the Roman Catholic Bishop of Greenburg (western Pennsylvania).

Constant Lambert (1905–1951), British composer, conductor, writer, and wit. A protégé of Ralph Vaughan Williams, he wrote a ballet for Diaghilev at age twenty and his most famous concert piece, *The Rio Grande*, at age twenty-two. He was later celebrated as a guest conductor at Covent Garden and the Royal Ballet, and as the author of *Music Ho! A Study of Music in Decline* (1934).

Wanda Landowska (1879–1959), Polish-born harpsichordist and pianist. After piano studies at the Warsaw Conservatory, she settled in Paris in 1900. Fascinated since her teens by the harpsichord music of Bach, Handel, Couperin, Scarlatti, and Rameau, she in 1912 commissioned Pleyel, the French piano manufacturer, to build her a harpsichord that was close in timbre to the instrument Bach used but that could also be heard in a modern concert hall. On this instrument she developed a recital repertoire that, after 1923, became a force in the international revival of early music. She also commissioned new music for her instrument from Poulenc and de Falla and composed her own cadenzas to Mozart's concertos.

Gloria Lane (b. 1930), American mezzo-soprano who created the role of Secretary of the Consulate for Menotti's *The Consul* (1949). From 1952 to 1961 she sang with the New York City Opera and on NBC television's *Opera Theatre*.

Hans Lange (1884–1960), Turkish-born violinist and conductor. He was assistant conductor of the New York Philharmonic (1927–36) and the Chicago Symphony (1936–43), principal conductor of the Chicago Symphony (1943–46), and founding director of the New Mexico Symphony Orchestra (1950–60).

Lucien K. Laporte (1900–1991), Belgian-born cellist. He played with the NBC and CBS orchestras before becoming a founding member of the Guilet String Quartet (1942–55) and the New World String Quartet (1956–60).

Joseph Lautner (1899–?), American tenor. He was a recent Harvard graduate and private voice teacher in Boston when, in May 1923, he, with Thomson at the piano, gave the American premiere of Satie's *Socrate* at a concert of the Harvard Musical Club. He had a long career as a soloist and as director of the Westminster Choir of Princeton, New Jersey.

Marjorie Lawrence (1907–1979), Australian soprano who sang Wagnerian roles with the Metropolitan Opera in 1936–41. Her autobiography, *Interrupted Melody* (1949), is an account of her slow recovery from poliomyelitis, which nearly ended her stage career in 1941.

Robert Lawrence (1912–1981), American conductor and music journalist. He was a member of the music staff of the *New York Herald Tribune* (1939–44) when Thomson arrived in 1940, and, after World War II, a freelance conductor specializing in French opera, especially Massenet and Berlioz.

Edward Lawton (1911–1967), American organist, bass, and choral conductor. After study at Harvard and with Malipiero in Venice, he for twenty-four years directed the chorus of the University of California–Berkeley (1939–63).

Denoe Leedy (1900–1964), American pianist and pedagogue. A professor of music at Mount Holyoke College (1937–64), he was for thirty years a fixture of the Boston concert scene.

Yvonne Léfébure (1898–1986), French pianist. A protégée of Alfred Cortot, she was a favorite soloist of conductors Pablo Casals and Wilhelm Furtwängler. She excelled in the modern French repertory, especially Ravel and Fauré.

Lotte Lehmann (1888–1976), German-born soprano. In 1916 she joined the Vienna State Opera, where, as prima donna for twenty-one years, she distinguished herself as an interpreter of Mozart, Puccini, and, especially, Richard Strauss. In 1937 she moved to New York, where she sang with the Metropolitan Opera from 1938 to 1945. As a recitalist she was one of her century's foremost interpreters of lieder.

René Leibowitz (1913–1972), Polish-born composer and conductor. After studies with Anton Webern, he became a leading French exponent of the twelve-tone method, which he analyzed in his influential book *Schoenberg et son ecole* ("Schoenberg and His School," 1947). He was a mentor to Pierre Boulez, his pupil in both composition and conducting.

Erich Leinsdorf (1912–1993), Austrian-born conductor. He was assistant to both Bruno Walter and Arturo Toscanini before he became head of German repertory at the Metropolitan Opera (1938–43). He was later music director of the Rochester Philharmonic (1947–55), the New York City Opera (1956–58), and the Boston Symphony Orchestra (1962–69) as well as a frequent conductor of the Metropolitan Opera (1957–83).

René Le Roy (1898–1985), French flutist and teacher. He toured internationally as a soloist and as a member of the Paris Instrumental Quintet (1922–45). He was also director of the Paris Society of Wind Instruments (1918–28) and, after 1971, a teacher at the Paris Conservatory.

Harold Alexander Leslie (1911–1955), American violinist and conductor. A protégé of Serge Koussevitzky, he was founder of the Pioneer Valley Youth Orchestra (Greenfield, Mass., 1939), the Pioneer Valley Symphony (Greenfield, 1940), and the Springfield (Mass.) Symphony Orchestra (1944).

Oscar Levant (1906–1972), American pianist, composer, writer, and entertainer. A Hollywood friend of George Gershwin, he later became one of Gershwin's foremost interpreters. A pupil of Schoenberg and Joseph Schillinger, he was a composer of difficult modern piano music but also wrote popular songs, including the standard "Blame It on My Youth" (1934). He was a comic entertainer on radio and television; a supporting actor in films, including *Rhapsody in Blue* (1945), *An American in Paris* (1951), and *The Band Wagon* (1953); and the best-selling author of the memoir *A Smattering of Ignorance* (1940).

Brenda Lewis (b. 1921), American soprano. She was a member of the New York City Opera from 1944 to 1964 and a frequent guest performer with the Metropolitan Opera from 1952 to 1965. In 1949 she created the role of Birdie for Marc Blitzstein's *Regina*.

Josef Lhévinne (1874–1944), Russian-born pianist. He studied at the Imperial Conservatory, Moscow, and there met his wife, Rosina (née Bessie) Lhévinne (1880–1976), with whom he would perform in a piano duo until 1942. The Lhévinnes opened a music studio in Berlin (1907–19) and, after emigrating to New York in 1922, continued their teaching at the Juilliard School. As a soloist and recitalist, Lhévinne was a leading interpreter of the Romantics, especially Chopin and Tchaikovsky. His *Principles in Pianoforte Playing* (1924) is a pedagogical classic.

William Lincer (1907–1997), principal violist of the Cleveland Orchestra (1941–43) and then, for nearly thirty years, of the New York Philharmonic (1943–72).

Ann Lipton (b. 1923), American soprano. She played Gabrielle in the Broadway version of Offenbach's *Vie Parisienne* (1941).

Emanuel List (1888–1967), Austrian-born bass. After a career in Berlin and London, he joined the Metropolitan Opera, where he distinguished himself in Wagnerian roles from 1933 to 1950.

Kurt List (1913–1970), Austrian-born composer, conductor, critic, and record producer.

Genrikh Litinsky (1901–1985), Russian violinist and composer. He wrote chamber music for strings, much of it based on folk tunes from his native Turkmenistan.

Tamara Livanova (1909–1986), Soviet composer and professor of music history at the University of Moscow.

George London (1920–1985), Canadian bass-baritone of Russian heritage. He sang mainly German repertory with the Metropolitan Opera for fifteen seasons (1951–66).

Avon Long (1910–1984), American singer, actor, and entertainer. He sang the role of Sportin' Life in the 1941 revival of Gershwin's *Porgy and Bess*.

Nikolai Lopatnikoff (1903–1976), Russian-born pianist and composer. Educated in Germany, he immigrated to the U.S. in 1941, becoming a professor of music at Carnegie Mellon Institute (1946–72) and a pillar of Pittsburgh's music community. Among his works are an opera (*Danton*, 1932), four symphonies, two piano concertos, and many pieces for solo piano.

Max Lorenz (1901–1970), German tenor. A favorite of Adolf Hitler, he sang lead roles for the Berlin State Opera and the Vienna State Opera from 1927 to 1954. From 1931 to 1949 he made fifty appearances with the Metropolitan Opera.

Estelle Loring (1925–2005), American soprano. After a decade-long career as a singer and actress on Broadway (1945–55), she reclaimed her birth name, Estelle Weinrib, and became a Jungian analyst.

Pierre Luboshutz (1891–1971), Russian-born pianist who, from 1937 to 1962, performed in a piano duo with his wife, Genia Nemenoff.

Otto Luening (1900–1996), American conductor and composer of German heritage. Born in Milwaukee and educated in Munich and Zurich, he at last settled in New York, where he conducted the premieres of Menotti's *The Medium* (1946) and Thomson's *The Mother of Us All* (1947). His compositions include an opera (*Evangeline*, 1948), some electronic music, and many art songs.

Boris Lyatoshinsky (1895–1968), Ukrainian pianist, composer, and conductor. His works include three operas, five symphonies, five string quartets, and many pieces for solo piano.

Werner Lywen (1909–2002), German-born violinist. He was concertmaster of the New York City Symphony, the Radio City Orchestra, and, for twenty years, the National Symphony Orchestra in Washington, D.C.

Jeanette MacDonald (1903–1965), American singer and actress. She was a Broadway chorus girl when, in 1929, she was cast in *The Love Parade*, the first of her twenty-nine movie musicals. In 1933 she signed a contract with M-G-M, for which she made eight immensely popular films costarring baritone Nelson Eddy (1935–42). After a year of lessons with Lotte Lehmann, she performed opera in Chicago, Cincinnati, Philadelphia, and Canada (1944–51). She retired from the stage in 1959.

Virginia MacWatters (1912–2005), American soprano. She enjoyed a twenty-year career as Broadway actress, concert soloist, and guest singer with American and London opera companies. From 1953 to 1959 she made thirteen appearances with the Metropolitan Opera in her signature role of Adele in *Die Fledermaus*. After 1957 she was artist-in-residence at Indiana University.

Bruno Maderna (1920–1973), Italian composer and conductor. In 1943–44 he studied with Gian Francesco Malipiero, who invited him to join the faculty of the Venice Conservatory. In 1963 he became a citizen of West Germany, where, as a proponent of the twelve-tone system, he presented programs of works by Schoenberg, Berg, and Stockhausen.

Fernand Maillet (1896–1963), French Roman Catholic priest and choir director. From 1924 to 1963 he led the Little Singers of Paris, an a cappella boys' choir founded in 1906, and in 1951 organized Pueri Cantores, the international organization of Roman Catholic children's choirs.

Gian Francesco Malipiero (1882–1973), Italian composer and music scholar. Largely self-taught, he studied composition by copying original manuscripts by Monteverdi at the Biblioteca Marciana, Venice. After lessons with Enrico Bossi, he taught composition in Parma, Padua, and Venice and embarked upon a sixteen-volume edition of Monteverdi's scores, published in 1926–42. As a composer he rejected the Austro-German tradition, embraced the music of the Italian Baroque, and paid close attention to modern French work. Among his works are seventeen symphonies, the opera *L'Orfeide*, and the string quartet *Rispetti e Strambotti*.

Leopold Mannes (1899–1964), Armenian-born pianist and inventor. The son of the founders of the Mannes School of Music, he studied piano from early youth but also nurtured a passion for science. From 1917 to 1934 he and the chemist Leopold Godowsky Jr. developed a new kind of color transparency that, with backing from Eastman Kodak, was perfected and marketed as Kodachrome (1935). After 1940 Mannes returned to music, both as president of the Mannes School of Music and as a solo pianist and accompanist.

Sylvia Marlowe (1908–1981), American harpsichordist. She performed the standard Baroque repertory but also, through her nonprofit Harpsichord Music Society (founded 1951), commissioned new work for the instrument from Elliott Carter, Alan Hovhaness, Henri Sauguet, and others.

Lois Marshall (1924–1997), Canadian soprano and mezzo-soprano. Though childhood polio restricted her mobility and kept her from the opera stage, she performed widely as a soloist, recitalist, and recording artist, often accompanied by her husband, pianist Weldon Kilburn.

Robert Marshall (fl. 1940s), American tenor of Italian heritage. He was a soloist with the Choral Ensemble of Radio City Music Hall.

Fernand Martel (1919–1995), Canadian-born bass. He made his debut at the New York City Opera in 1948 and sang with several North American companies through 1955. He then moved to Long Beach, California, where he performed locally in nightclubs, accompanying himself on the Hammond B3 organ.

Frank Martin (1890–1974), Swiss composer. Among his highly idiosyncratic works are the Petite Symphonie Concertante (1944) for harp, harpsichord, piano, and string orchestra; *Polyptique* (1973) for violin and two string orchestras; and *Golgotha* (1945–48), an oratorio for five voices, chorus, organ, and orchestra.

Wolfgang Martin (1899–1970), German-born conductor. He worked with theater and opera orchestras in Europe and the United States for twenty-eight years before becoming assistant director of German repertory for the Metropolitan Opera (1946–48). He then directed the Thornton Opera Program at the University of Southern California (1948–60).

Bohuslav Martinů (1890–1959), Czech composer. He studied violin, organ, and composition at the Prague Conservatory, and then moved to Paris in 1923. After 1940 he divided his time among the U.S., Prague, and Switzerland. His chief influences, early and late, were the neoclassicism of Stravinsky, American jazz, and the Bohemian folk tradition. Among his compositions are six symphonies, fifteen operas, fourteen ballets, and a large catalogue of orchestral, chamber, and vocal music.

Daniel Gregory Mason (1873–1953), Boston-born composer and writer on music. He was the son of the piano maker Henry Mason (1831–1890) and the grandson of American hymnist Lowell Mason (1792–1872). His German Romantic affinities were announced in the title of his first book, *From Grieg to Brahms* (1902). Educated at Harvard, he was lecturer in music history at Columbia University from 1905 to 1942.

Edward Matthews (1897–1954), American baritone. He created the roles of Saint Ignatius for Virgil Thomson's *Four Saints in Three Acts* (1934) and Jake the Fisherman for George Gershwin's *Porgy and Bess* (1935).

Dorothy Maynor (1910–1996), American soprano and educator. A protégée of Koussevitzky, she made her Town Hall debut in 1939. She enjoyed a twenty-year career as a soloist and recitalist in the U.S., Europe, and South America. In 1964 she founded the Harlem School of the Arts, which she directed through 1979.

Edwin McArthur (1907–1987), American pianist, conductor, and composer of art songs. He was accompanist to a roster of singers including Ezio Pinza, John Charles Thomas, and, from 1935 to 1955, Kirsten Flagstad. In 1941 he became the first American-born conductor to lead the orchestra of the Metropolitan Opera.

John McCormack (1884–1945), Irish tenor. He made his New York debut in 1909, and became a U.S. citizen in 1917. Although he was at home in the Italian operatic repertory, he was beloved as an interpreter of traditional and popular Irish song. One of the early stars of recorded music, his best sellers included "I Hear You Calling Me" (1908), "It's a Long Way to Tipperary" (1914), and "Keep the Home Fires Burning" (1917).

Harl McDonald (1899–1955), American composer, conductor, and pianist. Born in Boulder, Colorado, and educated at the University of California–Berkeley, his early work, including his Symphony No. 1 ("The Santa Fe Trail," 1933), is informed by the landscape and traditional melodies of the American West. His later work, written at the University of Pennsylvania, includes three further symphonies, several concertos, two piano trios, and choral music.

Colin McPhee (1900–1964), Canadian composer, percussionist, and ethnomusicologist. He lived most of his life in Bali and Java and was one of the first Western masters of gamelan music.

Nikolai Medtner (1880–1951), Russian-born pianist and composer long resident in London. His works include three piano concertos, fourteen piano sonatas, and many pieces for solo piano, including thirty-eight *Skazi* ("Fairy Tales").

Henri Médus (1904–1985), Algerian-born bass. He sang with the Paris Opéra from 1933 to 1959, and retired from the stage in 1979.

Lauritz Melchior (1890–1973), Danish-born tenor. After a career in Copenhagen and London, he made his U.S. debut in 1926 with the Metropolitan Opera in the role of Tannhäuser. He joined the company in 1928, and was its lead Wagnerian tenor through 1950.

James Melton (1904–1961), American tenor. He emerged in the 1920s as a radio singer, moving easily between popular and light classical fare. He later sang with the Chicago, St. Louis, and Philadelphia opera companies, and from 1942 to 1950 made eighty-four appearances with the Metropolitan Opera.

Arthur Mendel (1905–1979), Boston-born choral conductor and Bach scholar. After studies at Harvard and the American Conservatory, Fontainebleau, he was literary editor of G. Schirmer, Inc. (1930–38), and a teacher at the Dalcroze School of New York (1938–50). From 1936 to 1953 he led New York's Cantata Singers, which, with the Dessoff Choirs, was one of the first choral groups to give authentic performances of Baroque music. In 1952 he joined the faculty of Princeton University, where for twenty years he edited the works of J. S. Bach and, with Hans T. David, compiled *The Bach Reader: His Life in Letters and Documents* (1966). The Princeton music library is named in his honor.

Willem Mengelberg (1871–1951), Dutch conductor of German heritage. For seven years he was music director of the New York Philharmonic (1922–29), where he championed Mahler and Richard Strauss. For the rest of his career, which spanned 1895 to 1945, he was associated with the Amsterdam Concertgebouw Orchestra, for most years as principal conductor. Whether he welcomed or was politically indifferent to the Nazi occupation of Holland is a matter of dispute, but it is a fact that he conducted in Germany and the occupied countries throughout World War II. In 1945 the Netherlands' Honor Council for Music banned him from working in the Netherlands for six years. He died in Swiss exile two months before the ban expired.

Gian-Carlo Menotti (1911–2007), Italian-born composer and librettist. While a student at the Curtis Institute of Music, he wrote his first opera, the one-act *Amelia Goes to the Ball* (1936). His mature operas—for which he wrote both music and librettos—include *The Medium* (Pulitzer Prize, 1946), *The Telephone* (1947), *The Consul* (1950), *Amahl and the Night Visitors* (1951), and *The Saint of Bleecker Street* (Pulitzer Prize, 1954). He also wrote the librettos to two operas by his life partner, Samuel Barber. Thomson admired Menotti's "impeccable stage sense," his "fecund dramatic imagination," and his "strong librettos . . . in excellent American."

Yehudi Menuhin (1916–1999), American violinist and conductor. After studies with Georges Enesco and Adolf Busch he made a worldwide tour in 1934–35 that established him as a modern master. During World War II he played hundreds of concerts for the Allied Forces, and after the war resided in London. He was made an honorary Knight of the British Empire in 1965, and became a British subject in 1985.

Ruby Mercer (1906–1999), American-born soprano, broadcaster, and publisher. After a career in radio, on Broadway, and with the Metropolitan Opera (she sang Nedda in *Pagliacci*) she moved from New York to Toronto. There she founded the quarterly *Opera Canada* and was for thirty years host of CBC Radio's *Opera Time*.

Robert Merrill (1917–2004), American baritone. From 1945 to 1976 he made 769 appearances with the Metropolitan Opera, where his signature role was Germont in *La Traviata*. He was also a Los Vegas headliner, a favorite guest of Ed Sullivan, and for thirty years the opening-day singer of the national anthem at Yankee Stadium.

Olivier Messiaen (1908–1992), French composer and organist. In 1931, after studies with Paul Dukas and Marcel Dupré, he was named organist of the Roman Catholic Church of Sainte-Trinité, Paris, an appointment that lasted sixty years. His forays into Christian mysticism, non-Western music, and the patterns of birdsong are manifest in even his earliest compositions, which include many works for organ, for piano, and for voice. In 1936, with the composers André Jolivet, Daniel-Lesur, Pierre Schaeffer, and Yves Baudrier, he founded the group La Jeune France to counter what he saw as a lack of moral seriousness in Cocteau and his circle. As a soldier during World War II he was taken prisoner and interned at Görlitz; there he wrote his most widely performed work, *Quartet for the End of Time* (1941). After the war he taught harmony at the Paris Conservatory, where his students included Karl Stockhausen, Pierre Boulez, and the pianist Yvonne Loriod (whom he married in 1961). His *Turangalîla* (1946–48), a symphony in ten movements, is perhaps the epitome of his approach to composition, codified in his treatise *The Technique of My Musical Language* (1944).

Nikolai Miaskovsky (1881–1950), Russian composer whose twenty-seven symphonies (1908–49) helped define the Soviet style. His work was championed in the West by Frederick Stock, who commissioned his Symphony No. 21 (1940).

Janine Micheau (1914–1976), French soprano. She sang with the Paris Opéra and Opéra-Comique and in recital was a champion of the modern French song.

Arturo Benedetti Michelangeli (1920–1995), Italian pianist. He entered the Milan Conservatory at age ten, made his debut in Brussels at age eighteen, but did not appear in America until age twenty-eight. His repertoire included Mozart, Beethoven, Chopin, Liszt, Ravel, Debussy, and Italian folk songs in his own arrangements.

Francisco Mignone (1897–1986), Brazilian composer of Italian heritage. His orchestral music is of a "national" character, based on indigenous tunes and motifs, but his chamber music is indebted to the modern Italian school.

Zinka Milanov (1906–1989), Croatian-born soprano. She sang Italian repertory with the Metropolitan Opera for twenty-nine seasons (1937–66). Her signature roles were Verdi's Aida and Mascagni's Santuzza.

Darius Milhaud (1892–1974), French composer and pianist. After studies at the Paris Conservatory, he was accepted into the artists' circle of Satie, Cocteau, and Paul Claudel. A prolific composer whose works were widely performed even from his student days, he was one of a group of young French composers known as Les Six. In 1940 he immigrated to the U.S., where he found a teaching position at Mills College, in Oakland, California, his home for the rest of his life. He wrote in every traditional genre, but is best known for his contributions to the stage, including the jazz ballet *The Creation of the World* (to a scenario by Blaise Cendrars, 1923), the polytonal opera *Christoph Colomb* (to a libretto by Claudel, 1930), and the music for Claudel's adaptations of Aeschylus. His concert works include thirteen symphonies, eighteen string quartets, and the dance suite *Suadades do Brasil* (1921).

Charles Mills (1914–1982), American composer. His percussion-driven ballet *John Brown* (also known as *God's Angry Man: A Passion Play*, 1945) was written for the Erick Hawkins Dance Company.

Nathan Milstein (1904–1992), Russian-born violinist. After studies in St. Petersburg with Leopold Auer, he toured Russia from 1920 to 1926, often in joint recital with his friend Vladimir Horowitz. Emigrating first to Paris and then, in 1929, to the U.S., he quickly won an international reputation as a soloist, recitalist, and interpreter of the Romantic repertory. His violin compositions include *Paganiniana* (1954) and cadenzas to concertos by Beethoven and Brahms.

Dimitri Mitropoulos (1896–1960), Greek-born pianist and conductor. He was educated in Athens, Brussels, and Berlin, and from 1921 to 1935 was associated with the Berlin State Opera and the Berlin Philharmonic. He made his U.S. debut in 1936 as guest conductor with the Boston Symphony Orchestra, and from 1937 to 1949 was music director of the Minneapolis Symphony. A frequent guest of the New York Philharmonic throughout the 1940s, he was its principal conductor from 1949 to 1958. He was also a conductor for the Metropolitan Opera (1954–60), where, in 1958, he gave the world premiere of the Barber-Menotti *Vanessa* and, in 1959, added Berg's *Wozzeck* to the repertory.

Ernest Moeran (1894–1950), English composer of Irish heritage. His "symphonic impression" *In the Mountain Country* was composed in 1921. His other works include a symphony (1937), a violin concerto (1942), and a cello concerto (1945).

Mariquita Moll (1921–2000), American soprano. She sang regularly with the New York City Opera and, in 1954–58, appeared in Metropolitan Opera productions of *Das Rheingold* and *Die Walküre*.

Italo Montemezzi (1875–1952), Italian composer. Of his nine operas, only *The Love of Three Kings* (1913), performed sixty-seven times by the Metropolitan Opera from 1914 to 1948, has had any international currency.

Pierre Monteux (1875–1964), French-born conductor. As a conductor of Diaghilev's Ballets Russes (1911–14) he gave world premieres of *The Rite of Spring*, *Daphnis et Chloé*, and *Petrushka*. He was director of French repertory for the Metropolitan Opera (1917–19) and then principal conductor of the Boston Symphony Orchestra (1919–24), the Amsterdam Concertgebouw Orchestra (1924–34), the Orchestre Symphonique de Paris (1929–38), and the San Francisco Symphony (1936–52). He was also instrumental in developing and launching the NBC Symphony Orchestra, and directed its first broadcast, on November 13, 1937. An American citizen after 1942, he summered in Hancock, Maine, where in 1943 he founded the Pierre Monteux School for Conductors and Orchestra Musicians. His students included Neville Mariner, Lorin Maazel, Seiji Ozawa, and André Previn.

Douglas Moore (1893–1969), American composer of orchestral music, chamber works, and, above all, operas. His *The Devil and Daniel Webster* (1938) and *The Ballad of Baby Doe* (1956) have entered the international repertory. These operas, said Thomson, "have theatrical qualities and abundant melody."

Grace Moore (1898–1947), American soprano and actress. She began her career as a singer in the Irving Berlin Music Box Revues but soon left New York for Paris, where she performed at the Opéra-Comique. For eighteen seasons (1928–46) she sang with the Metropolitan Opera, where her signature role was Charpentier's Louise. She appeared in several feature films throughout the 1930s, starring in Columbia Pictures' opera-world romance *One Night of Love* (1934) and in Abel Gance's adaptation of *Louise* (1939). She died in a plane crash near Copenhagen, aged forty-eight.

Jean Morel (1903–1975), French-born conductor. He was for fifteen years an instructor at the American Conservatory, Fontainebleau, before he was a conductor at the New York City Opera (1946–51) and the head of French repertory at the Metropolitan Opera (1956–71). As professor of conducting at Juilliard he was a mentor to, among others, James Levine and Leonard Slatkin.

Erica Morini (1904–1995), Viennese-born violinist. The daughter of a music school principal, she made her professional debut at age twelve and her New York debut at age eighteen. From the 1920s until her retirement in 1976, she was a soloist with almost every major orchestra in Europe and the Americas.

Virginia Morley (1916–2013), American pianist. While a student at the American Conservatory, Fontainebleau, she formed a piano duo with fellow-student (and, later, husband) Livingston Gearhart, which toured widely in 1941–54. After 1954 she was the wife and business manager of choral director Fred Waring.

Nicola Moscona (1907–1975), Greek-born bass. He sang with the Metropolitan Opera for twenty-four seasons (1937–61) and was a favorite soloist of Toscanini and the NBC Symphony Orchestra.

Alexander Mossolov (1900–1973), Russian composer. His *Newspaper Advertisements* (a group of four art songs based on classified ads in *Izvestiya*, 1926) and his orchestral work *Iron Foundry* (a movement from his "futurist ballet" *Steel*, 1926–27) are the epitome of early Soviet music.

Charles Munch (1891–1968), Alsatian-born conductor and violinist. The son of an organ and voice instructor at the Strasbourg Conservatory, he was concertmaster of the conservatory's orchestra by age twenty-eight. In 1932 he relocated to Paris, where he studied conducting with Fritz Zweig and performed with the Orchestre Symphonique (1935–38). In 1937–46 he was principal conductor of the Paris Conservatory Orchestra. For exemplary conduct during the Occupation—he refused to program contemporary German works and protected Jewish colleagues from the Gestapo—he was awarded the Légion d'honneur in 1945. Munch made his U.S. debut with the Boston Symphony Orchestra in 1946, and was music director of the BSO from 1949 to 1962. In 1963 he returned to France as president of the École Normale de Musique.

Patrice Munsel (b. 1925), American soprano. When she made her debut with the Metropolitan Opera in 1943, "Princess Pat" was only seventeen—the youngest lead singer in Met history. She remained with the company through 1958, where her signature roles were Adele in *Die Fledermaus* and Rosina in *The Barber of Seville*.

Vano Muradeli (1908–1970), Soviet Georgian composer. Although he had won the Stalin Prize for his Symphony No. 2 (1946), he was condemned by the Soviets for mounting a Western-influenced opera (*The Great Friendship*, 1947) concerning Russian–Georgian relations at the time of the Revolution. He was rehabilitated by his symphonic poem *The Soviet Path to Victory*, which won the Stalin Prize in 1951.

Nicolas Nabokov (1903–1978), Russian-born composer and writer, first cousin of the novelist Vladimir Nabokov. In 1918 his family fled the Revolution, settling in Berlin and then in Paris. In 1933 he immigrated to the U.S., where from 1951 to 1963 he was secretary general of the Congress for Cultural Freedom. A prolific writer of magazine articles, he published two memoirs, *Old Friends and New Music* (1951) and *Bagazh: Memoirs of a Cosmopolitan* (1975). His compositions include the opera *Love's Labour's Lost* (with a libretto by W. H. Auden, 1973), six ballets, three symphonies, and many chamber pieces based on Russian folk songs.

Rosalind Nadell (b. 1922), or Rosalind Scheer, American soprano. She sang with the New York City Opera during its debut season, 1944–45.

Genia Nemenoff (1904–1989), Paris-born pianist who, from 1937 to 1962, performed in a piano duo with her husband, Pierre Luboshutz.

Ginette Neveu (1919–1949), French violinist. After studies with Georges Enesco and Carl Flesch, she enjoyed a fifteen-year career as a soloist. Both she and Jean-Paul Neveu, her brother and recital accompanist, died young in a plane crash in the Azores Islands.

Patricia Neway (1919–2012), American soprano and Broadway actress. Though she created the role of Magda Sorel for Menotti's *The Consul* (1950) and won a Tony as the Abbess in *The Sound of Music* (1960), she was best known as a pillar of the New York City Opera (1951–66).

Clifford Newdahl (1901–1950), American tenor, cabaret singer, and Broadway actor.

Riccardo Nielsen (1908–1982), Italian composer of Danish heritage. A writer of chamber music, operas, and musical plays for radio, his early work was inspired by the neoclassicism of Stravinsky, his work after 1943 by the serialism of Schoenberg.

Serge Nigg (1924–2008), French composer of ballets, cantatas, and chamber music. A protégé of René Leibowitz and an early adopter of the twelve-tone method, he later renounced atonality for Soviet-style "socialist realism."

Elena Nikolaidi (1909–2002), Greek-born contralto. After a ten-year career with the Vienna State Opera, she immigrated to New York in 1948. She made seventeen appearances with the Metropolitan Opera from 1951 to 1955.

Paul Nordoff (1909–1977), American composer who wrote ballets for Martha Graham and, in 1955, the popular neo-Romantic *Winter Symphony*. In the 1960s he developed, with his Bard College colleague Clive Robbins, the Nordoff-Robbins technique of childhood music therapy.

Alex North (1910–1991), American composer trained in Russia. He was the husband of choreographer Anna Sokolow, whose work immersed him in the worlds of film and theater music. In 1951 he wrote the music for Elia Kazan's *Streetcar Named Desire*, the first of his more than fifty film scores, fifteen of which received Oscar nominations. He also wrote popular songs, including the standard "Unchained Melody" (1955).

Guiomar Novaes (1897–1979), Brazilian pianist. A student of Isidor Philipp at the Paris Conservatory, she at age thirteen began a concert career that lasted well into her seventies. She was a leading twentieth-century interpreter of Chopin, Schumann, and Debussy.

Jarmila Novotná (1907–1994), Czech-born soprano and film actress. After a career in Prague and Berlin, she immigrated to New York in 1933. From 1940 to 1956, she made 208 appearances with the Metropolitan Opera. She also starred in Fred Zinneman's *The Search* (1948) and appeared in Richard Thorpe's *The Great Caruso* (1951).

Bernard Ocko (1902–1972), American violinist. He was a frequent soloist with the New York Philharmonic and the second violinist of both the Hartman String Quartet (1925–27) and the Musical Art Quartet (1927–31).

Helen Olheim (1905–1992), American mezzo-soprano. She sang supporting roles with the Metropolitan Opera in 1937–41.

Carl Orff (1895–1982), Munich-born composer who sought to strip German music of all traces of romanticism. Inspired by medieval mystery plays, Gregorian chant, and Stravinsky's *Rite of Spring*, he wrote the dramatic oratorio *Carmina Burana* (1935), a setting of secular poems about fate, fortune, and earthly passions drawn from a German manuscript of the twelfth century. As a pedagogue, he developed an immersive method of childhood musical education through exercises in singing, rhythm, and dance.

Eugene Ormandy (1899–1985), Hungarian-born conductor. A violin prodigy, he was admitted at age five to the Royal Academy of Budapest and joined the school's faculty at age fifteen. He emigrated to New York in 1921, where he established himself as a soloist and a guest conductor with the New York Philharmonic. He was music director of the Minneapolis Symphony Orchestra (1931–36) and then, with Leopold Stokowski, co-conductor of the Philadelphia Orchestra. Succeeding Stokowski in 1941, he led the Philadelphia Orchestra for thirty-nine consecutive seasons, until his retirement in 1980.

Leo Ornstein (1893–2002), Russian-born composer and pianist. He emigrated with his family from Petrograd to New York at age twelve and made his Town Hall debut at age eighteen. His avant-garde piano music, based on tone clusters that antedated Cowell's, created a sensation in 1910–25. "As modernism of yesterday," wrote Thomson in 1971, "his *Danse Sauvage* of 1915 . . . can still be listened to."

Robert Palmer (1915–2010), American composer and pianist. A protégé of Aaron Copland and Roy Harris, he wrote two symphonies, four string quartets, and many chamber pieces for piano. From 1943 to 1980 he taught theory and composition at Cornell University.

Alessio de Paolis (1893–1964), Italian-born tenor. He sang character roles with the Metropolitan Opera from 1938 to 1964.

Paul Paray (1886–1979), French conductor. After studies at the Paris Conservatory he enjoyed a long career with orchestras in France and in Monaco. From 1952 to 1963 he was music director of the Detroit Symphony Orchestra. He then returned to France and continued to conduct until the age of ninety-two.

Tony Parenti (1900–1972), American clarinetist and saxophonist. In the 1930s and '40s he was a staff musician for CBS radio. He also played New Orleans–style music with Ted Lewis, Eddie Condon, and his own Deans of Dixieland.

Léon Pascal (fl. 1930s–70s), French violist. He was a member of the Calvert Quartet (1931–38) before founding his own Pascal String Quartet (1941–73).

Bernhard Paumgartner (1887–1971), Austrian conductor and musicologist. He led the Vienna Composers' Orchestra (1914–17) and the Salzburg Mozarteum Orchestra (1917–52) and was later the founding conductor of the Camerata Academica (1952–71) and president of the Salzburg Festival (1960–71).

Peter Pears (1910–1986), English tenor. In 1934, while a member of the BBC Singers, he met Benjamin Britten, and by 1937 had become his lifelong partner and musical collaborator. Pears created the title roles for Britten's *Peter Grimes* (1945) and *Albert Herring* (1947) as well as Vere in *Billy Budd* (1951) and the Narrator/Peter Quint in *The Turn of the Screw* (1954). In 1974 he made his debut with the Metropolitan Opera as Aschenbach in Britten's *Death in Venice*. From 1937 to the early 1960s he also gave recitals, usually accompanied by Britten on piano. His repertoire included lieder, Schumann, Schubert, and art songs written for him by Britten.

James Pease (1916–1967), American bass-baritone. He sang with the New York City Opera (1946–60) and created the role of Balstrode for Benjamin Britten's *Peter Grimes* (1945).

Gerhard Pechner (1903–1969), German-born bass-baritone. After a decade with the Berlin State Opera, he emigrated to New York in

1939. After two years in San Francisco he joined the Metropolitan Opera, where he made 650 appearances from 1941 to 1966, usually in character roles.

Jan Peerce (1904–1984), American tenor of Polish heritage. He was a singer at the Radio City Music Hall when, in 1937, Toscanini tapped him as a soloist for the NBC Symphony Orchestra. In 1941 he joined the Metropolitan Opera, where he sang lead roles, usually in the Italian repertory, until 1966.

John Pennington (fl. 1920s–50s), English violinist. He was first violinist of the London String Quartet (1927–34, 1941–52) and concertmaster of the San Francisco Symphony (1934–52).

Henri Pensis (1900–1958), Luxembourg-born conductor, composer, and violinist. In 1933 he founded the Luxembourg Philharmonic Orchestra as a division of Radio Luxembourg. During World War II he lived in the U.S., where he was a guest conductor of the New York Philharmonic and the City Symphony.

Dorothea Persichetti (1919–1987), American pianist and educator. Born Dorothea Flanagan, she married composer Vincent Persichetti in 1941 and taught alongside him at both the Curtis Institute of Music and Juilliard. The couple frequently performed as a piano duo, for which Vincent wrote several compositions for four hands.

Vincent Persichetti (1915–1987), American composer, pianist, and educator. A native of Philadelphia, he first studied, then taught, at the Curtis Institute of Music, and later joined the faculty at Juilliard. Inspired by American jazz, he wrote many concert pieces for wind instruments. He also wrote liturgical music, including the well-known *Hymns and Responses for the Church Year* (1956). Thomson found that his work displayed "real grace and honest workmanship."

Yella Pessl (1906–1991), Austrian-born harpsichordist. As a soloist she was active for half a century, from 1928 to 1978. She was also founder and music director of the Bach Circle, a New York–based ensemble dedicated to lesser-known works by Bach and other Baroque composers.

Irra Petina (1908–2000), Russian-born contralto. She made 410 appearances with the Metropolitan Opera from 1933 to 1950, usually in supporting roles. Her Broadway credits include the operetta *Song of Norway* (1947) and Leonard Bernstein's *Candide* (1957).

Goffredo Petrassi (1904–2003), neoclassical Italian composer and conductor. His work is perhaps epitomized by his eight Concertos for Orchestra. He was the music director of the Venice opera house La Fenice and professor of composition at the Conservatory Santa Cecilia.

Frédérique Petrides (1903–1983), Belgian-born conductor and violinist. In 1932 she founded the Orchestrette Classique of New York, an ensemble of thirty to forty female musicians, which she led until 1943. The Orchestrette was devoted to new American music and presented six to eight concerts every season at Carnegie Hall.

Thomas Petrie (fl. 1900s–40s), second violinist of the London String Quartet (1908–34, 1941–52).

Isidor Philipp (1863–1958), Hungarian-born pianist, composer, and teacher. As a student at the Paris Conservatory he was a close friend of Debussy, and in later life was considered the foremost authority on his music. Though he began as a soloist and chamber player, he gave up the stage to devote himself to teaching at the Paris Conservatory (1893–1934) and at the American Conservatory, Fontainebleau (1921–33).

Edith Piaf (1915–1963), French chanteuse. Known as *La Môme Piaf* ("The Little Sparrow"), she was, from the 1940s, an international celebrity and best-selling recording artist. She wrote the lyrics to many of her songs, including "La vie en rose" (1945) and "Non, je ne regrette rien" (1961).

Mishel Piastro (1892–1970), Russian-born violinist and conductor. He was concertmaster of the New York Philharmonic under Toscanini (1931–43) and music director of radio's Longines Symphonette (1943–57).

Gregor Piatigorsky (1903–1976), Russian-born cellist. Named principal cellist of the Bolshoi Theater at age fifteen, he fled the country three years later to further his formal studies in Germany. While earning his tuition as a player in a café trio, he was heard by Wilhelm Furtwängler, who in 1921 hired him for the Berlin Philharmonic. He made his U.S. debut in 1929 and immigrated to the States in 1939. Widely considered, with Casals, as the foremost cellist of his generation, he played solo recitals, appeared with every major American and European orchestra, and formed a trio with Jascha Heifetz and Arthur Rubinstein. He also taught cello at the Curtis Institute of Music (1942–51), Boston University (1952–62), and the University of Southern California (1962–76).

Jane Pickens (1908–1992), American singer and actress. She was one of the Pickens Sisters, a popular vocal trio that in 1932–37 appeared on Broadway and in their own NBC radio series. She went on to a successful stage career, and in 1949 created the title role for Marc Blitzstein's *Regina*.

Willem Pijper (1894–1947), Dutch composer. Largely self-taught, he wrote three symphonies, many chamber works, and choral and song settings for Dutch texts. He favored the octotonic scale, sometimes called the Pijper scale.

Ezio Pinza (1892–1957), Italian-born bass. He sang at La Scala from 1922 to 1926, and then joined the Metropolitan Opera, where he made more than eight hundred appearances through 1948. His celebrated roles included Don Giovanni, Boris Godunov, and Mephistopheles in *Faust*. In 1949 he appeared on Broadway in *South Pacific* and in 1951–52 hosted a weekly NBC television variety show.

Walter Piston (1894–1976), American composer. After graduating from Harvard he studied in Paris with Nadia Boulanger and Paul Dukas. Upon returning to the U.S., in 1926, he was offered a position on the Harvard music faculty, where he remained for thirty-four years. He wrote mainly orchestral and chamber works, including many concertos and five string quartets, but is best known for his eight symphonies, of which the Third (1947) and the Seventh (1960) were awarded Pulitzer prizes. Thomson characterized him as "a neoclassical composer of Parisian cast, a skilled technician of the orchestra, [and] a valued pedagogue." His students included Leonard Bernstein, Elliott Carter, John Harbison, and Harold Shapero.

Ildebrando Pizzetti (1880–1968), Italian composer and conductor. His major works include twenty operas, many choral pieces, and a symphony. He frequently conducted the Italian Radio Symphony Orchestra and Chorus, Milan.

Eunice Podis (1922–2008), American pianist and teacher. A lifelong resident of Cleveland, Ohio, she made her debut as a soloist with the Cleveland Orchestra at age nineteen and performed with the orchestra every season until age seventy-five.

Leonid Polovinkin (1894–1949), Russian composer and pianist. His early works, including the piano series *Événements* ("Incidents," 1925) and the symphonic poem *Telescope* (1928), were written under the influence of Scriabin. He later adopted the Soviet style.

Lily Pons (1898–1976), French-born soprano, film actress, and glamour icon. She had a brief career with provincial French companies before joining the Metropolitan Opera in 1931. She sang lead roles for the next thirty years, most frequently Lakmé and Lucia di Lammermoor.

Gabriel Popov (1904–1972), Russian composer. His Symphony No. 1 (1935), admired by Shostakovich, was banned by the Soviet authorities for its "formalist tendencies." His later works more closely conformed to the Soviet style.

Lenore Portnoy (1919–?) American soprano. She sang with the New York City Opera in 1946–47.

Francis Poulenc (1899–1963), French composer and pianist. He was taught to play at home, by his mother, and by Spanish pianist Ricardo Viñes, a champion of Ravel and Debussy. Performances of his early works, in 1917–20, won him a place in a group of young French composers known as Les Six, and Diaghilev's production of his ballet *Les Biches* (1923) proved a popular as well as critical success. In 1926 he met baritone Pierre Bernac, a musical collaborator for whom he wrote many songs. He also wrote piano pieces, chamber works, sacred music, and the operas *Les Mamelles des Tirésias* (1947) and *Dialogue des Carmélites* (1957).

Marie Powers (1902–1973), American contralto and Broadway actress. She created two roles for Gian-Carlo Menotti: Madame Flora, in *The Medium* (1946), and the Mother, in *The Consul* (1950).

Fernando Previtali (1907–1985), Italian conductor. From 1936 to 1953 he was music director of Radio Italiana, for which he conducted the complete Verdi operas.

William Primrose (1904–1982), Scottish violist. He was a founding member of the London String Quartet (1930–34, 1941–46), first viola of the NBC Symphony Orchestra (1937–41), and one of the chamber musicians who augmented the Rubinstein-Heifetz-Piatigorsky trio. In 1953 he was created Commander of the Order of the British Empire by Queen Elizabeth II.

Jaro Prohaska (1891–1965), Austrian bass-baritone. He sang Wagnerian roles at the Berlin State Opera.

Sergei Prokofiev (1891–1953), Russian composer, pianist, and conductor. After studies in St. Petersburg with Rimsky-Korsakov, he lived for a decade in Paris, where he found fame through his early symphonies, his work for the Ballets Russes, and his operas *The Gambler* (1916) and *The Love for Three Oranges* (1921). After 1927, he strengthened his ties with his native country by accepting commissions from Soviet orchestras and writing scores for films, including *Lieutenant Kijé* (1933) and *Alexander Nevsky* (1938). In 1936, he moved permanently to the U.S.S.R., where, due to changing Soviet policy toward the arts, he was soon persecuted for his "formalist tendencies"—that is, his pursuit of art for art's sake rather than for the good of the Communist Party. His later works, including the operas *War and Peace* (1942) and *The Life of a Real Person* (1947), found little favor from the Soviet authorities.

Henri Rabaud (1873–1949), French composer and conductor. A composer of operas, oratorios, and music for the stage, he was music director of the Opéra-Comique (1908–14) and the Paris Opéra (1914–22) and director of the Paris Conservatory (1922–41).

Muriel Rahn (1911–1961), American soprano and Broadway actress. She began her career as a singer in Broadway revues and then, after studies at Juilliard, moved to the recital hall. She was one of two alternating leads in Oscar Hammerstein's *Carmen Jones* (1943) and created the role of Cora Lewis for the Jan Meyerowitz–Langston Hughes opera *The Barrier* (1949).

Torsten Ralf (1901–1954), Swedish tenor who enjoyed a mostly German career that spanned twenty-five years, from 1930 until his death in 1954. He sang Wagnerian leads with the Metropolitan Opera for three seasons (1945–48).

Edmond Rambaud (1887–1960), French tenor. He sang lead roles at the Paris Opéra from 1917 to 1946.

Nell Rankin (1924–2005), American mezzo-soprano. A protégée of Karin Branzell, she made her recital debut at Town Hall in 1947. For twenty-five seasons (1951–76) she sang with the Metropolitan Opera, where she excelled in the Italian repertory and as Bizet's Carmen.

Ernö Rapée (1891–1945), Hungarian-born conductor, arranger, and composer. He was music director of New York's Roxy Symphony Orchestra (1926–32) and its successor, the Radio City Symphony (1932–45).

George Reeves (1893–1960), American pianist and voice teacher. He was accompanist to a roster of singers, including Lotte Lehmann, Lauritz Melchior, Ezio Pinza, Maggie Teyte, and Jennie Tourel.

Fritz Reiner (1888–1963), Hungarian-born conductor. After studies at the Academy Franz Liszt, he directed operas in Budapest and Dresden. In 1922 he immigrated to the U.S., where he was music director of the Cincinnati Symphony (1922–31), the Pittsburgh Symphony (1938–48), and the Chicago Symphony (1953–63). He was also a conductor of German repertory for the Metropolitan Opera from 1949 to 1954.

Max Reiter (1905–1950), Italian-born conductor. After leading several orchestras in Germany and Italy he was music director of the San Antonio Symphony, a position he held from 1939 until his death, eleven years later, at age forty-five.

Regina Resnik (1922–2013), American mezzo-soprano. After her debut with the New Opera Company (1942) she sang with the Metropolitan Opera for thirty seasons, from 1944 to 1974. She later enjoyed a second career on Broadway, and in 1983 returned to the Met to reprise her role as the Marquise in Donizetti's *Daughter of the Regiment*.

Gertrude Ribla (1918–1980), American soprano. She made her national debut in 1943 performing Verdi arias for Toscanini's NBC Symphony Orchestra. She sang with the Metropolitan Opera for two seasons (1949–51) and appeared internationally through 1961.

Wallingford Riegger (1885–1961), American composer. He began as a writer of neo-Romantic orchestral and chamber music, experimented with atonality, and then wrote film scores and music for modern dance. Thomson said that "orchestral imagination and a poltergeist's musical wit give him a special place among U.S. composers. They even dominate the twelve-tone conformities of his middle-period."

Fritz Rikko (1903–1980), German-born violist, conductor, and concert impresario. He came to America in 1941, taught viola at Juilliard, and founded New York's Collegium Musicum, an early music ensemble that presented summer concerts in Washington Square Park from 1951 to 1974.

Jean Rivier (1896–1987), French composer. He wrote eight neoclassical symphonies, chamber pieces for flute and other wind instruments, and many frequently performed songs.

Artur Rodzinski (1892–1958), Polish-born conductor. After an apprenticeship in Warsaw he became musical assistant to Leopold Stokowski at the Philadelphia Orchestra (1925–29). He was then music director of the Los Angeles Philharmonic (1929–33) and the Cleveland Orchestra (1933–43) as well as a guest conductor of the New York Philharmonic in 1934 and 1937. He was named music director of the New York Philharmonic in 1943, an appointment that ended four years later due to differences with the orchestra's business manager, Arthur Judson. After a year as leader of the Chicago Symphony Orchestra he conducted operas in Italy, including the premiere of Prokofiev's *War and Peace* in Florence.

Bernard Rogers (1893–1968), American composer. He wrote five operas, including *The Warrior* (libretto by Norman Corwin), which received two performances by the Metropolitan Opera in 1947. He also wrote five symphonies, other orchestral pieces, three cantatas, and choral music.

Josef Roismann (1900–1974) was founding second violinist of the Budapest String Quartet (1927–32) and then first violinist (1936–74), replacing Emil Hauser.

Alexis Roland-Manuel (1891–1966), French composer. Although he composed primarily for stage and film, his best-known work is *Benedictiones* (1938), an a cappella song suite for women's or children's voices.

Stella Roman (1904–1992), Romanian soprano. After six years with Italian companies she joined the Metropolitan Opera, where she sang mostly Verdi from 1941 to 1951.

Leonard Rose (1918–1984), American cellist. After studies at the Curtis Institute of Music, he was principal cellist for the NBC Symphony, Cleveland, and New York Philharmonic orchestras. After 1951 he performed as a soloist and, from 1961 until his death, as a member of a trio with violinist Isaac Stern and pianist Eugene Istomin.

Charles Rosen (1927–2012), American pianist and polymath. He was a pupil at Juilliard from age six to eleven. In 1951, at twenty-four, he completed his Ph.D. in French at Princeton and made his New York debut in recital at Town Hall. He performed and recorded until the late 1960s and then turned to writing. He published criticism in *The New York of Review of Books* and, in 1971, published *The Classical Style* (1971; rev. 1997), the best known of his fifteen books.

Manuel Rosenthal (1904–2003), French composer and conductor.

A protégé of Maurice Ravel, he was music director of the French National Orchestra (1944–47), the Seattle Symphony (1948–51), and the Liège Symphony (1964–67). Among his works are the concert piece *Musique de table* (1941), the oratorio *Saint François d'Assise* (1936–39), and the orchestration of Offenbach's *Gaîté Parisienne*.

Hugh Ross (1898–1990), English-born choral conductor. Educated at Oxford and the Royal College of Music, he was director of the Winnipeg Choir when, in 1926, he was chosen to succeed Kurt Schindler as the second musical director of the Schola Cantorum, a position he held through 1971. The unofficial chorus of the New York Philharmonic, the Schola Cantorum also performed its own a cappella series at Town Hall and Carnegie Hall.

Artur Rubinstein (1887–1982), Polish-born pianist. He took his first lesson at age three, and by age eight was sent to Berlin for professional training. He made his German debut at eleven, his U.S. debut at eighteen. His early U.S. appearances were met with qualified praise— he often played from memory, missed notes, and improvised—but by the time of his tour of 1937 he was an acknowledged master, his only rival being Horowitz. He performed and recorded widely, and is remembered especially for his interpretations of Chopin and the Spanish masters. He wrote two volumes of memoirs, *My Young Years* (1973) and *My Many Years* (1980).

Beryl Rubinstein (1898–1952), American pianist, composer, and educator. A student of Ferruccio Busoni, he made his New York debut in 1916. He had a long career as a soloist and recitalist and published two piano concertos and many solo pieces. He was director of the Cleveland Institute of Music from 1932 until his death.

Carl Ruggles (1876–1971), American composer. He wrote few pieces, and those very slowly, and in old age disavowed works written before the age of forty-three as juvenilia. His most ambitious pieces include *Men and Mountains* (1924, revised 1936) and *Sun-Treader* (1926–31), for orchestra, and *Angels* (1921, revised 1940), for brass. "The auditory beauty of Ruggles's music is unique," said Thomson. "[It derives from] perfectly flexible melodies all perfectly placed so as to sound harmonious together, and along with these a consistently dissonant interval-texture, and a subtly irregular rhythm that avoids lilt."

François Ruhlmann (1868–1948), French conductor who from the 1890s until the mid-1940s worked with both the Paris Opéra and the Opéra-Comique.

Vincenz Ruzicka (1906–?), Austrian-born pianist. After studies at Juilliard with Josef Lhévinne, he performed in a piano duo with Celius Dougherty (1939–55). He was also a critic for *Musical America* magazine and a gifted watercolorist who frequently exhibited his work in New York City galleries.

Victor de Sabata (1892–1967), Italian conductor, composer, and violinist. After an apprenticeship in Rome and Monte Carlo, he was assistant conductor of the Cincinnati Orchestra (1927–28) and, from 1929, a pillar of the music staff at La Scala. He enjoyed a postwar career as guest conductor for many of the world's great orchestras, including the New York Philharmonic (1950–51). Though a severe heart attack in 1953 kept him from the podium, he continued to work as artistic advisor to La Scala until his death fourteen years later.

Evelyn Sachs (1924–2008), American mezzo-soprano. After making her debut in 1944 at the Chicago Civic Opera, she made twenty appearances with the Met in 1947–48. She was later a member of the New York City Opera.

Daniel Saidenberg (1906–1997), Canadian-born cellist and conductor. After studies at Juilliard and the Paris Conservatory, he performed with the Philadelphia Orchestra (1926–29) and the Chicago Symphony (1929–37). In 1938 he moved to New York, where he was a staff musician at NBC and founder of the Saidenberg Little Symphony, the house orchestra of the 92nd Street Y (1947–53).

Huguette St. Arnaud (fl. 1940s–50s), French mezzo-soprano long associated with the Paris Opéra and the Opéra-Comique.

Frank St. Leger (1890–1969), Madras-born conductor. After studies at the Royal Academy of Music, London, he enjoyed fifteen years with opera companies in Europe. Between 1929 and 1939 he held positions at the Chicago Civic Opera, the Houston Symphony, and Colorado's Central City Opera. He was then an assistant conductor for the Metropolitan Opera for eleven seasons (1939–50).

Carlos Salzedo (1885–1961), French harpist, pianist, composer, and conductor of Spanish heritage. He was harpist for the Monte Carlo Opera when, in 1909, Toscanini hired him for the orchestra of the Metropolitan Opera. He later worked as a soloist, founded several New York chamber ensembles, and taught harp at Juilliard, the Curtis Institute of Music, and his own Salzedo Harp Colony, in Camden, Maine.

Marjorie Call Salzedo (b. 1914), American harpist. In 1938, upon graduating from the Curtis Institute of Music, Marjorie Call married her teacher, Carlos Salzedo, with whom she toured in the Salzedo Harp Duo (1938–46).

Gyorgy Sandor (1912–2005), Hungarian-born pianist. He made his U.S. debut at Carnegie Hall in 1939. He was a leading interpreter of the piano works of his teachers Bartók and Kodály as well as of Liszt and Prokofiev.

Jesús María Sanromá (1902–1984), Puerto Rican pianist who at the age of eighteen was named principal pianist of the Boston Symphony

Orchestra (1920–40). In 1952 he returned to San Juan to direct the music department of the University of Puerto Rico.

Bidu Sayao (1902–1999), Brazilian soprano. A protégée of Villa-Lobos, she enjoyed a ten-year career in South America and Europe before joining the Metropolitan Opera (1937–52).

Nino Scattolini (fl. 1945–60), Italian tenor associated with the Teatro Lirico, Milan.

Maxim Schapiro (1899–1958), Russian-born pianist. After studies with Nikolai Medtner he enjoyed an international career as a soloist. He died of a heart attack suffered while performing Mozart's Coronation Concerto at the Carmel Bach Festival.

Walter Scheff (b. 1918), American baritone. A favorite of Marc Blitzstein, he recorded his song "Dusty Sun" (1942), sang at the premiere of the *Airborne Symphony* (1946), and played Gus Polock in the revival of *The Cradle Will Rock* (1947).

Hermann Scherchen (1891–1966), German-born conductor. From 1922 to 1950 he was the music director of the Winterthur Orchestra and the Zurich Opera.

Thomas Scherman (1917–1979), American conductor and composer. He was the founding director of the Little Orchestra Society, a forty to sixty-piece ensemble devoted to new and little-known music that during his tenure (1947–76) gave more than 250 New York premieres, usually at Town Hall.

Harold C. Schmidt (1910–1993), American choral conductor. From 1947 to 1975 he directed the Stanford University Chorus, which during his tenure doubled as the chorus of the San Francisco Symphony.

Florent Schmitt (1870–1958), French composer. After studies with Fauré and Massenet, he wrote music influenced by the German Romantics and by Wagner. His more frequently performed orchestral works include *Psalm 47* (with chorus, 1904), the suite from his ballet *Salomé* (1907), and *La Rêve* (1915).

E. Robert Schmitz (1889–1949), French-born pianist and composer. A protégé of Saint-Saëns, d'Indy, and Debussy, he enjoyed a ten-year career as a conductor in Paris before emigrating, in 1919, to New York. He was a leading interpreter of the piano works of Debussy, of which he left several recordings.

Artur Schnabel (1882–1951), Austrian-born pianist. After seven years as a pupil of Theodor Leschetizky, he made his debut in Vienna at age fifteen. He then enjoyed an international career as a soloist, in chamber groups, and, after 1905, in joint recital with his wife, contralto Therese Behr (1876–1959). In 1933 the Schnabels left Berlin for Italy and then, in 1939, immigrated to the U.S. He is remembered as a great interpreter of the Austro-Germany piano repertory, especially Beethoven.

Alexander Schneider (1908–1993), Lithuanian-born violinist and conductor. He was for twenty-four years the second violinist of the Budapest String Quartet (1932–44, 1955–67).

Mischa Schneider (1904–1985), Lithuanian-born cellist. The brother of Alexander Schneider, he was a member of the Budapest String Quartet (1930–67).

Arnold Schoenberg (1874–1951), Austrian-born composer. Born in Vienna, he was a largely self-taught musician whose innovations in composition earned the interest of Richard Strauss, Gustav Mahler, and the international musical avant-garde if not of the general public. His early works (1899–1907), often termed "Late Romantic," represent a highly idiosyncratic fusion of Brahms and Wagner. (See the string sextet *Verklärte Nacht*, 1899.) The works of his middle period (1908–22), often termed "atonal," are brief, dissonant, and free of key signatures and so of functional harmony. (See the song cycle *Pierrot Lunaire*, 1912.) The works of his late period (after 1923) are "dodecaphonic," or based on the twelve-tone method of composition. (See *Variations for Orchestra*, 1926–28, and String Quartet No. 4, 1936.) He left Austria in 1933 and settled in California in 1934. He taught at the University of Southern California and UCLA, where his students included John Cage and Lou Harrison.

Elmer Schoettle (1910–1973), American pianist and composer. As composer-in-residence at Fisk University and the University of Houston, he often played his own compositions in solo recital or in a piano duo with his wife, Mary Phillips Street.

Janos Scholz (1904–1993), Hungarian-born cellist. He was a member of the Roth String Quartet (1932–39) and, upon emigrating to New York, the New York City Symphony (1939–42). He was then a soloist and a private cello teacher whose students included Yo-Yo Ma.

William Schuman (1910–1992), American composer. As a teenager he played the double bass, joined a dance band, and wrote pop songs with his young friend, the lyricist Frank Loesser. At age nineteen he attended his first classical concert—Toscanini and the Philharmonic at Carnegie Hall—and resolved to become an orchestral composer. His most frequently performed works include the *American Festival Overture* (1939), Secular Cantata No. 2: *A Free Song* (Pulitzer Prize, 1943), the ballets *Undertow* (1945) and *Judith* (1949), and *New England Triptych* (1956). Thomson found him a composer "of highly individualized gesture [whose] music can be listened to." In 1945 he became president of the Juilliard School of Music and in 1961 the first president of Lincoln Center.

Carl Schuricht (1880–1967), German conductor. After studies with Max Reger and Engelbert Humperdinck he directed orchestras in Frankfurt (1909–22), Wiesbaden (1923–44), and throughout

Switzerland (1945–50s). He was also a frequent guest conductor with the Vienna Philharmonic, which he co-led on an American tour in 1956.

Joseph Schuster (1903–1969), Turkish-born cellist of Russian heritage. He was a member of the Berlin Philharmonic (1929–34) and the New York Philharmonic (1934–47) before becoming a Hollywood-based recitalist and soloist.

Philippa Duke Schuyler (1931–1967), American pianist and journalist. She was a media celebrity from childhood for her prodigious piano skills, precocious poise, and wealthy and eccentric mixed-race parents. By age thirty she had abandoned music for print journalism, and was killed in a helicopter crash while reporting from Da Nang for the *Manchester Union Leader*.

Albert Schweitzer (1875–1965), Alsatian-born medical missionary, writer, and organist. As a boy he took organ lessons from his father and from Eugene Munch of the Mulhouse Protestant Temple. In 1893 he moved to Paris and studied with Charles-Marie Widor and Isidor Philipp. He wrote books on the great organ builders, on the need for organ restoration, and on the life and work of J. S. Bach. In 1905 he founded the Bach Society of Paris and in the 1930s recorded his interpretations of Bach and César Franck.

Hazel Scott (1920–1981), Trinidad-born pianist, singer, and film actress. She moved easily between the classic repertory and jazz, and often performed her own swing arrangements of classical music melodies.

Norman Scott (1921–1968), American bass of Russian heritage. He sang character roles with the Metropolitan Opera from 1951 until his death, at age forty-six, in 1968.

Irmgard Seefried (1919–1988), German soprano whose international career, based at the Vienna State Opera, spanned 1940 to 1976. In 1953 she gave five performances as Susanna in *The Marriage of Figaro* with the Metropolitan Opera.

Andrés Segovia (1893–1987), Spanish guitarist who, through his virtuoso playing and transcriptions of the Baroque repertoire, revived the guitar as a concert instrument.

Carolina Segrera (1905–1998), Cuban-born soprano. After studies in Paris and Milan, she sang at La Scala throughout the 1930s. In 1937 she immigrated to the U.S., where she sang Italian repertory with the New York City Opera and Cuban and Spanish folk songs in recital halls and nightclubs.

Rudolf Serkin (1903–1991), Austrian-born pianist. Schooled in Vienna, he made his debut there at age twelve. In 1920 he moved to Berlin, where he performed as a recitalist and as pianist to Adolf Busch and his brothers. He made his New York debut at Carnegie Hall in 1937 and was soon known as a regular soloist with the New York

Philharmonic. In 1936 he became a teacher at the Curtis Institute of Music, and was director of the school from 1968 to 1976. He was also, in 1950, cofounder of the Marlboro School and Summer Music Festival, in Marlboro, Vermont.

Roger Sessions (1896–1985), American composer, teacher, and writer on music. After studies with Horatio Parker and Ernest Bloch, he taught composition at several schools, chiefly Princeton (1935–44, 1952–65). His music, at first neo-Romantic but later dense, idiosyncratic, and dissonant, includes three operas, eight symphonies, a concerto for orchestra (Pulitzer Prize, 1981), two string quartets, and several choral preludes for organ. Thomson found it "monumental . . . an emulation of Beethoven . . . work of a high viscosity, a stubborn obscurity, and some grandeur." Sessions also wrote a textbook on harmony and the essays and lectures collected in *The Music Experience* (1950), *Questions About Music* (1970), and *Roger Sessions on Music* (1979).

Fabien Sevitzky (1893–1967), né Koussevitzky, Russian-born conductor. A nephew and protégé of Serge Koussevitzky, he was music director of the Indianapolis Symphony Orchestra from 1937 to 1955.

Harold Shapero (1920–2013), American neoclassical composer. He was educated at Harvard and in Paris, where his teachers and mentors included Piston, Boulanger, Hindemith, and Stravinsky. His major work was the Symphony for Classical Orchestra (1947). He also wrote a great deal of chamber music for strings and piano. His overture *The Traveller* (1946) was revised as the Sinfonia in C minor for String Orchestra (1948).

Robert Shaw (1916–1999), American choral and orchestral conductor. After studies at Pomona College he moved to New York where he founded, in 1941, the Collegiate Chorale, a choir notable for its vocal excellence, its racial integration, and its use by Toscanini as the unofficial chorus of the NBC Symphony Orchestra. In 1948 he started a second choir, the Robert Shaw Chorale, which he led through 1953. He was then music director of the San Diego Symphony and, from 1957 to 1967, assistant conductor of the Cleveland Orchestra. From 1967 to 1988 he was music director of both the Atlanta Symphony and its chorus.

Vladimir Shcherbachov (1889–1952), Soviet Russian composer. He wrote five symphonies, many chamber works and solo piano pieces, and several film scores

Vissarion Shebalin (1902–1963), Soviet Russian composer and lifelong friend of Dmitri Shostakovich. He was a prolific writer of orchestral music but is better known for his operas, cantatas, choral works, and songs.

Arthur Shepherd (1880–1958), Utah-raised composer and conductor.

After studies at the New England Conservatory, he was assistant conductor of the Cleveland Orchestra from 1915 to 1927. His highly individualistic orchestral music includes *Overture to a Drama* (1919) and two symphonies evoking the landscape of the American West.

Dmitri Shostakovich (1906–1975), Soviet Russian composer and pianist. His Symphony No. 1, composed while he was still enrolled at the Petrograd Conservatory, received its world premiere in Berlin under Bruno Walter (1927), and its U.S. premiere under Leopold Stokowski (1928). He wrote his first opera, based on Gogol's *The Nose*, in 1929, and followed it with *Lady Macbeth of Mzensk* in 1934. The latter, popular with theatergoers but not with Stalin, was denounced in *Pravda* as petit-bourgeois formalism. Shostakovich was persona non grata until he "responded to just criticism" with his Symphony No. 5 (1937). Later works that have entered the repertory include his Piano Quintet, String Quartet No. 2, Symphony No. 7, and piano preludes.

Elie Siegmeister (1909–1991), American composer and folklorist. He collected American protest songs and wrote music for politically progressive texts, especially "outsider" poems in the American vernacular. He drew on jazz, blues, and cowboy songs for his chamber and choral works. He also wrote eight symphonies and many orchestral pieces, including *Abraham Lincoln Walks at Midnight* (1937) and *Western Suite* (1945).

Luigi Silva (1903–1961), Italian cellist and music historian. After studies in Bologna and Rome, he was principal cellist of the Rome Opera Orchestra. He was an internationally known soloist and chamber musician when he came to the U.S. in 1939. He taught cello at several institutions, including the Eastman School of Music, Juilliard, and Yale. He collected cello literature and made many transcriptions that have entered the instrument's repertory.

Graciela Silvain (1914–2006), Argentine-born soprano. She sang with the Teatro Colón of Buenos Aires before coming to the U.S. to teach at the Academy of Vocal Arts, Philadelphia. There she met her future husband, American tenor Frank Cappelli (1916–2007), with whom she performed in a recital duo.

Ginny Simms (1913–1994), American singer and film actress. She was an actress under contract to M-G-M (1939–50) and a singer for many West Coast–based bandleaders, including Paul Whiteman, Kay Kyser, and Woody Herman.

Martial Singher (1904–1990), French baritone. After eleven seasons with the Paris Opéra he sang with the Metropolitan Opera for another nine (1949–58).

Billy Singleton (fl. 1940s), American pianist. According to Thomson he was a jazz pianist associated with Willie "Bunk" Johnson during his year of residence in San Francisco (1943–44).

Alexander Smallens (1889–1972), Russian-born conductor. He came to America as a child and as a teenager studied at the Paris Conservatory. He was a conductor for many American music institutions including the Boston, Chicago, and Philadelphia orchestras and the Radio City Music Hall. He also conducted the premieres of Virgil Thomson's *Four Saints in Three Acts* (1934) and George Gershwin's *Porgy and Bess* (1935).

Jan Smeterlin (1892–1967), Polish pianist. He abandoned his law studies for a Viennese music education and did not make his professional debut until age twenty-eight. He was known for his interpretations of the music of his fellow-Poles, especially Chopin, Szymanowski, and his mentor Leopold Godowsky.

Leo Smit (1921–1999), American pianist and composer of Russian heritage. A protégé of Stravinsky and Nicolas Nabokov, he was a recitalist notable for his adventurous programming of Romantic, Russian, and new American works. He wrote two operas, two ballets, three symphonies, and more than a hundred songs, most of them settings of poems by Emily Dickinson.

Julia Smith (1905–1989), American pianist and composer. After studies at Juilliard she was pianist for Frédérique Petrides's Orchestrette Classique (1932–39) and head of the music department of the Hartt School, Hartford, Connecticut (1941–46). She wrote several operas, a symphony, some chamber music, and a number of songs and stage works for children.

Leonard B. Smith (1915–2002), American brass player and bandmaster. He played cornet with the Goldman Band (1934–40) and then trumpet with the Detroit Symphony Orchestra (1940–46). He founded and led both the Detroit Concert Band (1946–91) and the Cleveland Orchestra's Blossom Festival Concert Band (1972–97).

Muriel Smith (1923–1985), American singer and Broadway actress. A graduate of the Curtis Institute of Music, she was one of two alternating leads in Oscar Hammerstein's *Carmen Jones* (1943) and also played Ella Hammer in the 1947 revival of Marc Blitzstein's *The Cradle Will Rock*.

Utah Smith (1906–1965), American singer, electric guitarist, and traveling evangelist of the Church of God in Christ. A self-taught musician from Shreveport, Louisiana, he recorded his signature song, "I Want Two Wings," several times from 1945 to 1955. It has since become a gospel standard.

Cesare Sodero (1886–1947), Italian conductor, arranger, and pioneer of recorded and broadcast music. Born and educated in Naples, he emigrated to New York in 1906. He was music director, engineer, and chief of production at the Edison Phonograph Company (1913–25). He then was music director of the NBC (1925–34) and Mutual (1934–42) radio networks. In 1942 he joined the Metropolitan

Opera as director of Italian repertory, a position he enjoyed until his death five years later.

Ina Souez (1903–1992), American soprano. Born in Denver, she studied voice in Italy and sang with opera companies in Milan, London, Paris, and Rome (1928–41). She returned to the U.S. during World War II and was briefly a member of both the New Opera Company and the New York City Opera. A natural comedienne, she enjoyed a second career singing tour-de-force opera parodies for Spike Jones and His City Slickers (1945–55).

Gerard Souzay (1918–2004), French baritone. He was a philosophy student at the Sorbonne when he met his mentor, Pierre Bernac, who offered him private singing lessons and recommended him to the Paris Conservatory. He became one of his generation's leading interpreters of the French song but also mastered German lieder as a student of Lotte Lehmann.

Leo Sowerby (1895–1968), American composer, organist, and choral director. A largely self-taught musician, his Violin Concerto No. 1 was given its premiere by the Chicago Symphony Orchestra when he was eighteen. His first love was sacred music, and he was organist of Chicago's St. James Episcopal Church from 1927 to 1962. He published five symphonies, several cantatas, much choral music, and many works for organ.

Albert Spalding (1888–1953), American violinist. Son of Chicago sporting-goods tycoon J. W. Spalding, he studied in New York, Florence, Paris, and Bologna. He made his debut in Paris in 1906 and his New York debut in 1908. From 1919 to 1950 he made annual tours of the U.S. and gave premieres of concertos by Barber, Dohnányi, Elgar, and others.

Muggsy Spanier (1901–1967), Chicago-based American cornet player. His Ragtime Band played New Orleans–style jazz from the 1920s through the 1960s.

Tony Spargo (1897–1969), or Tony Sbarbaro, American drummer of Sicilian heritage. In 1917 he cofounded, with cornet player Nick LaRocca, the Original Dixieland Band. He led the group from the 1940s until its dissolution in the mid-1960s.

Tossy Spivakovsky (1906–1998), Russian-born violinist. He gave his first recital in Berlin at age ten and made his first European tour at age thirteen. He was touring Australia when Hitler came to power, and so made Melbourne his home from 1933 to 1939. He immigrated to the U.S. in 1940 and was concertmaster of the Cleveland Orchestra in 1942–45. He then established himself as a leading American soloist and gave premieres of works commissioned by him from Bartók, Diamond, Menotti, and Nielsen.

Eleanor Steber (1914–1990), American soprano. She sang mostly

German repertory with the Metropolitan Opera for twenty-one seasons (1940–61). A favorite of Samuel Barber, she commissioned his *Knoxville: Summer of 1915* (1947) and created the title role for his opera *Vanessa* (1958).

Maxine Stellman (1906–1972), American soprano. She sang supporting roles with the Metropolitan Opera for fourteen seasons (1936–50).

Isaac Stern (1920–2001), Russian-born violinist. He was one year old when his family moved from the Ukraine to California, and fifteen years old when he made his debut with the San Francisco Symphony. He quickly established himself as a soloist and as a member of a trio with pianist Eugene Istomin and cellist Leonard Rose. He was a prolific recording artist and a mentor and champion of many younger string players, including Yo-Yo Ma, Itzhak Perlman, and Pinchas Zukerman.

Eduard Steuermann (1892–1964), Austrian-born American pianist and conductor. His teachers included Busoni, Humperdinck, and, most important, Schoenberg, whose works he gave many world premieres. In 1938 he immigrated to the U.S., where he was renowned as a soloist and for his recitals of Beethoven's sonatas.

Risë Stevens (1913–2013), American mezzo-soprano of Norwegian heritage. A native New Yorker, she was discovered at age fourteen by Anna E. Schoen-René, a Juilliard voice instructor, who invited her to become her student. She sang with the Metropolitan Opera from 1938 to 1961 and is most closely associated with the role of Carmen.

Reginald Stewart (1900–1984), Scottish-born pianist and conductor. He was founding conductor of the Toronto Symphony Orchestra, which he led from 1934 to 1941. He was then the director of the Peabody Conservatory (1941–58) and music director of the Baltimore Symphony (1942–52).

Teresa Stich Randall (1927–2007), European-based American soprano. She made her debut in 1947 as Gertrude Stein in Virgil Thomson's *The Mother of Us All*. After several seasons as a soloist with the NBC Symphony Orchestra, she continued her career in Europe, mostly with the Vienna State Opera. From 1961 to 1966 she made twenty-four appearances with the Metropolitan Opera, as Fiordiligi in *Così fan tutte* or as Donna Anna in *Don Giovanni*.

Fritz Stiedry (1883–1968), Austrian conductor. While studying law at the University of Vienna he was hired as personal assistant to Gustav Mahler. He had conducted orchestras in Vienna, Kassel, and Berlin when, in 1933, he was named music director of the Leningrad Symphony Orchestra. In 1937 he came to the U.S. as music director of the New Friends of Music (1937–45) and was later a conductor of German repertory for the Metropolitan Opera (1946–58).

William Grant Still (1895–1978), American composer and arranger. Born in Little Rock, Arkansas, he was a self-taught musician who first found work as an arranger for jazz bands. In 1936, at a performance by the Los Angeles Symphony, he became the first African American to conduct a major U.S. orchestra. In 1934 he received a Guggenheim Fellowship to complete *Blue Steel*, the first of his eight operas. He published more than 150 musical works, including five symphonies and many songs.

Frederick Stock (1872–1942), German-born conductor. Trained as a violinist at the Cologne Conservatory, he was recruited at age twenty-three for the fledgling Chicago Symphony Orchestra. Ten years later, in 1905, he became music director, a position he held for thirty-seven years, until his death in 1942.

Albert Stoessel (1894–1943), American violinist, composer, and conductor. After studies in Munich, he toured Europe and the U.S. as second violinist of the Hess Quartet (1913–15) and then served in World War I. In 1921 he became music director of the New York Oratorio Society and one of the Northeast's leading guest conductors. He died of a heart attack, at age forty-eight, while leading a chamber performance at the annual meeting of the American Academy of Arts and Letters.

Leopold Stokowski (1882–1977), British conductor of Polish heritage. After graduating from the Royal College of Music, he continued his studies in Paris and New York and was briefly conductor of the Cincinnati Orchestra (1909–12). From 1912 to 1940 he was music director of the Philadelphia Orchestra, building it into a first-class ensemble and a pioneer in the fields of radio broadcasting and commercial recording. In 1936–40 he worked part-time in Hollywood, where he helped choose the program and conducted the music for Walt Disney's *Fantasia* (1940). He later held short-term and guest-conducting positions with dozens of American and European orchestras, including the New York Philharmonic and the New York City Symphony, the NBC Symphony Orchestra and Symphony of the Air, and the Metropolitan and New York City operas.

Polyna Stoska (1914–1999), American soprano of Lithuanian heritage whose international career spanned 1938 to 1959. She was a star of the New York City Opera when Kurt Weill invited her to create the role of Anna for *Street Scene* (1946). She sang with the Met from 1947 to 1950.

Richard Strauss (1864–1949), German composer and conductor. He received his early music education from his father, the principal horn player of the Court Opera, Munich. He was still in his teens when he became the personal assistant to Hans von Bülow, who, impressed by his early compositions, gave him lessons in conducting. He wrote very few solo and chamber pieces but instead, from the start, embarked on large-scale orchestral works. His tone poems *Till Eulenspiegel* and *Also Sprach Zarathustra* (both 1895) were among his first mature works. He is best known for his operas, including *Salomé* (1905), *Elektra* (1909), *Der Rosenkavalier* (1911), and *Ariadne auf Naxos* (1912), and during his lifetime was celebrated for his innovative work as codirector of the Vienna State Opera (1919–24). When Hitler came to power in 1933, he refused to join the Nazi Party but did accept a commission to write the "Hymn" for the Berlin Olympics of 1936. Among his last works were *Metamorphosen* (1945), a symphonic lament for war-torn Europe, and the elegiac *Vier letzte Lieder* ("Four Last Songs," 1948) for soprano and orchestra.

Igor Stravinsky (1882–1971), Russian-born composer, conductor, and pianist. The son of an operatic bass, he was immersed in the worlds of music and theater from infancy. He studied law and philosophy in St. Petersburg, but was encouraged to follow his vocation as a composer by Rimsky-Korsokov, who accepted him as a private pupil. In 1908 a performance of his orchestral *Scherzo Fantastique* so impressed Diaghilev that he hired him as a composer for the Ballets Russes, an arrangement that produced his first great works, *The Firebird* (1910) and *Petroushka* (1911). His dissonant ballet *Le Sacre du Printemps* ("The Rite of Spring") was given its premiere in Paris in May 1913 and instantly established him as the "disruptive" modern composer *par excellence*. At the outbreak of World War I, he moved to Switzerland, where he wrote the opera *Le Rosignol* ("The Nightingale," 1914) and the ballets *L'Histoire d'un Soldat* (1918), *Pulcinella* (1920), and *Les Noces* ("The Wedding," 1923). A long residency in France in the 1920s and '30s produced many neoclassical concert pieces and the opera-oratorio *Oedipus Rex* (1927). In 1939 he visited the United States to deliver the Norton lectures at Harvard and the following year settled permanently near Hollywood, California. His American works included *Circus Polka* (1942), commissioned by Ringling Bros.; *Ebony Concerto* (1945), commissioned by Woody Herman's big band; and *The Rake's Progress* (1951), an opera with libretto by W. H. Auden and Chester Kallman. After 1958, Stravinsky experimented with the twelve-tone system, composing a series of *Movements* (1959) for piano and *Variations* (1964) for orchestra. His final years were devoted to writing a series of autobiographical books in collaboration with his longtime musical and literary associate Robert Craft.

Soulima Stravinsky (1910–1994), Swiss-born pianist of Russian heritage. He was a significant interpreter of the works of his father, Igor Stravinksy, and a composer of virtuoso cadenzas to Mozart's piano concertos.

William Strickland (1914–1991), American conductor, composer, and organist. A champion of the American art song, he set the texts of many American poets to his own organ music and, at the end of his life, arranged songs by Charles Ives for electronic synthesizers.

Templeton Strong (1856–1948), or George Templeton Strong Jr., American-born Swiss composer. Born in New York City, he studied at the Leipzig Conservatory and after 1897 made his home in Vevey, on Lake Geneva. He wrote two Romantic symphonies and a number of orchestral and chamber pieces.

Brian Sullivan (1912–1969), American tenor. He sang with the Metropolitan Opera for thirteen seasons (1948–61), often in the lead roles of Peter Grimes and Lohengrin.

Maxine Sullivan (1911–1987), American singer and entertainer. She found a mass audience with the Claude Thornhill Orchestra's upbeat swing version of "Loch Lomond" (1937). Her career as a nightclub performer and recording artist spanned the 1930s to the 1980s.

Ralph Sutton (1922–2001), American pianist. An associate of Bob Scobey and Eddie Condon, he played stride piano in the early jazz tradition of James P. Johnson and Fats Waller.

Set Svanholm (1904–1964), Swedish tenor. In his youth a fixture of the Royal Opera House, Stockholm, he sang with the Metropolitan Opera for ten seasons (1946–56). He was noted for his Wagnerian roles, especially Tristan and Siegfried.

Alexander Sved (1906–1979), or Sándor Svéd, Hungarian-born baritone. He sang with the Metropolitan Opera for ten seasons (1940–50). His signature role was Scarpia in *Tosca*.

Alexander Sveshnikov (1890–1980), founder and director of the Soviet Union's State Academic Choir (1941–80) and the Moscow Choral College for Boys (1944–80).

Howard Swanson (1907–1978), American composer. He excelled at art songs, especially in collaborations with the poet Langston Hughes, including "The Negro Speaks of Rivers" and "Night Song" (both 1950). His orchestral music includes three symphonies and several concertos. Thomson called him "a songful composer of straightforward inspiration and rather wonderful simplicity."

Gladys Swarthout (1900–1969), American mezzo-soprano. After an apprenticeship in Chicago, she joined the Metropolitan Opera, where she sang for sixteen seasons (1929–45). She enjoyed a parallel career as a film star, a popular singer, and, after her retirement from the Met, a recitalist.

Enid Szantho (fl. 1930s–40s), Hungarian-born contralto long associated with the Vienna State Opera.

George Szell (1897–1970), Hungarian-born pianist and conductor. After studies in Vienna he became assistant conductor of the Berlin State Opera and a protégé of Richard Strauss. He made his U.S.

debut in 1930, immigrated to the States in 1939, and was a conductor of German repertory for the Metropolitan Opera from 1942 to 1946. In 1946 he became music director of the Cleveland Orchestra, which he conducted for twenty-four years, until his death in 1970.

Joseph Szigeti (1892–1973), Hungarian-born violinist. A childhood pupil of Jenö Hubay, he was playing professionally in Berlin at age thirteen. He was an internationally known soloist when he made his U.S. debut (1925) and was world famous when he immigrated to America in 1939. A proponent of new music, he commissioned music from Bartók, Bloch, and Diamond and gave American premieres of works by Stravinsky, Prokofiev, and others. In the 1950s he developed severe arthritis in his hands, and in 1960 retired to Geneva.

Ferruccio Tagliavini (1913–1975), Italian tenor whose career spanned 1938 to 1965. For six seasons (1947–53) he sang Italian repertory with the Metropolitan Opera. In 1962 he returned to the company to reprise his signature role, Rodolfo in *La Bohème*.

Alexandre Tansman (1897–1986), Polish-born French composer and pianist. A writer of neoclassical symphonies, chamber pieces, and ballets, he lived in New York from 1941 to 1946.

Leon Temerson (1904–1988), Paris-born violinist who came to the U.S. in 1941. He performed with the Pittsburgh and Chicago symphonies before enjoying a long career as a soloist and as a member of the New York Philharmonic (1946–72).

Maggie Teyte (1888–1976), English soprano. After childhood lessons at the Royal College of Music, she moved to Paris to study voice. In 1908, upon hearing her perform at the Opéra-Comique, Debussy personally coached her to succeed Mary Garden in that company's revival of his *Pelléas et Mélisande*. She then sang in London, and in Boston, Philadelphia, and Chicago, before going into semi-retirement until the 1930s. She reemerged as a recitalist and her generation's finest interpreter of French song.

Blanche Thebom (1915–2010), American mezzo-soprano. She sang for twenty-two seasons with the Metropolitan Opera (1944–66), where she excelled in Wagnerian roles and was eighty times Amneris in Verdi's *Aida*.

Jacques Thibaud (1889–1953), French violinist. After studies at the Paris Conservatory, where he won the premier prix in 1896, he earned his living as a café musician, slowly finding his way onto the concert stage. In 1903 he made his American debut as a soloist, and in the following year formed a long-lived trio (1904–37) with pianist Alfred Cortot and cellist Pablo Casals. His repertoire focused on Mozart, Beethoven, and contemporary French composers. He died, at age sixty-three, in a plane crash in the French Alps.

Helen Thigpen (1912–1966), American actress, singer, and concert soprano. She created the role of Serena for George Gershwin's *Porgy and Bess* (1935).

John Charles Thomas (1891–1960), American baritone. He was a popular and versatile performer on the radio, on Broadway, and in New York operetta for nearly a decade before decamping, in 1925, for Paris and an apprenticeship in opera. After singing for companies in Paris, Brussels, and London, he made his debut with the Metropolitan Opera in 1934. He sang with the Met for nine seasons, making 235 appearances in nine roles before retiring in 1943. Meanwhile, he cultivated a career as soloist and recitalist as well as a radio personality, culminating in NBC's weekly *Westinghouse Program Starring John Charles Thomas, America's Beloved Baritone* (1943–46).

Hugh Thompson (1916–2006), American baritone. He sang with the New York City Opera during its inaugural season and then, from 1944 to 1953, with the Metropolitan Opera.

Randall Thompson (1899–1984), American composer. He wrote three neo-Romantic symphonies, two string quartets, and the one-act opera *Solomon and Balkis* (1942). He is best known for his choral works, including *Allelulia* (1940) and *Requiem* (1959).

Kerstin Thorborg (1896–1970), Swedish-born contralto. She sang Wagnerian roles at the Berlin State Opera from 1924 to 1935 and then immigrated to America. She made her debut with the Metropolitan Opera in 1936 and then sang with the company for twelve seasons (1938–50). In 1950 she returned to Sweden, and was appointed royal court singer by King Gustav V.

Lawrence Tibbett (1896–1960), American baritone, radio singer, and film actor. He joined the Metropolitan Opera at the age of twenty-six and was a pillar of the company for twenty-seven seasons (1923–50). He excelled in Verdi roles, especially Ford in *Falstaff* and the name part in *Simon Boccanegra*.

Herbert Tichman (1922–2010), American clarinetist. After studies at Juilliard, he became a freelance soloist, chamber player, and jazz session artist as well as teacher at Juilliard and the Manhattan School of Music.

Armand Tokatyan (1894–1960), Bulgarian-born tenor of Armenian heritage. He sang Italian repertory with the Metropolitan Opera for nineteen nonconsecutive seasons (1922–46).

Julius Toldi (1892–1985), Austrian-born composer, arranger, and conductor. In 1933 he emigrated from Vienna to Hollywood, where he became staff violist in the scoring department at 20th Century–Fox.

Arturo Toscanini (1867–1957), Italian-born conductor. After cello studies at the Parma Conservatory, he joined the orchestra of the local opera company, for which he conducted *Aida* at age nineteen. He soon moved on to Milan, where he gave the premiere of *Pagliacci* in 1892, and Turin, where he did the same for *La Bohème* in 1896. As music director of La Scala (1898–1908, 1920–29), the Metropolitan Opera (1908–14), and, especially, the New York Philharmonic (1926–36), he enjoyed an international reputation as "The Maestro," the most famous conductor of opera and orchestral music of his time. After 1930 he became an American institution when CBS radio began its weekly broadcasts of Philharmonic concerts, the most listened-to classical music series in the country. In 1936 David Sarnoff, director of CBS's chief rival, the NBC radio network, invited the sixty-nine-year-old Toscanini to create and direct his own orchestra. Sarnoff built the Maestro a twelve-hundred-seat concert hall and broadcast facility—"Studio 8-H" at NBC headquarters, Radio City, in Rockefeller Center—and, in close consultation with him and his appointed deputies, hired the members of the NBC Symphony Orchestra. Under the terms of his contract, Toscanini made most of the programming decisions, including the choice of guest conductors, and was obliged to conduct ten concerts and one opera each season. He made his debut with the orchestra on Christmas Day, 1937, and his final appearance on April 4, 1954.

Roman Totenberg (1911–2012), Polish-born American violinist. After making his debut, at age eleven, with the Warsaw Philharmonic, he studied in Paris with Georges Enesco and Pierre Monteux. He made his U.S. debut in 1935 and immigrated to New York in 1938. He based his international career as soloist and chamber musician in Boston, where he taught violin and lectured at Boston University for nearly half a century.

Jennie Tourel (1900–1973), Belarusian-born mezzo-soprano. Forced to flee Russia during the Revolution, she settled in Paris, where she studied voice with Reynaldo Hahn and Anna El-Tour. From 1933 to 1940 she sang at the Opéra-Comique. Her association with the Metropolitan was brief: two appearances in 1937, eighteen in 1944–47, usually in the role of Mignon, or Carmen, or Adalgisa in Bellini's *Norma*. After the war, she sang mainly in recital, often accompanied by Leonard Bernstein on piano.

Maria von Trapp (1905–1987) was the musically gifted stepmother and matriarch of the Trapp Family Singers. Born Maria Kutschera, she was a schoolteacher and a postulant at a Benedictine nunnery in Salzburg when, in 1927, she met Austro-Hungarian naval officer Georg von Trapp, a widower who hired her as tutor to his oldest children. She soon became Trapp's second wife and—in collaboration with the children's replacement tutor, Father Franz Wasner—the leader of the Trapp Family Singers (1936–56), one of the best-loved concert attractions of the mid-twentieth century. Her autobiography, *The Story of the Trapp Family Singers* (1949), was the basis of the Rodgers and Hammerstein musical *The Sound of Music* (1959).

Helen Traubel (1899–1972), American soprano. She made her debut as a soloist with the St. Louis Symphony in 1923, and her operatic debut with the Metropolitan Opera in 1937. She joined the Met in 1939 and made 180 appearances through 1953, excelling in Wagnerian roles. After the Met she enjoyed a varied career on Broadway and in film, television, and cabaret. In 1959 she published her memoirs, *St. Louis Woman*.

Margaret Truman (1924–2008), American soprano. The only child of President Harry S Truman, she received professional voice lessons from age sixteen. She made her debut in 1947 with the Detroit Symphony Orchestra on ABC Radio's *Sunday Evening Hour*, but after three years of respectful but mixed reviews abandoned the concert stage.

Richard Tucker (1913–1975), Brooklyn-born tenor of Moldavian heritage. He was a cantor in Passaic, New Jersey, when Edward Johnson, who had heard of his singing abilities, invited him to audition for the Metropolitan Opera. He sang with the company for thirty seasons (1945–75), and is perhaps best remembered as Canio in Franco Zeffirelli's production of *Pagliacci* (1970).

Josephine Tumminia (1919–2004), American soprano. The untrained daughter of an Oakland barber, she sang with the San Francisco Opera (1935–38) and the Metropolitan Opera (1941–42). In 1937 she recorded a best-selling swing version of the *Blue Danube Waltz* with Jimmy Dorsey and His Orchestra.

Guido Turchi (1916–2010), Italian composer. His works, which are influenced by both the Italian Baroque and the atonality of Schoenberg, include a Concerto Breve for string quartet (1947) and a three-act opera based on Jaroslav Hašek's novel *The Good Soldier Švejk* (1962).

Rosalyn Tureck (1914–2003), Chicago-born pianist and harpsichordist. Renowned for her piano performances of Bach, she founded the International Bach Society (New York City, 1966) and the Tureck Bach Institute (Oxford, England, 1981) to promote performance of Bach's music and research into the composer's life and scores.

Ray Turner (1903–1976), American pianist and arranger. Long a member of the Paul Whiteman Orchestra, he later held the title "chief pianist" at Paramount Pictures.

Paul Ulanowsky (1908–1968), Austrian-born pianist. Though he performed with the Vienna Philharmonic from 1925 to 1936, he was known to Americans primarily as an accompanist. He worked mainly with the singers Enid Szantho, Martial Singher, and, from 1937 to 1951, Lotte Lehmann.

Alexander Uninsky (1910–1972), Russian-born pianist. Educated in Kiev and Paris, he immigrated to New York in 1933, where he enjoyed a reputation as an interpreter of the Romantic repertory, especially Chopin.

Theodor Uppman (1920–2005), American tenor of Swedish heritage. Although he sang with the Metropolitan Opera for twenty-three seasons (1955–78), he is perhaps best known as creator of the title role in Benjamin Britten's *Billy Budd* (1951).

Francesco Valentino (1907–1991), American baritone. A native New Yorker, he enjoyed a career in Italy and the United Kingdom before joining the Metropolitan Opera in 1940, where he made 407 appearances over the next twenty-two seasons.

Edgard Varèse (1883–1965), French-born composer. His preoccupations were not with melody and counterpoint but with timbre, rhythm, and volume. He did not claim to "compose" in the traditional sense but instead, in his phrase, to "organize sounds," to make richly textured complexes of interacting sonorities that are too intelligently structured to be called noise yet meet none of the listener's expectations of music. He wrote for orchestra, for percussion ensembles, and for electronic instruments. In 1971 Thomson called him "the most original composer of the last half century and one of the most powerfully communicative."

Astrid Varnay (1918–2006), Swedish-born soprano of Hungarian heritage. From 1941 to 1979 she made some two hundred appearances with the Metropolitan Opera, usually in Wagnerian roles. After 1950 she appeared regularly in Germany, in what she called her "second career, as a European mezzo-soprano."

Ralph Vaughan Williams (1872–1958), English composer of Welsh heritage. After studies at Cambridge and the Royal College of Music he became a collector of English hymns and folk songs. With the Anglican liturgist Percy Dearmer he edited the *English Hymnal* (1906), *Songs of Praise* (1926), and *The Oxford Book of Carols* (1928). His pursuit of an English national style based on folk elements and Tudor music is evident in the early orchestral works *Norfolk Rhapsodies* (1905–7), *Fantasia on a Theme by Thomas Tallis* (1910), and the *London Symphony* (1914). A prolific composer in every traditional genre, he wrote operas based on works by Bunyan (*The Pilgrim's Progress*) and Shakespeare (*The Merry Wives of Windsor*), song cycles to texts by George Herbert and A. E. Housman, film scores, incidental music, and orchestral, band, and chamber works. His sacred music includes an a cappella Mass in G major (1922), excerpts from which were sung at the coronation of Elizabeth II.

Sándor Végh (1912–1997), Hungarian-born violinist and conductor. After studies at the Academy Franz Liszt, Budapest, he began a career as soloist in 1927. He was a founding member of the Hungarian String Quartet (1934–40), which he left to found his own American group, the Végh Quartet (1940–70). In 1978 he left the U.S. for Austria to lead the Camerata Academica, the chamber orchestra of the Salzburg Mozarteum.

John Verrall (1908–2001), American violinist and composer. Born in Iowa and educated in Minnesota, he studied composition with Copland and Harris at Tanglewood and with Kodály in Budapest. He wrote four symphonies, a concerto for violin, a concerto for viola, seven string quartets, and many songs.

Heitor Villa-Lobos (1887–1959), Brazilian composer. He was a largely self-taught musician who from his early teens earned money playing guitar, cello, and clarinet in cafés and pickup groups. In 1913 he published the first of his more than two thousand compositions, the early works dominated by European concert-music tradition, the later by native folk songs and Brazilian popular music. He spent most of the 1920s in Paris, where he wrote his *Chôros* (1924–29), a series of sixteen pieces—one for solo guitar, another for solo piano, the rest for chamber groups or orchestra—that together form what the composer called a "*brasilophonia*" or sonic panorama of urban Brazilian street music. Other works include twelve symphonies, eighteen string quartets, and a series of nine *Bachianas Brasileiras*—Bach-inspired works in the South American idiom.

Ramón Vinay (1911–1996), Chilean tenor who from 1946 to 1966 made 171 appearances with the Metropolitan Opera. His signature role was Verdi's Otello, which he sang for Toscanini at La Scala (1946) and then on an NBC Symphony opera broadcast (1947). He also sang the role for the initial Met telecast, aired live on opening night of the 1948–49 season.

Thelma Votipka (1906–1972), American mezzo-soprano who excelled in character roles, especially in the Italian repertory. From 1935 to 1963, she made 1,422 appearances with the Metropolitan Opera, more than any other female performer in the company's history.

Bernard Wagenaar (1894–1971), Dutch-born composer, violinist, and teacher. In 1920 he came to America at the invitation of Leopold Stokowski, who hired him for the string section of the Philadelphia Orchestra. In 1925 he joined the staff of the Juilliard School, where he taught orchestration and composition through 1968. His music includes four neoclassical symphonies, several concertos, and many chamber works.

Frederic Waldman (1903–1995), Vienna-born American pianist and conductor. A protégé of George Szell, he was music director of the Juilliard Opera Theater from 1947 to 1967. He also founded and led Musica Aeterna (1957–85), a small orchestra dedicated to new music and the revival of forgotten works.

Alfred Wallenstein (1898–1983), Chicago-born cellist and conductor. He performed with the Los Angeles, San Francisco, and Chicago symphony orchestras before joining, at the invitation of Toscanini, the New York Philharmonic (1929–43). He conducted Hollywood Bowl summer concerts and from 1943 to 1956 was music director of the Los Angeles Philharmonic.

Bruno Walter (1876–1962), German-born pianist, composer, and conductor. After an apprenticeship in Hamburg under Gustav Mahler, he led several German orchestras and opera companies from 1900 to 1933. Expelled from Germany by the Nazi Party, he worked in Vienna, Amsterdam, and Paris before emigrating to the U.S. in 1939. Though based in Hollywood, he was a conductor of German repertory for the Metropolitan Opera from 1941 to 1949 and a frequent guest conductor through 1959. He also led the New York Philharmonic in 1947–49 and frequently appeared with the NBC Symphony and Philadelphia orchestras.

William Walton (1902–1983), English composer. The son of a choirmaster, he took piano and singing lessons but was self-taught as a composer. After studying prosody at Oxford, he was invited to write music to accompany the readings of his patron, the poet Edith Sitwell. From piano pieces and songs he quickly graduated to complex orchestral works. He also wrote the oratorio *Belshazzar's Feast* (1931), the opera *Troilus and Cressida* (1954), and scores for several films, including Olivier's *Henry V* (1944).

Sandra Warfield (1921–2009), American mezzo-soprano. She made 172 appearances with the Metropolitan Opera from 1953 to 1972. She was the wife of tenor James McCracken (1926–1988); together they sang the title roles of Saint-Saëns's *Samson and Delilah* at the Vienna State Opera, the Zurich Opera, and their farewell performance at the Met.

Leonard Warren (1911–1960), American baritone. Excelling in Italian roles, he was a lead singer with the Metropolitan Opera for twenty years—from 1939, at the age of twenty-seven, until his death from a stroke, at age forty-eight, during a performance of Verdi's *La forza del destino*.

Franz Wasner (1905–1992), Austrian choral director and Roman Catholic missionary. In 1936 he met the Austro-Hungarian naval officer Baron von Trapp, who hired him as the religious and academic tutor of his many young children. In collaboration with the children's stepmother, the musically gifted Maria von Trapp, he made the Trapp Family Singers (1938–56) one of the best-loved concert attractions of their time.

Ben Weber (1916–1979), American composer. Largely self-taught, he wrote chamber music and concertos that blended atonal and Romantic elements. Thomson described the work as "music of great sincerity and emotional depth couched in a modified serialism easily acceptable."

Beveridge Webster (1908–1999), American pianist. The son of the founder of the Pittsburgh Conservatory, he studied in France with Nadia Boulanger and Isidor Philipp. He was a leading interpreter of Ravel and Debussy and an ardent champion of contemporary American piano music.

Kurt Weill (1900–1950), German-born composer. After studies in Berlin with Ferruccio Busoni, for whom he composed some expressionistic chamber works, he began to write for the stage. In 1926 he forged a partnership with playwright Bertolt Brecht that resulted in, among other works, *Mahagonny* (1927; expanded 1930), *The Threepenny Opera* (1928), and the ballet-chanté *The Seven Deadly Sins* (1933). In 1935 he moved to New York, where he lived with the Austrian singer Lotte Lenya (1898–1981). His later works, most of them written for Broadway, include collaborations with Franz Werfel, Maxwell Anderson, Ira Gershwin, Ogden Nash, Elmer Rice, and Langston Hughes.

Carl Weinrich (1904–1991), American organist, choral director, and educator. The choirmaster and music director of Princeton's University Chapel from 1943 to 1973, he was a leader of the Baroque organ revival.

Ljuba Welitsch (1913–1996), Bulgarian-born soprano. After more than a decade with various German companies, she sang with the Metropolitan Opera for three seasons (1949–52) and then as a frequent guest star through 1972. Her signature role was Richard Strauss's Salomé, which she created for the composer in 1944.

Paul Whiteman (1890–1967), West Coast–based American composer and bandleader. Known from the 1920s as "The King of Jazz," he was, like Duke Ellington, a pioneer of "concert-hall swing," writing, commissioning, and arranging jazz-inspired works for the symphony orchestra, most notably George Gershwin's *Rhapsody in Blue.*

Emerson Whithorne (1884–1958), American pianist, composer, and ethnomusicologist. He wrote orchestral and chamber works, piano pieces, and songs that incorporated influences from Chinese music.

William Wilderman (1919–2004), German-born bass. He sang with the New York City Opera (1946–47) and the Metropolitan Opera (1958–64).

Healey Willan (1880–1968), London-born organist and composer. As music director of Toronto's Church of St. Mary Magdalene

(Anglican), he composed more than six hundred liturgical works for choir and for organ.

J. Finley Williamson (1887–1964), American choral director and educator. In 1920 he was appointed director of the choir of Westminster Presbyterian Church, Dayton, Ohio, which he quickly transformed into an elite touring group, the Westminster Choir. Six years later he founded Westminster Choir College, the first American institution dedicated to the education of church choirmasters and soloists. In 1939 he moved the school to Princeton, New Jersey, where it is now part of Rider University's Westminster College of the Arts.

Meredith Willson (1902–1984), American composer, songwriter, conductor, and playwright. During World War II, he worked as a bandleader, scriptwriter, and actor for U.S. Armed Forces Radio and for the Burns and Allen radio series. He later found fame as the author of the music, book, and lyrics for *The Music Man* (1957) and *The Unsinkable Molly Brown* (1960).

Erich Witte (1911–2008), German tenor. After seven years on the German stage, he sang for a season (1937–38) with the Metropolitan Opera. After the war he returned to Germany, where he enjoyed a long career with various state opera companies.

Stefan Wolpe (1902–1972), German-born composer. An early proponent of atonality, he also wrote workers' protest songs and, after immigrating to Palestine in 1934, tunes for the kibbutzim. In 1938 he moved to America where he befriended the Abstract Expressionists, taught at Black Mountain College, and, from 1957, was head of the music department at Long Island's C. W. Post College. Thomson called him "a remarkable teacher [and] a composer sometimes of high complexity, usually serial, always inspired."

G. Wallace Woodworth (1903–1969), American choral director and educator. A graduate of Harvard, he was the university's choirmaster for eighteen years, director of its Glee Club for twenty-five years, and director of the Radcliffe Choral Society for thirty-three years.

John W. Work (1901–1967), or John Wesley Work III, American choral director, composer, and ethnomusicologist. He was educated at Fisk University, Columbia, Juilliard, and Yale. In 1933 he joined the faculty at Fisk, where he founded the Fisk Jubilee Singers and compiled the anthology *American Negro Songs and Spirituals* (1940). His compositions include the string suite *Yenvalou* (1945), based on Haitian songs and dances.

Alexander Zakin (1903–1990), Russian-born pianist. For thirty-seven years (1940–77) he was accompanist to Isaac Stern.

Alfred Zighera (1898–1978), French-born cellist. Educated at the Paris Conservatory, he was recruited by Koussevitzky as principal cellist for the Boston Symphony Orchestra (1925–63). He founded, directed, and played viola da gamba in the Society of Ancient Instruments (1938–63), a Boston-based early music ensemble.

Bernard Zighera (1904–1984), French-born harpist and pianist. The brother of Alfred Zighera, he was principal harpist of the Boston Symphony Orchestra (1926–80) and piano accompanist to Koussevitzky in his infrequent double-bass recitals.

Efrem Zimbalist (1889–1985), Russian-born violinist, composer, and educator. The son of a conductor, he studied for eight years with violinist Leopold Auer. He immigrated to New York in 1911 and enjoyed a forty-year American career as a soloist. Among his compositions are the orchestral *American Rhapsody* (1936) and a violin concerto (1947). In 1928 he joined the faculty of the Curtis Institute of Music, and was the school's director from 1941 to 1968.

...revised by Nicola... *Grove Book of Opera*, by Stanley S... ...sity Press, 1996), and the *Oxford Dictionary of*... ...ion, edited by Michael and Joyce Kennedy with Tim Rutherfo... York: Oxford University Press, 2012). Quotations from Shakespeare... to G. Blakemore Evans, editor, *The Riverside Shakespeare* (Bosto... Mifflin, 1974). For further biographical detail than is contained in... ogy, see Kathleen Hoover and John Cage, *Virgil Thomson: His Life*... (New York: Thomas Yoseloff, 1959), Virgil Thomson, *Virgil Thom.*... York: Knopf, 1966), and Anthony Tommasini, *Virgil Thomson: Composer on the Aisle* (New York: Norton, 1997); also Tim Page and Vanessa Weeks Page, editors, *Selected Letters of Virgil Thomson* (New York: Summit Books, 1988), and Virgil Thomson, *A Virgil Thomson Reader* (Boston: Houghton Mifflin, 1981). The festschrift "A Tribute to Virgil Thomson on His Eighty-first Birthday," edited by Herbert Leibowitz (*Parnassus: Poetry in Review* 5:2, Spring/Summer 1977), collects memoirs by musical friends and acquaintances. For an annotated bibliography of Thomson's writings, as well as a list of his musical works and a discography, see Michael Meckna, *Virgil Thomson: A Bio-Bibliography* (Westport, CT: Greenwood Press, 1986). For an institutional history of the *New York Herald Tribune*, see Richard Kluger, *The Paper: The Life and Death of the New York Herald Tribune* (New York: Knopf, 1986). Grateful acknowledgement is made to G. Christopher Fish, Gino Francesconi, Gwendolyn Haverstock Freed, Jeffrey Herman, Vanessa Weeks Page, Charles Passy, Keenan Reesor, Jay Sullivan, Suzanne C. Taylor, Hillary Dyson Teachout, Anthony Tommasini, and Robert Tuggle for their assistance on this project.

THE MUSICAL SCENE

8.36–37 *De gustibus disputandum est*] Latin: In matters of taste there is dispute.

10.35–36 "I understand now . . . intellectual life."] In his volume of memoirs, *Virgil Thomson* (1966), Thomson identifies his longtime partner, the American painter Maurice Grosser (1903–1986), as the source of this remark.

12.4 Berkshire season] Since 1936, the Boston Symphony Orchestra has given a series of summer concerts at Tanglewood, near Lenox, in the Berkshire Mountains of western Massachusetts. See pages 716–18 of the present volume.

In the notes below, the reference numbers denote page and line
(line counts include desk-reference headings). No note is made
in standard desk-reference books, including *The Ox...*
York: Schirmer, 1993), *The G...*
Dictionary of Musicians, eighth edition ...

Car...

32.35   "C...
enne Gracie A...
1989). It was perfo...
and with Albert Coates ...
musical *Two Girls and a S...*

33.35-36   Leopold Stokowski ... Metropolitan Opera House, the Met orc... , and
the Collegiate Chorale, led by Robert Shaw, pe... *Matthew
Passion* while students from the School of American Ballet, ... direction
of George Balanchine, danced and mimed the parts of what was billed as "A
Modern Miracle Play." Actress Lillian Gish mimed the role of Mary Magdalene.

34.13   Bruno David Ussher] German-born American music critic (1897–1963)
who throughout the 1940s wrote program notes for concerts at the Hollywood
Bowl.

34.25   Ethel Waters ... *Laugh Time*] After tryouts on the West Coast, *Laugh
Time* (1943), a vaudeville revue, ran 126 performances on Broadway. It was a
showcase for actress and singer Ethel Waters (1896–1977), who reprised her hits
"Heat Wave," "Stormy Weather," and "Am I Blue?"

34.35-36   C.I.O. Hot Jazz Hall] CIO Hall, at 150 Golden Gate Avenue, was
the auditorium and meeting place of the San Francisco local of the Congress
of Industrial Organizations. Because the union was racially integrated, CIO
"Hot Jazz" Hall was a popular venue for integrated jazz bands in the 1930s and
'40s.

35.19   Rudi Blesh] American jazz critic and impresario (1899–1985). He was
a music reviewer for the *San Francisco Chronicle* and a Bay Area concert pro-
moter when, in 1944, Thomson hired him as jazz critic for the *Herald Tribune*.
He was author of, among other books, *They All Played Ragtime* (1950) and
the authorized life of Buster Keaton (1966). As cofounder of Circle Records

(1946–52) he rediscovered, recorded, and managed the career of ragtime pianist Eubie Blake (1887–1983).

37.30   Old Man] Nickname for Arturo Toscanini.

37.31   Mr. Petrillo] James Caesar Petrillo (1892–1984), strongman figure in the American Federation of Musicians, a labor union for professional musicians founded in 1896. Petrillo, originally a trumpet player, joined the Chicago local of the AFM in 1919 and was national president from 1940 to 1958. In 1942–44 he forbade union members to make commercial recordings until the AFM could negotiate better royalties for musicians from America's leading labels. This twenty-six-month musicians' strike was popularly known as the Petrillo Ban.

37.33   good Doctor] Nickname for Serge Koussevitzky, who in 1929 was presented by Harvard University with an honorary doctorate in music.

50.13   Mayor's boys] The New York City Symphony Orchestra, a public-funded institution founded in 1926, was, during the New Deal, sponsored by Mayor Fiorello LaGuardia and the WPA's Federal Music Project (see note 268.28).

70.10   according to Albert Schweitzer] Schweitzer published a two-volume life of J. S. Bach (1905, 1908) that in 1911 was translated into English by Ernest Newman (see note 790.2).

71.35–36   They did but they don't any more, as the ditty hath it.] Allusion to a marching song of World War I whose every bawdy verse begins "I used to work in Chicago / in a department store. / I used to work in Chicago, / I did but I don't any more."

72.9   John Peale Bishop . . . once rhymed so prettily] In "The New Mother Goose: The Famous Rhymes Revised to Conform to Modern Science and Morals" (*Vanity Fair*, July 1925), the American poet and wit John Peale Bishop (1892–1944) wrote: "What are little girls made of? / What are little girls made of? / Of Iphigenia's incestuous desires, / That's what little girls are made of."

72.27   Gluck-Piccinni quarrel] In 1776, Anne-Pierre-Jacques Devismes du Valgay, director of the Paris Opéra, set a challenge for the day's most popular composers, the German Christoph Willibald Gluck (1714–1787) and the Italian Niccolò Piccinni (1728–1800). Each was to compose a four-act opera based on the same source material, the *Iphigenia in Tauris* of Euripides. Gluck's opera, to a libretto by Nicholas-François Guillard, was given a successful premiere in May 1779. Piccinni's opera, to a libretto by Alphonse du Congé Dubreuil, was given a less well-received premiere in January 1881.

72.28   *querelle des bouffons*] "Quarrel of the Comic Actors" (1752–54), common name for a heated aesthetic debate among the French public about, in Thomson's phrase, "the respective virtues of the French and Italian operatic styles."

72.36–37   *Lettre ouverte . . . 1921*).] Claude Debussy's "Open Letter to M. le Chevalier W. Gluck" was included in his book *M. Croche, Anti-Dilettante*, a collection of reflections on music privately printed in 1921 by Librairie Dorbonaîné, Paris.

72.38–40 "*Entre nous . . . langue nuancée.*"] "Between us, your prosody is very bad; that is, you make French a language of emphasis when it is, on the contrary, a language of nuance."

74.3 Paul Henry Lang] Hungarian-born American music critic (1901–1991) and author of the standard college text *Music in Western Civilization* (1941). He succeeded Thomson as music critic at the *New York Herald Tribune* (1954–64).

75.23–24 "J'ai vu se tourner . . . mon père."] "I've seen turn against me / the gods, my homeland and my father" (Nicholas-François Guillard, *Iphigénie en Tauride* [1779] I:i).

81.34 Schikaneder's fairy tale] *Die Zauberflöte* ("The Magic Flute," 1791) was the last of several fairy-tale librettos written by the German poet, actor, and opera impresario Emanuel Schikaneder (1751–1812).

85.20–21 Rameau's and Fux's works on harmony] *Traité de l'harmonie* ("Treatise on Harmony," 1722), by French composer and music theorist Jean-Philippe Rameau (1683–1764), and *Gradus ad Parnassum* ("Steps toward Parnassus," 1725), by the Austrian composer and music teacher Johann Joseph Fux (1660–1741).

87.20 Manzoni] During the last five years of his life, Alessandro Manzoni (1785–1873), Italian poet and author of the novel *I promessi sposi* ("The Betrothed," 1828), was a close friend of the composer Giuseppe Verdi (1813–1901). Verdi's Requiem was first performed at the Church of San Marco, Milan, on May 22, 1874, the first anniversary of Manzoni's death.

88.28 Alma Gluck Zimbalist] Alma Gluck (1884–1938), Romanian-born American soprano, sang for the Metropolitan Opera for three seasons (1909–12). She married violinist Efrem Zimbalist in 1914, became one of the first stars of recorded music, and then retired from the stage in 1925. She died at age fifty-four, after a long battle with liver cancer, in New York's Roosevelt Hospital.

91.15 a recent correspondent] Ernst Křenek, recently arrived in New York from Vienna, had sent Thomson a letter regarding his review of Hindemith's Symphony No. 1 as performed by the New York Philharmonic under Dimitri Mitropoulos.

102.28–30 first-prize violin student . . . composed.] Samuel Dushkin was a first-prize violin student at the Paris Conservatory. Stravinsky wrote his Violin Concerto expressly for Dushkin and conducted him in the piece's premiere, with the Berlin Radio Orchestra, on October 23, 1931.

102.38 Mr. Balanchine] Russian-born dancer and choreographer George Balanchine (1904–1983) came to New York in 1933 to create, with Lincoln Kirstein (see note 491.26), the School of American Ballet (1934) and the New York City Ballet (1948). Balanchine remained ballet master of the school and principal choreographer of the company until his death.

105.31–32   opera about a Chinese emperor . . . nightingale] *Le Rossignol* ("The Nightingale," 1914), based on a fairy tale (1843) by Hans Christian Andersen.

120.6   first violin] Josef Roismann.

124.36–37   New York Music Critics' Circle] Organization founded in 1941 by Virgil Thomson and *New York Times* music critic Olin Downes to, in the words of its first press release, "award a testimonial to the American composer of a work . . . publicly performed for the first time in New York City during each season" and "encourage the establishment of an American repertory." Thomson and a membership of roughly thirty critics awarded prizes through the early 1960s, when the Critics' Circle was subsumed into the less parochial Music Critics Association of North America, founded in 1956.

131.31–32   His one film score] Roy Harris provided the score for *One-Tenth of Our Nation* (1940), a half-hour documentary on black education in the American South produced by the Rockefeller Foundation.

133.11   Will Geer] American actor and social activist (1902–1978). He created the role of Mr. Mister in Marc Blitzstein's *The Cradle Will Rock* (1937) and found late-life celebrity as Grandpa Zeb (1972–76) on CBS television's *The Waltons* (1972–81).

136.32–33   Music Critics Circle] See note 124.36–37.

142.21–22   Thirty-ninth Street] The "old" Metropolitan Opera House (1883–1967), at Thirty-ninth Street and Broadway.

143.28   *Twin Beds*] Farce in three acts (1914) by American playwrights Margaret Mayo (1882–1951) and Salisbury Field (1878–1936).

145.22   Frederick Kiesler] Austrian-born stage and costume designer (1890–1965) who from the late 1930s through the 1950s was on the theater faculty of both the Juilliard School and Columbia University.

147.32   "Ah, fors'e lui"] "Ah, perhaps he's the one . . ."

155.27–28   Inna Minnie] Perpetually exasperated ten-year-old cave-girl in the comic strip *Peter Piltdown* (1935–46), by Canadian cartoonist Mal Eaton (d. 1973). The strip appeared every Sunday in the *New York Herald Tribune*.

158.19–27   In the French version . . . loved him.] The libretto for the original version of Offenbach's *La Vie Parisienne* (1866) was written by Henri Mielhac and Ludovic Halévy. The book of the English version (1929) was freely adapted by *Punch* humorist A. P. Herbert. The Brentano-Verneuil-Farquhar version (1941), which closely follows Meilhac and Halévy, ran thirty-seven performances on Broadway.

159.8   Jean Cocteau] Avant-garde French poet, novelist, playwright, director, filmmaker, graphic artist, and editor (1889–1963).

159.9   Lutetian strand] Parisian riverfront.

159.17–20   "Repeuplons les salons . . . ," "Je veux m'en fourrer . . . ," "Je serai votre guide dans ce ville splendide."] "We repopulate the salons of the

Faubourg Saint-Germain," "I want to cram it all in," "I will be your guide to this beautiful city."

159.22   Mrs. Farquhar's rhymed lyrics] Marion Jones Farquhar (1879–1965) was a women's national tennis champion before she became a poet, translator, and private voice teacher. Her translations include not only Meilhac and Halévy's songs for *La Vie Parisienne* but also the libretto for Pergolesi's *La Serva Pedrona* and the poems of Victor Hugo.

159.32–33   in the Chéret manner] In the style of Jules Chéret (1836–1932), French draftsman and lithographer whose advertisements, especially for theaters and cabarets, helped define the graphic style of the Belle Époque poster.

159.38   Thirty-ninth Street crematorium] See note 142.21–22.

161.4   Charlotte Greenwood] American vaudeville entertainer (1890–1977) who, standing more than six feet tall on famously long legs, was billed as "the only woman in the world who could kick a giraffe in the eye."

163.20   Defrère] Belgian-born Désiré Defrère (1888–1964) joined the Metropolitan Opera as a baritone (1934–38) but found his true place in the company as a stage director (1935–63).

163.21–22   Hans Kautsky] Austrian-born artist (1864–1937) who was a set designer for the Vienna State Opera and the Bayreuth Festival before joining the staff of the Met in 1911.

164.31   Max Jacob] French poet, writer, and painter (1876–1944) whose early works were a shaping influence on the symbolist and surrealist movements in literature and art. Born into a Jewish family in Brittany, he converted to Chritianity in 1909 and became a Roman Catholic in 1915. He was arrested by the Germans during the occupation of France and died in the concentration camp at Drancy, near Paris.

164.37   Saint-Paul-Roux] French Symbolist poet, playwright, and librettist (1861–1940) who also published under his given name, Paul-Pierre Roux.

166.23   Richard Watts] American critic (1898–1981) who reviewed film and theater for the *New York Herald Tribune* (1936–42) and the *New York Post* (1946–74).

166.31   Madame Sans-Gêne] Cathérine Hübscher (1753–1835), "Madame Without-Reserve," vivacious French laundress who became, by a fortunate marriage, the Duchess of Danzig.

169.15   Little Eva] Evangeline St. Clare is the young daughter of a white slaveholder in Harriet Beecher Stowe's antislavery novel *Uncle Tom's Cabin* (1852). A holy innocent, she believed in the equality of all humankind, regardless of race.

170.27   Cheryl Crawford] Independent American theater producer (1902–1986) whose credits spanned four decades, from Clifford Odets's *Awake and Sing!* (1935) to Leah Napoli and Isaac Bashevis Singer's *Yentl* (1975).

170.29   Mamoulian] Rouben Mamoulian (1897–1987), Russian-born American film and theater director whose credits include the original production of George Gershwin's *Porgy and Bess* (1935).

175.3–4   Robinson's and Latouche's *Ballad for Americans*] Cantata (1938), with music by Earl Robinson (1910–1991) and words by John Latouche (1914–1956), written for *Sing for Your Supper* (1939), a "topical musical revue" presented by the WPA's Federal Theatre Project at the Adelphi Theater, New York. When, in late 1939, the CBS network broadcast the cantata, the performance, starring Paul Robeson, created a national sensation. In 1940 *Ballad for Americans* was recorded by Robeson, by Odetta, and Bing Crosby and was sung at the national conventions of both the Republican and U.S. Communist parties.

175.7   father Karamazov] Fyodor Pavlovich Karamazov, self-excoriating paterfamilias of Dostoevsky's novel *The Brothers Karamazov* (1880).

176.3   *Pieces of Eight*] Operatic comedy in two acts, with music by Bernard Wagenaar, book and lyrics by Edward Eager, which received five performances at Columbia University's Brander Matthews Theater, May 10–14, 1944.

194.2   Tilden or Budge] Bill Tilden (1893–1953) and Don Budge (1915–2000), dominant American tennis pros of, respectively, the 1920s and the 1930s.

200.26–27   Lawrence Gilman] American music critic (1878–1939) and for fourteen years Thomson's predecessor at the *New York Herald Tribune* (1925–39).

215.16   *"Peacock Pie"*] English poet Walter de la Mare (1873–1956) published *Peacock Pie*, his third book of children's verse, in 1913.

215.30   *tenue*] Bearing; deportment.

226.1   *bruits parasites*] Stray sounds; distracting peripheral noises.

226.32–33   what Sebastian Bach meant by the *stile francese*] See page 300 of the present volume.

228.26   reforms of Pope Pius X] See pages 772–73 of the present volume for Thomson's detailed analysis of Pius X's *Motu Proprio* of 1903.

231.27   *locum tenens*] Latin: placeholder; stand-in.

234.26–28   *Lady Macbeth of Mzensk* . . . Soviet government.] Thomson's sense is that when, in 1936, Stalin prohibited further performances of Shostakovich's popular but "bourgeois" opera *Lady Macbeth of Mzensk* (1934), he acted much as Pope Pius X did when, in 1903, he issued a *Motu Proprio* banning most sacred music composed since 1600 from use in the Roman Catholic liturgy.

237.3   *famille nombreuse*] French: large family.

239.30   Dr. Arne and Francis Hutchinson] Thomas Augustus Arne (1710–1778), composer of "Rule, Britannia!" (1740), and Francis Hutchinson (a.k.a. "Francis Ireland" or "Francis Hutcheson," 1721–1784), Irish songwriter.

243.31 *The Sacred Harp*] *The Sacred Harp: A Collection of Hymn Tunes, Odes, and Anthems, Selected from the Most Eminent Authors*, by Benjamin Franklin White (1800–1879) and Elisha J. King (1821?–1844) (Philadelphia: T. K. & P. G. Collins, for the Proprietors, B. F. White & E. J. King, Hamilton, Ga., 1844). The book went through three further editions during White's lifetime (1850, 1859, 1869) and has since gone through several more under various editors.

243.32 *Southern Harmony*] *The Southern Harmony, and Musical Companion: Containing a Choice Collection of Tunes, Hymns, Songs, Odes, and Anthems, Selected from the Most Eminent Authors in the United States*, by William Walker (1809–1875) (New Haven, CT: Nathan Whiting for the Author, 1835). The book went through four further editions (1840, 1847 [twice], 1854) during Walker's lifetime. The fifth edition, "Thoroughly Revised and Greatly Improved" (Philadelphia: E. W. Miller, 1854), was reprinted in 1939 (New York: Hastings House Publishers, for the WPA's Writers' Project of Kentucky) and has since become the standard.

244.6 George Pullen Jackson] American musicologist (1874–1953) whose *White Spirituals in the Southern Uplands: The Story of the Fasola Folk, Their Songs, Singings, and "Buckwheat Notes"* was published by the University of North Carolina Press in 1933.

246.9 Thurman Arnold] American antitrust lawyer (1891–1969) and author of *The Folklore of Capitalism* (1937), a study in "those ideas about our social and political system that are not generally regarded as folklore but popularly and usually erroneously accepted as fundamental principles of law and economics" —that is, as American *Realpolitik*.

250.14–15 published reports of Columbia University's Institute of Social Research reports] See, for example, Paul F. Lazarsfeld, Director of Radio Research, Columbia University, in his *Radio Research and Applied Psychology* (Special number of the *Journal of Applied Psychology*, December 1939) and *Radio and the Printed Page: An Introduction to the Study of Radio and Its Role in the Communication of Ideas* (New York: Duell, Sloan & Pearce, 1940).

255.18–19 *Silly Symphony* . . . the *William Tell* Overture] In Disney's Mickey Mouse short *The Band Concert* (1935), Mickey (not Donald Duck) conducts the *William Tell* Overture while Donald, playing "Turkey in the Straw" on a wooden flute, subverts the performance.

257.4 *The Great Dictator*] 1940 feature-length lampoon of Nazi Germany written and directed by Charlie Chaplin, and starring Chaplin and Paulette Goddard.

257.11 *City Lights*] Released in 1931, four years after the advent of sound, *City Lights* (like its successor, *Modern Times*, 1936) is a pantomime with a recorded-music soundtrack. *The Great Dictator*, by contrast, is a dialogue-driven "talkie," Chaplin's first.

258.32 *The Road to Life*] Soviet feature film (1931) written and directed by Nikolai Ekk (1902–1976). The screenplay is based on the life of Soviet pedagogue Anton Makarenko, headmaster of the Gorky Commune for Delinquent Youth.

258.33 René Clair] French filmmaker (1898–1981) whose early sound films include the comedy *À Nous la Liberté!* ("Freedom for Us!" 1931), with a score by Georges Auric.

259.17–18 Carl Van Doren] American literary historian (1885–1950) and Pulitzer Prize–winning biographer of Benjamin Franklin (1939).

260.12 Fredric March] American stage and film actor (1897–1975) who in 1931 won an Oscar for best actor in Rouben Mamoulian's *Dr. Jekyll and Mr. Hyde.*

266.1 United States Rubber Company] U.S. Rubber was the sponsor of the New York Philharmonic's Sunday afternoon broadcasts on CBS Radio from 1939 to 1947.

268.28 WPA orchestras] The Works Projects Administration (WPA), a New Deal agency that provided jobs for out-of-work Americans, employed composers, conductors, and other musicians through its Federal Music Project (1936–43) and related programs. More than twenty civic orchestras were either founded or funded under the WPA.

270.1 chamber opera troupes] See note 594.34.

278.1–3 mouth-organ . . . Town Hall] Jazz harmonica player Larry Adler (1914–2001) transcribed works by Debussy, Poulenc, Ravel, and others for his mixed pop and classical recitals.

278.5–6 national anthem . . . drinking glee?] The lyrics of "The Star-Spangled Banner" (1814), by Baltimore poet Francis Scott Key (1779–1843), were written to the melody of *To Anacreon in Heaven* (c. 1776), a drinking song by English composer John Stafford Smith (1750–1836).

279.7–8 Mrs. Astor's Four Hundred] Caroline Astor (1830–1908), the wife of businessman William Backhouse Astor Jr., was the arbiter of New York social life during the Gilded Age. According to her social secretary, Ward McAllister, only four hundred persons could be said to constitute New York's "fashionable society"—four hundred being the capacity of the ballroom in the Astors' townhouse at 350 Fifth Avenue.

THE ART OF JUDGING MUSIC

310.25–29 George Bernard Shaw . . . Hamlet soliloquies] In "Form and Design in Music" (*The World*, May 31, 1893), Shaw's "celebrated 'analysis' of Hamlet's soliloquy on suicide" parodies the methods of academic music criticism: "Shakespear, dispensing with the customary exordium, announces his subject at once in the infinitive, in which mood it is presently repeated after a short connecting passage in which, brief as it is, we recognise the alternative and negative forms on which so much of the significance of repetition depends. . . ."

313.3 *The Philharmonic Crisis*] On the evening of February 3, 1947, Artur Rodzinski, music director of the New York Philharmonic since 1943, resigned his position, effective October 1, after presenting earlier that day what he called a "state-of-the-orchestra report" to the executive committee of the board of directors, including Arthur Judson, business manager of the orchestra. Among the comments he made to the board were two that, at his home that night, he repeated for members of the press. "I told them," Rodzinski said, "that the three pillars of a soundly run orchestra were the board, the manager, and the musical director. As the New York Philharmonic is run, these three pillars are not of equal importance, as they must be. The board and the musical director [instead] revolve around the manager like satellites. I also told them that Columbia Concerts Inc., a concert management agency of which Mr. Judson is also president, is often more important than the New York Philharmonic-Symphony, which is treated as a subsidiary [of Columbia] on occasion." When *The New York Times* pressed Rodzinski for details of his dissatisfaction with Mr. Judson, whose Columbia Concerts Inc. had managed the conductor's American career from 1926 through 1945, he said that at the Philharmonic he was music director in name but not in fact. "[He] explained," wrote the *Times*, "that in organizations like the Boston Symphony Orchestra, the conductor, Serge Koussevitzky, had a vital voice in decisions relating to guest conductors, soloists, and such matters as who would conduct the orchestra in recording engagements. It was understood that Mr. Rodzinski's voice in these matters was not similarly controlling." Rodzinski's resignation, submitted by telegram, was accepted by the board on February 4, 1947. The Rodzinski-Judson clash held the public's imagination for months, and Rodzinski was featured on the cover of *Time* for February 17 above the caption "Conductor Rodzinski: Harmony Is Hand-Made."

317.26 Curzon line] Clifford Curzon, an English pianist who often performed in New Friends of Music concerts, was known for his interpretations of German composers, especially Mozart and Schubert. (The Curzon line was also the name of the border between Poland and the Soviet Union established in 1919–20.)

321.37 Frederick Ashton] Dancer, choreographer, and ballet master (1904–1988) long associated with the British Royal Ballet and its predecessor companies (1931–88).

331.15–16 M. A. De Wolfe Howe] A lifelong Bostonian, Howe (1864–1960) wrote many books of local literary history, including *The Atlantic Monthly and Its Makers* (1919) and *Memoirs of the Harvard War Dead* (1921). He also edited the letters of such New England figures as George Bancroft, Charles Eliot Norton, and John Jay Chapman.

331.19   Hugo Leichtentritt] Polish-born German-American musicologist (1874–1951). His *Music, History, and Ideas* (1938) was long a standard textbook in music history.

332.4–7   Justice Shientag . . . "irreparable harm."] In his opinion on *Koussevitzky v. Allen, Towne & Heath* (188 Misc. 479, 68 NYS 2d 779, Sup. Ct. 1947), Bernard L. Shientag (1887–1952) determined that *Koussevitzky*, by Moses Smith (1901–1964), contained "no so-called revelations of any intimate details which would tend to outrage public tolerance. There is nothing repugnant to one's sense of decency or that takes the book out of the realm of the legitimate dissemination of information on a subject of general interest."

379.7   *Carmen Jones*] All-black Broadway musical (1943) based on George Bizet's opera *Carmen* (1875), produced by Billy Rose and staged by Hassard Short. Bizet's music was adapted and arranged by Robert Russell Bennett, and the original French libretto, by Henri Meilhac and Ludovic Halévy, was freely adapted by Oscar Hammerstein II. *Carmen Jones* starred Muriel Rahn and Muriel Smith alternating in the title role. Joseph Littau conducted the orchestra, Robert Shaw directed the chorus, and Eugene Loring did the choreography. The show ran 503 performances at the Broadway Theatre in 1943–45.

385.20–21   "Nothing changes . . . looking at,"] Gertrude Stein (1874–1946), in "Composition as Explanation" (1925), wrote: "The only thing that is different from one time to another is what is seen and what is seen depends upon how everybody is doing everything. This makes the thing we are looking at very different and this makes what those who describe it make of it, it makes a composition, it confuses, it shows, it is, it looks, it likes it as it is, and this makes what is seen as it is seen. Nothing changes from generation to generation except the thing seen and that makes a composition."

388.18   Dr. Chevalier M. Jackson] American laryngologist, laryngeal surgeon, and pioneer of endoscopy (1865–1958).

391.11   Manuel García] Spanish baritone and voice teacher (1805–1906) who is traditionally credited with inventing, in 1854, the laryngoscope, a device for viewing the vocal cords.

394.23   Kirsten Flagstad's personal accompanist] Edwin McArthur.

401.7   Bobby Clark] American dancer, slapstick actor, and acrobatic clown (1888–1960) whose career spanned vaudeville, Hollywood, and the Ringling Bros. Circus.

402.9   Herbert Graf] Austrian-born opera director (1904–1973) who, after a successful career in Vienna, Geneva, and London, was a stage director at the Metropolitan Opera from 1936 to 1960. The son of musicologist Max Graf (see note 809.10), he was the "Little Hans" of Freud's famous case study *Analysis of a Phobia in a Five-Year-Old Boy* (1909).

406.13   Victor Hugo's play] Boito's libretto for *La Giaconda* (1876) is based on Hugo's drama *Angelo, Tyran de Padoue* ("Angelo, Tyrant of Padua," 1835).

410.21–22   Thirty-ninth Street] See note 142.21–22.

411.38   Foxy Grandpa] Protagonist of the pioneering Sunday comic strip *Foxy Grandpa* (1900–18), by American cartoonist Carl E. "Bunny" Schultze (1866–1939), in which a spry old man matched wits with his practical-joker grandsons.

413.12–13   Soglow's Little King] American cartoonist Otto Soglow (1900–1975) created the roly-poly pantomime character The Little King for *The New Yorker* (1931–33) and then continued his adventures in a syndicated Sunday strip (1933–75).

413.14   Zero Mostel] American comic actor (1915–1997) who, in the 1940s, was known as a nightclub comedian and the star of New York productions of Brecht and Molière. In 1964 he created the role of Tevye in Broadway's *Fiddler on the Roof*.

415.6   through the conventions of the Reinhardt baroque] That is, through the theatrical conventions established by the Austrian director Max Reinhardt (1873–1943), who in 1912 staged the premiere of *Ariadne auf Naxos* in Berlin in collaboration with composer Richard Strauss (1864–1949) and librettist Hugo von Hofmannsthal (1874–1929). Reinhardt, in the texts and music he chose or commissioned, delighted in creating aesthetic tension between the high and the low, the classical and the popular, the profound and the silly.

415.27   CARMEN JONES] See note 379.7.

416.12   Marion Farquhar] See note 159.22.

419.25–26   Horace Armistead] English-born American costume and set designer (1898–1980). He worked mainly on Broadway but also designed productions for the New York City Ballet and the Metropolitan Opera.

420.18–21   Helen Hayes . . . Stowe] American stage and film actress Hayes (1900–1993) played Harriet Beecher Stowe in *Harriet* (1943), a three-act play by Florence Ryerson and Colin Clements. Staged by Elia Kazan, it ran 377 performances on Broadway in 1943–44.

420.21–23   Gertrude Lawrence . . . *Lady in the Dark*] English actress and entertainer Gertrude Lawrence (1898–1952) played Liza Elliott, a fashion-magazine editor undergoing psychoanalysis, in *Lady in the Dark* (1941), a two-act musical with book by Moss Hart, music by Kurt Weill, and lyrics by Ira Gershwin. Staged by Hart, it ran 388 performances, on Broadway and on tour, in 1941–43.

420.34   "Paris qui Chante"] Short-lived cabaret (1943–45), at 62 West Forty-eighth Street, owned by Adolphe DeMilly, publisher of the New York–based French Resistance newspaper *La Voix de France* (1941–43).

420.37   "The Blue Angel"] Cabaret (1943–63), at 152 East Fifty-fifth Street, owned by Paris-born entrepreneur Herbert Jacoby and Village Vanguard founder Max Gordon.

421.3   "Casablanca"] Short-lived cabaret (1941–44) at 161 East Fifty-fourth Street.

433.30   *morceaux de genre*] French: genre pieces.

436.8   *The Art of Setting Words to Music*] Ninety-six-page pamphlet on prosody by Bainbridge Crist (New York: Carl Fischer, 1944).

443.32   Antony Tudor] English choreographer (1908–1987) who in 1938 founded the London Ballet and in 1940 joined and helped shape New York's Ballet Theater, later the American Ballet Theatre.

446.21   Norman Corwin] American writer, producer, director, and narrator of poetic, topical nonfiction radio programs (1910–2011), including the CBS series *Words Without Music* (1938–39), *The Pursuit of Happiness* (1939–40), and *The Columbia Workshop* (1941–42). His hour-long special "On a Note of Triumph," broadcast on May 8, 1945, the day World War II ended in Europe, was heard by some sixty million Americans.

448.3   Martha Graham] American modern dancer, choreographer, and provocateur (1894–1991), leader of the Martha Graham Dance Company, founded in 1926. She collaborated with and commissioned work from the leading composers of her day, including Barber, Copland, Dello Joio, and Schuman. Her work, which dramatized sexual, psychological, social, and political themes, attracted an audience larger than the usual one for modern dance.

448.14   Merce Cunningham] American avant-garde dancer and choreographer (1919–2009) who, after six years as a soloist in the Martha Graham Company (1939–45), became the life partner and frequent artistic collaborator of composer John Cage. In 1953 he formed the Merce Cunningham Dance Company, and remained its artistic director until his death.

452.20–21   Denis de Rougemont] Swiss-born poet and cultural historian (1906–1985) and disciple of the Protestant theologian Karl Barth. His book *L'Amour et l'Occident* ("Love and the Western World," 1939) is a classic history of the Western concept of romantic love.

454.6   Ida Rubinstein] Russian-born French actress, dancer, and ballet impresario (1885–1960) who was also a wealthy patron of the arts.

456.19   Lady Mendl] Elsie de Wolfe (1859–1950), wife of the British diplomat Sir Charles Mendl, was an American actress, food writer, interior designer, and arbiter of "good taste."

461.2–3   Miss Sokolow] American dancer and choreographer Anna Sokolow (1910–2000) was a member of Martha Graham's company (1929–35) before founding her own company, Dance Unit, in 1936. In 1939–48 she lived in

Mexico City, where she founded a new company that, under the sponsorship of the Mexican Ministry of Fine Arts, evolved into the country's National Academy of Dance. After 1950 she worked mainly for Broadway, where she created dances for Marc Blitzstein's *Regina* (1949), Bernstein's *Candide* (1956), and Joseph Papp's production of *Hair* (1968).

462.21   Curt Sachs] German-born ethnomusicologist and historian of musical instruments (1881–1959) who befriended Béla Bartók during his five years at Columbia University (1940–45).

466.11   Norman Corwin] See note 446.21.

466.13–14   Jean Cocteau's] See note 159.8.

466.14   radio American] On December 6, 1946, in a reply to a private letter from Norman Corwin regarding this review, Thomson wrote the following:

Dear Mr. Corwin:
    I thank you for the courteous letter. I still think that Cocteau's French is more elegant than the English, even though the latter may be based, as is Cocteau's text also, on Sophocles. I also think that the quality of elegance is one not inappropriate to this particular work. I believe it to have been, in effect, the primary conscious stylistic consideration of both Cocteau and Stravinsky. If I didn't find that quality in the English of the text spoken at City Center, that is merely one man's opinion. I grant you that calling the style of that text "radio American" is not quite clear. It did, all the same, seem to me to lack distinction of language in much the same way that a great many of our more ambitious literary broadcasts do. I should not consider the expressive powers of [Archibald] MacLeish, [Stephen Vincent] Benét, and [Carl] Sandburg to be characteristic of the radio, since these [American] poets came to the medium fully formed and lend themselves to it only occasionally. They are no more radio poets than I am a radio composer, though I have often written for radio too. Morton Gould, whose style was formed by radio work, could with more justice be said to write, musically speaking, in "radio American."
    It may be reactionary of me, but I do deplore the introduction of a public address system to circumstances that do not absolutely require it for clarity. I have heard speakers in the City Center make themselves perfectly clear to the top gallery, and I am sure your excellent diction would have needed no more than theirs a mechanical aid. Electrical devices are part and parcel of radio and of the spoken film, but mixing them with live music gives an effect not unlike that of placing colored reproductions of visual art beside real oil paintings in a museum. In short, wrong as I may be, the public address system did not seem to me the other evening to be either necessary or appropriate.
    Since we are on the subject, I also question the value of Americanizing the pronunciation of the leading character's name, since you pronounced all the others in Latin. "Oydipus" would have been consistent, and if

this were judged to be affected, "Eedipus" is the classical Anglicization, since the long vowel preserves the quantity of the original diphthong. "Eddipus" has, to my knowledge, no precedent in any scholastic usage. The point is a minor one. I only bring it up because it is typical of the tendency I reproached you with. I cannot see that folksiness of any sort helps the dissemination of so distinguished a work, since in the case of this particular work it is contrary to the basic stylistic conception that makes that work the kind of work it is.

475.4   Claudia Cassidy] Chicago-based cultural journalist (1900–1996) whose column "On the Aisle," covering music, theater, and dance, was a feature of the *Chicago Tribune* from 1942 to 1965. Her sustained attack on the talents of Désiré Defauw lasted the whole of his brief tenure as music director of the Chicago Symphony (1943–47).

478.14–15   "Tell it to Sweeney; the Stuyvesants will understand."] Advertising slogan of the New York *Daily News*, coined in 1922 by the tabloid's publisher, Richard Medill Patterson. The slogan made clear that Patterson's newspaper was for the city's "common man," not its "blue bloods."

480.8   Syria Mosque] Thirty-seven-hundred-seat auditorium (1916–91), at 4223 Bigelow Boulevard, Pittsburgh, Pennsylvania, which for forty-five seasons (1926–71) was home to the Pittsburgh Symphony Orchestra.

487.5   Carl Van Vechten] American writer and photographer (1880–1964) who was a patron of writers and artists of the Harlem Renaissance and the American avant-garde. The full name of the collection that he donated to Fisk University in 1947 is the George Gershwin Memorial Collection of Music and Musical Literature.

487.7   Lee J. Loventhal] Nashville businessman (1875–1940) and patron of educational and social welfare programs at Vanderbilt and Fisk universities and the Nashville YMHA.

491.26   Pvt. Lincoln Kirstein] In 1945 Lincoln Kirstein (1907–1996), co-founder, in 1933, of the School of American Ballet (see note 102.38), was a private first class in the U.S. Army, one of the so-called Monuments Men who during World War II helped protect and recover the art treasures of Europe.

491.28–31   *Les Clicquot . . . finest organs in France.*] *The Clicquots, Builders of Royal Organs, Being the History of a Family of Champagne-born Craftsmen Under the Ancien Régime* (1942), by the French organist and musicologist Norbert Dufourq (1904–1990), 88 pages.

492.1   The other brochure] *Le Grand Orgue du Palais de Chaillot*, by Norbert Dufourq (Paris: Théâtre National Populaire, 1943), 48 pages.

493.35   Cécile Sauvage] Olivier Messiaen's mother (1883–1927) was a widely published poet whose works explored the mystical aspects of nature, love, marriage, pregnancy, and motherhood. Messiaen published a setting of her poems, *Cécile Sauvage: Three Songs for Soprano*, in 1930.

498.37   Paul Claudel] French Catholic poet and dramatist (1868–1955) whose works include the poem cycle *Five Great Odes* (1910), the play *The Satin Slipper* (1924), and the text for *Joan of Arc at the Stake* (1938), an oratorio by Arthur Honegger.

499.2–3   *Nicolas de Flue* . . . Denis de Rougemont.] See note 452.20–21.

499.4–5   Ida Rubinstein] See note 454.6.

501.11   René Fauchois] French playwright, librettist, and actor (1882–1962) whose *Prenez garde à la Peinture* ("Look Out for Painting," 1932) was translated by American playwright Sidney Howard as *The Late Christopher Bean* (1933). In 1932 Jean Renoir wrote and directed a film based on his comedy *Boudu Saved from Drowning* (1919).

504.10   Alexandre Duval's poem] French dramatist and poet Alexandre-Vincent Pineux Duval (1767–1842) adapted his verse drama *Joseph et ses frères* (1806) for the libretto of Méhul's *Joseph*.

522.23   *The Nine Tailors*] Mystery novel (1934), by English writer Dorothy L. Sayers (1893–1957), in which Sayers's recurring protagonist, Lord Peter Wimsey, learns much about the English practice of bell ringing in the Fenland village of Fenchurch St. Paul.

525.19   Irish by birth] Maria Grandi, who performed under a succession of stage names and frequently falsified her personal history, was born Maria Gard, on Harwood Island, New South Wales, Australia, and was raised in Hobart, Tasmania.

535.16   USFET] United States Forces, European Theater.

538.23   Paul Strecker] German painter and set designer (1898–1950) long associated with the Berlin State Opera.

543.5   OWI] U.S. Office of War Information (1942–45).

551.3–4   Tovey . . . Hale . . . Gilman . . . Borowski] Donald Francis Tovey (1875–1940), British conductor and musicologist, wrote program notes for the Reid Orchestra of Edinburgh (1914–40), collected in the seven-volume series *Essays in Musical Analysis* (1935–44); Philip Hale (1854–1934), music critic for several Boston papers, wrote program notes for the Boston Symphony Orchestra (1901–34), collected posthumously in *Philip Hale's Boston Symphony Programme Notes* (1935); Lawrence Gilman (see note 200.26–27) wrote program notes for the Philadelphia and New York Philharmonic-Symphony orchestras (1921–39), collected posthumously in *Orchestral Music: An Armchair Guide* (1955); and Felix Borowski (1872–1956), British-born American composer and music critic for several Chicago papers, wrote program notes for the Chicago Symphony Orchestra (1908–56) and Civic Opera (1922–31), collected in the two-volume *Standard Opera and Concert Guide* (2nd ed., 1947).

552.6   United States Rubber Company] See note 266.1.

556.30   Inna Garsoian] Russian-born artist (1896–1984) who designed sets and costumes for Diaghilev's Ballets Russes and later painted oils of Nantucket townscapes.

558.9   *Joseph Osborne*] Russian-born American violinist (1905–?) and proprietor of a private violin studio in midtown Manhattan.

559.13   Leonard Liebling] American pianist and librettist (1874–1945) who was a columnist (1902–45) and after 1912 the editor of *The Musical Courier*, former trade journal of the American concert business (1880–1961).

560.31–32   only Schönberg, and that just once] In Variations on a Recitative for Organ, op. 40 (1941).

570.23–24   reflective article on the place of music in modern esthetics] "Silence Is Golden" ("Silence d'or"), by André Breton (1896–1966), translated from the French by Louise Varèse, in *Modern Music* 21:3 (March/April 1944), pages 150–54. Minna Lederman, the editor of *Modern Music*, solicited this essay from Breton, who lived in New York from 1941 to 1945. "Silence Is Golden" is reprinted in *What Is Surrealism? Selected Writings of André Breton*, edited by Franklin Rosemont (London: Pluto Press/Anchor Foundation, 1978).

571.8   "concourse of sweet sounds"] Or, in some editions, "concord"; *The Merchant of Venice* V.i.84.

571.13   "the food of love"] *Twelfth Night* I.i.1.

574.36   Alfred Einstein] German-born American music scholar (1880–1952) who edited and revised the Köchel catalogue of Mozart's works (1936). His best-selling works of music history include *A Short History of Music* (1917), *Greatness in Music* (1941), and *Mozart: His Character, His Works* (1945).

582.31   Saint Clement . . . debauchery."] See Book 2 of *Paedagogus* ("The Instructor," c. 198), by Clement of Alexandria (c. 150–215).

592.17   Mark Hopkins] American educator, Protestant theologian, and independent scholar (1802–1887) who was president of Williams College from 1836 to 1872.

594.16   New York Music Critics' Circle] See note 124.36–37.

594.34   Salmaggi and San Carlo troupes] Opera impresario Alfredo Salmaggi (1886–1975), often in partnership with Ringling Bros. & Barnum and Bailey, brought 99-cent opera to Brooklyn, Chicago, and the American provinces. The itinerant San Carlo Opera Company, under the direction of Fortune Gallo (1878–1970), barnstormed America from 1913 through the early 1950s.

596.31–32   MODERN MUSIC . . . Minna Lederman . . . League of Composers] *Modern Music* was for twenty-two years the quarterly journal of the League of Composers, an organization founded in New York in 1923 to, in the words of its mission statement, "produce the highest quality performances of new music, champion American composers in the United States and abroad, and introduce

American audiences to the best new music from around the world." (Since 1954 the League of Composers has been the U.S. chapter of the International Society of Contemporary Music.) Minna Lederman (1896–1995), a native New Yorker who had studied music and journalism at Barnard, was the editor of *Modern Music* for its entire run. She wrote a personal history of the journal, *The Life and Death of a Small Magazine: "Modern Music," 1924–1946* (Brooklyn: Institute of Music Studies of Brooklyn College, 1984).

MUSIC RIGHT AND LEFT

603.27–28   Ogden Reid . . . Geoffrey Parsons . . . Mrs. Reid] Ogden Mills Reid (1883–1947) was the son of *New York Tribune* founder Whitelaw Reid and, in 1912, his successor as publisher and editor-in-chief of the *Tribune*. In 1922 he bought the rival *New York Herald* and merged the two papers. Geoffrey Parsons (1879–1956), chief editorial writer of the *Herald Tribune* (1924–52; Pulitzer Prize, 1942) and the man in charge of its cultural coverage, was Thomson's boss and journalistic mentor. Helen Miles Rogers (1882–1970), the longtime social secretary to Mrs. Whitelaw Reid, married Ogden Reid in 1911. As Reid's alcoholism deepened during the 1910s, she emerged as the de facto head of the family business. She was vice-president of the *Herald Tribune* from 1922 to 1947, and president from 1947 to 1955.

603.30   Francis Perkins] American music journalist and editor (1898–1970) who was a member of the staff of the *New York Tribune* and *Herald Tribune* from 1919 to 1962.

605.32   "strangeness in the proportion"] Cf. "There is no excellent beauty that hath not some strangeness in the proportion," from the essay "Of Beauty" (1612), by Francis Bacon (1561–1626).

628.15   (d.v.)] Latin: *Deo volente*; God willing.

648.40   Yvette Guilbert, Polaire, and Damia) Guilbert (1865–1944), Polaire (Émelie-Marie Bouchard, 1874–1939), and Damia (Marie-Louise Damien, 1889–1978) were not only chanteuses but also silent film actresses and Paris style icons.

654.19–20   Lee Simonson's sets . . . Kautsky designs] In 1948 the American architect and stage designer Lee Simonson (1888–1967) created sets for the Metropolitan's Ring Cycle that remained in use through 1963. They replaced those of Hans Kautsky (see note 163.21–22), which had been in use since the 1910s.

666.18   Will Geer] See note 133.11.

666.35–36   Lillian Hellman's original play] Blitzstein's source for the story of *Regina* was *The Little Foxes* (1939), by the American playwright Lillian Hellman (1905–1984).

682.21   Paul Claudel] See note 498.37.

683.34   the film itself] *Entr'acte* (1924), twenty-minute black-and-white silent film by René Clair (see note 258.33) with a score by Erik Satie, created as the between-the-acts entertainment for the Ballets Suédois production of Satie's two-act ballet *Relâche* ("Show Cancelled"), presented at the Théâtre de Champs-Elysées in December 1924. Its surreal-comic scenario—a showcase for the slow-motion, stop-action, and lighting techniques of cinematographer Jimmy Berliet—was conceived by the Dada artist Francis Picabia (1879–1953). Its cast included dancers of the Ballets Suédois, choreographer Jean Börlin and prima ballerina Inge Frïss, as well as art-world figures Marcel Duchamp, Man Ray, Georges Auric, and Clair himself.

684.29   Max Jacob] See note 164.31.

685.1   Jean Cocteau] See note 159.8.

685.5   Frederick Kiesler] See note 145.22.

686.26   Aimee Semple McPherson] Los Angeles–based Pentecostal evangelist, radio broadcaster, and media celebrity (1890–1944) who, in 1927, founded the International Church of the Foursquare Gospel.

701.26   Rudi Blesh] See note 35.19.

703.8   *The Red Pony*] American feature film (1939), directed and produced by Lewis Milestone (1895–1980), with a script by John Steinbeck (1902–1968) based on his novella of 1933. The cast includes Robert Mitchum (Billy Buck, a stable hand), Myrna Loy (Alice Tiflin, a ranch owner), Shepperd Strudwick (Fred Tiflin, Alice's estranged husband), and Peter Miles (the Tiflins' young son, Tom).

713.17   *singspiel*] German folk opera or musical revue, usually short, episodic, satiric, and topical.

725.24   Syria Mosque] See note 480.8.

743.8–9   Boris Polyevoi . . . *The Life of a Real Person*] "Boris Polyevoi" was the pen name of Soviet journalist Boris Kampov (1908–1981), whose book *The Life of a Real Person* (or *A Story about a Real Man*, 1946) is an account of the life of Alexey Mareseyev (1916–2001), a Soviet fighter pilot whose plane was shot down over Nazi-occupied Russia in March 1942. Mareseyev, who lost his lower legs in the crash, somehow managed an eighteen-day crawl back to the Soviet line. After a year's recuperation he returned to the air, completing some eighty-six further missions and shooting down eleven German warplanes.

743.10   Mira Mendelssohn] Ukrainian writer (1915–1968) who, from 1939 to 1948, was Prokofiev's lover and artistic collaborator. She wrote the librettos for his operas *Betrothal in a Monastery* (1940), *War and Peace* (1942), and *The Life of a Real Person* (1947), none of which found favor with the Soviet authorities. She married the ailing Prokofiev in January 1948 and five weeks later was arrested on charges of espionage. She was not released by the Soviets until 1954, several months after Prokofiev's death.

747.17–18   Martha Graham] See note 448.3.

758.10–11   *Polyphonie*] Twelve numbers of *Polyphonie: Revue musicale trimes-trielle* ("Polyphony: A Quarterly Review of Music," 1947–54), each devoted to a single musical topic, were published irregularly in Paris and Geneva by Éditions Richard-Masse. *Polyphonie* No. 2 (1948) was titled *Le Rythme musical* and included Pierre Boulez's first published article, "Propositions." No. 4 (1949) was titled *Le Système dodécaphonique* and included Schoenberg's "La Composition à douze sons" as well as articles by Křenek, Dallapiccola, and René Leibowitz.

763.2–3   Music Critics' Circle of New York] See note 124.36–37.

765.14–15   *The Road to Mandalay*] Popular song (1907) by American composer Oley Speaks (1874–1948) with words freely adapted from Rudyard Kipling's poem "Mandalay" (in *Barrack-Room Ballads*, 1892).

772.32–33   *Motu Proprio*] Statement issued by the Pope "on his own impulse" and addressing a topic of pressing concern to the Church.

From MUSIC REVIEWED 1940–1954

779.4   Ogden Reid] See note 603.27–28.

779.11   Walter Lippman, Dorothy Thompson, Joseph Alsop] All three journalists wrote syndicated thrice-weekly columns of liberal political opinion: Lippman (1889–1974) "Today and Tomorrow" (1931–49, Pulitzer Prize 1942), Thompson (1893–1961) "On the Record" (1936–41), and Alsop (1910–1989), with his brother Stewart, "Matter of Fact" (1948–58).

779.12–13   Percy Hammond and Richard Watts . . . Walter Kerr] Hammond (1873–1936) was drama critic of the *Tribune* from 1921 to 1936, Watts (see note 166.23) from 1936 to 1942, and Kerr (1913–1996) from 1951 to 1966.

779.13   Royal Cortissoz . . . Emily Genauer] Cortissoz (1869–1948) was art critic of the *Tribune* from 1891 until his death, Genauer (1911–2002) from 1949 to 1966.

779.14–15   Henry Edward Krehbiel and Lawrence Gilman] Krehbiel (1854–1923) was music critic of the *Tribune* from 1884 until his death, Gilman (see notes 200.26–27 and 551.3–4) from 1925 to 1939.

779.19   Geoffrey Parsons] See note 603.27–28.

782.10   Sidney Finkelstein] New York–born music writer and record producer (1909–1974). He was a member of Thomson's music staff at the *Herald Tribune* during the 1940s and then, from 1951 to 1973, an executive at Vanguard Records.

790.2   Ernest Newman] Prolific English music critic and historian of music (1868–1959).

790.8   Paul Éluard] French surrealist poet (1895–1952).

791.6–9   *Age of Anxiety . . . W. H. Auden] The Age of Anxiety: A Baroque Eclogue* (1947), a book-length poem in six parts by Anglo-American poet W. H. Auden (1907–1973), won the Pulitzer Prize in Poetry in 1948. Written during World War II, it is a meditation on the fate of Western culture in the twentieth century in the form of a conversation among four strangers in a Third Avenue saloon.

801.32   Paul Claudel] See note 498.37.

804.34   Horace Armistead's set] See note 419.25–26.

807.32–33   Henry Pleasants III] American writer on music (1910–2000). He was music critic of the *Philadelphia Evening Bulletin* (1934–42), London-based music correspondent for *The New York Times* (1945–55) and the *International Herald Tribune* (1967–1999), and the author of many books, including *The Agony of Modern Music* (1955) and *The Great Singers* (1966).

808.16–17   Chorley . . . Fétis] English writer Henry Chorley (1808–1872) was music critic of London's *Athenaeum* magazine (1830–68). Belgian-born critic François-Joseph Fétis (1784–1871) was founding editor and chief contributor to the Paris newspaper *Revue Musicale* (1827–35).

809.10   Max Graf] Vienna-born writer (1873–1958) who was music critic of the *Neue Freie Presse* (1902–9), Paris music correspondent for the *Frankfurter Zeitung* (1909–38), and professor of music history at the New School, New York (1938–47). His *Composer and Critic: Two Hundred Years of Musical Criticism* was published in 1946.

810.19–20   Percy Hammond] See note 779.12–13.

815.1   Mr. Bing] Rudolf Bing assumed the position of general manager of the Metropolitan Opera on June 1, 1950. Thomson's "Spokesman for the Met" was published six months into Bing's twenty-two-year tenure.

817.11   so conservative a repertory] There were four new productions during Bing's first season at the Metropolitan Opera: Verdi's *Don Carlo*, Wagner's *Fliegende Holländer*, Strauss's *Fledermaus*, and *Cav* and *Pag* (see pages 804–5 of the present volume).

817.24–25   new Stravinsky opera] *The Rake's Progress* had received its premiere at the Teatro La Fenice, Venice, on September 11, 1951. It would receive its U.S. premiere at the Metropolitan Opera some seventeen months later, on February 14, 1953 (see pages 836–37 of the present volume).

821.32–33   piece . . . for twelve radio-receiving sets.] *Imaginary Landscape* No. 4 (1951), for twelve radios, twenty-four performers, and conductor. The score requires twelve pairs of performers, each controlling the tuner and volume knobs of an AM radio, to "play" the radios at prescribed frequencies and amplitudes, and for prescribed lengths of time, within the work's five-minute eleven-second duration.

822.8–9   *Music of Changes*] Work for solo piano (1951), composed by Cage with his associate David Tudor, in which sounds, durations, tempos, etc., are determined by the performer of the work in consultation with the *I Ching, or, Book of Changes*, as translated from the Chinese by Richard Wilhelm and Cary F. Baynes (Bollingen Series XIX; Princeton, NJ: Princeton University Press, 1950).

826.37   G. Ricordi and Co.] Italian music publishers, founded in Milan in 1808, whose catalogue includes the definitive scores of Giuseppe Verdi.

831.32–33   "not a part of New York's intellectual life."] See the bottom of page 10 in the present volume.

833.5   *The Dybbuk*] Opera in three acts (1933) by American composer David Tamkin (1906–1975), based on the play in Yiddish (1914) by Russian writer S. Ansky (1863–1920).

836.13   Horace Armistead] See note 419.25–26.

836.14   George Balanchine] See note 102.38.

836.18   Bedlam] London's Bethlem Royal Hospital (founded 1330), Europe's oldest hospital for the mentally ill.

836.24–25   Hogarth's engravings] English artist William Hogarth (1697–1764) painted a sequence of eight canvases, collectively titled *A Rake's Progress* (1732–33), that were made into a portfolio of captioned engravings in 1735.

837.23   If so, it will stay in the repertory.] The Met gave *The Rake's Progress* eight performances—six in 1951–52, two in 1952–53—and then dropped the opera from its repertory. In his memoirs, *A Knight at the Opera* (1981), Rudolf Bing remarks that, in terms of box office, programming Stravinsky was "perhaps the most serious mistake" he made as the company's general manager.

847.37   Éluard . . . Hugnet . . . Jacob] Paul Éluard (see note 790.8); Georges Hugnet (1906–1974), French surrealist poet and artist; Max Jacob (see note 164.31).

848.27   Christian Bérard] French painter and illustrator (1902–1949) who was production designer for Jean Cocteau's film *Beauty and the Beast* (1946).

852.18   John Ferren . . . Ralph Bates] Ferren (1905–1970) was an American abstract painter and sculptor, Bates (1899–2000) an English writer and Hispanophile best known for his novel *The Olive Field* (1936).

854.22   "human mind" . . . "human nature."] See Gertrude Stein, *The Geographical History of America, or The Relation of Human Nature to the Human Mind* (1936).

856.18   *Charley's Aunt*] Farce in three acts (1892) by English playwright Brandon Thomas (1848–1914).

862.23   Louis Kirstein] Boston-based retailer and philanthropist (1867–1942) who was president of Filene's department stores from 1911 to 1942. He was the father of Lincoln Kirstein (see note 491.26).

863.5   Mayor Charles Farnsley] Farnsley (1907–1990) was a native of Louisville, Kentucky, who, as mayor of the city (1948–53), did much to strengthen its arts and educational institutions, including the Louisville Symphony, the Free Public Library, and the University of Louisville.

866.14   Antony Tudor] See note 443.32.

866.31–32   Alma Morgenthau–Locust Valley Festival] Morgenthau (1887–1953), the daughter of a wealthy banker and philanthropist, was cofounder of the League of Composers and backer of Cos Cob Press (1929–38), publisher of scores by Copland, Harris, Thomson, and others. For three summers (1950–52) she hosted the Locust Valley Music Festival at her home, the Lattington Estate, in Locust Valley, Long Island.

872.16   A newspaper man] Geoffrey Parsons (see note 603.27–28).

873.18   "Damn braces; bless relaxes.") From "Proverbs of Hell," in *The Marriage of Heaven and Hell* (1793) by William Blake (1757–1827).

873.33   Olin Downes's public] Downes (1886–1955), American music journalist, lecturer, and writer, was music reviewer for the *Boston Post* (1906–24) before becoming chief music critic of *The New York Times* (1924–55). His books include two critical studies of Sibelius, whose work he championed, and the posthumous omnibus *Olin Downes on Music* (1957).

880.2   "all passion spent."] The last three words of *Samson Agonistes* (1671), by John Milton (1608–1674).

OTHER WRITINGS

887.15   Deems Taylor] American composer, music critic, and radio celebrity (1885–1946). A lifelong New Yorker, he was music critic for the New York *World* (1921–25), *Vanity Fair* (1926–28), and the New York *American* (1931–32); intermission commentator on the Philharmonic radio broadcasts (1936–1943); and Master of Ceremonies for Walt Disney's *Fantasia* (1940). His operas include *The King's Henchman* (1927), with a libretto by Edna St. Vincent Millay, the first American opera to be commissioned by the Met.

888.18–19   Marcel Duchamp . . . made a film . . .] *Anémic Cinéma* (1926), six-minute experimental black-and-white silent movie, animated by French artist Marcel Duchamp (1887–1968) in collaboration with Man Ray and Marc Allégret.

888.32   Martha Graham] See note 448.3.

889.22–23   what Miss Dorothy Thompson says] In a syndicated column of November 25, 1940, Thomson's *Herald Tribune* colleague Dorothy Thompson (see note 779.11) wrote that "if genius can be wholly destructive, then the *Fantasia* is a work of genius. Say, rather, that it is the work of [two] geniuses"— Walt Disney and Leopold Stokowski—"destroying genius . . . [They] out-genius genius in a supreme insult to the composers and to themselves. . . . I left the theater in a condition bordering on nervous breakdown. I felt as though I had been subjected to an assault, but [unlike other 'half-hysterical' reviewers] I had no desire to throw myself in adoration before the two masters who were responsible for the brutalization of sensibility in this remarkable nightmare."

890.5   cry "Nazism,"] Dorothy Thompson wrote: "All I could think to say of the 'experience' as I staggered out [of the theater] was that it was 'Nazi.' The word did not arise out of an obsession. Nazism is the abuse of power, the perverted betrayal of the best instincts, the genius of a race turned into black magical destruction, and so is the *Fantasia*. . . . If [Beethoven,] the man who turned against Napoleon[,] had lived to see the inside of a Nazi concentration camp, his torturers might have driven him mad by the performance of [the *Pastoral* Symphony by] Mr. Stokowski and Mr. Disney."

893.20–21   "the piano's martial blast."] British poet and librettist W. S. Gilbert (1836–1911), in "The Story of Prince Agib" (1868): "Let the piano's martial blast / Rouse the echoes of the past . . ."

899.9   WHITE AND NEGRO SPIRITUALS] *White and Negro Spirituals, Their Life-span and Kinship: Tracing 200 Years of Untrammeled Song-Making and Singing Among Our Country Folk, with 116 Songs as Sung by Both Races*, by George Pullen Jackson (see note 244.6).

900.5–6   He has analyzed . . . 550 of them.] See Jackson's *Spiritual Folk-Songs of Early America: 250 Tunes and Texts with an Introduction and Notes* (1937) and its sequel, *Down-East Spirituals and Others: 300 Songs Supplementary to "Spiritual Folk-Songs of Early America"* (1939).

908.28–31   The subject . . . royal household;] That is, the subject of Gilbert and Sullivan's *Iolanthe* (1882) may have less universal appeal than that of *H.M.S. Pinafore* (1878) or *The Mikado* (1885).

911.25–26   *The Circus*] Charlie Chaplin's silent feature film *The Circus* (1928) was reissued in 1947 with a recorded score commissioned by Chaplin from Hanns Eisler.

911.33   *Fourteen Ways of Describing Rain*] *Regen* ("Rain") is the name of the twelve-minute silent black-and-white nonfiction film made in 1929 by Dutch filmmaker Joris Ivens (1898–1989) with Mannus Franken (1899–1953). It is Hanns Eisler's music for the film, composed in 1941, that is titled *Vierzehn Arten den Regen zu beschreiben*.

921.5   Marie Dressler's travesty of *La Traviata*] In the Broadway comedy *Til-lie's Nightmare* (1910), a vehicle for American actress Marie Dressler (1868–1934), Tillie Blobb, a country girl only recently exposed to New York City's high culture, delivers her "hayseed" impression of Met soprano Luisa Tetrazzini (1871–1940).

929.35 familiar ode by Klopstock] "Die Auferstehung" ("The Resurrection," 1761), by the German poet Friedrich Gottlieb Klopstock (1724–1803). Mahler found the poem in *Des Knaben Wunderhorn* ("The Boy's Cornucopia," 1805), an anthology of "old German songs," edited by Achim von Arnim and Clemens Brentano, which was the source of texts for dozens of Mahler's songs.

931.12 Harold Teen] Bow-tied and brilliantined adolescent protagonist of *Harold Teen* (1919–59), daily and Sunday comic strip by American cartoonist Carl Ed (1890–1959) inspired by Booth Tarkington's best-selling comic novel *Seventeen* (1916).

943.12–15 Gertrude Stein . . . called him a name.] See Stein, "Poetry and Grammar" (1934), collected in her *Lectures in America* (1935).

946.35–37 A newspaper man] See note 872.16.

APPENDIX

960.16–17 We learned syncopation . . . Mexico.] When Thomson reprinted "Jazz" in *A Virgil Thomson Reader* (1981) he followed this sentence with a bracketed insert: "This is quite wrong; a Scottish source is more likely. V.T."

963.21 Mr. Downes] See note 873.33.

963.22 Mr. Taylor] See note 887.15.

964.3 Jackie Coogan] In 1925 Jackie Coogan (1914–1984) was Hollywood's leading child actor, the sidekick of Charlie Chaplin in *A Day's Pleasure* (1919) and *The Kid* (1921) and the star of Frank Lloyd's silent feature *Oliver Twist* (1922).

966.18 *pas seul*] French: solo dance.

973.28 Deems Taylor] See note 887.15.

974.14 Mr. Heyward] American writer DuBose Heyward (1885–1940), whose novel *Porgy* (1925), based on his observations of black life on the waterfront of his native Charleston, South Carolina, was the source material of Gershwin's *Porgy and Bess* (1935).

974.30 *Swanee River* and *Mighty Lak' a Rose*] "Swanee River" (or "The Old Folks at Home"), minstrel song (1851) by the American songwriter Stephen Foster (1826–1864); "Mighty Lak' a Rose," popular song (1901) with music by Ethelbert Nevin (1862–1901) and lyrics by Frank Lebby Stanton (1857–1927).

974.36 *Helen Retires*] Opera in three acts (1934) by George Antheil, with a libretto by John Erskine (1879–1951) from Erskine's novel *The Private Life of Helen of Troy* (1925).

976.3–5 If its eminence, as Shaw once said] Shaw, in the preface to his *Three Plays for Puritans* (1901), wrote that "Karl Marx said of John Stuart Mill that his eminence was due to the flatness of the surrounding country."

976.3–6   If its eminence . . . nonetheless real.] When Thomson reprinted
"George Gershwin" in *A Virgil Thomson Reader* (1981), the text of which is
used here, he cut the ending of the version that was published in *Modern Music*
in 1935. The essay originally ended as follows:

> If its eminence, as Shaw once said of John Stuart Mill, is due largely to
> the flatness of the surrounding country, it is none the less a real and vis-
> ible eminence. *Green Pastures*, the last act of *Run, Little Chillun*, *Four
> Saints in Three Acts*, and *Porgy and Bess* are little eminences on the flat
> horizon of American opera. But four operas that can be listened to and
> remembered is not very many.
>
> Two of these are straight folk-lore. The third is straight opera. *Porgy
> and Bess* is the least interesting of the four, because it is not straight any-
> thing. It is crooked folk-lore and half-way opera, a strong but crippled
> work. Like its hero, who didn't have a leg to stand on but who had some
> radiance in his face and a good deal of love in his heart.

977.14   *guindé*] French: staid; stilted.

982.25   Hugues Panassié's fine volume] Panassié (1912–1974), French music
critic and jazz enthusiast, was twenty-two years old when he wrote *Le Jazz Hot*
(1934). The author of several early books on jazz, including *La Musique de Jazz
et le Swing* (1943), he was also founding president of the musical association
Le Hot Club de France (1932) and, after 1937, co-owner of Swing Records,
which cut sides by Sidney Bechet, Tommy Ladnier, Benny Carter and other
American jazz musicians.

Index

*This book is set in 10 point ITC Galliard, a
face designed for digital composition by Matthew Carter
and based on the sixteenth-century face Granjon. The paper
is acid-free lightweight opaque and meets the requirements for
permanence of the American National Standards Institute.
The binding material is Brillianta, a woven rayon cloth
made by Van Heek-Scholco Textielfabrieken, Holland.
Composition by David Bullen Design. Printing and
binding by Edwards Brothers Malloy, Ann Arbor.
Designed by Bruce Campbell.*

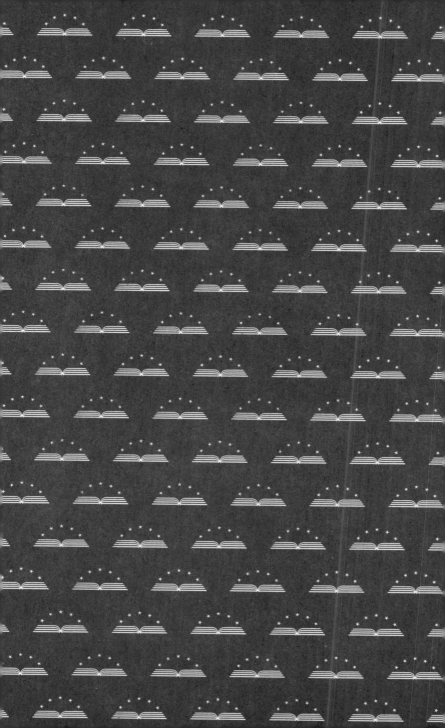